The Editor

G. R. THOMPSON is Professor of English and Comparative Literature at Purdue University. In addition to works on nineteenth-century literature, Romanticism, and the gothic tradition, he has published many works on or involving Edgar Allan Poe, including *Poe's Fiction: Romantic Irony in the Gothic Tales* and the Library of America edition of *Poe's Essays and Reviews*.

A NORTON CRITICAL EDITION

THE SELECTED WRITINGS
OF
EDGAR ALLAN POE

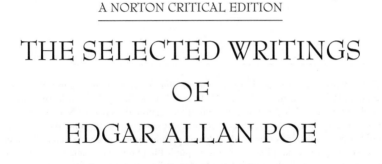

AUTHORITATIVE TEXTS
BACKGROUNDS AND CONTEXTS
CRITICISM

Selected and Edited by

G. R. Thompson

PURDUE UNIVERSITY

W. W. NORTON & COMPANY • *New York* • *London*

W. W. Norton & Company has been independent since its founding in 1923, when William Warder Norton and Mary D. Herter Norton first published lectures delivered at the People's Institute, the adult education division of New York City's Cooper Union. The Nortons soon expanded their program beyond the Institute, publishing books by celebrated academics from America and abroad. By mid-century, the two major pillars of Norton's publishing program—trade books and college texts—were firmly established. In the 1950s, the Norton family transferred control of the company to its employees, and today—with a staff of four hundred and a comparable number of trade, college, and professional titles published each year—W. W. Norton & Company stands as the largest and oldest publishing house owned wholly by its employees.

Composition by PennSet, Inc.
Manufacturing by the Courier Companies—Westford Division.
Production manager: Ben Reynolds.

Library of Congress Cataloging-in-Publication Data
Poe, Edgar Allan, 1809–1849.
 [Selections. 2004]
 The selected writings of Edgar Allan Poe: authoritative texts, background and contexts, criticism / selected and edited by G.R. Thompson.
 p. cm. — (A Norton critical edition)
 Includes bibliographical references.

ISBN 0-393-97285-2 (pbk.)

 1. Fantasy literature, American. 2. Poe, Edgar Allan, 1809–1849—Criticism and interpretation. 3. Fantasy literature, American—History and criticism. I. Thompson, Gary Richard, 1937– II. Title. III. Series.

PS2602.T3 2004
813'.3—dc22

 2003057042

W. W. Norton & Company, Inc., 500 Fifth Avenue, New York, N.Y. 10110-0017
www.wwnorton.com
W. W. Norton & Company Ltd., Castle House, 75/76 Wells Street,
London W1T 3QT

9 0

For Catherine Thompson Jordan

Contents

The Selected Writings of Edgar Allan Poe

Backgrounds and Contexts

Criticism 785

Edgar A. Poe: An American Life (1809–1849)

Edgar A. Poe died relatively young—at the age of forty—mysteriously—in the streets of Baltimore. With only fifty-some poems, a short novel, two novellas, about seventy short stories (and, in mass, a more or less equal volume of essays), Poe managed to exert a significant influence on American and world literature. For one thing, he was surely the most important influence from the English-speaking world on the development of three related literary movements in Continental Europe at the end of the nineteenth century and the beginning of the twentieth. In death, Poe became the contested icon of the art-for-art's-sake, symbolist, and surrealist movements, especially among those contradictorily aesthetic extremists and sociopolitical dissenters associated with France. For Charles Baudelaire, Poe was the *poète maudit*—the blighted or cursed poet of the Ideal, ground up in the crass machinery of a materialist culture. For Stéphane Mallarmé, Poe was a cultural-aesthetic hero, the poet of the transcendental, standing in opposition to the bourgeois values of a philistine America. Poe was for Paul Valéry a stunning skeptic, critical of traditional religious and philosophical assumptions, particularly those of his own Anglo-American heritage. The French had discerned a similarity between Poe as poet of the "transcendental" and "otherworldly," seeking escape from the material world, and Poe as prose critic—that is, someone who, giving vent to often acerbic cultural critique, stood in opposition to a materialist society.

The vogue of Poe in non-English-speaking countries in Europe continues to this day. His works hold special fascination for structuralist, poststructuralist, and deconstructionist critics and theorists and for other coteries of the avant-garde. Indeed, certain French intellectuals celebrate January 19, Poe's birthday, as a special occasion. But in America and Great Britain, with a few local exceptions, no such celebration is widely observed. In these countries, Poe presents a puzzle. The odd excesses of his style and his focus on the destructive aspect of the romantic life/death paradox, especially his addiction to gothic themes and grotesque modes, seem to many critics to put him outside the mainstream of the Anglo-American tradition. In fact, in English-speaking countries he is regarded by many as a sham artist, his works being more redolent of the carnival house of horrors than of the salons of serious art.

To those familiar with his American career, he has seemed quite

contradictory. Although he professed to be the poet of transcendental beauty, he was also deeply involved in the professional literary warfare of his time, which was exacerbated by differences between the North, where he was born, and the South, where he grew up. He was passionately ambitious to be a major player in the cultural scene of America, and indeed the world. And yet—although professionally he could be manipulative and sometimes deceptive, constantly wheeling and dealing in his efforts to establish a commercially successful magazine—he was also devoted to high standards of artistic merit and fiercely independent in his literary criticism. Such seeming oppositions—being both an elitist aesthete *and* a social critic, both a hack *and* a genius, both earnest *and* disingenuous at the same time—were to inform his personal life and professional career.

Poe's personality appears to have been strongly actuated by ambivalence and self-division, vigorously pursuing a desired goal and then self-destructing. In his fiction, he developed several stories around what he called "the perverse." By this term (which has both a theological and a psychological history antedating Poe's use of it) he meant to indicate a universal impulse to act in irrational opposition to one's own best interests. We can see this paradigm in both his creative works and in his life. Nevertheless, as a hard-working and ambitious professional, Poe tried all his adult life to invent himself as a Renaissance man of letters in nineteenth-century America. That is, he attempted to combine and unify the sophisticated and seemingly disparate roles of poet, writer of fiction, theoretical critic, practical critic, reviewer, journalist, editor, satirist, social critic, and philosopher.

Given the brevity of his career, his achievements are extraordinary. As a poet, Poe developed a mode of dramatized interior monologue and a lyric incantatory style aimed at suggesting a visionary state of supernal loveliness above or beyond the ordinary world. He tried to achieve this dreamlike perception through precise manipulation of sound and rhythm by means of hypnotic repetition. He developed a poetics that sought to reconcile the material and mental medium of language as sensuous sound that lifted the soul beyond the physical. At the same time that he sought a visionary spiritual beauty (tinged with loss and melancholy and glimpsed but indefinitely), he emphasized meticulous craftsmanship based on a pre-established pattern of total integration of all elements of a work.

As a practical critic, Poe unmasked carelessness, fraud, and literary theft while recognizing the talents of writers like Nathaniel Hawthorne. As a practicing journalist, Poe fought against the literary cliques that promoted inferior regional writing, especially those centered around the Northern periodicals. He defended the American struggle for literary independence from Europe. Yet, at the same time that he attacked slavish imitation of European models, he opposed the excesses of the American literary nationalism that forced critics into the dilemma of liking a stupid book because at least it represented an "American" stupidity. Although deeply involved in the literary warfare

of his times, Poe's quest was to establish a magazine of letters and culture freed from petty critical conflicts, social prejudice, and the prevailing moral bias of the age. Regarding the age's moral propensity, he even went so far as to propound the "heresy of the didactic." An overriding moral concern in a work of art, he said, was to be regarded as an offense against the ideals of art as art.

But it is Poe's achievement in the short story for which he is most famous. As he had with poetry, he codified an affective theory of the short story that aimed at an almost subliminal effect—one to be accomplished through a carefully predesigned and unified pattern. Every word, every phrase, and every sentence was essential to the reader's impression of the whole structure, an impression created not only by conscious responses but also by unconscious ones. He exemplified his theory in his practice, experimenting with proto-science fiction, visionary prose-poems, multileveled satire, and detective fiction. If he did not invent the detective story outright, he certainly brought it to new levels of "ratiocinative" analysis (reasoning logically and methodically). Simultaneously, he perfected the gothic tale of terror, horror, and mystery. Poe is an acknowledged master of external gothic atmosphere, but he is equally the master of the interior monologue of a profoundly disturbed mind. His fictional dramatizations of psychological turmoil operate on several levels, from gruesome physical shock, to spiritual anguish, to subtle manipulation of narrative point of view. The stories exhibit an architectural symmetry and proportion, reflecting his consistent attempt to integrate all details of setting, plot, and character into an indivisible whole.

Poe was a major advocate of one version of the romantic ideal of the organic wholeness of art. His romantic program was nothing less than to resolve all apparent contraries of the world into unity: the life and death impulses of existence; the apparent irradiation and collapse of a pulsating universe; the paradoxes of time and space, of matter and energy, of the rational and irrational; the seeming oppositions of the immaterial and material, of the serious and the comic, of imagination and logic, of poetry and science, of art and society. Although his critical reception has been marked by strong disagreement over the intrinsic merit of his writings, his achievements in poetry, criticism, magazine journalism, popular philosophy, and fiction are at the very least historically impressive. What cannot be denied is that in America he has had a major effect on the writing of fiction and the conception of the profession of letters.

Critical assessments of Poe's place in literature continue to be characterized by extreme division between the views of aesthetes and those of social activists. Until recently, the usual sketches of Edgar Poe's life and career have tended to psychoanalyze him according to simplistic Freudian models and to describe him in isolation from the social and political currents of his time. This critical tendency derives in part from Poe's habit of placing his narratives in some vague, often indeterminate setting. And Poe himself often affected the role of a visionary poet whose psychic existence takes form in a realm "out of

space—out of time." There is also his obsessive focus on *isolato* characters, who, even when not completely isolated from others, are often off in some dark place, alone in their own minds, watching themselves go to pieces. But Poe lived through a major period of formative sociopolitical and economic change. He was born into a country whose first president had been inaugurated only twenty years earlier. The events of recent American history and of his specific time and place played a more important role in his thinking and writing than is immediately apparent.

 The relation of Poe to the sociopolitical problems of his times is particularly interesting because, though he wrote about contemporary political, economic, and political issues, he was much more insistently "literary" than most of his famous contemporaries. Writers like James Fenimore Cooper, William Cullen Bryant, Washington Irving, Nathaniel Hawthorne, Ralph Waldo Emerson, Margaret Fuller, Henry David Thoreau, Lydia Maria Child, Catharine Sedgwick, Herman Melville, and Harriet Beacher Stowe engaged contemporary sociopolitical themes more overtly than did Poe. To him, science and ancient history and myth were of greater interest. He was particularly interested in astronomy, in the developing sciences of the brain, and in aberrant psychology. He was also concerned with the history and profession of letters per se—with literary professionalism and poetic vocation. Nevertheless, socioeconomic and political themes are present in many of his writings, particularly his political and social satires. Like his contemporaries, he exhibited a strong interest in things "American," but in a global rather than a provincial context. In the following biographical narrative, Poe's highly literary accomplishments are placed in the historical context of his country and times, framed by the inception of the United States as a unified nation-state and by the threatened break up of this new nation in civil war. The political events of Poe's turbulent America seem almost premonitory of his own divided self.

Historical Backgrounds: 1790–1815

By 1809, the year of Poe's birth, a number of momentous events had occurred in the life of the young American Republic. In the twenty years before Poe was born, the United States had rapidly become a world power; but Americans wanted to avoid being caught in the middle of European political conflicts. Although John Jay and Charles C. Pinckney had in 1794–95 negotiated a treaty with Great Britain that was favorable to American neutrality, tensions with the mother country remained high. Moreover, the American treaty with the British violated previous agreements with the French, leading to French naval aggression against American merchant vessels. Americans proposed a new treaty with France but were outraged by the XYZ Affair of 1797. It was discovered that the French foreign minister, Charles Maurice Talleyrand, had tried to extort £50,000 through three secret agents (X, Y, Z) as a "fee" before France would even talk to American emissaries

about a new treaty. America was finding it hard to remain neutral and uninvolved.

At home, struggling to enforce its centralized power, the new national government found itself in the throes of uncertain monetary and taxation policies. Representative are two events of 1791: the nationwide establishment of the First Bank of the United States and Alexander Hamilton's imposition of an excise tax on the manufacturing of whiskey as a federal prerogative. The former would set in motion a complicated series of national monetary crises that would extend over the next fifty years and would have a direct effect on the personal finances of the Poe family. The latter caused farmers in western Pennsylvania, who resented any extension of the power of the new central government over the economic interests of the states, to initiate the 1794 Whiskey Rebellion (cf. Shays's Rebellion in Massachusetts in 1786–87), forcing President Washington to send federal troops to put down the rioting. In 1798, four highly nationalistic congressional acts were passed into law. The so-called Alien and Sedition Acts were drafted by the Federalist Party, which advocated a strong (indeed, oppressive) central government, as a counter to the Jeffersonians, who represented a more decentralized position. The Alien Acts placed various restrictions on immigration and naturalization. More immediately alarming for intellectuals, writers, and political watchdogs was the restriction that the Sedition Acts put on American citizens' right to speak their minds. The Federalists were especially keen to suppress any expressions of opposition to them. The tension between a centralized federal power and individual state's rights, censorship and freedom of expression, would pervade Poe's lifetime.

At the beginning of the new century, the population had reached more than four million. The problems of central control over a burgeoning nation were intensified with the inauguration of Thomas Jefferson in 1801, whose administration had to face major issues of states' rights, economics, expansionism, and military power. In 1803, just as the Napoleonic Wars (1803–15) were beginning in Europe, Jefferson concluded the Louisiana Purchase, doubling the size of the country. Meanwhile, the international status of the United States was becoming even more pronounced. Repeated American victories from 1802 to 1805 over the Barbary Pirates (Algiers, Tunis, Tripoli) strengthened the position of the U.S. Navy. America's coming of age as a world sea power promoted increased exploration of both the Atlantic and the Pacific, including the distant Polar Regions, a topic that would absorb Poe. Another geographical event that would fascinate him was the Lewis and Clark Expedition. From 1804 to 1806, their party traveled up the Missouri River, across the Great Divide, to the Columbia River, and back. Overland explorations of the continent further increased expansionist sentiment among Americans—after all, there were fortunes to be made in the distant West. The establishment of the key fur-trading outpost in Astoria, Oregon, and a trading empire beyond, into the Pacific Ocean, Polynesia, and the Far East—a project Poe would write about in both fiction and nonfiction—would make

John Jacob Astor America's first bona fide multimillionaire. Driven by monetary interests, the widening expansionist view also brought increased federal regulation and taxation. By the time Poe was born in 1809, American nationalism was in full force both at home and abroad. Aaron Burr had recently been tried for treason against the nation, and the Embargo Act, aimed at curtailing British impressment of American sailors, had ratcheted up political tensions with England once again.

In 1810, Poe's second year of life, the Supreme Court under Chief Justice John Marshall, in a monumental legal step, declared that an act of the Georgia Legislature was unconstitutional. This decision (*Fletcher vs. Peck*) extended the precedent (*Marbury vs. Madison* in 1803) of federal jurisdiction over state laws and legislatures—that is, it affirmed the "implied powers" of the Court's judicial review of constitutionality. The sense of the formation of a new nation, under uniform federal law, which would extend farther and farther west, south, and north with exploration and annexation, was accelerating. Although there were counterforces to the expansion of federal powers, War Hawks began to advocate aggression in the Northwest (along the Canadian border) and the Southwest (near the Mexican border).

In 1811, when Poe was three years of age, William Henry Harrison's troops at Tippecanoe broke the power of the Indian Confederation (led by Tecumseh and The Prophet). This loose but powerful American Indian coalition had included an immense territory from the Great Lakes to the Gulf of Mexico. (Poe would satirize the politics of Indian warfare in several of his early stories.) Harrison's victory gave new impetus to American continental nationalism. But there were international problems on the horizon. British guns and ammunition were found among Indian supplies, fanning calls for another war with Britain, which, indeed, broke out in 1812.

Paradoxically, as the sentiment for a unique American tradition separate from European influences intensified, regional conflicts grew. And as the U.S. Supreme Court continued to enlarge its powers of judicial review over the states, the issue of the extension of slavery into new territories was heating up. While the North called for greater jurisdiction over all the states, in the South calls for a separate Southern Country began to appear. Moreover, when Congress failed to recharter the Bank of the United States, regional banks began to multiply rapidly; currencies became highly inflationary, adding economic flames to the coming political conflagration.

Such was the divided and somewhat precarious American world that Edgar Poe came into in 1809; and at the end of Poe's life, America would once again be heading toward revolution. Political, military, and economic crises framed the beginning of Poe's life; another war with the mother country and near financial disaster were central historical events of Poe's early boyhood; and shortly before he turned twenty, alienated from his foster father, Poe would leave the South and head North to join the U.S. Army, carrying with him a sheaf of unpublished romantic poems. At the beginning of the young poet's career, the

perennial economic instability of the early republic was beginning to come to a head—almost at the very moment that Poe, who would never know financial security, was striking out on his own to earn a living as a professional man of letters.

Poe's Early Years: 1809–27

In an American context of increasing divisiveness, Boston-born Edgar Poe, the orphaned son of impoverished itinerant actors, was to be brought up in Richmond, Virginia, as the foster son of a well-to-do Southern merchant. Although an acting career was regarded as rather disreputable, Poe's maternal grandmother, an English actress, had brought Poe's mother to America and immediately put her before the footlights. Young Elizabeth Arnold (c. 1787–1811) made her debut on the American stage at the age of nine. In 1802, at the age of fifteen or sixteen, Elizabeth married another actor, Charles Hopkins, who died three years later of unknown causes. The following spring Elizabeth Arnold Hopkins married David Poe Jr. (1784–1811?), the son of an Irish-born Revolutionary War patriot. David Poe had made his own acting debut at the end of 1803 at the age of nineteen. He was described by contemporaries as somewhat unstable and was reputed to be a heavy drinker. The oldest of the couple's three children, William Henry Leonard, was born on January 30, 1807; Edgar, the middle child, on January 19, 1809; and Rosalie, the youngest, on December 20, 1810. In 1811, the Poes found themselves in Richmond, where Elizabeth, in ill health, died on December 8. The children were promptly taken into the homes of various foster parents. Their father seems to have suddenly disappeared, though there are stories that he died shortly after Elizabeth.

Little Eddie was received into the childless home of a Richmond couple, John Allan (1779–1834) and Frances Keeling Valentine Allan (1785–1829). The Scots-born Allan was co-owner of a profitable import and export business (mainly tobacco and other domestic goods). Although not legally adopted by the couple, the boy was reared as the Allans' son and renamed Edgar Allan Poe. At first, John Allan seemed proud of Eddie's obvious intellect and precocious poetic gifts and used to take great pleasure in showing him off to neighbors. Later, as Eddie grew up and hit puberty, their relationship was to take a marked downward turn.

In 1812, just as the three Poe children were taken into foster homes, war with Britain broke out again. When the Peace of Ghent in 1814 proved advantageous to America, the quest for a national identity intensified. Almost simultaneously, the charter of the Second Bank of the United States forced regional banks to limit their currency issues and to pay full value for them. In 1815, seeking better business opportunities, John Allan took his family to Great Britain—first to Scotland for a brief period, and then to London, where they lived until 1820. The Allans made sure that young Edgar received the founda-

tions of a traditional classical education at British private schools. He first attended an academy run by the Misses Dubourg. In 1818, he became a boarding student at the Manor House School in the Stoke Newington section of suburban London, a site that would imagistically figure in "William Wilson," "The Fall of the House of Usher," and other tales.

While the Allan family was in England, cheap land in the American West had been made available to settlers, and the transportation system was improved. In 1817, work had begun on the Erie Canal with the purpose of connecting New York harbor to the Great Lakes. Westward roads (like the Wilderness Road, the Cumberland Road, the Lancaster Turnpike, and the Genessee Road) began to multiply rapidly. Meanwhile, the expansionist mood manifested itself in the deep South. As part of a conflict with Spain, war against the Seminole Indians in Florida broke out when General Andrew Jackson's troops seized Spanish forts on the peninsula, resulting in 1819 in the sale of Florida by the Spanish to the United States. (These Indian wars and Andrew Jackson would figure, like Harrison, Martin Van Buren, Richard M. Johnson, and others, in Poe's early satires a decade and a half later.)

Conflict over the slavery issue continued. When Missouri applied for admission to the Union in 1818, Congressman James Tallmadge proposed that admission of additional slave states should be prohibited and that the children of slave parents should be freed at the age of twenty-five. The Tallmadge Amendment passed in the House but was defeated in the Senate. The Missouri Compromise of 1820 dictated that slave and free states were to be equal in number. Missouri was to be admitted as a slave state along with Maine as a free state; slavery was to be excluded from Louisiana Purchase territory north of 36° 30', except in Missouri. Such was the intensifying political situation when the Allans returned to Richmond in July 1820.

The Allans saw to it that Edgar, now eleven years of age, continued to receive the best education available. They enrolled him in private academies in Richmond, where he excelled in languages (especially Latin), sports (especially swimming and jumping), amateur theatricals—and pranks. Records show that he composed several verse satires in couplets, all lost except for "O, Tempora! O, Mores!" During these years, he became devoted to Jane Stanard, the mother of a schoolboy friend; he described her later as "the first, purely ideal love of my soul" (she was the inspiration for his 1831 poem "To Helen"). In 1823–24, as Poe entered the middle of his teenage years, two important political events took place: the formulation of the Monroe Doctrine and the founding of the Democratic Party.

The Monroe Doctrine has a complicated history, going back to American efforts in the 1790s to avoid involvement in European politics; related political developments in the 1820s included the issues of nationalism, internationalism, isolationism, expansionism, and regionalism. By 1823 John Quincy Adams (then secretary of state) had become alarmed by the plans of Prince Metternich of Austria for the Quadruple Alliance (Great Britain, Austria, Prussia, and Russia) to re-

store the Spanish colonies in America to King Ferdinand of Spain. Adams was also concerned about the edict of Czar Alexander I extending the boundary of Alaska southward; the czar claimed all rights of exploration for Russia and announced the possible colonization of the western shore of North America. In response, President James Monroe declared that any attempts by European monarchies to expand farther into the American hemisphere would be considered a threat to the peace and safety of the United States. Nevertheless, Monroe and Adams declared, the United States would not interfere with any existing European colonies: the States had no interest in becoming entangled in any conflicts that European nations had with one another. In 1824, Andrew Jackson (nicknamed "Old Hickory" for his stiff military resolve) and several National Republican political leaders (John C. Calhoun, William Harris Crawford, Martin Van Buren) formed a splinter party. They took the name *Democrat* (from *demos*, government of the "people"). The Democrats were to dominate American political life for the next fourteen years.

It was also in 1824, following a two-year period of financial trouble, that John Allan's firm was dissolved. But the death of an uncle in 1825 soon made Allan a much richer man than he had been before. He bought a house in a fashionable quarter of Richmond, and young Edgar began to pay suit to Sarah Elmira Royster. Despite strong objections from both the Roysters and the Allans (in part because of their youth), they became engaged.

In 1826, Poe entered the University of Virginia at Charlottesville, established the preceding year by Thomas Jefferson. He again distinguished himself in ancient and modern romance languages. The rowdy students of the new university were given to heavy drinking, an activity in which Poe also seems to have distinguished himself. It was a problem that was to plague him for the rest of his life. (By an interesting coincidence, the American Temperance Society was formed in Boston in this same year.) The young man soon found the school allowance from his foster parent inadequate, especially if he were to participate in the gentlemanly art of gambling. Poe later claimed that he had to gamble because of Allan's miserliness, but he seems to have lost some $2,000, an enormous sum, equivalent to at least as much as fifteen times that amount today (probably more). Not unreasonably, Allan refused to pay the debt and withdrew him from the university. Poe returned to Richmond to find that he was no longer welcome in the Royster home. (Years later, he was to discover that Elmira's parents had intercepted his letters to her.)

Vituperative arguments between Poe and Allan broke out over various matters, leading eventually to their complete alienation. Indeed, Poe was later to abbreviate his middle name, diminishing *Allan* to the single initial *A*. Part of the problem seems to have been that Edgar had been brought up to expect the life of the son of a Virginia gentleman—or, if not quite an aristocrat, the next best to that—the son of a prosperous merchant. Allan, however, became more and more parsimonious as he became increasingly disaffected with his headstrong

ward. Despite Frances Allan's efforts at conciliation, Poe stormed out of the Allan household in March of 1827. In doing so, he forfeited family and class, perhaps perversely.

Nationalism, sectionalism, and regionalism—the young Poe was suspicious of all such politics. Southerner he was—American he would be—but, as he dreamed of a literary career, nothing less than worldwide fame would satisfy him. Under the alias of "Henri Le Rennet," he sailed for Boston and a larger world.

Cast Adrift: 1827–34

As the population of the United States neared thirteen million, transportation received special attention: the final phase of the Erie Canal began, and in 1827 the Baltimore & Ohio Rail Road received its charter. The second half of the decade of the 1820s also saw significant shifts in the relationship between political power and social class—changes of which the young Poe as a fledgling Virginia gentleman did not fully approve. During the administration of John Quincy Adams (1825–29), frontier democracy in the West eroded the power of money and privilege. At the same time, Northeastern laboring men (who had voting rights in every state but Rhode Island) campaigned for free public education, for the abolition of imprisonment for debt, for equitable mechanic's lien laws, and for the right to collective bargaining. Democratization and a version of socialism, suspect developments for most Southerners of station and means, were on the rise.

Such was the general condition of the country when in May 1827 young Poe, needful of an income, enlisted in the U.S. Army. He gave his name as "Edgar A. Perry," his age as twenty-two (he was eighteen), and his occupation as "clerk." He was assigned to a coastal artillery regiment at Fort Independence in Boston Harbor. By summer, he had somehow persuaded a young printer to publish his first book, *Tamerlane and Other Poems*—not by a Virginian, but by "a Bostonian." This was a thin volume of fewer than a dozen dreamy pieces. In addition to the title work, it included such poems as "Dreams," "Visit of the Dead," "Evening Star," and "Imitation" (later revised as "A Dream within a Dream").

In November 1827, Poe's unit was transferred to Fort Moultrie, on Sullivan's Island (the scene of "The Gold-Bug" years later), in the harbor of Charleston, South Carolina. After several rapid promotions, Poe reached the rank of sergeant major, the highest noncommissioned rank in the army. With a career as a commissioned officer in mind, he asked Allan to help him obtain an appointment to the Military Academy at West Point. Mrs. Allan was ill, and John Allan's attitude toward Edgar softened somewhat. The death of Frances Allan on February 28, 1829, prompted a temporary reconciliation between Poe and Allan. In April, having found a replacement enlistee, Poe was able to resign his noncommissioned position in the army. He went to live with various relatives in Baltimore to await word about his expected West Point

appointment. There is an unsubstantiated story (which some critics have taken as evidence of his Southern racism) that Poe may have acted as an agent for his paternal aunt, Maria Clemm, in the indenturing of a Negro slave named Edwin to one Henry Ridgway for a period of nine years.

During this time, Poe wrote Allan for money to subsidize a second volume of poems, seeking to mollify him by adding: "I have long given up Byron for a model." Allan refused to help him; nevertheless, *Al Aaraaf, Tamerlane and Minor Poems* was published by Hatch & Dunning of Baltimore in December 1829. This edition generally maintained the romantic, dreamy, and visionary quality of Poe's earlier poems, but the faint comic note of the first volume was now more noticeable. The *Al Aaraaf* volume contained a half-dozen new works added to the revised *Tamerlane* poems, including "Sonnet—To Science," "Fairy-Land," and a verse "Preface" (later to be expanded as the seriocomic "Introduction" for the 1831 edition of poems, and yet later to be reduced as "Romance"). Poe set the title poem (named for the Muslim limbo region of Al Aaraaf, where souls sleepily wait for yet another world) in a dreamlike star world out in space. Here poets and their poetic imaginings, banished from the earthly world, have ethereal existence.

In the more mundane world of the United States, Poe's appointment to West Point finally came through, and he entered the academy in May of 1830, where he once again excelled in languages. He soon became popular among cadets for his comic verses satirizing the officers. In October of the same year John Allan remarried and shortly afterward forever severed relations with his foster son, ostensibly because of an offensive letter (dated May 3, 1830) that Poe had sent to his army replacement in the enlisted corps, one Sergeant Samuel (Bully) Graves. In it Poe tried to explain his failure to send Graves the whole fee for standing in for him; his foster parent, he said, had not yet come forth with the money, adding that "Mr. A. is not very often sober." Graves wrote Allan for the money and apparently either enclosed Poe's letter or revealed its contents.

Once more Poe found himself without the kind of financial assistance a young Virginia gentleman might have come to expect. Embarrassed among the class of more or less aristocratic officer candidates, he intentionally disobeyed orders so as to obtain his release from the academy. These infractions consisted of absence from class, chapel, and roll call, though there is an unsubstantiated tradition that he also appeared in formation naked, wearing only the cross-straps of the uniform. In January 1831, he underwent the formality of what appears to have been a friendly court-martial and was expelled.

In February 1831, he relocated temporarily to New York City. With funds donated by fellow cadets, he was able in the spring to publish *Poems: Second Edition*, by "Edgar A. Poe," a volume he dedicated to "The U.S. Corps of Cadets." This work (in which the apocalyptic note is somewhat greater) included extensive revisions of "Tamerlane" and "Al Aaraaf" and a half-dozen new poems in much the same mode

as his previous lyrics: "To Helen," "Israfel," "The Doomed City" (later revised as "The City in the Sea"), "Irene" (later revised as "The Sleeper"), "A Paean" (revised as "Lenore"), and "The Valley Nis" (revised as "The Valley of Unrest"). In addition, the volume included his first published critical statement, a prose introduction titled "Letter to Mr ———." This somewhat complicated text was later revised as "Letter to Mr. B———," which satirizes romantic poetry and aesthetics while also expounding a high romantic view of literary art as passionate and yet otherworldly.

If Poe's life was a bit tumultuous in the late 1820s and early 1830s, the national life of the country was more so. Perhaps the single most sensational event in the South was Nat Turner's Rebellion in Poe's beloved Virginia. On August 21, 1831, Turner, a black slave, received what he considered a commandment from God and led a revolt that resulted in the deaths of sixty or more white people, including women and children, some of whom were brutally hacked to pieces. About one hundred black people were killed with equal brutality when the white population put down the rebellion. Evading capture for over six weeks, Turner and a dozen or so others were eventually caught and hanged. The episode rocked the foundations (and the mythology) of the "peculiar institution" of slavery in the South. But it also set back the work of emancipation groups. The state of Virginia had come to be regarded by abolitionists (both North and South) as the "breeding ground" for slavery (derogatorily called the "swamp" of blackness). This concern had caused the state legislature to debate the abolishment of slavery—the viability of which now came to an abrupt end. Given current critical interpretations of the implicit racism of some of Poe's texts, it is notable (one way or another) that he says nothing about this momentous and controversial event.

There were other major political controversies; the first administration of Andrew Jackson (1829–32) saw several. Some were of a more personal nature than others, involving assessments of the character of the president. These included the introduction of the "spoils system" (personal reward for political favors), the formation of the president's private personal council (the ad hoc "kitchen cabinet"), and the public scandal known as the "Eaton malaria" (see notes to "King Pest," pp. 148ff. herein). More purely political was the proposal to remove all American Indian tribes to an area west of the Mississippi River. Already in progress was the transfer of electoral powers from state legislators to representatives elected for the purpose. More dissension arose when Jackson disagreed with Calhoun over protective tariffs, majority rule, and states' rights. Calhoun was an advocate of Nullification—the issue of whether a state had the right to declare federal statutes null and void within its boundaries—a position that Jackson opposed. Jackson also clashed with Henry Clay. Jackson was opposed to the continuation of the National Bank of the United States, but in 1831 Clay persuaded Nicholas Biddle to apply to Congress for the renewal of the charter of the bank before its expiration date. In the Jackson–Clay campaign, Jackson would be re-elected. But in the

next five years, the unresolved monetary and banking policies stemming from the conflict would lead to a nationwide financial crash—one that would directly affect Poe and his family.

In this political climate, the penniless Poe left New York in May 1831 and took refuge in the Baltimore home of his aunt, Maria Clemm, a single mother with an eight-year-old daughter named Virginia. The household also included Poe's brother, William Henry (who was to die in August, probably of tuberculosis), and his grandmother Elizabeth Cairnes Poe, whose small pension from her late husband's Revolutionary War service helped keep the nearly destitute family afloat. While living in the Clemm household, Poe acted as a tutor to his little cousin Virginia and continued to pursue his writing career.

During this time, he submitted several tales to a contest announced by the Philadelphia *Saturday Courier*. The *Courier* published five of his tales at regular intervals from January to December in 1832: "Metzengerstein," "The Duke de L'Omelette," "A Tale of Jerusalem," "A Decided Loss" (the first version of "Loss of Breath"), and "The Bargain Lost" (the first version of "Bon-Bon"). With the possible exception of "Metzengerstein," these were all satiric parodies of popular genres and authors.

He also submitted six other stories for a prize announced in the Baltimore *Saturday Visiter*: "Some Passages in the Life of a Lion" (revised as "Lionizing"), "The Visionary" (revised as "The Assignation"), "Shadow," "Epimanes," "Siope" (revised as "Silence"), and "Ms. Found in a Bottle." Except for "Lionizing" (a satire on literary salons), these tales all seem to be, at least on the surface, serious romantic and visionary works, though a case has been made for a satiric component in each of them. "Ms.," based on the legend of the *Flying Dutchman* (the phantom ship doomed to roam the seas for eternity), won the first prize of $50. Poe also submitted the poem "The Coliseum," an evocation of the grandeur of the ancient world, which won an honorary second prize.

In May 1833, Poe wrote to the publishers of the *New England Magazine* about a unified volume of sequential tales he had tentatively titled "Eleven Tales of the Arabesque." He included a story-sketch that he thought was representative of the volume as a whole, "Epimanes" (later called "Four Beasts in One—The Homocameleopard"), an overtly comic work with many satiric thrusts at nineteenth-century concepts of progress and at American democracy as "mobocracy." This never-published volume Poe apparently intended as a large-scale parody. The whole series of tales and sketches, Poe explained in his letter to the editors, was not only an imitation of contemporary styles of tale writing, but also a burlesque of current modes of criticism:

> They are supposed to be read at table by the eleven members of a literary club, and are followed by the remarks of the company upon each. These remarks are intended as a burlesque upon criticism. In the whole, originality more than anything else has been attempted. . . . If you like the specimen which I have sent I will

forward the rest at your suggestion—but if you decide upon pub-
lishing all the tales, it would not be proper to print the one I now
send until it can be printed in its place with the others.

In October 1833, the *Visiter* published the prize-winning "Ms.
Found in a Bottle" and "The Coliseum," along with an advertisement
soliciting subscriptions to a volume to be called *Tales of the Folio
Club*. The "Folio Club" was an expansion of the scheme of the "Eleven
Tales of the Arabesque," also never published as an interconnected
whole. Many critics have come to regard the Folio Club plan as cen-
trally important for a full and balanced view of Poe's art in fiction. The
Folio Club survives in a fragmentary manuscript that contains only the
preface and the concluding tale, "Siope" ("Silence"). This manuscript
is all that remains of a relatively lengthy collection of tales that Poe
unsuccessfully sent to various publishers over the next three years.

He conceived of the Folio Club as a "Junto of Dunderheadism." The
club meets once a month at dinner for a reading by each member of "a
short tale of his own composition." The author of "the best tale" be-
comes "president for the month," while the author of "the worst tale"
provides dinner and wine for the next meeting. The writer of the pref-
ace represents himself as offering an exposé of the group after attend-
ing his first meeting. The intention of the club, the narrator says, is "to
abolish Literature, subvert the Press, and overturn the Government of
Nouns and Pronouns." The membership includes, besides the newly
elected author of the preface, ten "most remarkable men," such as
"Mr. Convolvulus Gondola," "De Rerum Natura, Esqr.," "Mr. Solomon
Seadrift who had every appearance of a fish," "Mr. Blackwood Black-
wood who had written certain articles for foreign magazines," and so
forth. A good deal of scholarly speculation has ensued about which of
the fictitious "authors" are to be assigned to the various tales (such as
Horribile Dictu to "Metzengerstein," Chronologos Chronology to "A
Tale of Jerusalem," Solomon Seadrift to "Ms. Found in a Bottle," and
so on). The document has also generated critical debate over the im-
plications of the Folio Club manuscript for Poe's overall intentions in
his earliest tales—that is, about how serious, satiric, comic, or ironic
these works were intended to be.

Back to Old Virginia: 1834–37

In January 1834, Poe's tale "The Visionary" appeared in *Godey's Lady's
Book*—his first publication in a journal of wide circulation. In March
1834 John Allan died. Although both legitimate and illegitimate chil-
dren were mentioned in his will, Poe was not. Fortunately, however,
one of the judges in the *Visiter* contest, John P. Kennedy, had taken an
interest in young Poe's career. But when Kennedy invited him to din-
ner, Poe was forced to decline, "for reasons of the most humiliating
nature in my personal appearance"—which prompted Kennedy to lend
him money for suitable clothes. Kennedy also recommended Poe to

Thomas White, the publisher of the new literary journal, the *Southern Literary Messenger*, back in Richmond.

White soon offered the young man a position with the magazine. Although Poe was not to move to Richmond until summer, he immediately began, from March 1835 forward, to contribute creative works and book reviews to the *Messenger*. These included several poems; the first part of a verse drama, *Politian*; and five new tales, "Morella," "Berenice," "King Pest," "Shadow," and his first long narrative, "Hans Phaall." Whereas *Politian*, "Morella," and "Shadow" appeared to be serious poetic evocations in the high dark-romantic style, the grotesque stories "Berenice" and "King Pest" were more problematic. "Berenice," by Poe's own testimony in a letter to Thomas White, seems to have been, gruesome as it is, a literary spoof of the kind of tale that was representative, in his opinion, of the popular literature of his time.

> The history of all Magazines shows plainly that those which have attained celebrity were indebted for it to articles *similar in nature—to Berenice*. . . . You ask me in what does the nature consist? In the ludicrous heightened into the grotesque: the fearful coloured into the horrible: the witty exaggerated into the burlesque: the singular wrought out into the strange and mystical.

"King Pest," misunderstood by many of Poe's contemporaries, was an allegorical satire (indeed, a somewhat vicious one) directed at Andrew Jackson and his Kitchen Cabinet, in which Poe suggested that the "reign" of King Andrew and his "court" has created a vile "*pest*ilence" in American political life (see notes to "King Pest," p. 148 herein).

In July 1835 Grandmother Poe died. In August, Edgar Poe went to Richmond, where he began to concentrate on becoming a professional "magazinist." He threw himself into his work. During his first nine months with the *Messenger*, he wrote a column on current literary events, and the number of his book reviews climbed to more than thirty. With this new vehicle of a vigorous southern magazine, he launched a campaign for a free and independent criticism—one that was to be on the world stage rather than a merely regional or national one. Although he noted that the South saw no "farther necessity for being ridden to death by New-England," he also commented that the real goal of American letters should be "a national as distinguished from a sectional literature." But even a national literature was not the true issue. He had earlier noted the many arguments in favor of maintaining a "proper nationality in American Letters." But "what this nationality is, or what is to be gained by it," he said, "has never been distinctly understood. That an American should confine himself to American themes, or even prefer them, is rather a political than a literary idea."

In addition to this cosmopolitan sensibility, Poe's outrage over the politics of publishing manifested itself in his first reviews in a sarcastic mode that seemed to some of his Northern contemporaries unnecessarily barbed. But these reviews helped sell copies of the *Messenger* and alerted Northern literary circles to the new, prickly tongued critic

from the Southern provinces. From his small platform in Richmond, Poe took direct aim at the Boston and New York literary establishments, especially for their habit of "puffing" the books of friends and colleagues. One of their favorite devices was to announce a new book by an anonymous writer of great talent, then to advertise the book in the papers they controlled with a guessing game about the author's identity.

Poe attacked this practice from the first. Noting that the New York *Mirror* had identified the author of the novel *Norman Leslie* as Theodore S. Fay and that Fay was an editor of the New York *Mirror*, Poe blasted the novel as the "silliest" book he had ever read. It was, he said, "a monstrous piece of absurdity and incongruity," with an incomprehensible plot and characters that "have no character." This satiric send-up of Fay's novel, precise and detailed, sounded a disturbing note in American criticism—one unafraid of the cliques and the publishing establishment. Poe's caustic reviews, combined with his continuing attacks on the Northern coteries that controlled both publishing and critical reviewing, quickly brought him and the *Messenger* to the attention of a wider audience. His sharpness of insight and acerbity of tone began to earn him the reputation of the "tomahawk man" from the South. With the increase in the circulation and reputation of the *Messenger* (though Poe was later to exaggerate the extent of both), White decided to hire Poe as an editorial assistant and made him the magazine's principal book reviewer.

Meanwhile, back in Baltimore, Maria Clemm was hinting that Virginia might move into the home of Neilson Poe, Edgar's second cousin, whom he regarded with apprehension. Whether Edgar Poe was suspicious of Neilson's character or suspected that Neilson did not approve of him, Poe promptly (almost hysterically) wrote to ask for Virginia's hand in marriage, protesting that if Virginia were taken into Neilson's home he might never see her again. In September, Poe went to Baltimore, where he may have secretly married Virginia, though a public ceremony would take place the following spring. In October 1835, with high hopes for the future, Poe returned to Richmond with Virginia and Mrs. Clemm. But Poe's drinking had already begun to cause problems, and White had written him a letter warning that any further episodes (especially drinking in the morning) would cost him his job. Poe apparently modified his drinking, for in December White offered him the editorship of the now flourishing magazine.

In a pattern that was to manifest itself during the rest of his life, Poe's improved position was not to last. For one thing, the country, like Poe himself, continually flirted with financial insolvency. During his second administration (1833–37), President Jackson had begun to remove federal deposits from the Bank of the United States and place them instead in selected regional banks. The country then experienced a rapid expansion of unsecured credit through state banks for investments in the land boom of 1835–36. Flushed with expansionist zeal, the Mexican province of Texas proclaimed its independence on the grounds that U.S. emigrants had settled it. But the bottom was

about to fall out of the U.S. economy. With inflation intensified by the influx of foreign investors, massive speculation took place. In 1836, Jackson issued the "Species Circular," which forbade federal land offices to take anything but approved specie in payment. Millennialists began to predict the imminent Second Coming of Christ at the same time that the State Asylum for the Insane was founded at Worcester, Massachusetts. The Great Panic of 1836–37 began when European creditors started to call in U.S. obligations; the Eastern banks called in their loans to Western and Southern banks; the national government called in its biggest depository obligations. By 1837, banks were closing or suspending specie payments. Factories and shops began to close. The country also experienced a massive crop failure.

It was in this unfortunate climate that Poe, with his usual mistiming, married Virginia Clemm in a public ceremony in May 1836, when she was not quite fourteen. Just as the economic situation of the country was at its worst, Poe moved, took a new job with an untried and underfinanced firm, and decided to marry. Although the fact that Mrs. Clemm was to live with Edgar and Virginia as housekeeper would alleviate some of the difficulties, Poe would now be responsible for two women.

Needing to provide for his little family—and ambitious for literary success—Poe worked even harder to make the *Messenger* a leading journal. One indication of his efforts is the large number of reviews he wrote in the course of 1836—over eighty. Among them was another scorching satire taking dead aim at the power groups in the big Northern cities. Indeed, Poe's superlative contempt for Fay's *Norman Leslie* would be exceeded by his disdain for Morris Matson's novel *Paul Ulric*. This book was another Northern clique-sponsored novel, and Poe observed that "when we called Norman Leslie the silliest book in the world we certainly had never seen Paul Ulric." Such books, he asserted, would "bring daily discredit upon our national literature."

A few months later, Poe scathingly responded to the outraged protests against this new "Southern wasp," which were running with increasing frequency in the New York *Mirror* and other Northern papers. He prefaced his assessment of the poems of Joseph Rodman Drake and Fitz-Greene Halleck with remarks on "the present state of American criticism," which, he suggested, was at a nadir. At one time, Americans "cringed to foreign opinion" and would not read an American book without European sanction. But now Americans have gone too far in the opposite direction: we "often find ourselves involved in the gross paradox of liking a stupid book the better, because, sure enough, its stupidity is American." Praise from personal, regional, or national bias brings no credit to American literature, he said. Only honest and unprejudiced criticism will gain the respect of the world. Other of his reviews included, besides attacks on writers now forgotten, two praising the earliest work of Dickens, along with exercises in critical definition. He also printed or reprinted (often with significant revisions) most of his stories and poems in the *Messenger's* pages.

Despite his position with the *Messenger*, Poe's family was still very

poor, in part due to the growing monetary crisis of the nation as a whole. Among the stratagems to improve their situation was a plan to borrow money from relatives for a boarding house to be run by Mrs. Clemm. Poe also planned a suit against the U.S. government to recover war loans made by his grandfather. Neither plan was successful. At this time, Poe was still trying to obtain a publisher for an integrated book-length volume of his tales. But despite the assistance of White and James Kirke Paulding, he was unable to find a publisher. The firm of Harper & Brothers wrote him that "readers in this country have a decided and strong preference for works . . . in which a single and connected story occupies the whole volume"—in other words, a novel.

Poe now became involved in disputes with White over editorial independence and his salary (approximately $10 a week). Perhaps Poe was insufficiently aware of the dire economic condition of the country: the panic of 1836–37 was about to wash over them. In any event, these disagreements led to his resignation from the *Messenger* in January 1837. Poe moved his small family to New York while he sought a new position. It was to be two years before he would find another editorship.

Return to New York: 1837–38

To help make ends meet, Mrs. Clemm managed a boarding house, while Poe did freelance editing and continued to write. He published several poems and stories, including the comic tale "Von Jung the Mystic," the two satiric companion stories "How to Write a Blackwood Article" and "The Scythe of Time" (later retitled "A Predicament"), and "Ligeia" (singled out by Poe as "my best tale"). Following the advice of Harper & Brothers, he resumed work on a long continuous narrative, two short installments of which had first appeared in the *Messenger*. This work became Poe's only full-length novel, *The Narrative of Arthur Gordon Pym*, detailing a journey to the South Pole, which Harper published in July 1838. Although he was himself fascinated by polar exploration, Poe was clearly seeking to capitalize on current excitement over the very recent Antarctic explorations of Americans like Jeremiah N. Reynolds and Charles Wilkes. Beginning in a more or less realistic mode, the story of *Pym* becomes increasingly fantastic, culminating in a mysterious indefinitive "revelation" at the Pole. Reviewers in America and Great Britain immediately questioned the credibility of the book: was it fictional or true? The controversy increased Poe's public visibility.

In the twentieth century, *Arthur Gordon Pym*—with its journey ever farther "south" and its insistent bifurcation between whiteness and blackness in the landscape and seascape of the nether world below the equator—would become a touchstone for highly speculative racialist interpretations. While Poe was associated with the *Southern Literary Messenger*, a favorable review of two books defending slavery appeared in its pages. Some twentieth-century critics have too confidently at-

tributed the so-called Drayton-Paulding review to Poe, whereas the available evidence strongly suggests that it was written by Nathaniel Beverley Tucker. These socially conscious critics have tried to use the review as a basis for interpreting *Pym* as a racist allegory of a divided America, told from an anxious and hostile "Southern" point of view. Even though the historical basis claimed for Poe's racism is not firm, the fact that the review was probably not Poe's does not totally negate such interpretations; and the review and several commentaries and interpretations are included in the present volume.

Philadelphia: 1839–43

In the last years of the 1830s, the Whigs had emerged as an important political group out of those National Republicans allied with Adams and Clay. They included anti-Jackson conservatives, native-born Americans hostile to foreign emigrants, and states' rights advocates angry with the Democrats because of Jackson's antinullification stand. The Whigs also blamed Jackson and Van Buren for the current economic depression. Despite Whig attempts to throw the election into the House of Representatives, Jackson's party and his candidate, Martin Van Buren, prevailed. Jacksonian Democrats would control the White House for another four years.

In July 1839 Poe moved his family to Philadelphia, where he continued to freelance. Poor and still unable to secure an editorship, he considered giving up literary work altogether. Desperate for money, he became involved in a dubious publishing venture, agreeing for $50 to let his name appear as author of another man's work, a shell-collecting manual by Thomas Wyatt, retitled *The Conchologist's First Book*. At this time he also began the first series of what were to be very popular solutions to cryptograms in *Alexander's Weekly Messenger*.

Poe's persistence in seeking an editorial position paid off when he made the acquaintance of William Burton, an actor and publisher, with whom he negotiated a job with the *Gentleman's Magazine*, to begin in May 1839. The major point that Burton insisted on was the acceptance of his policies as founder and owner of the magazine—a matter that later became an issue between the two. Another contractual point was that Poe was to contribute at least one signed feature for each issue and write most of the reviews. Among his first contributions were "The Man That Was Used Up" (another satire on the political "heroes" of the "Indian Wars") and two stories of doubles, "The Fall of the House of Usher" and "William Wilson."

Late in 1839, the Philadelphia firm of Lea and Blanchard published *Tales of the Grotesque and Arabesque* in two volumes. This work included the twenty-five stories Poe had written up to that time. Shortly afterward, serialization of the unsigned "Journal of Julius Rodman," a narrative of a journey into the far reaches of the American West, began in the January 1840 *Gentleman's Magazine*. But the long story ended abruptly in June. Poe left it unfinished because a quarrel with

Burton erupted over (among other things) editorial control, the very thing Burton had insisted on, and Burton summarily dismissed Poe. Deciding that he had to have total authority, or at least total editorial control, Poe printed up a subscription "Prospectus" for what he hoped would become his own magazine.

Since his *Messenger* days, Poe had campaigned for what he called a national "republic" of letters, in which unbiased assessments of contemporary literature would become the norm, rather than the current kowtowing to regional interests and large commercial publishing hegemonies. Poe's effort to shape the *Messenger* into his ideal of a literary magazine had, however, evoked Southern political opposition to his dictum of impartiality and resulted in interference with his editorial policies. When he moved north, the pattern repeated itself with two projected ventures: *The Penn Magazine* and its slightly later version, *The Stylus*. (*Penn* is a pun on *Pennsylvania* and *pen*; the word *stylus*, a sharp, pointed iron instrument, a kind of pen, continues the pun.) The revised prospectus for the *Stylus* promised "an absolutely independent criticism" guided "by the purest rules of Art," a criticism "aloof from all personal bias" and steadfastly opposed to "the arrogance of organized cliques." Poe's ideal magazine would "endeavor to support the general interests of the republic of letters, without reference to particular regions." To achieve these things, he had to be free from both Northern and Southern bias, while simultaneously encompassing both traditions—no easy task, but a necessary one given Poe's concept of the professional man of letters. Even America itself was too provincial a concept; instead, "the world at large" was "the true audience of the author." But neither *The Penn* nor *The Stylus* attracted enough subscribers to go into production.

In November 1840, Burton sold his magazine to George Graham, who united it with his own magazine, *The Casket*, to form *Graham's Magazine*. Despite their quarrel earlier in the year, Burton had apparently recommended Poe to Graham. Poe's relations with the new owner were at first cordial, and he was happier with Graham than he had been with Burton. In December 1840, Poe contributed "The Man of the Crowd," a dark tale about a mysterious urban wanderer, to the new magazine. The narrator thinks that he is able to "read" the various social classes and occupations of people in the crowded city, just by looking—except for one person who is singularly different and who remains unreadable. Early in 1841, Poe became an associate editor of *Graham's* at an annual salary of $800, just over $15 a week, which, beginning with the April 1841 issue, would be supplemented by extra payment for literary pieces. While in this position, Poe contributed several stories to *Graham's*, including the more or less visionary sketches "The Island of the Fay" and "The Colloquy of Monos and Una," and the curious "Never Bet the Devil Your Head." The "Devil" story, though told in the naive style of a children's fable, is an oblique and subtle satire on American Transcendentalism and on the transcendentalist style of writing.

Poe also contributed what appeared to be a new kind of fiction.

"The Murders in the Rue Morgue" and "A Descent into the Mael-ström" are the first specimens of what he called "tales of ratiocina-tion": mysteries in which one of the main interests is an explanation of or a solution to an inexplicable situation, which is arrived at step by step, carefully laid out in the narrative. In the case of the detective story per se, the solution is achieved by reasoning backward from an effect to a cause (from the crime to the criminal). In the course of de-veloping this genre, Poe created two main figures: the memorable French detective C. Auguste Dupin, who combines logical analysis with poetic intuition, and his less perceptive sidekick, a narrator friend who must have everything patiently explained to him. (This fictional mode and the two principal figures were developed more elaborately late in the nineteenth century by Arthur Conan Doyle into Sherlock Holmes and Dr. Watson.) Poe also created a small sensation when, in a review in the *Saturday Evening Post*, he correctly predicted the iden-tity of the murderer from the first installments of Charles Dickens's serialized mystery *Barnaby Rudge*. Later, during his American tour, Dickens met with Poe and expressed admiration for his ratiocinative abilities. The ratiocinative tales were especially popular, and by the end of the year, subscriptions to *Graham's* had risen noticeably (though, characteristically, Poe would exaggerate the numbers).

Throughout 1841, Poe not only continued to produce new works, like the visionary love story "Eleonora" (published in the Christmas annual, *The Gift*), but also developed various other special feature pieces. One of the most popular was his continuing series on cryptog-raphy; another was what he called "autography" (the analysis of auto-graphs of well-known people). Simultaneously, he turned again to the idea of editorial control of his own magazine, a project he rather naively hoped Graham would support financially. He asked Washing-ton Irving, James Fenimore Cooper, William Cullen Bryant, James P. Kennedy, and others for regular contributions.

In 1842, Poe's publications included the famous prose tone-poem evoking universal death and decay, "The Masque of the Red Death," and a complimentary review in *Graham's* of Hawthorne's *Twice-told Tales*—an essay that was to become a touchstone for the definition of the short story. In addition, he published a detective story based on newspaper accounts of a then unsolved real-life murder, "The Mystery of Marie Rogêt," along with a different kind of ratiocinative tale, "The Pit and the Pendulum," in which the protagonist attempts to figure out by careful logical analysis how he can escape from a sealed torture chamber. He also published a narrative sketch on the aesthetics of natural artifice, "The Landscape Garden"; the man-made garden is beautiful, but irreducible natural properties resist the artificial illu-sion.

On the one hand, things had never been better professionally. In 1842, at the age of thirty-two, he seemed to have his drinking under control, he was secure in his job, he was decently paid, he had edito-rial authority, he was productive, and he was well known and re-spected. On the other hand, the year also had a strong downside, and

most of the time he was anxious and generally depressed. In May, he quarreled with Graham over editorial control and resigned from the magazine. (He was succeeded by Rufus Wilmot Griswold, the man, who, after Poe's death, was to become his unscrupulous literary executor and detractor.) Unable to interest a publisher in an expanded edition of *Tales of the Grotesque and Arabesque,* Poe set to work on a new scheme: a revised two-volume collection of stories to be titled *Phantasy-Pieces* (in imitation of the German "*Phantasiestücke*"). But once again, he was unable to find a publisher for a collection of stories. More immediately important was Virginia's deteriorating health. In mid-January she had burst a blood vessel while singing, apparently a sign of the tuberculosis that was weakening her entire system. She never fully recovered. For the next five years, her health alternated between relatively good days and bouts of severe illness. Poe's letters record his anguish over her condition and their poverty (one winter Virginia apparently had only Edgar's greatcoat for a blanket and a large tortoiseshell cat to keep her chest warm).

During this time, Poe seems to have become quietly involved in Whig politics. He did volunteer work for the party, but his political affiliation was apparently somewhat nonconformist—and was perhaps opportunistic. Conservative in political orientation, Poe was skeptical of political motive and all claims of "progress," but he seems to have found compromise Whig leaders acceptable as an alternative to Jacksonianism, which struck him as the politics of mob rule and demogoguery. And yet Poe also found the political candidacy of noncontroversial war heroes somewhat absurd (see notes to "Loss of Breath," pp. 89ff. herein; "King Pest," pp. 148ff.; and "The Man That Was Used Up," pp. 190ff.). The Whig compromise candidate for president was the unprepossessing William Henry Harrison, hero of the Battle of Tippecanoe. Certainly the Whigs' public relations strategy was absurd enough. Knowing that they were perceived as affluent and privileged and more or less indifferent to the problems of the working classes, they tried to identify themselves as the party of "the people" by wearing coonskin caps, displaying models of log cabins, and drinking cider from barrels. The Whigs chose John Tyler of Virginia, an advocate of states' rights, as their compromise candidate for vice president. The campaign slogan of "Tippecanoe and Tyler, too" became famous, along with the label of the Hard Cider and Log Cabin Campaign. Harrison was elected the ninth president of the United States; when he died after only five weeks in office, Tyler became president in April 1841. Poe sensed a chance of getting a government post, for he was acquainted with Tyler's son, Robert. A government post would provide a secure income for his family and still leave him time to write (others were doing it, notably Hawthorne, as surveyor for the Salem Custom-House). Poe began to send out feelers to various friends and acquaintances who might put in a good word for him.

Tyler himself found the basic Whig positions too conservative, and he had made no secret of his own independently minded stance. Even

though disagreeing with certain Jacksonian principles, Tyler had earlier, albeit reluctantly, supported Jackson as the least objectionable of the various candidates. Now he tried to avoid being drawn into the attack on Jackson, then led by Clay and Daniel Webster. Henry Clay had announced the essential planks of the Whig platform in the election campaign: opposition to an independent treasury, formation of a new Bank of the United States, protective tariffs, and distribution to the states of money from sales of federal lands. Although Tyler eventually accepted a radically altered version of Clay's Program (thereby alienating many in his cabinet), he was so estranged that for a while he entertained the notion of a third party to be composed of disaffected Whigs and new Democrats. Some of the tensions were eased, however, when Tyler appointed Calhoun secretary of state. Meanwhile, difficulties with the British continued, even though the Webster-Ashburton Treaty had effected an international understanding on two important points; these were the controversy over the Canadian boundary with Maine and the issue of British searches of American ships suspected of engaging in the slave trade off the African coast. But the annexation of Texas was to be the major political issue for Tyler's administration. In an undeclared war, American troops defeated Santa Anna at the Battle of San Jacinto in 1843, and American calls for annexation of the Texas territory accelerated.

In the same year as Santa Anna's first major defeat by U.S. partisans, Poe was invited by James Russell Lowell to contribute regularly to his new magazine, *The Pioneer*. In its pages, he published the story "The Tell-Tale Heart," a study in the perversity of murder and guilt; the poem "Lenore"; and an essay on English versification later titled "The Rationale of Verse"; but the magazine failed after three issues. Following up on the successful inquiries he had made, Poe went to Washington, D.C., in March 1843 to be interviewed for a minor job in the Tyler administration (and to solicit subscriptions for *The Stylus*). Perversely, he went on a drunken binge, turned up disheveled with his cloak turned inside out, and thus ruined his chances for the position. Friends had to assist him to the train for his return trip to Philadelphia.

Despite this setback, he continued his large output of stories, poems, and reviews. Ever in need of money, he tried to borrow from Griswold and Lowell. In June, some relief came when "The Gold-Bug" won a $100 prize in the Philadelphia *Dollar Newspaper* contest. The story became an overnight sensation; multiple reprintings and a dramatized version gave Poe a taste of real fame for a time. Riding the crest of his current popularity, he was able to convince a publisher (the Philadelphia magazine agent William H. Graham) to announce a pamphlet series, *The Prose Romances of Edgar A. Poe*. The first number appeared in July (it included only two works, "The Murders in the Rue Morgue" and "The Man That Was Used Up"); but the series was not a success, and no further numbers were issued. "The Black Cat" (a classic tale of perversity) and "Diddling Considered as One of the Exact

Sciences" (a *jeu d'esprit* on con artists and con games) were published later in the year. In November 1843, Poe began a lecture circuit titled "The Poets and Poetry of America."

Return to the New York Literary Scene: 1844–47

On a rainy day in April 1844, Poe abruptly took Virginia, by train and steamboat, to New York City. On April 7, he wrote Maria Clemm (who would join them sometime in May) that they had found a boarding house ("the cheapest board I ever knew") where the food was excellent and abundant. It is one of Poe's most touching letters, full of hope, but clearly revealing their rather desperate circumstances:

> Last night, for supper, we had the nicest tea you ever drank, strong & hot—wheat bread & rye bread—cheese—tea-cakes (elegant) a great dish (2 dishes) of elegant ham, and 2 of cold veal, piled up like a mountain and large slices of the cakes, and every thing in the greatest profusion. No fear of starving here.

The letter twice mentions that Virginia ("Sissy") had coughed very little and continues the enumeration of the food and drink:

> For breakfast we had excellent-flavored coffe[e], hot & strong . . . veal cutlets, elegant ham & eggs & nice bread and butter. I never sat down to a more plentiful or a nicer breakfast. I wish you could have seen the eggs—and the great dishes of meat. I ate the first hearty breakfast I have eaten since I left our little home. Sis is delighted, and we are both in excellent spirits. She has coughed hardly any and had no night sweat. . . . The fire kept in all night.

Poe also comments on their cash supply and his drinking:

> We have now got 4 $ and a half left. Tomorrow I am going to try & borrow 3 $—so that I may have a fortnight to go upon. I feel in excellent spirits & have'nt drank a drop—so that I hope [soon] to get out of trouble. The very instant I scrape together enough money I will send it on.

On April 13, 1844, Poe pulled off a successful hoax in the New York *Sun* about a balloon journey across the Atlantic. A contemporary account described him standing in front of the editorial offices of the *Sun*, ironically warning the purchasers of the paper that the story was a fake. Still planning for *The Stylus* despite past frustrations, he envisaged a wide audience that would include the "well-educated men . . . among the innumerable plantations of our vast Southern & Western Countries." Although it is clear that he meant that he wanted a readership that went beyond the East Coast urban centers, it is striking that, having moved to New York, he now more or less perversely began to call for recognition of a literary stage and audience *not* centered in New York.

In response to a request from Lowell for autobiographical notes for use in a magazine article, Poe wrote a long letter that included his cur-

rent musings on the nature of existence: "I think that human exertion will have no appreciable effect upon humanity. . . . Man is now only more active—not more happy—nor more wise, than he was 6000 years ago." And yet his distrust of progress and criticism of abstract system were always counterbalanced by a fascination with new discoveries in physical science and mathematics.

Poe continued to contribute different kinds of fiction (though most involved unusual forms of death, strange encoffinings and sepultures) to a variety of magazines. As was his practice, he alternated comic and satiric tales with seemingly more serious occult tales. "A Tale of the Ragged Mountains" and "Mesmeric Revelation" explored psychic phenomena beyond the boundary of death. "The Premature Burial" and "The Angel of the Odd," however, were comic treatments of paranoia, both in literature and life. He followed these works with the ratiocinative "The Purloined Letter," in which his French detective, Dupin, plays an elaborate game of psychological cat and mouse. This tale was in turn followed by "Thou Art the Man," another coffin story, this time parodying the genre of the detective story that Poe had popularized over the last three years. In "The Oblong Box" he created a darker coffin-story mystery aboard a boat, with a seriocomic conclusion and explanation. In "The Spectacles" he spun out a light-hearted spoof on misperception, in which a near-sighted man falls in love with a very old woman at the theater, whom he takes to be a great beauty because he refuses to wear his glasses. These works were followed by "The Literary Life of Thingum Bob," a satire on authorship and on editors like Graham.

In October 1844, Poe joined the staff of New York *Evening Mirror*, to which he contributed articles on the literary marketplace, on contemporary authors, and on the lack of international copyright law. Poe angrily indicted the widespread practice among publishers of pirating popular British works for American publication. Since they did not have to pay royalties to foreign authors, American publishers were reluctant to publish native authors, who, of course, expected to be paid for their work. And like their American counterparts, European publishers were not legally bound to pay foreign authors for reprintings of their works. How could an American writer, or any writer for that matter, be a true professional under such economic conditions? In November, Poe began his "Marginalia" series in the *Democratic Review*; the "Marginalia" were composed of short, more or less random musings generated principally from his reading of the many books submitted for review. Throughout 1844, he had continued his lectures on American poetry and kept working on his "Critical History of American Literature"—but it was never completed.

On the political scene of 1844–45, the issues of nationalist expansionism and the extension of slavery westward were getting ever hotter. In the presidential campaign of 1844, Clay had sought to dislodge Van Buren, but the political maneuvering brought unlooked-for results. The Democrats passed over Van Buren (whom Poe had satirized in several tales) and chose James K. Polk, a pro-expansionist candi-

date. When antislavery Whigs voted against Clay and for James G. Bir-
ney of the Liberty Party instead, the way was cleared for the election
of Polk as president. Polk was in favor of the annexation of Texas
and the reoccupation of the Oregon territories. These were the very
regions that Poe had written about so extensively in his long 1837
review of Irving's *Astoria* and in his even longer 1840 tale "Julius
Rodman." (Public curiosity about the West and the expansionist fever
may be measured by the popularity of Francis Parkman's *The Oregon
Trail*, which was serialized in the *Knickerbocker Magazine* from 1847
to 1849 and then immediately issued in book form in 1849.)

In January 1845, "The Raven" appeared in the *Evening Mirror*. It
was an enormous success (comparing it to the popularity of "The
Gold-Bug," Poe was later to say that "the bird beat the bug—all hol-
low"), and with it, Poe began to break into New York literary society.
Mindful of keeping in the public eye, he initiated a number of ques-
tionable projects. One was a very public literary courtship in verse
with the poet Frances Sargent Osgood. Another was what he called
the "Little Longfellow War." From January to August 1845, he pub-
lished a series of five articles in which he accused Henry Wadsworth
Longfellow, one of the most popular literary figures of the day, of pla-
giarism. Although the ostensible subject was a stand against literary
piracy, Poe's essays largely constituted a campaign against Longfellow
as a symbol. Poe saw him as one of the most eminent members of the
insider literary cliques he detested. The articles brought him more
celebrity but alienated friends like Lowell. They also provoked a vigor-
ous print attack from one "Outis" (Greek for "no one"), whose literate
and literary castigation of Poe kept the controversy going. (Some
scholars suspect that Poe himself might have been Outis.)

At the same time that he was conducting literary warfare against the
New England "Brahmins" (as they were called, after the Hindu high-
est caste), Poe continued his campaign for an independent criticism.
In the *Broadway Journal*, he suggested that what is really appreciated
by the general public is a "pungent impartiality"; and he evidenced
this preference with reference to his having vastly increased the circu-
lation of *Graham's Magazine* in little over two years (once again exag-
gerating the numbers). As he had ten years before, he asserted that his
own practice as critic derived from a "set of principles" and was not
the product of bias or of a temperament given to habitual faultfinding.
Never, he wrote, had he rendered an opinion, positive or negative,
"without attempting, at least, to give it authority by something that
bore the semblance of a reason."

This point about the critic's responsibility to give reasons for his
judgments is one Poe had addressed three years earlier in "Exordium
to Critical Notices." The original concept of a book review, he wrote
then, was to "convey a just idea of its design"—that is, to "survey the
book to analyze its contents, and to pass judgment upon its merits or
defects." But present-day reviewers, hiding behind anonymity and paid
by the line, did little more than substitute a "digest" with "copious ex-
tracts" and "random comments." Perhaps worse, the "review" fre-

quently became a pretext for a "diffuse essay" on some other topic than the book. Although Poe admitted the value of "a good essay," these generalized effusions, he felt, had "nothing whatsoever" to do with "criticism." For criticism "is not, we think, an essay, nor a sermon, nor an oration, nor a chapter in history, nor a philosophical speculation, nor a prose-poem, nor an art-novel, nor a dialogue." Criticism is itself an art of high importance, a genre of "clearly ascertained limit"—which is "comment on Art." The critic's concern is with "the mode" of a book: and "it is only as the book that we subject it to review." The critic has "nothing to do" with "opinions" of a work except as they relate to the work itself. The true critic should judge a book's success only by its execution—not by its morality or politics, or its ideological or commercial connections.

In the early part of 1845, Poe met Evert Duyckinck, one of the editors of the *Literary World* and a person of great influence in the intellectual circles of New York, and initially made a good impression on him. In fact, Duyckinck selected twelve stories to be published as Poe's *Tales* by the firm of Wiley and Putnam in July. Since the volume was well received, in November the publishers brought out a companion volume, *The Raven and Other Poems*. During the course of the year, Poe had continued his remarkable productivity with several new stories. "The Thousand and Second Tale of Scheherazade" and "Some Words with a Mummy" were both satires on theories of progress and American technology and democracy. They were followed by "The Power of Words," a poetic and apocalyptic fantasy about the "actual" creation of worlds by words—being "spoken" into existence by an author/god. In "The Imp of the Perverse" he formulated his most elaborate articulation of the idea that we are possessed of an irrational impulse to do ourselves harm.

Poe had begun to contribute heavily to a new magazine, the *Broadway Journal*. In July 1845, he became one of its main editors. The editors soon quarreled, and Poe saw an opportunity. He borrowed heavily from Griswold, Fitzgreene Halleck, and Horace Greely and bought the *Broadway Journal* outright. At last he was the sole editor—and proprietor—of his own magazine. Needful of copy, he reprinted revised versions of most of his stories and poems, as well as contributing over sixty literary essays and reviews. Meanwhile, he published tales and poems in various other magazines—notably "The System of Dr. Tarr and Prof. Fether" (a satire on mental institutions and social and political issues) and "The Facts in the Case of M. Valdemar" (a tale of ambiguous survival after death in a state of suspended animation). He also published reviews in the *Messenger* and a substantial article, "American Drama," in the *American Whig Review*.

He continued to lecture and to give public performances. In May, he had again given the lecture "Poets and Poetry of America." In October, at the Boston Lyceum, instead of preparing a new work, Poe read his youthful poem, "Al Aaraaf." It was, he later said, a deliberately insulting gesture, implying that a poem by an adolescent had more than enough intellectual content for Bostonians (and after all, his first

book, written in adolescence, was "By a Bostonian"). The outraged newspaper accounts of this reading, and the subsequent jibes that Poe leveled at the Boston "Frogpondians," gained him further notoriety in the stronghold of Longfellow and Transcendentalism. Even though this incident made him still more widely known, it also did him damage, especially given (possibly scurrilous) reports that he was intoxicated when he gave his readings and lectures.

By the fall of 1845, Virginia's lingering illness had become critical. Poe experienced severe nervous depression, deepened by financial distress. He fell ill himself and was forced to cease publication of the *Broadway Journal* (which had lost money) after the issue of January 3, 1846. He moved his family to a cottage in Fordham, New York, where Virginia, now a semi-invalid, was nursed by Mrs. Marie Louise Shew, who brought them bedclothes and other essentials. He apparently left for a job interview in June 1846; in the second of only two known letters to Virginia, Poe wrote: "Keep up your heart in all hopefulness, and trust yet a little longer—In my last disappointment, I should have lost my courage but for you—my little darling wife you are my *greatest* and *only* stimulus now, to battle with this uncongenial, unsatisfactory and ungrateful life." Humiliatingly, the Poe family was mentioned as a charity case in various papers in New York and Pennsylvania.

Seriously ill most of 1846, Poe was yet able to publish "The Philosophy of Composition," an account of the step-by-step method by which he wrote "The Raven" (possibly half tongue-in-cheek) and to write reviews for *Godey's*. Midyear, still dreaming of his own magazine, he wrote Philip P. Cooke: "Touching "The Stylus":—this is the one great purpose of my literary life." He also continued the "Marginalia" series in *Graham's* and the *Democratic Review*.

In addition, in May he began, for *Godey's Lady's Book*, a series called "The Literati of New York City." These were sketches of well-known New York writers, some of them mildly satiric. One such sketch was of Thomas Dunn English, sometime friend, sometime antagonist. English replied angrily in the *Evening Mirror* and elsewhere and initiated a barrage of parodies of Poe's fiction and satiric portrayals of his character. English became intemperate, attacking Poe's sanity and character. Complicating the odd on-again off-again friendship of the two men was a tangled quarrel involving supposedly indiscreet letters that two women, Frances Osgood and Elizabeth Ellet, had sent Poe. English even went so far as to suggest in print that Poe was guilty of fraud, forgery, and philandering. When they encountered each other in the street one evening, their tempers exploded and they had a fistfight. Poe retorted in print and also brought an ultimately successful lawsuit against the *Mirror*, which had printed several other attacks on him. Godey cancelled the "Literati" feature with the sixth installment in November. Nevertheless, Poe wanted to continue to work on a book version of his "Literati" sketches, now to be titled *Literary America*. He hoped to incorporate in this work his analytic essays on versification as well as a revision of his Hawthorne review. But it was not to be. Virginia's health had continued to deteriorate throughout the year, and

Poe's mental and emotional stamina was being depleted. Perhaps the best news he received at this time was word of growing esteem in France, where translations of his work and a long essay on his *Tales* appeared.

As nationalist and racialist feeling increased in the United States, the country set about clarifying its borders. In 1845, America had peremptorily annexed Texas. The "Young America" wing of the Democratic Party adopted the slogan "Manifest Destiny," meaning that it was God's will that white Americans should possess the North American continent from sea to shining sea. In 1846, a treaty with Britain regarding Oregon established the entire border between the United States and Canada; and a treaty with Colombia established the right of way across the isthmus of Panama. The Wilmot Proviso, added to the Missouri Compromise, ensured that no slavery would exist in any territory acquired from Mexico either by purchase or by war. Also in 1846 the simmering conflicts with Mexico boiled into war. President Polk ordered General Zachary Taylor to advance to the Rio Grande. In California, the commodores Sloat and Stockton captured San Francisco, Monterey, and Los Angeles; settlers seized the town of Sonoma and raised the California Bear Flag; Captain Fremont then raised the Union flag over it. Colonel Kearney marched from Forth Leavenworth, Kansas, to San Diego, California. In November 1846, General Winfield Scott (who had been an acquaintance of John Allan) marched to Vera Cruz in preparation for an attack on Mexico City. The next year, Mormons would arrive in Utah while it was still a territory of Mexico; General Scott would score victories at Cerro Gordo and Chapultepec; and Mexico would agree to the Treaty of Guadalupe-Hidalgo. Poe must have looked on all this with a jaundiced eye—not believing in American progressivist slogans—indeed, he did not believe in social progress at all, as he had told Lowell back in 1844. Human beings were only more "active" not "progressive."

Poe concluded the year of 1846 with the publication of "The Cask of Amontillado," one of a series of revenge tales he would produce to the end of his life, culminating with "Hop-Frog" a scant three years later. "Amontillado" is a multilayered story in which Poe subtly interweaves a gothic tale of secret murder with nationalist, social, economic, and religious conflict. Although the story is set in Italy, current political affairs in America provide an extra resonance to the events of the tale. The Native American Party (no relation to Indian affairs) had been established in 1845 as a counter to the waves of immigrants from Germany and Ireland, who were perceived as taking low-paying jobs from people actually born in America. The main platform of the party was enactment of legislation to restrict the right to vote solely to "native-born" Americans. The party members became quite secretive, had cryptic gestures, and held meetings in out-of-the-way places. (They were so secretive that they became known in the next decade as the Know-Nothing Party.) Such sociopolitical turmoil served as an extratextual backdrop for American readers. In its depiction of a deadly encounter in the dark catacombs underneath the city streets, as the

masked ritual of Carnival plays out above and below, "Amontillado" evokes the conflicts between the old aristocracy and the nouveau riche, between the French and the Italians, and between the Catholics and the Protestants. Perceptive readers would have seen some relevance to the American political scene.

On January 30, 1847, Virginia died, of "pulmonary consumption." Almost immediately, in February, Poe was put through the ordeal of a court trial—his libel suit against the *Mirror*. Although he won (collecting $250), it must have been cold comfort. The months from the fall of 1845 to the beginning of 1847 had been debilitating. And 1847 was worse. He suffered from deep depression and sought solace in heavy drinking. He again fell gravely ill and again was nursed back to health by Mrs. Clemm and Mrs. Shew. This was Poe's least productive year; he was able to complete only four pieces. Two were quasi-revisions of earlier works: an expansion of the 1842 Hawthorne review and "The Domain of Arnheim." The "Arnheim" piece is an elaboration of the 1841 "Landscape Garden" into the aesthetic theory of which death intrudes its stony reality and the landscape architect himself dies. The other two works were poems, both poignantly personal. "To M. L. S." expressed his gratitude to Marie Louise Shew, who had nursed Virginia during her last illness. "Ulalume," which lyrically dramatizes the long repression of grief and then suddenly erupting agony of a lover who has lost his beloved, was published in December.

Last Years: 1848–49

Poe began the year 1848 in somewhat better health. In a letter to George W. Eveleth (January 4, 1848), he ascribed his past intermittent drinking to temporary insanity caused by constant fear of Virginia's death: "As a matter of course, my enemies referred the insanity to the drink rather than the drink to the insanity. . . . [I]t was the horrible never-ending oscillation between hope & despair which I could *not* longer have endured without total loss of reason. In the death of what was my life, then, I receive a new but—oh God! how melancholy an existence."

Meanwhile his interest in the ultimate nature of the universe, and the purpose of life and death within a cosmic plan, had led him to begin taking notes on contemporary cosmological theories. Throwing himself as usual into work, he began a series of lectures and readings, in part to raise money for *The Stylus*. The lecture "The Universe" that he gave at the New York Society Library in February 1848 was an abridged version of a long essay he had written on the principle of death and annihilation as part of the fundamental design of the universe. The full version, titled *Eureka: A Prose Poem*, was published as a book by Putnam in June–July 1848.

This was also a year in which Poe attempted a frantic series of more or less romantic liaisons—with Marie Louise Shew early in the year, with Mrs. Nancy ("Annie") Locke Heywood Richmond at midyear, and

with Sarah Helen Whitman at the end of the year. While speaking in
Lowell, Massachusetts, Poe formed an attachment to the married An-
nie Richmond, who quickly became a confidante on whom he relied
heavily for emotional support; this relationship resulted in stress with
the Richmonds and their friends and was broken off. Mrs. Whitman
was a wealthy, somewhat eccentric forty-five-year-old widow, a poet
and a mystic, who gave séances and wrapped her head in a gauzy flow-
ing shawl sometimes soaked in ether. Poe's courtship of her was short-
lived. When he rather precipitously proposed marriage, she resisted
because of rumors of his supposedly "unprincipled" character and the
"heretical" philosophical ideas he had expressed in *Eureka*. Temporar-
ily overcoming her doubts, Mrs. Whitman did become engaged to Poe
briefly; but she rescinded the commitment because of reports of Poe's
alcoholism and erratic behavior. In the fall, Poe fell into deep depres-
sion after a catastrophic trip to Mrs. Whitman's home in Providence,
Rhode Island. In importunate letters to her, he claimed he had taken a
very large dose of laudanum (an opium derivative) in a suicide attempt
but was so unfamiliar with the drug that he misjudged the size of the
dose and vomited it up. Mrs. Whitman seems to have wavered briefly
once again; but by the end of the year, the engagement was definitively
broken off.

Somehow, despite all the personal turmoil, Poe continued to work
and perform—mainly reading poems and lecturing on poetics. A long
theoretical essay, "The Rationale of Verse," and a tender poem, the
second "To Helen" (this time for Helen Whitman), were published
this year; and in December, he read "The Poetic Principle" as a lec-
ture.

It would be surprising, given all the grief and turmoil in his life, if
Poe had been very attentive to the political changes of the years
1848–49. And yet it seems he was. These years were marked by acer-
bic political conflicts between conservatives and liberals over women's
rights, over the rights of slaves versus freemen in the western territo-
ries, and over the illusory economics of get-rich-quick schemes.
Seneca Falls, New York, became the site of the first important
women's rights convention. Among the major indictments declared
against men were that married women were in general "civilly dead"
under the law, specifically that a married woman had no right to prop-
erty or even wages, which legally belonged to the husband. The New
York Married Women's Property Act of 1848 changed the prevailing
laws. Meanwhile, the slavery issue continued to intensify. During the
presidential election campaign of 1848, the Democratic Party had
been split by the Barn Burners and the Free Soilers, allowing the
Whigs to elect Zachary Taylor president. The precarious commerce of
westward migration—with implications for the extension of slavery—
was aggravated by the discovery of gold in the Sacramento Valley of
California. By the following year, as the population of the United
States approached twenty-three million, nearly a hundred thousand
Forty-Niners had been seduced into heading west.

Against this backdrop Poe's last works gain specific resonances. Poe

wrote two satires on the California gold craze. In a letter, he said that he wrote the tale "Von Kempelen and His Discovery" as a "check to the gold fever." It is a hoaxing news article in which metropolitan police come upon, in an abandoned urban apartment, the mysterious chemical apparatus of the scientist Von Kempelen; they discover that he has achieved the alchemists' dream of changing base metals into gold. The poem "Eldorado" features a "pilgrim shadow" who encourages a "gallant knight" to go in quest of the fabled Western City of Gold sought by the Conquistadors—to ride, boldly ride—into illusion and death. "Hop-Frog" (1849), the last work to be published in Poe's lifetime, is a gruesome "fairy tale" of oppression and revenge, told in a naive style similar to that of "Never Bet the Devil Your Head." Its narrative parable of the abuses inflicted by those in power—specifically the mistreatment of a beautiful Lilliputian woman and the misshapen dwarf who loves her—is obliquely suggestive of the issues of the rights of women and slaves.

During the last year of his life, Poe divided his time among the cities of New York, Richmond, and Baltimore. Despite his mental and physical deterioration, he remained productive. In February, he wrote to a friend: "Literature is the most noble of professions. In fact, it is about the only one fit for a man." In a rare indulgence of regionalist sentiment, he criticized Lowell's recently published A Fable for Critics for its omission of Southern writers, though his pique may have been aroused as much by Lowell's enduring satiric description of him:

> There comes Poe, with his raven, like Barnaby Rudge,
> Two-fifths of him genius and three-fifths sheer fudge.

That summer he traveled to Richmond to seek Southern financial support for The Stylus. On the way, ill and apparently mentally unstable, he seems to have sought help from acquaintances in Philadelphia, telling them a surrealistic story about being followed by murderers and having been imprisoned. George Lippard and John Sartain took him under their wing, and another friend, Charles Burr, paid the rest of his train fare to Richmond.

His summer stay in Richmond produced rapid changes in him, but the details are vague and ambiguous. He reunited with his sister, Rosalie, joined a temperance society, and became engaged to his childhood sweetheart, Sarah Elmira Royster (now the widowed Mrs. Shelton). Apparently intending to move his Aunt Maria Clemm from New York to Richmond, he sailed at the end of September for Baltimore on a packet steamer.

About a week later, in Baltimore, he seems to have gone on a drinking spree. He was found in strange clothes in a semiconscious state outside a polling booth on October 3. Taken to a nearby hospital, he lay in a comatose condition; he is reported to have drifted in and out of delirium. At one point, half waking, he is supposed to have called out the name "Reynolds!" Speculations on what this name meant to him vary. One of the more intriguing is the possibility that he was dreaming of the South Polar adventures of Jeremiah N. Reynolds for

the U.S. government, whose reports Poe had reviewed in the 1830s and made memorable use of in *The Narrative of Arthur Gordon Pym.* But the accounts of his last moments are not particularly trustworthy.

On Sunday morning, October 7, Poe was pronounced dead "of congestion of the brain" or a brain "lesion"—most likely a stroke, perhaps complicated by intestinal inflammation, a weak heart, and diabetes. Later conjectures about his death (mostly unfounded) vary widely. They range from the suggestions that he was kidnapped by a political gang (which is supposed to have disguised him and dragged him from one polling place to another to vote under different identities) to the rather improbable (but darkly appealing) idea that he was bitten by a rabid vampire bat.

Aftermath: 1849–61

Poe's death was immediately followed by two striking circumstances. One was the posthumous publication of two of his best-loved poems, both dealing with the final triumph of death. "Annabel Lee" was published in October and "The Bells" in November, in the "fall of the year." The other event was the almost immediate printing of Rufus Wilmot Griswold's slanderous obituary notice (signed "Ludwig"). Griswold actually had the audacity to defame Poe at the same time that he began work on a collected edition of his writings, not scrupling to alter Poe's letters to make him look worse than he was. Although immediately repudiated by Poe's defenders, Griswold's widely reprinted obituary notice adversely affected Poe's personal reputation for over a century. Griswold's edition of Poe's collected writings was published in four volumes by the New York firm of J. S. Redfield from 1850 to 1856; in it he insisted on reprinting and expanding his mean-spirited obituary notice.

Griswold's distortions—and the presumptions of a number of critics willing to accept easy paradigms—bring up important matters of biographical and historical interpretation. What might well be called the "Griswold tradition" mythologizes a rather unpleasant figure, one largely at variance with the facts. Poe is seen as ungenerous and self-absorbed, a backbiter, a debtor, a criminal, a racist, a drunkard, a drug addict, a misogynist, and even a pedophile.

Although Poe did not easily suffer fools and was not afraid to criticize stupidity, incompetence, and hypocrisy, many contemporary accounts mention his tender and generous side. Contemporaries record his devotion to his wife and his aunt. They describe his many kindnesses to colleagues and friends, his enjoyment of children at play, his love of music, and his love of animals. On the other hand, it is clear that he was habitually in debt, that he borrowed repeatedly and heavily from everyone, and that he did not always promptly pay back loans. His attitude toward money seems both desperate and cavalier. But there is little or no evidence that Poe intended to commit fraud or other criminal acts. Certainly he seems to have had a temper, which

sometimes erupted into some minor (reciprocated) aggression against male colleagues. But except for his fistfight with Thomas Dunn English, there is almost no reliable or any recorded evidence that he committed violent acts against anyone, male or female, or that he habitually wanted to do so against any specific persons even in his imagination—however much use he made of the scenes and themes of the popular sensational fiction of his times.

Poe may have had racist attitudes, but they do not seem to form a significant part of his writings or worldview except (possibly) symbolically. Recent scholarship is divided: a group of critics currently in the ascendant see Southern racism as central to Poe's world; others suggest that he was no more racist than the average white Northerner. Although now a contested issue, racial bias, while detectable, does not on the whole seem to figure as an obsessive theme in his writings. Indeed, given the number of separatist writings multiplying in the South and the increasing frequency of publications defending the "peculiar institution" of slavery, an argument may be made that Poe was actually less racist than the average white Southerner. Similarly, what seem to be occasional touches of anti-Semitism in his stories do not necessarily suggest a pervasive personal bigotry so much as a fictional stratagem, satirical jabs that he thought his main audience would find humorous.

That Poe had a drinking problem is clear. But it is not clear that he was habitually out of control; although he seems to have drunk something alcoholic nearly every day and although he went on intermittent binges, throughout his adult life he put in much more than what would be an average day's work for most people. It is hard to imagine that he could have edited, copyedited, set type, kept accounts, read so many books, written review after review after review, written hundreds of business and personal letters, and continually produced so many tales, poems, and essays—and been dead drunk all the time. As to drugs, the only recorded instance of his use of any is his failed suicide attempt, in which he betrayed such an abysmal lack of real-life knowledge of opium that he overdosed himself.

The charge of misogyny is a more complicated one. Poe was devoted to Maria Clemm (despite occasional annoyances with her), and he idealized women like Frances Allan, Jane Stanard, and Virginia Poe. His pursuit of women in the last years of his life suggests a rather desperate need for female influence. Yet dead or dying women, and violence, perversity, and madness, are features of his work familiar to every reader. But whatever we may surmise about Poe's personal psychological problems, it is important to remember that he was a self-conscious writer exploiting the popular taste of his time in an effort to become a success. Without denying his fascination with psychological aberration and violence, interpretations of Poe's portrayal of women need to include recognition that, as a crafty professional writer, he fashioned his materials for a specific literary objective in each text. His idealization of women in certain poems and essays (e.g., "To Helen," "The Poetic Principle") was counterpointed in fiction by female char-

acters who are subjected to violent physical assault ("The Murders in the Rue Morgue," "The Black Cat") or ravaged by disease ("Metzengerstein," "The Fall of the House of Usher"). In some works, he could parody a woman as vapid and absurd ("How to Write a Blackwood Article," "Mellonta Tauta"); in another, portray her intellectual genius ("Ligeia"); in others, hold her as the icon of ultimate sorrow ("The Raven," "Ulalume," "Annabel Lee"). While it is possible to extrapolate some obsessive concerns from the corpus of Poe's writings, such an inquiry should be accompanied by the awareness that there is no easy, direct correlation between an author's art and craft and his personal psychic life.

As to his supposed sexual interest in young girls, Poe confessed to a friend after Virginia's death that he had never consummated his marriage (leading twentieth-century Freudians to speculate that he was, contrariwise, impotent). The available biographical facts suggest that his marriage to his thirteen-year-old cousin was an attempt to keep the remnants of his shattered family together. Although he may not have been an average middle-class citizen, the Poe legend is based on a good deal of unfounded speculation and is fraught with assumption, presumption, conjecture, and error.

As Poe's life came to a close, war clouds were already beginning to gather over the Union. The 1850s saw America march steadily toward armed conflict between the North and the South. The stages of the growing war sentiment are poignantly represented in the pages of the most enduring of the magazines of the Old South, the *Southern Literary Messenger*, ever to be associated with the name of Edgar A. Poe. Despite the fact that the new Utah Territory brought further compromises on the issue of slavery, the division between proslavery and antislavery forces became sharper. The muddled Fugitive Slave Acts of 1850 required Northerners to assist in the return of escaped slaves to the South solely on the word of an "owner" (even if absent); and heavy penalties were imposed for disobeying. In 1851–52 Harriet Beecher Stowe began serial publication of *Uncle Tom's Cabin*, a book that fired controversy North and South. (Abraham Lincoln was to call Stowe "the little lady" whose book started the Civil War.) In 1853, through the Gadsden Purchase, the United States acquired the remaining California lands from Mexico, causing further debate on the extension of slavery into the new territories. Then in 1854, the year that the new Republican Party was formed, the Kansas-Nebraska Bill added further confusion to the Missouri Compromise of 1820 by creating two new territories instead of one, thus allowing for an interpretation that permitted slavery in one of them. Tempers flared on both sides.

In 1856, the first national convention of the new Republican Party was held. But the Republicans lost the presidential election to the Democrats, whose nominee, James Buchanan, became the fifteenth president of the United States in 1857. This was the same year that the Supreme Court announced its final decision on the much debated

Dred Scott case. The Court held that the federal government could not make laws against slavery in the new territories. Indeed, Chief Justice Roger B. Taney's written opinion held that the Missouri Compromise itself was unconstitutional.

In 1858, the Lincoln-Douglas debates began. In 1859, John Brown raided Harpers Ferry—in the name of freedom as he saw it. In 1860, the Republican nominee, Abraham Lincoln, was elected the sixteenth president of the United States. On December 20, 1860, South Carolina withdrew from the Union. By February of 1861, seven Southern states had seceded. In the spring of 1861, from April 12 to 14, Confederate troops bombarded Fort Sumter, South Carolina, the first engagement of the Civil War.

Fort Sumter stood at the head of Charleston harbor, near Fort Moultrie, where Poe had served as an enlisted soldier in the U.S. Army from 1827 to 1829. We can only wonder what the Bostonian reared in the South, who spent his life alternating between Northern and Southern cities, would have made of it all. Emotionally, he would likely have been drawn to the Southern cause. But he had served in the U.S. Army with distinction and had been a cadet at West Point. Despite his war against Northern power brokers, he saw the cities of Boston, New York, and Philadelphia as the seats of the literary culture and prestige to which he aspired. His life was divided almost equally between the North and the South. In a curious way, Poe's own internal division, his own civil war with himself, though springing from different sources, was mirrored in the dissension in American society that culminated, not long after his death, in a war with itself.

A Note on the Texts and Annotations

Texts

This Norton Critical Edition presents representative and provocative writings by and about Edgar Allan Poe, reprinting accurate texts and providing the student with materials necessary for an informed reading of them. The book represents major themes, genres, and styles in Poe's total corpus of work. These include short story, novel, literary parody, social satire, travel adventure, gothic romance, detective fiction, science fiction, landscape description, dramatic poem, lyric poem, visionary rhapsody, philosophical essay, critical review, theoretical essay, and so forth. In their surprisingly wide variety, Poe's writings present a number of problems for a modern selected edition. Moreover, he was an inveterate reviser and reprinted most of his works several times, sometimes with small changes, often with major changes. Some of his poems and tales exist in such radically different versions that they constitute separate works.

The most authoritative edition of Poe's poems and tales is the variorum *Collected Works of Edgar Allan Poe*, in three volumes (Cambridge, MA: Belknap Press of Harvard University Press, 1969–78), edited by Thomas Ollive Mabbott; and the simplest procedure would be to reprint directly from this edition. But Mabbott's choice of copy text does not always coincide with mine, sometimes because of differences in critical understanding. Furthermore, like other editors before him, Mabbott has a tendency to reprint from *The Works of the Late Edgar Allan Poe* (New York: Redfield, 1850–56) as edited by Rufus Wilmot Griswold. The textual principle in so doing is the idea that the latest revision constitutes the best text (one of several competing theories of textual editing). Griswold was Poe's literary executor, and it has been presumed that he had Poe's latest revisions. But Griswold is notorious for his attacks on Poe's character after his death, even going so far as to alter Poe's letters to cast him in a bad light. I see no compelling reason always to trust Griswold on the matter of final authorial revisions.

In addition, I do not find the notion of final revisions to be all-compelling. Who prefers Henry James's 1907 revision of *The American* to the first version of 1877? Many critics think he spoiled it, and most teachers use the early, not the late, version in class. Just as I have had to judge which of Poe's works best represent the scope and variety of his achievement as a writer, so I have had to use my best judgment

for what text is to be preferred. The introductory notes to each poem and tale identify the source of the text; when pertinent, significant variants are indicated in the notes. Sure typographical errors are in general corrected silently, though sometimes indicated by brackets. Otherwise, various nineteenth-century spellings and punctuation have been retained. With few exceptions, the texts of Poe's poems and tales reprinted herein are drawn from the original book, gift-album, magazine, and newspaper sources. The Mabbott edition is, however, used as the source for a small number of hard-to-find works. Harvard University Press has generously allowed us to reprint from Mabbott's edition the manuscript text of Poe's projected story cycle "The Tales of the Folio Club," Poe's prospectus for *The Penn Magazine*, and the self-review attributed to Poe, "A Reviewer Reviewed."

Poe's essays and reviews, unless otherwise indicated, follow original magazine sources. For a more comprehensive selection, see my edition of the *Essays and Reviews* for The Library of America. Reviews of Poe's works by others are from various scholarly sources, most notably *Edgar Allan Poe: The Critical Heritage* (London and New York: Routledge & Kegan Paul, 1986), edited by I. M. Walker, used by permission. We have also been granted permission to reprint from John Ward Ostrom's edition of *The Letters of Edgar Allan Poe* (originally published by Harvard in 1948; several times reprinted, with supplements, by various other publishers). Letters to and about Poe are principally from the *Works of Edgar Allan Poe* (New York: Thomas Y. Crowell, 1902), edited by James A. Harrison.

The text of Poe's only completed novel, *The Narrative of Arthur Gordon Pym of Nantucket*, is that of the American edition published by Harper & Brothers in 1838. The text of *Eureka* is that of the first American edition (New York: George P. Putnam, 1848).

Annotations

No attempt has been made to annotate each work with the same degree of thoroughness; that is not the goal of an anthology such as this. Rather, the point is to make the writings of Poe, which are often heavily allusive, as accessible as possible to students and to general readers who want a more thorough understanding of the texts. The presence of many footnotes can be interruptive of the reading experience, but sometimes it is a necessary evil (as in the case of Poe's obscure poem "Al Aaraaf"). At other times, dense footnotes are not required. With these guidelines in mind, I have tried to assess each tale and poem individually. For example, this volume contains a number of Poe's satires and parodies, and it has been necessary to annotate most of them in detail to identify Poe's targets and to suggest some of the exact satiric hits. Certain of Poe's works have generated heated interpretative debates (like "Ligeia," "The Fall of the House of Usher," *The Narrative of Arthur Gordon Pym*), and I have at times noted points of important

critical controversy. Other texts, such as Poe's reviews and essays and the discussions of poetry, philosophy, psychology, politics and the like by Poe's contemporaries, are less heavily annotated—as are the critical essays from the twentieth century.

Every editor who annotates the texts of a well-known author stands on the shoulders of predecessors, and that debt should be acknowledged. However, a seemingly recondite explanation of an allusion is not always the intellectual property of one researcher but of generations of scholars; I have not tried to trace the genealogy of a footnote, but I have tried to indicate my specific indebtedness when appropriate. My principal sources are Thomas Ollive Mabbott in the edition previously mentioned, the *Collected Works* (cited as "Mabbott"); *Poems of Edgar Allan Poe* (New York: Ginn, 1917), edited by Killis Campbell (cited as "Campbell"); *Edgar Allan Poe: Representative Selections*, revised edition (New York: Hill and Wang, 1962), edited by Margaret Alterton and Hardin Craig; and *The Short Fiction of Edgar Allan Poe*, revised edition (Urbana: University of Illinois Press, 1990), by Stuart G. Levine and Susan Levine (cited as "Levine"). Students are encouraged to consult the Mabbott edition as a magnificent work of antiquarian and biographical scholarship, but they should be aware that Mabbott's personal opinions abound and that not everything he says is to be taken as gospel. (In this regard, the volumes can be useful in giving a new generation a view of an older generation's taste and sensibilities.) The Levine edition contains sensible introductions to groups of tales and excellent (if sometimes offbeat) notes, along with maps and other pertinent illustrations, mainly from Poe's era. The student may also usefully consult two recent encyclopedic volumes: *A Companion to Poe Studies* (Westport, CT: Greenwood Press, 1996), edited by Eric W. Carlson, and *The Poe Encyclopedia* (Westport, CT: Greenwood Press, 1997), edited by Frederick S. Frank and Anthony Magistrale. Although both volumes contain a number of errors of fact and although some of the data and interpretations presented in one are colored by strong editorial bias, they nevertheless contain a wealth of biographical and critical information. The *Annotated Tales of Edgar Allan Poe* (New York: Avenel Books, 1981), edited by Stephen Peithman, though principally employing a pop culture approach, also provides useful glosses and references.

For the annotations of *The Narrative of Arthur Gordon Pym* I have followed the lead of previous editors, the principal of whom is Burton R. Pollin, who has continued the Mabbott edition under the title *Collected Writings of Edgar Allan Poe*. The first volume is titled *The Imaginary Voyages* (Boston: Twayne, 1981) and includes "Hans Pfaall," "The Journal of Julius Rodman," and *Pym*. It, too, is a variorum edition but sometimes silently emended to conform to modern spelling and punctuation and grammar. Pollin's notes are rich in detail if not always essential to the text at hand, though, as with Mabbott, they form a kind of antiquarian volume in themselves and can profitably be read almost independently. Other annotated editions of *Pym* include

those by Harold Beaver (New York: Penguin Classics, 1975), J. Gerald Kennedy (New York: Oxford University Press World Classics, 1994), and Richard Kopley (New York: Penguin Classics, 1999).

Preceding these scholar-editors are many others too numerous to acknowledge in detail. At one point, I felt that I was merely replicating the researches of Mabbott and the Levines. But as I came to see, they also depended heavily on their predecessors—and we are in fact involved in a cumulative discipline. As I read and reread, my admiration for many of the earlier editors grew with every endeavor. We have an enormous debt to our predecessors that we should not forget. But much of the annotation of this volume comes from my having read, over a period of more than thirty years, a very large number of critical and scholarly essays and books. I cannot at this remove properly acknowledge them all, but whenever I have felt a special debt I have tried to indicate it.

Each reader will have a slightly different interpretation of Poe's writings and career and life. I have my say mainly in the introductions; elsewhere in this volume I have generally steered a course, if not of complete objectivity, of some critical neutrality. That is, I have tried constantly to be aware of my own critical orientation and tried not to force an interpretation in the notes. Naturally, some biases will have crept in. I have, however, worked especially hard not to guide the student toward my own romantic-ironic readings of certain of the gothic and visionary works. In the essays in the last section of this Norton Critical Edition, I give a representative spread of various approaches—necessarily very general—including some that I strongly disagree with. Unfortunately, some of the very best works on Poe and his times are so specialized that only the advanced student would readily profit from them. But I have indicated many of these in the bibliographies. The criticism represented in this book is a sampler of ideas and approaches that I hope will stimulate further investigation into the riches of practical, historical, and theoretical criticism, the goal of which is to generate critical dialogue.

Acknowledgments

Several persons have been helpful—indeed, essential—in creating this volume. First, I wish to thank members of the W. W. Norton team. These include especially Allen Clawson, a field representative who recommended me for the Norton Critical Editions series, and the general editor of the series, Carol Stiles Bemis. One cannot say enough about Carol, who was unflaggingly encouraging, as patient as Job, and always understanding and insightful. I wish also to thank her assistant, Brian Baker, who oversaw production, and Candace Levy, who did a magnificent job of copyediting a very difficult manuscript. Like Carol, Grace Farrell of Butler University was steadfastly encouraging, offering me numerous critical/pedagogical insights as well as loaning me some of her personally annotated Poe texts. Beverly J. Reed, now of Stephen F. Austin State University, acted as my research assistant for some months and gathered many of the original materials from the magazines and gift books in which they were published, made photocopies, and pasted up texts; she also undertook, with a pedagogical eye, some of the initial annotations. The distinguished archeologist and ethnographer Robert C. Suggs offered several suggestions regarding the ancient language evoked at the end of *Arthur Gordon Pym*. My colleague at Purdue University, Robert Paul Lamb, who has won more teaching awards than anyone I know, made invaluable recommendations regarding the works—including the scholarly ones on Poe and his writings—that should be included for the student and general reader. Once again, I have to thank Elizabeth Boyd Thompson, who read and edited my introductions and other materials with acumen and put in long hours helping me assemble (and cut) the physical manuscript. This work could not have been completed without her patience, encouragement, and always incisive criticism.

THE SELECTED
WRITINGS OF
EDGAR ALLAN POE

Poems

Poe began his career as a poet, emulating Lord Byron, Percy Bysshe Shelley, and Thomas Moore. In his early nature lyrics, rather than try to picture the actualities of a worldly landscape, he employed an "indefinitive" imagery and diction. Instead, he reached toward a visionary state of "supernal beauty" evoked by the manipulation of sound and rhythm and, increasingly, by incantatory repetition. In both his practice and his aesthetic theory, Poe was more oriented toward the dark melancholy of Samuel Taylor Coleridge than toward the harmonious simplicity of the nature poetry of William Wordsworth.

Poe's first volume was the slender *Tamerlane and Other Poems* (1827). The longish title poem casts the Mongol conqueror as a prideful and tormented spirit brooding over his worldly ambition and his lost love (the latter a theme throughout Poe's poetry). The tone recalls Byronic world weariness; the imagery of dreams and distant stars, mist and night suggests a theme of infinite regress consequent to a dimming of perception. The nine shorter lyrics present an intensifying picture of the romantic agony of the persona of the lyric poet blighted by his very talent and tormented by brief glimpses of the supernal, which fade before he can justly transcribe them. The final poem, "The Lake," lyrically dramatizes the dark side of creativity. The isolated poet figure wanders around the shores of a remote lake (reputed to have poisonous waters) and finds that despite or because of its isolation he loves it: "So lovely was the loneliness / Of a wild lake, with black rock bound / And the tall pines that towered around." The "terror of the lone lake," he says, was "not fright, / But a tremulous delight." Although "Death was in that poisonous wave," his "lone imagining," his "solitary soul," makes "an Eden of that dim lake." A similar theme is found in "Alone," an uncollected poem dating from 1829. The speaker remembers that from childhood he has been different from others. The images of nature that most thrilled him were not so much gentle fountains but water in torrents, or the "red cliff of the mountain," or the tinted sunlight of autumn, or lightning and thunder, or a single cloud that when "the rest of Heaven was blue" took the form of "a demon in my view—."

In his second volume, *Al Aaraaf, Tamerlane, and Minor Poems* (1829), Poe added to the first collection the title poem and a half-dozen shorter works. "Al Aaraaf" is a key to one aspect of Poe's romanticism, but it is complex, obscure, and opaque—that is, deliberately indefinitive. The world of Al Aaraaf is an invented myth codifying the implications of earlier poems like "Evening Star," "Stanzas," and "A Dream." It anticipates such later prose-poem dialogues about the creation and destruction of the earth as "The Conversation of Eiros and Charmion" (1839), "The Colloquy of Monos and Una" (1841), and "The Power of Words" (1845). It anticipates as well his book-length cosmological treatise, also intended as a "poem," in prose, *Eureka* (1848); in this work, Poe attempts to reconcile various contraries of existence under the proposition that the fundamental paradox of existence is that annihilation is built into the very springing forth of life in both the individual and the cosmos.

3

The realm of Al Aaraaf contains both the terrible and the beautiful, where the "spirits" of poetic imaginings have a temporary existence between heaven and hell. Poe says that he has located this realm in "the celebrated star discovered by Tycho Brahe which appeared & disappeared so suddenly" in 1572–74. In *De Nova Stella* (Copenhagen, 1573) Tycho had described the star's appearance near a rectangle of four other stars in the constellation of Cassiopeia (which accounts for the four suns in the sky of the poem). The star seemed brighter than Venus and changed colors from white to yellow to red to leaden. After sixteen months it faded from view; while in its red phase, it generated terror that the end of the world was at hand. Poe writes that in his visionary poem this star "is represented as a messenger star of the Deity" on "an embassy to our world."

The distant star world of Al Aaraaf is a place where "nothing earthly" save the reflected ray of "Beauty's eye" is to be found and where imagination has fled from an earth bereft of poetry. The poem begins with an evocation of supernal beauty and ends in the destruction of the star. A similar theme, on a slightly more optimistic note, is found in the introductory "Sonnet—to Science." The speaker bemoans the impossibility of employing the old poetic myths now that science (the rational, analytic aspect of the mind) has destroyed such dream imaginings with its peering vulture eyes. But in the second part of the poem, in the very act of lamenting their passing, the speaker re-embodies the poetic legacy of the Elfin, Diana, the Hamadryad, and the Naiad. Thus "Sonnet—To Science" demonstrates poetic imagination triumphing over science's destruction of poetry.

Poe specifically indicates, in a letter, that he derived the dramatic world of the title poem from "the Al Aaraaf of the Arabians, a medium between Heaven & Hell where men suffer no punishment, but yet do not attain . . . tranquil and even happiness." Here they await entrance into yet another world, hoping to find the peace of soul that "they suppose" is to be found in a heaven. Poe echoes George Sale's "Preliminary Discourse" to his 1734 translation of the Koran, which says that among the inhabitants of the Muslim Al Aaraaf will be "angels in the form of men." Poe writes that he has "imagined some well known characters of the age of the star's appearance, as transferred to Al Aaraaf," principally the artist Michelangelo. Other Renaissance figures will, he suggests, be incorporated into a later version; but he never brought to completion the full design of the poem.

Sale remarks that some Muslim writers "place here such whose good and evil works are so equal that they exactly counterpoise each other, and therefore deserve neither reward nor punishment." On the last day, however—the Day of Judgment—they may be permitted into paradise "after they perform an act of adoration." But Poe writes that "one of the peculiarities" of his imagined star world is that those who choose it as their "residence" after death "do not enjoy immortality" but after "a second life of high excitement, sink into forgetfulness, & death." (He adds that the idea is taken from the story of Job, who said that he would "not live always.") Thus the poem presents a middle world in a series of infinitely regressive dreams of a higher reality—a half-realized Platonic idea of absolute Beauty—into the very origin of which destruction has been ordained.

At the beginning of the story, Nesace, the ruling angel of the star, bathing in the light of four suns, is preparing to pray. As the poem develops, the star world of Al Aaraaf moves from the drowsy dreamscape of the spirits of flowers, nymphs, and music floating upon the air to a disintegrating vision—one of desolation and ruin, as red winds burn and go out

in the heavens. We are first given a prevision of the divinely decreed destruction of earth, and then we see the actual final destruction as the star extinguishes. Thematically, the divine is known only through beauty via the imagination, which is the godlike part of man. But even in this "deep sky," as in the yet deeper heaven, the "terrible and fair, / in beauty vie," in an eternity of which we feel but the shadow. The spirit beings that dwell in Al Aaraaf have only dreamed of God's "Infinity" as a "model of their own" as they sleep the sleep of oblivion.

The goddess Nesace, as a messenger from God on high, awakes them. Nesace represents Beauty—and it is through Beauty and Harmony, represented by the spirit Ligeia, that the will of God is indefinitely communicated to human beings. Understanding of such things is but faint on earth; earthly science confuses truth and falsehood; and fuller knowledge is refracted, through death, from God's infinity. Dying, and dying again, though a melancholy necessity, brings human spirits close to ultimate spirituality beyond this world and beyond the next. The poetically imagined world of the angels hints of the true beauty beyond the "beyond," but even in this star world, Passion, which is too earthly for pure poetry and beauty, intrudes. Two lovers who have recently died have been given a new spiritual embodiment in Al Aaraaf, but their human love is too intense. The intrusion of earthly love destroys the two half-human, half-angelic spirits (almost as if this sense of the sinfulness of earthly desires were some hangover from Poe's lapsed Christianity). Thus, although the poem creates a cosmology of higher beauty, its world is also flawed; the only release from the tainted legacy of the earthly is to sink into oblivion.

Poems, Second Edition (1831) contains extensive revisions of the earlier poems along with a handful of new works, some of which feature an ambivalent self-irony. Otherwise, except for the idealized peace restored to the "weary, way-worn wanderer" of "To Helen," the implicit unrest of the first volume and the explicit apocalyptic vision of "Al Aaraaf" in the second volume have come to dominate the third. "The City in the Sea," for example, presents an indefinite double picture of doomed Sodom and Gomorrah at once visible under the waters yet about to sink into their waiting reflections. "The Sleeper" and "The Valley of Unrest" depict bizarre landscapes in which the human world shades into nightmare. The blighted vision of the earthly poet vainly seeking the otherworldly is intensified in "Israfel." The speaker claims that if he could but change places with the star god, "a bolder note," might swell from his "lyre within the sky" and Israfel "might not sing so wildly well— / A mortal melody."

For this volume, Poe wrote a new introduction, "Mysterious Star," which emphasizes the supernal loveliness of the star world of Al Aaraaf, with its dream gardens and dream maidens. All things, even sorrow, are gentle here: the "truest type of grief / Is the gently falling leaf," and "sorrow is not melancholy." But this new introduction to the volume as a whole also speaks of "eternal Condor years" falling on the visionary soul of the poet-narrator, robbing him of his ability to see the benign aspects of the world of spirit. The few calm hours that come to him must be spent grappling with some dimly perceived horror lurking beneath. Despite a wry portrait of the romanticist "dipt in folly" and "in love with melancholy," the new poem contains some of the most notorious lines in all of Poe's poetry:

> I could not love except where Death
> Was minging his with Beauty's breath—

Or Hymen, Time, and Destiny
Were stalking between her and me.

Biographical critics, especially those of a Freudian bent, have appropri-
ated these lines to demonstrate that Poe (the man) could not love *except*
when the woman was dead or dying. But these lines also suggest that
every time the young poet (not Poe, but a romantic persona) loved, the
beloved was *taken* from him—not that he could love *only* the dying.
Freudian readings also fail to take into account the conventions of Ro-
mantic melancholy and veiled vision, the artificed themes of recurrent
loss, self-abjuration, and egoistic pride so carefully constructed in the By-
ronic persona of Poe's earliest poems. The voice of these poems is a fictive
construct embodying the torment of the visionary spirit of the romantic
poet, racked by the vision of possible supernal loveliness in an other world
and the simultaneous recognition of the circumscription of the power of
poetic vision that earthly existence presents. This is the "ill demon" of the
world and the self as imaged in poems like "Alone." The vatic (prophetic)
poet is an uneasy mixture of external and internal, objective and subjec-
tive, mysteriously drawn "From ev'ry depth of good and ill."

Themes of ruin and apocalypse intensify in several poems of the early
1840s, one of which, "The Coliseum," retains the idea of poetic transcen-
dence found in "Sonnet—to Science." The speaker claims that the former
glory of the Roman coliseum is not entirely past; the poet feels it again
and re-creates it in his verse. "Dream-Land" returns to the trembling
world of "Al Aaraaf," evoking "bottomless vales" and "Mountains toppling
evermore / Into seas without a shore," seas that in turn surge into limitless
"lakes of fire." From this point on in Poe's poetry—except for the rather
charming verses addressed to various ladies and a number of self-
correcting parodies of Romantic poetic excess—the indefinitive visionary
aspect gives way almost entirely to the sense of loss, interior torment, infi-
nite regress, and the world of nightmare. The journey from the music and
song of bluebells, fountains, and woodland rills to the landscape of night-
mare is an incredibly rapid one, though hardly unlooked for, given the im-
plicit nightmare of even the earliest poems.

In a series of essays and reviews from 1831 to the end of his career, Poe
tried to develop a poetics of language as a medium of sensuous sound that
embodied the idea of the otherworldly. The earliest of these pieces is the
preface to *Poems* (1831), known as "Letter to B——," in which Poe distin-
guishes among the aims of poetry, music, and science and concludes that in-
definitiveness is the most poetic of effects. These ideas are refined in a
number of reviews and developed in such essays as "The Rationale of Verse"
(1848) and "The Poetic Principle" (1850). In notes for his unfinished *The
Living Writers of America*, Poe wrote that "distant subjects" are the "most
desirable." The "true poet is less affected by the absolute contemplation
than the *imagination* of a great landscape" (emphasis added), a vista bathed
in "the light that never was on land or sea." The paradoxical relation be-
tween mundane reality and the imagined otherworldly is also the subject ex-
plored in Poe's *Marginalia* note on Tennyson (December 1844) and in the
visionary sketch "Power of Words" (March 1846). At the same time that Poe
sought a visionary spiritual beauty, he emphasized meticulous craftmanship
and minute attention to detail. In his later poems, he transformed the dra-
matic monologue "Tamerlane" into brooding scenarios constructed around
the central issue of unconscious psychological revelation—especially the
perverse desire for self-torture in which one almost luxuriates in sorrow.

In "The Raven" (1845), for example, such a theme is clearly, yet am-
biguously, embodied in what was then (and continues to be) Poe's most
famous poem. Anguished by the death of his beloved Lenore and increas-
ingly aware that the raven can speak only a single word, the narrator com-
pulsively puts questions the answer to which heightens his pain. In "The
Philosophy of Composition" (1845). Poe purported to explain the calcu-
lated manner in which he constructed this poem. He reiterated his dictum
that a conception of overall effect and precise denouement must precede
actual writing. The first consideration, he said, was length: for unity of ef-
fect the poem must be brief enough to be read at a single sitting. The
effect sought in "The Raven" was a sustained tone of the melancholy
intrinsic to beauty; and the most "poetical" subject linking melancholy and
beauty was clearly the death of a beautiful woman. Among the most sig-
nificant aspects of "The Philosophy of Composition" is Poe's ability to
marshal his general ideas about poetry in the service of a specific strategy
for the revelation of character. The lover-narrator enacts "that species of
despair which delights in self-torture." He asks the bird questions that will
bring him the "luxury of sorrow, through the anticipated answer 'Never-
more.' " An "undercurrent" of meaning, Poe continues, one suggesting
the supernatural but not "overstepping the limits of the real," is designed
to heighten the effect, so that the reader feels the scene as does the
lover, even while maintaining aesthetic distance from the lover's point of
view.

Many of Poe's final poems deal with the loss of a beloved woman and
seem to have an obvious relevance to the loss of his wife, Virginia. In the
mysterious and initially opaque "Ulalume" (1847–49), the speaker is
warned by his companion, one "Psyche," not to continue his walk down a
cypress lane. He persists, however, and comes to the tomb of his cher-
ished Ulalume. Only by forgetting her existence has he repressed his grief
during the past year. Now his anguish erupts, like molten lava flowing
down an ice-locked volcano, to never-ending remembrance. Although in
ballad form, this poem too is cast as a psychodrama, a kind of dramatic
monologue in which the speaker is talking with himself (his psyche). The
final stanza is ambiguous, but it clearly suggests that the poem can be
read as a study of the compulsive desire to torture oneself.

Among Poe's last works are three more poems about the ultimate tri-
umph of death over loved ones. Each is heavily melodic and incantatory. A
tour de force in onomatopoeia, "The Bells" (1849) begins with the evoca-
tion of tinkling sleigh bells, suggesting childhood's happy and playful inno-
cence. The next section, developed at twice the length of the first, sounds
the golden notes of wedding bells. The third section, developed at three
times the length of the first, imitates "brazen" alarm bells signaling a life-
threatening fire blazing out of control. The last section, emulating
the "moaning" and the "groaning" of funeral bells, is developed at four
times the length of the original verse; the final phase of life belongs to the
"ghouls." In "For Annie" (1849), the speaker gives "thanks" that "the lin-
gering illness / Is over at last,— / And the fever called "Living" / Is con-
quered at last." He seems to be speaking of his lost love, Annie, but
he himself is lying "at full length." It is unclear if he is mourning the
dead woman in her coffin or if he is in his coffin and Annie is mourning
him; the poem surrealistically merges the lovers in life/death. A similar,
though clearer, situation is presented in "Annabel Lee" (1849); here the
bereaved speaker lies down beside his dead bride. He attributes the loss of
his beloved to covetous angels. The angels must have envied her beauty,

he says; for they came out of a cloud by night, "chilling and killing my Annabel Lee."

> And so, all the night-tide, I lie down by the side
> Of my darling, my darling, my life and my bride,
> In the sepulchre there by the sea,
> In her tomb by the sounding sea.

Angels or ghouls—this world or another—in Poe's poetry death finally always does come to mingle "his with Beauty's breath."

Tamerlane "Tamerlane" is the title poem of Poe's first collection, *Tamerlane and Other Poems. By a Bostonian* (Boston: Calvin F. S. Thomas, 1827), a small volume of barely forty pages. It is one of the rarest books in American letters; one of the few surviving copies recently sold for more than $200,000. Eight versions of the poem exist, some of them radically different. T. O. Mabbott in his Harvard edition of Poe's *Poems* (see "A Note on the Texts and Annotations" on p. xlix herein) reprints four versions (A, B, F, and H). The earliest version has notes appended, some of which are satiric and humorous. The version chosen here is Mabbott's H-text (without his emendations): the copy text is that of a photographically reproduced edition of *The Raven and Other Poems* (New York: Wiley and Putnam, 1845).

The preface to the 1827 edition contains some characteristic hyperbole, humor, and distortions of fact. It reads as follows:

> The greater part of the Poems which compose this little volume, were written in the year 1821–2, when the author had not completed his fourteenth year. They were of course not intended for publication; why they are now published concerns no one but himself. Of the smaller pieces very little need be said: they perhaps savour too much of Egotism; but they were written by one too young to have any knowledge of the world but from his own breast.
>
> In Tamerlane, he has endeavoured to express the folly of even *risk-ing* the best feelings of the heart at the shrine of Ambition. He is conscious that in this there are many faults, (besides that of the general character of the poem) which he flatters himself he could, with little trouble, have corrected, but unlike many of his predecessors, has been too fond of his early productions to amend them in his *old age.*
>
> He will not say that he is indifferent as to the success of these Poems—it might stimulate him to other attempts—but he can safely assert that failure will not at all influence him in a resolution already adopted. This is challenging criticism—let it be so. *Nos haeo novimus esse nihil.*

The Latin means that the author knows that the importance of what follows is next to nothing. Mabbott identifies the quotation as from the poems of the Roman satirist Martial (Marcus Valerius Martialis, 40–c. 104 C.E.), 13.2.8. Poe exaggerates the youthfulness of the teenage poet, enlarging the joke about authors who revise their works in their "old age."

Tamerlane.[1]

Kind solace in a dying hour![2]
 Such, father, is not (now) my theme—
I will not madly deem that power
 Of Earth may shrive me of the sin
 Unearthly pride hath revell'd in— 5
I have no time to dote or dream:
You call it hope—that fire of fire!
It is but agony of desire:
If I *can* hope—Oh God! I can—
 Its fount is holier—more divine— 10
I would not call thee fool, old man,
 But such is not a gift of thine.

Know thou the secret of a spirit
 Bow'd from its wild pride into shame.
O yearning heart! I did inherit 15
 Thy withering portion with the fame,
The searing glory which hath shone
Amid the Jewels of my throne,
Halo of Hell! and with a pain
Not Hell shall make me fear again— 20
O craving heart, for the lost flowers
And sunshine of my summer hours!
The undying voice of that dead time,
With its interminable chime,
Rings, in the spirit of a spell, 25
Upon thy emptiness—a knell.

I have not always been as now:
The fever'd diadem on my brow
 I claim'd and won usurpingly——
Hath not the same fierce heirdom given 30
 Rome to the Cæsar—this to me?
 The heritage of a kingly mind,

1. Tamerlane (1336–1405) was a conqueror from Kesh in central Asia (near Samarkand), who, according to widely disseminated legends, rose to power from lowly status but was distantly related to Genghis Khan. The first part of Poe's initial note to the 1827 version of the poem reads: "Of the history of Tamerlane little is known; and with that little, I have taken the full liberty of a poet.—That he was descended from the family of Zinghis Khan is more than probable—but he is vulgarly supposed to have been the son of a shepherd, and to have raised himself to the throne by his own address. He died in the year 1405, in the time of Pope Innocent VII." Tamerlane has been the subject of several literary treatments: by Christopher Marlowe (1587), Charles Saunders (1681), Nicholas Rowe (1702), Matthew G. Lewis (1811), and most notably (given Poe's early Byronism) Lord Byron in *The Deformed Transformed* (1824). Other Byronic influences on Poe's poem include *Childe Harold* (1812–18), "*The Bride of Abydos*" (1813), "*Manfred*" (1817), and *Don Juan* (1819–24). See the introduction pp. 3ff. herein.
2. The poem is a deathbed confession to a priest, a point made humorously clear in the second part of Poe's first note to the 1827 version: "How shall I account for giving him a 'friar,' as a death-bed confessor—I cannot exactly determine. He wanted some one to listen to his tale—and why not a friar? It does not pass the bounds of possibility—quite sufficient for my purpose—and I have at least good authority on my side for such innovations."

And a proud spirit which hath striven
 Triumphantly with human kind.

On mountain soil I first drew life: 35
 The mists of the Taglay[3] have shed
 Nightly their dews upon my head,
And, I believe, the winged strife
And tumult of the headlong air
Have nestled in my very hair. 40

So late from Heaven—that dew—it fell
 ('Mid dreams of an unholy night)
Upon me with the touch of Hell,
 While the red flashing of the light
From clouds that hung, like banners, o'er, 45
 Appeared to my half-closing eye
 The pageantry of monarchy,
And the deep trumpet-thunder's roar
 Came hurriedly upon me, telling
 Of human battle, where my voice, 50
 My own voice, silly child!—was swelling
 (O! how my spirit would rejoice,
And leap within me at the cry)
The battle-cry of Victory!

The rain came down upon my head 55
 Unshelter'd—and the heavy wind
 Rendered me mad and deaf and blind.
It was but man, I thought, who shed
 Laurels upon me: and the rush—
The torrent of the chilly air 60
Gurgled within my ear the crush
 Of empires—with the captive's prayer—
The hum of suitors—and the tone
Of flattery 'round a sovereign's throne.

My passions, from that hapless hour, 65
 Usurp'd a tyranny which men
Have deem'd, since I have reach'd to power,
 My innate nature[4]—be it so:
 But, father, there liv'd one who, then,
Then—in my boyhood—when their fire 70
 Burn'd with a still intenser glow
(For passion must, with youth, expire)
E'en *then* who knew this iron heart
In woman's weakness had a part.

3. Mountains in the clouds. Poe's note reads: "The mountains of Taglay are a branch of the Im-
 maus, in the southern part of independent Tartary.—They are celebrated for their singular
 wildness, and beauty of their vallies." "Immaus" is an ancient spelling of *Himalayas*.
4. By legend, Tamerlane is supposed to have been originally of gentle disposition, tolerant of
 Christians, and inclined to idealized romantic love.

I have no words—alas!—to tell 75
The loveliness of loving well!
Nor would I now attempt to trace
The more than beauty of a face
Whose lineaments, upon my mind,
Are——shadows on th' unstable wind: 80
Thus I remember having dwelt
 Some page of early lore upon,
With loitering eye, till I have felt
The letters—with their meaning—melt
 To fantasies—with none. 85

O, she was worthy of all love!
 Love—as in infancy was mine—
'Twas such as angel minds above
 Might envy;[5] her young heart the shrine
On which my every hope and thought 90
 Were incense—then a goodly gift,
 For they were childish and upright—
Pure——as her young example taught:
 Why did I leave it, and, adrift,
 Trust to the fire within, for light? 95

We grew in age—and love—together—
 Roaming the forest, and the wild;
My breast her shield in wintry weather—
 And, when the friendly sunshine smil'd,
And she would mark the opening skies, 100
I saw no Heaven—but in her eyes.

Young Love's first lesson is——the heart:
 For 'mid that sunshine, and those smiles,
When, from our little cares apart,
 And laughing at her girlish wiles, 105
I'd throw me on her throbbing breast,
 And pour my spirit out in tears—
There was no need to speak the rest—
 No need to quiet any fears
Of her—who ask'd no reason why, 110
But turn'd on me her quiet eye!

Yet *more* than worthy of the love
My spirit struggled with, and strove,
When, on the mountain peak, alone,
Ambition lent it a new tone— 115

5. Cf. "Annabel Lee" (pp. 75–76 herein). In the 1827 version of *Tamerlane* are several addi-
tional lines, including these: "We were still young: no purer thought / Dwelt in a seraph's
heart than *thine* . . . ," to which Poe appended a humorous note: "I must beg the reader's
pardon for making Tamerlane a Tartar of the fourteenth century, speak in the same language
as a Boston gentleman of the nineteenth: but of the Tartar mythology we have little infor-
mation." A "seraph" is a member of the highest of the nine orders of angelic beings. See
p. 33, l. 28, n. 2, and p. 38, n. 5 herein.

I had no being—but in thee:
 The world, and all it did contain
In the earth—the air—the sea—
 Its joy—its little lot of pain
That was new pleasure——the ideal, 120
 Dim, vanities of dreams by night—
And dimmer nothings which were real—
 (Shadows—and a more shadowy light!)
Parted upon their misty wings,
 And, so, confusedly, became 125
 Thine image and—a name—a name!
Two separate—yet most intimate things.

I was ambitious—have you known
 The passion, father? You have not:
A cottager, I mark'd a throne 130
Of half the world as all my own,
 And murmur'd at such lowly lot—
But, just like any other dream,
 Upon the vapor of the dew
My own had past, did not the beam 135
 Of beauty which did while[6] it thro'
The minute—the hour—the day—oppress
My mind with double loveliness.

We walk'd together on the crown
Of a high mountain which look'd down 140
Afar from its proud natural towers
 Of rock and forest, on the hills—
The dwindled hills! begirt with bowers
 And shouting with a thousand rills.

I spoke to her of power and pride, 145
 But mystically—in such guise
That she might deem it nought beside
 The moment's converse; in her eyes
I read, perhaps too carelessly—
 A mingled feeling with my own— 150
The flush on her bright cheek, to me
 Seem'd to become a queenly throne
Too well that I should let it be
 Light in the wilderness alone.

I wrapp'd myself in grandeur then 155
 And donn'd a visionary crown——
 Yet it was not that Fantasy
 Had thrown her mantle over me—
But that, among the rabble—men,
Lion ambition is chain'd down— 160

6. Here a verb, as in "to while away the hour."

And crouches to a keeper's hand—
Not so in deserts where the grand—
The wild—the terrible conspire
With their own breath to fan his fire.

Look 'round thee now on Samarcand![7]— 165
 Is she not queen of Earth? her pride
Above all cities? in her hand
 Their destinies? in all beside
Of glory which the world hath known
Stands she not nobly and alone? 170
Falling—her veriest stepping-stone
Shall form the pedestal of a throne—
And who her sovereign? Timour[8]—he
 Whom the astonished people saw
Striding o'er empires haughtily 175
 A diadem'd outlaw!

O, human love! thou spirit given,
On Earth, of all we hope in Heaven!
Which fall'st into the soul like rain
Upon the Siroc[9] -wither'd plain, 180
And, failing in thy power to bless,
But leav'st the heart a wilderness!
Idea! which bindest life around
With music of so strange a sound
And beauty of so wild a birth— 185
Farewell! for I have won the Earth.

When Hope, the eagle that tower'd, could see
 No cliff beyond him in the sky,
His pinions were bent droopingly—
 And homeward turn'd his soften'd eye, 190
'Twas sunset: when the sun will part
There comes a sullenness of heart
To him who still would look upon
The glory of the summer sun.
That soul will hate the ev'ning mist 195
So often lovely, and will list
To the sound of the coming darkness[1] (known

7. Or Samarkand, the capital of Timberlane's empire. Poe's 1827 note reads: "I believe it was after the battle of Angoria that Tamerlane made Samarcand his residence. It became for a time the seat of learning and the arts."

8. Poe notes that "He was called Timur Bek as well as Tamerlane." The Turkish version of his name is more usually spelled Timur Beg. Because he was lame, his Persian name was Timur-i-Leng (Timur the Lame). In the 1827 text of the poem, the protagonist is given the name Alexis and his lover is called Ada.

9. Hot desert wind; also called *sirocco*; cf. simoom.

1. Poe's 1827 note reads: "I have often fancied that I could distinctly hear the sound of darkness, as it steals over the horizon—a foolish fancy perhaps, but not more unintelligible than to see music—'The mind the music breathing from her face.'" Poe uses the first part of the note again in "Al Aaraaf," II.47 (see p. 34, n. 1 herein). The quotation is from Byron's "The Bride of Abydos," I.vi.22.

To those whose spirits harken) as one
Who, in a dream of night, *would* fly
But *cannot* from a danger nigh. 200

What tho' the moon—the white moon
Shed all the splendor of her noon,
Her smile is chilly—and *her* beam,
In that time of dreariness, will seem
(So like you gather in your breath) 205
A portrait taken after death.
And boyhood is a summer sun
Whose waning is the dreariest one—
For all we live to know is known
And all we seek to keep hath flown— 210
Let life, then, as the day-flower,[2] fall
With the noon-day beauty—which is all.

I reach'd my home—my home no more—
 For all had flown who made it so.
I pass'd from out its mossy door, 215
 And, tho' my tread was soft and low,
A voice came from the threshold stone
Of one whom I had earlier known—
 O, I defy thee, Hell, to show
 On beds of fire that burn below, 220
 An humbler heart—a deeper wo.

Father, I firmly do believe—
 I *know*—for Death who comes for me
 From regions of the blest afar,
Where there is nothing to deceive, 225
 Hath left his iron gate ajar,
 And rays of truth you cannot see
 Are flashing thro' Eternity——
I do believe that Eblis[3] hath
A snare in every human path— 230
Else how, when in the holy grove
I wandered of the idol, Love,
Who daily scents his snowy wings
With incense of burnt offerings
From the most unpolluted things, 235
Whose pleasant bowers are yet so riven
Above with trellie'd rays from Heaven
No mote may shun—no tiniest fly—

2. The 1827 version emphasizes the role of Time in frustrating Tamerlane's love and ambition. Poe glosses the allusion to the "day-flower" as follows: "There is a flow'r, (I have never known its botanic name,) vulgarly called the day flower. It blooms beautifully in the daylight, but withers towards evening, and by night its leaves appear totally shrivelled and dead. I have forgotten, however, to mention in the text, that it lives again in the morning. If it will not flourish in Tartary, I must be forgiven for carrying it thither."
3. Mabbott notes that "Eblis" is Mahomet's name for the prince of the jinn (genies) and of evil spirits in general. In William Beckford's novel *Vathek* (1786), it is the abode of the damned, whose hearts are aflame.

The light'ning of his eagle eye—
How was it that Ambition crept, 240
 Unseen, amid the revels there,
Till growing bold, he laughed and leapt
 In the tangles of Love's very hair?

Dreams[1]

Oh! that my young life were a lasting dream!
My spirit not awak'ning, till the beam
Of an Eternity should bring the morrow.
Yes! tho' that long dream were of hopeless sorrow,
'T were better than the cold reality 5
Of waking life, to him whose heart must be,
And hath been still, upon the lovely earth,
A chaos of deep passion, from his birth.
But should it be—that dream eternally
Continuing—as dreams have been to me 10
In my young boyhood—should it thus be giv'n,
'Twere folly still to hope for higher Heav'n.
For I have revell'd when the sun was bright
I' the summer sky, in dreams of living light,
And loveliness,—have left my very heart 15
Inclines of mine imaginary apart
From mine own home, with beings that have been
Of mine own thought—what more could I have seen?
'Twas once—and only once[2]—and the wild hour
From my remembrance shall not pass—some pow'r 20
Or spell had bound me—'twas the chilly wind
Came o'er me in the night, and left behind
Its image on my spirit—or the moon
Shone on my slumbers in her lofty noon
Too coldly—or the stars—howe'er it was 25
That dream was as that night-wind—let it pass.
I *have been* happy, tho' in a dream.
I have been happy—and I love the theme:
Dreams! in their vivid colouring of life
As in that fleeting, shadowy, misty strife 30
Of semblance with reality which brings
To the delirious eye, more lovely things.
Of Paradise and Love—and all our own![3]
Than young Hope in his sunniest hour hath known.

1. First published in *Tamerlane and Other Poems* (1827), the text followed here. Scholars have seen parallels to sentiments in Byron's "The Dream" and *Childe Harold*, in which visionary imagination is said to be able to conceive other worlds and people them with its own creations.
2. Apparently a single instance of full insight, causing recognition that ordinary experience in this world lacks something; one interpretation of the poem is that happiness resides only in this one fleeting moment of insight.
3. Created by poetic imagination; cf. line 18.

Spirits of the Dead[1]

I

Thy soul shall find itself alone
Mid dark thoughts of the gray tomb-stone—
Not one, of all the crowd, to pry
Into thine hour of secrecy:

II

Be silent in that solitude, 5
 Which is not loneliness—for then
The spirits of the dead who stood
 In life before thee are again
In death around thee—and their will
Shall overshadow thee: be still. 10

III

The night—tho' clear—shall frown—
And the stars shall look not down,
From their high thrones in the heaven,
With light like Hope to mortals given—
But their red orbs, without beam, 15
To thy weariness shall seem
As a burning and a fever
Which would cling to thee for ever.

IV

Now are thoughts thou shalt not banish—
Now are visions ne'er to vanish— 20
From thy spirit shall they pass
No more—like dew-drop from the grass.

V

The breeze—the breath of God—is still—
And the mist upon the hill
Shadowy—shadowy—yet unbroken, 25
Is a symbol and a token—
How it hangs upon the trees,
A mystery of mysteries!—

1. First published in *Tamerlane and Other Poems* (1827) as "Visit of the Dead," a somewhat shorter nonstanzaic poem. The version followed here is that of the July 1839 *Burton's Gentleman's Magazine*.

Evening Star[1]

'Twas noontide of summer,
 And mid-time of night;[2]
And stars, in their orbits,
 Shone pale, thro' the light
Of the brighter, cold moon,[3] 5
 'Mid planets her slaves,
Herself in the Heavens,
 Her beam on the waves.
 I gaz'd awhile
 On her cold smile; 10
Too cold—too cold for me—
 There pass'd, as a shroud,
 A fleecy cloud,
And I turn'd away to thee,
 Proud Evening Star, 15
 In thy glory afar,
And dearer thy beam shall be;
 For joy to my heart
 Is the proud part
Thou bearest in Heav'n at night, 20
 And more I admire
 Thy distant fire,
Than that colder, lowly light.

Imitation[1]

A dark unfathom'd tide
Of interminable pride—
A mystery, and a dream,
Should my early life seem;
I say that dream was fraught 5
With a wild, and waking thought
Of beings that have been,
Which my spirit hath not seen.
Had I let them pass me by,

1. First published in *Tamerlane and Other Poems* (1827), the text followed here. The poem shows some indebtedness to Thomas Moore's "While Gazing on the Moon's Light" from *Irish Melodies* (1808–34). The evening star is Venus, goddess of love. Poe uses her Phoenician name, Astarte, in other poems (see notes to "Ulalume").
2. Midnight. Cf. lines 1–10 of "Al Aaraaf," Part II (and notes). "Noontide": the tides are traditionally under the control of the moon (see line 5).
3. The goddess of the moon is Diana (or Luna), who, despite the association of moonlight with love and romance, is traditionally aloof, distant, cold. Moonlight is reflected light, not self-generated like starlight.
1. This work was revised over and over again and has a complicated publication history. The variations are so great that Mabbott reprints three versions as separate poems. Cf. the 1849 version, "A Dream within a Dream." For a discussion of the several variants, see G. R. Thompson, *Circumscribed Eden of Dreams: Dreamvision and Nightmare in Poe's Early Poetry*, pp. 33–37. The text is that of *Tamerlane and Other Poems* (1827). The "imitation" would seem to be of Lord Byron's lyrics; see the discussion of Romanticism in the Poems introduction on pp. 3ff.

With a dreaming eye! 10
Let none of earth inherit
That vision of my spirit;
Those thoughts I would controul,
As a spell upon his soul:
For that bright hope at last 15
And that light time have past,
And my worldly rest hath gone
With a sigh as it pass'd on:
I care not tho' it perish
With a thought I then did cherish. 20

[Stanzas][1]

How often we forget all time, when lone
Admiring Nature's universal throne;
Her woods—her wilds—her mountains—the intense
Reply of HERS to OUR intelligence![2]

1

In youth have I known one with whom the Earth
In secret communing held—as he with it,
In day light, and in beauty from his birth;
Whose fervid, flick'ring torch of life was lit
From the sun and stars, whence he had drawn forth 5
A passionate light—such for his spirit was fit—
And yet that spirit knew not—in the hour
Of its own fervor—what had o'er it power.

2

Perhaps it may be that my mind is wrought
To a ferver by the moon beam that hangs o'er, 10
But I will half believe that wild light fraught
With more of sov'reignty than ancient lore
Hath ever told—or is it of a thought
The unembodied essence and no more
That with a quick'ning[3] spell doth o'er us pass 15
As dew of the night-time, o'er the summer grass?

3

Doth o'er us pass, when, as th' expanding eye
To the loved object—so the tear to the lid

1. First published in *Tamerlane and Other Poems* (1827). Mabbott claims that this text contains "three incorrect readings," and he changes some of the punctuation; for a discussion of what may be his own incorrect reading, see G. R. Thompson, *Circumscribed Eden of Dreams: Dreamvision and Nightmare in Poe's Early Poetry*, pp. 37–39. Note especially "fervor" in l. 8 and "ferver" in l. 10; some scholars think that the latter should be "fever." The version printed here follows that of the *Tamerlane* volume. First printed without a title; in the edition of Poe's *Works* by Stedman and Woodberry, the poem was given the title "Stanzas"; other variants include "In Youth Have I Known" and the entire first line.
2. Appropriated from Lord Byron's "The Island" (1823), II.xvi.13–16.
3. Probably in the sense of life-giving, stimulating into life, as in the meaning of *quick* (alive) in the conventional phrase "the quick and the dead."

Will start, which lately slept in apathy?
And yet it need not be—(that object) hid 20
From us in life—but common—which doth lie
Each hour before us—but *then* only bid
With a strange sound, as of a harp-string broken
T'awake us—'Tis a symbol and a token,[4]

4

Of what in other worlds shall be—and giv'n 25
In beauty by our God, to those alone
Who otherwise would fall from life and Heav'n
Drawn by their heart's passion, and that tone,
That high tone of the spirit which hath striv'n
Tho' not with Faith—with godliness—whose throne 30
With desp'rate energy 't hath beaten down;
Wearing its own deep feeling as a crown.[5]

A Dream[1]

In visions of the dark night
 I have dreamed of joy departed—
But a waking dream of life and light
 Hath left me broken-hearted.

Ah! what is not a dream by day 5
 To him whose eyes are cast
On things around him with a ray
 Turned back upon the past?

That holy dream—that holy dream,
 While all the world were chiding, 10
Hath cheered me as a lovely beam
 A lonely spirit guiding.

What though that light, thro' storm and night,
 So trembled from afar—
What could there be more purely bright 15
 In Truth's day star?[2]

4. Cf. "Spirits of the Dead" (line 26). "Harp-string . . . awake us": possibly an allusion to Mem-
non, the mythical African-Egyptian-Trojan king, who was the son of Eos, the Dawn, and
Tithonus, a prince of Troy. Two enormous statues stood in Egyptian Thebes, one of which
(to the east) was said to make a sound like the breaking of a harp string when first struck by
the rays of the morning sun (see notes to "The Coliseum," pp. 53ff. herein). Mabbott notes
the myth of the sound emitted by the stone on which Apollo placed his lyre during the build-
ing of the walls of Megara in central Greece. This city was famous for its struggles against
the Persians and, in the mid-5th century B.C.E., against the Corinthians and its former allies,
the Athenians. The story of Apollo's harp stone is found in the *Metamorphoses* (VIII.14ff.),
by the Roman poet Ovid (43 B.C.E.–18 C.E.).
5. A regal crown or possibly a crown of thorns; see the discussion of Byronism in the introduc-
tion, p. 3 herein.
1. First published in *Tamerlane and Other Poems* (1827). The version followed here is that of
The Raven and Other Poems (1845).
2. The fainter light from a far star compared metaphorically and equivocally to the sun. Cf. the
similar observation about the star of Venus and the moon in "Evening Star" (p. 17 herein).

[The Happiest Day][1]

The happiest day—the happiest hour
 My sear'd and blighted heart hath known,
The highest hope of pride, and power,
 I feel hath flown.

Of power! said I? Yes! such I ween[2] 5
 But they have vanish'd long alas!
The visions of my youth have been—
 But let them pass.

And, pride, what have I now with thee?
 Another brow may ev'n inherit 10
The venom thou hast pour'd on me—
 Be still my spirit.

The happiest day—the happiest hour
 Mine eyes shall see—have ever seen
The brightest glance of pride and power 15
 I feel—have been:

But were that hope of pride and power
 Now offer'd, with the pain
Ev'n *then* I felt—that brightest hour
 I would not live again: 20

For on its wing was dark alloy[3]
 And as it flutter'd—fell
An essence—powerful to destroy
 A soul that knew it well.

The Lake—To ——— First published in *Tamerlane and Other Poems* (1827), the version followed here. The version printed in *The Raven and Other Poems* (1845) is divided into stanzas and shows minor changes of phrasing in lines 10–11, 15–16 (adding a line 17), 20–21. The setting is supposed by most scholars to be the Lake of the Dismal Swamp in Virginia (Drummond's Pond or Lake Drummond). Poe's poems shows some similarities to two of Thomas Moore's poems: "A Ballad: The Lake of the Dismal Swamp," based on his visit to Virginia in 1803, and "I Wish I Was by That Dim Lake," set in Donegal, Ireland, from *Irish Melodies* (1808–34) (see notes on Moore in "Al Aaraaf," pp. 22ff. *et passim*, "The

1. First published untitled in *Tamerlane and Other Poems* (1827), the version followed here. Interpretations of the poem vary: one of the more popular biographical readings is that when Poe returned to Richmond from the University of Virginia he realized that he had lost Elmira Royster and that, thus young, his happiest day had already passed. Nonbiographical readings focus on the Byronic lament for the curse of genius.
2. To think, to suppose; to think or suppose possible.
3. Element mixed with a thing of higher value or quality (as in metallurgy); anything that lowers the purity of something.

Assignation," pp. 116ff., and other of Poe's works herein.) By tradition, the lake was haunted by the ghosts of two lovers and its waters were said to be poisonous. Mabbott advocates a biographical interpretation that has many adherents; for a more literary reading in terms of Romanticism, see Thompson, *Circumscribed Eden of Dreams*, pp. 40–41; also see the Poems introduction, pp. 3ff. herein.

The Lake—To ————[1]

In spring of youth it was my lot
To haunt of the wide world a spot
The which I could not love the less—
So lovely was the loneliness
Of a wild lake, with black rock bound, 5
And the tall pines that towered around.

But when the Night had thrown her pall[2]
Upon that spot, as upon all,
And the mystic wind went by
Murmuring in melody— 10
Then—ah then I would awake
To the terror of the lone lake.

Yet that terror was not fright,
But a tremulous delight—
A feeling not the jewelled mine 15
Could teach or bribe me to define—
Nor Love—although the Love were thine.

Death was in that poisonous wave,
And in its gulf a fitting grave
For him who thence could solace bring 20
To his lone imagining—
Whose solitary soul could make
An Eden[3] of that dim lake.

Sonnet—To Science[1]

Science! true daughter of Old Time thou art!
 Who alterest all things with thy peering eyes.
Why preyest thou thus upon the poet's heart,
 Vulture, whose wings are dull realities?
How should he love thee? or how deem thee wise, 5

1. The identity of the person the poem is dedicated to is unknown.
2. A cover for a coffin; here, something that obscures, darkens, or depresses.
3. I.e., an original or unspoiled paradise.
1. First published in *Al Aaraaf, Tamerlane, and Minor Poems* (1829), where it stood as the introduction (see Poems introduction, pp. 3–5, and "Al Aaraaf," pp. 22ff. herein). As the epigraph to "The Island of the Fay," the poem has significant variants. The version followed here is that of *The Raven and Other Poems* (1845).

Who wouldst not leave him in his wandering
To seek for treasure in the jewelled skies,
 Albeit he soared with an undaunted wing?
Hast thou not dragged Diana[2] from her car?
 And driven the Hamadryad[3] from the wood 10
To seek a shelter in some happier star?[4]
 Hast thou not torn the Naiad[5] from her flood,
The Elfin[6] from the green grass, and from me
The summer dream beneath the tamarind tree?[7]

Al Aaraaf An "Extract from 'Al Aaraaf' an Unpublished Poem" was
published in the *Baltimore Gazette and Daily Advertiser*, May 18, 1829.
The whole poem appeared in book form later the same year: *Al Aaraaf,
Tamerlane and Minor Poems* (Hutch and Dunning). Poe made many
changes to this work in its different publications, including different "in-
troductions" that came to stand alone as separate poems. A version of "Ro-
mance" (p. 42, n.1 herein) was first published under the title "Preface" in
the 1829 edition; "Sonnet—to Science" (pp. 21–22 above) was also used
as an introduction. Yet another poem, "Mysterious Star" (not reprinted
herein), was substituted for the first fifteen lines of "Al Aaraaf" in 1831.
The text printed here follows that of *The Raven and Other Poems* (1845),
though Poe's annotations of the poem are treated slightly differently. From
its first publication, "Al Aaraaf" contained many notes referencing al-
lusions or offering personal comments (a convention of the time; cf.
"Tamerlane"). In the 1845 edition, Poe's notes are indicated by old
printer's notations (asterisks, daggers, double daggers, and the like) at the
beginning of particular lines. In this reprinting, Poe's notes are integrated
with the numbered editorial annotations of the Norton edition, and the
numerals are placed at the end of the line rather than the beginning. That
a note is Poe's is indicated in brackets: any additional annotations of Poe's
notes follow in the same note. Other editorial annotations occur in the
usual manner at the word or phrase glossed.
 "Al Aaraaf" is one of Poe's most highly allusive, complex, and opaque
works. The poem requires extensive annotation; in this matter, I have fol-
lowed the lead of previous commentators, principally Killis Campbell,
Margaret Alterton and Hardin Craig, Floyd Stovall, and Thomas Ollive
Mabbott. Campbell's 1917 edition of Poe's poems contained the most ex-
tensive glosses until that of Mabbott (1969), which builds on Campbell's
work (sometimes copying it verbatim). The most important of Poe's allu-
sions and sources are the Koran (Qu'ran) and Renaissance figures such as
Michelangelo, Christopher Marlowe, William Shakespeare, and John Mil-
ton, along with the Romantic poets Thomas Moore and Lord Byron. They

2. Goddess of the moon in Roman mythology, who rode her celestial chariot ("car") across the
 night sky.
3. In Greek mythology, a wood nymph.
4. In two versions (Philadelphia *Saturday Evening Post*, September 11, 1830; *The Casket*, Oc-
 tober 1830), this line read "Hast thou not spoilt a story in each star?"
5. A water nymph; in Greek mythology, Naias.
6. Poe's diminutive or plural for *elf*.
7. Arabic name of the Indian date tree, which has spreading branches covered with yellow
 flowers with red stripes; its fruit, used in both cooking and medicine, is bitter. As the epi-
 graph to "The Island of the Fay" (*Graham's Magazine*, June 1841), lines 13–14 read: "The
 elfin from the grass?—the danty *fay*, / The witch, the sprite, the goblin—where are they?"

may be said to be the presiding spirits of Poe's poem; indeed, Poe makes Michelangelo one of the characters of his story. Milton's great Puritan epic, *Paradise Lost* (1667), is perhaps the most pervasive Renaissance influence on Poe's poem. Poe invokes a grand Miltonic sense of admonition and of apocalyptic punishment of human sinfulness on a cosmic scale. The word *apocalypse* is most often used to mean impending doom—the final destruction of the world. But its root meaning is a final "discovery" (uncovering, unveiling) of a cosmic plan or story, a revelation that is left incomplete and obscure in Poe's poem. Although human sinfulness is a dominant motif in the poem, Poe's idea is not Puritan or even Christian. Nor is the vague possibility of salvation it hints at a Christian one. Instead it is aesthetic; sensitivity to supernal otherworldly Beauty is the only possible salvation, and even that is remote. (A thematic overview may be found in the Poetry introduction, pp. 3ff.)

The other most important influences are the major Romantic poets, especially Byron and Shelley, and in particular the Arabo-Oriental poems of Thomas Moore. Poe was fascinated by Moore's *Lalla Rookh* (1817) and *The Loves of the Angels* (1822); indeed, *Lalla Rookh*, an "Arabian" tale, is one of the most frequently cited works in Poe's whole body of work. Campbell's notes on Moore and Arabic sources for Poe are exemplary. He points out that in *Lalla Rookh* Moore makes specific references to George Sale's 1734 translation of the Koran, particularly to his introductory essay ("Preliminary Discourse"), in which certain Muslim religious ideas, stories, myths, and symbols, including the mysterious Al Aaraaf, are explained. Poe himself specifically indicates that the dramatic world of his poem is derived from the Al Aaraaf of the Arabians, conceived as "a medium between Heaven and Hell." *Al* is the Arabic definite article; *Aaraaf* (modern *Araf* or *Arâf*) is a veiled midregion between heaven and hell where souls await judgment. *Al Araf* (or *Al-Orf*) seems to be derived from the verb *Arafa*, which means "to distinguish between things or to separate them." In a note on chapter 7 of the Koran (titled "Al Arâf"), Sale describes the place as "a sort of purgatory for those who, though they deserve not to be sent to hell, yet have not merits sufficient to gain them immediate admittance into paradise, and will be tantalized here for a certain time." The point is made clearer by Campbell's quotation from the "Preliminary Discourse":

> The Mohammedan writers greatly differ as to the persons who are to be found on al Arâf. Some imagine it to be a sort of limbo, for the patriarchs and prophets, or for the martyrs and those who have been most eminent for sanctity, among whom they say there will be also angels in the form of men. Others place here such whose good and evil works are so equal that they exactly counterpoise each other and therefore deserve neither reward nor punishment; and these, they say, will on the last day be admitted into paradise, after they shall have performed an act of adoration, which will be imputed to them as a merit, and will make the scale of their good works to overbalance.

Sale notes that some have imagined Al Arâf as a wall between heaven and hell. But the "breadth of this partition wall cannot be supposed to be exceeding great, since not only those who shall stand thereon will hold conference with the inhabitants both of paradise and hell, but the blessed and the damned themselves will also be able to talk to one another."

Campbell observes that the "presence of sorrow in Al Aaraaf and the fate

of those who inhabit it" seems to be "an independent elaboration of Sale's note," made by Poe in "the interest of his story." He adds: "Original with Poe, too, no doubt, is the identification of Al Aaraaf with the star discovered by the . . . astronomer, Tycho Brahe." Poe based his story on a sixteenth-century astronomical event—apparently the explosion of a nova or supernova. It manifested itself for several months over Europe (see p. 24, n. 1 below). In Poe's poem, Al Aaraaf is an ephemeral star-island that suddenly appears in the night skies over the earth. Containing both the fearful and the beautiful, Al Aaraaf is the dwelling place of the spirits of poets and of poetic imaginings and other artistic creations; all have a transitory or interim existence between heaven and hell. In *The Loves of the Angels* (1822), Thomas Moore remarks that "a belief that the stars are either spirits, or the vehicles of spirits, was common to all the religions and heresies of the East." Poe's star world is peopled (in Campbell's words) "partly by the spirits of certain mortals who, in accordance with the Mohammedan tradition, were not good enough for heaven, but were too good for hell, and partly by certain angels who had dwelt from the beginning in Al Aaraaf." But the dwellers in Al Aaraaf are without divine knowledge or, as Campbell puts it, that "supreme knowledge possessed by the angels in heaven."

Al Aaraaf[1]

Part I[2]

O! NOTHING earthly save the ray
(Thrown back from flowers) of Beauty's eye,
As in those gardens where the day
Springs from the gems of Circassy[3]—
O! nothing earthly save the thrill 5
Of melody in woodland rill—
Or (music of the passion-hearted)

1. A star was discovered by Tycho Brahe which appeared suddenly in the heavens—attained, in a few days, a brilliancy surpassing that of Jupiter—then as suddenly disappeared, and has never been seen since [Poe's note]. The Danish astronomer Tycho (1546–1601) first observed the star in November 1572; it was visible for some sixteen months, fading away from view in 1574. (See the Poems introduction pp. 4–5 herein, for further details.) In the first printing of the "Extracts" in the *Baltimore Gazette*, Poe offered an "Introductory Note," similarly setting the scene of his poem but more explicitly announcing one of its major themes. "Michael Angelo is represented as transferred to this star, and speaking to the 'lady of his unearthly love' of the regions he had left." That is, although desiring knowledge of a realm beyond the earthly, he cannot give up his earthly ties and desires.
2. The dramatic situation of Part I may be summarized as follows. In an unearthly world floating in space, the goddess Nesace awakes in her temple. She is the presiding spirit of a star that resembles a fantastic island from ancient myth, with spectacular mountain vistas and luxuriant flowery gardens. Her silent prayer rises with the fragrance of flowers to yet more distant spheres. The prayer expresses the obedience of the star angels to God in seeking beauty rather than truth, for beauty belongs to the higher heaven. The form of God is unknown, though vaguely intimated by human science and art. The human mind, especially in its capacity to perceive beauty, comes closest to suggesting an image of God; but conceiving of the form of God in terms of the material world of earth is too limited, and giving God a human form (anthropomorphism) is an error. Nesace waits for a "sound of silence," which all nature speaks in tune with what "dreamy poets name the 'music of the spheres' " (i.e., cosmic harmony). But on the startled ear falls the "eternal voice of God" with a commandment. She is to "wing to other worlds" and admonish the "proud" beings that inhabit them of the danger of "falling" like the guilty race of earth. Al Aaraaf is thus a messenger star from God—warning that when the eternal voice of God shall pass by, red winds will wither in the sky.
3. Or Circassia; a region of the Caucasus famous for its precious gems and desirable light-skinned, light-haired women.

Joy's voice so peacefully departed
That like the murmur in the shell,
Its echo dwelleth and will dwell— 10
Oh, nothing of the dross[4] of ours—
Yet all the beauty—all the flowers
That list[5] our Love, and deck our bowers—
Adorn yon world afar, afar—
The wandering star. 15

 'Twas a sweet time for Nesace[6]—for there
Her world lay lolling on the golden air,
Near four bright suns[7]—a temporary rest—
An oasis in desert of the blest.
Away—away—'mid seas of rays that roll 20
Empyrean[8] splendor o'er th' unchained soul—
The soul that scarce (the billows are so dense)
Can struggle to its destin'd eminence—
To distant spheres, from time to time, she rode,
And late to ours, the favour'd one of God— 25
But, now, the ruler of an anchor'd realm,
She throws aside the sceptre—leaves the helm,
And, amid incense and high spiritual hymns,
Laves in quadruple light[9] her angel limbs.

 Now happiest, loveliest in yon lovely Earth, 30
Whence sprang the "Idea of Beauty" into birth,
(Falling in wreaths thro' many a startled star,
Like woman's hair 'mid pearls, until, afar,
It lit on hills Achaian,[1] and there dwelt)
She look'd into Infinity—and knelt. 35
Rich clouds, for canopies, about her curled—

4. Something impure, a waste product; valueless.
5. Listen to.
6. Campbell suggests that the meter of the poem requires pronunciation of the goddess's name in three syllables, with emphasis on the first and third and with a hard *c* at the end: NES-*a*-KE. Her name means "lady of the island" (*nesos*) according to Mabbott. The island–star comparison runs throughout the poem. Other scholars (including Campbell) have suggested that Nesace is a form of "Nausicaa," the courteous and desirable maiden at the beach in the *Odyssey* who rescues Odysseus from the sea and brings him to her father's fabulous palace.
7. A reference to the rectangle of four stars (now called Beta, Alpha, Gamma, and Kappa) in the constellation of Cassiopeia, where the supernova described by Tycho Brahe in the 16th century appeared (see the Poems introduction on pp. 4, 24 herein).
8. The farthest reaches of the sky: the outer orbit of celestial bodies—the realm of the stars—believed by many of the ancients to be composed of rings of fire. It is related to the "spherical" concept of the transparent crystal orbits of planets around the earth (Ptolemaic cosmology); see "Ulalume" (p. 63, n. 5 herein) and other poems. The words "unchained," "spheres," and "anchor'd" in lines 21, 24, and 26 seem to refer to the ancient idea that the earth is depended in space from a golden pendant chain anchored to the empyrean—an image that recurs in the poem. This in turn is related to the concept of the Great Chain of Being, wherein everything that exists has its own sphere, in a particular cosmic order, like the links in a chain.
9. Nesace bathes in the light of the four suns, or stars, previously mentioned (line 18).
1. In the 1829 version, the word is spelled *Archaian*, which indicates, in general, something ancient (archaic). Mabbott suggests that, spelled as it is here, the word implies something more specific—namely, Achaea in the Peloponnesus, thus a near synonym for "Hellenic."

Fit emblems of the model of her world[2]—
Seen but in beauty—not impeding sight
Of other beauty glittering thro' the light—
A wreath that twined each starry form around, 40
And all the opal'd air in color bound.

All hurriedly she knelt upon a bed
Of flowers: of lilies such as rear'd the head
On the fair Capo Deucato, and sprang[3]
So eagerly around about to hang 45
Upon the flying footsteps of——deep pride—
Of her who lov'd a mortal—and so died.[4]
The Sephalica, budding with young bees,[5]
Uprear'd its purple stem around her knees:
And gemmy flower, of Trebizond misnam'd[6]— 50
Inmate of highest stars, where erst it sham'd

2. The line suggests the rarefied ideal realm of Nesace's star world. Platonic idealism conceives
 of material existence as the "copy" of an "Idea" in a higher other world. Earthly art symboli-
 cally copies that copy and thus is circumscribed by material existence and stands farther
 from the Ideal unless it transcends the earthly. Here the astral island's clouds are a suitable
 "emblem" (symbol) of something else—of the "model" for the star world, which is itself but
 its copy or imitation. The passage is opaque, but the sequence suggests an infinite regressive
 series of worlds at various distances from the Godhead, with the material earth and human
 form at one of the far removes (cf. lines 104–05 of Part I).
3. On Santa Maura—olim Deucadia [Poe's note]. "Santa Maura": an island off the western
 coast of Greece. "Deucadia": ancient name for modern Leucas (Leucadia, Leucate, Lev-
 kadi), so called because of its white cliffs. Campbell notes that the place known as "cap de
 l'Epire" in French is called today the "Capo Ducato," the Italian name for its southern
 promontory, whereas Santa Maura is the Italian name of the island. Campbell quotes from
 Thomas Moore's notes to his "Evenings in Greece": "Now [called] Santa Maura—the island
 from whose cliffs Sappho leaped into the sea" (see n. 4 below).
4. Sappho [Poe's note]. One of the legends about the Greek lyric poet Sappho of Lesbos (early
 6th century B.C.E.), is that she supposedly leaped into the sea from the Leucadian Rock (or
 Deucadian; see previous note) because of the unrequited love of Phaon. The story as told in
 Ovid's 15th "Epistle" was translated by Alexander Pope as "Sappho to Phaon" and recounted
 in Thomas Moore's "Evenings in Greece." Citing the 1822 work *Corfu, Leucadia . . . [and]
 the Ionian Islands* by William Goodisson, Moore says that there are "scented lilies" still
 blooming on "that fearful place," marking the "immortal spot" where her last "bright foot-
 steps" passed. Moore's line seems to use the word *immortal* in the sense of eternally remem-
 bered, unforgotten. Poe's line plays with the tradition that love affairs between the gods and
 mortals tended to have tragic consequences. Although a real person, fragments of whose po-
 etry still survive, she was called the "tenth muse" by ancient writers like Plato. Since the
 muses (usually numbered as nine) are the goddesses of the sciences and the arts, Sappho
 would be (at least metaphorically) "immortal" while her lover, Phaon, was mortal.
5. In "The Veiled Prophet of Khorassan" episode in *Lalla Rookh*, II.155–59, Thomas Moore
 writes:

> the still sound
> Of falling waters, lulling as the song
> Of Indian bees at sunset, when they throng
> Around the fragrant Nilica, and deep
> In its blue blossoms hum themselves to sleep.

In a note Moore quotes Sir William Jones's "Botanical Observations on Select Indian Plants"
(reprinted 1807) to the effect that the plant known as the *Nilica* is called *Sephalica*, "thus
named because the bees are supposed to sleep on its blossoms."

6. This flower is much noticed by Lewenhoeck and Tournefort. The bee, feeding upon its blos-
 som, becomes intoxicated. [Poe's note]. Anton van Leeuwenhoek (1632–1723) was the in-
 ventor of the microscope. Joseph Pitton de Tournefort (1656–1708) was a French botanist.
 In the "Fire-Worshippers" section of *Lalla Rookh* (I.46–49), Thomas Moore writes:

> Ev'n as those bees of Trebizond,
> Which, from the sunniest flowers that glad
> With their pure smile the gardens round,
> Draw venom forth that drives men mad!

All other loveliness: its honied dew
(The fabled nectar that the heathen knew)
Deliriously sweet, was dropp'd from Heaven,
And fell on gardens of the unforgiven 55
In Trebizond[7]—and on a sunny flower
So like its own above that, to this hour,
It still remaineth, torturing the bee
With madness, and unwonted reverie:[8]
In Heaven, and all its environs, the leaf 60
And blossom of the fairy plant, in grief
Disconsolate linger—grief that hangs her head,
Repenting follies that full long have fled,
Heaving her white breast to the balmy air,
Like guilty beauty, chasten'd, and more fair: 65
Nyctanthes[9] too, as sacred as the light
She fears to perfume, perfuming the night:
 And Clytia pondering between many a sun,[1]
While pettish tears adown her petals run:
 And that aspiring flower that sprang on Earth[2]— 70
And died, ere scarce exalted into birth,
Bursting its odorous heart in spirit to wing
Its way to Heaven, from garden of a king:
 And Valisnerian lotus thither flown[3]

In a note, Moore paraphrases Tournefort's *Voyage into the Levant* (1791): "There is a kind of Rhododendros about Trebizonde, whose flowers the bee feeds upon, and the honey thence drives men mad." Animals, birds, and insects feeding on the plant were said to go temporarily mad, and honey made from it was said to be a poison. Campbell notes the somewhat parallel tradition of the asphodel, the pale white flower of Hades and the dead. He also notes Milton's treatment of a related tradition regarding the amaranth, which originally bloomed on earth but because of human sin was removed to a heavenly garden (*Paradise Lost*, III.353–57). Trebizond is the name of a city and a region in northeast Turkey by the Black Sea; the city in ancient times (post-8th century B.C.E.) was called Trapezus. Both the city and its environs were famous for gardens.

7. Mabbott speculates that the allusion to "the unforgiven / In Trebizond" is to Mithradates Eupator, king of Pontus (flourished 1st century B.C.E.). His dominions included Trapezus. He is supposed to have made himself immune to poisons by taking repeated small doses and indulging in magical practices. The Romans were his unforgiving enemies.

8. See n. 6, above.

9. Campbell observes that Thomas Moore, in a footnote to the "Veiled Prophet of Khorassen" section of *Lalla Rookh*, II.441–43, refers to "the sweet night flower" that perfumes the dark. Moore explains that the night flower is "the sorrowful nyctanthes, which begins to spread its rich odour after sunset." In observing that the sephalica is a species of nyctanthes. Moore may again have relied on Sir William Jones (see n. 5, above), who says that the botanist Linnaeus designates the sephalica as the "sorrowful nyctanthes." Also see Poe's "Letter to B——" (pp. 588ff. herein).

1. Clytia—The Chrysanthemum Peruvianum, or, to employ a better-known term, the turnsol—which turns continually towards the sun, covers itself, like Peru, the country from which it comes, with dewy clouds which cool and refresh its flowers during the most violent heat of the day.—*B. de St. Pierre* [Poe's note]. Poe's source is Henry Hunter's 1808 translation of *Études de la Nature* (Studies of Nature, 1784) by Jacques Henri Bernardin de Saint-Pierre (1737–1814).

2. There is cultivated in the king's garden at Paris, a species of serpentine aloes without prickles, whose large and beautiful flower exhales a strong odour of the vanilla, during the time of its expansion, which is very short. It does not blow till towards the month of July—you then perceive it gradually open its petals—expand them—fade and die.—*St. Pierre* [Poe's note]. Again from the Hunter translation of St. Pierre's *Studies of Nature*.

3. There is found, in the Rhone, a beautiful lily of the Valisnerian kind. Its stem will stretch to the length of three or four feet—thus preserving its head above water in the swellings of the river [Poe's note]. The source of this note is also Saint-Pierre's *Studies of Nature*. Mabbott observes that "Poe preserves the incorrect spelling of Vallisnerian as he does in his '1002nd Tale of Scheherezade.'" The Rhône River flows from a glacier of the same name in Switzerland

From struggling with the waters of the Rhone: 75
 And thy most lovely purple perfume, Zante![4]
Isola d'oro!—Fior di Levante!
 And the Nelumbo bud that floats for ever[5]
With Indian Cupid down the holy river—
Fair flowers, and fairy! to whose care is given 80
 To bear the Goddess' song, in odors, up to Heaven:[6]

 "Spirit! that dwellest where,
 In the deep sky,
 The terrible and fair,
 In beauty vie! 85
 Beyond the line of blue—
 The boundary of the star
 Which turneth at the view
 Of thy barrier and thy bar[7]—
 Of the barrier overgone 90
 By the comets who were cast
 From their pride, and from their throne
 To be drudges till the last—
 To be carriers of fire
 (The red fire of their heart)[8] 95
 With speed that may not tire
 And with pain that shall not part—
 Who livest—*that* we know—

into Lake Geneva and from there through southeast France, where it splits into a larger and a smaller stream and flows to the Mediterranean.

4. The Hyacinth [Poe's note]. "Zante" is the Italian name for an island off southern Greece in the Ionian sea; the word is a form of the Greek *Zacynthus*, which supposedly derives from *Hyacynthus*. François René, vicomte de Chateaubriand (1768–1848), in *Itinéraire de Paris à Jérusalem* (1811) observes that the "hyacinth came from Zante, and . . . this island received its name from the flower." Campbell connects the tradition that the island of Zante took its name from the hyacinth with the "Italian epithets which are applied to it"—*Isola d'oro* (Island of gold) and *Fior de Levante* (Flower of the Levant). See Poe's sonnet "To Zante" (1836), "To Helen" (1831; p. 47 herein) and "Irene" (1831) for other uses of the hyacinth. Even though Poe was fluent in French, Mabbott claims that he read Chateaubriand's work in F. Shoberl's translation, *Travels in Greece, Palestine, Egypt, and Barbary* (Philadelphia, 1813).
5. It is a fiction of the Indians, that Cupid was first seen floating in one of these down the river Ganges—and that he still loves the cradle of his childhood [Poe's note]. Thomas Moore writes in "The Light of the Harem" section of *Lalla Rookh* (see lines 587–92) that "bards have seen" the love god "in their dreams" floating and gliding "down the blue Ganges"— smiling and laughing "upon a rosy lotus wreath." In a note to this passage, Moore writes: "The Indians feign that Cupid was first seen floating down the Ganges on the Nymphaea Nelumbo. See Pennant." Thomas Pennant (1726–1798) was a Welsh naturalist and antiquarian. The image of the god of love and desire floating on the sacred lotus also occurs in a contemporary poem by the American poet Letitia E. Landon, whose works Poe reviewed. In "Manmadin," she writes: "Pillow'd on a lotus flower / . . . Rides he o'er the mountain wave." Mabbott adds that Manmatha (or Manmadin) is a variant of the names of Camdeo or Kamadeva," who is a "god of desire" and the Indian equivalent of the Greeks' Eros, the Romans' Cupid.
6. And golden vials full of odors which are the prayers of the saints—*Rev St. John* [Poe's note]. Close paraphrase of Revelation 5:8, a reference Poe himself glossed in 1829.
7. Campbell and others suggest that this phrase refers to the boundary that God has placed on the cosmic journey of Al Aaraaf, i.e., the messenger star cannot come any closer to the Godhead. It may, however, refer to the ultimate distancing from God of all created things.
8. The comets seem to be a reference to the fallen angels who sided with Lucifer against God; in Poe's poem they are punished by having to carry fire in their hearts. Cf. Milton's treatments of the story of the Revolt of the Angels in *Paradise Lost*, books, I, V, VI. In William Beckford's novel *Vathek* (1786), the damned wander Eblis with their hearts aflame: see p. 14, n. 3 herein.

 In Eternity—we feel—
But the shadow of whose brow 100
 What spirit shall reveal?
Tho' the beings whom thy Nesace,
 Thy messenger hath known
Have dream'd for thy Infinity
 A model of their own[9]— 105
Thy will is done, Oh, God!
 The star hath ridden high
Thro' many a tempest, but she rode
 Beneath thy burning eye;
And here, in thought, to thee— 110
 In thought that can alone
Ascend thy empire and so be
 A partner of thy throne[1]—
By winged Fantasy,[2]

9. [Poe's note:] The Humanitarians held that God was to be understood as having really a human form.—*Vide Clarke's Sermons*, vol. 1, page, 26, fol. edit.
 The drift of Milton's argument, leads him to employ language which would appear, at first sight, to verge upon their doctrine; but it will be seen immediately, that he guards himself against the charge of having adopted one of the most ignorant errors of the dark ages of the church.—*Dr. Sumner's Notes on Milton's Christian Doctrine.*
 This opinion, in spite of many testimonies to the contrary, could never have been very general. Andeus, a Syrian of Mesopotamia, was condemned for the opinion, as heretical. He lived in the beginning of the fourth century. His disciples were culled Anthropmorphites.—*Vide Du Pin.*
 Among Milton's minor poems are these lines:—

> Dicite sacrorum praesides nemorum Deae, &c.
> Quis ille primus cujus ex imagine
> Natura solers finxit humanum genus?
> Eternus, incorruptus, aequaevus polo,
> Unusque et universus exemplar Dei.—And afterwards,
> Non cui profundum Caecitas lumen dedit
> Dircaeus augur vidit hunc alto sinu, &c. [End of Poe's note.]

Poe's Latinate and abbreviated reference to the sermons of the Reverend Samuel Clarke reads: "see Clarke's Sermons, volume one, page twenty-six, folio [i.e., large page] edition." Campbell points out that Poe's references are to Charles R. Sumner's notes on Clarke's edition of John Milton's *Treatise of Christian Doctrine* (1825) and that Sumner's reference is to the 1738 edition of Clarke's *Works.* Poe referred to Sumner and Clarke again in a review of J. G. C. Brainard in *Graham's Magazine* for February 1842, in which he remarked that "bestowing upon Deity a human form is . . . low and most unideal." According to Mabbott, Poe's information about the obscure Andeus of Mesopotamia is correct; he founded his sect in Syria about 338 C.E. The French historian Louis-Ellies DuPin (1657–1719) wrote many works on both ancient and modern history. Poe apparently accidentally misspelled *anthropomophites*, leaving out the *o* after the first *p*. *Anthropomorphism* means conceiving of something, usually a deity, in human (*anthropo* = "man") shape or form (*morph*).
 The quoted verses, with omissions, are from John Milton's Latin poem "De idea platonica quemadmodum Aristoteles intellexit" (I.7–10, 25–26). The general sense is that the poet asks the sister goddesses, who guard the sacred groves, to tell him who, what, or where is the great eternal Being, the archetypal exemplar of humanity, that gave us our existence in the form of the god. He concludes that not even the seer whose blindness gave him greater sight (Tiresias of Thebes) could see Deity.

1. See p. 24, n. 2 herein.
2. Seltsamen Tochter Jovis
 Seinem Schosskinde
 Der Phantasie.—*Goethe* [Poe's note].

From Goethe's "Meine Göttin" (My Goddess, 1780), lines 7–9. Mabbott notes George Bancroft's "Life and Genius of Goethe" in the *North American Review* for October 1824, where he translates the lines loosely as: "Dearest in her father's eye. / Jove's own darling, Phantasy." More literally the lines read: Strange daughter of Jove / His beloved lap-child / Fantasy. Poe used the German quotation again in 1840 as a motto for *Tales of the Grotesque and Arabesque* and again in 1842 on the manuscript title page of his planned collection of stories *Phantasy-Pieces.* See the biographical sketch on p. xxxiv herein.

My embassy[3] is given, 115
Till secrecy shall knowledge be
In the environs of Heaven."

 She ceas'd—and buried then her burning cheek
Abash'd, amid the lilies there, to seek
A shelter from the fervour of His eye; 120
For the stars trembled at the Deity.[4]
She stirr'd not—breath'd not—for a voice was there
How solemnly pervading the calm air!
A sound of silence on the startled ear
Which dreamy poets name "the music of the sphere."[5] 125
Ours is a world of words: Quiet we call
"Silence"—which is the merest word of all.
All Nature speaks, and ev'n ideal things
Flap shadowy sounds from visionary wings—
But ah! not so when, thus, in realms on high 130
The eternal voice of God is passing by,
And the red winds are withering in the sky!

 "What tho' in worlds which sightless cycles run,[6]
Link'd to a little system, and one sun—
Where all my love is folly and the crowd 135
Still think my terrors but the thunder cloud,
The storm, the earthquake, and the ocean-wrath—
(Ah! will they cross me in my angrier path?)
What tho' in worlds which own a single sun
The sands of Time grow dimmer as they run, 140
Yet thine is my resplendency, so given
To bear my secrets thro' the upper Heaven.
Leave tenantless thy crystal[7] home, and fly,
With all thy train, athwart the moony sky—
Apart—like fire-flies in Sicilian night,[8] 145
And wing to other worlds another light!
Divulge the secrets of thy embassy
To the proud orbs that twinkle—and so be

3. For "embassy" as mission or message, Campbell references *Paradise Lost*, III.658.
4. Lesser creatures, whether angelic or mortal, traditionally cannot look directly at the dazzling face of Deity. W. B. Cairns suggests a parallel with Thomas Moore's "The Loves of the Angels," lines 932ff., and Campbell with lines 1653ff. (in the 1823 text).
5. A reference to the celestial music (imperceptible to the material ear of ordinary earthly beings) made by the planets and sun revolving around the earth in their crystal spheres (see p. 25, n. 8 herein). Campbell suggests a parallel with John Keats's *Endymion* II. 675: "Silence was music from the holy spheres." Also see Poe's prose sketch "Silence" (pp. 136ff. herein) and his poem "Sonnet—Silence" (p. 55). Cf. n. 7 below.
6. Sightless—too small to he seen.—*Legge* [Poe's note]. This usage is probably from a sermon of Edward Legge (1767–1827), bishop of Oxford. It is also found in Shakespeare's *Macbeth*.
7. The sphere of the fixed stars was called "crystalline," a concept to which Poe alludes in "Ulalume" and elsewhere (see p. 25, n. 8 and p. 63, n. 5 herein).
8. I have often noticed a peculiar movement of the fire-flies;—they will collect in a body and fly off, from a common centre, into innumerable radii [Poe's note].

To ev'ry heart a barrier and a ban
Lest the stars totter in the guilt of man!"[9] 150

 Up rose the maiden in the yellow night,
The single-mooned eve!—on Earth we plight
Our faith to one love—and one moon adore—
The birth-place of young Beauty had no more.
As sprang that yellow star from downy hours 155
Up rose the maiden from her shrine of flowers,
And bent o'er sheeny mountain and dim plain
Her way—but left not yet her Therasæan reign.[1]

9. The Deity's silent yet auditory reproach warns of an apocalypse, a disaster temporarily held
at bay by such star worlds as Al Aaraaf and emissaries as Nesace. Mabbott notes the well-
known apocalyptic description in Pope's *Essay on Man*, I.vii.251ff.

> Let earth unbalanced from her orbit fly,
> Planets and stars run lawless thro' the sky:
> Let ruling angels from their spheres be hurl'd,
> Being on being wreck'd, and world on world;
> Heav'n's whole foundations to their centre nod,
> And Nature tremble to the throne of God!

Campbell speculates that the "guilt of man" consists principally in conceiving of God as an-
thropomorphic and of God's attributes in terms of the material universe, ignoring the ways
in which Deity reveals itself in intellectual perception and in beauty (p. 32, n. 2 herein). Cf.
Percy Bysshe Shelley's "Hymn to Intellectual Beauty" (1817), which Poe singles out (in his
Drake-Halleck review, *Southern Literary Messenger*, April 1836) as a work most nearly de-
scribing the "ideality" of poetry. Shelley writes:

> The awful shadow of some unseen Power
> Floats unseen among us,—visiting
> This various world with as inconstant wing
> As summer winds that creep from flower to flower,—
> Like moonbeams . . . behind some piny mountain shower. . . .

This Power is indistinct, like the hue of evening, harmony, clouds in starlight, the memory of
music no longer heard. It is the "Spirit of Beauty," which passes away and leaves humankind
hopeless. It is Beauty alone that makes life worthy.

> Thy light alone—like mist o'er mountains driven,
> Or music by the night-wind sent
> Through strains of some still instrument,
> Or moonlight on a midnight stream,
> Gives grace and truth to life's unquiet dream.

1. Therasaea, or Therasea, the island mentioned by Seneca, which, in a moment, arose from
the sea to the eyes of astonished mariners [Poe's note]. According to Campbell, the account
of the creation of a new island by the Latin philosopher and dramatist Lucius Annaeus
Seneca (c. 3 B.C.E.–65 C.E.) is to be found in *Quaestionum naturalium libri septem*, VI, arti-
cle xxi. Mabbott observes that the island is said to have arisen near the island chain of the
Cyclades in the Aegean Sea. About to embark on her mission of divine warning, Nesace calls
her subjects together before leaving her star isle, which, like the island of Therasea, has ap-
peared suddenly (prophetically) in the sky seas above the earth.

Part II[2]

High on a mountain of enamell'd head—
Such as the drowsy shepherd[3] on his bed
Of giant pasturage lying at his ease,
Raising his heavy eyelid, starts and sees
With many a mutter'd "hope to be forgiven" 5
What time the moon is quadrated[4] in Heaven—
Of rosy head, that towering far away
Into the sunlit ether, caught the ray
Of sunken suns at eve—at noon of night,[5]

2. Part II opens with a description of a temple on a mountain that towers into sunlit ether at
 sunset (when the moon is at the "noon" of night; cf. p. 17, n. 2 herein). The smooth and re-
 flecting surface of the top of the mountain catches the ray of sunken suns. The moon
 dances with strange light and in the transparent air illuminates the gorgeous temple
 columns. A dome of "linked light" from Heaven sits on these columns. A circular diamond
 forms the dome's window, which looks out over the purple atmosphere. From God, rays
 shoot down in a meteor chain and hallow the beauty of the star world scene "twice again."
 But mortality lurks in Al Aaraaf as well as beauty. Ruined monuments of the earth are in-
 voked in association with the inevitable punishment of God. Punishment and destruction
 are anticipated, as a "sound" steals on the ear of one who sees darkness in the distance, like
 a cloud, with form and voice, palpable and resounding. The ominous sound, however, also
 brings music and "the rush of wings" as Nesace enters the temple to sing her summons to
 her subjects. She invokes Ligeia, the music of the harmony of nature, to awaken the sleep-
 ing spirits of Al Aaraaf. While the spirits gather, two lovers hold back, failing to hear the
 summons clearly because of their earthly passion for each other. One of these, named An-
 gelo, is the spirit of the earthly artist Michelangelo Buonarroti. Angelo bends his dark eye on
 earth and speaks to his lover, Ianthe, who is apparently an angelic native of the star world
 of Al Aaraaf. He tells her that such monuments as the Parthenon recall to him that there is
 more beauty in the intellect than in physical passion and that (or but that) he half wishes "to
 be again of men." Ianthe asks him why he feels this desire, while urging Angelo to ignore the
 goddess's summons and remain in the transitory world of Al Aaraaf. At this point, Angelo re-
 calls a sensation of falling rather than rising to the star of Al Aaraaf at the moment of his
 death. He also, he says, had a perception of the earth hurled into chaos; it was in a moment
 of apocalyptic destruction that he came to this "dread" star. The two spirits are likened to
 the "fire-fly of the night"; they simply come and go without asking any reason beyond the
 "angel-nod" of Nesace, who, in turn is responding to some summons from her God. Time, it
 is said, never unfurled a wing over a fairer world than earth, but when Al Aaraaf's beauty ap-
 peared in earth's sky, the star and the earth trembled reciprocally before the eye of God on
 the "guilty" heritage of humankind. The two lovers, not responding to Nesace's call, now
 seem to fall toward eternal sleep. Cf. "The Power of Words" (pp. 398ff.).
3. Scholars have suggested that, although the "drowsy shepherd" is a convention of earlier po-
 etry, Poe's description has particular resonances with James Thomson's *Seasons* ("Summer"),
 Milton's "Elegia," and Moore's *Lalla Rookh*.
4. Mabbott (having confirmed Poe's celestial setting with a professor of astronomy) states that
 "the moon is 'quadrated' when ninety degrees from the sun" and that " 'eve' [line 9] means
 after the sun has set" (see next note).
5. Mabbott: " 'Noon of night' is when the moon is at the zenith, as may occur at sunset (at sea
 level) only at the first quarter—" (cf. "Tamerlane," "Dreams," "Evening Star," "Israfel").
 Based on this understanding of the time of day, Mabbott summarizes the scene: "The shep-
 herd awakens . . . late in the afternoon; it is deep twilight where he lies, but he sees far off
 . . . a mountain's peak that catches the light of the sun sinking below the horizon . . . in the
 west. The most prominent things seen are the two lights, those of the moon and the moun-
 tain top. These are like partners in a dignified dance." "Campbell suggests resemblances in
 this description to *Paradise Lost*: "The opening line appears to have been suggested by the
 initial line of book II"; and the "lines immediately following resemble, both in content and in
 style, Milton's famous simile applied to Satan on first beholding the wonders of the terres-
 trial world" (III.542ff.). The "general description of Nesace's palace, with its gorgeous
 columns . . . was probably suggested by Milton's account of the building of Pandemonium"
 (I.710ff.). Poe's window of one circular diamond, through which a meteor chain of light was
 "admitted from the throne of God," may have been "suggested originally by the golden stair-
 way which Milton represents as let down on occasion from the environs of heaven to the
 roof of the world, or by the aperture through which this stairway passed" (III.501ff.). Camp-
 bell fails to mention that book III of *Paradise Lost* also describes Limbo as the "Paradise of
 Fools" and certain "middle Spirits" as taking existence "Betwixt th' angelical and human
 kind." The general parallels of scene, imagery, and theme are even greater.

While the moon danc'd with the fair stranger light— 10
Uprear'd upon such height arose a pile[6]
Of gorgeous columns on th' unburthen'd air,
Flashing from Parian marble[7] that twin smile
Far down upon the wave that sparkled there,
And nursled the young mountain in its lair. 15
Of molten stars their pavement, such as fall[8]
Thro' the ebon air, besilvering the pall
Of their own dissolution, while they die—
Adorning then the dwellings of the sky.
A dome, by linked[9] light from Heaven let down, 20
Sat gently on these columns as a crown—
A window of one circular diamond, there,
Look'd out above into the purple air,
And rays from God shot down that meteor chain[1]
And hallow'd all the beauty twice again, 25
Save when, between th' Empyrean and that ring,
Some eager spirit flapp'd his dusky wing.
But on the pillars Seraph[2] eyes have seen
The dimness of this world: that greyish green
That Nature loves the best for Beauty's grave 30
Lurk'd in each cornice, round each architrave[3]—
And every sculptur'd cherub[4] thereabout
That from his marble dwelling peeréd out,
Seem'd earthly in the shadow of his niche—
Achaian[5] statues in a world so rich? 35
Friezes from Tadmor and Persepolis[6]—

6. Not just a quantity of objects stacked together but used in the sense of a large, heavy, stone building and its foundations—frequently connoting the ruins of temples or churches.
7. Highly valued Parian marble from Mount Paros, outside Athens, used for the Parthenon.
8. Some star which, from the ruin'd roof
 Of shak'd Olympus, by mischance, did fall.—*Milton* [Poe's note].

 Imprecisely quoted from Milton's ode "On the Death of a Fair Infant." Campbell also suggests parallels with *Paradise Lost*, III.518–19, and especially the description of the floor of Heaven in III.362–64.
9. Probably a reference to the "golden chain" from which, in ancient myth, the earth is suspended (in another version spelled *linkéd*); here imaged as golden links of sunlight. See notes to Part I, especially, p. 25, n. 8 herein. See also Poe's "A Reviewer Reviewed" (1849; pp. 704ff. herein), in which as Mabbott observes, "Poe pointed out his own source in Pope's version of the *Iliad*, VIII, 25–26: 'Let down our golden everlasting chain, / Whose strong embrace holds Heaven and Earth and Main.' " Cf. *Paradise Lost*, II.1004ff.
1. See *Paradise Lost*, III.501ff.
2. Often used as a synonym for angel, the word specifically refers to a member of highest of the nine orders of spiritual beings called angelic. *Angel* derives from an ancient Greek word for "messenger," and angels are regarded as divine emissaries from God. The Seraphim, who have three sets of wings, guard the throne of God. Cf. "The Raven." "Empyrean": see p. 25, n. 8.
3. Can mean molding, usually around a door, but here is more likely used in the sense of classical architecture as the lowest part of an entablature that rests on the tops of columns. "Cornice": a horizontal molding (often projecting) at the top of the walls of a room or a building. An *entablature* is the overhead decoration of a room or building made up of three elements: the frieze (horizontal band along the upper part of a room), the cornice, and the architrave.
4. A member of the second order of angelic beings, usually depicted as a plump, winged child, with rosy cheeks.
5. See p. 25, n. 1 herein.
6. Voltaire, in speaking of Persepolis, says, "Je connois bien l'admiration qu'inspirent ces ruines—mais un palais erigé au pied d'une chaine des rochers sterils [*sic*]—peut il être un chef d'ouvre des arts!" [Poe's note]. Loosely quoted from chapter 5 of Voltaire's *"Essai sur les*

From Balbec,[7] and the stilly, clear abyss
Of beautiful Gomorrah! O, the wave[8]
Is now upon thee—but too late to save!

Sound loves to revel in a summer night: 40
Witness the murmur of the grey twilight
That stole upon the ear, in Eyraco,[9]
Of many a wild star-gazer long ago—
That stealeth ever on the ear of him
Who, musing, gazeth on the distance dim, 45
And sees the darkness coming as a cloud—
Is not its form—its voice—most palpable and loud?[1]

moeurs et l'esprit des nations" (Essay on the manners and the spirit of nations, 1742). The passage may be translated: "I know well what admiration those ruins inspire—but a palace built at the foot of a chain of barren rockcliffs—can it be a masterpiece of art?" Tadmor and Persepolis, along with Balbec (line 37), are famous ruined cities. Thomas Moore briefly describes the last two in the "Paradise of the Peri" episode in *Lalla Rookh*. Tadmor was built by Solomon (see 1 Kings 9:18; 2 Chronicles 8:4). Also called Tamar (place of palms), it acquired the name Palmyra. Its queen, Zenobia, taking the royal purple and the name Septimia Zenobia Augusta, revolted against Roman rule, causing the emperor Aurelian to attack the city in 272 C.E.; he took the queen prisoner and carried her back to Rome in chains (reputedly made of gold links). Persepolis was the capital of ancient Persia; Alexander the Great conquered and burned part of the city in 330 B.C.E.

7. Associated with sun worship; before the Romans colonized it, the Greeks had named it Heliopolis (*helios* = "sun"; *polis* = "city"), i.e., the city of the sun god. See notes to "MS. Found in a Bottle" (pp. 106ff. herein), "How to Write a Blackwood Article" (pp. 173ff.), and "Silence—a Fable" (pp. 136ff.).

8. [Poe's note at this point reads:] "Oh! the wave"—Ula Deguisi is the Turkish appellation; but, on its own shores, it is called Bahar Loth, or Almotanah. There were undoubtedly more than two cities engulphed in the "dead sea." In the valley of Siddim were five—Adrah, Zeboin, Zoar, Sodom and Gomorrah. Stephen of Byzantium mentions eight, and Strabo thirteen, (engulphed)—but the last is out of all reason.

 It is said, [Tacitus, Strabo, Josephus, Daniel of St. Saba, Nau, Maundrell, Troilo, D'Arvieux] that after an excessive drought, the vestiges of columns, walls, &c. are seen above the surface. At *any* season, such remains may be discovered by 'looking down into the transparent lake, and at such distances as would argue the existence of many settlements in the space now usurped by the 'Asphaltites' [end of Poe's note].

 The phrasing is from Chateaubriand's *Itinéraire* (see p. 28, n. 4 herein); two American editions of the Shoberl translation of Chateaubriand (Philadelphia, 1813; New York, 1814) both contain the misprint "deguisi" for "degnisi." Mabbott and others make several helpful observations on this note. The Turks sometimes speak of *Ölü deniz*, meaning "Dead Sea," but more usually call it *Lut denizi* (Lot's sea); the Arabic form is *Bahar Loth*, now usually written *Bahr Lut* (Sea of Lot). Another Arabic name for the sea is *Al-Buhairah Al-Muntinah*; the second phrase is from the root *ntn* (to stink). *Siddim* means "the large plains." *Lacus Asphaltites* is the Latin name of the Dead Sea. The names of some of the towns Poe mentions have suggestive etymologies: Sodom means "burning"; Gomorrah means "sunken"; Zoar, "littleness"; Zeboim, "place of hyenas, gazelles, or roes"; and Admah, "earth, fortress, or fruitful place." Ancient authorities give differing numbers for the destroyed cities. Strabo mentions thirteen and Stephen of Byzantium mentions ten (rather than eight, as Poe says). Mabbott gives the following specific references: Tacitus, *Historiae*, V.vii; Strabo, *Geographia*, XVI.ii; Josephus, *Bellum Judaicum*, IV.viii.4; Daniel, Abbot of St. Saba, a monastery near the Dead Sea (a "friend and informant" of Michel Nau); Michel Nau, *Voyage de la Terre Sainte* (1702): Henry Maundrell, *A Journey from Aleppo* (1697); Franz Ferdinand von Troilo, *Orientalische Reise* (1676); and Chevalier Lambert d'Arvieux, *Mémoires* (1735). Several lines at this point (38ff.), which Poe here omits, became the basis of his poem "The City in the Sea."

9. Eyraco—Chaldea [Poe's note]. Eyraco is an antiquated name for Iraq, a kingdom that included Babylonia and Chaldea. The Chaldeans were famous for astrology and magic, alluded to frequently in Poe's works.

1. I have often thought I could distinctly hear the sound of darkness as it stole over the horizon [Poe's note]. Poe uses essentially the same note toward the end of "Tamerlane." Apprehending or comparing one sense experience in terms of another—such as the blue buzz of a fly (sound as color) or as here the "sound" of fading "light"—is called *synaesthesia*. This kind of metaphoric play (which tends to break down normative categories of perception and thinking) became a favorite of 19th-century poets.

But what is this?—it cometh—and it brings
A music with it—'tis the rush of wings—
A pause—and then a sweeping, falling strain 50
And Nesace is in her halls again.
From the wild energy of wanton haste
 Her cheeks were flushing, and her lips apart;
And zone[2] that clung around her gentle waist
 Had burst beneath the heaving of her heart. 55
Within the centre of that hall to breathe
She paus'd and panted, Zanthe![3] all beneath,
The fairy light that kiss'd her golden hair
And long'd to rest, yet could but sparkle there!

 Young flowers were whispering in melody[4] 60
To happy flowers that night—and tree to tree;
Fountains were gushing music as they fell
In many a star-lit grove, or moon-lit dell;
Yet silence came upon material things—
Fair flowers, bright waterfalls and angel wings— 65
And sound alone that from the spirit sprang
Bore burthen to the charm[5] the maiden sang:
 " 'Neath blue-bell or streamer—
 Or tufted wild spray
 That keeps, from the dreamer, 70
 The moonbeam away[6]—
 Bright beings! that ponder,
 With half closing eyes,
 On the stars which your wonder
 Hath drawn from the skies, 75
 Till they glance thro' the shade, and
 Come down to your brow
 Like——eyes of the maiden
 Who calls on you now—
 Arise! from your dreaming 80
 In violet bowers,
 To duty beseeming
 These star-litten hours—
 And shake from your tresses

2. Old-fashioned word for a sash, usually associated with female sexual purity (her "virgin zone"). Nesace seems to respond to the voice of the Deity almost as a passionate lover.
3. Apparently a handmaiden of Nesace. The name recalls *Zante*, the name of the island mentioned in Part I, lines 75–76 (see p. 28, n. 4 herein), which derives from the hyacinth.
4. Fairies use flowers for their charactery.—*Merry Wives of Windsor* [Poe's note]. The reference is to V.v.77. Cf. the tradition of the so-called book of flowers, in which human characteristics or personalities are given in terms of conventionalized metaphors of flowers. Campbell suggests that this line and the several following recall *Paradise Lost*, IV.598ff.
5. From the Latin *carmen*, which may be a song, lyric poem, or magical incantation; here all three are pertinent. Cf. *Paradise Lost* IV. 642, and see previous notes on Milton. "Burthen": archaic for *burden*; here in the sense of the refrain of a song.
6. In Scripture is this passage—"The sun shall not harm thee by day, nor the moon by night." It is perhaps not generally known that the moon, in Egypt, has the effect of producing blindness to those who sleep with the face exposed to its rays, to which circumstance the passage evidently alludes [Poe's note]. See Psalms 121:6. Campbell cites as the probable model for the maiden's song certain scenes from Byron's *Deformed Transformed*, I.i; II.ii, which may also have influenced lines 80–83 of Poe's poem.

Encumber'd with dew 85
The breath of those kisses
 That cumber them too—
(O! how, without you, Love!
 Could angels be blest?)
Those kisses of true love 90
 That lull'd ye to rest!
Up!—shake from your wing
 Each hindering thing:
The dew of the night—
 It would weigh down your flight; 95
And true love caresses—
 O! leave them apart!
They are light on the tresses,
 But lead on the heart.

Ligeia![7] Ligeia! 100
 My beautiful one!
Whose harshest idea
 Will to melody run,
O! is it thy will
 On the breezes to toss? 105
Or, capriciously still,
 Like the lone Albatross,[8]
Incumbent[9] on night
 (As she on the air)
To keep watch with delight 110
 On the harmony there?

Ligeia! wherever
 Thy image may be,
No magic shall sever
 Thy music from thee. 115
Thou hast bound many eyes
 In a dreamy sleep—

7. In earlier versions there are quotation marks beginning this line and line 112 (conventional
 for new paragraphs in continuing quotations). But the line lengths (as well as the sense)
 make it clear that it is still the song begun at line 68. The name *Ligeia* is pronounced with a
 soft *g* sound [Lie-GEE-a] and rhymes with idea. It is the name of one of the Sirens, the sea
 nymphs (sometimes associated with mermaids) who sang so wildly well that their beautiful
 voices tempted passing sailors to shipwreck on the rocks of their island (as told in the
 Odyssey and elsewhere). The Roman poet Virgil (Publius Vergilius Maro, 70–19 B.C.E.) men-
 tions a nymph named Ligea in the *Georgics* (30 B.C.E.), as does Milton, spelling her name
 the same way in *Comus* (acted 1634, published in 1637). Mabbott notes that in a sketch of
 Poe in the *Saturday Museum* (March 4, 1843), Henry B. Hirst wrote that the name *Ligeia*
 was a Greek word for something melodic or high sounding and that Poe intended the nymph
 that Nesace addresses as "a personification of music." Most critics, however, take her to be
 the personification of cosmic harmony, symbolized in song. In Poe's prose story "Ligeia," the
 narrator says his beloved's speech is "melody more than mortal."
8. The Albatross is said to sleep on the wing [Poe's note]. Campbell points out a source in *Lalla
 Rookh*, where in a note to the "Fire-Worshippers," II.203–06, Moore says of the albatross,
 "These birds sleep in the air. They are most common about the Cape of Good Hope."
9. Cf. *Paradise Lost*, I.226: "Aloft, incumbent on the dusky air." *Incumbent* means lying, lean-
 ing, or resting on something, though its other meaning (metaphorically applied) of obliga-
 tion or duty is pertinent to the situation.

But the strains still arise
 Which *thy* vigilance keep—
The sound of the rain 120
 Which leaps down to the flower,
And dances again
 In the rhythm of the shower—
The murmur that springs[1]
 From the growing of grass 125
Are the music of things—
 But are modell'd, alas![2]—
Away, then my dearest,
 O! hie thee away
To springs that lie clearest 130
 Beneath the moon-ray—
To lone lake that smiles,
 In its dream of deep rest,
At the many star-isles
 That enjewel its breast[3]— 135
Where wild flowers, creeping,
 Have mingled their shade,
On its margin is sleeping
 Full many a maid—
Some have left the cool glade, and 140
 Have slept with the bee[4]—
Arouse them my maiden,
 On moorland and lea—
Go! breathe on their slumber,
 All softly in ear, 145

1. I met with this idea in an old English tale, which I am now unable to obtain and quote from memory:—"The verie essence and, as it were, springeheade and origine of all musiche is the verie pleasaunte sounde which the trees of the forest do make when they growe" [Poe's note]. Poe's source has not been found (if there is one—he may have invented it), though Campbell points to George Sale's "Preliminary Discourse" to the Koran for some general comments on the natural symbolism of harmony and melody. Sale remarks on the melodious voice of the angel Israfîl and suggests that the sounds of trees swaying in the wind in the gardens of Al Arâf, in addition to the sounds of bells in their branches, will "celebrate" the "harmony" of the Divine.
2. John Phelps Fruit in *The Mind and Art of Poe's Poetry* (1899), citing Plato's *Gorgias* and *Phaedo* (pp. 28ff.), takes these indefinite murmurings of nature in the song to Ligeia to be mere earthly imitations of divine prototypes; but such prototypes may be more questionable than he suggests (see p. 24, n. 2, and p. 26, n. 2 and p. 31; n. 9 herein).
3. Killis Campbell notes some parallel instances in Romantic poetry comparing stars with islands in the sea: e.g., Byron's *The Island*, canto II, xi.13–5, and *The Siege of Corinth*, xi.3–5, along with *The Pleasures of Hope*, II.206–07, by the Scots poet Thomas Campbell (1777–1844). Connecting these with allusions to starlike jewels adorning a woman's bodice, Killis Campbell hesitantly implies a connection between this imagery and the poem's theme of destruction via sexual passion; see the somewhat oblique references to Nesace's heaving breasts in *Al Aaraaf* Part II, lines 54–55 and 217, as well as Part I, lines 64–65.
4. The wild bee will not sleep in the shade if there be moonlight.
 The rhyme in this verse, as in one about sixty lines before, has an appearance of affectation. It is, however, imitated from Sir W. Scott, or rather from Cloud Halcro—in whose mouth I admired its effect:

> O! were there an island,
> Tho' ever so wild
> Where woman might smile, and
> No man be beguil'd, &c. [Poe's note].

Poe quotes the fourth stanza of a song called "Mary," from chapter xii of Sir Walter Scott's *The Pirate* (1822).

> The musical number
> They slumber'd to hear—
> For what can awaken
> An angel so soon
> Whose sleep hath been taken 150
> Beneath the cold moon,
> As the spell which no slumber
> Of witchery may test,
> The rhythmical number
> Which lull'd him to rest?" 155

Spirits in wing, and angels to the view,
A thousand seraphs burst th' Empyrean thro',
Young dreams still hovering on their drowsy flight—
Seraphs in all but "Knowledge,"[5] the keen light
That fell, refracted, thro' thy bounds, afar 160
O Death! from eye of God[6] upon that star:
Sweet was that error—sweeter still that death—
Sweet was that error—ev'n with *us* the breath
Of Science dims the mirror of our joy—
To them 'twere the Simoom,[7] and would destroy— 165
For what (to them) availeth it to know
That Truth is Falsehood—or that Bliss is Woe?
Sweet was their death—with them to die was rife
With the last ecstasy of satiate life—
Beyond that death no immortality— 170
But sleep that pondereth and is not "to be"—
And there—oh! may my weary spirit dwell—
Apart from Heaven's Eternity—and yet how far from Hell![8]

5. In the Christian mythos, four seraphim guard the throne of God; they have six wings each,
 veiling their faces with one pair and their feet with another; they rejoice in the "divine
 knowledge" that lesser creatures, even other angelic beings, do not have. Campbell suggests
 the influence of Moore's *The Loves of the Angels*, specifically, the 1823 preface and lines
 664ff. Mabbott observes that such stories go back to a work called *The Celestial Hierarchy*.
 The work used to be ascribed to Dionysius the Areopagite (1st century C.E.) but is now as-
 cribed to a later century and is cited usually as the work of "Pseudo-Dionysius." "Empyrean":
 p. 25, n. 8 herein.
6. See Ezra 5:5; here it is simply a general phrase rather than an allusion.
7. A destroying desert wind, sometimes considered poisonous or disorienting. See notes to
 "MS. Found in a Bottle" (p. 108, n. 3 herein).
8. [Poe's note here reads:] With the Arabians there is a medium between Heaven and Hell,
 where men suffer no punishment, but yet do not attain that tranquil and even happiness
 which they suppose to be characteristic of heavenly enjoyment.

> Un no rompido sueno—
> Un dia puro—allegre—libre
> Quiera—
> Libre de amor—de zelo—
> De odio—de esperanza—de rezelo.—*Luis Ponce de Leon.*

Sorrow is not excluded from "Al Aaraaf," but it is that sorrow which the living love to cher-
ish for the dead, and which, in some minds, resembles the delirium of opium. The passion-
ate excitement of Love and the buoyancy of spirit attendant upon intoxication are its less
holy pleasures—the price of which, to those souls who make choice of "Al Aaraaf" as their
residence after life, is final death and annihilation [end of Poe's note].

The passage on the realm between Heaven and Hell reflects Thomas Moore once again.
In "A Reviewer Reviewed," Poe quotes from *Lalla Rookh*: "to dwell / Full in the sight of Par-
adise / Beholding Heaven, yet feeling Hell." The quotation from "Vida Retirada" (Reclusive
life) by Fray Luís de León (1527–1591) is truncated and otherwise altered. Campbell gives
the correct verses:

What guilty spirit, in what shrubbery dim,
Heard not the stirring summons of that hymn? 175
But two: they fell: for Heaven no grace imparts
To those who hear not for their beating hearts.
A maiden-angel and her seraph-lover—
O! where (and ye may seek the wide skies over)
Was Love, the blind, near sober Duty known? 180
Unguided Love hath fallen—'mid "tears of perfect moan."⁹

He was a goodly spirit—he who fell:
A wanderer by moss-y-mantled well—
A gazer on the lights that shine above—
A dreamer in the moonbeam by his love: 185
What wonder? for each star is eye-like there,
And looks so sweetly down on Beauty's hair—
And they, and ev'ry mossy spring were holy
To his love-haunted heart and melancholy.
The night had found (to him a night of wo) 190
Upon a mountain crag, young Angelo¹—
Beetling it bends athwart the solemn sky,
And scowls on starry worlds that down beneath it lie.
Here sate he with his love—his dark eye bent
With eagle gaze along the firmament: 195
Now turn'd it upon her—but ever then
It trembled to the orb of EARTH again.

"Ianthe,² dearest, see! how dim that ray!
How lovely 'tis to look so far away!
She seem'd not thus upon that autumn eve 200
I left her gorgeous halls—nor mourn'd to leave.
That eve—that eve—I should remember well—
The sun-ray dropp'd, in Lemnos,³ with a spell
On th' Arabesque⁴ carving of a gilded hall

Un no rompido sueño,
Un dia, puro, alegre, libre quiero:
[Poe here omits eleven lines]
Libre de amor de zelo,
De odio, de esperanzas, de rezelo.

These lines may be rendered loosely as: An unbroken [uninterrupted] dream, / A day, pure, joyous, free [is what] I desire: / . . . / Free of love, of concern [care, zeal], / Of hatred, of hopes, of jealousy [suspicion].

9. There be tears of perfect moan
Wept for thee in Helicon.—*Milton* [Poe's note].

Slightly misquoted from John Milton's "Epitaph on the Marchioness of Winchester," lines 55–56. Helicon is a mountain in Boeotia, one of the legendary abodes of the Muses. Campbell suggests that the episode of the "maiden-angel" and the "seraph-lover" (line 178) is modeled on the "First Angel's Story" in Moore's *The Loves of the Angels.* Other of Poe's stories of angel lovers include "Eiros and Charmion" and "The Colloquy of Monos and Una" (pp. 279ff. herein).

1. The spirit of the artist Michelangelo Buonarroti (see pp. 22–23 herein, and p. 32, n.2). Campbell suggests a parallel with Moore's *Loves of the Angels,* lines 21ff. and 167ff.

2. Her name signifies hyacinth. Cf. Zante and Zanthe, above.

3. Or Limnos, an island off the west coast of Turkey, the place on which Vulcan is said to have fallen when hurled from Olympus by Jove.

4. Mabbott notes that in the text of 1831 Poe "put the word 'Arabesq' (*sic*) in quotation marks, as inappropriate to a Grecian isle, but in 1574 the island had been under Turkish dominion."

Wherein I sate, and on the draperied wall— 205
And on my eye-lids—O the heavy light!
How drowsily it weigh'd them into night!
On flowers, before, and mist, and love they ran
With Persian Saadi in his Gulistan:[5]
But O that light!—I slumber'd—Death, the while, 210
Stole o'er my senses in that lovely isle[6]
So softly that no single silken hair
A woke that slept—or knew that he was there.

The last spot of Earth's orb I trod upon
Was a proud temple call'd the Parthenon[7]— 215
More beauty clung around her column'd wall
Than ev'n thy glowing bosom beats withal,[8]
And when old Time my wing did disenthral
Thence sprang!—as the eagle from his tower,[9]
And years I left behind me in an hour. 220
What time upon her airy bounds I hung
One half the garden of her globe was flung
Unrolling as a chart unto my view—
Tenantless cities of the desert too!
Ianthe, beauty crowded on me then, 225
And half I wish'd to be again of men."

"My Angelo! and why of them to be?
A brighter dwelling-place is here for thee—
And greener fields than in yon world above,
And woman's loveliness—and passionate love." 230

"But, list, Ianthe! when the air so soft
Fail'd, as my pennon'd spirit leapt aloft,[1]

See the introduction to Tales and Sketches (pp. 77ff.) and notes on the word *Arabesque* in
"Ligeia" (pp. 167–68, n. 2 herein).
5. The Persian poet Saadi or Sadi (born c. 1184 C.E.) was known as the "bard of Shiraz." He is
 said to have lived to be 110. His best-known work is the *Gulistan* (Rose garden), a medley of
 prose and verse that has often been translated. Mabbott suggests that Poe may have known
 the English version of 1823 by James Ross.
6. In lines 200–04, the text seems to suggest that Michelangelo departed his earthly existence
 on the Greek isle of Lemnos in the fall of the year. Actually he died in Rome in the month
 of February (1563 or 1564). In Poe's poem, he dies while drifting off into sleep; his spirit
 wanders about among flowers and mists and rays of light and seems to visit several lovely
 spots on earth (the last being the Parthenon; see next note) before it flies to the star isle of
 Al Aaraaf. Campbell suggests a parallel in Moore's *Loves of the Angels* (lines 496ff.).
7. It was entire in 1687—the most elevated spot in Athens [Poe's note]. Mabbott suggests that
 Poe borrowed this note from the Shoberl version of Chateaubriand's *Itinéraire*, where it is
 said that the Parthenon "existed entire in 1687," the year during which it was badly damaged
 by an explosion of the gunpowder stored in it.
8. Shadowing more beauty in their airy brows
 Than have the white breasts of the Queen of Love.—*Marlowe* [Poe's note].

 From Christopher Marlowe's *Doctor Faustus* (performed c. 1588), I.150–51 of the 1616 edi-
 tion. See also p. 37, n. 3 herein.
9. Mabbott notes that it was the custom of the Romans to release an eagle from the top of the
 funeral pyre of an emperor, its flight symbolizing his spirit flying to Heaven. Campbell sug-
 gests that the lines immediately following (esp. 221–24) resemble *Paradise Lost*, III. 418ff.
1. Pennon—for pinion—*Milton* [Poe's note]. See *Paradise Lost*, II.933: "Flutt'ring his pennons,
 vain, plumb down he drops." Campbell notes that this unusual word occurs in Milton's ac-
 count of Satan's journey "up from the gates of hell to the rim of the world" in *Paradise Lost*,
 II.927ff., and that Poe's account of Angelo's flight in the next few lines echoes Milton.

Perhaps my brain grew dizzy—but the world
I left so late was into chaos hurl'd—
Sprang from her station, on the winds apart, 235
And roll'd, a flame, the fiery Heaven athwart.
Methought, my sweet one, then I ceased to soar
And fell—not swiftly as I rose before,
But with a downward, tremulous motion thro'
Light, brazen rays, this golden star unto! 240
Nor long the measure of my falling hours,
For nearest of all stars was thine to ours—
Dread star! that came, amid a night of mirth,
A red Dædalion[2] on the timid Earth.

"We came—and to thy Earth—but not to us 245
Be given our lady's bidding to discuss:
We came, my love; around, above, below,
Gay fire-fly of the night we come and go,
Nor ask a reason save the angel-nod
She grants to us, as granted by her God— 250
But, Angelo, than thine grey Time unfurl'd
Never his fairy wing o'er fairier world!
Dim was its little disk, and angel eyes
Alone could see the phantom in the skies,
When first Al Aaraaf knew her course to be 255
Headlong thitherward o'er the starry sea[3]—
But when its glory swell'd upon the sky,
As glowing Beauty's bust beneath man's eye,
We paus'd before the heritage of men,
And thy star trembled—as doth Beauty then!" 260

Thus, in discourse, the lovers whiled away
The night that waned and waned and brought no day.[4]
They fell: for Heaven to them no hope imparts
Who hear not for the beating of their hearts.

2. Misspelling of the adjective *daedalian*, here used as a noun. The usage is a little odd, but it is clearly a reference to the myth of Daedalus, the artificer of the labyrinth of Minos, who was imprisoned in a tower with his son, Icarus. With the waxen wings that Daedalus contrived, they flew out of the tower. Icarus in his passionate zeal flew too high; the sun melted his wings, and he plummeted into the sea and perished. The falling of Icarus would seem to be a secondary aspect of the allusion, and the winged flight of Daedalus the primary one; i.e., Angelo is one of the Daedalian band of winged beings. But, as the experience of the overweening Icarus suggests, human beings are always under the threat of a fall.
3. In a manuscript, Poe changed "Al Aaraaf" to "Tophet-Nour," a word that is a mixture of Hebrew and Arabic, meaning "Light of Hell" or "burning light" (cf. "Ulalume"). Elsewhere he called the star a phantom. The phrase "starry sea" continues the star/island and sky/sea imagery.
4. Cf. Byron's "Darkness," line 6: "Morn came and went—and came, and brought no day."

Introduction[1]

Romance, who loves to nod and sing,
With drowsy head and folded wing,
Among the green leaves as they shake
Far down within some shadowy lake,
To me a painted paroquet[2] 5
Hath been—a most familiar bird—
Taught me my alphabet to say—
To lisp my very earliest word
While in the wild-wood I did lie
A child—with a most knowing eye. 10

Succeeding years, too wild for song,
Then roll'd like tropic storms along,
Where, tho' the garish lights that fly
Dying along the troubled sky,
Lay bare, thro' vistas thunder-riven, 15
The blackness of the general Heaven,
That very blackness yet doth fling
Light on the lightning's silver wing.

For, being an idle boy lang syne,
Who read Anacreon,[3] and drank wine, 20
I early found Anacreon rhymes
Were almost passionate sometimes—
And by strange alchemy of brain
His pleasures always turn'd to pain—
His naivete to wild desire— 25
His wit to love—his wine to fire—
And so, being young and dipt in folly
I fell in love with melancholy,
And used to throw my earthly rest
And quiet all away in jest— 30
I could not love except where Death
Was mingling his with Beauty's breath—
Or Hymen, Time, and Destiny
Were stalking between her and me.[4]

O, then the eternal Condor years 35
So shook the very Heavens on high,
With tumult as they thunder'd by;
I had no time for idle cares,
Thro' gazing on the unquiet sky!

1. Published in this form in *Poems* (1831); the poem in this version uses the "Preface" (titled "Romance" in *The Raven and Other Poems*) to *Al Aaraaf* as lines 1–10 and 35–45, to which are added thirty-six new lines.
2. A parakeet or parrot. Mabbott thinks the reference is to a painted bird on an archery target, though he does not adequately explain the significance.
3. Greek lyric poet (flourished c. 520 B.C.E.) who extolled love and wine and combined humor with melancholy.
4. See the Poems introduction pp. 5–6 herein. Hymen was the goddess of marriage.

Or if an hour with calmer wing 40
Its down did on my spirit fling,
That little hour with lyre and rhyme
To while away—forbidden thing!
My heart half fear'd to be a crime
Unless it trembled with the string. 45
But *now* my soul hath too much room—
Gone are the glory and the gloom—
The black hath mellow'd into grey,
And all the fires are fading away.

My draught of passion hath been deep— 50
I revell'd, and I now would sleep—
And after-drunkenness of soul
Succeeds the glories of the bowl—
An idle longing night and day
To dream my very life away. 55

But dreams—of those who dream as I,
Aspiringly, are damned, and die:
Yet should I swear I mean alone,
By notes so very shrilly blown,
To break upon Time's monotone, 60
While yet my vapid joy and grief
Are tintless of the yellow leaf[5]—
Why not an imp the greybeard[6] hath,
Will shake his shadow in my path—
And even the greybeard will o'erlook 65
Connivingly[7] my dreaming-book.

Fairy-Land [1][1]

Dim vales—and shadowy floods—
And cloudy-looking woods,
Whose forms we can't discover
For the tears that drip all over.[2]
Huge moons there wax and wane— 5

5. A conventional metaphor for autumn, itself a traditional metaphor for the beginning of old age. "Vapid": empty, dull, stupid. The young speaker's joy and grief are empty of the experience of age.
6. A semicontemptuous term for an old man. "Imp": can connote both demons and pixies; i.e., both the sinister and the humorous.
7. Deceitfully, hypocritically, or lying.
1. First published in the *Yankee and Boston Literary Gazette* (September 1829) and reprinted frequently in various versions; the first complete version appears in *Al Aaraaf, Tamerlane and Minor Poems* (1829); the text followed here is that of *The Raven and Other Poems* (1845). The poem seems to be a parody of Romantic poets, particularly Thomas Moore (see notes to "Al Aaraaf" and other early poems, as well as "The Assignation"). The reference to fairies making their evening tents out of moonlight seems to be an allusion to Moore's *Lalla Rookh* (1817); the reference to the yellow albatross also seems to be a hit at Moore (see n. 3 following). For *Poems* (1831) Poe made so many revisions that this text gave rise to a new poem; reprinted on pp. 45–46 herein.
2. Cf. "Dream-Land," lines 9–12 (pp. 56–57 herein).

Again—again—again—
Every moment of the night—
Forever changing places—
And they put out the star-light
With the breath from their pale faces. 10
About twelve by the moon-dial
One more filmy than the rest
(A kind which, upon trial,
They have found to be the best)
Comes down—still down—and down 15
With its centre on the crown
Of a mountain's eminence,
While its wide circumference
In easy drapery falls
Over hamlets, over halls, 20
Wherever they may be—
O'er the strange woods—o'er the sea—
Over spirits on the wing—
Over every drowsy thing—
And buries them up quite 25
In a labyrinth of light—
And then, how deep!—O, deep!
Is the passion of their sleep.
In the morning they arise,
And their moony covering 30
Is soaring in the skies,
With the tempests as they toss,
Like—almost any thing—
Or a yellow Albatross.[3]
They use that moon no more 35
For the same end as before[4]—
Videlicet[5] a tent—
Which I think extravagant:
Its atomies, however,
Into a shower dissever, 40
Of which those butterflies,
Of Earth, who seek the skies,
And so come down again
(Never-contented things!)

3. In the *Al Aaraaf* volume of 1829 Poe's footnote reads: "Plagiarism—see the works of Thomas
Moore—*passim*—Edr." The Latin word *passim* means "throughout." *Edr.* is Poe's abbrevia-
tion for editor. The satiric point is apparently that Moore was inept and stole metaphors and
similes from everyone and everywhere, and that he would compare anything to anything,
whether appropriate or not. The albatross was reputed to sleep on the wing while flying long
distances; it is yellow presumably because of the moonlight or morning sunlight on its body.
4. Mabbott notes that the idea that the moon was created and destroyed each twenty-four
hours goes back at least to the Roman poet Lucretius (99–55 B.C.E.) in *De rerum natura* (On
the nature of things), V.731–736. If Mabbott's conjectural gloss on an allusion to Lucretius
is pertinent, Poe's satiric point might be surmised as something like the following: in creat-
ing such "new" moon metaphors, Romantic poets such as Moore reach for "extravagant" image-
ages; here a "tent" of moonlight.
5. Namely (Latin), used to introduce, specify, or exemplify something following; usually abbre-
viated *viz.* Here the earthly butterflies (evidently the poets) do not use the moon in the nor-
mal or traditional way: namely, they use it for a tent.

Have brought a specimen 45
Upon their quivering wings.

Fairy Land [2]¹

Sit down beside me, Isabel,²
Here, dearest, where the moonbeam fell
Just now so fairy-like and well.
Now thou art dress'd for paradise!
I am star-stricken with thine eyes! 5
My soul is lolling on thy sighs!
Thy hair is lifted by the moon
Like flowers by the low breath of June!
Sit down, sit down—how came we here?
Or is it all but a dream, my dear? 10

You know that most enormous flower—
That rose—that what d'ye call it—that hung
Up like a dog-star in this bower³—
To-day (the wind blew, and) it swung
So impudently in my face, 15
So like a thing alive you know,
I tore it from its pride of place
And shook it into pieces—so
Be all ingratitude requited.
The winds ran off with it delighted, 20
And, thro' the opening left, as soon
As she threw off her cloak, yon moon
Has sent a ray down with a tune.
And this ray is a *fairy* ray—
Did you not say so, Isabel? 25
How fantastically it fell
With a spiral twist and a swell,
And over the wet grass rippled away
With a tinkling like a bell!
In my own country all the way 30
We can discover a moon ray
Which thro' some tatter'd curtain pries
Into the darkness of a room,
Is by (the very source of gloom)
The motes, and dust, and flies. 35
On which it trembles and lies
Like joy upon sorrow!

1. Revised version of the 1829 "Fairy-Land"; published in *Poems* (1831), the text followed here. Lines 41–50 come, slightly changed, from the 1829 poem.
2. The speaker (gender uncertain) seems to be addressing a woman who is not very bright. Cf. "Introduction" (p. 42 herein), "How to Write a Blackwood Article" (p. 173), and "A Predicament" (p. 183).
3. Garden. The speaker thinks the "enormous flower" is a rose but is not sure. The point of the comparison to the dog star (Sirius) is unclear; maybe it is supposed to be absurd (see notes to "Fairy-Land [1]").

O, *when* will come the morrow?
Isabel! do you not fear
The night and the wonders here? 40
Dim vales! and shadowy floods!
And cloudy-looking woods
Whose forms we can't discover
For the tears that drip all over![4]

Huge moons—see! wax and wane 45
Again—again—again—
Every moment of the night—
Forever changing places!
How they put out the starlight
With the breath from their pale faces! 50

Lo! one is coming down
With its centre on the crown
Of a mountain's eminence!
Down—still down—and down—
Now deep shall be—O deep! 55
The passion of our sleep!
For that wide circumference
In easy drapery falls
Drowsily over halls—
Over ruin'd walls— 60
Over waterfalls,
(Silent waterfalls!)[5]
O'er the strange woods—o'er the sea—
Alas! over the sea!

[Alone][1]

From childhood's hour I have not been
As others were—I have not seen
As others saw—I could not bring
My passions from a common spring—
From the same source I have not taken 5
My sorrow—I could not awaken
My heart to joy at the same tone—
And all I lov'd—I lov'd alone—
Then—in my childhood—in the dawn
Of a most stormy life—was drawn 10

4. Close variants of these parodic lines are in the apparently serious "Dream-Land" (1844; pp. 56–57 herein).
5. Cf. the landscape descriptions in Part I of the seemingly intensely serious "Al Aaraaf" (pp. 24ff. herein).
1. Never published in Poe's lifetime; a manuscript version of "Alone" was found in a private album dating from 1829. It was published in 1875 and again in 1877 (in Eugene L. Didier's edition of Poe's poems), where it was given the present title. See the discussion of Byronism in the Poems introduction pp. 3, 6 herein.

From ev'ry depth of good and ill
The mystery which binds me still—
From the torrent, or the fountain—
From the red cliff of the mountain—
From the sun that 'round me roll'd 15
In its autumn tint of gold—
From the lightning in the sky
As it pass'd me flying by—
From the thunder, and the storm—
And the cloud that took the form 20
(When the rest of Heaven was blue)
Of a demon in my view—

To Helen[1]

Helen, thy beauty is to me
 Like those Nicéan[2] barks of yore,
That gently, o'er a perfumed sea,
 The weary, way-worn wanderer[3] bore
To his own native shore. 5

On desperate seas long wont to roam,
 Thy hyacinth hair, thy classic face,
Thy Naiad airs have brought me home
 To the glory that was Greece,
And the grandeur that was Rome. 10

Lo! in yon brilliant window-niche
 How statue-like I see thee stand,
The agate lamp[4] within thy hand!
 Ah, Psyche,[5] from the regions which
Are Holy-Land! 15

1. First published in *Poems* (1831). Reprinted frequently; the version followed here is that of *The Raven and Other Poems* (1845). Poe wrote to Sarah Helen Whitman (October 1, 1848) that "Helen Stanard" (i.e., Jane Stith Stanard, the mother of the close friend of his youth, Robert Stanard), whom he called the "first, purely ideal love of my soul," was the inspiration of this poem.
 Helen of Troy, a daughter of Zeus, was reputed to be the most beautiful woman of ancient Greece. One tradition suggests that she could appear in the form of, and with the voice of, a man's first love. She was also said to inspire poetry. Mabbott comments that she sometimes appeared in the heavens with her twin brothers, Castor and Pollux (the brothers, known as the Disocuri, who shared their immortality half in Heaven and half in Hell), as a third star to guide sailors at sea. The three were also associated with the phenomenon of "St. Elmo's fire," static electricity in ocean skies playing about the masts of ships (as in Herman Melville's *Moby-Dick*).
2. Presumably referring to Nike, goddess of victory, or possibly just to one of the ancient cities named Nicea.
3. Scholars have attempted to identify a specific classical myth for the wanderer: Bacchus, Dionysus, Menelaus, Odysseus, and others. Probably Poe's allusion is intended to have general reference.
4. In other versions of the poem the lamp was a scroll or a book. "Agate": made of marble banded with various swirling colors.
5. A mythical figure in classical literature. In Greek, the word means both "soul" and "butterfly"; see notes to "Ulalume" (pp. 61ff. herein) "How to Write a Blackwood Article" (pp. 173ff.); and other of Poe's works.

Israfel[1]

And the angel Israfel, whose heart-strings are a lute, and who has the
sweetest voice of all God's creatures. —KORAN.[2]

In Heaven a spirit doth dwell
 "Whose heart-strings are a lute;"
None sing so wildly well
As the angel Israfel,
And the giddy stars (so legends tell) 5
Ceasing their hymns, attend the spell
 Of his voice, all mute.

Tottering above
 In her highest noon,
 The enamoured moon 10
Blushes with love,
 While, to listen, the red levin[3]
 (With the rapid Pleiads,[4] even,
 Which were seven,)
Pauses in Heaven. 15

And they say (the starry choir
 And the other listening things)
That Israfeli's fire
Is owing to that lyre
 By which he sits and sings— 20
The trembling living wire
Of those unusual strings.

But the skies that angel trod,
 Where deep thoughts are a duty—
Where Love's a grown-up God[5]— 25
 Where the Houri[6] glances are
Imbued with all the beauty
 Which we worship in a star.

Therefore, thou art not wrong,
 Israfeli, who despisest 30
An unimpassioned song;

1. First published in *Poems* (1831). The version followed here is that of *The Raven and Other Poems* (1845), with emendations from Mabbott (the Lorimer Graham copy with Poe's revisions).
2. According to Mabbott, Poe's epigraph is not from the Koran directly but from George Sale's "Preliminary Discourse" to his translation of the Koran (see notes to "Al Aaraaf"), quoted by Thomas Moore in *Lalla Rookh* (1817). See Mabbott's discussion I.172–73.
3. Lightning (archaic).
4. A constellation of seven stars in Taurus; one is very faint, though sometimes visible. In classical mythology, they are sisters, one of which (the faintest) fell in love with a mortal and faded from sight.
5. Contrastive reference to Cupid in Roman mythology, who is pictured as a fat little boy with wings and bow and arrows.
6. The maidens tending men in the Muslim paradise. The word means "dark eyes" (cf. notes to "Ligeia," p. 161, n. 9 and n. 1 herein).

To thee the laurels belong,
 Best bard, because the wisest!
Merrily live, and long!

The ecstasies above 35
 With thy burning measures suit—
Thy grief, thy joy, thy hate, thy love,
 With the fervour of thy lute—
 Well may the stars be mute!

Yes, Heaven is thine; but this 40
 Is a world of sweets and sours;
 Our flowers are merely—flowers,
And the shadow of thy perfect bliss
 Is the sunshine of ours.

If I could dwell 45
Where Israfel
 Hath dwelt, and he where I,
He might not sing so wildly well
 A mortal melody,
While a bolder note than this might swell 50
 From my lyre within the sky.

The Sleeper[1]

At midnight, in the month of June,
I stand beneath the mystic moon.
An opiate vapour, dewy, dim,
Exhales from out her golden rim,
And, softly dripping, drop by drop, 5
Upon the quiet mountain top,
Steals drowsily and musically
Into the universal valley.
The rosemary nods upon the grave;
The lily[2] lolls upon the wave; 10
Wrapping the fog about its breast,
The ruin moulders, into rest;
Looking like Lethë,[3] see! the lake
A conscious slumber seems to take,
And would not, for the world, awake. 15
All Beauty sleeps!—and lo! where lies
Irenë, with her Destinies!

1. The first versions of what became "The Sleeper" are quite different. "Irene" (or as Mabbott would have it, "Irenë," as in the Greek Eirënë, the personification of Peace) was first printed in *Poems* (1831) and reprinted in the *Southern Literary Messenger* (May 1836) with a number of variants. The version known as "The Sleeper" was first published in the Philadelphia *Saturday Chronicle* (May 22, 1841) and reprinted several times. The text followed here is that of *The Raven and Other Poems* (1845), with emendations by Mabbott (the Lorimer J. Graham copy with Poe's handwritten revisions).
2. The funereal flower. "Rosemary": the herb of remembrance.
3. River of forgetfulness in Hades (Hell).

Oh, lady bright! can it be right—
This window open to the night?
The wanton airs, from the tree-top, 20
Laughingly through the lattice drop—
The bodiless airs, a wizard rout,
Flit through thy chamber in and out,
And wave the curtain canopy
So fitfully—so fearfully— 25
Above the closed and fringéd lid
'Neath which thy slumb'ring soul lies hid,[4]
That, o'er the floor and down the wall,
Like ghosts the shadows rise and fall!
Oh, lady dear, hast thou no fear? 30
Why and what art thou dreaming here?
Sure thou art come o'er far-off seas,
A wonder to these garden trees!
Strange is thy pallor! strange thy dress!
Strange, above all, thy length of tress,[5] 35
And this all solemn silentness!

The lady sleeps! Oh, may her sleep,
Which is enduring, so be deep!
Heaven have her in its sacred keep!
This chamber changed for one more holy, 40
This bed for one more melancholy,
I pray to God that she may lie
Forever with unopened eye,
While the pale sheeted ghosts go by!

My love, she sleeps! Oh, may her sleep, 45
As it is lasting, so be deep!
Soft may the worms about her creep!
Far in the forest, dim and old,
For her may some tall vault unfold—
Some vault that oft hath flung its black 50
And wingéd pannels fluttering back,
Triumphant, o'er the crested palls,
Of her grand family funerals—
Some sepulchre, remote, alone,
Against whose portal she hath thrown, 55
In childhood, many an idle stone—
Some tomb from out whose sounding door
She ne'er shall force an echo more,
Thrilling to think, poor child of sin!
It was the dead who groaned within. 60

4. I.e., the soul is hidden behind the lady's closed eye. The eyelid is fringed by eyelashes. Traditionally, the eyes are the "windows" to the soul.
5. Reference to the superstition that the hair continues to grow in the grave.

The Valley of Unrest[1]

Once it smiled a silent dell
Where the people did not dwell;
They had gone unto the wars,
Trusting to the mild-eyed stars,
Nightly, from their azure towers, 5
To keep watch above the flowers,
In the midst of which all day
The red sun-light lazily lay.
Now each visiter shall confess
The sad valley's restlessness. 10
Nothing there is motionless.
Nothing save the airs that brood
Over the magic solitude.
Ah, by no wind are stirred those trees
That palpitate like the chill seas 15
Around the misty Hebrides![2]
Ah, by no wind those clouds are driven
That rustle through the unquiet Heaven
Uneasily, from morn till even,
Over the violets there that lie 20
In myriad types of the human eye—
Over the lilies there that wave
And weep above a nameless grave!
They wave:—from out their fragrant tops
Eternal dews come down in drops. 25
They weep:—from off their delicate stems
Perennial tears descend in gems.

The City in the Sea First published as "The Doomed City" in
Poems (1831), this poem was frequently reprinted. Mabbott reprints both
the 1831 version (his A-text) and the version used in Griswold's edition of
Poe's *Works* (the H-text); the differences, like those of "The Valley Nis"
and "The Valley of Unrest" are illuminating. The text followed here is that
of *The Raven and Other Poems* (1845), which shows no variations from
Mabbott's H-text.

The basic allusion is to the doomed cities of Sodom and Gomorrah,
which the Bible says God sank (by earthquake or flood) into the Dead Sea
because of their excessive wickedness (see Genesis 19 for the story of
Lot). The Dead Sea is a lake of high-density saltwater 1,300 feet below sea

1. The first version, titled "The Valley Nis," was published in *Poems* (1831) and reprinted with
 substantial changes in the *Southern Literary Messenger* (February 1836). Scholars have spec-
 ulated that *nis* is a negative word from the late Middle Ages (appearing in Geoffrey
 Chaucer's times) or *sin* spelled backwards. There has also been speculation that the vague
 allusions in the poem refer to the story of a 17th-century Scots soldier who died at Boston
 Cottage on the road between Glasgow and Edinburgh (signaled by the reference to the He-
 brides in line 35). Poe shortened the poem, made it less specific and more indefinitive in
 1845, when it was several times reprinted as "The Valley of Unrest." The version followed
 here is that of *The Raven and Other Poems* (1845).
2. Foggy islands northwest of the Scottish mainland.

level on the border of Jordan and Israel—some forty-five miles long and
ten miles wide—and in places well over a 1,000 feet deep. It is also called
the Salt Sea, the East Sea, the Sea of the Plain, the *Bahr Lut* (Arabic for
the Sea of Lot), and the *Lacus Asphaltites* (Latin for the Lake of Asphalt,
or Bitumen). Sodom and Gomorrah were located on the southwest side of
the lake. See Part II of "Al Aaraaf" (p. 34, n. 8 herein), in which he men-
tions the two famous sunken cities along with a number of others (as
many as thirteen) that ancient commentators have suggested were "en-
gulphed." He also mentions that the ancient observers said that at times
the "vestiges of columns, walls &c. are seen above the surface" but that at
"*any* season, such remains may be discovered by looking down into the
transparent lake." Commentaries from ancient times also mention the
changeable colors of the lake's waters, as in the Jewish histories of Flavius
Josephus (37–95? C.E.). The Dead Sea area is rich in history and religion.
The famous Dead Sea Scrolls were first discovered in caves above the wa-
ters on the northwest side of the lake in 1947.

The City in the Sea

Lo! Death has reared himself a throne
In a strange city lying alone
Far down within the dim West,
Where the good and the bad and the worst and the best
Have gone to their eternal rest. 5
There shrines and palaces and towers
(Time-eaten towers that tremble not!)
Resemble nothing that is ours.
Around, by lifting winds forgot,
Resignedly beneath the sky 10
The melancholy waters lie.

No rays from the holy heaven come down
On the long night-time of that town;
But light from out the lurid sea
Streams up the turrets silently[1]— 15
Gleams up the pinnacles far and free
Up domes—up spires—up kingly halls—
Up fanes—up Babylon-like[2] walls—
Up shadowy long-forgotten bowers
Of sculptured ivy and stone flowers— 20
Up many and many a marvellous shrine
Whose wreathéd friezes intertwine
The viol, the violet, and the vine.[3]

1. Some critics have been puzzled that the light streams upward from the sea—perhaps it is
phosphorescence, perhaps the light from Hell, or perhaps a double reflection seen when
looking down into the waters. Poe's deliberate indefinitiveness makes it unclear if the cities
are already sunken or about to sink (possibly into their own reflections).
2. Another city notorious in the Bible for wickedness. Some critics have suggested that the city
Poe is describing is in fact Babylon, but others have pointed out that the hyphenated suffix
"-like" suggests a metaphoric comparison, not a literal reference, and that the phrase in gen-
eral suggests a city that is doomed for its wickedness.
3. Critics have looked for allegorical identifications, but the phrase seems more suggestive than
precise. Isaiah 14:11 mentions "pomp" being brought "down to the grave" along with the

Resignedly beneath the sky
The melancholy waters lie. 25
So blend the turrets and shadows there
That all seem pendulous in air,
While from a proud tower in the town
Death looks gigantically down.

There open fanes[4] and gaping graves 30
Yawn level with the luminous waves;
But not the riches there that lie
In each idol's diamond eye—
Not the gaily-jewelled dead
Tempt the waters from their bed; 35
For no ripples curl, alas!
Along that wilderness of glass—
No swellings tell that winds may be
Upon some far-off happier sea—
No heavings hint that winds have been 40
On seas less hideously serene.

But lo, a stir is in the air!
The wave—there is a movement there!
As if the towers had thrust aside,
In slightly sinking, the dull tide— 45
As if their tops had feebly given
A void within the filmy Heaven.
The waves have now a redder glow—
The hours are breathing faint and low—
And when, amid no earthly moans, 50
Down, down that town shall settle hence,
Hell, rising from a thousand thrones,[5]
Shall do it reverence.

The Coliseum[1]

Type of the antique Rome! Rich reliquary
Of lofty contemplation left to Time

noise of viols (stringed musical instruments). The hanging gardens of doomed Babylon were one of the seven wonders of the ancient world. "Wreathéd friezes": apparently vine-covered (whether real or carved) bas-reliefs around the tops of temple buildings.
4. Temples (archaic); the word Poe also used in "The Doomed City."
5. Mabbott observes that there are "very old" stories that "locate Hell directly under the Dead Sea." Also see Isaiah 14.
1. First published in the Baltimore Saturday Visiter (October 26, 1833). Submitted for the Visiter's prize contest, the poem was apparently considered the best of the entries, or so Poe was told. But the judges did not want to award both the fiction prize (won by Poe's "MS. Found in a Bottle") and the poetry prize to the same person—though the poetry winner, John H. Hewitt, happened to be the editor of the Visiter. The poem was frequently reprinted, with several variants, including incorporation as a soliloquy into the last scene of Poe's 1835 verse tragedy Politian (Poe's first two efforts in blank verse). Mabbott reprints (his M-text) from Works (1850); the text is from The Raven and Other Poems (1845), which shows only one variant (see p. 54, n. 5 herein) from Mabbott's M-text.
 The Coliseum in Rome (the amphitheater was finished in 80 C.E.) has attracted many poets, novelists, and other writers; among the more famous commentaries are Edward

By buried centuries of pomp and power!
At length—at length—after so many days
Of weary pilgrimage and burning thirst, 5
(Thirst for the springs of lore that in thee lie,)
I kneel, an altered and an humble man,
Amid thy shadows, and so drink within
My very soul thy grandeur, gloom, and glory!

Vastness! and Age! and Memories of Eld! 10
Silence! and Desolation! and dim Night!
I feel ye now—I feel ye in your strength—
O spells more sure than e'er Judæan king
Taught in the gardens of Gethsemane![2]
O charms more potent than the rapt Chaldee[3] 15
Ever drew down from out the quiet stars!

Here, where a hero fell, a column falls!
Here, where the mimic eagle glared in gold,[4]
A midnight vigil holds the swarthy bat!
Here, where the dames of Rome their gilded hair 20
Waved to the wind, now wave the reed and thistle!
Here, where on golden throne the monarch lolled,
Glides, spectre-like, unto his marble home,
Lit by the wan light of the hornéd moon,[5]
The swift and silent lizard of the stones! 25

But stay! these walls—these ivy-clad arcades—
These mouldering plinths[6]—these sad and
 blackened shafts—
These vague entablatures—this crumbling frieze—
These shattered cornices—this wreck—this ruin—
These stones—alas! these gray stones—are they 30
 all—
All of the famed, and the colossal left
By the corrosive Hours to Fate and me?

Gibbon's in *Decline and Fall of the Roman Empire* (6 vols., 1776–88) and Lord Byron's in "*Childe Harold*" (1812–18), IV.cxlii–cxlv, and *Manfred* (1817), III.iv.10–41. The parallels of Poe's poem with the lines in *Manfred* are manifest; the imagery and phrasing is similar. However, whereas Childe Harold sees the ruins indicating the decay of Roman civilization, Manfred, like Poe's narrator, finds inspiration in them (see Mabbott's discussion, I.226).

2. Suggestive allusions to supernatural power, not necessarily restricted to Jesus in the Garden of Gethsemane.

3. Refers to an astrologer-priest, a magician who could read the stars. The Chaldeans were a special class in Babylonia and Mesopotamia, dating from 1000 B.C.E., but they are associated principally with Nebuchadnezzar II in the 7th century B.C.E. and the invasion of Cyrus the Great, who sacked Babylon in the 6th century B.C.E. (see notes to "Loss of Breath," pp. 89ff. herein). Poe invokes the Chaldeans in other works; see "Al Aaraaf," II.42–43, (p. 34), and "Shadow" (p. 134).

4. Image of an eagle, gilded or in actual gold, at the top of a pole as the standard of the Roman legions, symbolizing the victories of Jupiter.

5. A crescent moon (see notes to "Ulalume," pp. 61ff. herein). "Wanlight" in *The Raven and Other Poems* was changed to "wan light" in the Lorimer Graham copy of *The Raven and Other Poems* and is followed here.

6. Rock-slab bases for pedestals, columns, or statues; also a bottom course of horizontal blocks meeting or supporting a vertical wall, often around an opening.

"Not all"—the Echoes answer me—"not all!
"Prophetic sounds and loud, arise forever
"From us, and from all Ruin, unto the wise, 35
"As melody from Memnon[7] to the Sun.
"We rule the hearts of mightiest men—we rule
"With a despotic sway all giant minds.
"We are not impotent—we pallid stones.
"Not all our power is gone—not all our fame— 40
"Not all the magic of our high renown—
"Not all the wonder that encircles us—
"Not all the mysteries that in us lie—
"Not all the memories that hang upon
"And cling around about us as a garment, 45
"Clothing us in a robe of more than glory."

Sonnet—Silence[1]

There are some qualities—some incorporate things,
 That have a double life, which thus is made
A type of that twin entity which springs
 From matter and light, evinced in solid and shade.
There is a two-fold *Silence*—sea and shore— 5
 Body and Soul. One dwells in lonely places,
 Newly with grass o'ergrown; some solemn graces,
Some human memories and tearful lore,
Render him terrorless: his name's "No more."
He is the corporate[2] Silence: dread him not! 10
 No power hath he of evil in himself;
But should some urgent fate (untimely lot!)
 Bring thee to meet his shadow (nameless elf,
That haunteth the lone regions where hath trod
No foot of man,) commend thyself to God! 15

7. Mythical African-Egyptian-Trojan king, the son of Eos, the Dawn, and Tithonus, prince of
Troy. (Eos was cursed by Aphrodite with insatiable desire for mortal men. She fell in love
with young Tithonus and asked Zeus to make him immortal so that they could be together
forever; but she forgot to ask for perpetual youth for him, and her lover aged and aged and
aged without the power to die.) Near Thebes in Egypt were two huge statues, one of which
(to the East) was said to make the sound like the breaking of a harp-string (an image Poe
uses elsewhere) when first struck by the rays of the morning sun. Although it was a statue of
King Amenophis III, also known as Amenhotep III, who reigned over the XVIII dynasty of
ancient Egypt (c. 1411–1372 B.C.E.), there was a tradition that it was of Memnon greeting
his mother with a sharp melodic salute. Cf. "Stanzas" (pp. 18–19 herein).
1. First published in the Philadelphia *Saturday Courier* (January 4, 1840). The text followed
here is that of *The Raven and Other Poems* (1845). The poem has fifteen rather than the
conventional fourteen lines, which Poe thought made it "a clever sonnet." It is a variant on
the Italian form, which is normally composed of an octave (8 lines) and a sestet (6 lines). In
its second publication, in *Burton's Gentleman's Magazine* (April 1840), it was divided into
three stanzas of four, five, and six lines.
2. Bodily.

Dream-Land[1]

By a route obscure and lonely,
Haunted by ill[2] angels only,
Where an Eidolon,[3] named Night,
On a black throne reigns upright,
I have reached these lands but newly 5
From an ultimate dim Thule[4]—
From a wild weird clime that lieth, sublime,
 Out of Space—out of Time.

 Bottomless vales and boundless floods,
 And chasms, and caves, and Titan woods,[5] 10
 With forms that no man can discover
For the dews that drip all over;[6]
Mountains toppling evermore
Into seas without a shore;
Seas that restlessly aspire, 15
Surging, unto skies of fire;
Lakes that endlessly outspread
Their lone waters—lone and dead,—
Their still waters—still and chilly
With the snows of the lolling lily. 20

By the lakes that thus outspread
Their lone waters, lone and dead,—
Their sad waters, sad and chilly
With the snows of the lolling lily,—
By the mountains—near the river 25
Murmuring lowly, murmuring ever,—
By the grey woods,—by the swamp
Where the toad and the newt encamp,—
By the dismal tarns and pools
 Where dwell the Ghouls,[7]— 30
By each spot the most unholy—
In each nook most melancholy,—
There the traveller meets aghast

1. First published in *Graham's Magazine* (June 1844). Mabbot's F-text, from the Richmond *Examiner* (October 23, 1849) shows no variants from that of *The Raven and Other Poems* (1845), followed here.
2. Probably in the sense of evil, ill-willed.
3. A phantom.
4. The Greek name (pronounced *Thu-lee*) for the then known farthest point of land in the north, described as an island and identified variously as what we know today as Iceland, Greenland, or even the Shetland Islands. The phrase "ultima Thule" (the farthest point) occurs in book I, line 30, of the *Georgics* (completed 30 B.C.E.) of the Roman poet Virgil (Publius Vergilius Maro, 70–19 B.C.E.). The phrase was used by subsequent poets to suggest the ultimate end point of the earth, at the North Pole, where a gigantic black rock jutted up into the sky; poetically, it means the farthest goal of human endeavor that can possibly be imagined.
5. Huge, like the Titans in classic mythology, who preceded the Olympian gods.
6. The next several lines echo "Fairy Land [2]." See notes to both "Fairy-Land [1]" (pp. 43–45 herein) and "Fairy Land [2]" (pp. 45–46).
7. Demons who prowl graveyards. In some myths, they are eaters of dead human flesh.

Sheeted Memories of the Past—
Shrouded forms that start and sigh 35
As they pass the wanderer by—
White-robed forms of friends long given,
In agony, to the Earth—and Heaven.[8]

For the heart whose woes are legion
'Tis a peaceful, soothing region— 40
For the spirit that walks in shadow
O! it is an Eldorado![9]
But the traveller, travelling through it,
May not—dare not openly view it;
Never its mysteries are exposed 45
To the weak human eye unclosed;
So wills its King, who hath forbid
The uplifting of the fringed lid;
And thus the sad Soul that here passes
Beholds it but through darkened glasses.[1] 50

By a route obscure and lonely,
Haunted by ill angels only,
Where an Eidolon, name NIGHT,
On a black throne reigns upright,
I have wandered home but newly 55
From this ultimate dim Thule.

The Raven Rapidly and repeatedly published in many magazines
and newspapers in the first weeks of 1845, "The Raven" continued to be
widely reprinted throughout the years 1845–49, with different line-length
experiments. The major influence on the rhythm and the stanza form of
"The Raven" was probably "Lady Geraldine's Courtship" (1844) by Eliza-
beth Barrett (Elizabeth Barrett Browning). Poe praised her poem in a re-
view (January 11, 1845) and dedicated *The Raven and Other Poems* (1845)
to her. This is the volume providing the text followed here; it differs from
Mabbott's choice, which represents the author's final intentions only in a
few instances of capitalization and punctuation, in italicizing the words
here in line 12 and *still* in line 103, and in diction only in lines 27 and 80
(see notes to these two lines herein). There were many parodies and imi-
tations during Poe's lifetime, going by such titles as "The Owl," "The
Craven," "The Turkey," and so on (Mabbott, I.352, gives a list). Poe explained
his technique and intent (possibly half tongue-in-cheek) in "The Philo-
sophy of Composition" (pp. 675ff. herein) the next year; see also the biogra-
phical sketch (pp. xxxviii–xxxix herein) and the Poems introduction (p. 7).

8. Ghosts of people and friends, who have been given in death to earthen graves but also thus
 to Heaven.
9. City of gold sought in the American West by the Spanish conquistadors (see also notes to
 "Eldorado," p. 74 herein).
1. The king of this otherworldly realm (of death or imagined half-death or of waking dream)
 forbids a direct view; one's eyes must be kept half-closed. The eyelashes and resultant
 oblique view are like darkened glasses, recalling 1 Corinthians 13:12: "For now we see
 through a glass, darkly."

The Raven

Once upon a midnight dreary, while I pondered, weak and weary,
Over many a quaint and curious volume of forgotten lore,
While I nodded, nearly napping, suddenly there came a tapping,
As of some one gently rapping, rapping at my chamber door.
" 'Tis some visiter," I muttered, "tapping at my chamber door— 5
 Only this, and nothing more."

Ah, distinctly I remember it was in the bleak December,
And each separate dying ember wrought its ghost upon the floor.
Eagerly I wished the morrow;—vainly I had sought to borrow
From my books surcease[1] of sorrow—sorrow for the lost 10
 Lenore—
For the rare and radiant maiden whom the angels name Lenore—
 Nameless here for evermore.[2]

And the silken sad uncertain rustling of each purple curtain
Thrilled me—filled me with fantastic terrors never felt before;
So that now, to still the beating of my heart, I stood repeating 15
" 'Tis some visiter entreating entrance at my chamber door—
Some late visiter entreating entrance at my chamber door;—
 This it is, and nothing more."

Presently my soul grew stronger; hesitating then no longer,
"Sir," said I, "or Madam, truly your forgiveness I implore; 20
But the fact is I was napping, and so gently you came rapping,
And so faintly you came tapping, tapping at my chamber door,
That I scarce was sure I heard you"—here I opened wide the door;—
 Darkness there, and nothing more.

Deep into that darkness peering, long I stood there wondering, 25
 fearing,
Doubting, dreaming dreams no mortal ever dared to dream before;
But the silence was unbroken, and the darkness[3] gave no token,
And the only word there spoken was the whispered word, "Lenore!"
This I whispered, and an echo murmured back the word, "Lenore!"
 Merely this, and nothing more. 30

Back into the chamber turning, all my soul within me burning,
Soon I heard again a tapping somewhat louder than before.
"Surely," said I, "surely that is something at my window lattice;
Let me see; then, what thereat[4] is, and this mystery explore—
Let my heart be still a moment and this mystery explore;— 35
 'Tis the wind and nothing more!"

1. Cessation.
2. Nameless *here* in Mabbott's print text: i.e., the bereaved narrator will not speak aloud, here
 on earth, the name of his deceased love.
3. In Mabbott's print text "stillness."
4. At a particular place or time (also by reason of).

Open here I flung the shutter, when, with many a flirt and flutter,
In there stepped a stately raven of the saintly days of yore;[5]
Not the least obeisance made he; not an instant stopped or
 stayed he;
But, with mien[6] of lord or lady perched above my chamber door— 40
Perched upon a bust of Pallas[7] just above my chamber door—
 Perched, and sat, and nothing more.

Then this ebony bird beguiling my sad fancy into smiling,
By the grave and stern decorum of the countenance it wore,
"Though thy crest be shorn and shaven, thou," I said, "art sure 45
 no craven,[8]
Ghastly grim and ancient raven wandering from the Nightly shore—
Tell me what thy lordly name is on the Night's Plutonian[9] shore!"
 Quoth the raven, "Nevermore."

Much I marvelled this ungainly fowl to hear discourse so plainly,
Though its answer little meaning—little relevancy bore; 50
For we cannot help agreeing that no living human being
Ever yet was blessed with seeing bird above his chamber door—
Bird or beast upon the sculptured bust above his chamber door,
 With such name as "Nevermore."

But the raven, sitting lonely on the placid bust, spoke only 55
That one word, as if his soul in that one word he did outpour.
Nothing farther then he uttered—not a feather then he fluttered—
Till I scarcely more than muttered "Other friends have flown before—
On the morrow *he* will leave me, as my hopes have flown before."
 Then the bird said "Nevermore." 60

5. Several ancient traditions regarding ravens exist. The Greeks considered them prophetic, and they were sacred to Apollo. They were regarded as prognostic of death because of their omnipresence after a war, scavenging the battlefields for carrion. In Roman myth, the raven was originally white; as punishment for an offense against the gods, its plumage was changed to black. There is an unsubstantiated story that Poe told Cornelius Mathews that the image of a raven, "that imp bird," pursued him "mentally, perpetually." He added: "I cannot rid myself of its presence . . . I hear its croak as I used to hear it at Stoke Newington [the young Poe's school in London], the flap of its wings in my ear" (quoted in Mabbott, I.354–55). Scholars are fond of suggesting multiple sources for Poe's use of the bird. One that may have more validity than some others is the raven Grip in Charles Dicken's *Barnaby Rudge* (1841), which Poe reviewed in 1842. Washington Irving's "Legend of Prince Ahmed Al Kamel; or, The Pilgrim of Love" in *The Alhambra* (1832) concisely sums up the reputation of ravens, and the situation bears some resemblance to that of the student lover in Poe's poem. Prince Ahmed, having learned the language of birds, speaks with an owl of his desire to seek an unknown love. The owl tells him to search out a certain raven belonging to "an Arabian magician" of Seville; the owl had once seen the magician "surrounded by his magic books and on his shoulder was perched his familiar, an ancient raven who had come with him from Egypt. . . . I would advise you, O prince, to seek that raven, for he is a soothsayer and a conjurer, and deals in the black art, for which all ravens, and especially those of Egypt, are renowned." The prince does so and addresses the raven as follows: "Pardon me, most ancient and darkly wise raven . . . if for a moment I interrupt those studies which are the wonder of the world. You behold before you a votary of love, who would fain seek your counsel how to obtain the object of his passion." To this the raven replies, the "harbinger of fate am I; who croak bodings of death from the chimney-top and flap my wings at the sick man's window. You must seek elsewhere for tidings of your unknown beauty."
6. A person's bearing, indicating attitude. "Obeisance": gesture showing respect, such as bowing.
7. A statue of the head and shoulders of Pallas Athena, goddess of wisdom and patroness of scholars; she was said to have sprung fully formed from the head of her father, Zeus.
8. Coward. Mabbott notes that sometimes cowardly knights had their heads shaved.
9. Of the realm of Pluto, king of the underworld (Greek, Hades), where the shades of the dead dwell.

Startled at the stillness broken by reply so aptly spoken,
"Doubtless," said I, "what it utters is its only stock and store
Caught from some unhappy master whom unmerciful Disaster[1]
Followed fast and followed faster till his songs one burden bore— 65
Till the dirges[2] of his Hope that melancholy burden bore
 Of 'Never—nevermore.' "

But the raven still beguiling all my sad soul into smiling,
Straight I wheeled a cushioned seat in front of bird, and bust and
 door;
Then, upon the velvet sinking, I betook myself to linking
Fancy unto fancy, thinking what this ominous bird of yore— 70
What this grim, ungainly, ghastly, gaunt, and ominous bird of yore
 Meant in croaking "Nevermore."

This I sat engaged in guessing, but no syllable expressing
To the fowl whose fiery eyes now burned into my bosom's core;
This and more I sat divining, with my head at ease reclining 75
On the cushion's velvet lining that the lamplight gloated[3] o'er,
But whose velvet violet lining with the lamplight gloating o'er,
 She shall press, ah, nevermore!

Then, methought, the air grew denser, perfumed from an unseen
 censer[4]
Swung by angels whose faint foot-falls tinkled on the tufted floor.[5] 80
"Wretch," I cried, "thy God hath lent thee—by these angels he
 hath sent thee
Respite—respite and nepenthe[6] from thy memories of Lenore!
Quaff, oh quaff this kind nepenthe and forget this lost Lenore!"
 Quoth the raven, "Nevermore."

"Prophet!" said I, "thing of evil!—prophet still, if bird or devil!— 85
Whether Tempter sent,[7] or whether tempest tossed thee here ashore,
Desolate yet all undaunted, on this desert land enchanted—
On this home by Horror haunted—tell me truly, I implore—
Is there—is there balm in Gilead?[8]—tell me—tell me, I implore!"
 Quoth the raven, "Nevermore." 90

1. The capitalization seems intended to call attention to the etymology of the word: *dis-aster*
 (unfavorable stars): i.e., an evil fate.
2. Funeral songs.
3. Reflected light from or on something (archaic).
4. Vessel for burning incense.
5. Mabbott's print text reads: "seraphim whose foot-falls." The phrase "whose foot-falls tinkled
 on the tufted floor" was criticized by Poe's sometime friend, sometime antagonist, Thomas
 Dunn English; he asked if Poe's angels had "bells on their toes." Poe claimed that the im-
 pression of the supernatural (or spiritual) was enhanced by the impossibility (or absurdity) of
 steps making a tinkling sound on a thick carpet. Poe is also said to have alluded in conver-
 sation to Isaiah 3:16, where the daughters of Zion make "a tinkling with their feet."
6. Pronounced as three syllables: *ne-PEN-thee*; any drug that induces a sense of oblivion to
 pain; in the *Odyssey*, IV.219–20, it is the drink that Helen produces to assuage grief (proba-
 bly an Egyptian opiate). "Respite": relief.
7. I.e., sent by the devil.
8. A figurative allusion to Genesis 37:25 and Jeremiah 8:22, meaning a curative, a healing oint-
 ment. In Genesis, the Ishmaelites are described as coming from Gilead (*GIL-lee-ad*) and
 bringing "spicery and balm and myrrh." In Jeremiah, the question quoted by Poe is specific.
 "Is there no balm in Gilead?" is followed by the question, "is there no physician" who can re-
 store the "health of the daughter" of the prophet's people?

"Prophet!" said I, "thing of evil—prophet still, if bird or devil!
By that Heaven that bends above us—by that God we both adore—
Tell this soul with sorrow laden if, within the distant Aidenn,[9]
It shall clasp a sainted maiden whom the angels name Lenore—
Clasp a rare and radiant maiden whom the angels name Lenore." 95
 Quoth the raven, "Nevermore."

"Be that word our sign of parting, bird or fiend!" I shrieked,
 upstarting—
"Get thee back into the tempest and the Night's Plutonian shore!
Leave no black plume as a token of that lie thy soul hath spoken!
Leave my loneliness unbroken!—quit the bust above my door! 100
Take thy beak from out my heart, and take thy form from off my
 door!"
 Quoth the raven, "Nevermore."

And the raven, never flitting, still is sitting, still[1] is sitting
On the pallid bust of Pallas just above my chamber door;
And his eyes have all the seeming of a demon's that is dreaming, 105
And the lamp-light o'er him streaming throws his shadow on the
 floor;
And my soul from out that shadow that lies floating on the floor
 Shall be lifted—nevermore!

Ulalume First published in the *American Review* (December 1847).
The text followed here is Mabbott's K-text, a manuscript version written
for Susan Ingram (dated September 10, 1849). Many readers have found
the poem difficult to follow; but Poe's friend and sometime fiancée Sarah
Helen Power Whitman (see the biographical sketch on pp. xlii–xliii
herein), gave a précis of it in the New York *Tribune* of October 13, 1875.
The spirit (or ghost) of the poem, she said, is Astarte (Aphrodite, Venus),
"the crescent star of hope and love," seen "after a night of horror." The
"forlorn heart" hails its appearance "as a harbinger of happiness yet to be,
hoping against hope"; but "when the planet was seen to be rising over the
tomb of a lost love, hope itself was rejected as a cruel mockery."

Ulalume—A Ballad[1]

The skies they were ashen and sober;
 The leaves they were crispéd and sere[2]—

9. Poe's spelling of *Adn*, Arabic for Eden; figuratively, Heaven.
1. Italicized in Mabbott's print text.
1. "Ulalume" (which rhymes with *tomb*) is a portmanteau word in which Poe has combined
ulalare (to wail or moan; Latin) with *lumen* (light)—so that the meaning is something like "sor-
row's light" or "sorrowful light" or "light out of sorrow" (or even the reverse). It is a favorite
scholars' game to adduce different etymologies, allusions, sources, and meanings; Mabbott
gives several (I.419–20). But the suggested basic meanings comport well with the dramatic sit-
uation and thematics of the poem. The self-tortured, bereaved lover, repressing the cause of
his sorrow, wandering in a "misty mid-region" of numbed forgetfulness, follows the light of a
star down an alley of cypress trees. At first, he trusts that the star is a benevolent sign of some
sort from the heavens; but his companion, Psyche (Greek for soul or mind), is mistrustful and
apprehensive. He persists and eventually arrives at the tomb of his lost love, whereupon the
subconscious agonies of the loss of his beloved burst forth into consciousness again.
2. Withered.

The leaves they were withering and sere:
It was night, in the lonesome October[3]
 Of my most immemorial[4] year: 5
It was hard by the dim lake of Auber,
 In the misty mid region of Weir:—
It was down by the dank tarn of Auber,
 In the ghoul-haunted woodland of Weir.[5]

Here once, through an alley Titanic,[6] 10
 Of cypress,[7] I roamed with my Soul—
 Of cypress, with Psyche,[8] my Soul.
These were days when my heart was volcanic
 As the scoriac[9] rivers that roll—
 As the lavas that restlessly roll 15
Their sulphurous currents down Yaanek,
 In the ultimate climes of the Pole—
That groan as they roll down Mount Yaanek,
 In the realms of the Boreal[1] Pole.

Our talk had been serious and sober, 20
 But our thoughts they were palsied and sere—
 Our memories were treacherous and sere;
For we knew not the month was October,
 And we marked not the night of the year—
 (Ah, night of all nights in the year!) 25
We noted not the dim lake of Auber,
 (Though once we had journeyed down here)
We remembered not the dank tarn of Auber,
 Nor the ghoul-haunted woodland of Weir.

3. Some critics have argued that Poe's specifying the month suggests Halloween (All Hallow's Eve), when demons roam before All Saint's Day (see "The Fall of the House of Usher," pp. 199, n.3 herein). Perhaps line 25 ("Ah, night of all nights in the year!") helps confirm this speculation, though it would seem more specifically to refer to the fact that it has been exactly one year since the death (or burial) of the speaker's lost loved one.

4. Word play on "least remembered," that which cannot be remembered (i.e., forgotten), and "worst remembered" (disastrous). The other meaning of "very old" may or may not apply.

5. Although scholars have made other suggestions, most likely these allusions are to the musical compositions of Daniel-François-Espirit Auber (1782–1871) and the paintings of Robert Walter Weir (1803–1889). Weir was an artist of the American Hudson River School, whose practitioners were generally romantic rather than realistic in their landscapes. "Ghoul": a demon who roams graveyards, said to feed on human flesh.

6. Gigantic, after the Titans, who preceded Olympian gods.

7. Symbolic of mourning; the traditional trees of graveyards. This is another clue to the basic dramatic situation of the poem.

8. Soul and butterfly (Greek); the latter a metaphor for the former (see notes to "How to Write a Blackwood Article," pp. 173ff. herein). The famous classical love story of the marriage of Psyche and Cupid, marred by distrust, is found in the cynical narrative *The Golden Ass*, by Lucius Apuleius (2nd century C.E.). Mabbott thinks it is significant that Apuleius's version of the myth is a soul/body fable and that Psyche distrusts her husband's mother, who is Venus; on the surface, however, these suggestive speculations seem a bit far afield.

9. Hardened molten flow lines from a volcano.

1. Normally means north, or the North Pole (Boreas, the North Wind). Mabbott, however, states that in French navigational terminology it also means the South Pole, which has its own magnetic field. Mount Yaanek, he suggests, may be a reference to Mount Erebus, an active volcano in the Antarctic; the name *Erebus* is associated with Hell. See Robert C. McLean's argument (pp. 798ff. herein) for an authoritative historical discussion of Poe's use of the names *Yaanek* and *Ulalume* for phonic and connotative suggestions.

And now, as the night was senescent,[2] 30
 And star-dials[3] pointed to morn—
 As the star-dials hinted of morn—
At the end of our path a liquescent
 And nebulous lustre was born,
Out of which a miraculous crescent 35
 Arose with a duplicate horn—
Astarte's[4] bediamonded crescent,
 Distinct with its duplicate horn.

And I said—"She is warmer than Dian;
 She rolls through an ether of sighs[5]— 40
 She revels in a region of sighs.
She has seen that the tears are not dry on
 These cheeks where the worm never dies,[6]
And has come past the stars of the Lion,[7]
 To point us the path to the skies— 45
 To the Lethean[8] peace of the skies—
Come up, in despite of the Lion,
 To shine on us with her bright eyes—
Come up, through the lair of the Lion,
 With love in her luminous eyes." 50

But Psyche, uplifting her finger,
 Said—"Sadly this star I mistrust—
 Her pallor I strangely mistrust—
Ah, hasten!—ah, let us not linger!
 Ah, fly!—let us fly!—for we must." 55
In terror she spoke; letting sink her

2. Growing old; i.e., the night is waning toward morning.
3. An invented night analogue for sundials.
4. The Phoenician equivalent of Aphrodite or Venus, goddess of love and fertility. In astrology, Venus is both the evening and the morning star. Mabbott seems to think that Poe deliberately confused or merged the moon (which can assume the aspect of a crescent) and the star Venus (which he says cannot). Poe may have had a different astronomical effect or constellation in mind. In contrast to the planet/goddess Venus, the moon is associated in myth both with madness (lunacy, from the goddess's other name, Luna) and with cold virginity and chastity (see next note). If one assumes that the death of Virginia Poe is the inspiration of the poem (see the biographical sketch, p. xlii herein), the autobiographical relevance of this paradox becomes powerfully suggestive. But the poem also dramatizes a general psychological theme of attraction/repulsion and subconscious/conscious forces.
5. The ancients conceived of outer space as filled with an invisible and impalpable gas, *ether*, from which we get the English word *ethereal* (or *etherial*), meaning "delicate, thin, weightless, unearthly." The ether was supposed to be an ineffably light, almost insubstantial gas between the crystalline spheres of the known planetary orbs (including that of the moon). As they revolved around the earth and around one another in more or less concentric orbits, they made "celestial music" (the "music of the spheres"). This poetic-scientific mythos is based on the idea of the earth-centered Ptolemaic universe. Ptolemy (2nd century C.E.) was a Greek mathematician, astronomer, and geographer. See also notes to "Loss of Breath" (pp. 89ff. herein). "Dian": Diana, goddess of the moon in classical mythology, was aloof, virginal, unattainable.
6. See the dark and unpleasant comments about the unruly dead in Isaiah 66:24 and Mark 9:48, where Hell is the region where the "worm does not die."
7. The constellation of Leo. Mabbott offers the following astrological interpretation: "Venus in Leo signifies lust or trouble in love." In 1847, "Venus left the sign of Leo and entered Virgo on July 30" and "remained in it until December; the latter sign is unfavorable to marriage" (I. 422).
8. A reference to the river Lethe in Hades, the waters of which bring forgetfulness.

Wings till they trailed in the dust—
 In agony sobbed; letting sink her
 Plumes till they trailed in the dust—
 Till they sorrowfully trailed in the dust. 60

I replied—"This is nothing but dreaming.
 Let us on, by this tremulous light!
 Let us bathe in this crystalline light!⁹
Its Sibyllic¹ splendor is beaming
 With Hope and in Beauty to-night— 65
 See!—it flickers up the sky through the night!
Ah, we safely may trust to its gleaming
 And be sure it will lead us aright—
We surely may trust to a gleaming
 That cannot but guide us aright 70
Since it flickers up to Heaven through the night."

Thus I pacified Psyche and kissed her,
 And tempted her out of her gloom—
 And conquered her scruples and gloom;
And we passed to the end of the vista— 75
 But were stopped by the door of a tomb—
 By the door of a legended tomb:²—
And I said—"What is written, sweet sister,
 On the door of this legended tomb?"
 She replied—"Ulalume—Ulalume!— 80
 'T is the vault of thy lost Ulalume!"

Then my heart it grew ashen and sober
 As the leaves that were crispéd and sere—
 As the leaves that were withering and sere—
And I cried—"It was surely October, 85
 On *this* very night of last year,
 That I journeyed—I journeyed down here!—
 That I brought a dread burden down³ here—
 On this night, of all nights in the year,
 Ah, what demon hath tempted me here? 90
Well I know, now, this dim lake of Auber—
 This misty mid region of Weir:—
Well I know, now, this dank tarn of Auber—
 This ghoul-haunted woodland of Weir."

Said we, then—the two, then—"Ah, can it⁴ 95
 Have been that the woodlandish ghouls—

9. See p. 63, n. 5, herein. Mabbott cites N. Bailey's *Dictionary* (1721) as restricting the word astronomically to the last celestial sphere, that of the stars.
1. Prophetic. A reference to the Sibyls, the prophetesses of Apollo.
2. I.e., one with an inscription ("legend") on it, apparently also implying something ancient, mythic, or archetypal (i.e., legendary).
3. Although some critics have seen an implication of murder in this phrase, it more clearly refers to bringing the body of the beloved to be buried.
4. This stanza is omitted in some versions of the poem; supposedly the omission was at the wish of Sarah Helen Whitman. It may have some autobiographical relevance, since she and

The pitiful, the merciful ghouls,[5]
To bar up our way and to ban it
From the secret that lies in these wolds[6]—
From the thing that lies hidden in these wolds— 100
Have drawn up the spectre of a planet
From the limbo of lunary souls[7]—
This sinfully scintillant[8] planet
From the Hell of the planetary souls?"

The Bells[1]

I.

Hear the sledges[2] with the bells—
 Silver bells!
What a world of merriment their melody foretells!
 How they tinkle, tinkle, tinkle,
 In the icy air of night! 5
 While the stars that oversprinkle
 All the Heavens, seem to twinkle
 With a crystalline[3] delight;
 Keeping time, time, time,
 In a sort of Runic rhyme,[4] 10
To the tintinabulation[5] that so musically wells
 From the bells, bells, bells, bells,
 Bells, bells, bells—
 From the jingling and the tinkling of the bells.

Poe were then engaged (see the biographical sketch on pp. xlii–xliii and notes to the second "To Helen" on pp. 68–70 herein). If so, the conclusion of the poem may be even darker or more melancholy than critics have suggested.
5. Probably bitterly ironic. However, Mabbott suggests that in this poem they are "friendly" to human beings; but neither context nor tradition seems to support this assertion. See notes to "The Bells" (immediately below) and the discussion of Byronism in the Poems introduction.
6. A word with contradictory meanings; it means both a plain without trees and a forested moor.
7. Souls of or beneath the moon; here apparently illuminated by moonlight, but suggesting the earthly as opposed to the heavenly (cf. the "sublunary lovers" in John Donne's "A Valediction: Forbidding Mourning") and possibly "lunacy" of some sort. "Limbo": a midregion between a positive and negative state, often with religious significance, as between Heaven and Hell.
8. Poe's neologistic form of *scintillating* or *scintillate*, i.e., giving off flashes of light. In astronomy, it indicates the rapid variation of light (twinkling) associated with stars, an effect caused by turbulence in the earth's atmosphere rather than by in anything in the supernal realm of the stars themselves. The word *scintillating* also carries the connotation of dazzling or radiant sexuality, which may explain the next phrase, "From the Hell of planetary souls." The implied meaning of it all may perhaps be glossed by the celestial drama of "Al Aaraaf," in which earthly love or passion destroys cosmic peace (see notes to "Al Aaraaf," pp. 22ff. herein, and the Poems introduction).
1. First printed in *Sartain's Union Magazine* (December 1849), the text followed here. Two much shorter versions from 1848 exist.
2. Horse-drawn snow sleighs.
3. See notes to "Ulalume" (pp. 61ff. herein).
4. Magical spell. Runes were among the earliest written characters of northern Europe and are associated with occult rites. Mabbott notes in passing that Thomas Gray (1716–1771) in the "Descent of Odin" mentions that "runic rhyme . . . wakes the dead."
5. Ringing. A surprising scholarly debate exists over whether Poe coined this word—surprising because it was well known in his time that the Romans used the onomatopoetic sound *tin-tin-nabula* for bells, and other usages in English existed before Poe's poem.

2.

Hear the mellow wedding bells— 15
 Golden bells!
What a world of happiness their harmony foretells!
 Through the balmy air of night
 How they ring out their delight!—
 From the molten-golden notes 20
 And all in tune,
 What a liquid ditty floats
To the turtle-dove that listens while she gloats[6]
 On the moon!
 Oh, from out the sounding cells 25
What a gush of euphony[7] voluminously wells!
 How it swells!
 How it dwells
 On the Future!—how it tells
 Of the rapture that impels 30
 To the swinging and the ringing
 Of the bells, bells, bells!—
Of the bells, bells, bells, bells,
 Bells, bells, bells—
To the rhyming and the chiming of the bells! 35

3.

Hear the loud alarum bells—
 Brazen[8] bells!
What tale of terror, now, their turbulency tells!
 In the startled ear of Night
 How they scream out their affright! 40
 Too much horrified to speak,
 They can only shriek, shriek,
 Out of tune,
In a clamorous appealing to the mercy of the fire—
In a mad expostulation[9] with the deaf and frantic fire, 45
 Leaping higher, higher, higher,
 With a desperate desire
 And a resolute endeavor
 Now—now to sit, or never,
By the side of the pale-faced moon. 50
 Oh, the bells, bells, bells!
 What a tale their terror tells
 Of despair!
 How they clang and clash and roar!
 What a horror they outpour 55
In the bosom of the palpitating air!

6. Normally, to regard with excessive satisfaction; here possibly used in its archaic sense of reflecting light (cf. "The Raven," p. 60, n. 3 herein). "Ditty": a little song with simple lyrics. "Turtle-dove": mourning dove.
7. Pleasing, agreeable sound.
8. Made of brass, but also suggesting a sharp, piercing sound, or aggressive conduct (brassy). "Alarum": alarm (archaic), usually military.
9. Strong reasoned argument, remonstrance, or protest.

Yet the ear, it fully knows,
 By the twanging
 And the clanging,
 How the danger ebbs and flows:— 60
Yes, the ear distinctly tells,
 In the jangling
 And the wrangling,
 How the danger sinks and swells,
By the sinking or the swelling in the anger of the bells— 65
 Of the bells—
 Of the bells, bells, bells, bells,
 Bells, bells, bells—
 In the clamor and the clangor of the bells.

<p style="text-align:center">4.</p>

Hear the tolling of the bells— 70
 Iron bells!
What a world of solemn thought their monody[1] compels!
 In the silence of the night
 How we shiver with affright
At the melancholy meaning of the tone! 75
 For every sound that floats
 From the rust within their throats
 Is a groan.
 And the people—ah, the people
 They that dwell up in the steeple 80
 All alone,
 And who, tolling, tolling, tolling,
 In that muffled monotone,
 Feel a glory in so rolling
 On the human heart a stone— 85
They are neither man nor woman—
They are neither brute nor human,
 They are Ghouls:[2]
And their king it is who tolls:—
And he rolls, rolls, rolls, rolls 90
 A Pæan[3] from the bells!
 And his merry bosom swells
 With the Pæan of the bells!
 And he dances and he yells;
Keeping time, time, time, 95
In a sort of Runic rhyme,
 To the Pæan of the bells—
 Of the bells:—
Keeping time, time, time,
In a sort of Runic rhyme, 100

1. Poetry or music for one voice (or something that has one simple theme); here probably suggesting that at the end there is only one final reality.
2. Demons associated with the dead. Poe originally indicated (in a canceled line) that the ghouls were "pestilential carcasses disparted [*sic*] from their souls."
3. Rolling note of music indicating praise, exultation, triumph.

> To the throbbing of the bells—
> Of the bells, bells, bells—
> To the sobbing of the bells:—
> Keeping time, time, time,
> As he knells,[4] knells, knells, 105
> In a happy Runic rhyme,
> To the rolling of the bells—
> Of the bells, bells, bells:—
> To the tolling of the bells—
> Of the bells, bells, bells, bells, 110
> Bells, bells, bells—
> To the moaning and the groaning of the bells.

To Helen Apparently first published in the *Union Magazine* for the issue dated November 1848, though a version appears in the New York *Tribune* for October 10, 1849. Mabbott reprints the text from Griswold's edition of Poe's *Works* (1850), which shows little revision and is followed here. It is one of the few examples of Poe's use of blank verse. The personal context of the poem is a little complicated, but basically it reflects Poe's incipient love interest in the widowed Sarah Helen Whitman of Providence, Rhode Island (see the biographical sketch on pp. xlii–xliii herein). Certain of the details are described by Mabbott, who reprints (I.442–43) Mrs. Whitman's poem, "To Edgar A. Poe," from the *Home Journal* (March 18, 1848). Her flattering and flirtatious poem seems to have stimulated Poe's own poetic response, which he had a mutual acquaintance deliver to her in June 1848.

To Helen[1]

> I saw thee once[2]—once only—years ago:
> I must not say *how* many—but *not* many.
> It was a July midnight; and from out
> A full-orbed moon, that, like thine own soul, soaring,
> Sought a precipitate[3] pathway up through heaven, 5
> There fell a silvery-silken veil of light,
> With quietude, and sultriness, and slumber,
> Upon the upturn'd faces of a thousand
> Roses that grew in an enchanted garden,
> Where no wind dared to stir, unless on tiptoe— 10
> Fell on the upturn'd faces of these roses
> That gave out, in return for the love-light,
> Their odorous souls in an ecstatic death—

4. The sound of bells, almost always funeral bells.
1. Poe's title is actually "To ———" but is usually known as the "second 'To Helen,' " for Sarah Helen Power Whitman. The first "To Helen" (1831; p. 47 herein) was for Jane Stith Stanard (see notes to that work).
2. Poe, walking with Mrs. Frances Osgood, glimpsed Mrs. Whitman in Providence, Rhode Island, in early July 1845 as she stood in front of her house and apparently was immediately taken with her.
3. Here a combination of several meanings: steep, rapid, or impulsive.

Fell on the upturn'd faces of these roses
That smiled and died in this parterre,[4] enchanted 15
By thee, and by the poetry of thy presence.

Clad all in white,[5] upon a violet bank
I saw thee half reclining; while the moon
Fell on the upturn'd faces of the roses,
And on thine own, upturn'd—alas, in sorrow! 20

Was it not Fate, that, on this July midnight—
Was it not Fate, (whose name is also Sorrow,)
That bade me pause before that garden-gate,
To breathe the incense of those slumbering roses?
No footstep stirred: the hated world all slept, 25
Save only thee and me. (Oh, Heaven!—oh, God!
How my heart beats in coupling those two words!)
Save only thee and me. I paused—I looked—
And in an instant all things disappeared.
(Ah, bear in mind this garden was enchanted!) 30
The pearly lustre of the moon went out:
The mossy banks and the meandering paths,
The happy flowers and the repining[6] trees,
Were seen no more: the very roses' odors
Died in the arms of the adoring airs. 35
All—all expired save thee—save less than thou:
Save only the divine light in thine eyes—
Save but the soul in thine uplifted eyes.
I saw but them—they were the world to me.
I saw but them—saw only them for hours— 40
Saw only them until the moon went down.
What wild heart-histories seemed to lie enwritten
Upon those crystalline, celestial spheres![7]
How dark a wo! yet how sublime a hope!
How silently serene a sea of pride! 45
How daring an ambition! yet how deep—
How fathomless a capacity for love!

But now, at length, dear Dian sank from sight,
Into a western couch of thunder-cloud;[8]
And thou, a ghost, amid the entombing trees 50
Didst glide away. *Only thine eyes remained.*
They *would not* go—they never yet have gone.
Lighting my lonely pathway home that night,
They have not left me (as my hopes have) since.

4. The bottom area, usually terraced, of a garden set aside especially for flowers.
5. Mrs. Whitman in her reminiscences of Poe says that she did have a rose garden and that in the summer she habitually wore white.
6. Literally, low in spirits, complaining; here probably the "sighing" of trees in the wind.
7. The planets were conceived in classical times to orbit the earth in crystal spheres, emitting heavenly music (the "music of the spheres") as they did so (see also notes to "Ulalume," pp. 61ff. herein).
8. Diana, the moon goddess (i.e., the moon), has disappeared into a cloud.

They follow me—they lead me through the years. 55
They are my ministers—yet I their slave.
Their office is to illumine and enkindle—
My duty, *to be saved* by their bright light,
And purified in their electric fire,[9]
And sanctified in their elysian fire.[1] 60
They fill my soul with Beauty (which is Hope,)
And are far up in Heaven—the stars I kneel to
In the sad, silent watches of my night;
While even in the meridian glare of day
I see them still—two sweetly scintillant 65
Venuses,[2] unextinguished by the sun!

A Dream within a Dream[1]

Take this kiss upon the brow!
And, in parting from you now,
Thus much let me avow—
You are not wrong, who deem
That my days have been a dream; 5
Yet if hope has flown away
In a night, or in a day,
In a vision, or in none,
Is it therefore the less *gone*?
All that we see or seem 10
Is but a dream within a dream.

I stand amid the roar
Of a surf-tormented shore,
And I hold within my hand
Grains of the golden sand— 15
How few! yet how they creep
Through my fingers to the deep,
While I weep—while I weep!
O God! can I not grasp
Them with a tighter clasp? 20
O God! can I not save
One from the pitiless wave?
Is *all* that we see or seem
But a dream within a dream?

9. Given the astronomical motif of the poem, probably lightning.
1. Allusion to the Elysium or the Elysian Fields, the meadows of the "happy isles" of mythology, the abode of the blessed after death.
2. See the end of "Ulalume," where Poe's phrase is "sinfully scintillant." Here Venus, the Roman goddess of love, is the morning star; thus the woman's eyes are flashing astral (starry) fire as bright as the sun's.
1. The final version of verses originally from *Tamerlane and Other Poems* (see "Imitation," pp. 17–18 herein) was published in the Boston *Flag of Our Union* (March 31, 1839). For a discussion of the relations of "Imitation," "To ——— (Should My Early Life Seem)" and this poem, see G. R. Thompson's *Circumscribed Eden of Dreams: Dreamvision and Nightmare in Poe's Early Poetry* (1984), pp. 33–37.

For Annie First printed in the Boston *Flag of Our Union* (April 28, 1849). Mabbott's G-text, which reprints the text of *Works* (1850), shows only a few spelling or punctuation variants from the version authorized by Poe for Griswold's *Poets and Poetry of America* (dated 1850 but published in 1849); it is the text followed here. The Annie of the poem is seemingly based on Mrs. Nancy Locke Heywood Richmond, whom Poe met on July 10, 1848, in Lowell, Massachusetts, where he was to give a lecture. They entered into a quasi-platonic literary flirtation, apparently without objection from her husband, Charles B. Richmond. Biographical critics interpret the poem as based on Poe's personal experience, specifically the incident of his failed suicide attempt; the speaker of the poem is seen as convalescing from an opium overdose (see the biographical sketch on p. xliii herein). In a letter to Mrs. Richmond (November 16, 1848), Poe told her that he had swallowed "about half of the laudanum" he had purchased but that "a friend was at hand" and "saved me." He told Mrs. Whitman, however, that he was so unacquainted with the drug that he took too much and his stomach rejected it; in the letter to Mrs. Richmond he says essentially the same thing, so that it is not clear how the friend "saved" him. More important is the dramatic situation of the poem. It is so obscure and oblique that it is hard to tell if the speaker is alive or dead or about to die—or whether it is Annie who is dead or dying, or some surreal combination of both (see the biographical introduction on pp. xlii–xliii). The poem may not be so much about suicide or the death of someone as (figuratively) about the extremity of world weariness or life sickness that was so popular in the writings of Lord Byron and other Romantic poets.

For Annie

Thank Heaven! the crisis—
 The danger is past,
And the lingering illness
 Is over at last—
And the fever called "Living" 5
 Is conquered at last.

Sadly, I know
 I am shorn of my strength,
And no muscle I move
 As I lie at full length— 10
But no matter!—I feel
 I am better at length.

And I rest so composedly,
 Now, in my bed,
That any beholder 15
 Might fancy me dead—
Might start at beholding me,
 Thinking me dead.

The moaning and groaning,
 The sighing and sobbing, 20

Are quieted now,
 With that horrible throbbing
At heart:—ah, that horrible,
 Horrible throbbing!

The sickness—the nausea— 25
 The pitiless pain—
Have ceased, with the fever
 That maddened my brain—
With the fever called "Living"
 That burned in my brain. 30

And oh! of all tortures
 That torture the worst
Has abated—the terrible
 Torture of thirst
For the napthaline[1] river 35
 Of Passion accurst:—
I have drank of a water
 That quenches all thirst:[2]—

Of a water that flows,
 With a lullaby sound,[3] 40
From a spring but a very few
 Feet under ground—
From a cavern not very far
 Down under ground.

And ah! let it never 45
 Be foolishly said
That my room it is gloomy
 And narrow my bed;
For man never slept
 In a different bed— 50
And, to *sleep*, you must slumber
 In just such a bed.

My tantalized[4] spirit
 Here blandly reposes,
Forgetting, or never 55
 Regretting its roses—

1. Flammable oil, made from rocks; in ancient times, produced from asphaltum around the
 Dead Sea for use in lamps (also spelled *napthalene*). Here the meaning is "fiery" and sug-
 gests Phlegethon, the river of fire in Hell.
2. Suggests death but may be a reference to everlasting life in the next world; see John 4:14.
3. Some critics have suggested that lines 39–40 are an allusion to Lethe, the river of forgetful-
 ness in Hell.
4. Tortured by desire, usually unsatisfied. The word comes from the myth of Tantalus, who, for
 an offense against the gods, was bound and placed up to his neck in water below a bunch of
 grapes (or other fruit) suspended just above his nose. He suffered dreadful thirst and
 hunger, but when he stretched his neck up to take the grapes in his mouth, they lifted just
 out of reach; and when he bent his head down toward the water to drink, it receded.

Its old agitations
 Of myrtles and roses:[5]

For now, while so quietly
 Lying, it[6] fancies 60
A holier odor
 About it, of pansies—
A rosemary odor,
 Commingled with pansies—
With rue and the beautiful 65
 Puritan pansies.[7]

And so it[8] lies happily,
 Bathing in many
A dream of the truth
 And the beauty of Annie— 70
Drowned in a bath
 Of the tresses of Annie.

She tenderly kissed me,
 She fondly caressed,
And then I fell gently 75
 To sleep on her breast—
Deeply to sleep
 From the heaven of her breast.

When the light was extinguished,
 She covered me warm, 80
And she prayed to the angels
 To keep me from harm—
To the queen of the angels[9]
 To shield me from harm.

And I lie so composedly, 85
 Now, in my bed,
(Knowing her love)
 That you fancy me dead—
And I rest so contentedly,
 Now in my bed, 90
(With her love at my breast)
 That you fancy me dead—
That you shudder to look at me,
 Thinking me dead:—

5. Flowers symbolic of love.
6. I.e., presumably, the speaker's spirit.
7. An unclear allusion, but Mabbott calls attention to Shakespeare's *Hamlet*, IV:v.175ff.,
 where Ophelia, picking flowers, mentions rosemary (remembrance), pansies (thought), and
 rue (regret) and calls the bouquet "herb-grace o' Sundays"; he also speculates that the term
 Puritan applies to Annie as a New Englander. "Rosemary": an herb traditionally symbolic of
 remembrance or revival (rebirth). "Rue": an herb symbolic of regret (as in the words *rue* and
 rueful).
8. Again, presumably, the speaker's spirit.
9. The Blessed Virgin, Mary, mother of Jesus, is called *regina angelorum*, the queen of angels.

But my heart it is brighter 95
 Than all of the many
Stars in the sky,
 For it sparkles with Annie—
It glows with the light
 Of the love of my Annie— 100
With the thought of the light
 Of the eyes of my Annie.

Eldorado[1]

Gaily bedight,
 A gallant knight,
In sunshine and in shadow,
 Had journeyed long,
 Singing a song, 5
In search of Eldorado.

But he grew old—
 This knight so bold—
And o'er his heart a shadow
 Fell, as he found 10
 No spot of ground
That looked like Eldorado.

And, as his strength
 Failed him at length
He met a pilgrim shadow— 15
 "Shadow," said he,
 "Where can it be—
This land of Eldorado?"

"Over the Mountains
 Of the Moon,[2] 20
Down the Valley of the Shadow,[3]
 Ride, boldly ride,"
 The shade replied,—
"If you seek for Eldorado!"

1. First printed in the Boston *Flag of Our Union* (April 21, 1849); the only variants are the use of double quotation marks in the dialogue at the end, in *Works* (1850). Eldorado was the city of gold sought by the Spanish conquistadors. Apparently an Indian king in 16th-century Colombia had himself covered with gold and thus was called "El Dorado," the "gilded one." He also seems to have tried to decorate everything in his capital city with gold. Mabbott points out that in Poe's time the term *Eldorado* (one word) was an American nickname for California. For Poe's satiric intentions in this work and in "Von Kempelen and His Discovery," both associated with the California Gold Rush, see the biographical sketch (p. xliv herein).
2. The snow-laden Montes Lunae of antiquity, long considered legendary, here meant to suggest something impossibly far away. According to Thomas Moore in *Lalla Rookh* (1817), one of the books Poe most often refers to (see notes to "Al Aaraaf," pp. 22ff. herein, and "Fairy-Land [1]," pp. 43–45), they were the source of the Nile River. Modern Europeans did not have actual proof of their existence until Sir Henry Stanley found them in 1888.
3. See Psalm 23:4: "valley of the shadow of death." Mabbott has a more complex translation and interpretation based on various sources (I.464–65, notes).

Annabel Lee Poe circulated this work in manuscript several times
in 1849, sometimes in partial payment of debt (autograph copies of his
works were becoming valuable). It was first printed in the late summer of
1849 in the Richmond *Examiner* (though it had been sold to *Sartain's
Union Magazine*, where it appeared in January 1850). It was picked up
immediately after Poe's death by the New York *Tribune* (October 9, 1849)
and shortly thereafter by the *Southern Literary Messenger* (November
1849). It was also published in Griswold's *Poets and Poetry of America*,
10th ed. (1850). Mabbott's A-text follows a manuscript sent to Griswold in
June 1849, which is now at Harvard; since it shows no overt forgeries (see
A Note on the Text, p. xlix herein), this is the version followed here. Al-
though most readers assume that the inspiration of the poem is the death
of Poe's wife, Virginia, one woman after another in Poe's life claimed that
he modeled the poem after her; for an extended account see Mabbott,
I. 468–75.

Annabel Lee

It was many and many a year ago,
 In a kingdom by the sea;
That a maiden there lived whom you may know
 By the name of Annabel Lee;—
And this maiden she lived with no other thought 5
 Than to love and be loved by me.

I was a child and *she* was a child,
 In this kingdom by the sea;
But we loved with a love that was more than love—
 I and my Annabel Lee— 10
With a love that the wingéd seraphs[1] in Heaven
 Coveted her and me.

And this was the reason that, long ago,
 In this kingdom by the sea,
A wind blew out of a cloud, chilling 15
 My beautiful Annabel Lee;
So that her high-born kinsmen came
 And bore her away from me,
To shut her up in a sepulchre,
 In this kingdom by the sea. 20

The angels, not half so happy in Heaven,
 Went envying her and me—
Yes!—that was the reason (as all men know,
 In this kingdom by the sea)
That the wind came out of the cloud by night, 25
 Chilling and killing my Annabel Lee.

1. Highest of the nine orders of angels: they have three pairs of wings (cf. p. 38, n. 5 herein).

But our love it was stronger by far than the love
 Of those who were older than we—
 Of many far wiser than we—
And neither the angels in Heaven above, 30
 Nor the demons down under the sea,
Can ever dissever my soul from the soul
 Of the beautiful Annabel Lee:—

For the moon never beams, without bringing me dreams
 Of the beautiful Annabel Lee; 35
And the stars never rise, but I feel the bright eyes
 Of the beautiful Annabel Lee:—
And so, all the night-tide, I lie down by the side
Of my darling—my darling—my life and my bride,
 In her sepulchre there by the sea— 40
 In her tomb by the sounding sea.

Tales and Sketches

The range of Romantic fiction—especially in its recurrent assaults on neoclassic decorum, on rules and restrictions, on forms, genres, and traditions—is so extensive that only a few highlights can be given here. Among the most important concepts for understanding Poe's fiction are the gothic, the grotesque, and the arabesque. The first two terms are still in wide use; the third requires special definition, particularly as understood in the Romantic era.

Gothic

Since 1765, when Horace Walpole appended to the second edition of his supernatural romance *The Castle of Otranto* the subtitle "A Gothic Story," the word has been a convenient critical term in English to describe certain kinds of subject matter and effects in fiction. As a literary term, *gothic* connotes sensationalism, violence, madness, terror, horror, fear of the supernatural, a foreboding sense of evil, a perception of awesome and sinister mystery. But the precise meaning of the word, like that of the word *romantic*, retains an ambiguous, even a contradictory quality. In history, *gothic* refers to northern European semibarbaric tribes of the Dark Ages that picked the Roman Empire to pieces. Yet these so-called barbarians (Vandals, Visigoths, Ostrogoths) merged with Latin-speaking peoples to produce a Christian culture that unified all of Europe in the Middle Ages. Indeed, in art history, *gothic* suggests the devotional quality of the elaborate architecture of cathedrals built by the peoples of medieval Europe. Yet the word was used in the eighteenth century not only to mean "medieval" in general but also to indicate disapproval of the Middle Ages' "barbarous" forms of architecture (since they were not in the pure classical style of Greece and Rome). The European eighteenth century, modeling itself after what it conceived to be the high point of classical culture in Rome under the rule of Augustus (63 B.C.E.–14 C.E.), saw itself as the new (neo) classical age. Nevertheless, it was to produce a neo-gothic movement in literature that became an integral part of the anti-classicist Romantic movement by the end of the century.

Thus in Anglo-American literature, the word *gothic* was associated, by the popularity of Walpole's story, not only with the medieval cathedral but also with various styles of medieval castles as appropriate settings for the new Romantic fiction that began to flood the presses in the 1780s and the 1790s. Bemusedly disapproving of these tales of terror and adventure, late neoclassicist critics seized on the word

gothic as a simple means of criticizing their lack of verisimilitude, their improbability and wild flights of fancy and imagination. But the gothicism of these works was enthusiastically embraced by the reading public. In fact, the subtitle "A Gothic Tale," especially if a work also purported to be an exotic translation, would stimulate greater sales than could be expected from the once popular sentimental and domestic tale. Didactic, satiric, and comic stories of domesticized people in a stable society were superseded by tales of mysterious, isolated personages committing vile deeds, then (melodramatically) brooding—alternately indulging forbidden lusts and narcissistically feeling intense remorse, which, paradoxically, further fed the fires of the passion. Sometimes these figures were supernaturally demonic; sometimes they were human beings undergoing a psychological breakdown.

Grotesque

Somewhat earlier, the related term *grotesque* emerged. In general, it suggests that which is "out of keeping," something jarring or distorted. The word comes from the Italian for *grotto*. In the early Renaissance, workers excavating the streets of Rome broke through to a lower level of the city dating to some 1500 years earlier. They found wall paintings and decorations in which realms of existence that are ordinarily perceived as separate or distinct in some way (like plants, animals, metals) were fused together. Plants had metal tools growing from their stems and leaves, or their stalks ended in human heads, and the like. The Roman engineer and architectural critic, Marcus Vitruvius Pollio (late 1st century B.C.E.–early 1st century C.E.), regarded them as abominations; in his *De Architectura*, Vitruvius wrote that they were bastard forms that had no locus in reality and violated natural decorum. These images became known in the Renaissance as "painters' dreams" (*sogni dei pittori*), indicating something that was disturbing, unreal, nightmarish. But they were more generally referred to as "grotto paintings": distortions or perversions of natural forms were said to be *grottesco*—that is, like those first-century figures found in the grottoes of Rome. And indeed, the word *nightmare* sums up the predominant meaning of *grotesque* in which surreal absurdity and horror are fused. In the eighteenth century, the word also began to acquire a comic meaning, so that one standard definition of *grotesque* became an uneasy combination of humor and horror.

Arabesque

Poe did not title his 1840 collection of stories "Gothic Tales" or "Tales of the Grotesque." He titled it *Tales of the Grotesque and Arabesque.* Precisely what he intended is a matter of critical speculation and debate, for the word *arabesque* has a history even more complex than that of *grotesque* and *gothic.*

Arabesque largely means "non-Western," indicating the "otherness" of things more or less Oriental—a source of both fascination and friction. The romanticized word *Araby* is closely associated. It conjures up

the "mysteries of the East" and images associated with North African lands like Egypt and Middle Eastern lands like Turkey and old Persia (modern Iran) and Iraq. But the concept of Araby or the arabesque is not confined to Arabia; it is a generalized term using the idea of exotic African and Middle Eastern lands as a metaphor for an even wider variety of more or less Arabic cultures. These extend from Mauritania and Morocco on the west coast of North Africa eastward through Algeria and Libya, to Egypt and the Sudan, thence farther eastward from north of the Caucasus southward to Turkey, Syria, Jordan, Lebanon, Egypt, Saudi Arabia—eastward across the great land bridge between West and East: from Europe to Iraq, Iran, Turkistan, Afghanistan, Pakistan, India, and even into western China—lands that reflect the spread of Islam over the centuries. During the hundred years between the middle of the eighteenth century and the middle of the nineteenth, the West became fascinated by aspects of the East that seemed different, strange. Postcolonial critics argue that, despite professed admiration for the cultures of the Other, Western Orientalism maintains a sense of the superiority of the West. Whether or not one accepts this view, historically speaking the infusion of Eastern art, architecture, landscape gardening, literature, religion, and philosophy into the West during this time was massive.

The terms *arabesque* and *Arabian* evoke the sense of place, the history, religion and philosophy, the cultural and social attitudes, and especially the arts of these regions: the geometric designs of architecture, textiles, costume, dance, and literature. Islamic tradition discourages the artistic reproduction of any natural forms that may be said to possess a soul; thus an art of almost purely geometrical forms developed, as may be seen in elaborately decorated mosques and textiles. In art and architecture, the term indicates an intricate design of flowing lines: small geometrical patterns within larger ones, both angular and curvilinear—with multiple shifting perspectives—sometimes in such proliferated array that one cannot immediately see the intrinsic symmetry. These arabesque (or Saracenic) designs are associated especially with carpets and tapestries and with walls, windows, and ceilings of mosques, but they also include landscape architecture and garden design and gates. They are most often distinguished by floral/leaf patterns. The reader will find variations on these elements in Poe's poetry and fiction.

In literature, between the 1750s and the 1850s, scores of "Oriental tales" were translated into English and then imitated. Among the most influential were the so-called Arabic tales from the *Book of the Thousand and One Nights*, which attained its present order about 1450. Early in the eighteenth century, it was translated into French (12 vols., 1704–17) and then into several English versions in the middle and late nineteenth century (the most famous being that of Sir Richard Burton, 1885–86). The *Arabian Nights*, as it is most generally known, contains stories of exotic adventure, including tales of genies, wizards, sorceresses, magic lamps; of sultans, caliphs, viziers, harems, eunuch guards, prohibited love; of hidden treasure, great sea and desert journeys

fraught with danger from sea monsters and giant birds; of saber-wielding Saracenic knights on horseback and of the Muslim Conquest and the Crusades; and of the deeds of great heroes like Sinbad the Sailor. These adventures are told through the medium of the beautiful Scheherazade as night after night she recounts them to the king of Baghdad, Harun-al-Rashid, withholding the conclusion of each until the next night. Her stories are often characterized by self-reference and self-reflexivity: framed stories within another frame within a frame.

In Germany, a Romantic aesthetic of the multilayered arabesque narrative developed toward the end of the eighteenth century and flourished during the first third of the nineteenth century. Under the particular influence of Friedrich von Schlegel (see pp. 727ff. herein), the elaborate and intricate structures of arabesque tales became meshed with a pervasive theory of *irony*. Humor, satire, and parody were seen as the tools of *Romantic irony*, which is neither just parodic or serious but both simultaneously, as in Cervantes's *Don Quixote* and the plays of Shakespeare. Thus Poe's title, *Tales of the Grotesque and Arabesque*, comes to have particularly suggestive and resonant implications for the mixture of serious gothic dread, exotic settings and themes, unnatural grotesqueries, comic distortions, and humor, satire, parody, and irony.

A special element in this regard is Poe's indebtedness to and satires on the popular fiction of his time as represented by tales in *Blackwood's Edinburgh Magazine* (founded in 1818). *Blackwood's* specialized in "sensation fiction" in which protagonists get themselves into a "predicament" (such as being buried alive) and then describe and analyze their sensations, all the while philosophizing on the mysteries of the universe and the human condition. Poe frequently caricatures the aspiring author-narrators of such tales and burlesques the various formulaic conventions of the genre (for selection from *Blackwood's*, see pp. 754ff. herein). Since many of Poe's gothic and grotesque works involve the same basic situations, the theory of multilayered and multitoned narrative as arabesque would seem to be particularly pertinent. Further discussion of these and related matters will be found in the notes to Poe's tales and in articles in the Criticism section. Also see Poe's plans for an interconnected sequence of stories framed by satiric sketches of putative "authors"; first titled "Eleven Tales of the Arabesque" (see the general biographical introduction, pp. xvff., xxv–xxvi; and letter 37, reprinted pp. 594–95 herein), the plan was soon expanded as "The Folio Club" (unfinished manuscript reprinted pp. 595–96 herein).

Poe's work is sometimes regarded as narrow by those who have read only the gothic tales, but the variety of his achievement in fiction is exemplified not only by his experiments in the grotesque and arabesque but also by his explorations in visionary prose-poems and philosophical "dialogues," by his verisimilitudinous travel-adventure stories and proto-science fiction, and by his innovations in detective fiction (see general introduction, pp. xv, xxv, xxxiii herein). In the last of these modes, he so distinguished himself that he has been given credit, though it is something of an exaggeration, for single-handedly creating a new genre.

Metzengerstein[1]

A Tale in Imitation of the German[2]

Pestis eram vivus—moriens tua mors ero.

Martin Luther.[3]

Horror and Fatality have been stalking abroad in all ages. Why then give a date to the story I have to tell? I will not. Besides, I have other reasons for concealment. Let it suffice to say, that at the period of which I speak, there existed, in the interior of Hungary, a settled although hidden belief in the doctrines of the Metempsychosis. Of the doctrines themselves—that is, of their falsity, or of their probability—I say nothing. I assert, however, that much of our incredulity—as La Bruyère says of all our unhappiness—"*vient de ne pouvoir etre seuls.*"[4] But there were some points in the Hungarian superstition which

1. Poe's first published story appeared January 14, 1832, in the Philadelphia *Saturday Courier*. The tale was one of a group of five that Poe submitted to the *Courier's* prize contest; he did not win, but the *Courier* published all five at intervals throughout 1832. The subtitle was added for its republication in the *Southern Literary Messenger* (January 1836), the text used here. Other reprintings, e.g., in *Tales of the Grotesque and Arabesque* (1840) and in the Griswold edition of *Works* (1850–56), omit the subtitle, several sentences, and a whole paragraph.
2. The subtitle would have alerted the contemporary reader that the tale was in the "mode" of gothic horror or in the fantastic "manner" of German writers like Ludwig Tieck (1773–1853), E. T. A. Hoffmann (1776–1822), and others represented in translated collections like Thomas Carlyle's well-known *German Romance* (1827). It could also, as an "imitation," have suggested that the tale was possibly not entirely serious (see notes to "Loss of Breath" pp. 89ff. herein). Whether or not one reads "Metzengerstein" as a parody, it is almost certainly one of stories in the never-published collection *Tales of the Folio Club* and would have been told by one of its oddly named members (see the introduction on p. xxvi and the "preface" to the *Tales of the Folio Club*, on pp. 595ff. herein). Gothic motifs like the spectral horse, the animated portrait, the destroying fire, the hereditary feud, the noble fall, mental instability, elongated life, and supernaturally linked destinies are standard in British gothic, e.g., in works like Horace Walpole's *The Castle of Otranto* (1765), Ann Radcliffe's *The Mysteries of Udolpho* (1794), Matthew G. Lewis's *The Monk* (1796), Charles Maturin's *Melmoth the Wanderer* (1820), and with variations and echoes in several of Sir Walter Scott's romances. The closest American source (or satiric target) would seem to be the senior Richard Henry Dana's once popular poem "The Buccanner" (1827), in which a spectral horse emerges from a fire and eventually carries the evil protagonist to his death.
3. Your plague was I living—your death shall I be dying (German). The terse, often repeated verse response of Martin Luther (1483–1546), leader of the Protestant Reformation, on the issues of the sovereignty of the Catholic Church and the authority of the pope.
4. Comes from not being able to be alone (French). A reference to "De l'homme" [On man], section 99, of *Les caractères* (1688) by Jean de la Bruyère (1645–1696). *Characters* is a didactic work celebrated among other things for its depiction of the degraded habits of the nobility. In the Griswold edition of *Works*, the following footnote (reproducing an item from Poe's 1836 *Pinakidia* series of "marginal notes" on his reading) was added after the quotation:

 *Mercier, in "L'an deux mille quatre cents quarante," seriously maintains the doctrines of Metempsychosis, and I.s D'Israeli says that "no system is so simple and so little repugnant to the understanding." Colonel Ethan Allen, the "Green Mountain Boy," is also said to have been a serious metempsychosist.

 Poe's references to these European commentaries on the transmigration and interpenetration of souls are to chapter 6 of *The Year 2440* (1770) by Louis-Sebastien Mercier (1740–1814) and to the chapter "Metempsychosis" in *Curiosities of Literature* (6 vols., 1791–1834) by Isaac D'Israeli (1776–1848). Ethan Allen (1738–1789), leader of the independent militia from Vermont (the Green Mountain Boys), was a thorough-going Deist and author of a tract titled "Reason the Only Oracle of Man" (1789); but Mabbott mentions a legend that Allen said that "he might live again in his great white horse" (II.30). Allen was also involved in land disputes after the Revolution.

were fast verging to absurdity. They—the Hungarians—differed very essentially from their Eastern authorities. For example. *"The soul,"* said the former—I give the words of an acute and intelligent Parisian—*ne demeure qu'un seul jois dans un corps sensible: au reste— un cheval, un chien, un homme même n' est que la ressemblance peu tangible de ces animaux."*[5]

The families of Berlifitzing and Metzengerstein had been at variance for centuries. Never before were two houses so illustrious mutually embittered by hostility so deadly. Indeed, at the era of this history, it was observed by an old crone of haggard and sinister appearance, that "fire and water might sooner mingle than a Berlifitzing clasp the hand of a Metzengerstein." The origin of this enmity seems to be found in the words of an ancient prophecy—"A lofty name shall have a fearful fall when, like the rider over his horse, the mortality of Metzengerstein shall triumph over the immortality of Berlifitzing."[6]

To be sure the words themselves had little or no meaning. But more trivial causes have given rise—and that no long while ago—to consequences equally eventful. Besides, the estates, which were contiguous, had long exercised a rival influence in the affairs of a busy government. Moreover, near neighbors are seldom friends—and the inhabitants of the Castle Berlifitzing might look, from their lofty buttresses, into the very windows of the Chateau Metzengerstein. Least of all was the more than feudal magnificence thus discovered calculated to allay the irritable feelings of the less ancient and less wealthy Berlifitzings. What wonder, then, that the words, however silly, of that prediction, should have succeeded in setting and keeping at variance two families already predisposed to quarrel by every instigation of hereditary jealousy? The prophecy seemed to imply—if it implied any thing—a final triumph on the part of the already more powerful house; and was of course remembered with the more bitter animosity on the side of the weaker and less influential.

Wilhelm, Count Berlifitzing, although honorably and loftily descended, was, at the epoch of this narrative, an infirm and doting old man, remarkable for nothing but an inordinate and inveterate personal antipathy to the family of his rival, and so passionate a love of horses, and of hunting, that neither bodily infirmity, great age, nor mental incapacity, prevented his daily participation in the dangers of the chase.

Frederick, Baron Metzengerstein, was, on the other hand, not yet of age. His father, the Minister G——, died young. His mother, the Lady

5. [The soul] resides only a single time in a sensate body: as for the rest—a horse, a dog, even a man, [the soul] is only a slightly tangible resemblance of these animals (French). The "Parisian" authority may be a topical allusion, the reference of which is lost, or Poe's invention to throw an air of arcane scholarly debate around the idea of the transmigration of souls.

6. The exact working out of vague, seemingly contradictory curses was a staple of much gothic fiction of the time. The paradox of this prophecy of "little or no meaning" (see next paragraph) is quite literally fulfilled at the end of the tale, as is the "silly explosion of hereditary pique" a few paragraphs later in the "curse" of the count's wife.

Mary, followed quickly after. Frederick was, at that time, in his fifteenth year. In a city fifteen years are no long period—a child may be still a child in his third lustrum: but in a wilderness—in so magnificent a wilderness as that old principality, fifteen years have a far deeper meaning.

The beautiful Lady Mary! How *could* she die?—and of consumption! But it is a path I have prayed to follow. I would wish all I love to perish of that gentle disease. How glorious! to depart in the hey-day of the young blood—the heart all passion—the imagination all fire—amid the remembrances of happier days—in the fall of the year—and so be buried up forever in the gorgeous autumnal leaves![7]

Thus died the Lady Mary. The young Baron Frederick stood without a living relative by the coffin of his dead mother. He placed his hand upon her placid forehead. No shudder came over his delicate frame—no sigh from his flinty bosom. Heartless, self-willed, and impetuous from his childhood, he had reached the age of which I speak through a career of unfeeling, wanton, and reckless dissipation; and a barrier had long since arisen in the channel of all holy thoughts and gentle recollections.

From some peculiar circumstances attending the administration of his father, the young Baron, at the decease of the former, entered immediately upon his vast possessions. Such estates were seldom held before by a nobleman of Hungary. His castles were without number—of these the chief in point of splendor and extent was the "Chateau Metzengerstein." The boundary line of his dominions was never clearly defined—but his principal park embraced a circuit of fifty miles.

Upon the succession of a proprietor so young—with a character so well known—to a fortune so unparalleled—little speculation was afloat in regard to his probable course of conduct. And, indeed, for the space of three days the behavior of the heir out-heroded Herod,[8] and fairly surpassed the expectations of his most enthusiastic admirers. Shameful debaucheries—flagrant treacheries—unheard-of atrocities—gave his trembling vassals quickly to understand that no servile submission on their part—no punctilios of conscience on his own—were thenceforward to prove any security against the remorseless and bloody fangs of a petty Caligula.[9] On the night of the fourth day, the stables of the Castle Berlifitzing were discovered to be on fire: and

7. This paragraph was omitted in the Griswold edition of *Works*, possibly a decision of the editor. Its silent omission somewhat muddies the overall tonality of the tale; the passage has been taken by differing critics as variously indicating Poe's morbid psychology, his undiscerning "purple prose," or his ironic parody. The Griswold edition also makes the young baron older (eighteen instead of fifteen years).

8. See *Hamlet* III.ii.16. Herod was the dynastic name of the ruling families of Palestine from about 65 B.C.E. to about 40 C.E., when their power began to ebb. Herod the Great (died 4 B.C.E.) was noted for profligacy and bloodthirstiness and in his later years was said to have become mentally unbalanced.

9. Little Boots (Latin, literal trans.). The nickname of Gaius Caesar Germanicus (12–41 C.E.), emperor of Rome from 37 to 41; his reign is noted for ruthless cruelty. By tradition, he is believed to have gone insane; among other things, he is said to have wanted to make his favorite horse a consul.

the unanimous opinion of the neighborhood instantaneously added the crime of the incendiary to the already hideous list of the Baron's misdemeanors and enormities.

But during the tumult occasioned by this occurrence, the young nobleman himself sat, apparently buried in meditation, in a vast and desolate upper apartment of the family palace of Metzengerstein. The rich although faded tapestry-hangings which swung gloomily upon the walls, represented the shadowy and majestic forms of a thousand illustrious ancestors. *Here*, rich-ermined priests, and pontifical dignitaries, familiarly seated with the autocrat and the sovereign, put a veto on the wishes of a temporal king—or restrained with the fiat of papal supremacy the rebellious sceptre of the Arch-Enemy. *There*, the dark, tall statures of the Princes Metzengerstein—their muscular war-coursers plunging over the carcass of a fallen foe—startled the steadiest nerves with their vigorous expression: and *here*, again, the voluptuous and swan-like figures of the dames of days gone by, floated away in the mazes of an unreal dance to the strains of imaginary melody.

But as the Baron listened, or affected to listen to the gradually increasing uproar in the stables of Berlifitzing—or perhaps pondered upon some more novel—some more decided act of audacity—his eyes became unwittingly rivetted to the figure of an enormous, and unnaturally colored horse, represented in the tapestry as belonging to a Saracen[1] ancestor of the family of his rival. The horse itself, in the foreground of the design, stood motionless and statue-like—while farther back its discomfitted rider perished by the dagger of a Metzengerstein.

On Frederick's lip arose a fiendish expression, as he became aware of the direction his glance had, without his consciousness, assumed. Yet he did not remove it. On the contrary he could by no means account for the singular, intense, and overwhelming anxiety which appeared falling like a shroud upon his senses. It was with difficulty that he reconciled his dreamy and incoherent feelings with the certainty of being awake. The longer he gazed, the more absorbing became the spell—the more impossible did it appear that he could ever withdraw his glance from the fascination of that tapestry. But the tumult without becoming suddenly more violent, with a kind of compulsory and desperate exertion he diverted his attention to the glare of ruddy light thrown full by the flaming stables upon the windows of the apartment.

The action, however, was but momentary—his gaze returned mechanically to the wall. To his extreme horror and astonishment the head of the gigantic steed had, in the meantime, altered its position. The neck of the animal, before arched, as if in compassion, over the

1. A term widely used in the Middle Ages to designate various Arabic peoples as well as Muslims in general. The Berlifitzings' Muslim ancestry as opposed to the Metzengersteins' Catholic ancestry suggests the religious conflict of the Crusades. Poe frequently uses the words *saracenic* and *arabesque* for their exotic historical and aesthetic resonances; but the latter also has specific aesthetic implications (see the Tales introduction on pp. 78–80).

prostrate body of its lord, was now extended, at full length, in the direction of the Baron. The eyes, before invisible, now wore an energetic and human expression, while they gleamed with a fiery and unusual red: and the distended lips of the apparently enraged horse left in full view his sepulchral and disgusting teeth.

Stupified with terror the young nobleman tottered to the door. As he threw it open, a flash of red light streaming far into the chamber, flung his shadow with a clear outline against the quivering tapestry; and he shuddered to perceive that shadow—as he staggered awhile upon the threshold—assuming the exact position, and precisely filling up the contour of the relentless and triumphant murderer of the Saracen Berlifitzing.

To lighten the depression of his spirits the Baron hurried into the open air. At the principal gate of the Chateau he encountered three equerries.[2] With much difficulty, and at the imminent peril of their lives, they were restraining the unnatural and convulsive plunges of a gigantic and fiery-colored horse.

"Whose horse? Where did you get him?" demanded the youth in a querulous and husky tone of voice, as he became instantly aware that the mysterious steed in the tapestried chamber was the very counterpart of the furious animal before his eyes.

"He is your own property, Sire"—replied one of the equerries—"at least he is claimed by no other owner. We caught him flying, all smoking and foaming with rage, from the burning stables of the Castle Berlifitzing. Supposing him to have belonged to the old Count's stud of foreign horses, we led him back as an estray. But the grooms there disclaim any title to the creature—which is strange, since he bears evident marks of having made a narrow escape from the flames."

"The letters W. V. B. are also branded very distinctly on his forehead"—interrupted a second equerry—"I supposed them, of course, to be the initials of Wilhelm Von Berlifitzing—but all at the Castle are positive in denying any knowledge of the horse."

"Extremely singular!" said the young Baron, with a musing air, and apparently unconscious of the meaning of his words—"He is, as you say, a remarkable horse—a prodigious horse! although, as you very justly observe, of a suspicious and untractable character——Let him be mine, however," he added, after a pause—"perhaps a rider like Frederick of Metzengerstein, may tame even the devil from the stables of Berlifitzing."

"You are mistaken, my lord—the horse, as I think we mentioned, is *not* from the stables of the Count. If such were the case, we know our duty better than to bring him into the presence of a noble of your family."

"True!" observed the Baron drily—and at that instant a page of the bed chamber came from the Chateau with a heightened color, and precipitate step. He whispered into his master's ear an account of the miraculous and sudden disappearance of a small portion of the tapestry,

2. Mounted servants, grooms or couriers.

in an apartment which he designated: entering, at the same time, into particulars of a minute and circumstantial character—but from the low tone of voice in which these latter were communicated, nothing escaped to gratify the excited curiosity of the equerries.

The young Frederick, during the conference, seemed agitated by a variety of emotions. He soon, however, recovered his composure, and an expression of determined malignancy settled upon his countenance, as he gave peremptory orders that a certain chamber should be immediately locked up, and the key placed in his own possession.

"Have you heard of the unhappy death of the old hunter Berlifitzing?" said one of his vassals to the Baron, as, after the affair of the page, the huge and mysterious steed which that nobleman had adopted as his own, plunged and curvetted, with redoubled and supernatural fury, down the long avenue which extended from the Chateau to the stables of Metzengerstein.

"No!"—said the Baron, turning abruptly towards the speaker— "dead! say you?"

"It is indeed true, my lord—and, to a noble of your name, will be, I imagine, no unwelcome intelligence."

A rapid smile of a peculiar and unintelligible meaning shot over the beautiful countenance of the listener—"How died he?"

"In his rash exertions to rescue a favorite portion of his hunting stud, he has himself perished miserably in the flames."

"I—n—d—e—e—d—!"—ejaculated the Baron, as if slowly and deliberately impressed with the truth of some exciting idea.[3]

"Indeed"—repeated the vassal.

"Shocking!" said the youth calmly, and turned quietly into the Chateau.

From this date a marked alteration took place in the outward demeanor of the dissolute young Baron Frederick Von Metzengerstein. Indeed his behaviour disappointed every expectation, and proved little in accordance with the views of many a manœuvering mamma—while his habits and manners, still less than formerly, offered any thing congenial with those of the neighboring aristocracy. He was never to be seen beyond the limits of his own domain, and, in this wide and social world, was utterly companionless—unless, indeed, that unnatural, impetuous, and fiery-colored horse, which he henceforward continually bestrode, had any mysterious right to the title of his friend.

Numerous invitations on the part of the neighborhood for a long time, however, periodically came in—"Will the Baron honor our festivals with his presence?" "Will the Baron join us in a hunting of the boar?" "Metzengerstein does not hunt"—"Metzengerstein will not attend"—were the haughty and laconic answers.

These repeated insults were not to be endured by an imperious no-

3. I.e., the young baron thinks that the soul of Count Berlifitzing has migrated by metempsychosis into Metzengerstein's tapestry horse, bringing it to life (marked with the count's initials just to make the point).

bility. Such invitations became less cordial—less frequent—in time they ceased altogether. The widow of the unfortunate Count Berlifitzing, was even heard to express a hope—"that the Baron might be at home when he did not wish to be at home, since he disdained the company of his equals: and ride when he did not wish to ride, since he preferred the society of a horse." This to be sure was a very silly explosion of hereditary pique; and merely proved how singularly unmeaning our sayings are apt to become, when we desire to be unusually energetic.

The charitable, nevertheless, attributed the alteration in the conduct of the young nobleman to the natural sorrow of a son for the untimely loss of his parents—forgetting, however, his atrocious and reckless behavior during the short period immediately succeeding that bereavement. Some there were, indeed, who suggested a too haughty idea of self-consequence and dignity. Others again—among whom may be mentioned the family physician—did not hesitate in speaking of morbid melancholy, and hereditary ill-heath: while dark hints, of a more equivocal nature, were current among the multitude.

Indeed the Baron's perverse attachment to his lately-acquired charger—an attachment which seemed to attain new strength from every fresh example of the animal's ferocious and demonlike propensities—at length became, in the eyes of all reasonable men, a hideous and unnatural fervor. In the glare of noon—at the dead hour of night—in sickness or in health[4]—in calm or in tempest—in moonlight or in shadow—the young Metzengerstein seemed rivetted to the saddle of that colossal horse, whose intractable audacities so well accorded with the spirit of his own.

There were circumstances, moreover, which, coupled with late events, gave an unearthly and portentous character to the mania of the rider, and to the capabilities of the steed. The space passed over in a single leap had been accurately measured, and was found to exceed by an astounding difference, the wildest expectations of the most imaginative. The Baron, besides, had no particular *name* for the animal, although all the rest in his extensive collection were distinguished by characteristic appellations. His stable, too, was appointed at a distance from the rest; and with regard to grooming and other necessary offices, none but the owner in person had ventured to officiate, or even to enter the enclosure of that particular stall. It was also to be observed, that although the three grooms, who had caught the horse as he fled from the conflagration at Berlifitzing, had succeeded in arresting his course, by means of a chain-bridle and noose—yet no one of the three could with any certainty affirm that he had, during that dangerous struggle, or at any period thereafter, actually placed his hand upon the body of the beast. Instances of peculiar intelligence in the demeanor of a noble and high spirited steed are not to be supposed capable of exciting unreasonable attention—especially among

4. From the wedding ceremony of the English Book of Common Prayer. The two enemies are wedded to each other.

men who, daily trained to the labors of the chase, might appear well acquainted with the sagacity of a horse—but there were certain circumstances which intruded themselves per force, upon the most skeptical and phlegmatic—and it is said there were times when this singular and mysterious animal, caused the gaping crowd who stood around to recoil in silent horror from the deep and impressive meaning of his terrible stamp—times when the young Metzengerstein turned pale and shrunk away from the rapid and searching expression of his intense and human-looking eye.

Among all the retinue of the Baron, however, none were found to doubt the ardor of that extraordinary affection which existed on the part of the young nobleman for the fiery qualities of his horse—at least, none but an insignificant and misshapen little page, whose deformities were in every body's way, and whose opinions were of the least possible importance. He—if his ideas are worth mentioning at all—had the effrontery to assert that his master never vaulted into the saddle, without an unaccountable and almost imperceptible shudder—and that, upon his return from every long-continued and habitual ride, an expression of triumphant malignity distorted every muscle in his countenance.

One tempestuous night, Metzengerstein, awaking from a heavy and oppressive slumber, descended like a maniac from his chamber, and mounting in great haste, bounded away into the mazes of the forest. An occurrence so common attracted no particular attention—but his return was looked for with intense anxiety on the part of his domestics, when, after some hour's absence, the stupendous and magnificent battlements of the Chateau Metzengerstein, were discovered crackling and rocking to their very foundation, under the influence of a dense and livid mass of ungovernable fire.

As the flames, when first seen, had already made so terrible a progress that all efforts to save any portion of the building were evidently futile, the astonished neighborhood stood idly around in silent and apathetic wonder. But a new and fearful object soon rivetted the attention of the multitude, and proved how much more intense is the excitement wrought in the feelings of a crowd by the contemplation of human agony, than that brought about by the most appalling spectacles of inanimate matter.

Up the long avenue of aged oaks which led from the forest to the main entrance of the Chateau Metzengerstein, a steed, bearing an unbonneted and disordered rider, was seen leaping with an impetuosity which outstripped the very Demon of the Tempest, and extorted from every stupified beholder the ejaculation—"horrible!"[5]

The career of the horseman was indisputably, on his own part, uncontrollable. The agony of his countenance—the convulsive struggle

5. The utterance of the word *horrible* may be an indication that the teller of the tale is Mr. Horribile Dictu (horrible to tell; Latin), a member of the Folio Club (see pp. 595ff. herein), who studied at the University of Göttingen in Germany. In its first publication, after the word *tempest*, the text read: "and called forth from every beholder an ejaculation of 'Azrael!'" Azrael is the Muslim angel of death, an allusion that continued the theme of religious (Saracen vs. Catholic) conflict.

of his frame—gave evidence of superhuman exertion: but no sound, save a solitary shriek, escaped from his lacerated lips, which were bitten through and through in the intensity of terror. One instant, and the clattering of hoofs resounded sharply and shrilly above the roaring of the flames and the shrieking of the winds—another, and, clearing at a single plunge the gateway and the moat, the steed bounded far up the tottering stair-cases of the Palace, and, with its rider, disappeared amid the whirlwind of chaotic fire.

The fury of the tempest immediately died away, and a dead calm sullenly succeeded. A white flame still enveloped the building like a shroud, and, streaming far away into the quiet atmosphere, shot forth a glare of preternatural light; while a cloud of smoke settled heavily over the battlements in the distinct collossal figure of—a horse.[6]

Loss of Breath[1]

A Tale a la Blackwood

O breathe not, &c.

—Moore's Melodies.[2]

The most notorious ill-fortune must, in the end, yield to the untiring courage of philosophy—as the most stubborn city to the ceaseless vigilance of an enemy. Salmanezer, as we have it in the holy writings, lay three years before Samaria: yet it fell.[3] Sardanapalus—see Diodorus—maintained himself seven in Nineveh: but to no purpose.[4] Troy expired at the close of the second lustrum: and Azoth, as Aristæus declares upon his honor as a gentleman, opened at last her

6. The last sentence is variously punctuated in different reprintings, and the word *horse* is italicized in the Griswold edition of *Works*. In the first printing, the horse is described as "motionless and colossal," followed by two concluding sentences: "Frederick, Baron Metzengerstein, was the last of a long line of princes. His family name is no longer to be found among the Hungarian aristocracy."

1. First published as "Decided Loss" in the Philadelphia *Saturday Courier* (November 10, 1832), this tale was reprinted under its present title in the *Southern Literary Messenger* (September 1835). At least three radically different versions exist; the *Messenger* version is reprinted here as most fully representative of Poe's satiric intent. One of his major targets, as the subtitle indicates, is the influential *Blackwood's Edinburgh Magazine*, founded in 1818 (a later version carried the subtitle, "A Tale Neither in Nor out of 'Blackwood' "). "Loss of Breath" may be most fully appreciated when read in conjunction with the selections from *Blackwood's* reprinted herein (pp. 754ff.) and Poe's metafictional satire on such fiction, "How to Write a Blackwood Article" (pp. 173ff. herein) and its companion piece "A Predicament" (pp. 183ff. herein).

2. The flippant epigraph alludes to a poem in *Irish Melodies* (1808–34) by Thomas Moore (1779–1852), a writer Poe frequently satirized. "Oh, breathe not his name! But let it sleep in the shade" is a memorial to Moore's friend Robert Emmet, leader of an Irish nationalist group, hanged in 1803.

3. In the shorter first version, the present opening passage was in the last paragraph. Shalmaneser V of Assyria died in 722 B.C.E. in the siege of Samaria, capital of Israel under King Hosea. Samaria fell to Sargon II of Assyria (died 705 B.C.E.) some three years after Shalmaneser's death. The story is briefly told in the early verses of 2 Kings 17; most of the rest of chapter 17 emphasizes the theme that the captured peoples brought into Samaria "know not the manner of the God of the land." "Every nation made gods of their own, and put them in the houses of the high places which the Samaritans had made" (2 Kings 17:29).

4. According to the Greek historian Diodorus Siculus (1st century B.C.E.). Nineveh, the capital city of King Sardanapalus I of Assyria (668–626 B.C.E.), withstood a long siege but eventually fell under the reign of his son.

gates to Psammitticus[5] after having barred them for the fifth part of a century.

"Thou wretch!—thou vixen!—thou shrew!"—said I to my wife on the morning after our wedding—"thou witch!—thou hag!—thou whippersnapper!—thou sink of iniquity!—thou fiery-faced quintessence of all that is abominable!—thou—thou—" Here standing upon tiptoe, seizing her by the throat, and placing my mouth close to her ear, I was preparing to launch forth a new and more decided epithet of opprobrium which should not fail, if ejaculated, to convince her of her insignificance, when, to my extreme horror and astonishment, I discovered that *I had lost my breath*.

The phrases "I am out of breath," "I have lost my breath," &c. are often enough repeated in common conversation, but it had never occurred to me that the terrible accident of which I speak could *bona fide* and actually happen! Imagine—that is if you have a fanciful turn—imagine I say, my wonder—my consternation—my despair!

There is a good genius,[6] however, which has never, at any time, entirely deserted me. In my most ungovernable moods I still retain a sense of propriety, *et le chemin des passions me conduit*—as Rousseau says it did him—*à la philosophie veritable*.[7]

Although I could not at first precisely ascertain to what degree the occurrence had affected me, I unhesitatingly determined to conceal at all events the matter from my wife until farther experience should discover to me the extent of this my unheard of calamity. Altering my countenance, therefore, in a moment, from its bepuffed and distorted appearance, to an expression of arch and coquettish benignity, I gave my lady a pat on the one cheek, and a kiss on the other, and without saying one syllable, (Furies! I could not,) left her astonished at my drollery, as I pirouetted out of the room in a *Pas de Zephyr*.[8]

Behold me then safely ensconced in my private *boudoir*, a fearful in-

5. Psammitticus I is said to have begun, in about 666 B.C.E. the siege of Ashdod, which lasted twenty-nine years. "Lustrum": five years. The fall of Troy, according to the *Iliad*, took ten years. Azoth was one of the five cities of the Philistine confederacy, also known as, or confused with, Azotus and Ashdod. Aristaeus is variously identified. Mabbott thinks Poe's reference is to Aristaeus of Proconnesus, "a half-fabulous poet" who was the source of the account of "the siege of Azoth" by the Greek historian Herodotus (c. 484–c. 425 B.C.E.). Levine suggests a courtier of the 3rd century B.C.E. thought to be the author of a document called *Aristeas to Philocrates*. There is also an Aristaeus in Greek mythology, associated with the keeping of bees. Poe's narrator is attempting to show off his erudition with this jumbled assemblage of allusions.
6. From Latin, usually indicating a "guardian spirit"; *Spiritus* = "Wind, air, breath" (thus a traditional metaphor for the invisible, impalpable anima). The Roman guardian *genius* was also associated with generation and birth.
7. The road of passions leads me . . . to the true philosophy (French). I.e., passion is superior to mere reason, a conventional Romantic declaration. Some scholars believe that this allusion to Jean-Jacques Rousseau's *Julie, ou la nouvelle Héloïse* (1761) is more pointedly a hit at Edward Bulwer-Lytton's novel *Pelham* (1828). In chapter 23, Bulwer translates the passage (from letter 3) as "It is the path of the passions which has conducted me to philosophy," a misreading that Poe may have ironically appropriated for the present tale.
8. A ballet position in which the dancer stands on one leg and moves the other forward and back. "Pirouette": a full rotation of the body while the dancer stands on one leg. Poe is making comic use of the fact that ballet dancers leap (the narrator is short and fat) through the "air" and thus plays on the word *Zephyr*, which in myth is the western wind, known for its gentleness (hence word play on "breath"). Kennedy suggests the pun "no wind" (*pas* in French is also a negative). Poe mentions other ballet steps toward the end of the tale.

stance of the ill consequences attending upon irascibility—alive with the qualifications of the dead—dead with the propensities of the living—an anomaly on the face of the earth—being very calm, yet breathless.

Yes! breathless. I am serious in asserting that my breath was entirely gone. I could not have stirred with it a feather if my life had been at issue, or sullied even the delicacy of a mirror. Hard fate!—yet there was some alleviation to the first overwhelming paroxysm of my sorrow. I found upon trial that the powers of utterance which, upon my inability to proceed in the conversation with my wife, I then concluded to be totally destroyed, were in fact only partially impeded, and I discovered that had I, at that interesting crisis, dropped my voice to a singularly deep guttural, I might still have continued to her the communication of my sentiments; this pitch of voice (the guttural) depending, I find, not upon the current of the breath, but upon a certain spasmodic action of the muscles of the throat.

Throwing myself upon a chair, I remained for some time absorbed in meditation. My reflections, be sure, wore of no consolatory kind. A thousand vague and lachrymatory[9] fancies took possession of my soul—and even the phantom Suicide flitted across my brain; but it is a trait in the perversity of human nature to reject the obvious and the ready, for the far-distant and equivocal. Thus I shudderd at self-murder as the most decided of atrocities, while the tabby cat purred strenuously upon the rug, and the very water-dog wheezed assiduously under the table, each taking to itself much merit for the strength of its lungs, and all obviously done in derision of my own pulmonary incapacity.

Oppressed with a tumult of vague hopes and fears, I at length heard the footstep of my wife descending the staircase. Being now assured of her absence, I returned with a palpitating heart to the scene of my disaster.

Carefully locking the door on the inside, I commenced a vigorous search. It was possible, I thought, that concealed in some obscure corner, or lurking in some closet or drawer, might be found the lost object of my inquiry. It might have a vapory—it might even have a tangible form. Most philosophers, upon many points of philosophy, are still very unphilosophical. William Godwin, however, says in his "Mandeville,"[1] that "invisible things are the only realities." This, all will allow, is a case in point. I would have the judicious reader pause before accusing such asseverations of an undue quantum of absurdity. Anaxagoras—it will be remembered—maintained that snow is black.[2] This I have since found to be the case.

Long and earnestly did I continue the investigation: but the

9. Tearful.
1. Godwin (1758–1836), *Mandeville: A Tale of the Seventeenth Century*, III.48 (1817 ed.).
2. Anaxagoras, Athenian philosopher (c. 500–428 B.C.E.), argued that the microstructure of white snow must contain black particles and was widely misunderstood to have said that snow is black (i.e., "philosophically" speaking, one can argue anything, such as white is black). In the earlier "A Decided Loss," Poe had included, as a further play on the motifs of light/dark and visible/invisible an allusion to a Peter Schlemihl, the title character of an 1814 story by the German writer Adelbert Chamisso (1781–1838), in which Schlemihl sells his shadow to the devil.

contemptible reward of my industry and perseverance proved to be only a set of false teeth, two pair of hips, an eye, and a bundle of *billets-doux*[3] from Mr. Windenough to my wife. I might as well here observe that this confirmation of my lady's partiality for Mr. W. occasioned me little uneasiness. That Mrs. Lacko'breath should admire any thing so dissimilar to myself was a natural and necessary evil. I am, it is well known, of a robust and corpulent appearance, and, at the same time somewhat diminutive in stature. What wonder then that the lath-like tenuity of my acquaintance, and his altitude which has grown into a proverb, should have met with all due estimation in the eyes of Mrs. Lacko'breath? It is by logic similar to this that true philosophy is enabled to set misfortune at defiance. But to return.

My exertions, as I have before said, proved fruitless. Closet after closet—drawer after drawer—corner after corner—were scrutinized to no purpose. At one time, however, I thought myself sure of my prize, having, in rummaging a dressing-case, accidentally demolished a bottle (I had a remarkably sweet breath) of Hewitt's "Seraphic and Highly Scented Extract of Heaven or Oil of Archangels"—which, as an agreeable perfume, I here take the liberty of recommending.

With a heavy heart I returned to my *boudoir*—there to ponder upon some method of eluding my wife's penetration, until I could make arrangements prior to my leaving the country, for to this I had already made up my mind. In a foreign climate, being unknown, I might, with some probability of success, endeavor to conceal my unhappy calamity—a calamity calculated, even more than beggary, to estrange the affections of the multitude, and to draw down upon the wretch the well-merited indignation of the virtuous and the happy. I was not long in hesitation. Being naturally quick, I committed to memory the entire tragedies of ——, and ——.[4] I had the good fortune to recollect that in the accentuation of these dramas, or at least of such portion of them as is allotted to their heroes, the tones of voice in which I found

3. Love letters (French). Some (more or less Freudian) critics have read sexual innuendo in the tale, based on the presumption that the phrase "loss of breath" was a traditional euphemism for loss of sexual potency. Mr. Lacko'breath (as the narrator is eventually named) and Mr. Windenough are not just competitors but also mirror images or inverse doubles. They resemble each other, but in reverse: one is fat and one thin; one with enough and one without any "wind" (spirit, afflatus, anima, power). Other "evidence" of a sexual theme includes recurrent references to the nose (a phallic symbol since the Middle Ages) and images of viscosity. The validity of such speculations on some sort of comic (and not-so-comic) sexual allegory is somewhat increased when the tale is read alongside "Some Passages in the Life of a Lion" ["Lionizing"]—see pp. 128ff. herein—the blatant sexual jokes of which Poe, as an editor, was able to publish without censorship in the *Southern Literary Messenger*. Cf. Herman Melville, who was able in 1855 to get an explicit sexual allegory. "The Tartarus of Maids," past the censors at *Harper's*, a large-circulation magazine aimed at a genteel audience.
4. In other versions, the "Indian tragedy" of *Metamora, or the Last of the Wampanoags* (1829), by John Augustus Stone (1800–1834), is specified. Metamora is one of the many variants on the name of the 17th-century chieftain Metacom or Metacomet, better known as King Philip, who died in battle against European colonists in 1676. Excoriated by American Puritan writers, King Philip was later celebrated as a noble and tragic figure by a number of American Romantic writers, including Washington Irving in *The Sketch-Book of Geoffrey Crayon* (1819–20) and James Fenimore Cooper in *The Wept of Wish-Ton-Wish* (1829). In the title role of Metamora, Edwin Forrest (1806–1872) made Stone's play one of the most popular on the American stage for decades (see next note). The succeeding sentences in this paragraph and the next burlesque Forrest's acting style, which consisted largely of stiff posturings and squintings, monotonal grunts and gutteral exclamations.

myself deficient were altogether unnecessary, and that the deep guttural was expected to reign monotonously throughout.

I practised for some time by the borders of a well-frequented marsh—herein, however, having no reference to a similar proceeding of Demosthenes,[5] but from a design peculiarly and conscientiously my own. Thus armed at all points, I determined to make my wife believe that I was suddenly smitten with a passion for the stage. In this I succeeded to a miracle; and to every question or suggestion found myself at liberty to reply in my most frog-like and sepulchral tones with some passage from the tragedies, any portion of which, as I soon took great pleasure in observing, would apply equally well to any particular subject. It is not to be supposed, however, that in the delivery of such passages I was found at all deficient in the looking asquint—the showing my teeth—the working my knees—the shuffling my feet—or in any of those unmentionable graces which are now justly considered the characteristics of a popular performer. To be sure they spoke of confining me in a straight jacket—but good God! they never suspected me of having lost my breath.

Having at length put my affairs in order, I took my seat very early one morning in the mail stage for ——, giving it to be understood among my acquaintances that business of the last importance required my immediate personal attendance.

The coach was crammed to repletion—but in the uncertain twilight the features of my companions could not be distinguished. Without making any effectual resistance I suffered myself to be placed between two gentlemen of colossal dimensions; while a third, of a size larger, requesting pardon for the liberty he was about to take, threw himself upon my body at full length, and falling asleep in an instant, drowned all my guttural ejaculations for relief, in a snore which would have put to the blush the roarings of a Phalarian bull.[6] Happily the state of my respiratory faculties rendered suffocation an accident entirely out of the question.

As however, the day broke more distinctly in our approach to the outskirts of the city, my tormentor arising and adjusting his shirt-collar, thanked me in a very friendly manner for my civility. Seeing that I remained motionless, (all my limbs were dislocated, and my head twisted on one side,) his apprehensions began to be excited; and arousing the rest of the passengers, he communicated, in a very decided manner, his opinion that a dead man had been palmed upon them during the night for a living *bona fide* and responsible fellow-traveller—here giving me a thump on the right eye by way of evidencing the truth of his suggestion.

5. An Athenian orator (384–322 B.C.E.), who is supposed to have practiced by filling his mouth with stones and trying to make himself heard above the ocean waves. "Marsh": possible satiric reference to Forrest, who is reputed to have practiced declaiming his lines in the Kentucky woods by a marsh (a property about which there may have been some financial irregularity).
6. Phalarus, dictator of Agrigentum in Sicily from c. 570 to c. 550 B.C.E., is supposed to have conducted human sacrifices in a brass vessel in the shape of a bull, heated to fiery temperature from below; the cries of the victims were said to resemble the bellowing of a sacrificial bull.

Thereupon all, one after another, (there were nine in company) believed it their duty to pull me by the ear. A young practising physician, too, having applied a pocket-mirror to my mouth, and found me without breath, the assertion of my persecutor was pronounced a true bill; and the whole party expressed their determination to endure tamely no such impositions for the future, and to proceed no farther with any such carcasses for the present.[7]

I was here accordingly thrown out at the sign of the "Crow," (by which tavern the coach happened to be passing) without meeting with any farther accident than the breaking of both my arms under the left hind wheel of the vehicle. I must besides do the driver the justice to state that he did not forget to throw after me the largest of my trunks, which, unfortunately falling on my head, fractured my skull in a manner at once interesting and extraordinary.

The landlord of the "Crow," who is a hospitable man, finding that my trunk contained sufficient to indemnify him for any little trouble he might take in my behalf, sent forthwith for a surgeon of his acquaintance, and delivered me to his care with a bill and receipt for five and twenty dollars.

The purchaser took me to his apartments and commenced operations immediately. Having, however, cut off my ears, he discovered signs of animation. He now rang the bell, and sent for a neighboring apothecary with whom to consult in the emergency. In case, however, of his suspicions with regard to my existence proving ultimately correct, he, in the meantime, made an incision in my stomach, and removed several of my viscera for private dissection.[8]

The apothecary had an idea that I was actually dead. This idea I endeavored to confute, kicking and plunging with all my might, and making the most furious contortions—for the operations of the surgeon had, in a measure, restored me to the possession of my faculties. All, however, was attributed to the effects of a new Galvanic Battery,[9] wherewith the apothecary, who is really a man of information, performed several curious experiments, in which, from my personal share in their fulfilment I could not help feeling deeply interested. It was a

7. The "predicaments" described in the next few paragraphs echo scenes and incidents from classic literary works and current popular fiction. The narrator's physical abuse, his state of inanimation, and his being thrown off the coach by passengers who object to riding with a "corpse" recall Henry Fielding's *Joseph Andrews* (1742). The predicament of being entombed alive reflects contemporary apprehensions in news accounts and fictional stories about mistaken diagnoses of death, suspended animation, catatonic states, and premature burial. See the Popular Fiction section and Kennedy, in Criticism.

8. This predicament of being physically abused and vivisected while yet fully conscious in a state of suspended animation occurs in Voltaire's *Candide* (1759) with the same kind of comic hyperbole.

9. A reference more particularly to the experiments with the properties of nerves and muscles conducted by Luigi Galvani (1737–1798), a professor of anatomy at the University of Bologna. Bringing together differently charged substances, Galvani touched the legs of dead frogs and observed spasmodic contractions; such movements led him to conclude that there was an electrical presence within animal tissue. Excited scientific theorists postulated an electromagnetic "fluid" connecting all phenomena and an electrochemical base to life, which further suggested the possibility of reanimation (cf. Victor Frankenstein's experiments). Alessandro Volta (1745–1827), however, produced electricity independent of living matter from two plates made of different metals suspended in an acid/salt solution (the Voltaic Pile). The names of these two Italian scientists are still present in many terms we use today: galvanized nails and voltage, for example.

source of mortification to me nevertheless, that although I made several attempts at conversation, my powers of speech were so entirely in *abeyance*, that I could not even open my mouth; much less then make reply to some ingenious but fanciful theories of which, under other circumstances, my minute acquaintance with the Hippocratian Pathology[1] would have afforded me a ready confutation.

Not being able to arrive at a conclusion, the practitioners remanded me for further examination. I was taken up into a garret; and the surgeon's lady having accommodated me with drawers and stockings, the surgeon himself fastened my hands, and tied up my jaws with a pocket handkerchief—then bolted the door on the outside as he hurried to his dinner, leaving me alone to silence and to meditation.

I now discovered to my extreme delight that I could have spoken had not my mouth been tied up by the pocket-handerchief. Consoling myself with this reflection, I was mentally repeating some passages of the ———,[2] as is my custom before resigning myself to sleep, when two cats, of a greedy and vituperative turn, entering at a hole in the wall, leaped up with a flourish *à la Catalani*,[3] and alighting opposite one another on my visage, betook themselves to unseemly and indecorous contention for the paltry consideration of my nose.

But, as the loss of his ears proved the means of elevating to the throne of Cyrus, the Magian or Mige-Gush of Persia, and as the cutting off his nose gave Zopyrus possession of Babylon,[4] so the loss of a few ounces of my countenance proved the salvation of my body. Aroused by the pain, and burning with indignation, I burst, at a single effort, the fastenings and the bandage. Stalking across the room I cast a glance of contempt at the belligerents, and throwing open the sash to their extreme horror and disappointment, precipitated myself—very dexterously—from the window.

The mail-robber W———,[5] to whom I bore a singular resemblance, was at this moment passing from the city jail to the scaffold erected

1. The basic theorem of Hippocrates (c. 460–c. 377 B.C.E.) was that all disease, rather than being the mysterious visitations of supernatural agency, had a natural cause, scientifically discoverable in the structures of physical existence. His explanation for gastrointestinal illness was that undigested food gave off a foul "air" that caused internal distress. Cf. the end of the tale.
2. In other versions, the work is specified as the long poem "The Omnipresence of Deity" (1828) by Robert Montgomery (1807–1855), a writer attacked for dullness by contemporaries like John Neal.
3. A punning reference to the Italian singer, Angelica Catalani (1779–1849). The two cats "sing" and "act" in the style "à la Cat-alani." See Poe's reference to her in "The Purloined Letter" (p. 381 herein).
4. The Persian accounts of the fate of the "throne of Cyrus," specifically the stories of the "Magian or Mige-Gush" and "Zopyrus," are from Herodotus. Cambyses, son of Cyrus the Great (died 529 B.C.E.), secretly killed his brother, Smerdis, to secure his position as king of Persia. When Cambyses himself was accidentally killed, the Persian magi (priests) secretly substituted a double for Smerdis; but the lookalike magian priest had no ears and was eventually executed as an impostor. Zopyrus was an officer of Darius I (died 486 B.C.E.), a distant cousin of Cambyses, at the siege of Babylon. Mutilating himself, he pretended to defect, claiming Darius had cut off his nose and ears. He was welcomed by the Babylonians and made commander of their army: thereupon he opened the gates of the city to Darius. The narrator gets the first story backward and cuts short the second.
5. In 1830 a pair of mail robbers were sentenced to hang in Philadelphia. One, named Wilson, received a reprieve and served prison time instead. Poe may be satirizing some, as yet unidentified, specific literary figures in the caricatures of W——— and Windenough.

for his execution in the suburbs. His extreme infirmity and long-continued ill health, had obtained him the privilege of remaining unmanacled; and habited in his gallows costume—a dress very similar to my own—he lay at full length in the bottom of the hangman's cart (which happened to be under the windows of the surgeon at the moment of my precipitation) without any other guard than the driver who was asleep, and two recruits of the sixth infantry, who were drunk.

As ill-luck would have it, I alit upon my feet within the vehicle. W——, who was an acute fellow, perceived his opportunity. Leaping up immediately he bolted out behind, and turning down an alley, was out of sight in the twinkling of an eye. The recruits aroused by the bustle, could not exactly comprehend the merits of the transaction. Seeing, however, a man, the precise counterpart of the felon, standing upright in the cart before their eyes, they were of opinion that "the rascal, (meaning W——) was after making his escape," (so they expressed themselves) and, having communicated this opinion to one another, they took each a dram, and then knocked me down with the but-ends of their muskets.

It was not long ere we arrived at the place of destination. Of course nothing could be said in my defence. Hanging was my inevitable fate. I resigned myself thereto, with a feeling half stupid, half acrimonious. Being little of a cynic, I had all the sentiments of a dog.[6] The hangman, however, adjusted the noose about my neck. The drop fell. My convulsions were said to be extraordinary. Several gentlemen swooned, and some ladies were carried home in hysterics. Pinxit, too, availed himself of the opportunity to retouch, from a sketch taken upon the spot, his admirable painting of the "Marsyas flayed alive."[7]

I will endeavor to depict my sensations upon the gallows. To write upon such a theme it is necessary to have been hanged. Every author should confine himself to matters of experience. Thus Mark Antony wrote a treatise upon drunkenness.[8]

6. The cynical philosophers of ancient Greece are said to have gotten their name, which means "doglike" (Latin: cynicus; Greek: kunikos), from their aggressive, snarling behavior toward others. The gymnasium where the founder of the school, Antisthenes of Athens (c. 444–c. 371 B.C.E.), taught was called the Kunosarge (Latin: Cynosarges). Antisthenes was a disciple of Socrates, but he and the cynics held that virtue was not just the highest good, as Socrates has said, but the only one. They advocated a life of poverty and were critical of those who did not practice self-denial. These traits led outsiders to regard them as suspicious of the motives of anyone but themselves and indifferent to the needs and sufferings of others: thus in later years the word cynicism came to suggest extreme skepticism regarding all value systems and human behavior.
7. "Pinxit": he painted [it] (Latin). Levine speculates that it is a reference to a poem titled "Written under the Engraving of a Portrait of Rafael Painted by Himself" (1816), under which appears "Leigh Hunt, pinxit," i.e., Hunt wrote ("painted") it. The jokes are a little complicated. Poe's comments on Hunt's work elsewhere tend to be negative. Marsysas was a satyr, who, finding a flute of Athena's, discovered that he could suddenly play beautifully. Succumbing to Pride (hubris or hybris), which the ancient Greeks considered the greatest of sins, Marsyas urged Apollo to a musical contest. He lost and, as punishment for challenging a god, was flayed alive. The story is the subject of a painting by the Renaissance painting master Raphael. Poe's satiric point seems to be that Hunt, drawing a parallel between himself and a master artist like Rafael, suffers from hubris; thus he may bring "flaying" upon himself (by critics like Poe) just as Disraeli has (who in Vivian Grey alludes to the story).
8. Antony's treatise on inebriation is referred to in the Natural History, XIV.28, of Pliny the Elder (c. 23–79 C.E.). Mabbott suggests that Poe's more likely reference is Horace Smith's Zillah: A Tale of the Holy City (1828), a book Poe parodies in "A Tale of Jerusalem."

Die I certainly did not. The sudden jerk given to my neck upon the falling of the drop, merely proved a corrective to the unfortunate twist afforded me by the gentleman in the coach. Although my body certainly *was*, I had, alas! no breath *to be* suspended; and but for the shaking of the rope, the pressure of the knot under my ear, and the rapid determination of blood to the brain, should, I dare say, have experienced very little inconvenience.

The latter feeling, however, grew momentarily more painful. I heard my heart beating with violence—the veins in my hands and wrists swelled nearly to bursting—my temples throbbed tempestuously—and I felt that my eyes were starting from their sockets. Yet when I say that in spite of all this my sensations were not absolutely intolerable, I will not be believed.

There were noises in my ears—first like the tolling of huge bells— then like the beating of a thousand drums—then, lastly, like the low, sullen murmurs of the sea. But these noises were very far from disagreeable.

Although, too, the powers of my mind were confused and distorted, yet I was—strange to say!—well aware of such confusion and distortion. I could, with unerring promptitude determine at will in what particulars my sensations were correct—and in what particulars I wandered from the path. I could even feel with accuracy *how far*—to *what very point*, such wanderings had misguided me, but still without the power of correcting my deviations. I took besides, at the same time, a wild delight in analyzing my conceptions.[9]

Memory, which, of all other faculties, should have first taken its departure, seemed on the contrary to have been endowed with quadrupled power. Each incident of my past life flitted before me like a shadow. There was not a brick in the building where I was born—not a dog-leaf in the primer I had thumbed over when a child—not a tree in the forest where I hunted when a boy—not a street in the cities I had traversed when a man—that I did not at that time most palpably behold. I could repeat to myself entire lines, passages, names, acts, chapters, books, from the studies of my earlier days; and while, I dare say, the crowd around me were blind with horror, or aghast with awe, I was alternately with Æschylus, a demi-god, or with Aristophanes,[1] a frog.

A dreamy delight now took hold upon my spirit, and I imagined that I had been eating opium, or feasting upon the Hashish of the old As-

9. The general reader will I dare say recognize, in these *sensations* of Mr. Lacko'breath, much of the absurd *metaphysicianism* of the redoubted Schelling [Poe's note]. The name of Friedrich Wilhelm Joseph Schelling (1775–1854) is associated with the Romantic concepts of *Naturphilosophie* and *Transcendentale Idealismus*. In several works circulated from about 1800 to 1803, he argued the probability of a conscious intelligence manifest and evolving in nature and the essential harmony and oneness of the realm of nonhuman nature with the human realm. Variations on Schelling's ideas had wide currency among American Transcendentalists like Ralph Waldo Emerson (1803–1882). See Transcendentalism and Alternative Romanticism herein.
1. Greek writer of comedies (c. 448–389 B.C.E.), one of whose works, *The Frogs*, is a literary satire that includes Aeschylus (525–456 B.C.E.), Greek tragedian and author of *Prometheus Bound*, among its targets.

sassins.[2] But glimpses of pure, unadulterated reason—during which I
was still buoyed up by the hope of finally escaping that death which
hovered, like a vulture above me—were still caught occasionally by my
soul.

By some unusual pressure of the rope against my face, a portion of
the cap was chafed away, and I found to my astonishment that my
powers of vision were not altogether destroyed. A sea of waving heads
rolled around me. In the intensity of my delight I eyed them with feel-
ings of the deepest commiseration, and blessed, as I looked upon the
haggard assembly, the superior benignity of *my* proper stars.

I now reasoned, rapidly I believe—profoundly I am sure—upon
principles of common law—propriety of that law especially, for which
I hung—absurdities in political economy which till then I had never
been able to acknowledge—dogmas in the old Aristotelians now gen-
erally denied, but not the less intrinsically true—detestable school for-
mulæ in Bourdon, in Garnier, in Lacroix—synonymes in Crabbe—
lunar-lunatic theories in St. Pierre—falsities in the Pelham novels—
beauties in Vivian Grey[3]—more than beauties in Vivian Grey—profun-
dity in Vivian Grey—genius in Vivian Grey—every thing in Vivian
Grey.

Then came, like a flood, Coleridge, Kant, Fitche, and Pantheism—
then like a deluge, the Academie, Pergola, La Scala, San Carlo, Faul,
Albert, Noblet, Ronzi Vestris, Fanny Bias, and Taglioni.[4]

A rapid change was now taking place in my sensations. The last
shadows of connection flitted away from my meditations. A storm—a
tempest of ideas, vast, novel, and soul-stirring, bore my spirit like a

2. The Assassins were an order of the Ismaili sect of Islam originating in Syria in the 11th cen-
tury C.E. They were an elite inner circle that carried out political executions (hence the mod-
ern meaning of the word *assassin*). They exerted power for about a hundred years, after
which they suffered a slow decline, but remnants are said still to exist today. The grand mas-
ter of the medieval order, Sheik al-Jabal, was known as the Old Man of the Mountain. He is
supposed to have rewarded his devoted executioners by taking them into his remote moun-
tain fortress to experience "earthly paradise," in which all forms of sensual pleasure were en-
hanced by hashish. The word *assassin* is, in fact, an Arabic variant of *hashish*, a mind-altering
drug made from hemp (a plant related to marijuana).
3. Poe is parodying ostentation in the pretentious literary publications of his day, especially the
"lists" of intellectuals, philosophers, scientists, authors, musicians, artists, and so forth
found in fashionable novels. Mabbott identifies Bourdon, Garnier, and Lacroix as contem-
porary French mathematicians. George Crabbe (1757–1823), author of grim narrative po-
ems on the realities of British rural life and of *English Synonymes Explained* (1816); cf.
p. 102, n. 7 herein. J.-H. Bernadin de St. Pierre (1737–1814), best known for his Romantic
idyll *Paul and Virginia* (1788), which was originally part of his voluminous *Studies of Nature*
(1784; trans. 1796), in which he argued that the moon did *not* affect the tides (hence the lu-
natic theories). Edward Bulwer-Lytton's *Pelham* (1828) and Benjamin Disraeli's *Vivian Grey*
(1826–27) were "novels of fashion," also known in the 1820s and 1830s as "novels of *ton*"
(social tone) or "silver fork" novels.
4. Poe continues the pretentious parade of learning that current writers were so fond of. The
British writer Samuel Taylor Coleridge (1772–1834) studied and translated the German
Transcendentalist philosophers, among whom (along with Schelling) are Immanuel Kant
(1724–1804) and Johann Gottlieb Fichte (1762–1814); see Hedge, pp. 720ff. herein. Kant's
notion of Transcendentalism, as Poe probably knew, was in some ways the opposite of
Fichte's, whose name is here misspelled Fitche, possibly for satiric effect (though the name
is so spelled elsewhere in Poe's works). "Pantheism": the idea that God is in everything that
exists, from human beings to dirt clods and stones. "Academie": or the Academie de
Musique, the opera at Paris. "Pergola": the opera at Florence. "La Scala": the opera at Mi-
lan. "San Carlo": the opera at Naples. Mabbott identifies Faul, Albert, Noblet, Ronzi Vestris,
Fanny Bias, and Taglioni as dancers and singers.

feather afar off. Confusion crowded upon confusion like a wave upon a wave. In a very short time Schelling himself would have been satisfied with my entire loss of self-identity.[5] The crowd became a mass of mere abstraction.

About this period I became aware of a heavy fall and shock—but, although the concussion jarred throughout my frame, I had not the slightest idea of its having been sustained in my own proper person; and thought of it as of an incident peculiar to some other existence—an idiosyncrasy belonging to some other Ens.[6]

It was at this moment—as I afterwards discovered—that having been suspended for the full term of execution, it was thought proper to remove my body from the gallows—this, the more especially as the real culprit had now been retaken and recognized.

Much sympathy was now exercised in my behalf—and as no one in the city appeared to identify my body, it was ordered that I should be interred in the public sepulchre early in the following morning. I lay, in the meantime, without signs of life—although from the moment, I suppose, when the rope was loosened from my neck, a dim consciousness of my situation oppressed me like the night-mare.

I was laid out in a chamber sufficiently small, and very much encumbered with furniture—yet to me it appeared of a size to contain the universe. I have never before or since, in body or in mind, suffered half so much agony as from that single idea. Strange! that the simple conception of abstract magnitude—of infinity—should have been accompanied with pain. Yet so it was. "With how vast a difference," said I, "in life and in death—in time and in eternity—here and hereafter, shall our merest sensations be imbodied!"

The day died away, and I was aware that it was growing dark—yet the same terrible conceit still overwhelmed me. Nor was it confined to the boundaries of the apartment—it extended, although in a more definite manner, to all objects, and, perhaps I will not be understood in saying that it extended also to all *sentiments*. My fingers as they lay cold, clammy, stiff, and pressing helplessly one against another, were, in my imagination, swelled to a size according with the proportions of the Antœus.[7] Every portion of my frame betook of their enormity. The pieces of money—I well remember—which being placed upon my eyelids, failed to keep them effectually closed, seemed huge, interminable chariot-wheels of the Olympia, or of the Sun.[8]

Yet it is very singular that I experienced no sense of weight—of gravity. On the contrary I was put to much inconvenience by that

5. Transcendentalist idea of the absorption of each individual ego into the absolute ego of the world soul; also the moment of epiphany wherein one has a perception of the harmonious oneness of the self with the universe, of the "me" with the "not-me." See Emerson's description of feeling like a "transparent eyeball" in chapter 1 of *Nature* (1836).
6. Existence.
7. A giant, son of Ge (the earth), whose strength was preserved and renewed when he was in contact with his mother. Hercules defeated him by lifting him into the air and holding him there, eventually strangling him.
8. Mabbott notes the description of the burning chariot wheels at the Olympic Games in Horace's *Odes*, I.i.3–6. "Pieces of money": coins were placed on the eyelids of the dead in part to hold them shut.

buoyancy—that tantalizing *difficulty of keeping down*, which is felt by the swimmer in deep water. Amid the tumult of my terrors I laughed with a hearty internal laugh to think what incongruity there would be—could I arise and walk—between the elasticity of my motion, and the mountain of my form.

The night came—and with it a new crowd of horrors. The consciousness of my approaching interment, began to assume new distinctness, and consistency—yet never for one moment did I imagine *that I was not actually dead.*

"This then"—I mentally ejaculated—"this darkness which is palpable, and oppresses with a sense of suffocation—this—this—is indeed *death.* This is death—this is death the terrible—death the holy. This is the death undergone by Regulus—and equally by Seneca.[9] Thus—thus, too, shall I always remain—always—always remain. Reason is folly, and Philosophy a lie. No one will know my sensations, my horror—my despair. Yet will men still persist in reasoning, and philosophiziog, and making themselves fools. There is, I find, no hereafter but this. This—this—this—is the only Eternity!—and what, O Baalzebub![1]—*what* an Eternity!—to lie in this vast—this awful void—a hideous, vague, and unmeaning anomaly—motionless, yet wishing for motion—powerless, yet longing for power—forever, forever, and forever!"

But the morning broke at length—and with its misty and gloomy dawn arrived in triple horror the paraphernalia of the grave. Then—and not till then—was I fully sensible of the fearful fate hanging over me. The phantasms of the night had faded away with its shadows, and the actual terrors of the yawning tomb left me no heart for the bugbear[2] speculations of Transcendentalism.

I have before mentioned that my eyes were but imperfectly closed—yet as I could not move them in any degree, those objects alone which crossed the direct line of vision were within the sphere of my comprehension. But across that line of vision spectral and stealthy figures were continually flitting, like the ghosts of Banquo.[3] They were making hurried preparations for my interment. First came the coffin which they placed quietly by my side. Then the undertaker with attendants

9. Seneca the Younger (Lucius Annaeus Seneca, c. 3 B.C.E.–65 C.E.), Roman philosopher, essayist, dramatist, and stateman, was the emperor Nero's teacher. He rose to great power, was eventually accused of conspiracy, and died the death of a "noble Roman," committing suicide at the emperor's bidding by "opening his veins." Marcus Atilius Regulus (died c. 250 B.C.E.), martyred Roman hero, was a general in the first Punic War. The Carthaginians captured him in 255 B.C.E. and sent him under a "parole" of honor back to Rome with an offer of peace. But the terms were humiliating, and Regulus urged the Romans to continue the war. True to his word, he returned to Carthage, where he is said to have been tortured to death.
1. Lord of the Flies. Originally a Babylonian god, Baal became associated with evil (cf. Poe's "Ligeia," pp. 159ff. herein) by the Hebrews because of "unspeakable" rites in his honor. Christians made Baal-zebub one of Satan's chief devils in the Revolt of the Angels, as in John Milton's *Paradise Lost* (1667); the name is sometimes used for Satan himself.
2. An object of obsessive concern or dread, a false apprehension. It is akin to the words *bugaboo* (used as an adjective) and *bogie* (boogie-man; American).
3. One of Macbeth's victims in his quest for the throne of Scotland. In Act III.iv of Shakespeare's 1606 play, Macbeth's guilty conscience conjures up Banquo's ghost. Ghosts, apparitions, shadows, shades, spirits, etc., are semitransparent, or "airy."

and a screw-driver. Then a stout man whom I could distinctly see and who took hold of my feet—while one whom I could only feel lifted me by the head and shoulders. Together they placed me in the coffin, and drawing the shroud up over my face proceeded to fasten down the lid. One of the screws, missing its proper direction, was screwed by the carelessness of the undertaker deep—deep—down into my shoulder. A convulsive shudder ran throughout my frame. With what horror, with what sickening of heart did I reflect that one minute sooner a similar manifestation of life, would, in all probability, have prevented my inhumation. But alas! it was now too late, and hope died away within my bosom as I felt myself lifted upon the shoulders of men—carried down the stairway—and thrust within the hearse.

During the brief passage to the cemetery my sensations, which for some time had been lethargic and dull, assumed, all at once, a degree of intense and unnatural vivacity for which I can in no manner account. I could distinctly hear the rustling of the plumes—the whispers of the attendants—the solemn breathings of the horses of death. Confined as I was in that narrow and strict embrace, I could feel the quicker or slower movement of the procession—the restlessness of the driver—the windings of the road as it led us to the right or to the left. I could distinguish the peculiar odor of the coffin—the sharp acid smell of the steel screws. I could see the texture of the shroud as it lay close against my face; and was even conscious of the rapid variations in light and shade which the flapping to and fro of the sable hangings occasioned within the body of the vehicle.

In a short time however, we arrived at the place of sculpture, and I felt myself deposited within the tomb. The entrance, was secured—they departed—and I was left alone. A line of Marston's "Malcontent,"

> "Death's a good fellow and keeps open house,"[4]

struck me at that moment as a palpable lie. Sullenly I lay at length, the quick among the dead—and *Anacharsis inter Scythas.*[5]

From what I overheard early in the morning, I was led to believe that the occasions when the vault was made use of were of very rare occurrence. It was probable that many months might elapse before the doors of the tomb would be again unbarred—and even should I survive until that period, what means could I have more than at present, of making known my situation or of escaping from the coffin? I resigned myself, therefore, with much tranquillity to my fate, and fell, after many hours, into a deep and deathlike sleep.

How long I remained thus is to me a mystery. When I awoke my limbs were no longer cramped with the cramp of death—I was no

4. The paraphrase from John Marston (1576–1634) is slightly misquoted and comically out of context. Scholars are fond of pointing out that Poe made a mistake: the lines alluded to are not from Marston's *The Malcontent* but from his *Antonio and Mellida* (1602). But Poe's "mistake" may be a deliberate one, a parody of the fake erudition of the typical sensation tale narrator.

5. Eurasian peoples who flourished from the 8th to the 4th century B.C.E. and were considered by the Greeks to be barbarians. Anacharsis was famous for being the only Scythian ever to go to Greece to study. The phrase "an Anacharsis among the Scythians" came to mean "one of a kind."

longer without the power of motion. A very slight exertion was suffi-
cient to force off the lid of my prison—for the dampness of the atmo-
sphere had already occasioned decay in the woodwork around the
screws.

My steps as I groped around the sides of my habitation were, how-
ever, feeble and uncertain, and I felt all the gnawings of hunger with
the pains of intolerable thirst. Yet, as time passed away, it is strange
that I experienced little uneasiness from these scourges of the earth,
in comparisons with the more terrible visitations of the fiend *Ennui*.[6]
Stranger still were the resources by which I endeavored to banish him
from my presence.

The sepulchre was large and subdivided into many compartments,
and I busied myself in examining the peculiarities of their construc-
tion. I determined the length and breadth of my abode. I counted and
recounted the stones of the masonry. But there were other methods by
which I endeavored to lighten the tedium of my hours. Feeling my way
among the numerous coffins ranged in order around, I lifted them
down, one by one, and breaking open their lids, busied myself in spec-
ulations about the mortality within.

"This," I reflected, tumbling over a carcass, puffy, bloated, and ro-
tund—"this has been, no doubt, in every sense of the word, an un-
happy—an unfortunate man. It has been his terrible lot not to walk,
but to waddle—to pass through life not like a human being, but like
an elephant—not like a man, but like a rhinoceros.

"His attempts at getting on have been mere abortions—and his cir-
cumgyratory[7] proceedings a palpable failure. Taking a step forward, it
has been his misfortune to take two towards the right, and three to-
wards the left. His studies have been confined to the Philosophy of
Crabbe.

"He can have had no idea of the wonders of a *Pirouette*. To him a
Pas de Papillon[8] has been an abstract conception.

"He has never ascended the summit of a hill. He has never viewed
from any steeple the glories of a metropolis.

"Heat has been his mortal enemy. In the dog-days[9] his days have
been the days of a dog. Therein, he has dreamed of flames and suffo-
cation—of mountains upon mountains—of Pelion upon Ossa.[1]

"He was short of breath—to say all in a word—he was short of
breath.

"He thought it extravagant to play upon wind instruments. He was

6. Weariness, especially in the sense of boredom (French), here comically raised to the status
of a demon (who infects stories like this one).
7. Pun on the name of George Crabbe (see end of paragraph); i.e., someone walking in a side-
ways circular manner like a crab.
8. Butterfly step (French, literal trans.), a diagonal jump with one foot crossing over the other.
Poe returns to the comic image of a fat ballet dancer introduced at the beginning.
9. The hot, humid interval from mid-July to the beginning of September in the Northern
Hemisphere—or, more precisely, the "dog star" days, because Sirius (the dog star) rises and
sets in time with the sun during this period. The reference recalls the previous allusion to
the cynic philosophers' penchant for personal discomfort.
1. Mountains in Thessaly, Greece. Ancient giants, warring against the gods, tried to gain the
summit of Mount Olympus by piling Mount Pelion upon Mount Ossa; the story is told by
Homer (8th century B.C.E.), Virgil (70–19 B.C.E.), and Ovid (43 B.C.E.–17 C.E.).

the inventor of self-moving fans—wind-sails—and ventilators. He patronized Du Pont the bellows-maker—and died miserably in attempting to smoke a cigar.

"His was a case in which I feel deep interest—a lot in which I sincerely sympathize."

"But here," said I—"here"—and I dragged spitefully from its receptacle a gaunt, tall, and peculiar-looking form, whose remarkable appearance struck me with a sense of unwelcome familiarity—"here," said I—"here is a wretch entitled to no earthly commiseration." Thus saying, in order to obtain a more distinct view of my subject, I applied my thumb and forefinger to his nose, and, causing him to assume a sitting position upon the ground, held him, thus, at the length of my arm, while I continued my soliloquy.

—"entitled," I repeated, "to no earthly commiseration. Who indeed would think of compassionating a shadow? Besides—has he not had his full share of the blessings of mortality? He was the originator of tall monuments—shot-towers—lightning-rods—lombardy-poplars. His treatize upon 'Shades and Shadows'[2] has immortalized him.

"He went early to college and studied Pneumatics.[3] He then came home—talked eternally—and played upon the French horn.

"He patronized the bag-pipes. Captain Barclay, who walked against Time,[4] would not walk against *him*. Windham and Allbreath[5] were his favorite writers. He died gloriously while inhaling gas—*levique flatu corrumpilur*, like the *fama pudicitiœ* in Hieronymus. He was indubitably a"——

"How *can* you?—how—*can*—you?"—interrupted the object of my animadversions, gasping for breath, and tearing off, with a desperate exertion, the bandage around his jaws—how *can* you, Mr. Lacko'breath, be so infernally cruel as to pinch me in that manner by the nose? Did you not see how they had fastened up my mouth—and you *must* know—if you know any thing—what a vast superfluity of breath I have to dispose of! If you do *not* know, however, sit down and you

2. Unidentified, though the story of Peter Schlemihl comes to mind. In other versions Poe references "South on the Bones," which Mabbott indentifies as the "cover title of some American reprints of *A Short Description of the Bones* (1825) by John Flint South, M.D." Despite scholarly guesses, the bellowsmaker remains unidentified. Poe sometimes made up sham references and quotations for effect. Note the air and noise imagery of the names and titles.
3. I.e., the science of air pressure.
4. Captain Robert Barclay-Allardyce of Scotland (1779–1856), famous for walking "against time"; he walked a thousand miles in a thousand hours in 1809.
5. *Tenera res in feminis fama pudicitiae et quasi flos pulcherrimus, cito ad levem marcessit aurum, levique flatu corrumpitur—maxime, &c.*—Hiero[n]ymus ad Salvinam [Poe's note]. The attribution references the famous letters of St. Jerome [Hieronymus, c. 347–c. 420 C.E.], one of the principal Church fathers (here from letter #79 to Salvinia). Jerome's scholarship provided the basis for the Vulgate Bible; he is also remembered for a tract advocating virginity and celibacy. The Latin may be paraphrased as saying that a woman's reputation for chastity, modesty, or respectability (i.e., avoiding "shame") is a delicate thing and, like a beautiful flower, may be easily destroyed by breezes or winds. The English words fail to convey the possible sexual innuendo intended (*pudicitiae/pudendus*, "causing shame"; *pudendum*, "genital region"). Mabbott observes that the speeches (hot air?) of a British statesman named William Wyndham (1750–1810) were reviewed in the *American Quarterly Review* in 1833. Whatever the contemporary references may or may not be, Wyndham and the unidentified Allbreath are clearly aerogaseous puns. In other versions of the tale, another such pun ("fizz") occurs when the narrator also mentions Phiz, the pseudonym of Hablot Knight Browne (1815–1882), the famous illustrator of Charles Dickens's early works.

shall see. In my situation it is really a great relief to be able to open one's mouth—to be able to expatiate—to be able to communicate with a person like yourself who do not think yourself called upon at every period to interrupt the thread of a gentleman's discourse. Interruptions are annoying and should undoubtedly be abolished—don't you think so?—no reply, I beg you,—one person is enough to be speaking at a time. I shall be done, by and bye, and then you may begin. How the devil, sir, did you get into this place?—not a word I beseech you— been here some time myself—terrible accident!—heard of it I suppose—awful calamity!—walking under your windows—some short while ago—about the time you were stage-struck—horrible occurrence! heard of 'catching one's breath,' eh?—hold your tongue I tell you!—I caught somebody else's!—had always too much of my own— met Blab at the corner of the street—would'nt give me a chance for a word—could'nt get in a syllable edgeways—attacked, consequently, with Epilepsis[6]—Blab made his escape—damn all fools!—they took me up for dead, and put me in this place—pretty doings all of them!— heard all you said about me—every word a lie—horrible!—wonderful!—outrageous!—hideous!—incomprehensible!—et cetera—et cetera— et cetera—et cetera"——

It is impossible to conceive my astonishment at so unexpected a discourse; or the extravagant joy with which I became gradually convinced that the breath so fortunately caught by the gentleman—whom I soon recognized as my neighbor Windenough—was, in fact, the identical expiration mislaid by myself in the conversation with my wife. Time—place—and incidental circumstances rendered it a matter beyond question. I did not however, immediately release my hold upon Mr. W.'s proboscis—not at least during the long period in which the inventor of lombardy poplars continued to favor me with his explanations. In this respect I was actuated by that habitual prudence which has ever been my predominating trait.

I reflected that many difficulties might still lie in the path of my preservation which extreme exertion on my part would be alone able to surmount. Many persons, I considered, are prone to estimate commodities in their possession—however valueless to the then proprietor—however troublesome, or distressing—in precise ratio with the advantages to be derived by others from their attainment—or by themselves from their abandonment. Might not this be the case with Mr. Windenough? In displaying anxiety for the breath of which he was at present so willing to get rid, might I not lay myself open to the exactions of his avarice? There are scoundrels in this world—I remembered with a sigh—who will not scruple to take unfair opportunities with even a next door neighbor—and (this remark is from

6. Epilepsy, popularly known as the "falling sickness," has several forms or degrees, one of which produces foaming at the mouth, another of which results in acute abdominal cramping and flatulence. The "corpse" (who turns out to be Mr. Windenough) suffers like Mr. Blab from an excess of flatulence or hot air that produces logorrhea (running off at the mouth, incessant chatter).

Epictetus)[7] it is precisely at that time when men are most anxious to throw off the burden of their own calamities that they feel the least desirous of relieving them in others.

Upon considerations similar to these, and still retaining my grasp upon the nose of Mr. W, I accordingly thought proper to model my reply.

"Monster!"—I began in a tone of the deepest indignation—"monster! and double-winded idiot!—Dost *thou* whom, for thine iniquities, it has pleased Heaven to accurse with a two-fold respiration—dost *thou*, I say, presume to address me in the familiar language of an old acquaintance?—'I lie,' forsooth!—and 'hold my tongue,' to be sure—pretty conversation, indeed, to a gentleman with a single breath!—all this, too, when I have it in my power to relieve the calamity under which thou dost so justly suffer—to curtail the superfluities of thine unhappy respiration." Like Brutus[8] I paused for a reply—with which, like a tornado, Mr. Windenough immediately overwhelmed me. Protestation followed upon protestation, and apology upon apology. There were no terms with which he was unwilling to comply, and there were none of which I failed to take the fullest advantage.

Preliminaries being at length arranged, my acquaintance delivered me the respiration—for which—having carefully examined it—I gave him afterwards a receipt.

I am aware that by many I shall be held to blame for speaking in a manner so cursory of a transaction so impalpable. It will be thought that I should have entered more minutely into the details of an occurrence by which—and all this is very true—much new light might be thrown upon a highly interesting branch of physical philosophy.

To all this, I am sorry, that I cannot reply. A hint is the only answer which I am permitted to make. There were circumstances—but I think it much safer upon consideration to say as little as possible about an affair so delicate—so *delicate*, I repeat, and at the same time involving the interests of a third party whose resentment I have not the least desire, at this moment, of incurring.

We were not long after this necessary arrangement in effecting an escape from the dungeons of the sepulchre. The united strength of our resuscitated voices was soon efficiently apparent. Scissors, the Whig Editor, republished a treatise upon "the nature and origin of subterranean noises."[9] A reply—rejoinder—confutation—and

7. Stoic philosopher (c. 50 B.C.E.–c. 38 C.E.), whose commentaries exist only in fragmentary notes by others. He taught that externals are of little value, that the highest good is to be found within, and that mankind is one vast brotherhood. But Poe's reference seems to be to his comment on fair-weather friends: in prosperity, it is very easy to find a friend; in adversity, very difficult (Fragment #122).

8. Marcus Junius Brutus (85?–42 B.C.E.) was the key assassin of Julius Caesar. Poe's reference is to Shakespeare's *Julius Caesar* (1599), III.ii.37. Brutus asks if any among the assembled "freedom-loving" citizens is so "base" as to be offended by his strike at tyranny. "I pause for a reply," he says. Hearing none, he leaves the scene, allowing Mark Antony to sway the crowd against him with his famous speech ("Friends, Romans, countrymen . . .").

9. The conservative American Whig Party in America emerged in the 1830s in opposition to the triumph of the ultra-liberal Jacksonian Democrats in the 1820s. Poe's references are a satiric slap at both politics and journalism. The name "Scissors" alludes to the reputation of editors for merciless abridging and rearranging of the work of their contributors. The treatise

justification followed in the columns of an ultra Gazette. It was not until the opening of the vault to decide the controversy, that the appearance of Mr. Windenough and myself proved both parties to have been decidedly in the wrong.

I cannot conclude these details of some very singular passages in a life at all times sufficiently eventful, without again recalling to the attention of the reader the merits of that indiscriminate philosophy which is a sure and ready shield against those shafts of calamity which can be neither seen, felt, nor fully understood. It was in the spirit of this wisdom that, among the ancient Hebrews, it was believed the gates of Heaven would be inevitably opened to that sinner, or saint, who with good lungs and implicit confidence, should vociferate the word "*Amen!*"[1] It was in the spirit of this wisdom that when a great plague raged at Athens, and every means had been in vain attempted for its removal, Epimenides—as Laertius relates in his second book of the life of that philosopher—advised the erection of a shrine and temple *to prostekonti Theo*—"to the proper God."[2]

Ms. Found in a Bottle[1]

Qui n'a plus qu'un moment à vivre
N'a plus rien à dissimuler.

—Quinault—Alys.[2]

Of my country and of my family I have little to say. Ill usage and length of years have driven me from the one, and estranged me from the other. Hereditary wealth afforded me an education of no common order, and a contemplative turn of mind enabled me to methodize the stores which early study very diligently garnered up.—Beyond all

on "subterranean noises" and the immediate rejoinder to it constitute a hit at those eager to offer opinions without determining the facts; it also continues the word play on *flatulence.*

1. Mabbott notes that Horace Smith mentions in *Zillah,* I.151, the notion of the ancient Jews that the gates of Heaven would open to one who shouted Amen "with all his might." But the point here is that it is "with all his breath."

2. Diogenes Laertes (3rd century C.E.), Greek biographer, not to be confused with the earlier Diogenes (c. 412–323 B.C.E.), Stoic philosopher famous for searching for an honest man at night with a lamp. The story of Epimenides (6th century B.C.E.) and the shrine to the "proper god" is given a backward twist by Poe's narrator. As recorded in Laertes' ten-volume *Lives of Eminent Philosophers,* Epimenides, a philosopher from Crete, was called to plague-stricken Athens to purify the city after a civic murder. He let loose a flock of sheep in the city; wherever one lay down to rest, the citizens were to offer a sacrifice to the "proper god" of the site (see p. 90, n. 6 herein). In other reprintings, Poe's tale ended with the signature "Lyttleton Barry," a pseudonym he used a number of times.

1. Winner of the prize contest sponsored by the *Baltimore Saturday Visiter* (*sic*), this tale was published in that newspaper on October 19, 1833, and republished frequently during Poe's lifetime, though not always with his authorization. Later versions reduce exaggerations (such as the size of the ship and the height of the great wave). The text used here is that of the *Broadway Journal* (October 11, 1845). Details of the storm and ship-handling techniques are similar to those found in Jane Porter's *Narrative of Sir Edward Seaward* (1831); some scholars think the parallels are satiric and assign the tale to the Folio Club author Solomon Seadrift.

2. The epigraph (added 1845) is from *Atys,* I.vi.15–16, a libretto by Philippe Quinault (1635–1688) for an opera by Jean Baptiste Lully (1632–1687). It can be translated as: "He who has only a moment to live no longer has anything to lie about." (The word *dissimuler* also has connotations of pretending.) Earliest versions carry a different epigraph, from an 1825 poem by Alan Cunningham (1784–1842): "A wet sheet and a flowing sea" (i.e., wet sails in a heavy sea).

things, the works of the German moralists[3] gave me great delight; not from any ill-advised admiration of their eloquent madness, but from the ease with which my habits of rigid thought enabled me to detect their falsities. I have often been reproached with the aridity of my genius; a deficiency of imagination has been imputed to me as a crime; and the Pyrrhonism[4] of my opinions has at all times rendered me notorious. Indeed, a strong relish for physical philosophy has, I fear, tinctured my mind with a very common error of this age—I mean the habit of referring occurrences, even the least susceptible of such reference, to the principles of that science. Upon the whole, no person could be less liable than myself to be led away from the severe precincts of truth by the *ignes fatui*[5] of superstition. I have thought proper to premise thus much, lest the incredible tale I have to tell should be considered rather the raving of a crude imagination, than the positive experience of a mind to which the reveries of fancy have been a dead letter and a nullity.

After many years spent in foreign travel, I sailed in the year 18——, from the port of Batavia, in the rich and populous island of Java, on a voyage to the Archipelago of the Sunda islands.[6] I went as passenger—having no other inducement than a kind of nervous restlessness which haunted me as a fiend.

Our vessel was a beautiful ship of about four hundred tons, copper-fastened,[7] and built at Bombay of Malabar teak. She was freighted with cotton-wool and oil, from the Lachadive islands.[8] We had also on board coir, jaggeree, ghee, cocoa-nuts, and a few cases of opium. The stowage was clumsily done, and the vessel consequently crank.[9]

3. The narrator is asserting his intellectual ability and coolness. German writers of the 18th and early 19th centuries, however, were celebrated not only for their moral and philosophical writings but also for their tales of terror and horror. See the Tales introduction pp. 77ff. herein and the notes to "Metzengerstein" (pp. 81ff.) and "Loss of Breath" (pp. 89ff.).
4. Complete skepticism. Paradoxically enough, the narrator is asserting his trustworthiness for the story that follows by alluding to one of the world's famous skeptics. Pyrrho of Elis (c. 360–270 B.C.E.) held that neither reason nor the senses were to be fully trusted, that logic and perception were hopelessly entangled, and that we can never truly know anything.
5. Things that mislead or deceive. From medieval Latin for "foolish fire," i.e., phosphorescent swamp gas (light emitted by gaseous decaying matter); also called a friar's lantern or a will-o'-the-wisp.
6. Batavia, named after ancient Germanic peoples who erected settlements in the Rhine delta in the 1st century B.C.E., was a fort built by the Dutch about 1619 next to the capital city of Djakarta (Jakarta), Indonesia. It was located across the Sunda strait from Sumatra on the northwest side of the island of Java, which lies southwest of Borneo, southeast of Sumatra, and just west of Bali. Ravaged over the years by war and natural disasters, the fort was intended to ensure control of Java and environs, in particular providing military protection for the operations of the Dutch East India Company (famous for exports like "Java" coffee). In addition to evoking exotic, romantic locales, Poe's emphasis on Dutch colonial enterprise sets up the story of the famous cursed ship the *Flying Dutchman* (see pp. 110–11, n. 8 herein).
7. A ship put together with a copper bottom and copper rivets instead of wood.
8. Coral atolls in the Arabian Sea, two hundred miles west of the Malabar coastline of India, lying some two thousand miles from the initial locations of the story.
9. Sick; i.e., a vessel with unbalanced cargo that is thus in danger of capsizing. The cargo specified has suggestive linkages in terms of coconut products. "Coir": a fiber produced from the husks of coconuts used to make rope and mats. "Jaggeree": or jaggery, a sugar product made from palm sap, sometimes mixed with coconut milk. "Ghee": clarified butter, traditionally made from water buffalo milk. It is made by heating the butter until the solids separate and turn brown; this increases the storage life of the butter and thus it was useful on long voyages. "Opium": made from the juice of poppies; also known as the "milk of paradise," it was a preferred narcotic (along with cocaine) of the 18th and 19th centuries. Elsewhere in Poe's

We got under way with a mere breath of wind, and for many days stood along the eastern coast of Java, without any other incident to beguile the monotony of our course than the occasional meeting with some of the small grabs[1] of the Archipelago to which we were bound.

One evening, leaning over the taffrail, I observed a very singular, isolated cloud, to the N. W. It was remarkable, as well for its color, as from its being the first we had seen since our departure from Batavia. I watched it attentively until sunset, when it spread all at once to the eastward and westward, girting in the horizon with a narrow strip of vapor, and looking like a long line of low beach. My notice was soon afterwards attracted by the dusky-red appearance of the moon, and the peculiar character of the sea. The latter was undergoing a rapid change, and the water seemed more than usually transparent. Although I could distinctly see the bottom, yet, heaving the lead, I found the ship in fifteen fathoms. The air now became intolerably hot, and was loaded with spiral exhalations similar to those arising from heated iron. As night came on, every breath of wind died away, and a more entire calm it is impossible to conceive. The flame of a candle burned upon the poop without the least perceptible motion, and a long hair, held between the finger and thumb, hung without the possibility of detecting a vibration. However, as the captain said he could perceive no indication of danger, and as we were drifting in bodily to shore, he ordered the sails to be furled, and the anchor let go. No watch was set, and the crew, consisting principally of Malays,[2] stretched themselves deliberately upon deck. I went below—not without a full presentiment of evil. Indeed, every appearance warranted me in apprehending a Simoom.[3] I told the captain my fears; but he paid no attention to what I said, and left me without deigning to give a reply. My uneasiness, however, prevented me from sleeping, and about midnight I went upon deck.—As I placed my foot upon the upper step of the companion-ladder, I was startled by a loud, humming noise, like that occasioned by the rapid revolution of a mill-wheel, and before I could ascertain its meaning, I found the ship quivering to its centre. In the next instant, a wilderness of foam hurled us upon our beam-ends, and, rushing over us fore and aft, swept the entire decks from stem to stern.

The extreme fury of the blast proved, in a great measure, the salvation of the ship. Although completely water-logged, yet, as her masts had gone by the board, she rose, after a minute, heavily from the sea, and, staggering awhile beneath the immense pressure of the tempest, finally righted.

By what miracle I escaped destruction, it is impossible to say.

fiction, the mention of such a drug or alcohol often has a bearing on the narrator's trustworthiness in reporting events.

1. Shallow-draft sailing ships, typical of the coastal East India trade.
2. Various peoples of Southeast Asia, especially from the Malayan Peninsula and adjacent islands. Also used as an alternative general term for *Indonesian*.
3. Or simoon, a strong, hot, and densely sand-laden wind from the Sahara and Arabian deserts (Arabic: *samum* = "poisonous"; from Aramaic: *samma* = "drug"). Poe's agitated narrator applies the word to a torrential, possibly apparitional storm at sea.

Stunned by the shock of the water, I found myself, upon recovery, jammed in between the stern-post and rudder. With great difficulty I gained my feet, and looking dizzily around, was, at first, struck with the idea of our being among breakers; so terrific, beyond the wildest imagination, was the whirlpool of mountainous and foaming ocean within which we were engulfed. After a while, I heard the voice of an old Swede, who had shipped with us at the moment of our leaving port. I hallooed to him with all my strength, and presently he came reeling aft. We soon discovered that we were the sole survivors of the accident. All on deck, with the exception of ourselves, had been swept overboard;—the captain and mates must have perished as they slept, for the cabins were deluged with water. Without assistance, we could expect to do little for the security of the ship, and our exertions were at first paralyzed by the momentary expectation of going down. Our cable[4] had, of course, parted like pack-thread, at the first breath of the hurricane, or we should have been instantaneously overwhelmed. We scudded with frightful velocity before the sea, and the water made clear breaches over us. The framework of our stern was shattered excessively, and, in almost every respect, we had received considerable injury; but to our extreme joy we found the pumps unchoked, and that we had made no great shifting of our ballast.—The main fury of the blast had already blown over, and we apprehended little danger from the violence of the wind; but we looked forward to its total cessation with dismay; well believing, that, in our shattered condition, we should inevitably perish in the tremendous swell which would ensue. But this very just apprehension seemed by no means likely to be soon verified. For five entire days and nights—during which our only subsistence was a small quantity of jaggeree, procured with great difficulty from the forecastle—the hulk flew at a rate defying computation, before rapidly succeeding flaws of wind, which, without equalling the first violence of the Simoom, were still more terrific than any tempest I had before encountered. Our course for the first four days was, with trifling variations, S. E. and by S.; and we must have run down the coast of New Holland.[5] On the fifth day the cold became extreme, although the wind had hauled round a point more to the northward.— The sun arose with a sickly yellow lustre, and clambered a very few degrees above the horizon—emitting no decisive light. There were no clouds apparent, yet the wind was upon the increase, and blew with a fitful and unsteady fury. About noon, as nearly as we could guess, our attention was again arrested by the appearance of the sun. It gave out no light, properly so called, but a dull and sullen glow without reflection, as if all its rays were polarized. Just before sinking within the turgid sea, its central fires suddenly went out, as if hurriedly extinguished by some unaccountable power. It was a dim, silver-like rim, alone, as it rushed down the unfathomable ocean.

We waited in vain for the arrival of the sixth day—that day to me

4. I.e., anchor cable or chain.
5. An older name for Australia (once again pointing up the Dutch connection).

has not arrived—to the Swede, never did arrive. Thenceforward we were enshrouded in pitchy darkness, so that we could not have seen an object at twenty paces from the ship. Eternal night continued to envelop us, all unrelieved by the phosphoric sea-brilliancy to which we had been accustomed in the tropics. We observed too, that, although the tempest continued to rage with unabated violence, there was no longer to be discovered the usual appearance of surf, or foam, which had hitherto attended us. All around were horror, and thick gloom, and a black sweltering desert of ebony.—Superstitious terror crept by degrees into the spirit of the old Swede, and my own soul was wrapped up in silent wonder. We neglected all care of the ship, as worse than useless, and securing ourselves, as well as possible, to the stump of the mizen-mast, looked out bitterly into the world of ocean. We had no means of calculating time, nor could we form any guess of our situation. We were, however, well aware of having made farther to the southward than any previous navigators, and felt great amazement at not meeting with the usual impediments of ice. In the meantime every moment threatened to be our last—every mountainous billow hurried to overwhelm us. The swell surpassed anything I had imagined possible, and that we were not instantly buried is a miracle. My companion spoke of the lightness of our cargo, and reminded me of the excellent qualities of our ship; but I could not help feeling the utter hopelessness of hope itself, and prepared myself gloomily for that death which I thought nothing could defer beyond an hour, as, with every knot[6] of way the ship made, the swelling of the black stupendous seas became more dismally appalling. At times we gasped for breath at an elevation beyond the albatross—at times became dizzy with the velocity of our descent into some watery hell, where the air grew stagnant, and no sound disturbed the slumbers of the kraken.[7]

We were at the bottom of one of these abysses, when a quick scream from my companion broke fearfully upon the night. "See!" see!" cried he, shrieking in my ears, "Almighty God! see! see!" As he spoke, I became aware of a dull, sullen glare of red light which streamed down the sides of the vast chasm where we lay, and threw a fitful brilliancy upon our deck. Casting my eyes upwards, I beheld a spectacle which froze the current of my blood. At a terrific height directly above us, and upon the very verge of the precipitous descent, hovered a gigantic ship of, perhaps, four thousand tons. Although upreared upon the summit of a wave more than a hundred times her own altitude, her apparent size still exceeded that of any ship of the line or East Indiaman[8] in existence. Her huge hull was of a deep dingy black,

6. Nautical miles per hour.
7. In Norse myth, a sea beast, reputedly as large as an island, that slumbers in the deep and arises once in an eon. It is frequently imaged as a giant octopus or squid that grasps entire ships in its tentacles and drags them down. The albatross was thought to glide in the air (often "sleeping upon the wing") at very great heights for great distances.
8. A very large ship engaged in the East India trade. "Ship of the line": a large war ship. The gigantic ship the narrator sees at the crest of the wave from deep in its trough is many times larger. Here Poe begins to evoke the legend of the *Flying Dutchman*, a phantom ship doomed to roam the seas forever because of a blasphemous oath on the part of its captain. One of the legends surrounding it is that it appears, full rigged, when another ship is about

unrelieved by any of the customary carvings of a ship. A single row of brass cannon protruded from her open ports, and dashed from their polished surfaces the fires of innumerable battle-lanterns, which swung to and fro about her rigging. But what mainly inspired us with horror and astonishment, was that she bore up under a press of sail[9] in the very teeth of that supernatural sea, and of that ungovernable hurricane. When we first discovered her, her bows were alone to be seen, as she rose slowly from the dim and horrible gulf beyond her. For a moment of intense terror she paused upon the giddy pinnacle, as if in contemplation of her own sublimity, then trembled and tottered, and—came down.

At this instant, I know not what sudden self-possession came over my spirit. Staggering as far aft as I could, I awaited fearlessly the ruin that was to overwhelm. Our own vessel was at length ceasing from her struggles, and sinking with her head to the sea. The shock of the descending mass struck her, consequently, in that portion of her frame which was already under water, and the inevitable result was to hurl me, with irresistible violence, upon the rigging of the stranger.

As I fell, the ship hove in stays, and went about;[1] and to the confusion ensuing I attributed my escape from the notice of the crew. With little difficulty I made my way unperceived to the main hatchway, which was partially open, and soon found an opportunity of secreting myself in the hold.[2] Why I did so I can hardly tell. An indefinite sense of awe, which at first sight of the navigators of the ship had taken hold of my mind, was perhaps the principle of my concealment. I was unwilling to trust myself with a race of people who had offered, to the cursory glance I had taken, so many points of vague novelty, doubt, and apprehension. I therefore thought proper to contrive a hiding-place in the hold. This I did by removing a small portion of the shifting-boards,[3] in such a manner as to afford me a convenient retreat between the huge timbers of the ship.

I had scarcely completed my work, when a footstep in the hold forced me to make use of it. A man passed by my place of concealment with a feeble and unsteady gait. I could not see his face, but had an opportunity of observing his general appearance. There was about it an evidence of great age and infirmity. His knees tottered beneath a load of years, and his entire frame quivered under the burthen. He muttered to himself, in a low broken tone, some words of a language which I could not understand, and groped in a corner among a pile of

to founder. Since the *Dutchman* is traditionally seen off the Cape of Good Hope, at the southernmost tip of Africa, it would seem that the narrator's ship has been carried off course some three thousand miles to the southwest. Thus it would be on course toward the Weddell Sea, which, along with the Ross Sea (in the opposite direction); was the farthest known penetration of the ocean waters into the ice-laden shores of Antarctica. Poe makes use of such suggestions again in *The Narrative of Arthur Gordon Pym* (1838).

9. I.e., the ship has its principal sails up in spite of the heavy winds.

1. I.e., in the act of tacking (zigzagging against winds and currents to sail a straight course), the ship turns too far and goes in the opposite direction.

2. Finding oneself confined in a dark place somewhere "below" is a recurrent feature in Poe's writings. Cf. Arthur Gordon Pym's confinement in the dark hold of the ship *Grampus*.

3. According to Levine, these are removable partitions in the hold to keep the cargo from shifting.

singular-looking instruments, and decayed charts of navigation. His manner was a wild mixture of the peevishness of second childhood, and the solemn dignity of a God. He at length went on deck, and I saw him no more.

A feeling, for which I have no name, has taken possession of my soul—a sensation which will admit of no analysis, to which the lessons of by-gone time are inadequate, and for which I fear futurity itself will offer me no key. To a mind constituted like my own, the latter consideration is an evil. I shall never—I know that I shall never—be satisfied with regard to the nature of my conceptions. Yet it is not wonderful that these conceptions are indefinite, since they have their origin in sources so utterly novel. A new sense—a new entity is added to my soul.

It is long since I first trod the deck of this terrible ship, and the rays of my destiny are, I think, gathering to a focus. Incomprehensible men! Wrapped up in meditations of a kind which I cannot divine, they pass me by unnoticed. Concealment is utter folly on my part, for the people *will not* see. It was but just now that I passed directly before the eyes of the mate—it was no long while ago that I ventured into the captain's own private cabin, and took thence the materials with which I write, and have written. I shall from time to time continue this journal. It is true that I may not find an opportunity of transmitting it to the world, but I will not fail to make the endeavour. At the last moment I will enclose the MS. in a bottle, and cast it within the sea.

An incident has occurred which has given me new room for meditation. Are such things the operation of ungoverned Chance? I had ventured upon deck and thrown myself down, without attracting any notice, among a pile of ratlin-stuff and old sails, in the bottom of the yawl.[4] While musing upon the singularity of my fate, I unwittingly daubed with a tar-brush the edges of a neatly-folded studding-sail[5] which lay near me on a barrel. The studding-sail is now bent upon the ship, and the thoughtless touches of the brush are spread out into the word DISCOVERY.

I have made many observations lately upon the structure of the vessel. Although well armed, she is not, I think, a ship of war. Her rigging, build, and general equipment, all negative a supposition of this kind. What she *is not*, I can easily perceive—what she *is* I fear it is impossible to say. I know not how it is, but in scrutinizing her strange model and singular cast of spars, her huge size and overgrown suits of canvass, her severely simple bow and antiquated stern; there will occasionally flash across my mind a sensation of familiar things, and there

4. A small boat. "Ratlin-stuff": material for small rope ladders.
5. A small sail set beyond the vertical edges of a principal sail (used in fair weather for extra thrust).

is always mixed up with such indistinct shadows of recollection, an unaccountable memory of old foreign chronicles and ages long ago.[6]

I have been looking at the timbers of the ship. She is built of a material to which I am a stranger. There is a peculiar character about the wood which strikes me as rendering it unfit for the purpose to which it has been applied. I mean its extreme *porousnses*, considered independently of the worm-eaten condition which is a consequence of navigation in these seas, and apart from the rottenness attendant upon age. It will appear perhaps an observation somewhat over-curious, but this wood would have every characteristic of Spanish oak, if Spanish oak were distended by any unnatural means.

In reading the above sentence a curious apothegm of an old weather-beaten Dutch navigator comes full upon my recollection. "It is as sure," he was wont to say, when any doubt was entertained of his veracity, "as sure as there is a sea where the ship itself will grow in bulk like the living body of the seaman."

About an hour ago, I made bold to thrust myself among a group of the crew. They paid me no manner of attention, and, although I stood in the very midst of them all, seemed utterly unconscious of my presence. Like the one I had at first seen in the hold, they all bore about them the marks of a hoary old age. Their knees trembled with infirmity; their shoulders were bent double with decrepitude; their shrivelled skins rattled in the wind; their voices were low, tremulous and broken; their eyes glistened with the rheum of years; and their gray hairs streamed terribly in the tempest. Around them, on every part of the deck, lay scattered mathematical instruments of the most quaint and obsolete construction.

I mentioned some time ago the bending of a studding-sail. From that period the ship, being thrown dead off the wind, has continued her terrific course due south, with every rag of canvass packed upon her, from her trucks to her lower studding-sail booms, and rolling every moment her top-gallant yard-arms[7] into the most appalling hell of water which it can enter into the mind of man to imagine. I have just left the deck, where I find it impossible to maintain a footing, although the crew seem to experience little inconvenience. It appears to me a miracle of miracles that our enormous bulk is not swallowed up at once and forever. We are surely doomed to hover continually upon the brink of Eternity, without taking a final plunge into the abyss. From billows a thousand times more stupendous than any I have ever seen, we glide away with the facility of the arrowy sea-gull; and the colossal waters rear their heads above us like demons of the deep, but

6. It is left unclear (perhaps deliberately) if the word *Discovery* in the preceding paragraph appears as a supernatural portent of things to come or if it merely reflects the narrator's growing apprehensions (his disordered state of mind). In any case, it is clear that at this point he begins to recall legends like that of the *Flying Dutchman*.
7. A pole running at right angles to the mast from which the sail is hung on a square-rigged ship. "Top-gallant": the highest mast, sails, or rigging.

like demons confined to simple threats and forbidden to destroy. I am led to attribute these frequent escapes to the only natural cause which can account for such effect.—I must suppose the ship to be within the influence of some strong current or impetuous under-tow.[8]

I have seen the captain face to face, and in his own cabin—but, as I expected, he paid me no attention. Although in his appearance there is, to a casual observer, nothing which might bespeak him more or less than man—still a feeling of irrepressible reverence and awe mingled with the sensation of wonder with which I regarded him. In stature he is nearly my own height; that is, about five feet eight inches. He is of a well-knit and compact frame of body, neither robust nor remarkably otherwise. But it is the singularity of the expression which reigns upon the face—it is the intense, the wonderful, the thrilling evidence of old age so utter, so extreme, which excites within my spirit a sense—a sentiment ineffable. His forehead, although little wrinkled, seems to bear upon it the stamp of a myriad of years.—His gray hairs are records of the past, and his grayer eyes are Sybils[9] of the future. The cabin floor was thickly strewn with strange, iron-clasped folios, and mouldering instruments of science, and obsolete long-forgotten charts. His head was bowed down upon his hands, and he pored, with a fiery unquiet eye, over a paper which I took to be a commission, and which, at all events, bore the signature of a monarch. He muttered to himself, as did the first seaman whom I saw in the hold, some low peevish syllables of a foreign tongue, and although the speaker was close at my elbow, his voice seemed to reach my ears from the distance of a mile.

The ship and all in it are imbued with the spirit of Eld. The crew glide to and fro like the ghosts of buried centuries; their eyes have an eager and uneasy meaning; and when their figures fall athwart my path in the wild glare of the battle-lanterns, I feel as I have never felt before, although I have been all my life a dealer in antiquities, and have imbibed the shadows of fallen columns at Balbec, and Tadmor, and Persepolis,[1] until my very soul has become a ruin.

8. Drifting farther and farther south on strong undercurrents and the "dashing of a cataract" (four paragraphs below) are also features of the ending of *Arthur Gordon Pym*. Poe seems to make reference to the contemporary theory that deep ocean currents circulated to and through the North and South Poles. See also p. 115, n. 4, and pp. 429–31 herein.
9. Or sibyls; women, usually of great age, whom the Greeks and Romans thought endowed with the gift of prophecy.
1. Ruined cities of ancient Arabia. Baalbek (usual spelling) was a city in what is now Lebanon, lying north-northwest of Damascus. It was devoted to Baal (or Bel), who was originally a sun god but who came to be regarded as evil because of child sacrifices practiced in his honor (see notes to "Ligeia," pp. 159ff. herein). The Greeks called it Heliopolis (city of the sun). The Romans chose it as the site for two temples celebrated in antiquity: one to Bacchus (the god of wine) and one to Jupiter (the king of the gods). Sacked by numerous invading armies over the centuries, Baalbek was destroyed by earthquake in 1759. Tadmor is the biblical name of Palmyra (city of palms) in what is now central Syria; it was said to have been founded by King Solomon. The city came under Roman protection in the 1st century C.E. but was later taken by the Arabs and eventually sacked by Tamerlane (or Timur Leng, 1336–1404). It too is famous for a shrine to Baal. Persepolis was the ceremonial capital of the Persian kings, beginning as early as the reign of Darius I (521–486 B.C.E.). Alexander the Great looted the inner citadel containing its fabulous treasury. The ruins of Persepolis lie on a huge platform constructed from the limestone of the adjacent mountains; scattered over

When I look around me I feel ashamed of my former apprehensions. If I trembled at the blast which has hitherto attended us, shall I not stand aghast at a warring of wind and ocean, to convey any idea of which the words tornado and simoom are trivial and ineffective! All in the immediate vicinity of the ship is the blackness of eternal night, and a chaos of foamless water; but, about a league on either side of us, may be seen, indistinctly and at intervals, stupendous ramparts of ice, towering away into the desolate sky, and looking like the walls of the universe.

As I imagined, the ship proves to be in a current; if that appellation can properly be given to a tide which, howling and shrieking by the white ice, thunders on to the southward with a velocity like the headlong dashing of a cataract.

To conceive the horror of my sensations is, I presume, utterly impossible; yet a curiosity to penetrate the mysteries of these awful regions, predominates even over my despair, and will reconcile me to the most hideous aspect of death. It is evident that we are hurrying onwards to some exciting knowledge—some never-to-be-imparted secret, whose attainment is destruction. Perhaps this current leads us to the southern pole itself.[2] It must be confessed that a supposition apparently so wild has every probability in its favor.

The crew pace the deck with unquiet and tremulous step; but there is upon their countenances an expression more of the eagerness of hope than of the apathy of despair.

In the meantime the wind is still in our poop,[3] and, as we carry a crowd of canvass, the ship is at times lifted bodily from out the sea————Oh, horror upon horror! the ice opens suddenly to the right, and to the left, and we are whirling dizzily, in immense concentric circles, round and round the borders of a gigantic amphitheatre, the summit of whose walls is lost in the darkness and the distance. But little time will be left me to ponder upon my destiny—the circles rapidly grow small—we are plunging madly within the grasp of the whirlpool—and amid a roaring, and bellowing, and thundering of ocean and of tempest, the ship is quivering, oh God! and—going down.[4]

the plains are the remains of other Persian cities (such as Estakhr) and temples (e.g., to the legendary Persian hero Rustam). Buried under the desert surface are red ocher murals dating from 4000 B.C.E.

2. The South Pole was the subject of much excited speculation and the object of several expeditions by the United States in the 1830s. Poe wrote several essays on the Wilkes expedition.
3. The superstructure of the stern of a ship (hence a poop deck is the aftermost deck on a ship).
4. The "Ms. Found in a Bottle," was originally published in 1831; and it was not until many years afterwards that I became acquainted with the maps of Mercator, in which the ocean is represented as rushing, by four mouths, into the (northern) Polar Gulf, to be absorbed into the bowels of the earth; the Pole itself being represented by a black rock, towering to a prodigious height [Note added to the posthumous version of 1850].
 So far as we know, however, Poe's tale was first published in 1833 rather than in 1831. Gerardus Mercator was the pseudonym of Gerhard Kremer (1512–1594), a mapmaker famous for the Mercator projection, which attempted to represent proportionately on a flat surface the land masses of a round earth. As this added note makes clear, the whirlpool in

The Assignation[1]

Stay for me there! I will not fail
To meet thee in that hollow vale.
[Exequy on the death of his wife, by Henry King, Bishop of Chichester.][2]

Ill-fated and mysterious man!—bewildered in the brilliancy of thine
own imagination, and fallen in the flames of thine own youth! Again in
fancy I behold thee! Once more thy form hath risen before me!—
not—oh not as thou art—in the cold valley and shadow—but as thou
shouldst be—squandering away a life of magnificent meditation in that
city of dim visions, thine own Venice—which is a star-beloved Elysium
of the sea, and the wide windows of whose Palladian[3] palaces look
down with a deep and bitter meaning upon the secrets of her silent
waters. Yes! I repeat it—as thou *shouldst be*. There are surely other
worlds than this—other thoughts than the thoughts of the multi-
tude—other speculations than the speculations of the sophist.[4] Who
then shall call thy conduct into question? who blame thee for thy
visionary hours, or denounce those occupations as a wasting away
of life, which were but the overflowings of thine everlasting
energies?[5]

the tale is more than just an ordinary one. Poe is doubtless alluding not only to the current
theory of cartographers like Mercator, but also to the well-known hollow earth propositions
of John Cleves Symmes (1780–1829). In the fantasy novel *Symzonia: A Voyage of Discovery;
by "Adam Seaborn"* (1820; see notes and illustration to *Narrative of Arthur Gordon Pym*
pp. 429–31 herein), sometimes attributed to Nathaniel Ames but more usually to Symmes
himself, the entrances to the interior world are at the North and South Poles. The oceans
circulate around the exterior shell of the earth, drift to one of the poles, disappear into the
interior of the globe, and then emerge again at the other Pole. The interior world in
Symmes's romance is inhabited by an entire subterranean culture, eons old.

1. First published in the *Lady's Book* (January 1834) as "The Visionary." The text followed here
 is from the *Broadway Journal* (June 7, 1845).
2. The epigraph (repeated toward the end of the tale) is from "Exequy on the Death of a
 Beloved Wife" (1657) by Henry King (1592–1669). Exequies are funeral rites; thus the
 opening motto anticipates the revelation at the end. The earliest version of the tale had two
 epigraphs from German literature. The first was: "Ich habe gelebt, und geliebet.—*Schiller's
 Wallenstein*. I have lived, and I have loved." Mabbott suggests that this reference is not to
 Friedrich Schiller's dramatic trilogy (1798–99) but to Adelbert von Chamisso's *Frauen Liebe
 und Leben* (Lives and loves of women; 1830). The second German motto reads: "Und ster-
 bich denn, so sterbich doch / Durch sie, durch sie.—*Goethe*. And if I die, at least I die / With
 her—with her." Mabbott identifies the lines as from Johann Wolfgang von Goethe's ballad,
 "Das Veilchen" (The violet), lines 19–20, and suggests that Poe got it from George Ban-
 croft's "Life and Genius of Goethe," *North American Review* (October 1824). Poe comically
 distorts these very lines in "A Predicament" (p. 190 herein).
3. In the style of the Italian architect Andrea Palladio (1518–1580). "Elysium": a place of ideal
 happiness; in Greek myth, the abode of the blessed after death (also Elysian Fields).
4. One skilled at devious argument (but cf. the philosophical school of Greek Sophists in the
 notes to "Loss of Breath," pp. 89ff. herein).
5. Two coyly ambiguous paragraphs preceded this one in the 1834 version. Calling attention to
 his status as a "writer," the narrator comments on literary conventions and clichés, insisting
 that he does not indulge in cheap tricks (even as he in fact does so). It is he who knows the
 true circumstances surrounding the death of a literary genius—one much misunderstood by
 others—indeed, maliciously lied about. He will tell the story, but the immortal name of this
 bright talent, for special reasons, must be concealed from the public eye. Nor will the narra-
 tor use a false suggestively similar name to tease the public with the identity of the protago-
 nist of the story. For, while like some architects, popular writers need a famous name for the
 "key-stone to the arch of their narrations," our narrator is not such an author. Thus the nar-
 rator ironically hints that his tale might be a *roman à clef* (story with a key); and part of the
 fun is speculating on not only the identity of the protagonist (and his lover) but also guess-

It was at Venice, beneath the covered archway there called the *Ponte di Sospiri*,[6] that I met for the third or fourth time the person of whom I speak. It is with a confused recollection that I bring to mind the circumstances of that meeting. Yet I remember—ah! how should I forget?—the deep midnight, the Bridge of Sighs, the beauty of woman, and the Genius of Romance[7] that stalked up and down the narrow canal.

It was a night of unusual gloom. The great clock of the Piazza[8] had sounded the fifth hour of the Italian evening. The square of the Campanile lay silent and deserted, and the lights in the old Ducal Palace were dying fast away. I was returning home from the Piazetta, by way of the Grand Canal. But as my gondola arrived opposite the mouth of the canal San Marco,[9] a female voice from its recesses broke suddenly upon the night, in one wild, hysterical, and long continued shriek. Startled at the sound, I sprang upon my feet: while the gondolier, letting slip his single oar, lost it in the pitchy darkness beyond a chance of recovery, and we were consequently left to the guidance of the current which here sets from the greater into the smaller channel. Like some huge and sable-feathered condor, we were slowly drifting down towards the Bridge of Sighs, when a thousand flambeaux flashing from the windows, and down the staircases of the Ducal Palace, turned all at once that deep gloom into a livid and preternatural[1] day.

A child, slipping from the arms of its own mother, had fallen from an upper window of the lofty structure into the deep and dim canal. The quiet waters had closed placidly over their victim; and, although my own gondola was the only one in sight, many a stout swimmer, already in the stream, was seeking in vain upon the surface, the treasure which was to be found, alas! only within the abyss. Upon the broad black marble flagstones at the entrance of the palace, and a few steps above the water, stood a figure which none who then saw can have ever since forgotten. It was the Marchesa Aphrodite—the adoration of all Venice—the gayest of the gay—the most lovely where all were beautiful—but still the young wife of the old and intrigu-

ing that of the narrator. Among the Folio Club members (see p. 596 herein), "Mr. Convolvulus Gondola, a young gentleman who had travelled a good deal," is immediately suggested for the narrator. The tale takes place in Venice, the city of canals, famous for romantic travel by gondola.

6. Bridge of Sighs (Italian); so named because it was said that the sighs of condemned prisoners could be heard as they crossed the bridge over the narrow canal between the prison and the palace of the Venetian doge (duke). Poe's tale is full of "Byronic" echoes and innuendoes; cf. the famous lines, "I stood in Venice on the Bridge of Sighs / A palace and a prison on each hand" from Lord Byron's *Childe Harold* (1812–18), IV.i.1–2.

7. Originally meaning something out of the ordinary round of everyday life (adventures, supernatural encounters, etc.). By the 18th century, the word *romance* came also to have almost a separate definition as a love intrigue. "Genius": either spirit or demon.

8. A city square.

9. The area described is St. Mark's Square (Piazza di San Marco), one of the central squares of Venice, dominated by St. Mark's Church, the Bell Tower ("Campanile"), and the palace of the doge of Venice. The street that goes from St. Mark's past the palace and a smaller square to the waterside comes to the juncture of the Grand Canal and St. Mark's Canal. The prison and the Bridge of Sighs are just to the east of the palace, not far from the open water leading out to sea.

1. Highly unusual; outside of natural causes as commonly understood. In other versions, the word used is *supernatural*, i.e., above or beyond natural cause (occult). "Flambeaux": torches.

ing[2] Mentoni, and the mother of that fair child, her first and only one who now deep beneath the murky water, was thinking in bitterness of heart upon her sweet caresses, and exhausting its little life in struggles to call upon her name.

She stood alone. Her small, bare, and silvery feet gleamed in the black mirror of marble beneath her. Her hair, not as yet more than half loosened for the night from its ball-room array, clustered, amid a shower of diamonds, round and round her classical head, in curls like those of the young hyacinth. A snowy-white and gauze-like drapery seemed to be nearly the sole covering to her delicate form; but the mid-summer and midnight air was hot, sullen, and still, and no motion in the statue-like form itself, stirred even the folds of that raiment of very vapor which hung around it as the heavy marble hangs around the Niobe.[3] Yet—strange to say!—her large lustrous eyes were not turned downwards upon that grave wherein her brightest hope lay buried—but riveted in a widely different direction! The prison of the Old Republic is, I think, the statliest building in all Venice—but how could that lady gaze so fixedly upon it, when beneath her lay stifling her only child? Yon dark, gloomy niche, too, yawns right opposite her chamber window—what, then, *could* there be in its shadows—in its architecture—in its ivy-wreathed and solemn cornices—that the Marchesa di Mentoni had not wondered at a thousand times before? Nonsense!—Who does not remember that, at such a time as this, the eye, like a shattered mirror, multiplies the images of its sorrow, and sees in innumerable far off places, the wo which is close at hand?[4]

Many steps above the Marchesa, and within the arch of the water-gate, stood, in full dress, the Satyr-like[5] figure of Mentoni himself. He was occasionally occupied in thrumming a guitar, and seemed *ennuyé*[6] to the very death, as at intervals he gave directions for the recovery of his child. Stupified and aghast, I had myself no power to move from the upright position I had assumed upon first hearing the shriek, and must have presented to the eyes of the agitated group a spectral and ominous appearance, as with pale countenance and rigid limbs, I floated down among them in that funereal gondola.

All efforts proved in vain. Many of the most energetic in the search were relaxing their exertions, and yielding to a gloomy sorrow. There seemed but little hope for the child; (how much less than for the mother!) but now, from the interior of that dark niche which has been already mentioned as forming a part of the Old Republican prison, and as fronting the lattice of the Marchesa, a figure muffled in a

2. In the sense of "plotting" (making devious plans) or possibly in the sense of having secret flirtations or petty love affairs. "Marchesa": marchioness, feminine of marquess, a noble rank above a count and below a prince or duke. The name of Aphrodite for old Mentoni's young wife suggests her beauty and desirability. Aphrodite is the Greek name of the Roman love goddess Venus. (In the first version of the tale, the marchesa's name is Bianca.)
3. In Greek myth, after her children are killed, Niobe is turned to stone, from which tears flow. The reference here is to a group of marble figures.
4. Possibly more Byronic echoes. Cf. *Childe Harold*, III.xxxii.1–3: "Even as a broken mirror, which the glass / In every fragment multiplies; and makes / A thousand images of one that was."
5. In Greek myth, satyrs were half-men half-goat demigods associated with carnal lust.
6. A bored person (French).

cloak, stepped out within reach of the light, and, pausing a moment upon the verge of the giddy descent, plunged headlong into the canal. As, in an instant afterwards, he stood with the still living and breathing child within his grasp, upon the marble flagstones by the side of the Marchesa, his cloak, heavy with the drenching water, became unfastened, and, falling in folds about his feet, discovered to the wonder-stricken spectators the graceful person of a very young man, with the sound of whose name the greater part of Europe was then ringing.[7]

No word spoke the deliverer. But the Marchesa! She will now receive her child—she will press it to her heart—she will cling to its little form, and smother it with her caresses. Alas! *another's* arms have taken it from the stranger—*another's* arms have taken it away, and borne it afar off, unnoticed, into the palace! And the Marchesa! Her lip—her beautiful lip trembles: tears are gathering in her eyes—those eyes which, like Pliny's acanthus, are "soft and almost liquid."[8] Yes: tears are gathering in those eyes—and see! the entire woman thrills throughout the soul, and the statue has started into life! The pallor of the marble countenance, the swelling of the marble bosom, the very purity of the marble feet, we behold suddenly flushed over with a tide of ungovernable crimson; and a slight shudder quivers about her delicate frame, as a gentle air at Napoli[9] about the rich silver lilies in the grass.

Why *should* that lady blush! To this demand there is no answer—except that, having left, in the eager haste and terror of a mother's heart, the privacy of her own *boudoir*, she has neglected to enthral her tiny feet in their slippers, and utterly forgotten to throw over her Venitian shoulders that drapery which is their due. What other possible reason could there have been for her so blushing?—for the glance of those wild appealing eyes?—for the unusual tumult of that throbbing bosom?—for the convulsive pressure of that trembling hand?—that hand which fell, as Mentoni turned into the palace, accidentally, upon the hand of the stranger. What reason could there have been for the low—the singularly low tone of those unmeaning words which the lady uttered hurriedly in bidding him adieu? "Thou hast conquered"—

7. The heroics of the enigmatic stranger are quite Byronic, and the tale reeks of Byronism. Lord Byron created in *Childe Harold* and other works a defiant and sardonic, world-weary and lonely hero, whose mysterious past hints of some great offense or crime. But Poe's tale goes beyond a general literary evocation of Byronism. Some scholars, notably Richard P. Benton, have pointed out parallels between the protagonist and George Gordon Noel Byron (1788–1824) himself. Lord Byron lived in a Venetian palazzo for a time, where he was visited by his friend and biographer Thomas Moore (1779–1852). Byron had an affair with the Venetian countess Teresa Guiccioli, whose older husband threatened him. Some of the art works the narrator will soon encounter in the stranger's palazzo have specific Byronic associations. The poem that the stranger later recites has similarities to a poem by Byron to his early love Mary Chaworth (see p. 126, n. 8 herein). Benton argues that the narrator is a burlesque caricature of Moore, whose adulatory *Letters and Journals of Lord of Byron, with Notices of His Life* (2 vols.) appeared in 1830—and whom Poe lampoons elsewhere.
8. Levine observes that the leaves of the acanthus plant "provide a decorative motif in Corinthian columns" but claims that nothing in the *Natural History* of Pliny the Older (c. 23–79 C.E.) matches this description of the plant as "soft and almost liquid." Mabbott, however, cites the *Letters* V.vi.16, of Pliny the Younger (c. 62–113 C.E.) and notes the very same phrasing in Horace Smith's *Zillah* (1828), III.220, one of Poe's favorite satiric targets. See notes to Poe's "Loss of Breath" (pp. 89ff. herein).
9. Naples, Italy.

she said, or the murmurs of the water deceived me—"thou hast conquered—one hour after sunrise—we shall meet—so let it be!"

The tumult had subsided, the lights had died away within the palace, and the stranger, whom I now recognised, stood alone upon the flags. He shook with inconceivable agitation, and his eye glanced around in search of a gondola. I could not do less than offer him the service of my own; and he accepted the civility. Having obtained an oar at the water-gate, we proceeded together to his residence, while he rapidly recovered his self-possession, and spoke of our former slight acquaintance in terms of great apparent cordiality.

There are some subjects upon which I take pleasure in being minute. The person of the stranger—let me call him by this title, who to all the world was still a stranger—the person of the stranger is one of these subjects. In height he might have been below rather than above the medium size: although there were moments of intense passion when his frame actually *expanded* and belied the assertion. The light, almost slender symmetry of his figure, promised more of that ready activity which he evinced at the Bridge of Sighs, than of that Herculean strength which he has been known to wield without an effort, upon occasions of more dangerous emergency. With the mouth and chin of a deity—singular, wild, full, liquid eyes, whose shadows varied from pure hazel to intense and brilliant jet—and a profusion of curling, black hair, from which a forehead of unusual breadth gleamed forth at intervals all light and ivory—his were features than which I have seen none more classically regular, except, perhaps, the marble ones of the Emperor Commodus.[1] Yet his countenance was, nevertheless, one of those which all men have seen at some period of their lives, and have never afterwards seen again. It had no peculiar—it had no settled predominant expression to be fastened upon the memory; a countenance seen and instantly forgotten—but forgotten with a vague and never-ceasing desire of recalling it to mind. Not that the spirit of each rapid passion failed, at any time, to throw its own distinct image upon the mirror of that face—but that the mirror, mirror-like, retained no vestige of the passion, when the passion had departed.

Upon leaving him on the night of our adventure, he solicited me, in what I thought an urgent manner, to call upon him *very* early the next morning. Shortly after sunrise, I found myself accordingly at his Palazzo, one of those huge structures of gloomy, yet fantastic pomp, which tower above the waters of the Grand Canal in the vicinity of the Rialto.[2] I was shown up a broad winding staircase of mosaics, into an

1. Emperor Lucius Aelius Aurelius Commodus (161–192 C.E.), licentious and arrogant emperor of Rome from 180 to 192, was the son of Marcus Aurelius (121–180), the Stoic philosopher, famous for his book of *Meditations*. (In the first version of the tale, the comparison was not to Commodus but to the profiles found on ancient Hebrew medallions, an allusion also used in "Ligeia.") The description of the stranger conforms generally to the descriptions of Byron by Thomas Moore and others.
2. The Palazzo Mocenigo where Byron lived was on the Grand Canal, down the water and around the great loop from the famous Rialto Bridge. Richard Benton, noting similar descriptive language in Thomas Moore's biographical notices of Byron, suggests that the paragraph is a parody.

apartment whose unparalleled splendor burst through the opening door with an actual glare, making me blind and dizzy with luxuriousness.

I knew my acquaintance to be wealthy. Report had spoken of his possessions in terms which I had even ventured to call terms of ridiculous exaggeration. But as I gazed about me, I could not bring myself to believe that the wealth of any subject in Europe could have supplied the princely magnificence which burned and blazed around.

Although, as I say, the sun had arisen, yet the room was still brilliantly lighted up. I judged from this circumstance, as well as from an air of exhaustion in the countenance of my friend, that he had not retired to bed during the whole of the preceding night. In the architecture and embellishments of the chamber, the evident design had been to dazzle and astound. Little attention had been paid to the *decora* of what is technically called *keeping*, or to the proprieties of nationality.[3] The eye wandered from object to object, and rested upon none—neither the *grotesques* of the Greek painters, nor the sculptures of the best Italian days, nor the huge carvings of untutored Egypt.[4] Rich draperies in every part of the room trembled to the vibration of low, melancholy music, whose origin was not to be discovered. The senses were oppressed by mingled and conflicting perfume reeking up from strange convolute consers,[5] together with multitudinous flaring and flickering tongues of emerald and violet fire. The rays of the newly risen sun poured in upon the whole, through windows formed each of a single pane of crimson-tinted glass. Glancing to and fro, in a thousand reflections, from curtains which rolled from their cornices like cataracts of molten silver, the beams of natural glory mingled at length fitfully with the artificial light, and lay weltering in subdued masses upon a carpet of rich, liquid-looking cloth of Chili gold.[6]

"Ha! ha! ha!—ha! ha! ha!"—laughed the proprietor, motioning me to

3. The theory of *decorum* (pl. *decora*) is usually associated with neoclassicism as distinguished from Romanticism. It is the idea that certain forms, images, styles, etc. are appropriate to and must be "in keeping with" certain subjects. In dramatic literature, for example, there is a long tradition that nobles speak in poetry (elevated language) and commoners in prose (low language), as befits their different stations in life.

4. The profusion of different art objects in different styles that the mysterious stranger has brought together from different countries (Greece, Italy, and Egypt) does not conform to the principle of decorum. The idea of the "grotesque" goes in the opposite direction from decorum; it suggests that which is out of keeping, jarring, or distorted or something unnaturally bonded or fused together (see the Tales introduction pp. 77ff.). One standard definition of *grotesque* became the uneasy combination of humor and horror—a meaning obviously appropriate to the attitude of the stranger in Poe's tale.

5. Vessels to hold burning incense, often wrought of interlooping metal strands or carved extravagantly out of stone or molded in clay. Some (as here) were designed to throw intricate patterns of glowing light on the floor, walls, and ceiling of a room. To be *convoluted* means rolled, coiled, or twisted back on itself. In the first version of the tale, the censers were called *arabesque* (as they are later in this version). The term indicates geometric "Arab-like" designs of great intricacy, such as those of Persian carpets. The light source was also originally said to lie "in the recesses" of a "crimson trellis-work which tapestried the ceiling."

6. Previous commentators have suggested the Chili province of northern China, celebrated for its carpets. In the first version were two anti-decorum (pro-Romantic) sentences at this point: "Here then had the hand of genius been.—A wilderness—a chaos of beauty was before me; a sense of dreamy and incoherent grandeur took possession of my soul, and I remained speechless."

a seat as I entered the room, and throwing himself back at full length upon an ottoman.[7] "I see," said he, perceiving that I could not immediately reconcile myself to the *bienséance*[8] of so singular a welcome— "I see you are astonished at my apartment—at my statues—my pictures—my originality of conception in architecture and upholstery—absolutely drunk, eh? with my magnificence. But pardon me, my dear sir, (here his tone of voice dropped to the very spirit of cordiality,) pardon me for my uncharitable laughter. You appeared so *utterly* astonished. Besides, some things are so completely ludicrous that a man *must* laugh or die. To die laughing must be the most glorious of all glorious deaths! Sir Thomas More[9]—a very fine man was Sir Thomas More—Sir Thomas More died laughing, you remember. Also in the *Absurdities* of Ravisius Textor,[1] there is a long list [of] characters who came to the same magnificent end. "Do you know, however," continued he musingly, "that at Sparia (which is now Palæochori), at Sparta, I say, to the west of the citadel, among a chaos of scarcely visible ruins, is a kind of *socle* upon which are still legible the letters ΛΑΞΜ. They are undoubtedly part of ΓΕΛΑΞΜΑ.[2] Now at Sparta were a thousand temples and shrines to a thousand different divinities. How exceedingly strange that the altar of Laughter should have survived all the others! But in the present instance," he resumed, with a singular alteration of voice and manner, "I have no right to be merry at your expense. You might well have been amazed. Europe cannot produce anything so fine as this, my little regal cabinet. My other apartments are by no means of the same order; mere *ultras*[3] of fashionable insipidity. This is better than fashion—is it not? Yet this has but to be seen to become the rage—that is, with those who could afford it at the cost of their entire patrimony. I have guarded, however, against any such profanation. With one exception you are the only human being besides myself and my *valet*, who has been admitted within

7. A low upholstered sofa without arms; also a cushioned foot rest, frequently in arabesque style.
8. Here something like conventional expectations, i.e., the question of the propriety of the mysterious stranger's effusiveness.
9. More (1478–1535), later canonized, was lord chancellor under King Henry VIII of England. Famous as the author of *Utopia* (1516), he is also celebrated as a martyr to his faith. He was beheaded for refusing to sign the Act of Supremacy, which impugned the authority of the pope and asserted Henry VIII as head of the Church of England. More is said to have been "cheerful" at his execution and to have made jokes on the platform; he is recorded as saying that his neck was very short and therefore the headsman should take extra care to make sure his ax stroke did not go awry. The thrice-repeated name, according to the Benton thesis, is a clue to Poe's satire on the 19th-century Thomas Moore.
1. Presumably an allusion to the French humanist, Jean Textier, signeur de Ravisy (died 1524). Mabbott cites a handbook on classical lore, *Theatrum Poetarum . . . sive Officina Io. Ravisii Textoris* (1520), in which a comment about laughing at death occurs. Levine remarks that no work of his called *Absurdities* has been discovered but notes that Robert Southey, in his novel *The Doctor* (1834)—which Poe reviewed in 1836—retells two stories from Textier about men "making merry in defiance of Death."
2. Plutarch (c. 46–c. 120 C.E.) in *Parallel Lives* mentions a statue or altar to ΓΕΛΑΞΜΑ (laughter) in his life of Lycurgus. Mabbott believes that Francois René Chateaubriand is Poe's more direct source, however, because Chateaubriand claimed to have found the altar and also used the word *socle* in his *Itinéraire de Paris à Jerusalem* (1811). Ancient Sparta was the capital of Laconia in Greece, founded before the 7th century B.C.E. "Palæochori": old site. "*Socle*": a pedestal for a statue or bust (from Latin through the Italian for "shoe").
3. Of fashionable insipidity. Ultimates or extremes in taste (or tastelessness), deriving from a self-conscious sense of being avant-garde.

the mysteries of these imperial precincts, since they have been be-dizzened[4] as you see!"

I bowed in acknowledgment: for the overpowering sense of splendor and perfume, and music, together with the unexpected eccentricity of his address and manner, prevented me from expressing, in words, my appreciation of what I might have construed into a compliment.

"Here," he resumed, arising and leaning on my arm as he sauntered around the apartment, "here are paintings from the Greeks to Cimabue,[5] and from Cimabue to the present hour. Many are chosen, as you see, with little deference to the opinions of Virtû.[6] They are all, however, fitting tapestry for a chamber such as this. Here too, are some *chéf d'oeuvres* of the unknown great—and here unfinished de-signs by men, celebrated in their day, whose very names the perspicac-ity[7] of the academies has left to silence and to me. "What think you," said he, turning abruptly as he spoke—"what think you of this Madonna della Pietà?"[8]

"It is Guido's own!" I said with all the enthusiasm of my nature, for I had been poring intently over its surpassing loveliness. "It is Guido's own!—how *could* you have obtained it?—she is undoubtedly in paint-ing what the Venus is in sculpture."

"Ha!" said he thoughtfully, "the Venus—the beautiful Venus?—the Venus of the Medici?[9]—she of the diminutive head and the gilded hair? Part of the left arm (here his voice dropped so as to be heard with difficulty), and all the right are restorations, and in the coquetry[1] of that right arm lies, I think, the quintessence of all affectation. Give *me* the Canova![2] The Apollo, too!—is a copy—there can be no doubt of it—blind fool that I am, who cannot behold the boasted inspiration of the Apollo! I cannot help—pity me!—I cannot help preferring the Antinous.[3] Was it not Socrates who said that the statuary found his

4. Vulgarly or tastelessly ornamented.
5. Giovanni Cimabue (1240–1320?), Florentine artist associated with the new style of painting in the early Renaissance.
6. Knowledge of the fine arts; taste, connoisseurship.
7. Insightfulness, acuteness of perception. "*Chéf d'œuvres*": masterpieces.
8. Mabbott suggests that this reference is to the huge painting of the Madonna by Guido Reni of Bologna (1573–1642), which measures over ten by twenty feet. Levine, however, suggests the *Virgin and Child* of Guido de Siena (flourished 1250–1275) because he was the founder of a "neo-Byzantine school" and his paintings are very rare. Whichever it is, the reference to the Madonna reifies the first term of a Virgin/Venus conjunction that recurs throughout the tale.
9. The second term of the Virgin/Venus theme. In the original version of the tale, the *Venus de Medici* is attributed to "Cleomenes, the son of the Athenian! As much as it is a work of my own hand." A letter from Byron to his publisher contains similar language, and Poe could have read it in Moore's edition of the *Letters*. Moore's account of his visit to Byron's palazzo in Venice records their conversation on art and reveals Byron's unconventional aesthetics. Although Poe may not have known it, the inscription on the pedestal ("Cleomenes, son of Apollodorus the Athenian") is supposed to be a Renaissance forgery. The Byronic stranger repeatedly mentions copies and fakes, which may have a bearing on the Madonna/Venus theme.
1. Affected modesty while yet inviting sexual overtures. The stranger may be mistaking genuine modesty for coy flirtatiousness.
2. The *Venus* (1805) of Antonio Canova (1757–1822), which depicts a nude woman on a lion's back, replaced the Medici *Venus* when it was taken to Paris, but the old pedestal inscription remained. Byron mentions Canova with exorbitant praise in *Childe Harold*.
3. Antinoüs (flourished 110–130 C.E.), the subject of a painting by Canova, was the beloved friend of the Roman emperor Hadrian (76–138), who caused likenesses of Antinoüs to be placed on statues and coins. The *Apollo Belvidere* in the Vatican is supposed to be a copy;

statue in the block of marble? Then Michæl Angelo was by no means original in his couplet—

> 'Non ha l'ottimo artista alcun concetto
> Chè un marmo solo in se nou circunscriva.' "[4]

It has been, or should be remarked, that, in the manner of the true gentleman, we are always aware of a difference from the bearing of the vulgar, without being at once precisely able to determine in what such difference consists. Allowing the remark to have applied in its full force to the outward demeanor of my acquaintance, I felt it, on that eventful morning, still more fully applicable to his moral temperament and character. Nor can I better define that peculiarity of spirit which seemed to place him so essentially apart from all other human beings, than by calling it a *habit* of intense and continual thought, pervading even his most trivial actions—intruding upon his moments of dalliance—and interweaving itself with his very flashes of merriment—like adders which writhe from out the eyes of the grinning masks in the cornices around the temples of Persepolis.[5]

I could not help, however, repeatedly observing, through the mingled tone of levity and solemnity with which he rapidly descanted upon matters of little importance, a certain air of trepidation—a degree of nervous *unction* in action and in speech—an unquiet excitability of manner which appeared to me at all times unaccountable, and upon some occasions even filled me with alarm. Frequently, too, pausing in the middle of a sentence whose commencement he had apparently forgotten, he seemed to be listening in the deepest attention, as if either in momentary expectation of a visiter, or to sounds which must have had existence in his imagination alone.

It was during one of these reveries or pauses of apparent abstraction, that, in turning over a page of the poet and scholar Politian's beautiful tragedy "The Orfeo," (the first native Italian tragedy,)[6] which

many people have been struck by its strong resemblance to Byron. The stranger's rejection of his own image as false constitutes a complex joke, according to Richard Benton.

4. The great Renaissance painter and sculptor Michelangelo Buonorroti (1475–1564), made this famous statement in a sonnet. It may be loosely translated as: "The best of artists has no concept that the marble block does not already circumscribe." That is, the statue is already in the stone; the artist's job is to release it. Diogenes Laertius (early 3rd century C.E.), in his *Lives of the Eminent Philosophers*, II.xvi, quotes an ambiguous remark, attributed to Socrates, about how sculptors, careless of their own looks, are very careful in cutting an image out of the stone.

5. The capital of ancient Persia, burned by Alexander the Great in 330 B.C.E. It is one of the most famous of ruined cities and monuments—a major motif in the poetry and fiction of the late 18th century and of the Romantic era. "Cornices": the horizontal moldings between walls and ceiling, frequently used for decoration.

6. Politian is the anglicized name of Angelo Poliziano (1454–1494), also known as Politianus, a Florentine dramatist and poet. He is the author of a tragedy based on the myth of Orpheus, *La Favola d'Orfeo* (1488). Orpheus was the greatest mortal musician in Greek myth. His skill was so great that even trees and stones wept when he played. His name became a symbol of supreme artistry, and one can sometimes still run across the adjective *orphic*. When his wife, Eurydice, was killed, Hades claimed her. Orpheus braved the dangers of Hell, descended to the depths, and confronted Hades (or Pluto), god of the underworld. He played so beautifully that Hades allowed Eurydice to follow her husband back up to the upper world, but he set one condition: Orpheus, no matter what demons and terrors they encountered on the journey, was not to look back at his beloved until they were both in sunlight again. He reached the mouth of Hell and stepped into the light, Eurydice just be-

lay near me upon an ottoman, I discovered a passage underlined in pencil. It was a passage towards the end of the third act—a passage of the most heart-stirring excitement—a passage which, although tainted with impurity,[7] no man shall read without a thrill of novel emotion—no woman without a sigh. The whole page was blotted with fresh tears, and, upon the opposite interleaf, were the following English lines, written in a hand so very different from the peculiar characters of my acquaintance, that I had some difficulty in recognising it as his own.

> Thou wast that all to me, love,
> For which my soul did pine—
> A green isle in the sea, love,
> A fountain and a shrine,
> All wreathed with fairy fruits and flowers;
> And all the flowers were mine.
>
> Ah, dream too bright to last;
> Ah, starry Hope that didst arise
> But to be overcast!
> A voice from out the Future cries
> "Onward!"—but o'er the Past
> (Dim gulf!) my spirit hovering lies,
> Mute, motionless, aghast!
>
> For alas! alas! with me
> The light of life is o'er.
> "No more—no more—no more,"
> (Such language holds the solemn sea
> To the sands upon the shore.)
> Shall bloom the thunder-blasted tree,
> Or the stricken eagle soar!
>
> Now all my hours are trances;
> And all my nightly dreams
> Are where thy dark eye glances,
> And where thy footstep gleams,
> In what ethereal dances,
> By what Italian streams.
>
> Alas! for that accursed time
> They bore thee o'er the billow,
> From Love to titled age and crime,

hind him. In his eagerness, Orpheus turned too soon: she was at the entrance, but half in sun and half in shadow. He watched her fade before his eyes. Orpheus went mad, roaming the forests like a savage beast, where eventually the wild women of the woods, the Bacchantes (or Maenads), tore him to pieces. Poe refers to Politian several times in his writings, and his only verse drama is titled *Politian* (1835; left unfinished).

7. According to Mabbott, the passage in *Orfeo* is where Orpheus proclaims that without Eurydice he has no place in this world. In his "Pinakidia" series (*Southern Literary Messenger*, August 1836), Poe offers a translation of Politian's 32nd "Greek Epigram" (see Mabbott I.216). The speaker asks for "fruit" from his beloved (physical love), but she will give him only "flowers" (platonic love) while on earth; their love will be consummated in another realm. (Note the fruit and flower allusions in the first stanza of the "English lines" below; see next note.) The narrator's comment that a passage from Politian is "tainted with impurity" may be to show this work instead of his Orpheus play; in any case, it continues the Virgin/Venus motif.

And an unholy pillow—
From me, and from our misty clime,
Where weeps the silver willow![8]

That these lines were written in English—a language with which I had not believed their author acquainted—afforded me little matter for surprise. I was too well aware of the extent of his acquirements, and of the singular pleasure he took in concealing them from observation, to be astonished at any similar discovery; but the place of date, I must confess, occasioned me no little amazement. It had been originally written *London*, and afterwards carefully overscored—not, however, so effectually as to conceal the word from a scrutinizing eye. I any this occasioned me no little amazement; for I well remember that, in a former conversation with my friend, I particularly inquired if he had at any time met in London the Marchesa di Mentoni, (who for some years previous to her marriage had resided in that city,) when his answer, if I mistake not, gave me to understand that he had never visited the metropolis of Great Britain. I might as well here mention, that I have more than once heard, (without of course giving credit to a report involving so many improbabilities,) that the person of whom I speak was not only by birth, but in education, an *Englishman*.[9]

"There is one painting," said he, without being aware of my notice of the tragedy—"there is still one painting which you have not seen." And throwing aside a drapery, he discovered a full length portrait of the Marchesa Aphrodite.

Human art could have done no more in the delineation of her superhuman beauty. The same ethereal figure which stood before me the preceding night upon the steps of the Ducal Palace, stood before me once again. But in the expression of the countenance, which was beaming all over with smiles, there still lurked (incomprehensible anomaly!) that fitful stain of melancholy which will ever be found inseparable from the perfection of the beautiful. Her right arm lay folded over her bosom. With her left she pointed downward to a curiously fashioned vase. One small, fairy foot, alone visible, barely touched the earth—and, scarcely discernible in the brilliant atmosphere which seemed to encircle and enshrine her loveliness, floated a pair of the most delicately imagined wings. My glance fell from the painting to the figure of my friend, and the vigorous words of Chapman's *Bussy D'Ambois* quivered instinctively upon my lips:

8. These lines were also used as a separate publication (with the present fifth stanza omitted), reprinted several times under the titles "To Ianthe in Heaven" and "To One in Paradise." Scholars have argued that there is a resemblance to some lines that Byron wrote to Mary Chaworth on the eve of her wedding to another (Poe published the sketch "Byron and Miss Chaworth" in 1844). In Byron's poem, the speaker says that hopes of future bliss are over and that both regret and hope are in vain; but in Poe's tale, the mysterious stranger hopes to be united with his beloved in an afterlife.
9. More mystification and teasing about the identity of the stranger as Lord Byron.

"He is up
There like a Roman statue! He will stand
Till Death hath made him marble!"[1]

"Come!" he said at length, turning towards a table of richly enam-
elled and massive silver, upon which were a few goblets fantastically
stained, together with two large Etruscan vases, fashioned in the same
extraordinary model as that in the foreground of the portrait, and filled
with what I supposed to be Johannisberger.[2] "Come!" he said abruptly,
"let us drink! It is early—but let us drink. It is *indeed* early," he con-
tinued, musingly, as a cherub with a heavy golden hammer, made the
apartment ring with the first hour after sunrise—"It is *indeed* early but
what matters it? let us drink! Let us pour out an offering to yon
solemn sun which these gaudy lamps and censers are so eager to sub-
due!" And, having made me pledge him in a bumper,[3] he swallowed in
rapid succession several goblets of the wine.

"To dream," he continued, resuming the tone of his desultory con-
versation, as he held up to the rich light of a censer one of the mag-
nificent vases—"to dream has been the business of my life. I have
therefore framed for myself, as you see, a bower of dreams. In the
heart of Venice could I have erected a better! You behold around you,
it is true, a medley of architectural embellishments. The chastity of Io-
nia is offended by antediluvian devices, and the sphynxes of Egypt[4] are
outstretched upon carpets of gold. Yet the effect is incongruous to the
timid alone. Proprieties of place, and especially of time, are the bug-
bears which terrify mankind from the contemplation of the magnifi-
cent. Once I was myself a decorist: but that sublimation of folly has
palled upon my soul. All this is now the fitter for my purpose. Like
these arabesque censers, my spirit is writhing in fire, and the delirium
of this scene is fashioning me for the wilder visions of that land of real
dreams whither I am now rapidly departing." He here paused abruptly,
bent his head to his bosom, and seemed to listen to a sound which I
could not hear.[5] At length, erecting his frame, he looked upwards and
ejaculated the lines of the Bishop of Chichester:—

1. George Chapman (1559?–1634), *The Tragedie of Busye D'Amboise* (1607). The courtier
 Bussy is attacked for his affair with a count's wife; mortally wounded, he uses his sword as a
 support so that he can die standing. Poe has adapted the original quotation (V.iv.95–98).
2. A Rhine wine from Hesse in Germany. The Etruscans were the most highly developed civi-
 lization in Italy before the Romans, renowned, among other things, for governance, for in-
 troducing chariot racing, and for their work with gold and pottery. They were different from
 the indigenous peoples of Tuscany and constituted an elite class. Gradually evolving in the
 8th and 7th centuries B.C.E. their domination was established by 500 B.C.E.
3. A vessel filled to the brim. I.e., drink a generous toast.
4. Structures regarded as coming from a different kind of creative imagination—one that
 creates powerful grotesque beings; here also associated with gorgeously elaborated
 arabesque carpets. Ionia is perhaps the most ancient of Greek civilizations, dating from be-
 fore 1000 B.C.E. It occupied a narrow coastal region in the eastern Mediterranean (western
 Turkey). The Ionic order is a standard of classic simplicity; Ionic columns supporting the
 roofs of older temples are of slender proportion and mathematically calculated. The Byronic
 stranger's point is that this mix is incongruous only by conventional standards observing
 decorum, not to a dreaming visionary like himself.
5. The stranger is not only a visionary in art but also seems to the narrator to have another kind
 of visionary experience, as though having received an occult message.

Stay for me there! I will not fail
To meet thee in that hollow vale.

In the next instant, confessing the power of the wine, he threw himself at full length upon an ottoman.

A quick step was now heard upon the staircase, and a loud knock at the door rapidly succeeded. I was hastening to anticipate a second disturbance, when a page of Mentoni's household burst into the room, and faltered out, in a voice choking with emotion, the incoherent words, "My mistress!—my mistress!—poisoned!—poisoned! Oh beautiful—oh beautiful Aphrodite!"

Bewildered, I flew to the ottoman, and endeavored to arouse the sleeper to a sense of the startling intelligence. But his limbs were rigid—his lips were livid—his lately beaming eyes were riveted in *death*. I staggered back towards the table—my hand fell upon a cracked and blackened goblet—and a consciousness of the entire and terrible truth flashed suddenly over my soul.[6]

Some Passages in the Life of a Lion[1]

————All people went
Upon their ten toes in wild wonderment.
 Bishop Hall's Satires.[2]

I am—that is to say I *was*—a great man; but I am neither the author of Junius nor the man in the mask; for my name, I believe, is Robert Jones, and I was born somewhere in the city of Fum-Fudge.[3]

The first action of my life was the taking hold of my nose with both hands. My mother saw this and called me a genius:—my father wept for joy and presented me with a treatise on Nosology.[4] This I mastered before I was breeched.[5]

6. The goblet is made of Venetian glass, which according to tradition was chemically treated to test for poisons. When the narrator sees that the goblet is cracked and discolored, he realizes that the Byronic stranger and the marchesa have a lovers' assignation in death: a mutual suicide pact at an appointed hour.

1. First published in the *Southern Literary Messenger* (May 1835) as "Lionizing. A Tale." The text followed here is that of the *Broadway Journal* (March 15, 1845).

2. The epigraph is adapted from Bishop Hall's *Satires* (1597). Instead of "All people," the original reads "Genus and Species long since."

3. Possibly a reference to Thomas Moore's *The Fudge Family in Paris* (1818); here the word *fudge* indicates nonsense. Junius is the pseudonym for the author(s) of a series of celebrated political letters, published in a London periodical from 1769 to 1772. "Man in the mask": a reference to a mysterious prisoner incarcerated in the Bastille for some thirty-four years by Louis XIV (1638–1715), supposedly for having revealed some intimate secret about the grand Sun King. The prisoner is said to have been treated with great deference until eventually put into a leather or iron mask. His actual identity is still the subject of scholarly debate, the most likely candidate being one Eustache D[aunger] de Cavoir (died 1703). Alexandre Dumas made him a central figure of tragedy in the last installment of his trilogy of popular romances about the musketeers (royal bodyguards), the "Man in the Iron Mask" section of *The Vicompte de Bragellone* (1848–50). In earlier versions, Poe's narrator is Thomas rather than Robert Jones.

4. The study of the classification of diseases (Greek: *nosos* = "disease"). The joke here is that it is treated as the study of noses—which involves a complex series of literary and sexual allusions, including popular British and American literary salons; the English and Scots magazine wars; the British writers Laurence Sterne (1713–1768), Lord Byron (1788–1824), Thomas Moore (1779–1852), Francis Jeffrey (1773–1850), Marguerite, countess of Blessington (1789–1849), and Edward Bulwer-Lytton (1803–1873); the American writer Nathaniel Parker Willis (1806–1867); and various philosophers, theologians, and intellectuals over the centuries.

5. Wearing grown-up pants; also a pun on being born.

I now began to feel my way in the science; and soon came to understand that, provided a man had a nose sufficiently conspicuous, he might, by merely following it, arrive at a Lionship.[6] But my attention was not confined to theories alone. Every morning I gave my proboscis a couple of pulls and swallowed a half dozen of drams.[7]

When I came of age my father asked me, one day, if I would step with him into his study.

"My son," said he, when we were seated, "what is the chief end of your existence?"[8]

"My father," I answered, "it is the study of Nosology."

"And what, Robert," he inquired, "is Nosology?"

"Sir," I said, "it is the Science of Noses."

"And can you tell me," he demanded, "what is the meaning of a nose?"

"A nose, my father," I replied, greatly softened, "has been variously defined by about a thousand different authors."[9] [Here I pulled out my watch.] "It is now noon or thereabouts—We shall have time enough to get through with them all before midnight. To commence then:—The nose, according to Bartholinus, is that protuberance—that bump— that excrescence—that—" —"Will do, Robert," interrupted the good old gentleman. "I am thunderstruck at the extent of your information—I am positively—upon my soul." [Here he closed his eyes and placed his hand upon his heart.] "Come here!" [Here he took me by the arm.] "Your education may now be considered as finished—it is high time you should scuffle for yourself—and you cannot do a better thing than merely follow your nose—so—so—so—" [Here he kicked me down stairs, and out of the door.]—"so get out of my house and God bless you!"

As I felt within me the divine *afflatus*,[1] I considered this accident rather fortunate than otherwise. I resolved to be guided by the paternal advice. I determined to follow my nose. I gave it a pull or two upon the spot, and wrote a pamphlet on Nosology forthwith.

6. Comic twisting of the words, *lion* and *lionize*. A social lion is someone given overblown celebrity status. To lionize suggests that adulatory admirers pursue the social lions so that they can bathe in a (reflected) social glory.

7. A dram is small unit of fluid, as in a dram of liqueur: also an apothecary's (druggist's) weight (60 grains). "Proboscis": the nose; in folk and literary tradition, a metaphor for the penis. The *Edinburgh Review* for June 1827 noted that "every man has his own *style* . . . like his own *nose*" and facetiously noted the association of the male member with the nose in the Slawkenbergius episodes (books III–IV) of Laurence Sterne's *Tristram Shandy* (1760–67).

8. Discreet pun on *end* by altered allusion to the Westminster Catechism: "What is the chief end of man?"

9. In the first version of the tale, some are specifically named: "Pliny, Aristotle, Alexander Ross, Minutius Felix, Hermanus Pictorius, Del Rio, Villarêt, Bartholinus, and Sir Thomas Browne." Some names are distorted versions of real persons. Mabbott notes that these people did in fact all have something to say about the human nose—so that part of the satire is that the sham erudition has a solid base to it.

1. Divine inspiration as the creative imagination. The word comes from the Latin: *afflare* = "to breathe on"; *flare* = "to blow." The word *spirit* comes from the Latin *spiritus* = "wind, air, or breath." To be inspired means to be "inspirited," to have the "ethereal" presence of the divine within oneself. Aristotle posited the idea that nature abhors a vacuum; there must be an insensible, impalpable something even out in the space between the planets and the stars. Thus we have the *ether*, an infinitely thin gaseous element. Medically, *afflatus* means gas, i.e., flatulence. Poe's joke is that Jones's creative inspiration is intestinal gas, the smell of which he follows with his nose. Cf. "Loss of Breath" (pp. 89ff. herein).

All Fum-Fudge was in an uproar.

"Wonderful genius!" said the Quarterly.

"Superb physiologist!" said the Westminster.

"Clever fellow!" said the Foreign.

"Fine writer!" said the Edinburgh.

"Profound thinker!" said the Dublin.

"Great man!" said Bentley.

"Divine soul!" said Fraser.

"One of us!" said Blackwood.[2]

"Who can he be?" said Mrs. Bas-Bleu.[3]

"What can he be?" said big Miss Bas-Bleu.

"Where can he be?" said little Miss Bas-Bleu.—But I paid these people no attention whatever—I just stepped into the shop of an artist.

The Duchess of Bless-my-soul[4] was sitting for her portrait; the Marquis of So-and-So was holding the Duchess' poodle; the Earl of This-and-That was flirting with her salts; and his Royal Highness of Touch-me-Not was leaning upon the back of her chair.[5]

I approached the artist and turned up my nose.

"Oh, beautiful!" sighed her Grace.

"Oh my!" lisped the Marquis.

"Oh shocking!" groaned the Earl.

"Oh abominable!" growled his Royal Highness.

"What will you take for it?" asked the artist.

"For his *nose!*" shouted her Grace.

"A thousand pounds," said I, sitting down.

"A thousand pounds?" inquired the artist, musingly.

"A thousand pounds," said I.

"Do you warrant it?" he asked, turning the nose to the light.

"I do," said I, blowing it well.

"Is it *quite* original?" inquired he, touching it with reverence.

"Humph!" said I, twisting it to one side.

2. The British journals named (in short title) are all real ones.

3. A bluestocking, i.e., a person regarded as pedantic and excessively artsy, suggesting literary and artistic affectation and snobbery. The name comes from a predominately female intellectual and social club of 18th-century London; it was given the name The Blue Stocking Society in derision, with reference to the blue worsted stockings worn by some of its members.

4. A reference to the countess of Blessington, famous for her artistic salons and sexual escapades, such as her liaison with her stepdaughter's husband, the count d'Orsay, with whom she established a celebrated salon in Kensington. Lady Blessington wrote several novels, but her best remembered work is *Conversations with Lord Byron* (1834), who was also famous for sexual exploits.

5. The list of guests with comic names suggests a satiric hit at Nathaniel Parker Willis (1806–1867), a contemporary American magazine editor and writer. Poe had contempt for Willis and satirized him on more than one occasion, notably as the pretentious dandy in "The Duke de L'Omelette" (1832). In his magazine, the New York *Mirror*, Willis described his own lionization at Almack's, where Lady Blessington held some of her salons, and presented himself as one of the Almack inner circle. Willis painted this picture again in *Pencillings by the Way Side* (1835), a collection of sketches, somewhat breathlessly listing Lady Blessington's distinguished guests. A similar picture is found in *Pelham* (1828), by Edward Bulwer-Lytton, who was also a member of Lady Blessington's Almack circle. In chapter 33, Lord Russelton (a representation of the ultimate of dandies, Beau Brummel) observes that the secret to being courted by society was to be scornful and arrogant (to turn up one's nose). In chapter 45, young Pelham, in a conversation about Almack's, is initiated "into the newest scandal and satire" and favored with a "list" of the notable guests.

"Has *no* copy been taken?" he demanded, surveying it through a microscope.

"None," said I, turning it up.

"*Admirable!*" he ejaculated, thrown quite off his guard by the beauty of the manœuvre.

"A thousand pounds,"[6] said I.

"A *thousand* pounds?" said he.

"Precisely," said I.

"A thousand *pounds?*" said he.

"Just so," said I.

"You shall have them," said he, "what a piece of *virtu!*"[7]—So he drew me a check upon the spot, and took a sketch of my nose. I engaged rooms in Jermyn street, and sent her Majesty the ninety-ninth edition of the "Nosology" with a portrait of the proboscis. That sad little rake, the Prince of Wales, invited me to dinner.[8]

We were all lions and *recherchés*.[9]

There was a modern Platonist. He quoted Porphyry, Iamblicus, Plotinus, Proclus, Hierocles, Maximus Tyrius, and Syrianus.[1]

There was a human-perfectibility man. He quoted Turgot, Price, Priestly, Condorcet, De Stael, and the "Ambitious Student in Ill Health."[2]

There was Sir Positive Paradox. He observed that all fools were philosophers, and that all philosophers were fools.

There was Æstheticus Ethix. He spoke of fire, unity, and atoms; bipart and pre-existent soul; affinity and discord; primitive intelligence and homeomeria.[3]

There was Theologos Theology. He talked of Eusebius and Arianus; heresy and the Council of Nice; Puseyism and consubstantialism; Homousios and Homouioisios.[4]

6. The repetitions of "a thousand pounds" probably allude to Thomas Moore's demand that the publishing house of Longmans make him an advance of 3000 guineas for his poem *Lallah Rookh* (1817), sight unseen—a record sum.

7. Artistic taste.

8. "His majesty" in the first version was changed to "her majesty" after Victoria ascended the throne in 1837 (the reference to the Prince of Wales was added as well). Jermyn Street was a fashionable district of London, with many clubs.

9. Unusual in some way; the avant-garde; or the odd and eccentric. Of the guests who are listed in the following paragraphs, some suggest caricatures of Poe's contemporaries like Bulwer-Lytton and Willis, and others are generalized burlesques of erudite pretenders—the philosophe, the idealist, the skeptic, the transcendentalist, the Western theologian, the gourmet, the wine connoisseur, the art connoisseur, the academic scholar-administrator, the foreign traveler, the Muslim theologian, the multilingual classicist, the geologist-mineralist. Note the resemblance to the members of the Folio Club (see pp. 595ff. herein). Except for the comic names of the twelve guests, the allusions are to real people, places, things, and ideas.

1. All philosophers who flourished from about 150 B.C.E. to 485 C.E. Mabbot identified the specific list as from a passage in Benjamin Disraeli's *Vivian Grey*, book I, chapter 6, a book Poe was fond of lampooning. See notes to "Loss of Breath" (pp. 89ff. herein).

2. By Bulwer-Lytton. Poe repeats most of the list of such believers in perfectibility in other of his works, such as "The Domain of Arnheim." Bulwer's views were being circulated in a series of "Conversations" in the London *New Monthly* in 1831–32.

3. The idea that the whole and its individual elements or parts are one and reflect one another in their elementary composition.

4. Of *same* essence and of *like* essence. "Theologos Theology": a reference to those debating the nature of God, specifically the relation of the beings of the Trinity (God, Father, Holy Spirit). "Puseyism": derogatory reference to the Oxford Movement, which was an attempt by John Keble (1792–1856), John Henry Newman (1801–1890), Edward Bouverie Pusey (1800–1882), and others to reinspire the Church of England with higher standards of worship and belief and to promote a return to high church ceremony. In the 1830s and 1840s,

There was Fricassée from the Rocher de Cancale. He mentioned Muriton of red tongue; cauliflowers with *velouté* sauce; veal *à la* St. Menehoult; marinade *à la* St. Florentin; and orange jellies *enmosäiques*.[5]

There was Bibulus O'Bumper. He touched upon Latour and Markbrünen; upon Mousseux and Chambertin; upon Richbourg and St. George; upon Haubrion, Leonville, and Medoc; upon Barac and Preignac; upon Grave, and upon St. Peray. He shook his head at Clos de Vougeot, and told, with his eyes shut, the difference between Sherry and Amontillado.

There was Signor Tintontintino from Florence. He discoursed of Cimbabué, Arpino, Carpaccio, and Argostino—of the gloom of Caravaggio, of the amenity of Albano, of the colors of Titian, of the frows of Rubens, and of the waggeries of Jan Steen.

There was the President of the Fum-Fudge University. He was of opinion that the moon was called Bendis in Thrace, Bubastis in Egypt, Dian in Rome, and Artemis in Greece.

There was a grand Turk from Stamboul. He could not help thinking that the angels were horses, cocks and bulls; that somebody in the sixth heaven had seventy thousand heads; and that the earth was supported by a sky-blue cow with an incalculable number of green horns.

There was Delphinus Polyglott. He told us what had become of the eighty-three lost tragedies of Æschylus; of the fifty-four orations of Isœus; of the three hundred and ninety-one speeches of Lysias; of the hundred and eighty treatises of Theophrastus; of the eighth book of the Conic Sections of Apollonius; of Pindar's hymns and dithyrambics; and of the five and forty tragedies of Homer Junior.

There was Ferdinand Fitz-Fossillus Feltspar. He informed us all about internal fires and tertiary formations; about äeriforms, fluidiforms, and solidiforms; about quartz and marl; about schist and schorl; about gypsum and trap; about talc and calc; about blende and horn-blende; about mica-slate and pudding-stone; about cyanite and lepidolite; about hœmatite and tremolite; about antimony and calcedony; about manganese and whatever you please.

There was myself. I spoke of myself;—of myself, of myself, of myself;—of Nosology, of my pamphlet, and of myself. I turned up my nose and spoke of myself.

"Marvellous clever man!" said the Prince.

"Superb!" said his guests; and next morning her Grace of Bless-my-soul paid me a visit.

"Will you go to Almacks, pretty creature?" she said, tapping me under the chin.

Pusey published several "tracts for the times" in which he advocated the doctrine of "Real Presence," i.e., the idea that the Eucharist is actual and not symbolic. Transubstantiation is the belief that the bread and blood of the communion ritual is in fact mystically transformed into the body and blood of Christ; it differs from "consubstantiation," in which the bread and wine are taken to be merely symbolic of the crucifixion of Jesus and the hope of resurrection for believers.

5. The various delicacies, along with the wines, may suggest more hits at Willis, who wrote a precious magazine column in which he represented himself as a man of exquisite taste. The text progresses from consubstantiation to food (in this paragraph) and to wine in the next.

"Upon honor," said I.

"Nose and all?" she asked.

"As I live," I replied.

"Here then is a card, my life, shall I say you *will* be there?"

"Dear Duchess, with all my heart."

"Pshaw, no!—but with all your nose?"

"Every bit of it my love," said I:—so I gave it a twist or two and found myself at Almacks.

The rooms were crowded to suffocation.

"He is coming!" said somebody on the staircase.

"He is coming!" said somebody farther up.

"He is coming!" said somebody farther still.

"He is come!" exclaimed the Duchess—"he is come, the little love!"—and seizing me firmly by both hands, she kissed me thrice upon the nose.

A marked sensation immediately ensued.

"*Diavolo!*" cried Count Capricornutti.

"*Mille tonnerres!*" ejaculated the Prince de Grenouille.

"*Tousand teufel!*"[6] growled the Elector of Bluddennuff.

This was not to be borne. I grew angry. I turned short upon Bluddennuff.

"Sir," said I, "you are a baboon."

"Sir," he replied, after a pause. "*Donner und Blitzen.*"[7]

This was all that could be desired. We exchanged cards. At Chalk-Farm,[8] the next morning, I shot off his nose—and then called upon my friends.

"*Béte!*" said the first.

"Fool!" said the second.

"Dolt!" said the third.

"Ass!" said the fourth.

"Ninny!" said the fifth.

"Noodle!" said the sixth.

"Be off!" said the seventh.

At all this I felt mortified, and so called upon my father.

"Father," I said, "what is the chief end of my existence?"

"My son," he replied, "it is still the study of Nosology; but in shooting off the Elector's nose you have overshot your mark. You have a fine nose, it is true; but then Bluddeanuff has none. You are damned, and he has become the hero of the day. I grant you that in Fum-Fudge the greatness of a lion is in proportion to the size of his proboscis—but, Good Heavens! there is no competing with a lion who has no proboscis at all."

6. Devil! Thousand thunders! Thousand devils!

7. Thunder and lightning!

8. The place where an absurd duel between Thomas Moore and Francis Jeffrey took place in 1806. Because of incompetent seconds and such things as a missing pistol ball, the incident became a stock anecdote of the time. Jeffrey was a founder and editor of the *Edinburgh Review*, which had criticized one of Byron's earliest works, *Hours of Idleness* (1806–07), prompting Byron's satiric reply in "English Bards and Scotch Reviewers" (1809), which lampoons Jeffrey and Moore among others.

Shadow—A Parable[1]

Yea! though I walk through the valley of the *Shadow:*
—*Psalm of David.*[2]

Ye who read are still among the living; but I who write shall have long since gone my way into the region of shadows. For indeed strange things shall happen, and secret things be known, and many centuries shall pass away, ere these memorials be seen of men. And, when seen, there will be some to disbelieve, and some to doubt, and yet a few who will find much to ponder upon in the characters here graven with a stylus of iron.

The year had been a year of terror, and of feelings more intense than terror for which there is no name upon the earth. For many prodigies and signs had taken place, and far and wide, over sea and land, the black wings of the Pestilence were spread abroad. To those, nevertheless, cunning in the stars, it was not unknown that the heavens wore an aspect of ill; and to me, the Greek Oinos,[3] among others, it was evident that now had arrived the alternation of that seven hundred and ninety-fourth year when, at the entrance of Aries, the planet Jupiter is conjoined with the red ring of the terrible Saturnus.[4] The peculiar spirit of the skies, if I mistake not greatly, made itself manifest, not only in the physical orb of the earth, but in the souls, imaginations, and meditations of mankind.

Over some flasks of the red Chian wine, within the walls of a noble hall, in a dim city called Ptolemais,[5] we sat, at night, a company of

1. First published in the *Southern Literary Messenger* (September 1835) as "Shadow / A Fable." The text reprinted here is that of the *Broadway Journal* (May 31, 1845). Mabbott calls the "historical setting" of this portentous piece "surprisingly correct." The "action takes place in the twilight of the Greco-Roman civilization in Egypt, where even older cultures had flourished and were no more." Mabbott also suggests that the "Pestilence" in the story may be the plague that "first appeared at the port of Pelusium in the Nile Delta during the reign of Justinian, A.D., 542." Scholars have identified two works as important sources for or influences on the tale: Thomas Moore's romantic novel *The Epicurean* (1827) and Jacob Bryant's capriciously fanciful work of "scholarship" *A New System . . . of Antient Mythology* (3rd ed., 1807).
2. The lines from Psalm 23 in the King James translation of the Bible read: "Yea, though I walk through the valley of the shadow of death, I will fear no evil: for thou art with me."
3. A Greek word with two meanings: "one" and "wine." Levine observes that Jacob Bryant (whom Poe paraphrases and even quotes without attribution) free-associates a Greek Oinas (spelled with an *a*) with Ion, Ionah (Jonah), and Noah. He thereby identifies the dove of the Ark with Oinas as the divine messenger or interpreter of the will of the gods. Bryant further identifies Oinas with Eanus as Janus, the two-faced god, guardian of gates and doors, who looks both backward (where you have been: the past) and forward (where you are going: the future).
4. The astrological conjunction of Jupiter and Saturn in the sign of the Ram predicts violent change. Mabbott points out that its occurrence there once in 794 years is mentioned in Bielfeld, Poe's favorite encyclopedia. Aries (Greek god of war) is the planet Mars. Levine points out that Mars and Saturn signal the end of one time period and the beginning of another and that in religious rites celebrating the end of winter and the beginning of spring Saturn was associated with Dionysus (forest god of death, rebirth, and fertility). They suggest that the rites of spring symbolize the continuity (oneness) of life and death, that ritual sacrifices involved ceremonial wine, and that an alternative name for Dionysus was Oinos (Woinos).
5. In honor of the Macedonian dynasty of ancient Egypt several cities were named after the Ptolemies. Poe probably has reference either to the Hellenistic metropolis in upper Egypt at the Nile north of Abydos or to the small town of Ptolemais Theron on the Red Sea, where,

seven. And to our chamber there was no entrance save by a lofty door of brass: and the door was fashioned by the artizan Corinnos,[6] and, being of rare workmanship, was fastened from within. Black draperies, likewise, in the gloomy room, shut out from our view the moon, the lurid stars, and the peopleless streets—but the boding and the memory of Evil, they would not be so excluded. There were things around us and about of which I can render no distinct account—things material and spiritual—heaviness in the atmosphere—a sense of suffocation—anxiety—and, above all, that terrible state of existence which the nervous experience when the senses are keenly living and awake, and meanwhile the powers of thought lie dormant. A dead weight hung upon us. It hung upon our limbs—upon the household furniture—upon the goblets from which we drank; and all things were depressed, and borne down thereby—all things save only the flames of the seven iron lamps[7] which illumined our revel. Uprearing themselves in tall slender lines of light, they thus remained burning all pallid and motionless; and in the mirror which their lustre formed upon the round table of ebony at which we sat, each of us there assembled beheld the pallor of his own countenance, and the unquiet glare in the downcast eyes of his companions. Yet we laughed and were merry in our proper way—which was hysterical; and sang the songs of Anacreon[8]—which are madness; and drank deeply—although the purple wine reminded us of blood. For there was yet another tenant of our chamber in the person of young Zoilus.[9] Dead, and at full length he lay, enshrouded;—the genius and the demon of the scene. Alas! he bore no portion in our mirth, save that his countenance, distorted with the plague, and his eyes in which Death had but half extinguished the fire of the pestilence, seemed to take such interest in our merriment as the dead may haply take in the merriment of those who are to die. But although I, Oinos, felt that the eyes of the departed were upon me, still I forced myself not to perceive the bitterness of their expression, and, gazing down steadily into the depths of the ebony mirror, sang with a loud and sonorous voice the songs of the son of Teios.[1] But gradually my songs they ceased, and their echoes, rolling afar off among the sable draperies of the chamber, became weak, and

Mabbott observes, "the Sun casts no shadow at noon during the summer solstice" (Pliny, *Natural History*, II.lxxv, VI.xxxiii). Chios is the capital city of the island of Chios (Khios), which lies just west of Asia Minor in the Aegean sea. Wine from Chios is mentioned in both Jacob Bryant's *Mythology* and the *Natural History* (book XIV) of Pliny the Elder (c. 23–79 C.E.). In some traditions, Chios is the birthplace of Homer.

6. Some scholars suggest that this is a made-up name, probably to suggest an artisan from Corinth, a city famed for its brass objets d'art inlaid with gold and silver. Mabbott suggests it is the name of a legendary poet who lived at the time of the Trojan War.

7. Cf. "The Masque of the Red Death" (pp. 299ff. herein) another story of pestilence. Milton mentions seven lamps of the zodiac representing the heavenly fires (*Paradise Lost*, XII. 255ff.).

8. Greek poet (c. 563–c. 478 B.C.E.) whose verses celebrate love and wine. The Irish writer Thomas Moore (1779–1852), whom Poe lampoons on several occasions (see, e.g., "The Assignation" pp. 116ff. herein) was nicknamed Anacreon Moore. Cf. Poe's poem "Introduction" (p. 42 herein).

9. Although the name suggests someone who is overly critical (after a 4th-century B.C.E. writer notorious for his criticism of the revered writings of Homer), Levine suggests that Poe got the name from Jacob Bryant, who wrote that one "Coilus" was a sacred or heavenly person.

1. Anacreon was born at Teos in Ionia (region on the Aegean coast of present-day Turkey).

undistinguishable, and so faded away. And lo! from among those sable draperies where the sounds of the song departed, there came forth a dark and undefined shadow—a shadow such as the moon, when low in heaven, might fashion from the figure of a man: but it was the shadow neither of man, nor of God, nor of any familiar thing. And, quivering awhile among the draperies of the room, it at length rested in full view upon the surface of the door of brass. But the shadow was vague, and formless, and indefinite, and was the shadow neither of man nor of God—neither God of Greece, nor God of Chaldæa,[2] nor any Egyptian God. And the shadow rested upon the brazen doorway, and under the arch of the entablature of the door, and moved not, nor spoke any word, but there became stationary and remained. And the door whereupon the shadow rested was, if I remember aright, over against the feet of the young Zoilus enshrouded. But we, the seven there assembled, having seen the shadow as it came out from among the draperies, dared not steadily behold it, but cast down our eyes, and gazed continually into the depths of the mirror of ebony. And at length I, Oinos, speaking some low words, demanded of the shadow its dwelling and its appellation. And the shadow answered, "I am SHADOW, and my dwelling is near to the Catacombs of Ptolemais, and hard by those dim plains of Helusion which border upon the foul Charonian canal."[3] And then did we, the seven, start from our seats in horror, and stand trembling, and shuddering, and aghast: for the tones in the voice of the shadow were not the tones of any one being, but of a multitude of beings, and, varying in their cadences from syllable to syllable, fell duskily upon our ears in the well remembered and famil-iar accents of many thousand departed friends.

Silence.—A Fable First published in the *Baltimore Book*, a gift an-nual for 1838, as "Siope. A Fable," with the further subtitle "In the man-ner of the Psychological Autobiographists." The text reprinted here is that of the *Broadway Journal* (September 6, 1845). Siope is a town near Chal-cedon, an ancient Greek city of Asia Minor on the Bosporus, founded by the inhabitants of the city of Megara opposite Byzantium in 685 B.C.E.

2. Strictly, of the southernmost part of the valley of the Tigris and Euphrates Rivers; more gen-erally, of Babylonia and all of southern Mesopotamia. Chaldean civilization dates from be-fore 1000 B.C.E. but is associated principally with the 7th-century B.C.E. reign of Nebuchadnezzar II and with the 6th-century B.C.E. invasion of Cyrus the Great, who sacked Babylon in 539 B.C.E. (see notes to "Loss of Breath," pp. 89ff. herein) The Chaldeans devel-oped the theory of astrology (a method of occult divination by means of reckoning the posi-tions of the stars) in the 7th and 6th centuries B.C.E., and the word *Chaldee* came to be a synonym for *astrologer*.
3. "Helusian" is a variant spelling of Elysian (Elysium), which usually refers to the Greek no-tion of the Happy Isles, the resting place for the departed souls of heroes (Elysian Fields) or to the Roman notion of a comfortable place in the underworld for the souls of the righteous. The word can also indicate one of two vast plains in Egypt or Libya famous for shrines to Amon Ra, the chief Egyptian god (derived from Amon, the chief god of Thebes, and later as-sociated with the Greek Zeus and Roman Jupiter). Levine notes that Jacob Bryant writes that the "Elysian plain, near the Catacombs in Egypt, stood upon the foul Charonian canal" (*Mythology*, I.34). Charon in classical myth is the ferryman who carries the dead across the river Styx to Hades. "Catacombs": underground chambers for burial of the dead (cf. notes to "Loss of Breath," pp. 89ff).

The city is better known as the site of the Council of Chalcedon in 451 C.E., when theologians agreed on a definition of the person of Jesus Christ (two distinct natures, one human, one divine). Poe may have had in mind the hermit saint of Siope, Auxintius (died 470 C.E.), who was said to live without eating. By "psychological autobiographists" Poe seems to have meant currently popular writers like Edward Bulwer-Lytton (1803–1873) and Thomas De Quincey (1785–1859) and maybe Benjamin Disraeli (1804–1881) and James Hogg (1770–1835), whose narrators often wrote of their mental stress in a portentous, evocative, prophetic, and elliptical style. The work of Bulwer's most like "Silence" is "Monos and Daimonos," published in the London *New Monthly* (May 1830). In the first publication of "Silence" as "Siope," there was a reference to the "dreams of the daughters of Delos," which Poe seems to have picked up from Bulwer's "A Manuscript Found in a Madhouse" (see notes to "Ligeia," pp. 159ff.). Levine argues that Poe also made use of ideas, scenes, and phrases from Jacob Bryant's *A New System of . . . Antient Mythology*, 3rd ed. (1807); see notes to "Shadow" (pp. 134–37). "Siope" was part of the manuscript fragment for the *Folio Club Tales* (see introduction on pp. xxv–xxvi) and thus seems to have been written by 1833.

Silence.—A Fable

Ἐνδουσιν δ' ορεων κορυφαι τε καὶ φάραγγες
Πρώονές τε καὶ Χαράδραι.

ALCMAN.

The mountain pinnacles slumber; valleys, crags and caves *are silent.*[1]

"Listen to *me*," said the Demon,[2] as he placed his hand upon my head. "The region of which I speak is a dreary region in Libya, by the borders of the river Zäire.[3] And there is no quiet there, nor silence.

"The waters of the river have a saffron and sickly hue; and they flow not onwards to the sea, but palpitate forever and forever beneath the red eye of the sun with a tumultous and convulsive motion. For many miles on either side of the river's oozy bed is a pale desert of gigantic water-lilies. They sigh one unto the other in that solitude, and stretch

1. The motto is from the Greek poet Alcman (flourished mid-7th century B.C.E.), whose works exist only in fragments quoted and commented on by other later writers like Apollonius (1st century B.C.E.) in his *Homeric Lexicon*. The Greek in the *Broadway Journal* has several typographical errors; the version here follows the text as corrected in Mabbott. The English under the Greek is Poe's loose translation. Levine points out that an English version of the Greek fragment by the Scottish Romantic poet Thomas Campbell (1777–1854), glosses Poe's tale:

> The mountain summits sleep: glens, cliffs, and caves
> Are silent—all the earth's reptile brood—
> The bees—the wild beasts of the mountain wood:
> In depths beneath the dark red ocean's waves
> Its monsters rest, whilst wrapped in bower and spray
> Each bird is hush'd that stretch'd its pinions to the day.

For the *Baltimore Book* publication, the motto was composed of two lines from Poe's "Al Aaraaf" (1829): "Ours is a world of words: Quiet we call / *Silence*—which is the merest word of all."
2. Jacob Bryant wrote in his *Mythology* that ancient religions consisted of the worship of dead souls (demons or daemons), who are the "guardians of mankind."
3. Portuguese name for the Congo. Libya was the name the Greeks used for all Africa.

towards the heaven their long and ghastly necks, and nod to and fro their everlasting heads. And there is an indistinct murmur which cometh out from among them like the rushing of subterrene water. And they sigh one unto the other.

"But there is a boundary to their realm—the boundary of the dark, horrible, lofty forest. There, like the waves about the Hebrides,[4] the low underwood is agitated continually. But there is no wind throughout the heaven. And the tall primeval trees rock eternally hither and thither with a crashing and mighty sound. And from their high summits, one by one, drop everlasting dews. And at the roots strange poisonous flowers lie writhing in perturbed slumber. And overhead, with a rustling and loud noise, the gray clouds rush westwardly forever, until they roll, a cataract, over the fiery wall of the horizon. But there is no wind throughout the heaven. And by the shores of the river Zäire there is neither quiet nor silence.[5]

"It was night, and the rain fell; and, falling, it was rain, but, having fallen, it was blood. And I stood in the morass among the tall lilies, and the rain fell upon my head—and the lilies sighed one unto the other in the solemnity of their desolation.

"And, all at once, the moon arose through the thin ghastly mist, and was crimson in color. And mine eyes fell upon a huge gray rock which stood by the shore of the river, and was lighted by the light of the moon. And the rock was gray, and ghastly, and tall,—and the rock was gray. Upon its front were characters engraven in the stone; and I walked through the morass of water-lilies, until I came close unto the shore, that I might read the characters upon the stone. But I could not decypher them. And I was going back into the morass, when the moon shone with a fuller red, and I turned and looked again upon the rock, and upon the characters;—and the characters were DESOLATION.

"And I looked upwards, and there stood a man upon the summit of the rock; and I hid myself among the water-lilies that I might discover the actions of the man. And the man was tall and stately in form, and was wrapped up from his shoulders to his feet in the toga of old Rome. And the outlines of his figure were indistinct—but his features were the features of a deity; for the mantle of the night, and of the mist, and of the moon, and of the dew, had left uncovered the features of his face. And his brow was lofty with thought, and his eye wild with care; and, in the few furrows upon his cheek I read the fables of sorrow, and weariness, and disgust with mankind, and a longing after solitude.

"And the man sat upon the rock, and leaned his head upon his hand, and looked out upon the desolation. He looked down into the low unquiet shrubbery, and up into the tall primeval trees, and up higher at the rustling heaven, and into the crimson moon. And I lay close within shelter of the lilies, and observed the actions of the man. And the man trembled in the solitude;—but the night waned, and he sat upon the rock.

4. Also known as the Western Islands; some five hundred islands west and northwest of Scotland.
5. Cf. similar descriptions in Poe's poems "The Valley Nis" (1831) and "Out of Space—Out of Time" (1844–49) and in the *Narrative of Arthur Gordon Pym* (1838), chapters 2 and 25.

"And the man turned his attention from the heaven, and looked out upon the dreary river Zäire, and upon the yellow ghastly waters, and upon the pale legions of the water-lilies. And the man listened to the sighs of the water lilies, and to the murmur that came up from among them. And I lay close within my covert and observed the actions of the man. And the man trembled in the solitude;—but the night waned and he sat upon the rock.[6]

"Then I went down into the recesses of the morass, and waded afar in among the wilderness of the lilies, and called unto the hippopotami which dwelt among the fens in the recesses of the morass. And the hippopotami heard my call, and came, with the behemoth,[7] unto the foot of the rock, and roared loudly and fearfully beneath the moon. And I lay close within my covert and observed the actions of the man. And the man trembled in the solitude;—but the night waned and he sat upon the rock.

"Then I cursed the elements with the curse of tumult; and a frightful tempest gathered in the heaven where, before, there had been no wind. And the heaven became livid with the violence of the tempest— and the rain beat upon the head of the man—and the floods of the river came down—and the river was tormented into foam—and the waterlilies shrieked within their beds—and the forest crumbled before the wind—and the thunder rolled—and the lightning fell—and the rock rocked to its foundation. And I lay close within my covert and observed the actions of the man. And the man trembled in the solitude;—but the night waned and he sat upon the rock.

"Then I grew angry and cursed, with the curse of *silence*, the river, and the lilies, and the wind, and the forest, and the heaven, and the thunder, and the sighs of the water-lilies. And they became accursed, and *were still*. And the moon ceased to totter up its pathway to heaven—and the thunder died away—and the lightning did not flash—and the clouds hung motionless—and the waters sunk to their level and remained—and the trees ceased to rock—and the water-lilies sighed no more—and the murmur was heard no longer from among them, nor any shadow of sound throughout the vast illimitable desert. And I looked upon the characters of the rock, and they were changed;—and the characters were SILENCE.

"And mine eyes fell upon the countenance of the man, and his countenance was wan with terror. And, hurriedly, he raised his head from his hand, and stood forth upon the rock and listened. But there was no voice throughout the vast illimitable desert, and the characters upon the rock were SILENCE. And the man shuddered, and turned

6. In *Mythology*, Jacob Bryant writes a fanciful narrative about the tradition of worshiping on a high rocky place and hypothesizes the linguistic changes of the word *petra* from the name of a *sun god* to the word for *temple* (on a rock) to the word for *rock* itself.
7. The giant land beast sent by God as an instrument of destruction in Job 40:15–24; its companion is Leviathan, the gigantic sea-beast. By tradition Leviathan is the whale and Behemoth the hippopotamus, but Poe seems to have some other animal in mind. Jacob Bryant explains that "the crocodile and the hippopotamus were emblems of the Ark; because during the inundation of the Nile they rose with the waters." The Lotus (a water lily), he says, has the same significance, and he mentions that in other rites of ancient Egypt there is "a person preserved in the midst of waters" (Levine, p. 111).

his face away, and fled afar off, in haste, so that I beheld him no more."

Now there are fine tales in the volumes of the Magi[8]—in the iron-bound, melancholy volumes of the Magi. Therein, I say, are glorious histories of the Heaven, and of the Earth, and of the mighty sea—and of the Genii[9] that over-ruled the sea, and the earth, and the lofty heaven. There was much lore too in the sayings which were said by the Sybils;[1] and holy, holy things were heard of old by the dim leaves that trembled around Dodona—but, as Allah liveth, that fable which the demon told me as he sat by my side in the shadow of the tomb,[2] I hold to be the most wonderful of all! And as the Demon made an end of his story, he fell back within the cavity of the tomb and laughed. And I could not laugh with the Demon, and he cursed me because I could not laugh. And the lynx[3] which dwelleth forever in the tomb, came out therefrom, and lay down at the feet of the Demon, and looked at him steadily in the face.

Berenice[1]

Dicebant mihi sodales, si sepulchrum amicæ visitarem, curas meas aliquantulum fore levatas.

—*Ebn Zaiot.*[2]

Misery is manifold. The wretchedness of earth is multiform. Over-reaching the wide horizon as the rainbow,[3] its hues are as various as

8. Persian priests famed for magic.
9. Middle Eastern spirits, some benign, some malign; also spelled Jinns or Djinns.
1. Greek or Roman prophetesses.
2. The phrasing is similar to that of Jacob Bryant's *Mythology*. Dodona is the site of the grove of Zeus in Epirus, about fifty miles east of Corcyra, on the Ionian Sea, west of Macedonia (present-day northwest Greece and southern Albania), and was also sacred to Dione. It is the oldest oracle in the ancient Greek religion; according to legend, a black dove from Egyptian Thebes settled on the branches of an old oak tree, investing it with prophetic powers. When the wind blew, the priests of Zeus interpreted the rustling and rattling of leaves and the clanging of brass containers tied to the tree's branches as messages from the god. (They also divined from the cooings of doves in the tree.) "Allah": the Arabic name of God. It predated Islam in polytheistic Arabia, but when the prophet Mohammed introduced monotheism, Allah became the name of the one and only God.
3. Sacred to Apollo and thus a symbol of prophecy, but also a symbol for sharp-eyedness and cunning.
1. First published in the *Southern Literary Messenger* (March 1835). The text reproduced here is that of the *Broadway Journal* (April 5, 1845), which lacks a gruesome passage found in earlier printings (see p. 146, n. 8 herein). After hearing of complaints from readers of the *Messenger*, Poe wrote to T. W. White, the magazine's owner, that the "subject is far too horrible" but that the tale "originated in a bet that I could produce nothing effective on a subject so singular, provided I treated it seriously." He apologized for approaching "the very verge of bad-taste" and promised not to "sin quite so egregiously again." Scholars have found sources for the incident that is the basis of the tale, in particular an account of robbing graves for dentists in the Baltimore *Saturday Visiter* (February 23, 1833).
2. In an early printing, Poe translates the motto as "My companions told me I might find some little alleviation of my misery, in visiting the grave of my beloved." Ben Zaïat was the pen name of Abou Giafar Mohammed ben Abdalmalek ben Abban of Baghdad (died c. 218 C.E.); among other things he wrote a poem about the loss of a beloved slave girl. The only known version of the sentence in question is in French, not Latin.
3. The symbol of hope and of God's covenant with Noah not to destroy the world by water again.

the hues of that arch,—as distinct too, yet as intimately blended. Overreaching the wide horizon as the rainbow! How is it that from beauty I have derived a type of unloveliness?—from the covenant of peace a simile of sorrow? But as, in ethics, evil is a consequence of good, so, in fact, out of joy is sorrow born. Either the memory of past bliss is the anguish of to-day, or the agonies which *are* have their origin in the ecstasies which *might have been.*

My baptismal name is Egæus;[4] that of my family I will not mention. Yet there are no towers in the land more time-honored than my gloomy, gray, hereditary hails. Our line has been called a race of visionaries; and in many striking particulars—in the character of the family mansion—in the frescos of the chief saloon—in the tapestries of the dormitories—in the chiselling of some butresses in the armory—but more especially in the gallery of antique paintings—in the fashion of the library chamber—and, lastly, in the very peculiar nature of the library's contents, there is more than sufficient evidence to warrant the belief.

The recollection of my earliest years are connected with that chamber, and with its volumes—of which latter I will say no more. Here died my mother. Herein was I born. But it is mere idleness to say that I had not lived before—that the soul has no previous existence. You deny it?—let us not argue the matter. Convinced myself, I seek not to convince. There is, however, a remembrance of aerial forms—of spiritual and meaning eyes—of sounds, musical yet sad—a remembrance which will not be excluded; a memory like a shadow, vague, variable, indefinite, unsteady; and like a shadow, too, in the impossibility of my getting rid of it while the sunlight of my reason shall exist.

In that chamber was I born. Thus awaking from the long night of what seemed, but was not, nonentity, at once into the very regions of fairy-land—into a palace of imagination—into the wild dominions of monastic thought and erudition—it is not singular that I gazed around me with a startled and ardent eye—that I loitered away my boyhood in books, and dissipated my youth in reverie; but it *is* singular that as years rolled away, and the noon of manhood found me still in the mansion of my fathers—it *is* wonderful what stagnation there fell upon the springs of my life—wonderful how total an inversion took place in the character of my commonest thought. The realities of the world affected me as visions, and as visions only, while the wild ideas of the land of dreams became, in turn,—not the material of my everyday existence—but in very deed that existence utterly and solely in itself.

Berenice and I were cousins, and we grew up together in my paternal halls. Yet differently we grew—I ill of health and buried in gloom—she agile, graceful, and overflowing with energy—hers the ramble on the hill-side—mine the studies of the cloister—I living within my own heart, and addicted body and soul to the most intense and painful

4. Mabbott suggests a source in, or a reference to, Hermia's father in Shakespeare's *A Midsummer Night's Dream* (1595), a man who "failed to understand love." The parallels seem rather thin, however, and Shakespeare's source might prove more to the point.

meditation—she roaming carelessly through life with no thought of the shadows in her path, or the silent flight of the raven winged hours. Berenice!—I call upon her name—Berenice!—and from the gray ruins of memory a thousand tumultuous recollections are startled at the sound! Ah! vividly is her image before me now, as in the early days of her light-heartedness and joy! Oh! gorgeous yet fantastic beauty! Oh! sylph amid the shrubberies of Arnheim![5]—Oh! Naiad among its fountains!—and then—then all is mystery and terror, and a tale which should not be told. Disense—a fatal disease—fell like the simoom[6] upon her frame, and, even while I gazed upon her, the spirit of change swept over her, pervading her mind, her habits, and her character, and, in a manner the most subtle and terrible, disturbing even the identity of her person! Alas! the destroyer came and went, and the victim—where was she? I knew her not—or knew her no longer as Berenice.

Among the numerous train of maladies superinduced by that fatal and primary one which effected a revolution of so horrible a kind in the moral and physical being of my cousin, may be mentioned as the most distressing and obstinate in its nature, a species of epilepsy[7] not unfrequently terminating in *trance* itself—trance very nearly resembling positive dissolution, and from which her manner of recovery was, in most instances, startlingly abrupt. In the mean time my own disease—for I have been told that I should call it by no other appellation—my own disease, then, grew rapidly upon me, and assumed finally a monomaniac character of a novel and extraordinary form—hourly and momently gaining vigor—and at length obtaining over me the most incomprehensible ascendancy. This monomania,[8] if I must so term it, consisted in a morbid irritability of those properties of the mind in metaphysical science termed the *attentive*. It is more than probable that I am not understood; but I fear, indeed, that it is in no manner possible to convey to the mind of the merely general reader, an adequate idea of that nervous *intensity of interest* with which, in my case, the powers of meditation (not to speak technically) busied and buried themselves, in the contemplation of even the most ordinary objects of the universe.

To muse for long unwearied hours with my attention riveted to some frivolous device[9] on the margin, or in the typography of a book; to become absorbed for the better part of a summer's day in a quaint shadow falling aslant upon the tapestry, or upon the floor; to lose myself for an entire night in watching the steady flame of a lamp, or the

5. See Poe's tale "The Domain of Arnheim" (1847). One theory is that the allusion is to a character in Sir Walter Scott's *Anne of Geierstein* (1829), chapters 11 and 21. But the parallels are not very strong.
6. Or simoon, a hot Araby wind, mythically deadly.
7. Strictly speaking, a nervous disorder characterized by recurrent malfunctioning of sensory and/or motor or mental processes. Poe seems to intend by it a general cessation of normal responses. Cf. the "catalepsy" of Madeline Usher (see notes to "The Fall of the House of Usher," pp. 199ff. herein); which is supposed to involve cessation of breathing and rigidity of flesh and body, thus leading to premature burial, a phobia of the times.
8. Pathological obsession with one idea; a fixed idea (*idée fixe*); associated with paranoia.
9. Printer's mark.

embers of a fire; to dream away whole days over the perfume of a flower; to repeat monotonously some common word, until the sound, by dint of frequent repetition, ceased to convey any idea whatever to the mind; to lose all sense of motion or physical existence, by means of absolute bodily quiescence long and obstinately persevered in;— such were a few of the most common and least pernicious vagaries[1] induced by a condition of the mental faculties, not, indeed, altogether unparalleled, but certainly bidding defiance to anything like analysis or explanation.

Yet let me not be misapprehended.—The undue, earnest, and morbid attention thus excited by objects in their own nature frivolous, must not be confounded in character with that ruminating propensity common to all mankind, and more especially indulged in by persons of ardent imagination. It was not even, as might be at first supposed, an extreme condition, or exaggeration of such propensity, but primarily and essentially distinct and different. In the one instance, the dreamer, or enthusiast, being interested by an object usually *not* frivolous, imperceptibly loses sight of this object in a wilderness of deductions and suggestions issuing therefrom, until, at the conclusion of a day dream *often replete with luxury*, he finds the *incitamentum* or first cause of his musings entirely vanished and forgotten. In my case the primary object was *invariably frivolous*, although assuming, through the medium of my distempered vision, a refracted and unreal importance. Few deductions, if any, were made; and those few pertinaciously returning in upon the original object as a centre. The meditations were *never* pleasurable; and, at the termination of the reverie, the first cause, so far from being out of sight, had attained that supernaturally exaggerated interest which was the prevailing feature of the disease. In a word, the powers of mind more particularly exercised were, with me, as I have said before, the *attentive*, and are, with the day-dreamer, the *speculative*.

My books, at this epoch, if they did not actually serve to irritate the disorder, partook, it will be perceived, largely, in their imaginative and inconsequential nature, of the characteristic qualities of the disorder itself. I well remember, among others, the treatise of the noble Italian Cœlius Secundus Curio "*de Amplitudine Beati Regni Dei:*" St. Austin's great work, the "City of God;" and Tertullian "*de Carne Christi,*" in which the paradoxical sentence "*Mortuus est Dei filius; credibile est quia ineptum est: et sepultus resurrexit; certum est quia impossible est*"[2] occupied my undivided time, for many weeks of laborious and fruitless investigation.

1. Wandering ideas: erratic; extravagant.
2. Tertullian (c. 165–220 C.E.) in *On the Flesh of Christ* (202–08) argued that the more logically absurd a thing seems, the more God values those who believe in it. Poe's quotation translates as: "The Son of God is dead, believable because absurd; and buried he is risen again, certain because impossible." Poe alludes to this passage more than once in his works. Ceolius Secundus Curio (1503–1569) argued in *De Amplitudine beati Regni Dei* (1550) that Heaven contains more souls than does Hell. Poe probably got the quotation from the "Hell" section of Isaac D'Israeli's *Curiosities of Literature*. St. Austin is Saint Augustine (354–430 C.E.), who, in *The City of God* (413–26), argued that the earthly city of Rome (humankind) will give way to the City of God on earth.

Thus it will appear that, shaken from its balance only by trivial things, my reason bore resemblance to that ocean-crag spoken of by Ptolemy Hephestion, which steadily resisting the attacks of human violence, and the fiercer fury of the waters and the winds, trembled only to the touch of the flower called Asphodel.[3] And although, to a careless thinker, it might appear a matter beyond doubt, that the alteration produced by her unhappy malady, in the *moral* condition of Berenice, would afford me many objects for the exercise of that intense and abnormal meditation whose nature I have been at some trouble in explaining, yet such was not in any degree the case. In the lucid intervals of my infirmity, her calamity, indeed, gave me pain, and, taking deeply to heart that total wreck of her fair and gentle life, I did not fail to ponder frequently and bitterly upon the wonder-working means by which so strange a revolution had been so suddenly brought to pass. But these reflections partook not of the idiosyncrasy of my disease, and where such as would have occurred, under similar circumstances, to the ordinary mass of mankind. True to its own character, my disorder revelled in the less important but more startling changes wrought in the *physical* frame of Berenice—in the singular and most appalling distortion of her personal identity.

During the brightest days of her unparalleled beauty, most surely I had never loved her. In the strange anomaly of my existence, feelings with me, *had never been* of the heart, and my passions *always were* of the mind. Through the gray of the early morning—among the trellised shadows of the forest at noon-day—and in the silence of my library at night, she had flitted by my eyes, and I had seen her—not as the living and breathing Berenice, but as the Berenice of a dream—not as a being of the earth, earthy, but as the abstraction of such a being—not as a thing to admire, but to analyze—not as an object of love, but as the theme of the most abstruse although desultory speculation. And *now*—now I shuddered in her presence, and grew pale at her approach: yet bitterly lamenting her fallen and desolate condition, I called to mind that she had loved me long, and, in an evil moment, I spoke to her of marriage.

And at length the period of our nuptials was approaching, when, upon an afternoon in the winter of the year,—one of those unseasonably warm, calm, and misty days which are the nurse of the beautiful Halcyon,[4]—I sat, (and sat, as I thought, alone,) in the inner apartment

3. A symbol of death; the meadows of Hades are supposed to be covered with them. Ptolemy Hephestion is Ptolemy or Ptolomaeus Chennos, the son of Hephestion. He is referred to by Jacob Bryant in his discussion of a rock (Petra Gigonia) that can be swayed by a blade of grass (in his *Mythology*; see notes to "Silence," pp. 136ff. herein).
4. For as Jove, during the winter season, gives twice seven days of warmth, men have called this clement and temperate time the nurse of the beautiful Halcyon.—Simonides [Poe's note]. Simonides of Ceos (c. 556–c. 469 B.C.E.) was a Greek poet, fragments of whose works are preserved in the writings of Aristotle. In myth, Halcyon is a bird (traditionally the kingfisher) that calmed the ocean and the wind to nest on the waters. "Twice seven days" here means the week before and the week after the winter solstice. Mabbott cites the *Natural History* of Pliny the Elder (c. 23–79 C.E.) for this event at the summer solstice. The English word *halcyon* means calm, peaceful, or "golden" in the sense of a benign or prosperous time. Poe is apparently creating an irony around the theme of horror out of beauty (see p. 140, paragraph 1 and n. 3, and p. 141 herein) by having a horrible event take place on a beautiful day.

of the library. But uplifting my eyes I saw that Berenice stood before me.

Was it my own excited imagination—or the misty influence of the atmosphere—or the uncertain twilight of the chamber—or the gray draperies which fell around her figure—that caused in it so vacillating and indistinct an outline? I could not tell. She spoke no word, and I— not for worlds could I have uttered a syllable. An icy chill ran through my frame; a sense of insufferable anxiety oppressed me; a consuming curiosity pervaded my soul; and sinking back upon the chair, I remained for some time breathless and motionless, with my eyes riveted upon her person. Alas! its emaciation was excessive, and not one vestige of the former being, lurked in any single line of the contour. My burning glances at length fell upon the face.

The forehead was high, and very pale, and singularly placid; and the once jetty hair fell partially over it, and overshadowed the hollow temples with innumerable ringlets now of a vivid yellow, and jarring discordantly, in their fantastic character, with the reigning melancholy of the countenance. The eyes were lifeless, and lustreless, and seemingly pupil-less, and I shrank involuntarily from their glassy stare to the contemplation of the thin and shrunken lips. They parted; and in a smile of peculiar meaning, *the teeth* of the changed Berenice disclosed themselves slowly to my view. Would to God that I had never beheld them, or that, having done so, I had died!

The shutting of a door disturbed me, and, looking up, I found that my cousin had departed from the chamber. But from the disordered chamber of my brain, had not, alas! departed, and would not be driven away, the white and ghastly *spectrum*[5] of the teeth. Not a speck on their surface—not a shade on their enamel—not an indenture in their edges—but what that brief period of her smile had sufficed to brand in upon my memory. I saw them *now* even more unequivocally than I beheld them *then*. The teeth!—the teeth!—they were here, and there, and every where, and visibly and palpably before me; long, narrow, and excessively white, with the pale lips writhing about them, as in the very moment of their first terrible development. Then came the full fury of my *monomania*, and I struggled in vain against its strange and irresistible influence. In the multiplied objects of the external world I had no thoughts but for the teeth. For these I longed with a phrenzied desire. All other matters and all different interests became absorbed in their single contemplation. They—they alone were present to the mental eye, and they, in their sole individuality, became the essence of my mental life. I held them in every light. I turned them in every attitude. I surveyed their characteristics. I dwelt upon their peculiarities. I pondered upon their conformation. I mused upon the alteration in their nature. I shuddered as I assigned to them in imagination a sensitive and sentient power, and even when unassisted by the lips, a capability of moral expression. Of Mad'selle Sallé it has been well said,

5. The range of the distribution of basic elements, such as color or brightness.

"que tous ses pas etaient des sentiments," and of Berenice I more seriously believed *que tous ses dents etaient: des idées.*[6] *Des idées!*—ah here was the idiotic thought that destroyed me! *Des idées!*—ah *therefore* it was that I coveted them so madly! I felt that their possession could alone ever restore me to peace, in giving me back to reason.

And the evening closed in upon me thus—and then the darkness came, and tarried, and went—and the day again dawned—and the mists of a second night were now gathering around—and still I sat motionless in that solitary room, and still I sat buried in meditation, and still the *phantasma*[7] of the teeth maintained its terrible ascendancy as, with the most vivid and hideous distinctness, it floated about amid the changing lights and shadows of the chamber. At length there broke in upon my dreams a cry as of horror and dismay; and thereunto, after a pause, succeeded the sound of troubled voices, intermingled with many low moanings of sorrow, or of pain. I arose from my seat, and, throwing open one of the doors of the library, saw standing out in the antechamber a servant maiden, all in tears, who told me that Berenice was—no more. She had been seized with epilepsy in the early morning, and now, at the closing in of the night, the grave was ready for its tenant, and all the preparations for the burial were completed.[8]

I found myself sitting in the library, and again sitting there alone. It seemed that I had newly awakened from a confused and exciting dream. I knew that it was now midnight, and I was well aware that

6. The ballerina Marie Sallé (1714–1756), a friend of Voltaire, was thought to be such a wonderful dancer that the *Reçueil des Operas* (1734) said that "her every step was a sentiment." According to Mabbott, Poe would have gotten the quotation from Bielfield's encyclopedia. Egæus's insane alteration reads "that all her teeth were ideas."
7. Appearances, illusions; here the images of the teeth as ideas.
8. In this version, Poe omitted a long passage that some found in especially bad taste. In the *Southern Literary Messenger* and *Tales of the Grotesque and Arabesque,* the following grim details were given:

> With a heart full of grief, yet reluctantly, and oppressed with awe, I made my way to the bed-chamber of the departed. The room was large, and very dark, and at every step within its gloomy precincts I encountered the paraphernalia of the grave. The coffin, so a menial told me, lay surrounded by the curtains of yonder bed, and in that coffin, he whisperingly assured me, was all that remained of Berenice. Who was it asked me would I not look upon the corpse? I had seen the lips of no one move, yet the question had been demanded, and the echo of the syllables still lingered in the room. It was impossible to refuse; and with a sense of suffocation I dragged myself to the side of the bed. Gently I uplifted the sable draperies of the curtains.
>
> As I let them fall they descended upon my shoulders, and shutting me thus out from the living, enclosed me in the strictest communion with the deceased.
>
> The very atmosphere was redolent of death. The peculiar smell of the coffin sickened me; and I fancied a deleterious odor was already exhaling from the body. I would have given worlds to escape—to fly from the pernicious influence of mortality—to breathe once again the pure air of the eternal heavens. But I had no longer the power to move—my knees tottered beneath me—and I remained rooted to the spot, and gazing upon the frightful length of the rigid body as it lay outstretched in the dark coffin without a lid.
>
> God of heaven!—is it possible? Is it my brain that reeled—or was it indeed the finger of the enshrouded dead that stirred in the white cerement that bound it? Frozen with unutterable awe I slowly raised my eyes to the countenance of the corpse. There had been a band around the jaws, but, I know not how, it was broken asunder. The livid lips were wreathed in a species of smile, and, through the enveloping gloom, once again there glared upon me in too palpable a reality, the white and glistening, and ghastly teeth of Berenice. I sprang convulsively from the bed, and, uttering no word, rushed forth a maniac from that apartment of triple horror, and mystery, and death.

since the setting of the sun Berenice had been interred. But of that dreary period which intervened I had no positive—at least no definite comprehension. Yet its memory was replete with horror—horror more horrible from being vague, and terror more terrible from ambiguity. It was a fearful page in the record of my existence, written all over with dim, and hideous, and unintelligible recollections. I strived to decypher them, but in vain; while ever and anon, like the spirit of a departed sound, the shrill and piercing shriek of a female voice seemed to be ringing in my ears. I had done a deed—what was it? I asked myself the question aloud, and the whispering echoes of the chamber answered me, *"what was it?"*

On the table beside me burned a lamp, and near it lay a little box. It was of remarkable character, and I had seen it frequently before, for it was the property of the family physician; but how came it *there*, upon my table, and why did I shudder in regarding it? These things were in no manner to be accounted for, and my eyes at length dropped to the open pages of a book, and to a sentence underscored therein. The words were the singular but simple ones of the poet Ebn Zaiat, *"Dicebant mihi sodales si sepulchrum amicae visitarem, curas meas aliquantulum fore levatas."*[9] Why then, as I perused them, did the hairs of my head erect themselves on end, and the blood of my body become congealed within my veins?

There came a light tap at the library door, and pale as the tenant of a tomb, a menial entered upon tiptoe. His looks were wild with terror, and he spoke to me in a voice tremulous, husky, and very low. What said he?—some broken sentences I heard. He told of a wild cry disturbing the silence of the night—of the gathering together of the household—of a search in the direction of the sound;—and then his tones grew thrillingly distinct as he whispered me of a violated grave—of a disfigured body enshrouded, yet still breathing, still palpitating, *still alive!*

He pointed to my garments;—they were muddy and clotted with gore. I spoke not, and he took me gently by the hand;—it was indented with the impress of human nails. He directed my attention to some object against the wall;—I looked at it for some minutes;—it was a spade. With a shriek I bounded to the table, and grasped the box that lay upon it. But I could not force it open; and in my tremor it slipped from my hands, and fell heavily, and burst into pieces; and from it, with a rattling sound, there rolled out some instruments of dental surgery, intermingled with thirty-two small, white and ivory-looking substances that were scattered to and fro about the floor.

9. This is the epigraph to the tale. See p. 140, n.2, for Poe's translation.

King Pest[1]

A Tale Containing an Allegory

The gods do bear and well allow in kings
The things which they abhor in rascal routes.
Buckhurst's Tragedy of Ferrex and Porrex.[2]

About twelve o'clock, one night in the month of October, and during the chivalrous reign of the third Edward,[3] two seamen belonging to the crew of the "Free and Easy," a trading schooner plying between Sluys and the Thames, and then at anchor in that river, were much astonished to find themselves seated in the tap-room of an ale-house in the parish of St. Andrews, London—which ale-house bore for sign the portraiture of a "Jolly Tar."[4]

The room, although ill-contrived, smoke-blackened, low-pitched, and in every other respect agreeing with the general character of such places at the period—was, nevertheless, in the opinion of the grotesque groups scattered here and there within it, sufficiently well adapted to its purpose.

Of these groups our two seamen formed, I think, the most interesting, if not the most conspicuous.

The one who appeared to be the elder, and whom his companion

1. First published in the *Southern Literary Messenger* (September 1835). The text reprinted here is that of the *Broadway Journal* (October 18, 1845), which was signed with the pseudonym Littleton Barry. The original title was "King Pest the First. A Tale containing an Allegory." The nature of the allegory has been debated. One suggestion is that the tale is a parody of the party scene in book 6, chapter 1 of Benjamin Disraeli's *Vivian Grey* (1826–27), a novel Poe frequently satirized. Another is that the physically bizarre characters are various types of social pests (a do-nothing highbrow, a big-mouthed gossip, a person who pokes her nose into everything, and so forth). More pointed is the interpretation that Andrew Jackson (1767–1845), seventh president of the United States (1829–37), and his circle are the targets of political satire and that the tale is in the mode of the *roman à clef* (a story with a key). There is, of course, no reason why it cannot be all these.

2. The epigraph is from the play, *Gorboduc* (1561, 1563), the first English tragedy in blank verse, written principally by Thomas Sackville (1536–1608), earl of Dorset, who became Baron Buckhurst in 1567, and by Thomas Norton (1532–1538). It is subtitled *Ferrex and Porrex*, which are the names of King Gorboduc's two sons, between whom he divides his kingdom. The sons quarrel; Porrex is murdered by his mother who wants her other son to rule; the people rise up in outrage and execute the queen and king; the nobility retaliates; and civil war breaks out. Thus the mistakes of the legendary king and his court (mentioned in Geoffrey of Monmouth's history of England) may apply to "King Andrew" (Jackson) and his "court," with the dire prediction of civil unrest.

3. Edward III ruled 1327–77, during which time the plague devastated England at least three times.

4. Sailor (slang). The name of the ship, the *Free and Easy*, may allude to the somewhat sleazy reputation of some of Jackson's circle and of certain aspects of Jacksonian politics (see the biographical introduction, pp. xxivff.). Sluis is a town in Holland, near where Edward III won a great naval victory against the French. The Thames is the major river running through London; Levine suggests that Poe specifically works in its name as part of the political satire. The "Battle of the Thames" in 1813 was part of the Canadian Campaign in the War of 1812; Richard M. Johnson (1781–1850), a Jackson supporter, who was widely thought to have killed the great Indian chief Tecumseh, was celebrated as the hero of the Thames. Johnson was nominated for vice president by the new Democratic Party on the same ticket with Martin Van Buren; the May 1835 convention was held in Baltimore at a time when Poe was in that city. (Poe seems to have Johnson in mind as one of the main satiric targets of "The Man That Was Used Up," pp. 190ff. herein). St. Andrews is near where Poe lived with the Allans as a young boy. The name Andrew seems to offer a solid clue to the political allegory.

addressed by the characteristic appellation of "Legs,"[5] was at the same time much the taller of the two. He might have measured six feet and a half, and an habitual stoop in the shoulders seemed to have been the necessary consequence of an altitude so enormous.—Superfluities in height were, however, more than accounted for by deficiencies in other respects. He was exceedingly thin; and might, as his associates asserted, have answered, when drunk, for a pennant at the masthead, or, when sober, have served for a jib-boom.[6] But these jests, and others of a similar nature, had evidently produced, at no time, any effect upon the cachinnatory[7] muscles of the tar. With high cheek-bones, a large hawk-nose, retreating chin, fallen under-jaw, and huge protruding white eyes, the expression of his countenance, although tinged with a species of dogged indifference to matters and things in general, was not the less utterly solemn and serious beyond all attempts at imitation or description.

The younger seaman was, in all outward appearance, the converse of his companion.[8] His stature could not have exceeded four feet. A pair of stumpy bow-legs supported his squat, unwieldly figure, while his unusually short and thick arms, with no ordinary fists at their extremities, swung off dangling from his sides like the fins of a sea-turtle. Small eyes, of no particular color, twinkled far back in his head. His nose remained buried in the mass of flesh which enveloped his round, full, and purple face; and his thick upper-lip rested upon the still thicker one beneath with an air of complacent self-satisfaction, much heightened by the owner's habit of licking them at intervals. He evidently regarded his tall shipmate with a feeling half-wondrous, half-quizzical; and stared up occasionally in his face as the red setting sun stares up at the crags of Ben Nevis.[9]

Various and eventful, however, had been the peregrinations of the worthy couple in and about the different tap-houses of the neighbourhood during the earlier hours of the night. Funds even the most

5. Perhaps a caricature of Major Jack Downing, a literary persona created by the American humorist Seba Smith (1792–1868), but more likely the American horticulturist and author of books on landscape gardening (a subject of great interest to Poe), Andrew Jackson Downing (1815–1852). The coincidence of Downing's first two names with the name of the U.S. president perhaps suggested to Poe the idea of creating a physical resemblance between Legs and the "president" of the grotesque group the two sailors are about to meet.
6. A spar (pole) used to shift the jib sail from one side of the ship to the other to change the angle of progress of the ship as it tacks into the wind (a jib is a triangular sail that stretches from the foretopmast to the bow or to a boom).
7. Laughing loud and hard, to guffaw; here Poe makes up a comic adjective to describe the jaw muscles' function in convulsively laughing.
8. Scholars have suggested that the younger sailor (named Hugh Tarpaulin below) represents Martin Van Buren (1782–1862), who was Jackson's secretary of state from 1829 to 1831. He resigned to force other resignations so Jackson could clear his cabinet of the supporters of John C. Calhoun (1782–1850). Calhoun was an advocate of Nullification—the right of a state to declare federal statutes null within its boundaries. Although Jackson's strong Unionist stand in the tariff controversy of 1828 (which favored the North) angered the Southern states, Van Buren was elected vice president under Jackson in 1832 and remained one of Jackson's most influential allies. When Van Buren became the eighth president of the United States in 1837 (with Richard M. Johnson as his vice president), he announced that he would continue Jacksonian policies. But he immediately faced a major economic crisis—the Panic of 1837. Hard times made Van Buren unpopular with the common man, and he was not reelected.
9. In Inverness, Scotland, the tallest mountain in Great Britain (4,400 feet). The red face of the sun perhaps suggests habitual indulgence in alcoholic drink.

ample, are not always everlasting: and it was with empty pockets our friends had ventured upon the present hostelrie.

At the precise period, then, when this history properly commences, Legs, and his fellow Hugh Tarpaulin, sat, each with both elbows resting upon the large oaken table in the middle of the floor, and with a hand upon either cheek. They were eyeing, from behind a huge flagon of unpaid-for "humming-stuff," the portentous words, "No Chalk,"[1] which to their indignation and astonishment were scored over the doorway by means of that very mineral whose presence they purported to deny. Not that the gift of decyphering written characters—a gift among the commonalty of that day considered little less cabalistical than the art of inditing[2]—could, in strict justice, have been laid to the charge of either disciple of the sea; but there was, to say the truth, a certain twist in the formation of the letters—an indescribable lee-lurch about the whole—which foreboded, in the opinion of both seamen, a long run of dirty weather; and determined them at once, in the allegorical words of Legs himself, to "pump ship, clew up all sail, and scud[3] before the wind."

Having accordingly disposed of what remained of the ale, and looped up the points of their short doublets, they finally made a bolt for the street. Although Tarpaulin rolled twice into the fire-place, mistaking it for the door, yet their escape was at length happily effected— and half after twelve o'clock found our heroes ripe for mischief, and running for life down a dark alley in the direction of St. Andrew's Stair,[4] hotly pursued by the landlady of the "Jolly Tar."

At the epoch of this eventful tale, and periodically, for many years before and after, all England, but more especially the metropolis, re-sounded with the fearful cry of "Plague!"[5] The city was in a great

1. No credit given (not chalked up on a tally board). "Humming-stuff": strong drink (so called probably from the effect of a drunken humming in the head).
2. Writing. The cabala is a system of interpreting scripture that developed in the 7th century C.E. but whose adherents claimed for it a more ancient lineage. Cabalistic interpretation of scripture is based on the belief that every word, letter, number, and even accent has a mystical meaning accessible to those who know the secret. The cabala as "secret writing" became associated with medieval magic.
3. To run before a gale with little or no sail. "Lee": the side of a ship opposite the direction from which the wind is blowing. "Pump ship": remove excess seawater. "Clew up": raise the lower corners of a sail by using the lines tied to cleats (clews) below and running up to the mast or yard.
4. Possibly the steps to St. Andrews Church. Critics note the repetition of the name Andrew as a clue to political allegory.
5. The ravages of the Black Death were described in article titled "The Great Plague in the Fourteenth Century," *Fraser's Magazine* (May 1832). Poe seems to be paralleling the Black Death with recent cholera epidemics in Baltimore and Washington, D.C., during the election campaign of 1832—thus thoroughly associating Jackson's two terms as president with pestilence. Not only did Southerners dislike Jackson's tariff policy and anti-Nullification position but also many people, North and South, criticized Jackson for his stand against the central Bank of the United States, for his Spoils System (political and economic patronage to Jackson's friends and supporters), and for his Kitchen Cabinet. In the early years of his administration, Jackson limited his cabinet secretaries and department heads to the performance of their official duties and sought policy advice from a group of personal friends, most of whom at that time had no official status. The Kitchen Cabinet included Francis P. Blair Sr., Duff Green, Isaac Hill, Amos Kendall, William H. Lewis, John H. Eaton, and later Martin Van Buren. These were mainly journalists and editors of influential newspapers, who vigorously defended his policies to the public. In general, Jackson's personal and political associates were considered by his critics and opponents to be vulgar rabble given to drunken parties and of "free and easy" morality. Early in 1835 Jackson's friends honored him on the

measure depopulated—and in those horrible regions, in the vicinity of the Thames, where amid the dark, narrow, and filthy lanes and alleys, the Demon of Disease was supposed to have had his nativity, Awe, Terror, and Superstition were alone to be found stalking abroad.

By authority of the king such districts were placed *under ban*, all persons forbidden, under pain of death, to intrude upon their dismal solitude. Yet neither the mandate of the monarch, nor the huge barriers erected at the entrances of the streets, nor the prospect of that loathsome death which, with almost absolute certainty, overwhelmed the wretch whom no peril could deter from the adventure, prevented the unfurnished and untenanted dwellings from being stripped, by the hand of nightly rapine, of every article, such as iron, brass, or lead-work, which could in any manner be turned to a profitable account.

Above all, it was usually found, upon the annual winter opening of the barriers, that locks, bolts, and secret cellars, had proved but slender protection to those rich stores of wines and liquors which, in consideration of the risk and trouble of removal, many of the numerous dealers having shops in the neighbourhood had consented to trust, during the period of exile, to so insufficient a security.

But there were very few of the terror-stricken people who attributed these doings to the agency of human hands. Pest-spirits, plague-goblins, and fever-demons, were the popular imps of mischief; and tales so blood-chilling were hourly told, that the whole mass of forbidden buildings was, at length, enveloped in terror as in a shroud, and the plunderer himself was often scared away by the horrors his own depredations had created; leaving the entire vast circuit of prohibited district to gloom, silence, pestilence, and death.

It was by one of the terrific barriers already mentioned, and which indicated the region beyond to be under the Pest-ban, that, in scrambling down an alley, Legs and the worthy Hugh Tarpaulin found their progress suddenly impeded. To return was out of the question, and no time was to be lost, as their pursuers were close upon their heels. With thorough-bred seamen to clamber up the roughly fashioned plank-work was a trifle; and, maddened with the twofold excitement of exercise and liquor, they leaped unhesitatingly down within the enclosure, and holding on their drunken course with shouts and yellings, were soon bewildered in its noisome and intricate recesses.

Had they not, indeed, been intoxicated beyond moral sense, their reeling footsteps must have been palsied by the horrors of their situation. The air was cold and misty. The paving-stones, loosened from their beds, lay in wild disorder amid the tall, rank grass, which sprang up around the feet and ankles. Fallen houses choked up the streets. The most fetid and poisonous smells everywhere prevailed;—and by the aid of that ghastly light which, even at midnight, never fails to emanate from a vapory and pestilential atmosphere, might be discerned lying in the by-paths and alleys, or rotting in the windowless

anniversary of his victory at the Battle of New Orleans with a banquet celebrated for the "free and easy" flow of liquor.

habitations, the carcass of many a nocturnal plunderer arrested by the hand of the plague in the very perpetration of his robbery.

—But it lay not in the power of images, or sensations, or impediments such as these, to stay the course of men who, naturally brave, and at that time especially, brimful of courage and of "humming-stuff!" would have reeled, as straight as their condition might have permitted, undauntedly into the very jaws of Death. Onward—still onward stalked the grim Legs, making the desolate solemnity echo and re-echo with yells like the terrific war-whoop of the Indian: and onward, still onward rolled the dumpy Tarpaulin, hanging on to the doublet of his more active companion, and far surpassing the latter's most strenuous exertions in the way of vocal music, by bull-roarings *in basso*, from the profundity of his stentorian[6] lungs.

They had now evidently reached the strong hold of the pestilence. Their way at every step or plunge grew more noisome and more horrible—the paths more narrow and more intricate. Huge stones and beams falling momently from the decaying roofs above them, gave evidence, by their sullen and heavy descent, of the vast height of the surrounding houses; and while actual exertion became necessary to force a passage through frequent heaps of rubbish, it was by no means seldom that the hand fell upon a skeleton or rested upon a more fleshey corpse.

Suddenly, as the seamen stumbled against the entrance of a tall and ghastly-looking building, a yell more than usually shrill from the throat of the excited Legs, was replied to from within, in a rapid succession of wild, laughter-like, and fiendish shrieks. Nothing daunted at sounds which, of such a nature, at such a time, and in such a place, might have curdled the very blood in hearts less irrevocably on fire, the drunken couple rushed headlong against the door, burst it open, and staggered into the midst of things with a volley of curses.

The room within which they found themselves proved to be the shop of an undertaker; but an open trap-door, in a corner of the floor near the entrance, looked down upon a long range of wine-cellars, whose depths the occasional sound of bursting bottles proclaimed to be well stored with their appropriate contents. In the middle of the room stood a table—in the centre of which again arose a huge tub of what appeared to be punch. Bottles of various wines and cordials, together with jugs, pitchers, and flagons of every shape and quality, were scattered profusely upon the board. Around it, upon coffin-tressels, was seated a company of six. This company I will endeavor to delineate one by one.

Fronting the entrance, and elevated a little above his companions, sat a personage who appeared to be the president of the table. His stature was gaunt and tall, and Legs was confounded to behold in him a figure more emaciated than himself. His face was as yellow as saffron—but no feature excepting one alone, was sufficiently marked to merit a particular description. This one consisted in a forehead so un-

6. After Stentor, the loud herald in Homer's *Iliad*. "*In basso*": in a bass voice and very loud.

usually and hideously lofty, as to have the appearance of a bonnet, or crown of flesh superseded upon the natural head.[7] His mouth was puckered and dimpled into an expression of ghastly affability, and his eyes, as indeed the eyes of all at table, were glazed over with the fumes of intoxication. This gentleman was clothed from head to foot in a richly-embroidered black silk-velvet pall, wrapped negligently around his form after the fashion of a Spanish cloak.—His head was stuck full of sable hearse-plumes, which he nodded to and fro with a jaunty and knowing air; and, in his right hand, he held a huge human thigh-bone, with which he appeared to have been just knocking down some member of the company for a song.[8]

Opposite him, and with her back to the door, was a lady of no whit the less extraordinary character. Although quite as tall as the person just described, she had no right to complain of his unnatural emaciation. She was evidently in the last stage of a dropsy;[9] and her figure resembled nearly that of the huge puncheon of October beer which stood, with the head driven in, close by her side, in a corner of the chamber. Her face was exceedingly round, red, and full; and the same peculiarity, or rather want of peculiarity, attached itself to her countenance, which I before mentioned in the case of the president—that is to say, only one feature of her face was sufficiently distinguished to need a separate characterization: indeed the acute Tarpaulin immediately observed that the same remark might have applied to each individual person of the party, every one of whom seemed to possess a monopoly of some particular portion of physiognomy. With the lady in question this portion proved to be the mouth. Commencing at the right ear, it swept with a terrific chasm to the left—the short pendants which she wore in either auricle continually bobbing into the aperture. She made however, every exertion to keep her mouth closed and look dignified, in a dress consisting of a newly starched and ironed shroud coming up close under her chin, with a crimpled ruffle of cambric muslin.

At her right hand sat a diminutive young lady whom she appeared to patronise.[1] This delicate little creature, in the trembling of her wasted fingers, in the livid hue of her lips, and in the slight hectic spot which

7. The physical description (tall, thin, high forehead) parallels that of President Andrew Jackson.
8. I.e., He is gaveling the club to order.
9. A disease in which the body and limbs become quite swollen. Mabbott notes that it also is an obsolete term for unquenchable thirst. This tall fat lady, with a red face and huge mouth, who wears a shroud, is later named Queen Pest, the club president's "Serene Consort." She may represent Rachel Jackson, Jackson's wife. She married Jackson before her divorce from her first husband was legally in effect; and although the marriage ceremony was later conducted a second time, Jackson's opponents tried to use the incident to smear him as an immoral man with an immoral wife.
1. The diminutive, consumptive young lady with the long waggily nose is later named the Arch-Duchess Ana-pest. This personage would seem to be Peggy Eaton (Margaret O'Neil Timberlake Eaton, c. 1796–1879), the second wife of the president's secretary of war, John H. Eaton (1790–1856). Eaton's first wife was Andrew Jackson's ward and thus socially acceptable, but Margaret O'Neill was the daughter of a Washington tavern owner, thus considered ill-bred. She was rumored to have been intimate with Eaton before they were married and even before her first husband's death. She was snubbed by the wives of the other cabinet secretaries—a situation that disrupted the cabinet and led as well to a rift in Jackson's inner circle. Mrs. John C. Calhoun, in particular, took exception to Peggy Eaton's presence socially, which intensified the antagonism between Jackson and Calhoun and played a part in Jackson's increasing reliance on Van Buren.

tinged her otherwise leaden complexion, gave evident indications of a galloping consumption. An air of extreme *haut ton*, however, pervaded her whole appearance; she wore in a graceful and *degagé* manner, a large and beautiful winding-sheet of the finest India lawn;[2] her hair hung in ringlets over her neck; a soft smile played about her mouth; but her nose, extremely long, thin, sinuous, flexible and pimpled, hung down far below her under lip, and in spite of the delicate manner in which she now and then moved it to one side or the other with her tongue, gave to her countenance a somewhat equivocal expression.

Over against her, and upon the left of the dropsical lady, was seated a little puffy, wheezing, and gouty old man, whose cheeks reposed upon the shoulders of their owner, like two huge bladders of Oporto wine.[3] With his arms folded, and with one bandaged leg deposited upon the table, he seemed to think himself entitled to some consideration. He evidently prided himself much upon every inch of his personal appearance, but took more especial delight in calling attention to his gaudy-colored surtout.[4] This, to say the truth, must have cost him no little money, and was made to fit him exceedingly well—being fashioned from one of the curiously embroidered silken covers appertaining to those glorious escutcheons which, in England and elsewhere, are customarily hung up, in some conspicuous place, upon the dwellings of departed aristocracy.

Next to him, and at the right hand of the president, was a gentleman in long white hose and cotton drawers.[5] His frame shook, in a ridiculous manner, with a fit of what Tarpaulin called "the horrors." His jaws, which had been newly shaved, were tightly tied up by a bandage of muslin; and his arms being fastened in a similar way at the wrists, prevented him from helping himself too freely to the liquors upon the table; a precaution rendered necessary, in the opinion of Legs, by the peculiarly sottish and wine-bibbing cast of his visage. A pair of prodigious ears, nevertheless, which it was no doubt found impossible to confine, towered away into the atmosphere of the apartment, and were occasionally pricked up in a spasm, at the sound of the drawing of a cork.

Fronting him, sixthly and lastly, was situated a singularly stiff-looking personage, who, being afflicted with paralysis, must, to speak seriously,

2. An expensive, thin, very fine fabric of cotton or linen. *"Haut ton"*: socially high toned. *"Degagé"*: easy in the sense of assured. Levine suggests that it continues the word play on "free and easy." "Winding-sheet": funeral shroud.
3. I.e., port wine. The gouty old man whose sagging cheeks rest on his shoulders is later named His Grace, the Arch-Duke Pest-Iferous, a pun on "pestiferous" (breeding disease, infected; also morally diseased, evil). One suggested identification is Colonel Thomas Hart Benton (1782–1858), like Jackson originally from Tennessee but at first a personal enemy of his. Reconciling in 1824, they became stout friends, and Benton thereafter was one of Jackson's strongest supporters.
4. Overcoat.
5. The alcoholic man with the big ears that prick up at the sound of a wine cork being removed is apparently His Grace the Duke Pest-Ilential (named below). Francis Blair Sr. (1791–1876) has been suggested for this figure. In 1830, he established the Washington *Globe*, a paper that almost immediately became known as the "court journal of King Andrew"; the paper exerted great pro-administration influence through the end of Van Buren's term (1841).

have felt very ill at ease in his unaccommodating habiliments.[6] He was habited, somewhat uniquely, in a new and handsome mahogany coffin. Its top or head-piece pressed upon the skull of the wearer, and extended over it in the fashion of a hood; giving to the entire face an air of indescribable interest. Arm-holes had been cut in the sides, for the sake not more of elegance than of convenience; but the dress, nevertheless, prevented its proprietor from sitting as erect as his associates; and as he lay reclining against his tressel, at an angle of forty-five degrees, a pair of huge goggle eyes rolled up their awful whites towards the ceiling in absolute amazement at their own enormity.

Before each of the party lay a portion of a skull, which was used as a drinking cup. Overhead was suspended a human skeleton, by means of a rope tied round one of the legs and fastened to a ring in the ceiling. The other limb confined by no such fetter, stuck off from the body at right angles, causing the whole loose and rattling frame to dangle and twirl about at the caprice of every occasional puff of wind which found its way into the aparment. In the cranium of this hideous thing lay a quantity of ignited charcoal, which threw a fitful but vivid light over the entire scene; while coffins, and other wares appertaining to the shop of an undertaker, were piled high up around the room, and against the windows, preventing any ray from escaping into the street.[7]

At sight of this extraordinary assembly, and of their still more extraordinary paraphernalia, our two seamen did not conduct themselves with that degree of decorum which might have been expected. Legs, leaning against the wall near which he happened to be standing, dropped his lower law still lower than usual, and spread open his eyes to their fullest extent: while Hugh Tarpaulin, stooping down so as to bring his nose upon a level with the table, and spreading out a palm upon either knee, burst into a long, loud, and obstreprons roar of very ill-timed and immoderate laughter.

Without, however, taking offence at behaviour so excessively rude, the tall president smiled very graciously upon the intruders—nodded to them in a dignified manner with his head of sable plumes—and, arising, took each by an arm, and led him to a seat which some others of the company had placed in the meantime for his accommodation. Legs to all this offered not the slightest resistance, but sat down as he was directed; while the gallant Hugh, removing his coffin tressel from its station near the head of the table, to the vicinity of the little consumptive lady in the winding sheet, plumped down by her side in high glee, and pouring out a skull of red wine, quaffed it to their better acquaintance. But at this presumption the stiff gentleman in the coffin seemed exceedingly nettled; and serious consequences might have ensued, had not the president, rapping upon the table with his

6. The man with huge goggle eyes wearing his coffin is apparently His Grace the Duke Tempest (named below). Both Amos Kendall (1789–1869) and William H. Crawford (1772–1834) have been suggested as the political figure represented. Kendall helped Jackson outline his policies and write his speeches; he was perhaps Jackson's greatest apologist, writing one defense after another in Blair's *Globe*.

7. Cf. the censers and coffins in other Poe stories, such as "The Assignation" (pp. 116ff. herein), "Ligeia" (pp. 159ff.) and "The Fall of the House of Usher" (pp. 199ff.).

truncheon, diverted the attention of all present to the following speech:

"It becomes our duty upon the present happy occasion"———

"Avast there!" interrupted Legs, looking very serious, "avast there a bit, I say, and tell us who the devil ye all are, and what business ye have here, rigged off like the foul fiends, and swilling the snug blue ruin stowed away for the winter by my honest shipmate, Will Wimble[8] the undertaker!"

At this unpardonable piece of ill-breeding, all the original company half started to their feet, and uttered the same rapid succession of wild fiendish shrieks which had before caught the attention of the seamen. The president, however, was the first to recover his composure, and at length, turning to Legs with great dignity, recommenced:

"Most willingly will we gratify any reasonable curiosity on the part of guests so illustrious, unbidden though they be. Know then that in these dominions I am monarch, and here rule with undivided empire under the title of 'King Pest the First.'[9]

"This apartment, which you no doubt profanely suppose to be the shop of Will Wimble the undertaker—a man whom we know not, and whose plebeian appellation has never before this night thwarted our royal ears—this apartment, I say, is the Dais-Chamber of our Palace, devoted to the councils of our kingdom, and to other sacred and lofty purposes.

"The noble lady who sits opposite is Queen Pest, our Serene Consort. The other exalted personages whom you behold are all of our family, and wear the insignia of the blood royal under the respective titles of 'His Grace the Arch Duke Pest-Iferous'—'His Grace the Duke Pest-Ilential'—'His Grace the Duke Tem-Pest'—and 'Her Serene Highness the Arch Duchess Ana-Pest.'[1]

"As regards," continued he, "your demand of the business upon which we sit here in council, we might be pardoned for replying that it concerns, and concerns *alone*, our own private and regal interest, and is in no manner important to any other than ourself. But in consideration of those rights to which as guests and strangers you may feel yourselves entitled, we will furthermore explain that we are here this night, prepared by deep research and accurate investigation, to examine, analyze, and thoroughly determine the indefinable spirit—the incomprehensible qualities and nare[2]—of those inestimable treasures of the palate, the wines, ales, and liqueurs of this goodly metropolis: by so doing to advance not more our own designs than the true welfare of that unearthly sovereign whose reign is over us all, whose dominions are unlimited, and whose name is 'Death,' "

"Whose name is Davy Jones!"[3] ejaculated Tarpaulin, helping the

8. A character in Joseph Addison and Richard Steele's *Spectator Papers* (1712). Levine points out that a *wimble* is also "a kind of a drill for boring in soft earth." "Avast": nautical term meaning to desist. "Blue ruin": a specially fermented gin drink, available at little cost.
9. Poe seems to be equating the democratic U.S. president (the people's president) with the tyranny of the British kings.
1. "Ana-Pest" is a pun on the word *pest*; here a poetic measure: the *anapest*, a three-syllable measure composed of two unaccented syllables and a final accented one.
2. Nostril (Latin); here apparently the smells of wines, ales, and liqueurs.
3. Death at sea. The folk-mythic fiend Davy Jones keeps the bodies of drowned sailors in his underwater "locker."

lady by his side to a skull of liqueur, and pouring out a second for himself.

"Profane varlet!" said the president, now turning his attention to the worthy Hugh, "profane and execrable wretch!—we have said, that in consideration of those rights which, even in thy filthy person, we feel no inclination to violate, we have condescended to make reply to thy rude and unseasonable inquiries.[4] We nevertheless, for your unhallowed intrusion upon our councils, believe it our duty to mulct thee and thy companion in each a gallon of Black Strap[5] having imbibed which to the prosperity of our kingdom—at a single draught—and upon your bended knees—ye shall be forthwith free either to proceed upon your way, or remain and be admitted to the privileges of our table, according to your respective and individual pleasures."

"It would be a matter of utter unpossibility" replied Legs, whom the assumptions and dignity of King Pest the First had evidently inspired with some feelings of respect, and who arose and steadied himself by the table as he spoke—"it would, please your majesty, be a matter of utter unpossibility to stow away in my hold even one-fourth part of that same liquor which your majesty has just mentioned. To say nothing of the stuffs placed on board in the forenoon by way of ballast, and not to mention the various ales and liqueurs shipped this evening at different sea-ports, I have, at present, a full cargo of 'humming stuff' taken in and duly paid for at the sign of the 'Jolly Tar.' You will, therefore, please your majesty, be so good as to take the will for the deed—for by no manner of means either can I or will I swallow another drop—least of all a drop of that villanous bilge-water that answers to the hail of 'Black Strap.' "

"Belay that!" interrupted Tarpaulin, astonished not more at the length of his companion's speech than at the nature of his refusal— "Belay that you lubber!—and I say, Legs, none of your palaver![6] My hull is still light, although I confess you yourself seem to be a little top-heavy; and as for the matter of your share of the cargo, why rather than raise a squall I would find stowage-room for it myself, but"[7]——

"This proceeding," interposed the President, "is by no means in accordance with the terms of the mulct or sentence, which is in its nature Median,[8] and not to be altered or recalled. The conditions we have imposed must be fulfilled to the letter, and that without a moment's hesitation—in failure of which fulfilment we decree that you

4. Probably an allusion to the inquiries into the alleged scandals of Jackson's friends and associates.
5. Black strap molasses was used to make industrial alcohol, but Mabbott glosses it as inferior thick port wine. "Mulct": to pay a penalty or to demand a fine. The fine demanded is that the sailors must each drink a gallon all at once, without stopping, while kneeling.
6. As with other of the sailor's speeches, the paragraph proceeds by a series of comic nautical phrases and metaphors. "Belay": secure, make fast; here stop what one is doing or saying. "Lubber": as in landlubber, a clumsy, inexperienced sailor. "Palaver": insignificant talk, idle chatter.
7. Hugh Tarpaulin's "hull is . . . light" (he is not filled up), but Legs seems "top-heavy" (like a ship about to list too far over; i.e., he's dizzy from drink). Rather than fuss ("raise a squall"), Hugh will make room in his belly ("stowage-room") for Legs's share of black strap. A squall is a small storm.
8. According to the custom of the ancient Medes, mentioned several times in the Bible for their unalterable or inflexible laws. That is, the fine is not to be altered.

do here be tied neck and heels together, and duly drowned as rebels in yon hogshead of October beer!"

"A sentence!—a sentence!—a righteous and just sentence!—a glorious decree!—a most worthy and upright, and holy condemnation!" shouted the Pest family altogether. The king elevated his forehead into innumerable wrinkles; the gouty little old man puffed like a pair of bellows; the lady of the winding sheet waved her nose to and fro; the gentleman in the cotton drawers pricked up his ears; she of the shroud gasped like a dying fish; and he of the coffin looked stiff and rolled up his eyes.

"Ugh! ugh! ugh!" chuckled Tarpaulin without heeding the general excitation, "ugh! ugh! ugh!—ugh! ugh! ugh! ugh!—ugh! ugh! ugh!—I was saying," said he, "I was saying when Mr. King Pest poked in his marlin-spike, that as for the matter of two or three gallons more or less of Black Strap, it was a trifle to a tight seaboat like myself not overstowed—but when it comes to drinking the health of the Devil (whom God assoilzie[9]) and going down upon my marrow bones to his ill-favored majesty there, whom I know as well as I know myself to be a sinner, to be nobody in the whole world, but Tim Hurlygurly the stage-player—why! it's quite another guess sort of a thing, and utterly and altogether past my comprehension."

He was not allowed to finish this speech in tranquility. At the name of Tim Hurlygurly the whole assembly leaped from their seats.

"Treason!" shouted his Majesty King Pest the First.

"Treason!" said the little man with the gout.

"Treason!" screamed the Arch Duchess Ana-Pest.

"Treason!" muttered the gentleman with his jaws tied up.

"Treason!" growled he of the coffin.

"Treason! treason!" shrieked her majesty of the mouth; and, seizing by the hinder part of his breeches the unfortunate Tarpaulin, who had just commenced pouring out for himself a skull of liqueur, she lifted him high into the air, and let him fall without ceremony into the huge open puncheon of his beloved ale. Bobbing up and down, for a few seconds, like an apple in a bowl of toddy, he, at length, finally disappeared amid the whirlpool of foam which, in the already effervescent liquor, his struggles easily succeeded in creating.

Not tamely, however, did the tall seaman behold the discomfiture of his companion. Jostling King Pest through the open trap, the valiant Legs slammed the door down upon him with an oath, and strode towards the centre of the room. Here tearing down the skeleton which swung over the table, he laid it about him with so much energy and good will, that, as the last glimpses of light died away within the apartment, he succeeded in knocking out the brains of the little gentleman with the gout. Rushing then with all his force against the fatal hogshead full of October ale and Hugh Tarpaulin, he rolled it over and over in an instant. Out burst a deluge of liquor so fierce—so impetuous—so overwhelming—that the room was flooded from wall to

9. Absolve.

wall—the loaded table was overturned—the tressels were thrown upon their backs—the tub of punch into the fire-place—and the ladies into hysterics. Piles of death-furniture floundered about. Jugs, pitchers, and carboys mingled promiscuously in the *melée*, and wicker flagons encountered desperately with bottles of junk.[1] The man with the horrors was drowned upon the spot—the little stiff gentleman floated off in his coffin—and the victorious Legs, seizing by the waist the fat lady in the shroud, rushed out with her into the street, and made a bee-line for the "Free and Easy,"[2] Followed under easy sail by the redoubtable Hugh Tarpaulin, who, having sneezed three or four times, panted and puffed after him with the Arch Duchess Ana-Pest.

Ligeia[1]

And the will therein lieth, which dieth not. Who knoweth the mysteries of the will, with its vigor? For God is but a great will pervading all things by nature of its intentness. Man doth not yield himself to the angels, nor unto death utterly, save only through the weakness of his feeble will.

—JOSEPH GLANVILL.[2]

I cannot, for my soul, remember how, when, or even precisely where, I first became acquainted with the lady Ligeia. Long years have since elapsed, and my memory is feeble through much suffering. Or, perhaps, I cannot *now* bring these points to mind, because, in truth, the character of my beloved, her rare learning, her singular yet placid cast of beauty, and the thrilling and enthralling eloquence of her low musical language, made their way into my heart by paces so steadily and stealthily progressive that they have been unnoticed and unknown. Yet I believe that I met her first and most frequently in some large, old, decaying city near the Rhine. Of her family—I have surely heard her speak. That it is of a remotely ancient date cannot be doubted. Ligeia! Ligeia! Buried in studies of a nature more than all else adapted to deaden impressions of the outward world, it is by that sweet word alone—by Ligeia—that I bring before mine eyes in fancy the image of her who is no more. And now, while I write, a recollection flashes upon me that I have *never known* the paternal name of her who was my friend and my betrothed, and who became the

1. Bottles made of thick dark glass. "Melée": confused scene; free-for-all.
2. "Free and Easy" repeated at the end in conjunction with carrying off the women again suggests the questionable reputations of the Jacksonian women.
1. First published in the *Baltimore American Museum* (September 1848); the text followed here is that of the *Broadway Journal* (September 27, 1845). Mabbott observes that the name (which Poe also uses in "Al Aaraaf") comes from a Homeric Greek word meaning high-sounding and clear-toned, or (contradictorily) shrill. He also notes also that a dryad in Virgil's *Georgics* (30 B.C.E.) and a siren in Milton's *Comus* (1634, 1637) bear the name "Ligeia."
2. Scholars have searched unsuccessfully for the source of this epigraph in the writings of Joseph Glanvill or Glanvil (1636–1680), English clergyman and philosopher. The apparently fabricated quotation is very much in the mode of Glanvil, who was associated with the Cambridge Platonists, a school of philosophers centered around that university in the second half of the 17th century. In reaction to the mechanistic theories of Thomas Hobbes (1588–1679) and others, they revived Platonic and Neoplatonic ideas concerning the relation of the human soul to God.

partner of my studies, and finally the wife of my bosom. Was it a playful charge on the part of my Ligeia? or was it a test of my strength of affection, that I should institute no inquiries upon this point? or was it rather a caprice of my own—a wildly romantic offering on the shrine of the most passionate devotion? I but indistinctly recall the fact itself—what wonder that I have utterly forgotten the circumstances which originated or attended it? And, indeed, if ever that spirit which is entitled *Romance*[3]—if ever she, the wan and the misty-winged *Ashtophet*[4] of idolatrous Egypt, presided, as they tell, over marriages illomened, then most surely she presided over mine.

There is one dear topic, however, on which my memory fails me not. It is the *person* of Ligeia. In stature she was tall, somewhat slender, and, in her latter days, even emaciated. I would in vain attempt to portray the majesty, the quiet ease, of her demeanor, or the incomprehensible lightness and elasticity of her footfall. She came and departed as a shadow. I was never made aware of her entrance into my closed study save by the dear music of her low sweet voice, as she placed her marble hand upon my shoulder. In beauty of face no maiden ever equalled her. It was the radiance of an opium dream—an airy and spirit-lifting vision more wildly divine than the phantasies which hovered about the slumbering souls of the daughters of Delos.[5] Yet her features were not of that regular mould which we have been falsely taught to worship in the classical labors of the heathen. "There is no exquisite beauty," says Bacon, Lord Verulam, speaking truly of all the forms and *genera* of beauty, "without some *strangeness* in the proportion."[6] Yet, although I saw that the features of Ligeia were not of a classic regularity—although I perceived that her loveliness was indeed "exquisite," and felt that there was much of "strangeness" pervading it, yet I have tried in vain to detect the irregularity and to trace home my

3. A tale of the unusual, the exotic, the extraordinary, the marvelous; derived from the word *roman*, meaning in the "Roman" tongue rather than in Latin (i.e., in the language of the ordinary Roman populace rather than the refined Latin of the educated). Aimed at a popular audience, the romance of the Middle Ages was a vernacular tale (written in the romance languages derived from Roman). The medieval romance was a story or a series of stories of chivalry and daring deeds and unusual events. The romance as simply or mainly a love story is a more recent development.

4. A Phoenician goddess associated with the ancient city of Sidon (founded before 1400 B.C.E. in what is now Lebanon), parent of the more famous city-colony of Tyre (south of Sidon), whose descendents built the still more famous city of Carthage on the coast of North Africa. The Sidonian sarcophagus (stone coffin) of Eshmunzar lists fertility deities like Baal and Ashtoreth. Baal was originally a sun god and thus considered the source of life; he was worshiped in Canaan (the territory between Jordan, the Dead Sea, and the Mediterranean Sea), i.e., ancient Palestine, the Promised Land of the Hebrews, who conquered Canaan after their escape from Egypt. But the Phoenician cult of Baal had developed rites of holy prostitution and child sacrifice, and thus Baal became abhorrent to the Hebrews. The cognates *Beel* and *Bel* can be seen in the name Beelzebub (Baal-zebub), often a synonym for Satan, and in the name of the famous courtesan of Tyre, Jezebel (Jeze-baal). Ashtoreth (Astorath, Ashtaroth) is the Hebrew form of the Semitic goddess Astarte (Babylonian Ishtar, Greek Aphrodite, Roman Venus), the most important of the Phoenician female deities. She is the goddess of erotic love, frequently disastrous in its consequences, whose very name the Jews were forbidden to utter.

5. An island off Greece in the Aegean Sea, which flourished from before 500 B.C.E. to after 88 B.C.E., presided over by the sibling gods Apollo and Artemis.

6. Francis Bacon (1561–1626), Lord Verulam and Viscount St. Albans, writes in "Of Beauty" in *Essays* (1597–1625): "There is no excellent beauty that hath not some strangeness in the proportion" (Essay 43).

own perception of "the strange." I examined the contour of the lofty and pale forehead—it was faultless—how cold indeed that word when applied to a majesty so divine!—the skin rivalling the purest ivory, the commanding extent and repose, the gentle prominence of the regions above the temples;[7] and then the raven-black, the glossy, the luxuriant and naturally-curling tresses, setting forth the full force of the Homeric epithet, "hyacinthine!" I looked at the delicate outlines of the nose—and nowhere but in the graceful medallions of the Hebrews had I beheld a similar perfection. There were the same luxurious smoothness of surface, the same scarcely perceptible tendency to the aquiline, the same harmoniously curved nostrils speaking the free spirit. I regarded the sweet mouth. Here was indeed the triumph of all things heavenly—the magnificent turn of the short upper lip—the soft, voluptuous slumber of the under—the dimples which sported, and the color which spoke—the teeth glancing back, with a brilliancy almost startling, every ray of the holy light which fell upon them in her serene and placid, yet most exultingly radiant of all smiles. I scrutinized the formation of the chin—and here, too, I found the gentleness of breadth, the softness and the majesty, the fullness and the spirituality, of the Greek—the contour which the God Apollo revealed but in a dream, to Cleomenes, the son of the Athenian.[8] And then I peered into the large eyes of Ligeia.

For eyes we have no models in the remotely antique. It might have been, too, that in these eyes of my beloved lay the secret to which Lord Verulam alludes. They were, I must believe, far larger than the ordinary eyes of our own race. They were even fuller than the fullest of the gazelle eyes of the tribe of the valley of Nourjahad.[9] Yet it was only at intervals—in moments of intense excitement—that this peculiarity became more than slightly noticeable in Ligeia. And at such moments was her beauty—in my heated fancy thus it appeared perhaps—the beauty of beings either above or apart from the earth—the beauty of the fabulous Houri[1] of the Turk. The hue of the orbs was the most brilliant of black, and, far over them, hung jetty lashes of great length. The brows, slightly irregular in outline, had the same tint. The "strangeness," however, which I found in the eyes, was of a nature distinct from the formation, or the color, or the brilliancy of

7. Scholars have noted that Poe's facial portrait is phrenologically accurate. Phrenology was a popular pseudo-science of the time that purported to be able to read character and abilities from the contours and configurations of the skull (reading "bumps" on the head). It was paralleled by "physiognomy," the pseudo-science of reading character from facial configurations (see the introduction to Sciences of the Mind, herein, especially the phrenological chart, p. 747). The prominence of the area above the temples phrenologically suggests "love of life." But nearby is the area of "alimentiveness"; the alimentary canal is for digestion—in other words, there may be some suggestion that the mysterious Ligeia is some kind of a "heavy feeder" (i.e., vampiristic).

8. This Cleomenes was the son of the more famous Apollodorus, Athenian painter of the 5th century B.C.E. who was called the Shadower because of his innovative use of light and shadow to suggest form. Cleomenes' statue of Venus was supposedly inspired by a divine vision.

9. Title of an "Oriental" novel, The History of Nourjahad (1767) by Frances Sheridan (pseudonym, Sidney Biddulph). The female slaves of exquisite beauty sought by Prince Nourjahad all had large eyes. Mabbott notes the play Illusion, or the Trance of Nourjahad, performed in 1813, which may have given further contemporary resonance to Poe's allusion.

1. In Muslim mythology, maidens waiting on men in Heaven. They have very large dark eyes (houri), by which name they are known. They seem sensual but are ethereal.

the features, and must, after all, be referred to the *expression*. Ah, word of no meaning! behind whose vast latitude of mere sound we intrench our ignorance of so much of the spiritual. The expression of the eyes of Ligeia! How for long hours have I pondered upon it! How have I, through the whole of a midsummer night, struggled to fathom it! What was it—that something more profound than the well of Democritus[2]—which lay far within the pupils of my beloved? What *was* it? I was possessed with a passion to discover. Those eyes! those large, those shining, those divine orbs! they became to me twin stars of Leda, and I to them devoutest of astrologers.[3]

There is no point, among the many incomprehensible anomalies of the science of mind, more thrillingly exciting than the fact—never, I believe, noticed in the schools—that, in our endeavors to recall to memory something long forgotten, we often find ourselves *upon the very verge* of remembrance, without being able, in the end, to remember. And thus how frequently, in my intense scrutiny of Ligeia's eyes, have I felt approaching the full knowledge of their expression—felt it approaching—yet not quite be mine—and so at length entirely depart! And (strange, oh strangest mystery of all!) I found, in the commonest objects of the universe, a circle of analogies to that expression. I mean to say that, subsequently to the period when Ligeia's beauty passed into my spirit, there dwelling as in a shrine, I derived, from many existences in the material world, a sentiment such as I felt always around within me by her large and luminous orbs. Yet not the more could I define that sentiment, or analyze, or even steadily view it. I recognized it, let me repeat, sometimes in the survey of a rapidly-growing vine—in the contemplation of a moth, a butterfly, a chrysalis, a stream of running water. I have felt it in the ocean; in the falling of a meteor. I have felt it in the glances of unusually aged people. And there are one or two stars in heaven—(one especially, a star of the sixth magnitude, double and changeable, to be found near the large star in Lyra[4]) in a telescopic scrutiny of which I have been made aware of the feeling. I have been filled with it by certain sounds from stringed instruments, and not unfrequently by passages from books. Among innumerable other instances, I well remember something in a volume of Joseph Glanvill,[5] which (perhaps merely from its quaintness—who shall say?) never failed to inspire me with the sentiment;—"And the will therein lieth, which dieth not. Who knoweth the mysteries of the will, with its

2. Greek philosopher (c. 460–c. 370 B.C.E.), father of atomic theory. He is supposed to have said that truth lies in the "depths," traditionally translated as "at the bottom of a well."
3. Those who practice astrology, the study of stars (*astra*), in an effort to predict the future and the will of the gods (cf. notes to "Shadow," pp. 134–36 herein). "Twin stars": named after the twins Castor and Pollux (the "Dioscuri").
4. Bright star in the constellation Alpha Lyrae, known as Vega. It is actually a multiple star cluster, the brightness of which frequently changes.
5. See p. 159, n. 2 herein. Although a proponent of scientific method and the absolute sovereignty of God in all events, Glanvil also believed in the reality of witchcraft and in 1666 published *Philosophical Considerations Touching Witches and Witchcraft*, a book countering skeptics. It was later revised under the title *Saducismus Triumphatus* (1681), suggesting a "triumph over Sadducees" (loosely, from a Christian point of view, unbelievers). Whether Poe meant Ligeia to be taken as some sort of witch or vampire has been the subject of critical debate.

vigor? For God is but a great will pervading all things by nature of its intentness. Man doth not yield him to the angels, nor unto death utterly, save only through the weakness of his feeble will."

Length of years, and subsequent reflection, have enabled me to trace, indeed, some remote connection between this passage in the English moralist and a portion of the character of Ligeia. An *intensity* in thought, action, or speech, was possibly, in her, a result, or at least an index, of that gigantic volition which, during our long intercourse, failed to give other and more immediate evidence of its existence. Of all the women whom I have ever known, she, the outwardly calm, the ever-placid Ligeia, was the most violently a prey to the tumultuous vultures of stern passion. And of such passion I could form no estimate, save by the miraculous expansion of those eyes which at once so delighted and appalled me—by the almost magical melody, modulation, distinctness and placidity of her very low voice—and by the fierce energy (rendered doubly effective by contrast with her manner of utterance) of the wild words which she habitually uttered.

I have spoken of the learning of Ligeia: it was immense—such as I have never known in woman. In the classical tongues was she deeply proficient, and as far as my own acquaintance extended in regard to the modern dialects of Europe, I have never known her at fault. Indeed upon any theme of the most admired, because simply the most abstruse of the boasted erudition[6] of the academy, have I *ever* found Ligeia at fault? How singularly—how thrillingly, this one point in the nature of my wife has forced itself, at this late period only, upon my attention! I said her knowledge was such as I have never known in woman—but where breathes the man who has traversed, and successfully, *all* the wide areas of moral, physical, and mathematical science? I saw not then what I now clearly perceive, that the acquisitions of Ligeia were gigantic, were astounding; yet I was sufficiently aware of her infinite supremacy to resign myself, with a child-like confidence, to her guidance through the chaotic world of metaphysical investigation at which I was most busily occupied during the earlier years of our marriage. With how vast a triumph—with how vivid a delight— with how much of all that is ethereal in hope—did I *feel*, as she bent over me in studies but little sought—but less known—that delicious vista by slow degrees expanding before me, down whose long, gorgeous, and all untrodden path, I might at length pass onward to the goal of a wisdom too divinely precious not to be forbidden!

How poignant, then, must have been the grief with which, after some years, I beheld my well grounded expectations take wings to themselves and fly away! Without Ligeia I was but as a child groping benighted. Her presence, her readings alone, rendered vividly luminous the many mysteries of the transcendentalism in which we were immersed.[7] Wanting the radiant lustre of her eyes, letters, lambent and golden, grew duller than Saturnian lead. And now those eyes shone less

6. Learnedness. "Abstruse": abstract and complicated.
7. Ligeia, as a German occultist and mystic, is apparently a student of German idealist philosophy—specifically of Transcendentalism. This was a more or less coherent body of ideas

and less frequently upon the pages over which I pored. Ligeia grew ill. The wild eyes blazed with a too—too glorious effulgence; the pale fingers became of the transparent waxen hue of the grave, and the blue veins upon the lofty forehead swelled and sank impetuously with the tides of the most gentle emotion. I saw that she must die—and I struggled desperately in spirit with the grim Azrael.[8] And the struggles of the passionate wife were, to my astonishment, even more energetic than my own. There had been much in her stern nature to impress me with the belief that, to her, death would have come without its terrors;—but not so. Words are impotent to convey any just idea of the fierceness of resistance with which she wrestled with the Shadow. I groaned in anguish at the pitiable spectacle. I would have soothed—I would have reasoned; but, in the intensity of her wild desire for life,—for life—*but* for life—solace and reason were alike the uttermost of folly. Yet not until the last instance, amid the most convulsive writhings of her fierce spirit, was shaken the external placidity of her demeanor. Her voice grew more gentle—grew more low—yet I would not wish to dwell upon the wild meaning of the quietly uttered words. My brain reeled as I hearkened entranced, to a melody more than mortal—to assumptions and aspirations which mortality had never before known.

That she loved me I should not have doubted; and I might have been easily aware that, in a bosom such as hers, love would have reigned no ordinary passion. But in death only, was I fully impressed with the strength of her affection. For long hours, detaining my hand, would she pour out before me the overflowing of a heart whose more than passionate devotion amounted to idolatry. How had I deserved to be so blessed by such confessions?—how had I deserved to be so cursed with the removal of my beloved in the hour of her making them? But upon this subject I cannot bear to dilate.[9] Let me say only, that in Ligeia's more than womanly abandonment to a love, alas! all unmerited, all unworthily bestowed, I at length recognized the principle of her longing with so wildly earnest a desire for the life which was now fleeing so rapidly away. It is this wild longing—it is this eager vehemence of desire for life—*but* for life—that I have no power to portray—no utterance capable of expressing.

centered about the new "nature philosophy" (*Naturphilosophie*) that was debated by various philosophers from the end of the 18th century to the middle of the 19th century (see the introduction to Transcendentalism and Alternative Romanticism, pp. 717–20 herein). Proponents held different, even opposite, opinions concerning the power or feebleness of the human mind and will. It is possible, however, that Poe here has reference to an older tradition of transcendent knowledge—that of the alchemists. Alchemy is thought to have originated in early Egypt or China in the 5th to 3rd centuries B.C.E.. It was early associated with astrology. The alchemical program of turning base metals into gold (the highest and purest metal) was seen by Hellenistic Greeks as part of the general, natural impulse of all things toward perfection. The sacred purpose of the "science" (Latin for "knowledge") of alchemy was to attain ultimate or transcendent knowledge. The purpose of the profane alchemists was to produce gold for wealth and power (see notes to "The Gold-Bug," pp. 321ff.). By the 8th century C.E., alchemical lore, heavily infused with magic, had reached the Arabs. By the Middle Ages, alchemy was generally regarded with suspicion and fear. European alchemists became very secretive and wrote up their experiments in cryptic symbols; and their chemistry experiments became associated in the public mind with the "black arts."

8. Muslim angel of death.
9. To expand on; develop.

At high noon of the night in which she departed, beckoning me, peremptorily, to her side, she bade me repeat certain verses[1] composed by herself not many days before. I obeyed her.—They were these:

Lo! 'tis a gala night
 Within the lonesome latter years!
An angel throng, bewinged, bedight
 In veils, and drowned in tears,
Sit in a theatre, to see
 A play of hopes and fears,
While the orchestra breathes fitfully
 The music of the spheres.[2]

Mimes,[3] in the form of God on high,
 Mutter and mumble low,
And hither and thither fly—
 Mere puppets they, who come and go
At bidding of vast formless things
 That shift the scenery to and fro,
Flapping from out their Condor wings
 Invisible Wo!

That motley drama!—oh, be sure
 It shall not be forgot!
With its Phantom chased forevermore,
 By a crowd that seize it not,
Through a circle that ever returneth in
 To the self-same spot,
And much of Madness and more of Sin,
 And Horror the soul of the plot.

But see, amid the mimic rout,
 A crawling shape intrude!
A blood-red thing that writhes from out
 The scenic solitude!
It writhes!—it writhes!—with mortal pangs
 The mimes become its food,
And the seraphs sob at vermin[4] fangs
 In human gore imbued.

Out—out are the lights—out all!
 And over each quivering form,
The curtain, a funeral pall,
 Comes down with the rush of a storm,
And the angels, all pallid and wan,
 Uprising, unveiling, affirm

1. "The Conqueror Worm" was first published in *Graham's Magazine* in January 1843 as a separate poem; it appeared as part of "Ligeia" in the New York *New World* (February 15, 1845).
2. Reference to the idea that the earth-centered universe was composed of ethereal yet crystalline concentric spheres that made celestial music as they revolved around one another.
3. Imitators; actors who grotesquely or comically mimic ordinary human actions without making sounds.
4. Predatory, lower-life forms like rats or snakes or certain insects. Here three levels of existence are invoked: "seraphs" (angels) weep to see vermin sink their fangs into humans.

That the play is the tragedy, "Man,"
And its hero the Conqueror Worm.

"O God!" half shrieked Ligeia, leaping to her feet and extending her arms aloft with a spasmodic movement, as I made an end of these lines—"O God! O Divine Father!—shall these things be undeviatingly so?—shall this Conqueror be not once conquered? Are we not part and parcel in Thee? Who—who knoweth the mysteries of the will with its vigor? Man doth not yield him to the angels, *nor unto death utterly*, save only through the weakness of his feeble will."

And now, as if exhausted with emotion, she suffered her white arms to fall, and returned solemnly to her bed of Death. And as she breathed her last sighs, there came mingled with them a low murmur from her lips. I bent to them my ear and distinguished, again, the concluding words of the passage in Glanvill—*"Man doth not yield him to the angels, nor unto death utterly, save only through the weakness of his feeble will."*

She died;—and I, crushed into the very dust with sorrow, could no longer endure the lonely desolation of my dwelling in the dim and decaying city by the Rhine. I had no lack of what the world calls wealth. Ligeia had brought me far more, very far more than ordinarily falls to the lot of mortals. After a few months, therefore, of weary and aimless wandering, I purchased, and put in some repair, an abbey, which I shall not name, in one of the wildest and least frequented portions of fair England. The gloomy and dreary grandeur of the building, the almost savage aspect of the domain, the many melancholy and time-honored memories connected with both, had much in unison with the feelings of utter abandonment which had driven me into that remote and unsocial region of the country. Yet although the external abbey, with its verdant decay hanging about it, suffered but little alteration, I gave way, with a child-like perversity, and perchance with a faint hope of alleviating my sorrows, to a display of more than regal magnificence within.— For such follies, even in childhood, I had imbibed a taste and now they came back to me as if in the dotage of grief. Alas, I feel how much even of incipient madness might have been discovered in the gorgeous and fantastic draperies, in the solemn carvings of Egypt, in the wild cornices and furniture, in the Bedlam[5] patterns of the carpets of tufted gold! I had become a bounden slave in the trammels of opium,[6] and my labors and my orders had taken a coloring from my dreams. But these absurdities I must not pause to detail. Let me speak only of that one chamber, ever accursed, whither in a moment of mental alienation, I led from the altar as my bride—as the successor of the unforgotten Ligeia—the fair-haired and blue-eyed Lady Rowena Trevanion, of Tremaine.[7]

5. Turmoil, agitated disturbance, confusion verging on madness; derived from the short appellation for Bethlehem Royal Hospital (pronounced *Bed'lam*), the oldest establishment for the care and confinement of the mentally ill in England, converted from a 13th-century priory about 1400.
6. A literary staple of 19th-century gothic stories, usually indicating evil, debauchery, or madness; commonly smoked or mixed with alcohol, though it could be taken whole (i.e., eaten).
7. This name has been variously glossed as a reference to the blond heroine Rowena in Sir Walter Scott's novel *Ivanhoe* (1820), as a Cornish line of medieval magicians, and even as the family name of Byron's grandmother. But perhaps most suggestive is the possibility of a reference to the gothic novel *Trevanion; or Matrimonial Errors* (1800).

There is no individual portion of the architecture and decoration of that bridal chamber which is not now visibly before me. Where were the souls of the haughty family of the bride, when, through thirst of gold, they permitted to pass the threshold of an apartment *so* bedecked, a maiden and a daughter so beloved? I have said that I minutely remember the details of the chamber—yet I am sadly forgetful on topics of deep moment—and here there was no system, no keeping, in the fantastic display, to take hold upon the memory. The room lay in a high turret of the castellated abbey, was pentagonal[8] in shape, and of capacious size. Occupying the whole southern face of the pentagon was the sole window—an immense sheet of unbroken glass from Venice[9]—a single pane, and tinted of a leaden hue, so that the rays of either the sun or moon, passing through it, fell with a ghastly lustre on the objects within. Over the upper portion of this huge window, extended the trellice-work of an aged vine, which clambered up the massy walls of the turret. The ceiling, of gloomy-looking oak, was excessively lofty, vaulted, and elaborately fretted with the wildest and most grotesque specimens of a semi-Gothic, semi-Druidical[1] device. From out the most central recess of this melancholy vaulting, depended, by a single chain of gold with long links, a huge censer of the same metal, Saracenic[2] in pattern, and with

8. The shape of the room is significant. In occult lore, the pentagon is the internal five-sided figure that is created by drawing a five-pointed star without lifting pencil or chalk. This star is composed of straight lines connecting the vertices of a pentagon and enclosing the internal pentagon. The figure is thus capable of infinite multiplication of infinite regress. Known as the *pentacle* (or pentagram), it is one of the most powerful figures in sorcery; it is the physical and psychic "gateway" to the occult realm. Levine illustrates it thus:
9. Certain Venetian glasses were associated with magic, and one kind of Venetian glass was said to reveal poison in a drink by cracking and turning black (cf. notes to "The Assignation," p. 128, n.6 herein).

1. The Druids were a priestly upper class among ancient Celtic peoples, associated in particular with Great Britain and Gaul (approximately the region of modern France and Belgium). Worshiping various nature deities, they performed magical rituals in forests, woods, and groves; some traditions hold that they performed ritual sacrifices. They regarded the oak tree (note the ceiling in the story) and especially its mistletoe as sacred. "Grotesque": something distorted or deformed beyond the norms of a subject or domain, often indicating the fusion of normally discrete realms (e.g., animal and plant); see notes to "The Assignation" (pp. 116ff. herein) and discussion in the Tales introduction (pp. 77–80). The Goths were a loose collective of pagan tribes of northern Europe in the 3rd to 5th centuries C.E. (Visigoths, Ostrogoths, and others). Their barbaric and superstitious ways caused neoclassic writers to apply the term *gothic* to the kinds of art and literature that evoked horror, terror, and mystery.
2. Arabesque or Arabian; here indicating intricate geometric designs that fold or loop back upon one another. Although basically nonrepresentational, Islamic architecture and textile

many perforations so contrived that there writhed in and out of them, as if endued with a serpent vitality, a continual succession of parti-colored fires.

Some few ottomans and golden candelabra, of Eastern figure, were in various stations about—and there was the couch, too—the bridal couch—of an Indian model, and low, and sculptured of solid ebony, with a pall-like[3] canopy above. In each of the angles of the chamber stood on end a gigantic sarcophagus of black granite, from the tombs of the kings over against Luxor, with their aged lids full of immemorial sculpture.[4] But in the draping of the apartment lay, alas! the chief phantasy of all. The lofty walls, gigantic in height—even unpropor-tionably so—were hung from summit to foot, in vast folds, with a heavy and massive-looking tapestry—tapestry of a material which was found alike as a carpet on the floor, as a covering for the ottomans and the ebony bed as a canopy for the bed, and as the gorgeous volutes[5] of the curtains which partially shaded the window. The material was the richest cloth of gold. It was spotted all over, at irregular intervals, with arabesque figures, about a foot in diameter, and wrought upon the cloth in patterns of the most jetty black. But these figures partook of the true character of the arabesque only when regarded from a single point of view. By a contrivance now common, and indeed, traceable to a very remote period of antiquity, they were made changeable in as-pect. To one entering the room, they bore the appearance of simple monstrosities; but upon a farther advance, this appearance gradually departed; and step by step, as the visiter moved his station in the chamber, he saw himself surrounded by an endless succession of the ghastly forms which belong to the superstition of the Norman, or arise in the guilty slumbers of the monk.[6] The phantasmagoric effect was vastly heightened by the artificial introduction of a strong continual current of wind behind the draperies—giving a hideous and uneasy animation to the whole.

In halls such as these—in a bridal chamber such as this—I passed, with the Lady of Tremaine, the unhallowed hours of the first month of our marriage—passed them with but little disquietude. That my wife dreaded the fierce moodiness of my temper—that she shunned me and loved me but little—I could not help perceiving; but it gave me

designs usually reflect a residual abstract motif of entwined leaves, flowers, and vines. The flickering flames of the gigantic censer are like the moving patterns of light thrown on the floor, walls, and ceiling of the palace of the Byronic stranger in "The Assignation" (pp. 116ff. herein; see notes).

3. Resembling a cover for a coffin or a tomb. "Ottoman": a cushioned footstool or sofa (with-out arms or back).

4. The lids of the coffins are carved with designs from a time before human memory (im-memorial). "Sarcophagus": a stone coffin (from the Greek stem *sark* = "flesh" and *oisophagos* = "gullet": thus a "flesh-eater"). Luxor is an ancient city on the Nile in central Egypt. Along with Karnak, it occupies part of the site of the great city of Thebes (before 3000 B.C.E.). Temples at all three sites contain many monuments to the dynasties of the Pharaohs.

5. Spiral or twisted ornamentation, usually on a vertical column; here of the hanging folds of the drapery.

6. Monk: a solitary, commonly a member of a religious fraternity, in the West usually Christian, living isolated from outside society (i.e., in a monastery). The Normans were northern sav-ages of the European Dark Ages who were regarded in later centuries as hopelessly mired in superstitious demonology. "Guilty slumbers": probably refers to anguish of conscience, prompting dreams of Hell.

rather pleasure than otherwise. I loathed her with a hatred belonging more to demon than to man. My memory flew back, (oh, with what intensity of regret!) to Ligeia, the beloved, the august, the beautiful, the entombed. I revelled in recollections of her purity, of her wisdom, of her lofty, her ethereal nature, of her passionate, her idolatrous love. Now, then, did my spirit fully and freely burn with more than all the fires of her own. In the excitement of my opium dreams (for I was habitually fettered in the shackles of the drug)[7] I would call aloud upon her name, during the silence of the night, or among the sheltered recesses of the glens by day, as if, through the wild eagerness, the solemn passion, the consuming ardor of my longing for the departed, I could restore her to the pathway she had abandoned—ah, *could* it be forever?—upon the earth.

About the commencement of the second month of the marriage, the Lady Rowena was attacked with sudden illness, from which her recovery was slow. The fever which consumed her rendered her nights uneasy; and in her pertubed state of half-slumber, she spoke of sounds, and of motions, in and about the chamber of the turret, which I concluded had no origin save in the distemper of her fancy, or perhaps in the phantasmagoric influences of the chamber itself. She became at length convalescent—finally well. Yet but a brief period elapsed, ere a second more violent disorder again threw her upon a bed of suffering; and from this attack her frame, at all times feeble, never altogether recovered. Her illnesses were, after this epoch, of alarming character, and of more alarming recurrence, defying alike the knowledge and the great exertions of her physicians. With the increase of the chronic disease which had thus, apparently, taken too sure hold upon her constitution to be eradicated by human means, I could not fail to observe a similar increase in the nervous irritation of her temperament, and in her excitability by trivial causes of fear. She spoke again, and now more frequently and pertinaciously, of the sounds—of the slight sounds—and of the unusual motions among the tapestries, to which she had formerly alluded.

One night, near the closing in of September, she pressed this distressing subject with more than usual emphasis upon my attention. She had just awakened from an unquiet slumber, and I had been watching, with feelings half of anxiety, half of a vague terror, the workings of her emaciated countenance. I sat by the side of her ebony bed,

7. The repeated references to opium and dreams (including an early description of Ligeia's face) have from the very first suggested to some readers that the narrator's experiences are delusional. Mabbott notes that in a reprinting of the story in the New York *New World* (February 15, 1845) the magazine carried an interpretative notice. After praising Poe's force and boldness, the reviewer writes: "Mark the exquisite art, which keeps constantly before the reader the ruined and spectre-haunted mind of the narrator, and so suggests a *possible explanation* of the marvels of the story, without in the least weakening its vigor as an exposition of the mystical *thesis* which the tale is designed to illustrate and enforce." Although insisting on supernatural reading of the tale, Mabbott points out the close similarity of the dramatic situation and even of the opening paragraph to Charles Dickens's "A Madman's Manuscript," chapter 11 of *Pickwick Papers* (1836–37). He also notes that the phrase "daughters of Delos," may have been borrowed from Edward Bulwer-Lytton's "Manuscript Found in a Madhouse," a story in his *Conversations with an Ambitious Student in Ill Health, with Other Pieces* (1835), where the reference is to divinely inspired visions or dreams.

upon one of the ottomans of India. She partly arose, and spoke, in an earnest low whisper, of sounds which she *then* heard, but which I could not hear—of motions which she *then* saw, but which I could not perceive. The wind was rushing hurriedly behind the tapestries, and I wished to show her (what, let me confess it, I could not *all* believe) that those almost inarticulate breathings, and those very gentle variations of the figures upon the wall, were but the natural effects of that customary rushing of the wind. But a deadly pallor, over-spreading her face, had proved to me that my exertions to reassure her would be fruitless. She appeared to be fainting, and no attendants were within call. I remembered where was deposited a decanter of light wine which had been ordered by her physicians, and hastened across the chamber to procure it. But, as I stepped beneath the light of the censer, two circumstances of a startling nature attracted my attention. I had felt that some palpable although invisible object had passed lightly by my person; and I saw that there lay upon the golden carpet, in the very middle of the rich lustre thrown from the censer, a shadow—a faint, indefinite shadow of angelic aspect—such as might be fancied for the shadow of a shade. But I was wild with the excitement of an immoderate dose of opium, and heeded these things but little, nor spoke of them to Rowena. Having found the wine, I recrossed the chamber, and poured out a goblet-ful, which I held to the lips of the fainting lady. She had now partially recovered, however, and took the vessel herself, while I sank upon an ottoman near me, with my eyes fastened upon her person. It was then that I became distinctly aware of a gentle foot-fall upon the carpet, and near the couch; and in a second thereafter, as Rowena was in the act of raising the wine to her lips, I saw, or may have dreamed that I saw, fall within the goblet, as if from some invisible spring in the atmosphere of the room, three or four large drops of a brilliant and ruby colored fluid.[8] If this I saw—not so Rowena. She swallowed the wine unhesitatingly, and I forbore to speak to her of a circumstance which must, after all, I considered, have been but the suggestion of a vivid imagination, rendered morbidly active by the terror of the lady, by the opium, and by the hour.

Yet I cannot conceal it from my own perception that, immediately subsequent to the fall of the ruby-drops, a rapid change for the worse took place in the disorder of my wife; so that, on the third subsequent night, the hands of her menials prepared her for the tomb, and on the fourth, I sat alone, with her shrouded body, in that fantastic chamber which had received her as my bride.—Wild visions, opium-engendered, flitted, shadow-like, before me. I gazed with unquiet eye upon the sarcophagi in the angles of the room, upon the varying figures of the drapery, and upon the writhing of the parti-colored fires in the censer overhead. My eyes then fell, as I called to mind the circumstances of a former night, to the spot beneath the glare of the censer where I had seen the faint traces of the shadow. It was there,

8. Critics have disagreed whether these drops are poison administered by the crazed narrator or are the transformed spirit of Ligeia as the alchemical "elixir of life" entering a new corporeal existence.

however, no longer; and breathing with greater freedom, I turned my glances to the pallid and rigid figure upon the bed. Then rushed upon me a thousand memories of Ligeia—and then came back upon my heart, with the turbulent violence of a flood, the whole of that unutterable wo with which I had regarded *her* thus enshrouded. The night waned; and still, with a bosom full of bitter thoughts of the one only and supremely beloved, I remained gazing upon the body of Rowena.

It might have been midnight, or perhaps earlier, or later, for I had taken no note of time, when a sob, low, gentle, but very distinct, startled me from my revery.—I *felt* that it came from the bed of ebony—the bed of death. I listened in an agony of superstitious terror—but there was no repetition of the sound. I strained my vision to detect any motion in the corpse—but there was not the slightest perceptible. Yet I could not have been deceived. I *had* heard the noise, however faint, and my soul was awakened within me. I resolutely and perseveringly kept my attention riveted upon the body. Many minutes elapsed before any circumstance occurred tending to throw light upon the mystery. At length it became evident that a slight, a very feeble, and barely noticeable tinge of color had flushed up within the cheeks, and along the sunken small veins of the eyelids. Through a species of unutterable horror and awe, for which the language of mortality has no sufficiently energetic expression, I felt my heart cease to beat, my limbs grow rigid where I sat. Yet a sense of duty finally operated to restore my self-possession. I could no longer doubt that we had been precipitate in our preparations—that Rowena still lived. It was necessary that some immediate exertion be made; yet the turret was altogether apart from the portion of the abbey tenanted by the servants—there were none within call—I had no means of summoning them to my aid without leaving the room for many minutes—and this I could not venture to do. I therefore struggled alone in my endeavors to call back the spirit still hovering. In a short period it was certain, however, that a relapse had taken place; the color disappeared from both eyelid and cheek, leaving a wanness even more than that of marble; the lips became doubly shrivelled and pinched up in the ghastly expression of death; a repulsive clamminess and coldness overspread rapidly the surface of the body; and all the usual rigorous stiffness immediately supervened. I fell back with a shudder upon the couch from which I had been so startingly aroused, and again gave myself up to passionate waking visions of Ligeia.

An hour thus elapsed when (could it be possible?) I was a second time aware of some vague sound issuing from the region of the bed. I listened—in extremity of horror. The sound came again—it was a sigh. Rushing to the corpse, I saw—distinctly saw—a tremor upon the lips. In a minute afterward they relaxed, disclosing a bright line of the pearly teeth. Amazement now struggled in my bosom with the profound awe which had hitherto reigned there alone. I felt that my vision grew dim, that my reason wandered; and it was only by a violent effort that I at length succeeded in nerving myself to the task which duty thus once more had pointed out. There was now a partial glow

upon the forehead and upon the cheek and throat; a perceptible warmth pervaded the whole frame; there was even a slight pulsation at the heart. The lady *lived*; and with redoubled ardor I betook myself to the task of restoration. I chafed and bathed the temples and the hands, and used every exertion which experience, and no little medical reading, could suggest. But in vain. Suddenly, the color fled, the pulsation ceased, the lips resumed the expression of the dead, and, in an instant afterward, the whole body took upon itself the icy chilliness, the livid hue, the intense rigidity, the sunken outline, and all the loathsome peculiarities of that which has been, for many days, a tenant of the tomb.

And again I sunk into visions of Ligeia—and again, (what marvel that I shudder while I write?) *again* there reached my ears a low sob from the region of the ebony bed. But why shall I minutely detail the unspeakable horrors of that night? Why shall I pause to relate how, time after time, until near the period of the gray dawn, this hideous drama of revivication was repeated; how each terrific relapse was only into a sterner and apparently more irredeemable death; how each agony wore the aspect of a struggle with some invisible foe; and how each struggle was succeeded by I know not what of wild change in the personal appearance of the corpse? Let me hurry to a conclusion.

The greater part of the fearful night had worn away, and she who had been dead, once again stirred—and now more vigorously than hitherto, although arousing from a dissolution more appalling in its utter hopelessness than any. I had long ceased to struggle or to move, and remained sitting rigidly upon the ottoman, a helpless prey to a whirl of violent emotions, of which extreme awe was perhaps the least terrible, the least consuming. The corpse, I repeat, stirred, and now more vigorously than before. The hues of life flushed up with unwonted energy into the countenance—the limbs relaxed—and, save that the eyelids were yet pressed heavily together, and that the bandages and draperies of the grave still imparted their charnel character to the figure, I might have dreamed that Rowena had indeed shaken off, utterly, the fetters of Death. But if this idea was not, even then, altogether adopted, I could at least doubt no longer, when, arising from the bed, tottering, with feeble steps, with closed eyes, and with the manner of one bewildered in a dream, the thing that was enshrouded advanced boldly and palpably into the middle of the apartment.

I trembled not—I stirred not—for a crowd of unutterable fancies connected with the air, the stature, the demeanor of the figure, rushing hurridly through my brain, had paralyzed—had chilled me into stone. I stirred not—but gazed upon the apparition. There was a mad disorder in my thoughts—a tumult unappeasable. Could it, indeed, be the *living* Rowena who confronted me? Could it indeed be Rowena *at all*—the fair-haired, the blue-eyed Lady Rowena Trevanion of Tremaine? Why, *why* should I doubt it? The bandage lay heavily about the mouth—but then might it not be the mouth of the breathing Lady of Tremaine? And the cheeks—there were the roses as in her noon of life—yes, these might indeed be the fair cheeks of the living Lady of

Tremaine. And the chin, with its dimples, as in health, might it not be hers?—but *had she then grown taller since her malady?* What inexpressible madness seized me with that thought? One bound, and I had reached her feet! Shrinking from my touch, she let fall from her head, unloosened, the ghastly cerements which had confined it, and there streamed forth, into the rushing atmosphere of the chamber, huge masses of long and dishevelled hair; *it was blacker than the raven wings of the midnight!* And now slowly opened *the eyes* of the figure which stood before me. "Here then, at least," I shrieked aloud, "can I never—can I never be mistaken—these are the full, and the black, and the wild eyes—of my lost love—of the lady—of the LADY LIGEIA!"

How to Write a Blackwood Article This work was published under different titles and subtitles and in different formats. It was first published in the Baltimore *American Museum* (November 1838) as "The Signora Psyche Zenobia" with a companion tale, "The Scythe of Time," which was supposed to be the result of Psyche Zenobia's following the instructions of a successful magazine editor. The text reprinted here is that of the *Broadway Journal* (July 12, 1845), where it was set up as one story including the other ("The Scythe of Time" was retitled "A Predicament," as though a comment on the main title). *Blackwood's Edinburgh Magazine*, founded 1817–18, almost immediately became famous for its "sensation" tales, which Poe defines quite precisely in this parodic work. See the Tales introduction pp. 77–80 herein) for further discussion; a sampling of sensation tales from *Blackwood's* is included in this volume (pp. 754–66).

How to Write a Blackwood Article

> "In the name of the Prophet—figs!!"
> *Cry of the Turkish fig-pedler.*[1]

I presume every body has heard of me. My name is the Signora Psyche Zenobia. This I know to be a fact. No body but my enemies ever calls me Suky Snobbs.[2] I have been assured that Suky is but a vulgar

1. Mabbott suggests that the motto is an allusion to *Rejected Addresses: or The New Theatrum Poetarum* (1812), a parody of poets like Wordsworth, Scott, Coleridge, and Byron, published by Horace Smith and James Smith. This particular passage is from a speech attributed to Dr. Samuel Johnson's ghost: "A swelling opening is too often succeeded by an insignificant conclusion," as when street venders in Constantinople used to cry out "in the name of the Prophet—figs." That is, a big promise (name of the prophet of God) has little result (figs). Mabbott does not remark that the word *figs* is also an ancient street metaphor accompanied by an obscene gesture. The allusion also implicates Horace Smith's novel *Zillah: A Tale of the Holy City* (1828), a book that Poe lampoons elsewhere (especially in "A Tale of Jerusalem"; see notes to "Loss of Breath," pp. 89ff. herein).
2. "Zenobia" is a classic name for a woman of great beauty and intelligence, an allusion to the queen of Palmyra (c. 268–272) who sought to extend her power over the Roman Empire in the East. She was defeated by Emperor Aurelian, who brought her fettered and manacled in shackles of gold back to Rome (though she was allowed to live in a villa in Tivoli). The narrator's contrasting class status is indicated by the mispronunciation of her name by her enemies: Psyche (with a long *i* sound) becomes Suky, and Zenobia (with a long *o*) becomes Snobbs in an apparent pun on *snob*. See Mabbott, II, 357, for possible satiric targets.

corruption of Psyche, which is good Greek, and means "the soul" (that's me, I'm *all* soul) and sometimes "a butterfly," which latter meaning undoubtedly alludes to my appearance in my new crimson satin dress, with the sky-blue Arabian *mantelet*, and the trimmings of green *agraffas*, and the seven flounces of orange-colored *auriculas*.[3] As for Snobbs—any person who should look at me would be instantly aware that my name wasn't Snobbs. Miss Tabitha Turnip propagated that report through sheer envy. Tabitha Turnip indeed! Oh the little wretch! But what can we expect from a turnip? Wonder if she remembers the old adage about "blood out of a turnip, &c." [Mem: put her in mind of it the first opportunity.] [Mem again—pull her nose.] Where was I? Ah! I have been assured that Snobbs is a mere corruption of Zenobia, and that Zenobia was a queen—(So am I. Dr. Moneypenny, always calls me the Queen of Hearts)—and that Zenobia, as well as Psyche, is good Greek, and that my father was "a Greek,"[4] and that consequently I have a right to our patronymic, which is Zenobia, and not by any means Snobbs. Nobody but Tabitha Turnip calls me Suky Snobbs. I am the Signora Psyche Zenobia.

As I said before, every body has heard of me. I am that very Signora Psyche Zenobia, so justly celebrated as corresponding secretary to the "*Philadelphia, Regular, Exchange, Tea, Total, Young, Belles, Lettres, Universal, Experimental, Bibliographical, Association, To, Civilize, Humanity.*" Dr. Moneypenny made the title for us, and says he chose it because it sounded big like an empty rum-puncheon. (A vulgar man that sometimes—but he's deep.) We all sign the initials of the society after our names, in the fashion of the R.S.A., Royal Society of Arts[5]— the S.D.U.K., Society for the Diffusion of Useful Knowledge, &c. &c. Dr. Moneypenny says that S stands for *stale*, and that D.U.K. spells duck, (but it don't,) and that S.D.U.K. stands for Stale Duck, and not for Lord Brougham's society[6]—but then Dr. Moneypenny is such a queer man that I am never sure when he is telling me the truth. At any rate we always add to our names the initials P.R.E.T.T.Y. B.L.U.E.B.A.T.C.H.—that is to say, Philadelphia, Regular, Exchange, Tea, Total, Young, Belles, Lettres, Universal, Experimental, Bibliographical, Association, To, Civilize, Humanity—one letter for each word, which is a decided improvement upon Lord Brougham. Dr. Moneypenny will have it that our initials give our true character—but for my life I can't see what he means.

3. Flowers of the primrose family. "*Mantelet*": a short cloak. "*Agraffas*": ornamental clasps. Psyche does mean "soul" in Greek; it is a metaphor from the butterfly, which passes through several stages of metamorphosis from an earthbound creature (larvae state) to a beautiful winged creature of the skies. Miss Zenobia's outlandish attire suggests her attempt to be "*all* soul."

4. A hard drinker or a gambler (old slang, according to Mabbott); thus she unknowingly suggests that her father was a wastrel. Levine suggests that Dr. Moneypenny equals Ralph Waldo Emerson; but the satire seems general, aimed at editors as a type. Queen of Hearts: Psyche fell in love with Eros (Roman Cupid), the god of love, and married him, after which Zeus made her immortal.

5. A British society founded in 1754.

6. Lord Henry Brougham (1778–1868), political, social, and educational reformer who was connected with the *Edinburgh Review*. Brougham established the Society for the Diffusion of Useful Knowledge (S.D.U.K.) to provide inexpensive publications on useful subjects.

Notwithstanding the good offices of the Doctor, and the strenuous exertions of the association to get itself into notice, it met with no very great success until I joined it. The truth is, members indulged in too flippant a tone of discussion. The papers read every Saturday evening were characterized less by depth than buffoonery. They were all whipped syllabub.[7] There was no investigation of first causes, first principles. There was no investigation of anything at all. There was no attention paid to that great point the "fitness of things." In short there was no fine writing like this. It was all low—very! No profundity, no reading, no metaphysics—nothing which the learned call spirituality, and which the unlearned choose to stigmatise as cant. [Dr. M. says I ought to spell "cant" with a capital K—but I know better.]

When I joined the society it was my endeavour to introduce a better style of thinking and writing, and all the world knows how well I have succeeded. We get up as good papers now in the P.R.E.T.T.Y.B.L.U.E. B.A.T.C.H. as any to be found even in Blackwood.[8] I say, Blackwood, because I have been assured that the finest writing, upon every subject, is to be discovered in the pages of that justly celebrated Magazine. We now take it for our model upon all themes, and are getting into rapid notice accordingly. And, after all, it's not so very difficult a matter to compose an article of the genuine Blackwood stamp, if one only goes properly about it. Of course I don't speak of the political articles. Every body knows how *they* are managed, since Dr. Moneypenny explained it. Mr. Blackwood has a pair of tailor's-shears, and three apprentices who stand by him for orders. One hands him the "Times," another the "Examiner," and a third a "Gulley's New Compendium of Slang-Whang."[9] Mr. B. merely cuts out and intersperses. It is soon done—nothing but Examiner, Slang-Whang, and Times— then Times, Slang-Whang, and Examiner—and then Times, Examiner, and Slang-Whang.

But the chief merit of the Magazine lies in its miscellaneous articles; and the best of these come under the head of what Dr. Moneypenny calls the *bizarreries* (whatever they may mean) and what every body else calls the *intensities*. This is a species of writing which I have long known how to appreciate, although it is only since my late visit to Mr. Blackwood (deputed by the society) that I have been made aware of the exact method of composition. This method is very simple, but not so much so as the politics. Upon my calling at Mr. B.'s, and making known to him the wishes of the society, he received me with great civility, took me into his study, and gave me a clear explanation of the whole process.

"My dear madam," said he, evidently struck with my majestic

7. A dessert of milk or cream mixed with wine or cider that is either whipped until frothy or boiled until solid.
8. A slam at the intellectual pretensions of *Blackwood's* and the whole society of Bluestockings (see notes to "Lionizing," pp. 128ff. herein.)
9. John Gully (1783–1868), English boxer, legislator, horse owner, and manager of a coal business. "Slang-Whang": according to Levine, may come from a piece in the *New York Mirror* dealing with a Chinese editor who drinks too much brandy. The *Times* was the most distinguished and respected London paper of this period. The *Examiner* was another London paper.

appearance, for I had on the crimson satin, with the green *agraffas*, and orange-coloured *auriculas*, "My *dear* madam," said he, "sit down. The matter stands thus. In the first place, your writer of intensities must have very black ink, and a very big pen, with a very blunt nib. And, mark me, Miss Psyche Zenobia!" he continued, after a pause, with the most impressive energy and solemnity of manner, "mark me!— *that pen—must—never be mended!* Herein, madam, lies the secret, the soul, of intensity. I assume it upon myself to say, that no individual, of however great genius, ever wrote with a good pen,—understand me,— a good article. You may take it for granted, that when manuscript can be read it is never worth reading. This is a leading principle in our faith, to which if you cannot readily assent, our conference is at an end."

He paused. But, of course, as I had no wish to put an end to the conference, I assented to a proposition so very obvious, and one, too, of whose truth I had all along been sufficiently aware. He seemed pleased, and went on with his instructions.

"It may appear invidious in me, Miss Psyche Zenobia, to refer you to any article, or set of articles, in the way of model or study; yet perhaps I may as well call your attention to a few cases. Let me see. There was 'The Dead Alive,'[1] a capital thing!—the record of a gentleman's sensations when entombed before the breath was out of his body—full of taste, terror, sentiment, metaphysics, and erudition. You would have sworn that the writer had been born and brought up in a coffin. Then we had the 'Confessions of an Opium-eater'[2]—fine, very fine!—glorious imagination—deep philosophy—acute speculation—plenty of fire and fury, and a good spicing of the decidedly unintelligible. That was a nice bit of flummery, and went down the throats of the people delightfully. They would have it that Coleridge wrote the paper—but not so. It was composed by my pet baboon, Juniper, over a rummer of Hollands[3] and water, 'hot, without sugar.'" [This I could scarcely have believed had it been any body but Mr. Blackwood, who assured me of it.] "Then there was 'The Involuntary Experimentalist,'[4] all about a gentleman who got baked in an oven, and came out alive and well, although certainly done to a turn. And then there was 'The Diary of a Late Physician,'[5] where the merit lay in good rant, and indifferent Greek—both of them taking things, with the public. And then there was 'The Man

1. Appeared in *Fraser's Magazine* in 1833–34, but the story as described is that of "The Buried Alive" in *Blackwood's* (October 1821; reprinted on pp. 759ff. herein).
2. First published, anonymously, in the *London Magazine* in 1821, giving rise to advertising hype about who the author might be. It was published as a book in 1822. Although the publishers and reviewers encouraged speculation on its authorship, the secret was not well kept, and many knew that the author was Thomas De Quincey (1785–1859). Poe's description (below) of this nightmarish narrative of drug addiction as "flummery" (pudding) that the public swallowed easily and his having Mr. Blackwood attribute its authorship to his "pet baboon" are satiric hits on several targets, including Coleridge, De Quincey, the publishers, *Blackwood's*, the reviewers, and the reading public.
3. A variety of gin. "Rummer": a tall glass without a stem.
4. A story that appeared in *Blackwood's* in October 1837 about a man who gets trapped in a giant metal vat (rather than a literal oven) which then becomes heated.
5. A serial by Samuel Warren (1807–1877) that appeared in *Blackwood's* in 1830 and was published as a book in 1838.

in the Bell,'[6] a paper by-the-bye, Miss Zenobia, which I cannot suffi-
ciently recommend to your attention. It is the history of a young per-
son who goes to sleep under the clapper of a church bell, and is
awakened by its tolling for a funeral. The sound drives him mad, and,
accordingly, pulling out his tablets, he gives a record of his sensations.
Sensations are the great things after all. Should you ever be drowned
or hung, be sure and make a note of your sensations—they will be
worth to you ten guineas a sheet. If you wish to write forcibly, Miss
Zenobia, pay minute attention to the sensations."

"That I certainly will, Mr. Blackwood," said I.

"Good!" he replied. "I see you are a pupil after my own heart. But I
must put you *au fait*[7] to the details necessary in composing what may
be denominated a genuine Blackwood article of the sensation stamp—
the kind which you will understand me to say I consider the best for
all purposes.

"The first thing requisite is to get yourself into such a scrape as no
one ever got into before. The oven, for instance,—that was a good hit.
But if you have no oven, or big bell, at hand, and if you cannot conve-
niently tumble out of a balloon, or be swallowed up in an earthquake, or
get stuck fast in a chimney, you will have to be contented with simply
imagining some similar misadventure. I should prefer, however, that you
have the actual fact to bear you out. Nothing so well assists the fancy, as
an experimental knowledge of the matter in hand. 'Truth is strange,' you
know, 'stranger than fiction'—besides being more to the purpose."

Here I assured him I had an excellent pair of garters, and would go
and hang myself forthwith.

"Good!" he replied, "do so;—although hanging is somewhat hack-
nied. Perhaps you might do better. Take a dose of Brandreth's pills,[8]
and then give us your sensations. However, my instructions will apply
equally well to any variety of misadventure, and in your way home you
may easily get knocked in the head, or run over by an omnibus, or bit-
ten by a mad dog, or drowned in a gutter. But, to proceed.

"Having determined upon your subject, you must next consider the
tone, or manner, of your narration. There is the tone didactic, the tone
enthusiastic, the tone natural—all common-place enough. But then
there is the tone laconic, or curt, which has lately come much into
use. It consists in short sentences. Somehow thus. Can't be too brief.
Can't be too snappish. Always a full stop. And never a paragraph.

"Then there is the tone elevated, diffusive, and interjectional. Some
of our best novelists patronize this tone. The words must be all in a
whirl, like a humming-top, and make a noise very similar, which an-
swers remarkably well instead of meaning. This is the best of all possi-
ble styles where the writer is in too great a hurry to think.

6. A story by William Maginn that appeared in *Blackwood's* in November 1821. (Reprinted
pp. 762ff. herein.)
7. I.e., make you privy to, bring you up to date.
8. A well-known laxative from Britain, widely used in America. According to Mabbott, the pills
were said to remove "acrimonious humors," the source of all illnesses. See "A Predicament"
(pp. 187–88, n. 2 herein) and "Some Words with a Mummy" (p. 397, n. 7).

"The tone metaphysical is also a good one. If you know any big words this is your chance for them. Talk of the Ionic and Eleatic schools—of Archytas, Gorgias and Alcmœon.[9] Say something about objectivity and subjectivity. Be sure and abuse a man called Locke.[1] Turn up your nose at things in general, and when you let slip anything a little *too* absurd, you need not be at the trouble of scratching it out, but just add a foot-note, and say that you are indebted for the above profound observation to the '*Kritik der reinem Vernunft,*' or to the '*Metaphysische Anfangsgrunde der Naturwissenschaft.*'[2] This will look erudite and—and—and frank.[3]

"There are various other tones of equal celebrity, but I shall mention only two more—the tone transcendental and the tone heterogeneous. In the former the merit consists in seeing into the nature of affairs a very great deal farther than any body else. This second sight is very efficient when properly managed. A little reading of the 'Dial'[4] will carry you a great way. Eschew, in this case, big words; get them as small as possible, and write them upside down. Look over Channing's poems and quote what he says about a 'fat little man with a delusive show of Can.'[5] Put in something about the Supernal Oneness. Don't say a syl-

9. There is more than one Alcmæon or Alcmœon in myth and history; this one appears to be a natural philosopher who lived in Crotona in the 6th century B.C.E. and was a pupil a Pythagoras. (Not to be confused with Alcman, the 7th-century B.C.E. Greek lyric poet.) "Ionic [school]": founded by philosopher Thales of Miletus (c. 636–c. 546 B.C.E.) in Asiatic Ionia, who believed that there was one basic source of all things, namely, water. "Eleatic school": founded by the Greek philosopher Parmenides (born c. 514 B.C.E.) and later developed by his pupil Zeno of Elea (c. 490–c. 430 B.C.E.). They claimed that reason should have priority over the senses and were highly skeptical of so-called common sense. Parmenides posited the basic physical existence of all being and then deconstructed notions of change and motion as illusions of the senses. One of Zeno's most famous arguments was against the possibility of motion consistent with the notion of infinitely divisible physical parts (known as the Paradox of Achilles and the Tortoise). Zeno of Elea is to be distinguished from Zeno of Citium (334–c. 262 B.C.E.), who is associated with the Stoic school of Greek philosophers (see notes to "Loss of Breath," pp. 89ff. herein). Archytas (mid-4th century B.C.E.), Pythagorean mathematician and philosopher. Gorgias (5th century B.C.E.), Sicilian orator and Sophist who appears as a character in Plato's *Meno*.
1. John Locke (1632–1704), founder of British philosophical empiricism. Rejecting the notion of innate ideas, he argued that all knowledge derives from the experience of the five senses, which write on the human mind as on a *tabula rasa* (blank tablet). The question of objectivity and subjectivity is one of recurrent debate among the philosophers of the later 18th century and the earlier 19th century, as well as among the literary Romantics (see next note).
2. *Critique of Pure Reason* (1781) and *Metaphysical Foundations of Natural Science* (1786), written by the German philosopher Immanuel Kant (1724–1804). He rejected the systems of empirical philosophers like David Hume (1711–1776) who had tried to press the implications of Lockean philosophy to a logical extreme of skepticism. Kant suggested that there is within the mind a power to intuit things transcending the finite limitations of reason and sense experience. He argued that objective reality can be understood only insofar as sense experience conforms to the essential "knowing" powers or subjective structures of the mind. Beyond the phenomena of the physical world lie the "noumena" of another realm, unknowable but yet compelling acknowledgment (the categorical imperative of his system of ethics). See Transcendentalism and Alternative Romanticism, pp. 717–27 herein.
3. A continuation of the satire on pretended learning rampant in the magazines of Poe's time.
4. The chief magazine, which ran from 1840 to 1844, of the American Transcendentalists. Fuller and Emerson each edited it. Several scholars have assumed that Miss Zenobia is Margaret Fuller (1810–1850), a prolific writer and an aggressive advocate of women's rights and other more or less liberal causes. But Poe was probably satirizing not her so much as an empty-headed amateur writer for whom writing was not a vocation but an avocation. The references to *The Dial* were not included until 1845, as part of Poe's general satire on at the Transcendentalist group in America.
5. The poet William Ellery Channing (1818–1901), nephew of William Ellery Channing (1780–1842), the Unitarian minister. A volume of the younger Channing's *Poems* was pub-

lable about the Infernal Twoness. Above all, study inuendo. Hint every thing—assert nothing. If you feel inclined to say 'bread and butter' do not by any means say it outright. You may say anything and every thing *approaching* to 'bread and butter.' You may hint at buck-wheat cake, or you may even go so far as to insinuate oat-meal porridge, but if bread and butter be your real meaning, be cautious, my *dear* Miss Psyche, not on any account to say 'bread and butter!' "

I assured him that I should never say it again as long as I lived. He kissed me and continued:

"As for the tone heterogeneous, it is merely a judicious mixture, in equal proportions, of all the other tones in the world, and is consequently made up of everything deep, great, odd, piquant, pertinent, and pretty.

"Let us suppose now you have determined upon your incidents and tone. The most important portion,—in fact the soul of the whole business, is yet to be attended to—I allude to *the filling up*. It is not to be supposed that a lady or gentleman either has been leading the life of a bookworm. And yet above all things it is necessary that your article have an air of erudition, or at least afford evidence of extensive general reading. Now I'll put you in the way of accomplishing this point. See here!" (pulling down some three or four ordinary looking volumes, and opening them at random.) "By casting your eye down almost any page of any book in the world, you will be able to perceive at once a host of little scraps of either learning or *bel-esprit-ism*,[6] which are the very thing for the spicing of a Blackwood article. You might as well note down a few while I read them to you. I shall make two divisions: first, *Piquant Facts for the Manufacture of Similes*; and second, *Piquant Expressions to be introduced as occasion may require*. Write now!—" and I wrote as he dictated.

"Piquant facts for similes. 'There were originally but three Muses—Melete, Mneme, and Aœde[7]—meditation, memory, and singing.' You may make a great deal of that little fact if properly worked. You see it is not generally known, and looks *recherché*.[8] You must be careful and give the thing with a downright improviso air.[9]

"Again. 'The river Alpheus[1] passed beneath the sea, and emerged without injury to the purity of its waters.' Rather stale that, to be sure,

lished in 1842–43, which Poe reviewed unfavorably in *Graham's* in August 1843. Channing was widely criticized by reviewers for his sloppy composition and awkward lines. This twisted quotation refers to Channing's lines: "Thou meetest a common man, / With a delusive show of *can*." Channing was also a friend of Emerson.

6. Poe's neologism. *Bel esprit* is frequently used in French to suggest wit; also, loosely, the practice of letters. Here a joke: Mr. Blackwood would make an affected bel-esprit-ist out of Zenobia, i.e., someone who makes a "profession" out of one's taste.

7. In Greek mythology, the patron goddesses of the arts. There are several versions of the myth; Blackwood's list is just one, and not the most standard one. Here Melete is muse of meditation; Mneme, of memory; and Aoede, of song. One account says the muses were the daughters of Zeus and Mnemosyne; originally three, they eventually became nine. A standard version of the nine arts they represent is epic poetry and eloquence (Calliope), music and lyric poetry (Euterpe), love poetry (Erato), sacred poetry and oratory (Polyhymnia or Polymnia), history (Clio), tragedy (Melpomene), comedy (Thalia), choral song and dance (Terpsichore), astronomy (Urania).

8. Uncommon; esoteric; studied; mannered.

9. Improvised, offhand (the opposite of *recherché*).

1. In "Kubla Khan," Coleridge refers to Kubla's "pleasure dome . . . where Alph, the sacred river, ran / Through caverns measureless to man / Down to a sunless sea." Alpheus is usually

but, if properly dressed and dished up, will look quite as fresh as ever.
"Here is something better. 'The Persian Iris[2] appears to some per-
sons to possess a sweet and very powerful perfume, while to others it
is perfectly scentless.' Fine that, and very delicate! Turn it about a lit-
tle, and it will do wonders. We'll have something else in the botanical
line. There's nothing goes down so well, especially with the help of a
little Latin. Write!

" 'The Epidendrum Flos Aeris, of Java,[3] bears a very beautiful flower,
and will live when pulled up by the roots. The natives suspend it by a
cord from the ceiling, and enjoy its fragrance for years.' That's capital!
That will do for the similes. Now for the Piquant Expressions.

PIQUANT EXPRESSIONS. 'The venerable Chinese novel Ju-Kiao-Li.'[4]
Good! By introducing these few words with dexterity you will evince your
intimate acquaintance with the language and literature of the Chinese.
With the aid of this you may possibly get along without either Arabic, or
Sanscrit, or Chickasaw. There is no passing muster, however, without
Spanish, Italian, German, Latin, and Greek. I must look you out a little
specimen of each. Any scrap will answer, because you must depend upon
your own ingenuity to make it fit into your article. Now write!

" 'Aussi tendre que Zaire'—as tender as Zaire[5]—French. Alludes to
the frequent repetition of the phrase, la tendre Zaire, in the French
tragedy of that name. Properly introduced, will show not only your
knowledge of the language, but your general reading and wit. You can
say, for instance, that the chicken you were eating (write an article
about being choked to death by a chicken-bone) was not altogether
aussi tendre que Zaire. Write!

> 'Van muerte tan escondida,
> Que no te sienta venir,
> Porque e! plazer del morir
> No me torne a dar la vida.'

That's Spanish—from Miguel de Cervantes, 'Come quickly O death!
but be sure and don't let me see you coming, lest the pleasure I shall
feel at your appearance should unfortunately bring me back again to
life.'[6] This you may slip in quite à propos when you are struggling in
the last agonies with the chicken-bone. Write!

identified as the river of the Peloponnesus in southern Greece that flows to the Ionian Sea.
 Its course at several places runs underground. This feature seems to have given rise to the
 myth of the river god Alpheus who pursued the nymph Arethusa through subterranean
 chambers. Artemis changed her into the fountain of Arethusa on the island Ortygia at Syra-
 cuse; but Alpheus chased after her even under the sea, trying to merge his waters with those
 of the fountain.
2. A plant whose flowers have white upper and brown lower petals.
3. An island near the main island of Indonesia (see notes to "Ms. Found in Bottle," pp. 106ff.
 herein). "Flos Aeris": flower of the air (Latin).
4. A Chinese novel by an unknown author written during the late Ming Dynasty (1368–1644).
 It was translated into French, German, and English in the 1820s and created a small stir in
 American papers when it was published. It is also known also as "The Beautiful Couple" or
 "The Two Fair Cousins" (subtitle).
5. The tragedy Zaire (1732) is by Voltaire.
6. These lines are quoted by Cervantes (1547–1616) in Don Quixote (1605–15), II.xxxviii, and
 are attributed to Valencian Escrivá. The translation is a bit loose. Blackwood's imprecisions
 will be compounded by Miss Zenobia in her use of his suggestions in the companion tale
 that follows.

'Il pover 'huomo che non se'n era accorto,
Andava combattendo, e era morto.'

That's Italian, you perceive,—from Ariosto.[7] It means that a great hero, in the heat of combat, not perceiving that he had been fairly killed, continued to fight valiantly, dead as he was. The application of this to your own case is obvious—for I trust, Miss Psyche, that you will not neglect to kick for at least an hour and a half after you have been choked to death by that chicken-bone. Please to write!

'Und sterb' ich doch, no sterb' ich denn
Durch sie—durch sie!'

That's German—from Schiller.[8] 'And if I die, at least I die—for thee— for thee!' Here it is clear that you are apostrophising the *cause* of your disaster, the chicken. Indeed what gentleman (or lady either) of sense, *would'nt* die, I should like to know, for a well fattened capon of the right Molucca breed, stuffed with capers and mushrooms, and served up in a salad-bowl, with orange-jellies *en mosäiques*.[9] Write! (You can get them that way at Tortoni's,)[1]—Write, if you please!

"Here is a nice little Latin phrase, and rare too, (one can't be too *recherché* or brief in one's Latin, it's getting so common,)—*ignoratio elenchi*.[2] He has committed an *ignoratio elenchi*—that is to say, he has understood the words of your proposition, but not the ideas. The man was a *fool*, you see. Some poor fellow whom you addressed while choking with that chicken-bone, and who therefore didn't precisely understand what you were talking about. Throw the *ignoratio elenchi* in his teeth, and, at once, you have him annihilated. If he dare to re- ply, you can tell him from Lucan (here it is) that speeches are mere *anemonae verborum*,[3] anemone words. The anemone, with great bril- liancy, has no smell. Or, if he begin to bluster, you may be down upon him with *insomnia Jovis*, reveries of Jupiter[4]—a phrase which Silius Italicus (see here!) applies to thoughts pompous and inflated. This will be sure and cut him to the heart. He can do nothing but roll over and die. Will you be kind enough to write?

"In Greek we must have something pretty—from Demosthenes,[5] for

7. Another imprecision of Blackwood's. The lines are not from the *Orlando Furioso* of Ludovico Ariosto (1474–1535), which was a continuation of the medieval epic of Roland as told in Matteo Maria Boiardo's *Orlando Innamorato* (1st complete ed., 1506), but from the once popular revision of Boiardo by Francesco Berni (1497?–1535).

8. Not from Johann Christoph Friedrich von Schiller (1759–1805) but from the ballad "Das Veilchen" (The violet, or modesty) by Johann Wolfgang von Goethe (1749–1832). The mis- quoted word *no* should be *so*.

9. Jellies presented in a mosaic pattern. According to Levine, there is no Molucca breed of capon. The Moluccas are a group of islands, formerly known as the Spice Islands, located in East Indonesia, which were colonized both by the Portuguese and the Dutch.

1. A famous restaurant located in Paris. Another of that name was in New York.

2. The technique (a logical fallacy) of arguing against a point that the other party has not pro- posed; an irrelevant refutation or conclusion.

3. Unsubstantial flowers of speech (Latin). Not from Lucan (38–65 C.E.), the Roman poet who wrote the epic *Pharsalia*, but from "Lexiphones" by Lucian (flourished 2nd century C.E.), a Greek satirist.

4. Mabbott suggests that the "reveries of Jupiter" actually comes from a Latin version of *On the Sublime* by the Greek aesthetician Longinus (flourished 1st century C.E.).

5. Greek orator (384–322 B.C.E.) who is best known for his *Philippics*. Being reprimanded for running away from Philip of Macedonia at the Battle of Chaeronea, he responded with the

example. *Ανηρ ο φευγων και παλιν μαχησεται.* [Aner o pheogon kai palin makesetai.] There is a tolerably good translation of it in Hudibras—

> For he that flies may fight again,
> Which he can never do that's slain.[6]

In a Blackwood article nothing makes so fine a show as your Greek. The very letters have an air of profundity about them. Only observe, madam, the astute look of that Epsilon. That Phi ought certainly to be a bishop! Was ever there a smarter fellow than that Omicron? Just twig that Tau![7] In short, there is nothing like Greek for a genuine sensation-paper. In the present case your application is the most obvious thing in the world. Rap out the sentence, with a huge oath, and by way of *ultimatum*, at the good-for-nothing dunder-headed villain who couldn't understand your plain English in relation to the chickenbone. He'll take the hint and be off, you may depend upon it."

These were all the instructions Mr. B. could afford me upon the topic in question, but I felt they would be entirely sufficient. I was, at length, able to write a genuine Blackwood article, and determined to do it forthwith. In taking leave of me, Mr. B. made a proposition for the purchase of the paper when written; but as he could offer me only fifty guineas a sheet, I thought it better to let our society have it, than sacrifice it for so paltry a sum. Notwithstanding this niggardly spirit, however, the gentleman showed his consideration for me in all other respects, and indeed treated me with the greatest civility. His parting words made a deep impression upon my heart, and I hope I shall always remember them with gratitude.

"My dear Miss Zenobia," he said, while the tears stood in his eyes, "is there *any*thing else I can do to promote the success of your laudable undertaking? Let me reflect! It is just possible that you may not be able, so soon as convenient, to—to—get yourself drowned, or—choked with a chicken-bone, or—or hung,—or—bitten by a—but stay! Now I think me of it, there are a couple of very excellent bull dogs in the yard—fine fellows, I assure you—savage, and all that—indeed just the thing for your money—they'll have you eaten up, *auriculas* and all, in less than five minutes (here's my watch!)—and then only think of the sensations! Here! I say—Tom!—Peter!—Dick, you villain!—let out those"—but as I was really in a great hurry, and had not another moment to spare, I was reluctantly forced to expedite my departure, and accordingly took leave *at once*—somewhat more abruptly, I admit, than strict courtesy would have, otherwise, allowed.

It was my primary object, upon quitting Mr. Blackwood, to get into some immediate difficulty, pursuant to his advice, and with this view I

words quoted in the text. Poe includes a transliteration for those who don't read Greek, so that the garblings of Miss Zenobia's version in the tale that follows will be clearer. The erroneous Greek spellings in the following quotation were corrected by Poe in the *Phantasy-Pieces* manuscript but not in the printed versions of the tale; the versions given here is from Mabbott.

6. Slightly misquoted from the anti-Puritan *Hudibras* (1663–78), a comic epic poem by the English satirist Samuel Butler (1612–1680).

7. Epsilon, Σ; phi, Φ; omicron, O; and tau, T.

spent the greater part of the day in wandering about Edinburgh, seeking for desperate adventures—adventures adequate to the intensity of my feelings, and adapted to the vast character of the article I intended to write. In this excursion I was attended by my negro-servant Pompey, and my little lap-dog Diana, whom I had brought with me from Philadelphia. It was not, however, until late in the afternoon that I fully succeeded in my arduous undertaking. An important event then happened, of which the following Blackwood article,[8] in the tone heterogeneous is the substance and result.

A Predicament

What chance, good lady, hath bereft you thus?

—Comus.[9]

It was a quiet and still afternoon when I strolled forth in the goodly city of Edina. The confusion and bustle in the streets were terrible. Men were talking. Women were screaming. Children were choking. Pigs were whistling. Carts they rattled. Bulls they bellowed. Cows they lowed. Horses they neighed. Cats they caterwauled. Dogs they danced. *Danced!* Could it then be possible? *Danced!* Alas, thought I, *my* dancing days are over! Thus it is ever. What a host of gloomy recollections will ever and anon be awakened in the mind of genius and imaginative contemplation, especially of a genius doomed to the everlasting, and eternal, and continual, and, as one might say, the—*continued*—yes, the *continued and continuous*, bitter, harassing, disturbing, and, if I may be allowed the expression, the *very* disturbing influence of the serene, and godlike, and heavenly, and exalting, and elevated, and purifying effect of what may be rightly termed the most enviable, the most *truly* enviable—nay! the most benignly beautiful, the most deliciously ethereal, and, as it were, the most *pretty* (if I may use so bold an expression) *thing* (pardon me, gentle reader!) in the word—but I am led away by my feelings. In *such* a mind, I repeat, what a host of recollections are stirred up by a trifle! The dogs danced! I—I *could* not! They frisked—I wept. They capered—I sobbed aloud. Touching circumstances! which cannot fail to bring to the recollection of the classical reader that exquisite passage in relation to the fitness of things, which is to be found in the commencement of the third volume of that admirable and venerable Chinese novel, the *Jo-Go-Slow.*

In my solitary walk through the city I had two humble but faithful companions. Diana, my poodle! sweetest of creatures! She had a quantity of hair over her one eye, and a blue ribband tied fashionably around her neck. Diana was not more than five inches in height, but her head was somewhat bigger than her body, and her tail, being cut off exceedingly close, gave an air of injured innocence to the interesting animal which rendered her a favorite with all.

8. In her imitation of the *Blackwood's* style of tale, Psyche Zenobia produces "A Predicament," formerly titled "The Scythe of Time." Most of the allusions she makes (in garbled fashion) are explained in the Blackwood frame-story (see the headnote on p. 173).
9. The epigraph is from John Milton's *Comus* (1634), line 277.

And Pompey, my negro!—sweet Pompey! how shall I ever forget
thee? I had taken Pompey's arm. He was three feet in height (I like to
be particular) and about seventy, or perhaps eighty, years of age. He
had bow-legs and was corpulent. His mouth should not be called
small, nor his ears short. His teeth, however, were like pearl, and his
large full eyes were deliciously white. Nature had endowed him with
no neck, and had placed his ankles (as usual with that race) in the
middle of the upper portion of the feet. He was clad with a striking
simplicity. His sole garments were a stock of nine inches in height,
and a nearly-new drab overcoat which had formerly been in the ser-
vice of the tall, stately, and illustrious Dr. Moneypenny. It was a good
overcoat. It was well cut. It was well made. The coat was nearly new.
Pompey held it up out of the dirt with both hands.[1]

There were three persons in our party, and two of them have already
been the subject of remark. There was a third—that third person was
myself. I am the Signora Psyche Zenobia. I am *not* Suky Snobbs. My
appearance is commanding. On the memorable occasion of which I
speak I was habited in a crimson satin dress, with a sky-blue Arabian
mantelet. And the dress had trimmings of green agraffas, and seven
graceful flounces of the orange colored auricula. I thus formed the
third of the party. There was the poodle. There was Pompey. There was
myself. We were *three*. Thus it is said there were originally but three
Furies—Melty, Nimmy and Hetty—Meditation, Memory, and Fid-
dling.

Leaning upon the arm of the gallant Pompey, and attended at a re-
spectful distance by Diana, I proceeded down one of the populous and
very pleasant streets of the now deserted Edina. On a sudden, there
presented itself to view a church—a Gothic cathedral—vast, venera-
ble, and with a tall steeple, which towered into the sky. What madness
now possessed me? Why did I rush upon my fate? I was seized with an
uncontrollable desire to ascend the giddy pinnacle, and thence survey
the immense extent of the city. The door of the cathedral stood invit-
ingly open. My destiny prevailed. I entered the ominous archway.
Where then was my guardian angel?—if indeed such angels there be.
If! Distressing monosyllable! what a world of mystery, and meaning,
and doubt, and uncertainty is there involved in thy two letters! I en-
tered the ominous archway! I entered; and, without injury to my
orange-colored auriculas, passed beneath the portal, and emerged
within the vestibule! Thus it is said the immense river Alfred passed,
unscathed, and unwetted, beneath the sea.

I thought the staircases would never have an end. *Round!* Yes, they
went round and up, and round and up and round and up, until I could
not help surmising, with the sagacious Pompey, upon whose support-
ing arm I leaned in all the confidence of early affection—I *could* not

1. This burlesque description is taken by many critics as an example of Poe's Southern racism.
 Whether that is true or not, it should be noted that he is parodying such writings; he not
 only caricatures a stock minstrel figure but also mercilessly lampoons the white authoress as
 an idiotic bluestocking (see notes to "Lionizing," pp. 128ff. herein).

help surmising that the upper end of the continuous spiral ladder had been accidentally, or perhaps designedly, removed. I paused for breath; and, in the meantime, an incident occurred of too momentous a nature in a moral, and also in a metaphysical point of view, to be passed over without notice. It appeared to me—indeed I was quite confident of the fact—I could not be mistaken—no! I had, for some moments, carefully and anxiously observed the motions of my Diana—I say that *I could not be* mistaken—Diana *smelt a rat!* At once I called Pompey's attention to the subject, and he—he agreed with me. There was then no longer any reasonable room for doubt. The rat had been smelled— and by Diana. Heavens! shall I ever forget the intense excitement of that moment? Alas! what is the boasted intellect of man? The rat!—it was there—that is to say, it was somewhere. Diana smelled the rat. *I*— I *could* not! Thus it is said the Prussian Isis has, for some persons, a sweet and very powerful perfume, while to others it is perfectly scentless.

The staircase had been surmounted, and there were now only three or four more upward steps intervening between us and the summit. We still ascended, and now only one step remained. One step! One little, little step! Upon one such little step in the great staircase of human life how vast a sum of human happiness or misery often depends! I thought of myself, then of Pompey, and then of the mysterious and inexplicable destiny which surrounded us. I thought of Pompey!—alas, I thought of love! I thought of the many false *steps* which have been taken, and may be taken again. I resolved to be more cautious, more reserved. I abandoned the arm of Pompey, and, without his assistance, surmounted the one remaining step, and gained the chamber of the belfry. I was followed immediately afterwards by my poodle. Pompey alone remained behind. I stood at the head of the staircase, and encouraged him to ascend. He stretched forth to me his hand, and unfortunately in so doing was forced to abandon his firm hold upon the overcoat. Will the gods never cease their persecution? The overcoat it dropped, and, with one of his feet, Pompey stepped upon the long and trailing skirt of the overcoat. He stumbled and fell—this consequence was inevitable. He fell forwards, and, with his accursed head, striking me full in the——in the breast, precipitated me headlong, together with himself, upon the hard, filthy and detestable floor of the belfry. But my revenge was sure, sudden and complete. Seizing him furiously by the wool with both hands, I tore out a vast quantity of the black, and crisp, and curling material, and tossed it from me with every manifestation of disdain. It fell among the ropes of the belfry and remained. Pompey arose, and said no word. But he regarded me piteously with his large eyes and—sighed. Ye gods—that sigh! It sunk into my heart. And the hair—the wool! Could I have reached that wool I would have bathed it with my tears, in testimony of regret. But alas! it was now far beyond my grasp. As it dangled among the cordage of the bell, I fancied it still alive. I fancied that it stood on end with indignation. Thus the *happy dandy Flos Aeris* of Java, bears, it is said, a

beautiful flower, which will live when pulled up by the roots. The natives suspend it by a cord from the ceiling and enjoy its fragrance for years.

Our quarrel was now made up, and we looked about the room for an aperture through which to survey the city of Edina. Windows there were none. The sole light admitted into the gloom chamber proceeded from a square opening, about a foot in diameter, at a height of about seven feet from the floor. Yet what will the energy of true genius not effect? I resolved to chamber up to this hole. A vast quantity of wheels, pinions, and other cabalistic-looking machinery stood opposite the hole, close to it; and through the hole there passed an iron rod from the machinery. Between the wheels and the wall where the hole lay, there was barely room for my body—yet I was desperate, and determined to persevere. I called Pompey to my side.

"You perceive that aperture, Pompey. I wish to look through it. You will stand here just beneath the hole—so. Now, hold out one of your hands, Pompey, and let me step upon it—thus. Now, the other hand, Pompey, and with its aid I will get upon your shoulders."

He did everything I wished, and I found, upon getting up, that I could easily pass my head and neck through the aperture. The prospect was sublime. Nothing could be more magnificent. I merely paused a moment to bid Diana behave herself, and assure Pompey that I would be considerate and bear as lightly as possible upon his shoulders. I told him I would be tender of his feelings—*ossi tender que beefsteak*. Having done this justice to my faithful friend, I gave myself up with great zest and enthusiasm to the enjoyment of the scene with so obligingly spread itself out before my eyes.

Upon this subject, however, I shall forbear to dilate. I will not describe the city of Edinburgh. Every one has been to Edinburgh—the classic Edina. I will confine myself to the momentous details of my own lamentable adventure. Having, in some measure, satisfied my curiosity in regard to the extent, situation, and general appearance of the city, I had leisure to survey the church in which I was, and the delicate architecture of the steeple. I observed that the aperture through which I had thrust my head was an opening in the dial-plate of a gigantic clock, and must have appeared, from the street, as a large keyhole, such as we see in the face of French watches. No doubt the true object was to admit the arm of an attendant, to adjust, when necessary, the hands of the clock from within. I observed also, with surprise, the immense size of these hands, the longest of which could not have been less than ten feet in length, and, where broadest, eight or nine inches in breadth. They were of solid steel apparently, and their edges appeared to be sharp. Having noticed these particulars, and some others, I again turned my eyes upon the glorious prospect below and soon became absorbed in contemplation.

From this, after some minutes, I was aroused by the voice of Pompey, who declared he could stand it no longer, and requested that I would be so kind as to come down. This was unreasonable, and I told him so in a speech of some length. He replied, but with an evident

misunderstanding of my ideas upon the subject. I accordingly grew angry, and told him in plain words that he was a fool, that he had committed an *ignoramus e-clench-eye*, that his notions were mere *insommary Bovis*, and his words little better than *an enemy-werrybor'em*. With this he appeared satisfied, and I resumed my contemplations.

It might have been half an hour after this altercation when, as I was deeply absorbed in the heavenly scenery beneath me, I was startled by something very cold which pressed with a gentle pressure upon the back of my neck. It is needless to say that I felt inexpressibly alarmed. "I knew that Pompey was beneath my feet, and that Diana was sitting, according to my explicit directions, upon her hind legs in the farthest corner of the room. What could it be? Alas! I but too soon discovered. Turning my head gently to one side, I perceived, to my extreme horror, that the huge, glittering, scimetar-like minute-hand of the clock, had, in the course of its hourly revolution, *descended upon my neck*. There was, I knew, not a second to be lost. I pulled back at once—but it was too late. There was no chance of forcing my head through the mouth of that terrible trap in which it was so fairly caught, and which grew narrower and narrower with a rapidity too horrible to be conceived. The agony of that moment is not to be imagined. I threw up my hands and endeavoured, with all my strength, to force upwards the ponderous iron bar. I might as well have tried to lift the cathedral itself. Down, down, down it came, closer, and yet closer. I screamed to Pompey for aid: but he said that I had hurt his feelings by calling him "an ignorant old squint eye." I yelled to Diana; but she only said "bow-wow-wow," and that "I had told her on no account to stir from the corner." Thus I had no relief to expect from my associates.

Meantime the ponderous and terrific *Scythe of Time* (for I now discovered the literal import of that classical phrase) had not stopped, nor was it likely to stop, in its career. Down and still down, it came. It had already buried its sharp edge a full inch in my flesh, and my sensations grew indistinct and confused. At one time I fancied myself in Philadelphia with the stately Dr. Moneypenny, at another in the back parlor of Mr. Blackwood receiving his invaluable instructions. And then again the sweet recollection of better and earlier times came over me, and I thought of that happy period when the world was not all a desert, and Pompey not altogether cruel.

The ticking of the machinery amused me. *Amused me*, I say, for my sensations now bordered upon perfect happiness, and the most trifling circumstances afforded me pleasure. The eternal *click-clack, click-clack, click-clack*, of the clock was the most melodious of music in my ears, and occasionally even put me in mind of the grateful sermonic harangues of Dr. Ollapod.[2] Then there were the great figures upon the

2. A character in *The Poor Gentleman*, a popular farce written by George Colman Jr. (1762–1836). In 1839–40, Poe worked as assistant to William E. Burton (1804–60), owner and editor of the *Gentleman's Magazine*. Burton, a popular comic actor, played the part of Dr. Ollapod and became more or less permanently associated with this character. While in Burton's employ, Poe changed the name in the next printing of his story to Dr. Morphine; but after he left *Burton's* and had control of his own magazine (the *Broadway Journal*), he changed it back to Ollapod. In the farce, Ollapod is a quack who wants to overdose everyone

dial-plate—how intelligent, how intellectual, they all looked! And presently they took to dancing the Mauzurka, and I think it was the figure V who performed the most to my satisfaction. She was evidently a lady of breeding. None of your swaggerers, and nothing at all indelicate in her motions. She did the pirouette to admiration—whirling round upon her apex. I made an endeavor to hand her a chair, for I saw that she appeared fatigued with her exertions—and it was not until then that I fully perceived my lamentable situation. Lamentable indeed! The bar had buried itself two inches in my neck. I was aroused to a sense of exquisite pain. I prayed for death, and, in the agony of the moment, could not help repeating those exquisite verses of the poet Miguel De Cervantes:

> Vanny Buren, tan escondida
> Query no te senty venny
> Pork and pleasure, delly morry
> Nommy, tomy, darry, widdy![3]

But now a new horror presented itself, and one indeed sufficient to startle the strongest nerves. My eyes, from the cruel pressure of the machine, were absolutely starting from their sockets. While I was thinking how I should possibly manage without them, one actually tumbled out of my head, and, rolling down the steep side of the steeple, lodged in the rain gutter which ran along the eaves of the main building. The loss of the eye was not so much as the insolent air of independence and contempt with which it regarded me after it was out. There it lay in the gutter just under my nose, and the airs it gave itself would have been ridiculous had they not been disgusting. Such a winking and blinking were never before seen. This behaviour on the part of my eye in the gutter was not only irritating on account of its manifest insolence and shameful ingratitude, but was also exceedingly inconvenient on account of the sympathy which always exists between two eyes of the same head, however far apart. I was forced, in a manner, to wink and to blink, whether I would or not, in exact concert with the scoundrelly thing that lay just under my nose. I was presently relieved, however, by the dropping out of the other eye. In falling it took the same direction (possibly a concerted plot) as its fellow. Both rolled out of the gutter together, and in truth I was very glad to get rid of them.

The bar was now four inches and a half deep in my neck, and there was only a little bit of skin to cut through. My sensations were those of entire happiness, for I felt that in a few minutes, at farthest, I should be relieved from my disagreeable situation. And in this expec-

on cathartics/laxatives (see p. 177, n. 8 herein). Willis Clark of the *Knickerbocker* magazine, with whom Poe had some difficulties, wrote under the pseudonym of Ollapod (Spanish: *olla prodrida*, "hodgepodge"), possibly providing Poe with even more incentive to change the name back.

3. A mangling of the quotation from Cervantes (see p. 180). The nonsensical reference to "pork" is to the financial deals of politicians, in this case to those of Martin Van Buren. Cf. Poe's satiric hits on Van Buren in "King Pest" (pp. 148ff. herein) and "The Man That Was Used Up" pp. 190ff.).

tation I was not at all deceived. At twenty-five minutes past five in the afternoon precisely, the huge minute-hand had proceeded sufficiently far on its terrible revolution to sever the small remainder of my neck. I was not sorry to see the head which had occasioned me so much embarrassment at length make a final separation from my body. It first rolled down the side of the steeple, then lodged, for a few seconds, in the gutter, and then made its way, with a plunge, into the middle of the street.[4]

I will candidly confess that my feelings were now of the most singular—nay of the most mysterious, the most perplexing and incomprehensible character. My senses were here and there at one and the same moment. With my head I imagined, at one time, that I the head, was the real Signora Psyche Zenobia—at another I felt convinced that myself, the body, was the proper identity. To clear my ideas upon this topic I felt in my pocket for my snuff-box, but, upon getting it, and endeavoring to apply a pinch of its grateful contents in the ordinary manner, I became immediately aware of my peculiar deficiency, and threw the box at once down to my head. It took a pinch with great satisfaction, and smiled me an acknowledgement in return. Shortly afterwards it made me a speech, which I could hear but indistinctly without ears. I gathered enough, however, to know that it was astonished at my wishing to remain alive under such circumstances. In the concluding sentences it quoted the noble words of Ariosto—

> Il pover hommy che non sera corty
> And have a combat tenty erry morty.

thus comparing me to the hero who, in the heat of the combat, not perceiving that he was dead, continued to contest the battle with inextinguishable valor. There was nothing now to prevent my getting down from my elevation, and I did so. What it was that Pompey saw so *very* peculiar in my appearance I have never yet been able to find out. The fellow opened his mouth from ear to ear, and shut his two eyes as if he were endeavoring to crack nuts between the lids. Finally, throwing off his overcoat, he made one spring for the staircase and disappeared. I hurled after the scoundrel those vehement words of Demosthenes—

> Andrew O'Phlegethon, you really make haste to fly,[5]

and then turned to the darling of my heart, to the one-eyed! the shaggy-haired Diana. Alas! what horrible vision affronted my eyes? *Was* that a rat I saw skulking into his hole? *Are* these the picked bones of the little angel who has been cruelly devoured by the monster? Ye Gods! and what *do* I behold—is that the departed spirit, the shade, the ghost of my beloved puppy, which I perceive sitting with a grace so melancholy, in the corner? Harken! for she speaks, and, heavens! it is in the German of Schiller—

4. This predicament may owe something to the examinations done during the French Revolution to assess consciousness after decapitation—the so-called blinking experiments.
5. See p. 182 and n. 6 herein.

"Unt stubby duk, so stubby dun
Duk she! duk she!"

Alas!—and are not her words too true?

And if I died at least I died
For thee—for thee.

Sweet creature! she *too* has sacrificed herself in my behalf. Dogless, niggerless, headless, what *now* remains for the unhappy Signora Psyche Zenobia? Alas—*nothing!* I have done.

The Man That Was Used Up First published in *Burton's Gentleman's Magazine* (August 1839). The text reprinted here is from the *Broadway Journal* (August 9, 1845). William Whipple has argued that the story is a political satire aimed at Richard M. Johnson, Indian fighter, politician, and vice president of the United States (1837–41) under Martin Van Buren. In the Canadian Battle of the Thames in 1813, Johnson had killed the great Indian chief Tecumseh, sustaining repeated wounds (see notes to "King Pest," pp. 148ff. herein) A contemporary described him as "a man upon crutches; his frame all mutilated: moving with difficulty." In his 1836 campaign, Van Buren exploited Johnson's status as a national hero to garner votes. In Van Buren's 1840 campaign, a song used by his opponents begins "Van, Van's a Used Up Man." The phrase *used up* in Poe's time could mean not only burnt out or exhausted but also someone who is ridiculed or parodied; both senses are here comically literalized.

The Man That Was Used Up

A Tale of the Late Bugaboo and Kickapoo[1] Campaign

Pleurez, pleurez, mes yeux, et fondez vous en eau!
La moitié de ma vie a mis l' autre au tombeau.
CORNEILLE[2]

I cannot just now remember when or where I first made the acquaintance of that truly fine-looking fellow, Brevet Brigadier General John A. B. C. Smith. Some one *did* introduce me to the gentleman, I am sure—at some public meeting, I know very well—held about something of great importance, no doubt—at some place or other, I feel convinced,—whose name I have unaccountably forgotten.[3] The truth is—that the introduction was attended, upon my part, with a degree of

1. Indian tribe involved in the Florida Indian Wars of the late 1830s. "Bugaboo": bogeyman, false fear.
2. The epigraph is from *Le Cid* (1637) by Pierre Corneille (1606–1684), French Renaissance tragedian. Poe provides a loose translation of the lines elsewhere ("Pinakidia" 20): "Weep, weep, my eyes! It is no time to laugh / For half myself has buried the other half."
3. Presumably Vice President Johnson, though any such general type of war-hero politician fits the satire. Cf. the opening lines of "Ligeia" (p. 159 herein) and the descriptions of the faces of Ligeia and Roderick Usher. Another suggestion involves the trial, about the time of Poe's writing this tale, of Captain Daniel Mann for conspiracy and dueling. A Captain Mann is mentioned later in the tale, with insider jokes on the word or name *man*.

anxious embarrassment which operated to prevent any definite impression of either time or place. I am constitutionally nervous—this, with me, is a family failing, and I can't help it. In especial, the slightest appearance of mystery—of any point I cannot exactly comprehend—puts me at once into a pitiable state of agitation.

There was something, as it were, remarkable—yes, *remarkable*, although this is but a feeble term to express my full meaning—about the entire individuality of the personage in question. He was, perhaps, six feet in height, and of a presence singularly commanding. There was an *air distingué* pervading the whole man, which spoke of high breeding, and hinted at high birth. Upon this topic—the topic of Smith's personal appearance—I have a kind of melancholy satisfaction in being minute. His head of hair would have done honor to a Brutus;[4]—nothing could be more richly flowing, or possess a brighter gloss. It was of a jetty black;—which was also the color, or more properly the no color, of his unimaginable whiskers. You perceive I cannot speak of these latter without enthusiasm; it is not too much to say that they were the handsomest pair of whiskers under the sun. At all events, they encircled, and at times partially overshadowed, a mouth utterly unequalled. Here were the most entirely even, and the most brilliantly white of all conceivable teeth. From between them, upon every proper occasion, issued a voice of surpassing clearness, melody, and strength. In the matter of eyes, also, my acquaintance was preeminently endowed. Either one of such a pair was worth a couple of the ordinary ocular organs. They were of a deep hazel, exceedingly large and lustrous; and there was perceptible about them, ever and anon, just that amount of interesting obliquity which gives pregnancy to expression.[5]

The bust of the General was unquestionably the finest bust I ever saw. For your life you could not have found a fault with its wonderful proportion. This rare peculiarity set off to great advantage a pair of shoulders which would have called up a blush of conscious inferiority into the countenance of the marble Apollo. I have a passion for fine shoulders, and may say that I never beheld them in perfection before. The arms altogether were admirably modelled. Nor were the lower limbs less superb. These were, indeed, the *ne plus ultra*[6] of good legs. Every connoisseur in such matters admitted the legs to be good. There was neither too much flesh, nor too little,—neither rudeness nor fragility. I could not imagine a more graceful curve than that of the *os femoris*, and there was just that due gentle prominence in the rear of the *fibula*[7] which goes to the conformation of a properly proportioned calf. I wish to God my young and talented friend Chiponchipino,[8]

4. Marcus Junius Brutus (85?–42 B.C.E.), one of the chief assassins of Julius Caesar. Mabbott notes that although the Roman hero most celebrated for beautiful hair was Cincinnatus, there may been some theatrical tradition of playing Brutus with long hair.
5. In the four preceding publications of this tale, the parallel to "Ligeia" was more pointed: ". . . gives force to the pregnant observation of Francis Bacon—that 'there is no exquisite beauty existing in the world without a certain degree of *strangeness* in the expression.' "
6. The best or utmost (Latin).
7. Long bone on the outer side of the lower leg. "*Os femoris*": femur; thigh bone.
8. Punning made-up name for a typical Italian sculptor (chipping) with a polysyllabic name.

the sculptor, had but seen the legs of Brevet Brigadier General John A. B. C. Smith.

But although men so absolutely fine-looking are neither as plenty as reasons or blackberries, still I could not bring myself to believe that *the remarkable* something to which I alluded just now,—that the odd air of *je ne sais quoi*[9] which hung about my new acquaintance,—lay altogether, or indeed at all, in the supreme excellence of his bodily endowments. Perhaps it might be traced to the *manner*;—yet here again I could not pretend to be positive. There *was* a primness, not to say stiffness, in his carriage—a degree of measured, and, if I may so express it, of rectangular precision, attending his every movement, which, observed in a more diminutive figure, would have had the least little savor in the world, of affectation, pomposity or constraint, but which, noticed in a gentleman of his undoubted dimension, was readily placed to the account of reserve, *hauteur*[1]—of a commendable sense, in short, of what is due to the dignity of colossal proportion.

The kind friend who presented me to General Smith whispered in my ear some few words of comment upon the man. He was a *remarkable* man—a *very* remarkable man—indeed one of the *most* remarkable men of the age. He was an especial favorite, too, with the ladies—chiefly on account of his high reputation for courage.

"In *that* point he is unrivalled—indeed he is a perfect desperado—a down-right fire-eater, and no mistake," said my friend, here dropping his voice excessively low, and thrilling me with the mystery of his tone.

"A downright fire-eater, and *no* mistake. Showed *that*, I should say, to some purpose, in the late tremendous swamp-fight away down South, with the Bugaboo and Kickapoo Indians."[2] [Here my friend opened his eyes to some extent.] "Bless my soul!—blood and thunder, and all that!—*prodigies* of valor!—heard of him of course?—you know he's the man"——

"Man alive, how *do* you do? why how *are* ye? *very* glad to see ye, indeed!" here interrupted the General himself, seizing my companion by the hand as he drew near, and bowing stiffly, but profoundly, as I was presented. I then thought, (and I think so still,) that I never heard a clearer nor a stronger voice, nor beheld a finer set of teeth: but I *must* say that I was sorry for the interruption just at that moment, as, owing to the whispers and insinuations aforesaid, my interest had been greatly excited in the hero of the Bugaboo and Kickapoo campaign.

However, the delightfully luminous conversation of Brevet Brigadier General John A. B. C. Smith soon completely dissipated this chagrin. My friend leaving us immediately, we had quite a long *tête-à-tête*,[3] and I was not only pleased but *really*—instructed. I never heard a more fluent talker, or a man of greater general information. With becoming

9. I know not what (French).
1. Haughtiness (French).
2. Part of the joke is that Tecumseh was not a Kickapoo but a Shawnee, famous not in the South but in the North. Poe comically associates the words Kickapoo and bugaboo.
3. Head to head (French, literal trans.); a private conversation.

modesty, he forebore, nevertheless, to touch upon the theme I had just then most at heart—I mean the mysterious circumstances attending the Bugaboo war—and, on my own part, what I conceive to be a proper sense of delicacy forbade me to broach the subject; although, in truth, I was exceedingly tempted to do so. I perceived, too, that the gallant soldier preferred topics of philosophical interest, and that he delighted, especially, in commenting upon the rapid march of mechanical invention. Indeed, lead him where I would, this was a point to which he invariably came back.

"There is nothing at all like it," he would say; "we are a wonderful people, and live in a wonderful age, Parachutes and rail-roads—man-traps and spring-guns![4] Our steam-boats are upon every sea, and the Nassau balloon packet is about to run regular trips (fare either way only twenty pounds sterling) between London and Timbuctoo. And who shall calculate the immense influence upon social life—upon arts—upon commerce—upon literature—which will be the immediate result of the great principles of electro-magnetics? Nor is this all, let me assure you! There is really no end to the march of invention. The most wonderful—the most ingenious—and let me add, Mr.—Mr.—Thompson, I believe, is your name—let me add, I say, the most *useful*—the most truly *useful* mechanical contrivances, are daily springing up like mushrooms, if I may so express myself, or, more figuratively, like—ah—grasshoppers—like grasshoppers, Mr. Thompson—about us and ah—ah—ah—around us!"

Thompson, to be sure, is not my name; but it is needless to say that I left General Smith with a heightened interest in the man, with an exalted opinion of his conversational powers, and a deep sense of the valuable privileges we enjoy in living in this age of mechanical invention. My curiosity, however, had not been altogether satisfied, and I resolved to prosecute immediate inquiry among my acquaintances touching the Brevet Brigadier General himself, and particularly respecting the tremendous events *quorum pars magna fuit*,[5] during the Bugaboo and Kickapoo campaign.

The first opportunity which presented itself, and which (*horresco referens*) I did not in the least scruple to seize, occurred at the Church of the Reverend Doctor Drummummupp, where I found myself established, one Sunday just at sermon time, not only in the pew, but by the side, of that worthy and communicative little friend of mine, Miss Tabitha T.[6] Thus seated, I congratulated myself, and with much reason, upon the very flattering state of affairs. If any person knew anything about Brevet Brigadier General John A. B. C. Smith, that

4. Preset self-actuated weapons to ward off intruders. Levine notes that these can be the means of inadvertent self-destruction and that many of the allusions to historical and literary figures in Poe's story are to self-destructive characters.
5. In which he bore a large part (Latin); from Virgil's *Aeneid*, II.6.
6. Levine notes that a Tabitha Titmouse is a character in a popular novel by Samuel Warren (1807–1877), *Ten Thousand a Year* (1841). But Poe might have had in mind Tabitha Tenney (1762–1837), who wrote a satire on silly, self-absorbed women with romantic ideas, *Female Quixoticism: Exhibited in the Romantic Opinions and Extravagant Adventures of Dorcasina Shelton* (1801). "*Horresco referens*": I shudder at the memory (Latin); Aeneid, II.204. "Drummummupp": i.e., drum 'em up.

person, it was clear to me, was Miss Tabitha T. We telegraphed a few signals, and then commenced, *sotto voce*,[7] a brisk *tête-à-tête*.

"Smith!" said she, in reply to my very earnest inquiry; "Smith!—why, not General John A. B. C.? Bless me, I thought you *knew* all about *him!* This is a wonderfully inventive age! Horrid affair that!—a bloody set of wretches, those Kickapoos!—fought like a hero—prodigies of valor—immortal renown. Smith!—Brevet Brigadier General John A. B. C.!—why, you know he's the man"——

"Man," here broke in Doctor Drummummupp, at the top of his voice, and with a thump that came near knocking the pulpit about our ears; "man that is born of a woman hath but a short time to live; he cometh up and is cut down like a flower!"[8] I started to the extremity of the pew, and perceived by the animated looks of the divine, that the wrath which had nearly proved fatal to the pulpit had been excited by the whispers of the lady and myself. There was no help for it; so I submitted with a good grace, and listened, in all the martyrdom of dignified silence, to the balance of that very capital discourse.

Next evening found me a somewhat late visitor at the Rantipole theatre, where I felt sure of satisfying my curiosity at once, by merely stepping into the box of those exquisite specimens of affability and omniscience, the Misses Arabella and Miranda Cognoscenti.[9] That fine tragedian, Climax, was doing Iago to a very crowded house, and I experienced some little difficulty in making my wishes understood; especially as our box was next the slips,[1] and completely overlooked the stage.

"Smith?" said Miss Arabella, as she at length comprehended the purport of my query; "Smith?—why, not General John A. B. C.?"

"Smith?" inquired Miranda, musingly. "God bless me, did you ever behold a finer figure?"

"Never, madam, but *do* tell me"——

"Or so inimitable grace?"

"Never, upon my word!—but pray inform me"——

"Or so just an appreciation of stage effect?"

"Madam!"

"Or a more delicate sense of the true beauties of Shakespeare? Be so good as to look at that leg!"

"The devil!" and I turned again to her sister.

"Smith?" said she, "why, not General John A. B. C.? Horrid affair that, wasn't it?—great wretches, those Bugaboos—savage and so on—but we live in a wonderfully inventive age!—Smith!—O yes! great man!—perfect desperado—immortal renown—prodigies of valor! *Never heard!*" [This was given in a scream.] "Bless my soul!—why he's the man"——

7. Low voiced, whispered.

8. Garbled passages from *Macbeth* and elsewhere, still playing on the word *man*.

9. The word *cognoscenti* means those in the know about something (usually social, political, or artsy). "Rantipole Theater": apparently a pun on the word *rant*, which means to speak or perform a part to excess. Rather than Edwin Forrest, whom Poe pokes fun at in "Loss of Breath," William Burton, publisher, editor, and actor, may be the satiric target here (or any such type of ranting ham actor).

1. Sides of the theater gallery.

"———mandragora
Nor all the drowsy syrups of the world
Shall ever medicine thee to that sweet sleep
Which thou owd'st yesterday!"[2]

here roared out Climax just in my ear, and shaking his fist in my face all the time, in a way that I *couldn't* stand, and I *wouldn't*. I left the Misses Cognoscenti immediately, went behind the scenes forthwith, and gave the beggarly scoundrel such a thrashing as I trust he will remember to the day of his death.

At the *soirée* of the lovely widow, Mrs. Kathleen O'Trump, I was confident that I should meet with no similar disappointment. Accordingly, I was no sooner seated at the card table, with my pretty hostess for a *vis-à-vis*,[3] than I propounded those questions the solution of which had become a matter so essential to my peace.

"Smith?" said my partner, "why, not General John A. B. C.? Horrid affair that, wasn't it?—diamonds, did you say?—terrible wretches those Kickapoos!—we are playing *whist*, if you please, Mr. Tattle— however, this is the age of invention, most certainly—*the* age; one may say—*the* age *par excellence*—speak French?—oh, quite a hero—perfect desperado!—*no hearts*, Mr. Tattle? I don't believe it!—immortal renown and all that—prodigies of valor! *Never heard!!*—why, bless me, he's the man"———

"Mann?—*Captain* Mann?" here screamed some little feminine interloper from the farthest corner of the room. "Are you talking about Captain Mann and the duel?—oh, I *must* hear—do tell—go on; Mrs. O'Trump!—do now go on!" And go on Mrs. O'Trump did—all about a certain Captain Mann who was either shot or hung, or should have been both shot and hung. Yes! Mrs. O'Trump, she went on, and I—I went off. There was no chance of hearing anything farther that evening in regard to Brevet Brigadier General John A. B. C. Smith.

Still I consoled myself with the reflection that the tide of ill luck would not run against me forever, and so determined to make a bold push for information at the rout of that bewitching little angel, the graceful Mrs Pirouette.

"Smith?" said Mrs. P., as we twirled about together in a *pas de zephyr*,[4] "Smith?—why not General John A. B. C.? Dreadful business that of the Bugaboos, wasn't it?—terrible creatures those Indians!—*do* turn out your toes! I really am ashamed of you—man of great courage, poor fellow!—but this is a wonderful age for invention—O dear me, I'm out of breath—quite a desperado—prodigies of valor—*never*

2. More garbled passages. "Not poppy, nor mandragora" are the beginning words of Iago's speech in act III of Shakespeare's *Othello* (1602), where Iago plans to ruin Othello by attacking his manhood by planting suspicion that his wife, Desdemona, has been unfaithful to him. The roots of the mandrake plant ("mandragora") were thought to resemble a man; it was used to produce a drug. The mandrake was said to "scream" when pulled up by the roots. The poppy is a source of opium (and symbolizes the sleep of forgetfulness).
3. Here a face-to-face talk.
4. A ballet step; see notes to "Loss of Breath" on the ballet terms (p. 90, n. 8 herein) that Poe uses for wordplay.

heard!!—can't believe it—I shall have to sit down and enlighten you—
Smith! why he's the man"——

"Man-*Fred*, I tell you!" here bawled out Miss Bas-Bleu, as I led Mrs.
Pirouette to a seat. "Did ever anybody hear the like? It's Man-*Fred*, I
say, and not at all by any means Man-*Friday*." Here Miss Bas-Bleu
beckoned to me in a very peremptory manner; and I was obliged, will I
nill I, to leave Mrs. P. for the purpose of deciding a dispute touching
the title of a certain poetical drama of Lord Byron's. Although I pro-
nounced, with great promptness, that the true title was Man-*Friday*,
and not by any means Man-*Fred*, yet when I returned to seek Mrs.
Pirouette she was not to be discovered, and I made my retreat from
the house in a very bitter spirit of animosity against the whole race of
the Bas-Bleus.[5]

Matters had now assumed a really serious aspect, and I resolved to
call at once upon my particular friend, Mr. Theodore Sinivate,[6] for I
knew that here at least I should get something like definite informa-
tion.

"Smith?" said he, in his well known peculiar way of drawling out his
syllables; "Smith?—why, not General John A—B—C? Savage affair
that with the Kickapo-o-o-os, wasn't it? Say! don't you think so?—per-
fect despera-a-ado—great pity, 'pon my honor!—wonderfully inventive
age!—pro-o-odigies of valor! By the by, did you ever hear about Cap-
tain Ma-a-a-n?"

"Captain Mann be d—d!" said I, "please to go on with your story."

"Hem!—oh well!—quite *la même cho-o-ose*,[7] as we say in France.
Smith, eh? Brigadier General John A—B—C? I say"—[here Mr. S.
thought proper to put his finger to the side of his nose]—"I say, you
don't mean to insinuate now, really, and truly, and conscientiously,
that you don't know all about that affair of Smith's, as well as I do, eh?
Smith? John A—B—C.? Why bless me, he's the ma-a-an"——

"*Mr.* Sinivate," said I imploringly, "*is* he the man in the mask?"[8]

"No-o-o!" said he, looking wise, "nor the man in the mo-o-o-on."

This reply I considered a pointed and positive insult, and so left the
house at once in high dudgeon, with a firm resolve to call my friend,
Mr. Sinivate, to a speedy account for his ungentlemanly conduct and
ill breeding.

In the meantime, however, I had no notion of being thwarted touch-
ing the information I desired. There was one resource left me yet. I
would go to the fountain head. I would call forthwith upon the Gen-
eral himself, and demand, in explicit terms, a solution of this abom-
inable piece of mystery. Here at least there should be no chance for

5. Bluestocking, a person with artistic pretensions (usually female); cf. "Lionizing" (p. 130,
n. 3 herein). Along with the references to Captain Mann, these titles and names play on the
word *man*. Byron's *Manfred* (1817) is a poetic drama about a man who is tormented by self-
hatred. Mabbott notes that a burlesque of Byron's play was produced about 1834: "Man-
Fred" by Gilbert A'Beckett features a heroic chimneysweep, who appeared in blackface.
"Man-Friday": a servant or faithful sidekick of lower stature than the hero, so named from
the character Friday in *Robinson Crusoe* (1719) by Daniel Defoe (1660?–1731).
6. Slang pronunciation for *insinuate*.
7. *La même chose*: the same thing (French).
8. See "Lionizing," p. 128, n. 3.

equivocation. It would be plain, positive, peremptory—as short as pie-crust—as concise as Tacitus or Montesquieu.[9]

It was early when I called, and the general was dressing; but I pleaded urgent business, and was shown at once into his bed-room by an old negro valet, who remained in attendance during my visit. As I entered the chamber, I looked about, of course, for the occupant, but did not immediately perceive him. There was a large and exceedingly odd looking bundle of something which lay close by my feet on the floor, and, as I was not in the best humor in the world, I gave it a kick out of the way.

"Hem! ahem! rather civil that, I should say!" said the bundle, in one of the smallest, and altogether the funniest little voices, between a squeak and a whistle, that I ever heard in all the days of my existence.

"Ahem! rather civil that, I should observe."

I fairly shouted with terror, and made off, at a tangent, into the far-thest extremity of the room.

"God bless me! my dear fellow," here again whistled the bundle "what—what—what—why, what *is* the matter? I really believe you don't know me at all."

What *could* I say to all this—what *could* I? I staggered into an arm-chair, and, with staring eyes and open mouth, awaited the solution of the wonder.

"Strange you shouldn't know me though, isn't it?" presently re-squeaked the nondescript, which I now perceived was performing, upon the floor, some inexplicable evolution, very analagous to the drawing on of a stocking. There was only a single leg, however, apparent.

"Strange you shouldn't know me, though, isn't it? Pompey, bring me that leg!" Here Pompey[1] handed the bundle a very capital cork leg, all ready dressed, which it screwed on in a trice; and then it stood upright before my eyes.

"And a bloody action it *was*," continued the thing, as if in a soliloquy; "but then one mustn't fight with the Bugaboos and Kickapoos, and think of coming off with a mere scratch. Pompey, I'll thank you now for that arm. Thomas" [turning to me] "is decidedly the best hand at a cork leg; but if you should ever want an arm, my dear fellow, you must really let me recommend you to Bishop." Here Pompey screwed on an arm.

"We had rather hot work of it, that you may say. Now, you dog, slip on my shoulders and bosom! Pettitt makes the best shoulders, but for a bosom you will have to go to Ducrow."[2]

9. Charles de Secondat, baron de la Brède et de Montesquieu (1689–1755), celebrated for his concise ironic and sarcastic witticisms. Cornelius Tacitus (c. 55–c. 117 C.E.), Roman histo-rian who made a statement about a ruler that became famous for concision: "he was fit to rule only had he never ruled." Mabbott suggests Poe conjoined the two because Hugh Blair does so in his *Lectures on Rhetoric* (1783), a book that had a major influence on Poe and other writers of the time.
1. The name of the black servant in "How to Write a Blackwood Article: A Predicament." Part of the racism of the day was to give black slaves and servants incongruous classical names. Cneius Pompeius Magnus (106–48 B.C.E.), Pompey the Great, was the Roman general whose heroic exploits made him Julius Caesar's greatest political and military rival in the quest for leadership of Rome.
2. The manufacturers of artificial human parts here and in the next few paragraphs may not all be real, but scholars have identified several of them. John F. Thomas was an artificial-limb

"Bosom!" said I.

"Pompey, will you *never* be ready with that wig? Scalping is a rough process after all; but then you can procure such a capital scratch at De L'Orme's."[3]

"Scratch!"

"Now, you nigger, my teeth! For a *good* set of these you had better go to Parmly's at once; high prices, but excellent work. I swallowed some very capital articles, though, when the big Bugaboo rammed me down with the butt end of his rifle."

"Butt end! ram down!! my eye!!!"

"O yes, by the by, my eye—here, Pompey, you scamp, screw it in! Those Kickapoos are not so very slow at a gouge;[4] but he's a belied man, that Dr. Williams, after all; you can't imagine how well I see with the eyes of his make."

I now began very clearly to perceive that the object before me was nothing more nor less than my new acquaintance, Brevet Brigadier General John A. B. C. Smith. The manipulations of Pompey had made, I must confess, a very striking difference in the appearance of the personal man. The voice, however, still puzzled me no little; but even this apparent mystery was speedily cleared up.

"Pompey, you black rascal," squeaked the General, "I really do believe you would let me go out without my palate."

Hereupon the negro, grumbling out an apology, went up to his master, opened his mouth with the knowing air of a horse-jockey, and adjusted therein a somewhat singular-looking machine, in a very dexterous manner, that I could not altogether comprehend. The alteration, however, in the entire expression of the General's countenance was instantaneous and surprising. When he again spoke, his voice had resumed all that rich melody and strength which I had noticed upon our original introduction.

"D——n the vagabonds!" said he, in so clear a tone that I positively started at the change, "D——n the vagabonds! they not only knocked in the roof of my mouth, but took the trouble to cut off at least seven-eighths of my tongue. There isn't Bonfanti's equal, however, in America, for really good articles of this description. I can recommend you to him with confidence," [here the General bowed,] "and assure you that I have the greatest pleasure in so doing."

I acknowledged his kindness in my best manner, and took leave of him at once, with a perfect understanding of the true state of affairs—

maker in Philadelphia. A certain Nicholas Pettit was a Philadelphia tailor in the 1830s. An Andrew Ducrow, a famous London equestrian showman (died 1842), was noted for his fine chest according to Mabbott. Levine notes a reference to him in John Wilson's *Noctes Ambrosianae* (1822–35), where one of the characters in the dialogue makes fun of the mythic centaur (a man-horse combination). L. S. Parmley wrote *On the Natural History and Management of the Teeth* (1838). Dr. Williams may be Dr. John Williams, an oculist in Philadelphia in the 1830s. He had the reputation of being a quack and was sued by a patient who went blind under his care. A Joseph Bonfanti sold talking dolls in New York.

3. A name Poe uses elsewhere—possibly an allusion to Victor Hugo's play, *Marion de Lorme* (1831), or to G. P. R. James's novel, *De l'Orme* (1830). "Scratch": wig (slang).

4. Not only to scoop out something violently but also to con money from someone by swindle or by overcharging for incompetent work.

with a full comprehension of the mystery which had troubled me so long. It was evident. It was a clear case. Brevet Brigadier General John A. B. C. Smith was the man——was *the man that was used up.*

The Fall of the House of Usher[1]

> Son cœur est un luth suspendu;
> Sitôt qu'on le touche il résonne.
> *De Béranger.*[2]

[handwritten: Crack in house – divided]

[handwritten: house w/u Civil War]

During the whole of a dull, dark, and soundless day in the autumn of the year,[3] when the clouds hung oppressively low in the heavens, I had been passing alone, on horseback, through a singularly dreary tract of country; and at length found myself, as the shades of the evening drew on, within view of the melancholy House of Usher. I know not how it was—but, with the first glimpse of the building, a sense of insufferable gloom pervaded my spirit. I say insufferable; for the feeling was unrelieved by any of that half-pleasurable, because poetic, sentiment, with which the mind usually receives even the sternest natural images of the desolate or terrible.[4] I looked upon the scene before me—upon the mere house, and the simple landscape features of the domain—upon the bleak walls—upon the vacant eye-like windows—upon a few rank sedges—and upon a few white trunks of decayed trees—with an utter depression of soul which I can compare to no earthly sensation more properly than to the after-dream of the reveller upon opium—the bitter lapse into everyday life—the hideous dropping off the veil.[5] There was an iciness, a sinking, a sickening of the heart—an unredeemed dreariness of thought which no goading of the imagination could torture into aught of the sublime. What was it—I paused to think—what was it that so unnerved me in the contemplation of the House of Usher? It was a mystery all insoluble; nor could I grapple with the shadowy fancies that crowded upon

1. First published in *Burton's Gentleman's Magazine, and Monthly Review* (September 1839); the text here is that of *Tales* (1845).
2. Poe slightly alters lines from the then celebrated lyric poet Pierre Jean de Béranger (1780–1857). The word "my" (*mon*) becomes "his" (*son*). The epigraph may be translated as: "His heart is like a suspended [hanging or taut] lute; as soon as it is touched it resonates."
3. Some scholars have speculated that Poe is obliquely suggesting that the narrator arrives at the House of Usher just before All Hallow's Eve, a time when demons, ghosts, and witches are given free reign. But fall/winter is a common seasonal setting for gothic stories.
4. Poe is alluding to the tradition of romantic melancholy associated with architectural ruins and sublimely blasted landscapes celebrated by late-18th-century and early-19th-century poets. The present view of the House of Usher and its environs has none of this pleasurable effect for the narrator; rather it makes him quite nervous.
5. It was the custom for Romantic writers to allude to opium (sometimes called "the milk of paradise"); various opiates were supposed to open the channels of the mind to another world more "ideal" than this material one. When the opiate wears off, the drug-induced veil over our mundane reality drops away and the discrepancy between the supernal and the everyday can drive the reveler mad. Although suggestive, the reference does not necessarily indicate that the narrator is a user of opium. Nor does it with regard to Roderick Usher—even though the narrator later mentions the drug in connection with him. "Beneath the veil" was a favored phrase of Romantic writers; it suggests seeing the truth and specifically alludes to the tradition that in ancient Egypt the priests of Isis who peered beneath the veil of the goddess to see her actual face were driven mad.

me as I pondered. I was forced to fall back upon the unsatisfactory conclusion, that while, beyond doubt, there *are* combinations of very simple natural objects which have the power of thus affecting us, still the analysis of this power lies among considerations beyond our depth.[6] It was possible, I reflected, that a mere different arrangement of the particulars of the scene, of the details of the picture, would be sufficient to modify, or perhaps to annihilate its capacity for sorrowful impression; and, acting upon this idea, I reined my horse to the precipitous brink of a black and lurid tarn that lay in unruffled lustre by the dwelling, and gazed down—but with a shudder even more thrilling than before—upon the remodelled and inverted images of the gray sedge, and the ghastly tree-stems, and the vacant and eye-like windows.

Nevertheless, in this mansion of gloom I now proposed to myself a sojourn of some weeks. Its proprietor, Roderick Usher, had been one of my boon companions in boyhood; but many years had elapsed since our last meeting. A letter, however, had lately reached me in a distant part of the country—a letter from him—which, in its wildly importunate nature, had admitted of no other than a personal reply. The MS. gave evidence of nervous agitation. The writer spoke of acute bodily illness—of a mental disorder which oppressed him—and of an earnest desire to see me, as his best, and indeed his only personal friend, with a view of attempting, by the cheerfulness of my society, some alleviation of his malady. It was the manner in which all this, and much more, was said—it was the apparent *heart* that went with his request—which allowed me no room for hesitation; and I accordingly obeyed forthwith what I still considered a very singular summons.

Although, as boys, we had been even intimate associates, yet I really knew little of my friend. His reserve had been always excessive and habitual. I was aware, however, that his very ancient family had been noted, time out of mind, for a peculiar sensibility of temperament, displaying itself, through long ages, in many works of exalted art, and manifested, of late, in repeated deeds of munificent yet unobtrusive charity, as well as in a passionate devotion to the intricacies, perhaps even more than to the orthodox and easily recognisable beauties, of musical science. I had learned, too, the very remarkable fact, that the stem of the Usher race, all time-honored as it was, had put forth, at no period, any enduring branch; in other words, that the entire family lay in the direct line of descent,[7] and had always, with very trifling and very temporary variation, so lain. It was this deficiency, I considered,

6. A Romantic as opposed to a Neoclassic notion. Just why certain combinations of purely natural objects should have the power to generate indefinite fantasies is, according to the conventions of the time, beyond the rational powers. The word *fancy* had other important meanings; and elsewhere Poe engages in the Neoclassic/Romantic debate on the difference between "imagination" and "fancy"; see Criticism, pp. 789ff. (Stovall essay).

7. I.e., the Usher family is extremely inbred and has been so for generations. Incest was a popular motif with Romantic writers, partly for its shock effect (Romantic revolt against bourgeois values), partly for its implications regarding the nature of identity. Incest was associated with hemophilia and with madness; bleeding and mental instability were "royal" diseases in the public mind. Inbreeding decreases the variability of characteristics within the gene pool (increasing the possibility for the expression of recessive genes): thus Roderick Usher's precarious state of mind and heightened sensitivities to sound and light.

while running over in thought the perfect keeping of the character of the premises with the accredited character of the people, and while speculating upon the possible influence which the one, in the long lapse of centuries, might have exercised upon the other—it was this deficiency, perhaps, of collateral issue, and the consequent undeviating transmission, from sire to son, of the patrimony with the name, which had, at length, so identified the two as to merge the original title of the estate in the quaint and equivocal appellation of the "House of Usher"—an appellation which seemed to include, in the minds of the peasantry who used it, both the family and the family mansion.[8]

I have said that the sole effect of my somewhat childish experiment—that of looking down within the tarn—had been to deepen the first singular impression. There can be no doubt that the consciousness of the rapid increase of my superstition—for why should I not so term it?—served mainly to accelerate the increase itself. Such, I have long known, is the paradoxical law of all sentiments having terror as a basis.[9] And it might have been for this reason only, that, when I again uplifted my eyes to the house itself, from its image in the pool, there grew in my mind a strange fancy—a fancy so ridiculous, indeed, that I but mention it to show the vivid force of the sensations which oppressed me. I had so worked upon my imagination as really to believe that about the whole mansion and domain there hung an atmosphere peculiar to themselves and their immediate vicinity—an atmosphere which had no affinity with the air of heaven, but which had reeked up from the decayed trees, and the gray wall, and the silent tarn—a pestilent and mystic vapor,[1] dull, sluggish, faintly discernible, and leaden-hued.

Shaking off from my spirit what *must* have been a dream, I scanned more narrowly the real aspect of the building. Its principal feature seemed to be that of an excessive antiquity. The discoloration of ages had been great. Minute fungi over-spread the whole exterior, hanging in a fine tangled web-work from the caves. Yet all this was apart from any extraordinary dilapidation. No portion of the masonry had fallen; and there appeared to be a wild inconsistency between its still perfect adaptation of parts, and the crumbling condition of the individual stones. In this there was much that reminded me of the specious totality of old wood-work which has rotted for long years in some neglected vault, with no disturbance from the breath of the external air. Beyond this indication of extensive decay, however, the fabric gave little token of instability. Perhaps the eye of a scrutinizing observer

8. The narrator senses something puzzling or uncertain in the naming of the house as physical building and the "house" as family. His statement sets up the theme of the "sameness" of Roderick and Madeline Usher (twins with the same sensibilities) and introduces the idea of an occult relation between the family of Usher and the seemingly sentient physical building, which is mysteriously tied in with their fate (see p. 204, n. 6 herein).
9. The idea that consciousness of a phobia or a fear serves only to increase its intensity is recurrent in Poe and in gothic writings. This idea goes in the opposite direction from Freudian psychoanalysis, which contends that it is by confronting one's demons (neuroses, phobias, etc.) that one conquers them.
1. There were theories current in Poe's time regarding the poisonous and/or hallucinatory properties of marsh gas (the product of masses of decaying matter in swamps and other watery areas without egress). Marsh gas can also be highly combustible.

might have discovered a barely perceptible fissure, which, extending from the roof of the building in front, made its way down the wall in a zigzag direction, until it became lost in the sullen waters of the tarn.

Noticing these things, I rode over a short causeway to the house. A servant in waiting took my horse, and I entered the Gothic archway of the hall. A valet, of stealthy step, thence conducted me, in silence, through many dark and intricate passages in my progress to the *studio* of his master. Much that I encountered on the way contributed, I know not how, to heighten the vague sentiments of which I have already spoken. While the objects around me—while the carvings of the ceilings, the sombre tapestries of the walls, the ebon blackness of the floors, and the phantasmagoric armorial trophies which rattled as I strode, were but matters to which, or to such as which, I had been accustomed from my infancy—while I hesitated not to acknowledge how familiar was all this—I still wondered to find how unfamiliar were the fancies which ordinary images were stirring up. On one of the staircases, I met the physician of the family. His countenance, I thought, wore a mingled expression of low cunning and perplexity. He accosted me with trepidation and passed on. The valet now threw open a door and ushered me into the presence of his master.

The room in which I found myself was very large and lofty. The windows were long, narrow, and pointed, and at so vast a distance from the black oaken floor as to be altogether inaccessible from within. Feeble gleams of encrimsoned light made their way through the trellissed panes, and served to render sufficiently distinct the more prominent objects around; the eye, however, struggled in vain to reach the remoter angles of the chamber, or the recesses of the vaulted and fretted ceiling. Dark draperies hung upon the walls. The general furniture was profuse, comfortless, antique, and tattered. Many books and musical instruments lay scattered about, but failed to give any vitality to the scene. I felt that I breathed an atmosphere of sorrow. An air of stern, deep, and irredeemable gloom hung over and pervaded all.

Upon my entrance, Usher arose from a sofa on which he had been lying at full length, and greeted me with a vivacious warmth which had much in it, I at first thought, of an overdone cordiality—of the constrained effort of the *ennuyé* man of the world.[2] A glance, however, at his countenance, convinced me of his perfect sincerity. We sat down; and for some moments, while he spoke not, I gazed upon him with a feeling half of pity, half of awe. Surely, man had never before so terribly altered, in so brief a period, as had Roderick Usher! It was with difficulty that I could bring myself to admit the identity of the wan being before me with the companion of my early boyhood. Yet the character of his face had been at all times remarkable. A cadaverousness of complexion; an eye large, liquid, and luminous beyond comparison; lips somewhat thin and very pallid, but of a surpassingly beautiful curve; a nose of a delicate Hebrew model, but with a breadth

2. I.e., restrained or obligatory attempts at cordiality by someone who is world-weary ("ennuyé," cf. *ennui*) from excessive sophistication.

of nostril unusual in similar formations; a finely moulded chin, speaking, in its want of prominence, of a want of moral energy;[3] hair of a more than web-like softness and tenuity; these features, with an inordinate expansion above the regions of the temple, made up altogether a countenance not easily to be forgotten. And now in the mere exaggeration of the prevailing character of these features, and of the expression they were wont to convey, lay so much of change that I doubted to whom I spoke. The now ghastly pallor of the skin, and the now miraculous lustre of the eye, above all things startled and even awed me. The silken hair, too, had been suffered to grow all unheeded, and as, in its wild gossamer texture, it floated rather than fell about the face, I could not, even with effort, connect its Arabesque[4] expression with any idea of simple humanity.

In the manner of my friend I was at once struck with an incoherence—an inconsistency; and I soon found this to arise from a series of feeble and futile struggles to overcome an habitual trepidancy—an excessive nervous agitation. For something of this nature I had indeed been prepared, no less by his letter, than by reminiscences of certain boyish traits, and by conclusions deduced from his peculiar physical conformation and temperament. His action was alternately vivacious and sullen. His voice varied rapidly from a tremulous indecision (when the animal spirits seemed utterly in abeyance) to that species of energetic concision—that abrupt, weighty, unhurried, and hollow-sounding enunciation—that leaden, self-balanced, and perfectly modulated guttural utterance, which may be observed in the lost drunkard, or the irreclaimable eater of opium,[5] during the periods of his most intense excitement.

It was thus that he spoke of the object of my visit, of his earnest desire to see me, and of the solace he expected me to afford him. He entered, at some length, into what he conceived to be the nature of his malady. It was, he said, a constitutional and a family evil, and one for which he despaired to find a remedy—a mere nervous affection, he immediately added, which would undoubtedly soon pass off. It displayed itself in a host of unnatural sensations. Some of these, as he detailed them, interested and bewildered me; although, perhaps, the terms, and the general manner of the narration had their weight. He suffered much from a morbid acuteness of the senses; the most insipid food was alone endurable; he could wear only garments of

3. According to contemporary physiognomy theory Usher's weak chin indicates a weak will. The most famous of writers on how moral and psychological characteristics are indicated by the physical features of the face was Johann Kaspar Lavater (1741–1801), Swiss theologian and mystic. An American edition of his work was published in Boston in 1794 as J. C. Lavater's *Essays on Physiognomy* (see pp. 742–43 herein). Physiognomic reading is related to phrenology (see notes to "Ligeia," pp. 159ff. and the phrenological chart, p. 747).

4. Possibly meaning exotic (Arab-like, Middle Eastern), though equally in the sense of intricate intertwined lines characteristic of Islamic art. The reference of the antecedent is ambiguous, grammatically entwining Usher's face and hair. In the Romantic era, the words *arabesque* and *grotesque* were sometimes used interchangeably, but important distinctions existed in aesthetic theory of the time (see the Tales introduction on pp. 77ff.).

5. The narrator now seems to interpret Usher's mental state in terms of alcohol or opium usage (cf. p. 199, n. 5 herein). The notorious *Confessions of an English Opium-Eater* (1821–22), thought at first to be by Samuel Taylor Coleridge but actually by Thomas De Quincey (1785–1859), contains depictions of opium dreams. Cf. "Ligeia."

this life was given to him.' Commenting on divide in Civil War

certain texture; the odors of all flowers were oppressive; his eyes were tortured by even a faint light; and there were but peculiar sounds, and these from stringed instruments, which did not inspire him with horror.

To an anomalous species of terror I found him a bounden slave. "I shall perish," said he, "I *must* perish in this deplorable folly. Thus, thus, and not otherwise, shall I be lost. I dread the events of the future, not in themselves, but in their results. I shudder at the thought of any, even the most trivial, incident, which may operate upon this intolerable agitation of soul. I have, indeed, no abhorrence of danger, except in its absolute effect—in terror. In this unnerved—in this pitiable condition—I feel that the period will sooner or later arrive when I must abandon life and reason together, in some struggle with the grim phantasm, FEAR."

The house is cursed

I learned, moreover, at intervals, and through broken and equivocal hints, another singular feature of his mental condition. He was enchained by certain superstitious impressions in regard to the dwelling which he tenanted, and whence, for many years, he had never ventured forth—in regard to an influence whose supposititious force was conveyed in terms too shadowy here to be re-stated—an influence which some peculiarities in the mere form and substance of his family mansion, had, by dint of long sufferance, he said, obtained over his spirit—an effect which the *physique* of the gray walls and turrets, and of the dim tarn into which they all looked down, had, at length, brought about upon the *morale* of his existence.[6]

He admitted, however, although with hesitation, that much of the peculiar gloom which thus afflicted him could be traced to a more natural and far more palpable origin—to the severe and long-continued illness—indeed to the evidently approaching dissolution—of a tenderly beloved sister—his sole companion for long years—his last and only relative on earth. "Her decease," he said, with a bitterness which I can never forget, "would leave him (him the hopeless and the frail) the last of the ancient race of the Ushers." While he spoke, the lady Madeline (for so was she called) passed slowly through a remote portion of the apartment, and, without having noticed my presence, disappeared. I regarded her with an utter astonishment not unmingled with dread—and yet I found it impossible to account for such feelings. A sensation of stupor oppressed me, as my eyes followed her retreating steps. When a door, at length, closed upon her, my

sister

6. A version of the theory of continuity developed by Gottfried Wilhelm von Leibniz (1646–1714), German mathematician and philosopher, famous for inventing a calculus system before Isaac Newton. Leibniz was both celebrated and satirized for his claim that the totality of the harmoniously designed and completely integrated universe is "the best of all possible worlds" (in which, however, evil is a necessary ingredient). The basic building blocks of this universe Leibniz called *monads*, which he conceived of as immaterial, psychic atoms. He theorized that all monads have some degree of sentience and consciousness but that certain forms or collocations of monads have rational or logical consciousness. Poe's narrator continues the theme of continuity between the outer (the "physique") and the inner (the "morale"). Here it is not just between the outer appearance of one's face and one's character (physiognomy theory) but also between the organic (the Ushers) and the inorganic (the house), connected by vegetation in various degrees of sentience and decay. Usher seems to believe that by long, continuous, and intimate habitation by the same inbred family a psychic relationship between the physical house and the Ushers has developed (see p. 201, n. 8, and p. 209, n. 3 herein).

glance sought instinctively and eagerly the countenance[7] of the brother—but he had buried his face in his hands, and I could only perceive that a far more than ordinary wanness had overspread the emaciated fingers through which trickled many passionate tears.

The disease of the lady Madeline had long baffled the skill of her physicians. A settled apathy, a gradual wasting away of the person, and frequent although transient affections of a partially cataleptical character,[8] were the unusual diagnosis. Hitherto she had steadily borne up against the pressure of her malady, and had not betaken herself finally to bed; but, on the closing in of the evening of my arrival at the house, she succumbed (as her brother told me at night with inexpressible agitation) to the prostrating power of the destroyer; and I learned that the glimpse I had obtained of her person would thus probably be the last I should obtain—that the lady, at least while living, would be seen by me no more.

For several days ensuing, her name was unmentioned by either Usher or myself: and during this period I was busied in earnest endeavors to alleviate the melancholy of my friend. We painted and read together; or I listened, as if in a dream, to the wild improvisations of his speaking guitar.[9] And thus, as a closer and still closer intimacy admitted me more unreservedly into the recesses of his spirit, the more bitterly did I perceive the futility of all attempt at cheering a mind from which darkness, as if an inherent positive quality, poured forth upon all objects of the moral and physical universe, in one unceasing radiation of gloom.

I shall ever bear about me a memory of the many solemn hours I thus spent alone with the master of the House of Usher. Yet I should fail in any attempt to convey an idea of the exact character of the studies, or of the occupations, in which he involved me, or led me the way. An excited and highly distempered ideality[1] threw a sulphureous lustre over all. His long improvised dirges will ring forever in my ears. Among other things, I hold painfully in mind a certain singular perversion and amplification of the wild air of the last waltz of Von Weber.[2] From the paintings over which his elaborate fancy brooded, and which grew, touch by touch, into vaguenesses at which I shuddered the more

7. In the earlier versions of the story, Poe emphasizes the resemblance of Roderick and Madeline: "Her figure, her hair, her features—all, in their very minutest development were those—were identically (I can use no other sufficient term) were identically those of the Roderick Usher who sat beside me."
8. Catalepsy (or catalency) is a nervous disorder related to epilepsy, schizophrenia, and hysteria in which the sufferer falls into a deep, narcotic sleep, has no response to external stimuli, shows no visible sign of breathing, and is stiff and rigid to the touch. Later Roderick begins to suspect that Madeline has not died but is in a cataleptic coma or trance.
9. I.e., singing guitar, melodious (cf. epigraph, p. 199 and n. 2 herein).
1. Romantic term indicating an aesthetic or intellectual heightening that transcends mere earthly reality; the "poetic." Also the realm of "ideas" beyond this world in which mental concepts and images exist in a state of perfection (cf. "idealism" and "neoplatonism"). Here Roderick Usher's typical excess distorts or makes sick his very ideality.
2. Carl Maria von Weber (1786–1826), German composer better known for his operatic works than his instrumental works, regarded as having laid down the foundation for German Romantic opera, in which the supernatural plays a large part. His dance and concert pieces (1819–21) are in the virtuoso style. Shortly before his death, Weber copied out a "Last Waltz" now attributed to his friend Karl Gottlieb Reissiger (1798–1859); since the surviving manuscript was in Weber's hand, it was long thought to be his.

thrillingly, because I shuddered knowing not why;—from these paint-
ings (vivid as their images now are before me) I would in vain en-
deavor to educe more than a small portion which should lie within the
compass of merely written words. By the utter simplicity, by the
nakedness of his designs, he arrested and overawed attention. If ever
mortal painted an idea, that mortal was Roderick Usher. For me at
least—in the circumstances then surrounding me—there arose out of
the pure abstractions which the hypochondriac contrived to throw
upon his canvass, an intensity of intolerable awe, no shadow of which
felt I ever yet in the contemplation of the certainly glowing yet too
concrete reveries of Fuseli.[3]

One of the phantasmagoric conceptions of my friend, partaking not
so rigidly of the spirit of abstraction, may be shadowed forth, although
feebly, in words. A small picture presented the interior of an im-
mensely long and rectangular vault or tunnel, with low walls, smooth,
white, and without interruption or device. Certain accessory points of
the design served well to convey the idea that this excavation lay at an
exceeding depth below the surface of the earth. No outlet was ob-
served in any portion of its vast extent, and no torch, or other artificial
source of light was discernible; yet a flood of intense rays rolled
throughout, and bathed the whole in a ghastly and inappropriate
splendor.

I have just spoken of that morbid condition of the auditory nerve
which rendered all music intolerable to the sufferer, with the excep-
tion of certain effects of stringed instruments. It was, perhaps, the
narrow limits to which he thus confined himself upon the guitar,
which gave birth, in great measure, to the fantastic character of his
performances. But the fervid *facility* of his *impromptus*[4] could not be
so accounted for. They must have been, and were, in the notes, as well
as in the words of his wild fantasias[5] (for he not unfrequently accom-
panied himself with rhymed verbal improvisations), the result of that

3. Among the most famous paintings of Henry Fuseli (1741–1845), an Anglo-Swiss artist
whose work contains a good deal of the supernatural and demonic, are a series of works in
the 1770s generally known as "Nightmare." Dissatisfied with the overall effect, he reworked
the same subject several times. In the best-known of his renditions, Fuseli reliteralizes the
metaphor of the "night mare," a horse that comes in the night and treads on sleepers. In the
upper left corner of the picture appears the head of a dark horse with glowing white eyes
and flared nostrils. The mare observes the actions of another disturbing nighttime oppressor:
a demon with sunken eyes, bulbous nose, thick lips, pointed ears, and an apelike body sits
on the abdomen of a sleeping woman in a diaphanous white gown. Her upper body is arched
backward over the top of a disarrayed bed; her head depends upside down from an elongated
white neck stretched over the end of the bed so that her hair cascades perpendicularly
down. Her right hand disappears into her hair, while her long left arm stretches languidly or
helplessly down to the floor.

The hunched over creature is an *incubus*, the male form of a bisexual demon; in its female
form it is called a *succubus*. As succubus, the demon comes to sleeping men, causing an
erotic but nightmarish dream and gathers their sperm. The sperm undergoes a demonic
transformation, and the succubus changes into the male form. It comes to sleeping women,
again causing disturbing erotic dreams and impregnates them with the demon seed. In both
cases, the sleepers experience a sense of heavy oppression, as if something were sitting on
their abdomens and chests, so that the dreamers gasp for breath. According to Poe's narra-
tor, Usher's paintings surpass Fuseli's in intensity and awesomeness, for Fuseli's "glowing"
pictures are yet too concrete, while Usher's have a sick ethereality (or "ideality").
4. Musical compositions made on the spot, extemporaneous.
5. A free-form musical work structured according to the composer's fancy or fantasy.

intense mental collectedness and concentration to which I have previously alluded as observable only in particular moments of the highest artificial excitement. The words of one of these rhapsodies[6] I have easily remembered. I was, perhaps, the more forcibly impressed with it, as he gave it, because, in the under or mystic current of its meaning, I fancied that I perceived, and for the first time, a full consciousness on the part of Usher, of the tottering of his lofty reason upon her throne. The verses, which were entitled "The Haunted Palace,"[7] ran very nearly, if not accurately, thus:

I.

In the greenest of our valleys,
 By good angels tenanted,
Once a fair and stately palace—
 Radiant palace—reared its head.
In the monarch Thought's dominion—
 It stood there!
Never seraph[8] spread a pinion
 Over fabric half so fair.

II.

Banners yellow, glorious, golden,
 On its roof did float and flow;
(This—all this—was in the olden
 Time long ago)
And every gentle air that dallied,
 In that sweet day,
Along the ramparts plumed and pallid,
 A winged odor went away.

III.

Wanderers in that happy valley
 Through two luminous windows saw
Spirits moving musically
 To a lute's well-tunéd law,
Round about a throne, where sitting
 (Porphyrogene!)[9]

6. A musical piece free or irregular in form, often improvised. In general usage, the word means an impassioned speech, work, or performance, often excessively so.
7. Published separately in April 1839 in the Baltimore *American Museum of Science, Literature and the Arts.* Poe is said to have submitted it to the *United States Magazine and Democratic Review,* whose editor, J. L. O'Sullivan, rejected the poem because he did not understand it. But the allegory is quite straightforward: the architectural structure resembles a human face. Poe wrote to Rufus Wilmot Griswold that the palace is meant "to imply a mind haunted by phantoms—a disordered brain." The narrator, who has previously announced his theory of the psychology of fear, here perceives that Usher himself is afraid he is losing his mind. The poem also recalls the opening description of the house, connecting house and owner more closely. Some critics have argued that Poe was employing the iconographic tradition of the "Mouth of Hell" from the Middle Ages and the Renaissance. Frequently, the entrance to hell was set in the facelike structure of a building. See the cover of this Norton Critical Edition.
8. Highest of the nine orders of angels.
9. Purple, the color of royal vestments.

In state his glory well befitting,
The ruler of the realm was seen.

IV.

And all with pearl and ruby glowing
Was the fair palace door,
Through which came flowing, flowing, flowing,
And sparkling evermore.
A troop of Echoes whose sweet duty
Was but to sing,
In voices of surpassing beauty,
The wit and wisdom of their king.

V.

But evil things, in robes of sorrow,
Assailed the monarch's high estate;
(Ah, let us mourn, for never morrow
Shall dawn upon him, desolate!)
And, round about his home, the glory
That blushed and bloomed
Is but a dim-remembered story
Of the old time entombed.

VI.

And travellers now within that valley,
Through the red-litten windows, see
Vast forms that move fantastically
To a discordant melody;
While, like a rapid ghastly river,
Through the pale door,
A hideous throng rush out forever,
And laugh—but smile no more.[1]

I well remember that suggestions arising from this ballad, led us into a train of thought wherein there became manifest an opinion of Usher's which I mention not so much on account of its novelty, (for other men[2] have thought thus,) as on account of the pertinacity with which he maintained it. This opinion, in its general form, was that of the sentience of all vegetable things. But, in his disordered fancy, the

1. I.e., uncontrolled laughter indicates that the palace of thought is no longer under the direction of calm reason; cf. the Neoclassic idea of the "sweet smile of reason," observable in many Enlightenment portrait paintings.
2. Watson, Dr. Percival, Spallanzani, and especially the Bishop Landaff.—See "Chemical Essays," vol. v [Poe's note]. Richard Watson (1737–1816), a British chemist, became the bishop of Llandaff in Wales. Thus, rather than being a mistake (taking the bishop as a separate person from Watson), Poe's note appears to emphasize his importance: Watson, Percival, Spallanzani—and especially Watson. This chemist, botanist, and natural philosopher claimed that the sentience (perceptiveness, feeling, consciousness) of the vegetable kingdom indicates the basic organic oneness of all matter. His *Essay on the Subjects of Chemistry* (1771) was reprinted in volume 5 of his *Chemical Essays* (1787). The Abbé Lazzaro Spallanzani (1729–1799), author of *Dissertations Relative to the Natural History of Animals and Vegetables*, was professor of natural philosophy at the University of Pavia (Lombardy, northern Italy); the work was translated into English in 1784. Poe's note suggests that there is some scientific and medical credibility to Usher's ideas.

idea had assumed a more daring character, and trespassed, under certain conditions, upon the kingdom of inorganization.[3] I lack words to express the full extent, or the earnest *abandon* of his persuasion. The belief, however, was connected (as I have previously hinted) with the gray stones of the home of his forefathers. The conditions of the sentience had been here, he imagined, fulfilled in the method of collocation of these stones—in the order of their arrangement, as well as in that of the many *fungi* which overspread them, and of the decayed trees which stood around—above all, in the long undisturbed endurance of this arrangement, and in its reduplication in the still waters of the tarn. Its evidence—the evidence of the sentience—was to be seen, he said, (and I here started as he spoke,) in the gradual yet certain condensation of an atmosphere of their own about the waters and the walls. The result was discoverable, he added, in that silent, yet importunate and terrible influence which for centuries had moulded the destinies of his family, and which made *him* what I now saw him— what he was. Such opinions need no comment, and I will make none.

Our books—the books which, for years, had formed no small portion of the mental existence of the invalid—were, as might be supposed, in strict keeping with this character of phantasm. We pored together over such works as the Ververt et Chartreuse of Gresset; the Belphegor of Machiavelli; the Heaven and Hell of Swedenborg; the Subterranean Voyage of Nicholas Klimm by Holberg; the Chiromancy of Robert Flud, of Jean D'Indaginé, and of De la Chambre; the Journey into the Blue Distance of Tieck; and the City of the Sun of Campanella.[4] One favorite volume was a small octavo edition of the

Some scholars have taken the reference to Dr. Percival to be to James Gates Percival (1795–1856), an American physician and poet. The suggestion is that he may have been a model for Usher because he was noted for his hypersensitivities. He is described as having a cloud of blondish hair floating about his thin face—a speculation that may be more likely than the idea that Poe's pen portrait of Usher is actually a self-portrait (Poe had dark hair). Even more likely, however, is Mabbott's suggestion that the reference is to Dr. Thomas Percival, who wrote an essay on the "perceptive power" of vegetables in 1785.

3. Inanimate (inorganic) world of minerals and rocks and other such materials. Usher's studies have caused him to believe that the world's elemental constituents are linked in a continuous sentient chain to one another; i.e., as suggested in previous notes, even nonorganic substances have sense perception, feeling, and consciousness. Usher thinks that the house is alive ("sentient") and that its fate is linked in an occult way to that of the last of the Usher family line (cf. p. 201, n. 8, and p. 204, n. 6 herein).

4. These books in Usher's library, contrary to the claims of some scholars, are not made up; they are all real. Poe probably got most of the references from the encyclopedia by Baron Bielfeld, *L'Erudition Universelle*. Most of them have to do with journeys to and from other worlds (notably the underworld) and vigils and prayers for the dead. Jean-Baptiste-Louis Gresset (1709–1777) wrote a poem about a talking parrot "Ververt" (1734) that speaks both nonsense and religious truths. The bird is expelled from his convent into the larger world and later returns to die in the walled-in world of the convent; like the other poems collected in *La Chartreuse*, it is partly comic and satiric. Niccolò Machiavelli (1469–1527), in his satire *Belphegor* (c. 1515) has a fallen archangel come to earth to look into the claim that women cause the damnation of men; the angel marries, gets entangled with several other women, and finally escapes his scheming wife by returning to Hell. Sir David Brewster (1781–1868), world-renowned Edinburgh scientist who experimented with optics and pioneered research into polarized light. Emanuel Swedenborg (1688–1772), Swedish philosopher and mystic, in his *Heaven and Hell* (1758), described these two "other worlds" in detail. Ludwig Holberg (1684–1754), Danish historian and dramatist, told the story of a voyage to a world inside the world in the *Subterranean Voyage of Nicholas Klimm* (*Iter Subterraneum*). Cf. Poe's use of *Symzonia* in the *Narrative of Arthur Gordon Pym* (pp. 429ff. herein) and "Ms. Found in a Bottle" (pp. 106ff. herein).

Directorium Inquisitorium, by the Dominican Eymeric de Gironne; and there were passages in Pomponius Mela, about the old African Satyrs and Œgipans,[5] over which Usher would sit dreaming for hours. His chief delight, however, was found in the perusal of an exceedingly rare and curious book in quarto Gothic—the manual of a forgotten church—the *Vigiliae Mortuorum secundum Chorum Ecclesiae Maguntinae.*[6]

I could not help thinking of the wild ritual of this work, and of its probable influence upon the hypochondriac, when, one evening, having informed me abruptly that the lady Madeline was no more, he stated his intention of preserving her corpse for a fortnight, (previously to its final interment,) in one of the numerous vaults within the main walls of the building. The worldly reason, however, assigned for this singular proceeding, was one which I did not feel at liberty to dispute. The brother had been led to his resolution (so he told me) by consideration of the unusual character of the malady of the deceased, of certain obtrusive and eager inquiries on the part of her medical men, and of the remote and exposed situation of the burial-ground of the family. I will not deny that when I called to mind the sinister countenance of the person whom I met upon the staircase, on the day of my arrival at the house, I had no desire to oppose what I regarded as at best but a harmless, and by no means an unnatural, precaution.[7]

Mabbott points out that the next three references are all from a single entry in Bielfeld. Robert Flud or Fludd (1574–1637) was an English physician and member of the reemergent Rosicrucians, or the Ancient Mystic Order Rosae Crucis (AMORC), the order of the "rosy-crucifix" (i.e., red or bloody cross); the original founder is supposed to have been a 15th-century friar named Christian Rosenkreutz. The Rosicrucians were mystic philosopher-theologians who looked for divine guidance from ancient sacred texts of the Middle East (Arabesque works). Flud published a work on water divination by wooden branches (geomancy) in 1687. "Chiromancy": palmistry, the art (or "science") of reading of palms to discover character and to predict the past and the future. It typically adduces an astrological relation between the patterns of the palm and the patterns of the stars. Jean D'Indaginé (Johannes ab Indagine of Steinheim) published an introduction to chiromancy in 1522, and Marin Cureau de la Chambre published a discourse on the principles of chiromancy in 1653.

Ludwig Tieck (1773–1853) was a major figure in the foundation of German Romanticism, noted for drama, fiction, and poetry in a new key. The *Journey into the Blue Distance* (1834), was long thought by American scholars to be Poe's invention. But it is the second part of the title of Tieck's *The Old Book* (full title: *Das alte Buch und die Reise ins blaue hinein*) that tells of a paradisiacal land inside a mountain where the souls of artists both great and inconsequential have gone. Tommaso Campanella (1569–1639) wrote of a utopian world in *City of the Sun* (*Civitas Solis,* 1623).

5. Pomponius Mela (1st century) was a Roman geographer who described strange beasts and strange men in strange lands in his *De Situ Orbis* (eventually published 1471). He mentions "Œgipans" (aegipans or goat-pans) and describes fields full of pans and satyrs. Pan is one of the chief pastoral gods of the Romans; he was supposed to make the herds of cattle and goats fertile; in this role he became a rough equivalent of the Greek deity Dionysus, the forest god of wine and procreation. Dionysian festivals were drunken and orgiastic, sometimes followed by violence and death. Both deities are frequently pictured as having the horns, ears, legs, and genitals of a goat. Satyrs are also depicted as half-man and half-goat and as extremely lustful. In 1356, de Gironne (Gerone) became the inquisitor-general of Castile in Spain; his *Directorium Inquisitorium* (1503), which contains a list of forbidden books, is a set of procedures for interrogating heretics.

6. The title may be translated as The vigils of the dead according to the . . . Church of Mainz (published in Basel, c. 1500). "Quarto": a book composed of pages the size of which has been determined by folding a printer's sheet into four leaves—thus distinguishing it from the other most common size, *octavo* (eight folds). "Gothic": black letter type, a heavy broad type with thick ornamental serifs (vertical or horizontal finish lines); also known as Church Text or Old English.

7. Madeline has an especially interesting rare disease; therefore Usher and the narrator fear body snatching, i.e., digging up a fresh corpse from a recent grave to sell to medical students

At the request of Usher, I personally aided him in the arrangements for the temporary entombment. The body having been encoffined, we two alone bore it to its rest. The vault in which we placed it (and which had been so long unopened that our torches, half smothered in its oppressive atmosphere, gave us little opportunity for investigation) was small, damp, and entirely without means of admission for light; lying, at great depth, immediately beneath that portion of the building in which was my own sleeping apartment. It had been used, apparently, in remote feudal times, for the worst purposes of a donjon-keep; and, in later days, as a place of deposit for powder,[8] or some other highly combustible substance, as a portion of its floor, and the whole interior of a long archway through which we reached it, were carefully sheathed with copper. The door, of massive iron, had been, also, similarly protected. Its immense weight caused an unusually sharp grating sound, as it moved upon its hinges.

Having deposited our mournful burden upon tressels within this region of horror, we partially turned aside the yet unscrewed lid of the coffin, and looked upon the face of the tenant. A striking similitude between the brother and sister now first arrested my attention; and Usher, divining, perhaps, my thoughts, murmured out some few words from which I learned that the deceased and himself had been twins, and that sympathies of a scarcely intelligible nature had always existed between them.[9] Our glances, however, rested not long upon the dead—for we could not regard her unawed. The disease which had thus entombed the lady in the maturity of youth, had left, as usual in all maladies of a strictly cataleptical character, the mockery of a faint blush upon the bosom and the face, and that suspiciously lingering smile upon the lip which is so terrible in death. We replaced and screwed down the lid, and, having secured the door of iron, made our way, with toil, into the scarcely less gloomy apartments of the upper portion of the house.

And now, some days of bitter grief having elapsed, an observable change came over the features of the mental disorder of my friend. His ordinary manner had vanished. His ordinary occupations were neglected or forgotten. He roamed from chamber to chamber with hurried, unequal, and objectless step. The pallor of his countenance had assumed, if possible, a more ghastly hue—but the luminousness of his eye had utterly gone out. The once occasional huskiness of his tone was heard no more; and a tremulous quaver, as if of extreme terror, habitually characterized his utterance. There were times, indeed, when I thought his unceasingly agitated mind was laboring with some

and physicians for dissection. The narrator earlier remarks on the look of low cunning and perplexity on the face of the family physician (p. 202 herein). Such grave robbers were also known ironically as "resurrection men."

8. Although dampish, this dungeon prison ("donjon keep") has been used to store highly combustible materials like gunpowder (despite all the highly conductive metal surrounding it); the "worst purposes" of an earlier time were presumably torture and execution.

9. See p. 201, n. 8 herein. Although it is biologically impossible for twins of the opposite sex to be identical, it would be possible, because of the inbreeding of the family line, for Roderick and Madeline to look exactly alike. One folk tradition surrounding identical twins is that they can share feelings and thoughts telepathically.

oppressive secret, to divulge which he struggled for the necessary courage. At times, again, I was obliged to resolve all into the mere inexplicable vagaries of madness, for I beheld him gazing upon vacancy for long hours, in an attitude of the profoundest attention, as if listening to some imaginary sound. It was no wonder that his condition terrified—that it infected me. I felt creeping upon me, by slow yet certain degrees, the wild influences of his own fantastic yet impressive superstitions.

It was, especially, upon retiring to bed late in the night of the seventh or eighth day after the placing of the lady Madeline within the donjon, that I experienced the full power of such feelings. Sleep came not near my couch—while the hours waned and waned away. I struggled to reason off the nervousness which had dominion over me. I endeavored to believe that much, if not all of what I felt, was due to the bewildering influence of the gloomy furniture of the room—of the dark and tattered draperies, which, tortured into motion by the breath of a rising tempest, swayed fitfully to and fro upon the walls, and rustled uneasily about the decorations of the bed. But my efforts were fruitless. An irrepressible tremor gradually pervaded my frame; and, at length, there sat upon my very heart an incubus of utterly causeless alarm.[1] Shaking this off with a gasp and a struggle, I uplifted myself upon the pillows, and, peering earnestly within the intense darkness of the chamber, harkened—I know not why, except that an instinctive spirit prompted me—to certain low and indefinite sounds which came, through the pauses of the storm, at long intervals, I knew not whence. Overpowered by an intense sentiment of horror, unaccountable yet unendurable, I threw on my clothes with haste (for I felt that I should sleep no more during the night), and endeavored to arouse myself from the pitiable condition into which I had fallen, by pacing rapidly to and fro through the apartment.

I had taken but few turns in this manner, when a light step on an adjoining staircase arrested my attention. I presently recognised it as that of Usher. In an instant afterward he rapped, with a gentle touch, at my door, and entered, bearing a lamp. His countenance was, as usual, cadaverously wan—but, moreover, there was a species of mad hilarity in his eyes—an evidently restrained *hysteria* in his whole demeanor. His air appalled me—but anything was preferable to the solitude which I had so long endured, and I even welcomed his presence as a relief.

"And you have not seen it?" he said abruptly, after having stared about him for some moments in silence—"you have not then seen it?—but, stay! you shall." Thus speaking, and having carefully shaded his lamp, he hurried to one of the casements, and threw it freely open to the storm.

The impetuous fury of the entering gust nearly lifted us from our feet. It was, indeed, a tempestuous yet sternly beautiful night, and one

1. Poe's narrator uses the allusion to the incubus myth to suggest that the apprehensiveness he feels is imaginary (paradoxically raising the possibility it is not).

wildly singular in its terror and its beauty. A whirlwind had apparently
collected its force in our vicinity; for there were frequent and violent
alterations in the direction of the wind; and the exceeding density of
the clouds (which hung so low as to press upon the turrets of the
house) did not prevent our perceiving the life-like velocity with which
they flew careering from all points against each other, without passing
away into the distance. I say that even their exceeding density did not
prevent our perceiving this—yet we had no glimpse of the moon or
stars—nor was there any flashing forth of the lightning.[2] But the un-
der surfaces of the huge masses of agitated vapor, as well as all terres-
trial objects immediately around us, were glowing in the unnatural
light of a faintly luminous and distinctly visible gaseous exhalation
which hung about and enshrouded the mansion.

"You must not—you shall not behold this!" said I, shudderingly, to
Usher, as I led him, with a gentle violence, from the window to a seat.
"These appearances, which bewilder you, are merely electrical phe-
nomena not uncommon—or it may be that they have their ghastly ori-
gin in the rank miasma of the tarn. Let us close this casement;—the
air is chilling and dangerous to your frame. Here is one of your fa-
vorite romances.[3] I will read, and you shall listen;—and so we will pass
away this terrible night together."

The antique volume which I had taken up was the "Mad Trist" of
Sir Launcelot Canning;[4] but I had called it a favorite of Usher's more
in sad jest than in earnest; for, in truth, there is little in its uncouth
and unimaginative prolixity which could have had interest for the lofty
and spiritual ideality of my friend. It was, however, the only book im-
mediately at hand; and I indulged a vague hope that the excitement
which now agitated the hypochondriac, might find relief (for the his-
tory of mental disorder is full of similar anomalies) even in the ex-
tremeness of the folly which I should read. Could I have judged,
indeed, by the wild overstrained air of vivacity with which he hark-
ened, or apparently harkened, to the words of the tale, I might well
have congratulated myself upon the success of my design.

I had arrived at that well-known portion of the story where
Ethelred; the hero of the Trist, having sought in vain for peaceable ad-
mission into the dwelling of the hermit, proceeds to make good an en-
trance by force. Here, it will be remembered, the words of the
narrative run thus:

"And Ethelred, who was by nature of a doughty[5] heart, and who was
now mighty withal, on account of the powerfulness of the wine which

2. The grammar of the sentence may be deliberately ambiguous. In some interpretations of this
 tale, the existence or nonexistence of lightning is important. If something like sheet light-
 ning is present, then there are possible natural explanations for what seems to be the super-
 natural fate of the house at the end—which in turn may have a bearing on what actually
 happens to its inhabitants in the final scene.
3. In the sense of narratives of the exotic, the unusual, or the extraordinary—often distin-
 guished from novels, which deal with the familiar, the everyday, the ordinary.
4. So far as is known, this work is a fabrication of Poe's—the only one of Usher's books that is
 not real. "Trist": a meeting—as between two knights—not a *tryst* in the sense of a lover's
 meeting, though that meaning of the word may not be completely irrelevant.
5. Courageous.

he had drunken, waited no longer to hold parley with the hermit, who, in sooth, was of an obstinate and maliceful turn, but, feeling the rain upon his shoulders, and fearing the rising of the tempest, uplifted his mace outright, and, with blows, made quickly room in the plankings of the door for his gauntleted hand; and now pulling therewith sturdily, he so cracked, and ripped, and tore all asunder that the noise of the dry and hollow-sounding wood alarummed[6] and reverberated throughout the forest."

At the termination of this sentence I started, and for a moment, paused; for it appeared to me (although I at once concluded that my excited fancy had deceived me)—it appeared to me that, from some very remote portion of the mansion, there came, indistinctly, to my ears, what might have been, in its exact similarity of character, the echo (but a stifled and dull one certainly) of the very crackling and ripping sound which Sir Launcelot had so particularly described. It was, beyond doubt, the coincidence alone which had arrested my attention; for, amid the rattling of the sashes of the casements, and the ordinary commingled noises of the still increasing storm, the sound, in itself, had nothing, surely, which should have interested or disturbed me. I continued the story:

"But the good champion Ethelred, now entering within the door, was sore enraged and amazed to perceive no signal of the maliceful hermit; but, in the stead thereof, a dragon of a scaly and prodigious demeanor, and of a fiery tongue, which sate in guard before a palace of gold, with a floor of silver; and upon the wall there hung a shield of shining brass with this legend enwritten—

> Who entereth herein, a conqueror hath bin;
> Who slayeth the dragon, the shield he shall win;[7]

And Ethelred uplifted his mace, and struck upon the head of the dragon, which fell before him, and gave up his pesty breath, with a shriek so horrid and harsh, and withal so piercing, that Ethelred had fain to close his ears with his hands against the dreadful noise of it, the like whereof was never before heard."

Here again I paused abruptly, and now with a feeling of wild amazement—for there could be no doubt whatever that, in this instance, I did actually hear (although from what direction it proceeded I found it impossible to say) a low and apparently distant, but harsh, protracted, and most unusual screaming or grating sound—the exact counterpart of what my fancy had already conjured up for the dragon's unnatural shriek as described by the romancer.

Oppressed, as I certainly was, upon the occurrence of this second and most extraordinary coincidence, by a thousand conflicting sensations, in which wonder and extreme terror were predominant, I still retained sufficient presence of mind to avoid exciting, by any observa-

6. Alarmed (archaic), but normally signifying a call to arms.
7. Among the traditional symbolic meanings of the dragon is fear; thus to slay the dragon can mean to conquer one's fear. The dragon also traditionally symbolizes evil, and Satan is often pictured as a dragon or serpent.

tion, the sensitive nervousness of my companion. I was by no means certain that he had noticed the sounds in question; although, assuredly, a strange alteration had, during the last few minutes, taken place in his demeanor. From a position fronting my own, he had gradually brought round his chair, so as to sit with his face to the door of the chamber; and thus I could but partially perceive his features, although I saw that his lips trembled as if he were murmuring inaudibly. His head had dropped upon his breast—yet I knew that he was not asleep, from the wide and rigid opening of the eye as I caught a glance of it in profile. The motion of his body, too, was at variance with this idea—for he rocked from side to side with a gentle yet constant and uniform sway. Having rapidly taken notice of all this, I resumed the narrative of Sir Launcelot, which thus proceeded:

"And now, the champion, having escaped from the terrible fury of the dragon, bethinking himself of the brazen shield, and of the breaking up of the enchantment which was upon it, removed the carcass from out of the way before him, and approached valorously over the silver pavement of the castle to where the shield was upon the wall; which in sooth tarried not for his full coming, but fell down at his feet upon the silver floor, with a mighty great and terrible ringing sound."

No sooner had these syllables passed my lips, than—as if a shield of brass had indeed, at the moment, fallen heavily upon a floor of silver—I became aware of a distinct, hollow, metallic, and clangorous, yet apparently muffled reverberation. Completely unnerved, I leaped to my feet; but the measured rocking movement of Usher was undisturbed. I rushed to the chair in which he sat. His eyes were bent fixedly before him, and throughout his whole countenance there reigned a stony rigidity. But, as I placed my hand upon his shoulder, there came a strong shudder over his whole person; a sickly smile quivered about his lips; and I saw that he spoke in a low, hurried, and gibbering murmur, as if unconscious of my presence. Bending closely over him, I at length drank in the hideous import of his words.

"Not hear it?—yes, I hear it, and *have* heard it. Long—long—long— *the sounds* many minutes, many hours, many days, have I heard it—yet I dared not—oh, pity me, miserable wretch that I am!—I dared not—I *dared* not speak! We have put her living in the tomb! Said I not that my senses were acute? I *now* tell you that I heard her first feeble movements in the hollow coffin. I heard them—many, many days ago—yet I dared not—*I dared not speak!* And now—to-night—Ethelred—ha! ha!—the breaking of the hermit's door, and the death-cry of the dragon, and the clangor of the shield!—say, rather, the rending of her coffin, and the grating of the iron hinges of her prison, and her struggles within the coppered archway of the vault! Oh whither shall I fly? Will she not be here anon? Is she not hurrying to upbraid me for my haste? Have I not heard her footstep on the stair? Do I not distinguish that heavy and horrible beating of her heart? Madman!"—here he sprang furiously to his feet, and shrieked out his syllables, as if in the effort he were giving up his soul—"*Madman! I tell you that she now stands without the door!*"

acute senses are also in the tell-tale heart —hearing the beating of her heart

As if in the superhuman energy of his utterance there had been found the potency of a spell—the huge antique pannels to which the speaker pointed, threw slowly back, upon the instant, their ponderous and ebony jaws. It was the work of the rushing gust—but then without those doors there *did* stand the lofty and enshrouded figure of the lady Madeline of Usher. There was blood upon her white robes, and the evidence of some bitter struggle upon every portion of her emaciated frame. For a moment she remained trembling and reeling to and fro upon the threshold—then, with a low moaning cry, fell heavily inward upon the person of her brother, and in her violent and now final death-agonies, bore him to the floor a corpse, and a victim to the terrors he had anticipated.

From that chamber, and from that mansion, I fled aghast. The storm was still abroad in all its wrath as I found myself crossing the old causeway. Suddenly there shot along the path a wild light, and I turned to see whence a gleam so unusual could have issued; for the vast house and its shadows were alone behind me. The radiance was that of the full, setting, and blood-red moon, which now shone vividly through that once barely-discernible fissure, of which I have before spoken as extending from the roof of the building, in a zigzag direction, to the base. While I gazed, this fissure rapidly widened—there came a fierce breath of the whirlwind—the entire orb of the satellite burst at once upon my sight—my brain reeled as I saw the mighty walls rushing asunder—there was a long tumultuous shouting sound like the voice of a thousand waters[8]—and the deep and dank tarn at my feet closed sullenly and silently over the fragments of the *"House of Usher."*

William Wilson[1]

What say of it? what say CONSCIENCE grim,
That spectre in my path?

CHAMBERLAIN'S PHARONNIDA[2]

Let me call myself, for the present, William Wilson. The fair page now lying before me need not be sullied with my real appellation. This

8. The phrasing and imagery of the end echoes some apocalyptic passages in Psalms and the Book of Revelation. In Psalm 93, a great flood lifts up with a roaring greater than the thunders of many waters. In Revelation 12 a great dragon appears, and the end of the earth is nigh; and in Revelation 14.2 the prophet hears a voice from heaven like the sound of many waters or like thunder.
1. First published in 1839 in *The Gift: a Christmas and New Year's Present for 1840*. The text reprinted here is that of the *Broadway Journal* (August 30, 1845). In a letter to Washington Irving (October 12, 1839), Poe acknowledged a debt to his "An Unwritten Drama of Lord Byron," in which Irving outlines the plan of a play (based on an old Spanish drama) that Byron at one time contemplated writing. Irving concludes by saying that the "foregoing sketch of the plot may hereafter suggest rich theme to a poet or dramatist of the Byron school." Poe seems to have directly followed up on this invitation; there are many parallels between the two pieces, including the basic plot.
2. Although attributed to *Pharonnida* (1659), a verse romance by William Chamberlayne, this epigraph does not appear in it; a somewhat similar passage, however, appears in his *Love's Victory* (1658). "Conscience waits on me like the frighting shades / Of ghosts when gastly [*sic*], messengers of death." These two works were published together in three volumes in 1820.

has been already too much an object for the scorn—for the horror—
for the detestation of my race. To the uttermost regions of the globe
have not the indignant winds bruited its unparalleled infamy? Oh,
outcast of all outcasts most abandoned!—to the earth art thou not for-
ever dead? to its honors, to its flowers, to its golden aspirations?—and
a cloud, dense, dismal, and limitless, does it not hang eternally be-
tween thy hopes and heaven?

I would not, if I could, here or to-day, embody a record of my later
years of unspeakable misery, and unpardonable crime. This epoch—
these later years—took unto themselves a sudden elevation in tur-
pitude, whose origin alone it is my present purpose to assign.
Men usually grow base by degrees. From me, in an instant, all virtue
dropped bodily as a mantle. From comparatively trivial wickedness I
passed, with the stride of a giant, into more than the enormities of an
Elah-Gabalus.[3] What chance—what one event brought this evil thing
to pass, bear with me while I relate. Death approaches; and the
shadow which foreruns him has thrown a softening influence over my
spirit. I long, in passing through the dim valley, for the sympathy—I
had nearly said for the pity—of my fellow men. I would fain have them
believe that I have been, in some measure, the slave of circumstances
beyond human control. I would wish them to seek out for me, in the
details I am about to give, some little oasis of *fatality* amid a wilder-
ness of error. I would have them allow—what they cannot refrain from
allowing—that, although temptation may have erewhile existed as
great, man was never *thus*, at least, tempted before—certainly, never
thus fell. And is it therefore that he has never thus suffered? Have I
not indeed been living in a dream? And am I not now dying a victim to
the horror and the mystery of the wildest of all sublunary visions?

I am the descendant of a race whose imaginative and easily ex-
citable temperament has at all times rendered them remarkable; and,
in my earliest infancy, I gave evidence of having fully inherited the
family character. As I advanced in years it was more strongly devel-
oped; becoming, for many reasons, a cause of serious disquietude to
my friends, and of positive injury to myself. I grew self-willed, addicted
to the wildest caprices, and a prey to the most ungovernable passions.
Weak-minded, and beset with constitutional infirmities akin to my
own, my parents could do but little to check the evil propensities
which distinguished me. Some feeble and ill-directed efforts resulted
in complete failure on their part, and, of course, in total triumph on
mine. Thenceforward my voice was a household law; and at an age
when few children have abandoned their leading-strings, I was left to
the guidance of my own will, and became, in all but name, the master
of my own actions.

My earliest recollections of a school-life, are connected with a large,

3. Elagabalus or Heliogabalus (c. 205–222 C.E.), Roman Emperor (218–22) and priest of the
sun god. Known as a monster of depravity, he is notorious for conducting disgusting and in-
decent religious rites, including the worship of Baal (see notes to "Loss of Breath," pp. 89ff.
herein, and "Ligeia," pp. 159ff.). In contempt of the state, he gave high offices to an actor, a
charioteer, and a barber. Heliogabalus was murdered along with his mother in an uprising of
the Praetorian Guard.

rambling, Elizabethan house, in a misty-looking village of England, where were a vast number of gigantic and gnarled trees, and where all the houses were excessively ancient. In truth, it was a dream-like and spirit-soothing place, that venerable old town. At this moment, in fancy, I feel the refreshing chilliness of its deeply-shadowed avenues, inhale the fragrance of its thousand shrubberies, and thrill anew with undefinable delight, at the deep hollow note of the church-bell, breaking, each hour, with sullen and sudden roar, upon the stillness of the dusky atmosphere in which the fretted Gothic steeple lay imbedded and asleep.

It gives me, perhaps, as much of pleasure as I can now in any manner experience, to dwell upon minute recollections of the school and its concerns. Steeped in misery as I am—misery, alas! only too real—I shall be pardoned for seeking relief, however slight and temporary, in the weakness of a few rambling details. These, moreover, utterly trivial, and even ridiculous in themselves, assume, to my fancy, adventitious importance, as connected with a period and a locality when and where I recognise the first ambiguous monitions of the destiny which afterwards so fully overshadowed me. Let me then remember.

The house, I have said, was old and irregular. The grounds were extensive, and a high and solid brick wall, topped with a bed of mortar and broken glass, encompassed the whole. This prison-like rampart formed the limit of our domain; beyond it we saw but thrice a week— once every Saturday afternoon, when, attended by two ushers, we were permitted to take brief walks in a body through some of the neighbouring fields—and twice during Sunday, when we were paraded in the same formal manner to the morning and evening service in the one church of the village. Of this church the principal of our school was pastor. With how deep a spirit of wonder and perplexity was I wont to regard him from our remote pew in the gallery, as, with step solemn and slow, he ascended the pulpit! This reverend man, with countenance so demurely benign, with robes so glossy and so clerically flowing, with wig so minutely powdered, so rigid and so vast,— could this be he who, of late, with sour visage, and in snuffy habiliments, administered, ferule in hand, the Draconian[4] laws of the academy? Oh, gigantic paradox, too utterly monstrous for solution!

At an angle of the ponderous wall frowned a more ponderous gate. It was riveted and studded with iron bolts, and surmounted with jagged iron spikes. What impressions of deep awe did it inspire! It was never opened save for the three periodical egressions and ingressions already mentioned; then, in every creak of its mighty hinges, we found a plenitude of mystery—a world of matter for solemn remark, or for more solemn meditation.

4. Severe—from the harsh laws of the Athenian politician, Draco (fl. 621 B.C.E.), whose usual penalty was death even for trivial crimes. The description of the house bears some resemblance to the Manor House School of the Reverend John Bransby at Stoke Newington in England, which Poe attended. Scholars have speculated that Poe's character (named the Reverend Dr. Bransby four paragraphs below) is based on a composite of Bransby and the Reverend George Gaskin, a rector of St. Mary's Church and a secretary of the Society for Promoting Christian Knowledge.

The extensive enclosure was irregular in form, having many capacious recesses. Of these, three or four of the largest constituted the play-ground. It was level, and covered with fine hard gravel. I well remember it had no trees, nor benches, nor any thing similar within it. Of course it was in the rear of the house. In front lay a small parterre, planted with box and other shrubs; but through this sacred division we passed only upon rare occasions indeed—such as a first advent to school or final departure thence, or perhaps, when a parent or friend having called for us, we joyfully took our way home for the Christmas or Midsummer holydays.

But the house!—how quaint an old building was this!—to me how veritably a palace of enchantment! There was really no end to its windings—to its incomprehensible subdivisions. It was difficult, at any given time, to say with certainty upon which of its two stories one happened to be. From each room to every other there were sure to be found three or four steps either in ascent or descent. Then the lateral branches were innumerable—inconceivable—and so returning in upon themselves, that our most exact ideas in regard to the whole mansion were not very far different from those with which we pondered upon infinity. During the five years of my residence here, I was never able to ascertain with precision, in what remote locality lay the little sleeping apartment assigned to myself and some eighteen or twenty other scholars.

The school-room was the largest in the house—I could not help thinking, in the world. It was very long, narrow, and dismally low, with pointed Gothic windows and a ceiling of oak. In a remote and terror-inspiring angle was a square enclosure of eight or ten feet, comprising the *sanctum*, "during hours," of our principal, the Reverend Dr. Bransby. It was a solid structure, with massy door, sooner than open which in the absence of the "Dominie," we would all have willingly perished by the *peine forte et dure*.[5] In other angles were two other similar boxes, far less reverenced, indeed, but still greatly matters of awe. One of these was the pulpit of the "classical" usher, one of the "English and mathematical." Interspersed about the room, crossing and re-crossing in endless irregularity, were innumerable benches and desks, black, ancient, and time-worn, piled desperately with much-bethumbed books, and so beseamed with initial letters, names at full length, grotesque figures, and other multiplied efforts of the knife, as to have entirely lost what little of original form might have been their portion in days long departed. A huge bucket with water stood at one extremity of the room, and a clock of stupendous dimensions at the other.

Encompassed by the massy walls of this venerable academy, I passed, yet not in tedium or disgust, the years of the third lustrum[6] of my life. The teeming brain of childhood requires no external world of incident to occupy or amuse it; and the apparently dismal monotony

5. Pain strong and long in duration (French). A capital punishment by which the individual is usually pressed to death with heavy weights. "Dominie": master.
6. A period of five years.

of a school was replete with more intense excitement than my riper
youth has derived from luxury, or my full manhood from crime. Yet I
must believe that my first mental development had in it much of the
uncommon—even much of the *outré*.[7] Upon mankind at large the
events of very early existence rarely leave in mature age any definite
impression. All is gray shadow—a weak and irregular remembrance—
an indistinct regathering of feeble pleasures and phantasmagoric
pains. With me this is not so. In childhood I must have felt with the
energy of a man what I now find stamped upon memory in lines as
vivid, as deep, and as durable as the *exergues* of the Carthaginian
medals.[8]

Yet in fact—in the fact of the world's view—how little was there to
remember! The morning's awakening, the nightly summons to bed;
the connings,[9] the recitations; the periodical half-holidays, and peram-
bulations; the play-ground, with its broils, its pastimes, its intrigues;—
these, by a mental sorcery long forgotten, were made to involve a
wilderness of sensation, a world of rich incident, an universe of varied
emotion, of excitement the most passionate and spirit-stirring. "*Oh, le
bon temps, que ce siecle de fer!*"[1]

In truth, the ardor, the enthusiasm, and the imperiousness of my
disposition, soon rendered me a marked character, among my school-
mates, and by slow, but natural gradations, gave me an ascendancy
over all not greatly older than myself;—over all with a single excep-
tion. This exception was found in the person of a scholar, who,
although no relation, bore the same Christian and surname as my-
self;—a circumstance, in fact, little remarkable; for, notwithstand-
ing a noble descent, mine was one of those every-day appellations
which seem, by prescriptive right, to have been, time out of mind, the
common property of the mob. In this narrative I have therefore desig-
nated myself as William Wilson,—a fictitious title not very dissimilar
to the real. My namesake alone, of those who in school phraseology
constituted "our set," presumed to compete with me in the studies of
the class—in the sports and broils of the play-ground—to refuse im-
plicit belief in my assertions, and submission to my will—indeed, to
interfere with my arbitrary dictation in any respect whatsoever. If
there is on earth a supreme and unqualified despotism, it is the des-
potism of a master mind in boyhood over the less energetic spirits of
its companions.

Wilson's rebellion was to me a source of the greatest embarrass-
ment;—the more so as, in spite of the bravado with which in public I
made a point of treating him and his pretensions, I secretly felt that I
feared him, and could not help thinking the equality which he main-

7. Strange, extreme (French).
8. From the French *médaille*; here a coin no longer current. "*Exergues*": inscribed below
 (French); term relating to the portion beneath the figures of a coin where information is im-
 printed. Carthaginian: of the city of Carthage, Rome's African rival.
9. Learning by memorizing. Students often softly read or whispered their studies over and over
 to themselves.
1. Oh, the good old days, that Iron Age (French). The quotation, an ironic comment on those
 who indulge in nostalgia, is from one of Voltaire's satires, *Le Mondain*.

tained so easily with myself, a proof of his true superiority; since not to be overcome cost me a perpetual struggle. Yet this superiority—even this equality—was in truth acknowledged by no one but myself; our associates, by some unaccountable blindness, seemed not even to suspect it. Indeed, his competition, his resistance, and especially his impertinent and dogged interference with my purposes, were not more pointed than private. He appeared to be destitute alike of the ambition which urged, and of the passionate energy of mind which enabled me to excel. In his rivalry he might have been supposed actuated solely by a whimsical desire to thwart, astonish, or mortify myself; although there were times when I could not help observing, with a feeling made up of wonder, abasement, and pique, that he mingled with his injuries, his insults, or his contradictions, a certain most inappropriate, and assuredly most unwelcome *affectionateness* of manner. I could only conceive this singular behavior to arise from a consummate self-conceit assuming the vulgar airs of patronage and protection.

Perhaps it was this latter trait in Wilson's conduct, conjoined with our identity of name, and the mere accident of our having entered the school upon the same day, which set afloat the notion that we were brothers, among the senior classes in the academy. These do not usually inquire with much strictness into the affairs of their juniors. I have before said, or should have said, that Wilson was not, in the most remote degree, connected with my family. But assuredly if we *had* been brothers we must have been twins; for, after leaving Dr. Bransby's, I casually learned that my namesake was born on the nineteenth of January, 1813—and this is a somewhat remarkable coincidence; for the day is precisely that of my own nativity.

It may seem strange that in spite of the continual anxiety occasioned me by the rivalry of Wilson, and his intolerable spirit of contradiction, I could not bring myself to hate him altogether. We had, to be sure, nearly every day a quarrel in which, yielding me publicly the palm of victory, he, in some manner, contrived to make me feel that it was he who had deserved it; yet a sense of pride on my part, and a veritable dignity on his own, kept us always upon what are called "speaking terms," while there were many points of strong congeniality in our tempers, operating to awake in me a sentiment which our position alone, perhaps, prevented from ripening into friendship. It is difficult, indeed, to define, or even to describe, my real feelings towards him. They formed a motley and heterogeneous admixture;—some petulant animosity, which was not yet hatred, some esteem, more respect, much fear, with a world of uneasy curiosity. To the moralist it will be unnecessary to say, in addition, that Wilson and myself were the most inseparable of companions.

It was no doubt the anomalous state of affairs existing between us, which turned all my attacks upon him, (and they were many, either open or covert) into the channel of banter or practical joke (giving pain while assuming the aspect of mere fun) rather than into a more serious and determined hostility. But my endeavours on this head were by no means uniformly successful, even when my plans were the most

wittily concocted; for my namesake had much about him, in character, of that unassuming and quiet austerity which, while enjoying the poignancy of its own jokes, has no heel of Achilles in itself, and absolutely refuses to be laughed at. I could find, indeed, but one vulnerable point, and that, lying in a personal peculiarity, arising, perhaps, from constitutional disease, would have been spared by any antagonist less at his wit's end than myself;—my rival had a weakness in the faucial or guttural organs, which precluded him from raising his voice at any time *above a very low whisper*. Of this defect I did not fail to take what poor advantage lay in my power.

Wilson's retaliations in kind were many; and there was one form of his practical wit that disturbed me beyond measure. How his sagacity first discovered at all that so petty a thing would vex me, is a question I never could solve; but, having discovered, he habitually practised the annoyance. I had always felt aversion to my uncourtly patronymic, and its very common, if not plebeian prænomen. The words were venom in my ears; and when, upon the day of my arrival, a second William Wilson came also to the academy, I felt angry with him for bearing the name, and doubly disgusted with the name because a stranger bore it, who would be the cause of its twofold repetition, who would be constantly in my presence, and whose concerns, in the ordinary routine of the school business, must inevitably, on account of the detestable coincidence, be often confounded with my own.

The feeling of vexation thus engendered grew stronger with every circumstance tending to show resemblance, moral or physical, between my rival and myself. I had not then discovered the remarkable fact that we were of the same age; but I saw that we were of the same height, and I perceived that we were even singularly alike in general contour of person and outline of feature. I was galled, too, by the rumor touching a relationship, which had grown current in the upper forms.[2] In a word, nothing could more seriously disturb me, (although I scrupulously concealed such disturbance,) than any allusion to a similarity of mind, person, or condition existing between us. But, in truth, I had no reason to believe that (with the exception of the matter of relationship, and in the case of Wilson himself,) this similarity had ever been made a subject of comment, or even observed at all by our schoolfellows. That *he* observed it in all its bearings, and as fixedly as I, was apparent; but that he could discover in such circumstances so fruitful a field of annoyance, can only be attributed, as I said before, to his more than ordinary penetration.

His cue, which was to perfect an imitation of myself, lay both in words and in actions; and most admirably did he play his part. My dress it was an easy matter to copy; my gait and general manner were, without difficulty, appropriated; in spite of his constitutional defect, even my voice did not escape him. My louder tones were, of course, unattempted, but then the key, it was identical; *and his singular whisper, it grew the very echo of my own.*

2. Upper classes or grades.

How greatly this most exquisite portraiture harassed me, (for it could not justly be termed a caricature,) I will not now venture to describe. I had but one consolation—in the fact that the imitation, apparently, was noticed by myself alone, and that I had to endure only the knowing and strangely sarcastic smiles of my namesake himself. Satisfied with having produced in my bosom the intended effect, he seemed to chuckle in secret over the sting he had inflicted, and was characteristically disregardful of the public applause which the success of his witty endeavours might have so easily elicited. That the school, indeed, did not feel his design, perceive its accomplishment, and participate in his sneer, was, for many anxious months, a riddle I could not resolve. Perhaps the *gradation* of his copy rendered it not so readily perceptible; or, more possibly, I owed my security to the masterly air of the copyist, who, disdaining the letter, (which in a painting is all the obtuse can see,) gave but the full spirit of his original for my individual contemplation and chagrin.

I have already more than once spoken of the disgusting air of patronage which he assumed toward me, and of his frequent officious interference with my will. This interference often took the ungracious character of advice; advice not openly given, but hinted or insinuated. I received it with a repugnance which gained strength as I grew in years. Yet, at this distant day, let me do him the simple justice to acknowledge that I can recall no occasion when the suggestions of my rival were on the side of those errors or follies so usual to his immature age and seeming inexperience; that his moral sense, at least, if not his general talents and worldly wisdom, was far keener than my own; and that I might, to-day, have been a better, and thus a happier man, had I less frequently rejected the counsels embodied in those meaning whispers which I then but too cordially hated and too bitterly despised.

As it was, I at length grew restive in the extreme under his distasteful supervision, and daily resented more and more openly what I considered his intolerable arrogance. I have said that, in the first years of our connexion as schoolmates, my feelings in regard to him might have been easily ripened into friendship; but, in the latter months of my residence at the academy, although the intrusion of his ordinary manner had, beyond doubt, in some measure, abated, my sentiments, in nearly similar proportion, partook very much of positive hatred. Upon one occasion he saw this, I think, and afterwards avoided, or made a show of avoiding me.

It was about the same period, if I remember aright, that, in an altercation of violence with him, in which he was more than usually thrown off his guard, and spoke and acted with an openness of demeanor rather foreign to his nature, I discovered, or fancied I discovered, in his accent, his air, and general appearance, a something which first startled, and then deeply interested me, by bringing to mind dim visions of my earliest infancy—wild, confused and thronging memories of a time when memory herself was yet unborn. I cannot better describe the sensation which oppressed me than by saying that

I could with difficulty shake off the belief of my having been acquainted with the being who stood before me, at some epoch very long ago—some point of the past even infinitely remote. The delusion, however, faded rapidly as it came; and I mention it at all but to define the day of the last conversation I there held with my singular namesake.

The huge old house, with its countless subdivisions, had several large chambers communicating with each other, where slept the greater number of the students. There were, however, (as must necessarily happen in a building so awkwardly planned,) many little nooks or recesses, the odds and ends of the structure; and these the economic ingenuity of Dr. Bransby had also fitted up as dormitories; although, being the merest closets, they were capable of accommodating but a single individual. One of these small apartments was occupied by Wilson.

One night, about the close of my fifth year at the school, and immediately after the altercation just mentioned, finding every one wrapped in sleep, I arose from bed, and, lamp in hand, stole through a wilderness of narrow passages from my own bedroom to that of my rival. I had long been plotting one of those ill-natured pieces of practical wit at his expense in which I had hitherto been so uniformly unsuccessful. It was my intention, now, to put my scheme in operation, and I resolved to make him feel the whole extent of the malice with which I was imbued. Having reached his closet, I noiselessly entered, leaving the lamp, with a shade over it, on the outside. I advanced a step, and listened to the sound of his tranquil breathing. Assured of his being asleep, I returned, took the light, and with it again approached the bed. Close curtains were around it, which, in the prosecution of my plan, I slowly and quietly withdrew, when the bright rays fell vividly upon the sleeper, and my eyes, at the same moment, upon his countenance. I looked;—and a numbness, an iciness of feeling instantly pervaded my frame. My breast heaved, my knees tottered, my whole spirit became possessed with an objectless yet intolerable horror. Gasping for breath, I lowered the lamp in still nearer proximity to the face. Were these—*these* the lineaments of William Wilson? I saw, indeed, that they were his, but I shook as if with a fit of the ague in fancying they were not. What *was* there about them to confound me in this manner? I gazed;—while my brain reeled with a multitude of incoherent thoughts. Not thus he appeared—assuredly not *thus*—in the vivacity of his waking hours. The same name! the same contour of person! the same day of arrival at the academy! And then his dogged and meaningless imitation of my gait, my voice, my habits, and my manner! Was it, in truth, within the bounds of human possibility, that *what I now saw* was the result, merely, of the habitual practice of this sarcastic imitation? Awe-stricken, and with a creeping shudder, I extinguished the lamp, passed silently from the chamber, and left, at once, the halls of that old academy, never to enter them again.

After a lapse of some months, spent at home in mere idleness, I

found myself a student at Eton. The brief interval had been sufficient to enfeeble my remembrance of the events at Dr. Bransby's, or at least to effect a material change in the nature of the feelings with which I remembered them. The truth—the tragedy—of the drama was no more. I could now find room to doubt the evidence of my senses; and seldom called up the subject at all but with wonder at the extent of human credulity, and a smile at the vivid force of the imagination which I hereditarily possessed. Neither was this species of skepticism likely to be diminished by the character of the life I led at Eton. The vortex of thoughtless folly into which I there so immediately and so recklessly plunged, washed away all but the froth of my past hours, engulfed at once every solid or serious impression, and left to memory only the veriest levities of a former existence.

I do not wish, however, to trace the course of my miserable profligacy here—a profligacy which set at defiance the laws, while it eluded the vigilance of the institution. Three years of folly, passed without profit, had but given me rooted habits of vice, and added, in a somewhat unusual degree, to my bodily stature, when, after a week of soulless dissipation, I invited a small party of the most dissolute students to a secret carousal in my chambers. We met at a late hour of the night; for our debaucheries were to be faithfully protracted until morning. The wine flowed freely, and there were not wanting other and perhaps more dangerous seductions; so that the grey dawn had already faintly appeared in the east, while our delirious extravagance was at its height. Madly flushed with cards and intoxication, I was in the act of insisting upon a toast of more than wonted profanity, when my attention was suddenly diverted by the violent, although partial unclosing of the door of the apartment, and by the eager voice of a servant from without. He said that some person, apparently in great haste, demanded to speak with me in the hall.

Wildly excited with wine, the unexpected interruption rather delighted than surprised me. I staggered forward at once, and a few steps brought me to the vestibule of the building. In this low and small room there hung no lamp; and now no light at all was admitted, save that of the exceedingly feeble dawn which made its way through the semi-circular window. As I put my foot over the threshold, I became aware of the figure of a youth about my own height, and habited in a white kerseymere[3] morning frock, cut in the novel fashion of the one I myself wore at the moment. This the faint light enabled me to perceive; but the features of his face I could not distinguish. Upon my entering he strode hurriedly up to me, and, seizing me by the arm with a gesture of petulant impatience, whispered the words "William Wilson!" in my ear.

I grew perfectly sober in an instant.

There was that in the manner of the stranger, and in the tremulous shake of his uplifted finger, as he held it between my eyes and the light, which filled me with unqualified amazement; but it was not this

3. Cashmere.

which had so violently moved me. It was the pregnancy of solemn admonition in the singular, low, hissing utterance; and, above all, it was the character, the tone, *the key*, of those few, simple, and familiar, yet *whispered* syllables, which came with a thousand thronging memories of by-gone days, and struck upon my soul with the shock of a galvanic battery. Ere I could recover the use of my senses he was gone.

Although this event failed not of a vivid effect upon my disordered imagination, yet was it evanescent as vivid. For some weeks, indeed, I busied myself in earnest inquiry, or was wrapped in a cloud of morbid speculation. I did not pretend to disguise from my perception the identity of the singular individual who thus perseveringly interfered with my affairs, and harassed me with his insinuated counsel. But who and what was this Wilson?—and whence came he?—and what were his purposes? Upon neither of these points could I be satisfied; merely ascertaining, in regard to him, that a sudden accident in his family had caused his removal from Dr. Bransby's academy on the afternoon of the day in which I myself had eloped. But in a brief period I ceased to think upon the subject; my attention being all absorbed in a contemplated departure for Oxford. Thither I soon went; the uncalculating vanity of my parents furnishing me with an outfit, and annual establishment, which would enable me to indulge at will in the luxury already so dear to my heart,—to vie in profuseness of expenditure with the haughtiest heirs of the wealthiest earldoms in Great Britain.

Excited by such appliances to vice, my constitutional temperament broke forth with redoubled ardor, and I spurned even the common restraints of decency in the mad infatuation of my revels. But it were absurd to pause in the detail of my extravagance. Let it suffice, that among spendthrifts I out-Heroded Herod,[4] and that, giving name to a multitude of novel follies, I added no brief appendix to the long catalogue of vices then usual in the most dissolute university of Europe.

It could hardly be credited, however, that I had, even here, so utterly fallen from the gentlemanly estate, as to seek acquaintance with the vilest arts of the gambler by profession, and, having become an adept in his despicable science, to practise it habitually as a means of increasing my already enormous income at the expense of the weak-minded among my fellow collegians. Such, nevertheless, was the fact. And the very enormity of this offence against all manly and honourable sentiment proved, beyond doubt, the main if not the sole reason of the impunity with which it was committed. Who, indeed, among my most abandoned associates, would not rather have disputed the clearest evidence of his senses, than have suspected of such courses, the gay, the frank, the generous William Wilson—the noblest and most liberal commoner at Oxford—him whose follies (said his parasites) were but the follies of youth and unbridled fancy—whose

4. From *Hamlet*, III.ii.16, where it means to rant violently, but also to outdo someone who does or has done something in extremity. Herod the Great (died 4 B.C.E.), who ruled Palestine, promoted Hellenization by elaborately adorning the cities of his rule, especially Jerusalem.

errors but inimitable whim—whose darkest vice but a careless and dashing extravagance?

I had been now two years successfully busied in this way, when there came to the university a young *parvenu* nobleman, Glendinning—rich, said report, as Herodes Atticus[5]—his riches, too, as easily acquired. I soon found him of weak intellect, and, of course, marked him as a fitting subject for my skill. I frequently engaged him in play, and contrived, with a gambler's usual art, to let him win considerable sums, the more effectually to entangle him in my snares. At length, my schemes being ripe, I met him (with the full intention that this meeting should be final and decisive) at the chambers of a fellow-commoner, (Mr. Preston,) equally intimate with both, but who, to do him justice, entertained not even a remote suspicion of my design. To give to this a better coloring, I had contrived to have assembled a party of some eight or ten, and was solicitously careful that the introduction of cards should appear accidental, and originate in the proposal of my contemplated dupe himself. To be brief upon a vile topic, none of the low finesse was omitted, so customary upon similar occasions that it is a just matter for wonder how any are still found so besotted as to fall its victim.

We had protracted our sitting far into the night, and I had at length effected the manœuvre of getting Glendinning as my sole antagonist. The game, too, was my favorite *écarté*.[6] The rest of the company, interested in the extent of our play, had abandoned their own cards, and were standing around us as spectators. The *parvenu*, who had been induced by my artifices in the early part of the evening, to drink deeply, now shuffled, dealt, or played, with a wild nervousness of manner for which his intoxication, I thought, might partially, but could not altogether account. In a very short period he had become my debtor to a large amount, when, having taken a long draught of port, he did precisely what I had been coolly anticipating—he proposed to double our already extravagant stakes. With a well-feigned show of reluctance, and not until after my repeated refusal had seduced him into some angry words which gave a color of *pique* to my compliance, did I finally comply. The result, of course, did but prove how entirely the prey was in my toils; in less than an hour he had quadrupled his debt. For some time his countenance had been losing the florid tinge lent it by the wine; but now, to my astonishment, I perceived that it had grown to a pallor truly fearful. I say to my astonishment. Glendinning had been represented to my eager inquiries as immeasurably wealthy; and the sums which he had as yet lost, although in themselves vast, could not, I supposed, very seriously annoy, much less so violently affect him. That he was overcome by the wine just swallowed, was the idea which most readily presented itself; and, rather with a view to the preservation of my own character in the eyes of my associates, than from any less interested motive, I was about to insist, peremptorily, upon a discontinuance of

5. Greek rhetorician (fl. 2nd century C.E.). A patron of learning and the arts, he spent his fortune adorning Athens along with other Greek cities. "*Parvenu*": newly rich (French).
6. Card game for two individuals.

the play, when some expressions at my elbow from among the company, and an ejaculation evincing utter despair on the part of Glendinning, gave me to understand that I had effected his total ruin under circumstances which, rendering him an object for the pity of all, should have protected him from the ill offices even of a fiend.

What now might have been my conduct it is difficult to say. The pitiable condition of my dupe had thrown an air of embarrassed gloom over all; and, for some moments, a profound silence was maintained, during which I could not help feeling my cheeks tingle with the many burning glances of scorn or reproach cast upon me by the less abandoned of the party. I will even own that an intolerable weight of anxiety was for a brief instant lifted from my bosom by the sudden and extraordinary interruption which ensued. The wide, heavy folding doors of the apartment were all at once thrown open, to their full extent, with a vigorous and rushing impetuosity that extinguished, as if by magic, every candle in the room. Their light, in dying, enabled us just to perceive that a stranger had entered, about my own height, and closely muffled in a cloak. The darkness, however, was now total; and we could only *feel* that he was standing in our midst. Before any one of us could recover from the extreme astonishment into which this rudeness had thrown all, we heard the voice of the intruder.

"Gentlemen," he said, in a low, distinct, and never-to-be-forgotten *whisper* which thrilled to the very marrow of my bones, "Gentlemen, I make no apology for this behaviour, because in thus behaving, I am not fulfilling a duty. You are, beyond doubt, uninformed of the true character of the person who has to-night won at *écarté* a large sum of money from Lord Glendinning. I will therefore put you upon an expeditious and decisive plan of obtaining this very necessary information. Please to examine, at your leisure, the inner linings of the cuff of his left sleeve, and the several little packages which may be found in the somewhat capacious pockets of his embroidered morning wrapper."[7]

While he spoke, so profound was the stillness that one might have heard a pin drop upon the floor. In ceasing, he departed at once, and as abruptly as he had entered. Can I—shall I describe my sensations?—must I say that I felt all the horrors of the damned? Most assuredly I had little time given for reflection. Many hands roughly seized me upon the spot, and lights were immediately reprocured. A search ensued. In the lining of my sleeve were found all the court cards essential in *écarté*, and, in the pockets of my wrapper, a number of packs, fac-similes of those used at our sittings, with the single exception that mine were of the species called, technically, *arrondées*;[8] the honors being slightly convex at the ends, the lower cards slightly convex at the sides. In this disposition, the dupe who cuts, as customary, at the length of the pack, will invariably find that he cuts his antagonist an honor; while the gambler, cutting at the breadth, will, as

7. The situation resembles that of "The Gamesters," part of the "Old Bachelor" series of sketches published in book form in 1814 under the supervision of William Wirt.
8. Rounded (French).

certainly, cut nothing for his victim which may count in the records of the game.[9]

Any burst of indignation upon this discovery would have affected me less than the silent contempt, or the sarcastic composure, with which it was received.

"Mr. Wilson," said our host, stooping to remove from beneath his feet an exceedingly luxurious cloak of rare furs, "Mr. Wilson, this is your property." (The weather was cold; and, upon quitting my own room, I had thrown a cloak over my dressing wrapper, putting it off upon reaching the scene of play.) "I presume it is supererogatory to seek here (eyeing the folds of the garment with a bitter smile) for any farther evidence of your skill. Indeed, we have had enough. You will see the necessity, I hope, of quitting Oxford—at all events, of quitting instantly my chambers."

Abased, humbled to the dust as I then was, it is probable that I should have resented this galling language by immediate personal violence, had not my whole attention been at the moment arrested by a fact of the most startling character. The cloak which I had worn was of a rare description of fur; how rare, how extravagantly costly, I shall not venture to say. Its fashion, too, was of my own fantastic invention; for I was fastidious to an absurd degree of coxcombry, in matters of this frivolous nature. When, therefore, Mr. Preston reached me that which he had picked up upon the floor, and near the folding doors of the apartment, it was with an astonishment nearly bordering upon terror, that I perceived my own already hanging on my arm, (where I had no doubt unwittingly placed it,) and that the one presented me was but its exact counterpart in every, in even the minutest possible particular. The singular being who had so disastrously exposed me, had been muffled, I remembered, in a cloak; and none had been worn at all by any of the members of our party with the exception of myself. Retaining some presence of mind, I took the one offered me by Preston; placed it, unnoticed, over my own; left the apartment with a resolute scowl of defiance; and, next morning ere dawn of day, commenced a hurried journey from Oxford to the continent, in a perfect agony of horror and of shame.

I *fled in vain*. My evil destiny pursued me as if in exultation, and proved, indeed, that the exercise of its mysterious dominion had as yet only begun. Scarcely had I set foot in Paris ere I had fresh evidence of the detestable interest taken by this Wilson in my concerns. Years flew, while I experienced no relief. Villain!—at Rome, with how untimely, yet with how spectral an officiousness, stepped he in between me and my ambition! At Vienna, too—at Berlin—and at Moscow! Where, in truth, had I *not* bitter cause to curse him within my heart? From his inscrutable tyranny did I at length flee, panic-stricken, as from a pestilence; and to the very ends of the earth I *fled in vain*.

And again, and again, in secret communion with my own spirit, would I demand the questions "Who is he?—whence came he?—and

9. I.e., the cards are marked and shaved (slightly rounded at one end).

what are his objects?" But no answer was there found. And now I scrutinized, with a minute scrutiny, the forms, and the methods, and the leading traits of his impertinent supervision. But even here there was very little upon which to base a conjecture. It was noticeable, indeed, that, in no one of the multiplied instances in which he had of late crossed my path, had he so crossed it except to frustrate those schemes, or to disturb those actions, which, if fully carried out, might have resulted in bitter mischief. Poor justification this, in truth, for an authority so imperiously assumed! Poor indemnity for natural rights of self-agency so pertinaciously, so insultingly denied!

I had also been forced to notice that my tormentor, for a very long period of time, (while scrupulously and with miraculous dexterity maintaining his whim of an identity of apparel with myself,) had so contrived it, in the execution of his varied interference with my will, that I saw not, at any moment, the features of his face. Be Wilson what he might, *this*, at least, was but the veriest of affectation, or of folly. Could he, for an instant, have supposed that, in my admonisher at Eton—in the destroyer of my honor at Oxford,—in him who thwarted my ambition at Rome, my revenge at Paris, my passionate love at Naples, or what he falsely termed my avarice in Egypt,—that in this, my arch-enemy and evil genius, I could fail to recognise the William Wilson of my schoolboy days,—the namesake, the companion, the rival,—the hated and dreaded rival at Dr. Bransby's? Impossible!—But let me hasten to the last eventful scene of the drama.

Thus far I had succumbed supinely to this imperious domination. The sentiment of deep awe with which I habitually regarded the elevated character, the majestic wisdom, the apparent omnipresence and omnipotence of Wilson, added to a feeling of even terror, with which certain other traits in his nature and assumptions inspired me, had operated, hitherto, to impress me with an idea of my own utter weakness and helplessness, and to suggest an implicit, although bitterly reluctant submission to his arbitrary will. But, of late days, I had given myself up entirely to wine; and its maddening influence upon my hereditary temper rendered me more and more impatient of control. I began to murmur,—to hesitate,—to resist. And was it only fancy which induced me to believe that, with the increase of my own firmness, that of my tormentor underwent a proportional diminution? Be this as it may, I now began to feel the inspiration of a burning hope, and at length nurtured in my secret thoughts a stern and desperate resolution that I would submit no longer to be enslaved.

It was at Rome, during the Carnival of 18—, that I attended a masquerade in the palazzo of the Neapolitan Duke Di Broglio. I had indulged more freely than usual in the excesses of the wine-table; and now the suffocating atmosphere of the crowded rooms irritated me beyond endurance. The difficulty, too, of forcing my way through the mazes of the company contributed not a little to the ruffling of my temper; for I was anxiously seeking, (let me not say with what unworthy motive) the young, the gay, the beautiful wife of the aged and

doting Di Broglio. With a too unscrupulous confidence she had previously communicated to me the secret of the costume in which she would be habited, and now, having caught a glimpse of her person, I was hurrying to make my way into her presence.—At this moment I felt a light hand placed upon my shoulder, and that ever-remembered, low, damnable *whisper* within my ear.

In an absolute phrenzy of wrath, I turned at once upon him who had thus interrupted me, and seized him violently by the collar. He was attired, as I had expected, in a costume altogether similar to my own; wearing a Spanish cloak of blue velvet, begirt about the waist with a crimson belt sustaining a rapier. A mask of black silk entirely covered his face.

"Scoundrel!" I said, in a voice husky with rage, while every syllable I uttered seemed as new fuel to my fury, "scoundrel! impostor! accursed villain! you shall not—you *shall not* dog me unto death! Follow me, or I stab you where you stand!"—and I broke my way from the ballroom into a small ante-chamber adjoining—dragging him unresistingly with me as I went.

Upon entering, I thrust him furiously from me. He staggered against the wall, while I closed the door with an oath, and commanded him to draw. He hesitated but for an instant; then, with a slight sigh, drew in silence, and put himself upon his defence.

The contest was brief indeed. I was frantic with every species of wild excitement, and felt within my single arm the energy and power of a multitude. In a few seconds I forced him by sheer strength against the wainscoting, and thus, getting him at mercy, plunged my sword, with brute ferocity, repeatedly through and through his bosom.

At that instant some person tried the latch of the door. I hastened to prevent an intrusion, and then immediately returned to my dying antagonist. But what human language can adequately portray *that* astonishment, *that* horror which possessed me at the spectacle then presented to view? The brief moment in which I averted my eyes had been sufficient to produce, apparently, a material change in the arrangements at the upper or farther end of the room. A large mirror,—so at first it seemed to me in my confusion—now stood where none had been perceptible before; and, as I stepped up to it in extremity of terror, mine own image, but with features all pale and dabbled in blood, advanced to meet me with a feeble and tottering gait.

Thus it appeared I say, but was not. It was my antagonist—it was Wilson, who then stood before me in the agonies of his dissolution. His mask and cloak lay, where he had thrown them, upon the floor. Not a thread in all his raiment—not a line in all the marked and singular lineaments of his face which was not, even in the most absolute identity, *mine own!*[1]

1. A key line in Irving's "Unwritten Drama of Lord Byron" reads: "The spectre is an allegorical being, the personification of conscience, or of the passions." Poe, in his 1842 review of *Twice-told Tales*, claims that passages parallel with the end of "William Wilson" occur in Hawthorne's "Howe's Masquerade" and implies that they are plagiarized. But there is almost no resemblance, and Hawthorne's tale was published over a year before Poe's.

It was Wilson; but he spoke no longer in a whisper, and I could have fancied that I myself was speaking while he said:

"*You have conquered, and I yield. Yet, henceforward art thou also dead—dead to the World, to Heaven and to Hope! In me didst thou exist—and, in my death, see by this image, which is thine own, how utterly thou hast murdered thyself.*"

The Man of the Crowd[1]

Ce grand malheur, de ne pouvoir être seul.

La Bruyère[2]

IT was well said of a certain German book that "*er lasst sich nicht lesen*"—it does not permit itself to be read.[3] There are some secrets which do not permit themselves to be told. Men die nightly in their beds, wringing the hands of ghostly confessors, and looking them piteously in the eyes—die with despair of heart and convulsion of throat, on account of the hideousness of mysteries which will not *suffer themselves* to be revealed. Now and then, alas, the conscience of man takes up a burthen so heavy in horror that it can be thrown down only into the grave. And thus the essence of all crime is undivulged.

Not long ago, about the closing in of an evening in autumn, I sat at the large bow window of the D—— Coffee-House in London. For some months I had been ill in health, but was now convalescent, and, with returning strength, found myself in one of those happy moods which are so precisely the converse of *ennui*—moods of the keenest appetency, when the film from the mental vision departs—the αχλυς υς πριν επηεν—and the intellect, electrified, surpasses as greatly its every-day condition, as does the vivid yet candid reason of Leibnitz, the mad and flimsy rhetoric of Gorgias.[4] Merely to breathe was enjoyment; and I derived positive pleasure even from many of the legitimate sources of pain. I felt a calm but inquisitive interest in every thing. With a cigar in my mouth and a newspaper in my lap, I had been amusing myself for the greater part of the afternoon, now in poring over advertisements, now in observing the promiscuous company

1. First published in December 1840 simultaneously in the Philadelphia *Casket* and *Burton's Gentleman's Magazine.* The text reprinted here is from *Tales* (1845). Scholars have seen sources for the tale in Charles Dickens's *Sketches by Boz* (1836), notably "The Drunkard's Death" and "Gin Shops."
2. This great misfortune of not being able to be alone (French). The epigraph is from "De L'Homme" in *Les Caractères* by Jean de la Bruyère (1645–1696).
3. This quotation reappears at the end of the tale (see p. 239, n. 6 herein). According to most critics, Poe meant that the book was too shocking to be read. But the literal translation of the German can be applied to the situation of the narrator trying to "read" (understand) the old man; he will not "permit" himself to be read.
4. A Greek statesman and rhetorician (c. 483–375 B.C.E.) during the time of Plato; his style was so elaborate that it bordered on absurdity. The Greek can be translated as "the mist that previously was upon [them]" (*Iliad,* V.127). Athene helped Diomedes to distinguish the gods in battle by removing the haze from his eyes. Gottfried Wilhelm von Leibniz (1646–1716) was a German philosopher and mathematician who, among other things, proposed the metaphysical theory that we live in a totally interconnected world that is "the best of all possible worlds." In earlier versions, Poe alluded to George Combe (1778–1858), moral philosopher and phrenologist. Phrenology was an attempt to "read" personality and character from the contours of the head (see "Ligeia," p. 161, n. 7 and Sciences of the Mind, pp. 742ff. herein).

in the room, and now in peering through the smoky panes into the street.

This latter is one of the principal thoroughfares of the city, and had been very much crowded during the whole day. But, as the darkness came on, the throng momently increased; and, by the time the lamps were well lighted, two dense and continuous tides of population were rushing past the door. At this particular period of the evening I had never before been in a similar situation, and the tumultuous sea of human heads filled me, therefore, with a delicious novelty of emotion. I gave up, at length, all care of things within the hotel, and became absorbed in contemplation of the scene without.

At first my observations took an abstract and generalizing turn. I looked at the passengers in masses, and thought of them in their aggregate relations. Soon, however, I descended to details, and regarded with minute interest the innumerable varieties of figure, dress, air, gait, visage, and expression of countenance.

By far the greater number of those who went by had a satisfied business-like demeanor, and seemed to be thinking only of making their way through the press. Their brows were knit, and their eyes rolled quickly; when pushed against by fellow-wayfarers they evinced no symptom of impatience, but adjusted their clothes and hurried on. Others, still a numerous class, were restless in their movements, had flushed faces, and talked and gesticulated to themselves, as if feeling in solitude on account of the very denseness of the company around. When impeded in their progress, these people suddenly ceased muttering, but redoubled their gesticulations, and awaited, with an absent and overdone smile upon the lips, the course of the persons impeding them. If jostled, they bowed profusely to the jostlers, and appeared overwhelmed with confusion.—There was nothing very distinctive about these two large classes beyond what I have noted. Their habiliments belonged to that order which is pointedly termed the decent. They were undoubtedly noblemen, merchants, attorneys, tradesmen, stock-jobbers—the Eupatrids[5] and the common-places of society— men of leisure and men actively engaged in affairs of their own—conducting business upon their own responsibility. They did not greatly excite my attention.

The tribe of clerks was an obvious one and here I discerned two remarkable divisions. There were the junior clerks of flash houses[6]— young gentlemen with tight coats, bright boots, well-oiled hair, and supercilious lips. Setting aside a certain dapperness of carriage, which may be termed *deskism* for want of a better word, the manner of these persons seemed to me an exact facsimile of what had been the perfection of *bon ton*[7] about twelve or eighteen months before. They wore the cast-off graces of the gentry;—and this, I believe, involves the best definition of the class.

The division of the upper clerks of staunch firms, or of the "steady

5. Persons belonging to the aristocracy.
6. Firms engaging in new, speculative lines of business.
7. Fashionable style.

old fellows," it was not possible to mistake. These were known by their coats and pantaloons of black or brown, made to sit comfortably, with white cravats and waistcoats, broad solid-looking shoes, and thick hose or gaiters.—They had all slightly bald heads, from which the right ears, long used to pen-holding, had an odd habit of standing off on end. I observed that they always removed or settled their hats with both hands, and wore watches, with short gold chains of a substantial and ancient pattern. Theirs was the affectation of respectability;—if indeed there be an affectation so honorable.

There were many individuals of dashing appearance, whom I easily understood as belonging to the race of swell pick-pockets, with which all great cities are infested. I watched these gentry with much inquisitiveness, and found it difficult to imagine how they should ever be mistaken for gentlemen by gentlemen themselves. Their voluminousness of wristband, with an air of excessive frankness, should betray them at once.

The gamblers, of whom I descried not a few, were still more easily recognisable. They wore every variety of dress, from that of the desperate thimble-rig bully,[8] with velvet waistcoat, fancy neckerchief, gilt chains, and filagreed buttons, to that of the scrupulously inornate clergyman, than which nothing could be less liable to suspicion. Still all were distinguished by a certain sodden swarthiness of complexion, a filmy dimness of eye, and pallor and compression of lip. There were two other traits, moreover, by which I could always detect them;— a guarded lowness of tone in conversation, and a more than ordinary extension of the thumb in a direction at right angles with the fingers.—Very often, in company with these sharpers, I observed an order of men somewhat different in habits, but still birds of a kindred feather. They may be defined as the gentlemen who live by their wits. They seem to prey upon the public in two battalions—that of the dandies and that of the military men. Of the first grade the leading features are long locks and smiles; of the second frogged coats and frowns.

Descending in the scale of what is termed gentility, I found darker and deeper themes for speculation. I saw Jew pedlars, with hawk eyes flashing from countenances whose every other feature wore only an expression of abject humility; sturdy professional street beggars scowling upon mendicants of a better stamp, whom despair alone had driven forth into the night for charity; feeble and ghastly invalids, upon whom death had placed a sure hand, and who sidled and tottered through the mob, looking every one beseechingly in the face, as if in search of some chance consolation, some lost hope; modest young girls returning from long and late labor to a cheerless home, and shrinking more tearfully than indignantly from the glances of ruffians, whose direct contact, even, could not be avoided; women of the town of all kinds and of all ages—the unequivocal beauty in the prime of her womanhood, putting one in mind of the statue in Lucian, with

8. A shell game run by a con artist; the victim guesses which thimble a pea is hidden under.

the surface of Parian marble,[9] and the interior filled with filth—the loathsome and utterly lost leper in rags—the wrinkled, bejewelled and paint-begrimed beldame, making a last effort at youth—the mere child of immature form, yet, from long association, an adept in the dreadful conquetries of her trade, and burning with a rabid ambition to be ranked the equal of her elders in vice; drunkards innumerable and indescribable—some in shreds and patches, reeling, inarticulate, with bruised visage and lack-lustre eyes—some in whole although filthy garments, with a slightly unsteady swagger, thick sensual lips, and hearty-looking rubicund faces—others clothed in materials which had once been good, and which even now were scrupulously well brushed—men who walked with a more than naturally firm and springy step, but whose countenances were fearfully pale, whose eyes hideously wild and red, and who clutched with quivering fingers, as they strode through the crowd, at every object which came within their reach; beside these, pie-men, porters, coal-heavers, sweeps; organ-grinders, monkey-exhibiters and ballad mongers, those who vended with those who sang; ragged artizans and exhausted laborers of every description, and all full of a noisy and inordinate vivacity which jarred discordantly upon the ear, and gave an aching sensation to the eye.

As the night deepened, so deepened to me the interest of the scene; for not only did the general character of the crowd materially alter (its gentler features retiring in the gradual withdrawal of the more orderly portion of the people, and its harsher ones coming out into bolder relief, as the late hour brought forth every species of infamy from its den,) but the rays of the gas-lamps, feeble at first in their struggle with the dying day, had now at length gained ascendancy, and threw over every thing a fitful and garish lustre. All was dark yet splendid—as that ebony to which has been likened the style of Tertullian.[1]

The wild effects of the light enchained me to an examination of individual faces; and although the rapidity with which the world of light flitted before the window, prevented me from casting more than a glance upon each visage, still it seemed that, in my then peculiar mental state, I could frequently read, even in that brief interval of a glance, the history of long years.

With my brow to the glass, I was thus occupied in scrutinizing the mob, when suddenly there came into view a countenance (that of a decrepid old man, some sixty-five or seventy years of age,)—a countenance which at once arrested and absorbed my whole attention, on account of the absolute idiosyncracy of its expression. Any thing even remotely resembling that expression I had never seen before. I well remember that my first thought, upon beholding it, was that

9. Marble from Paros, well known for its fine white statuary marble. In his *Somnium* (Dream), Lucian of Samosata (c. 125–c. 200 C.E.), Greek satiric writer, contrasted the exterior beauty of Greek statues with the inner structure that hides that which is unsightly.

1. A church writer (c. 150–c. 220 C.E.) known for his vigorous denunciation of worldliness. Although the context does not directly support the idea, Levine speculates that the word "ebony" signals a satiric hit at the *Blackwood's* style. For ebony is black wood, and *Ebony* was a code name used by one of the coterie writers for *Blackwood's*.

Retzch,[2] had he viewed it, would have greatly preferred it to his own pictural incarnations of the fiend. As I endeavored, during the brief minute of my original survey, to form some analysis of the meaning conveyed, there arose confusedly and paradoxically within my mind, the ideas of vast mental power, of caution, of penuriousness, of avarice, of coolness, of malice, of blood-thirstiness, of triumph, of merriment, of excessive terror, of intense—of supreme despair. I felt singularly aroused, startled, fascinated. "How wild a history," I said to myself, "is written within that bosom!" Then came a craving desire to keep the man in view—to know more of him. Hurriedly putting on an overcoat, and seizing my hat and cane, I made my way into the street, and pushed through the crowd in the direction which I had seen him take; for he had already disappeared. With some little difficulty I at length came within sight of him, approached, and followed him closely, yet cautiously, so as not to attract his attention.

I had now a good opportunity of examining his person. He was short in stature, very thin, and apparently very feeble. His clothes, generally, were filthy and ragged; but as he came, now and then, within the strong glare of a lamp, I perceived that his linen, although dirty, was of beautiful texture; and my vision deceived me, or, through a rent in a closely-buttoned and evidently second-handed *roquelaire*[3] which enveloped him, I caught a glimpse both of a diamond and of a dagger. These observations heightened my curiosity, and I resolved to follow the stranger whithersoever he should go.

It was now fully night-fall, and a thick humid fog hung over the city, soon ending in a settled and heavy rain. This change of weather had an odd effect upon the crowd, the whole of which was at once put into new commotion, and overshadowed by a world of umbrellas. The waver, the jostle, and the hum increased in a tenfold degree. For my own part I did not much regard the rain—the lurking of an old fever in my system rendering the moisture somewhat too dangerously pleasant. Tying a handkerchief about my mouth, I kept on. For half an hour the old man held his way with difficulty along the great thoroughfare; and I here walked close at his elbow through fear of losing sight of him. Never once turning his head to look back, he did not observe me. By and bye he passed into a cross street, which, although densely filled with people, was not quite so much thronged as the main one he had quitted. Here a change in his demeanor became evident. He walked more slowly and with less object than before—more hesitatingly. He crossed and re-crossed the way repeatedly without apparent aim; and the press was still so thick that, at every such movement, I was obliged to follow him closely. The street was a narrow and long one, and his course lay within it for nearly an hour, during which the passengers had gradually diminished to about that number which is ordinarily seen at noon in Broadway near the Park—so vast a difference is there between a London populace and that of the most frequented Ameri-

2. Friedrich August Moritz Retzsch (1779–1857), German painter, etcher, and designer noted for his illustrations of the works of Goethe, Schiller, and Shakespeare.
3. Short cloak.

can city. A second turn brought us into a square, brilliantly lighted, and overflowing with life. The old manner of the stranger re-appeared. His chin fell upon his breast, while his eyes rolled wildly from under his knit brows, in every direction, upon those who hemmed him in. He urged his way steadily and perseveringly. I was surprised, however, to find, upon his having made the circuit of the square, that he turned and retraced his steps. Still more was I astonished to see him repeat the same walk several times—once nearly detecting me as he came round with a sudden movement.

In this exercise he spent another hour, at the end of which we met with far less interruption from passengers than at first. The rain fell fast; the air grew cool; and the people were retiring to their homes. With a gesture of impatience, the wanderer passed into a bye-street comparatively deserted. Down this, some quarter of a mile long, he rushed with an activity I could not have dreamed of seeing in one so aged, and which put me to much trouble in pursuit. A few minutes brought us to a large and busy bazaar, with the localities of which the stranger appeared well acquainted, and where his original demeanor again became apparent, as he forced his way to and fro, without aim, among the host of buyers and sellers.

During the hour and a half, or thereabouts, which we passed in this place, it required much caution on my part to keep him within reach without attracting his observation. Luckily I wore a pair of caoutchouc[4] over-shoes, and could move about in perfect silence. At no moment did he see that I watched him. He entered shop after shop, priced nothing, spoke no word, and looked at all objects with a wild and vacant stare. I was now utterly amazed at his behaviour, and firmly resolved that we should not part until I had satisfied myself in some measure respecting him.

A loud-toned clock struck eleven, and the company were fast deserting the bazaar. A shop-keeper, in putting up a shutter, jostled the old man, and at the instant I saw a strong shudder come over his frame. He hurried into the street, looked anxiously around him for an instant, and then ran with incredible swiftness through many crooked and people-less lanes, until we emerged once more upon the great thoroughfare whence we had started—the street of the D—— Hotel. It no longer wore, however, the same aspect. It was still brilliant with gas; but the rain fell fiercely, and there were few persons to be seen. The stranger grew pale. He walked moodily some paces up the once populous avenue, then, with a heavy sigh, turned in the direction of the river, and, plunging through a great variety of devious ways, came out, at length, in view of one of the principal theatres. It was about being closed, and the audience were thronging from the doors. I saw the old man gasp as if for breath while he threw himself amid the crowd; but I thought that the intense agony of his countenance had, in some measure, abated. His head again fell upon his breast; he appeared as I had seen him at first. I observed that he now took the course in which

4. Rubber.

had gone the greater number of the audience—but, upon the whole, I was at a loss to comprehend the waywardness of his actions.

As he proceeded, the company grew more scattered, and his old uneasiness and vacillation were resumed. For some time he followed closely a party of some ten or twelve roisterers; but from this number one by one dropped off, until three only remained together, in a narrow and gloomy lane little frequented. The stranger paused, and, for a moment, seemed lost in thought; then, with every mark of agitation, pursued rapidly a route which brought us to the verge of the city, amid regions very different from those we had hitherto traversed. It was the most noisome quarter of London, where every thing wore the worst impress of the most deplorable poverty, and of the most desperate crime. By the dim light of an accidental lamp, tall, antique, worm-eaten, wooden tenements were seen tottering to their fall, in directions so many and capricious that scarce the semblance of a passage was discernible between them. The paving-stones lay at random, displaced from their beds by the rankly-growing grass. Horrible filth festered in the dammed-up gutters. The whole atmosphere teemed with desolation. Yet, as we proceeded, the sounds of human life revived by sure degrees, and at length large bands of the most abandoned of a London populace were seen reeling to and fro. The spirits of the old man again flickered up, as a lamp which is near its death-hour. Once more he strode onward with elastic tread. Suddenly a corner was turned, a blaze of light burst upon our sight, and we stood before one of the huge suburban temples of Intemperance—one of the palaces of the fiend, Gin.

It was now nearly day-break; but a number of wretched inebriates still pressed in and out of the flaunting entrance. With a half shriek of joy the old man forced a passage within, resumed at once his original bearing, and stalked backward and forward, without apparent object, among the throng. He had not been thus long occupied, however, before a rush to the doors gave token that the host was closing them for the night. It was something even more intense than despair that I then observed upon the countenance of the singular being whom I had watched so pertinaciously. Yet he did not hesitate in his career, but, with a mad energy, retraced his steps at once, to the heart of the mighty London. Long and swiftly he fled, while I followed him in the wildest amazement, resolute not to abandon a scrutiny in which I now felt an interest all-absorbing. The sun arose while we proceeded, and, when we had once again reached that most thronged mart of the populous town, the street of the D—— Hotel, it presented an appearance of human bustle and activity scarcely inferior to what I had seen on the evening before. And here, long, amid the momently increasing confusion, did I persist in my pursuit of the stranger. But, as usual, he walked to and fro, and during the day did not pass from out the turmoil of that street. And, as the shades of the second evening came on, I grew wearied unto death, and, stopping fully in front of the wanderer, gazed at him steadfastly in the face. He noticed me not, but resumed his solemn walk, while I, ceasing to follow, remained absorbed

in contemplation. "This old man," I said at length, "is the type and the genius of deep crime. He refuses to be alone. *He is the man of the crowd.* It will be in vain to follow; for I shall learn no more of him, nor of his deeds. The worst heart of the world is a grosser book than the 'Hortulus Animæ,'⁵ and perhaps it is but one of the great mercies of God that '*er lasst sich nicht lesen.*' "⁶

The Murders in the Rue Morgue First published in *Graham's Magazine* (April 1841). The text reprinted here is from *Tales* (1845). The tale is sometimes mistakenly called the first detective story. There are many literary precedents for the method of Poe's philosophical detective. One of the earliest and most important is Voltaire's *Zadig, or Destiny* (1748), a work Poe mentions in "Hop-Frog." Zadig is a wealthy Babylonian of philosophical temperament who recurrently discovers that in this world there is no good without evil. Zadig's method of inference was renowned. In one instance he "deduces" (actually induces) from jumbled tracks in the sand that an animal made them, that it was a female dog that had recently had puppies, that she had long ears, and that she was lame. His deductive powers are repeated later in regard to the king's horse, which had been lost. He seems to know so much about the horse that he is accused of stealing it. He explains that although he has never seen it he can describe it because of his powers of observation. The marks of the horseshoes are all equidistant apart, suggesting that it gallops perfectly. The dust on the trees along a narrow road only seven feet wide is brushed off both right and left three and half feet from the center of the road; therefore the horse's tail was three and half feet long. Leaves on the tree branches above the road have been worn into an arch five feet high; since some have been knocked down, the horse must be fifteen hands high. Regarding what Poe called the "ratiocinative" method of his detective stories, see his letter to Philp Pendleton Cooke (August 9, 1846; p. 684 herein).

In 1838–39, as Poe was negotiating an associate editorship with the magazine, *Burton's Gentleman's Magazine* published a series of stories titled "Unpublished Passages in the Life of Vidocq" by one "J. M. B." François-Eugène Vidocq (1775–1857) was head of the Parisian detective bureau under Napoleon. He was an ex-convict and engaged other ex-convicts for services to the bureau; some suspicion attached to him, including the possibility that he had staged certain crimes in order to "solve" them. Two of the *Burton's* Vidocq series in particular have been proposed as direct influences on Poe's story: "Marie Laurente" (September 1838) and "Dr. Arsac" (October 1838). Vidocq is specifically mentioned in "Murders in the Rue Morgue." In regard to the solution, Mabbott lists several articles and stories before "Murders" in which trained animals commit acts of theft.

Although some of the details of the streets and buildings of Paris are accurate enough, there are also many errors. Morgue Street is Poe's

5. The *Hortulus Animæ cum Oratiunculis Aliquibus Superadditis* of Grünninger [Poe's note]. Johann Reinhart Grünninger (c. 1455–c. 1533) published this book of "prayers" in 1500.
6. Mabbott follows most critics in suggesting that Poe meant that the book was too profound (or shocking) to be read, which conforms to the narrator's sense of cosmic mystery about the man of the crowd. The literal translation of the German also applies to the disoriented narrator's futile attempts to "read" (understand) the old man; a further twist is that the book may have been so badly printed that it could not be read.

invention. In earlier versions of the tale, the narrator speculates in the opening paragraph that phrenology would uncover an "organ of *analysis.*" For discussion of phrenology, see the introduction to Sciences of the Mind, pp. 743–47 herein; see especially the phrenological chart of the head, p. 747, and the notes to "Ligeia" (p. 161, n. 7) and "The Fall of the House of Usher" (p. 203, n. 3). Also see p. 242, n. 7 in "Murders."

The Murders in the Rue Morgue

> What song the Syrens sang, or what name Achilles assumed when he hid himself among women, although puzzling questions, are not beyond *all* conjecture.
>
> *Sir Thomas Browne*[1]

THE mental features discoursed of as the analytical, are, in themselves, but little susceptible of analysis. We appreciate them only in their effects. We know of them, among other things, that they are always to their possessor, when inordinately possessed, a source of the liveliest enjoyment. As the strong man exults in his physical ability, delighting in such exercises as call his muscles into action, so glories the analyst in that moral activity which *disentangles.* He derives pleasure from even the most trivial occupations bringing his talent into play. He is fond of enigmas, of conundrums, of hieroglyphics; exhibiting in his solutions of each a degree of *acumen*[2] which appears to the ordinary apprehension præternatural. His results, brought about by the very soul and essence of method, have, in truth, the whole air of intuition.

The faculty of re-solution is possibly much invigorated by mathematical study, and especially by that highest branch of it which, unjustly, and merely on account of its retrograde operations, has been called, as if *par excellence*, analysis. Yet to calculate is not in itself to analyse. A chess-player, for example, does the one without effort at the other. It follows that the game of chess, in its effects upon mental character, is greatly misunderstood. I am not now writing a treatise, but simply prefacing a somewhat peculiar narrative by observations very much at random; I will, therefore, take occasion to assert that the higher powers of the reflective intellect are more decidedly and more usefully tasked by the unostentatious game of draughts[3] than by all the elaborate frivolity of chess. In this latter, where the pieces have different and *bizarre* motions, with various and variable values, what is only complex is mistaken (a not unusual error) for what is profound. The *attention* is here called powerfully into play. If it flag for an instant, an oversight is committed, resulting in injury or defeat. The possible moves being not only manifold but involute, the chances of such oversights are multiplied; and in nine cases out of ten it is the more concentrative rather than the more acute player who conquers. In

1. The epigraph is from *Hydriotaphia, or Urn-Burial*, an essay by Sir Thomas Browne (1605–1682); it refers to the difficult questions the emperor puts to scholars, questions that are not totally beyond solution.
2. Mental sharpness.
3. Checkers.

draughts, on the contrary, where the moves are *unique* and have but little variation, the probabilities of inadvertence are diminished, and the mere attention being left comparatively unemployed, what advantages are obtained by either party are obtained by superior *acumen*. To be less abstract—Let us suppose a game of draughts where the pieces are reduced to four kings, and where, of course, no oversight is to be expected. It is obvious that here the victory can be decided (the players being at all equal) only by some *recherché*[4] movement, the result of some strong exertion of the intellect. Deprived of ordinary resources, the analyst throws himself into the spirit of his opponent, identifies himself therewith, and not unfrequently sees thus, at a glance, the sole methods (sometimes indeed absurdly simple ones) by which he may seduce into error or hurry into miscalculation.

Whist[5] has long been noted for its influence upon what is termed the calculating power; and men of the highest order of intellect have been known to take an apparently unaccountable delight in it, while eschewing chess as frivolous. Beyond doubt there is nothing of a similar nature so greatly tasking the faculty of analysis. The best chess-player in Christendom *may* be little more than the best player of chess; but proficiency in whist implies capacity for success in all those more important undertakings where mind struggles with mind. When I say proficiency, I mean that perfection in the game which includes a comprehension of *all* the sources whence legitimate advantage may be derived. These are not only manifold but multiform, and lie frequently among recesses of thought altogether inaccessible to the ordinary understanding. To observe attentively is to remember distinctly; and, so far, the concentrative chess-player will do very well at whist; while the rules of Hoyle[6] (themselves based upon the mere mechanism of the game) are sufficiently and generally comprehensible. Thus to have a retentive memory, and to proceed by "the book," are points commonly regarded as the sum total of good playing. But it is in matters beyond the limits of mere rule that the skill of the analyst is evinced. He makes, in silence, a host of observations and inferences. So, perhaps, do his companions; and the difference in the extent of the information obtained, lies not so much in the validity of the inference as in the quality of the observation. The necessary knowledge is that of *what* to observe. Our player confines himself not at all; nor, because the game is the object, does he reject deductions from things external to the game. He examines the countenance of his partner, comparing it carefully with that of each of his opponents. He considers the mode of assorting the cards in each hand; often counting trump by trump, and honor by honor, through the glances bestowed by their holders upon each. He notes every variation of face as the play progresses, gathering a fund of thought from the differences in the expression of certainty,

4. Rare, recondite,
5. A card game for four players in two partnerships, a predecessor of modern bridge.
6. Sir Edmund Hoyle (1672–1769) wrote on the rules of indoor games, especially card games (thus the phrase, "according to Hoyle," which has come to mean by the rules, on the up and up).

of surprise, of triumph, or of chagrin. From the manner of gathering up a trick he judges whether the person taking it can make another in the suit. He recognises what is played through feint, by the air with which it is thrown upon the table. A casual or inadvertent word; the accidental dropping or turning of a card, with the accompanying anxiety or carelessness in regard to its concealment; the counting of the tricks, with the order of their arrangement; embarrassment, hesitation, eagerness or trepidation—all afford, to his apparently intuitive perception, indications of the true state of affairs. The first two or three rounds having been played, he is in full possession of the contents of each hand, and thenceforward puts down his cards with as absolute a precision of purpose as if the rest of the party had turned outward the faces of their own.

The analytical power should not be confounded with simple ingenuity; for while the analyst is necessarily ingenious, the ingenious man is often remarkably incapable of analysis. The constructive or combining power, by which ingenuity is usually manifested, and to which the phrenologists[7] (I believe erroneously) have assigned a separate organ, supposing it a primitive faculty, has been so frequently seen in those whose intellect bordered otherwise upon idiocy, as to have attracted general observation among writers on morals. Between ingenuity and the analytic ability there exists a difference far greater, indeed, than that between the fancy and the imagination, but of a character very strictly analogous. It will be found, in fact, that the ingenious are always fanciful, and the *truly* imaginative never otherwise than analytic.

The narrative which follows will appear to the reader somewhat in the light of a commentary upon the propositions just advanced.

Residing in Paris during the spring and part of the summer of 18—, I there became acquainted with a Monsieur C. Auguste Dupin.[8] This young gentleman was of an excellent—indeed of an illustrious family, but, by a variety of untoward events, had been reduced to such poverty that the energy of his character succumbed beneath it, and he ceased to bestir himself in the world, or to care for the retrieval of his fortunes. By courtesy of his creditors, there still remained in his possession a small remnant of his patrimony; and, upon the income arising from this, he managed, by means of a rigorous economy, to procure the necessaries of life, without troubling himself about its superfluities. Books, indeed, were his sole luxuries, and in Paris these are easily obtained.

7. Those who believed that different sections of the brain were linked to various mental faculties and that by studying the shape of the skull, they could determine the development of each faculty. See the Sciences of the Mind section herein.
8. Poe's detective hero also appears in "The Mystery of Marie Rogêt" and "The Purloined Letter" (pp. 367ff. herein). Scholars are fond of speculating on the sources of the detective's name. Among the more persuasive are the following. "C. Auguste" was the given name of a Monsieur Dubouchet, an acquaintance of Poe, who in 1841 was seeking a position as a French teacher. André-Marie-Jean-Jacques Dupin (1783–1865) was a well-known French politician, described by Mabbott as a "person of antithetical qualities, a living encyclopedia, and a lover of legal methods." He was the author of *Sketches of Living Characters of France*, translated by J. M. Walsh in 1841, reviewed by Poe in the same issue of *Graham's* with his story. Later on, the minister of police is called G——, which may be a reference to Henri-Joseph Guisquet, who served in that capacity in Paris from 1831 to 1836.

Our first meeting was at an obscure library in the Rue Montmartre, where the accident of our both being in search of the same very rare and very remarkable volume, brought us into closer communion. We saw each other again and again. I was deeply interested in the little family history which he detailed to me with all that candor which a Frenchman indulges whenever mere self is his theme. I was astonished, too, at the vast extent of his reading; and, above all, I felt my soul enkindled within me by the wild fervor, and the vivid freshness of his imagination. Seeking in Paris the objects I then sought, I felt that the society of such a man would be to me a treasure beyond price; and this feeling I frankly confided to him. It was at length arranged that we should live together during my stay in the city; and as my worldly circumstances were somewhat less embarrassed than his own, I was permitted to be at the expense of renting, and furnishing in a style which suited the rather fantastic gloom of our common temper, a time-eaten and grotesque mansion, long deserted through superstitions into which we did not inquire, and tottering to its fall in a retired and desolate portion of the Faubourg St. Germain.

Had the routine of our life at this place been known to the world, we should have been regarded as madmen—although, perhaps, as madmen of a harmless nature. Our seclusion was perfect. We admitted no visitors. Indeed the locality of our retirement had been carefully kept a secret from my own former associates; and it had been many years since Dupin had ceased to know or be known in Paris. We existed within ourselves alone.

It was a freak of fancy in my friend (for what else shall I call it?) to be enamored of the Night for her own sake; and into this *bizarrerie*, as into all his others, I quietly fell; giving myself up to his wild whims with a perfect *abandon*. The sable divinity would not herself dwell with us always; but we could counterfeit her presence. At the first dawn of the morning we closed all the massy shutters of our old building; lighting a couple of tapers which, strongly perfumed, threw out only the ghastliest and feeblest of rays. By the aid of these we then busied our souls in dreams—reading, writing, or conversing, until warned by the clock of the advent of the true Darkness. Then we sallied forth into the streets, arm in arm, continuing the topics of the day, or roaming far and wide until a late hour, seeking, amid the wild lights and shadows of the populous city, that infinity of mental excitement which quiet observation can afford.

At such times I could not help remarking and admiring (although from his rich ideality I had been prepared to expect it) a peculiar analytic ability in Dupin. He seemed, too, to take an eager delight in its exercise—if not exactly in its display—and did not hesitate to confess the pleasure thus derived. He boasted to me, with a low chuckling laugh, that most men, in respect to himself, wore windows in their bosoms, and was wont to follow up such assertions by direct and very startling proofs of his intimate knowledge of my own. His manner at these moments was frigid and abstract; his eyes were vacant in expression; while his voice, usually a rich tenor, rose into a treble which

would have sounded petulantly but for the deliberateness and entire distinctness of the enunciation. Observing him in these moods, I often dwelt meditatively upon the old philosophy of the Bi-Part Soul,[9] and amused myself with the fancy of a double Dupin—the creative and the resolvent.

Let it not be supposed, from what I have just said, that I am detailing any mystery, or penning any romance. What I have described in the Frenchman, was merely the result of an excited, or perhaps of a diseased intelligence. But of the character of his remarks at the periods in question an example will best convey the idea.

We were strolling one night down a long dirty street, in the vicinity of the Palais Royal.[1] Being both, apparently, occupied with thought, neither of us had spoken a syllable for fifteen minutes at least. All at once Dupin broke forth with these words:

"He is a very little fellow, that's true, and would do better for the *Théâtre des Variétés*."[2]

"There can be no doubt of that," I replied unwittingly, and not at first observing (so much had I been absorbed in reflection) the extraordinary manner in which the speaker had chimed in with my meditations. In an instant afterward I recollected myself, and my astonishment was profound.

"Dupin," said I, gravely, "this is beyond my comprehension. I do not hesitate to say that I am amazed, and can scarcely credit my senses. How was it possible you should know I was thinking of———?" Here I paused, to ascertain beyond a doubt whether he really knew of whom I thought.

———"of Chantilly," said he, "why do you pause? You were remarking to yourself that his diminutive figure unfitted him for tragedy."

This was precisely what had formed the subject of my reflections. Chantilly was a *quondam*[3] cobbler of the Rue St. Denis, who, becoming stage-mad, had attempted the *rôle* of Xerxes, in Crébillon's tragedy so called, and been notoriously Pasquinaded[4] for his pains.

"Tell me, for Heaven's sake," I exclaimed, "the method—if method there is—by which you have been enabled to fathom my soul in this matter." In fact I was even more startled than I would have been willing to express.

"It was the fruiterer," replied my friend, "who brought you to the conclusion that the mender of soles was not of sufficient height for Xerxes *et id genus omne*."[5]

9. See notes to "Lionizing" (pp. 128ff.), "Usher" (pp. 199ff.), and "William Wilson" (pp. 216ff.).
1. Jacques Lemercier designed this building for Cardinal Richelieu (chief minister for Louis XIII) in 1629–34; it later served as the residence for the princes of Orléans. The Palais Royal is a hollow rectangle of long, plain exterior walls that enclose a park with gardens and galleries.
2. A theater for variety shows.
3. Former.
4. Publicly lampooned; from "Pasquino," the nickname of an ancient statue in Rome on which lampoons were posted in the Renaissance. "Crébillon": pseudonym of Prosper Jolyot (1674–1762), a French dramatist and rival to Voltaire; he wrote *Xerxes* in 1714. Poe's narrator is amused at the thought of a humble cobbler playing a heroic character based on Xerxes the Great (c. 519–c. 465 B.C.E.), a Persian king. ("The Purloined Letter" concludes with a reference to Crébillon's *Atrée*.)
5. And all that sort of thing (Latin).

"The fruiterer!—you astonish me—I know no fruiterer whomsoever."

"The man who ran up against you as we entered the street—it may have been fifteen minutes ago."

I now remembered that, in fact, a fruiterer, carrying upon his head a large basket of apples, had nearly thrown me down, by accident, as we passed from the Rue C—— into the thoroughfare where we stood; but what this had to do with Chantilly I could not possibly understand.

There was not a particle of *charlatânerie*[6] about Dupin. "I will explain," he said, "and that you may comprehend all clearly, we will first retrace the course of your meditations, from the moment in which I spoke to you until that of the *rencontre*[7] with the fruiterer in question. The larger links of the chain[8] run thus—Chantilly, Orion, Dr. Nichols, Epicurus, Stereotomy, the street stones, the fruiterer."

There are few persons who have not, at some period of their lives, amused themselves in retracing the steps by which particular conclusions of their own minds have been attained. The occupation is often full of interest; and he who attempts it for the first time is astonished by the apparently illimitable distance and incoherence between the starting-point and the goal. What, then, must have been my amazement when I heard the Frenchman speak what he had just spoken, and when. I could not help acknowledging that he had spoken the truth. He continued:

"We had been talking of horses, if I remember aright, just before leaving the Rue C——. This was the last subject we discussed. As we crossed into this street, a fruiterer, with a large basket upon his head, brushing quickly past us, thrust you upon a pile of paving-stones collected at a spot where the causeway is undergoing repair. You stepped upon one of the loose fragments, slipped, slightly strained your ankle, appeared vexed or sulky, muttered a few words, turned to look at the pile, and then proceeded in silence. I was not particularly attentive to what you did; but observation has become with me, of late, a species of necessity.

"You kept your eyes upon the ground—glancing, with a petulant expression, at the holes and ruts in the pavement, (so that I saw you were still thinking of the stones,) until we reached the little alley called Lamartine, which has been paved, by way of experiment, with the overlapping and riveted blocks. Here your countenance brightened up, and, perceiving your lips move, I could not doubt that you murmured the word 'stereotomy,'[9] a term very affectedly applied to this species of pavement. I knew that you could not say to yourself

6. Charlatanism, fakery.
7. Encounter.
8. Dupin explains the series of links in the paragraphs immediately following—except for Dr. Nichols. John Pringle Nichol (1804–1859), Regius Professor of astronomy at Glasgow University, published *Views of the Architecture of the Heavens in a Series of Letters to a Lady* (1837). This work presented the findings and theories of current astronomy, growing out of the discoveries of Sir William Herschel, his son John, and their contemporaries. Poe cites this work frequently (see, e.g., *Eureka*).
9. The art of cutting solid materials, such as stones for masonry.

'stereotomy' without being brought to think of atomies, and thus of the theories of Epicurus;[1] and since, when we discussed this subject not very long ago, I mentioned to you how singularly, yet with how little notice, the vague guesses of that noble Greek had met with confirmation in the late nebular cosmogony, I felt that you could not avoid casting your eyes upward to the great *nebula* in Orion,[2] and I certainly expected that you would do so. You did look up; and I was now assured that I had correctly followed your steps. But in that bitter *tirade* upon Chantilly, which appeared in yesterday's '*Musée*,' the satirist, making some disgraceful allusions to the cobbler's change of name upon assuming the buskin,[3] quoted a Latin line about which we have often conversed. I mean the line

<center>Perdidit antiquum litera prima sonum[4]</center>

I had told you that this was in reference to Orion, formerly written Urion; and, from certain pungencies connected with this explanation, I was aware that you could not have forgotten it. It was clear, therefore, that you would not fail to combine the two ideas of Orion and Chantilly. That you did combine them I saw by the character of the smile which passed over your lips. You thought of the poor cobbler's immolation. So far, you had been stooping in your gait; but now I saw you draw yourself up to your full height. I was then sure that you reflected upon the diminutive figure of Chantilly. At this point I interrupted your meditations to remark that as, in fact, he *was* a very little fellow—that Chantilly—he would do better at the *Théâtre des Variétés*."

Not long after this, we were looking over an evening edition of the "Gazette des Tribunaux," when the following paragraphs arrested our attention.

"EXTRAORDINARY MURDERS.—This morning, about three o'clock, the inhabitants of the Quartier St. Roch were aroused from sleep by a succession of terrific shrieks, issuing, apparently, from the fourth story of a house in the Rue Morgue, known to be in the sole occupancy of one Madame L'Espanaye, and her daughter, Mademoiselle Camille L'Espanaye. After some delay, occasioned by a fruitless attempt to procure admission in the usual manner, the gateway was broken in with a crowbar, and eight or ten of the neighbors entered, accompanied by two *gendarmes*. By this time the cries had ceased; but, as the party rushed up the first flight of stairs, two or more rough voices, in angry contention, were distinguished, and seemed to proceed from the upper part of the house. As the second landing was reached, these

1. Greek philosopher (341–270 B.C.E.) who subscribed to the theory of Democritus (c. 460–c. 370 B.C.E.) that everything, both material and spiritual, consists of small indivisible particles called atoms. Poe refers to Epicurus in *Eureka* and elsewhere.
2. The Orion nebula was discovered in 1610 by Nicholas-Claude Fabri de Peiresc, although Ptolemy (Claudius Ptolemaeus, flourished c. 125–c. 150 C.E.) had cataloged the brightest stars within it. This nebula became the starting point in 1774 for William and John Herschel's survey of the skies. Nichol (see p. 245, n. 8) often quotes the Herschels.
3. A type of boot associated with actors in tragedies. "*Musée*": a newspaper.
4. The first letter has lost its original sound. According to Mabbott, this quotation is from Ovid's *Fasti* and concerns the birth of the Bœotian Orion (or Urion).

sounds, also, had ceased, and everything remained perfectly quiet. The party spread themselves, and hurried from room to room. Upon arriving at a large back chamber in the fourth story, (the door of which, being found locked, with the key inside, was forced open,) a spectacle presented itself which struck every one present not less with horror than with astonishment.

"The apartment was in the wildest disorder—the furniture broken and thrown about in all directions. There was only one bedstead; and from this the bed had been removed, and thrown into the middle of the floor. On a chair lay a razor, besmeared with blood. On the hearth were two or three long and thick tresses of grey human hair, also dabbled in blood, and seeming to have been pulled out by the roots. Upon the floor were found four Napoleons, an ear-ring of topaz, three large silver spoons, three smaller of *métal d'Alger*,[5] and two bags, containing nearly four thousand francs in gold. The drawers of a *bureau*, which stood in one corner, were open, and had been, apparently, rifled, although many articles still remained in them. A small iron safe was discovered under the *bed* (not under the bedstead). It was open, with the key still in the door. It had no contents beyond a few old letters, and other papers of little consequence.

"Of Madame L'Espanaye no traces were here seen; but an unusual quantity of soot being observed in the fire-place, a search was made in the chimney, and (horrible to relate!) the corpse of the daughter, head downward, was dragged therefrom; it having been thus forced up the narrow aperture for a considerable distance. The body was quite warm. Upon examining it, many excoriations were perceived, no doubt occasioned by the violence with which it had been thrust up and disengaged. Upon the face were many severe scratches, and, upon the throat, dark bruises, and deep indentations of finger nails, as if the deceased had been throttled to death.

"After a thorough investigation of every portion of the house, without farther discovery, the party made its way into a small paved yard in the rear of the building, where lay the corpse of the old lady, with her throat so entirely cut that, upon an attempt to raise her, the head fell off. The body, as well as the head, was fearfully mutilated—the former so much so as scarcely to retain any semblance of humanity.

"To this horrible mystery there is not as yet, we believe, the slightest clew."

The next day's paper had these additional particulars.

"*The Tragedy in the Rue Morgue.* Many individuals have been examined in relation to this most extraordinary and frightful affair." [The word '*affaire*' has not yet, in France, that levity of import which it conveys with us,] "but nothing whatever has transpired to throw light upon it. We give below all the material testimony elicited.

"*Pauline Dubourg*, laundress, deposes that she has known both the deceased for three years, having washed for them during that period.

5. The metal of Algiers (French); a combination of lead, tin, and antimony. "Napoleons": French 20-franc gold coins.

The old lady and her daughter seemed on good terms—very affection-
ate towards each other. They were excellent pay. Could not speak in
regard to their mode or means of living. Believed that Madame L. told
fortunes for a living. Was reputed to have money put by. Never met
any persons in the house when she called for the clothes or took them
home. Was sure that they had no servant in employ. There appeared to
be no furniture in any part of the building except in the fourth story.

"*Pierre Moreau*, tobacconist, deposes that he has been in the habit
of selling small quantities of tobacco and snuff to Madame L'Espanaye
for nearly four years. Was born in the neighborhood, and has always
resided there. The deceased and her daughter had occupied the house
in which the corpses were found, for more than six years. It was for-
merly occupied by a jeweller, who under-let the upper rooms to vari-
ous persons. The house was the property of Madame L. She became
dissatisfied with the abuse of the premises by her tenant, and moved
into them herself, refusing to let any portion. The old lady was child-
ish. Witness had seen the daughter some five or six times during the
six years. The two lived an exceedingly retired life—were reputed to
have money. Had heard it said among the neighbors that Madame L.
told fortunes—did not believe it. Had never seen any person enter the
door except the old lady and her daughter, a porter once or twice, and
a physician some eight or ten times.

"Many other persons, neighbors, gave evidence to the same effect.
No one was spoken of as frequenting the house. It was not known
whether there were any living connexions of Madame L. and her
daughter. The shutters of the front windows were seldom opened.
Those in the rear were always closed, with the exception of the large
back room, fourth story. The house was a good house—not very old.

"*Isidore Musèt, gendarme*, deposes that he was called to the house
about three o'clock in the morning, and found some twenty or thirty
persons at the gateway, endeavoring to gain admittance. Forced it
open, at length, with a bayonet—not with a crowbar. Had but little dif-
ficulty in getting it open, on account of its being a double or folding
gate, and bolted neither at bottom nor top. The shrieks were contin-
ued until the gate was forced—and then suddenly ceased. They
seemed to be screams of some person (or persons) in great agony—
were loud and drawn out, not short and quick. Witness led the way up
stairs. Upon reaching the first landing, heard two voices in loud and
angry contention—the one a gruff voice, the other much shriller—a
very strange voice. Could distinguish some words of the former, which
was that of a Frenchman. Was positive that it was not a woman's
voice. Could distinguish the words '*sacré*' and '*diable*.' The shrill voice
was that of a foreigner. Could not be sure whether it was the voice of
a man or of a woman. Could not make out what was said, but believed
the language to be Spanish. The state of the room and of the bodies
was described by this witness as we described them yesterday.

"*Henri Duval*, a neighbor, and by trade a silver-smith, deposes that
he was one of the party who first entered the house. Corroborates the
testimony of Musèt in general. As soon as they forced an entrance,

they reclosed the door, to keep out the crowd, which collected very fast, notwithstanding the lateness of the hour. The shrill voice, this witness thinks, was that of an Italian. Was certain it was not French. Could not be sure that it was a man's voice. It might have been a woman's. Was not acquainted with the Italian language. Could not distinguish the words, but was convinced by the intonation that the speaker was an Italian. Knew Madame L. and her daughter. Had conversed with both frequently. Was sure that the shrill voice was not that of either of the deceased.

"—— *Odenheimer, restaurateur.* This witness volunteered his testimony. Not speaking French, was examined through an interpreter. Is a native of Amsterdam. Was passing the house at the time of the shrieks. They lasted for several minutes—probably ten. They were long and loud—very awful and distressing. Was one of those who entered the building. Corroborated the previous evidence in every respect but one. Was sure that the shrill voice was that of a man—of a Frenchman. Could not distinguish the words uttered. They were loud and quick—unequal—spoken apparently in fear as well as in anger. The voice was harsh—not so much shrill as harsh. Could not call it a shrill voice. The gruff voice said repeatedly '*sacré*,' '*diable*,' and once '*mon Dieu.*'

"*Jules Mignaud,* banker, of the firm of Mignaud et Fils, Rue Deloraine. Is the elder Mignaud. Madame L'Espanaye had some property. Had opened an account with his banking house in the spring of the year—— (eight years previously). Made frequent deposits in small sums. Had checked for nothing until the third day before her death, when she took out in person the sum of 4000 francs. This sum was paid in gold, and a clerk sent home with the money.

"*Adolphe Le Bon,* clerk to Mignaud et Fils, deposes that on the day in question, about noon, he accompanied Madame L'Espanaye to her residence with the 4000 francs, put up in two bags. Upon the door being opened, Mademoiselle L. appeared and took from his hands one of the bags, while the old lady relieved him of the other. He then bowed and departed. Did not see any person in the street at the time. It is a bye-street—very lonely.

"*William Bird,* tailor, deposes that he was one of the party who entered the house. Is an Englishman. Has lived in Paris two years. Was one of the first to ascend the stairs. Heard the voices in contention. The gruff voice was that of a Frenchman. Could make out several words, but cannot now remember all. Heard distinctly '*sacré*' and '*mon Dieu.*' There was a sound at the moment as if of several persons struggling—a scraping and scuffling sound. The shrill voice was very loud—louder than the gruff one. Is sure that it was not the voice of an Englishman. Appeared to be that of a German. Might have been a woman's voice. Does not understand German.

"Four of the above-named witnesses, being recalled, deposed that the door of the chamber in which was found the body of Mademoiselle L. was locked on the inside when the party reached it. Every thing was perfectly silent—no groans or noises of any kind. Upon

forcing the door no person was seen. The windows, both of the back and front room, were down and firmly fastened from within. A door between the two rooms was closed, but not locked. The door leading from the front room into the passage was locked, with the key on the inside. A small room in the front of the house, on the fourth story, at the head of the passage, was open, the door being ajar. This room was crowded with old beds, boxes, and so forth. These were carefully removed and searched. There was not an inch of any portion of the house which was not carefully searched. Sweeps were sent up and down the chimneys. The house was a four story one, with garrets (*mansardes*.) A trap-door on the roof was nailed down very securely— did not appear to have been opened for years. The time elapsing between the hearing of the voices in contention and the breaking open of the room door, was variously stated by the witnesses. Some made it as short as three minutes—some as long as five. The door was opened with difficulty.

"*Alfonzo Garcio*, undertaker, deposes that he resides in the Rue Morgue. Is a native of Spain. Was one of the party who entered the house. Did not proceed up stairs. Is nervous, and was apprehensive of the consequences of agitation. Heard the voices in contention. The gruff voice was that of a Frenchman. Could not distinguish what was said. The shrill voice was that of an Englishman—is sure of this. Does not understand the English language, but judges by the intonation.

"*Alberto Montani*, confectioner, deposes that he was among the first to ascend the stairs. Heard the voices in question. The gruff voice was that of a Frenchman. Distinguished several words. The speaker appeared to be expostulating. Could not make out the words of the shrill voice. Spoke quick and unevenly. Thinks it the voice of a Russian. Corroborates the general testimony. Is an Italian. Never conversed with a native of Russia.

"Several witnesses, recalled, here testified that the chimneys of all the rooms on the fourth story were too narrow to admit the passage of a human being. By 'sweeps' were meant cylindrical sweeping-brushes, such as are employed by those who clean chimneys. These brushes were passed up and down every flue in the house. There is no back passage by which any one could have descended while the party proceeded up stairs. The body of Mademoiselle L'Espanaye was so firmly wedged in the chimney that it could not be got down until four or five of the party united their strength.

"*Paul Dumas*, physician, deposes that he was called to view the bodies about day-break. They were both then lying on the sacking of the bedstead in the chamber where Mademoiselle L. was found. The corpse of the young lady was much bruised and excoriated. The fact that it had been thrust up the chimney would sufficiently account for these appearances. The throat was greatly chafed. There were several deep scratches just below the chin, together with a series of livid spots which were evidently the impression of fingers. The face was fearfully discolored, and the eye-balls protruded. The tongue had been partially bitten through. A large bruise was discovered upon the pit of the stom-

ach, produced, apparently, by the pressure of a knee. In the opinion of M. Dumas, Mademoiselle L'Espanaye had been throttled to death by some person or persons unknown. The corpse of the mother was horribly mutilated. All the bones of the right leg and arm were more or less shattered. The left *tibia*[6] much splintered, as well as all the ribs of the left side. Whole body dreadfully bruised and discolored. It was not possible to say how the injuries had been inflicted. A heavy club of wood, or a broad bar of iron—a chair—any large, heavy, and obtuse weapon would have produced such results, if wielded by the hands of a very powerful man. No woman could have inflicted the blows with any weapon. The head of the deceased, when seen by witness, was entirely separated from the body, and was also greatly shattered. The throat had evidently been cut with some very sharp instrument—probably with a razor.

"*Alexandre Etienne*, surgeon, was called with M. Dumas to view the bodies. Corroborated the testimony, and the opinions of M. Dumas.

"Nothing farther of importance was elicited, although several other persons were examined. A murder so mysterious, and so perplexing in all its particulars, was never before committed in Paris—if indeed a murder has been committed at all. The police are entirely at fault—an unusual occurrence in affairs of this nature. There is not, however, the shadow of a clew apparent."

The evening edition of the paper stated that the greatest excitement still continued in the Quartier St. Roch—that the premises in question had been carefully re-searched, and fresh examinations of witnesses instituted, but all to no purpose. A postscript, however, mentioned that Adolphe Le Bon had been arrested and imprisoned—although nothing appeared to criminate him, beyond the facts already detailed.

Dupin seemed singularly interested in the progress of this affair—at least so I judged from his manner, for he made no comments. It was only after the announcement that Le Bon had been imprisoned, that he asked me my opinion respecting the murders.

I could merely agree with all Paris in considering them an insoluble mystery. I saw no means by which it would be possible to trace the murderer.

"We must not judge of the means," said Dupin, "by this shell of an examination. The Parisian police, so much extolled for *acumen*, are cunning, but no more. There is no method in their proceedings, beyond the method of the moment. They make a vast parade of measures; but, not unfrequently, these are so ill adapted to the objects proposed, as to put us in mind of Monsieur Jourdain's calling for his *robe-de-chambre—pour mieux entendre la musique*.[7] The results attained by them are not unfrequently surprising, but, for the most part,

6. Shinbone.
7. To understand the music better. The phrase is from *Le bourgeois gentilhomme* (1670), a satiric comedy by Jean Baptiste Poquelin Molière (1622–1673), in which the nouveau riche Jourdain calls for his "*robe-de-chambre*" (dressing gown; chamber robe) to understand "chamber music" better. Dupin is sarcastically commenting on the incompetence of the Parisian police.

are brought about by simple diligence and activity. When these qualities are unavailing, their schemes fail. Vidocq,[8] for example, was a good guesser, and a persevering man. But, without educated thought, he erred continually by the very intensity of his investigations. He impaired his vision by holding the object too close. He might see, perhaps, one or two points with unusual clearness, but in so doing he, necessarily, lost sight of the matter as a whole. Thus there is such a thing as being too profound. Truth is not always in a well.[9] In fact, as regards the more important knowledge, I do believe that she is invariably superficial. The depth lies in the valleys where we seek her, and not upon the mountain-tops where she is found. The modes and sources of this kind of error are well typified in the contemplation of the heavenly bodies. To look at a star by glances—to view it in a sidelong way, by turning toward it the exterior portions of the *retina* (more susceptible of feeble impressions of light than the interior), is to behold the star distinctly—is to have the best appreciation of its lustre—a lustre which grows dim just in proportion as we turn our vision *fully* upon it. A greater number of rays actually fall upon the eye in the latter case, but, in the former, there is the more refined capacity for comprehension. By undue profundity we perplex and enfeeble thought; and it is possible to make even Venus herself vanish from the firmament by a scrutiny too sustained, too concentrated, or too direct.

"As for these murders, let us enter into some examinations for ourselves, before we make up an opinion respecting them. An inquiry will afford us amusement," [I thought this an odd term, so applied, but said nothing] "and, besides, Le Bon once rendered me a service for which I am not ungrateful. We will go and see the premises with our own eyes. I know G———, the Prefect of Police, and shall have no difficulty in obtaining the necessary permission."

The permission was obtained, and we proceeded at once to the Rue Morgue. This is one of those miserable thoroughfares which intervene between the Rue Richelieu and the Rue St. Roch. It was late in the afternoon when we reached it; as this quarter is at a great distance from that in which we resided. The house was readily found; for there were still many persons gazing up at the closed shutters, with an objectless curiosity, from the opposite side of the way. It was an ordinary Parisian house, with a gateway, on one side of which was a glazed watch-box, with a sliding panel in the window, indicating a *loge de concierge*.[1] Before going in we walked up the street, turned down an alley, and then, again turning, passed in the rear of the building—Dupin, meanwhile, examining the whole neighborhood, as well as the house, with a minuteness of attention for which I could see no possible object.

Retracing our steps, we came again to the front of the dwelling, rang, and, having shown our credentials, were admitted by the agents

8. François-Eugène Vidocq, the French minister of police under Napoleon I; see the headnote to "Murders" (p. 239 herein).
9. Reference to Democritus's statement (known as "the well of Democritus") that "Of truth we know nothing, for truth lies in an abyss." Poe also alludes to this phrase in "A Descent into the Maelström" (p. 266) and elsewhere.
1. A doorkeeper's apartment.

in charge. We went up stairs—into the chamber where the body of Mademoiselle L'Espanaye had been found, and where both the deceased still lay. The disorders of the room had, as usual, been suffered to exist. I saw nothing beyond what had been stated in the "Gazette des Tribunaux." Dupin scrutinized every thing—not excepting the bodies of the victims. We then went into the other rooms, and into the yard; a *gendarme* accompanying us throughout. The examination occupied us until dark, when we took our departure. On our way home my companion stepped in for a moment at the office of one of the daily papers.

I have said that the whims of my friend were manifold, and that *Je les ménagais:*[2]—for this phrase there is no English equivalent. It was his humor, now, to decline all conversation on the subject of the murder, until about noon the next day. He then asked me, suddenly, if I had observed any thing *peculiar* at the scene of the atrocity.

There was something in his manner of emphasizing the word "peculiar," which caused me to shudder, without knowing why.

"No, nothing *peculiar*," I said; "nothing more, at least, than we both saw stated in the paper."

"The 'Gazette,'" he replied, "has not entered, I fear, into the unusual horror of the thing. But dismiss the idle opinions of this print. It appears to me that this mystery is considered insoluble, for the very reason which should cause it to be regarded as easy of solution—I mean for the *outré*[3] character of its features. The police are confounded by the seeming absence of motive—not for the murder itself—but for the atrocity of the murder. They are puzzled, too, by the seeming impossibility of reconciling the voices heard in contention, with the facts that no one was discovered up stairs but the assassinated Mademoiselle L'Espanaye, and that there were no means of egress without the notice of the party ascending. The wild disorder of the room; the corpse thrust, with the head downward, up the chimney; the frightful mutilation of the body of the old lady; these considerations, with those just mentioned, and others which I need not mention, have sufficed to paralyze the powers, by putting completely at fault the boasted *acumen*, of the government agents. They have fallen into the gross but common error of confounding the unusual with the abstruse. But it is by these deviations from the plane of the ordinary, that reason feels its way, if at all, in its search for the true. In investigations such as we are now pursuing, it should not be so much asked 'what has occurred,' as 'what has occurred that has never occurred before.' In fact, the facility with which I shall arrive, or have arrived, at the solution of this mystery, is in the direct ratio of its apparent insolubility in the eyes of the police."

I stared at the speaker in mute astonishment.

"I am now awaiting," continued he, looking toward the door of our apartment—"I am now awaiting a person who, although perhaps not

2. The narrator is right; there is no literal English equivalent for this highly idiomatic French phrase. What it means is, "I handled them [Dupin's whims] with kid gloves"; tactfully.
3. Strange, bizarre.

the perpetrator of these butcheries, must have been in some measure implicated in their perpetration. Of the worst portion of the crimes committed, it is probable that he is innocent. I hope that I am right in this supposition; for upon it I build my expectation of reading the entire riddle. I look for the man here—in this room—every moment. It is true that he may not arrive; but the probability is that he will. Should he come, it will be necessary to detain him. Here are pistols; and we both know how to use them when occasion demands their use."

I took the pistols, scarcely knowing what I did, or believing what I heard, while Dupin went on, very much as if in a soliloquy. I have already spoken of his abstract manner at such times. His discourse was addressed to myself; but his voice, although by no means loud, had that intonation which is commonly employed in speaking to some one at a great distance. His eyes, vacant in expression, regarded only the wall.

"That the voices heard in contention," he said, "by the party upon the stairs, were not the voices of the women themselves, was fully proved by the evidence. This relieves us of all doubt upon the question whether the old lady could have first destroyed the daughter, and afterward have committed suicide. I speak of this point chiefly for the sake of method; for the strength of Madame L'Espanaye would have been utterly unequal to the task of thrusting her daughter's corpse up the chimney as it was found; and the nature of the wounds upon her own person entirely preclude the idea of self-destruction. Murder, then, has been committed by some third party; and the voices of this third party were those heard in contention. Let me now advert—not to the whole testimony respecting these voices—but to what was *peculiar* in that testimony. Did you observe any thing peculiar about it?"

I remarked that, while all the witnesses agreed in supposing the gruff voice to be that of a Frenchman, there was much disagreement in regard to the shrill, or, as one individual termed it, the harsh voice.

"That was the evidence itself," said Dupin, "but it was not the peculiarity of the evidence. You have observed nothing distinctive. Yet there *was* something to be observed. The witnesses, as you remark, agreed about the gruff voice; they were here unanimous. But in regard to the shrill voice, the peculiarity is—not that they disagreed—but that, while an Italian, an Englishman, a Spaniard, a Hollander, and a Frenchman attempted to describe it, each one spoke of it as that *of a foreigner*. Each is sure that it was not the voice of one of his own countrymen. Each likens it—not to the voice of an individual of any nation with whose language he is conversant—but the converse. The Frenchman supposes it the voice of a Spaniard, and 'might have distinguished some words *had he been acquainted with the Spanish.*' The Dutchman maintains it to have been that of a Frenchman; but we find it stated that '*not understanding French this witness was examined through an interpreter.*' The Englishman thinks it the voice of a German, and '*does not understand German.*' The Spaniard 'is sure' that it was that of an Englishman, but 'judges by the intonation' altogether, '*as he has no knowledge of the English.*' The Italian believes it the voice

of a Russian, but '*has never conversed with a native of Russia.*' A second Frenchman differs, moreover, with the first, and is positive that the voice was that of an Italian; but, *not being cognizant of that tongue*, is, like the Spaniard, 'convinced by the intonation.' Now, how strangely unusual must that voice have really been, about which such testimony as this *could* have been elicited!—in whose *tones*, even, denizens of the five great divisions of Europe could recognise nothing familiar! You will say that it might have been the voice of an Asiatic—of an African. Neither Asiatics nor Africans abound in Paris; but, without denying the inference, I will now merely call your attention to three points. The voice is termed by one witness 'harsh rather than shrill.' It is represented by two others to have been 'quick and *unequal.*' No words— no sounds resembling words—were by any witness mentioned as distinguishable.

"I know not," continued Dupin, "what impression I may have made, so far, upon your own understanding; but I do not hesitate to say that legitimate deductions even from this portion of the testimony—the portion respecting the gruff and shrill voices—are in themselves sufficient to engender a suspicion which should give direction to all farther progress in the investigation of the mystery. I said 'legitimate deductions;' but my meaning is not thus fully expressed. I designed to imply that the deductions are the *sole* proper ones, and that the suspicion arises *inevitably* from them as the single result. What the suspicion is, however, I will not say just yet. I merely wish you to bear in mind that, with myself, it was sufficiently forcible to give a definite form—a certain tendency—to my inquiries in the chamber.

"Let us now transport ourselves, in fancy, to this chamber. What shall we first seek here? The means of egress employed by the murderers. It is not too much to say that neither of us believe in præter-natural events. Madame and Mademoiselle L'Espanaye were not destroyed by spirits. The doers of the deed were material, and escaped materially. Then how? Fortunately, there is but one mode of reasoning upon the point, and that mode *must* lead us to a definite decision.— Let us examine, each by each, the possible means of egress. It is clear that the assassins were in the room where Mademoiselle L'Espanaye was found, or at least in the room adjoining, when the party ascended the stairs. It is then only from these two apartments that we have to seek issues. The police have laid bare the floors, the ceilings, and the masonry of the walls, in every direction. No *secret* issues could have escaped their vigilance. But, not trusting to *their* eyes, I examined with my own. There were, then, *no* secret issues. Both doors leading from the rooms into the passage were securely locked, with the keys inside. Let us turn to the chimneys. These, although of ordinary width for some eight or ten feet above the hearths, will not admit, throughout their extent, the body of a large cat. The impossibility of egress, by means already stated, being thus absolute, we are reduced to the windows. Through those of the front room no one could have escaped without notice from the crowd in the street. The murderers *must* have passed, then, through those of the back room. Now, brought to this

conclusion in so unequivocal a manner as we are, it is not our part, as reasoners, to reject it on account of apparent impossibilities. It is only left for us to prove that these apparent 'impossibilities' are, in reality, not such.

"There are two windows in the chamber. One of them is unobstructed by furniture, and is wholly visible. The lower portion of the other is hidden from view by the head of the unwieldy bedstead which is thrust close up against it. The former was found securely fastened from within. It resisted the utmost force of those who endeavored to raise it. A large gimlet-hole had been pierced in its frame to the left, and a very stout nail was found fitted therein, nearly to the head. Upon examining the other window, a similar nail was seen similarly fitted in it; and a vigorous attempt to raise this sash, failed also. The police were now entirely satisfied that egress had not been in these directions. And, *therefore*, it was thought a matter of supererogation to withdraw the nails and open the windows.

"My own examination was somewhat more particular, and was so for the reason I have just given—because here it was, I knew, that all apparent impossibilities *must* be proved to be not such in reality.

"I proceeded to think thus—*à posteriori*.[4] The murderers *did* escape from one of these windows. This being so, they could not have refastened the sashes from the inside, as they were found fastened;— the consideration which put a stop, through its obviousness, to the scrutiny of the police in this quarter. Yet the sashes *were* fastened. They *must*, then, have the power of fastening themselves. There was no escape from this conclusion. I stepped to the unobstructed casement, withdrew the nail with some difficulty, and attempted to raise the sash. It resisted all my efforts, as I had anticipated. A concealed spring must, I now knew, exist; and this corroboration of my idea convinced me that my premises, at least, were correct, however mysterious still appeared the circumstances attending the nails. A careful search soon brought to light the hidden spring. I pressed it, and, satisfied with the discovery, forbore to upraise the sash.

"I now replaced the nail and regarded it attentively. A person passing out through this window might have reclosed it, and the spring would have caught—but the nail could not have been replaced. The conclusion was plain, and again narrowed in the field of my investigations. The assassins *must* have escaped through the other window. Supposing, then, the springs upon each sash to be the same, as was probable, there *must* be found a difference between the nails, or at least between the modes of their fixture. Getting upon the sacking of the bedstead, I looked over the head-board minutely at the second casement. Passing my hand down behind the board, I readily discovered and pressed the spring, which was, as I had supposed, identical in character with its neighbor. I now looked at the nail. It was as stout as the other, and apparently fitted in the same manner—driven in nearly up to the head.

4. After the fact; to argue back from the evidence of the case rather than forward from beginning assumptions.

"You will say that I was puzzled; but, if you think so, you must have misunderstood the nature of the inductions. To use a sporting phrase, I had not been once 'at fault.' The scent had never for an instant been lost. There was no flaw in any link of the chain. I had traced the secret to its ultimate result,—and that result was *the nail*. It had, I say, in every respect, the appearance of its fellow in the other window; but this fact was an absolute nullity (conclusive as it might seem to be) when compared with the consideration that here, at this point, terminated the clew. 'There *must* be something wrong,' I said, 'about the nail.' I touched it; and the head, with about a quarter of an inch of the shank, came off in my fingers. The rest of the shank was in the gimlet-hole, where it had been broken off. The fracture was an old one (for its edges were incrusted with rust), and had apparently been accomplished by the blow of a hammer, which had partially imbedded, in the top of the bottom sash, the head portion of the nail. I now carefully replaced this head portion in the indentation whence I had taken it, and the resemblance to a perfect nail was complete—the fissure was invisible. Pressing the spring, I gently raised the sash for a few inches; the head went up with it, remaining firm in its bed. I closed the window, and the semblance of the whole nail was again perfect.

"The riddle, so far, was now unriddled. The assassin had escaped through the window which looked upon the bed. Dropping of its own accord upon his exit (or perhaps purposely closed), it had become fastened by the spring; and it was the retention of this spring which had been mistaken by the police for that of the nail,—farther inquiry being thus considered unnecessary.

"The next question is that of the mode of descent. Upon this point I had been satisfied in my walk with you around the building. About five feet and a half from the casement in question there runs a lightning-rod. From this rod it would have been impossible for any one to reach the window itself, to say nothing of entering it. I observed, however, that the shutters of the fourth story were of the peculiar kind called by Parisian carpenters *ferrades*—a kind rarely employed at the present day, but frequently seen upon very old mansions at Lyons and Bourdeaux. They are in the form of an ordinary door, (a single, not a folding door) except that the lower half is latticed or worked in open trellis—thus affording an excellent hold for the hands. In the present instance these shutters are fully three feet and a half broad. When we saw them from the rear of the house, they were both about half open—that is to say, they stood off at right angles from the wall. It is probable that the police, as well as myself, examined the back of the tenement; but, if so, in looking at these *ferrades* in the line of their breadth (as they must have done), they did not perceive this great breadth itself, or, at all events, failed to take it into due consideration. In fact, having once satisfied themselves that no egress could have been made in this quarter, they would naturally bestow here a very cursory examination. It was clear to me, however, that the shutter belonging to the window at the head of the bed, would, if swung fully back to the wall, reach to within two feet of the lightning-rod. It was

also evident that, by exertion of a very unusual degree of activity and courage, an entrance into the window, from the rod, might have been thus effected.—By reaching to the distance of two feet and a half (we now suppose the shutter open to its whole extent) a robber might have taken a firm grasp upon the trellis-work. Letting go, then, his hold upon the rod, placing his feet securely against the wall, and springing boldly from it, he might have swung the shutter so as to close it, and, if we imagine the window open at the time, might even have swung himself into the room.

"I wish you to bear especially in mind that I have spoken of a *very* unusual degree of activity as requisite to success in so hazardous and so difficult a feat. It is my design to show you, first, that the thing might possibly have been accomplished:—but, secondly and *chiefly*, I wish to impress upon your understanding the *very extraordinary*—the almost præternatural character of that agility which could have accomplished it.

"You will say, no doubt, using the language of the law, that 'to make out my case,' I should rather undervalue, than insist upon a full estimation of the activity required in this matter. This may be the practice in law, but it is not the usage of reason. My ultimate object is only the truth. My immediate purpose is to lead you to place in juxta-position, that *very unusual* activity of which I have just spoken, with that *very peculiar* shrill (or harsh) and *unequal* voice, about whose nationality no two persons could be found to agree, and in whose utterance no syllabification could be detected."

At these words a vague and half-formed conception of the meaning of Dupin flitted over my mind. I seemed to be upon the verge of comprehension, without power to comprehend—as men, at times, find themselves upon the brink of remembrance, without being able, in the end, to remember. My friend went on with his discourse.

"You will see," he said, "that I have shifted the question from the mode of egress to that of ingress. It was my design to convey the idea that both were effected in the same manner, at the same point. Let us now revert to the interior of the room. Let us survey the appearances here. The drawers of the bureau, it is said, had been rifled, although many articles of apparel still remained within them. The conclusion here is absurd. It is a mere guess—a very silly one—and no more. How are we to know that the articles found in the drawers were not all these drawers had originally contained? Madame L'Espanaye and her daughter lived an exceedingly retired life—saw no company—seldom went out—had little use for numerous changes of habiliment. Those found were at least of as good quality as any likely to be possessed by these ladies. If a thief had taken any, why did he not take the best— why did he not take all? In a word, why did he abandon four thousand francs in gold to encumber himself with a bundle of linen? The gold *was* abandoned. Nearly the whole sum mentioned by Monsieur Mignaud, the banker, was discovered, in bags, upon the floor. I wish you, therefore, to discard from your thoughts the blundering idea of *motive*, engendered in the brains of the police by that portion of the evi-

dence which speaks of money delivered at the door of the house. Co-
incidences ten times as remarkable as this (the delivery of the money,
and murder committed within three days upon the party receiving it),
happen to all of us every hour of our lives, without attracting even mo-
mentary notice. Coincidences, in general, are great stumbling-blocks
in the way of that class of thinkers who have been educated to know
nothing of the theory of probabilities—that theory to which the most
glorious objects of human research are indebted for the most glorious
of illustration. In the present instance, had the gold been gone, the
fact of its delivery three days before would have formed something
more than a coincidence. It would have been corroborative of this idea
of motive. But, under the real circumstances of the case, if we are to
suppose gold the motive of this outrage, we must also imagine the per-
petrator so vacillating an idiot as to have abandoned his gold and his
motive together.

"Keeping now steadily in mind the points to which I have drawn your
attention—that peculiar voice, that unusual agility, and that startling ab-
sence of motive in a murder so singularly atrocious as this—let us
glance at the butchery itself. Here is a woman strangled to death by
manual strength, and thrust up a chimney, head downward. Ordinary
assassins employ no such modes of murder as this. Least of all, do they
thus dispose of the murdered. In the manner of thrusting the corpse up
the chimney, you will admit that there was something *excessively outré*—
something altogether irreconcilable with our common notions of human
action, even when we suppose the actors the most depraved of men.
Think, too, how great must have been that strength which could have
thrust the body *up* such an aperture so forcibly that the united vigor of
several persons was found barely sufficient to drag it *down*!

"Turn, now, to other indications of the employment of a vigor most
marvellous. On the hearth were thick tresses—very thick tresses—of
grey human hair. These had been torn out by the roots. You are aware
of the great force necessary in tearing thus from the head even twenty
or thirty hairs together. You saw the locks in question as well as my-
self. Their roots (a hideous sight!) were clotted with fragments of the
flesh of the scalp—sure token of the prodigious power which had been
exerted in uprooting perhaps half a million of hairs at a time. The
throat of the old lady was not merely cut, but the head absolutely sev-
ered from the body: the instrument was a mere razor. I wish you also
to look at the *brutal* ferocity of these deeds. Of the bruises upon the
body of Madame L'Espanaye I do not speak. Monsieur Dumas, and
his worthy coadjutor Monsieur Etienne, have pronounced that they
were inflicted by some obtuse instrument; and so far these gentlemen
are very correct. The obtuse instrument was clearly the stone pave-
ment in the yard, upon which the victim had fallen from the window
which looked in upon the bed. This idea, however simple it may now
seem, escaped the police for the same reason that the breadth of the
shutters escaped them—because, by the affair of the nails, their per-
ceptions had been hermetically sealed against the possibility of the
windows having ever been opened at all.

"If now, in addition to all these things, you have properly reflected upon the odd disorder of the chamber, we have gone so far as to combine the ideas of an agility astounding, a strength superhuman, a ferocity brutal, a butchery without motive, a *grotesquerie* in horror absolutely alien from humanity, and a voice foreign in tone to the ears of men of many nations, and devoid of all distinct or intelligible syllabification. What result, then, has ensued? What impression have I made upon your fancy?"

I felt a creeping of the flesh as Dupin asked me the question. "A madman," I said, "has done this deed—some raving maniac, escaped from a neighboring *Maison de Santé*."[5]

"In some respects," he replied, "your idea is not irrelevant. But the voices of madmen, even in their wildest paroxysms, are never found to tally with that peculiar voice heard upon the stairs. Madmen are of some nation, and their language, however incoherent in its words, has always the coherence of syllabification. Besides, the hair of a madman is not such as I now hold in my hand. I disentangled this little tuft from the rigidly clutched fingers of Madame L'Espanaye. Tell me what you can make of it."

"Dupin!" I said, completely unnerved; "this hair is most unusual—this is no *human* hair."

"I have not asserted that it is," said he; "but, before we decide this point, I wish you to glance at the little sketch I have here traced upon this paper. It is a *fac-simile* drawing of what has been described in one portion of the testimony as 'dark bruises, and deep indentations of finger nails,' upon the throat of Mademoiselle L'Espanaye, and in another, (by Messrs. Dumas and Etienne,) as a 'series of livid spots, evidently the impression of fingers.'

"You will perceive," continued my friend, spreading out the paper upon the table before us, "that this drawing gives the idea of a firm and fixed hold. There is no *slipping* apparent. Each finger has retained—possibly until the death of the victim—the fearful grasp by which it originally imbedded itself. Attempt, now, to place all your fingers, at the same time, in the respective impressions as you see them."

I made the attempt in vain.

"We are possibly not giving this matter a fair trial," he said. "The paper is spread out upon a plane surface; but the human throat is cylindrical. Here is a billet of wood, the circumference of which is about that of the throat. Wrap the drawing around it, and try the experiment again."

I did so; but the difficulty was even more obvious than before. "This," I said, "is the mark of no human hand."

"Read now," replied Dupin, "this passage from Cuvier."[6]

5. Sanitarium; here an insane asylum.
6. Georges Cuvier (1769–1832), French naturalist, systematist, and comparative anatomist whose classification of animals was one of the standard guides of his time. In his *Lessons in Comparative Anatomy* (1800–1805), Cuvier devised a method that divided the skull with a vertical and a longitudinal section and obtained a sliding gradation from the European to the Negro to the orangutan ("ourang-outang") to the monkey. But, unlike Linnaeus who placed man in the same order with the ape, Cuvier, in *The Animal Kingdom* (1817), classified man

It was a minute anatomical and generally descriptive account of the large fulvous Ourang-Outang of the East Indian Islands. The gigantic stature, the prodigious strength and activity, the wild ferocity, and the imitative propensities of these mammalia are sufficiently well known to all. I understood the full horrors of the murder at once.

"The description of the digits," said I, as I made an end of reading, "is in exact accordance with this drawing. I see that no animal but an Ourang-Outang, of the species here mentioned, could have impressed the indentations as you have traced them. This tuft of tawny hair, too, is identical in character with that of the beast of Cuvier. But I cannot possibly comprehend the particulars of this frightful mystery. Besides, there were *two* voices heard in contention, and one of them was unquestionably the voice of a Frenchman."

"True; and you will remember an expression attributed almost unanimously, by the evidence, to this voice,—the expression, '*mon Dieu!*' This, under the circumstances, has been justly characterized by one of the witnesses (Montani, the confectioner,) as an expression of remonstrance or expostulation. Upon these two words, therefore, I have mainly built my hopes of a full solution of the riddle. A Frenchman was cognizant of the murder. It is possible—indeed it is far more than probable—that he was innocent of all participation in the bloody transactions which took place. The Ourang-Outang may have escaped from him. He may have traced it to the chamber; but, under the agitating circumstances which ensued, he could never have re-captured it. It is still at large. I will not pursue these guesses—for I have no right to call them more—since the shades of reflection upon which they are based are scarcely of sufficient depth to be appreciable by my own intellect, and since I could not pretend to make them intelligible to the understanding of another. We will call them guesses then, and speak of them as such. If the Frenchman in question is indeed, as I suppose, innocent of this atrocity, this advertisement, which I left last night, upon our return home, at the office of 'Le Monde,' (a paper devoted to the shipping interest, and much sought by sailors,) will bring him to our residence."

He handed me a paper, and I read thus:

CAUGHT—*In the Bois de Boulogne, early in the morning of the ——— inst., (the morning of the murder,) a very large, tawny Ourang-Outang of the Bornese species. The owner, (who is ascertained to be a sailor, belonging to a Maltese vessel,) may have the animal again, upon identifying it satisfactorily, and paying a few charges arising from its capture and keeping. Call at No.———, Rue ———, Faubourg St. Germain—au troisième.*[7]

"How was it possible," I asked, "that you should know the man to be a sailor, and belonging to a Maltese vessel?"

in a separate order (the "bimana") from apes and monkeys (the "quadrumana") based on man's distinguishing characteristics (i.e., a biped gait as opposed to walking on all fours). A description of the orangutan appears under the classification of *quadruman* in Thomas Wyatt's *A Synopsis of Natural History* (1839), a book that Poe helped edit.
7. The third floor; but the fourth floor to Americans. Many European countries do not "number" the ground floor.

"I do *not* know it," said Dupin. "I am not *sure* of it. Here, however, is a small piece of ribbon, which from its form, and from its greasy appearance, has evidently been used in tying the hair in one of those long *queues* of which sailors are so fond. Moreover, this knot is one which few besides sailors can tie, and is peculiar to the Maltese. I picked the ribbon up at the foot of the lightning-rod. It could not have belonged to either of the deceased. Now if, after all, I am wrong in my induction from this ribbon, that the Frenchman was a sailor belonging to a Maltese vessel, still I can have done no harm in saying what I did in the advertisement. If I am in error, he will merely suppose that I have been misled by some circumstance into which he will not take the trouble to inquire. But if I am right, a great point is gained. Cognizant although innocent of the murder, the Frenchman will naturally hesitate about replying to the advertisement—about demanding the Ourang-Outang. He will reason thus:—'I am innocent; I am poor; my Ourang-Outang is of great value—to one in my circumstances a fortune of itself—why should I lose it through idle apprehensions of danger? Here it is, within my grasp. It was found in the Bois de Boulogne—at a vast distance from the scene of that butchery. How can it ever be suspected that a brute beast should have done the deed? The police are at fault—they have failed to procure the slightest clew. Should they even trace the animal, it would be impossible to prove me cognizant of the murder, or to implicate me in guilt on account of that cognizance. Above all, *I am known*. The advertiser designates me as the possessor of the beast. I am not sure to what limit his knowledge may extend. Should I avoid claiming a property of so great value, which it is known that I possess, I will render the animal at least, liable to suspicion. It is not my policy to attract attention either to myself or to the beast. I will answer the advertisement, get the Ourang-Outang, and keep it close until this matter has blown over.' "

At this moment we heard a step upon the stairs.

"Be ready," said Dupin, "with your pistols, but neither use them nor show them until at a signal from myself."

The front door of the house had been left open, and the visiter had entered, without ringing, and advanced several steps upon the staircase. Now, however, he seemed to hesitate. Presently we heard him descending. Dupin was moving quickly to the door, when we again heard him coming up. He did not turn back a second time, but stepped up with decision, and rapped at the door of our chamber.

"Come in," said Dupin, in a cheerful and hearty tone.

A man entered. He was a sailor, evidently,—a tall, stout, and muscular-looking person, with a certain dare-devil expression of countenance, not altogether unprepossessing. His face, greatly sunburnt, was more than half hidden by whisker and *mustachio*. He had with him a huge oaken cudgel,[8] but appeared to be otherwise unarmed. He

8. Short, heavy club.

bowed awkwardly, and bade us "good evening," in French accents, which, although somewhat Neufchatelish,[9] were still sufficiently indicative of a Parisian origin.

"Sit down, my friend," said Dupin. "I suppose you have called about the Ourang-Outang. Upon my word, I almost envy you the possession of him; a remarkably fine, and no doubt a very valuable animal. How old do you suppose him to be?"

The sailor drew a long breath, with the air of a man relieved of some intolerable burden, and then replied, in an assured tone:

"I have no way of telling—but he can't be more than four or five years old. Have you got him here?"

"Oh no; we had no conveniences for keeping him here. He is at a livery stable in the Rue Dubourg, just by. You can get him in the morning. Of course you are prepared to identify the property?"

"To be sure I am, sir."

"I shall be sorry to part with him," said Dupin.

"I don't mean that you should be at all this trouble for nothing, sir," said the man. "Couldn't expect it. Am very willing to pay a reward for the finding of the animal—that is to say, any thing in reason."

"Well," replied my friend, "that is all very fair, to be sure. Let me think!—what should I have? Oh! I will tell you. My reward shall be this. You shall give me all the information in your power about these murders in the Rue Morgue."

Dupin said the last words in a very low tone, and very quietly. Just as quietly, too, he walked toward the door, locked it, and put the key in his pocket. He then drew a pistol from his bosom and placed it, without the least flurry, upon the table.

The sailor's face flushed up as if he were struggling with suffocation. He started to his feet and grasped his cudgel; but the next moment he fell back into his seat, trembling violently, and with the countenance of death itself. He spoke not a word. I pitied him from the bottom of my heart.

"My friend," said Dupin, in a kind tone, "you are alarming yourself unnecessarily—you are indeed. We mean you no harm whatever. I pledge you the honor of a gentleman, and of a Frenchman, that we intend you no injury. I perfectly well know that you are innocent of the atrocities in the Rue Morgue. It will not do, however, to deny that you are in some measure implicated in them. From what I have already said, you must know that I have had means of information about this matter—means of which you could never have dreamed. Now the thing stands thus. You have done nothing which you could have avoided—nothing, certainly, which renders you culpable. You were not even guilty of robbery, when you might have robbed with impunity. You have nothing to conceal. You have no reason for concealment. On the other hand, you are bound by every principle of honor to confess all

9. Uncouth, countrified behavior, according to Mabbott, since the people of Neufchatel are Protestants rather than Roman Catholic and speak an acquired French enmeshed with a local dialect.

you know. An innocent man is now imprisoned, charged with that crime of which you can point out the perpetrator."

The sailor had recovered his presence of mind, in a great measure, while Dupin uttered these words; but his original boldness of bearing was all gone.

"So help me God," said he, after a brief pause, "I *will* tell you all I know about this affair;—but I do not expect you to believe one half I say—I would be a fool indeed if I did. Still, I *am* innocent, and I will make a clean breast if I die for it."

What he stated was, in substance, this. He had lately made a voyage to the Indian Archipelago. A party, of which he formed one, landed at Borneo, and passed into the interior on an excursion of pleasure. Himself and a companion had captured the Ourang-Outang. This companion dying, the animal fell into his own exclusive possession. After great trouble, occasioned by the intractable ferocity of his captive during the home voyage, he at length succeeded in lodging it safely at his own residence in Paris, where, not to attract toward himself the unpleasant curiosity of his neighbors, he kept it carefully secluded, until such time as it should recover from a wound in the foot, received from a splinter on board ship. His ultimate design was to sell it.

Returning home from some sailors' frolic on the night, or rather in the morning of the murder, he found the beast occupying his own bed-room, into which it had broken from a closet adjoining, where it had been, as was thought, securely confined. Razor in hand, and fully lathered, it was sitting before a looking-glass, attempting the operation of shaving, in which it had no doubt previously watched its master through the key-hole of the closet. Terrified at the sight of so dangerous a weapon in the possession of an animal so ferocious, and so well able to use it, the man, for some moments, was at a loss what to do. He had been accustomed, however, to quiet the creature, even in its fiercest moods, by the use of a whip, and to this he now resorted. Upon sight of it, the Ourang-Outang sprang at once through the door of the chamber, down the stairs, and thence, through a window, unfortunately open, into the street.

The Frenchman followed in despair; the ape, razor still in hand, occasionally stopping to look back and gesticulate at its pursuer, until the latter had nearly come up with it. It then again made off. In this manner the chase continued for a long time. The streets were profoundly quiet, as it was nearly three o'clock in the morning. In passing down an alley in the rear of the Rue Morgue, the fugitive's attention was arrested by a light gleaming from the open window of Madame L'Espanaye's chamber, in the fourth story of her house. Rushing to the building, it perceived the lightning-rod, clambered up with inconceivable agility, grasped the shutter, which was thrown fully back against the wall, and, by its means, swung itself directly upon the headboard of the bed. The whole feat did not occupy a minute. The shutter was kicked open again by the Ourang-Outang as it entered the room.

The sailor, in the meantime, was both rejoiced and perplexed. He had strong hopes of now recapturing the brute, as it could scarcely es-

cape from the trap into which it had ventured, except by the rod, where it might be intercepted as it came down. On the other hand, there was much cause for anxiety as to what it might do in the house. This latter reflection urged the man still to follow the fugitive. A lightning-rod is ascended without difficulty, especially by a sailor; but, when he had arrived as high as the window, which lay far to his left, his career was stopped; the most that he could accomplish was to reach over so as to obtain a glimpse of the interior of the room. At this glimpse he nearly fell from his hold through excess of horror. Now it was that those hideous shrieks arose upon the night, which had startled from slumber the inmates of the Rue Morgue. Madame L'Espanaye and her daughter, habited in their night clothes, had apparently been occupied in arranging some papers in the iron chest already mentioned, which had been wheeled into the middle of the room. It was open, and its contents lay beside it on the floor. The victims must have been sitting with their backs toward the window; and, from the time elapsing between the ingress of the beast and the screams, it seems probable that it was not immediately perceived. The flapping-to of the shutter would naturally have been attributed to the wind.

As the sailor looked in, the gigantic animal had seized Madame L'Espanaye by the hair, (which was loose, as she had been combing it,) and was flourishing the razor about her face, in imitation of the motions of a barber. The daughter lay prostrate and motionless; she had swooned. The screams and struggles of the old lady (during which the hair was torn from her head) had the effect of changing the probably pacific purposes of the Ourang Outang into those of wrath. With one determined sweep of its muscular arm it nearly severed her head from her body. The sight of blood inflamed its anger into phrenzy. Gnashing its teeth, and flashing fire from its eyes, it flew upon the body of the girl, and imbedded its fearful talons in her throat, retaining its grasp until she expired. Its wandering and wild glances fell at this moment upon the head of the bed, over which the face of its master, rigid with horror, was just discernible. The fury of the beast, who no doubt bore still in mind the dreaded whip, was instantly converted into fear. Conscious of having deserved punishment, it seemed desirous of concealing its bloody deeds, and skipped about the chamber in an agony of nervous agitation; throwing down and breaking the furniture as it moved, and dragging the bed from the bedstead. In conclusion, it seized first the corpse of the daughter, and thrust it up the chimney, as it was found; then that of the old lady, which it immediately hurled through the window headlong.

As the ape approached the casement with its mutilated burden, the sailor shrank aghast to the rod, and, rather gliding than clambering down it, hurried at once home—dreading the consequences of the butchery, and gladly abandoning, in his terror, all solicitude about the fate of the Ourang-Outang. The words heard by the party upon the staircase were the Frenchman's exclamations of horror and affright, commingled with the fiendish jabberings of the brute.

I have scarcely anything to add. The Ourang-Outang must have

escaped from the chamber, by the rod, just before the breaking of the door. It must have closed the window as it passed through it. It was subsequently caught by the owner himself, who obtained for it a very large sum at the *Jardin des Plantes*.[1] Le Bon was instantly released, upon our narration of the circumstances (with some comments from Dupin) at the *bureau* of the Prefect of Police. This functionary, however well disposed to my friend, could not altogether conceal his chagrin at the turn which affairs had taken, and was fain to indulge in a sarcasm or two, about the propriety of every person minding his own business.

"Let him talk," said Dupin, who had not thought it necessary to reply. "Let him discourse; it will ease his conscience. I am satisfied with having defeated him in his own castle. Nevertheless, that he failed in the solution of this mystery, is by no means that matter for wonder which he supposes it; for, in truth, our friend the Prefect is somewhat too cunning to be profound. In his wisdom is no *stamen*. It is all head and no body, like the pictures of the Goddess Laverna[2]—or, at best, all head and shoulders, like a codfish. But he is a good creature after all. I like him especially for one master stroke of cant, by which he has attained his reputation for ingenuity. I mean the way he has '*de nier ce qui est, et d'expliquer ce qui n'est pas.*' "[3]

A Descent into the Maelström[1]

> The ways of God in Nature, as in Providence, are not as *our* ways; nor are the models that we frame any way commensurate to the vastness, profundity, and unsearchableness of His works, *which have a depth in them greater than the well of Democritus.*
>
> *Joseph Glanville.*[2]

WE had now reached the summit of the loftiest crag. For some minutes the old man seemed too much exhausted to speak.

"Not long ago," said he at length, "and I could have guided you on this route as well as the youngest of my sons; but, about three years past, there happened to me an event such as never happened before to

1. The botanical garden (garden of plants) in Paris.
2. The Roman goddess of thieves, imposters, and frauds.
3. Rousseau—Nouvelle Heloise [Poe's note]. The French reads: of denying what is, and explaining what is not. It is the conclusion of a discussion of Plato's explanation of apparitions in Jean-Jacques Rousseau's *Julie ou la Nouvelle Héloise* (1760). The full sentence is: "It is a common mania of philosophers of all eras to deny what is and explain what is not."
1. First published in *Graham's Magazine* (May 1841). The text printed here is from *Tales* (1845). Mabbott and others have noted that Poe fuses together into a single unified story several different sources. The most notable are Edward Wilson Landor's "The Maelstrom: A Fragment" in *Fraser's Magazine* (September 1834); "Maelstrom" in the *Encyclopaedia Britannica* (3rd to 6th eds.), an article taken from *The Natural History of Norway* (1775); *The Mariner's Chronicle* (1834), a compilation of narratives of disasters at sea (including the whole of the *Britannica* article). Ironically, Poe's story subsequently became a "source" for a later encyclopedia entry on whirlpools.
2. The epigraph is slightly altered from *Essays on Several Important Subjects in Philosophy and Religion* (1676) by Joseph Glanvill (1636–1680), an English essayist. Democritus (c. 460–c. 360 B.C.E.) was a materialist philosopher. The "well of Democritus" refers to his statement that "of truth we know nothing, for truth is in an abyss." Poe also refers to this well of truth in "The Murders in the Rue Morgue" (p. 252, n. 9 herein) and elsewhere.

mortal man—or at least such as no man ever survived to tell of—and the six hours of deadly terror which I then endured have broken me up body and soul. You suppose me a *very* old man—but I am not. It took less than a single day to change these hairs from a jetty black to white, to weaken my limbs, and to unstring my nerves, so that I tremble at the least exertion, and am frightened at a shadow. Do you know I can scarcely look over this little cliff without getting giddy?"

The "little cliff," upon whose edge he had so carelessly thrown himself down to rest that the weightier portion of his body hung over it, while he was only kept from falling by the tenure of his elbow on its extreme and slippery edge—this "little cliff" arose, a sheer unobstructed precipice of black shining rock, some fifteen or sixteen hundred feet from the world of crags beneath us. Nothing would have tempted me to within half a dozen yards of its brink. In truth so deeply was I excited by the perilous position of my companion, that I fell at full length upon the ground, clung to the shrubs around me, and dared not even glance upward at the sky—while I struggled in vain to divest myself of the idea that the very foundations of the mountain were in danger from the fury of the winds. It was long before I could reason myself into sufficient courage to sit up and look out into the distance.

"You must get over these fancies," said the guide, "for I have brought you here that you might have the best possible view of the scene of that event I mentioned—and to tell you the whole story with the spot just under your eye."

"We are now," he continued, in that particularizing manner which distinguished him—"we are now close upon the Norwegian coast—in the sixty-eighth degree of latitude—in the great province of Nordland—and in the dreary district of Lofoden.[3] The mountain upon whose top we sit is Helseggen, the Cloudy. Now raise yourself up a little higher—hold on to the grass if you feel giddy—so—and look out, beyond the belt of vapor beneath us, into the sea."

I looked dizzily, and beheld a wide expanse of ocean, whose waters wore so inky a hue as to bring at once to my mind the Nubian geographer's account of the *Mare Tenebrarum*.[4] A panorama more deplorably desolate no human imagination can conceive. To the right and left, as far as the eye could reach, there lay outstretched, like ramparts of the world, lines of horridly black and beetling cliff, whose character of gloom was but the more forcibly illustrated by the surf which reared high up against it its white and ghastly crest, howling and shrieking for ever. Just opposite the promontory upon whose apex we were placed, and at a distance of some five or six miles out at sea, there was visible a small, bleak-looking island; or, more properly, its position was discernible through the wilderness of surge in which it was enveloped.

3. Or, Lofoten, an island group, off the northwest coast of Norway, located within the Arctic Circle. The narrator and the fisherman are on an actual promontory nearly 2,000 feet high.
4. The account that follows is from Jacob Bryant's *Antient Mythology* (3rd ed., 1807). Bryant refers to the "Nubian geographer," al Idrisi, who wrote the *Geographia nubiensis*. Poe also refers to al Idrisi in "Eleonora," "Mellonta Tauta," and *Eureka*. This geographer consistently uses the phrase "Mare Tenebrarum" (Sea of Darkness) for the Atlantic Ocean.

About two miles nearer the land, arose another of smaller size, hideously craggy and barren, and encompassed at various intervals by a cluster of dark rocks.

The appearance of the ocean, in the space between the more distant island and the shore, had something very unusual about it. Although, at the time, so strong a gale was blowing landward that a brig in the remote offing lay to under a double-reefed trysail, and constantly plunged her whole hull out of sight, still there was here nothing like a regular swell, but only a short, quick, angry cross dashing of water in every direction—as well in the teeth of the wind as otherwise. Of foam there was little except in the immediate vicinity of the rocks.

"The island in the distance," resumed the old man, "is called by the Norwegians Vurrgh. The one midway is Moskoe. That a mile to the northward is Ambaaren. Yonder are Islesen, Hotholm, Keildhelm, Suarven, and Buckholm. Farther off—between Moskoe and Vurrgh—are Otterholm, Flimen, Sandflesen, and Stockholm.[5] These are the true names of the places—but why it has been thought necessary to name them at all, is more than either you or I can understand. Do you hear any thing? Do you see any change in the water?"

We had now been about ten minutes upon the top of Helseggen, to which we had ascended from the interior of Lofoden, so that we had caught no glimpse of the sea until it had burst upon us from the summit. As the old man spoke, I became aware of a loud and gradually increasing sound, like the moaning of a vast herd of buffaloes upon an American prairie; and at the same moment I perceived that what seamen term the *chopping* character of the ocean beneath us, was rapidly changing into a current which set to the eastward. Even while I gazed, this current acquired a monstrous velocity. Each moment added to its speed—to its headlong impetuosity. In five minutes the whole sea, as far as Vurrgh, was lashed into ungovernable fury; but it was between Moskoe and the coast that the main uproar held its sway. Here the vast bed of the waters, seamed and scarred into a thousand conflicting channels, burst suddenly into phrensied convulsion—heaving, boiling, hissing—gyrating in gigantic and innumerable vortices, and all whirling and plunging on to the eastward with a rapidity which water never elsewhere assumes except in precipitous descents.

In a few minutes more, there came over the scene another radical alteration. The general surface grew somewhat more smooth, and the whirlpools, one by one, disappeared, while prodigious streaks of foam became apparent where none had been seen before. These streaks, at length, spreading out to a great distance, and entering into combination, took unto themselves the gyratory motion of the subsided vortices, and seemed to form the germ of another more vast. Suddenly—very suddenly—this assumed a distinct and definite existence, in a circle of more than a mile in diameter. The edge of the whirl was represented by a broad belt of gleaming spray; but no particle of this slipped into the mouth of the terrific funnel, whose interior, as far as

5. All of the islands mentioned are part of the Lofoten group.

the eye could fathom it, was a smooth, shining, and jet-black wall of water, inclined to the horizon at an angle of some forty-five degrees, speeding dizzily round and round with a swaying and sweltering motion, and sending forth to the winds an appalling voice, half shriek, half roar, such as not even the mighty cataract of Niagara ever lifts up in its agony to Heaven.

The mountain trembled to its very base, and the rock rocked. I threw myself upon my face, and clung to the scant herbage in an excess of nervous agitation.

"This," said I at length, to the old man—"this *can* be nothing else than the great whirlpool of the Maelström."

"So it is sometimes termed," said he. "We Norwegians call it the Moskoe-ström, from the island of Moskoe in the midway."

The ordinary accounts of this vortex had by no means prepared me for what I saw. That of Jonas Ramus,[6] which is perhaps the most circumstantial of any, cannot impart the faintest conception either of the magnificence, or of the horror of the scene—or of the wild bewildering sense of *the novel* which confounds the beholder. I am not sure from what point of view the writer in question surveyed it, nor at what time; but it could neither have been from the summit of Helseggen, nor during a storm. There are some passages of his description, nevertheless, which may be quoted for their details, although their effect is exceedingly feeble in conveying an impression of the spectacle.

"Between Lofoden and Moskoe," he says, "the depth of the water is between thirty-six and forty fathoms; but on the other side, toward Ver (Vurrgh) this depth decreases so as not to afford a convenient passage for a vessel, without the risk of splitting on the rocks, which happens even in the calmest weather. When it is flood, the stream runs up the country between Lofoden and Moskoe with a boisterous rapidity; but the roar of its impetuous ebb to the sea is scarce equalled by the loudest and most dreadful cataracts; the noise being heard several leagues off, and the vortices or pits are of such an extent and depth, that if a ship comes within its attraction, it is inevitably absorbed and carried down to the bottom, and there beat to pieces against the rocks; and when the water relaxes, the fragments thereof are thrown up again. But these intervals of tranquillity are only at the turn of the ebb and flood and in calm weather, and last but a quarter of an hour, its violence gradually returning. When the stream is most boisterous, and its fury heightened by a storm, it is dangerous to come within a Norway mile[7] of it. Boats, yachts, and ships have been carried away by not guarding against it before they were within its reach. It likewise happens frequently, that whales come too near the stream, and are overpowered by its violence; and then it is impossible to describe their howlings and bellowings in their fruitless struggles to disengage

6. Ramus (1649–1718) wrote *Ulysses et Otinus Unus & idem sive Disquisitio & Historica Geographica* (1702), in which he proposes that Odysseus (Ulysses) had his adventure with Scylla and Charybdis (a giant whirlpool and clashing rocks in the *Odyssey*) in the Maelström off the Norwegian coast. Levine suggests that Poe took his account from the *Britannica*, which had copied a natural history of Norway.
7. Equal to approximately 4.5 miles.

themselves. A bear once, attempting to swim from Lofoden to Moskoe, was caught by the stream and borne down, while he roared terribly, so as to be heard on shore. Large stocks of firs and pine trees, after being absorbed by the current, rise again broken and torn to such a degree as if bristles grew upon them. This plainly shows the bottom to consist of craggy rocks, among which they are whirled to and fro. This stream is regulated by the flux and reflux of the sea—it being constantly high and low water every six hours. In the year 1645, early in the morning of Sexagesima Sunday,[8] it raged with such noise and impetuosity that the very stones of the houses on the coast fell to the ground."

In regard to the depth of the water, I could not see how this could have been ascertained at all in the immediate vicinity of the vortex. The "forty fathoms" must have reference only to portions of the channel close upon the shore either of Moskoe or Lofoden. The depth in the centre of the Moskoe-ström must be immeasurably greater; and no better proof of this fact is necessary than can be obtained from even the sidelong glance into the abyss of the whirl which may be had from the highest crag of Helseggen. Looking down from this pinnacle upon the howling Phlegethon[9] below, I could not help smiling at the simplicity with which the honest Jonas Ramus records, as a matter difficult of belief, the anecdotes of the whales and the bears; for it appeared to me, in fact, a self-evident thing, that the largest ship of the line in existence, coming within the influence of that deadly attraction, could resist it as little as a feather the hurricane, and must disappear bodily and at once.

The attempts to account for the phenomenon—some of which, I remember, seemed to me sufficiently plausible in perusal—now wore a very different and unsatisfactory aspect. The idea generally received is that this, as well as three smaller vortices among the Ferroe islands,[1] "have no other cause than the collision of waves rising and falling, at flux and reflux, against a ridge of rocks and shelves, which confines the water so that it precipitates itself like a cataract; and thus the higher the flood rises, the deeper must the fall be, and the natural result of all is a whirlpool or vortex, the prodigious suction of which is sufficiently known by lesser experiments."—These are the words of the Encyclopædia Britannica. Kircher[2] and others imagine that in the centre of the channel of the Maelström is an abyss penetrating the globe, and issuing in some very remote part—the Gulf of Bothnia being somewhat decidedly named in one instance. This opinion, idle in itself, was the one to which, as I gazed, my imagination most readily assented; and, mentioning it to the guide, I was rather surprised to hear him say that, although it was the view almost universally enter-

8. The second Sunday before Lent.
9. Fiery river in Hades.
1. Located between Iceland and northern Scotland.
2. According to Mabbott, Pontoppidan (London, 1755) states that Athanasius Kircher (1602–1680) asserted the Maelström was "a sea-vortex, attracting the flood under the shore of Norway, where, through another abyss, it is discharged into the gulph of Bothnia." Cf. the theory of "polar holes" through which the oceans circulate in *Narrative of Arthur Gordon Pym*, pp. 429–31 herein. Located between Sweden and Finland, the Gulf of Bothnia is an opening of the Baltic Sea.

tained of the subject by the Norwegians, it nevertheless was not his own. As to the former notion he confessed his inability to comprehend it; and here I agreed with him—for, however conclusive on paper, it becomes altogether unintelligible, and even absurd, amid the thunder of the abyss.

"You have had a good look at the whirl now," said the old man, "and if you will creep round this crag, so as to get in its lee, and deaden the roar of the water, I will tell you a story that will convince you I ought to know something of the Moskoe-ström."

I placed myself as desired, and he proceeded.

"Myself and my two brothers once owned a schooner-rigged smack[3] of about seventy tons burthen, with which we were in the habit of fishing among the islands beyond Moskoe, nearly to Vurrgh. In all violent eddies at sea there is good fishing, at proper opportunities, if one has only the courage to attempt it; but among the whole of the Lofoden coastmen, we three were the only ones who made a regular business of going out to the islands, as I tell you. The usual grounds are a great way lower down to the southward. There fish can be got at all hours, without much risk, and therefore these places are preferred. The choice spots over here among the rocks, however, not only yield the finest variety, but in far greater abundance; so that we often got in a single day, what the more timid of the craft could not scrape together in a week. In fact, we made it a matter of desperate speculation—the risk of life standing instead of labor, and courage answering for capital.

"We kept the smack in a cove about five miles higher up the coast than this; and it was our practice, in fine weather, to take advantage of the fifteen minutes' slack to push across the main channel of the Moskoe-ström, far above the pool, and then drop down upon anchorage somewhere near Otterholm, or Sandflesen, where the eddies are not so violent as elsewhere. Here we used to remain until nearly time for slack-water again, when we weighed and made for home. We never set out upon this expedition without a steady side wind for going and coming—one that we felt sure would not fail us before our return—and we seldom made a mis-calculation upon this point. Twice, during six years, we were forced to stay all night at anchor on account of a dead calm, which is a rare thing indeed just about here; and once we had to remain on the grounds nearly a week, starving to death, owing to a gale which blew up shortly after our arrival, and made the channel too boisterous to be thought of. Upon this occasion we should have been driven out to sea in spite of everything, (for the whirlpools threw us round and round so violently, that, at length, we fouled our anchor and dragged it) if it had not been that we drifted into one of the innumerable cross currents—here to-day and gone to-morrow—which drove us under the lee of Flimen, where, by good luck, we brought up.

"I could not tell you the twentieth part of the difficulties we encountered 'on the grounds'—it is a bad spot to be in, even in good

3. A small sailing ship (such as a sloop or a cutter) used chiefly in coastal fishing.

weather—but we made shift always to run the gauntlet of the Moskoe-ström itself without accident; although at times my heart has been in my mouth when we happened to be a minute or so behind or before the slack. The wind sometimes was not as strong as we thought it at starting, and then we made rather less way than we could wish, while the current rendered the smack unmanageable. My eldest brother had a son eighteen years old, and I had two stout boys of my own. These would have been of great assistance at such times, in using the sweeps, as well as afterward in fishing—but, somehow, although we ran the risk ourselves, we had not the heart to let the young ones get into the danger—for, after all is said and done, it *was* a horrible danger and that is the truth.

"It is now within a few days of three years since what I am going to tell you occurred. It was on the tenth day of July, 18—, a day which the people of this part of the world will never forget—for it was one in which blew the most terrible hurricane that ever came out of the heavens. And yet all the morning, and indeed until late in the afternoon, there was a gentle and steady breeze from the south-west, while the sun shone brightly, so that the oldest seaman among us could not have foreseen what was to follow.

"The three of us—my two brothers and myself—had crossed over to the islands about two o'clock P.M., and had soon nearly loaded the smack with fine fish, which, we all remarked, were more plenty that day than we had ever known them. It was just seven, *by my watch*, when we weighed and started for home, so as to make the worst of the Ström at slack water, which we knew would be at eight.

"We set out with a fresh wind on our starboard quarter, and for some time spanked along at a great rate, never dreaming of danger, for indeed we saw not the slightest reason to apprehend it. All at once we were taken aback by a breeze from over Helseggen. This was most un-usual—something that had never happened to us before—and I began to feel a little uneasy, without exactly knowing why. We put the boat on the wind, but could make no headway at all for the eddies, and I was upon the point of proposing to return to the anchorage, when, looking astern, we saw the whole horizon covered with a singular copper-colored cloud that rose with the most amazing velocity.

"In the meantime the breeze that had headed us off fell away, and we were dead becalmed, drifting about in every direction. This state of things, however, did not last long enough to give us time to think about it. In less than a minute the storm was upon us—in less than two the sky was entirely overcast—and what with this and the driving spray, it became suddenly so dark that we could not see each other in the smack.

"Such a hurricane as then blew it is folly to attempt describing. The oldest seaman in Norway never experienced any thing like it. We had let our sails go by the run before it cleverly took us; but, at the first puff, both our masts went by the board as if they had been sawed off—the mainmast taking with it my youngest brother, who had lashed himself to it for safety.

"Our boat was the lightest feather of a thing that ever sat upon water. It had a complete flush deck, with only a small hatch near the bow, and this hatch it had always been our custom to batten down when about to cross the Ström, by way of precaution against the chopping seas. But for this circumstance we should have foundered at once—for we lay entirely buried for some moments. How my elder brother escaped destruction I cannot say, for I never had an opportunity of ascertaining. For my part, as soon as I had let the foresail run, I threw myself flat on deck, with my feet against the narrow gunwale of the bow, and with my hands grasping a ring-bolt near the foot of the foremast. It was mere instinct that prompted me to do this—which was undoubtedly the very best thing I could have done—for I was too much flurried to think.

"For some moments we were completely deluged, as I say, and all this time I held my breath, and clung to the bolt. When I could stand it no longer I raised myself upon my knees, still keeping hold with my hands, and thus got my head clear. Presently our little boat gave herself a shake, just as a dog does in coming out of the water, and thus rid herself, in some measure, of the seas. I was now trying to get the better of the stupor that had come over me, and to collect my senses so as to see what was to be done, when I felt somebody grasp my arm. It was my elder brother, and my heart leaped for joy, for I had made sure that he was overboard—but the next moment all this joy was turned into horror—for he put his mouth close to my ear, and screamed out the word '*Moskoe-ström!*'

"No one ever will know what my feelings were at that moment. I shook from head to foot as if I had had the most violent fit of the ague. I knew what he meant by that one word well enough—I knew what he wished to make me understand. With the wind that now drove us on, we were bound for the whirl of the Ström, and nothing could save us!

"You perceive that in crossing the Ström *channel*, we always went a long way up above the whirl, even in the calmest weather, and then had to wait and watch carefully for the slack—but now we were driving right upon the pool itself, and in such a hurricane as this! 'To be sure,' I thought, 'we shall get there just about the slack—there is some little hope in that'—but in the next moment I cursed myself for being so great a fool as to dream of hope at all. I knew very well that we were doomed, had we been ten times a ninety-gun ship.

"By this time the first fury of the tempest had spent itself, or perhaps we did not feel it so much, as we scudded before it, but at all events the seas, which at first had been kept down by the wind, and lay flat and frothing, now got up into absolute mountains. A singular change, too, had come over the heavens. Around in every direction it was still as black as pitch, but nearly overhead there burst out, all at once, a circular rift of clear sky—as clear as I ever saw—and of a deep bright blue—and through it there blazed forth the full moon with a lustre that I never before knew her to wear. She lit up every thing about us with the greatest distinctness—but, oh God, what a scene it was to light up!

"I now made one or two attempts to speak to my brother—but, in some manner which I could not understand, the din had so increased that I could not make him hear a single word, although I screamed at the top of my voice in his ear. Presently he shook his head, looking as pale as death, and held up one of his fingers, as if to say '*listen!*'

"At first I could not make out what he meant—but soon a hideous thought flashed upon me. I dragged my watch from its fob. It was not going. I glanced at its face by the moonlight, and then burst into tears as I flung it far away into the ocean. *It had run down at seven o'clock! We were behind the time of the slack, and the whirl of the Ström was in full fury!*

"When a boat is well built, properly trimmed, and not deep laden, the waves in a strong gale, when she is going large, seem always to slip from beneath her—which appears very strange to a landsman—and this is what is called *riding*, in sea phrase. Well, so far we had ridden the swells very cleverly; but presently a gigantic sea happened to take us right under the counter, and bore us with it as it rose—up—up—as if into the sky. I would not have believed that any wave could rise so high. And then down we came with a sweep, a slide, and a plunge, that made me feel sick and dizzy, as if I was falling from some lofty mountain-top in a dream. But while we were up I had thrown a quick glance around—and that one glance was all sufficient. I saw our exact position in an instant. The Moskoe-ström whirlpool was about a quarter of a mile dead ahead—but no more like the every-day Moskoe-ström, than the whirl as you now see it is like a mill-race. If I had not known where we were, and what we had to expect, I should not have recognised the place at all. As it was, I involuntarily closed my eyes in horror. The lids clenched themselves together as if in a spasm.

"It could not have been more than two minutes afterward until we suddenly felt the waves subside, and were enveloped in foam. The boat made a sharp half turn to larboard, and then shot off in its new direction like a thunderbolt. At the same moment the roaring noise of the water was completely drowned in a kind of shrill shriek—such a sound as you might imagine given out by the waste-pipes of many thousand steam-vessels, letting off their steam all together. We were now in the belt of surf that always surrounds the whirl; and I thought, of course, that another moment would plunge us into the abyss—down which we could only see indistinctly on account of the amazing velocity with which we were borne along. The boat did not seem to sink into the water at all, but to skim like an air-bubble upon the surface of the surge. Her starboard side was next the whirl, and on the starboard arose the world of ocean we had left. It stood like a huge writhing wall between us and the horizon.

"It may appear strange, but now, when we were in the very jaws of the gulf, I felt more composed than when we were only approaching it. Having made up my mind to hope no more, I got rid of a great deal of that terror which unmanned me at first. I suppose it was despair that strung my nerves.

"It may look like boasting—but what I tell you is truth—I began to

reflect how magnificent a thing it was to die in such a manner, and how foolish it was in me to think of so paltry a consideration as my own individual life, in view of so wonderful a manifestation of God's power. I do believe that I blushed with shame when this idea crossed my mind. After a little while I became possessed with the keenest curiosity about the whirl itself. I positively felt a *wish* to explore its depths, even at the sacrifice I was going to make; and my principal grief was that I should never be able to tell my old companions on shore about the mysteries I should see. These, no doubt, were singular fancies to occupy a man's mind in such extremity—and I have often thought since, that the revolutions of the boat around the pool might have rendered me a little light-headed.

"There was another circumstance which tended to restore my self-possession; and this was the cessation of the wind, which could not reach us in our present situation—for, as you saw yourself, the belt of surf is considerably lower than the general bed of the ocean, and this latter now towered above us, a high, black, mountainous ridge. If you have never been at sea in a heavy gale, you can form no idea of the confusion of mind occasioned by the wind and spray together. They blind, deafen, and strangle you, and take away all power of action or reflection. But we were now, in a great measure, rid of these annoyances—just as death condemned felons in prison are allowed petty indulgences, forbidden them while their doom is yet uncertain.

"How often we made the circuit of the belt it is impossible to say. We careered round and round for perhaps an hour, flying rather than floating, getting gradually more and more into the middle of the surge, and then nearer and nearer to its horrible inner edge. All this time I had never let go of the ring-bolt. My brother was at the stern, holding on to a small empty water-cask which had been securely lashed under the coop of the counter, and was the only thing on deck that had not been swept overboard when the gale first took us. As we approached the brink of the pit he let go his hold upon this, and made for the ring, from which, in the agony of his terror, he endeavored to force my hands, as it was not large enough to afford us both a secure grasp. I never felt deeper grief than when I saw him attempt this act—although I knew he was a madman when he did it—a raving maniac through sheer fright. I did not care, however, to contest the point with him. I knew it could make no difference whether either of us held on at all; so I let him have the bolt, and went astern to the cask. This there was no great difficulty in doing; for the smack flew round steadily enough, and upon an even keel—only swaying to and fro, with the immense sweeps and swelters of the whirl. Scarcely had I secured myself in my new position, when we gave a wild lurch to starboard, and rushed headlong into the abyss. I muttered a hurried prayer to God, and thought all was over.

"As I felt the sickening sweep of the descent. I had instinctively tightened my hold upon the barrel, and closed my eyes. For some seconds I dared not open them—while I expected instant destruction, and wondered that I was not already in my death-struggles with the water.

But moment after moment elapsed. I still lived. The sense of falling had ceased; and the motion of the vessel seemed much as it had been before, while in the belt of foam, with the exception that she now lay more along. I took courage, and looked once again upon the scene.

"Never shall I forget the sensations of awe, horror, and admiration with which I gazed about me. The boat appeared to be hanging, as if by magic, midway down, upon the interior surface of a funnel vast in circumference, prodigious in depth, and whose perfectly smooth sides might have been mistaken for ebony, but for the bewildering rapidity with which they spun around, and for the gleaming and ghastly radiance they shot forth, as the rays of the full moon, from that circular rift amid the clouds which I have already described, streamed in a flood of golden glory along the black walls, and far away down into the inmost recesses of the abyss.

"At first I was too much confused to observe anything accurately. The general burst of terrific grandeur was all that I beheld. When I recovered myself a little, however, my gaze fell instinctively downward. In this direction I was able to obtain an unobstructed view, from the manner in which the smack hung on the inclined surface of the pool. She was quite upon an even keel—that is to say, her deck lay in a plane parallel with that of the water—but this latter sloped at an angle of more than forty-five degrees, so that we seemed to be lying upon our beam-ends. I could not help observing, nevertheless, that I had scarcely more difficulty in maintaining my hold and footing in this situation, than if we had been upon a dead level; and this, I suppose, was owing to the speed at which we revolved.

"The rays of the moon seemed to search the very bottom of the profound gulf; but still I could make out nothing distinctly, on account of a thick mist in which everything there was enveloped, and over which there hung a magnificent rainbow, like that narrow and tottering bridge which Mussulmen[4] say is the only pathway between Time and Eternity. This mist, or spray, was no doubt occasioned by the clashing of the great walls of the funnel, as they all met together at the bottom—but the yell that went up to the Heavens from out of that mist, I dare not attempt to describe.

"Our first slide into the abyss itself, from the belt of foam above, had carried us a great distance down the slope; but our farther descent was by no means proportionate. Round and round we swept—not with any uniform movement—but in dizzying swings and jerks, that sent us sometimes only a few hundred yards—sometimes nearly the complete circuit of the whirl. Our progress downward, at each revolution, was slow, but very perceptible.

"Looking about me upon the wide waste of liquid ebony on which we were thus borne, I perceived that our boat was not the only object in the embrace of the whirl. Both above and below us were visible fragments of vessels, large masses of building timber and trunks of trees, with many smaller articles, such as pieces of house furniture,

4. Muslims.

broken boxes, barrels and staves. I have already described the unnatu-
ral curiosity which had taken the place of my original terrors. It ap-
peared to grow upon me as I drew nearer and nearer to my dreadful
doom. I now began to watch, with a strange interest, the numerous
things that floated in our company. I *must* have been delirious—for I
even sought *amusement* in speculating upon the relative velocities of
their several descents toward the foam below. 'This fir tree,' I found
myself at one time saying, 'will certainly be the next thing that takes
the awful plunge and disappears,'—and then I was disappointed to
find that the wreck of a Dutch merchant ship overtook it and went
down before. At length, after making several guesses of this nature,
and being deceived in all—this fact—the fact of my invariable miscal-
culation—set me upon a train of reflection that made my limbs again
tremble, and my heart beat heavily once more.

"It was not a new terror that thus affected me, but the dawn of a
more exciting *hope*. This hope arose partly from memory, and partly
from present observation. I called to mind the great variety of buoyant
matter that strewed the coast of Lofoden, having been absorbed and
then thrown forth by the Moskoe-ström. By far the greater number of
the articles were shattered in the most extraordinary way—so chafed
and roughened as to have the appearance of being stuck full of splin-
ters—but then I distinctly recollected that there were *some* of them
which were not disfigured at all. Now I could not account for this dif-
ference except by supposing that the roughened fragments were the
only ones which had been *completely absorbed*—that the others had
entered the whirl at so late a period of the tide, or, for some reason,
had descended so slowly after entering, that they did not reach the
bottom before the turn of the flood came, or of the ebb, as the case
might be. I conceived it possible, in either instance, that they might
thus be whirled up again to the level of the ocean, without undergoing
the fate of those which had been drawn in more early, or absorbed
more rapidly. I made, also, three important observations. The first was,
that, as a general rule, the larger the bodies were, the more rapid their
descent—the second, that, between two masses of equal extent, the
one spherical, and the other *of any other shape*, the superiority in
speed of descent was with the sphere—the third, that, between two
masses of equal size, the one cylindrical and the other of any other
shape, the cylinder was absorbed the more slowly. Since my escape, I
have had several conversations on this subject with an old school-
master of the district; and it was from him that I learned the use of the
words 'cylinder' and 'sphere.' He explained to me—although I have for-
gotten the explanation—how what I observed was, in fact, the natural
consequence of the forms of the floating fragments—and showed me
how it happened that a cylinder, swimming in a vortex, offered more
resistance to its suction, and was drawn in with greater difficulty than
an equally bulky body, of any form whatever.[5]

5. See Archimedes, *De Incidentibus in Fluido.*—lib. 2 [Poe's note]. Archimedes (c. 287–212
 B.C.E.), a Greek mathematician and practical scientist, is most famous for one particular in-
 cident. Having noticed that the volume of water displaced by his body in his bath contained

"There was one startling circumstance which went a great way in enforcing these observations, and rendering me anxious to turn them to account, and this was that, at every revolution, we passed something like a barrel, or else the yard or the mast of a vessel, while many of these things, which had been on our level when I first opened my eyes upon the wonders of the whirlpool, were now high up above us, and seemed to have moved but little from their original station.

"I no longer hesitated what to do. I resolved to lash myself securely to the water cask upon which I now held, to cut it loose from the counter, and to throw myself with it into the water. I attracted my brother's attention by signs, pointed to the floating barrels that came near us, and did everything in my power to make him understand what I was about to do. I thought at length that he comprehended my design—but, whether this was the case or not, he shook his head despairingly, and refused to move from his station by the ring-bolt. It was impossible to reach him; the emergency admitted of no delay; and so, with a bitter struggle, I resigned him to his fate, fastened myself to the cask by means of the lashings which secured it to the counter, and precipitated myself with it into the sea, without another moment's hesitation.

"The result was precisely what I had hoped it might be. As it is myself who now tell you this tale—as you see that I *did* escape—and as you are already in posession of the mode in which this escape was effected, and must therefore anticipate all that I have farther to say—I will bring my story quickly to conclusion. It might have been an hour, or thereabout, after my quitting the smack, when, having descended to a vast distance beneath me, it made three or four wild gyrations in rapid succession, and, bearing my loved brother with it, plunged headlong, at once and forever, into the chaos of foam below. The barrel to which I was attached sunk very little farther than half the distance between the bottom of the gulf and the spot at which I leaped overboard, before a great change took place in the character of the whirlpool. The slope of the sides of the vast funnel became momently less and less steep. The gyrations of the whirl grew, gradually, less and less violent. By degrees, the froth and the rainbow disappeared, and the bottom of the gulf seemed slowly to uprise. The sky was clear, the winds had gone down, and the full moon was setting radiantly in the west, when I found myself on the surface of the ocean, in full view of the shores of Lofoden, and above the spot where the pool of the Moskoe-ström *had been*. It was the hour of the slack—but the sea still heaved in mountainous waves from the effects of the hurricane. I was borne violently into the channel of the Ström, and in a few minutes was hurried down the coast into the 'grounds' of the fishermen. A boat picked me up—exhausted from fatigue—and (now that the danger was removed) speechless from the memory of its horror. Those who drew me on

the key to a mathematical problem he was grappling with, he ran naked through the streets shouting "Eureka!" (I have found it!). Note the name of Poe's treatise on the universe, *Eureka* (1848). But no references to how the objects in the present story react in water have been found in the ambiguously titled work cited by Poe.

board were my old mates and daily companions—but they knew me no more than they would have known a traveller from the spirit-land. My hair which had been raven-black the day before, was as white as you see it now. They say too that the whole expression of my countenance had changed. I told them my story—they did not believe it. I now tell it to *you*—and I can scarcely expect you to put more faith in it than did the merry fishermen of Lofoden."

The Colloquy of Monos and Una[1]

Μελλοντα ταυτα

Sophocles—Antig:

These things are in the future.[2]

Una. "Born again?"[3]

Monos. Yes, fairest and best beloved Una, "born again." These were the words upon whose mystical meaning I had so long pondered, rejecting the explanations of the priesthood, until Death himself resolved for me the secret.

Una. Death!

Monos. How strangely, sweet Una, you echo my words! I observe, too, a vacillation in your step—a joyous inquietude in your eyes. You are confused and oppressed by the majestic novelty of the Life Eternal. Yes, it was of Death I spoke. And here how singularly sounds that word which of old was wont to bring terror to all hearts—throwing a mildew upon all pleasures!

Una. Ah, Death, the spectre which sate at all feasts! How often, Monos, did we lose ourselves in speculations upon its nature! How mysteriously did it act as a check to human bliss—saying unto it "thus far, and no farther!" That earnest mutual love, my own Monos, which burned within our bosoms—how vainly did we flatter ourselves, feeling happy in its first upspringing, that our happiness would strengthen with its strength! Alas! as it grew, so grew in our hearts the dread of that evil hour which was hurrying to separate us forever! Thus, in time, it became painful to love. Hate would have been mercy then.

Monos. Speak not here of these griefs, dear Una—mine, mine forever now!

Una. But the memory of past sorrow—is it not present joy? I have much to say yet of the things which have been. Above all, I burn to

1. First published in *Graham's Magazine* (August 1841). The text reprinted here is from *Tales* (1845). The names are the Greek masculine ("Monos") and the feminine Latin ("Una") for *one*. See notes to "Silence" (pp. 136ff., herein). "Colloquy": a conversation.
2. The Greek, from the *Antigone* of Sophocles (c. 496–406 B.C.E.), translates as given.
3. John 3:3: "Except a man be born again, he cannot see the kingdom of God." Mabbott identifies in this tale what he considers other echoes of the New Testament, along with allusions to Genesis, Job, the *Aeneid*, Shakespeare's *Hamlet*, Milton's *Paradise Lost*, Pope's "Essay on Man," D'Israeli's *Curiosities of Literature*, Bulwer-Lytton's *Rienzi*, and other works. But many of these echoes are rather faint.

know the incidents of your own passage through the dark Valley and Shadow.[4]

Monos. And when did the radiant Una ask anything of her Monos in vain? I will be minute in relating all—but at what point shall the weird narrative begin?

Una. At what point?

Monos. You have said.

Una. Monos, I comprehend you. In Death we have both learned the propensity of man to define the indefinable. I will not say, then, commence with the moment of life's cessation—but commence with that sad, sad instant when, the fever having abandoned you, you sank into a breathless and motionless torpor, and I pressed down your pallid eyelids with the passionate fingers of love.

Monos. One word first, my Una, in regard to man's general condition at this epoch. You will remember that one or two of the wise among our forefathers—wise in fact, although not in the world's esteem—had ventured to doubt the propriety of the term "improvement," as applied to the progress of our civilization. There were periods in each of the five or six centuries immediately preceding our dissolution, when arose some vigorous intellect, boldly contending for those principles whose truth appears now, to our disenfranchised reason, so utterly obvious—principles which should have taught our race to submit to the guidance of the natural laws, rather than attempt their control. At long intervals some master-minds appeared, looking upon each advance in practical science as a retro-gradation in the true utility. Occasionally the poetic intellect—that intellect which we now feel to have been the most exalted of all—since those truths which to us were of the most enduring importance could only be reached by that *analogy* which speaks in proof-tones to the imagination alone, and to the unaided reason bears no weight—occasionally did this poetic intellect proceed a step farther in the evolving of the vague idea of the philosophic, and find in the mystic parable that tells of the tree of knowledge, and of its forbidden fruit, death-producing, a distinct intimation that knowledge was not meet for man in the infant condition of his soul. And these men—the poets—living and perishing amid the scorn of the "utilitarians"[5]—of rough pedants, who arrogated to themselves a title which could have been properly applied only to the scorned—these men, the poets, pondered piningly, yet not unwisely, upon the ancient days when our wants were not more simple than our enjoyments were keen—days when *mirth* was a word unknown, so solemnly deep-toned was happiness—holy, august and blissful days, when blue rivers ran undammed, between hills unhewn, into far forest solitudes, primæval, odorous, and unexplored.

Yet these noble exceptions from the general misrule served but to

4. Psalm 23: "Yea, though I walk through the valley of the shadow of death, I will fear no evil."
5. Jeremy Bentham (1748–1832), English social theorist, formulated in his *Introduction to the Principles of Morals and Legislation* (1789) the principle of utility, whereby a beneficial social action is measured by its overall tendency to promote the greatest happiness for the greatest number of people.

strengthen it by opposition. Alas! we had fallen upon the most evil of all our evil days. The great "movement"—that was the cant term— went on: a diseased commotion, moral and physical. Art—the Arts— arose supreme, and, once enthroned, cast chains upon the intellect which had elevated them to power. Man, because he could not but ac- knowledge the majesty of Nature, fell into childish exultation at his acquired and still-increasing dominion over her elements. Even while he stalked a God in his own fancy, an infantine imbecility came over him. As might be supposed from the origin of his disorder, he grew in- fected with system, and with abstraction. He enwrapped himself in generalities. Among other odd ideas, that of universal equality gained ground; and in the face of analogy and of God—in despite of the loud warning voice of the laws of *gradation* so visibly pervading all things in Earth and Heaven—wild attempts at an omni-prevalent Democracy were made. Yet this evil sprang necessarily from the leading evil, Knowledge. Man could not both know and succumb.[6] Meantime huge smoking cities arose, innumerable. Green leaves shrank before the hot breath of furnaces. The fair face of Nature was deformed as with the ravages of some loathsome disease. And methinks, sweet Una, even our slumbering sense of the forced and of the far-fetched might have arrested us here. But now it appears that we had worked out our own destruction in the perversion of our *taste*, or rather in the blind ne- glect of its culture in the schools. For, in truth, it was at this crisis that taste alone—that faculty which, holding a middle position between the pure intellect and the moral sense, could never safely have been disregarded—it was now that taste alone[7] could have led us gently back to Beauty, to Nature, and to Life. But alas for the pure contem- plative spirit and majestic intuition of Plato! Alas for the μουσικη which he justly regarded as an all-sufficient education for the soul! Alas for him and for it!—since both were most desperately needed when both were most entirely forgotten or despised.[8]

Pascal, a philosopher whom we both love, has said, how truly!— *"que tout notre raisonnement se rèduit à cèder au sentiment;"*[9] and it is not impossible that the sentiment of the natural, had time permitted

6. The sense would seem to indicate that a second *not* has been dropped before *succumb*.
7. Based on the formulation of Immanuel Kant (1724–1804), who maintained that taste (aes- thetics) is the interface between the understanding (intellectual knowledge) and the moral sense (virtue, ethics). See the introduction to Transcendentalism and Alternative Romanti- cism, herein.
8. "It will be hard to discover a better [method of education] than that which the experience of so many ages has already discovered; and this may be summed up as consisting in gymnas- tics for the body, and *music* for the soul."—Repub. lib. 2. "For this reason is a musical edu- cation most essential; since it causes Rhythm and Harmony to penetrate most intimately into the soul, taking the strongest hold upon it, filling it with *beauty* and making the man *beautiful-minded*. . . . He will praise and admire *the beautiful*; will receive it with joy into his soul, will feed upon it, and *assimilate his own condition with it.*—Ibid. lib. 3. Music (μουσικη) had, however, among the Athenians, a far more comprehensive signification than with us. It included not only the harmonies of time and of tune, but the poetic diction, sen- timent and creation, each in its widest sense. The study of *music* was with them, in fact, the general cultivation of the taste—of that which recognizes the beautiful—in contra- distinction from reason, which deals only with the true [Poe's note]. The quotations are from Plato's *Republic*, books II and III.
9. That all our reasoning reduces itself to giving way to sentiment (French). From Blaise Pas- cal (1623–1662), *Pensées* (Thoughts), VII. 4. *Sentiment* here in the sense of feeling or intu- ition.

it, would have regained its old ascendancy over the harsh mathematical reason of the schools. But this thing was not to be. Prematurely induced by intemperance of knowledge, the old age of the world drew on. This the mass of mankind saw not, or, living lustily although unhappily, affected not to see. But, for myself, the Earth's records had taught me to look for widest ruin as the price of highest civilization. I had imbibed a prescience of our Fate from comparison of China the simple and enduring, with Assyria the architect, with Egypt the astrologer, with Nubia, more crafty than either, the turbulent mother of all Arts.[1] In history[2] of these regions I met with a ray from the Future. The individual artificialities of the three latter[3] were local diseases of the Earth, and in their individual overthrows we had seen local remedies applied; but for the infected world at large I could anticipate no regeneration save in death. That man, as a race, should not become extinct, I saw that he must be "*born again*."[4]

And now it was, fairest and dearest, that we wrapped our spirits, daily, in dreams. Now it was that, in twilight, we discoursed of the days to come, when the Art-scarred surface of the Earth, having undergone that purification[5] which alone could efface its rectangular obscenities, should clothe itself anew in the verdure and the mountain-slopes and the smiling waters of Paradise, and be rendered at length a fit dwelling-place for man:—for man the Death-purged—for man to whose now exalted intellect there should be poison in knowledge no more—for the redeemed, regenerated, blissful, and now immortal, but still for the *material*, man.

Una. Well do I remember these conversations, dear Monos; but the epoch of the fiery overthrow was not so near at hand as we believed, and as the corruption you indicate did surely warrant us in believing. Men lived; and died individually. You yourself sickened, and passed into the grave; and thither your constant Una speedily followed you. And though the century which has since elapsed, and whose conclusion brings us thus together once more, tortured our slumbering senses with no impatience of duration, yet, my Monos, it was a century still.

Monos. Say, rather, a point in the vague infinity. Unquestionably, it was in the Earth's dotage[6] that I died. Wearied at heart with anxieties which had their origin in the general turmoil and decay, I succumbed to the fierce fever. After some few days of pain, and many of dreamy delirium replete with ecstasy, the manifestations of which you mistook for pain; while I longed but was impotent to undeceive you—after

1. "Astrologer": see notes to "Shadow" (pp. 134ff.) "Ligeia" (pp. 159ff.) and "The Fall of the House of Usher" (pp. 199ff.). "Prescience": intuition, preknowledge.
2. "History," from ιστορειμ, to contemplate [Poe's note].
3. Mabbott notes the general impression of the day that the culture of Nubia/Ethiopia was older than that of Egypt and the others mentioned.
4. Although the phrase echoes the Christian doctrine of rebirth as a regenerate person, in this context it is the race of humankind that is to be reborn, not the individual.
5. The word *purification* seems here to be used with reference to its root in the Greek πυρ, fire [Poe's note]. "Art-scarred": probably a reference to the etymological root of the word *art*, meaning artificed, made, constructed, as instanced in the "rectangular obscenities," i.e., buildings.
6. Old age.

some days there came upon me, as you have said, a breathless and motionless torpor; and this was termed *Death* by those who stood around me.

Words are vague things. My condition did not deprive me of sentience.[7] It appeared to me not greatly dissimilar to the extreme quiescence of him, who, having slumbered long and profoundly, lying motionless and fully prostrate in a midsummer noon, begins to steal slowly back into consciousness, through the mere sufficiency of his sleep, and without being awakened by external disturbances.

I breathed no longer. The pulses were still. The heart had ceased to beat. Volition[8] had not departed, but was powerless. The senses were unusually active, although eccentrically so—assuming often each other's functions at random.[9] The taste and the smell were inextricably confounded, and became one sentiment, abnormal and intense. The rose-water with which your tenderness had moistened my lips to the last, affected me with sweet fancies of flowers—fantastic flowers, far more lovely than any of the old Earth, but whose prototypes we have here blooming around us. The eyelids, transparent and bloodless, offered no complete impediment to vision. As volition was in abeyance, the balls could not roll in their sockets—but all objects within the range of the visual hemisphere were seen with more or less distinctness; the rays which fell upon the external retina, or into the corner of the eye, producing a more vivid effect than those which struck the front or interior surface. Yet, in the former instance, this effect was so far anomalous that I appreciated it only as *sound*—sound sweet or discordant as the matters presenting themselves at my side were light or dark in shade—curved or angular in outline. The hearing, at the same time, although excited in degree, was not irregular in action—estimating real sounds with an extravagance of precision, not less than of sensibility. Touch had undergone a modification more peculiar. Its impressions wore tardily received, but pertinaciously[1] retained, and resulted always in the highest physical pleasure. Thus the pressure of your sweet fingers upon my eyelids, at first only recognised through vision, at length, long after their removal, filled my whole being with a sensual delight immeasurable. I say with a sensual delight. *All* my perceptions were purely sensual. The materials furnished the passive brain by the senses were not in the least degree wrought into shape by the deceased understanding. Of pain there was some little; of pleasure there was much; but of moral pain or pleasure none at all. Thus your wild sobs floated into my ear with all their mournful cadences and were appreciated in their every variation of sad tone; but they were soft musical sounds and no more; they conveyed to the extinct reason no intimation of the sorrows which gave them birth; while the large and constant tears which fell upon my face, telling the bystanders of a

7. Physical awareness; feeling.
8. Power of choosing, deciding, acting; will power.
9. The next several sentences literalize the metaphor of *synaesthesia*, the description of one kind of sense experience in terms of another (e.g., hearing color).
1. Persistently, holding firm.

heart which broke, thrilled every fibre of my frame with ecstasy alone. And this was in truth the *Death* of which these bystanders spoke reverently, in low whispers—you, sweet Una, gaspingly, with loud cries.

They attired me for the coffin—three or four dark figures which flitted busily to and fro. As these crossed the direct line of my vision they affected me as *forms*; but upon passing to my side their images impressed me with the idea of shrieks, groans, and other dismal expressions of terror, of horror, or of wo. You alone, habited in a white robe, passed in all directions musically about me.

The day waned; and, as its light faded away, I became possessed by a vague uneasiness—an anxiety such as the sleeper feels when sad real sounds fall continuously within his ear—low distant bell-tones, solemn, at long but equal intervals, and commingling with melancholy dreams. Night arrived; and with its shadows a heavy discomfort. It oppressed my limbs with the oppression of some dull weight, and was palpable. There was also a moaning sound, not unlike the distant reverberation of surf, but more continuous, which, beginning with the first twilight, had grown in strength with the darkness. Suddenly lights were brought into the room, and this reverberation became forthwith interrupted into frequent unequal bursts of the same sound, but less dreary and less distinct. The ponderous oppression was in a great measure relieved; and, issuing from the flame of each lamp, (for there were many,) there flowed unbrokenly into my ears a strain of melodious monotone. And when now, dear Una, approaching the bed upon which I lay outstretched, you sat gently by my side, breathing odor from your sweet lips, and pressing them upon my brow, there arose tremulously within my bosom, and mingling with the merely physical sensations which circumstances had called forth, a something akin to sentiment itself—a feeling that, half appreciating, half responded to your earnest love and sorrow; but this feeling took no root in the pulseless heart, and seemed indeed rather a shadow than a reality, and faded quickly away, first into extreme quiescence, and then into a purely sensual pleasure as before.

And now, from the wreck and the chaos of the usual senses, there appeared to have arisen within me a sixth, all perfect. In its exercise I found a wild delight—yet a delight still physical, inasmuch as the understanding had in it no part. Motion in the animal frame had fully ceased. No muscle quivered; no nerve thrilled; no artery throbbed. But there seemed to have sprung up in the brain, *that* of which no words could convey to the merely human intelligence even an indistinct conception. Let me term it a mental pendulous pulsation. It was the moral embodiment of man's abstract idea of *Time*. By the absolute equalization of this movement—or of such as this—had the cycles of the firmamental orbs themselves, been adjusted. By its aid I measured the irregularities of the clock upon the mantel, and of the watches of the attendants. Their tickings came sonorously to my ears. The slightest deviations from the true proportion—and these deviations were omniprævalent—affected me just as violations of abstract truth were wont,

on earth, to affect the moral sense. Although no two of the time-pieces in the chamber struck the individual seconds accurately together, yet I had no difficulty in holding steadily in mind the tones, and the respective momentary errors of each. And this—this keen, perfect, self-existing sentiment of *duration*—this sentiment existing (as man could not possibly have conceived it to exist) independently of any succession of events—this idea—this sixth sense, upspringing from the ashes of the rest, was the first obvious and certain step of the intemporal[2] soul upon the threshold of the temporal Eternity.

I was midnight; and you still sat by my side. All others had departed from the chamber of Death. They had deposited me in the coffin. The lamps burned flickeringly; for this I knew by the tremulousness of the monotonous strains. But, suddenly these strains diminished in distinctness and in volume. Finally they ceased. The perfume in my nostrils died away. Forms affected my vision no longer. The oppression of the Darkness uplifted itself from my bosom. A dull shock like that of electricity pervaded my frame, and was followed by total loss of the idea of contact. All of what man has termed sense was merged in the sole consciousness of entity, and in the one abiding sentiment of duration. The mortal body had been at length stricken with the hand of the deadly *Decay*.

Yet had not all of sentience departed; for the consciousness and the sentiment remaining supplied some of its functions by a lethargic intuition. I appreciated the direful change now in operation upon the flesh, and, as the dreamer is sometimes aware of the bodily presence of one who leans over him, so, sweet Una, I still dully felt that you sat by my side. So, too, when the noon of the second day came, I was not unconscious of those movements which displaced you from my side, which confined me within the coffin, which deposited me within the hearse, which bore me to the grave, which lowered me within it, which heaped heavily the mould upon me, and which thus left me, in blackness and corruption, to my sad and solemn slumbers with the worm.

And here, in the prison-house which has few secrets to disclose, there rolled away days and weeks and months; and the soul watched narrowly each second as it flew, and, without effort, took record of its flight—without effort and without object.

A year passed. The consciousness of *being* had grown hourly more indistinct, and that of mere *locality* had, in great measure, usurped its position. The idea of entity was becoming merged in that of *place*. The narrow space immediately surrounding what had been the body, was now growing to be the body itself. At length, as often happens to the sleeper (by sleep and its world alone is *Death* imaged)—at length, as sometimes happened on Earth to the deep slumberer, when some flitting light half startled him into awaking, yet left him half enveloped in dreams—so to me, in the strict embrace of the *Shadow*, came *that* light which alone might have had power to startle—the light of

2. Not subject to time. Cf. "Shadow."

enduring *Love*. Men toiled at the grave in which I lay darkling. They upthrew the damp earth. Upon my mouldering bones there descended the coffin of Una.

And now again all was void. That nebulous light had been extinguished. That feeble thrill had vibrated itself into quiescence. Many *lustra*[3] had supervened. Dust had returned to dust.[4] The worm had food no more. The sense of being had at length utterly departed, and there reigned in its stead—instead of all things—dominant and perpetual—the autocrats *Place* and *Time*. For *that* which *was not*—for that which had no form—for that which had no thought—for that which had no sentience—for that which was soulless, yet of which matter formed no portion—for all this nothingness, yet for all this immortality, the grave was still a home, and the corrosive hours, comates.

Never Bet the Devil Your Head[1]

A Tale with a Moral.

"*Con tal que las costumbres de un autor,*" says Don Thomas De Las Torres, in the preface to his "Amatory Poems" "*sean puras y castas, importo muy poco que no sean igualmente severas sus obras*"—meaning, in plain English, that, provided the morals of an author are pure, personally, it signifies nothing what are the morals of his books.[2] We presume that Don Thomas is now in Purgatory for the assertion. It would be a clever thing, too, in the way of poetical justice, to keep him there until his "Amatory Poems" get out of print, or are laid definitely upon the shelf through lack of readers. Every fiction *should have* a moral; and, what is more to the purpose, the critics have discovered that every fiction *has*.[3] Philip Melancthon, some time ago, wrote a commentary upon the "Batrachomyomachia" and proved that the poet's object was to excite a distaste for sedition. Pierre La Seine, going a step farther, shows that the intention was to recommend to young men temperance in eating and drinking. Just so, too, Jacobus Hugo has satisfied himself

3. A *lustrum* is a period of five years. The word comes from the ceremonial "purification" that ancient Romans undertook after each five-year census and is etymologically associated with the lustrous light of the moon.

4. Cf. "dust thou art, and unto dust shalt thou return" (Genesis 3:19).

1. First published in *Graham's* (September 1841) as "Never Bet Your Head," this "tale with a moral" is one of Poe's most vigorous attacks on the prevalence of didacticism in American literature, which was especially insisted on by New England writers. Mabbott speculates that a source is a passage in chapter 2 of Charles Dickens's *Pickwick Papers* (which Poe reviewed in the *Southern Literary Messenger* in November 1836), where a "loquacious stranger" warns Mr. Pickwick's party: "Heads, heads, take care of your heads," as they pass under a low archway, converted in Poe's story to an American covered bridge. The text reprinted here is that of the *Broadway Journal* (August 16, 1845).

2. "Torres": Probably Tomás Hermenegildo de Las Torres, author of *Cuentos en verso castellano* (1828). The sense of the Spanish may be more accurately rendered: "if it be that the [personal] habits an author are pure and chaste, it matters very little that his works may not be equally so strict."

3. Poe several times in his career observed that valuing a work of literature primarily for its moral was a heresy against art—the "heresy of the Didactic" (see, e.g., "The Poetic Principle"). For Poe, the artistic element was what was important and any moral instruction should exist only as a deep "undercurrent" (cf. p 287, n. 8 herein).

that, by Euenis, Homer meant to insinuate John Calvin; by Antinöus, Martin Luther; by the Lotophagi, Protestants in general; and, by the Harpies, the Dutch.[4] Our more modern Scholiasts,[5] are equally acute. These fellows demonstrate a hidden meaning in "The Antediluvians," a parable in "Powhatan," new views in "Cock Robin," and transcendentalism in "Hop O' My Thumb."[6] In short, it has been shown that no man can sit down to write without a very profound design. Thus to authors in general much trouble is spared. A novelist, for example, need have no care of his moral. It is there—that is to say it is somewhere—and the moral and the critics can take care of themselves. When the proper time arrives, all that the gentleman intended, and all that he did not intend, will be brought to light, in the "Dial," or the "Down-Easter,"[7] together with all that he ought to have intended, and the rest that he clearly meant to intend:—so that it will all come very straight in the end.

There is no just ground, therefore, for the charge brought against me by certain ignoramuses—that I have never written a moral tale, or, in more precise words, a tale with a moral. They are not the critics predestined to bring me out, and *develop* my morals:—that is the secret. By and by the "North American Quarterly Humdrum"[8] will make them ashamed of their stupidity. In the meantime, by way of staying execution—by way of mitigating the accusations against me—I offer the sad history appended;—a history about whose obvious moral there can be no question whatever, since he who runs may read it in the

4. Mabbott points out that these references come from H. N. Coleridge's *Introductions to the Study of the Classic Poets* (1831), a book Poe quotes from in his "Pinakidia" series of reader's notes in the *Southern Literary Messenger* in 1836. Philip Melancthon (1497–1560) was second only to Martin Luther (c. 1483–1546) as the most important of the new theological scholars of the Protestant Reformation. Coleridge reads his 1542 commentary on the *Batrachomyomachia* (The Battle of the Frogs and Mice), a Greek comic poem, as a moral tract against sedition (language or actions inciting defiance of official authority). But he notes that Pierre La Seine, or Pietro Lasena (died 1636), an Italian scholar of French descent, sees a different moral: a warning to young men about intemperance in eating and drinking. Jacobus Hugo (Jacques Hugues) in his *True History of Rome* (1655) sees several prefigurings of later history in Homer's *Iliad* and *Odyssey*. For Hugo, the Greek epic poet Homer was in the 9th century B.C.E. prophesying the advent in the 16th century C.E. of Jean Calvin (1509–1564), a French Protestant reformer. (Hugo's "Euenis" reference is unclear but may be to Evenus, who defeated suitors for his virgin daughter in a chariot race; the price was to have their heads cut off; see *Iliad*, IX.) For Hugo, Antinous, the most arrogant of the suitors for Queen Penelope's hand in the *Odyssey*, was Homer's anticipation of Martin Luther; and the Lotophagi, the "lotus eaters" of North Africa (*Odyssey*, Book IX), who drift into a state of forgetfulness after eating the plant, prefigured Lutheran Protestants in general. The Harpies, who in ancient Greek myth were ugly female creatures—part bird of prey and part human who tormented the souls of the departed—anticipated the Dutch as unpleasant carping Protestants. Poe's satiric point about reading into texts meanings that are patently not there and the practice of inane moral criticism is illustrated by these absurd examples.
5. Older commentators on classical texts.
6. The last is a fairy tale. *The Antediluvians, or the World Destroyed* (1839–40) is an epic narrative poem by the American writer James MacHenry. In the July 1841 issue of *Graham's*, Poe unfavorably reviewed *Powhatan: A Metrical Romance in Seven Cantos* by Seba Smith (Jack Downing). "Who Killed Cock Robin" is a nursery rhyme.
7. Most likely *The Yankee and Boston Literary Gazette* (elsewhere in Poe called "Down-East Review"), the editor of which, John Neal, wrote a novel called *The Down-Easters* (1833). *Down-East* is colloquial for the northern Atlantic coast region. "Dial": the principal Transcendentalist magazine (edited at different times by Ralph Waldo Emerson and Margaret Fuller), which Poe parodies in "How to Write a Blackwood Article" (pp. 173ff. herein) and other stories.
8. Probably the *North American Review*, which Poe satirizes elsewhere and criticizes for seeing literature as primarily an instrument for inculcating morality.

large capitals which form the title of the tale.[9] I should have credit for this arrangement—a far wiser one than that of La Fontaine[1] and others, who reserve the impression to be conveyed until the last moment, and thus sneak it in at the fag end of their fables.

Defuncti injuriâ ne afficiantur was a law of the twelve tables, and *De mortuis nil nisi bonum*[2] is an excellent injunction—even if the dead in question be nothing but dead small beer. It is not my design, therefore, to vituperate my deceased friend, Toby Dammit. He was a sad dog, it is true, and a dog's death[3] it was that he died; but he himself was not to blame for his vices. They grew out of a personal defect in his mother. She did her best in the way of flogging him while an infant—for duties to her well-regulated mind were always pleasures, and babies, like tough steaks, or the modern Greek olive trees, are invariably the better for beating—but, poor woman! she had the misfortune to be left-handed,[4] and a child flogged left-handedly had better be left unflogged. The world revolves from right to left. It will not do to whip a baby from left to right. If each blow in the proper direction drives an evil propensity out, it follows that every thump in an opposite one knocks its quota of wickedness in. I was often present at Toby's chastisements, and, even by the way in which he kicked, I could perceive that he was getting worse and worse every day. At last I saw, through the tears in my eyes, that there was no hope of the villain at all, and one day when he had been cuffed until he grew so black in the face that one might have mistaken him for a little African, and no effect had been produced beyond that of making him wriggle himself into a fit, I could stand it no longer, but went down upon my knees forthwith, and, uplifting my voice, made prophecy of his ruin.

The fact is that his precocity in vice was awful. At five months of age he used to get into such passions that he was unable to articulate. At six months, I caught him gnawing a pack of cards. At seven months he was in the constant habit of catching and kissing the female babies. At eight months he peremptorily refused to put his signature to the Temperance pledge.[5] Thus he went on increasing in iniquity, month after month, until, at the close of the first year, he not only insisted upon wearing *moustaches*, but had contracted a propensity for cursing and swearing, and for backing his assertions by bets.

9. One critic suggests that Poe's "tale" is a parodic fable, the chief character of which is a dog and that the title puns on "head" and "tail."
1. Jean de La Fontaine (1621–1695), author of *Fables choisies* (Selected fables: 1668–94), a collection of modern satiric verse tales based on the classical fable, which is traditionally an animal story illustrating a moral, as in Aesop's *Fables* (6th century B.C.E.).
2. *Defuncti injuriâ ne afficiantur*: let the dead suffer no injury (Latin). "Law of the twelve tables": early Roman law (actually the origin of the saying is not known). *De mortuis nil nisi bonum*: Of the dead nothing [should be said] but good (Latin). This maxim is said by Plutarch (46–c. 120 C.E.) to be one of the laws of Solon (c. 639–c. 559 B.C.E.), the founder of Athenean democracy. It is attributed by Diogenes Laertius (fl. early 3rd century C.E.) to an early Greek philosopher called Chilo.
3. A metaphor for a miserable, dishonorable death.
4. In heraldry, a lance or baton rising to the left is the sign of a bastard; see the last paragraph of the story (p. 295).
5. A promise that one would not consume alcoholic beverages. Temperance societies were on the rise in mid-19th-century America.

Through this latter most ungentlemanly practice, the ruin which I
had predicted to Toby Dammit overtook him at last. The fashion had
"grown with his growth and strengthened with his strength,"[6] so that,
when he came to be a man, he could scarcely utter a sentence without
interlarding it with a proposition to gamble. Not that he actually *laid*
wagers—no. I will do my friend the justice to say that he would as
soon have laid eggs. With him the thing was a mere formula—nothing
more. His expressions on this head had no meaning attached to them
whatever. They were simple if not altogether innocent expletives—
imaginative phrases wherewith to round off a sentence. When he said
"I'll bet you so and so," nobody ever thought of taking him up; but still
I could not help thinking it my duty to put him down. The habit was
an immoral one, and so I told him. It was a vulgar one—this I begged
him to believe. It was discountenanced by society—here I said nothing
but the truth. It was forbidden by act of Congress—here I had not the
slightest intention of telling a lie. I remonstrated—but to no purpose.
I demonstrated—in vain. I entreated—he smiled. I implored—he
laughed. I preached—he sneered. I threatened—he swore. I kicked
him—he called for the police. I pulled his nose—he blew it, and of-
fered to bet the Devil his head that I would not venture to try that ex-
periment again.

Poverty was another vice which the peculiar physical deficiency of
Dammit's mother had entailed upon her son. He was detestably poor;
and this was the reason, no doubt, that his expletive expressions about
betting, seldom took a pecuniary turn. I will not be bound to say that
I ever heard him make use of such a figure of speech as "I'll bet you a
dollar." It was usually "I'll bet you what you please," or "I'll bet you
what you dare," or "I'll bet you a trifle," or else, more significantly still,
"I'll bet the Devil my head."

This latter form seemed to please him best:—perhaps because it in-
volved the least risk; for Dammit had become excessively parsimo-
nious. Had any one taken him up, his head was small, and thus his
loss would have been small too. But these are my own reflections, and
I am by no means sure that I am right in attributing them to him. At
all events the phrase in question grew daily in favor, notwithstanding
the gross impropriety of a man's betting his brains like bank-notes:—
but this was a point which my friend's perversity of disposition would
not permit him to comprehend. In the end, he abandoned all other
forms of wager, and gave himself up to *"I'll bet the Devil my head,"*
with a pertinacity and exclusiveness of devotion that displeased not
less than it surprised me. I am always displeased by circumstances for
which I cannot account. Mysteries force a man to think, and so injure
his health. The truth is, there was something in *the air* with which Mr.
Dammit was wont to give utterance to his offensive expression—some-
thing in his *manner* of enunciation—which at first interested, and

6. Slightly altered from Pope's *Essay on Man*, II.136. Death presents a paradox, it must "subdue
[man] at length" and thus "Grows with his growth, and strengthens with his strength." Poe
also uses this allusion in "The Colloquy of Monos and Una" (pp. 279ff. herein) and "The
Black Cat" (pp. 348ff.).

afterwards made me very uneasy—something which, for want of a more definite term at present, I must be permitted to call *queer*; but which Mr. Coleridge would have called mystical, Mr. Kant pantheistical, Mr. Carlyle twistical, and Mr. Emerson[7] hyperquizzitistical. I began not to like it at all. Mr. Dammit's soul was in a perilous state. I resolved to bring all my eloquence into play to save it. I vowed to serve him as St. Patrick, in the Irish chronicle, is said to have served the toad, that is to say, "awaken him to a sense of his situation."[8] I addressed myself to the task forthwith. Once more I betook myself to remonstrance. Again I collected my energies for a final attempt at expostulation.

When I had made an end of my lecture, Mr. Dammit indulged himself in some very equivocal behaviour. For some moments he remained silent, merely looking me inquisitively in the face. But presently he threw his head to one side, and elevated his eyebrows to great extent. Then he spread out the palms of his hands and shrugged up his shoulders. Then he winked with the right eye. Then he repeated the operation with the left. Then he shut them both up very tight. Then he opened them both so very wide that I became seriously alarmed for the consequences. Then, applying his thumb to his nose, he thought proper to make an indescribable movement with the rest of his fingers. Finally, setting his arms a-kimbo,[9] he condescended to reply.

I can call to mind only the heads of his discourse. He would be obliged to me if I would hold my tongue. He wished none of my advice. He despised all my insinuations. He was old enough to take care of himself. Did I still think him baby Dammit? Did I mean to say anything against his character? Did I intend to insult him? Was I a fool? Was my maternal parent aware, in a word, of my absence from the domicilliary residence? He would put this latter question to me as to a man of veracity, and he would bind himself to abide by my reply. Once more he would demand explicitly if my mother knew that I was out. My confusion, he said, betrayed me, and he would be willing to bet the Devil his head that she did not.

Mr. Dammit did not pause for my rejoinder. Turning upon his heel, he left my presence with undignified precipitation. It was well for him that he did so. My feelings had been wounded. Even my anger had been aroused. For once I would have taken him up upon his insulting wager. I would have won for the Arch-Enemy Mr. Dammit's little head—for the fact is, my mamma *was* very well aware of my merely temporary absence from home.

But *Khoda shefa midêhed*—Heaven gives relief—as the Mussel-

7. Famous writers associated with Transcendentalism, mysticism, and Romanticism. Samuel Taylor Coleridge (1772–1834), Immanuel Kant (1724–1804), Thomas Carlyle (1795–1881), and Ralph Waldo Emerson (1803–1882).

8. St. Patrick is supposed to have driven snakes and other "vermin" out of Ireland—moralizing that paradise has no creatures as frogs, scorpions, dragons, and such—thus presumably "awakening" these loathsome creatures to their base condition. Poe uses the same idea elsewhere.

9. Standing with hands on hips, elbows extended sharply outward and slightly forward—a typical stance of someone about to deliver a disapproving opinion. The word derives from Anglo-Saxon words for "a keen bow" (sharply bent bow).

men[1] say when you tread upon their toes. It was in pursuance of my duty that I had been insulted, and I bore the insult like a man. It now seemed to me, however, that I had done all that could be required of me, in the case of this miserable individual, and I resolved to trouble him no longer with my counsel, but to leave him to his conscience and himself. But although I forebore to intrude with my advice, I could not bring myself to give up his society altogether. I even went so far as to humor some of his less reprehensible propensities; and there were times when I found myself lauding his wicked jokes, as epicures do mustard, with tears in my eyes:[2]—so profoundly did it grieve me to hear his evil talk.

One fine day, having strolled out together arm in arm, our route led us in the direction of a river. There was a bridge, and we resolved to cross it. It was roofed over, by way of protection from the weather, and the arch-way, having but few windows, was thus very uncomfortably dark. As we entered the passage, the contrast between the external glare, and the interior gloom, struck heavily upon my spirits. Not so upon those of the unhappy Dammit, who offered to bet the Devil his head that I was hipped.[3] He seemed to be in an unusual good humor. He was excessively lively—so much so that I entertained I know not what of uneasy suspicion. It is not impossible that he was affected with the transcendentals.[4] I am not well enough versed, however, in the diagnosis of this disease to speak with decision upon the point; and unhappily there were none of my friends of the "Dial" present. I suggest the idea, nevertheless, because of a certain species of austere Merry-Andrewism which seemed to beset my poor friend, and caused him to make quite a Tom-Fool of himself.[5] Nothing would serve him but wriggling and skipping about under and over everything that came in his way; now shouting out, and now lisping out, all manner of odd little and big words, yet preserving the gravest face in the world all the time. I really could not make up my mind whether to kick or to pity him. At length, having passed nearly across the bridge, we approached the termination of the foot-way, when our progress was impeded by a turnstile of some height. Through this I made my way quietly, pushing it around as usual. But this turn would not serve the turn of Mr. Dammit. He insisted upon leaping the stile, and said he could cut a pigeon-wing[6] over it in the air. Now this, conscientiously

1. Muslims (believers in Islam). The Persian reads "God gives healing."
2. "Epicures": people of refined taste in wine or food. Poe's jest is that, although the narrator laughs intensely at Toby's crude jokes, the tears that come to his eyes are like the tears that mustard can bring to the eyes of an epicure (i.e., affecting the narrator's "delicate" moral sensibilities).
3. Morbidly depressed, affected with hypochondria (OED).
4. Poe's comic phrase for Transcendental moments of inspiration—intense sensitivity to cosmic order—epiphanies such as Emerson's on Boston Common when he says he felt the "Universal Being" circulate through him so that he became an all-seeing "transparent eyeball" (Nature, 1836, chapter 1).
5. May indicate an idiot or insane person or buffoon. A "Merry-Andrew" is a circus or puppet-theater clown or fool.
6. A dance step in which, with arms akimbo, one jumps straight up and clicks one's feet together. A turnstile is a revolving gate typically constructed as a series of horizontal bars projecting from a central vertical post. The word "stile" by itself usually indicates a series of steps on both sides of a fence (allowing human beings to get over but not farm animals).

speaking, I did not think he could do. The best pigeon-winger over all kinds of style,[7] was my friend Mr. Carlyle, and as I knew *he* could not do it, I would not believe it could be done by Toby Dammit. I therefore told him, in so many words, that he was a braggadocio, and could not do what he said. For this, I had reason to be sorry afterwards;—for he straightway offered to *bet the Devil his head* that he could.

I was about to reply, notwithstanding my previous resolutions, with some remonstrance against his impiety, when I heard, close at my elbow, a slight cough, which sounded very much like the ejaculation "*ahem!*" I started, and looked about me in surprise. My glance at length fell into a nook of the frame-work of the bridge, and upon the figure of a little lame[8] old gentleman of venerable aspect. Nothing could be more reverend than his whole appearance; for, he not only had on a full suit of black, but his shirt was perfectly clean and the collar turned very neatly down over a white cravat, while his hair was parted in front like a girl's. His hands were clasped pensively together over his stomach, and his two eyes were carefully rolled up into the top of his head.[9]

Upon observing him more closely, I perceived that he wore a black silk apron over his small-clothes; and this was a thing which I thought very odd. Before I had time to make any remark, however, upon so singular a circumstance, he interrupted me with a second "*ahem!*"

To this observation I was not immediately prepared to reply. The fact is, remarks of this laconic nature are nearly unanswerable. I have known a Quarterly Review *non-plused* by the word "*Fudge!*"[1] I am not ashamed to say, therefore, that I turned to Mr. Dammit for assistance.

"Dammit," said I, "what are you about? don't you hear?—the gentleman says '*ahem!*' " I looked sternly at my friend while I thus addressed him; for, to say the truth, I felt particularly puzzled, and when a man is particularly puzzled he must knit his brows and look savage, or else he is pretty sure to look like a fool.

"Dammit," observed I—although this sounded very much like an oath, than which nothing was farther from my thoughts—"Dammit," I suggested—"the gentleman says '*ahem!*' "

I do not attempt to defend my remark on the score of profundity; I did not think it profound myself; but I have noticed that the effect of our speeches is not always proportionate with their importance in our own eyes; and if I had shot Mr. D. through and through with a Paix-

7. Here the word *stile* is altered punningly to *style*.
8. Traditionally, the devil is lame (presumably because he is cloven-footed like a goat).
9. Mabbott suggests that Poe's description is an allusion (1) to John Neal's comment in the *Yankee* (December 1829) that a portrait of the poet Robert Montgomery (1807–1855) made him "look like a hero of a French cookery-book-with his hair parted in the middle like a girl's"; and (2) to such a drawing of him in *Fraser's Magazine* (January 1832)—but with his hands on his stomach and his eyes rolled up. The picture was labeled "The author of Satan," in reference to Montgomery's *Satan, or the Intellect without God* (1830).
1. I.e., nonsense. The reference may have something to do with Thomas Moore's popular books on the travels of the "Fudge Family" in Europe (see notes to "The Assignation," pp. 116ff. herein, and "Lionizing" ["Some Passages in the Life of a Lion"], pp. 128ff.).

han bomb, or knocked him in the head with the "Poets and Poetry of America,"[2] he could hardly have been more discomfited than when I addressed him with those simple words—"Dammit, what are you about?—don't you hear?—the gentleman says '*ahem!*' "

"You don't say so?" gasped he at length, after turning more colors than a pirate runs up,[3] one after the other, when chased by a man-of-war. "Are you quite sure he said *that?* Well, at all events I am in for it now, and may as well put a bold face upon the matter. Here goes, then—*ahem!*"

At this the little old gentleman seemed pleased—God only knows why. He left his station at the nook of the bridge, limped forward with a gracious air, took Dammit by the hand and shook it cordially, looking all the while straight up in his face with an air of the most unadulterated benignity which it is possible for the mind of man to imagine.

"I am quite sure you will win it, Dammit," said he with the frankest of all smiles, "but we are obliged to have a trial you know, for the sake of mere form."

"Ahem!" replied my friend, taking off his coat with a deep sigh, tying a pocket-hankerchief around his waist, and producing an unaccountable alteration in his countenance by twisting up his eyes, and bringing down the corners of his mouth—"ahem!" And "ahem," said he again, after a pause; and not another word more than "ahem!" did I ever know him to say after that. "Aha!" thought I, without expressing myself aloud—"this is quite a remarkable silence on the part of Toby Dammit, and is no doubt a consequence of his verbosity upon a previous occasion. One extreme induces another. I wonder if he has forgotten the many unanswerable questions which he propounded to me so fluently on the day when I gave him my last lecture? At all events, he is cured of the transcendentals."

"Ahem!" here replied Toby, just as if he had been reading my thoughts, and looking like a very old sheep in a reverie.

The old gentleman now took him by the arm, and led him more into the shade of the bridge—a few paces back from the turnstile. "My good fellow," said he, "I make it a point of conscience to allow you this much run. Wait here, till I take my place by the stile, so that I may see whether you go over it handsomely, and transcendentally, and don't omit any flourishes of the pigeon-wing. A mere form, you know. I will say 'one, two, three, and away.'[4] Mind you start at the word 'away.' "

Here he took his position by the stile, paused a moment as if in profound reflection, then *looked up* and, I thought, smiled very slightly, then tightened the strings of his apron, then took a long look at Dammit, and finally gave the word as agreed upon—

One—two—three—and away!

2. A large collection edited by Rufus Wilmot Griswold, with whom Poe had an odd on-again, off-again professional relation (see the biographical introduction, especially p. xlv, herein). "Paixhan bomb": reference to Henri Joseph Paixhans (1783–1854), French artillery officer, inventor of a field cannon that shot explosive shells (used in the Napoleonic Wars).
3. Flags. Pirates used to fly different national flags to deceive other ships.
4. See Poe's characterization of transcendental and "elevated" styles of writing in his satire "How to Write a Blackwood Article" (pp. 173ff. herein)

Punctually, at the word "away," my poor friend set off in a strong gallop. The stile was not very high, like Mr. Lord's[5]—nor yet very low, like that of Mr. Lord's reviewers, but upon the whole I made sure that he would clear it. And then what if he did not?—ah, that was the question—what if he did not? "What right," said I, "had the old gentleman to make any other gentleman jump? The little old dot-and-carry-one![6] who is *he*? If he asks *me* to jump, I won't do it, that's flat, and I don't care who *the devil he is*." The bridge, as I say, was arched and covered in, in a very ridiculous manner, and there was a most uncomfortable echo about it at all times—an echo which I never before so particularly observed as when I uttered the four last words of my remark.[7]

But what I said, or what I thought, or what I heard, occupied only an instant. In less than five seconds from his starting, my poor Toby had taken the leap. I saw him run nimbly, and spring grandly from the floor of the bridge, cutting the most awful flourishes with his legs as he went up. I saw him high in the air, pigeon-winging it to admiration just over the top of the stile; and of course I thought it an unusually singular thing that he did not *continue* to go over. But the whole leap was the affair of a moment, and, before I had a chance to make any profound reflections, down came Mr. Dammit on the flat of his back, on the same side of the stile from which he had started. In the same instant I saw the old gentleman limping off at the top of his speed, having caught and wrapped up in his apron something that fell heavily into it from the darkness of the arch just over the turnstile. At all this I was much astonished; but I had no leisure to think, for Mr. Dammit lay particularly still, and I concluded that his feelings had been hurt, and that he stood in need of my assistance. I hurried up to him and found that he had received what might be termed a serious injury. The truth is, he had been deprived of his head, which after a close search I could not find anywhere;—so I determined to take him home, and send for the homœo-pathists.[8] In the mean time a thought struck me, and I threw open an adjacent window of the bridge; when the sad truth flashed upon me at once. About five feet just above the top of the turnstile, and crossing the arch of the foot-path so as to constitute a brace, there extended a flat iron bar, lying with its breadth horizontally, and forming one of a series that served to strengthen the structure throughout its extent. With the edge of this brace it appeared evident that the neck of my unfortunate friend had come precisely in contact.

5. William Wilburforce Lord (1819–1907), American poet and clergyman. In the earlier version of this tale, Poe used Hugh A. Pue, a grammarian. The change may have been prompted by Lord's parody of "The Raven" in 1845.
6. Old style of addition. According to Peithman, the phrase was used to indicate a person with a wooden, shorter, or lame leg.
7. I.e., "the devil he is."
8. Doctors who subscribe to a system of medicine based on the idea of similarity—that "like can be cured by like." At the beginning of the 19th century, Samuel Hahnemann of Leipzig, Germany, advocated the practice of homeopathy, distinguishing it from its opposite, allopathy (the idea that the cure must be different from the disease). In homeopathy, when a medicine produced the same symptoms as a disease, small doses of it were used as a cure. Quinine, for example, produced very weak symptoms of malaria and so became the standard treatment for the disease (cf. cowpox inoculation for smallpox).

He did not long survive his terrible loss. The homœopathists did not give him little enough physic,[9] and what little they did give him he hesitated to take. So in the end he grew worse, and at length died, a lesson to all riotous livers. I bedewed his grave with my tears, worked a *bar* sinister[1] on his family escutcheon, and, for the general expenses of his funeral, sent in my very moderate bill to the transcendendalists. The scoundrels refused to pay it, so I had Mr. Dammit dug up at once, and sold him for dog's meat.[2]

The Oval Portrait First published in *Graham's* (April 1842) as "Life in Death." The earlier version contained a motto in Italian purporting to be an "Inscription beneath an Italian picture of St. Bruno," which in translation reads: "He is alive and would speak did he not observe the rule of silence." Saint Bruno of Cologne (1030?, 1046?–1101) was the founder of the Carthusian order of monks, which often required the brothers to keep silent. Poe severely cut the story for its reprinting in the *Broadway Journal* (April 26, 1845), the text reprinted here. The omissions radically change the emphasis and increase the ambiguity of the story. Among the most important of these cuts is the opening paragraph of "Life in Death":

> My fever had been excessive and of long duration. All the remedies attainable in this wild Appennine region had been exhausted to no purpose. My valet and sole attendant in the lonely chateau, was too nervous and too grossly unskilful to venture upon letting blood—of which indeed I had already lost too much in the affray with the banditti. Neither could I safely permit him to leave me in search of assistance. At length I bethought me of a little pacquet of opium which lay with my tobacco in the hookahcase; for at Constantinople I had acquired the habit of smoking the weed with the drug. Pedro handed me the case. I sought and found the narcotic. But when about to cut off a portion I felt the necessity of hesitation. In smoking it was a matter of little importance *how much* was employed. Usually, I had half filled the bowl of the hookah with opium and tobacco cut and mingled intimately, half and half. Sometimes when I had used the whole of this mixture I experienced no very peculiar effects; at other times I would not have smoked the pipe more than two-thirds out, when symptoms of mental derangement, which were even alarming, warned me to desist. But the effect proceeded with an easy gradation which deprived the indulgence of all danger. Here, however, the case was different. I had never *swallowed* opium before. Laudanum and morphine I had occasionally used, and about *them* should have had no reason to hesitate. But the solid drug I had never seen employed. Pedro knew no more respecting the proper quantity to be taken, than myself—and thus, in the sad emergency, I was left altogether to

9. In earlier times any medicinal drug; later, the word was used for drugs that induce vomiting or evacuation of the bowels (i.e., purging the whole system).
1. *Sinister* means left; here the "heraldic" signs of the bastard; note the earlier reference to the hero's beatings by a left-handed mother (p. 288 herein).
2. Offal, waste parts, especially of a butchered animal, edible only to dogs or vermin. See p. 288, n. 9 herein for the speculation that the tale is an animal fable and Toby a "Transcendentalist" dog.

conjecture. Still I felt no especial uneasiness; for I resolved to pro-
ceed *by degrees*. I would take a *very* small dose in the first instance.
Should this prove impotent, I would repeat it; and so on, until I
should find an abatement of the fever, or obtain that sleep which was
so pressingly requisite, and with which my reeling senses had not
been blessed for now more than a week. No doubt it was this very
reeling of my senses—it was the dull delirium which already op-
pressed me—that prevented me from perceiving the incoherence of
my reason—which blinded me to the folly of defining any thing as ei-
ther large or small where I had no preconceived standard of compari-
son. I had not, at the moment, the faintest idea that what I conceived
to be an exceedingly small dose of solid opium might, in fact, be an
excessively large one. On the contrary I well remember that I judged
confidently of the quantity to be taken by reference to the entire
quantity of the lump in possession. The portion which, in conclusion,
I swallowed, and swallowed without fear, was no doubt a very small
proportion *of the piece which I held in my hand*.

Compare the opening of "The Buried Alive" in *Blackwood's* (October
1821; p. 759 herein). Probably the most famous use of the phrase "life in
death" in English is that of Samuel Taylor Coleridge in the *Rime of the An-
cient Mariner* (1798).

The Oval Portrait

The chateau into which my valet had ventured to make forcible en-
trance, rather than permit me, in my desperately wounded condition,
to pass a night in the open air, was one of those piles of commingled
gloom and grandeur which have so long frowned among the Appenines,
not less in fact than in the fancy of Mrs. Radcliffe.[1] To all appearance
it had been temporarily and very lately abandoned. We established our-
selves in one of the smallest and least sumptuously furnished apart-
ments. It lay in a remote turret of the building. Its decorations were
rich, yet tattered and antique. Its walls were hung with tapestry and be-
decked with manifold and multiform armorial trophies, together with
an unusually great number of very spirited modern paintings in frames
of rich golden arabesque.[2] In these paintings, which depended from
the walls not only in their main surfaces, but in very many nooks which
the bizarre architecture of the chateau rendered necessary—in these
paintings my incipient delirium, perhaps, had caused me to take deep
interest; so that I bade Pedro to close the heavy shutters of the room—

1. Ann Radcliffe (1764–1823) is the author of popular gothic novels featuring a sensitive hero-
ine beleaguered by malign forces in desolate castles high in the mountains, such as the
Apennines, which run the entire length of Italy. Seeming supernatural occurrences in her
works are eventually given natural explanations, as in *The Romance of the Forest* (1791), *The
Mysteries of Udolpho* (1794), and *The Italian* (1797). "Piles": in this sense, heavy masses of
stones laid one atop another to form castles, fortresses, or cathedrals in the Middle Ages and
early Renaissance.
2. An art term indicating the geometrical ornament and design of Arabic architecture, painting,
textiles, and the like, based on spiraling flowers and leaves. The arabesque also appears in
elaborate frames in carpets, in and around paintings, and in literary works. See the Tales and
Sketches introduction (pp. 77–80) and notes to several other tales (e.g., "The Fall of the
House of Usher"); see also p. 297, n. 5 herein.

since it was already night—to light the tongues of a tall candelabrum which stood by the head of my bed—and to throw open far and wide the fringed curtains of black velvet which enveloped the bed itself. I wished all this done that I might resign myself, if not to sleep, at least alternately to the contemplation of these pictures, and the perusal of a small volume which had been found upon the pillow, and which purported to criticise and describe them.

Long—long I read—and devoutly, devotedly I gazed.[3] Rapidly and gloriously the hours flew by, and the deep midnight came. The position of the candelabrum displeased me, and outreaching my hand with difficulty, rather than disturb my slumbering valet, I placed it so as to throw its rays more fully upon the book.

But the action produced an effect altogether unanticipated. The rays of the numerous candles (for there were many) now fell within a niche of the room which had hitherto been thrown into deep shade by one of the bed-posts. I thus saw in vivid light a picture all unnoticed before. It was the portrait of a young girl just ripening into womanhood. I glanced at the painting hurriedly, and then closed my eyes. Why I did this was not at first apparent even to my own perception. But while my lids remained thus shut, I ran over in mind my reason for so shutting them. It was an impulsive movement to gain time for thought—to make sure that my vision had not deceived me—to calm and subdue my fancy for a more sober and more certain gaze. In a very few moments I again looked fixedly at the painting.

That I now saw aright I could not and would not doubt; for the first flashing of the candles upon that canvas had seemed to dissipate the dreamy stupor which was stealing over my senses, and to startle me at once into waking life.

The portrait, I have already said, was that of a young girl. It was a mere head and shoulders, done in what is technically termed a *vignette* manner; much in the style of the favorite heads of Sully.[4] The arms, the bosom and even the ends of the radiant hair, melted imperceptibly into the vague yet deep shadow which formed the background of the whole. The frame was oval, richly gilded and filagreed in *Moresque*.[5] As a thing of art nothing could be more admirable than the painting itself. But it could have been neither the execution of the work, nor the immortal beauty of the countenance, which had so suddenly and so vehemently moved me. Least of all, could it have been that my fancy, shaken from its half slumber, had mistaken the head for

3. At this point (after the word *gazed*), "Life in Death" contained the following sentences: "I felt meantime, the voluptuous narcotic stealing its way to my brain. I felt that in its magical influence lay much of the gorgeous richness and variety of the frames—much of the ethereal hue that gleamed from the canvas—and much of the wild interest of the book which I perused. Yet this consciousness rather strengthened than impaired the delight of the illusion, while it weakened the illusion itself."
4. Probably the well-known artist Thomas Sully (1783–1872), but possibly his son, Robert, who is supposed to have painted a near-life-size oval portrait of Julia Sully of Richmond, Virginia. Robert Sully was a friend of Poe. "*Vignette* manner": an art technique to soften the edges of a picture so that it shades off into the borders or frames, blurring the distinction between picture and frame. It is often associated with an unenclosed decorative design at the beginning of a book or a chapter or the margins of pages.
5. In the arabesque style of the Moors, who conquered Spain in the 8th century.

that of a living person. I saw at once that the peculiarities of the design, of the *vignetting*, and of the frame, must have instantly dispelled such idea—must have prevented even its momentary entertainment. Thinking earnestly upon these points, I remained, for an hour perhaps, half sitting, half reclining, with my vision riveted upon the portrait. At length, satisfied with the true secret of its effect, I fell back within the bed. I had found the spell of the picture in an absolute *lifelikeliness* of expression, which at first startling, finally confounded, subdued and appalled me. With deep and reverent awe I replaced the candelabrum in its former position. The cause of my deep agitation being thus shut from view, I sought eagerly the volume which discussed the paintings and their histories. Turning to the number which designated the oval portrait, I there read the vague and quaint words which follow:

"She was a maiden of rarest beauty, and not more lovely than full of glee. And evil was the hour when she saw, and loved, and wedded the painter. He, passionate, studious, austere, and having already a bride in his Art: she a maiden of rarest beauty, and not more lovely than full of glee: all light and smiles, and frolicksome as the young fawn: loving and cherishing all things: hating only the Art which was her rival: dreading only the pallet and brushes and other untoward instruments which deprived her of the countenance of her lover. It was thus a terrible thing for this lady to hear the painter speak of his desire to pourtray even his young bride. But she was humble and obedient, and sat meekly for many weeks in the dark high turret-chamber where the light dripped upon the pale canvas only from overhead. But he, the painter, took glory in his work, which went on from hour to hour and from day to day. And he was a passionate, and wild and moody man, who became lost in reveries; so that he *would* not see that the light which fell so ghastlily in that lone turret withered the health and the spirits of his bride, who pined visibly to all but him. Yet she smiled on and still on, uncomplainingly, because she saw that the painter, (who had high renown,) took a fervid and burning pleasure in his task, and wrought day and night to depict her who so loved him, yet who grew daily more dispirited and weak. And in sooth some who beheld the portrait spoke of its resemblance in low words, as of a mighty marvel, and a proof not less of the power of the painter than of his deep love for her whom he depicted so surpassingly well. But at length, as the labor drew nearer to its conclusion, there were admitted none into the turret; for the painter had grown wild with the ardor of his work, and turned his eyes from the canvas rarely, even to regard the countenance of his wife. And he *would* not see that the tints which he spread upon the canvas were drawn from the cheeks of her who sate beside him. And when many weeks had passed, and but little remained to do, save one brush upon the mouth and one tint upon the eye, the spirit of the lady again flickered up as the flame within the socket of the lamp. And then the brush was given, and then the tint was placed; and, for one moment, the painter stood entranced before the work which he had wrought; but in the next, while he yet gazed, he grew tremulous and

very pallid, and aghast, and crying with a loud voice 'This is indeed *Life* itself!' turned suddenly to regard his beloved:—*She was dead.*"[6]

The Masque of the Red Death First published in *Graham's* (May 1842) under the title "The Mask of the Red Death." The text reprinted here is that of the *Broadway Journal* (July 19, 1845), where it appeared under the present title. By changing the spelling to "masque," Poe evokes the medieval tradition not only of libidinous yet sinister masked festival but also of the literary form of the Renaissance courtly *masque*, in which static emblems and ritual elements from myth and legendary history came together in tableaux and dance. It was the custom to perform masked balls and plays that symbolized the interpenetration of the realms of Heaven, Earth, and Hell. Poe may have had in mind the name of the magician Prospero in Shakespeare's *The Tempest* (c. 1611), a play that, despite its grotesque creatures and characters, is ultimately in the tradition of the *comedia*. At one point, the magician's half-monster half-human servant, Caliban, utters a curse inflicting the "red plague." Toward the end, Prospero causes a masque in progress to cease as an illusory and useless show. Poe's Prospero, fleeing the plague, retreats with a thousand courtiers and ladies to the seeming security of a fortified abbey, which he then seals up; but they are all trapped within—so that the name of the "prosperous" prince becomes ironic. The plague and the prince's Italian name also evoke the *Decameron* (1351–53) of Giovanni Boccaccio (1313?–1375). In this work, a group of young people flee the Black Death raging in 14th-century Florence to a castle outside the city—a plague Poe transforms into the fictive Red Death. In Poe's lifetime, there were several outbreaks of cholera and yellow fever in America and Europe. In 1832, in the New York *Mirror* (June 2), Nathaniel Parker Willis described a masque ball during the cholera epidemic in Paris that year in which some of the jesting masqueraders danced the "cholera-waltz" and one very tall man wore a costume representing the "walking pestilence" of "the *Cholera* itself."

The Masque of the Red Death

The "Red Death" had long devastated the country. No pestilence had ever been so fatal, or so hideous. Blood was its Avator[1] and its seal—the redness and the horror of blood. There were sharp pains, and sudden dizziness, and then profuse bleeding at the pores, with dissolution. The scarlet stains upon the body and especially upon the face of the victim, were the pest ban which shut him out from the aid and from the sympathy of his fellow-men. And the whole seizure,

6. After the word *suddenly*, instead of the text that follows here, the "Life in Death" text reads: "round to his beloved—who *was* dead. The painter then added—'But is this indeed Death?' "

1. From a Sanskrit word indicating the descent to earth of a deity in human or animal form— an incarnation of a god, most especially Vishnu, who, beginning as one of the three supreme gods, became the Supreme Being, superior even to Brahma, the creator. In his avatars, he appears nine times, with one last avatar prophesied but not yet manifest. He is usually pictured as dark blue. The word has come to mean in English the concrete manifestation of an abstraction or of something outside of or above the natural world.

progress and termination of the disease, were the incidents of half an hour.

But the Prince Prospero was happy and dauntless and sagacious. When his dominions were half depopulated, he summoned to his presence a thousand hale and light-hearted friends from among the knights and dames of his court, and with these retired to the deep seclusion of one of his castellated abbeys. This was an extensive and magnificent structure, the creation of the prince's own eccentric yet august taste. A strong and lofty wall girdled it in. This wall had gates of iron. The courtiers, having entered, brought furnaces and massy hammers and welded the bolts. They resolved to leave means neither of ingress or egress to the sudden impulses of despair or of frenzy from within. The abbey was amply provisioned. With such precautions the courtiers might bid defiance to contagion. The external world could take care of itself. In the meantime it was folly to grieve, or to think. The prince had provided all the appliances of pleasure. There were buffoons, there were improvisatori,[2] there were ballet-dancers, there were musicians, there was Beauty, there was wine. All these and security were within. Without was the "Red Death."

It was toward the close of the fifth or sixth month of his seclusion, and while the pestilence raged most furiously abroad, that the Prince Prospero entertained his thousand friends at a masked ball of the most unusual magnificence.

It was a voluptuous scene, that masquerade. But first let me tell of the rooms in which it was held. There were seven—an imperial suite. In many palaces, however, such suites form a long and straight vista, while the folding doors slide back nearly to the walls on either hand, so that the view of the whole extent is scarcely impeded. Here the case was very different; as might have been expected from the duke's love of the *bizarre*. The apartments were so irregularly disposed that the vision embraced but little more than one at a time. There was a sharp turn at every twenty or thirty yards, and at each turn a novel effect. To the right and left, in the middle of each wall, a tall and narrow Gothic window looked out upon a closed corridor which pursued the windings of the suite. These windows were of stained glass whose color varied in accordance with the prevailing hue of the decorations of the chamber into which it opened. That at the eastern extremity was hung, for example, in blue—and vividly blue were its windows. The second chamber was purple in its ornaments and tapestries, and here the panes were purple. The third was green throughout, and so were the casements. The fourth was furnished and lighted with orange—the fifth with white—the sixth with violet. The seventh apartment was closely shrouded in black velvet tapestries that hung all over the ceiling and down the walls, falling in heavy folds upon a carpet of the same material and hue. But in this chamber only, the color of the windows failed to correspond with the decorations. The panes here were scarlet—a deep blood

2. Individuals who improvise songs.

color.[3] Now in no one of the seven apartments was there any lamp or candelabrum, amid the profusion of golden ornaments that lay scattered to and fro or depended from the roof. There was no light of any kind emanating from lamp or candle within the suite of chambers. But in the corridors that followed the suite, there stood, opposite to each window, a heavy tripod, bearing a brazier of fire that projected its rays through the tinted glass and so glaringly illumined the room. And thus were produced a multitude of gaudy and fantastic appearances. But in the western or black chamber the effect of the fire-light that streamed upon the dark hangings through the blood-tinted panes, was ghastly in the extreme, and produced so wild a look upon the countenances of those who entered, that there were few of the company bold enough to set foot within its precincts at all.

It was in this apartment, also, that there stood against the western wall, a gigantic clock of ebony. Its pendulum swung to and fro with a dull, heavy, monotonous clang; and when the minute-hand made the circuit of the face, and the hour was to be stricken, there came from the brazen lungs of the clock a sound which was clear and loud and deep and exceedingly musical, but of so peculiar a note and emphasis that, at each lapse of an hour, the musicians of the orchestra were constrained to pause, momentarily, in their performance to harken to the sound; and thus the waltzers perforce ceased their evolutions; and there was a brief disconcert of the whole gay company; and, while the chimes of the clock yet rang, it was observed that the giddiest grew pale, and the more aged and sedate passed their hands over their brows as if in confused reverie or meditation. But when the echoes had fully ceased, a light laughter at once pervaded the assembly; the musicians looked at each other and smiled as if at their own nervousness and folly, and made whispering vows, each to the other, that the next chiming of the clock should produce in them no similar emotion; and then, after the lapse of sixty minutes, (which embrace three thousand and six hundred seconds of the Time that flies,) there came yet another chiming of the clock, and then were the same disconcert and tremulousness and meditation as before.

But, in spite of these things, it was a gay and magnificent revel. The tastes of the duke were peculiar. He had a fine eye for colors and effects. He disregarded the *decora*[4] of mere fashion. His plans were bold and fiery, and his conceptions glowed with barbaric lustre. There are some who would have thought him mad. His followers felt that he was not. It was necessary to hear and see and touch him to be *sure* that he was not.

He had directed, in great part, the moveable embellishments of the

3. One of the favorite pastimes of critics is trying to identify the symbolic meaning of the colors of the seven rooms. Speculation includes the seven ages of man, the seven days of the week, the seven deadly sins, the seven Christian sacraments, and so forth. Some readers have noted that the rooms proceed from east to west, blue at one end and black at the other, suggesting the cycle of a day from night to night. Mabbott notes the absence of yellow and that "blue and red are the poles of a compass—the beginning and the end." In Revelation seven seals are broken, letting forth the apocalyptic final destruction of the earth.
4. Plural of *decorum* (see notes on the theory of decorum in "The Assignation," pp. 116ff. herein).

seven chambers, upon occasion of this great *fête*;[5] and it was his own guiding taste which had given character to the masqueraders. Be sure they were grotesque.[6] There were much glare and glitter and piquancy and phantasm—much of what has been since seen in "Hernani."[7] There were arabesque[8] figures with unsuited limbs and appointments. There were delirious fancies such as the madman fashions. There was much of the beautiful, much of the wanton, much of the *bizarre*, something of the terrible, and not a little of that which might have excited disgust. To and fro in the seven chambers there stalked, in fact, a multitude of dreams. And these—the dreams—writhed in and about, taking hue from the rooms, and causing the wild music of the orchestra to seem as the echo of their steps. And, anon, there strikes the ebony clock which stands in the hall of the velvet. And then, for a moment, all is still, and all is silent save the voice of the clock. The dreams are stiff-frozen as they stand. But the echoes of the chime die away—they have endured but an instant—and a light, half-subdued laughter floats after them as they depart. And now again the music swells, and the dreams live, and writhe to and fro more merrily than ever, taking hue from the many tinted windows through which stream the rays from the tripods. But to the chamber which lies most westwardly of the seven, there are now none of the maskers who venture: for the night is waning away; and there flows a ruddier light through the blood-colored panes; and the blackness of the sable drapery appals; and to him whose foot falls upon the sable carpet, there comes from the near clock of ebony a muffled peal more solemnly emphatic than any which reaches *their* ears who indulge in the more remote gaieties of the other apartments.

But these other apartments were densely crowded, and in them beat feverishly the heart of life. And the revel went whirlingly on, until at length there commenced the sounding of midnight upon the clock. And then the music ceased, as I have told; and the evolutions of the waltzers were quieted; and there was an uneasy cessation of all things as before. But now there were twelve strokes to be sounded by the bell of the clock; and thus it happened, perhaps, that more of thought crept, with more of time, into the meditations of the thoughtful among those who revelled. And thus, too, it happened, perhaps, that before the last echoes of the last chime had utterly sunk into silence, there were many individuals in the crowd who had found leisure to become aware of the presence of a masked figure which had arrested the attention of no single individual before. And the rumor of this new presence having spread itself whisperingly around, there arose at

5. A lavish festival.
6. Distorted, unnatural, combining elements that are normally discrete or separated (see the Tales and Sketches introduction, pp. 77–80 herein).
7. An 1830 tragic play by Victor Hugo that precipitated an uproar between the Classicists and Romanticists because it merged incompatible opposites (like humor and horror, tragedy and comedy), violating the classic rules of decorum.
8. A reference to geometrical Arabic art forms based on abstract representations of flowers and leaves and vines (see the Tales and Sketches introduction, pp. 77–80 herein and the notes to "The Oval Portrait," pp. 295–97). The word was also sometimes used to suggest *grotesque* or *gothic* (see notes to "Ligeia," pp. 159ff.).

length from the whole company a buzz, or murmur, expressive of dis-approbation and surprise—then, finally, of terror, of horror, and of dis-gust.

In an assembly of phantasms such as I have painted, it may well be supposed that no ordinary appearance could have excited such sensa-tion. In truth the masquerade license of the night was nearly unlim-ited; but the figure in question had out-Heroded Herod,[9] and gone beyond the bounds of even the prince's indefinite decorum. There are chords in the hearts of the most reckless which cannot be touched without emotion. Even with the utterly lost, to whom life and death are equally jests, there are matters of which no jest can be made. The whole company, indeed, seemed now deeply to feel that in the cos-tume and bearing of the stranger neither wit nor propriety existed. The figure was tall and gaunt, and shrouded from head to foot in the ha-biliments of the grave. The mask which concealed the visage was made so nearly to resemble the countenance of a stiffened corpse that the closest scrutiny must have had difficulty in detecting the cheat. And yet all this might have been endured, if not approved, by the mad revellers around. But the mummer[1] had gone so far as to assume the type of the Red Death. His vesture was dabbled in *blood*—and his broad brow, with all the features of the face, was besprinkled with the scarlet horror.

When the eyes of Prince Prospero fell upon this spectral image (which with a slow and solemn movement, as if more fully to sustain its *rôle*, stalked to and fro among the waltzers) he was seen to be con-vulsed, in the first moment with a strong shudder either of terror or distaste; but, in the next, his brow reddened with rage.

"Who dares?" he demanded hoarsely of the courtiers who stood near him—"who dares insult us with this blasphemous mockery? Seize him and unmask him—that we may know whom we have to hang at sunrise, from the battlements!"

It was in the eastern or blue chamber in which stood the Prince Prospero as he uttered these words. They rang throughout the seven rooms loudly and clearly—for the prince was a bold and robust man, and the music had become hushed at the waving of his hand.

It was in the blue room where stood the prince, with a group of pale courtiers by his side. At first, as he spoke, there was a slight rushing movement of this group in the direction of the intruder, who at the moment was also near at hand, and now, with deliberate and stately step, made closer approach to the speaker. But from a certain name-less awe with which the mad assumptions of the mummer had in-spired the whole party, there were found none who put forth hand to seize him; so that, unimpeded, he passed within a yard of the prince's person; and, while the vast assembly, as if with one impulse, shrank from the centres of the rooms to the walls, he made his way uninter-

9. From *Hamlet*, III.ii.16, and used elsewhere by Poe (e.g., "Metzengerstein" and "William Wil-son"). Herod the Great (died 4 B.C.E.), who ruled Palestine, elaborately adorned the cities of his rule, especially Jerusalem; he was also known for his bloodthirstiness. See p. 226, n. 4 herein.
1. A performer in a pantomime.

ruptedly, but with the same solemn and measured step which had dis-
tinguished him from the first, through the blue chamber to the pur-
ple—through the purple to the green—through the green to the
orange—through this again to the white—and even thence to the vio-
let, ere a decided movement had been made to arrest him.[2] It was
then, however, that the Prince Prospero, maddening with rage and the
shame of his own momentary cowardice, rushed hurriedly through the
six chambers, while none followed him on account of a deadly terror
that had seized upon all. He bore aloft a drawn dagger, and had ap-
proached, in rapid impetuosity, to within three or four feet of the re-
treating figure, when the latter, having attained the extremity of the
velvet apartment, turned suddenly and confronted his pursuer. There
was a sharp cry—and the dagger dropped gleaming upon the sable
carpet, upon which, instantly afterwards, fell prostrate in death the
Prince Prospero. Then, summoning the wild courage of despair, a
throng of the revellers at once threw themselves into the black apart-
ment, and, seizing the mummer, whose tall figure stood erect and mo-
tionless within the shadow of the ebony clock, gasped in unutterable
horror at finding the grave-cerements and corpse-like mask which they
handled with so violent a rudeness, untenanted by any tangible form.

And now was acknowledged the presence of the Red Death. He had
come like a thief in the night.[3] And one by one dropped the revellers
in the blood-bedewed halls of their revel, and died each in the de-
spairing posture of his fall. And the life of the ebony clock went out
with that of the last of the gay. And the flames of the tripods expired.
And Darkness and Decay and the Red Death held illimitable dominion
over all.[4]

The Pit and the Pendulum First published in *The Gift: a Christ-
mas and New Year's Present, MDCCCXLIII* (actually 1842). The text
reprinted here is that of the *Broadway Journal* (May 17/19, 1845). Among
the likely influences and sources for Poe's tale are a review in the *Philadel-
phia Museum of Foreign Literature and Sciences* for April 1833 (reprinted
from the *British Critic* for January 1827) of Juan Antonio Llorente's
History of the Inquisition (1827) and several stories from *Blackwood's*:
"The Man in the Bell" (pp. 762ff. herein), "The Involuntary Experimental-
ist," and "The Iron Shroud" (see Poe's satire "How to Write a Blackwood
Article" [pp. 176–77]). Other suggestions include "Singular Recovery

2. The figure first appears in the eastern room and moves west; some readers see this as a fig-
 uration of the process of life (the passage of a day, birth to death, the stages of life marked
 by the tolling of the clock).
3. 1 Thessalonians 5:2–3: "For you yourselves know perfectly that the day of the Lord so
 cometh as a thief in the night. For when they shall say, Peace and safety; then sudden
 destruction cometh upon them . . . and they shall not escape." The phrase also occurs in
 2 Peter 3:10: "But the day of the Lord will come as a thief in the night; in the which the
 heavens shall pass away with a great noise, and the elements shall melt with fervent heat.—"
 Cf. Luke 12:39–40.
4. Some readers have heard echoes of Alexander Pope's *The Dunciad* (1728, last revision 1743)
 in these final lines. A satire on the "dunces" of the day, the poem concludes: "Lo! Thy dread
 empire, CHAOS! is restored; / Light dies before thy uncreating word: / Thy hand, great An-
 arch! Lets the curtain fall; / And universal darkness buries All."

from Death," *Blackwood's* (December 1821), Thomas Dick's *Philosophy of Religion* (1825), James Brown's article "The Inquisition of Spain," *Blackwood's* (July–August 1826), Charles Brockden Brown's novel *Edgar Huntly* (1799), and Charles Maturin's novel *Melmoth the Wanderer* (1820).

The Pit and the Pendulum

> Impia tortorum longas hic turba furores
> Sanguinis innocui, non satiata, aluit.
> Sospite nunc patrià, fracto nunc funeris antro,
> Mors ubi dira fuit vita salusque patent.

[*Quatrain composed for the gates of a Market to be erected upon the site of the Jacobin Club House at Paris.*][1]

I was sick—sick unto death with that long agony; and when they at length unbound me, and I was permitted to sit, I felt that my senses were leaving me. The sentence—the dread sentence of death—was the last of distinct accentuation which reached my ears. After that, the sound of the inquisitorial[2] voices seemed merged in one dreamy indeterminate hum. It conveyed to my soul the idea of *revolution*—perhaps from its association in fancy with the burr of a millwheel. This only for a brief period; for presently I heard no more. Yet, for a while, I saw; but with how terrible an exaggeration! I saw the lips of the black-robed judges. They appeared to me white—whiter than the sheet upon which I trace these words—and thin even to grotesqueness; thin with the intensity of their expression of firmness—of immoveable resolution—of stern contempt of human torture. I saw that the decrees of what to me was Fate, were still issuing from those lips. I saw them writhe with a deadly locution. I saw them fashion the syllables of my name; and I shuddered because no sound succeeded. I saw, too, for a few moments of delirious horror, the soft and nearly imperceptible waving of the sable draperies which enwrapped the walls of the apartment. And then my vision fell upon the seven tall candles upon the table.[3] At first they wore the aspect of charity, and seemed white slen-

1. The motto may be paraphrased:

 > Here the furious mob, unsatisfied, long harbored hatred of innocent blood. Now that the fatherland is saved, and the cave of death destroyed, wholesome life appears where grim death has been.

 After the French Revolution, the Jacobin Club House in Paris was razed and the Marché St. Honoré built over it. Led by Maximillien Marie Isadore Robespierre (1758–1794), the Jacobins, a radical democratic group during the Revolution, were largely responsible for the Reign of Terror (1793–94), in which several thousands were guillotined. Poe parallels the conservative tyranny of the Spanish Inquisition with the liberal tyranny of the French Revolution (note the italicized word *revolution* in the first paragraph).
2. The Spanish Inquisition (1478–1834) was established by the Spanish monarchs to punish heretics, such as Jews and Muslims. Supposedly, some two thousand people were burned at the stake in 1483, the initial year of the reign of Tomás de Torquemada (1420–1498) as grand inquisitor of Castile and Aragon. Torquemada was in charge of centralizing the Inquisition in Spain and ridding the country of heretics; in 1492 (the year Columbus discovered the Americas), he achieved the expulsion of unconverted Jews and Moors. The public executions lasted almost three centuries, the last being recorded in Seville in 1781.
3. On the significance of the number seven, cf. notes to "The Masque of the Red Death," especially p. 301, n. 3 herein.

der angels who would save me; but then, all at once, there came a most deadly nausea over my spirit, and I felt every fibre in my frame thrill as if I had touched the wire of a galvanic battery,[4] while the angel forms became meaningless spectres, with heads of flame, and I saw that from them there would be no help. And then there stole into my fancy, like a rich musical note, the thought of what sweet rest there must be in the grave. The thought came gently and stealthily, and it seemed long before it attained full appreciation; but just as my spirit came at length properly to feel and entertain it, the figures of the judges vanished, as if magically, from before me; the tall candles sank into nothingness; their flames went out utterly; the blackness of darkness supervened; all sensations appeared swallowed up in a mad rushing descent as of the soul into Hades. Then silence, and stillness, and night were the universe.

I had swooned; but still will not say that all of consciousness was lost. What of it there remained I will not attempt to define, or even to describe; yet all was not lost. In the deepest slumber—no! In delirium—no! In a swoon—no! In death—no! even in the grave all *is not* lost. Else there is no immortality for man. Arousing from the most profound of slumbers, we break the gossamer web of *some* dream.[5] Yet in a second afterward, (so frail may that web have been) we remember not that we have dreamed. In the return to life from the swoon there are two stages; first, that of the sense of mental or spiritual; secondly, that of the sense of physical, existence. It seems probable that if, upon reaching the second stage, we could recall the impressions of the first, we should find these impressions eloquent in memories of the gulf beyond. And that gulf is—what? How at least shall we distinguish its shadows from those of the tomb? But if the impressions of what I have termed the first stage, are not, at will, recalled, yet, after long interval, do they not come unbidden, while we marvel whence they come? He who has swooned, is not he who finds strange palaces and wildly familiar faces in coals that glow; is not he who beholds floating in mid-air the sad visions that the many may not view; is not he who ponders ever the perfume of some novel flower—is not he whose brain grows bewildered with the meaning of some musical cadence which has never before arrested his attention.

Amid frequent and thoughtful endeavors to remember; amid earnest struggles to regather some token of the state of seeming nothingness into which my soul had lapsed, there have been moments when I have dreamed of success; there have been brief, very brief periods when I have conjured up remembrances which the lucid reason of a later epoch assures me could have had reference only to that condition of seeming unconsciousness. These shadows of memory tell, indistinctly, of tall figures that lifted and bore me in silence down—down—still down—till a hideous dizziness oppressed me at the mere idea of the interminableness of the descent. They tell also of a vague horror at my

4. Chemical generator of electricity.
5. See Poe's other speculations on dream states and stages (e.g., *Marginalia* 150, in *Graham's*, March 1846) and Richard Wilbur's essay "The House of Poe" (pp. 807ff. herein).

heart, on account of that heart's unnatural stillness. Then comes a sense of sudden motionlessness throughout all things; as if those who bore me (a ghastly train!) had outrun, in their descent, the limits of the limitless, and paused from the wearisomeness of their toil. After this I call to mind flatness and dampness; and then all is *madness*—the madness of a memory which busies itself among forbidden things.

Very suddenly there came back to my soul motion and sound—the tumultuous motion of the heart, and, in my ears, the sound of its beating, Then a pause in which all is blank. Then again sound, and motion, and touch—a tingling sensation pervading my frame. Then the mere consciousness of existence, without thought—a condition which lasted long. Then, very suddenly, *thought*, and shuddering terror, and earnest endeavor to comprehend my true state. Then a strong desire to lapse into insensibility. Then a rushing revival of soul and a successful effort to move. And now a full memory of the trial, of the judges, of the sable draperies, of the sentence, of the sickness, of the swoon. Then entire forgetfulness of all that followed; of all that a later day and much earnestness of endeavor have enabled me vaguely to recall.

So far, I had not opened my eyes. I felt that I lay upon my back, unbound. I reached out my hand, and it fell heavily upon something damp and hard. There I suffered it to remain for many minutes, while I strove to imagine where and *what* I could be. I longed, yet dared not to employ my vision. I dreaded the first glance at objects around me. It was not that I feared to look upon things horrible, but that I grew aghast lest there should be *nothing* to see. At length, with a wild desperation at heart, I quickly unclosed my eyes. My worst thoughts, then, were confirmed. The blackness of eternal night encompassed me. I struggled for breath. The intensity of the darkness seemed to oppress and stifle me. The atmosphere was intolerably close. I still lay quietly, and made effort to exercise my reason. I brought to mind the inquisitorial proceedings, and attempted from that point to deduce my real condition. The sentence had passed; and it appeared to me that a very long interval of time had since elapsed. Yet not for a moment did I suppose myself actually dead. Such a supposition, notwithstanding what we read in fiction, is altogether inconsistent with real existence;—but where and in what state was I? The condemned to death, I knew, perished usually at the *auto-da-fes*,[6] and one of these had been held on the very night of the day of my trial. Had I been remanded to my dungeon, to await the next sacrifice, which would not take place for many months? This I at once saw could not be. Victims had been in immediate demand. Moreover, my dungeon, as well as all the condemned cells at Toledo,[7] had stone floors, and light was not altogether excluded.

A fearful idea now suddenly drove the blood in torrents upon my

6. Acts of faith, i.e., ceremonial execution (as a public act of the faith) of heretics during the Spanish Inquisition, most often by burning at the stake by civil authorities after a judgment of heresy by the Church. The accused wore yellow robes with a red cross on the front and the back and a tall pointed hood with peaks front and back.
7. City that became the center of the Inquisition in Spain.

heart, and for a brief period, I once more relapsed into insensibility. Upon recovering, I at once started to my feet, trembling convulsively in every fibre. I thrust my arms wildly above and around me in all directions. I felt nothing; yet dreaded to move a step, lest I should be impeded by the walls of a *tomb*. Perspiration burst from every pore, and stood in cold big beads upon my forehead. The agony of suspense, grew at length intolerable, and I cautiously moved forward, with my arms extended, and my eyes straining from their sockets, in the hope of catching some faint ray of light. I proceeded for many paces; but still all was blackness and vacancy. I breathed more freely. It seemed evident that mine was not, at least, the most hideous of fates.[8]

And now, as I still continued to step cautiously onward, there came thronging upon my recollection a thousand vague rumors of the horrors of Toledo. Of the dungeons there had been strange things narrated—fables I had always deemed them—but yet strange, and too ghastly to repeat, save in a whisper. Was I left to perish of starvation in this subterranean world of darkness; or what fate, perhaps even more fearful, awaited me? That the result would be death, and a death of more than customary bitterness, I knew too well the character of my judges to doubt. The mode and the hour were all that occupied or distracted me.

My outstretched hands at length encountered some solid obstruction. It was a wall, seemingly of stone masonry—very smooth, slimy, and cold. I followed it up; stepping with all the careful distrust with which certain antique narratives had inspired me. This process, however, afforded me no means of ascertaining the dimensions of my dungeon; as I might make its circuit, and return to the point whence I set out, without being aware of the fact; so perfectly uniform seemed the wall. I therefore sought the knife which had been in my pocket, when led into the inquisitorial chamber; but it was gone; my clothes had been exchanged for a wrapper of coarse serge.[9] I had thought of forcing the blade in some minute crevice of the masonry, so as to identify my point of departure. The difficulty, nevertheless, was but trivial; although, in the disorder of my fancy, it seemed at first insuperable. I tore a part of the hem from the robe and placed the fragment at full length, and at right angles to the wall. In groping my way around the prison, I could not fail to encounter this rag upon completing the circuit. So, at least I thought: but I had not counted upon the extent of the dungeon, or upon my own weakness. The ground was moist and slippery. I staggered onward for some time, when I stumbled and fell. My excessive fatigue induced me to remain prostrate; and sleep soon overtook me as I lay.

Upon awaking, and stretching forth an arm, I found beside me a loaf and a pitcher with water. I was too much exhausted to reflect upon this circumstance, but ate and drank with avidity. Shortly afterward, I resumed my tour around the prison, and with much toil, came at last upon the fragment of the serge. Up to the period when I fell I

8. I.e., burial alive.
9. A twilled cloth of firmly textured and compactly twisted woolen yarn.

had counted fifty-two paces, and upon resuming my walk, I had counted forty-eight more;—when I arrived at the rag. There were in all, then, a hundred paces; and, admitting two paces to the yard, I presumed the dungeon to be fifty yards in circuit. I had met, however, with many angles in the wall, and thus I could form no guess at the shape of the vault; for vault I could not help supposing it to be.

I had little object—certainly no hope—in these researches; but a vague curiosity prompted me to continue them. Quitting the wall, I resolved to cross the area of the enclosure. At first I proceeded with extreme caution, for the floor, although seemingly of solid material, was treacherous with slime. At length, however, I took courage, and did not hesitate to step firmly; endeavoring to cross in as direct a line as possible. I had advanced some ten or twelve paces in this manner, when the remnant of the torn hem of my robe became entangled between my legs. I stepped on it, and fell violently on my face.

In the confusion attending my fall, I did not immediately apprehend a somewhat startling circumstance, which yet, in a few seconds afterward, and while I still lay prostrate, arrested my attention. It was this— my chin rested upon the floor of the prison, but my lips and the upper portion of my head, although seemingly at a less elevation than the chin, touched nothing. At the same time my forehead seemed bathed in a clammy vapor, and the peculiar smell of decayed fungus arose to my nostrils. I put forward my arm, and shuddered to find that I had fallen at the very brink of a circular pit, whose extent, of course, I had no means of ascertaining at the moment. Groping about the masonry just below the margin, I succeeded in dislodging a small fragment, and let it fall into the abyss. For many seconds I hearkened to its reverberations as it dashed against the sides of the chasm in its descent; at length there was a sullen plunge into water, succeeded by loud echoes. At the same moment there came a sound resembling the quick opening, and as rapid closing of a door overhead, while a faint gleam of light flashed suddenly through the gloom, and as suddenly faded away.

I saw clearly the doom which had been prepared for me, and congratulated myself upon the timely accident by which I had escaped. Another step before my fall, and the world had seen me no more. And the death just avoided, was of that very character which I had regarded as fabulous and frivolous in the tales respecting the Inquisition. To the victims of its tyranny, there was the choice of death with its direst physical agonies, or death with its most hideous moral horrors.[1] I had been reserved for the latter. By long suffering my nerves had been unstrung, until I trembled at the sound of my own voice, and had become in every respect a fitting subject for the species of torture which awaited me.

Shaking in every limb, I groped my way back to the wall; resolving there to perish rather than risk the terrors of the wells, of which my imagination now pictured many in various positions about the dungeon. In other conditions of mind I might have had courage to end my

1. I.e., spiritual or psychical horrors, as distinguished from physical horrors.

misery at once by a plunge into one of these abysses; but now I was the veriest of cowards. Neither could I forget what I had read of these pits—that the *sudden* extinction of life formed no part of their most horrible plan.

Agitation of spirit kept me awake for many long hours; but at length I again slumbered. Upon arousing, I found by my side, as before, a loaf and pitcher of water. A burning thirst consumed me, and I emptied the vessel at a draught. It must have been drugged; for scarcely had I drunk, before I became irresistibly drowsy. A deep sleep fell upon me—a sleep like that of death. How long it lasted of course, I know not; but when, once again, I unclosed my eyes, the objects around me were visible. By a wild sulphurous[2] lustre, the origin of which I could not at first determine, I was enabled to see the extent and aspect of the prison.

In its size I had been greatly mistaken. The whole circuit of its walls did not exceed twenty-five yards. For some minutes this fact occasioned me a world of vain trouble; vain indeed! for what could be of less importance, under the terrible circumstances which environed me, than the mere dimensions of my dungeon? But my soul took a wild interest in trifles, and I busied myself in endeavors to account for the error I had committed in my measurement. The truth at length flashed upon me. In my first attempt at exploration I had counted fifty-two paces, up to the period when I fell; I must then have been within a pace or two of the fragment of serge; in fact, I had nearly performed the circuit of the vault. I then slept, and upon awaking, I must have returned upon my steps—thus supposing the circuit nearly double what it actually was. *My* confusion of mind prevented me from observing that I began my tour with the wall to the left, and ended it with the wall to the right.

I had been deceived, too, in respect to the shape of the enclosure. In feeling my way I had found many angles, and thus deduced an idea of great irregularity; so potent is the effect of total darkness upon one arousing from lethargy or sleep! The angles were simply those of a few slight depressions, or niches, at odd intervals. The general shape of the prison was square. What I had taken for masonry seemed now to be iron, or some other metal, in huge plates, whose sutures or joints occasioned the depression. The entire surface of this metallic enclosure was rudely daubed in all the hideous and repulsive devices to which the charnel superstition of the monks has given rise. The figures of fiends in aspects of menace, with skeleton forms, and other more really fearful images, overspread and disfigured the walls. I observed that the outlines of these monstrosities were sufficiently distinct, but that the colors seemed faded and blurred, as if from the effects of a damp atmosphere. I now noticed the floor, too, which was of stone. In the centre yawned the circular pit from whose jaws I had escaped; but it was the only one in the dungeon.

2. Sulfur, by tradition, suggests Hell—as does the word *abyss*, though here also suggesting the void of nothingness (see paragraphs 1 and 5 of the story).

All this I saw indistinctly and by much effort: for my personal condition had been greatly changed during slumber. I now lay upon my back, and at full length, on a species of low framework of wood. To this I was securely bound by a long strap resembling a surcingle.[3] It passed in many convolutions about my limbs and body, leaving at liberty only my head, and my left arm to such extent that I could, by dint of much exertion, supply myself with food from an earthen dish which lay by my side on the floor. I saw, to my horror, that the pitcher had been removed. I say to my horror; for I was consumed with intolerable thirst. This thirst it appeared to be the design of my persecutors to stimulate: for the food in the dish was meat pungently seasoned.

Looking upward, I surveyed the ceiling of my prison. It was some thirty or forty feet overhead, and constructed much as the side walls. In one of its panels a very singular figure riveted my whole attention. It was the painted figure of Time as he is commonly represented, save that, in lieu of a scythe, he held what, at a casual glance, I supposed to be the pictured image of a huge pendulum such as we see on antique clocks.[4] There was something, however, in the appearance of this machine which caused me to regard it more attentively. While I gazed directly upward at it (for its position was immediately over my own) I fancied that I saw it in motion. In an instant afterward the fancy was confirmed. Its sweep was brief, and of course slow. I watched it for some minutes, somewhat in fear, but more in wonder. Wearied at length with observing its dull movement, I turned my eyes upon the other objects in the cell.

A slight noise attracted my notice, and, looking to the floor, I saw several enormous rats traversing it. They had issued from the well, which lay just within view to my right. Even then, while I gazed, they came up in troops, hurriedly, with ravenous eyes, allured by the scent of the meat. From this it required much effort and attention to scare them away.

It might have been half an hour, perhaps even an hour, (for I could take but imperfect note of time) before I again cast my eyes upward. What I then saw confounded and amazed me. The sweep of the pendulum had increased in extent by nearly a yard. As a natural consequence, its velocity was also much greater. But what mainly disturbed me was the idea that it had perceptibly *descended*. I now observed— with what horror it is needless to say—that its nether extremity was formed of a crescent of glittering steel, about a foot in length from horn to horn; the horns upward, and the under edge evidently as keen as that of a razor. Like a razor also, it seemed massy and heavy, tapering from the edge into a solid and broad structure above. It was appended to a weighty rod of brass, and the whole *hissed* as it swung through the air.

I could no longer doubt the doom prepared for me by monkish ingenuity in torture. My congnizance of the pit had become known to

3. Leather belt for a clerical cassock or a horse's saddle.
4. The Grim Reaper is traditionally represented as a skeletal figure wielding a scythe to mow down not grain but people, here altered to a machine.

the inquisitorial agents—*the pit* whose horrors had been destined for so bold a recusant as myself—*the pit*, typical of hell, and regarded by rumor as the Ultima Thule[5] of all their punishments. The plunge into this pit I had avoided by the merest of accidents, and I knew that surprise, or entrapment into torment, formed an important portion of all the grotesquerie of these dungeon deaths. Having failed to fall, it was no part of the demon plan to hurl me into the abyss; and thus (there being no alternative) a different and a milder destruction awaited me. Milder! I half smiled in my agony as I thought of such application of such a term.

What boots it to tell of the long, long hours of horror more than mortal, during which I counted the rushing vibrations of the steel! Inch by inch—line by line—with a descent only appreciable at intervals that seemed ages—down and still down it came! Days passed—it might have been that many days passed—ere it swept so closely over me as to fan me with its acrid breath. The odor of the sharp steel forced itself into my nostrils. I prayed—I wearried heaven with my prayer for its more speedy descent. I grew frantically mad, and struggled to force myself upward against the sweep of the fearful scimitar. And then I fell suddenly calm, and lay smiling at the glittering death, as a child at some rare bauble.

There was another interval of utter insensibility; it was brief; for, upon again lapsing into life there had been no perceptible descent in the pendulum. But it might have been long; for I knew there were demons who took note of my swoon, and who could have arrested the vibration at pleasure. Upon my recovery, too, I felt very—oh, inexpressibly sick and weak, as if through long inanition. Even amid the agonies of that period, the human nature craved food. With painful effort I outstretched my left arm as far as my bonds permitted, and took possession of the small remnant which had been spared me by the rats. As I put a portion of it within my lips, there rushed to my mind a half formed thought of joy—of hope. Yet what business had *I* with hope? It was, as I say, a half formed thought—man has many such which are never completed. I felt that it was of joy—of hope; but I felt also that it had perished in its formation. In vain I struggled to perfect—to regain it. Long suffering had nearly annihilated all my ordinary powers of mind. I was an imbecile—an idiot.

The vibration of the pendulum was at right angles to my length. I saw that the crescent was designed to cross the region of the heart. It would fray the serge of my robe—it would return and repeat its operations—again—and again. Notwithstanding its terrifically wide sweep (some thirty feet or more) and the hissing vigor of its descent, sufficient to sunder these very walls of iron, still the fraying of my robe would be all that, for several minutes, it would accomplish. And at

5. End of the world, ultimate reach of the known, as mentioned in Virgil's *Georgics*, I.30 (see notes to "Dream-Land," pp. 56ff. herein); here meaning the extreme limit of Inquisitorial punishment. "Recusant": Poe may mean either someone who returns to heretical thinking after recanting or someone who refuses to recant.

this thought I paused. I dared not go farther than this reflection. I dwelt upon it with a pertinacity of attention—as if, in so dwelling, I could arrest *here* the descent of the steel. I forced myself to ponder upon the sound of the crescent as it should pass across the garment—upon the peculiar thrilling sensation which the friction of cloth produces on the nerves. I pondered upon all this frivolity until my teeth were on edge.

Down—steadily down it crept. I took a frenzied pleasure in contrasting its downward with its lateral velocity. To the right—to the left—far and wide—with the shriek of a damned spirit; to my heart with the stealthy pace of the tiger! I alternately laughed and howled as the one or the other idea grew predominant.

Down—certainly, relentlessly down! It vibrated within three inches of my bosom! I struggled violently, furiously, to free my left arm. This was free only from the elbow to the hand. I could reach the latter, from the platter beside me, to my mouth, with great effort, but no farther. Could I have broken the fastenings above the elbow, I would have seized and attempted to arrest the pendulum. I might as well have attempted to arrest an avalanche!

Down—still unceasingly—still inevitably down! I gasped and struggled at each vibration. I shrunk convulsively at its every sweep. My eyes followed its outward or upward whirls with the eagerness of the most unmeaning despair; they closed themselves spasmodically at the descent, although death would have been a relief, oh! how unspeakable! Still I quivered in every nerve to think how slight a sinking of the machinery would precipitate that keen, glistening axe upon my bosom. It was *hope* that prompted the nerve to quiver—the frame to shrink. It was *hope*—the hope that triumphs on the rack—that whispers to the death-condemned even in the dungeons of the Inquisition.

I saw that some ten or twelve vibrations would bring the steel in actual contact with my robe, and with this observation there suddenly came over my spirit all the keen, collected calmness of despair. For the first time during many hours—or perhaps days—I *thought*. It now occurred to me that the bandage, or surcingle, which enveloped me, was *unique*.[6] I was tied by no separate cord. The first stroke of the razor-like crescent athwart any portion of the band, would so detach it that it might be unwound from my person by means of my left hand. But how fearful, in that case, the proximity of the steel! The result of the slightest struggle how deadly! Was it likely, moreover, that the minions of the torturer had not foreseen and provided for this possibility! Was it probable that the bandage crossed my bosom in the track of the pendulum? Dreading to find my faint, and, as it seemed, my last hope frustrated, I so far elevated my head as to obtain a distinct view of my breast. The surcingle enveloped my limbs and body close in all directions—*save in the path of the destroying crescent.*

6. Poe apparently means the strap is all of one piece (*uni-*) and therefore of uniform thickness and consistency, rather than made up of different pieces.

Scarcely had I dropped my head back into its original position, when there flashed upon my mind what I cannot better describe than as the unformed half of that idea of deliverance to which I have previously alluded, and of which a moiety[7] only floated indeterminately through my brain when I raised food to my burning lips. The whole thought was now present—feeble, scarcely sane, scarcely definite,—but still entire. I proceeded at once, with the nervous energy of despair, to attempt its execution.

For many hours the immediate vicinity of the low framework upon which I lay, had been literally swarming with rats. They were wild, bold, ravenous; their red eyes glaring upon me as if they waited but for motionlessness on my part to make me their prey. "To what food," I thought, "have they been accustomed in the well."

They had devoured, in spite of all my efforts to prevent them, all but a small remnant of the contents of the dish. I had fallen into an habitual see-saw, or wave of the hand about the platter: and, at length, the unconscious uniformity of the movement deprived it of effect. In their voracity the vermin frequently fastened their sharp fangs in my fingers. With the particles of the oily and spicy viand which now remained, I thoroughly rubbed the bundage wherever I could reach it; then, raising my hand from the floor, I lay breathlessly still.

At first the ravenous animals were startled and terrified at the change—at the cessation of movement. They shrank alarmedly back; many sought the well. But this was only for a moment. I had not counted in vain upon their voracity. Observing that I remained without motion, one or two of the boldest leaped upon the frame-work, and smelt at the surcingle. This seemed the signal for a general rush. Forth from the well they hurried in fresh troops. They clung to the wood—they overran it, and leaped in hundreds upon my person. The measured movement of the pendulum disturbed them not at all. Avoiding its strokes they busied themselves with the anointed bandage. They pressed—they swarmed upon me in ever accumulating heaps. They writhed upon my throat; their cold lips sought my own; I was half stifled by their thronging pressure; disgust, for which the world has no name, swelled my bosom, and chilled, with a heavy clamminess, my heart. Yet one minute, and I felt that the struggle would be over. Plainly I perceived the loosening of the bandage. I knew that in more than one place it must be already severed. With a more than human resolution I lay *still*.

Nor had I erred in my calculations—nor had I endured in vain. I at length felt that I was *free*. The surcingle hung in ribands from my body. But the stroke of the pendulum already pressed upon my bosom. It had divided the serge of the robe. It had cut through the linen beneath. Twice again it swung, and a sharp sense of pain shot through every nerve. But the moment of escape had arrived. At a wave of my hand my deliverers hurried tumultuously away. With a steady move-

7. Half of something, or an indefinite portion thereof.

ment—cautious, sidelong, shrinking, and slow—I slid from the embrace of the bandage and beyond the the reach of the scimitar. For the moment, at least, *I was free.*

Free!—and in the grasp of the Inquisition! I had scarcely stepped from my wooden bed of horror upon the stone floor of the prison, when the motion of the hellish machine ceased and I beheld it drawn up, by some invisible force, through the ceiling. This was a lesson which I took desperately to heart. My every motion was undoubtedly watched. Free!—I had but escaped death in one form of agony, to be delivered unto worse than death in some other. With that thought I rolled my eyes nervously around on the barriers of iron that hemmed me in. Something unusual—some change which, at first, I could not appreciate distinctly—it was obvious, had taken place in the apartment. For many minutes of a dreamy and trembling abstraction, I busied myself in vain, unconnected conjecture. During this period, I became aware, for the first time, of the origin of the sulphurous light which illumined the cell. It proceeded from a fissure, about half an inch in width, extending entirely around the prison at the base of the walls, which thus appeared, and were, completely separated from the floor. I endeavored, but of course in vain, to look through the aperture.

As I arose from the attempt, the mystery of the alteration in the chamber broke at once upon my understanding. I have observed that, although the outlines of the figures upon the walls were sufficiently distinct, yet the colours seemed blurred and indefinite. These colors had now assumed, and were momentarily assuming, a startling and most intense brilliancy, that gave to the spectral and fiendish portraitures an aspect that might have thrilled even firmer nerves than my own. Demon eyes, of a wild and ghastly vivacity, glared upon me in a thousand directions, where none had been visible before, and gleamed with the lurid lustre of a fire that I could not force my imagination to regard as unreal.

Unreal!—Even while I breathed there came to my nostrils the breath of the vapour of heated iron! A suffocating odour pervaded the prison! A deeper glow settled each moment in the eyes that glared at my agonies! A richer tint of crimson diffused itself over the pictured horrors of blood. I panted! I gasped for breath! There could be no doubt of the design of my tormentors—oh! most unrelenting! oh! most demoniac of men! I shrank from the glowing metal to the centre of the cell. Amid the thought of the fiery destruction that impended, the idea of the coolness of the well came over my soul like balm. I rushed to its deadly brink. I threw my straining vision below. The glare from the enkindled roof illumined its inmost recesses. Yet, for a wild moment, did my spirit refuse to comprehend the meaning of what I saw. At length it forced—it wrestled its way into my soul—it burned itself in upon my shuddering reason.—Oh! for a voice to speak!—oh! horror!—oh! any horror but this! With a shriek, I rushed from the margin, and buried my face in my hands—weeping bitterly.

The heat rapidly increased, and once again I looked up, shuddering

as with a fit of the ague.[8] There had been a second change in the cell—and now the change was obviously in the *form*. As before, it was in vain that I, at first, endeavoured to appreciate or understand what was taking place. But not long was I left in doubt. The Inquisitorial vengeance had been hurried by my two-fold escape, and there was to be no more dallying with the King of Terrors. The room had been square. I saw that two of its iron angles were now acute—two, consequently, obtuse. The fearful difference quickly increased with a low rumbling or moaning sound. In an instant the apartment had shifted its form into that of a lozenge. But the alteration stopped not here—I neither hoped nor desired it to stop. I could have clasped the red walls to my bosom as a garment of eternal peace. "Death," I said, "any death but that of the pit!" Fool! might I have not known that *into the pit* it was the object of the burning iron to urge me? Could I resist its glow? or, if even that, could I withstand its pressure? And now, flatter and flatter grew the lozenge, with a rapidity that left me no time for contemplation. Its centre, and of course, its greatest width, came just over the yawning gulf. I shrank back—but the closing walls pressed me resistlessly onward. At length for my seared and writhing body there was no longer an inch of foothold on the firm floor of the prison. I struggled no more, but the agony of my soul found vent in one loud, long, and final scream of despair. I felt that I tottered upon the brink—I averted my eyes—

There was a discordant hum of human voices! There was a loud blast as of many trumpets! There was a harsh grating as of a thousand thunders! The fiery walls rushed back! An outstretched arm caught my own as I fell, fainting, into the abyss. It was that of General Lasalle.[9] The French army had entered Toledo. The Inquisition was in the hands of its enemies.

The Tell-Tale Heart First published in the *Boston Pioneer* (January 1843). The text reprinted here is that of the *Broadway Journal* (August 23, 1845). Mabbott points to Daniel Webster's account of the April 6, 1830 murder of Joseph White by Richard Crowninshield Jr., who had been hired by John Francis Knapp to do the deed. Crowninshield killed himself, but Knapp was brought to trial, which took place in July and August 1830. Webster, a special prosecutor, published his *Argument of the Trial* the same year. In it, he describes the slow, step-by-step murder, tells how the calmness of the accused little by little gave way, and dramatizes the building pressure (indeed, compulsion) to confess. Another source for Poe's tale would seem to be Charles Dickens's "Confession Found in a Prison in the Time of Charles the Second," collected in *Master Humphrey's Clock and Other Early Stories and Sketches*, which Poe re-

8. A condition in which the symptoms of chills, fever, and sweating alternate.
9. Antoine, comte de Lasalle (1775–1809), one of Napoleon's most successful generals, entered the city of Toledo in 1808. The Napoleonic wars brought the Inquisition to a temporary halt; but after the French had been expelled, the Inquisition falteringly began again in the second decade of the 19th century. Although this reference to the count of Lasalle is a historical allusion, it may not be insignificant that *la salle* in French means "the room."

viewed in *Graham's* (May 1841). The narrator tells how he murdered his nephew (whom he could not bear to look in the eye) and placed a chair over the burial site in front of two visitors. The body was discovered when bloodhounds appeared on the scene. The first version of the story carried as a motto the fourth stanza of Henry Wadsworth Longfellow's "A Psalm of Life" (1838), which contains the phrases: "our hearts . . . like muffled drums, are beating / Funeral marches to the grave."

The Tell-Tale Heart

True!—nervous—very, very dreadfully nervous I had been and am; but why *will* you say that I am mad? The disease had sharpened my senses—not destroyed—not dulled them. Above all was the sense of hearing acute. I heard all things in the heaven and in the earth.[1] I heard many things in hell. How, then, am I mad? Hearken! and observe how healthily—how calmly I can tell you the whole story.[2]

It is impossible to say how first the idea entered my brain; but once conceived, it haunted me day and night. Object there was none. Passion there was none. I loved the old man. He had never wronged me. He had never given me insult. For his gold I had no desire. I think it was his eye! yes, it was this! He had the eye of a vulture—a pale blue eye, with a film over it. Whenever it fell upon me, my blood ran cold; and so by degrees—very gradually—I made up my mind to take the life of the old man, and thus rid myself of the eye forever.

Now this is the point. You fancy me mad. Madmen know nothing. But you should have seen *me*. You should have seen how wisely I proceeded—with what caution—with what foresight—with what dissimulation I went to work! I was never kinder to the old man than during the whole week before I killed him. And every night, about midnight, I turned the latch of his door and opened it—oh so gently! And then, when I had made an opening sufficient for my head, I put in a dark lantern, all closed, closed, so that no light shone out, and then I thrust in my head. Oh, you would have laughed to see how cunningly I thrust it in! I moved it slowly—very, very slowly, so that I might not disturb the old man's sleep. It took me an hour to place my whole head within the opening so far that I could see him as he lay upon his bed. Ha!—would a madman have been so wise as this? And then, when my head was well in the room, I undid the lantern cautiously—oh, so cautiously—cautiously (for the hinges creaked)—I undid it just so much that a single thin ray fell upon the vulture eye. And this I did for seven long nights—every night just at midnight—but I found the eye always closed; and so it was impossible to do the work; for it was not the old man who vexed me, but his Evil Eye.[3] And every morning,

1. Cf. Philippians 2:10: "Things in heaven, and things in earth, and things under the earth."
2. In his account "The Trial of James Wood" in *Alexander's Weekly Messenger* (April 1, 1840), Poe mentions that the extreme calmness of the murderer suggested that the man was insane rather than the reverse.
3. The old man's disturbingly abnormal eye has been transformed by the narrator into the Evil Eye of superstition—often conceived as an instrument of a demon or the devil. Traditionally,

when the day broke, I went boldly into the chamber, and spoke coura-
geously to him, calling him by name in a hearty tone,[4] and inquiring
how he had passed the night. So you see he would have been a very
profound old man, indeed, to suspect that every night, just at twelve, I
looked in upon him while he slept.

Upon the eighth night I was more than usually cautious in opening
the door. A watch's minute hand moves more quickly than did mine.
Never before that night, had I *felt* the extent of my own powers—of
my sagacity. I could scarcely contain my feelings of triumph. To think
that there I was, opening the door, little by little, and he not even to
dream of my secret deeds or thoughts. I fairly chuckled at the
idea; and perhaps he heard me; for he moved on the bed suddenly, as
if startled. Now you may think that I drew back—but no. His room
was as black as pitch with the thick darkness, (for the shutters were
close fastened, through fear of robbers,) and so I knew that he could
not see the opening of the door, and I kept pushing it on steadily,
steadily.

I had my head in, and was about to open the lantern, when my
thumb slipped upon the tin fastening, and the old man sprang up in
the bed, crying out—"Who's there?"

I kept quite still and said nothing. For a whole hour I did not move
a muscle, and in the meantime I did not hear him lie down. He was
still sitting up in the bed listening;—just as I have done, night after
night, hearkening to the death watches in the wall.[5]

Presently I heard a slight groan, and I knew it was the groan of mor-
tal terror. It was not a groan of pain or of grief—oh, no!—it was the
low stifled sound that arises from the bottom of the soul when over-
charged with awe. I knew the sound well. Many a night, just at mid-
night, when all the world slept, it has welled up from my own bosom,
deepening, with its dreadful echo, the terrors that distracted me. I say
I knew it well. I knew what the old man felt, and pitied him, although
I chuckled at heart. I knew that he had been lying awake ever since
the first slight noise, when he had turned in the bed. His fears had
been ever since growing upon him. He had been trying to fancy them
causeless, but could not. He had been saying to himself—"It is noth-
ing but the wind in the chimney—it is only a mouse crossing the
floor," or "it is merely a cricket which has made a single chirp." Yes, he
has been trying to comfort himself with these suppositions: but he had
found all in vain. *All in vain*; because Death, in approaching him had
stalked with his black shadow before him, and enveloped the victim.
And it was the mournful influence of the unperceived shadow that

a person with the Evil Eye is said to have the power to inflict pain or injury, cause ill luck, or
 cast a spell by the fixed stare of the eye.
4. Since the narrator calls the old man "by name," it seems unlikely that he is addressing his
 father, as some critics have suggested.
5. Two or more species of beetle that gnaw in walls and old furniture. During their mating sea-
 son, they signal by bumping their heads against solid objects, the sound of which supersti-
 tiously came to be called the "death watch," foretelling the death of someone in the house.
 (Poe's narrator night after night conducts his own kind of death watch.) Contemporary de-
 scriptions of the rhythmic sounds of these beetles, as well as of crickets and cicadas, note
 how the cadences seem to match the rhythms of one's own pulse.

caused him to feel—although he neither saw nor heard—to *feel* the presence of my head within the room.

When I had waited a long time, very patiently, without hearing him lie down, I resolved to open a little—a very, very little crevice in the lantern. So I opened it—you cannot imagine how stealthily, stealthily—until, at length a single dim ray, like the thread of the spider, shot from out the crevice and fell full upon the vulture eye.

It was open—wide, wide open—and I grew furious as I gazed upon it. I saw it with perfect distinctness—all a dull blue, with a hideous veil over it that chilled the very marrow in my bones; but I could see nothing else of the old man's face or person: for I had directed the ray as if by instinct, precisely upon the damned spot.

And have I not told you that what you mistake for madness is but over acuteness of the senses?[6]—now, I say, there came to my ears a low, dull, quick sound, such as a watch makes when enveloped in cotton. I knew *that* sound well, too. It was the beating of the old man's heart. It increased my fury, as the beating of a drum stimulates the soldier into courage.

But even yet I refrained and kept still. I scarcely breathed. I held the lantern motionless. I tried how steadily I could maintain the ray upon the eye. Meantime the hellish tattoo of the heart increased. It grew quicker and quicker, and louder and louder every instant. The old man's terror *must* have been extreme! It grew louder, I say, louder every moment!—do you mark me well? I have told you that I am nervous: so I am. And now at the dead hour of the night, amid the dreadful silence of that old house, so strange a noise as this excited me to uncontrollable terror. Yet, for some minutes longer I refrained and stood still. But the beating grew louder, louder! I thought the heart must burst. And now a new anxiety seized me—the sound would be heard by a neighbour! The old man's hour had come! With a loud yell, I threw open the lantern and leaped into the room. He shrieked once—once only. In an instant I dragged him to the floor, and pulled the heavy bed over him. I then smiled gaily, to find the deed so far done. But, for many minutes, the heart beat on with a muffled sound. This, however, did not vex me; it would not be heard through the wall. At length it ceased. The old man was dead. I removed the bed and examined the corpse. Yes, he was stone, stone dead. I placed my hand upon the heart and held it there many minutes. There was no pulsation. He was stone dead. His eye would trouble me no more.

If still you think me mad, you will think so no longer when I describe the wise precautions I took for the concealment of the body. The night waned, and I worked hastily, but in silence. First of all I dismembered the corpse. I cut off the head and the arms and the legs.

I then took up three planks from the flooring of the chamber, and deposited all between the scantlings.[7] I then replaced the boards so

6. Cf. Roderick Usher (see notes to "The Fall of the House of Usher," pp. 199ff. herein).
7. Small timbers supporting a floor.

cleverly, so cunningly, that no human eye—not even *his*—could have detected any thing wrong. There was nothing to wash out—no stain of any kind—no blood-spot whatever. I had been too wary for that. A tub had caught all—ha! ha!

When I had made an end of these labors, it was four o'clock—still dark as midnight. As the bell sounded the hour, there came a knocking at the street door. I went down to open it with a light heart,—for what had I *now* to fear? There entered three men, who introduced themselves, with perfect suavity, as officers of the police. A shriek had been heard by a neighbour during the night; suspicion of foul play had been aroused; information had been lodged at the police office, and they (the officers) had been deputed to search the premises.

I smiled,—for *what* had I to fear? I bade the gentlemen welcome. The shriek, I said, was my own in a dream. The old man, I mentioned, was absent in the country. I took my visitors all over the house. I bade them search—search *well*. I led them, at length, to *his* chamber. I showed them his treasures, secure, undisturbed. In the enthusiasm of my confidence, I brought chairs into the room, and desired them *here* to rest from their fatigues, while I myself, in the wild audacity of my perfect triumph, placed my own seat upon the very spot beneath which reposed the corpse of the victim.

The officers were satisfied. My *manner* had convinced them. I was singularly at ease. They sat, and while I answered cheerily, they chatted of familiar things. But, ere long, I felt myself getting pale and wished them gone. My head ached, and I fancied a ringing in my ears: but still they sat and still chatted. The ringing became more distinct:—it continued and became more distinct: I talked more freely to get rid of the feeling: but it continued and gained definitiveness—until, at length, I found that the noise was *not* within my ears.

No doubt I now grew *very* pale;—but I talked more fluently, and with a heightened voice. Yet the sound increased—and what could I do? It was *a low, dull, quick sound—much such a sound as a watch makes when enveloped in cotton.* I gasped for breath—and yet the officers heard it not. I talked more quickly—more vehemently; but the noise steadily increased. I arose and argued about trifles, in a high key and with violent gesticulations; but the noise steadily increased. Why *would* they not be gone? I paced the floor to and fro with heavy strides, as if excited to fury by the observations of the men—but the noise steadily increased. Oh God! what *could* I do? I foamed—I raved—I swore! I swung the chair upon which I had been sitting, and grated it upon the boards, but the noise arose over all and continually increased. It grew louder—louder—*louder!* And still the men chatted pleasantly, and smiled. Was it possible they heard not? Almighty God!—no, no! They heard!—they suspected!—they *knew!*—they were making a mockery of my horror!—this I thought, and this I think. But anything was better than this agony! Anything was more tolerable than this derision! I could bear those hypocritical smiles no longer! I felt that I must scream or die!—and now—again!—hark! louder! louder! louder! *louder!*—

"Villains!" I shrieked, "dissemble no more! I admit the deed!—tear up the planks!—here, here!—it is the beating of his hideous heart!"

The Gold-Bug First published in two parts in the Philadelphia *Dollar Newspaper* (June 21 and 28, 1843) as the $100 winning entry in a contest. The text reprinted here is from *Tales* (1845); minor revisions occur in the J. Lorimer Graham copy of *Tales* (cf. Mabbott). Poe was capitalizing on the contemporary popularity of puzzles and cryptograms in mass-market publications. The story includes the decoding of a mysterious cryptogram that is supposed to lead to the discovery of buried pirate treasure, specifically that of the famous Captain Kidd (William Kidd, c. 1645–1701), though in reprints the code contains errors. In *Alexander's Weekly Messenger* for December 18, 1839, Poe issued a challenge: he would decipher any cryptogram sent him. Also see his piece in *Graham's* for July 1841, where he claimed to have solved every cryptogram he received save one that was nonsense. Just how good a cryptographer Poe was is a matter of continuing scholarly debate. The present story is one of Poe's tales of "ratiocination," in which we follow the "solution" of a mystery via a somewhat credulous or slow-witted narrator (see notes to "The Murders in the Rue Morgue," pp. 239ff. herein and "The Purloined Letter, pp. 367ff.). Among the more likely influences is Washington Irving's "The Money Diggers" section of *Tales of a Traveler* (1824), though other stories of pirate treasure abounded. "The Gold-Bug" was extremely popular; it was turned into a play the same year as its first publication, and Poe claimed that it was one of his most frequently reprinted pieces.

The Gold-Bug

> What ho! what ho! this fellow is dancing mad!
> He hath been bitten by the Tarantula.
> > *All in the Wrong.*[1]

MANY years ago, I contracted an intimacy with a Mr. William Legrand. He was of an ancient Huguenot family,[2] and had once been wealthy; but a series of misfortunes had reduced him to want. To avoid the mortification consequent upon his disasters, he left New Orleans, the city of his forefathers, and took up his residence at Sullivan's Island, near Charleston, South Carolina.

This Island is a very singular one. It consists of little else than the sea sand, and is about three miles long. Its breadth at no point exceeds a quarter of a mile. It is separated from the main land by a scarcely

1. According to Mabbott and others, this quotation is not from Arthur Murphy's comedy, *All in the Wrong* (1761), but is Poe's own composition. The poisonous bite of the tarantula spider is supposed to have sent the victim into spasms and twitches; frenzied dancing (there is an Italian folk dance called the tarantella) was supposed to ensue, though in some legends the "dancing" is said to be a curative. In any event, the words *tarantula* and *bug* suggest the onset of madness; the phrase "gold-bug" may have suggested the growing gold craze of the 1840s in America (cf. Poe's ironic poem "Eldorado," p. 74 herein, and his satiric tale "Von Kempelen and His Discovery," both written at the time of the California gold rush).
2. Fundamentalist French Protestants (Calvinists), who, having been driven out of France, settled in the Netherlands, Switzerland, Great Britain, and America.

perceptible creek, oozing its way through a wilderness of reeds and slime, a favorite resort of the marsh-hen. The vegetation, as might be supposed, is scant, or at least dwarfish. No trees of any magnitude are to be seen. Near the western extremity, where Fort Moultrie[3] stands, and where are some miserable frame buildings, tenanted, during summer, by the fugitives from Charleston dust and fever, may be found, indeed, the bristly palmetto; but the whole island, with the exception of this western point, and a line of hard, white beach on the sea-coast, is covered with a dense undergrowth of the sweet myrtle, so much prized by the horticulturists of England. The shrub here often attains the height of fifteen or twenty feet, and forms an almost impenetrable coppice, burthening the air with its fragrance.

In the inmost recesses of this coppice, not far from the eastern or more remote end of the island, Legrand had built himself a small hut, which he occupied when I first, by mere accident, made his acquaintance. This soon ripened into friendship—for there was much in the recluse to excite interest and esteem. I found him well educated, with unusual powers of mind, but infected with misanthropy,[4] and subject to perverse moods of alternate enthusiasm and melancholy. He had with him many books, but rarely employed them. His chief amusements were gunning and fishing, or sauntering along the beach and through the myrtles, in quest of shells or entomological specimens;—his collection of the latter might have been envied by a Swammerdamm.[5] In these excursions he was usually accompanied by an old negro, called Jupiter,[6] who had been manumitted before the reverses of the family, but who could be induced, neither by threats nor by promises, to abandon what he considered his right of attendance upon the footsteps of his young "Massa Will." It is not improbable that the relatives of Legrand, conceiving him to be somewhat unsettled in intellect, had contrived to instil this obstinacy into Jupiter, with a view to the supervision and guardianship of the wanderer.

The winters in the latitude of Sullivan's Island are seldom very severe, and in the fall of the year it is a rare event indeed when a fire is considered necessary. About the middle of October, 18—, there oc-

3. Where, from November 1827 to December 1828, Poe was stationed. It is on the western end of Sullivan's Island, not far off the coast at Charleston, South Carolina; thus Poe knew the island and the Charleston area well.
4. Hatred or mistrust of mankind.
5. Jan Swammerdamm (1637–1680), a Dutch entomologist who wrote a history of insects (posthumously published 1737–38; translated 1758).
6. The first of several references suggesting a coded alchemical allegory in the story. In medieval alchemy and astrology, there were seven metals corresponding to the seven orbits of the known planets and the moon and sun. In this system, tin = Jupiter, lead = Saturn, mercury = Mercury, iron = Mars, copper = Venus, silver = the moon, and gold = the sun. The alchemist or "natural philosopher," writing his experiments in a secret code, tried to turn base metals, such as tin and lead, into gold by symbolically progressing upward through the seven branches of the cylindrical alchemical tree, at the bottom of which lay buried the mixed bones of animals (usually a wolf) and human beings. At the moment of transmutation, the metallic mixture became the philosopher's "stone," in an iridescent flash of many-colored lights called the "peacock's tail." Profane alchemy sought simply wealth; the goal of sacred alchemy was enlightenment, the transfiguration not just of metals but of the philosopher himself (see notes on alchemy in other of Poe's stories). In the present tale, which is in part satiric, the black slave, Jupiter, a freed slave ("manumitted"), climbs up the smooth metallic trunk of the tulip tree to its seventh branch and prattles about tin and gold.

curred, however, a day of remarkable chilliness. Just before sunset I scrambled my way through the evergreens to the hut of my friend, whom I had not visited for several weeks—my residence being, at that time, in Charleston, a distance of nine miles from the Island, while the facilities of passage and re-passage were very far behind those of the present day. Upon reaching the hut I rapped, as was my custom, and getting no reply, sought for the key where I knew it was secreted, unlocked the door and went in. A fine fire was blazing upon the hearth. It was a novelty, and by no means an ungrateful one. I threw off an overcoat, took an arm-chair by the crackling logs, and awaited patiently the arrival of my hosts.

Soon after dark they arrived, and gave me a most cordial welcome. Jupiter, grinning from ear to ear, bustled about to prepare some marsh-hens for supper. Legrand was in one of his fits—how else shall I term them?—of enthusiasm. He had found an unknown bivalve, forming a new genus, and, more than this, he had hunted down and secured, with Jupiter's assistance, a *scarabæus*[7] which he believed to be totally new, but in respect to which he wished to have my opinion on the morrow.

"And why not to-night?" I asked, rubbing my hands over the blaze, and wishing the whole tribe of *scarabæi* at the devil.

"Ah, if I had only known you were here!" said Legrand, "but it's so long since I saw you; and how could I foresee that you would pay me a visit this very night of all others? As I was coming home I met Lieutenant G——, from the fort, and, very foolishly, I lent him the bug; so it will be impossible for you to see it until the morning. Stay here to-night, and I will send Jup down for it at sunrise. It is the loveliest thing in creation!"

"What?—sunrise?"

"Nonsense! no!—the bug. It is of a brilliant gold color—about the size of a large hickory-nut—with two jet black spots near one extremity of the back, and another, somewhat longer, at the other. The *antennæ*[8] are—"

"Dey aint *no* tin in him, Massa Will, I keep a tellin on you," here interrupted Jupiter; "de bug is a goole bug, solid, ebery bit of him, inside and all, sep him wing—neber feel half so hebby a bug in my life."

"Well, suppose it is, Jup," replied Legrand, somewhat more earnestly, it seemed to me, than the case demanded, "is that any reason for your letting the birds burn? The color"—here he turned to me—"is really almost enough to warrant Jupiter's idea. You never saw a more brilliant metallic lustre than the scales emit—but of this you cannot judge till to-morrow. In the mean time I can give you some idea of the shape." Saying this, he seated himself at a small table, on which were a pen and ink, but no paper. He looked for some in a drawer, but found none.

7. An Old World genus of beetle. The ancient Egyptians regarded certain species as sacred and used the carved image of the scarab in amulets. Poe seems to have combined the physical characteristics of two species of beetles found on Sullivan's Island.
8. Pronounced in Southern dialects "*ann-tinny*" (Mabbott); possibly a pun on *tin*.

"Never mind," said he at length, "this will answer;" and he drew from his waistcoat pocket a scrap of what I took to be very dirty foolscap,[9] and made upon it a rough drawing with the pen. While he did this, I retained my seat by the fire, for I was still chilly. When the design was complete, he handed it to me without rising. As I received it, a loud growl was heard, succeeded by a scratching at the door. Jupiter opened it, and a large Newfoundland, belonging to Legrand, rushed in, leaped upon my shoulders, and loaded me with caresses; for I had shown him much attention during previous visits. When his gambols were over, I looked at the paper, and, to speak the truth, found myself not a little puzzled at what my friend had depicted.

"Well!" I said, after contemplating it for some minutes, "this *is* a strange *scarabæus*, I must confess: new to me: never saw anything like it before—unless it was a skull, or a death's-head—which it more nearly resembles than anything else that has come under *my* observation."

"A death's-head!" echoed Legrand—"Oh—yes—well, it has something of that appearance upon paper, no doubt. The two upper black spots look like eyes, eh? and the longer one at the bottom like a mouth—and then the shape of the whole is oval."

"Perhaps so," said I; "but, Legrand, I fear you are no artist. I must wait until I see the beetle itself, if I am to form any idea of its personal appearance."

"Well, I don't know," said he, a little nettled, "I draw tolerably—*should* do it at least—have had good masters, and flatter myself that I am not quite a blockhead."

"But, my dear fellow, you are joking then," said I, "this is a very passable *skull*—indeed, I may say that it is a very *excellent* skull, according to the vulgar notions about such specimens of physiology—and your *scarabæus* must be the queerest *scarabæus* in the world if it resembles it. Why, we may get up a very thrilling bit of superstition upon this hint. I presume you will call the bug *scarabæus caput hominis*,[1] or something of that kind—there are many similar titles in the Natural Histories. But where are the *antennæ* you spoke of?"

"The *antennæ!*" said Legrand, who seemed to be getting unaccountably warm upon the subject; "I am sure you must see the *antennæ*. I made them as distinct as they are in the original insect, and I presume that is sufficient."

"Well, well," I said, "perhaps you have—still I don't see them;" and I handed him the paper without additional remark, not wishing to ruffle his temper; but I was much surprised at the turn affairs had taken; his ill humor puzzled me—and, as for the drawing of the beetle, there were positively *no antennæ* visible, and the whole *did* bear a very close resemblance to the ordinary cuts of a death's-head.

9. Sheet of writing paper measuring approximately thirteen by sixteen inches.
1. The man's-head beetle (Latin); i.e., with the apparent figuration of a skull on its back.

He received the paper very peevishly, and was about to crumple it, apparently to throw it in the fire, when a casual glance at the design seemed suddenly to rivet his attention. In an instant his face grew violently red—in another as excessively pale. For some minutes he continued to scrutinize the drawing minutely where he sat. At length he arose, took a candle from the table, and proceeded to seat himself upon a sea-chest in the farthest corner of the room. Here again he made an anxious examination of the paper; turning it in all directions. He said nothing, however, and his conduct greatly astonished me; yet I thought it prudent not to exacerbate the growing moodiness of his temper by any comment. Presently he took from his coat pocket a wallet, placed the paper carefully in it, and deposited both in a writing-desk, which he locked. He now grew more composed in his demeanor; but his original air of enthusiasm had quite disappeared. Yet he seemed not so much sulky as abstracted. As the evening wore away he became more and more absorbed in reverie, from which no sallies of mine could arouse him. It had been my intention to pass the night at the hut, as I had frequently done before, but, seeing my host in this mood, I deemed it proper to take leave. He did not press me to remain, but, as I departed, he shook my hand with even more than his usual cordiality.

It was about a month after this (and during the interval I had seen nothing of Legrand) when I received a visit, at Charleston, from his man, Jupiter. I had never seen the good old negro look so dispirited, and I feared that some serious disaster had befallen my friend.

"Well, Jup," said I, "what is the matter now?—how is your master?"

"Why, to speak de troof, massa, him not so berry well as mought be."

"Not well! I am truly sorry to hear it. What does he complain of?"

"Dar! dat's it!—him neber plain of notin—but him berry sick for all dat."

"*Very* sick, Jupiter!—why didn't you say so at once? Is he confined to bed?"

"No, dat he aint!—he aint find nowhar—dat's just whar de shoe pinch—my mind is got to be berry hebby bout poor Massa Will."

"Jupiter, I should like to understand what it is you are talking about. You say your master is sick. Hasn't he told you what ails him?"

"Why, massa, taint worf while for to git mad about de matter—Massa Will say noffin at all aint de matter wid him—but den what make him go about looking dis here way, wid he head down and he soldiers up, and as white as a gose? And den he keep a syphon all de time—"

"Keeps a what, Jupiter?"

"Keeps a syphon[2] wid de figgurs on de slate—de queerest figgurs I ebber did see. Ise gittin to be skeered, I tell you. Hab for to keep mighty tight eye pon him noovers.[3] Todder day he gib me slip fore de sun

2. Jupiter confuses the word *cipher* with the word *syphon*.
3. Probably, maneuvers.

up and was gone de whole ob de blessed day. I had a big stick ready cut for to gib him deuced good beating[4] when he did come— but Ise sich a fool dat I hadn't de heart arter all—he look so berry poorly."

"Eh?—what?—ah yes!—upon the whole I think you had better not be too severe with the poor fellow—don't flog him, Jupiter—he can't very well stand it—but can you form no idea of what has occasioned this illness, or rather this change of conduct? Has anything unpleasant happened since I saw you?"

"No, massa, dey aint bin noffin onpleasant *since* den—'twas *fore* den I'm feared—'twas de berry day you was dare."

"How? what do you mean?"

"Why, massa, I mean de bug—dare now."

"The what?"

"De bug—I'm berry sartain dat Massa Will bin bit somewhere bout de head by dat goole-bug."

"And what cause have you, Jupiter, for such a supposition?"

"Claws enuff, massa, and mouff too. I nebber did see sich a deuced bug—he kick and he bite ebery ting what cum near him. Massa Will cotch him fuss, but had for to let him go gin mighty quick, I tell you— den was de time he must ha got de bite. I did n't like de look ob de bug mouff, myself, no how, so I would n't take hold ob him wid my finger, but I cotch him wid a piece ob paper dat I found. I rap him up in de paper and stuff piece ob it in he mouff—dat was de way."

"And you think, then, that your master was really bitten by the bee- tle, and that the bite made him sick?"

"I do n't tink noffin about it—I nose it. What make him dream bout de goole so much, if taint cause he bit by de goole-bug? Ise heerd bout dem goole-bugs fore dis."

"But how do you know he dreams about gold?"

"How I know? why cause he talk about it in he sleep—dat's how I nose."

"Well, Jup, perhaps you are right; but to what fortunate circum- stance am I to attribute the honor of a visit from you to-day?"

"What de matter, massa?"

"Did you bring any message from Mr. Legrand?"

"No, massa, I bring dis here pissel;"[5] and here Jupiter handed me a note which ran thus:

MY DEAR——

Why have I not seen you for so long a time? I hope you have not been so foolish as to take offence at any little *brusquerie*[6] of mine; but no, that is improbable.

Since I saw you I have had great cause for anxiety. I have something

4. A traditional "therapy" for persons considered hysterical or temporarily mad—still a common concept (cf. a slap across the face to "bring people to their senses"); here apparently a cultural joke (a black man beating a white man in the South). The characters of Jupiter and Pompey ("How to Write a Blackwood Article: A Predicament") have been seen by some critics as exam- ples of Poe's racism (but see Terence Whalen's essay, "Average Racism" (pp. 920ff. herein).
5. Jupiter's mispronunciation of *epistle* (letter).
6. Brusqueness or abruptness, which could be misunderstood as coldness or rudeness.

to tell you, yet scarcely know how to tell it, or whether I should tell it at all.

I have not been quite well for some days past, and poor old Jup annoys me, almost beyond endurance, by his well-meant attentions. Would you believe it?—he had prepared a huge stick, the other day, with which to chastise me for giving him the slip, and spending the day, *solus*, among the hills on the main land. I verily believe that my ill looks alone saved me a flogging.

I have made no addition to my cabinet since we met.

If you can, in any way, make it convenient, come over with Jupiter. *Do* come. I wish to see you *to-night*, upon business of importance. I assure you that it is of the *highest* importance.

> Ever yours, WILLIAM LEGRAND.

There was something in the tone of this note which gave me great uneasiness. Its whole style differed materially from that of Legrand. What could he be dreaming of? What new crotchet possessed his excitable brain? What "business of the highest importance" could *he* possibly have to transact? Jupiter's account of him boded no good. I dreaded lest the continued pressure of misfortune had, at length, fairly unsettled the reason of my friend. Without a moment's hesitation, therefore, I prepared to accompany the negro.

Upon reaching the wharf, I noticed a scythe and three spades, all apparently new, lying in the bottom of the boat in which we were to embark.

"What is the meaning of all this, Jup?" I inquired.

"Him syfe, massa, and spade."

"Very true; but what are they doing here?"

"Him de syfe and de spade what Massa Will sis pon my buying for him in de town, and de debbils own lot of money I had to gib for em."

"But what, in the name of all that is mysterious, is your 'Massa Will' going to do with scythes and spades?"

"Dat's more dan *I* know, and debbil take me if I don't blieve 'tis more dan he know, too. But it's all cum ob de bug."

Finding that no satisfaction was to be obtained of Jupiter, whose whole intellect seemed to be absorbed by "de bug," I now stepped into the boat and made sail. With a fair and strong breeze we soon ran into the little cove to the northward of Fort Moultrie, and a walk of some two miles brought us to the hut. It was about three in the afternoon when we arrived. Legrand had been awaiting us in eager expectation. He grasped my hand with a nervous *empressement*[7] which alarmed me and strengthened the suspicions already entertained. His countenance was pale even to ghastliness, and his deep-set eyes glared with unnatural lustre. After some inquiries respecting his health, I asked him, not knowing what better to say, if he had yet obtained the *scarabæus* from Lieutenant G——.

"Oh, yes," he replied, coloring violently, "I got it from him the next morning. Nothing should tempt me to part with that *scarabæus*. Do you know that Jupiter is quite right about it?"

7. Pressure.

"In what way?" I asked, with a sad foreboding at heart.

"In supposing it to be a bug of *real gold*." He said this with an air of profound seriousness, and I felt inexpressibly shocked.

"This bug is to make my fortune," he continued, with a triumphant smile, "to reinstate me in my family possessions. Is it any wonder, then, that I prize it? Since Fortune has thought fit to bestow it upon me, I have only to use it properly and I shall arrive at the gold of which it is the index. Jupiter, bring me that *scarabæus!*"

"What! de bug, massa? I'd rudder not go for trubble dat bug—you mus git him for your own self." Hereupon Legrand arose, with a grave and stately air, and brought me the beetle from a glass case in which it was enclosed. It was a beautiful *scarabæus*, and, at that time, unknown to naturalists—of course a great prize in a scientific point of view. There were two round, black spots near one extremity of the back, and a long one near the other. The scales were exceedingly hard and glossy, with all the appearance of burnished gold. The weight of the insect was very remarkable, and, taking all things into consideration, I could hardly blame Jupiter for his opinion respecting it; but what to make of Legrand's concordance with that opinion, I could not, for the life of me, tell.

"I sent for you," said he, in a grandiloquent[8] tone, when I had completed my examination of the beetle, "I sent for you, that I might have your counsel and assistance in furthering the views of Fate and of the bug"—

"My dear Legrand," I cried, interrupting him, "you are certainly unwell, and had better use some little precautions. You shall go to bed, and I will remain with you a few days, until you get over this. You are feverish and"—

"Feel my pulse," said he.

I felt it, and, to say the truth, found not the slightest indication of fever.

"But you may be ill and yet have no fever. Allow me this once to prescribe for you. In the first place, go to bed. In the next"—

"You are mistaken," he interposed, "I am as well as I can expect to be under the excitement which I suffer. If you really wish me well, you will relieve this excitement."

"And how is this to be done?"

"Very easily. Jupiter and myself are going upon an expedition into the hills, upon the main land, and, in this expedition, we shall need the aid of some person in whom we can confide. You are the only one we can trust. Whether we succeed or fail, the excitement which you now perceive in me will be equally allayed."

"I am anxious to oblige you in any way," I replied; "but do you mean to say that this infernal beetle has any connection with your expedition into the hills?"

"It has."

"Then, Legrand, I can become a party to no such absurd proceeding."

8. Pompous or bombastic speech or expression.

"I am sorry—very sorry—for we shall have to try it by ourselves."

"Try it by yourselves! The man is surely mad!—but stay!—how long do you propose to be absent?"

"Probably all night. We shall start immediately, and be back, at all events, by sunrise."

"And will you promise me, upon your honor, that when this freak of yours is over, and the bug business (good God!) settled to your satisfaction, you will then return home and follow my advice implicitly, as that of your physician?"

"Yes; I promise; and now let us be off, for we have no time to lose."

With a heavy heart I accompanied my friend. We started about four o'clock—Legrand, Jupiter, the dog, and myself. Jupiter had with him the scythe and spades—the whole of which he insisted upon carrying—more through fear, it seemed to me, of trusting either of the implements within reach of his master, than from any excess of industry or complaisance. His demeanor was dogged in the extreme, and "dat deuced bug" were the sole words which escaped his lips during the journey. For my own part, I had charge of a couple of dark lanterns, while Legrand contented himself with the *scarabæus*, which he carried attached to the end of a bit of whip-cord; twirling it to and fro, with the air of a conjuror, as he went. When I observed this last, plain evidence of my friend's aberration of mind, I could scarcely refrain from tears. I thought it best, however, to humor his fancy, at least for the present, or until I could adopt some more energetic measures with a chance of success. In the mean time I endeavored, but all in vain, to sound him in regard to the object of the expedition. Having succeeded in inducing me to accompany him, he seemed unwilling to hold conversation upon any topic of minor importance, and to all my questions vouchsafed no other reply than "we shall see!"

We crossed the creek at the head of the island by means of a skiff, and, ascending the high grounds on the shore of the main land, proceeded in a northwesterly direction, through a tract of country excessively wild and desolate, where no trace of a human footstep was to be seen. Legrand led the way with decision; pausing only for an instant, here and there, to consult what appeared to be certain landmarks of his own contrivance upon a former occasion.

In this manner we journeyed for about two hours, and the sun was just setting when we entered a region infinitely more dreary than any yet seen. It was a species of table land, near the summit of an almost inaccessible hill, densely wooded from base to pinnacle, and interpersed with huge crags that appeared to lie loosely upon the soil, and in many cases were prevented from precipitating themselves into the valleys below, merely by the support of the trees against which they reclined. Deep ravines, in various directions, gave an air of still sterner solemnity to the scene.

The natural platform to which we had clambered was thickly overgrown with brambles, through which we soon discovered that it would have been impossible to force our way but for the scythe; and Jupiter, by direction of his master, proceeded to clear for us a path to the foot

of an enormously tall tulip-tree, which stood, with some eight or ten oaks, upon the level, and far surpassed them all, and all other trees which I had then ever seen, in the beauty of its foliage and form, in the wide spread of its branches, and in the general majesty of its appearance. When we reached this tree, Legrand turned to Jupiter, and asked him if he thought he could climb it. The old man seemed a little staggered by the question, and for some moments made no reply. At length he approached the huge trunk, walked slowly around it, and examined it with minute attention. When he had completed his scrutiny, he merely said,

"Yes, massa, Jup climb any tree he ebber see in he life."

"Then up with you as soon as possible, for it will soon be too dark to see what we are about."

"How far mus go up, massa?" inquired Jupiter.

"Get up the main trunk first, and then I will tell you which way to go—and here—stop! take this beetle with you."

"De bug, Massa Will!—de goole bug!" cried the negro, drawing back in dismay—"what for mus tote de bug way up de tree?—d—n if I do!"

"If you are afraid, Jup, a great big negro like you, to take hold of a harmless little dead beetle, why you can carry it up by this string—but, if you do not take it up with you in some way, I shall be under the necessity of breaking your head with this shovel."

"What de matter now, massa?" said Jup, evidently shamed into compliance; "always want for to raise fuss wid old nigger. Was only funnin any how. Me feered de bug! what I keer for de bug?" Here he took cautiously hold of the extreme end of the string, and, maintaining the insect as far from his person as circumstances would permit, prepared to ascend the tree.

In youth, the tulip-tree, or *Liriodendron Tulipiferum,*[9] the most magnificent of American foresters, has a trunk peculiarly smooth, and often rises to a great height without lateral branches; but, in its riper age, the bark becomes gnarled and uneven, while many short limbs make their appearance on the stem. Thus the difficulty of ascension, in the present case, lay more in semblance than in reality. Embracing the huge cylinder, as closely as possible, with his arms and knees, seizing with his hands some projections, and resting his naked toes upon others, Jupiter, after one or two narrow escapes from falling, at length wriggled himself into the first great fork, and seemed to consider the whole business as virtually accomplished. The *risk* of the achievement was, in fact, now over, although the climber was some sixty or seventy feet from the ground.

"Which way mus go now, Massa Will?" he asked.

"Keep up the largest branch—the one on this side," said Legrand. The negro obeyed him promptly, and apparently with but little trouble; ascending higher and higher, until no glimpse of his squat figure could

9. I.e., *Liriodendron tulipifera,* the tulip tree, related to the magnolia, popularly associated with the unrelated yellow poplar (or balm of Gilead tree). By changing the ending of the species name to *-ferum* Poe may be punning on *ferrum,* Latin for "iron." See p. 322, n. 6 herein.

be obtained through the dense foliage which enveloped it. Presently his voice was heard in a sort of halloo.

"How much fudder is got for go?"

"How high up are you?" asked Legrand.

"Ebber so fur," replied the negro; "can see de sky fru de top ob de tree."

"Never mind the sky, but attend to what I say. Look down the trunk and count the limbs below you on this side. How many limbs have you passed?"

"One, two, tree, four, fibe—I done pass fibe big limb, massa, pon dis side."

"Then go one limb higher."

In a few minutes the voice was heard again, announcing that the seventh limb[1] was attained.

"Now, Jup," cried Legrand, evidently much excited, "I want you to work your way out upon that limb as far as you can. If you see anything strange, let me know."

By this time what little doubt I might have entertained of my poor friend's insanity, was put finally at rest. I had no alternative but to conclude him stricken with lunacy, and I became seriously anxious about getting him home. While I was pondering upon what was best to be done, Jupiter's voice was again heard.

"Mos feerd for to ventur pon dis limb berry far—tis dead limb putty much all de way."

"Did you say it was a *dead* limb, Jupiter?" cried Legrand in a quavering voice.

"Yes, massa, him dead as de door-nail—done up for sartain—done departed dis here life."

"What in the name of heaven shall I do?" asked Legrand, seemingly in the greatest distress.

"Do!" said I, glad of an opportunity to interpose a word, "why come home and go to bed. Come now!—that's a fine fellow. It's getting late, and, besides, you remember your promise."

"Jupiter," cried he, without heeding me in the least, "do you hear me?"

"Yes, Messa Will, hear you ebber so plain."

"Try the wood well, then, with your knife, and see if you think it *very* rotten."

"Him rotten, massa, sure nuff," replied the negro in a few moments, "but not so berry rotten as mought be. Mought ventur out leetle way pon de limb by myself, dat's true."

"By yourself!—what do you mean?"

"Why I mean de bug. 'Tis *berry* hebby bug. Spose I drop him down fuss, and den de limb won't break wid just de weight ob one nigger."

"You infernal scoundrel!" cried Legrand, apparently much relieved, "what do you mean by telling me such nonsense as that? As sure as you drop that beetle I'll break your neck. Look here, Jupiter, do you hear me?"

1. See p. 322, n. 6 herein.

"Yes, massa, needn't hollo at poor nigger dat style."

"Well! now listen!—if you will venture out on the limb as far as you think safe, and not let go the beetle, I'll make you a present of a silver dollar as soon as you get down."

"I'm gwine, Massa Will—deed I is," replied the negro very promptly—"mos out to the eend now."

"*Out to the end!*" here fairly screamed Legrand, "do you say you are out to the end of that limb?"

"Soon be to de eend, massa,—o-o-o-o-oh! Lor-gol-a-marcy! what *is* dis here pon de tree?"

"Well!" cried Legrand, highly delighted, "what is it?"

"Why taint noffin but a skull—somebody bin lef him head up de tree, and de crows done gobble ebery bit ob de meat off."

"A skull, you say!—very well!—how is it fastened to the limb?—what holds it on?"

"Sure nuff, massa; mus look. Why dis berry curous sarcumstance, pon my word—dare's a great big nail in de skull, what fastens ob it on to de tree."

"Well now, Jupiter, do exactly as I tell you—do you hear?"

"Yes, massa."

"Pay attention, then!—find the left eye of the skull."

"Hum! hoo! dat's good! why dare aint no eye lef at all."

"Curse your stupidity! do you know your right hand from your left?"

"Yes, I nose dat—nose all bout dat—tis my lef hand what I chops de wood wid."

"To be sure! you are left-handed; and your left eye is on the same side as your left hand. Now, I suppose, you can find the left eye of the skull, or the place where the left eye has been. Have you found it?"

Here was a long pause. At length the negro asked,

"Is de lef eye of de skull pon de same side as de lef hand of de skull, too?—cause de skull aint got not a bit ob a hand at all—nebber mind! I got de lef eye now—here de lef eye! what mus do wid it?"

"Let the beetle drop through it, as far as the string will reach—but be careful and not let go your hold of the string."

"All dat done, Massa Will; mighty easy ting for to put de bug fru de hole—look out for him dare below!"

During this colloquy no portion of Jupiter's person could be seen; but the beetle, which he had suffered to descend, was now visible at the end of the string, and glistened, like a globe of burnished gold, in the last rays of the setting sun, some of which still faintly illumined the eminence upon which we stood. The *scarabæus* hung quite clear of any branches, and, if allowed to fall, would have fallen at our feet. Legrand immediately took the scythe, and cleared with it a circular space, three or four yards in diameter, just beneath the insect, and, having accomplished this, ordered Jupiter to let go the string and come down from the tree.

Driving a peg, with great nicety, into the ground, at the precise spot where the beetle fell, my friend now produced from his pocket a tape-measure. Fastening one end of this at that point of the trunk of the

tree which was nearest the peg, he unrolled it till it reached the peg, and thence farther unrolled it, in the direction already established by the two points of the tree and the peg, for the distance of fifty feet— Jupiter clearing away the brambles with the scythe. At the spot thus attained a second peg was driven, and about this, as a centre, a rude circle, about four feet in diameter, described. Taking now a spade himself, and giving one to Jupiter and one to me, Legrand begged us to set about digging as quickly as possible.

To speak the truth, I had no especial relish for such amusement at any time, and, at that particular moment, would most willingly have declined it; for the night was coming on, and I felt much fatigued with the exercise already taken; but I saw no mode of escape, and was fearful of disturbing my poor friend's equanimity by a refusal. Could I have depended, indeed, upon Jupiter's aid, I would have had no hesitation in attempting to get the lunatic home by force; but I was too well assured of the old negro's disposition, to hope that he would assist me, under any circumstances, in a personal contest with his master. I made no doubt that the latter had been infected with some of the innumerable Southern superstitions about money buried, and that his phantasy had received confirmation by the finding of the *scarabæus*, or, perhaps, by Jupiter's obstinacy in maintaining it to be "a bug of real gold." A mind disposed to lunacy would readily be led away by such suggestions—especially if chiming in with favorite preconceived ideas—and then I called to mind the poor fellow's speech about the beetle's being "the index of his fortune." Upon the whole, I was sadly vexed and puzzled, but, at length, I concluded to make a virtue of necessity—to dig with a good will, and thus the sooner to convince the visionary, by ocular demonstration, of the fallacy of the opinions he entertained.

The lanterns having been lit, we all fell to work with a zeal worthy a more rational cause; and, as the glare fell upon our persons and implements, I could not help thinking how picturesque a group we composed, and how strange and suspicious our labors must have appeared to any interloper who, by chance, might have stumbled upon our whereabouts.

We dug very steadily for two hours. Little was said; and our chief embarrassment lay in the yelpings of the dog, who took exceeding interest in our proceedings. He, at length, became so obstreperous[2] that we grew fearful of his giving the alarm to some stragglers in the vicinity;—or, rather, this was the apprehension of Legrand;—for myself, I should have rejoiced at any interruption which might have enabled me to get the wanderer home. The noise was, at length, very effectually silenced by Jupiter, who, getting out of the hole with a dogged air of deliberation, tied the brute's mouth up with one of his suspenders, and then returned, with a grave chuckle, to his task.

When the time mentioned had expired, we had reached a depth of five feet, and yet no signs of any treasure became manifest. A general pause ensued, and I began to hope that the farce was at an end.

2. Aggressively boisterous, animated and loud.

Legrand, however, although evidently much disconcerted, wiped his brow thoughtfully and recommenced. We had excavated the entire circle of four feet diameter, and now we slightly enlarged the limit, and went to the farther depth of two feet. Still nothing appeared. The gold-seeker, whom I sincerely pitied, at length clambered from the pit, with the bitterest disappointment imprinted upon every feature, and proceeded, slowly and reluctantly, to put on his coat, which he had thrown off at the beginning of his labor. In the mean time I made no remark. Jupiter, at a signal from his master, began to gather up his tools. This done, and the dog having been unmuzzled, we turned in profound silence towards home.

We had taken, perhaps, a dozen steps in this direction, when, with a loud oath, Legrand strode up to Jupiter, and seized him by the collar. The astonished negro opened his eyes and mouth to the fullest extent, let fall the spades, and fell upon his knees.

"You scoundrel," said Legrand, hissing out the syllables from between his clenched teeth—"you infernal black villain!—speak, I tell you!—answer me this instant, without prevarication!—which—which is your left eye?"

"Oh, my golly, Massu Will! aint dis here my lef eye for sartain?" roared the terrified Jupiter, placing his hand upon his *right* organ of vision, and holding it there with a desperate pertinacity, as if in immediate dread of his master's attempt at a gouge.

"I thought so!—I knew it! hurrah!" vociferated Legrand, letting the negro go, and executing a series of curvets and caracols,[3] much to the astonishment of his valet, who, arising from his knees, looked, mutely, from his master to myself, and then from myself to his master.

"Come! we must go back," said the latter, "the game's not up yet;" and he again led the way to the tulip-tree.

"Jupiter," said he, when we reached its foot, "come here! was the skull nailed to the limb with the face outwards, or with the face to the limb?"

"De face was out, massa, so dat de crows could get at de eyes good, without any trouble."

"Well, then, was it this eye or that through which you dropped the beetle?"—here Legrand touched each of Jupiter's eyes.

"'Twas dis eye, massa—de lef eye—jis as you tell me," and here it was his right eye that the negro indicated.

"That will do—we must try it again."

Here my friend, about whose madness I now saw, or fancied that I saw, certain indications of method, removed the peg which marked the spot where the beetle fell, to a spot about three inches to the westward of its former position. Taking, now, the tape-measure from the nearest point of the trunk to the peg, as before, and continuing the extension in a straight line to the distance of fifty feet, a spot was indicated, re-

3. Terms used in horsemanship. "Curvets": prancing leaps into the air. "Caracols": capering half-turns to the right or left.

moved, by several yards, from the point at which we had been digging. Around the new position a circle, somewhat larger than in the former instance, was now described, and we again set to work with the spades. I was dreadfully weary, but, scarcely understanding what had occasioned the change in my thoughts, I felt no longer any great aversion from the labor imposed. I had become most unaccountably interested—nay, even excited. Perhaps there was something, amid all the extravagant demeanor of Legrand—some air of forethought, or of deliberation, which impressed me. I dug eagerly, and now and then caught myself actually looking, with something that very much resembled expectation, for the fancied treasure, the vision of which had demented my unfortunate companion. At a period when such vagaries of thought most fully possessed me, and when we had been at work perhaps an hour and a half, we were again interrupted by the violent howlings of the dog. His uneasiness, in the first instance, had been, evidently, but the result of playfulness or caprice, but he now assumed a bitter and serious tone. Upon Jupiter's again attempting to muzzle him, he made furious resistance, and, leaping into the hole, tore up the mould frantically with his claws. In a few seconds he had uncovered a mass of human bones, forming two complete skeletons,[4] intermingled with several buttons of metal, and what appeared to be the dust of decayed woollen. One or two strokes of a spade upturned the blade of a large Spanish knife, and, as we dug farther, three or four loose pieces of gold and silver coin came to light.

At sight of these the joy of Jupiter could scarcely be restrained, but the countenance of his master wore an air of extreme disappointment. He urged us, however, to continue our exertions, and the words were hardly uttered when I stumbled and fell forward, having caught the toe of my boot in a large ring of iron that lay half buried in the loose earth.

We now worked in earnest, and never did I pass ten minutes of more intense excitement. During this interval we had fairly unearthed an oblong chest of wood, which, from its perfect preservation and wonderful hardness, had plainly been subjected to some mineralizing process—perhaps that of the Bi-chloride of Mercury.[5] This box was three feet and a half long, three feet broad, and two and a half feet deep. It was firmly secured by bands of wrought iron, riveted, and forming a kind of open trelliswork over the whole. On each side of the chest, near the top, were three rings of iron—six in all—by means of which a firm hold could be obtained by six persons. Our utmost united endeavors served only to disturb the coffer very slightly in its bed. We at once saw the impossibility of removing so great a weight. Luckily, the sole fastenings of the lid consisted of two sliding bolts. These we drew back—trembling and panting with anxiety. In an instant, a treasure of incalculable value lay gleaming before us. As the rays of the

4. See p. 322, n. 6 herein; and note the dog's name, Wolf (see p. 340 herein).
5. A lethal mixture used to preserve museum pieces and wood from rot (the reference also continues the alchemical suggestions).

lanterns fell within the pit, there flashed upwards a glow and a glare, from a confused heap of gold and of jewels, that absolutely dazzled our eyes.

I shall not pretend to describe the feelings with which I gazed. Amazement was, of course, predominant. Legrand appeared exhausted with excitement, and spoke very few words. Jupiter's countenance wore, for some minutes, as deadly a pallor as it is possible, in the nature of things, for any negro's visage to assume. He seemed stupified—thunderstricken. Presently he fell upon his knees in the pit, and, burying his naked arms up to the elbows in gold, let them there remain, as if enjoying the luxury of a bath. At length, with a deep sigh, he exclaimed, as if in a soliloquy,

"And dis all cum ob de goole-bug! de putty goole-bug! de poor little goole-bug, what I boosed[6] in dat sabage kind ob style! Aint you shamed ob yourself, nigger?—answer me dat!"

It became necessary, at last, that I should arouse both master and valet to the expediency of removing the treasure. It was growing late, and it behooved us to make exertion, that we might get every thing housed before daylight. It was difficult to say what should be done, and much time was spent in deliberation—so confused were the ideas of all. We, finally, lightened the box by removing two thirds of its contents, when we were enabled, with some trouble, to raise it from the hole. The articles taken out were deposited among the brambles, and the dog left to guard them, with strict orders from Jupiter neither, upon any pretence, to stir from the spot, nor to open his mouth until our return. We then hurriedly made for home with the chest; reaching the hut in safety, but after excessive toil, at one o'clock in the morning. Worn out as we were, it was not in human nature to do more immediately. We rested until two, and had supper; starting for the hills immediately afterwards, armed with three stout sacks, which, by good luck, were upon the premises. A little before four we arrived at the pit, divided the remainder of the booty, as equally as might be, among us, and, leaving the holes unfilled, again set out for the hut, at which, for the second time, we deposited our golden burthens, just as the first faint streaks of the dawn gleamed from over the tree-tops in the East.

We were now thoroughly broken down; but the intense excitement of the time denied us repose. After an unquiet slumber of some three or four hours' duration, we arose, as if by preconcert, to make examination of our treasure.

The chest had been full to the brim, and we spent the whole day, and the greater part of the next night, in a scrutiny of its contents. There had been nothing like order or arrangement. Every thing had been heaped in promiscuously. Having assorted all with care, we found ourselves possessed of even vaster wealth than we had at first supposed. In coin there was rather more than four hundred and fifty thousand dollars—estimating the value of the pieces, as accurately as we could, by the tables of the period. There was not a particle of silver.

6. Jupiter's mispronunciation of *abused*.

All was gold of antique date and of great variety—French, Spanish, and German money, with a few English guineas, and some counters,[7] of which we had never seen specimens before. There were several very large and heavy coins, so worn that we could make nothing of their inscriptions. There was no American money. The value of the jewels we found more difficulty in estimating. There were diamonds—some of them exceedingly large and fine—a hundred and ten in all, and not one of them small; eighteen rubies of remarkable brilliancy;—three hundred and ten emeralds, all very beautiful; and twenty-one sapphires, with an opal. These stones had all been broken from their settings and thrown loose in the chest. The settings themselves, which we picked out from among the other gold, appeared to have been beaten up with hammers, as if to prevent identification. Besides all this, there was a vast quantity of solid gold ornaments;—nearly two hundred massive finger and ear rings;—rich chains—thirty of these, if I remember;—eighty-three very large and heavy crucifixes;—five gold censers[8] of great value;—a prodigious golden punchbowl, ornamented with richly chased vine-leaves and Bacchanalian[9] figures; with two sword-handles exquisitely embossed, and many other smaller articles which I cannot recollect. The weight of these valuables exceeded three hundred and fifty pounds avoirdupois;[1] and in this estimate I have not included one hundred and ninety-seven superb gold watches; three of the number being worth each five hundred dollars, if one. Many of them were very old, and as time keepers valueless; the works having suffered, more or less, from corrosion—but all were richly jewelled and in cases of great worth. We estimated the entire contents of the chest, that night, at a million and a half of dollars; and, upon the subsequent disposal of the trinkets and jewels (a few being retained for our own use), it was found that we had greatly undervalued the treasure.

When, at length, we had concluded our examination, and the intense excitement of the time had, in some measure, subsided, Legrand, who saw that I was dying with impatience for a solution of this most extraordinary riddle, entered into a full detail of all the circumstances connected with it.[2]

"You remember," said he, "the night when I handed you the rough sketch I had made of the *scarabæus*. You recollect also, that I became quite vexed at you for insisting that my drawing resembled a death's-head. When you first made this assertion I thought you were jesting; but afterwards I called to mind the peculiar spots on the back of the insect, and admitted to myself that your remark had some little foundation in fact. Still, the sneer at my graphic powers irritated me—for I am considered a good artist—and, therefore, when you handed me the

7. Valuable tokens or coins, but of uncertain weight (archaic measure).
8. Containers for burning incense, especially during religious services.
9. Frenzied, ecstatic, or wild in nature. Bacchus was the Roman god of wine; he is associated with orgiastic celebrations involving the wild women of the forest, the Maenads.
1. A system of weights and measures based on 1 pound containing 16 ounces or 7,000 grains and equal to 453.59 grams.
2. The first installment in the *Dollar Newspaper* ended here.

scrap of parchment, I was about to crumple it up and throw it angrily into the fire."

"The scrap of paper, you mean," said I.

"No; it had much of the appearance of paper, and at first I supposed it to be such, but when I came to draw upon it, I discovered it, at once, to be a piece of very thin parchment. It was quite dirty, you remember. Well, as I was in the very act of crumpling it up, my glance fell upon the sketch at which you had been looking, and you may imagine my astonishment when I perceived, in fact, the figure of a death's-head just where, it seemed to me, I had made the drawing of the beetle. For a moment I was too much amazed to think with accuracy. I knew that my design was very different in detail from this—although there was a certain similarity in general outline. Presently I took a candle, and seating myself at the other end of the room, proceeded to scrutinize the parchment more closely. Upon turning it over, I saw my own sketch upon the reverse, just as I had made it. My first idea, now, was mere surprise at the really remarkable similarity of outline—at the singular coincidence involved in the fact, that unknown to me, there should have been a skull upon the other side of the parchment, immediately beneath my figure of the *scarabæus*, and that this skull, not only in outline, but in size, should so closely resemble my drawing. I say the singularity of this coincidence absolutely stupified me for a time. This is the usual effect of such coincidences. The mind struggles to establish a connexion—a sequence of cause and effect—and, being unable to do so, suffers a species of temporary paralysis. But, when I recovered from this stupor, there dawned upon me gradually a conviction which startled me even far more than the coincidence. I began distinctly, positively, to remember that there had been *no* drawing upon the parchment when I made my sketch of the *scarabæus*. I became perfectly certain of this; for I recollected turning up first one side and then the other, in search of the cleanest spot. Had the skull been then there, of course I could not have failed to notice it. Here was indeed a mystery which I felt it impossible to explain; but, even at that early moment, there seemed to glimmer, faintly, within the most remote and secret chambers of my intellect, a glow-worm-like conception of that truth which last night's adventure brought to so magnificent a demonstration. I arose at once, and putting the parchment securely away, dismissed all farther reflection until I should be alone.

"When you had gone, and when Jupiter was fast asleep, I betook myself to a more methodical investigation of the affair. In the first place I considered the manner in which the parchment had come into my possession. The spot where we discovered the *scarabæus* was on the coast of the main land, about a mile eastward of the island, and but a short distance above high water mark. Upon my taking hold of it, it gave me a sharp bite, which caused me to let it drop. Jupiter, with his accustomed caution, before seizing the insect, which had flown towards him, looked about him for a leaf, or something of that nature, by which to take hold of it. It was at this moment that his eyes, and

mine also, fell upon the scrap of parchment, which I then supposed to be paper. It was lying half buried in the sand, a corner sticking up. Near the spot where we found it, I observed the remnants of the hull of what appeared to have been a ship's long boat. The wreck seemed to have been there for a very great while; for the resemblance to boat timbers could scarcely be traced.

"Well, Jupiter picked up the parchment, wrapped the beetle in it, and gave it to me. Soon afterwards we turned to go home, and on the way met Lieutenant G——. I showed him the insect, and he begged me to let him take it to the fort. Upon my consenting, he thrust it forthwith into his waistcoat pocket, without the parchment in which it had been wrapped, and which I had continued to hold in my hand during his inspection. Perhaps he dreaded my changing my mind, and thought it best to make sure of the prize at once—you know how enthusiastic he is on all subjects connected with Natural History. At the same time, without being conscious of it, I must have deposited the parchment in my own pocket.

"You remember that when I went to the table, for the purpose of making a sketch of the beetle, I found no paper where it was usually kept. I looked in the drawer, and found none there. I searched my pockets, hoping to find an old letter, when my hand fell upon the parchment. I thus detail the precise mode in which it came into my possession; for the circumstances impressed me with peculiar force.

"No doubt you will think me fanciful—but I had already established a kind of *connexion*. I had put together two links of a great chain. There was a boat lying upon a sea-coast, and not far from the boat was a parchment—*not a paper*—with a skull depicted upon it. You will, of course, ask 'where is the connection?' I reply that the skull, or death's-head, is the well-known emblem of the pirate. The flag of the death's-head is hoisted in all engagements.

"I have said that the scrap was parchment, and not paper. Parchment is durable—almost imperishable. Matters of little moment are rarely consigned to parchment; since, for the mere ordinary purposes of drawing or writing, it is not nearly so well adapted as paper. This reflection suggested some meaning—some relevancy—in the death's-head. I did not fail to observe, also, the *form* of the parchment. Although one of its corners had been, by some accident, destroyed, it could be seen that the original form was oblong. It was just such a slip, indeed, as might have been chosen for a memorandum—for a record of something to be long remembered and carefully preserved."

"But," I interposed, "you say that the skull was *not* upon the parchment when you made the drawing of the beetle. How then do you trace any connexion between the boat and the skull—since this latter, according to your own admission, must have been designed (God only knows how or by whom) at some period subsequent to your sketching the *scarabæus?*"

"Ah, hereupon turns the whole mystery; although the secret, at this point, I had comparatively little difficulty in solving. My steps were sure, and could afford but a single result. I reasoned, for example,

thus: When I drew the *scarabæus*, there was no skull apparent upon the parchment. When I had completed the drawing I gave it to you, and observed you narrowly until you returned it. *You,* therefore, did not design the skull, and no one else was present to do it. Then it was not done by human agency. And nevertheless it was done.

"At this stage of my reflections I endeavored to remember, and *did* remember, with entire distinctness, every incident which occurred about the period in question. The weather was chilly (oh rare and happy accident!), and a fire was blazing upon the hearth. I was heated with exercise and sat near the table. You, however, had drawn a chair close to the chimney. Just as I placed the parchment in your hand, and as you were in the act of inspecting it, Wolf, the Newfoundland, entered, and leaped upon your shoulders. With your left hand you caressed him and kept him off, while your right, holding the parchment, was permitted to fall listlessly between your knees, and in close proximity to the fire. At one moment I thought the blaze had caught it, and was about to caution you, but, before I could speak, you had withdrawn it, and were engaged in its examination. When I considered all these particulars, I doubted not for a moment that *heat* had been the agent in bringing to light, upon the parchment, the skull which I saw designed upon it. You are well aware that chemical preparations exist, and have existed time out of mind, by means of which it is possible to write upon either paper or vellum, so that the characters shall become visible only when subjected to the action of fire.[3] Zaffre, digested in *aqua regia,*[4] and diluted with four times its weight of water, is sometimes employed; a green tint results. The regulus[5] of cobalt, dissolved in spirit of nitre, gives a red. These colors disappear at longer or shorter intervals after the material written upon cools, but again become apparent upon the re-application of heat.

"I now scrutinized the death's-head with care. Its outer edges—the edges of the drawing nearest the edge of the vellum—were far more *distinct* than the others. It was clear that the action of the caloric[6] had been imperfect or unequal. I immediately kindled a fire, and subjected every portion of the parchment to a glowing heat. At first, the only effect was the strengthening of the faint lines in the skull; but upon perserving in the experiment, there became visible, at the corner of the slip, diagonally opposite to the spot in which the death's-head was delineated, the figure of what I at first supposed to be a goat. A closer scrutiny, however, satisfied me that it was intended for a kid."

"Ha! ha!" said I, "to be sure I have no right to laugh at you—a million and a half of money is too serious a matter for mirth—but you are not about to establish a third link in your chain—you will not find any

3. According to Mabbott, the information about invisible writing fluid comes from an article titled "Ink" in Abraham Rees's *Cyclopaedia* (1819).
4. Terms from alchemical tradition. "Zaffre": an impure oxide of cobalt, used to make a blue pigment. "*Aqua regia*": a corrosive, fuming, volatile mixture of hydrochloric and nitric acids, used for testing and dissolving metals like gold.
5. The impure metallic mass that sinks to the bottom of a furnace or crucible during smelting.
6. Heat (archaic); here in the alchemical sense of a "fluid" thought to be responsible for heat (until James Prescott Joule, 1818–1889, a British physicist, proved that heat is itself a form of energy).

especial connexion between your pirates and a goat—pirates, you know, have nothing to do with goats; they appertain to the farming interest."

"But I have just said that the figure was *not* that of a goat."

"Well, a kid then—pretty much the same thing."

"Pretty much, but not altogether," said Legrand. "You may have heard of one *Captain* Kidd. I at once looked upon the figure of the animal as a kind of punning or hieroglyphical signature. I say signature; because its position upon the vellum suggested this idea. The death's-head at the corner diagonally opposite, had, in the same manner, the air of a stamp, or seal. But I was sorely put out by the absence of all else—of the body to my imagined instrument—of the text for my context."

"I presume you expected to find a letter between the stamp and the signature."

"Something of that kind. The fact is, I felt irresistibly impressed with a presentiment of some vast good fortune impending. I can scarcely say why. Perhaps, after all, it was rather a desire than an actual belief;—but do you know that Jupiter's silly words, about the bug being of solid gold, had a remarkable effect upon my fancy? And then the series of accidents and coincidences—these were so *very* extraordinary. Do you observe how mere an accident it was that these events should have occurred upon the *sole* day of all the year in which it has been, or may be, sufficiently cool for fire, and that without the fire, or without the intervention of the dog at the precise moment in which he appeared, I should never have become aware of the death's-head, and so never the possessor of the treasure?"

"But proceed—I am all impatience."

"Well; you have heard, of course, the many stories current—the thousand vague rumors afloat about money buried, somewhere upon the Atlantic coast, by Kidd and his associates. These rumors must have had some foundation in fact. And that the rumors have existed so long and so continuous, could have resulted, it appeared to me, only from the circumstance of the buried treasure still *remaining* entombed. Had Kidd concealed his plunder for a time, and afterwards reclaimed it, the rumors would scarcely have reached us in their present unvarying form. You will observe that the stories told are all about money-seekers, not about money-finders. Had the pirate recovered his money, there the affair would have dropped. It seemed to me that some accident—say the loss of a memorandum indicating its locality—had deprived him of the means of recovering it, and that this accident had become known to his followers, who otherwise might never have heard that treasure had been concealed at all, and who, busying themselves in vain, because unguided attempts, to regain it, had given first birth, and then universal currency, to the reports which are now so common. Have you ever heard of any important treasure being unearthed along the coast?"

"Never."

"But that Kidd's accumulations were immense, is well known. I took

it for granted, therefore, that the earth still held them; and you will scarcely be surprised when I tell you that I felt a hope, nearly amounting to certainty, that the parchment so strangely found, involved a lost record of the place of deposit."

"But how did you proceed?"

"I held the vellum again to the fire, after increasing the heat; but nothing appeared. I now thought it possible that the coating of dirt might have something to do with the failure; so I carefully rinsed the parchment by pouring warm water over it, and, having done this, I placed it in a tin pan, with the skull downwards, and put the pan upon a furnace of lighted charcoal. In a few minutes, the pan having become thoroughly heated, I removed the slip, and, to my inexpressible joy, found it spotted, in several places, with what appeared to be figures arranged in lines. Again I placed it in the pan, and suffered it to remain another minute. Upon taking it off, the whole was just as you see it now."

Here Legrand, having re-heated the parchment, submitted it to my inspection. The following characters were rudely traced, in a red tint, between the death's-head and the goat:[7]

53‡‡†305))6*;4826)4‡.)4‡);806*;48†8¶60))85;1‡(;:¶‡*8†83(88)5
*†;46(;88*96*?;8)*‡(;485);5*†2:*‡(;4956*2(5*—4)8¶8*;4069285);)
6†8)4‡‡;1(‡9;48081;8:8‡1;48†85;4)485†528806*81(‡9;48;(88;4
(‡?34;48)4‡;161;:188;‡?;

"But," said I, returning him the slip, "I am as much in the dark as ever. Were all the jewels of Golconda[8] awaiting me upon my solution of this enigma, I am quite sure that I should be unable to earn them."

"And yet," said Legrand, "the solution is by no means so difficult as you might be lead to imagine from the first hasty inspection of the characters. These characters, as any one might readily guess, form a cipher—that is to say, they convey a meaning; but then, from what is known of Kidd, I could not suppose him capable of constructing any of the more abstruse cryptographs. I made up my mind, at once, that this was of a simple species—such, however, as would appear, to the crude intellect of the sailor, absolutely insoluble without the key."

"And you really solved it?"

"Readily; I have solved others of an abstruseness ten thousand times greater. Circumstances, and a certain bias of mind, have led me to take interest in such riddles, and it may well be doubted whether human ingenuity can construct an enigma of the kind which human in-

7. Poe seems to have used William Blair's article, titled "Cipher," from Rees's *Cyclopædia*. Peithman notes an article ("Cryptographica Denudata") in the *Gentleman's Magazine* for 1742 by David Arnold Conradus. Mabbott notes similar articles in the *Encyclopædia Britannica* (3rd–6th eds., 1798–1836) and the *Encyclopædia Americana* (1836), adding that the code was correct in the first printing of Poe's story but contained errors thereafter (some scholars speculate that Poe deliberately introduced errors of coding, angles, chemistry, and the like into the story as part of his gold-fever hoax).
8. An ancient city in India once known for its riches, especially its legendary treasure troves of diamonds.

genuity may not, by proper application, resolve. In fact, having once established connected and legible characters, I scarcely gave a thought to the mere difficulty of developing their import.

"In the present case—indeed in all cases of secret writing—the first question regards the *language* of the cipher; for the principles of solution, so far, especially, as the more simple ciphers are concerned, depend upon, and are varied by, the genius of the particular idiom. In general, there is no alternative but experiment (directed by probabilities) of every tongue known to him who attempts the solution, until the true one be attained. But, with the cipher now before us, all difficulty was removed by the signature. The pun upon the word 'Kidd' is appreciable in no other language than the English. But for this consideration I should have begun my attempts with the Spanish and French, as the tongues in which a secret of this kind would most naturally have been written by a pirate of the Spanish main. As it was, I assumed the cryptograph to be English.

"You observe there are no divisions between the words. Had there been divisions, the task would have been comparatively easy. In such case I should have commenced with a collation and analysis of the shorter words, and, had a word of a single letter occurred, as is most likely, (*a* or *I*, for example,) I should have considered the solution as assured. But, there being no division, my first step was to ascertain the predominant letters, as well as the least frequent. Counting all, I constructed a table, thus:

Of the character 8 there are 33.

;	"	26.
4	"	19.
‡)	"	16.
*	"	13.
5	"	12.
6	"	11.
† 1	"	8.
0	"	6.
9 2	"	5.
: 3	"	4.
?	"	3.
¶	"	2.
—.	"	1.

"Now, in English, the letter which most frequently occurs is *e*. Afterwards, the succession runs thus: *a o i d h n r s t u y c f g l m w b k p q x z*. E predominates so remarkably that an individual sentence of any length is rarely seen, in which it is not the prevailing character.

"Here, then, we have, in the very beginning, the groundwork for something more than a mere guess. The general use which may be made of the table is obvious—but, in this particular cipher, we shall only very partially require its aid. As our predominant character is 8, we will commence by assuming it as the *e* of the natural alphabet. To verify the supposition, let us observe if the 8 be seen often in couples—for *e* is doubled with great frequency in English—in such words,

for example, as 'meet,' 'fleet,' 'speed,' 'seen,' been,' 'agree,' &c. In the present instance we see it doubled no less than five times, although the cryptograph is brief.

"Let us assume 8, then, as *e*. Now, of all *words* in the language, 'the' is most usual; let us see, therefore, whether there are not repetitions of any three characters, in the same order of collocation, the last of them being 8. If we discover repetitions of such letters, so arranged, they will most probably represent the word 'the.' Upon inspection, we find no less than seven such arrangements, the characters being ;18. We may, therefore, assume that ; represents *t*, 4 represents *h*, and 8 represents *e*—the last being now well confirmed. Thus a great step has been taken.

"But, having established a single word, we are enabled to establish a vastly important point; that is to say, several commencements and terminations of other words. Let us refer, for example, to the last instance but one, in which the combination ;48 occurs—not far from the end of the cipher. We know that the ; immediately ensuing is the commencement of a word, and, of the six characters succeeding this 'the,' we are cognizant of no less than five. Let us set these characters down, thus, by the letters we know them to represent, leaving a space for the unknown—

<p align="center">t eeth.</p>

"Here we are enabled, at once, to discard the '*th*,' as forming no portion of the word commencing with the first *t*; since, by experiment of the entire alphabet for a letter adapted to the vacancy, we perceive that no word can be formed of which this *th* can be a part. We are thus narrowed into

<p align="center">t ee,</p>

and, going through the alphabet, if necessary, as before, we arrive at the word 'tree,' as the sole possible reading. We thus gain another letter, *r*, represented by (, with the words 'the tree' in juxtaposition.

"Looking beyond these words, for a short distance, we again see the combination ;48, and employ it by way of *termination* to what immediately precedes. We have thus this arrangement:

<p align="center">the tree ;4(‡?34 the,</p>

or, substituting the natural letters, where known, it reads thus:

<p align="center">the tree thr‡?3h the.</p>

"Now, if, in place of the unknown characters, we leave blank spaces, or substitute dots, we read thus:

<p align="center">the tree thr . . . h the,</p>

when the word '*through*' makes itself evident at once. But this discovery gives us three new letters, *o*, *u* and *g*, represented by ‡ ? and 3.

"Looking now, narrowly, through the cipher for combinations of known characters, we find, not very far from the beginning, this arrangement,

<p align="center">83(88, or egree,</p>

which, plainly, is the conclusion of the word 'degree,' and gives us another letter, *d*, represented by †.

"Four letters beyond the word 'degree,' we perceive the combination

<p align="center">;48(;88.</p>

"Translating the known characters, and representing the unknown by dots, as before, we read thus:

th rtee.

an arrangement immediately suggestive of the word 'thirteen,' and again furnishing us with two new characters, *i* and *n*, represented by 6 and *.

"Referring, now, to the beginning of the cryptograph, we find the combination,

53‡‡†.

"Translating, as before, we obtain

. good,

which assures us that the first letter is A, and that the first two words are 'A good.'

"It is now time that we arrange our key, as far as discovered, in a tabular form, to avoid confusion. It will stand thus:

5	represents	a
†	"	d
8	"	e
3	"	g
4	"	h
6	"	i
*	"	n
‡	"	o
("	r
;	"	t

"We have, therefore, no less than ten of the most important letters represented, and it will be unnecessary to proceed with the details of the solution. I have said enough to convince you that ciphers of this nature are readily soluble, and to give you some insight into the *rationale* of their development. But be assured that the specimen before us appertains to the very simplest species of cryptograph. It now only remains to give you the full translation of the characters upon the parchment, as unriddled. Here it is:

'*A good glass in the bishop's hostel in the devil's seat forty-one degrees and thirteen minutes northeast and by north main branch seventh limb east side shoot from the left eye of the death's-head a bee line from the tree through the shot fifty feet out.*' "

"But," said I, "the enigma seems still in as bad a condition as ever. How is it possible to extort a meaning from all this jargon about 'devil's seats,' 'death's-heads,' and 'bishop's hotels?' "

"I confess," replied Legrand, "that the matter still wears a serious aspect, when regarded with a casual glance. My first endeavor was to divide the sentence into the natural division intended by the cryptographist."

"You mean, to punctuate it?"

"Something of that kind."

"But how was it possible to effect this?"

"I reflected that it had been a *point* with the writer to run his words together without division, so as to increase the difficulty of solution.

Now, a not over-acute man, in pursuing such an object, would be nearly certain to overdo the matter. When, in the course of his composition, he arrived at a break in his subject which would naturally require a pause, or a point, he would be exceedingly apt to run his characters, at this place, more than usually close together. If you will observe the MS., in the present instance, you will easily detect five such cases of unusual crowding. Acting upon this hint, I made the division thus:

'A good glass in the Bishop's hostel in the Devil's seat—forty-one degrees and thirteen minutes—northeast and by north—main branch seventh limb east side—shoot from the left eye of the death's-head—a bee-line from the tree through the shot fifty feet out.' "

"Even this division," said I, "leaves me still in the dark."

"It left me also in the dark," replied Legrand, "for a few days; during which I made diligent inquiry, in the neighborhood of Sullivan's Island, for any building which went by the name of the 'Bishop's Hotel;' for, of course, I dropped the obsolete word 'hostel.' Gaining no information on the subject, I was on the point of extending my sphere of search, and proceeding in a more systematic manner, when, one morning, it entered into my head, quite suddenly, that this 'Bishop's Hostel' might have some reference to an old family, of the name of Bessop, which, time out of mind, had held possession of an ancient manor-house, about four miles to the northward of the Island. I accordingly went over to the plantation, and re-instituted my inquiries among the older negroes of the place. At length one of the most aged of the women said that she had heard of such a place as *Bessop's Castle*, and thought that she could guide me to it, but that it was not a castle, nor a tavern, but a high rock.

"I offered to pay her well for her trouble, and, after some demur, she consented to accompany me to the spot. We found it without much difficulty, when, dismissing her, I proceeded to examine the place. The 'castle' consisted of an irregular assemblage of cliffs and rocks—one of the latter being quite remarkable for its height as well as for its insulated and artificial appearance. I clambered to its apex, and then felt much at a loss as to what should be next done.

"While I was busied in reflection, my eyes fell upon a narrow ledge in the eastern face of the rock, perhaps a yard below the summit upon which I stood. This ledge projected about eighteen inches, and was not more than a foot wide, while a niche in the cliff just above it, gave it a rude resemblance to one of the hollow-backed chairs used by our ancestors. I made no doubt that here was the 'devil's-seat' alluded to in the MS., and now I seemed to grasp the full secret of the riddle.

"The 'good glass,' I knew, could have reference to nothing but a telescope; for the word 'glass' is rarely employed in any other sense by seamen. Now here, I at once saw, was a telescope to be used, and a definite point of view, *admitting no variation*, from which to use it. Nor did I hesitate to believe that the phrases, 'forty-one degrees and thirteen minutes,' and 'northeast and by north,' were intended as directions for the levelling of the glass. Greatly excited by these discoveries, I hurried home, procured a telescope, and returned to the rock.

"I let myself down to the ledge, and found that it was impossible to retain a seat upon it except in one particular position. This fact confirmed my preconceived idea. I proceeded to use the glass. Of course, the 'forty-one degrees and thirteen minutes' could allude to nothing but elevation above the visible horizon, since the horizontal direction was clearly indicated by the words, 'northeast and by north.' This latter direction I at once established by means of a pocket-compass; then, pointing the glass as nearly at an angle of forty-one degrees of elevation as I could do it by guess, I moved it cautiously up or down, until my attention was arrested by a circular rift or opening in the foliage of a large tree that overtopped its fellows in the distance. In the centre of this rift I perceived a white spot, but could not, at first, distinguish what it was. Adjusting the focus of the telescope, I again looked, and now made it out to be a human skull.

"Upon this discovery I was so sanguine as to consider the enigma solved; for the phrase 'main branch, seventh limb, east side,' could refer only to the position of the skull upon the tree, while 'shoot from the left eye of the death's-head' admitted, also, of but one interpretation, in regard to a search for buried treasure. I perceived that the design was to drop a bullet from the left eye of the skull, and that a bee-line, or, in other words, a straight line, drawn from the nearest point of the trunk through 'the shot,' (or the spot where the bullet fell,) and thence extended to a distance of fifty feet, would indicate a definite point—and beneath this point I thought it at least *possible* that a deposit of value lay concealed."

"All this," I said, "is exceedingly clear, and, although ingenious, still simple and explicit. When you left the Bishop's Hotel, what then?"

"Why, having carefully taken the bearings of the tree, I turned homewards. The instant that I left 'the devil's seat,' however, the circular rift vanished; nor could I get a glimpse of it afterwards, turn as I would. What seems to me the chief ingenuity in this whole business, is the fact (for repeated experiment has convinced me it *is* a fact) that the circular opening in question is visible from no other attainable point of view than that afforded by the narrow ledge upon the face of the rock.

"In this expedition to the 'Bishop's Hotel' I had been attended by Jupiter, who had, no doubt, observed, for some weeks past, the abstraction of my demeanor, and took especial care not to leave me alone. But, on the next day, getting up very early, I contrived to give him the slip, and went into the hills in search of the tree. After much toil I found it. When I came home at night my valet proposed to give me a flogging. With the rest of the adventure I believe you are as well acquainted as myself."

"I suppose," said I, "you missed the spot, in the first attempt at digging, through Jupiter's stupidity in letting the bug fall through the right instead of through the left eye of the skull."

"Precisely. This mistake made a difference of about two inches and a half in the 'shot'—that is to say, in the position of the peg nearest the tree; and had the treasure been *beneath* the 'shot,' the error would

have been of little moment; but 'the shot,' together with the nearest point of the tree, were merely two points for the establishment of a line of direction; of course the error, however trivial in the beginning, increased as we proceeded with the line, and by the time we had gone fifty feet, threw us quite off the scent. But for my deep-seated impressions that treasure was here somewhere actually buried, we might have had all our labor in vain."

"But your grandiloquence, and your conduct in swinging the beetle—how excessively odd! I was sure you were mad. And why did you insist upon letting fall the bug, instead of a bullet, from the skull?"

"Why, to be frank, I felt somewhat annoyed by your evident suspicions touching my sanity, and so resolved to punish you quietly, in my own way, by a little bit of sober mystification. For this reason I swung the beetle, and for this reason I let it fall it from the tree. An observation of yours about its great weight suggested the latter idea."

"Yes, I perceive; and now there is only one point which puzzles me. What are we to make of the skeletons found in the hole?"

"That is a question I am no more able to answer than yourself. There seems, however, only one plausible way of accounting for them—and yet it is dreadful to believe in such atrocity as my suggestion would imply. It is clear that Kidd—if Kidd indeed secreted this treasure, which I doubt not—it is clear that he must have had assistance in the labor. But this labor concluded, he may have thought it expedient to remove all participants in his secret. Perhaps a couple of blows with a mattock were sufficient, while his coadjutors were busy in the pit; perhaps it required a dozen—who shall tell?"

The Black Cat First published in the Philadelphia *United States Saturday Post* (August 19, 1843). The text reprinted here is from *Tales* (1845). This story contains an important definition and illustration of Poe's concept of the "perverse," which should be supplemented with his "The Imp of the Perverse" (1845; pp. 401ff. herein). Compare the confessions of the walling-up of another person in "The Cask of Amontillado" (1846; pp. 415ff.) and the burial under the floor in "The Tell-Tale Heart" (1843; pp. 316ff.). Mabbott, although he regards the cat as real, feels compelled to note that Poe would have read in Sir Walter Scott's *Letters on Demonology* (1830) the account of a man who tells his physician the following: "I found myself . . . embarrassed by the presence of a large cat, which came and disappeared I could not exactly tell how. . . . I was compelled to regard it [as having] no existence save in my deranged visual organs, or depraved imagination."

The Black Cat

FOR the most wild, yet most homely narrative which I am about to pen, I neither expect nor solicit belief. Mad indeed would I be to expect it, in a case where my very senses reject their own evidence. Yet,

mad am I not—and very surely do I not dream. But to-morrow I die, and to-day I would unburthen my soul. My immediate purpose is to place before the world, plainly, succinctly, and without comment, a series of mere household events. In their consequences, these events have terrified—have tortured—have destroyed me. Yet I will not attempt to expound them. To me, they have presented little but Horror—to many they will seem less terrible than *barroques*.[1] Hereafter, perhaps, some intellect may be found which will reduce my phantasm to the common-place—some intellect more calm, more logical, and far less excitable than my own, which will perceive, in the circumstances I detail with awe, nothing more than an ordinary succession of very natural causes and effects.

From my infancy I was noted for the docility and humanity of my disposition. My tenderness of heart was even so conspicuous as to make me the jest of my companions. I was especially fond of animals, and was indulged by my parents with a great variety of pets. With these I spent most of my time, and never was so happy as when feeding and caressing them. This peculiarity of character grew with my growth, and, in my manhood, I derived from it one of my principal sources of pleasure. To those who have cherished an affection for a faithful and sagacious[2] dog, I need hardly be at the trouble of explaining the nature or the intensity of the gratification thus derivable. There is something in the unselfish and self-sacrificing love of a brute, which goes directly to the heart of him who has had frequent occasion to test the paltry friendship and gossamer fidelity of mere *Man*.

I married early, and was happy to find in my wife a disposition not uncongenial with my own. Observing my partiality for domestic pets, she lost no opportunity of procuring those of the most agreeable kind. We had birds, gold-fish, a fine dog, rabbits, a small monkey, and *a cat*.

This latter was a remarkably large and beautiful animal, entirely black, and sagacious to an astonishing degree. In speaking of his intelligence, my wife, who at heart was not a little tinctured with superstition, made frequent allusion to the ancient popular notion, which regarded all black cats as witches in disguise. Not that she was ever *serious* upon this point—and I mention the matter at all for no better reason than that it happens, just now, to be remembered.

Pluto[3]—this was the cat's name—was my favorite pet and playmate. I alone fed him, and he attended me wherever I went about the house. It was even with difficulty that I could prevent him from following me through the streets.

Our friendship lasted, in this manner, for several years, during which my general temperament and character—through the instrumentality of the Fiend Intemperance[4]—had (I blush to confess it) experienced a radical alteration for the worse. I grew, day by day, more moody, more irritable, more regardless of the feelings of others. I suf-

1. Incidents characterized by grotesqueness and extravagance.
2. Here probably meaning having keen perception.
3. The name in some myths of the ruler of Hell (or Hades, which is another name for its ruler).
4. Excessive consumption of alcohol.

fered myself to use intemperate language to my wife. At length, I even offered her personal violence. My pets, of course, were made to feel the change in my disposition. I not only neglected, but ill-used them. For Pluto, however, I still retained sufficient regard to restrain me from maltreating him, as I made no scruple of maltreating the rabbits, the monkey, or even the dog, when by accident, or through affection, they came in my way. But my disease grew upon me—for what disease is like Alcohol!—and at length even Pluto, who was now becoming old, and consequently somewhat peevish—even Pluto began to experience the effects of my ill temper.

One night, returning home, much intoxicated, from one of my haunts about town, I fancied that the cat avoided my presence. I seized him; when, in his fright at my violence, he inflicted a slight wound upon my hand with his teeth. The fury of a demon instantly possessed me. I knew myself no longer. My original soul seemed, at once, to take its flight from my body; and a more than fiendish malevolence, gin-nurtured, thrilled every fibre of my frame. I took from my waistcoat-pocket a pen-knife, opened it, grasped the poor beast by the throat, and deliberately cut one of its eyes from the socket! I blush, I burn, I shudder, while I pen the damnable atrocity.

When reason returned with the morning—when I had slept off the fumes of the night's debauch—I experienced a sentiment half of horror, half of remorse, for the crime of which I had been guilty; but it was, at best, a feeble and equivocal feeling, and the soul remained untouched. I again plunged into excess, and soon drowned in wine all memory of the deed.

In the meantime the cat slowly recovered. The socket of the lost eye presented, it is true, a frightful appearance, but he no longer appeared to suffer any pain. He went about the house as usual, but, as might be expected, fled in extreme terror at my approach. I had so much of my old heart left, as to be at first grieved by this evident dislike on the part of a creature which had once so loved me. But this feeling soon gave place to irritation. And then came, as if to my final and irrevocable overthrow, the spirit of PERVERSENESS. Of this spirit philosophy takes no account. Yet I am not more sure that my soul lives, than I am that perverseness is one of the primitive impulses of the human heart—one of the indivisible primary faculties, or sentiments, which give direction to the character of Man.[5] Who has not, a hundred times, found himself committing a vile or a silly action, for no other reason than because he knows he should *not*? Have we not a perpetual inclination, in the teeth of our best judgment, to violate that which is *Law*, merely because we understand it to be such? This spirit of perverseness, I say, came to my final overthrow. It was this unfathomable longing of the soul *to vex itself*—to offer violence to its own nature—to do wrong for the wrong's sake only—that urged me to continue and finally to consummate the injury I had inflicted upon the unoffending brute. One

5. Cf. "The Imp of the Perverse" (pp. 401ff. herein) in which some of the language is much the same. Originally, Poe included some references to phrenology (see notes to "Imp").

morning, in cool blood, I slipped a noose about its neck and hung it to the limb of a tree;—hung it with the tears streaming from my eyes, and with the bitterest remorse at my heart;—hung it *because* I knew that it had loved me, and *because* I felt it had given me no reason of offence;—hung it *because* I knew that in so doing I was committing a sin—a deadly sin that would so jeopardize my immortal soul as to place it—if such a thing were possible—even beyond the reach of the infinite mercy of the Most Merciful and Most Terrible God.

On the night of the day on which this cruel deed was done, I was aroused from sleep by the cry of fire. The curtains of my bed were in flames. The whole house was blazing. It was with great difficulty that my wife, a servant, and myself, made our escape from the conflagration. The destruction was complete. My entire worldly wealth was swallowed up, and I resigned myself thenceforward to despair.

I am above the weakness of seeking to establish a sequence of cause and effect, between the disaster and the atrocity. But I am detailing a chain of facts—and wish not to leave even a possible link imperfect. On the day succeeding the fire, I visited the ruins. The walls, with one exception, had fallen in. This exception was found in a compartment wall, not very thick, which stood about the middle of the house, and against which had rested the head of my bed. The plastering had here, in great measure, resisted the action of the fire—a fact which I attributed to its having been recently spread. About this wall a dense crowd were collected, and many persons seemed to be examining a particular portion of it with very minute and eager attention. The words "strange!" "singular!" and other similar expressions, excited my curiosity. I approached and saw, as if graven in *bas relief*[6] upon the white surface, the figure of a gigantic *cat*. The impression was given with an accuracy truly marvellous. There was a rope about the animal's neck.

When I first beheld this apparition—for I could scarcely regard it as less—my wonder and my terror were extreme. But at length reflection came to my aid. The cat, I remembered, had been hung in a garden adjacent to the house. Upon the alarm of fire, this garden had been immediately filled by the crowd—by some one of whom the animal must have been cut from the tree and thrown, through an open window, into my chamber. This had probably been done with the view of arousing me from sleep. The falling of other walls had compressed the victim of my cruelty into the substance of the freshly-spread plaster; the lime of which, with the flames, and the *ammonia* from the carcass, had then accomplished the portraiture as I saw it.

Although I thus readily accounted to my reason, if not altogether to my conscience, for the startling fact just detailed, it did not the less fail to make a deep impression upon my fancy. For months I could not rid myself of the phantasm of the cat; and, during this period, there came back into my spirit a half-sentiment that seemed, but was not, remorse. I went so far as to regret the loss of the animal, and to look about me, among the vile haunts which I now habitually frequented,

6. Low-relief sculpture; i.e., the design projects very little from the background.

for another pet of the same species, and of somewhat similar appearance, with which to supply its place.

One night as I sat, half stupified, in a den of more than infamy, my attention was suddenly drawn to some black object, reposing upon the head of one of the immense hogsheads[7] of Gin, or of Rum, which constituted the chief furniture of the apartment. I had been looking steadily at the top of this hogshead for some minutes, and what now caused me surprise was the fact that I had not sooner perceived the object thereupon. I approached it, and touched it with my hand. It was a black cat—a very large one—fully as large as Pluto, and closely resembling him in every respect but one. Pluto had not a white hair upon any portion of his body; but this cat had a large, although indefinite splotch of white, covering nearly the whole region of the breast.

Upon my touching him, he immediately arose, purred loudly, rubbed against my hand, and appeared delighted with my notice. This, then, was the very creature of which I was in search. I at once offered to purchase it of the landlord; but this person made no claim to it—knew nothing of it—had never seen it before.

I continued my caresses, and, when I prepared to go home, the animal evinced a disposition to accompany me. I permitted it to do so; occasionally stooping and patting it as I proceeded. When it reached the house it domesticated itself at once, and became immediately a great favorite with my wife.

For my own part, I soon found a dislike to it arising within me. This was just the reverse of what I had anticipated; but—I know not how or why it was—its evident fondness for myself rather disgusted and annoyed. By slow degrees, these feelings of disgust and annoyance rose into the bitterness of hatred. I avoided the creature; a certain sense of shame, and the remembrance of my former deed of cruelty, preventing me from physically abusing it. I did not, for some weeks, strike, or otherwise violently ill use it; but gradually—very gradually—I came to look upon it with unutterable loathing, and to flee silently from its odious presence, as from the breath of a pestilence.

What added, no doubt, to my hatred of the beast, was the discovery, on the morning after I brought it home, that, like Pluto, it also had been deprived of one of its eyes. This circumstance, however, only endeared it to my wife, who, as I have already said, possessed, in a high degree, that humanity of feeling which had once been my distinguishing trait, and the source of many of my simplest and purest pleasures.

With my aversion to this cat, however, its partiality for myself seemed to increase. It followed my footsteps with a pertinacity which it would be difficult to make the reader comprehend. Whenever I sat, it would crouch beneath my chair, or spring upon my knees, covering me with its loathsome caresses. If I arose to walk it would get between my feet and thus nearly throw me down, or, fastening its long and sharp claws in my dress, clamber, in this manner, to my breast. At such times, although I longed to destroy it with a blow, I was yet with-

7. A barrel whose capacity is anywhere from 62.5 to 140 gallons.

held from so doing, partly by a memory of my former crime, but chiefly—let me confess it at once—by absolute *dread* of the beast.

This dread was not exactly a dread of physical evil—and yet I should be at a loss how otherwise to define it. I am almost ashamed to own— yes, even in this felon's cell, I am almost ashamed to own—that the terror and horror with which the animal inspired me, had been heightened by one of the merest chimæras[8] it would be possible to conceive. My wife had called my attention, more than once, to the character of the mark of white hair, of which I have spoken, and which constituted the sole visible difference between the strange beast and the one I had destroyed. The reader will remember that this mark, although large, had been originally very indefinite; but, by slow de- grees—degrees nearly imperceptible, and which for a long time my Reason struggled to reject as fanciful—it had, at length, assumed a rigorous distinctness of outline. It was now the representation of an object that I shudder to name—and for this, above all, I loathed, and dreaded, and would have rid myself of the monster *had I dared*—it was now, I say, the image of a hideous—of a ghastly thing—of the GAL- LOWS!—oh, mournful and terrible engine of Horror and of Crime—of Agony and of Death!

And now was I indeed wretched beyond the wretchedness of mere Humanity. And *a brute beast*—whose fellow I had contemptuously de- stroyed—*a brute beast* to work out for *me*—for me a man, fashioned in the image of the High God—so much of insufferable wo! Alas! neither by day nor by night knew I the blessing of Rest any more! During the former the creature left me no moment alone; and, in the latter, I started, hourly, from dreams of unutterable fear, to find the hot breath of *the thing* upon my face, and its vast weight—an incarnate Night- Mare that I had no power to shake off—incumbent eternally upon my *heart!*[9]

Beneath the pressure of torments such as these, the feeble remnant of the good within me succumbed. Evil thoughts became my sole inti- mates—the darkest and most evil of thoughts. The moodiness of my usual temper increased to hatred of all things and of all mankind; while, from the sudden, frequent, and ungovernable outbursts of a fury to which I now blindly abandoned myself, my uncomplaining wife, alas! was the most usual and the most patient of sufferers.

One day she accompanied me, upon some household errand, into the cellar of the old building which our poverty compelled us to in- habit. The cat followed me down the steep stairs, and, nearly throwing me headlong, exasperated me to madness. Uplifting an axe, and for- getting, in my wrath, the childish dread which had hitherto stayed my hand, I aimed a blow at the animal which, of course, would have proved instantly fatal had it descended as I wished. But this blow was arrested by the hand of my wife. Goaded, by the interference, into a rage more than demoniacal, I withdrew my arm from her grasp and

8. Imaginary monsters, most often composed of grotesquely disparate parts.
9. The Night Mare of myth was a dream horse that trampled people in their sleep, its great weight causing a sense of suffocation (see notes to "Usher," especially p. 206, n. 3 herein).

buried the axe in her brain. She fell dead upon the spot, without a groan.

This hideous murder accomplished, I set myself forthwith, and with entire deliberation, to the task of concealing the body. I knew that I could not remove it from the house, either by day or by night, without the risk of being observed by the neighbors. Many projects entered my mind. At one period I thought of cutting the corpse into minute fragments, and destroying them by fire. At another, I resolved to dig a grave for it in the floor of the cellar. Again, I deliberated about casting it in the well in the yard—about packing it in a box, as if merchandize, with the usual arrangements, and so getting a porter to take it from the house. Finally I hit upon what I considered a far better expedient than either of these. I determined to wall it up in the cellar—as the monks of the middle ages are recorded to have walled up their victims.

For a purpose such as this the cellar was well adapted. Its walls were loosely constructed, and had lately been plastered throughout with a rough plaster, which the dampness of the atmosphere had prevented from hardening. Moreover, in one of the walls was a projection, caused by a false chimney, or fireplace, that had been filled up, and made to resemble the rest of the cellar. I made no doubt that I could readily displace the bricks at this point, insert the corpse, and wall the whole up as before, so that no eye could detect any thing suspicious.

And in this calculation I was not deceived. By means of a crow-bar I easily dislodged the bricks, and, having carefully deposited the body against the inner wall, I propped it in that position, while, with little trouble, I re-laid the whole structure as it originally stood. Having procured mortar, sand, and hair, with every possible precaution, I prepared a plaster which could not be distinguished from the old, and with this I very carefully went over the new brick-work. When I had finished, I felt satisfied that all was right. The wall did not present the slightest appearance of having been disturbed. The rubbish on the floor was picked up with the minutest care. I looked around triumphantly, and said to myself—"Here at least, then, my labor has not been in vain."

My next step was to look for the beast which had been the cause of so much wretchedness; for I had, at length, firmly resolved to put it to death. Had I been able to meet with it, at the moment, there could have been no doubt of its fate; but it appeared that the crafty animal had been alarmed at the violence of my previous anger, and forebore to present itself in my present mood. It is impossible to describe, or to imagine, the deep, the blissful sense of relief which the absence of the detested creature occasioned in my bosom. It did not make its appearance during the night—and thus for one night at least, since its introduction into the house, I soundly and tranquilly slept; aye, *slept* even with the burden of murder upon my soul!

The second and the third day passed, and still my tormentor came not. Once again I breathed as a freeman. The monster, in terror, had fled the premises forever! I should behold it no more! My happiness was supreme! The guilt of my dark deed disturbed me but little. Some

few inquiries had been made, but these had been readily answered. Even a search had been instituted—but of course nothing was to be discovered. I looked upon my future felicity as secured.

Upon the fourth day of the assassination, a party of the police came, very unexpectedly, into the house, and proceeded again to make rigorous investigation of the premises. Secure, however, in the inscrutability of my place of concealment, I felt no embarrassment whatever. The officers bade me accompany them in their search. They left no nook or corner unexplored. At length, for the third or fourth time, they descended into the cellar. I quivered not in a muscle. My heart beat calmly as that of one who slumbers in innocence. I walked the cellar from end to end. I folded my arms upon my bosom, and roamed easily to and fro. The police were thoroughly satisfied and prepared to depart. The glee at my heart was too strong to be restrained. I burned to say if but one word, by way of triumph, and to render doubly sure their assurance of my guiltlessness.

"Gentlemen," I said at last, as the party ascended the steps, "I delight to have allayed your suspicions. I wish you all health, and a little more courtesy. By the bye, gentlemen, this—this is a very well constructed house." [In the rabid desire to say something easily, I scarcely knew what I uttered at all.]—"I may say an *excellently* well constructed house. These walls—are you going, gentlemen?—these walls are solidly put together"; and here, through the mere phrenzy of bravado, I rapped heavily, with a cane which I held in my hand, upon that very portion of the brick-work behind which stood the corpse of the wife of my bosom.

But may God shield and deliver me from the fangs of the Arch-Fiend! No sooner had the reverberation of my blows sunk into silence, than I was answered by a voice from within the tomb!—by a cry, at first muffled and broken, like the sobbing of a child, and then quickly swelling into one long, loud, and continuous scream, utterly anomalous and inhuman—a howl—a wailing shriek, half of horror and half of triumph, such as might have arisen only out of hell, conjointly from the throats of the damned in their agony and of the demons that exult in the damnation.

Of my own thoughts it is folly to speak. Swooning, I staggered to the opposite wall. For one instant the party upon the stairs remained motionless, through extremity of terror and of awe. In the next, a dozen stout arms were toiling at the wall. It fell bodily. The corpse, already greatly decayed and clotted with gore, stood erect before the eyes of the spectators. Upon its head, with red extended mouth and solitary eye of fire, sat the hideous beast whose craft had seduced me into murder, and whose informing voice had consigned me to the hangman. I had walled the monster up within the tomb!

The Premature Burial First published in the Philadelphia *Dollar Newspaper* (July 31, 1844); the text reprinted here is that of the *Broadway Journal* (June 14, 1845). The subject of premature burial was frequently featured in newspaper articles and stories, and Poe was exploiting (and satirizing) their popularity. In fact, two extracts from Poe's tale (paragraphs 4–7 and 14–19) were immediately reprinted in an article in the *New York Rover* ("Burying Alive," August 1844). In the 1820s, some European cemeteries had guardians, trained in "reviving" medicine, who watched over the newly dead for at least three days to ensure that they were not still living. In 1839, George Alfred Walker published *Gatherings from Grave Yards*, a compendium of anecdotes and narratives of burials and revivals. It seems that some people, having fallen into a deep coma, were actually interred alive—the limited medical knowledge of the time failing to detect faint signs of life. In 1843 a "life-preserving coffin" with some of the features of the coffin in Poe's tale was exhibited at the annual fair of the American Institute of New York City.

The Premature Burial

There are certain themes of which the interest is all-absorbing, but which are too entirely horrible for the purposes of legitimate fiction. These the mere romanticist must eschew, if he do not wish to offend, or to disgust. They are with propriety handled, only when the severity and majesty of Truth sanctify and sustain them. We thrill, for example, with the most intense of "pleasurable pain,"[1] over the accounts of the Passage of the Beresina, of the Earthquake at Lisbon, of the Plague at London, of the Massacre of St. Bartholomew, or of the stifling of the hundred and twenty-three prisoners in the Black Hole at Calcutta.[2] But, in these accounts, it is the fact—it is the reality—it is the history which excites. As inventions, we should regard them with simple abhorrence.

I have mentioned some few of the more prominent and august calamities on record; but, in these, it is the extent, not less than the character of the calamity, which so vividly impresses the fancy. I need not remind the reader that, from the long and weird catalogue of human miseries, I might have selected many individual instances more

1. Writers have for centuries remarked on the intermingling of pleasure and pain, musing on why we find enjoyment in hearing or reading about pain and danger; here the narrator seems to be implying that this is a factual article, not fiction.
2. A reference to a notorious incident in the mid-18th century. On June 29, 1756, the Nawáb of Bengal took the city of Calcutta and imprisoned the British garrison; 146 people were placed in a small airless enclosure only eighteen feet square. By the next morning, 123 had died of suffocation; the British retook Calcutta in 1757. Napoleon's Grand Army crossed the Bersina River November 26–28, 1812, and thereby escaped total annihilation by the Russian forces, though 20,000 men were lost; by mid-December less than 100,000 of an original force of over 600,000 had escaped the Russian winter and the guerrilla assaults of the Cossacks. More than 300,000 of Napoleon's troops had been killed and over 100,000 captured; another 100,000 had deserted. The Lisbon earthquake of November 1, 1755, killed over 30,000 people and left the Portuguese capital in ruins. The London plague of April 1655 was the last of several great plagues to sweep through the city (see notes to "King Pest," pp. 148ff. herein). The Saint Bartholomew's Day Massacre was the slaughter of some 30,000 French Huguenot Protestants on August 24, 1572, by order of Charles IX, resulting in the resumption of civil war in France.

replete with essential suffering than any of these vast generalities of disaster. The true wretchedness, indeed—the ultimate woe—is particular, not diffuse. That the ghastly extremes of agony are endured by man the unit, and never by man the mass—for this let us thank a merciful God!

To be buried while alive, is, beyond question, the most terrific of these extremes which has ever fallen to the lot of mere mortality. That it has frequently, very frequently, so fallen, will scarcely be denied by those who think. The boundaries which divide Life from Death, are at best shadowy and vague. Who shall say where the one ends, and where the other begins! We know that there are diseases in which occur total cessations of all the apparent functions of vitality, and yet in which these cessations are merely suspensions, properly so called. They are only temporary pauses in the incomprehensible mechanism. A certain period elapses, and some unseen mysterious principle again sets in motion the magic pinions and the wizard wheels. The silver cord was not forever loosed, nor the golden bowl irreparably broken.[3] But where, meantime, was the soul?[4]

Apart, however, from the inevitable conclusion, *à priori*,[5] that such causes must produce such effects—that the well known occurrence of such cases of suspended animation must naturally give rise, now and then, to premature interments—apart from this consideration, we have the direct testimony of medical and ordinary experience, to prove that a vast number of such interments have actually taken place. I might refer at once, if necessary, to a hundred well authenticated instances. One of very remarkable character, and of which the circumstances may be fresh in the memory of some of my readers, occurred, not very long ago, in the neighboring city of Baltimore, where it occasioned a painful, intense, and widely extended excitement. The wife of one of the most respectable citizens—a lawyer of eminence and a member of Congress—was seized with a sudden and unaccountable illness, which completely baffled the skill of her physicians. After much suffering she died, or was supposed to die. No one suspected, indeed, or had reason to suspect, that she was not actually dead. She presented all the ordinary appearances of death. The face assumed the usual pinched and sunken outline. The lips were of the usual marble pallor. The eyes were lustreless. There was no warmth. Pulsation had ceased. For three days the body was preserved unburied, during which it had acquired a stony rigidity. The funeral, in short, was hastened, on account of the rapid advance of what was supposed to be decomposition.

The lady was deposited in her family vault, which, for three subse-

3. Cf Ecclesiastes 12:6–8: "Or ever the silver cord be loosed, or the golden bowl be broken, or the pitcher be broken or the fountain, or the wheel broken at the cistern. Then shall the dust return to the earth as it was: and the spirit shall return unto God who gave it. Vanity of vanities, saith the preacher; all is vanity."
4. According to some occultists of Poe's day, the soul wanders abroad when one is in an unconscious state or hypnotic trance.
5. Deductive; not dependent on empirical observation: an effect deduced from an assumed cause.

quent years, was undisturbed. At the expiration of this term, it was opened for the reception of a sarcophagus;—but, alas! how fearful a shock awaited the husband, who, personally, threw open the door. As its portals swung outwardly back, some white-apparrelled object fell rattling within his arms. It was the skeleton of his wife in her yet un-mouldered shroud.

A careful investigation rendered it evident that she had revived within two days after her entombment—that her struggles within the coffin had caused it to fall from a ledge, or shelf, to the floor, where it was so broken as to permit her escape. A lamp which had been acci-dentally left, full of oil, within the tomb, was found empty; it might have been exhausted, however, by evaporation. On the uppermost of the steps which led down into the dread chamber, was a large frag-ment of the coffin, with which it seemed that she had endeavored to arrest attention, by striking the iron door. While thus occupied, she probably swooned, or possibly died, through sheer terror; and, in falling, her shroud became entangled in some iron-work which pro-jected interiorly. Thus she remained, and thus she rotted, erect.[6]

In the year 1810, a case of living inhumation happened in France, attended with circumstances which go far to warrant the assertion that truth is, indeed, stranger than fiction. The heroine of the story was a Mademoiselle Victorine Lafourcade, a young girl of illustrious family, of wealth, and of great personal beauty. Among her numerous suitors was Julien Bossuet, a poor *littérateur*, or journalist, of Paris. His talents and general amiability had recommended him to the notice of the heiress, by whom he seems to have been truly beloved; but her pride of birth decided her, finally, to reject him, and to wed a Mon-sieur Rénelle, a banker, and a diplomatist of some eminence. After marriage, however, this gentleman neglected, and, perhaps, even more positively ill-treated her. Having passed with him some wretched years, she died,—at least her condition so closely resembled death as to deceive every one who saw her. She was buried—not in a vault—but in an ordinary grave in the village of her nativity. Filled with de-spair, and still inflamed by the memory of a profound attachment, the lover journeys from the capital to the remote province in which the village lies, with the romantic purpose of disinterring the corpse, and possessing himself of its luxuriant tresses. He reaches the grave. At midnight he unearths the coffin, opens it, and is in the act of detach-ing the hair, when he is arrested by the unclosing of the beloved eyes. In fact, the lady had been buried alive. Vitality had not altogether de-parted; and she was aroused, by the caresses of her lover, from the lethargy which had been mistaken for death. He bore her frantically to his lodgings in the village. He employed certain powerful restoratives suggested by no little medical learning.[7] In fine, she revived. She rec-

6. Scholars have noted parallels with "The Lady Buried Alive" in the *Philadelphia Casket* (later *Graham's*) for September 1827. This story in turn echoes two 18th-century accounts: one by Domenico Maria Manni (1690–1788), author of *Istoria de Decamerone di Giovanni Boccac-cio* (1742), involving an incident of the plague in Florence, Italy, in 1460; and one by Gayot de Pitivol in *Causes célèbres et intéressantes* (1737).

7. The most common procedure was to try to "revive" consciousness as a test for signs of life by

ognized her preserver. She remained with him until, by slow degrees, she fully recovered her original health. Her woman's heart was not adamant, and this last lesson of love sufficed to soften it. She bestowed it upon Bossuet. She returned no more to her husband, but concealing from him her resurrection, fled with her lover to America. Twenty years afterwards, the two returned to France, in the persuasion that time had so greatly altered the lady's appearance that her friends would be unable to recognize her. They were mistaken, however; for, at the first meeting, Monsieur Rénelle did actually recognize and make claim to his wife. This claim she resisted; and a judicial tribunal sustained her in her resistance; deciding that the peculiar circumstances, with the long lapse of years, had extinguished, not only equitably but legally, the authority of the husband.

The "Chirurgical Journal"[8] of Leipsic—a periodical, of high authority and merit, which some American bookseller would do well to translate and republish—records, in a late number, a very distressing event of the character in question.

An officer of artillery, a man of gigantic stature and of robust health, being thrown from an unmanageable horse, received a very severe contusion upon the head, which rendered him insensible at once; the skull was slightly fractured; but no immediate danger was apprehended. Trepanning[9] was accomplished successfully. He was bled, and many other of the ordinary means of relief were adopted. Gradually, however, he fell into a more and more hopeless state of stupor; and, finally, it was thought that he died.

The weather was warm; and he was buried, with indecent haste, in one of the public cemeteries. His funeral took place on Thursday. On the Sunday following, the grounds of the cemetery were, as usual, much thronged with visitors; and, about noon, an intense excitement was created by the declaration of a peasant that, while sitting upon the grave of the officer; he had distinctly felt a commotion of the earth, as if occasioned by some one struggling beneath. At first little attention was paid to the man's asseveration;[1] but his evident terror, and the dogged obstinacy with which he persisted in his story, had, at length, their natural effect upon the crowd. Spades were hurriedly procured, and the grave, which was shamefully shallow, was, in a few minutes, so far thrown open that the head of its occupant appeared. He was then, seemingly, dead; but he sat nearly erect within his coffin, the lid of which, in his furious struggles, he had partially uplifted.

He was forthwith conveyed to the nearest Hospital, and there pronounced to be still living, although in an asphytic condition.[2] After

means of smelling salts (spirits of ammonia). The names of the personages in Poe's account of Madame Lafourcade seem to be a jumble of fiction and miscellaneous reportage.
8. No such surgical journal is known, though scholars have found a *Zeitschrift für Chirurgen*, published in Poland 1841–46.
9. Cutting an opening in the skull to relieve pressure from swelling of the brain (or from a tumor or bleeding).
1. Vigorous affirmation, assertion.
2. Lack of oxygen in the blood leading to coma. In Poe's time the phrase suggested "suspension of life, with all the appearance of death," as N. P. Willis wrote in the *New York Mirror*

some hours he revived, recognized individuals of his acquaintance, and, in broken sentences, spoke of his agonies in the grave.

From what he related, it was clear that he must have been conscious of life for more than an hour, while inhumed, before lapsing into insensibility. The grave was carelessly and loosely filled with an exceedingly porous soil; and thus some air was necessarily admitted. He heard the footsteps of the crowd overhead, and endeavored to make himself heard in turn. It was the tumult within the grounds of the cemetery, he said, which appeared to awaken him from a deep sleep—but no sooner was he awake than he became fully aware of the awful horrors of his position.

This patient, it is recorded, was doing well, and seemed to be in a fair way of ultimate recovery, but fell a victim to the quackeries of medical experiment. The galvanic battery was applied; and he suddenly expired in one of those ecstatic paroxysms[3] which, occasionally, it superinduces.

The mention of the galvanic battery, nevertheless, recalls to my memory a well known and very extraordinary case in point,[4] where its action proved the means of restoring to animation a young attorney of London who had been interred for two days. This occurred in 1831, and created, at the time, a very profound sensation wherever it was made the subject of converse.

The patient, Mr. Edward Stapleton, had died, apparently, of typhus fever, accompanied with some anomalous symptoms which had excited the curiosity of his medical attendants. Upon his seeming decease, his friends were requested to sanction a *post mortem* examination, but declined to permit it. As often happens when such refusals are made, the practitioners resolved to disinter the body and dissect it at leisure, in private. Arrangements were easily effected with some of the numerous corps of body-snatchers[5] with which London abounds; and, upon the third night after the funeral, the supposed corpse was unearthed from a grave eight feet deep, and deposited in the operating chamber of one of the private hospitals.

An incision of some extent had been actually made in the abdomen, when the fresh and undecayed appearance of the subject suggested an application of the battery. One experiment succeeded another, and the customary effects supervened, with nothing to characterize them in any respect, except, upon one or two occasions, a more than ordinary degree of life-likeliness in the convulsive action.

It grew late. The day was about to dawn; and it was thought expedi-

(November 18, 1843). The word is related to *asphyxia*, death by suffocation (oxygen deprivation); see notes to "Some Words with a Mummy" (pp. 382ff. herein).

3. Sudden convulsions. "Galvanic battery": battery that produced electricity chemically (named after Luigi Galvani). The term *galvanism* referred more specifically to the stimulation of a nerve or muscle (even after death) into twitching or jumping by electrical shock (administered externally by a conductive wire); see notes to "Loss of Breath" (pp. 89ff. herein) and "Some Words with a Mummy" (pp. 383ff.).

4. See "The Buried Alive," *Blackwood's* (October 1821) (pp. 759ff. herein) and the reference to "The Dead Alive" in Poe's "How to Write a Blackwood Article" (p. 176 herein).

5. Grave robbers who dug up bodies for medical research (cf. "The Fall of the House of Usher," pp. 199ff. herein). The Burial Act of 1857 finally made it a punishable crime.

ent, at length, to proceed at once to the dissection. A student, however, was especially desirous of testing a theory of his own, and insisted upon applying the battery to one of the pectoral muscles. A rough gash was made, and a wire hastily brought in contact; when the patient, with a hurried but quite unconvulsive movement, arose from the table, stepped into the middle of the floor, gazed about him uneasily for a few seconds, and then—spoke. What he said was unintelligible; but words were uttered; the syllabification was distinct. Having spoken, he fell heavily to the floor.

For some moments all were paralyzed with awe—but the urgency of the case soon restored them their presence of mind. It was seen that Mr. Stapleton was alive, although in a swoon. Upon exhibition of ether he revived and was rapidly restored to health, and to the society of his friends—from whom, however, all knowledge of his resuscitation was withheld, until a relapse was no longer to be apprehended. Their wonder—their rapturous astonishment—may be conceived.

The most thrilling peculiarity of this incident, nevertheless, is involved in what Mr. S. himself asserts. He declares that at no period was he altogether insensible—that, dully and confusedly, he was aware of every thing which happened to him, from the moment in which he was pronounced *dead* by his physicians, to that in which he fell swooning to the floor of the Hospital. "I am alive" were the uncomprehended words which, upon recognizing the locality of the dissecting-room, he had endeavored, in his extremity, to utter.

It were an easy matter to multiply such histories as these—but I forbear—for, indeed, we have no need of such to establish the fact that premature interments occur. When we reflect how very rarely, from the nature of the case, we have it in our power to detect them, we must admit that they may *frequently* occur without our cognizance. Scarcely, in truth, is a graveyard ever encroached upon, for any purpose, to any great extent, that skeletons are not found in postures which suggest the most fearful of suspicions.[6]

Fearful indeed the suspicion—but more fearful the doom! It may be asserted, without hesitation, that *no* event is no terribly well adapted to inspire the supremeness of bodily and of mental distress, as is burial before death. The unendurable oppression of the lungs—the stifling fumes from the damp earth—the clinging of the death garments—the rigid embrace of the narrow house—the blackness of the absolute Night—the silence like a sea that overwhelms—the unseen but palpable presence of the Conqueror Worm—these things, with thoughts of the air and grass above, with memory of dear friends who would fly to save us if but informed of our fate, and with consciousness that of this fate they can *never* be informed—that our hopeless portion is that of the really dead—these considerations, I say, carry into the heart, which still palpitates, a degree of appalling and intolerable horror from which the most daring imagination must re-

6. The different positions of the corpse causes the "suspicion" that the "deceased" has been buried alive.

coil. We know of nothing so agonizing upon Earth—we can dream of nothing half so hideous in the realms of the nethermost Hell. And thus all narratives upon this topic have an interest profound; an interest, nevertheless, which, through the sacred awe of the topic itself, very properly and very peculiarly depends upon our conviction of the *truth* of the matter narrated. What I have now to tell, is of my own actual knowledge—of my own positive and personal experience.

For several years I had been subject to attacks of the singular disorder which physicians have agreed to term catalepsy,[7] in default of a more definitive title. Although both the immediate and the predisposing causes, and even the actual diagnosis, of this disease, are still mysteries, its obvious and apparent character is sufficiently well understood. Its variations seem to be chiefly of degree. Sometimes the patient lies, for a day only, or even for a shorter period, in a species of exaggerated lethargy. He is senseless and externally motionless; but the pulsation of the heart is still faintly perceptible; some traces of warmth remain; a slight color lingers within the centre of the cheek; and, upon application of a mirror to the lips, we can detect a torpid, unequal, and vacillating action of the lungs. Then again the duration of the trance is for weeks—even for months; while the closest scrutiny, and the most rigorous medical tests, fail to establish any material distinction between the state of the sufferer and what we conceive of absolute death. Very usually, he is saved from premature interment solely by the knowledge of his friends that he has been previously subject to catalepsy, by the consequent suspicion excited, and, above all, by the non-appearance of decay. The advances of the malady are, luckily, gradual. The first manifestations, although marked, are unequivocal. The fits grow successively more and more distinctive, and endure each for a longer term than the preceding. In this lies the principal security from inhumation. The unfortunate whose *first* attack should be of the extreme character which is occasionally seen, would almost inevitably be consigned alive to the tomb.

My own case differed in no important particular from those mentioned in medical books. Sometimes, without any apparent cause, I sank, little by little, into a condition of hemi-syncope,[8] or half swoon; and, in this condition, without pain, without ability to stir, or, strictly speaking, to think, but with a dull lethargic consciousness of life and of the presence of those who surrounded my bed, I remained, until the crisis of the disease restored me, suddenly, to perfect sensation. At other times I was quickly and impetuously smitten. I grew sick, and numb, and chilly, and dizzy, and so fell prostrate at once. Then, for weeks, all was void, and black, and silent, and Nothing became the universe. Total annihilation could be no more. From these latter attacks I awoke, however, with a gradation slow in proportion to the suddenness of the seisure. Just as the day dawns to the friendless and

7. An unconscious state in which the body becomes immobile and rigid (see notes to "The Fall of the House of Usher," pp. 199ff. herein, and "Some Words with a Mummy," pp. 382ff.).
8. Persistent printing error in this tale for *semi-syncope*, a fainting spell. A *syncope* (chopping off) is a sudden loss (cutting off) of consciousness.

houseless beggar who roams the streets throughout the long desolate winter night—just so tardily—just so wearily—just so cheerily came back the light of the Soul to me.

Apart from the tendency to trance, however, my general health appeared to be good; nor could I perceive that it was at all affected by the one prevalent malady—unless, indeed, an idiosyncrasy in my ordinary *sleep* may be looked upon as superinduced. Upon awaking from slumber, I could never gain, at once, thorough possession of my senses, and always remained, for many minutes, in much bewilderment and perplexity;—the mental faculties in general, but the memory in especial, being in a condition of absolute abeyance.

In all that I endured there was no physical suffering, but of moral distress an infinitude. My fancy grew charnal. I talked "of worms, of tombs and epitaphs."[9] I was lost in reveries of death, and the idea of premature burial held continual possession of my brain. The ghastly Danger to which I was subjected, haunted me day and night. In the former, the torture of meditation was excessive—in the latter, supreme. When the grim Darkness overspread the Earth, then, with very horror of thought, I shook—shook as the quivering plumes upon the hearse. When Nature could endure wakefulness no longer, it was with a struggle that I consented to sleep—for I shuddered to reflect that, upon awaking, I might find myself the tenant of a grave. And when, finally, I sank into slumber, it was only to rush at once into a world of phantasms, above which, with vast, sable, overshadowing wings, hovered, predominant, the one sepulchral Idea.

From the innumerable images of gloom which thus oppressed me in dreams, I select for record but a solitary vision. Methought I was immersed in a cataleptic trance of more than usual duration and profundity. Suddenly there came an icy hand upon my forehead, and an impatient, gibbering voice whispered the word "Arise!" within my ear.

I sat erect. The darkness was total. I could not see the figure of him who had aroused me. I could call to mind neither the period at which I had fallen into the trance, nor the locality in which I then lay. While I remained motionless, and busied in endeavors to collect my thoughts, the cold hand grasped me fiercely by the wrist, shaking it petulantly, while the gibbering voice said again:

"Arise! did I not bid thee arise?"

"And who," I demanded, "art thou?"

"I have no name in the regions which I inhabit," replied the voice mournfully; "I was mortal, but am fiend. I was merciless, but am pitiful. Thou dost feel that I shudder.—My teeth chatter as I speak, yet it is not with the chilliness of the night—of the night without end. But this hideousness is insufferable. How canst *thou* tranquilly sleep? I cannot rest for the cry of these great agonies. These sights are more than I can bear. Get thee up! Come with me into the outer Night, and let me unfold to thee the graves. Is not this a spectacle of woe?—Behold!"

9. See Shakespeare's *Richard II*, III.ii.145: "Let's talk of graves, of worms, and epitaphs."

I looked; and the unseen figure, which still grasped me by the wrist, had caused to be thrown open the graves of all mankind; and from each issued the faint phosphoric radiance of decay;[1] so that I could see into the innermost recesses, and there view the shrouded bodies in their sad and solemn slumbers with the worm. But, alas! the real sleepers were fewer, by many millions, than those who slumbered not at all; and there was a feeble struggling; and there was a general sad unrest; and from out the depths of the countless pits there came a melancholy rustling from the garments of the buried. And, of those who seemed tranquilly to repose, I saw that a vast number had changed, in a greater or less degree, the rigid and uneasy position in which they had originally been entombed. And the voice again said to me, as I gazed:

"Is it not—oh, is it *not* a pitiful sight?"—but, before I could find words to reply, the figure had ceased to grasp my wrist, the phosphoric lights expired, and the graves were closed with a sudden violence, while from out them arose a tumult of despairing cries, saying again— "Is it not—oh, God! is it *not* a very pitiful sight?"

Phantasies such as these, presenting themselves at night, extended their terrific influence far into my waking hours.—My nerves became thoroughly unstrung, and I fell a prey to perpetual horror. I hesitated to ride, or to walk, or to indulge in any exercise that would carry me from home. In fact I no longer dared trust myself out of the immediate presence of those who were aware of my proneness to catalepsy, lest, falling into one of my usual fits, I should be buried before my real condition could be ascertained. I doubted the care, the fidelity of my dearest friends. I dreaded that, in some trance of more than customary duration, they might be prevailed upon to regard me as irrecoverable. I even went so far as to fear that, as I occasioned much trouble, they might be glad to consider any very protracted attack as sufficient excuse for getting rid of me altogether. It was in vain they endeavored to reassure me by the most solemn promises. I exacted the most sacred oaths, that under no circumstances they would bury me until decomposition had so materially advanced as to render farther preservation impossible. And, even then, my mortal terrors would listen to no reason—would accept no consolation. I entered into a series of elaborate precautions. Among other things, I had the family vault so remodelled as to admit of being readily opened from within. The slightest pressure upon a long lever that extended far into the tomb would cause the iron portals to fly back. There were arrangements also for the free admission of air and light, and convenient receptacles for food and water, within immediate reach of the coffin intended for my reception. This coffin was warmly and softly padded; and was provided with a lid, fashioned upon the principle of the vault-door, with the addition of springs so contrived that the feeblest movement of the body would be sufficient to set it at liberty. Besides all this, there was suspended from the roof of the tomb, a large bell, the rope of which, it was designed,

1. Bacteria and fungi on rotting flesh or wood can produce an eerie glow.

should extend through a hole in the coffin, and so be fastened to one of the hands of the corpse.[2] But, alas! what avails the vigilance against the Destiny of man? Not even these well contrived securities sufficed to save from the uttermost agonies of living inhumation, a wretch to these agonies foredoomed!

There arrived an epoch—as often before there had arrived—in which I found myself emerging from total unconsciousness into the first feeble and indefinite sense of existence.—Slowly—with a tortoise gradation—approached the faint gray dawn of the psychal day. A torpid uneasiness. An apathetic endurance of dull pain. No care—no hope—no effort. Then, after long interval, a ringing in the ears; then, after a lapse still longer, a pricking or tingling sensation in the extremities; then a seemingly eternal period of pleasurable quiescence, during which the awakening feelings are struggling into thought; then a brief re-sinking into non-entity; then a sudden recovery. At length the slight quivering of an eyelid, and immediately thereupon, an electric shock of a terror, deadly and indefinite, which sends the blood in torrents from the temples to the heart. And now the first positive effort to think. And now the first endeavor to remember. And now a partial and evanescent success. And now the memory has so far regained its dominion that, in some measure, I am cognizant of my state. I feel that I am not awaking from ordinary sleep. I recollect that I have been subject to catalepsy. And now, at last, as if by the rush of an ocean, my shuddering spirit is overwhelmed by the one grim Danger—by the one spectral and ever-prevalent Idea.

For some minutes after this fancy possessed me, I remained without motion. And why? I could not summon courage to move. I dared not make the effort which was to satisfy me of my fate—and yet there was something at my heart which whispered me it *was sure*. Despair—such as no other species of wretchedness ever calls into being—despair alone urged me, after long irresolution, to uplift the heavy lids of my eyes. I uplifted them. It was dark—all dark. I knew that the fit was over. I knew that the crisis of my disorder had long passed. I knew that I had now fully recovered the use of my visual faculties—and yet it was dark—all dark—the intense and utter raylessness of the Night that endureth for evermore.

I endeavored to shriek; and my lips and my parched tongue moved convulsively together in the attempt—but no voice issued from the cavernous lungs, which, oppressed as if by the weight of some incumbent mountain, gasped and palpitated, with the heart, at every elaborate and struggling inspiration.

The movement of the jaws, in this effort to cry aloud, showed me that they were bound up, as is usual with the dead. I felt, too, that I lay upon some hard substance; and by something similar my sides were, also, closely compressed. So far, I had not ventured to stir any of my limbs—

2. For the details of this paragraph, see the description of the "life-preserving coffin" by N. P. Willis in the *New York Mirror* for November 1843 (see p. 356 herein); also see Thomas Hood's "The Death Watch" (*The Rover*, June 1843) and a poem on the New York life coffin by Mrs. Seba Smith in the *Columbian Lady's and Gentleman's Magazine* (January 1845).

but now I violently threw up my arms, which had been lying at length, with the wrists crossed. They struck a solid wooden substance, which extended above my person at an elevation of not more than six inches from my face. I could no longer doubt that I reposed within a coffin at last.

And now, amid all my infinite miseries, came sweetly the cherub Hope—for I thought of my precautions. I writhed, and made spasmodic exertions to force open the lid: it would not move. I felt my wrists for the bell-rope: it was not to be found. And now the Comforter fled forever, and a still sterner Despair reigned triumphant; for I could not help perceiving the absence of the paddings which I had so carefully prepared—and then, too, there came suddenly to my nostrils the strong peculiar odor of moist earth. The conclusion was irresistible. I was *not* within the vault. I had fallen into a trance while absent from home—while among strangers—when, or how, I could not remember—and it was they who had buried me as a dog—nailed up in some common coffin—and thrust, deep, deep, and forever, into some ordinary and nameless *grave*.

As this awful conviction forced itself, thus, into the innermost chambers of my soul, I once again struggled to cry aloud. And in this second endeavor I succeeded. A long, wild, and continuous shriek, or yell, of agony, resounded through the realms of the subterrene Night.

"Hillo! hillo, there!" said a gruff voice in reply.

"What the devil's the matter now!" said a second.

"Get out o' that!" said a third.

"What do you mean by yowling in that ere kind of style, like a cattymount!"[3] said a fourth; and hereupon I was seized and shaken without ceremony, for several minutes, by a junto of very rough-looking individuals. They did not arouse me from my slumber—for I was wide awake when I screamed—but they restored me to the full possession of my memory.

This adventure occurred near Richmond, in Virginia. Accompanied by a friend, I had proceeded, upon a gunning expedition, some miles down the banks of James River. Night approached, and we were overtaken by a storm. The cabin of a small sloop lying at anchor in the stream, and laden with garden mould, afforded us the only available shelter. We made the best of it, and passed the night on board. I slept in one of the only two berths in the vessel—and the berths of a sloop of sixty or seventy tons, need scarcely be described. That which I occupied had no bedding of any kind. Its extreme width was eighteen inches. The distance of its bottom from the deck overhead, was precisely the same. I found it a matter of exceeding difficulty to squeeze myself in. Nevertheless, I slept soundly; and the whole of my vision—for it was no dream, and no nightmare—arose naturally from the circumstances of my position—from my ordinary bias of thought—and from the difficulty, to which I have alluded, of collecting my senses, and especially of regaining my memory, for a long time after awaking from slumber. The men who shook me were the crew of the sloop, and

3. Or catamount; mountain lion.

some laborers engaged to unload it. From the load itself came the earthy smell. The bandage about the jaws was a silk handkerchief in which I had bound up my head, in default of my customary nightcap. The tortures endured, however, were indubitably quite equal, for the time, to those of actual sepulture. They were fearfully—they were inconceivably hideous; but out of Evil proceeded Good; for their very excess wrought in my spirit an inevitable revulsion. My soul acquired tone—acquired temper. I went abroad. I took vigorous exercise. I breathed the free air of Heaven. I thought upon other subjects than Death. I discarded my medical books. "Buchan"[4] I burned. I read no "Night Thoughts"—no fustian about churchyards—no bugaboo[5] tales— *such as this*. In short, I became a new man, and lived a man's life. From that memorable night, I dismissed forever my charnal apprehensions, and with them vanished the cataleptic disorder, of which, perhaps, they had been less the consequence than the cause.

There are moments when, even to the sober eye of Reason, the world of our sad Humanity may assume the semblance of a Hell—but the imagination of man is no Carathis, to explore with impunity its every cavern. Alas! the grim legion of sepulchral terrors cannot be regarded as altogether fanciful—but, like the Demons in whose company Afrasiab made his voyage down the Oxus, they must sleep, or they will devour us—they must be suffered to slumber, or we perish.[6]

The Purloined Letter[1]

Nil sapientiæ odiosius acumine nimio.

Seneca.[2]

Paris, just after dark one gusty evening in the autumn of 18—, I was enjoying the twofold luxury of meditation and a meerschaum, in com-

4. Probably William Buchan (1729–1805), who wrote the popular *Domestic Medicine; or The Family Physician* (1769; reprinted twenty-one times by 1813 and twenty-nine times by 1854). Levine notes another possibility: Peter Buchan (1790–1854), author of *Witchcraft Detected and Prevented, or the School of Black Art Newly Opened* (1826).
5. Fairy-tale fright or terror. The English slang word is related to the Welsh, Scots, Cornish *bogie, bogle, hygus, buccaboo* (demon, boogyman, ghost, giant) and the Old French *bugibus*; see notes to "The Man That Was Used Up" (pp. 190ff. herein). *The Complaint: or, Night-Thoughts on Life, Death, & Immortality* (1742; 1745–46) was a long popular poem by Edward Young (1683–1765) that set the trend for the Graveyard School of poetry in English literature. *Fustian*: pretentious, pompous speech or writing.
6. The whole paragraph echoes two passages from Horace Binney Wallace's novel, *Stanley* (1838). Carathis is the witch mother in William Beckford's Arabo-Oriental gothic romance *Vathek* (1786), who is given a day to roam Hell as she wishes before suffering eternal torture. The Oxus River (the ancient name of the Amu Darya) is the scene of many battles in Persian history; it flows some fifteen hundred miles through central Asia to the Aral Sea. The legendary Afrasiab was the king of Turân (now western Turkistan), deadly enemy of the Persian hero Rustum. Levine notes that Afrasiab is a recurrent figure in the Persian epic, *Shâh-náma* (or *Shah Nameh*) by Abdul Kasim Mansur Firdausi (c. 950–c. 1020), who is more generally known as simply "Firdusi." Somewhat later in the 19th century, Matthew Arnold memorialized Rustum in his epic poem *Sohrab and Rustrum* (1853).
1. First published in *The Gift: a Christmas, New Year, and Birthday Present* (dated 1845 but published in September 1844), this story was frequently reprinted and pirated, with unauthorized variants and abridgements. The text reprinted here is from *Tales* (1845).
2. Nothing is more hateful to sense than too much cunning (Latin). Seneca the Younger: Lucius Annaeus Seneca (c. 3 B.C.E.–65 C.E.), Stoic Roman philosopher, playwright, and statesman, author of *Moral Letters*; cf. p. 100, n. 9.

pany with my friend C. Auguste Dupin, in his little back library, or book-closet, *au troisiême*,[3] *No. 33, Rue Dunôt, Faubourg St. Germain.* For one hour at least we had maintained a profound silence; while each, to any casual observer, might have seemed intently and exclusively occupied with the curling eddies of smoke that oppressed the atmosphere of the chamber. For myself, however, I was mentally discussing certain topics which had formed matter for conversation between us at an earlier period of the evening; I mean the affair of the Rue Morgue, and the mystery attending the murder of Marie Rogêt. I looked upon it, therefore, as something of a coincidence, when the door of our apartment was thrown open and admitted our old acquaintance, Monsieur G——, the Prefect of the Parisian police.

We gave him a hearty welcome; for there was nearly half as much of the entertaining as of the contemptible about the man, and we had not seen him for several years. We had been sitting in the dark, and Dupin now arose for the purpose of lighting a lamp, but sat down again, without doing so, upon G.'s saying that he had called to consult us, or rather to ask the opinion of my friend, about some official business which had occasioned a great deal of trouble.

"If it is any point requiring reflection," observed Dupin, as he forebore to enkindle the wick, "we shall examine it to better purpose in the dark."

"That is another of your odd notions," said the Prefect, who had a fashion of calling every thing "odd" that was beyond his comprehension, and thus lived amid an absolute legion of "oddities."

"Very true," said Dupin, as he supplied his visiter with a pipe, and rolled towards him a comfortable chair.

"And what is the difficulty now?" I asked. "Nothing more in the assassination way, I hope?"

"Oh no; nothing of that nature. The fact is, the business is *very* simple indeed, and I make no doubt that we can manage it sufficiently well ourselves; but then I thought Dupin would like to hear the details of it, because it is so excessively *odd*."

"Simple and odd," said Dupin.

"Why, yes; and not exactly that, either. The fact is, we have all been a good deal puzzled because the affair *is* so simple, and yet baffles us altogether."

"Perhaps it is the very simplicity of the thing which puts you at fault," said my friend.

"What nonsense you *do* talk!" replied the Prefect, laughing heartily.

"Perhaps the mystery is a little *too* plain," said Dupin.

"Oh, good heavens! who ever heard of such an idea?"

"A little *too* self-evident."

"Ha! ha! ha!—ha! ha! ha!—ho! ho! ho!" roared our visiter, profoundly amused, "oh, Dupin, you will be the death of me yet!"

3. The third floor (French), but the fourth floor to Americans; European countries normally designate what Americans call the "first" floor as the "ground" floor and begin numbering with the next one up from there. "Meerschaum": a fine, compact, and usually white claylike material; also a pipe made from it.

"And what, after all, *is* the matter on hand?" I asked.

"Why, I will tell you," replied the Prefect, as he gave a long, steady, and contemplative puff, and settled himself in his chair. "I will tell you in a few words; but, before I begin, let me caution you that this is an affair demanding the greatest secrecy, and that I should most probably lose the position I now hold, were it known that I confided it to any one."

"Proceed," said I.

"Or not," said Dupin.

"Well, then; I have received personal information, from a very high quarter, that a certain document of the last importance, has been purloined from the royal apartments. The individual who purloined it is known; this beyond a doubt; he was seen to take it. It is known, also, that it still remains in his possession."

"How is this known?" asked Dupin.

"It is clearly inferred," replied the Prefect, "from the nature of the document, and from the non-appearance of certain results which would at once arise from its passing *out* of the robber's possession;— that is to say, from his employing it as he must design in the end to employ it."

"Be a little more explicit," I said.

"Well, I may venture so far as to say that the paper gives its holder a certain power in a certain quarter where such power is immensely valuable." The Prefect was fond of the cant of diplomacy.

"Still I do not quite understand," said Dupin.

"No? Well; the disclosure of the document to a third person, who shall be nameless, would bring in question the honor of a personage of most exalted station; and this fact gives the holder of the document an ascendancy over the illustrious personage whose honor and peace are so jeopardized."

"But this ascendancy," I interposed, "would depend upon the robber's knowledge of the loser's knowledge of the robber. Who would dare—"

"The thief," said G., "is the Minister D——, who dares all things, those unbecoming as well as those becoming a man. The method of the theft was not less ingenious than bold. The document in question—a letter, to be frank—had been received by the personage robbed while alone in the royal *boudoir*. During its perusal she was suddenly interrupted by the entrance of the other exalted personage from whom especially it was her wish to conceal it. After a hurried and vain endeavor to thrust it in a drawer, she was forced to place it, open as it was, upon a table. The address, however, was uppermost, and, the contents thus unexposed, the letter escaped notice. At this juncture enters the Minister D——. His lynx eye immediately perceives the paper, recognises the handwriting of the address, observes the confusion of the personage addressed, and fathoms her secret. After some business transactions, hurried through in his ordinary manner, he produces a letter somewhat similar to the one in question, opens it, pretends to read it, and then places it in close juxtaposition to the

other. Again he converses, for some fifteen minutes, upon the public affairs. At length, in taking leave, he takes also from the table the letter to which he had no claim. Its rightful owner saw, but, of course, dared not call attention to the act, in the presence of the third personage who stood at her elbow. The minister decamped; leaving his own letter—one of no importance—upon the table."

"Here, then," said Dupin to me, "you have precisely what you demand to make the ascendancy complete—the robber's knowledge of the loser's knowledge of the robber."

"Yes," replied the Prefect; "and the power thus attained has, for some months past, been wielded, for political purposes, to a very dangerous extent. The personage robbed is more thoroughly convinced, every day, of the necessity of reclaiming her letter. But this, of course, cannot be done openly. In fine, driven to despair, she has committed the matter to me."

"Than whom," said Dupin, amid a perfect whirlwind of smoke, "no more sagacious agent could, I suppose, be desired, or even imagined."

"You flatter me," replied the Prefect; "but it is possible that some such opinion may have been entertained."

"It is clear," said I, "as you observe, that the letter is still in possession of the minister; since it is this possession, and not any employment of the letter, which bestows the power. With the employment the power departs."

"True," said G.; "and upon this conviction I proceeded. My first care was to make thorough search of the minister's hotel; and here my chief embarrassment lay in the necessity of searching without his knowledge. Beyond all things, I have been warned of the danger which would result from giving him reason to suspect our design."

"But," said I, "you are quite *au fait*[4] in these investigations. The Parisian police have done this thing often before."

"O yes; and for this reason I did not despair. The habits of the minister gave me, too, a great advantage. He is frequently absent from home all night. His servants are by no means numerous. They sleep at a distance from their master's apartment, and, being chiefly Neapolitans, are readily made drunk. I have keys, as you know, with which I can open any chamber or cabinet in Paris. For three months a night has not passed, during the greater part of which I have not been engaged, personally, in ransacking the D—— Hotel. My honor is interested, and, to mention a great secret, the reward is enormous. So I did not abandon the search until I had become fully satisfied that the thief is a more astute man than myself. I fancy that I have investigated every nook and corner of the premises in which it is possible that the paper can be concealed."

"But is it not possible," I suggested, "that although the letter may be in possession of the minister, as it unquestionably is, he may have concealed it elsewhere than upon his own premises?"

"This is barely possible," said Dupin. "The present peculiar condi-

4. Well-informed.

tion of affairs at court, and especially of those intrigues in which D——is known to be involved, would render the instant availability of the document—its susceptibility of being produced at a moment's no-tice—a point of nearly equal importance with its possession."

"Its susceptibility of being produced?" said I.

"That is to say, of being *destroyed*," said Dupin.

"True," I observed; "the paper is clearly then upon the premises. As for its being upon the person of the minister, we may consider that as out of the question."

"Entirely," said the Prefect. "He has been twice waylaid, as if by footpads, and his person rigorously searched under my own inspec-tion."

"You might have spared yourself this trouble," said Dupin. "D——, I presume, is not altogether a fool, and, if not, must have anticipated these waylayings, as a matter of course."

"Not *altogether* a fool," said G., "but then he's a poet, which I take to be only one remove from a fool."

"True," said Dupin, after a long and thoughtful whiff from his meer-schaum, "although I have been guilty of certain doggrel myself."

"Suppose you detail," said I, "the particulars of your search."

"Why the fact is, we took our time, and we searched *every where*. I have had long experience in these affairs. I took the entire building, room by room; devoting the nights of a whole week to each. We exam-ined, first, the furniture of each apartment. We opened every possible drawer; and I presume you know that, to a properly trained police agent, such a thing as a *secret* drawer is impossible. Any man is a dolt who permits a 'secret' drawer to escape him in a search of this kind. The thing is *so* plain. There is a certain amount of bulk—of space—to be accounted for in every cabinet. Then we have accurate rules. The fiftieth part of a line could not escape us. After the cabinets we took the chairs. The cushions we probed with the fine long needles you have seen me employ. From the tables we removed the tops."

"Why so?"

"Sometimes the top of a table, or other similarly arranged piece of furniture, is removed by the person wishing to conceal an article; then the leg is excavated, the article deposited within the cavity, and the top replaced. The bottoms and tops of bedposts are employed in the same way."

"But could not the cavity be detected by sounding?" I asked.

"By no means, if, when the article is deposited, a sufficient wadding of cotton be placed around it. Besides, in our case, we were obliged to proceed without noise."

"But you could not have removed—you could not have taken to pieces *all* articles of furniture in which it would have been possible to make a deposit in the manner you mention. A letter may be com-pressed into a thin spiral roll, not differing much in shape or bulk from a large knitting-needle, and in this form it might be inserted into the rung of a chair, for example. You did not take to pieces all the chairs?"

"Certainly not; but we did better—we examined the rungs of every chair in the hotel, and, indeed, the jointings of every description of furniture, by the aid of a most powerful microscope. Had there been any traces of recent disturbance we should not have failed to detect it instantly. A single grain of gimlet-dust, for example, would have been as obvious as an apple. Any disorder in the glueing—any unusual gaping in the joints—would have sufficed to insure detection."

"I presume you looked to the mirrors, between the boards and the plates, and you probed the beds and the bed-clothes, as well as the curtains and carpets."

"That of course; and when we had absolutely completed every particle of the furniture in this way, then we examined the house itself. We divided its entire surface into compartments, which we numbered, so that none might be missed; then we scrutinized each individual square inch throughout the premises, including the two houses immediately adjoining, with the microscope, as before."

"The two houses adjoining!" I exclaimed; "you must have had a great deal of trouble."

"We had; but the reward offered is prodigious."

"You include the *grounds* about the houses?"

"All the grounds are paved with brick. They gave us comparatively little trouble. We examined the moss between the bricks, and found it undisturbed."

"You looked among D——'s papers, of course, and into the books of the library?"

"Certainly; we opened every package and parcel; we not only opened every book, but we turned over every leaf in each volume, not contenting ourselves with a mere shake, according to the fashion of some of our police officers. We also measured the thickness of every book-*cover*, with the most accurate admeasurement, and applied to each the most jealous scrutiny of the microscope. Had any of the bindings been recently meddled with, it would have been utterly impossible that the fact should have escaped observation. Some five or six volumes, just from the hands of the binder, we carefully probed, longitudinally, with the needles."

"You explored the floors beneath the carpets?"

"Beyond doubt. We removed every carpet, and examined the boards with the microscope."

"And the paper on the walls?"

"Yes."

"You looked into the cellars?"

"We did."

"Then," I said, "you have been making a miscalculation, and the letter is *not* upon the premises, as you suppose."

"I fear you are right there," said the Prefect. "And now, Dupin, what would you advise me to do?"

"To make a thorough re-search of the premises."

"That is absolutely needless," replied G——. "I am not more sure that I breathe than I am that the letter is not at the Hotel."

"I have no better advice to give you," said Dupin. "You have, of course, an accurate description of the letter?"

"Oh yes!"—And here the Prefect, producing a memorandum-book, proceeded to read aloud a minute account of the internal, and especially of the external appearance of the missing document. Soon after finishing the perusal of this description, he took his departure, more entirely depressed in spirits than I had ever known the good gentleman before.

In about a month afterwards he paid us another visit, and found us occupied very nearly as before. He took a pipe and a chair and entered into some ordinary conversation. At length I said,—

"Well, but G——, what of the purloined letter? I presume you have at last made up your mind that there is no such thing as overreaching the Minister?"

"Confound him, say I—yes; I made the re-examination, however, as Dupin suggested—but it was all labor lost, as I knew it would be."

"How much was the reward offered, did you say?" asked Dupin.

"Why, a very great deal—a *very* liberal reward—I don't like to say how much, precisely; but one thing I *will* say, that I wouldn't mind giving my individual check for fifty thousand francs to any one who could obtain me that letter. The fact is, it is becoming of more and more importance every day; and the reward has been lately doubled. If it were trebled, however, I could do no more than I have done."

"Why, yes," said Dupin, drawlingly, between the whiffs of his meerschaum, "I really—think, G——, you have not exerted yourself—to the utmost in this matter. You might—do a little more, I think, eh?"

"How?—in what way?"

"Why—puff, puff—you might—puff, puff—employ counsel in the matter, eh?—puff, puff, puff. Do you remember the story they tell of Abernethy?"

"No; hang Abernethy!"

"To be sure! hang him and welcome. But, once upon a time, a certain rich miser conceived the design of spunging upon this Abernethy for a medical opinion. Getting up, for this purpose, an ordinary conversation in a private company, he insinuated his case to the physician, as that of an imaginary individual.

" 'We will suppose,' said the miser, 'that his symptoms are such and such; now, doctor, what would *you* have directed him to take?'

" 'Take!' said Abernethy, 'why, take *advice*, to be sure.' "

"But," said the Prefect, a little discomposed, "I am *perfectly* willing to take advice, and to pay for it. I would *really* give fifty thousand francs to any one who would aid me in the matter."

"In that case," replied Dupin, opening a drawer, and producing a check-book, "you may as well fill me up a check for the amount mentioned. When you have signed it, I will hand you the letter."

I was astounded. The Prefect appeared absolutely thunder-stricken. For some minutes he remained speechless and motionless, looking incredulously at my friend with open mouth, and eyes that seemed starting from their sockets; then, apparently recovering himself in some

measure, he seized a pen, and after several pauses and vacant stares, finally filled up and signed a check for fifty thousand francs, and handed it across the table to Dupin. The latter examined it carefully and deposited it in his pocket-book; then, unlocking an *escritoire*,[5] took thence a letter and gave it to the Prefect. This functionary grasped it in a perfect agony of joy, opened it with a trembling hand, cast a rapid glance at its contents, and then, scrambling and struggling to the door, rushed at length unceremoniously from the room and from the house, without having uttered a syllable since Dupin had requested him to fill up the check.

When he had gone, my friend entered into some explanations.

"The Parisian police," he said, "are exceedingly able in their way. They are persevering, ingenious, cunning, and thoroughly versed in the knowledge which their duties seem chiefly to demand. Thus, when G—— detailed to us his mode of searching the premises at the Hotel D——, I felt entire confidence in his having made a satisfactory investigation—so far as his labors extended."

"So far as his labors extended?" said I.

"Yes," said Dupin. "The measures adopted were not only the best of their kind, but carried out to absolute perfection. Had the letter been deposited within the range of their search, these fellows would, beyond a question, have found it."

I merely laughed—but he seemed quite serious in all that he said.

"The measures, then," he continued, "were good in their kind, and well executed; their defect lay in their being inapplicable to the case, and to the man. A certain set of highly ingenious resources are, with the Prefect, a sort of Procrustean bed,[6] to which he forcibly adapts his designs. But he perpetually errs by being too deep or too shallow, for the matter in hand; and many a schoolboy is a better reasoner than he. I knew one about eight years of age, whose success at guessing in the game of 'even and odd' attracted universal admiration. This game is simple, and is played with marbles. One player holds in his hand a number of these toys, and demands of another whether that number is even or odd. If the guess is right, the guesser wins one; if wrong, he loses one. The boy to whom I allude won all the marbles of the school. Of course he had some principle of guessing; and this lay in mere observation and admeasurement[7] of the astuteness of his opponents. For example, an arrant simpleton is his opponent, and, holding up his closed hand, asks, 'are they even or odd?' Our schoolboy replies, 'odd,' and loses; but upon the second trial he wins, for he then says to himself, 'the simpleton had them even upon the first trial, and his amount of cunning is just sufficient to make him have them odd upon the second; I will therefore guess odd';—he guesses odd, and wins. Now, with a simpleton a degree above the first, he would have reasoned thus:

5. Writing desk.
6. In mythology, Procrustes (see Ovid's *Metamorphoses*, VII), tied travelers to a bed and made them fit: if their legs were too short, he stretched them; if their legs were too long, he cut them off. Procrustes has been used as a symbol both for tyranny and for revolution.
7. Here, to divide and distribute proportionally.

'This fellow finds that in the first instance I guessed odd, and, in the second, he will propose to himself, upon the first impulse, a simple variation from even to odd, as did the first simpleton; but then a second thought will suggest that this is too simple a variation, and finally he will decide upon putting it even as before. I will therefore guess even;'—he guesses even, and wins. Now this mode of reasoning in the schoolboy, whom his fellows termed 'lucky,'—what, in its last analysis, is it?"

"It is merely," I said, "an identification of the reasoner's intellect with that of his opponent."

"It is," said Dupin; "and, upon inquiring of the boy by what means he effected the *thorough* identification in which his success consisted, I received answer as follows: 'When I wish to find out how wise, or how stupid, or how good, or how wicked is any one, or what are his thoughts at the moment, I fashion the expression of my face, as accurately as possible, in accordance with the expression of his, and then wait to see what thoughts or sentiments arise in my mind or heart, as if to match or correspond with the expression.' This response of the schoolboy lies at the bottom of all the spurious profundity which has been attributed to Rochefoucault, to La Bougive, to Machiavelli, and to Campanella."[8]

"And the identification," I said, "of the reasoner's intellect with that of his opponent, depends, if I understand you aright, upon the accuracy with which the opponent's intellect is admeasured."

"For its practical value it depends upon this," replied Dupin; "and the Prefect and his cohort fail so frequently, first, by default of this identification, and, secondly, by ill-admeasurement, or rather through non-admeasurement, of the intellect with which they are engaged. They consider only their *own* ideas of ingenuity; and, in searching for anything hidden, advert only to the modes in which *they* would have hidden it. They are right in this much—that their own ingenuity is a faithful representative of that of *the mass*; but when the cunning of the individual felon is diverse in character from their own, the felon foils them, of course. This always happens when it is above their own, and very usually when it is below. They have no variation of principle in their investigations; at best, when urged by some unusual emergency—by some extraordinary reward—they extend or exaggerate their old modes of *practice*, without touching their principles. What, for example, in this case of D——, has been done to vary the principle of action? What is all this boring, and probing, and sounding, and scrutinizing with the microscope, and dividing the surface of the building into registered square

8. Tommaso Campanella (1568–1639), Italian philosopher and Dominican monk, who wrote *Philosophy Demonstrated by the Senses* (1591) and the *City of the Sun* (written 1602; published in 1623), the first of which caused his imprisonment for heresy. François, duc de la Rochefoucauld (1613–1680), prince de Marsillac, was a well-known French moralist and courtier. In *Réflexions, ou Sentences et Maximes Morales* (1665), he proposes that self-love is the prime motive for all human actions. According to Mabbott, "La Bougive" (the candle) is the result of a printer's misreading of Poe's manuscript and Poe instead intended Jean de la Bruyère (1645–1696). Niccolò Machiavelli (1469–1527), Italian philosopher known for his political treatise *The Prince* (1513); his name is associated with political expediency, deceit, and cunning.

inches—what is it all but an exaggeration *of the application* of the one principle or set of principles of search, which are based upon the one set of notions regarding human ingenuity, to which the Prefect, in the long routine of his duty, has been accustomed? Do you not see he has taken it for granted that *all* men proceed to conceal a letter,—not exactly in a gimlet-hole bored in a chair-leg—but, at least, in *some* out-of-the-way hole or corner suggested by the same tenor of thought which would urge a man to secrete a letter in a gimlet-hole bored in a chair-leg? And do you not see also, that such *recherchés*[9] nooks for concealment are adapted only for ordinary occasions, and would be adopted only by ordinary intellects; for, in all cases of concealment, a disposal of the article concealed—a disposal of it in this *recherché* manner,—is, in the very first instance, presumable and presumed; and thus its discovery depends, not at all upon the acumen, but altogether upon the mere care, patience, and determination of the seekers; and where the case is of importance—or, what amounts to the same thing in the policial eyes, when the reward is of magnitude,—the qualities in question have *never* been known to fail. You will now understand what I meant in suggesting that, had the purloined letter been hidden any where within the limits of the Prefect's examination—in other words, had the principle of its concealment been comprehended within the principles of the Prefect—its discovery would have been a matter altogether beyond question. This functionary, however, has been thoroughly mystified; and the remote source of his defeat lies in the supposition that the Minister is a fool, because he has acquired renown as a poet. All fools are poets; this the Prefect *feels*; and he is merely guilty of a *non distributio medii*[1] in thence inferring that all poets are fools."

"But is this really the poet?" I asked. "There are two brothers, I know; and both have attained reputation in letters. The Minister I believe has written learnedly on the Differential Calculus. He is a mathematician, and no poet."

"You are mistaken; I know him well; he is both. As poet *and* mathematician, he would reason well; as mere mathematician, he could not have reasoned at all, and thus would have been at the mercy of the Prefect."

9. Rare, strange, choice, or elaborate.
1. Undistributed middle (Latin); a common logical fallacy. The conclusion of a syllogistic argument is invalid when the middle term (the one that appears in both the major and minor premises) needs to include *all* the members of a class (be distributed to all) but really does not. The argument here can be stated as: All fools are poets (major premise); the minister is a poet (minor premise); therefore, the minister is a fool. But nothing is asserted about *all* poets (the term that appears in both the major and the minor premises), only about all fools. It should be noted that the logic of the proposition does not depend on the truth of the claims (whether or not all fools are poets). Even though all the fools we know of might be poets, it still does not follow that all the poets we know are fools; i.e., by the terms of the first premise, *some* poets might *not* be fools. This kind of careless thinking is guilt by association. Two examples:

- All goats have beards; Santa Claus has a beard; therefore, Santa Claus is a goat. The conclusion is invalid because nothing is categorically asserted by the middle term—bearded creatures; i.e., not *all* creatures with a beard are goats.
- All three of the shoplifters arrested yesterday belonged to a certain sorority; Mary also belongs to this sorority; therefore, she must also be a shoplifter. This conclusion is not valid because nothing has been categorically asserted in the main premise about *all* members of the sorority. Mary may or may not be a shoplifter.

"You surprise me," I said, "by these opinions, which have been contradicted by the voice of the world. You do not mean to set at naught the well-digested idea of centuries. The mathematical reason has long been regarded as *the* reason *par excellence*."

" '*Il y a à parièr*,' " replied Dupin, quoting from Chamfort, " '*que toute idée publique, toute convention reçue, est une sottise, car elle a convenue au plus grand nombre*.'² The mathematicians, I grant you, have done their best to promulgate the popular error to which you allude, and which is none the less an error for its promulgation as truth. With an art worthy a better cause, for example, they have insinuated the term 'analysis' into application to algebra. The French are the originators of this particular deception; but if a term is of any importance—if words derive any value from applicability—then 'analysis' conveys 'algebra' about as much as, in Latin, '*ambitus*' implies 'ambition,' '*religio*' 'religion,' or '*homines honesti*,'³ a set of *honorable* men."

"You have a quarrel on hand, I see," said I, "with some of the algebraists of Paris; but proceed."

"I dispute the availability, and thus the value, of that reason which is cultivated in any especial form other than the abstractly logical. I dispute, in particular, the reason educed by mathematical study. The mathematics are the science of form and quantity; mathematical reasoning is merely logic applied to observation upon form and quantity. The great error lies in supposing that even the truths of what is called *pure* algebra, are abstract or general truths. And this error is so egregious that I am confounded at the universality with which it has been received. Mathematical axioms are *not* axioms of general truth. What is true of *relation*—of form and quantity—is often grossly false in regard to morals, for example. In this latter science it is very usually *un*true that the aggregated parts are equal to the whole. In chemistry also the axiom fails. In the consideration of motive it fails; for two motives, each of a given value, have not, necessarily, a value when united, equal to the sum of their values apart. There are numerous other mathematical truths which are only truths within the limits of *relation*. But the mathematician argues, from his *finite truths*, through habit, as if they were of an absolutely general applicability—as the world indeed imagines them to be. Bryant,⁴ in his very learned 'Mythology,' mentions an analogous source of error, when he says that 'although the Pagan fables are not believed, yet we forget ourselves continually, and make inferences from them as existing realities.' With the algebraists, however, who are Pagans themselves, the 'Pagan fa-

2. It is safe to wager that [or the odds are that] every idea that is public property [popular], that every accepted convention, is a bit of stupidity [nonsense,] for it has suited [itself to] the majority [opinion]. According to Mabbott, Poe is quoting from *Maximes de Pensées*, II.42, written by the French cynic Sébastien-Roch Nicholas (c. 1740–1794), known as Chamfort.
3. According to Levine, distinguished rather than absolutely honest; i.e., one can be distinguished in society without being totally honest. "*Ambitus*": going about in search of something. Levine suggests that this includes paying for things like votes. "*Religio*": duty, ranging from the demands of established religion to personal conscience.
4. Jacob Bryant (1715–1804), an English antiquarian. The quotation is from his *A New System, or an Analysis of Antient Mythology* (1774–76). Cf. "Eleonora," "Shadow," "Four Beasts in One," *Eureka*, and references in the "Pinakidia," a miscellaneous collection Poe put together in 1836.

bles' *are* believed, and the inferences are made, not so much through lapse of memory, as through an unaccountable addling of the brains. In short, I never yet encountered the mere mathematician who could be trusted out of equal roots, or one who did not clandestinely hold it as a point of his faith that $x^2 + px$ was absolutely and unconditionally equal to q. Say to one of these gentlemen, by way of experiment, if you please, that you believe occasions may occur where $x^2 + px$ is *not* altogether equal to q, and, having made him understand what you mean, get out of his reach as speedily as convenient, for, beyond doubt, he will endeavor to knock you down.[5]

"I mean to say," continued Dupin, while I merely laughed at his last observations, "that if the Minister had been no more than a mathematician, the Perfect would have been under no necessity of giving me this check. I knew him, however, as both mathematician and poet, and my measures were adapted to his capacity, with reference to the circumstances by which he was surrounded. I knew him as a courtier, too, and as a bold *intriguant*.[6] Such a man, I considered, could not fail to be aware of the ordinary policial modes of action. He could not have failed to anticipate—and events have proved that he did not fail to anticipate—the waylayings to which he was subjected. He must have foreseen, I reflected, the secret investigations of his premises. His frequent absences from home at night, which were hailed by the Prefect as certain aids to his success, I regarded only as *ruses*, to afford opportunity for thorough search to the police, and thus the sooner to impress them with the conviction to which G——, in fact, did finally arrive—the conviction that the letter was not upon the premises. I felt, also, that the whole train of thought, which I was at some pains in detailing to you just now, concerning the invariable principle of policial action in searches for articles concealed—I felt that this whole train of thought would necessarily pass through the mind of the Minister. It would imperatively lead him to despise all the ordinary *nooks* of concealment. *He* could not, I reflected, be so weak as not to see that the most intricate and remote recess of his hotel would be as open as his commonest closets to the eyes, to the probes, to the gimlets, and to the microscopes of the Prefect. I saw, in fine, that he would be driven, as a matter of course, to *simplicity*, if not deliberately induced to it as a matter of choice. You will remember, perhaps, how desperately the Prefect laughed when I suggested, upon our first interview, that it was just possible this mystery troubled him so much on account of its being so *very* self-evident."

"Yes," said I, "I remember his merriment well. I really thought he would have fallen into convulsions."

"The material world," continued Dupin, "abounds with very strict analogies to the immaterial; and thus some color of truth has been given to the rhetorical dogma, that metaphor, or simile, may be made to strengthen an argument, as well as to embellish a description. The

5. I.e., they are absolutely convinced *their* formula or equation is correct and stubbornly defend it.
6. Intriguer.

principle of the *vis inertiæ*,[7] for example, seems to be identical in physics and metaphysics. It is not more true in the former, that a large body is with more difficulty set in motion than a smaller one, and that its subsequent *momentum* is commensurate with this difficulty, than it is, in the latter, that intellects of the vaster capacity, while more forcible, more constant, and more eventful in their movements than those of inferior grade, are yet the less readily moved, and more embarrassed and full of hesitation in the first few steps of their progress. Again: have you ever noticed which of the street signs, over the shop-doors, are the most attractive of attention?"

"I have never given the matter a thought," I said.

"There is a game of puzzles," he resumed, "which is played upon a map. One party playing requires another to find a given word—the name of town, river, state or empire—any word, in short, upon the motley and perplexed surface of the chart. A novice in the game generally seeks to embarrass his opponents by giving them the most minutely lettered names; but the adept selects such words as stretch, in large characters, from one end of the chart to the other. These, like the over-largely lettered signs and placards of the street, escape observation by dint of being excessively obvious; and here the physical oversight is precisely analogous with the moral inapprehension by which the intellect suffers to pass unnoticed those considerations which are too obtrusively and too palpably self-evident. But this is a point, it appears, somewhat above or beneath the understanding of the Prefect. He never once thought it probable, or possible, that the Minister had deposited the letter immediately beneath the nose of the whole world, by way of best preventing any portion of that world from perceiving it.

"But the more I reflected upon the daring, dashing, and discriminating ingenuity of D——; upon the fact that the document must always have been *at hand*, if he intended to use it to good purpose; and upon the decisive evidence, obtained by the Prefect, that it was not hidden within the limits of that dignitary's ordinary search—the more satisfied I became that, to conceal this letter, the Minister had resorted to the comprehensive and sagacious expedient of not attempting to conceal it at all.

"Full of these ideas, I prepared myself with a pair of green spectacles, and called one fine morning, quite by accident, at the Ministerial hotel. I found D—— at home, yawning, lounging, and dawdling, as usual, and pretending to be in the last extremity of *ennui*.[8] He is, perhaps, the most really energetic human being now alive—but that is only when nobody sees him.

"To be even with him, I complained of my weak eyes, and lamented the necessity of the spectacles, under cover of which I cautiously and thoroughly surveyed the whole apartment, while seemingly intent only upon the conversation of my host.

"I paid especial attention to a large writing-table near which he sat,

7. Power of inertia. In physics, the tendency of a body to stay at rest or in motion until some force is applied to it.
8. Listlessness and dissatisfaction resulting from a lack of interest; boredom.

and upon which lay confusedly, some miscellaneous letters and other papers, with one or two musical instruments and a few books. Here, however, after a long and very deliberate scrutiny, I saw nothing to excite particular suspicion.

"At length my eyes, in going the circuit of the room, fell upon a trumpery fillagree card-rack of pasteboard, that hung dangling by a dirty blue ribbon, from a little brass knob just beneath the middle of the mantel-piece. In this rack, which had three or four compartments, were five or six visiting cards and a solitary letter. This last was much soiled and crumpled. It was torn nearly in two, across the middle—as if a design, in the first instance, to tear it entirely up as worthless, had been altered, or stayed, in the second. It had a large black seal, bearing the D—— cipher *very* conspicuously, and was addressed, in a diminutive female hand, to D——, the minister, himself. It was thrust carelessly, and even, as it seemed, contemptuously, into one of the uppermost divisions of the rack.

"No sooner had I glanced at this letter, than I concluded it to be that of which I was in search. To be sure, it was, to all appearance, radically different from the one of which the Prefect had read us so minute a description. Here the seal was large and black, with the D—— cipher; there it was small and red, with the ducal arms of the S—— family. Here, the address, to the Minister, was diminutive and feminine; there the superscription, to a certain royal personage, was markedly bold and decided; the size alone formed a point of correspondence. But, then, the *radicalness* of these differences, which was excessive; the dirt; the soiled and torn condition of the paper, so inconsistent with the *true* methodical habits of D——, and so suggestive of a design to delude the beholder into an idea of the worthlessness of the document; these things, together with the hyperobtrusive situation of this document, full in the view of every visiter, and thus exactly in accordance with the conclusions to which I had previously arrived; these things, I say, were strongly corroborative of suspicion, in one who came with the intention to suspect.

"I protracted my visit as long as possible, and, while I maintained a most animated discussion with the Minister, upon a topic which I knew well had never failed to interest and excite him, I kept my attention really riveted upon the letter. In this examination, I committed to memory its external appearance and arrangement in the rack; and also fell, at length, upon a discovery which set at rest whatever trivial doubt I might have entertained. In scrutinizing the edges of the paper, I observed them to be more *chafed* than seemed necessary. They presented the *broken* appearance which is manifested when a stiff paper, having been once folded and pressed with a folder, is refolded in a reversed direction, in the same creases or edges which had formed the original fold. This discovery was sufficient. It was clear to me that the letter had been turned, as a glove, inside out, re-directed, and resealed. I bade the Minister good morning, and took my departure at once, leaving a gold snuff-box upon the table.

"The next morning I called for the snuff-box, when we resumed,

quite eagerly, the conversation of the preceding day, While thus engaged, however, a loud report, as if of a pistol, was heard immediately beneath the windows of the hotel, and was succeeded by a series of fearful screams, and the shoutings of a terrified mob. D—— rushed to a casement, threw it open, and looked out. In the meantime, I stepped to the card-rack, took the letter, put it in my pocket, and replaced it by a *fac-simile*, (so far as regards externals,) which I had carefully prepared at my lodgings—imitating the D—— cipher, very readily, by means of a seal formed of bread.

"The disturbance in the street had been occasioned by the frantic behavior of a man with a musket. He had fired it among a crowd of women and children. It proved, however, to have been without ball, and the fellow was suffered to go his way as a lunatic or a drunkard. When he had gone, D—— came from the window, whither I had followed him immediately upon securing the object in view. Soon afterwards I bade him farewell. The pretended lunatic was a man in my own pay."

"But what purpose had you," I asked, "in replacing the letter by a *fac-simile?* Would it not have been better, at the first visit, to have seized it openly, and departed?"

"D——," replied Dupin, "is a desperate man, and a man of nerve. His hotel, too, is not without attendants devoted to his interests. Had I made the wild attempt you suggest, I might never have left the Ministerial presence alive. The good people of Paris might have heard of me no more. But I had an object apart from these considerations. You know my political prepossessions. In this matter, I act as a partisan of the lady concerned. For eighteen months the Minister has had her in his power. She has now him in hers—since, being unaware that the letter is not in his possession, he will proceed with his exactions as if it was. Thus will he inevitably commit himself, at once, to his political destruction. His downfall, too, will not be more precipitate than awkward. It is all very well to talk about the *facilis descensus Averni*; but in all kinds of climbing, as Catalani[9] said of singing, it is far more easy to get up than to come down. In the present instance I have no sympathy—at least no pity—for him who descends. He is that *monstrum horrendum*,[1] an unprincipled man of genius. I confess, however, that I should like very well to know the precise character of his thoughts, when, being defied by her whom the Prefect terms 'a certain personage,' he is reduced to opening the letter which I left for him in the card-rack."

"How? did you put any thing particular in it?"

"Why—it did not seem altogether right to leave the interior blank—

9. Angelica Catalani (1779–1849), famous Italian operatic singer. See the pun on her name in "Loss of Breath" (p. 95, n. 3 herein). *"Facilis descenstis Avern"*: The descent to Hades is easy (from Virgil's *Aeneid*. VII.126). Avernus ("Averni" appears to be a deliberate plural by Poe) is literally a smoking crater in Italy: its aspect was so daunting that it came to be figured as one of the main entrances to Hell. When Aeneas asks the sibyl of Cumae to allow him to descend into the underworld to visit his father, she warns him: "The descent into hell is easy—all night and day the gate of dark city of Dis stands open. But to retrace your steps and come again into upper air—this is the burden—this is your task."

1. A terrifying monster (*Aeneid*, III.658).

that would have been insulting. D——, at Vienna once, did me an evil turn, which I told him, quite good-humoredly, that I should remember. So, as I knew he would feel some curiosity in regard to the identity of the person who had outwitted him, I thought it a pity not to give him a clue. He is well acquainted with my MS., and I just copied into the middle of the blank sheet the words—

" '—— ——Un dessein si funeste,
 S'il n'est digne d'Atrée, est digne de Thyeste.²

They are to be found in Crébillon's 'Atrée.' "

Some Words with a Mummy The text reprinted here is that of the *Broadway Journal* (November 1, 1845). The story was first published some six months earlier (April 13, 1845) in the *American Review: A Whig Journal* (usually referred to as the *American Whig Review*), and there are puns on wigs and Whigs in the story. The American Whig Party (not to be confused with the British Whigs) became an important political force in the second quarter of the nineteenth century. The Whigs originated in opposition to what they considered the excessive power of the government under Andrew Jackson and his followers. In the campaign against Martin Van Buren in 1840—with the slogan "Tippecanoe and Tyler too"—they succeeded in putting their candidate, William Henry Harrison, in the White House (see the biographical introduction on p. xxxi and pp. xxxiv–xxxv herein; cf. notes to "The Man That Was Used Up," pp. 190ff.). But Poe is primarily satirizing (and exploiting) the Egyptology craze in America after European scholars began to decipher the Rosetta Stone.

This stone is a basalt slab inscribed by the priests of Ptolemy V (reigned 205–180 B.C.E.). Napoleon's troops had taken it from the Egyptian town of Rosetta (in Arabic, Rashid) in 1799; in 1801 it was captured by the British and taken to England, where it resides in the British Museum in London. The stone contains fragments of the same text in three languages. One was in unknown pictographs or ideograms (picture writing)—the famous Egyptian hieroglyphics (*hieros* = sacred; *glyph* = carved = stone writing). But the other two languages were known: Greek and late demotic Egyptian. (Demotic was originally derived from hieroglyphics but had evolved so radically as to be a separate language with different linguistic principles.) With two known versions of the same text, Jean François Champollion (1790–1832) began the laborious process of translating the old Egyptian pictographs, which were much more complex than expected. His first efforts were published as early as 1814; as more and more hieroglyphs were interpretatively rendered into English and French, the stock of known hieroglyphic characters grew (though even today it is still incomplete).

The nineteenth century felt that great historical and occult secrets were on the verge of revelation; and innumerable studies of ancient Egypt were generated. Among those that Poe had ready access to the following are the

2. So malevolent a plan, if unworthy of Atreus, is yet worthy of Thyestes; from the revenge tragedy *Atrée et Thyeste* (1707), by Prosper Jolyot de Crébillon (1674–1762). It is based in part on the *Oresteia* (Orestes) trilogy, which chronicles the fall of the House of Atreus, by the ancient Greek tragedian Aeschylus. Crébillon's Thyestes seduces the wife of his brother Atreus and puts in motion a scheme to murder him. But Atreus slaughters Thyestes' three sons, carves them up, cooks them, and serves them to their father at a banquet in honor of the family of Atreus. Cf. reference to Crébillon in "Rue Morgue" (p. 244 herein).

most directly pertinent: "A Letter from a Revived Mummy." New York *Mirror* (January 21, 1832); Sir James Wilkinson, *Manners and Customs of the Ancient Egyptians* (vol. 1, 1837; vol. 2, 1841); a review of three works (including Wilkinson's) on Egyptian monuments, history, and customs in the *New York Journal of Commerce* for September 2, 1841, and in the *New York Tribune* of December 21, 1841 (abstracted from the *Westminster Review* for July 1841); articles on mummies and embalming in the *Encyclopædia Americana* (1836 ed.); and George Robins Gliddon's *Appeal to the Antiquaries of Europe, on the Destruction of the Monuments of Egypt* (1841) and *Ancient Egypt* (1843), which contained revisions of the popular lectures he had given in Boston (December 1842 to January 1843) comparing biblical history with new findings in Egyptian history. (For details and other possible sources, see Mabbott, III.1175–77.) The idea that ancient civilizations possessed a superior knowledge of science and the occult arts, now lost in a degenerate present age, is an old one; specific applications to Egypt date at least from the mid-eighteenth century.

Some Words with a Mummy

The symposium[1] of the preceding evening had been a little too much for my nerves. I had a wretched headache, and was desperately drowsy. Instead of going out, therefore, to spend the evening as I had proposed, it occurred to me that I could not do a wiser thing than just eat a mouthful of supper and go immediately to bed.

A *light* supper of course. I am exceedingly fond of Welsh rabbit.[2] More than a pound at once, however, may not at all times be advisable. Still, there can be no material objection to two. And really between two and three, there is merely a single unit of difference. I ventured, perhaps, upon four. My wife will have it five;—but, clearly, she has confounded two very distinct affairs. The abstract number, five, I am willing to admit; but, concretely, it has reference to bottles of Brown Stout, without which, in the way of condiment, Welsh rabbit is to be eschewed.[3]

Having thus concluded a frugal meal, and donned my night-cap, with the serene hope of enjoying it till noon the next day, I placed my head upon the pillow, and through the aid of a capital conscience, fell into a profound slumber forthwith.

But when were the hopes of humanity fulfilled? I could not have completed my third snore when there came a furious ringing at the street-door bell, and then an impatient thumping at the knocker, which awakened me at once. In a minute afterward, and while I was

1. In classical times, a gathering of friends and intellectuals for wine, food, and intellectual exchange.
2. A dish made of melted cheese on toast (sometimes spelled "rarebit") as a substitute for a meat dish the Welsh poor supposedly could not afford. It was generally considered hard to digest and likely to produce nightmares.
3. Avoided. "Brown Stout": a dark thick ale, with a higher alcohol content than ordinary beer. Poe satirically plays with overeating, drinking, indigestion, flatulence, constipation, diarrhea, and bad dreams in other works; see, e.g., the notes to "Loss of Breath" (pp. 89ff. herein) and "The Angel of the Odd" (not reprinted here).

still rubbing my eyes, my wife thrust in my face a note from my old friend, Doctor Ponnonner.[4] It ran thus:

Come to me by all means, my dear good friend, as soon as you receive this. Come and help us to rejoice. At last, by long persevering diplomacy, I have gained the assent of the Directors of the City Museum, to my examination of the Mummy—you know the one I mean. I have permission to unswathe it and open it, if desirable. A few friends only will be present—you, of course. The Mummy is now at my house, and we shall begin to unroll it at eleven to-night.

<div style="text-align:right">Yours ever,
PONNONNER.</div>

By the time I had reached the "Ponnonner," it struck me that I was as wide awake as a man need be. I leaped out of bed in an ecstasy, overthrowing all in my way; dressed myself with a rapidity truly marvellous; and set off, at the top of my speed, for the Doctor's.

There I found a very eager company assembled. They had been awaiting me with much impatience; the Mummy was extended upon the dining table; and the moment I entered, its examination was commenced.

It was one of a pair brought several years previously, by Captain Arthur Sabretash, a cousin of Ponnonner's, from a tomb near Eleithias, in the Lybian Mountains, a considerable distance above Thebes on the Nile.[5] The grottoes at this point, although less magnificent than the Theban sepulchres, are of higher interest, on account of affording more numerous illustrations of the private life of the Egyptians. The chamber from which our specimen was taken, was said to be very rich in such illustrations; the walls being completely covered with fresco paintings and bas-reliefs, while statues, vases, and Mosaic work of rich patterns, indicated the vast wealth of the deceased.

The treasure had been deposited in the Museum precisely in the same condition in which Captain Sabretash had found it;—that is to say, the coffin had not been disturbed. For eight years it had thus stood, subject only externally to public inspection. We had now, therefore, the complete Mummy at our disposal; and to those who are aware how very rarely the unransacked antique reaches our shores, it will be evident, at once, that we had great reason to congratulate ourselves upon our good fortune.

4. See the end of the story where Ponnonner's "lozenges" (apparently Poe's invention) are linked with Brandreth's pills, a well-known laxative of the time.
5. The reference to the Lybian Mountains is not to mountains in Libya but apparently to hills outside Thebes, an ancient city in central Egypt on the Nile River, which flows northward to the Mediterranean Sea up the eastern side of Egypt parallel to the Red Sea. Although Thebes had originated long before, it was around 1230 B.C.E. that the city began to rise to prominence as a seat of royalty and a site of the worship of the god Amon. The necropolis (city of the dead) was composed of crypts for Egyptian nobility carved into cliffs on the west bank of the Nile. Most of the details here and in the next paragraphs come from the article "Mummies," *Encyclopædia Americana* (1836), IX.89–90; Mabbott reproduces a long segment in Poe's *Works*, III.1196–97. "Sabretash": a comic name appearing in British and American magazine columns of the time (Captain Saber-Pocket, i.e., an officer with his sword sheathed in a leather pouch). The ancient Egyptian city of Nuben was called Eileithyia ("Eleithias") by the Greeks.

Approaching the table, I saw on it a large box, or case, nearly seven feet long, and perhaps three feet wide, by two feet and a half deep. It was oblong—not coffin-shaped. The material was at first supposed to be the wood of the sycamore (*platanus*), but, upon cutting into it, we found it to be pasteboard, or more properly, *papier maché*, composed of papyrus.[6] It was thickly ornamented with paintings, representing funeral scenes, and other mournful subjects, interspersed among which in every variety of position, were certain series of hieroglyphical characters intended, no doubt, for the name of the departed. By good luck, Mr. Gliddon formed one of our party; and he had no difficulty in translating the letters, which were simply phonetic, and represented the word, *Allamistakeo*.[7]

We had some difficulty in getting this case open without injury, but, having at length accomplished the task, we came to a second, coffin-shaped, and very considerably less in size than the exterior one, but resembling it precisely in every other respect. The interval between the two was filled with resin, which had, in some degree, defaced the colors of the interior box.

Upon opening this latter (which we did quite easily,) we arrived at a third case, also coffin-shaped, and varying from the second one in no particular, except in that of its material, which was cedar, and still emitted the peculiar and highly aromatic odor of that wood. Between the second and the third case there was no interval; the one fitting accurately within the other.

Removing the third case, we discovered and took out the body itself. We had expected to find it, as usual, enveloped in frequent rolls, or bandages, of linen, but, in place of these, we found a sort of sheath, made of papyrus, and coated with a layer of plaster, thickly gilt and painted. The paintings represented subjects connected with the various supposed duties of the soul, and its presentation to different divinities, with numerous identical human figures, intended, very probably, as portraits of the persons embalmed. Extending from head to foot, was a columnar, or perpendicular inscription in phonetic hieroglyphics,[8] giving again his name and titles, and the names and titles of his relations.

Around the neck thus ensheathed, was a collar of cylindrical glass beads, diverse in color, and so arranged as to form images of deities, of

6. Possibly elaborate puns indicating misinformation of various kinds. Poe's narrator gives the Latin name for the American sycamore tree, not the Egyptian plant used to make papyrus (paper made by laborious slicing, soaking, stretching, and drying). Fibrous papyrus is not very suitable for making papier mâché, which is made of wood pulp.
7. As the tale progresses, several references to and scenes out of music hall burlesque develop. The mummy's name is a somewhat flat play on *all-a-mistake*, but it also plays on the sacred name of Allah. The reference to "Mr. Gliddon" is doubtless to George Robins Gliddon (1809–1857) the famous contemporary Egyptologist mentioned in the headnote (p. 383 herein). Poe alludes to him in his 1837 review of John Stephens's *Arabia Petraea*. In 1842, Gliddon pledged a mummy case to the newly proposed Smithsonian Institution in Washington, D.C.
8. Although we tend to think of Egyptian hieroglyphics principally as pictographs, there was also a parallel phonetic system for sounds involving the same picture symbols; e.g., the hieroglyph for *owl* also meant the sound *m*, because the sound for the word for owl had an *m* as its principal consonant.

the scarabæus, etc., with the winged globe.[9] Around the small of the waist was a similar collar, or belt.

Stripping off the papyrus, we found the flesh in excellent preservation, with no perceptible odor. The color was reddish. The skin was hard, smooth and glossy. The teeth and hair were in good condition. The eyes (it seemed) had been removed, and glass ones substituted, which were very beautiful and wonderfully life-like, with the exception of somewhat too determined a stare. The finger and the nails were brilliantly gilded.

Mr. Gliddon was of opinion, from the redness of the epidermis, that the embalment had been effected altogether by asphaltum,[1] but, on scraping the surface with a steel instrument, and throwing into the fire some of the powder thus obtained, the flavor of camphor and other sweet-scented gums became apparent.

We searched the corpse very carefully for the usual openings through which the entrails are extracted, but, to our surprise, we could discover none. No member of the party was at that period aware that entire or unopened mummies are not unfrequently met. The brain it was customary to withdraw through the nose; the intestines through an incision in the side; the body was then shaved, washed, and salted; then laid aside for several weeks, when the operation of embalming, properly so called, began.

As no trace of an opening could be found, Doctor Ponnonner was preparing his instruments for dissection, when I observed that it was then past two o'clock. Hereupon it was agreed to postpone the internal examination until the next evening; and we were about to separate for the present, when some one suggested an experiment or two with the Voltaic pile.[2]

The application of electricity to a Mummy three or four thousand years old at the least, was an idea, if not very sage, still sufficiently original, and we all caught at it at once. About one tenth in earnest and nine tenths in jest, we arranged a battery in the Doctor's study, and conveyed thither the Egyptian.

It was only after much trouble that we succeeded in laying bare some portions of the temporal muscle which appeared of less stony rigidity than other parts of the frame, but which, as we had anticipated, of course, gave no indication of galvanic susceptibility[3] when brought in contact with the wire. This the first trial, indeed, seemed

9. The winged disk is one of a group of related Egyptian symbols that represent the disk of the sun and the life-death cycle; the complicated symbolism of the shape and behavior of the "beetle" ("scarabæus") and the daily progress of the sun-disk across the sky were associated with burial and resurrection. The dung beetle rolling its recycled ball of nutriments back to its underground lair was associated with the sun god Khepri (*khepes* = create), who rolled the sun-disk across the heavens into the darkness of night, to emerge again the next day. For more on the scarab beetle, see notes to "The Gold-Bug," pp. 321ff.
1. A dark bituminous substance that is found naturally where petroleum has oozed and dried.
2. A chemical battery named after its inventor, Count Alessandro Volta (1745–1825); see the next note and notes to "Loss of Breath," pp. 89ff. herein.
3. The galvanic battery, named for its inventor Luigi Galvani (1737–1798), produced direct electricity chemically; here the reference is to the physiological effect on nerves and muscles produced by electric shock. Galvani was involved in technical disputes over electricity and its effects with Count Volta.

decisive, and, with a hearty laugh at our own absurdity, we were bidding each other good night, when my eyes, happening to fall upon those of the Mummy, were there immediately riveted in amazement. My brief glance, in fact, had sufficed to assure me that the orbs which we had all supposed to be glass, and which were originally noticeable for a certain wild stare, were now so far covered by the lids that only a small portion of the *tunica albuginea*[4] remained visible.

With a shout I called attention to the fact, and it became immediately obvious to all.

I cannot say that I was *alarmed* at the phenomenon, because "alarmed" is, in my case, not exactly the word. It is possible, however, that, but for the Brown Stout, I might have been a little nervous. As for the rest of the company, they really made no attempt at concealing the downright fright which possessed them. Doctor Ponnonner was a man to be pitied. Mr. Gliddon, by some peculiar process, rendered himself invisible. Mr. Silk Buckingham,[5] I fancy, will scarcely be so bold as to deny that he made his way, upon all fours, under the table.

After the first shock of astonishment, however, we resolved, as a matter of course, upon farther experiment forthwith. Our operations were now directed against the great toe of the right foot. We made an incision over the outside of the exterior *os sesamoideum pollicis pedis*, and thus got at the root of the *abductor*[6] muscle. Re-adjusting the battery, we now applied the fluid to the bisected nerves—when, with a movement of exceeding life-likeness, the Mummy first drew up its right knee so as to bring it nearly in contact with the abdomen, and then, straightening the limb with inconceivable force, bestowed a kick upon Doctor Ponnonner which had the effect of discharging that gentleman, like an arrow from a catapult, through a window into the street below.[7]

We rushed out *en masse* to bring in the mangled remains of the victim, but had the happiness to meet him upon the staircase, coming up in an unaccountable hurry, brimfull of the most ardent philosophy, and more than ever impressed with the necessity of prosecuting our experiments with rigor and with zeal.

It was by his advice, accordingly, that we made, upon the spot, a profound incision into the tip of the subject's nose, while the Doctor himself, laying violent hands upon it, pulled it into vehement contact with the wire.

4. A dense white collagenous membrane that forms the whites of the eyes.
5. James Silk Buckingham (1786–1855) worked as a British journalist in India and traveled extensively in the Near East, publishing travel books on Palestine, Syria, and Mesopotamia from 1822 to 1827 and a volume on Assyria, Media, and Persia in 1830. After serving in Parliament, he published a series of books on America and Canada in the early 1840s, in which he was quite critical of slavery in the American South (see especially *The Slave States of America*, 1842).
6. In physiology to abduct is to draw away from the median line of a bone or a muscle or a body part. "Os . . . pedis": sesamoid bone of the big toe. A sesamoid is formed of small rounded masses in tendons and joints. The "fluid" referred to in the next sentence is an older metaphor for the electrical "current" from the battery.
7. In Poe's time, numerous stories circulated about the violent physiological reactions of cadavers after the electrical stimulation of the galvanic battery. (Similar stories persisted regarding newly hanged or guillotined bodies; see notes to "Loss of Breath," pp. 89ff. herein and "A Predicament," pp. 183ff.)

Morally and physically—figuratively and literally—was the effect electric. In the first place, the corpse opened its eyes and winked very rapidly for several minutes, as does Mr. Barnes[8] in the pantomime; in the second place, it sneezed; in the third, it sat upon end; in the fourth, it shook its fist in Doctor Ponnonner's face; in the fifth, turning to Messieurs Gliddon and Buckingham, it addressed them, in very capital Egyptian, thus:

"I must say, gentlemen, that I am as much surprised as I am mortified, at your behaviour. Of Doctor Ponnonner nothing better was to be expected. He is a poor little fat fool who *knows* no better. I pity and forgive him. But you, Mr. Gliddon—and you, Silk—who have travelled and resided in Egypt until one might imagine you to the manor born—you, I say, who have been so much among us that you speak Egyptian fully as well, I think, as you write your mother tongue—you, whom I have always been led to regard as the firm friend of the mummies—I really did anticipate more gentlemanly conduct from *you*. What am I to think of your standing quietly by and seeing me thus unhandsomely used? What am I to suppose by your permitting Tom, Dick and Harry to strip me of my coffins, and my clothes, in this wretchedly cold climate? In what light (to come to the point) am I to regard your aiding and abetting that miserable little villain, Doctor Ponnonner, in pulling me by the nose?"

It will be taken for granted, no doubt, that upon hearing this speech under the circumstances, we all either made for the door, or fell into violent hysterics, or went off in a general swoon. One of these three things was, I say, to be expected. Indeed each and all of these lines of conduct might have been very plausibly pursued. And, upon my word, I am at a loss to know how or why it was that we pursued neither the one or the other. But, perhaps, the true reason is to be sought in the spirit of the age, which proceeds by the rule of contraries altogether, and is now usually admitted as the solution of everything in the way of paradox and impossibility. Or, perhaps, after all, it was only the Mummy's exceedingly natural and matter-of-course air that divested his words of the terrible. However this may be, the facts are clear, and no member of our party betrayed any very particular trepidation, or seemed to consider that any thing had gone very especially wrong.

For my part I was convinced it was all right, and merely stepped aside, out of the range of the Egyptian's fist. Doctor Ponnonner thrust his hands into his breeches' pockets, looked hard at the Mummy, and grew excessively red in the face. Mr. Gliddon stroked his whiskers and drew up the collar of his shirt. Mr. Buckingham hung down his head, and put his right thumb into the left corner of his mouth.

The Egyptian regarded him with a severe countenance for some minutes, and at length, with a sneer, said:

"Why don't you speak, Mr. Buckingham? Did you hear what I asked you, or not? *Do* take your thumb out of your mouth!"

8. John Barnes (1761–1841), an English actor at the Park Theatre in New York from about 1816 on, was noted for his achievement in low comedy.

Mr. Buckingham, hereupon, gave a slight start, took his right thumb out of the left corner of his mouth, and, by way of indemnification, inserted his left thumb in the right corner of the aperture above-mentioned.

Not being able to get an answer from Mr. B., the figure turned peevishly to Mr. Gliddon, and, in a peremptory tone, demanded in general terms what we all meant.

Mr. Gliddon replied at great length, in phonetics; and but for the deficiency of American printing-offices in hieroglyphical type, it would afford me much pleasure to record here, in the original, the whole of his very excellent speech.

I may as well take this occasion to remark, that all the subsequent conversation in which the Mummy took a part, was carried on in primitive Egyptian, through the medium (so far as concerned myself and other untravelled members of the company)—through the medium, I say, of Messieurs Gliddon and Buckingham, as interpreters. These gentlemen spoke the mother-tongue of the mummy with inimitable fluency and grace; but I could not help observing that (owing, no doubt, to the introduction of images entirely modern, and, of course, entirely novel to the stranger,) the two travelers were reduced, occasionally, to the employment of sensible forms for the purpose of conveying a particular meaning. Mr. Gliddon, at one period, for example, could not make the Egyptian comprehend the term "politics," until he sketched upon the wall, with a bit of charcoal, a little carbuncle-nosed gentleman, out at elbows, standing upon a stump, with his left leg drawn back, his right arm thrown forward, with the fist shut, the eyes rolled up toward Heaven, and the mouth open at an angle of ninety degrees.[9] Just in the same way Mr. Buckingham failed to convey the absolutely modern idea, "wig," until, (at Doctor Ponnonner's suggestion,) he grew very pale in the face, and consented to take off his own.[1]

It will be readily understood that Mr. Gliddon's discourse turned chiefly upon the vast benefits accruing to science from the unrolling and disembowelling of mummies; apologizing, upon this score, for any disturbance that might have been occasioned *him*, in particular, the individual Mummy called Allamistakeo; and concluding with a mere hint, (for it could scarcely be considered more,) that, as these little matters were now explained, it might be as well to proceed with the investigation intended. Here Doctor Ponnonner made ready his instruments.

In regard to the latter suggestions of the orator, it appears that Allamistakeo had certain scruples of conscience, the nature of which I did not distinctly learn; but he expressed himself satisfied with the apologies tendered, and, getting down from the table, shook hands with the company all round.

9. A caricature of a politician with a nose like a large red boil orating atop a tree stump (apparently the origin of the verb form of political "stumping" in a campaign).
1. In 1841 a New York paper reprinted an English article about a very large wig found in Thebes that was then on display in England. It reminded the author of the wigs worn by elected officials and judges in his native country (later reprintings of Poe's story actually spelled it "whig").

When this ceremony was at an end, we immediately busied our-
selves in repairing the damages which our subject had sustained from
the scalpel. We sewed up the wound in his temple, bandaged his foot,
and applied a square inch of black plaster to the tip of his nose.

It was now observed that the Count, (this was the title, it seems, of
Allamistakeo,) had a slight fit of shivering—no doubt from the cold.
The doctor immediately repaired to his wardrobe, and soon returned
with a black dress coat, made in Jennings' best manner, a pair of sky-
blue plaid pantaloons with straps, a pink gingham *chemise*, a flapped
vest of brocade, a white sack overcoat, a walking cane with a hook, a
hat with no brim, patent-leather boots, straw-colored kid gloves, an
eye-glass, a pair of whiskers, and a waterfall cravat.[2] Owing to the dis-
parity of size between the Count and doctor, (the proportion being as
two to one,) there was some little diffi[culty] in adjusting these habili-
ments upon the person of the Egyptian; but when all was arranged, he
might have been said to be dressed. Mr. Gliddon, therefore, gave him
his arm, and led him to a comfortable chair by the fire, while the doc-
tor rang the bell upon the spot and ordered a supply of cigars and wine.

The conversation soon grew animated. Much curiosity was, of
course, expressed in regard to the somewhat remarkable fact of Al-
lamistakeo's still remaining alive.

"I should have thought," observed Mr. Buckingham, "that it is high
time you were dead."

"Why," replied the Count, very much astonished, "I am little more
than seven hundred years old! My father lived a thousand, and was by
no means in his dotage when he died."

Here ensued a brisk series of questions and computations, by means
of which it became evident that the antiquity of the Mummy had been
grossly misjudged. It had been five thousand and fifty years, and some
months, since he had been consigned to the catacombs at Eleithias.

"But my remark," resumed Mr. Buckingham, "had no reference to
your age at the period of interment; (I am willing to grant, in fact, that
you are still a young man,) and my allusion was to the immensity of
time during which, by your own showing, you must have been done up
in asphaltum."

"In what?" said the Count.

"In asphaltum," persisted Mr. B.

"Ah, yes; I have some faint notion of what you mean; it might be
made to answer, no doubt,—but in my time we employed scarcely any-
thing else than the Bichloride of Mercury."[3]

"But what we are especially at a loss to understand," said Doctor
Ponnonner, "is how it happens that, having been dead and buried in
Egypt five thousand years ago, you are here to-day all alive, and look-
ing so delightfully well."

2. Also known as a waterfall neck cloth or mail-coach necktie; a tie of large folds of (usually
 white) cloth that spread down over the knot like a waterfall. It was a common part of men's
 attire from 1818 to the 1830s. Jennings was apparently a contemporary tailor.
3. Used in the preservation of museum specimens and wood, but see p. 335, n. 5 herein. Poe
 takes this detail from the speculations of the *Americana* article on mummies.

"Had I been, as you say, *dead*," replied the Count, "it is more than probable that dead I should still be; for I perceive you are yet in the infancy of Galvanism,[4] and cannot accomplish with it what was a common thing among us in the old days. But the fact is, I fell into catalepsy,[5] and it was considered by my best friends that I was either dead or should be; they accordingly embalmed me at once—I presume you are aware of the chief principle of the embalming process?"

"Why, not altogether."

"Ah, I perceive;—a deplorable condition of ignorance! Well, I cannot enter into details just now: but it is necessary to explain that to embalm, (properly speaking,) in Egypt, was to arrest indefinitely *all* the animal functions subjected to the process. I use the word "animal" in its widest sense, as including the physical not more than the moral and *vital* being. I repeat that the leading principle of embalment consisted, with us, in the immediately arresting, and holding in perpetual *abeyance, all* the animal functions subjected to the process. To be brief, in whatever condition the individual was, at the period of embalment, in that condition he remained. Now, as it is my good fortune to be of the blood of the Scarabæus, I was embalmed *alive*, as you see me at present."

"The blood of the Scarabæus!" exclaimed Doctor Ponnonner.

"Yes. The Scarabæus was the *insignium*, or the "arms," of a very distinguished and a very rare patrician family. To be "of the blood of the Scarabæus," is merely to be one of that family of which the Scarabæus is the *insignium*. I speak figuratively."

"But what has this to do with your being alive?"

"Why it is the general custom, in Egypt, to deprive a corpse, before embalmment, of its bowels and brains; the race of the Scarabæus alone did not coincide with the custom. Had I not been a Scarabæus, therefore, I should have been without bowels and brains; and without either it is inconvenient to live."

"I perceive that" said Mr. Buckingham, "and I presume that all the *entire* mummies that come to hand are of the race of Scarabæus."

"Beyond doubt."

"I thought," said Mr. Gliddon very meekly, "that the Scarabæus was one of the Egyptian gods."

"One of the Egyptian *what?*" exclaimed the Mummy, starting to its feet.

"Gods!" repeated the traveler.

"Mr. Gliddon I really am ashamed to hear you talk in this style," said the Count, resuming his chair. "No nation upon the face of the earth has ever acknowledged more than *one* god. The Scarabæus, the Ibis,

4. Here again the reference is to muscle movements generated by external application of electricity.
5. A condition of suspended animation whereby the limbs remain in whatever position they are placed. Levine, noting that "a peculiar form of catalepsy" called *Catochus* was popular with writers of Poe's day, quotes from the *Boston Miscellany of Literature and Fashion* (June 1842): the "patient retains the use of his various senses, while the power of motion is entirely suspended, and presents an appearance which may be easily mistaken for death." Cf. "The Fall of the House of Usher" (p. 205, n. 8 herein).

etc., were with us, (as similar creatures have been with others) the symbols, or *media*, through which we offered worship to a Creator too august to be more directly approached."[6]

There was here a pause. At length the colloquy was renewed by Doctor Ponnonner.

"It is not improbable, then, from what you have explained," said he, "that among the catacombs near the Nile, there may exist other mummies of the Scarabæus tribe, in a condition of vitality."

"There can be no question of it," replied the Count; all the Scarabæus embalmed accidentally while alive, are alive now. Even some of those *purposely* so embalmed, may have been overlooked by their executors, and still remain in the tombs."

"Will you be kind enough to explain," I said, "what you mean by 'purposely so embalmed?' "

"With great pleasure," answered the Mummy, after surveying me leisurely through his eye-glass—for it was the first time I had ventured to address him a direct question.

"With great pleasure," said he. "The usual duration of man's life, in my time, was about eight hundred years. Few men died, unless by most extraordinary accident, before the age of six hundred; few lived longer than a decade of centuries; but eight were considered the natural term.[7] After the discovery of the embalming principle, as I have already described it to you, it occurred to our philosophers that a laudable curiosity might be gratified, and, at the same time, the interests of science much advanced, by living this natural term in instalments. In the case of history, indeed, experience demonstrated that something of this kind was indispensable. An historian, for example, having attained the age of five hundred, would write a book with great labor and then get himself carefully embalmed; leaving instructions to his executors *pro tem.*,[8] that they should cause him to be revivified after the lapse of a certain period—say five or six hundred years. Resuming existence at the expiration of this term, he would invariably find his great work converted into a species of hap-hazard notebook—that is to say, into a kind of literary arena for the conflicting guesses, riddles, and personal squabbles of whole herds of exasperated commentators. These guesses, etc., which passed under the name of annotations or emendations, were found so completely to have enveloped, distorted, and overwhelmed the text, that the author had to

6. The count corrects the American's "mistaken" notion that Egypt was polytheistic. The sacred animals were not gods in themselves but intermediaries for human beings to approach somewhat nearer to the august (high, awesome) Creator. "Ibis": a wading bird with a long curved bill, descending in a crescent shape, found in the warm regions of both hemispheres. The black-and-white sacred Ibis of Egypt was connected to Thebes, especially in the persons of Amun-Ra (or Re) and Atum-Ra (or Re), who were in turn associated with the sun as one over-deity, who came to incorporate lesser or regional gods. In 1375 B.C.E., the court of Amenophis IV established the idea of one god as the official religion, symbolized as the disk of the sun. In 1380 B.C.E., the king took the name Akhennaten (Servant of the Sun Disk), by which he is best known. Some thirty years later, after the death of Tutankhamen (1357–1347 B.C.E.), Egypt returned to polytheism. (Tutankhamen was unknown in Poe's time; his tomb was not discovered until 1922.)
7. See Genesis 5 for the long lives of the ancients.
8. Abbreviation for *pro tempore*, meaning "for the time being, temporarily."

go about with a lantern to discover his own book. When discovered, it was never worth the trouble of the search. After re-writing it throughout, it was regarded as the bounden duty of the historian to set himself to work, immediately, in correcting from his own private knowledge and experience, the traditions of the day concerning the epoch at which he had originally lived. Now this process of rescription and personal rectification, pursued by various individual sages, from time to time, had the effect of preventing our history from degenerating into absolute fable."

"I beg your pardon," said Doctor Ponnonner at this point, laying his hand gently upon the arm of the Egyptian—"I beg your pardon, sir, but may I presume to interrupt you for one moment?"

"By all means, sir," replied the Count, drawing up.

"I merely wished to ask you a question," said the Doctor. "You mentioned the historian's personal correction of *traditions* respecting his own epoch. Pray, sir, upon an average, what proportion of these Kabbala[9] were usually found to be right?"

"The Kabbala, as you properly term them, sir, were generally discovered to be precisely on a par with the facts recorded in the un-re-written histories themselves;—that is to say, not one individual iota of either, was ever known, under any circumstances, to be not totally and radically wrong."

"But since it is quite clear," resumed the Doctor, "that at least five thousand years have elapsed since your entombment, I take it for granted that your histories at that period, if not your traditions, were sufficiently explicit on that one topic of universal interest, the Creation, which took place, as I presume you are aware, only about ten centuries before."[1]

"Sir!" said Count Allamistakeo.

The Doctor repeated his remarks, but it was only after much additional explanation, that the foreigner could be made to comprehend them. The latter at length said, hesitatingly:

"The ideas you have suggested are to me, I confess, utterly novel. During my time I never knew any one to entertain so singular a fancy as that the universe (or this world if you will have it so) ever had a beginning at all. I remember, once, and once only, hearing something remotely hinted, by a man of many speculations, concerning the origin *of the human race*; and by this individual the very word *Adam*, (or Red

9. Or Cabbala or Cabala; often used to evoke esoteric, occult, or secret knowledge. More specifically it indicates Jewish interpretations of the Old Testament, especially the Torah, in the "tradition of Abraham," by which every word, letter, number—every detail of the sacred text—was believed to contain secret revelations that could be divined only by those schooled in Abrahamic tradition. Kabbalistic practice arose in the Middle Ages, reaching its zenith in the 12th century. Christians viewed it with suspicion as Jewish occultism and magic (see notes to "Ligeia," pp. 159ff. herein; "Usher," pp. 199 ff.; and other stories.) The Egyptian count is suggesting that everyone has gotten both history and revealed truth wrong.

1. I.e., about 4000 B.C.E. Dr. Ponnonner alludes to the controversy over the dating of the creation (one that still persists today). Archbishop James Ussher of Armaah (1581–1656) proposed a scheme of biblical chronology (relying especially on Genesis) that placed the creation in 4004 B.C.E. In the 19th century, Ussher's long-accepted chronology came under scrutiny because of new geological and archaeological data that were regularly being discovered. These scientific observations strongly suggested that the earth was actually millions of years old.

Earth)[2] which you make use of, was employed. He employed it, however, in a generical sense, with reference to the spontaneous germination from rank soil (just as a thousand of the lower *genera* of creatures are germinated)—the spontaneous germination, I say, of five vast hordes of men, simultaneously upspringing in five distinct and nearly equal divisions of the globe."[3]

Here, in general, the company shrugged their shoulders, and one or two of us touched our foreheads with a very significant air. Mr. Silk Buckingham, first glancing slightly at the occiput and then at the siniciput[4] of Allamistakeo, spoke as follows:—

"The long duration of human life in your time, together with the occasional practice of passing it, as you have explained, in instalments, must have had, indeed, a strong tendency to the general development and conglomeration of knowledge. I presume, therefore, that we are to attribute the marked inferiority of the old Egyptians in all particulars of science, when compared with the moderns, and more especially with the Yankees, altogether to the superior solidity of the Egyptian skull."

"I confess again," replied the Count with much suavity, "that I am somewhat at a loss to comprehend you; pray, to what particulars of science do you allude?"

Here our whole party, joining voices, detailed, at great length, the assumptions of phrenology and the marvels of animal magnetism.[5]

Having heard us to an end, the Count proceeded to relate a few anecdotes, which rendered it evident that prototypes of Gall and Spurzheim had flourished and faded in Egypt so long ago as to have been nearly forgotten, and that the manœuvres of Mesmer were really very contemptible tricks when put in collation with the positive miracles of the Theban *savans*,[6] who created lice and a great many other similar things.

I here asked the Count if his people were able to calculate eclipses. He smiled rather contemptuously, and said they were.

2. In Hebrew *Adam* means "human being" (man). In a work that Poe frequently echoes, *The Deformed Transformed* (1824), Lord Byron observes that the meaning of *Adam* is "Red Earth" (I.i.385). Gliddon, in his *Ancient Egypt* (see p. 383 herein), writes that "in Hebrew, ADAM, the first man," means "both man and red earth, or clay" (pp. 28–29) and cites Isaiah 64:8. The word also seems to be related to the Assyrian word *admu:* "child, a being created by God."

3. Johann Blumenbach (1752–1840) of Göttingen University, founder of physical anthropology, named five "varieties" of humans (Caucasian, Asiatic, American, Ethiopian, and Malay) in his *On the Natural Variety of Mankind* (2nd ed., 1781); not only did Blumenbach add a fifth race, Malay, to classification system of plants, animals, and minerals of Carolus Linnaeus (1707–1778) but he also coined the term *Caucasian*. "Spontaneous germination": the belief held in ancient Greece and Rome that new living organisms were generated spontaneously out of mud or feces by the heat of the sun (thus accounting for the sudden appearance of lice, maggots, flies, worms, and even larger vermin, where there had been none the day before). See the 1st-century Latin poet Lucretius's *De Rerum Natura* (On the nature of things), V.797–98.

4. The front part of the head or skull. "Occiput": the back part of the head or skull.

5. Franz (Friedrich) Anton Mesmer (1733?–1815) claimed that via the mysterious force of fluid "animal magnetism" he could hypnotize his patients and heal them—hence the word *mesmerized.* Mesmer made elaborate hand gestures ("passes") in the air around the heads and bodies of his patients.

6. Persons of great knowledge. But cf. the account of the Egyptian magi and lice in Exodus 8. For Gall and Spurzheim, see the introduction to Sciences of the Mind (pp. 742–43 herein).

This put me a little out, but I began to make other inquiries in regard to his astronomical knowledge, when a member of the company, who had never as yet opened his mouth, whispered in my ear that, for information on this head, I had better consult Ptolemy, (whoever Ptolemy is) as well as one Plutarch *de facie lunæ*.[7]

I then questioned the Mummy about burning-glasses and lenses, and, in general, about the manufacture of glass; but I had not made an end of my queries before the silent member again touched me quietly on the elbow, and begged me for God's sake to take a peep at Diodorus Siculus.[8] As for the Count, he merely asked me, in the way of reply, if we moderns possessed any such microscopes as would enable us to cut cameos in the style of the Egyptians. While I was thinking how I should answer this question, little Doctor Ponnonner committed himself in a very extraordinary way.

"Look at our architecture!" he exclaimed, greatly to the indignation of both the travelers, who pinched him black and blue to no purpose.

"Look," he cried with enthusiasm, "at the Bowling-Green Fountain in New York![9] or if this be too vast a contemplation, regard for a moment the Capitol at Washington, D. C.!"—and the good little medical man went on to detail very minutely the proportions of the fabric to which he referred. He explained that the portico alone was adorned with no less than four and twenty columns, five feet in diameter, and ten feet apart.

The Count said that he regretted not being able to remember, just at that moment, the precise dimensions of any one of the principal buildings of the city of Aznac,[1] whose foundations were laid in the night of Time, but the ruins of which were still standing, at the epoch of his entombment, in a vast plain of sand to the westward of Thebes. He recollected, however, (talking of porticoes) that one affixed to an inferior palace in a kind of suburb called Carnac,[2] consisted of a hundred and forty-four columns, thirty-seven feet each in circumference, and twenty-five feet apart. The approach to this portico, from the Nile, was through an avenue two miles long, composed of sphynxes, statues and obelisks, twenty, sixty, and a hundred feet in height. The palace itself (as well as he could remember) was, in one direction, two miles

7. Poe takes material in this paragraph and the next from the *Westminster Review* article cited in the headnote (p. 383 herein). Claudius Ptolemaeus was a 2nd-century C.E. Alexandrian astronomer, mathematician, and geographer of Greek and Egyptian ancestry. In his *Almagest*, he describes a geocentric system of astronomy and geography, in which the earth stands at the center, surrounded by eight spheres. Plutarch (46–120 C.E.), a Roman historian and biographer, is apparently not the author of a study concerning the face of the moon ("*de facie lunæ*"). The word *lunacy* comes from Luna, goddess of the moon.
8. A 1st-century B.C.E. Sicilian historian, who wrote a forty-volume history of the world that included much unreliable material. The *Westminster Review* article suggests that the eighteenth Theban dynasty was technologically more advanced than the present, as suggested by Diodorus Siculus's account of Theban artisans' ability to refine glass for lenses of various kinds.
9. A controversial monument erected in 1843, much reviled and mocked. Poe made fun of it in the first letter of his *Doings of Gotham [New York]* (May 18, 1844) and in a review (*Aristidean*, March 1845) of George Jones's *Ancient America*. It was asymmetrical, crooked, and apparently lit at night by sixteen "bat wing" gas lights. The comparison to the U.S. capitol building (next sentence) continues the satire on the mistaken conviction of American national superiority.
1. Seems to be an imagined city.
2. Or Karnac; one mile east of Luxor on a part of the site of the original Thebes.

long, and might have been, altogether, about seven in circuit. Its walls were richly painted all over, within and without, with hieroglyphics. He would not pretend to *assert* that even fifty or sixty of the Doctor's Capitols might have been built within these walls, but he was by no means sure that two or three hundred of them might not have been squeezed in with some trouble. That palace at Carnac was an insignificant little building after all. He, (the Count) however, could not conscientiously refuse to admit the ingenuity, magnificence, and superiority of the Fountain at the Bowling-Green, as described by the Doctor. Nothing like it, he was forced to allow, had ever been seen in Egypt or elsewhere.

I here asked the Count what he had to say to our railroads.

"Nothing," he replied, "in particular." They were rather slight, rather ill-conceived, and clumsily put together. They could not be compared, of course, with the vast, level, direct, iron-grooved causeways, upon which the Egyptians conveyed entire temples and solid obelisks of a hundred and fifty feet in altitude.

I spoke of our gigantic mechanical forces.

He agreed that we knew something in that way, but inquired how I should have gone to work in getting up the imposts on the lintels of even the little palace at Carnac.

This question I concluded not to hear, and demanded if he had any idea of Artesian wells; but he simply raised his eye-brows; while Mr. Gliddon, winked at me very hard, and said, in a low tone, that one had been recently discovered by the engineers employed to bore for water in the Great Oasis.

I then mentioned our steel; but the foreigner elevated his nose, and asked me if our steel could have executed the sharp curved work seen on the obelisks, and which was wrought altogether by edge-tools of copper.[3]

This disconcerted us so greatly that we thought it advisable to vary the attack to Metaphysics. We sent for a copy of a book called the "Dial,"[4] and read out of it a chapter or two about something which is not very clear, but which the Bostonians call the Great Movement or Progress.

The Count merely said that Great Movements were awfully common things in his day, and as for Progress it was at one time quite a nuisance, but it never progressed.

We then spoke of the great beauty and importance of Democracy, and were at much trouble in impressing the Count with a due sense of the advantages we enjoyed in living where there was suffrage *ad libitum*,[5] and no king.

3. The details about copper tools down to Hero and Solomon de Caus (eight paragraphs below) are from the *Westminster Review* article.
4. The major publication of the Transcendentalists, which ran from 1840 to 1844; at different times Margaret Fuller and Ralph Waldo Emerson served as editor. Poe repeatedly satirized not only American Transcendentalism and the *Dial* but also both of the editors; see especially the notes to "How to Write a Blackwood Article" (pp. 173ff. herein).
5. Freely; here extending voting rights to everyone. See Poe's satiric comments on progress and mob democracy in "Monos and Una" (pp. 279ff. herein) and the biographical introduction (*passim*).

He listened with marked interest, and in fact seemed not a little amused. When we had done, he said that, a great while ago, there had occurred something of a very similar sort. Thirteen Egyptian provinces determined all at once to be free, and so set a magnificent example to the rest of mankind. They assembled their wise men, and concocted the most ingenious constitution it is possible to conceive. For a while they managed remarkably well; only their habit of bragging was prodigious. The thing ended, however, in the consolidation of the thirteen states, with some fifteen or twenty others, into the most odious and insupportable despotism that ever was heard of upon the face of the Earth.

I asked what was the name of the usurping tyrant.

As well as the Count could recollect, it was *Mob*.

Not knowing what to say to this, I raised my voice, and deplored the Egyptian ignorance of steam.

The Count looked at me with much astonishment, but made no answer. The silent gentleman, however, gave me a violent nudge in the ribs with his elbows—told me I had sufficiently exposed myself for once—and demanded if I was really such a fool as not to know that the modern steam engine is derived from the invention of Hero, through Solomon de Caus.[6]

We were now in imminent danger of being discomfited; but, as good luck would have it, Doctor Ponnonner, having rallied, returned to our rescue, and inquired if the people of Egypt would seriously pretend to rival the moderns in the all-important particular of dress.

The Count, at this, glanced downward to the straps of his pantaloons, and then, taking hold of the end of one of his coat-tails, held it up close to his eyes for some minutes. Letting it fall, at last, his mouth extended itself very gradually from ear to ear; but I do not remember that he said anything in the way of reply.

Hereupon we recovered our spirits, and the Doctor, approaching the mummy with great dignity, desired it to say candidly, upon its honor as a gentleman, if the Egyptians had comprehended, at *any* period, the manufacture of either Ponnonner's lozenges, or Brandreth's pills.[7]

We looked, with profound anxiety, for an answer;—but in vain. It was not forthcoming. The Egyptian blushed and hung down his head. Never was triumph more consummate; never was defeat borne with so ill a grace. Indeed I could not endure the spectacle of the poor Mummy's mortification.[8] I reached my hat, bowed to him stiffly, and took leave.

Upon getting home I found it past four o'clock, and went immediately to bed. It is now ten, A. M. I have been up since seven, penning

6. Solomon (Salomon) de Caus (Caux) was a Norman engineer (1576–1626), who worked on the theory of steam power and planned an engine described in a work on the causes of moving forces with various machines in 1615. Hero of Alexandria (c. 170 B.C.E.) is alleged to have built a type of steam engine.
7. A well-known and widely advertised laxative. Levine notes a reference in *Moby-Dick:* "How to cure . . . a whale's dyspepsia it were hard to say, unless by administering three or four boat loads of Brandreth's pills, and then running out of harm's way, as laborers do in blasting rocks."
8. The second such playful usage in association with the mummy.

these memoranda for the benefit of my family and of mankind. The former I shall behold no more. My wife is a shrew. The truth is, I am heartily sick of this life and of the nineteenth century in general. I am convinced that everything is going wrong. Besides, I am anxious to know who will be President in 2045.[9] As soon, therefore, as I shave and swallow a cup of coffee, I shall just step over to Ponnonner's and get embalmed for a couple of hundred years.

The Power of Words[1]

Oinos.—Pardon, Agathos,[2] the weakness of a spirit new-fledged with immortality!

Agathos.—You have spoken nothing, my Oinos, for which pardon is to be demanded. Not even here is knowledge a thing of intuition. For wisdom ask of the angels freely, that it may be given!

Oinos.—But in this existence, I dreamed that I should be at once cognizant of all things, and thus at once happy in being cognizant of all.

Agathos.—Ah, not in knowledge is happiness, but in the acquisition of knowledge! In for ever knowing, we are for ever blessed; but to know all were the curse of a fiend.[3]

Oinos.—But does not The Most High know all?

Agathos.—*That* (since he is The Most Happy) must be still the *one* thing unknown even to HIM.

Oinos.—But, since we grow hourly in knowledge, must not *at last* all things be known?

Agathos.—Look down into the abysmal distances!—attempt to force the gaze down the multitudinous vistas of the stars, as we sweep slowly through them thus—and thus—and thus! Even the spiritual vision, is it not at all points arrested by the continuous golden walls of the universe?—the walls of the myriads of the shining bodies that mere number has appeared to blend into unity?

Oinos.—I clearly perceive that the infinity of matter is no dream.

Agathos.—There are *no* dreams in Aidenn[4]—but it is here whispered that, of this infinity of matter, the *sole* purpose is to afford infinite springs, at which the soul may allay the thirst *to know* which is for

9. I.e., two hundred years in the future.
1. First published in the *Democratic Review* (June 1845). The text reprinted here is that of the *Broadway Journal* (October 25, 1845). The idea that every action, whether physical or mental, including spoken words, sets up an infinite "physical" vibration in the universe is also found in Poe's *Eureka* (1848). The idea that happiness does not result from *attainment* of ultimate knowledge but rather from the infinite *process* of acquiring knowledge is a recurrent theme in Romantic literature. A notable antecedent is the "Second Angel's Story" in Thomas Moore's *The Loves of the Angels* (see notes to "Al Aaraaf," pp. 22ff. herein and n. 3 following). On the creative power of words, also see Poe's *Marginalia* 150 (*Graham's*, March 1846).
2. Good (Greek). "*Oinos*": one. See notes to "Shadow" (pp. 134–36 herein), where Poe seems to pun on the word for *wine*, though Levine speculates that Poe is punning on a Hebrew derivation from the word for *man* (i.e., *oinos*, pronounced *ee-nos: Enos*).
3. Cf. Thomas Moore's "Second Angel's Story": "The wish to know—that endless thirst— / Which even by quenching is awaked, / And which becomes or blest or curst / As is the fount whereat 'tis slaked— / Still urged me onward, with desire / Insatiate, to explore, inquire."
4. Poe's spelling of the Arabic *Adn* or *Aden*, a variant of *Eden* (see especially "The Raven," p. 61 herein).

ever unquenchable within it—since to quench it would be to extinguish the soul's self. Question me then, my Oinos, freely and without fear. Come! we will leave to the left the loud harmony of the Pleiades, and swoop outward from the throne into the starry meadows beyond Orion, where, for pansies and violets, and heart's-ease, are the beds of the triplicate and triple-tinted suns.[5]

Oinos.—And now, Agathos, as we proceed, instruct me! speak to me in the earth's familiar tones! I understood not what you hinted to me, just now, of the modes or of the methods of what, during mortality, we were accustomed to call Creation. Do you mean to say that the Creator is not God?

Agathos.—I mean to say that the Deity does not create.

Oinos.—Explain!

Agathos.—In the beginning *only*, he created. The seeming creatures which are now, throughout the universe, so perpetually springing into being, can only be considered as the mediate or indirect, not as the direct or immediate results of the Divine creative power.

Oinos.—Among men, my Agathos, this idea would be considered heretical in the extreme.

Agathos.—Among angels, my Oinos, it is seen to be simply true.

Oinos.—I can comprehend you thus far—that certain operations of what we term Nature, or the natural laws, will, under certain conditions, give rise to that which has all the *appearance* of creation. Shortly before the final overthrow of the earth, there were, I well remember, many very successful experiments in what some philosophers were weak enough to denominate the creation of animalculæ.[6]

Agathos.—The cases of which you speak were, in fact, instances of the secondary creation—and of the *only* species of creation which has ever been, since the first word spoke into existence the first law.

5. Cf. the star world cosmos of "Al Aaraaf" (pp. 22ff. herein). In the present tale, the two angels will leave the dissonance of the nearer stars to those beings left behind while they themselves swoop farther outward to more ethereal heavens beyond the incredibly distant constellation Orion. The word *harmony* suggests the old idea of the "music of the spheres," which the Pythagoreans believed to be produced by the regular mathematical movements of the heavenly bodies in their orbs, a concept of the cosmos that endured through the Middle Ages. This music could not be heard by ordinary human beings; thus Agathos and Oinos, finding even the star music of the distant Pleiades loud, are more ethereal than those gifted beings (artists, poets, spirits) that do hear the celestial music. Yet Poe's angels are limited, and the world that Agathos has created is doomed in some way (again cf. "Al Aaraaf"). In Greek myth, Orion the hunter pursues seven sisters, the Pleiades, daughters of Atlas, transformed into stars. In astronomy, the Pleiades are an open star cluster in the constellation Taurus, six of which are visible to the naked eye. There is an allusion to the Pleiades and Orion in Job 9, where verses 2–11 acknowledge an unseen superior power that creates, judges, and destroys: "I know it is so of a truth: but how should a man be just with God? If he will contend with him, he cannot answer him one of a thousand. He is wise in heart, and mighty in strength. . . . Which removeth the mountains, and they know not; which overturneth them in his anger. Which shaketh the earth out of her place, and the pillars thereof tremble. Which commandeth the sun, and it riseth not; and sealeth up the stars. Which alone spreadeth out the heavens, and treadeth upon the waves of the sea. Which maketh Arcturus, Orion, and Pleiades, and the chambers of the south. Which doeth great things past finding out; yea, and wonders without number. Lo, he goeth by me, and I see him not: he passeth on also, but I perceive him not."
6. Minute animals. Andrew Crosse in 1837 performed a series of experiments in electrocrystalization that resulted in what was excitedly thought to be a newly created microorganism. Mabbott notes that for his tale "Some Words with a Mummy" Poe used an article on ancient Egyptians in the *Westminster Review* (July 1841) in which Crosse's experiments are mentioned.

Oinos.—Are not the starry worlds that, from the abyss of nonentity, burst hourly forth into the heavens—are not these stars, Agathos, the immediate handiwork of the King?

Agathos.—Let me endeavor, my Oinos, to lead you, step by step, to the conception I intend. You are well aware that, as no thought can perish, so no act is without infinite result. We moved our hands, for example, when we were dwellers on the earth, and, in so doing, we gave vibration to the atmosphere which engirdled it. This vibration was indefinitely extended, till it gave impulse to every particle of the earth's air, which thence-forward, *and for ever*, was actuated by the one movement of the hand. This fact the mathematicians of our globe well knew. They made the special effects, indeed, wrought in the fluid by special impulses, the subject of exact calculation—so that it became easy to determine in what precise period an impulse of given extent would engirdle the orb, and impress (for ever) every atom of the atmosphere circumambient.[7] Retrograding,[8] they found no difficulty, from a given effect, under given conditions, in determining the value of the original impulse. Now the mathematicians who saw that the results of any given impulse were absolutely endless—and who saw that a portion of these results were accurately traceable through the agency of algebraic analysis—who saw, too, the facility of the retrogradation—these men saw, at the same time, that this species of analysis itself, had within itself a capacity for indefinite progress—that there were no bounds conceivable to its advancement and applicability, except within the intellect of him who advanced or applied it. But at this point our mathematicians paused.

Oinos.—And why, Agathos, should they have proceeded?

Agathos.—Because there were some considerations of deep interest, beyond. It was deducible from what they knew, that to a being of infinite understanding—one to whom the *perfection* of the algebraic analysis lay unfolded—there could be no difficulty in tracing every impulse given the air—and the ether through the air—to the remotest consequences at any even infinitely remote epoch of time. It is indeed demonstrable that every such impulse *given the air*, must, *in the end*, impress every individual thing that exists *within the universe*;—and the being of infinite understanding—the being whom we have imagined —might trace the remote undulations of the impulse—trace them upward and onward in their influences upon all particles of all matter—upward and onward for ever in their modifications of old forms—or in in other words, *in their creation of new*—until he found them reflected—unimpressive *at last*—back from the throne of the Godhead. And not only could such a being do this, but at any epoch, should a given result be afforded him—should one of these numberless comets, for example, be presented to his inspection,—he could have no difficulty in determining, by the analytic retrogradation, to what original impulse it was due. This power of retrogradation in its absolute ful-

7. The atmosphere circulating around the planet. According to Poe's scenario, once set in motion, a physical event would vibrate or oscillate forever.
8. Working backwards astronomically; reversing.

ness and perfection—this faculty of referring at *all* epochs, *all* effects to *all* causes—is of course the prerogative of the Deity alone—but in every variety of degree, short of the absolute perfection, is the power itself exercised by the whole host of the Angelic Intelligences.

Oinos.—But you speak merely of impulses upon the air.

Agathos.—In speaking of the air, I referred only to the earth:—but the general proposition has reference to impulses upon the ether[9]— which, since it pervades, and alone pervades all space, is thus the great medium of *creation.*

Oinos.—Then all motion, of whatever nature, creates.

Agathos.—It must: but a true philosophy has long taught that the source of all motion is thought—and the source of all thought is—

Oinos.—God.

Agathos.—I have spoken to you, Oinos, as to a child of the fair Earth which lately perished—of impulses upon the atmosphere of the Earth.

Oinos.—You did.

Agathos.—And while I thus spoke, did there not cross your mind some thought of the *physical power of words?* Is not every word an impulse on the air?

Oinos.—But why, Agathos, do you weep?—and why—oh why do your wings droop as we hover above this fair star—which is the greenest and yet most terrible of all we have encountered in our flight? Its brilliant flowers look like a fairy dream—but its fierce volcanoes like the passions of a turbulent heart.

Agathos.—They *are!*—they *are!* This wild star—it is now three centuries since with clasped hands, and with streaming eyes, at the feet of my beloved—I spoke it—with a few passionate sentences—into birth. Its brilliant flowers *are* the dearest of all unfulfilled dreams, and its raging volcanoes *are* the passions of the most turbulent and unhallowed of hearts.[1]

The Imp of the Perverse The text printed here is that of the first publication: *Graham's Magazine* (July 1845). The two later versions of the text have some significant variations from the first. Mabbott suggests that the means of the murder in Poe's tale may have been suggested by an article in the *New Monthly*, a magazine Poe read regularly and borrowed from for other works, though the idea had been around for centuries. In *Marginalia* 52 (*Democratic Review* for December 1844) Poe had noted a passage in Lady Georgiana Fullerton's novel *Ellen Middleton* (1844) in which heroine is said to have a strong "organ of destructiveness." Other of Poe's

9. Reflecting the scientific conceptions of his time, Aristotle had declared that "nature abhors a vacuum," and ancient natural philosophers posited a physical medium between the planets and stars in space—*ether*—an infinitely refined gas, physical, yet imperceptible to human observation. Thus in Poe's monistic universe, everything (both the physical and the seemingly nonphysical) is linked in one continuum.

1. Levine suggests that the last two paragraphs contrast an ordinary or commonsense perception that something is *like* something else (i.e., a simile or metaphor) with a Romantic-symbolic tenet that there is a mystical *identity* of words and things. The poet is thus a kind of lesser divinely creative angel or god. Cf. "Al Aaraaf."

works in which the concept of the perverse is important include *Arthur Gordon Pym* (1838), "William Wilson" (1839), and "The Black Cat" (1843). The narrator of "The Black Cat" defines the perverse as the "longing of the soul *to vex itself*—to offer violence to its own nature—to do wrong for the wrong's sake only" (p. 350 herein). A preexistent theological meaning is fallen, unregenerate.

The Imp of the Perverse

IN the consideration of the faculties and impulses—of the *prima mobilia* of the human soul, the phrenologists[1] have failed to make room for a propensity which, although obviously existing as a radical, primitive, irreducible sentiment, has been equally overlooked by the moralists who have preceded them. In the pure arrogance of the reason we have all overlooked it. We have suffered its existence to escape our senses solely through want of belief—of faith—whether it be faith in Revelation or faith in the inner teachings of the spirit.[2] Its idea has not occurred to us, simply because of its seeming supererogation.[3] We saw no *need* for the propensity in question. We could not perceive its necessity. We could not understand—that is to say, we could not have understood, had the notion of this *primum mobile* ever obtruded itself—in what manner it might be made to further the objects of humanity, either temporal or eternal. It cannot be denied that all metaphysicianism has been concocted *à priori*.[4] The intellectual or logical man, rather than the understanding or observant man, set himself to imagine designs—to dictate purposes to God. Having thus fathomed to his satisfaction the intentions of Jehovah, out of these intentions he reared his innumerable systems of Mind. In the matter of Phrenology, for example, we first determined, naturally enough, that it was the design of Deity that man should eat. We then assigned to man an organ of Alimentiveness,[5] and this organ is the scourge by which Deity compels man to his food. Again, having settled it to be God's will that man should continue his species, we discovered an organ of Amativeness forthwith. And so with Combativeness, with Ideality, with Causality, with Constructiveness; so, in short, with every organ, whether representing a propensity, a moral sentiment, or a faculty of the pure intellect. And in these arrangements of the *principia* of human action, the Spurzheimites,[6] whether right or wrong, in part, or upon the whole,

1. People who believed that different areas (or "organs") of the brain were linked to various mental faculties and thus by studying the shape of the skull (its bumps), they thought that they could determine the development of each faculty (see the Sciences of the Mind section of this volume). "*Prima mobilia*": prime movers (Latin); first causes.
2. The final version reads "faith in the Kabbala." The Cabala (or Cabbala) is a mystic Hebrew philosophy derived from scripture that arose in the Middle Ages (see notes to "Usher," pp. 199ff. herein) and "Some Words with a Mummy" (p. 393, n. 9).
3. Here in the sense of unwarranted, something more than what is needed.
4. Reasoning from a cause to an effect, knowledge does not depend on experience or observation. "Metaphysicianism": or metaphysics; the study of the ultimate nature of reality, speculation on questions that cannot be answered through scientific analysis.
5. A phrenological "organ" concerned with digestion.
6. Along with Dr. Franz Josef Gall, Dr. Johann Kaspar Spurzheim (1776–1832) founded and promoted the pseudoscience of phrenology and eventually came to America. Poe was inter-

have but followed, in principle, the footsteps of their predecessors; deducing and establishing every thing from the preconceived destiny of man, and upon the ground of the *objects* of his Creator.

It would have been safer—if classify we must—to classify upon the basis of what man usually or occasionally did, and was always occasionally doing, rather than upon the basis of what we took it for granted the Deity intended him to do. If we cannot comprehend God in his visible works, how then in his inconceivable thoughts that call the works into being? If we cannot understand him in his objective creatures, how then in his substantive moods and phases of creation?

Induction *à posteriori*[7] would have brought Phrenology to admit, as an innate and primitive principle of human action, a paradoxical something which for want of a better term, we may call *Perverseness*. In the sense I intend, it is, in fact, a *mobile* without motive—a motive not *motivirt*.[8] Through its promptings we act without comprehensible object. Or if this shall be understood as a contradiction in terms, we may so far modify the proposition as to say that through its promptings we act for the reason that we should *not*. In theory, no reason can be more unreasonable, but in reality there is none so strong. With certain minds, under certain circumstances, it becomes absolutely irresistible. I am not more sure that I breathe, than that the conviction of the wrong or impolicy of an action is often the one unconquerable *force* which impels us, and alone impels us, to its prosecution. Nor will this overwhelming tendency to do wrong for the wrong's sake, admit of analysis, or resolution into ulterior elements. It is a radical, a primitive impulse—elementary. It will be said, I am aware, that when we persist in acts because we feel that we should *not* persist in them, our conduct is but a modification of that which ordinarily springs from the Combativeness of Phrenology. But a glance will show the fallacy of this idea. The phrenological Combativeness has for its essence the necessity of self-defence. It is our safeguard against injury. Its principle regards our well-being; and thus the desire to be well must be excited simultaneously with any principle which shall be merely a modification of Combativeness. But in the case of that something which I term Perverseness, the desire to be well is not only *not* aroused, but a strongly antagonistical sentiment prevails.

An appeal to one's own heart is, after all, the best reply to the sophistry[9] just noticed. No one who trustingly consults his own soul will be disposed to deny the entire radicalness of the propensity in question. It is not more incomprehensible than distinct. There lives no man who, at some period, has not been tormented, for example, by an earnest desire to tantalize a listener by circumlocution. The speaker, in such case, is aware that he displeases; he has every intention to please; he is usually curt, precise, and clear; the most laconic and lu-

ested in phrenology early in his career but came to be less confident about its scientific validity, even satirizing it. See the Sciences of the Mind section of this volume.

7. Reasoning from experience or observation to a cause; the reverse of *à priori*.
8. An innate cause rather than a particular motivation.
9. A seemingly plausible but misleading argument.

minous language is struggling for utterance upon his tongue; it is only
with difficulty that he restrains himself from giving it flow; he dreads
and deprecates the anger of him whom he addresses; yet a shadow
seems to flit across the brain, and suddenly the thought strikes that,
by certain involutions and parentheses, anger may be engendered.
That single thought is enough. The impulse increases to a wish—the
wish to a desire—the desire to an uncontrollable longing—and the
longing, in defiance of all consequences, is indulged.

Again:—We have a task before us which must be speedily per-
formed. We know that it will be ruinous to make delay. The most im-
portant crisis of our life calls, trumpet-tongued, for immediate energy
and action. We glow—we are consumed with eagerness to commence
the work, and our whole souls are on fire with anticipation of the glo-
rious result. It must—it shall be undertaken to-day—and yet we put it
off until to-morrow. And why? There is no answer except that we feel
perverse—employing the word with no comprehension of the princi-
ple. To-morrow arrives, and with it a more impatient anxiety to do our
duty; but with this very increase of anxiety arrives, also, a nameless—
a positively fearful, because unfathomable, craving for delay. This
craving gathers strength as the moments fly. The last hour for action is
at hand. We tremble with the violence of the conflict within us—of
the definite with the indefinite—of the Substance with the Shadow;
but, if the contest have proceeded thus far, it is the Shadow which
prevails. We struggle in vain. The clock strikes and is the knell of our
welfare, but at the same time is the chanticleer-note to the Thing that
has so long overawed us. It flies. It disappears. We are free. The old
energy returns. We will labor *now*—alas, it is *too late!*

And yet again:—We stand upon the brink of a precipice. We peer
into the abyss. We grow sick and dizzy. Our first impulse is to shrink
from the danger, and yet, unaccountably, we remain. By slow degrees
our sickness, and dizziness, and horror, become merged in a cloud of
unnameable feeling. By gradations still more imperceptible this cloud
assumes shape, as did the vapor from the bottle out of which arose the
Genius[1] in the Arabian Nights. But out of this *our* cloud on the
precipice's edge, there grows into palpability a shape far more terrible
than any Genius or any Demon of a tale. And yet it is but a *Thought*,
although one which chills the very marrow of our bones with the
fierceness of the delight of its horror. It is merely the idea of what
would be our sensations during the sweeping precipitancy of a fall
from such a height. And this fall—this rushing annihilation—for the
very reason that it involves that one most ghastly and loathsome of all
the most ghastly and loathsome images of death and suffering which
have ever presented themselves to our imagination—*for this very cause*
do we now the most impetuously desire it. And because our reason
most strenuously deters us from the brink, *therefore* do we the more
unhesitatingly approach it. There is no passion in Nature of so [de-

1. I.e., genie. See the "Tale of the Fisherman" in the *Arabian Nights* for the story of the bottle
imp.

monic] an impatience as the passion of him who, shuddering upon the edge of a precipice, thus meditates a plunge. To indulge, even for a moment, in any attempt at *thought*, is to be inevitably lost; for reflection but urges us to forbear, and *therefore* it is, I say, that we *cannot*. If there be no friendly arm to check us, or if we fail in a sudden effort to throw ourselves backward from the danger, and so out of its sight, we plunge and are destroyed.

Examine these and similar actions as we will, we shall find them resulting solely from the spirit of the *Perverse*. We perpetrate them merely because we feel that we should *not*. Beyond or behind this there is no principle that men, in their fleshly nature, can understand; and were it not occasionally known to operate in furtherance of good, we might deem the anomalous feeling a direct instigation of the Arch-fiend.

I have premised thus much that I may be able, in some degree, to give an intelligible answer to your queries—that I may explain to you why I am here—that I may assign something like a reason for my wearing these fetters and tenanting the cell of the condemned. Had I not been thus prolix,[2] you might either have misunderstood me altogether, or, with the rabble, you might have fancied me mad.

It is impossible that any deed could have been wrought with more thorough deliberation. For weeks—for months—I pondered upon the means of the murder. I rejected a thousand schemes because their accomplishment involved a *chance* of detection. At length, in reading some French memoirs, I found an account of a nearly fatal illness that occurred to Madame Pilau, through the agency of a candle accidentally poisoned.[3] The idea struck my fancy at once. I know my victim's habit of reading in bed. I knew, too, that his apartment was narrow and ill-ventilated. But I need not vex you with impertinent details. I need not describe the easy artifices by which I substituted, in his candle-stand, a wax-light of my own making for the one which I there found. The next morning he was dead in his bed, and the verdict was "Death by the visitation of God."

Having inherited his estate, all went merrily with me for years. The idea of detection never obtruded itself. Of the remains of the fatal taper I had myself carefully disposed, nor had I left the shadow of a clue by which it would be possible to convict or even to suspect me of the crime.

It is inconceivable how rich a sentiment of satisfaction arose in my bosom as I reflected upon my *absolute* security. For a very long period of time I reveled in this sentiment. It afforded me, I believe, more real delight than all the mere worldly advantages accruing from my sin.

There arrived at length an epoch, after which this pleasurable feeling took to itself a new tone, and grew, by scarcely perceptible gradations, into a haunting and harassing thought—a thought that harassed because it haunted.

2. Wordy.
3. According to Catherine F. Gore's "An Oddity of the Seventeenth Century" (*New Monthly Magazine*, December 1839), the eighty-six-year-old Madame Pilau nearly died from a poisoned candle.

I could scarcely get rid of it for an instant. It is quite a common thing to be thus annoyed by the ringing in our ears, or memories, of the burden of an ordinary song, or some unimpressive snatches from an opera. Nor will we be the less tormented though the song in itself be good, or the opera-air meritorious. In this manner, at last, I would perpetually find myself pondering upon my impunity and security, and very frequently would catch myself repeating, in a low, under-tone, the phrases "I am safe—I am safe."

One day, while sauntering listlessly about the streets, I arrested myself in the act of murmuring, half aloud, these customary syllables. In a fit of petulance at my indiscretion I remodeled them thus:—"I am safe—I am safe—yes, *if I do not prove fool enough to make open confession.*"

No sooner had I uttered these words, than I felt an icy chill creep to my heart. I had had (long ago, during childhood) some experience in those fits of Perversity whose nature I have been at so much trouble in explaining, and I remembered that in no instance had I successfully resisted their attacks. And now my own casual self-suggestion—that I might possibly prove fool enough to make open confession—confronted me, as if the very ghost of him I had murdered, and beckoned me on to death.

At first I made strong effort to shake off this nightmare of the soul. I whistled—I laughed aloud—I walked vigorously—faster and still faster. At length I saw—or fancied that I saw—a vast and formless shadow that seemed to dog my footsteps, approaching me from behind, with a cat-like and stealthy pace. It was then that I *ran.* I felt a wild desire to shriek aloud. Every succeeding wave of thought overwhelmed me with new terror—for alas! I understood too well that *to think,* in my condition, was to be undone. I still quickened my steps. I bounded like a madman through the crowded thoroughfares. But now the populace took alarm and pursued. Then—then I felt the consummation of my Fate. Could I have torn out my tongue I would have done it. But a rough voice from some member of the crowd now resounded in my ears, and a rougher grasp seized me by the arm. I turned—I gasped for breath. For a moment I experienced all the pangs of suffocation—I became blind, and deaf, and giddy—and at this instant it was no mortal hand, I knew, that struck me violently with a broad and massive palm upon the back. At that blow the long imprisoned secret burst forth from my soul.

They say that I spoke with distinct enunciation, but with emphasis and passionate hurry, as if in dread of interruption before concluding the brief but pregnant sentences that consigned me to the hangman and to Hell.[4]

4. The final version adds two short paragraphs:

> Having related all that was necessary for the fullest judicial conviction, I fell prostrate in a swoon.
> But why should I say more? To-day I wear these chains, and am *here.* To-morrow I shall be fetterless!—*but where?*

The Facts in the Case of M. Valdemar First published as "The Facts of M. Valdemar's Case" in the *American Review: A Whig Journal* (December 1845). This conservative magazine was usually referred to as the *Whig Review*. The text printed here is that of the *Broadway Journal* (December 20, 1845); it contains a few printer's errors, which have been corrected. Poe's tale created a minor sensation as both American and British papers speculated on its truth. Poe prefaced the version printed here with some journalistic banter supposedly by "Ed. B. J." (i.e., the editor of the *Broadway Journal*). He later admitted that the piece was a hoax—that he was taking advantage of the public interest in possible life-and-death intersections revealed by hypnotism. Poe had read Chauncey Hare Townsend's *Facts in Mesmerism* (1840, 4th ed. 1844), and in 1844 he had published "Mesmeric Revelation," a tale about a man in suspended animation who communicates to his listeners a vision of the cosmos that in some ways parallels Poe's book-length essay, *Eureka* (1848). A letter from a doctor describing surgery performed while the patient was in a trance state (and thus feeling no pain) was printed in the *Broadway Journal* in February 1845. An American edition of Justinius Andreas Kerner's German Romance involving a woman in a life-death trance, *The Seeress of Prevorst*, was advertised in the *Broadway Journal* in August 1845. Earlier, the name Valdemar or Waldemar had turned up in translations of Romantic German stories and plays, and in the 1830s a drama titled *Valdemar* was playing in America.

The Facts in the Case of M. Valdemar

> An article of ours, thus entitled, was published in the last number of Mr. Colton's "American Review," and has given rise to some discussion—especially in regard to the truth or falsity of the statements made. It does not become us, of course, to offer one word on the point at issue. We have been requested to reprint the article, and do so with pleasure. We leave it to speak for itself. We may observe, however, that there are a certain class of people who pride themselves upon Doubt, as a profession.
>
> —*Ed. B. J.*

Of course I shall not pretend to consider it any matter for wonder, that the extraordinary case of M. Valdemar has excited discussion. It would have been a miracle had it not—especially under the circumstances. Through the desire of all parties concerned, to keep the affair from the public, at least for the present, or until we had farther opportunities for investigation—through our endeavors to effect this—a garbled or exaggerated account made its way into society, and became the source of many unpleasant misrepresentations, and, very naturally, of a great deal of disbelief.

It is now rendered necessary that I give the *facts*—as far as I comprehend them myself. They are, succinctly, these:

My attention, for the last three years, had been repeatedly drawn to the subject of Mesmerism;[1] and, about nine months ago, it occurred

1. An early form of hypnosis believed to be induced by "animal magnetism." The term *mesmerism* originates with its founder, the Austrian physician Franz Mesmer (1734–1815), who

to me, quite suddenly, that in the series of experiments made hitherto, there had been a very remarkable and most unaccountable omission:—no person had as yet been mesmerized *in articulo mortis*.[2] It remained to be seen, first, whether, in such condition, there existed in the patient any susceptibility to the magnetic influence; secondly, whether, if any existed, it was impaired or increased by the condition; thirdly, to what extent, or for how long a period, the encroachments of Death might be arrested by the process. There were other points to be ascertained, but these most excited my curiosity—the last in especial, from the immensely important character of its consequences.

In looking around me for some subject by whose means I might test these particulars, I was brought to think of my friend, M. Ernest Valdemar, the well-known compiler of the "Bibliotheca Forensica," and author (under the *nom de plume* of Issachar Marx) of the Polish versions of "Wallenstein" and "Gargantua."[3] M. Valdemar, who has resided principally at Harlaem, N. Y., since the year 1839, is (or was) particularly noticeable for the extreme spareness of his person—his lower limbs much resembling those of John Randolph,[4] and, also, for the whiteness of his whiskers, in violent contrast to the blackness of his hair—the latter, in consequence, being very generally mistaken for a wig. His temperament was markedly nervous, and rendered him a good subject for mesmeric experiment. On two or three occasions I had put him to sleep with little difficulty, but was disappointed in other results which his peculiar constitution had naturally led me to anticipate. His will was at no period positively, or thoroughly, under my control, and in regard to *clairvoyance*,[5] I could accomplish with him nothing to be relied upon. I always attributed my failure at these points to the disordered state of his health. For some months previous to my becoming acquainted with him, his physicians had declared him in a confirmed phthisis.[6] It was his custom, indeed, to speak calmly of his approaching dissolution, as of a matter neither to be avoided nor regretted.

When the ideas to which I have alluded first occurred to me, it was of course very natural that I should think of M. Valdemar. I knew the

sought to treat disease through electromagnetic hypnotism, which involved much passing of the hands around the patient's body. Cf. p. 394, n. 5 herein.

2. In the grasp of death (Latin). A British version of Poe's story was pirated and published under the title *Mesmerism "in articulo mortis,"* with the subtitle *Astounding & Horrifying Narrative, shewing the extraordinary power of mesmerism in arresting the Progress of Death* (1846).

3. "Biblioteca Forensica": made-up title of a fictive collection of legal works. The fictitious name (*nom de plume*, or "pen name") and the other works of its fictitious compiler is the beginning of an elaborate joke. "Issachar" in Hebrew means something like "bringer of gifts," but according to Genesis 49:14, Jacob, while blessing his sons, stated that Issachar was the name of a sturdy ass weighed down between two burdens. *Wallenstein* is a tragedy by Johann Christoph Friedrich von Schiller (1759–1805), and *Gargantua* (1534) is a reference to one of the five volumes collectively called *Gargantua and Pantagruel*, a satire by François Rabelais (c. 1483–1553). The Polish translations, then, would seem to be the two burdens of the asinine writer Issachar, i.e., Valdemar, whose further gift would seem to be the revelation of the trance state between the two burdens of life and death.

4. A Virginia politician (1773–1833), whose liberalism contrasted with Poe's political orientation. He is said to have had a cadaverous appearance and odd-shaped legs.

5. Power to see what cannot be perceived by any of the senses.

6. Tuberculosis.

steady philosophy of the man too well to apprehend any scruples from *him*; and he had no relatives in America who would be likely to interfere. I spoke to him frankly upon the subject; and, to my surprise, his interest seemed vividly excited. I say to my surprise; for, although he had always yielded his person freely to my experiments, he had never before given me any tokens of sympathy with what I did. His disease was of that character which would admit of exact calculation in respect to the epoch of its termination in death; and it was finally arranged between us that he would send for me about twenty-four hours before the period announced by his physicians as that of his decease.

It is now rather more than seven months since I received, from M. Valdemar himself, the subjoined note:

MY DEAR P——,

You may as well come *now*. D—— and F—— are agreed that I cannot hold out beyond to-morrow midnight; and I think they have hit the time very nearly.[7]

VALDEMAR.

I received this note within half an hour after it was written, and in fifteen minutes more I was in the dying man's chamber. I had not seen him for ten days, and was appalled by the fearful alteration which the brief interval had wrought in him. His face wore a leaden hue; the eyes were utterly lustreless; and the emaciation was so extreme that the skin had been broken through by the cheek-bones. His expectoration was excessive. The pulse was barely perceptible. He retained, nevertheless, in a very remarkable manner, both his mental power and a certain degree of physical strength. He spoke with distinctness— took some palliative medicines without aid—and, when I entered the room, was occupied in penciling memoranda in a pocket-book. He was propped up in the bed by pillows. Doctors D—— and F—— were in attendance.

After pressing Valdemar's hand, I took these gentlemen aside, and obtained from them a minute account of the patient's condition. The left lung had been for eighteen months in a semi-osseous or cartilaginous state, and was, of course, entirely useless for all purposes of vitality. The right, in its upper portion, was also partially, if not thoroughly, ossified, while the lower region was merely a mass of purulent tubercles, running one into another. Several extensive perforations existed; and, at one point, permanent adhesion to the ribs had taken place. These appearances in the right lobe were of comparatively recent date. The ossification had proceeded with very unusual rapidity; no sign of it had been discovered a month before, and the adhesion had only been observed during the three previous days. Independently of the phthisis, the patient was suspected of aneurism of

7. Scholars have speculated that P—— is Poe (as also, supposedly, in "Mesmeric Revelation"), that D—— is John W. Draper, and that F—— is John W. Francis; both of the latter were celebrated physicians known to Poe. No one has identified Mr. Theodore L——l, the medical student who shows up three paragraphs later.

the aorta;[8] but on this point the osseous symptoms rendered an exact diagnosis impossible. It was the opinion of both physicians that M. Valdemar would die about midnight on the morrow (Sunday). It was then seven o'clock on Saturday evening.

On quitting the invalid's bed-side to hold conversation with myself, Doctors D—— and F—— had bidden him a final farewell. It had not been their intention to return; but, at my request, they agreed to look in upon the patient about ten the next night.

When they had gone, I spoke freely with M. Valdemar on the subject of his approaching dissolution, as well as, more particularly, of the experiment proposed. He still professed himself quite willing and even anxious to have it made, and urged me to commence it at once. A male and a female nurse were in attendance; but I did not feel myself altogether at liberty to engage in a task of this character with no more reliable witnesses than these people, in case of sudden accident, might prove. I therefore postponed operations until about eight the next night, when the arrival of a medical student with whom I had some acquaintance, (Mr. Theodore L——l,) relieved me from farther embarrassment. It had been my design, originally, to wait for the physicians; but I was induced to proceed, first, by the urgent entreaties of M. Valdemar, and secondly, by my conviction that I had not a moment to lose, as he was evidently sinking fast.

Mr. L——l was so kind as to accede to my desire that he would take notes of all that occurred; and it is from his memoranda that what I now have to relate is, for the most part, either condensed or copied *verbatim*.

It wanted about five minutes of eight when, taking the patient's hand, I begged him to state, as distinctly as he could, to Mr. L——l, whether he (M. Valdemar) was entirely willing that I should make the experiment of mesmerizing him in his then condition.

He replied feebly, yet quite audibly, "Yes, I wish to be mesmerized"—adding immediately afterwards, "I fear you have deferred it too long."

While he spoke thus, I commenced the passes which I had already found most effectual in subduing him. He was evidently influenced with the first lateral stroke of my hand across his forehead; but although I exerted all my powers, no farther perceptible effect was induced until some minutes after ten o'clock, when Doctors D—— and F—— called, according to appointment. I explained to them, in a few words, what I designed, and as they opposed no objection, saying that the patient was already in the death agony, I proceeded without hesitation—exchanging, however, the lateral passes for downward ones, and directing my gaze entirely into the right eye of the sufferer.

By this time his pulse was imperceptible and his breathing was stertorous,[9] and at intervals of half a minute.

This condition was nearly unaltered for a quarter of an hour. At the

8. The main artery from the left chamber of the heart. An aneurism is the dilation and thinning of a blood vessel, which, if it ruptures, frequently causes instant death.
9. Respiration that sounds like heavy snoring.

expiration of this period, however, a natural although a very deep sigh escaped the bosom of the dying man, and the stertorous breathing ceased—that is to say, its stertorousness was no longer apparent; the intervals were undiminished. The patient's extremities were of an icy coldness.

At five miutes before eleven I perceived unequivocal signs of the mesmeric influence. The glassy roll of the eye was changed for that expression of uneasy *inward* examination which is never seen except in cases of sleep-waking,[1] and which it is quite impossible to mistake. With a few rapid lateral passes I made the lids quiver, as in incipient sleep, and with a few more I closed them altogether. I was not satisfied, however, with this, but continued the manipulations vigorously, and with the fullest exertion of the will, until I had completely stiffened the limbs of the slumberer, after placing them in a seemingly easy position. The legs were at full length; the arms were nearly so, and reposed on the bed at a moderate distance from the loins. The head was very slightly elevated.

When I had accomplished this, it was fully midnight, and I requested the gentlemen present to examine M. Valdemar's condition. After a few experiments, they admitted him to be in an unusually perfect state of mesmeric trance. The curiosity of both the physicians was greatly excited. Dr. D—— resolved at once to remain with the patient all night, while Dr. F—— took leave with a promise to return at daybreak. Mr. L——l and the nurses remained.

We left M. Valdemar entirely undisturbed until about three o'clock in the morning, when I approached him and found him in precisely the same condition as when Dr. F—— went away—that is to say, he lay in the same position; the pulse was imperceptible; the breathing was gentle (scarcely noticeable, unless through the application of a mirror to the lips); the eyes were closed naturally; and the limbs were as rigid and as cold as marble. Still, the general appearance was certainly not that of death.

As I approached M. Valdemar I made a kind of half effort to influence his right arm into pursuit of my own, as I passed the latter gently to and fro above his person. In such experiments with this patient I had never perfectly succeeded before, and assuredly I had little thought of succeeding now; but to my astonishment, his arm very readily, although feebly, followed every direction I assigned it with mine. I determined to hazard a few words of conversation.

"M. Valdemar," I said, "are you asleep?" He made no answer, but I perceived a tremor about the lips, and was thus induced to repeat the question, again and again. At its third repetition, his whole frame was agitated by a very slight shivering; the eye-lids unclosed themselves so far as to display a white line of the ball; the lips moved sluggishly, and from between them, in a barely audible whisper, issued the words:

"Yes;—asleep now. Do not wake me!—let me die so!"

1. A trance state, in which the mesmerized person is both asleep and awake at the same time—not the same thing as sleepwalking.

I here felt the limbs and found them as rigid as ever. The right arm, as before, obeyed the direction of my hand. I questioned the sleep-waker again:

"Do you still feel pain in the breast, M. Valdemar?"

The answer now was immediate, but even less audible than before: "No pain—I am dying."

I did not think it advisable to disturb him farther just then, and nothing more was said or done until the arrival of Dr. F——, who came a little before sunrise, and expressed unbounded astonishment at finding the patient still alive. After feeling the pulse and applying a mirror to the lips, he requested me to speak to the sleep-waker again. I did so, saying:

"M. Valdemar, do you still sleep?"

As before, some minutes elapsed ere a reply was made; and during the interval the dying man seemed to be collecting his energies to speak. At my fourth repetition of the question, he said very faintly, almost inaudibly:

"Yes; still asleep—dying."

It was now the opinion, or rather the wish, of the physicians, that M. Valdemar should be suffered to remain undisturbed in his present apparently tranquil condition, until death should supervene—and this, it was generally agreed, must now take place within a few minutes. I concluded, however, to speak to him once more, and merely repeated my previous question.

While I spoke, there came a marked change over the countenance of the sleep-waker. The eyes rolled themselves slowly open, the pupils disappearing upwardly; the skin generally assumed a cadaverous hue, resembling not so much parchment as white paper; and the circular hectic spots which, hitherto, had been strongly defined in the centre of each cheek, *went out* at once. I use this expression, because the suddenness of their departure put me in mind of nothing so much as the extinguishment of a candle by a puff of the breath. The upper lip, at the same time, writhed itself away from the teeth, which it had previously covered completely; while the lower jaw fell with an audible jerk, leaving the mouth widely extended, and disclosing in full view the swollen and blackened tongue. I presume that no member of the party then present had been unaccustomed to death-bed horrors; but so hideous beyond conception was the appearance of M. Valdemar at this moment, that there was a general shrinking back from the region of the bed.

I now feel that I have reached a point of this narrative at which every reader will be startled into positive disbelief. It is my business, however, simply to proceed.

There was no longer the faintest sign of vitality in M. Valdemar; and concluding him to be dead, we were consigning him to the charge of the nurses, when a strong vibratory motion was observable in the tongue. This continued for perhaps a minute. At the expiration of this period, there issued from the distended and motionless jaws a voice—such as it would be madness in me to attempt describing. There are,

indeed, two or three epithets which might be considered as applicable to it in part; I might say, for example, that the sound was harsh, and broken and hollow; but the hideous whole is indescribable, for the simple reason that no similar sounds have ever jarred upon the ear of humanity. There were two particulars, nevertheless, which I thought then, and still think, might fairly be stated as characteristic of the intonation—as well adapted to convey some idea of its unearthly peculiarity. In the first place, the voice seemed to reach our ears—at least mine—from a vast distance, or from some deep cavern within the earth. In the second place, it impressed me (I fear, indeed, that it will be impossible to make myself comprehended) as gelatinous or glutinous matters impress the sense of touch.

I have spoken both of "sound" and of "voice." I mean to say that the sound was one of distinct—of even wonderfully, thrillingly distinct—syllabification. M. Valdemar *spoke*—obviously in reply to the question I had propounded to him a few minutes before. I had asked him, it will be remembered, if he still slept. He now said:

"Yes;—no;—I *have been* sleeping—and now—now—*I am dead.*"

No person present even affected to deny, or attempted to repress, the unutterable, shuddering horror which these few words, thus uttered, were so well calculated to convey. Mr. L——l (the student) swooned. The nurses immediately left the chamber, and could not be induced to return. My own impressions I would not pretend to render intelligible to the reader. For nearly an hour, we busied ourselves, silently—without the utterance of a word—in endeavors to revive Mr. L——l. When he came to himself, we addressed ourselves again to an investigation of M. Valdemar's condition.

It remained in all respects as I have last described it, with the exception that the mirror no longer afforded evidence of respiration. An attempt to draw blood from the arm failed. I should mention, too, that this limb was no farther subject to my will. I endeavored in vain to make it follow the direction of my hand. The only real indication, indeed, of the mesmeric influence, was now found in the vibratory movement of the tongue, whenever I addressed M. Valdemar a question. He seemed to be making an effort at reply, but had no longer sufficient volition. To queries put to him by any other person than myself he seemed utterly insensible—although [I] endeavored to place each member of the company in mesmeric *rapport* with him. I believe that I have now related all that is necessary to an understanding of the sleep-waker's state at this epoch. Other nurses were procured; and at ten o'clock I left the house in company with the two physicians and Mr. L——l.

In the afternoon we all called again to see the patient. His condition remained precisely the same. We had now some discussion as to the propriety and feasibility of awakening him; but we had little difficulty in agreeing that no good purpose would be served by so doing. It was evident that, so far, death (or what is usually termed death) had been arrested by the mesmeric process. It seemed clear to us all that to

awaken M. Valdemar would be merely to insure his instant, or at least his speedy dissolution.

From this period until the close of last week—*an interval of nearly seven months*—we continued to make daily calls at M. Valdemar's house, accompanied, now and then, by medical and other friends. All this time the sleep-waker remained *exactly* as I have last described him. The nurses' attentions were continual.

It was on Friday last that we finally resolved to make the experiment of awakening, or attempting to awaken him; and it is the (perhaps) unfortunate result of this latter experiment which has given rise to so much discussion in private circles—to so much of what I cannot help thinking unwarranted popular feeling.

For the purpose of relieving M. Valdemar from the mesmeric trance, I made use of the customary passes. These, for a time, were unsuccessful. The first indication of revival was afforded by a partial descent of the iris. It was observed, as especially remarkable, that this lowering of the pupil was accompanied by the profuse out-flowing of a yellowish ichor[2] (from beneath the lids) of a pungent and highly offensive odor.

It now was suggested that I should attempt to influence the patient's arm, as heretofore. I made the attempt and failed. Dr. F—— then intimated a desire to have me put a question. I did so as follows:

"M. Valdemar, can you explain to us what are your feelings or wishes now?"

There was an instant return of the hectic circles on the cheeks; the tongue quivered, or rather rolled violently in the mouth (although the jaws and lips remained rigid as before;) and at length the same hideous voice which I have already described, broke forth:

"For God's sake!—quick!—quick!—put me to sleep—or, quick!—waken me!—quick!—*I say to you that I am dead!*"

I was thoroughly unnerved, and for an instant remained undecided what to do. At first I made an endeavor to re-compose the patient; but, failing in this through total abeyance of the will, I retraced my steps and as earnestly struggled to awaken him. In this attempt I soon saw that I should be successful—or at least I soon fancied that my success would be complete—and I am sure that all in the room were prepared to see the patient awaken.

For what really occurred, however, it is quite impossible that any human being could have been prepared.

As I rapidly made the mesmeric passes amid ejaculations of "dead! dead!" absolutely *bursting* from the tongue and not from the lips of the sufferer, his whole frame at once—within the space of a single minute, or even less, shrunk—crumbled—absolutely *rotted* away beneath my hands. Upon the bed, before that whole company, there lay a nearly liquid mass of loathsome—of detestable putrescence.

2. Here a thin, sour-smelling fluid discharge, as from a wound or ulcer.

The Cask of Amontillado[1]

THE thousand injuries of Fortunato I had borne as I best could, but when he ventured upon insult I vowed revenge. You, who so well know the nature of my soul, will not suppose, however, that I gave utterance to a threat.[2] At *length* I would be avenged; this was a point definitively settled—but the very definitiveness with which it was resolved precluded the idea of risk. I must not only punish but punish with impunity.[3] A wrong is unredressed when retribution overtakes its redresser. It is equally unredressed when the avenger fails to make himself felt as such to him who has done the wrong.

It must be understood that neither by word nor deed had I given Fortunato cause to doubt my good will. I continued, as was my wont, to smile in his face, and he did not perceive that my smile *now* was at the thought of his immolation.

He had a weak point—this Fortunato—although in other regards he was a man to be respected and even feared. He prided himself upon his connoisseurship in wine. Few Italians have the true virtuoso spirit. For the most part their enthusiasm is adopted to suit the time and opportunity, to practice imposture upon the British and Austrian *millionaires*. In painting and gemmary, Fortunato, like his countrymen, was a quack,[4] but in the matter of old wines he was sincere. In this respect I did not differ from him materially;—I was skilful in the Italian vintages myself, and bought largely whenever I could.

It was about dusk, one evening during the supreme madness of the carnival[5] season, that I encountered my friend. He accosted me with

1. The text reprinted here is that of the first publication in *Godey's Lady's Book* (November 1846). The subject of living immurement, like premature burial, was popular in Poe's day; see Mabbott, III, 1252–56.
2. Most readers have taken this address to be an apostrophe in the "Dear Reader" style of so many 18th- and 19th-century stories. But since the reader does not yet know the nature of the narrator's soul, it suggests that the story is being told to an implied listener.
3. These words and the rest of this paragraph anticipate the narrator's family motto (quoted in the middle of the tale). "*Impunity*": from *punto*, *puntor*, "to punish or correct." A *punitor* is an avenger. *Impunity* means "without punishment" (i.e., to get away with it), one of two conditions the narrator is about to specify for successful revenge. To "impugn" someone also means to slander them, to call into question their honor. Some readers have found the indefiniteness of Fortunato's "insult" to the narrator both chilling and problematic; but there are clues to more than one possible insult.
4. Quack: a fake, an incompetent posing as an expert. Mabbott observes that in Poe's day Italy was a center for foisting off bogus art works on foreign visitors. The phrase the narrator uses to describe Fortunato ("like *his* countrymen") puts immediate distance between them, suggesting among other things that the narrator is not of Italian ancestry.
5. Spring festival of the fleshly appetites (Latin: *carne*, "flesh"), celebrated for centuries in Europe. It originated out of folk celebrations of the mysteries of Dionysus in Greece (god of fertility and regeneration) and Osiris in Egypt (god of fertility and vegetation, associated with the renewal of life brought by the yearly flooding of the Nile). Carnival is traditionally characterized by parades, pageants, masquerades, singing, dancing, and general revelry, much of it drunken and bawdy. The Roman carnivals of Bacchanalia, Saturnalia, and Lupercalia evolved into Christian feasts in the Middle Ages: notably the Feast of the Ass, which continued the old pagan bawdiness, and the Feast of the Fools, which featured blasphemous impersonations of the clergy and a mock Mass. In the 14th through the 16th centuries, the Roman Catholic Church took steps to associate Carnival more closely with the spiritual aspects of Christian holy days, connecting it with Lent (the forty days of penance before Easter, symbolic of the forty days of Jesus's fasting in the desert). Americans know the rites of Carnival from Mardi Gras as celebrated in New Orleans, Louisiana. *Mardi gras* means something like "fat Tuesday"; the people are allowed a day to indulge fleshly appetites

excessive warmth, for he had been drinking much. The man wore motley. He had on a tight-fitting parti-striped dress, and his head was surmounted by the conical cap and bells.[6] I was so pleased to see him that I thought I should never have done wringing his hand.

I said to him—"My dear Fortunato, you are luckily met. How remarkably well you are looking to-day. But I have received a pipe of what passes for Amontillado,[7] and I have my doubts."

"How?" said he. "Amontillado! A pipe! Impossible! And in the middle of the carnival!"

"I have my doubts," I replied; "and I was silly enough to pay the full Amontillado price without consulting you in the matter. You were not to be found, and I was fearful of losing a bargain."

"Amontillado!"

"I have my doubts."

"Amontillado!"

"And I must satisfy them."

"Amontillado!"

"As you are engaged, I am on my way to Luchresi. If any one has a critical turn it is he. He will tell me——"

"Luchresi cannot tell Amontillado from Sherry."[8]

"And yet some fools will have it that his taste is a match for your own."

"Come, let us go."

"Whither?"

"To your vaults."

"My friend, no; I will not impose upon your good nature. I perceive you have an engagement. Luchresi——"

"I have no engagement;—come."

"My friend, no. It is not the engagement, but the severe cold with which I perceive you are afflicted. The vaults are insufferably damp. They are encrusted with nitre."[9]

"Let us go, nevertheless. The cold is merely nothing. Amontillado! You have been imposed upon. And as for Luchresi, he cannot distinguish Sherry from Amontillado."

Thus speaking, Fortunato possessed himself of my arm; and putting on a mask of black silk and drawing a *roquelaire*[1] closely about my person, I suffered him to hurry me to my palazzo.

and let off steam against authority. Some critics see the action of Poe's tale as playing out these symbolic ceremonies in a perverse way: the linguistic repetitions are both darkly comic and ritualistic, suggesting that the narrator is conducting a mock Mass for the dead as part of a satanic crucifixion and burial. Followed by Ash Wednesday (the first day of Lent), Mardi Gras is also called Shrove Tuesday; the last day before confessing to a priest, doing penance, and seeking forgiveness for one's sins (being "shriven").

6. Fortunato is wearing the traditional clown's or jester's costume of the Feast of Fools.
7. A light, semisweet sherry from the south of Spain, prized by connoisseurs. "Pipe": a large cask. Some critics have suggested that in this scene Poe erred regarding the origin and genre of Amontillado, mistaking it for an Italian vintage rather than a Spanish one. But the situation is being manipulated by the narrator; his intent is to trick Fortunato by appealing to his pride, his sense of superior connoisseurship.
8. Fortunato (rather than Poe) here reveals his ignorance; as the narrator says, in the connoisseurship of wines Fortunato was, like the narrator, "sincere" (not necessarily expert).
9. Potassium nitrate, a gray-white mineral deposit used in making gunpowder; also called saltpeter (salt rock).
1. A cape or small cloak. In contrast to Fortunato's fool's costume, Montresor's mask and a cape suggest the costume of a stage villain (a "masked avenger").

There were no attendants at home; they had absconded to make merry in honour of the time. I had told them that I should not return until the morning, and had given them explicit orders not to stir from the house. These orders were sufficient, I well knew, to insure their immediate disappearance, one and all, as soon as my back was turned.

I took from their sconces two flambeaux,[2] and giving one to Fortunato, bowed him through several suites of rooms to the archway that led into the vaults. I passed down a long and winding staircase, requesting him to be cautious as he followed. We came at length to the foot of the descent, and stood together upon the damp ground of the catacombs of the Montresors.[3]

The gait of my friend was unsteady, and the bells upon his cap jingled as he strode.

"The pipe," said he.

"It is farther on," said I; "but observe the white web-work which gleams from these cavern walls."

He turned towards me, and looked into my eyes with two filmy orbs that distilled the rheum of intoxication.

"Nitre?" he asked, at length.

"Nitre," I replied. "How long have you had that cough?"

"Ugh! ugh! ugh!—ugh! ugh! ugh!—ugh! ugh! ugh!—ugh! ugh! ugh!—ugh! ugh! ugh!"

My poor friend found it impossible to reply for many minutes.

"It is nothing," he said, at last.

"Come," I said, with decision, "we will go back; your health is precious. You are rich, respected, admired, beloved; you are happy, as once I was. You are a man to be missed. For me it is no matter.[4] We will go back; you will be ill, and I cannot be responsible. Besides, there is Luchresi——"

"Enough," he said; "the cough is a mere nothing; it will not kill me. I shall not die of a cough."

"True—true," I replied; "and, indeed, I had no intention of alarming you unnecessarily—but you should use all proper caution. A draught of this Medoc[5] will defend us from the damps."

Here I knocked off the neck of a bottle which I drew from a long row of its fellows that lay upon the mould.

2. A "sconce" is a decorative bracket for candles or torches ("flambeaux"), usually recessed in the wall; from the Latin *absconsus*, past participle of *abscondere*, "to hide away." Sconce is also an informal usage for "skull." A rough German equivalent, *Schanze*, is an earthen-work concavity, a fortification, paralleling the Italian *scanso*, "a defense."

3. "Catacombs": underground burial crypts, connected by labyrinthine passageways, descending down to sixty feet or more underground. The catacombs outside Rome (from the 1st century C.E.) are full of niches and cubicles designed as a Christian sanctorum for the dead, i.e., to protect the bodies from desecration. Living Christians also used them as a place of refuge from religious persecution. The name Montresor (some critics are in the habit of spelling it Montressor) heightens the multileveled word play. It suggests the narrator's French, rather than Italian, ancestry. In French, *mon tresor* means "my treasure." The name Fortunato in Italian suggests "fortune" (he is wealthy) and "fortunate" (obviously not) along with "fated." The name of the other Italian connoisseur, Luchresi, suggests *lucre* (Latin: money). Griswold's edition changes it to Luchesi (the name of a contemporary writer) for reasons that are not entirely clear.

4. Montresor's irony provides another hint of the nature of the insult.

5. Wine believed to have medicinal properties.

"Drink," I said, presenting him the wine.

He raised it to his lips with a leer. He paused and nodded to me familiarly, while his bells jingled.

"I drink," he said, "to the buried that repose around us."

"And I to your long life."

He again took my arm, and we proceeded.

"These vaults," he said, "are extensive."

"The Montresors," I replied, "were a great and numerous family."

"I forget your arms."

"A huge human foot d'or, in a field azure; the foot crushes a serpent rampant whose fangs are imbedded in the heel."[6]

"And the motto!"

"*Nemo me impune lacessit.*"[7]

"Good!" he said.

The wine sparkled in his eyes and the bells jingled. My own fancy[8] grew warm with the Medoc. We had passed through long wells of piled skeletons, with casks and puncheons[9] intermingling, into the inmost recesses of the catacombs. I paused again, and this time I made bold to seize Fortunato by an arm above the elbow.

"The nitre!" I said; "see, it increases. It hangs like moss upon the vaults. We are below the river's bed. The drops of moisture trickle among the bones. Come, we will go back ere it is too late. Your cough——"

"It is nothing," he said; "let us go on. But first, another draught of the Medoc."

I broke and reached him a flaçon of De Grâve.[1] He emptied it at a breath. His eyes flashed with a fierce light. He laughed and threw the bottle upwards with a gesticulation I did not understand.

I looked at him in surprise. He repeated the movement—a grotesque one.

"You do not comprehend!" he said.

"Not I," I replied.

"Then you are not of the brotherhood."

"How!"

6. The Montresors were once great and numerous, now no longer; unforgivably, Fortunato has "forgotten" the nobleman's family coat of arms. As the present Montresor explains, the coat of arms portrays a foot of gold ("d'or") against a blue background ("field azure") in the act of crushing a serpent: the serpent, risen up to strike ("rampant"), has embedded its fangs in the heel of the foot. It is left unclear whether the Montresors are the avenging foot or the avenging serpent. (But see Genesis 3:15.)

7. No one is allowed to impugn me (Latin); or paraphrased as "no one offends me with impunity." It is the well-known motto of the Scottish Royal Coat of Arms, and some scholars surmise that there is thus a coded reference to *Blackwood's Edinburgh Magazine* in the tale. This interpretation focuses on John Wilson (1785–1854), known as "Christopher North," who was a professor of philosophy at the University of Edinburgh and an early contributing editor of *Blackwood's*. He was noted for acerbity, and William Hazlitt (1778–1830) is supposed to have explained the "thistle" in Wilson's family crest by reference to the motto. Although there may well be some kind of payback in terms of the literary warfare of the day, this reading tends to push the story rather far toward a *roman à clef* (story with a "key").

8. Imagination; from the Greek root for fantasy (*phantasein*).

9. Casks that each hold approximately eighty-four gallons.

1. Wine from the Bordeaux region of France. Montresor's pun is obvious. "Flaçon": a stoppered bottle.

"You are not of the masons."[2]

"Yes, yes," I said; "yes, yes."

"You? Impossible! A mason!"

"A mason," I replied.

"A sign," he said, "a sign."

"It is this," I answered, producing from beneath the folds of my *roquelaire* a trowel.

"You jest," he exclaimed, recoiling a few paces. "But let us proceed to the Amontillado."

"Be it so," I said, replacing the tool beneath the cloak and again offering him my arm. He leaned upon it heavily. We continued our route in search of the Amontillado. We passed through a range of low arches, descended, passed on, and descending again, arrived at a deep crypt, in which the foulness of the air caused our flambeaux rather to glow than flame.

At the most remote end of the crypt there appeared another less spacious. Its walls had been lined with human remains, piled to the vault overhead, in the fashion of the great catacombs of Paris.[3] Three sides of this interior crypt were still ornamented in this manner. From the fourth side the bones had been thrown down, and lay promiscuously upon the earth, forming at one point a mound of some size. Within the wall thus exposed by the displacing of the bones, we perceived a still interior crypt or recess, in depth about four feet, in width three, in height six or seven. It seemed to have been constructed for no especial use within itself, but formed merely the interval between two of the colossal supports of the roof of the catacombs, and was backed by one of their circumscribing walls of solid granite.

It was in vain that Fortunato, uplifting his dull torch, endeavoured to pry into the depth of the recess. Its termination the feeble light did not enable us to see.

"Proceed," I said; "herein is the Amontillado. As for Luchresi——"

"He is an ignoramus," interrupted my friend, as he stepped unsteadily forward, while I followed immediately at his heels. In an instant he had reached the extremity of the niche, and finding his progress arrested by the rock, stood stupidly bewildered. A moment more and I had fettered him to the granite. In its surface were two iron staples, distant from each other about two feet, horizontally. From one of these depended a short chain, from the other a padlock. Throwing the links about his waist, it was but the work of a few seconds to secure it. He was too much astounded to resist. Withdrawing the key I stepped back from the recess.

2. Those who build or work with stone or brick. Fortunato means to indicate the Brotherhood of the Masons, a late-medieval trade guild originating in Scotland and England. Over the centuries, the Masons became an international secret society: Protestant or Deist in religious orientation and strongly opposed by the Catholic Church. By the end of the 18th century, all the major countries of Europe had Masonic societies. Fortunato's gesture is a secret sign unrecognized by Montresor, who produces a trowel (see below) as an ironic portent of his real intentions.
3. Like the earlier and more famous Christian catacombs of Rome, these are underground burial crypts and passages; the reference to the Parisian "fashion" of piling corpses to the ceiling tends to confirm Montresor's French origins.

"Pass your hand," I said, "over the wall; you cannot help feeling the nitre. Indeed, it is *very* damp. Once more let me *implore* you to return. No! Then I must positively leave you. But I will first render you all the little attentions in my power."

"The Amontillado!" ejaculated my friend, not yet recovered from his astonishment.

"True," I replied; "the Amontillado.[4]

As I said those words I busied myself among the pile of bones of which I have before spoken. Throwing them aside, I soon uncovered a quantity of building stone and mortar. With these materials and with the aid of my trowel, I began vigorously to wall up the entrance of the niche.

I had scarcely laid the first tier of the masonry when I discovered that the intoxication of Fortunato had in great measure worn off. The earliest indication I had of this was a low moaning cry from the depth of the recess. It was *not* the cry of a drunken man. There was then a long and obstinate silence. I laid the second tier, and the third, and the fourth; and then I heard the furious vibration of the chain. The noise lasted for several minutes, during which, that I might hearken to it with the more satisfaction, I ceased my labours and sat down upon the bones. When at last the clanking subsided, I resumed the trowel, and finished without interruption the fifth, the sixth, and the seventh tier. The wall was now nearly upon a level with my breast. I again paused, and holding the flambeaux over the mason-work, threw a few feeble rays upon the figure within.

A succession of loud and shrill screams, bursting suddenly from the throat of the chained form, seemed to thrust me violently back. For a brief moment I hesitated, I trembled. Unsheathing my rapier, I began to grope with it about the recess; but the thought of an instant reassured me. I placed my hand upon the solid fabric of the catacombs, and felt satisfied. I reapproached the wall. I replied to the yells of him who clamoured. I re-echoed, I aided, I surpassed them in volume and in strength. I did this, and the clamourer grew still.

It was now midnight, and my task was drawing to a close. I had completed the eighth, the ninth and the tenth tier. I had finished a portion of the last and the eleventh; there remained but a single stone to be fitted and plastered in. I struggled with its weight; I placed it partially in its destined position. But now there came from out the niche a low laugh that erected the hairs upon my head. It was succeeded by a sad voice, which I had difficulty in recognizing as that of the noble Fortunato. The voice said—

"Ha! ha! ha!—he! he! he!—a very good joke, indeed—an excellent jest. We will have many a rich laugh about it at the palazzo—he! he! he!—over our wine—he! he! he!"

"The Amontillado!" I said.

"He! he! he!—he! he! he!—yes, the Amontillado. But is it not getting

4. Possibly a reference to the "wine" of revenge.

late? Will not they be awaiting us at the palazzo—the Lady Fortunato and the rest? Let us be gone."

"Yes," I said, "let us be gone."

"For the love of God, Montresor!"

"Yes," I said, "for the love of God!"[5]

But to these words I hearkened in vain for a reply. I grew impatient. I called aloud—

"Fortunato!"

No answer. I called again—

"Fortunato!"

No answer still. I thrust a torch through the remaining aperture and let it fall within. There came forth in return only a jingling of the bells. My heart grew sick; it was the dampness of the catacombs that made it so.[6] I hastened to make an end of my labour. I forced the last stone into its position; I plastered it up. Against the new masonry I re-erected the old rampart of bones. For the half of a century no mortal has disturbed them. *In pace requiescat!*[7]

Hop-Frog; or, The Eight Chained Ourang-Outangs[1]

I never knew any one so keenly alive to a joke as the king was. He seemed to live only for joking. To tell a good story of the joke kind, and to tell it well, was the surest road to his favor. Thus it happened that his seven ministers were all noted for their accomplishments as jokers. They all took after the king, too, in being large, corpulent, oily men, as well as inimitable jokers. Whether people grow fat by joking, or whether there is something in fat itself which predisposes to a joke, I have never been quite able to determine; but certain it is that a lean joker is a *rara avis in terris.*[2]

5. Some critics have seen the repetition of this phrase as especially significant, arguing that a Protestant–Catholic conflict lies at the heart of the insult.

6. In the Griswold version, these words are rendered: "—on account of the dampness of the catacombs." The dash was used perhaps to suggest more strongly a hurried afterthought, a disingenuous denial that the narrator has been moved by the horror of his deed. By Catholic doctrine, if Montresor is *not* penitent, he cannot receive absolution, and his soul will go to Hell; on the other hand, if he *is* remorseful, then one of the two stated conditions for successful revenge in the first paragraph has not been fulfilled.

7. The last two sentences hint at Montresor's present age and would seem to have special relevance to his problematic spiritual and psychological state. The Latin is the final burial prayer: "Rest in peace." It is unclear whether the reference is to Fortunato or to himself—or if in fact it is Montresor's utterance at all.

1. The text reprinted here follows that of the first publication in the *Flag of Our Union* (March 17, 1849). This tale was the last to be published during Poe's lifetime. It may have been inspired by the story of the accidental burning death of several aristocrats in the court of Charles VI of France at a masquerade party in 1385, as told by Jean Froissart (1337?–1410?) in chapter 138 of his *Chronicles* of the Hundred Years War (written over a thirty-year period from 1369 to about 1400). This incident was summarized in an article published in the *Broadway Journal* for February 1, 1845. In "Barbarities of the Theatre," Evert A. Duyckinck, an editor of the influential New York *Literary World*, likened the recent death of a young dancer in London, whose costume caught fire from the gas lights illuminating the stage, to Froissart's account.

2. A rare bird on earth (Latin); a famous phrase of Juvenal (Decimus Junius Juvenalis, 1st–2nd century C.E.), Roman satirist.

About the refinements, or, as he called them, the 'ghosts' of wit, the king troubled himself very little. He had an especial admiration for *breadth* in a jest, and would often put up with *length*, for the sake of it. Over-niceties wearied him. He would have preferred Rabelais's 'Gargantua,' to the 'Zadig' of Voltaire:[3] and, upon the whole, practical jokes suited his taste far better than verbal ones.

At the date of my narrative, professing jesters had not altogether gone out of fashion at court. Several of the great continental 'powers' still retained their 'fools,' who wore motley,[4] with caps and bells, and who were expected to be always ready with sharp witticisms, at a moment's notice, in consideration of the crumbs that fell from the royal table.

Our king, as a matter of course, retained his 'fool.' The fact is, he *required* something in the way of folly—if only to counterbalance the heavy wisdom of the seven wise men who were his ministers—not to mention himself.

His fool, or professional jester, was not *only* a fool, however. His value was trebled in the eyes of the king, by the fact of his being also a dwarf and a cripple. Dwarfs were as common at court, in those days, as fools; and many monarchs would have found it difficult to get through their days (days are rather longer at court than elsewhere) without both a jester to laugh *with*, and a dwarf to laugh *at*. But, as I have already observed, your jesters, in ninety-nine cases out of a hundred, are fat, sound and unwieldy—so that it was no small source of self-gratulation with our king that, in Hop-Frog (this was the fool's name), he possessed a triplicate treasure in one person.

I believe the name 'Hop-Frog' was *not* that given to the dwarf by his sponsors at baptism, but it was conferred upon him, by general consent of the seven ministers, on account of his inability to walk as other men do. In fact, Hop-Frog could only get along by a sort of interjectional gait—something between a leap and a wriggle—a movement that afforded illimitable amusement, and of course consolation, to the king; for (notwithstanding the protuberance of his stomach and a constitutional swelling of the head) the king, by his whole court, was accounted a capital figure.

But although Hop-Frog, through the distortion of his legs, could move only with great pain and difficulty along a road or floor, the prodigious muscular power which nature seemed to have bestowed upon his arms, by way of compensation for deficiency in the lower limbs, enabled him to perform many feats of wonderful dexterity, where trees or ropes were in question, or anything else to climb. At such exercises he certainly much more resembled a squirrel, or a small monkey, than a frog.

3. François Rabelais (c. 1483–1553) in *Gargantua and Pantgruel*, written from 1532 to about 1552, told the contemporary adventures of two giants from French folklore. Rabelais's figures are loud, crude, and sensual, and the humor of the book is famous for its obscenity. The *Zadig* (1748) of François Marie Arouet de Voltaire (1694–1778), on the other hand, features a refined, philosophical, analytical hero (see headnote to "Murders in the Rue Morgue," p. 239 herein).
4. Heterogeneous, often used to mean many colored, especially in the attire of a court jester.

I am not able to say, with precision, from what country Hop-Frog originally came. It was from some barbarous region, however, that no person ever heard of—a vast distance from the court of our king. Hop-Frog, and a young girl very little less dwarfish than himself (although of exquisite proportions, and a marvellous dancer), had been forcibly carried off from their respective homes in adjoining provinces, and sent as presents to the king, by one of his ever-victorious generals.

Under these circumstances, it is not to be wondered at that a close intimacy arose between the two little captives. Indeed, they soon became sworn friends. Hop-Frog, who, although he made a great deal of sport, was by no means popular, had it not in his power to tender Trippetta many services; but *she*, on account of her grace and exquisite beauty (although a dwarf), was universally admired and petted: so she possessed much influence; and never failed to use it, whenever she could, for the benefit of Hop-Frog.

On some grand state occasion—I forget what—the king determined to have a masquerade; and whenever a masquerade, or anything of that kind, occurred at our court, then the talents both of Hop-Frog and Trippetta were sure to be called in play. Hop-Frog, in especial, was so inventive in the way of getting up pageants, suggesting novel characters, and arranging costumes, for masked balls, that nothing could be done, it seems, without his assistance.

The night appointed for the *fête*[5] had arrived. A gorgeous hall had been fitted up, under Trippetta's eye, with every kind of device which could possibly give *éclât*[6] to a masquerade. The whole court was in a fever of expectation. As for costumes and characters, it might well be supposed that everybody had come to a decision on such points. Many had made up their minds (as to what *rôles* they should assume) a week, or even a month, in advance, and, in fact, there was not a particle of indecision anywhere—except in the case of the king and his seven ministers. Why *they* hesitated I never could tell, unless they did it by way of a joke. More probably, they found it difficult, on account of being so fat, to make up their minds. At all events, time flew; and, as a last resource, they sent for Trippetta and Hop-Frog.

When the two little friends obeyed the summons of the king, they found him sitting at his wine with the seven members of his cabinet council; but the monarch appeared to be in a very ill humor. He knew that Hop-Frog was not fond of wine; for it excited the poor cripple almost to madness; and madness is no comfortable feeling.[7] But the king loved his practical jokes, and took pleasure in forcing Hop-Frog to drink and (as the king called it) 'to be merry.'

'Come here, Hop-Frog,' said he, as the jester and his friend entered the room: 'swallow this bumper[8] to the health of your absent friends [here Hop-Frog sighed], and then let us have the benefit of your invention. We want characters—*characters*, man—something novel—

5. Festival.
6. Figuratively, high tone, brilliancy, or splendor.
7. Critics are fond of interpreting this tale biographically.
8. A glass filled to the brim.

out of the way. We are wearied with this everlasting sameness. Come, drink! the wine will brighten your wits.'

Hop-Frog endeavored, as usual, to get up a jest in reply to these advances from the king; but the effort was too much. It happened to be the poor dwarf's birthday, and the command to drink to his 'absent friends' forced the tears to his eyes. Many large, bitter drops fell into the goblet as he took it, humbly, from the hand of the tyrant.

'Ah! ha! ha! ha!' roared the latter, as the dwarf reluctantly drained the beaker.—"See what a glass of good wine can do! Why, your eyes are shining already!'

Poor fellow! his large eyes *gleamed*, rather than shone; for the effect of wine on his excitable brain was not more powerful than instantaneous. He placed the goblet nervously on the table, and looked round upon the company with a half-insane stare. They all seemed highly amused at the success of the king's *'joke.'*

'And now to business,' said the prime minister, a *very* fat man.

'Yes,' said the king; 'come, Hop-Frog, lend us your assistance. Characters, my fine fellow; we stand in need of characters—all of us—ha! ha! ha!' and as this was seriously meant for a joke, his laugh was chorused by the seven.

Hop-Frog also laughed, although feebly and somewhat vacantly.

'Come, come,' said the king, impatiently, 'have you nothing to suggest?'

'I am endeavoring to think of something *novel*,' replied the dwarf, abstractedly, for he was quite bewildered by the wine.

'Endeavoring!' cried the tyrant, fiercely; 'what do you mean by *that*? Ah, I perceive. You are sulky, and want more wine. Here, drink this!' and he poured out another goblet full and offered it to the cripple, who merely gazed at it, gasping for breath.

'Drink, I say!' shouted the monster, 'or by the fiends—'

The dwarf hesitated. The king grew purple with rage. The courtiers smirked. Trippetta, pale as a corpse, advanced to the monarch's seat, and, falling on her knees before him, implored him to spare her friend.

The tyrant regarded her, for some moments, in evident wonder at her audacity. He seemed quite at a loss what to do or say—how most becomingly to express his indignation. At last, without uttering a syllable, he pushed her violently from him, and threw the contents of the brimming goblet in her face.

The poor girl got up as best she could, and, not daring even to sigh, resumed her position at the foot of the table.

There was a dead silence for about half a minute, during which the falling of a leaf, or of a feather, might have been heard. It was interrupted by a low, but harsh and protracted *grating* sound which seemed to come at once from every corner of the room.

'What—what—*what* are you making that noise for?' demanded the king, turning furiously to the dwarf.

The latter seemed to have recovered, in great measure, from his intoxication, and looking fixedly but quietly into the tyrant's face, merely ejaculated:

'I—I? How could it have been me?'

'The sound appeared to come from without,' observed one of the courtiers. 'I fancy it was the parrot at the window, whetting his bill upon the cage-wires.'

'True,' replied the monarch, as if much relieved by the suggestion; 'but on the honor of a knight, I could have sworn that it was the gritting of this vagabond's teeth.'

Hereupon the dwarf laughed (the king was too confirmed a joker to object to any one's laughing), and displayed a set of large, powerful, and very repulsive teeth. Moreover, he avowed his perfect willingness to swallow as much wine as desired. The monarch was pacified; and having drained another bumper, with no very perceptible ill effect, Hop-Frog entered at once, and with spirit, into the plans for the masquerade.

'I cannot tell what was the association of idea,' observed he, very tranquilly, and as if he had never tasted wine in his life, 'but *just after* your majesty had struck the girl and thrown the wine in her face—*just after* your majesty had done this, and while the parrot was making that odd noise outside the window, there came into my mind a capital diversion—one of my own country frolics—often enacted among us, at our masquerades: but here it will be new altogether. Unfortunately, however, it requires a company of eight persons, and—'

'Here we *are!*' cried the king, laughing at his acute discovery of the coincidence; 'eight to a fraction—I and my seven ministers. Come! what is the diversion?'

'We call it,' replied the cripple, 'the Eight Chained Ourang-Outangs, and it really is excellent sport if well enacted.'

'*We* will enact it,' remarked the king, drawing himself up, and lowering his eyelids.

'The beauty of the game,' continued Hop-Frog, 'lies in the fright it occasions among the women.'

'Capital!' roared in chorus the monarch and his ministry.

'*I* will equip you as ourang-outangs,' proceeded the dwarf; 'leave all that to me. The resemblance shall be so striking, that the company of masqueraders will take you for real beasts—and of course, they will be as much terrified as astonished.'

'O, this is exquisite!' exclaimed the king. 'Hop-Frog! I will make a man of you.'

'The chains are for the purpose of increasing the confusion by their jangling. You are supposed to have escaped, *en masse*, from your keepers. Your majesty cannot conceive the *effect* produced, at a masquerade, by eight chained ourang-outangs, imagined to be real ones by most of the company; and rushing in, with savage cries, among the crowd of delicately and gorgeously habited men and women. The *contrast* is inimitable.'

'It *must* be,' said the king: and the council arose hurriedly (as it was growing late), to put in execution the scheme of Hop-Frog.

His mode of equipping the party as ourang-outangs was very simple, but effective enough for his purposes. The animals in question had, at

the epoch of my story, very rarely been seen in any part of the civilized world; and as the imitations made by the dwarf were sufficiently beast-like and more than sufficiently hideous, their truthfulness to nature was thus thought to be secured.

The king and his ministers were first encased in tight-fitting stockinet shirts and drawers. They were then saturated with tar. At this stage of the process, some one of the party suggested feathers; but the suggestion was at once overruled by the dwarf, who soon convinced the eight, by ocular demonstration, that the hair of such a brute as the ourang-outang was much more efficiently represented by *flax*.[9] A thick coating of this latter was accordingly plastered upon the coating of tar. A long chain was now procured. First, it was passed about the waist of the king, *and tied*; then about another of the party, and also tied; then about all successively, in the same manner. When this chaining arrangement was complete, and the party stood as far apart from each other as possible, they formed a circle; and, to make all things appear natural, Hop-Frog passed the residue of the chain, in two diameters, at right angles, across the circle, after the fashion adopted, at the present day, by those who capture Chimpanzees, or other large apes, in Borneo.

The grand salon in which the masquerade was to take place, was a circular room, very lofty, and receiving the light of the sun only through a single window at top. At night (the season for which the apartment was especially designed) it was illuminated principally by a large chandelier, depending by a chain from the centre of the skylight, and lowered, or elevated, by means of a counter-balance as usual; but (in order not to look unsightly) this latter passed outside the cupola[1] and over the roof.

The arrangements of the room had been left to Trippetta's superintendence; but, in some particulars, it seems, she had been guided by the calmer judgment of her friend the dwarf. At his suggestion it was that, on this occasion, the chandelier was removed. Its waxen drippings (which, in weather so warm, it was quite impossible to prevent) would have been seriously detrimental to the rich dresses of the guests, who, on account of the crowded state of the salon, could not *all* be expected to keep from out its centre; that is to say, from under the chandelier. Additional sconces were set in various parts of the hall, out of the way; and a flambeau emitting sweet odor was placed in the right hand of each of the Caryatides[2] that stood against the wall; some fifty or sixty altogether.

The eight ourang-outangs, taking Hop-Frog's advice, waited patiently until midnight (when the room was thoroughly filled with masqueraders) before making their appearance. No sooner had the clock ceased striking, however, than they rushed, or rather rolled in, all to-

9. A fine-stemmed plant used in textiles (its seeds yield linseed oil).
1. Dome.
2. Columns in the form of women holding up the cornices and roofs of buildings. Mabbott suggests that these decorations are especially appropriate since the king in this tale is cruel to women and the captive Caryae women of Laconia were condemned by the Spartans to carry heavy burdens as punishment for supporting the Persian invasion of Greece. "Sconces": wall brackets for lights, frequently in hollowed-out recesses. "Flambeau": a torch.

gether; for the impediment of their chains caused most of the party to fall, and all to stumble as they entered.

The excitement among the masqueraders was prodigious, and filled the heart of the king with glee. As had been anticipated, there were not a few of the guests who supposed the ferocious-looking creatures to be beasts of *some* kind in reality, if not precisely ourang-outangs. Many of the women swooned with affright; and had not the king taken the precaution to exclude all weapons from the salon, his party might soon have expiated[3] their frolic in their blood. As it was, a general rush was made for the doors; but the king had ordered them to be locked immediately upon his entrance; and, at the dwarf's suggestion, the keys had been deposited with *him*.

While the tumult was at its height, and each masquerader attentive only to his own safety—(for, in fact, there was much *real* danger from the pressure of the excited crowd), the chain by which the chandelier ordinarily hung, and which had been drawn up on its removal, might have been seen very gradually to descend, until its hooked extremity came within three feet of the floor.

Soon after this, the king and his seven friends, having reeled about the hall in all directions, found themselves, at length, in its centre, and, of course, in immediate contact with the chain. While they were thus situated, the dwarf, who had followed closely at their heels, inciting them to keep up the commotion, took hold of their own chain at the intersection of the two portions which crossed the circle diametrically and at right angles. Here, with the rapidity of thought, he inserted the hook from which the chandelier had been wont to depend; and, in an instant, by some unseen agency, the chandelier-chain was drawn so far upward as to take the hook out of reach, and, as an inevitable consequence, to drag the ourang-outangs together in close connection, and face to face.

The masqueraders, by this time, had recovered, in some measure, from their alarm; and, beginning to regard the whole matter as a well-contrived pleasantry, set up a loud shout of laughter at the predicament of the apes.

'Leave them to *me!*' now screamed Hop-Frog; his shrill voice making itself easily heard through all the din. 'Leave them to *me*. I fancy *I* know them. If I can only get a good look at them, I can soon tell who they are!'

Here, scrambling over the heads of the crowd, he managed to get to the wall; when, seizing a flambeau from one of the Caryatides, he returned, as he went, to the centre of the room; leaping, with the agility of a monkey, upon the king's head, and thence clambered a few feet up the chain; holding down the torch to examine the group of ourang-outangs, and still screaming '*I* shall soon find out who they are!'

And now, while the whole assembly (the apes included) were con-

3. Atoned for; redressed or purged. Here a sarcastic way of saying that the king's men, if they had had weapons at hand, might have purged the crowd by violence.

vulsed with laughter, the jester suddenly uttered a shrill whistle; when the chain flew violently up for about thirty feet; dragging with it the dismayed and struggling ourang-outangs, and leaving them suspended in midair between the sky-light and the floor. Hop-Frog, clinging to the chain as it rose, still maintaining his relative position in respect to the eight maskers,[4] and still (as if nothing were the matter) continued to thrust his torch down towards them, as though endeavoring to discover who they were.

So thoroughly astonished were the whole company at this ascent, that a dead silence, of about a minute's duration, ensued. It was broken by just such a low, harsh, *grating* sound as had before attracted the attention of the king and his councillors, when the former threw the wine in the face of Trippetta. But, on the present occasion, there could be no question as to *whence* the sound issued. It came from the fang-like teeth of the dwarf, who ground them and gnashed them as he foamed at the mouth, and glared, with an expression of maniacal rage, into the upturned countenances of the king and his seven companions.

'Ah, ha!' said at length the infuriated jester. 'Ah, ha! I begin to see who these people *are*, now.' Here, pretending to scrutinize the king more closely, he held the flambeau to the flaxen coat which enveloped him, and which instantly burst into a sheet of vivid flame. In less than half a minute the whole eight ourang-outangs were blazing fiercely, amid the shrieks of the multitude who gazed at them from below, horror-stricken, and without the power to render them the slightest assistance.

At length the flames, suddenly increasing in virulence, forced the jester to climb higher up the chain, to be out of their reach; and, as he made this movement, the crowd again sank, for a brief instant, into silence. The dwarf seized his opportunity and once more spoke:

'I now see *distinctly*,' he said, 'what manner of people these maskers are. They are a great king and his seven privy councillors—a king who does not scruple to strike a defenceless girl, and his seven councillors who abet him in the outrage. As for myself, I am simply Hop-Frog, the jester—and *this is my last jest.*'

Owing to the high combustibility of both the flax and the tar to which it adhered, the dwarf had scarcely made an end of his brief speech before the work of vengeance was complete. The eight corpses swung in their chains, a fetid, blackened, hideous, and indistinguishable mass. The cripple hurled his torch at them, clambered leisurely to the ceiling, and disappeared through the sky-light.

It is supposed that Trippetta, stationed on the roof of the salon, had been the accomplice of her friend in his fiery revenge, and that, together, they effected their escape to their own country: for neither was seen again.

4. Masqueraders.

The Narrative of
Arthur Gordon Pym

Harper published *Pym* in New York in July 1838. Wily and Putnam printed an unauthorized version of the book in October 1838 in England (the last paragraph was omitted and a report of the sudden death of Pym added to the preface). The American edition is the text reprinted here; sure typographical errors in this printing are silently corrected; other emendations are enclosed in brackets; standard nineteenth-century variant spellings and punctuation have been allowed to stand. The American edition includes two different chapters numbered XXIII (here identified as XXIII-a and XXIII-b) preceding the final chapter—for a total of twenty-five chapters in all.

These chapters are preceded by a "preface" by the fictional author (Arthur Gordon Pym) and followed by a fictional publisher's or editor's final "note." Two installments had appeared in the *Southern Literary Messenger* (*SLM*) in January and February 1837; Poe was in the process of leaving the magazine and no further portions of the *Pym* narrative appeared in its pages. Reference to these two installments occurs in the book preface with a fictionalized twist. Differences between the *SLM* version of these passages and that of the Harper book-length edition are minimal. The fact that Poe was in the process of moving to another city and other stressful aspects of his life in 1837–38 have suggested to some critics that he hurried his story rather than giving it the careful, detailed attention that was his trademark; and a favorite critical pastime is to point out errors or inconsistencies in the texts. But the hoaxical elements and the epistemological questions raised by the narrative are so insistent that readers should be cautious in attributing simple error (see comments in the notes to the story).

The title page of the book carried the following provocative summary of the "true" adventures related therein, all in larger and smaller capitals, and centered on the page:

> The Narrative of Arthur Gordon Pym. Of Nantucket. Comprising the details of a mutiny and atrocious butchery on board the American brig Grampus, on her way to the South Seas, in the month of June, 1827. With an account of the recapture of the vessel by the survivers; their shipwreck and subsequent horrible sufferings from famine; their deliverance by means of the British schooner Jane Guy; the brief cruise of this latter vessel in the Antarctic ocean; her capture, and the massacre of her crew among a group of islands in the eighty-fourth parallel of Southern latitude; together with the incredible adventures and discoveries still farther South to which that distressing calamity gave rise.

Poe used many works of travel literature (both fiction and nonfiction) in writing this narrative of a haphazard journey to the end of the world. Some of the principal ones are Captain James Cook and James King, *A*

Voyage to the Pacific (1784); the retrospective *History of the Expedition under the Command of Capts. Lewis and Clark* (1814); William Scoresby Jr., *An Account of the Arctic Regions with a History and Description of the Northern Whale-Fishery* (1820); *Symzonia: A Voyage of Discovery by Captain Adam Seaborn* (1820–22), a futuristic fantasy presumably written by John Cleves Symmes Jr.; Jane Porter's novel *Narrative of Sir Edward Seaward* (1831); Benjamin Morrell, *A Narrative of Four Voyages to the South Sea, North and South Pacific Ocean, Chinese Sea, Ethiopic and Southern Atlantic Ocean, Indian and Antarctic Ocean. From the Year 1812 to 1832* (1832), supposedly rewritten by Samuel Woodworth; Washington Irving, *Astoria* (1835), which Poe reviewed; R. Thomas, *Remarkable Shipwrecks and Remarkable Events* (1836); J. N. Reynolds, *Address, on the Subject of a Surveying and Exploring Expedition to the Pacific Ocean and the South Seas* (1836), which Poe reviewed; John Stephens, *Incidents of Travel in Egypt, Arabia Petraea, and the Holy Land* (1837), which Poe also reviewed; and Reynolds's "Leaves from an Unpublished Journal," published three months before *Pym* in the New York *Mirror* (April 21, 1838). A number of Poe's specific borrowings from these and other works are indicated in the notes; differences between Poe's narrative and quoted or paraphrased passages are suggestive regarding Poe's thematic intent. Many of the nautical terms are glossed in the notes to "Ms. Found in a Bottle" (pp. 106ff.).

Of special interest is the narrative *Symzonia*, for it seems to provide a mythic context for Pym's journey into the vaporous waters at the end of the world, the mysterious rock writings, and the obscure larger-than-life figure that rises out of the mists at the South Pole. In 1820, a small volume titled *Symzonia: A Voyage of Discovery* appeared as the work of one Captain Adam Seaborn. The book has on occasion been attributed to Nathaniel Ames, but the title points to John Cleves [or Cleve] Symmes (1780?–1829), who propounded a theory of a hollow earth, formed of concentric spheres, with surface entrances to its interior lands at the North and South Poles. In this cosmography, the great ocean currents flow to the poles, plunge downward inside the outer shell of the earth, circulate to the opposite pole, and reemerge. Symmes's theory of "holes at the poles" struck many as not only improbable but laughable. Yet it had its adherents—or at least those willing to entertain the possibility—including the American naval officer Jeremiah N. Reynolds (1799–1858). Reynolds petitioned the U.S. Congress to fund an Antarctic expedition, part of the aim of which was to locate Symmes's hole. Poe reviewed Reynold's reports and gave him strong support for leading the expedition.

The full text of *Symzonia* tells the story of a ship that penetrates the Great Ice Barrier of the Antarctic and discovers (as in *Pym*) a warm sea at the Pole. The adventurers then locate an entrance to the interior of the earth, proceed cautiously inward, and discover different island civilizations. They learn that certain warring and unworthy peoples had been cast out of the interior word—exiled to the external world, barred from returning. Like Jonathan Swift's *Gulliver's Travels* (1726) and other imaginary sea voyages, *Symzonia* particularizes measurements, ship's tonnage, compass directions, sea currents, and latitudes and longitudes in a realistic mode, then propels the reader into a fantasyland, where a critique of modern society is launched. Nineteenth-century Eurocentric society suffers a negative comparison with the society of the interior dwellers—the "Symzonians." The simplified chart on p. 431—representing the concentric structure of the earth in terms of degrees of the supposed declination of the sun—was the frontispiece of the 1820 volume.

SECTIONAL VIEW OF THE EARTH.

SHOWING THE
OPENINGS AT THE POLES.

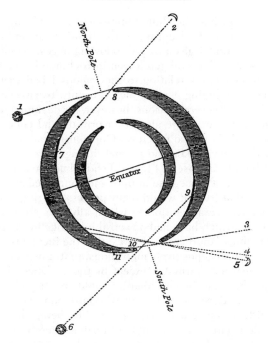

EXPLANATION OF THE PLATE.

Fig. 1.—Rays of the sun when in the equator, refracted 3 degrees.

2.—Moon's rays in 28° north declination.

3.—Sun's rays in 9° south declination

4.—Sun's rays in 23° do

5.—Moon's rays in 28° do

6.—Sun's rays in 23° 27′ south declination, refracted 3°.

7.—Supposed place of Belzubia.

8.—Place of exile.

9.—Symzonia.

10.—Token Island.

11 —Seaborn's Land.

The Narrative of Arthur Gordon Pym

Preface

Upon my return to the United States a few months ago, after the extraordinary series of adventure in the South Seas and elsewhere, of which an account is given in the following pages, accident threw me into the society of several gentlemen in Richmond, Va., who felt deep interest in all matters relating to the regions I had visited, and who were constantly urging it upon me, as a duty, to give my narrative to the public. I had several reasons, however, for declining to do so, some of which were of a nature altogether private, and concern no person but myself; others not so much so. One consideration which deterred me was, that, having kept no journal during a greater portion of the time in which I was absent, I feared I should not be able to write, from mere memory, a statement so minute and connected as to have the *appearance* of that truth it would really possess, barring only the natural and unavoidable exaggeration to which all of us are prone when detailing events which have had powerful influence in exciting the imaginative faculties. Another reason was, that the incidents to be narrated were of a nature so positively marvellous, that, unsupported as my assertions must necessarily be (except by the evidence of a single individual, and he a half-breed Indian), I could only hope for belief among my family, and those of my friends who have had reason, through life, to put faith in my veracity—the probability being that the public at large would regard what I should put forth as merely an impudent and ingenious fiction. A distrust in my own abilities as a writer was, nevertheless, one of the principal causes which prevented me from complying with the suggestions of my advisers.

Among those gentlemen in Virginia who expressed the greatest interest in my statement, more particularly in regard to that portion of it which related to the Antarctic Ocean, was Mr. Poe, lately editor of the Southern Literary Messenger, a monthly magazine, published by Mr. Thomas W. White, in the city of Richmond. He strongly advised me, among others, to prepare at once a full account of what I had seen and undergone, and trust to the shrewdness and common sense of the public—insisting, with great plausibility, that however roughly, as regards mere authorship, my book should be got up, its very uncouthness, if there were any, would give it all the better chance of being received as truth.

Notwithstanding this representation, I did not make up my mind to do as he suggested. He afterward proposed (finding that I would not stir in the matter) that I should allow him to draw up, in his own words, a narrative of the earlier portion of my adventures, from facts afforded by myself, publishing it in the Southern Messenger *under the garb of fiction.* To this, perceiving no objection, I consented, stipulating only that my real name should be retained. Two numbers of the pretended fiction appeared, consequently, in the Messenger for January and February (1837), and, in order that it might certainly be re-

garded as fiction, the name of Mr. Poe was affixed to the articles in the table of contents of the magazine.[1]

The manner in which this *ruse* was received has induced me at length to undertake a regular compilation and publication of the adventures in question; for I found that, in spite of the air of fable which had been so ingeniously thrown around that portion of my statement which appeared in the Messenger (without altering or distorting a single fact), the public were still not at all disposed to receive it as fable, and several letters were sent to Mr. P.'s address distinctly expressing a conviction to the contrary. I thence concluded that the facts of my narrative would prove of such a nature as to carry with them sufficient evidence of their own authenticity, and that I had consequently little to fear on the score of popular incredulity.

This *exposé* being made, it will be seen at once how much of what follows I claim to be my own writing; and it will also be understood that no fact is misrepresented in the first few pages which were written by Mr. Poe. Even to those readers who have not seen the Messenger, it will be unnecessary to point out where his portion ends and my own commences; the difference in point of style will be readily perceived.[2]

A. G. PYM.

New-York, July, 1838.

Narrative of A. Gordon Pym
[Chapter I]

My name is Arthur Gordon Pym. My father was a respectable trader in sea-stores at Nantucket, where I was born. My maternal grandfather was an attorney in good practice. He was fortunate in everything, and had speculated very successfully in stocks of the Edgarton[3] New-Bank, as it was formerly called. By these and other means he had managed to lay by a tolerable sum of money. He was more attached to myself, I believe, than to any other person in the world, and I expected to inherit the most of his property at his death. He sent me, at six years of age, to the school of old Mr. Ricketts, a gentleman with only one arm, and of eccentric manners—he is well known to almost every person who has visited New Bedford. I stayed at his school until I was sixteen,[4] when I left him for Mr. E. Ronald's academy on the hill. Here

1. See headnote p. 429 herein and notes to Chapters II and IV.
2. This accounting for the *SLM* narrative having appeared as fiction under the name of Poe seems to have the dual purpose of perpetrating a tongue-in-cheek hoax while giving greater verisimilitude to the narrative. That is, we now have the "real" account by Mr. Pym, not a mere "fiction" by Mr. Poe. Some critics suggest that this declaration is one of a number of ironic observations about the craft of writing found in the text: the contradictory circularity of the argument is deliberately absurd. The first partial publication was a "pretended fiction," but what is now presented is actually "true"; therefore, the previous pretense to fiction "confirms" its truth. In addition to these logical games, there is no readily perceived difference of style after the third paragraph of Chapter IV, where the *SLM* installments cease.
3. On Martha's Vineyard, an island close to Nantucket Island, where Pym supposedly grew up.
4. Fourteen in the *SLM* version.

I became intimate with the son of Mr. Barnard, a sea captain, who generally sailed in the employ of Lloyd and Vredenburgh—Mr. Barnard is also very well known in New Bedford, and has many relations, I am certain, in Edgarton. His son was named Augustus, and he was nearly two years older than myself. He had been on a whaling voyage with his father in the John Donaldson, and was always talking to me of his adventures in the South Pacific Ocean. I used frequently to go home with him, and remain all day, and sometimes all night. We occupied the same bed, and he would be sure to keep me awake until almost light, telling me stories of the natives of the Island of Tinian, and other places he had visited in his travels. At last I could not help being interested in what he said, and by degrees I felt the greatest desire to go to sea. I owned a sail-boat called the Ariel,[5] and worth about seventy-five dollars. She had a half-deck or cuddy, and was rigged sloop[6] fashion—I forget her tonnage, but she would hold ten persons without much crowding. In this boat we were in the habit of going on some of the maddest freaks in the world; and, when I now think of them, it appears to me a thousand wonders that I am alive to-day.

I will relate one of these adventures by way of introduction to a longer and more momentous narrative.[7] One night there was a party at Mr. Barnard's, and both Augustus and myself were not a little intoxicated towards the close of it. As usual, in such cases, I took part of his bed in preference to going home. He went to sleep, as I thought, very quietly (it being near one when the party broke up), and without saying a word on his favourite topic. It might have been half an hour from the time of our getting in bed, and I was just about falling into a doze, when he suddenly started up, and swore with a terrible oath that he would not go to sleep for any Arthur Pym in Christendom, when there was so glorious a breeze from the southwest. I never was so astonished in my life, not knowing what he intended, and thinking that the wines and liquors he had drunk had set him entirely beside himself. He proceeded to talk very coolly, however, saying he knew that I supposed him intoxicated, but that he was never more sober in his life. He was only tired, he added, of lying in bed on such a fine night like a dog, and was determined to get up and dress, and go out on a frolic with the boat. I can hardly tell what possessed me, but the words were no sooner out of his mouth than I felt a thrill of the greatest excitement and pleasure, and thought his mad idea one of the most delightful and most reasonable things in the world. It was blowing almost a gale, and the weather was very cold—it being late in October. I sprang out of bed, nevertheless, in a kind of ecstasy, and told him I was quite as brave as himself, and quite as tired as he was of lying in bed like a dog, and quite as ready for any fun or frolic as any Augustus Barnard in Nantucket.

5. Contemporary newspaper accounts of the wreck of the Norfolk ship the *Ariel* may have suggested the opening (e.g., Norfolk *Beacon*, February 18, 1836; Norfolk *Herald*, February 19, 1836). Critics have also suggested a biblical allusion to Jerusalem (see Isaiah 29:1) and to the sprite Ariel in Shakespeare's *The Tempest* (c. 1611). The name Ariel is also found in John Milton's *Paradise Lost* (1667) and James Fenimore Cooper's *The Pilot* (1823).
6. A single-masted fore- and aft-rigged sailing ship. "Cuddy": small cabin or the cook's galley.
7. A sentence added for the book-length version.

We lost no time in getting on our clothes and hurrying down to the boat. She was lying at the old decayed wharf by the lumber-yard of Pankey & Co., and almost thumping her sides out against the rough logs. Augustus got into her and bailed her, for she was nearly half full of water. This being done, we hoisted jib and mainsail, kept full, and started boldly out to sea.

The wind, as I before said, blew freshly from the southwest. The night was very clear and cold. Augustus had taken the helm, and I stationed myself by the mast, on the deck of the cuddy. We flew along at a great rate—neither of us having said a word since casting loose from the wharf. I now asked my companion what course he intended to steer, and what time he thought it probable we should get back. He whistled for a few minutes, and then said crustily, "I am going to sea— you may go home if you think proper." Turning my eyes upon him, I perceived at once that, in spite of his assumed *nonchalance*, he was greatly agitated. I could see him distinctly by the light of the moon— his face was paler than any marble, and his hand shook so excessively that he could scarcely retain hold of the tiller. I found that something had gone wrong, and became seriously alarmed. At this period I knew little about the management of a boat, and was now depending entirely upon the nautical skill of my friend. The wind, too, had suddenly increased, as we were fast getting out of the lee of the land—still I was ashamed to betray any trepidation, and for almost half an hour maintained a resolute silence. I could stand it no longer, however, and spoke to Augustus about the propriety of turning back. As before, it was nearly a minute before he made answer, or took any notice of my suggestion. "By-and-by," said he at length—"time enough—home by-and-by." I had expected a similar reply, but there was something in the tone of these words which filled me with an indescribable feeling of dread. I again looked at the speaker attentively. His lips were perfectly livid, and his knees shook so violently together that he seemed scarcely able to stand. "For God's sake, Augustus," I screamed, now heartily frightened, "what ails you?—what is the matter?—what *are* you going to do?" "Matter!" he stammered, in the greatest apparent surprise, letting go the tiller at the same moment, and falling forward into the bottom of the boat—"matter!—why, nothing is the—matter— going home—d—d—don't you see?" The whole truth now flashed upon me. I flew to him and raised him up. He was drunk—beastly drunk—he could no longer either stand, speak, or see. His eyes were perfectly glazed; and as I let him go in the extremity of my despair, he rolled like a mere log into the bilge-water from which I had lifted him. It was evident that, during the evening, he had drunk far more than I suspected, and that his conduct in bed had been the result of a highly-concentrated state of intoxication—a state which, like madness, frequently enables the victim to imitate the outward demeanour of one in perfect possession of his senses. The coolness of the night air, however, had had its usual effect—the mental energy began to yield before its influence—and the confused perception which he no doubt then had of his perilous situation had assisted in hastening the catastrophe.

He was now thoroughly insensible, and there was no probability that he would be otherwise for many hours.

It is hardly possible to conceive the extremity of my terror. The fumes of the wine lately taken had evaporated, leaving me doubly timid and irresolute. I knew that I was altogether incapable of managing the boat, and that a fierce wind and strong ebb tide were hurrying us to destruction. A storm was evidently gathering behind us; we had neither compass nor provisions; and it was clear that, if we held our present course, we should be out of sight of land before daybreak. These thoughts, with a crowd of others equally fearful, flashed through my mind with a bewildering rapidity, and for some moments paralyzed me beyond the possibility of making any exertion. The boat was going through the water at a terrible rate—full before the wind— no reef in either jib or mainsail—running her bows completely under the foam. It was a thousand wonders she did not broach to—Augustus having let go the tiller, as I said before, and I being too much agitated to think of taking it myself. By good luck, however, she kept steady, and gradually I recovered some degree of presence of mind. Still the wind was increasing fearfully; and whenever we rose from a plunge forward, the sea behind fell combing over our counter, and deluged us with water. I was so utterly benumbed, too, in every limb, as to be nearly unconscious of sensation. At length I summoned up the resolution of despair, and rushing to the mainsail, let it go by the run. As might have been expected, it flew over the bows, and, getting drenched with water, carried away the mast short off by the board. This latter accident alone saved me from instant destruction. Under the jib[8] only, I now boomed along before the wind, shipping heavy seas occasionally over the counter, but relieved from the terror of immediate death. I took the helm, and breathed with greater freedom as I found that there yet remained to us a chance of ultimate escape. Augustus still lay senseless in the bottom of the boat; and as there was imminent danger of his drowning (the water being nearly a foot deep just where he fell), I contrived to raise him partially up, and keep him in a sitting position, by passing a rope round his waist, and lashing it to a ringbolt in the deck of the cuddy. Having thus arranged everything as well as I could in my chilled and agitated condition, I recommended myself to God, and made up my mind to bear whatever might happen with all the fortitude in my power.

Hardly had I come to this resolution, when, suddenly, a loud and long scream or yell, as if from the throats of a thousand demons, seemed to pervade the whole atmosphere around and above the boat. Never while I live shall I forget the intense agony of terror I experienced at that moment. My hair stood erect on my head—I felt the blood congealing in my veins—my heart ceased utterly to beat, and without having once raised my eyes to learn the source of my alarm, I

8. A triangular sail stretching from the foretopmast toward the bow, fastened to a jib boom in large ships or to the bowsprit or bow itself in smaller vessels. In an 1838 review questioning *Pym*'s veracity and realism, William Burton observed that since the mast has been "carried away," there is nothing to support the jib.

tumbled headlong and insensible upon the body of my fallen companion.

I found myself, upon reviving, in the cabin of a large whaling-ship (the Penguin)[9] bound to Nantucket. Several persons were standing over me, and Augustus, paler than death, was busily occupied in chafing my hands. Upon seeing me open my eyes, his exclamations of gratitude and joy excited alternate laughter and tears from the rough-looking personages who were present. The mystery of our being in existence was now soon explained. We had been run down by the whaling-ship, which was close hauled, beating up to Nantucket with every sail she could venture to set, and consequently running almost at right angles to our own course. Several men were on the look-out forward, but did not perceive our boat until it was an impossibility to avoid coming in contact—their shouts of warning upon seeing us were what so terribly alarmed me. The huge ship, I was told, rode immediately over us with as much ease as our own little vessel would have passed over a feather, and without the least perceptible impediment to her progress. Not a scream arose from the deck of the victim—there was a slight grating sound to be heard mingling with the roar of wind and water, as the frail bark which was swallowed up rubbed for a moment along the keel of her destroyer—but this was all. Thinking our boat (which it will be remembered was dismasted) some mere shell cut adrift as useless, the captain (Captain E. T. V. Block of New London) was for proceeding on his course without troubling himself further about the matter. Luckily, there were two of the look-out who swore positively to having seen some person at our helm, and represented the possibility of yet saving him. A discussion ensued, when Block grew angry, and, after a while, said that "it was no business of his to be eternally watching for egg-shells; that the ship should *not* put about for any such nonsense; and if there was a man run down, it was nobody's fault but his own—he might drown and be d—d," or some language to that effect. Henderson, the first mate, now took the matter up, being justly indignant, as well as the whole ship's crew, at a speech evincing so base a degree of heartless atrocity. He spoke plainly, seeing himself upheld by the men, told the captain he considered him a fit subject for the gallows, and that he would disobey his orders if he were hanged for it the moment he set his foot on shore. He strode aft, jostling Block (who turned very pale and made no answer) on one side, and seizing the helm, gave the word, in a firm voice, *Hard-a-lee!*[1] The men flew to their posts, and the ship went cleverly about. All this had occupied nearly five minutes, and it was supposed to be hardly within the bounds of possibility that any individual could

9. An American ship named the *Penguin* journeyed to the South Seas in 1829–30. J. N. Reynolds wrote of their experiences in two works: "Leaves from an Unpublished Journal" (April 21, 1838) and "Mocha Dick" (May 1839), an account of a notorious ship-sinking whale that was one of the sources for Melville's white whale, which he renamed Moby-Dick. Poe mentions Reynolds several times in *Pym* and elsewhere, and he reviewed with great approbation Reynolds's arguing the cause of further South Seas exploration by the U.S. government.

1. A sharp turn out of the wind. "Lee": the off-windward side.

be saved—allowing any to have been on board the boat. Yet, as the reader has seen, both Augustus and myself were rescued; and our deliverance seemed to have been brought about by two of those almost inconceivable pieces of good fortune which are attributed by the wise and pious to the special interference of Providence.

While the ship was yet in stays, the mate lowered the jolly-boat and jumped into her with the very two men, I believe, who spoke up as having seen me at the helm. They had just left the lee of the vessel (the moon still shining brightly) when she made a long and heavy roll to windward, and Henderson, at the same moment, starting up in his seat, bawled out to his crew to *back water*. He would say nothing else—repeating his cry impatiently, *back water! back water!* The men put back as speedily as possible; but by this time the ship had gone round, and gotten fully under headway, although all hands on board were making great exertions to take in sail. In despite of the danger of the attempt, the mate clung to the main-chains as soon as they came within his reach. Another huge lurch now brought the starboard side of the vessel out of water nearly as far as her keel, when the cause of his anxiety was rendered obvious enough. The body of a man was seen to be affixed in the most singular manner to the smooth and shining bottom (the Penguin was coppered and copper-fastened), and beating violently against it with every movement of the hull. After several ineffectual efforts, made during the lurches of the ship, and at the imminent risk of swamping the boat, I was finally disengaged from my perilous situation and taken on board—for the body proved to be my own. It appeared that one of the timber-bolts having started and broken a passage through the copper, it had arrested my progress as I passed under the ship, and fastened me in so extraordinary a manner to her bottom. The head of the bolt had made its way through the collar of the green baize jacket I had on, and through the back part of my neck, forcing itself out between two sinews and just below the right ear. I was immediately put to bed—although life seemed to be totally extinct. There was no surgeon on board. The captain, however, treated me with every attention—to make amends, I presume, in the eyes of his crew, for his atrocious behaviour in the previous portion of the adventure.

In the meantime, Henderson had again put off from the ship, although the wind was now blowing almost a hurricane. He had not been gone many minutes when he fell in with some fragments of our boat, and shortly afterward one of the men with him asserted that he could distinguish a cry for help at intervals amid the roaring of the tempest. This induced the hardy seamen to persevere in their search for more than half an hour, although repeated signals to return were made them by Captain Block, and although every moment on the water in so frail a boat was fraught to them with the most imminent and deadly peril. Indeed, it is nearly impossible to conceive how the small jolly they were in could have escaped destruction for a single instant. She was built, however, for the whaling service, and was fitted, as I

have since had reason to believe, with air-boxes, in the manner of some life-boats used on the coast of Wales.

After searching in vain for about the period of time just mentioned, it was determined to get back to the ship. They had scarcely made this resolve when a feeble cry arose from a dark object which floated rapidly by. They pursued and soon overtook it. It proved to be the entire deck of the Ariel's cuddy. Augustus was struggling near it, apparently in the last agonies. Upon getting hold of him it was found that he was attached by a rope to the floating timber. This rope, it will be remembered, I had myself tied round his waist, and made fast to a ringbolt, for the purpose of keeping him in an upright position, and my so doing, it appeared, had been ultimately the means of preserving his life. The Ariel was slightly put together, and in going down her frame naturally went to pieces; the deck of the cuddy, as might be expected, was lifted, by the force of the water rushing in, entirely from the main timbers, and floated (with other fragments, no doubt) to the surface—Augustus was buoyed up with it, and thus escaped a terrible death.

also
saved
each
other

It was more than an hour after being taken on board the Penguin before he could give any account of himself, or be made to comprehend the nature of the accident which had befallen our boat. At length he became thoroughly aroused, and spoke much of his sensations while in the water. Upon his first attaining any degree of consciousness, he found himself beneath the surface, whirling round and round with inconceivable rapidity, and with a rope wrapped in three or four folds tightly about his neck. In an instant afterward he felt himself going rapidly upward, when, his head striking violently against a hard substance, he again relapsed into insensibility. Upon once more reviving he was in fuller possession of his reason—this was still, however, in the greatest degree clouded and confused. He now knew that some accident had occurred, and that he was in the water, although his mouth was above the surface, and he could breathe with some freedom. Possibly, at this period, the deck was drifting rapidly before the wind, and drawing him after it, as he floated upon his back. Of course, as long as he could have retained this position, it would have been nearly impossible that he should be drowned. Presently a surge threw him directly athwart the deck; and this post he endeavoured to maintain, screaming at intervals for help. Just before he was discovered by Mr. Henderson, he had been obliged to relax his hold through exhaustion, and, falling into the sea, had given himself up for lost. During the whole period of his struggles he had not the faintest recollection of the Ariel, nor of any matters in connexion with the source of his disaster. A vague feeling of terror and despair had taken entire possession of his faculties. When he was finally picked up, every power of his mind had failed him; and, as before said, it was nearly an hour after getting on board the Penguin before he became fully aware of his condition. In regard to myself—I was resuscitated from a state bordering very nearly upon death (and after every other means had been tried in vain for three hours and a half) by vigorous friction with

flannels bathed in hot oil—a proceeding suggested by Augustus. The wound in my neck, although of an ugly appearance, proved of little real consequence, and I soon recovered from its effects.

The Penguin got into port about nine o'clock in the morning, after encountering one of the severest gales ever experienced off Nantucket. Both Augustus and myself managed to appear at Mr. Barnard's in time for breakfast—which, luckily, was somewhat late, owing to the party over night. I suppose all at the table were too much fatigued themselves to notice our jaded appearance—of course, it would not have borne a very rigid scrutiny. Schoolboys, however, can accomplish wonders in the way of deception, and I verily believe not one of our friends in Nantucket had the slightest suspicion that the terrible story told by some sailors in town of their having run down a vessel at sea and drowned some thirty or forty poor devils, had reference either to the Ariel, my companion, or myself. We two have since very frequently talked the matter over—but never without a shudder. In one of our conversations Augustus frankly confessed to me, that in his whole life he had at no time experienced so excruciating a sense of dismay, as when on board our little boat he first discovered the extent of his intoxication, and felt himself sinking beneath its influence.

Chapter II

In no affairs of mere prejudice, pro or con, do we deduce inferences with entire certainty even from the most simple data. It might be supposed that a catastrophe such as I have just related would have effectually cooled my incipient passion for the sea. On the contrary, I never experienced a more ardent longing for the wild adventures incident to the life of a navigator than within a week after our miraculous deliverance. This short period proved amply long enough to erase from my memory the shadows, and bring out in vivid light all the pleasurably exciting points of colour, all the picturesqueness of the late perilous accident. My conversations with Augustus grew daily more frequent and more intensely full of interest. He had a manner of relating his stories of the ocean (more than one half of which I now suspect to have been sheer fabrications) well adapted to have weight with one of my enthusiastic temperament, and somewhat gloomy, although glowing imagination. It is strange, too, that he most strongly enlisted my feelings in behalf of the life of a seaman, when he depicted his more terrible moments of suffering and despair. For the bright side of the painting I had a limited sympathy. My visions were of shipwreck and famine; of death or captivity among barbarian hordes; of a lifetime dragged out in sorrow and tears, upon some gray and desolate rock, in an ocean unapproachable and unknown. Such visions or desires—for they amounted to desires—are common, I have since been assured, to the whole numerous race of the melancholy among men—at the time of which I speak I regarded them only as prophetic glimpses of a destiny which I felt myself in a measure bound to fulfil. Augustus thoroughly entered into my state of mind. It is probable, indeed, that our

intimate communion had resulted in a partial interchange of character.

About eighteen months after the period of the Ariel's disaster, the firm of Lloyd and Vredenburgh (a house connected in some manner with the Messieurs Enderby, I believe, of Liverpool) were engaged in repairing and fitting out the brig Grampus[2] for a whaling voyage. She was an old hulk, and scarcely seaworthy when all was done to her that could be done. I hardly know why she was chosen in preference to other good vessels belonging to the same owners—but so it was. Mr. Barnard was appointed to command her, and Augustus was going with him. While the brig was getting ready, he frequently urged upon me the excellency of the opportunity now offered for indulging my desire of travel. He found me by no means an unwilling listener—yet the matter could not be so easily arranged. My father made no direct opposition; but my mother went into hysterics at the bare mention of the design; and, more than all, my grandfather, from whom I expected much, vowed to cut me off with a shilling if I should ever broach the subject to him again. These difficulties, however, so far from abating my desire, only added fuel to the flame. I determined to go at all hazards; and, having made known my intention to Augustus, we set about arranging a plan by which it might be accomplished. In the meantime I forbore speaking to any of my relations in regard to the voyage, and, as I busied myself ostensibly with my usual studies, it was supposed that I had abandoned the design. I have since frequently examined my conduct on this occasion with sentiments of displeasure as well as of surprise. The intense hypocrisy I made use of for the furtherance of my project—an hypocrisy pervading every word and action of my life for so long a period of time—could only have been rendered tolerable to myself by the wild and burning expectation with which I looked forward to the fulfilment of my long-cherished visions of travel.

In pursuance of my scheme of deception, I was necessarily obliged to leave much to the management of Augustus, who was employed for the greater part of every day on board the Grampus, attending to some arrangements for his father in the cabin and cabin hold. At night, however, we were sure to have a conference, and talk over our hopes. After nearly a month passed in this manner, without our hitting upon any plan we thought likely to succeed, he told me at last that he had determined upon everything necessary. I had a relation living in New Bedford, a Mr. Ross, at whose house I was in the habit of spending occasionally two or three weeks at a time. The brig was to sail about the middle of June (June, 1827), and it was agreed that, a day or two before her putting to sea, my father was to receive a note, as usual, from Mr. Ross, asking me to come over and spend a fortnight with

2. A member of the genus of marine mammals (cetaceans) that includes dolphins and whales. Strictly speaking, *grampus* means the roundhead (or beakless) gray dolphin but can also indicate certain whales like the *orca* (killer whale). There is a ship named the *Grampus* in Joseph C. Hart's popular narrative *Miriam Coffin, or The Whale-Fisherman* (1834), which also seems to have influenced in some degree Melville's *Moby-Dick*. "Brig": short for *brigantine*, a two-masted ship with fore and aft mainsails, usually square-rigged (i.e., the square sails are horizontally at right angles to the length of the ship).

Robert and Emmet (his sons). Augustus charged himself with the en-diting of this note and getting it delivered. Having set out, as sup-posed, for New Bedford, I was then to report myself to my companion, who would contrive a hiding-place for me in the Grampus. This hid-ing-place, he assured me, would be rendered sufficiently comfortable for a residence of many days, during which I was not to make my ap-pearance. When the brig had proceeded so far on her course as to make any turning back a matter out of question, I should then, he said, be formally installed in all the comforts of the cabin; and as to his father, he would only laugh heartily at the joke. Vessels enough would be met with by which a letter might be sent home explaining the adventure to my parents.[3]

The middle of June at length arrived, and everything had been ma-tured. The note was written and delivered, and on a Monday morning I left the house for the New Bedford packet, as supposed. I went, however, straight to Augustus, who was waiting for me at the corner of a street. It had been our original plan that I should keep out of the way until dark, and then slip on board the brig; but, as there was now a thick fog in our favour, it was agreed to lose no time in secreting me. Augustus led the way to the wharf, and I followed at a little distance, enveloped in a thick seaman's cloak, which he had brought with him, so that my person might not be easily recognised. Just as we turned the second corner, after passing Mr. Edmund's well, who should ap-pear, standing right in front of me, and looking me full in the face, but old Mr. Peterson, my grandfather. "Why, bless my soul, Gordon," said he, after a long pause, "why, why—*whose* dirty cloak is that you have on?" "Sir!" I replied, assuming, as well as I could, in the exigency of the moment, an air of offended surprise, and talking in the gruffest of all imaginable tones—"sir! you are a sum'mat mistaken—my name, in the first place, bee'nt nothing at all like Goddin,[4] and I'd want you for to know better, you blackguard, than to call my new obercoat a darty one!" For my life I could hardly refrain from screaming with laughter at the odd manner in which the old gentleman received this handsome rebuke. He started back two or three steps, turned first pale and then excessively red, threw up his spectacles, then, putting them down, ran full tilt at me, with his umbrella uplifted. He stopped short, however, in his career, as if struck with a sudden recollection; and presently, turning round, hobbled off down the street, shaking all the while with rage, and muttering between his teeth, "Won't do—new glasses—thought it was Gordon—d——d good-for-nothing salt water Long Tom."[5]

After this narrow escape we proceeded with greater caution, and ar-rived at our point of destination in safety. There were only one or two of the hands on board, and these were busy forward, doing something to the fore-castle combings. Captain Barnard, we knew very well, was

3. The first portion of the *SLM* version stops here.
4. I.e., Gordon, mispronounced; possibly a comic allusion to Goddin's Tavern in Richmond.
5. A gun (naval slang). There is also a character in James Fenimore Cooper's novel *The Pilot* (1823) named Long Tom Coffin. "D——d": damned; the partially blanked-out word is typi-cal of 19th-century squeamish aversion to spelling out swear words; cf. pp. 435 and 437.

engaged at Lloyd and Vredenburg's, and would remain there until late in the evening, so we had little to apprehend on his account. Augustus went first up the vessel's side, and in a short while I followed him, without being noticed by the men at work. We proceeded at once into the cabin, and found no person there. It was fitted up in the most comfortable style—a thing somewhat unusual in a whaling-vessel. There were four very excellent staterooms, with wide and convenient berths. There was also a large stove, I took notice, and a remarkably thick and valuable carpet covering the floor of both the cabin and staterooms. The ceiling was full seven feet high, and, in short, everything appeared of a more roomy and agreeable nature than I had anticipated. Augustus, however, would allow me but little time for observation, insisting upon the necessity of my concealing myself as soon as possible. He led the way into his own stateroom, which was on the starboard side of the brig, and next to the bulkheads. Upon entering, he closed the door and bolted it. I thought I had never seen a nicer little room than the one in which I now found myself. It was about ten feet long, and had only one berth, which, as I said before, was wide and convenient. In that portion of the closet nearest the bulkheads there was a space of four feet square, containing a table, a chair, and a set of hanging shelves full of books, chiefly books of voyages and travels. There were many other little comforts in the room, among which I ought not to forget a kind of safe or refrigerator, in which Augustus pointed out to me a host of delicacies, both in the eating and drinking department.

He now pressed with his knuckles upon a certain spot of the carpet in one corner of the space just mentioned, letting me know that a portion of the flooring, about sixteen inches square, had been neatly cut out and again adjusted. As he pressed, this portion rose up at one end sufficiently to allow the passage of his finger beneath. In this manner he raised the mouth of the trap (to which the carpet was still fastened by tacks), and I found that it led into the after hold. He next lit a small taper by means of a phosphorus match, and, placing the light in a dark lantern, descended with it through the opening, bidding me follow. I did so, and he then pulled the cover upon the hole, by means of a nail driven into the under side—the carpet, of course, resuming its original position on the floor of the stateroom, and all traces of the aperture being concealed.

The taper gave out so feeble a ray, that it was with the greatest difficulty I could grope my way through the confused mass of lumber among which I now found myself. By degrees, however, my eyes became accustomed to the gloom, and I proceeded with less trouble, holding on to the skirts of my friend's coat. He brought me, at length, after creeping and winding through innumerable narrow passages, to an iron-bound box, such as is used sometimes for packing fine earthenware. It was nearly four feet high, and full six long, but very narrow. Two large empty oil-casks lay on the top of it, and above these, again, a vast quantity of straw matting, piled up as high as the floor of the cabin. In every other direction around was wedged as closely as possi-

ble, even up to the ceiling, a complete chaos of almost every species of ship-furniture, together with a heterogenous medley of crates, hampers, barrels, and bales, so that it seemed a matter no less than miraculous that we had discovered any passage at all to the box. I afterward found that Augustus had purposely arranged the stowage in this hold with a view to affording me a thorough concealment, having had only one assistant in the labour, a man not going out in the brig.

My companion now showed me that one of the ends of the box could be removed at pleasure. He slipped it aside and displayed the interior, at which I was excessively amused. A mattress from one of the cabin berths covered the whole of its bottom, and it contained almost every article of mere comfort which could be crowded into so small a space, allowing me, at the same time, sufficient room for my accommodation, either in a sitting position or lying at full length. Among other things, there were some books, pen, ink, and paper, three blankets, a large jug full of water, a keg of sea-biscuit, three or four immense Bologna sausages, an enormous ham, a cold leg of roast mutton, and half a dozen bottles of cordials and liqueurs. I proceeded immediately to take possession of my little apartment, and this with feelings of higher satisfaction, I am sure, than any monarch ever experienced upon entering a new palace. Augustus now pointed out to me the method of fastening the open end of the box, and then, holding the taper close to the deck, showed me a piece of dark whipcord lying along it. This, he said, extended from my hiding-place throughout all the necessary windings among the lumber, to a nail which was driven into the deck of the hold, immediately beneath the trapdoor leading into his stateroom. By means of this cord I should be enabled readily to trace my way out without his guidance, provided any unlooked-for accident should render such a step necessary. He now took his departure, leaving with me the lantern, together with a copious supply of tapers and phosphorus, and promising to pay me a visit as often as he could contrive to do so without observation. This was on the seventeenth of June.

I remained three days and nights[6] (as nearly as I could guess) in my hiding-place without getting out of it at all, except twice for the purpose of stretching my limbs by standing erect between two crates just opposite the opening. During the whole period I saw nothing of Augustus; but this occasioned me little uneasiness, as I knew the brig was expected to put to sea every hour, and in the bustle he would not easily find opportunities of coming down to me. At length I heard the trap open and shut, and presently he called in a low voice, asking if all was well, and if there was anything I wanted. "Nothing," I replied; "I am as comfortable as can be; when will the brig sail?" "She will be under weigh in less than half an hour," he answered. "I came to let you know, and for fear you should be uneasy at my absence. I shall not have a chance of coming down again for some time—perhaps for three

6. A good deal of critical speculation focuses on the possible symbolism of Pym's three-day "entombment" and later "resurrection."

or four days more. All is going on right aboveboard. After I go up and close the trap, do you creep along by the whipcord to where the nail is driven in. You will find my watch there—it may be useful to you, as you have no daylight to keep time by. I suppose you can't tell how long you have been buried—only three days—this is the twentieth. I would bring the watch to your box, but am afraid of being missed." With this he went up.

In about an hour after he had gone I distinctly felt the brig in motion, and congratulated myself upon having at length fairly commenced a voyage. Satisfied with this idea, I determined to make my mind as easy as possible, and await the course of events until I should be permitted to exchange the box for the more roomy, although hardly more comfortable, accommodations of the cabin. My first care was to get the watch. Leaving the taper burning, I groped along in the dark, following the cord through windings innumerable, in some of which I discovered that, after toiling a long distance, I was brought back within a foot or two of a former position. At length I reached the nail, and, securing the object of my journey, returned with it in safety. I now looked over the books which had been so thoughtfully provided, and selected the expedition of Lewis and Clarke to the mouth of the Columbia.[7] With this I amused myself for some time, when, growing sleepy, I extinguished the light with great care, and soon fell into a sound slumber.

Upon awaking I felt strangely confused in mind, and some time elapsed before I could bring to recollection all the various circumstances of my situation. By degrees, however, I remembered all. Striking a light, I looked at the watch; but it was run down, and there were, consequently, no means of determining how long I had slept. My limbs were greatly cramped, and I was forced to relieve them by standing between the crates. Presently, feeling an almost ravenous appetite, I bethought myself of the cold mutton, some of which I had eaten just before going to sleep, and found excellent. What was my astonishment at discovering it to be in a state of absolute putrefaction! This circumstance occasioned me great disquietude; for, connecting it with the disorder of mind I experienced upon awaking, I began to suppose that I must have slept for an inordinately long period of time. The close atmosphere of the hold might have had something to do with this, and might, in the end, be productive of the most serious results. My head ached excessively; I fancied that I drew every breath with difficulty; and, in short, I was oppressed with a multitude of gloomy feelings. Still I could not venture to make any disturbance by opening the trap

7. In 1814, an edited version of the journals of the expedition led by Meriwether Lewis and William Clark overland to the Pacific Ocean was published as the *History of the Expedition under the Command of Capts. Lewis and Clark* (to the "Sources of the Missouri, Then across the Rocky Mountains and down the River Columbia to the Pacific Ocean, Performed during the Years 1804–5–6 by Order of the Government of the United States"). Poe wrote a narrative of an overland expedition westward toward the Pacific, which he called "The Journal of Julius Rodman," some of the details of which are also derived from Washington Irving's *Astoria* (1835). Six chapters of a planned twelve for the complete *Julius Rodman* appeared in *Burton's Gentleman's Magazine* (1840); but Poe left the magazine and did not finish the narrative.

or otherwise, and, having wound up the watch, contented myself as well as possible.

Throughout the whole of the next tedious twenty-four hours no person came to my relief, and I could not help accusing Augustus of the grossest inattention. What alarmed me chiefly was, that the water in my jug was reduced to about half a pint, and I was suffering much from thirst, having eaten freely of the Bologna sausages after the loss of my mutton. I became very uneasy, and could no longer take any interest in my books. I was overpowered, too, with a desire to sleep, yet trembled at the thought of indulging it, lest there might exist some pernicious influence, like that of burning charcoal, in the confined air of the hold. In the mean time the roll of the brig told me that we were far in the main ocean, and a dull humming sound, which reached my ears as if from an immense distance, convinced me no ordinary gale was blowing. I could not imagine a reason for the absence of Augustus. We were surely far enough advanced on our voyage to allow of my going up. Some accident might have happened to him—but I could think of none which would account for his suffering me to remain so long a prisoner, except, indeed, his having suddenly died or fallen overboard, and upon this idea I could not dwell with any degree of patience. It was possible that we had been baffled by head winds, and were still in the near vicinity of Nantucket. This notion, however, I was forced to abandon; for, such being the case, the brig must have frequently gone about; and I was entirely satisfied, from her continual inclination to the larboard, that she had been sailing all along with a steady breeze on her starboard quarter. Besides, granting that we were still in the neighbourhood of the island, why should not Augustus have visited me and informed me of the circumstance? Pondering in this manner upon the difficulties of my solitary and cheerless condition, I resolved to wait yet another twenty-four hours, when, if no relief were obtained, I would make my way to the trap, and endeavour either to hold a parley with my friend, or get at least a little fresh air through the opening, and a further supply of water from his stateroom. While occupied with this thought, however, I fell, in spite of every exertion to the contrary, into a state of profound sleep, or rather stupor. My dreams were of the most terrific description. Every species of calamity and horror befell me. Among other miseries, I was smothered to death between huge pillows, by demons of the most ghastly and ferocious aspect. Immense serpents held me in their embrace, and looked earnestly in my face with their fearfully shining eyes. Then deserts, limitless, and of the most forlorn and awe-inspiring character, spread themselves out before me. Immensely tall trunks of trees, gray and leafless, rose up in endless succession as far as the eye could reach. Their roots were concealed in wide-spreading morasses, whose dreary water lay intensely black, still, and altogether terrible, beneath. And the strange trees seemed endowed with a human vitality, and, waving to and fro their skeleton arms, were crying to the silent waters for mercy, in the shrill and piercing accents of the most acute agony and despair. The scene changed; and I stood, naked and alone, amid the

burning sand-plains of Zahara. At my feet lay crouched a fierce lion of the tropics. Suddenly his wild eyes opened and fell upon me. With a convulsive bound he sprang to his feet, and laid bare his horrible teeth. In another instant there burst from his red throat a roar like the thunder of the firmament, and I fell impetuously to the earth. Stifling in a paroxysm of terror, I at last found myself partially awake. My dream, then, was not all a dream. Now, at least, I was in possession of my senses. The paws of some huge and real monster were pressing heavily upon my bosom—his hot breath was in my ear—and his white and ghastly fangs were gleaming upon me through the gloom.

Had a thousand lives hung upon the movement of a limb or the utterance of a syllable, I could have neither stirred nor spoken. The beast, whatever it was, retained his position without attempting any immediate violence, while I lay in an utterly helpless, and, I fancied, a dying condition beneath him. I felt that my powers of body and mind were fast leaving me—in a word, that I was perishing, and perishing of sheer fright. My brain swam—I grew deadly sick—my vision failed—even the glaring eyeballs above me grew dim. Making a last strong effort, I at length breathed a faint ejaculation to God, and resigned myself to die. The sound of my voice seemed to arouse all the latent fury of the animal. He precipitated himself at full length upon my body; but what was my astonishment, when, with a long and low whine, he commenced licking my face and hands with the greatest eagerness, and with the most extravagant demonstrations of affection and joy! I was bewildered, utterly lost in amazement—but I could not forget the peculiar whine of my Newfoundland dog Tiger,[8] and the odd manner of his caresses I well knew. It was he. I experienced a sudden rush of blood to my temples—a giddy and overpowering sense of deliverance and reanimation. I rose hurriedly from the mattress upon which I had been lying, and, throwing myself upon the neck of my faithful follower and friend, relieved the long oppression of my bosom in a flood of the most passionate tears.

As upon a former occasion, my conceptions were in a state of the greatest indistinctness and confusion after leaving the mattress. For a long time I found it nearly impossible to connect any ideas—but, by very slow degrees, my thinking faculties returned, and I again called to memory the several incidents of my condition. For the presence of Tiger I tried in vain to account; and after busying myself with a thousand different conjectures respecting him, was forced to content myself with rejoicing that he was with me to share my dreary solitude, and render me comfort by his caresses. Most people love their dogs—but for Tiger I had an affection far more ardent than common; and never, certainly, did any creature more truly deserve it. For seven years he had been my inseparable companion, and in a multitude of instances had given evidence of all the noble qualities for which we

8. See ch. IX, p. 485, n. 5 herein. Some critics question whether the dog begets the dream of the lion or the dream begets Pym's hallucination of the sudden appearance of his dog Tiger. Walter Bezanson has even suggested that the rest of the narrative is Pym's long dream—unfolding in a "troubled sleep."

value the animal. I had rescued him, when a puppy, from the clutches of a malignant little villain in Nantucket, who was leading him, with a rope around his neck, to the water; and the grown dog repaid the obligation, about three years afterward, by saving me from the bludgeon of a street-robber.

Getting now hold of the watch, I found, upon applying it to my ear, that it had again run down; but at this I was not at all surprised, being convinced, from the peculiar state of my feelings, that I had slept, as before, for a very long period of time; how long, it was of course impossible to say. I was burning up with fever, and my thirst was almost intolerable. I felt about the box for my little remaining supply of water; for I had no light, the taper having burnt to the socket of the lantern, and the phosphorus-box not coming readily to hand. Upon finding the jug, however, I discovered it to be empty—Tiger, no doubt, having been tempted to drink it, as well as to devour the remnant of mutton, the bone of which lay, well picked, by the opening of the box. The spoiled meat I could well spare, but my heart sank as I thought of the water. I was feeble in the extreme—so much so that I shook all over, as with an ague, at the slightest movement or exertion. To add to my troubles, the brig was pitching and rolling with great violence, and the oil-casks which lay upon my box were in momentary danger of falling down, so as to block up the only way of ingress or egress. I felt, also, terrible sufferings from sea-sickness. These considerations determined me to make my way, at all hazards, to the trap, and obtain immediate relief, before I should be incapacitated from doing so altogether. Having come to this resolve, I again felt about for the phosphorus-box and tapers. The former I found after some little trouble; but, not discovering the tapers as soon as I had expected (for I remembered very nearly the spot in which I had placed them), I gave up the search for the present, and bidding Tiger lie quiet, began at once my journey towards the trap.

In this attempt my great feebleness became more than ever apparent. It was with the utmost difficulty I could crawl along at all, and very frequently my limbs sank suddenly from beneath me; when, falling prostrate on my face, I would remain for some minutes in a state bordering on insensibility. Still I struggled forward by slow degrees, dreading every moment that I should swoon amid the narrow and intricate windings of the lumber, in which event I had nothing but death to expect as the result. At length, upon making a push forward with all the energy I could command, I struck my forehead violently against the sharp corner of an iron-bound crate. The accident only stunned me for a few moments; but I found, to my inexpressible grief, that the quick and violent roll of the vessel had thrown the crate entirely across my path, so as effectually to block up the passage. With my utmost exertions I could not move it a single inch from its position, it being closely wedged in among the surrounding boxes and ship-furniture. It became necessary, therefore, enfeebled as I was, either to leave the guidance of the whipcord and seek out a new passage, or to climb over the obstacle, and resume the path on the other

side. The former alternative presented too many difficulties and dangers to be thought of without a shudder. In my present weak state of both mind and body, I should infallibly lose my way if I attempted it, and perish miserably amid the dismal and disgusting labyrinths of the hold. I proceeded, therefore, without hesitation, to summon up all my remaining strength and fortitude, and endeavour, as I best might, to clamber over the crate.

Upon standing erect, with this end in view, I found the undertaking even a more serious task than my fears had led me to imagine. On each side of the narrow passage arose a complete wall of various heavy lumber, which the least blunder on my part might be the means of bringing down upon my head; or, if this accident did not occur, the path might be effectually blocked up against my return by the descending mass, as it was in front by the obstacle there. The crate itself was a long and unwieldy box, upon which no foothold could be obtained. In vain I attempted, by every means in my power, to reach the top, with the hope of being thus enabled to draw myself up. Had I succeeded in reaching it, it is certain that my strength would have proved utterly inadequate to the task of getting over, and it was better in every respect that I failed. At length, in a desperate effort to force the crate from its ground, I felt a strong vibration in the side next me. I thrust my hand eagerly to the edge of the planks, and found that a very large one was loose. With my pocket-knife, which luckily I had with me, I succeeded, after great labour, in prying it entirely off; and, getting through the aperture, discovered, to my exceeding joy, that there were no boards on the opposite side—in other words, that the top was wanting, it being the bottom through which I had forced my way. I now met with no important difficulty in proceeding along the line until I finally reached the nail. With a beating heart I stood erect, and with a gentle touch pressed against the cover of the trap. It did not rise as soon as I had expected, and I pressed it with somewhat more determination, still dreading lest some other person than Augustus might be in his stateroom. The door, however, to my astonishment, remained steady, and I became somewhat uneasy, for I knew that it had formerly required little or no effort to remove it. I pushed it strongly—it was nevertheless firm: with all my strength—it still did not give way: with rage, with fury, with despair—it set at defiance my utmost efforts; and it was evident, from the unyielding nature of the resistance, that the hole had either been discovered and effectually nailed up, or that some immense weight had been placed upon it, which it was useless to think of removing.

My sensations were those of extreme horror and dismay. In vain I attempted to reason on the probable cause of my being thus entombed. I could summon up no connected chain of reflection, and, sinking on the floor, gave way, unresistingly, to the most gloomy imaginings, in which the dreadful deaths of thirst, famine, suffocation, and premature interment, crowded upon me as the prominent disasters to be encountered. At length there returned to me some portion of presence of mind. I arose, and felt with my fingers for the seams or cracks

of the aperture. Having found them, I examined them closely to ascertain if they emitted any light from the stateroom; but none was visible. I then forced the penblade of my knife through them, until I met with some hard obstacle. Scraping against it, I discovered it to be a solid mass of iron, which, from its peculiar wavy feel as I passed the blade along it, I concluded to be a chain-cable. The only course now left me was to retrace my way to the box, and there either yield to my sad fate, or try so to tranquillize my mind as to admit of my arranging some plan of escape. I immediately set about the attempt, and succeeded, after innumerable difficulties, in getting back. As I sank, utterly exhausted, upon the mattress, Tiger threw himself at full length by my side, and seemed as if desirous, by his caresses, of consoling me in my troubles, and urging me to bear them with fortitude.

The singularity of his behaviour at length forcibly arrested my attention. After licking my face and hands for some minutes, he would suddenly cease doing so, and utter a low whine. Upon reaching out my hand towards him, I then invariably found him lying on his back, with his paws uplifted. This conduct, so frequently repeated, appeared strange, and I could in no manner account for it. As the dog seemed distressed, I concluded that he had received some injury; and, taking his paws in my hands, I examined them one by one, but found no sign of any hurt. I then supposed him hungry, and gave him a large piece of ham, which he devoured with avidity—afterward, however, resuming his extraordinary manœuvres. I now imagined that he was suffering, like myself, the torments of thirst, and was about adopting this conclusion as the true one, when the idea occurred to me that I had as yet only examined his paws, and that there might possibly be a wound upon some portion of his body or head. The latter I felt carefully over, but found nothing. On passing my hand, however, along his back, I perceived a slight erection of the hair extending completely across it. Probing this with my finger, I discovered a string, and, tracing it up, found that it encircled the whole body. Upon a closer scrutiny, I came across a small slip of what had the feeling of letter paper, through which the string had been fastened in such a manner as to bring it immediately beneath the left shoulder of the animal.

Chapter III

The thought instantly occurred to me that the paper was a note from Augustus, and that some unaccountable accident having happened to prevent his relieving me from my dungeon, he had devised this method of acquainting me with the true state of affairs. Trembling with eagerness, I now commenced another search for my phosphorus matches and tapers. I had a confused recollection of having put them carefully away just before falling asleep; and, indeed, previously to my last journey to the trap, I had been able to remember the exact spot where I had deposited them. But now I endeavoured in vain to call it to mind, and busied myself for a full hour in a fruitless and vexatious

search for the missing articles; never, surely, was there a more tanta-
lizing state of anxiety and suspense. At length, while groping about,
with my head close to the ballast, near the opening of the box, and
outside of it, I perceived a faint glimmering of light in the direction of
the steerage. Greatly surprised, I endeavoured to make my way to-
wards it, as it appeared to be but a few feet from my position. Scarcely
had I moved with this intention, when I lost sight of the glimmer en-
tirely, and, before I could bring it into view again, was obliged to feel
along by the box until I had exactly resumed my original situation.
Now, moving my head with caution to and fro, I found that, by pro-
ceeding slowly, with great care, in an opposite direction to that in
which I had at first started, I was enabled to draw near the light, still
keeping it in view. Presently I came directly upon it (having squeezed
my way through innumerable narrow windings), and found that it pro-
ceeded from some fragments of my matches lying in an empty barrel
turned upon its side. I was wondering how they came in such a place,
when my hand fell upon two or three pieces of taperwax, which had
been evidently mumbled by the dog. I concluded at once that he had
devoured the whole of my supply of candles, and I felt hopeless of be-
ing ever able to read the note of Augustus. The small remnants of the
wax were so mashed up among other rubbish in the barrel, that I
despaired of deriving any service from them, and left them as they
were. The phosphorus, of which there was only a speck or two, I gath-
ered up as well as I could, and returned with it, after much difficulty,
to my box, where Tiger had all the while remained.

What to do next I could not tell. The hold was so intensely dark that
I could not see my hand, however close I would hold it to my face.
The white slip of paper could barely be discerned, and not even that
when I looked at it directly; by turning the exterior portions of the
retina towards it, that is to say, by surveying it slightly askance, I found
that it became in some measure perceptible. Thus the gloom of my
prison may be imagined, and the note of my friend, if indeed it were a
note from him, seemed only likely to throw me into further trouble, by
disquieting to no purpose my already enfeebled and agitated mind.
In vain I revolved in my brain a multitude of absurd expedients for
procuring light—such expedients precisely as a man in the perturbed
sleep occasioned by opium would be apt to fall upon for a similar pur-
pose—each and all of which appear by turns to the dreamer the most
reasonable and the most preposterous of conceptions, just as the rea-
soning or imaginative faculties flicker, alternately, one above the other.
At last an idea occurred to me which seemed rational, and which gave
me cause to wonder, very justly, that I had not entertained it before. I
placed the slip of paper on the back of a book, and, collecting the frag-
ments of the phosphorus matches which I had brought from the bar-
rel, laid them together upon the paper. I then, with the palm of my
hand, rubbed the whole over quickly yet steadily. A clear light diffused
itself immediately throughout the whole surface; and had there been
any writing upon it, I should not have experienced the least difficulty,

I am sure, in reading it. Not a syllable was there, however—nothing but a dreary and unsatisfactory blank; the illumination died away in a few seconds, and my heart died away within me as it went.[9]

I have before stated more than once that my intellect, for some period prior to this, had been in a condition nearly bordering on idiocy. There were, to be sure, momentary intervals of perfect sanity, and, now and then, even of energy; but these were few. It must be remembered that I had been, for many days certainly, inhaling the almost pestilential atmosphere of a close hold in a whaling vessel, and a long portion of that time but scantily supplied with water. For the last fourteen or fifteen hours I had none—nor had I slept during that time. Salt provisions of the most exciting kind had been my chief, and, indeed, since the loss of the mutton, my only supply of food, with the exception of the sea-biscuit; and these latter were utterly useless to me, as they were too dry and hard to be swallowed in the swollen and parched condition of my throat. I was now in a high state of fever, and in every respect exceedingly ill. This will account for the fact that many miserable hours of despondency elapsed after my last adventure with the phosphorus, before the thought suggested itself that I had examined only one side of the paper. I shall not attempt to describe my feelings of rage (for I believe I was more angry than anything else) when the egregious oversight I had committed flashed suddenly upon my perception. The blunder itself would have been unimportant, had not my own folly and impetuosity rendered it otherwise—in my disappointment at not finding some words upon the slip, I had childishly torn it in pieces and thrown it away, it was impossible to say where.

From the worst part of this dilemma I was relieved by the sagacity of Tiger. Having got, after a long search, a small piece of the note, I put it to the dog's nose, and endeavoured to make him understand that he must bring me the rest of it. To my astonishment (for I had taught him none of the usual tricks for which his breed are famous), he seemed to enter at once into my meaning, and, rummaging about for a few moments, soon found another considerable portion. Bringing me this, he paused a while, and, rubbing his nose against my hand, appeared to be waiting for my approval of what he had done. I patted him on the head, when he immediately made off again. It was now some minutes before he came back—but when he did come, he brought with him a large slip, which proved to be all the paper missing—it having been torn, it seems, only into three pieces. Luckily, I had no trouble in finding what few fragments of the phosphorus were left—being guided by the indistinct glow one or two of the particles still emitted. My difficulties had taught me the necessity of caution, and I now took time to reflect upon what I was about to do. It was very probable, I considered, that some words were written upon that side of the paper which had not been examined—but which side was that? Fitting the pieces together gave me no clew in this respect, although it assured me that

9. Later, in an apparent contradiction, Pym tells us that Augustus wrote on the back of the letter (see Chapter V and cf. Chapter II). Critics have debated whether this is simply an error or a metafictional sleight-of-hand.

the words (if there were any) would be found all on one side, and con-
nected in a proper manner, as written. There was the greater necessity
of ascertaining the point in question beyond a doubt, as the phospho-
rus remaining would be altogether insufficient for a third attempt,
should I fail in the one I was now about to make. I placed the paper
on a book as before, and sat for some minutes thoughtfully revolving
the matter over in my mind. At last I thought it barely possible that the
written side might have some unevenness on its surface, which a deli-
cate sense of feeling might enable me to detect. I determined to make
the experiment, and passed my finger very carefully over the side
which first presented itself—nothing however, was perceptible, and I
turned the paper, adjusting it on the book. I now again carried my
forefinger cautiously along, when I was aware of an exceedingly slight,
but still discernible glow, which followed as it proceeded. This, I
knew, must arise from some very minute remaining particles of the
phosphorus with which I had covered the paper in my previous at-
tempt. The other, or under side, then, was that on which lay the writ-
ing, if writing there should finally prove to be. Again I turned the note,
and went to work as I had previously done. Having rubbed in the
phosphorus, a brilliancy ensued as before—but this time several lines
of MS. in a large hand, and apparently in red ink, became distinctly
visible. The glimmer, although sufficiently bright, was but momentary.
Still, had I not been too greatly excited, there would have been ample
time enough for me to peruse the whole three sentences before me—
for I saw there were three. In my anxiety, however, to read all at once,
I succeeded only in reading the seven concluding words, which thus
appeared: "*blood—your life depends upon lying close.*"

Had I been able to ascertain the entire contents of the note—the
full meaning of the admonition which my friend had thus attempted
to convey, that admonition, even although it should have revealed a
story of disaster the most unspeakable, could not, I am firmly con-
vinced, have imbued my mind with one tithe of the harrowing and yet
indefinable horror with which I was inspired by the fragmentary warn-
ing thus received. And "*blood*" too, that word of all words—so rife at
all times with mystery, and suffering, and terror—how trebly full of
import did it now appear—how chillily and heavily (disjointed, as it
thus was, from any foregoing words to qualify or render it distinct) did
its vague syllables fall, amid the deep gloom of my prison, into the in-
nermost recesses of my soul!

Augustus had, undoubtedly, good reasons for wishing me to remain
concealed, and I formed a thousand surmises as to what they could
be—but I could think of nothing affording a satisfactory solution of
the mystery. Just after returning from my last journey to the trap, and
before my attention had been otherwise directed by the singular con-
duct of Tiger, I had come to the resolution of making myself heard at
all events by those on board, or, if I could not succeed in this directly,
of trying to cut my way through the orlop deck.[1] The half certainty

1. The lowest deck of a ship, though the term is usually applied to warships.

which I felt of being able to accomplish one of these two purposes in
the last emergency, had given me courage (which I should not other-
wise have had) to endure the evils of my situation. The few words I
had been able to read, however, had cut me off from these final re-
sources, and I now, for the first time, felt all the misery of my fate. In
a paroxysm of despair I threw myself again upon the mattress, where,
for about the period of a day and night, I lay in a kind of stupor, re-
lieved only by momentary intervals of reason and recollection.

At length I once more arose, and busied myself in reflection upon
the horrors which encompassed me. For another twenty-four hours it
was barely possible that I might exist without water—for a longer time
I could not do so. During the first portion of my imprisonment I had
made free use of the cordials with which Augustus had supplied me,
but they only served to excite fever, without in the least degree assuag-
ing my thirst. I had now only about a gill left, and this was of a species
of strong peach liqueur at which my stomach revolted. The sausages
were entirely consumed; of the ham nothing remained but a small
piece of the skin; and all the biscuit, except a few fragments of one,
had been eaten by Tiger. To add to my troubles, I found that my
headache was increasing momentarily, and with it the species of delir-
ium which had distressed me more or less since my first falling asleep.
For some hours past it had been with the greatest difficulty I could
breathe at all, and now each attempt at so doing was attended with the
most distressing spasmodic action of the chest. But there was still an-
other and very different source of disquietude, and one, indeed, whose
harassing terrors had been the chief means of arousing me to exertion
from my stupor on the mattress. It arose from the demeanour of the
dog.

I first observed an alteration in his conduct while rubbing in the
phosphorus on the paper in my last attempt. As I rubbed, he ran his
nose against my hand with a slight snarl; but I was too greatly excited
at the time to pay much attention to the circumstance. Soon after-
ward, it will be remembered, I threw myself on the mattress, and fell
into a species of lethargy. Presently I became aware of a singular hiss-
ing sound close at my ears, and discovered it to proceed from Tiger,
who was panting and wheezing in a state of the greatest apparent ex-
citement, his eyeballs flashing fiercely through the gloom. I spoke to
him, when he replied with a low growl, and then remained quiet.
Presently I relapsed into my stupor, from which I was again awakened
in a similar manner. This was repeated three or four times, until fi-
nally his behaviour inspired me with so great a degree of fear that I be-
came fully aroused. He was now lying close by the door of the box,
snarling fearfully, although in a kind of under tone, and grinding his
teeth as if strongly convulsed. I had no doubt whatever that the want
of water or the confined atmosphere of the hold had driven him mad,
and I was at a loss what course to pursue. I could not endure the
thought of killing him, yet it seemed absolutely necessary for my own
safety. I could distinctly perceive his eyes fastened upon me with an
expression of the most deadly animosity, and I expected every instant

that he would attack me. At last I could endure my terrible situation no longer, and determined to make my way from the box at all hazards, and despatch him, if his opposition should render it necessary for me to do so. To get out, I had to pass directly over his body, and he already seemed to anticipate my design—raising himself upon his fore legs (as I perceived by the altered position of his eyes), and displaying the whole of his white fangs, which were easily discernible. I took the remains of the ham-skin, and the bottle containing the liqueur, and secured them about my person, together with a large carving-knife which Augustus had left me—then, folding my cloak as closely around me as possible, I made a movement towards the mouth of the box. No sooner did I do this than the dog sprang with a loud growl towards my throat. The whole weight of his body struck me on the right shoulder, and I fell violently to the left, while the enraged animal passed entirely over me. I had fallen upon my knees, with my head buried among the blankets, and these protected me from a second furious assault, during which I felt the sharp teeth pressing vigorously upon the woollen which enveloped my neck—yet, luckily, without being able to penetrate all the folds. I was now beneath the dog, and a few moments would place me completely in his power. Despair gave me strength, and I rose bodily up, shaking him from me by main force, and dragging with me the blankets from the mattress. These I now threw over him, and before he could extricate himself I had got through the door and closed it effectually against his pursuit. In this struggle, however, I had been forced to drop the morsel of ham-skin, and I now found my whole stock of provisions reduced to a single gill[2] of liqueur. As this reflection crossed my mind, I felt myself actuated by one of those fits of perverseness[3] which might be supposed to influence a spoiled child in similar circumstances, and, raising the bottle to my lips, I drained it to the last drop, and dashed it furiously upon the floor.

Scarcely had the echo of the crash died away, when I heard my name pronounced in an eager but subdued voice, issuing from the direction of the steerage. So unexpected was anything of the kind, and so intense was the emotion excited within me by the sound, that I endeavoured in vain to reply. My powers of speech totally failed, and, in an agony of terror lest my friend should conclude me dead, and return without attempting to reach me, I stood up between the crates near the door of the box, trembling convulsively, and gasping and struggling for utterance. Had a thousand worlds depended upon a syllable, I could not have spoken it. There was a slight movement now audible among the lumber somewhere forward of my station. The sound presently grew less distinct, then again less so, and still less. Shall I ever forget my feelings at this moment? He was going—my friend— my companion, from whom I had a right to expect so much—he was

2. An old-fashioned unit of liquid measure, about 4 ounces American or about 5 ounces British; cf. p. 454.
3. The idea of perversity was not only a long-standing theological concept (indicating original sin or "depravity") but also in Poe's time a psychological concept, indicating a propensity to harm oneself physically, mentally, socially, and of course spiritually. See "The Black Cat" (p. 350 herein) and the essay tale, "The Imp of the Perverse" (pp. 401ff.).

going—he would abandon me—he was gone! He would leave me to perish miserably, to expire in the most horrible and loathsome of dungeons—and one word—one little syllable would save me—yet that single syllable I could not utter! I felt, I am sure, more than ten thousand times the agonies of death itself. My brain reeled, and I fell, deadly sick, against the end of the box.

As I fell, the carving-knife was shaken out from the waistband of my pantaloons, and dropped with a rattling sound to the floor. Never did any strain of the richest melody come so sweetly to my ears! With the intensest anxiety I listened to ascertain the effect of the noise upon Augustus—for I knew that the person who called my name could be no one but himself. All was silent for some moments. At length I again heard the word *Arthur!* repeated in a low tone, and one full of hesitation. Reviving hope loosened at once my powers of speech, and I now screamed, at the top of my voice, "*Augustus! oh Augustus!*" "Hush—for God's sake be silent!" he replied, in a voice trembling with agitation; "I will be with you immediately—as soon as I can make my way through the hold." For a long time I heard him moving among the lumber, and every moment seemed to me an age. At length I felt his hand upon my shoulder, and he placed at the same moment a bottle of water to my lips. Those only who have been suddenly redeemed from the jaws of the tomb, or who have known the insufferable torments of thirst under circumstances as aggravated as those which encompassed me in my dreary prison, can form any idea of the unutterable transports which that one long draught of the richest of all physical luxuries afforded.

When I had in some degree satisfied my thirst, Augustus produced from his pocket three or four cold boiled potatoes, which I devoured with the greatest avidity. He had brought with him a light in a dark lantern, and the grateful rays afforded me scarcely less comfort than the food and drink. But I was impatient to learn the cause of his protracted absence, and he proceeded to recount what had happened on board during my incarceration.

Chapter IV

The brig put to sea, as I had supposed, in about an hour after he had left the watch. This was on the twentieth of June. It will be remembered that I had then been in the hold for three days; and, during this period, there was so constant a bustle on board, and so much running to and fro, especially in the cabin and staterooms, that he had had no chance of visiting me without the risk of having the secret of the trap discovered. When at length he did come, I had assured him that I was doing as well as possible; and, therefore, for the two next days he felt but little uneasiness on my account—still, however, watching an opportunity of going down. It was not *until the fourth day* that he found one. Several times during this interval he had made up his mind to let his father know of the adventure, and have me come up at once; but we were still within reaching distance of Nantucket,

and it was doubtful, from some expressions which had escaped Captain Barnard, whether he would not immediately put back if he discovered me to be on board. Besides, upon thinking the matter over, Augustus, so he told me, could not imagine that I was in immediate want, or that I would hesitate, in such case, to make myself heard at the trap. When, therefore, he considered everything, he concluded to let me stay until he could meet with an opportunity of visiting me unobserved. This, as I said before, did not occur until the fourth day after his bringing me the watch, and the seventh since I had first entered the hold. He then went down without taking with him any water or provisions, intending in the first place merely to call my attention, and get me to come from the box to the trap—when he would go up to the stateroom and thence hand me down a supply. When he descended for this purpose he found that I was asleep, for it seems that I was snoring very loudly. From all the calculations I can make on the subject, this must have been the slumber into which I fell just after my return from the trap with the watch, and which, consequently, must have lasted *for more than three entire days and nights* at the very least. Latterly, I have, had reason, both from my own experience and the assurance of others, to be acquainted with the strong soporific effects of the stench arising from old fish-oil when closely confined; and when I think of the condition of the hold in which I was imprisoned, and the long period during which the brig had been used as a whaling vessel, I am more inclined to wonder that I awoke at all, after once falling asleep, than that I should have slept uninterruptedly for the period specified above.

Augustus called to me at first in a low voice and without closing the trap—but I made him no reply. He then shut the trap, and spoke to me in a louder, and finally in a very loud tone—still I continued to snore. He was now at a loss what to do. It would take him some time to make his way through the lumber to my box, and in the mean while his absence would be noticed by Captain Barnard, who had occasion for his services every minute, in arranging and copying papers connected with the business of the voyage. He determined, therefore, upon reflection, to ascend, and await another opportunity of visiting me. He was the more easily induced to this resolve, as my slumber appeared to be of the most tranquil nature, and he could not suppose that I had undergone any inconvenience from my incarceration. He had just made up his mind on these points when his attention was arrested by an unusual bustle, the sound of which proceeded apparently from the cabin. He sprang through the trap as quickly as possible, closed it, and threw open the door of his stateroom. No sooner had he put his foot over the threshold than a pistol flashed in his face, and he was knocked down, at the same moment, by a blow from a handspike.

A strong hand held him on the cabin floor, with a tight grasp upon his throat—still he was able to see what was going on around him. His father was tied hand and foot, and lying along the steps of the companion-way with his head down, and a deep wound in the forehead, from which the blood was flowing in a continued stream. He

spoke not a word, and was apparently dying. Over him stood the first mate, eying him with an expression of fiendish derision, and deliberately searching his pockets, from which he presently drew forth a large wallet and a chronometer. Seven of the crew (among whom was the cook, a negro) were rummaging the staterooms on the larboard for arms, where they soon equipped themselves with muskets and ammunition. Besides Augustus and Captain Barnard, there were nine men altogether in the cabin, and these among the most ruffianly of the brig's company. The villains now went upon deck, taking my friend with them, after having secured his arms behind his back. They proceeded straight to the forecastle, which was fastened down—two of the mutineers standing by it with axes—two also at the main hatch. The mate called out in a loud voice, "Do you hear there below? tumble up with you—one by one, now, mark that—and no grumbling." It was some minutes before any one appeared: at last an Englishman, who had shipped as a raw hand, came up, weeping piteously, and entreating the mate in the most humble manner to spare his life. The only reply was a blow on the forehead from an axe. The poor fellow fell to the deck without a groan, and the black cook lifted him up in his arms as he would a child, and tossed him deliberately into the sea. Hearing the blow and the plunge of the body, the men below could now be induced to venture on deck neither by threats nor promises, until a proposition was made to smoke them out. A general rush then ensued, and for a moment it seemed possible that the brig might be retaken. The mutineers, however, succeeded at last in closing the forecastle effectually before more than six of their opponents could get up. These six, finding themselves so greatly outnumbered and without arms, submitted after a brief struggle. The mate gave them fair words—no doubt with a view of inducing those below to yield, for they had no difficulty in hearing all that was said on deck. The result proved his sagacity, no less than his diabolical villany. All in the forecastle presently signified their intention of submitting, and, ascending one by one, were pinioned and thrown on their backs together with the first six—there being in all, of the crew who were not concerned in the mutiny, twenty-seven.[4]

A scene of the most horrible butchery ensued. The bound seamen were dragged to the gangway. Here the cook stood with an axe, striking each victim on the head as he was forced over the side of the vessel by the other mutineers. In this manner twenty-two perished, and Augustus had given himself up for lost, expecting every moment his own turn to come next. But it seemed that the villains were now either weary, or in some measure disgusted with their bloody labour; for the four remaining prisoners, together with my friend, who had been thrown on the deck with the rest, were respited while the mate sent below for rum, and the whole murderous party held a drunken carouse, which lasted until sunset. They now fell to disputing in regard to the fate of the survivers, who lay not more than four paces off,

4. The second *SLM* portion of the story stops here.

and could distinguish every word said. Upon some of the mutineers the liquor appeared to have a softening effect, for several voices were heard in favour of releasing the captives altogether, on condition of joining the mutiny and sharing the profits. The black cook, however (who in all respects was a perfect demon, and who seemed to exert as much influence, if not more, than the mate himself), would listen to no proposition of the kind, and rose repeatedly for the purpose of resuming his work at the gangway. Fortunately, he was so far overcome by intoxication as to be easily restrained by the less blood-thirsty of the party, among whom was a line-manager,[5] who went by the name of Dirk Peters. This man was the son of an Indian squaw of the tribe of Upsarokas, who live among the fastnesses of the Black Hills near the source of the Missouri. His father was a fur-trader, I believe, or at least connected in some manner with the Indian trading-posts on Lewis river. Peters himself was one of the most purely ferocious-looking men I ever beheld. He was short in stature—not more than four feet eight inches high—but his limbs were of the most Herculean mould. His hands, especially, were so enormously thick and broad as hardly to retain a human shape. His arms, as well as legs, were *bowed* in the most singular manner, and appeared to possess no flexibility whatever. His head was equally deformed, being of immense size, with an indentation on the crown (like that on the head of most negroes), and entirely bald. To conceal this latter deficiency, which did not proceed from old age, he usually wore a wig formed of any hair-like material which presented itself—occasionally the skin of a Spanish dog or American grizzly bear. At the time spoken of he had on a portion of one of these bearskins; and it added no little to the natural ferocity of his countenance, which betook of the Upsaroka character. The mouth extended nearly from ear to ear; the lips were thin, and seemed, like some other portions of his frame, to be devoid of natural pliancy, so that the ruling expression never varied under the influence of any emotion whatever. This ruling expression may be conceived when it is considered that the teeth were exceedingly long and protruding, and never even partially covered, in any instance, by the lips. To pass this man with a casual glance, one might imagine him to be convulsed with laughter—but a second look would induce a shuddering acknowledgment, that if such an expression were indicative of merriment, the merriment must be that of a demon. Of this singular being many anecdotes were prevalent among the seafaring men of Nantucket. These anecdotes went to prove his prodigious strength when under excitement, and some of them had given rise to a doubt of his sanity. But on board the Grampus, it seems, he was regarded at the time of the mutiny with feelings more of derision than of anything else. I have been thus particular in speaking of Dirk Peters, because, ferocious as he appeared, he proved the main instrument in preserving the life of Augustus, and because I shall have frequent occasion to mention him

5. The man who works the coil of a line tied to the harpoon. Poe derives some of the description from Irving's *Astoria*, which he reviewed in 1837.

hereafter in the course of my narrative—a narrative, let me here say, which, in its latter portions, will be found to include incidents of a nature so entirely out of the range of human experience, and for this reason so far beyond the limits of human credulity, that I proceed in utter hopelessness of obtaining credence for all that I shall tell, yet confidently trusting in time and progressing science to verify some of the most important and most improbable of my statements.

After much indecision and two or three violent quarrels, it was determined at last that all the prisoners (with the exception of Augustus, whom Peters insisted in a jocular manner upon keeping as his clerk) should be set adrift in one of the smallest whaleboats. The mate went down into the cabin to see if Captain Barnard was still living—for, it will be remembered, he was left below when the mutineers came up. Presently the two made their appearance, the captain pale as death, but somewhat recovered from the effects of his wound. He spoke to the men in a voice hardly articulate, entreated them not to set him adrift, but to return to their duty, and promising to land them wherever they chose, and to take no steps for bringing them to justice. He might as well have spoken to the winds. Two of the ruffians seized him by the arms and hurled him over the brig's side into the boat, which had been lowered while the mate went below. The four men who were lying on the deck were then untied and ordered to follow, which they did without attempting any resistance—Augustus being still left in his painful position, although he struggled and prayed only for the poor satisfaction of being permitted to bid his father farewell. A handful of sea-biscuit and a jug of water were now handed down; but neither mast, sail, oar, nor compass. The boat was towed astern for a few minutes, during which the mutineers held another consultation—it was then finally cut adrift. By this time night had come on—there were neither moon nor stars visible—and a short and ugly sea was running, although there was no great deal of wind. The boat was instantly out of sight, and little hope could be entertained for the unfortunate sufferers who were in it. This event happened, however, in latitude 35° 30' north, longitude 61° 20' west, and consequently at no very great distance from the Bermuda Islands. Augustus therefore endeavoured to console himself with the idea that the boat might either succeed in reaching the land, or come sufficiently near to be fallen in with by vessels off the coast.

All sail was now put upon the brig, and she continued her original course to the southwest—the mutineers being bent upon some piratical expedition, in which, from all that could be understood, a ship was to be intercepted on her way from the Cape Verd Islands to Porto Rico.[6] No attention was paid to Augustus, who was untied and suffered to go about anywhere forward of the cabin companion-way. Dirk Peters treated him with some degree of kindness, and on one occasion saved him from the brutality of the cook. His situation was still one of the most precarious, as the men were continually intoxicated, and

6. Old-fashioned spellings for Cape Verde and Puerto Rico.

there was no relying upon their continued good-humour or careless-
ness in regard to himself. His anxiety on my account he represented,
however, as the most distressing result of his condition; and, indeed, I
had never reason to doubt the sincerity of his friendship. More than
once he had resolved to acquaint the mutineers with the secret of my
being on board, but was restrained from so doing, partly through rec-
ollection of the atrocities he had already beheld, and partly through a
hope of being able soon to bring me relief. For the latter purpose he
was constantly on the watch; but, in spite of the most constant vigi-
lance, three days elapsed after the boat was cut adrift before any
chance occurred. At length, on the night of the third day, there came
on a heavy blow from the eastward, and all hands were called up to
take in sail. During the confusion which ensued, he made his way be-
low unobserved, and into the stateroom. What was his grief and horror
in discovering that the latter had been rendered a place of deposite for
a variety of sea-stores and ship-furniture, and that several fathoms of
old chain-cable, which had been stowed away beneath the companion-
ladder, had been dragged thence to make room for a chest, and were
now lying immediately upon the trap! To remove it without discovery
was impossible, and he returned on deck as quickly as he could. As he
came up the mate seized him by the throat, and demanding what he
had been doing in the cabin, was about flinging him over the larboard
bulwark, when his life was again preserved through the interference of
Dirk Peters. Augustus was now put in handcuffs (of which there were
several pairs on board), and his feet lashed tightly together. He was
then taken into the steerage, and thrown into a lower berth next to the
forecastle bulkheads, with the assurance that he should never put his
foot on deck again "until the brig was no longer a brig." This was the
expression of the cook, who threw him into the berth—it is hardly pos-
sible to say what precise meaning was intended by the phrase. The
whole affair, however, proved the ultimate means of my relief, as will
presently appear.

Chapter V

For some minutes after the cook had left the forecastle, Augustus
abandoned himself to despair, never hoping to leave the berth alive.
He now came to the resolution of acquainting the first of the men who
should come down with my situation, thinking it better to let me take
my chance with the mutineers than perish of thirst in the hold—for it
had been ten days since I was first imprisoned, and my jug of water
was not a plentiful supply even for four. As he was thinking on this
subject, the idea came all at once into his head that it might be possi-
ble to communicate with me by the way of the main hold. In any other
circumstances, the difficulty and hazard of the undertaking would
have prevented him from attempting it; but now he had, at all events,
little prospect of life, and consequently little to lose—he bent his
whole mind, therefore, upon the task.

His handcuffs were the first consideration. At first he saw no

method of removing them, and feared that he should thus be baffled in the very outset; but, upon a closer scrutiny, he discovered that the irons could be slipped off and on at pleasure with very little effort or inconvenience, merely by squeezing his hands through them—this species of manacle being altogether ineffectual in confining young persons, in whom the smaller bones readily yield to pressure. He now untied his feet, and, leaving the cord in such a manner that it could easily be readjusted in the event of any person's coming down, proceeded to examine the bulkhead where it joined the berth. The partition here was of soft pine board, an inch thick, and he saw that he should have little trouble in cutting his way through. A voice was now heard at the forecastle companion-way, and he had just time to put his right hand into its handcuff (the left had not been removed), and to draw the rope in a slipknot around his ankle, when Dirk Peters came below, followed by Tiger, who immediately leaped into the berth and lay down. The dog had been brought on board by Augustus, who knew my attachment to the animal, and thought it would give me pleasure to have him with me during the voyage. He went up to our house for him immediately after first taking me into the hold, but did not think of mentioning the circumstance upon his bringing the watch. Since the mutiny, Augustus had not seen him before his appearance with Dirk Peters, and had given him up for lost, supposing him to have been thrown overboard by some of the malignant villains belonging to the mate's gang. It appeared afterward that he had crawled into a hole beneath a whaleboat, from which, not having room to turn round, he could not extricate himself. Peters at last let him out, and with a species of good feeling which my friend knew well how to appreciate, had now brought him to him in the forecastle as a companion, leaving at the same time some salt junk and potatoes, with a can of water; he then went on deck, promising to come down with something more to eat on the next day.

When he had gone, Augustus freed both hands from the manacles and unfastened his feet. He then turned down the head of the mattress on which he had been lying, and with his penknife (for the ruffians had not thought it worth while to search him) commenced cutting vigorously across one of the partition planks, as closely as possible to the floor of the berth. He chose to cut here, because, if suddenly interrupted, he would be able to conceal what had been done by letting the head of the mattress fall into its proper position. For the remainder of the day, however, no disturbance occurred, and by night he had completely divided the plank. It should here be observed, that none of the crew occupied the forecastle as a sleeping-place, living altogether in the cabin since the mutiny, drinking the wines, and feasting on the seastores of Captain Barnard, and giving no more heed than was absolutely necessary to the navigation of the brig. These circumstances proved fortunate both for myself and Augustus; for, had matters been otherwise, he would have found it impossible to reach me. As it was, he proceeded with confidence in his design. It was near daybreak, however, before he completed the second division of the board (which

was about a foot above the first cut), thus making an aperture quite large enough to admit his passage through with facility to the main orlop deck. Having got here, he made his way with but little trouble to the lower main hatch, although in so doing he had to scramble over tiers of oil-casks piled nearly as high as the upper deck, there being barely room enough left for his body. Upon reaching the hatch, he found that Tiger had followed him below, squeezing between two rows of the casks. It was now too late, however, to attempt getting to me before dawn, as the chief difficulty lay in passing through the close stowage in the lower hold. He therefore resolved to return, and wait till the next night. With this design he proceeded to loosen the hatch, so that he might have as little detention as possible when he should come again. No sooner had he loosened it than Tiger sprang eagerly to the small opening produced, snuffed for a moment, and then uttered a long whine, scratching at the same time, as if anxious to remove the covering with his paws. There could be no doubt, from his behaviour, that he was aware of my being in the hold, and Augustus thought it possible that he would be able to get to me if he put him down. He now hit upon the expedient of sending the note, as it was especially desirable that I should make no attempt at forcing my way out, at least under existing circumstances, and there could be no certainty of his getting to me himself on the morrow as he intended. After events proved how fortunate it was that the idea occurred to him as it did: for, had it not been for the receipt of the note, I should undoubtedly have fallen upon some plan, however desperate, of alarming the crew, and both our lives would most probably have been sacrificed in consequence.

Having concluded to write, the difficulty was now to procure the materials for so doing. An old toothpick was soon made into a pen; and this by means of feeling altogether, for the between-decks were as dark as pitch. Paper enough was obtained from the back of a letter—a duplicate of the forged letter from Mr. Ross. This had been the original draught; but the handwriting not being sufficiently well imitated, Augustus had written another, thrusting the first, by good fortune, into his coat-pocket, where it was now most opportunely discovered.[7] Ink alone was thus wanting, and a substitute was immediately found for this by means of a slight incision with the penknife on the back of a finger just above the nail—a copious flow of blood ensuing, as usual from wounds in that vicinity. The note was now written, as well as it could be in the dark and under the circumstances. It briefly explained that a mutiny had taken place; that Captain Barnard was set adrift; and that I might expect immediate relief as far as provisions were concerned, but must not venture upon making any disturbance. It con-

7. This scene is supposed to contain the previously mentioned error of Poe's regarding the letter. Pym says that down in the hold he saw a note on paper that was blank on one side but had Augustus's message on the other side; but now there would seem to be writing on both sides. Letters in the early 19th century were folded over and the address written on the back. But was the flawed original addressed? Or was this the forgery? Did Augustus write on the same side as the text of the letter, perhaps below it? Is all this Poe's error or is it thematically significant for the epistemological issues of the novel?

cluded with these words, "*I have scrawled this with blood—your life de-pends upon lying close.*"

The slip of paper being tied upon the dog, he was now put down the hatchway, and Augustus made the best of his way back to the forecas-tle, where he found no reason to believe that any of the crew had been in his absence. To conceal the hole in the partition, he drove his knife in just above it, and hung up a pea-jacket which he found in the berth. His handcuffs were then replaced, and also the rope around his an-kles.

These arrangements were scarcely completed when Dirk Peters came below, very drunk, but in excellent humour, and bringing with him my friend's allowance of provision for the day. This consisted of a dozen large Irish potatoes roasted, and a pitcher of water. He sat for some time on a chest by the berth, and talked freely about the mate, and the general concerns of the brig. His demeanour was exceedingly capricious and even grotesque. At one time Augustus was much alarmed by his odd conduct. At last, however, he went on deck, mut-tering a promise to bring his prisoner a good dinner on the morrow. During the day two of the crew (harpooners) came down, accompa-nied by the cook, all three in nearly the last stage of intoxication. Like Peters, they made no scruple of talking unreservedly about their plans. It appeared that they were much divided among themselves as to their ultimate course, agreeing in no point except the attack on the ship from the Cape Verd Islands, with which they were in hourly expecta-tion of meeting. As far as could be ascertained, the mutiny had not been brought about altogether for the sake of booty; a private pique of the chief mate's against Captain Barnard having been the main insti-gation. There now seemed to be two principal factions among the crew—one headed by the mate, the other by the cook. The former party were for seizing the first suitable vessel which should present it-self, and equipping it at some of the West India Islands for a piratical cruise. The latter division, however, which was the stronger, and in-cluded Dirk Peters among its partisans, were bent upon pursuing the course originally laid out for the brig into the South Pacific; there ei-ther to take whale, or act otherwise, as circumstances should suggest. The representations of Peters, who had frequently visited these re-gions, had great weight, apparently, with the mutineers, wavering as they were between half-engendered notions of profit and pleasure. He dwelt on the world of novelty and amusement to be found among the innumerable islands of the Pacific, on the perfect security and free-dom from all restraint to be enjoyed, but, more particularly, on the de-liciousness of the climate, on the abundant means of good living, and on the voluptuous beauty of the women. As yet, nothing had been ab-solutely determined upon; but the pictures of the hybrid line-manager were taking strong hold upon the ardent imaginations of the seamen, and there was every probability that his intentions would be finally carried into effect.

The three men went away in about an hour, and no one else entered the forecastle all day. Augustus lay quiet until nearly night. He then

freed himself from the rope and irons, and prepared for his attempt. A bottle was found in one of the berths, and this he filled with water from the pitcher left by Peters, storing his pockets at the same time with cold potatoes. To his great joy he also came across a lantern, with a small piece of tallow candle in it. This he could light at any moment, as he had in his possession a box of phosphorus matches. When it was quite dark, he got through the hole in the bulkhead, having taken the precaution to arrange the bedclothes in the berth so as to convey the idea of a person covered up. When through, he hung up the pea-jacket on his knife, as before, to conceal the aperture—this manœuvre being easily effected, as he did not readjust the piece of plank taken out until afterward. He was now on the main orlop deck, and proceeded to make his way, as before, between the upper deck and the oil-casks to the main hatchway. Having reached this, he lit the piece of candle, and descended, groping with extreme difficulty among the compact stowage of the hold. In a few moments he became alarmed at the insufferable stench and the closeness of the atmosphere. He could not think it possible that I had survived my confinement for so long a period breathing so oppressive an air. He called my name repeatedly, but I made him no reply, and his apprehensions seemed thus to be confirmed. The brig was rolling violently, and there was so much noise in consequence, that it was useless to listen for any weak sound, such as those of my breathing or snoring. He threw open the lantern, and held it as high as possible, whenever an opportunity occurred, in order that, by observing the light, I might, if alive, be aware that succour was approaching. Still nothing was heard from me, and the supposition of my death began to assume the character of certainty. He determined, nevertheless, to force a passage, if possible, to the box, and at least ascertain beyond a doubt the truth of his surmises. He pushed on for some time in a most pitiable state of anxiety, until, at length, he found the pathway utterly blocked up, and that there was no possibility of making any farther way by the course in which he had set out. Overcome now by his feelings, he threw himself among the lumber in despair, and wept like a child. It was at this period that he heard the crash occasioned by the bottle which I had thrown down. Fortunate, indeed, was it that the incident occurred—for, upon this incident, trivial as it appears, the thread of my destiny depended. Many years elapsed, however, before I was aware of this fact. A natural shame and regret for his weakness and indecision prevented Augustus from confiding to me at once what a more intimate and unreserved communion afterward induced him to reveal.[8] Upon finding his further progress in the hold impeded by obstacles which he could not overcome, he had resolved to abandon his attempt at reaching me, and return at once to the forecastle. Before condemning him entirely on this head, the ha-

8. Another supposed error by Poe. Many years are said to elapse before Pym learns of Augustus's almost calling off the search, and Augustus dies shortly after this scene. Some critics point out, however, that Pym could easily have learned the details from others, like Dirk Peters. The text merely states, not that *Augustus* informed Pym many years later, but that Pym became fully "aware" of the fact much later.

rassing circumstances which embarrassed him should be taken into consideration. The night was fast wearing away, and his absence from the forecastle might be discovered; and, indeed, would necessarily be so, if he should fail to get back to the berth by daybreak. His candle was expiring in the socket, and there would be the greatest difficulty in retracing his way to the hatchway in the dark. It must be allowed, too, that he had every good reason to believe me dead; in which event no benefit could result to me from his reaching the box, and a world of danger would be encountered to no purpose by himself. He had repeatedly called, and I had made him no answer. I had been now eleven days and nights with no more water than that contained in the jug which he had left with me, a supply which it was not at all probable I had hoarded in the beginning of my confinement, as I had had every cause to expect a speedy release. The atmosphere of the hold, too, must have appeared to him, coming from the comparatively open air of the steerage, of a nature absolutely poisonous, and by far more intolerable than it had seemed to me upon my first taking up my quarters in the box—the hatchways at that time having been constantly open for many months previous. Add to these considerations that of the scene of bloodshed and terror so lately witnessed by my friend; his confinement, privations, and narrow escapes from death; together with the frail and equivocal tenure by which he still existed—circumstances all so well calculated to prostrate every energy of mind—and the reader will be easily brought, as I have been, to regard his apparent falling off in friendship and in faith with sentiments rather of sorrow than of anger.

The crash of the bottle was distinctly heard, yet Augustus was not sure that it proceeded from the hold. The doubt, however, was sufficient inducement to persevere. He clambered up nearly to the orlop deck by means of the stowage, and then watching for a lull in the pitchings of the vessel, he called out to me in as loud a tone as he could command—regardless, for the moment, of the danger of being overheard by the crew. It will be remembered that on this occasion the voice reached me, but I was so entirely overcome by violent agitation as to be incapable of reply. Confident, now, that his worst apprehensions were well founded, he descended, with a view of getting back to the forecastle without loss of time. In his haste some small boxes were thrown down, the noise occasioned by which I heard, as will be recollected. He had made considerable progress on his return when the fall of the knife again caused him to hesitate. He retraced his steps immediately, and, clambering up the stowage a second time, called out my name, loudly as before, having watched for a lull. This time I found voice to answer. Overjoyed at discovering me to be still alive, he now resolved to brave every difficulty and danger in reaching me. Having extricated himself as quickly as possible from the labyrinth of lumber by which he was hemmed in, he at length struck into an opening which promised better, and finally, after a series of struggles, arrived at the box in a state of utter exhaustion.

Chapter VI

The leading particulars of this narration were all that Augustus communicated to me while we remained near the box. It was not until afterward that he entered fully into all the details. He was apprehensive of being missed, and I was wild with impatience to leave my detested place of confinement. We resolved to make our way at once to the hole in the bulkhead, near which I was to remain for the present, while he went through to reconnoitre. To leave Tiger in the box was what neither of us could endure to think of; yet, how to act otherwise was the question. He now seemed to be perfectly quiet, and we could not even distinguish the sound of his breathing upon applying our ears closely to the box. I was convinced that he was dead, and determined to open the door. We found him lying at full length, apparently in a deep stupor, yet still alive. No time was to be lost, yet I could not bring myself to abandon an animal who had now been twice instrumental in saving my life, without some attempt at preserving him. We therefore dragged him along with us as well as we could, although with the greatest difficulty and fatigue; Augustus, during part of the time, being forced to clamber over the impediments in our way with the huge dog in his arms—a feat to which the feebleness of my frame rendered me totally inadequate. At length we succeeded in reaching the hole, when Augustus got through, and Tiger was pushed in afterward. All was found to be safe, and we did not fail to return sincere thanks to God for our deliverance from the imminent danger we had escaped. For the present it was agreed that I should remain near the opening, through which my companion could readily supply me with a part of his daily provision, and where I could have the advantages of breathing an atmosphere comparatively pure.

In explanation of some portions of this narrative wherein I have spoken of the stowage of the brig, and which may appear ambiguous to some of my readers who may have seen a proper or regular stowage, I must here state that the manner in which this most important duty had been performed on board the Grampus was a most shameful piece of neglect on the part of Captain Barnard, who was by no means as careful or as experienced a seaman as the hazardous nature of the service on which he was employed would seem necessarily to demand. A proper stowage cannot be accomplished in a careless manner, and many most disastrous accidents, even within the limits of my own experience, have arisen from neglect or ignorance in this particular. Coasting vessels, in the frequent hurry and bustle attendant upon taking in or discharging cargo, are the most liable to mishap from the want of a proper attention to stowage. The great point is to allow no possibility of the cargo or ballast's shifting position even in the most violent rollings of the vessel. With this end, great attention must be paid, not only to the bulk taken in, but to the nature of the bulk, and whether there be a full or only a partial cargo. In most kinds of freight the stowage is accomplished by means of a screw. Thus, in a load of tobacco or flour, the whole is screwed so tightly into the hold of the

vessel that the barrels or hogsheads upon discharging are found to be completely flattened, and take some time to regain their original shape. This screwing, however, is resorted to principally with a view of obtaining more room in the hold; for in a *full* load of any such commodities as flour or tobacco, there can be no danger of any shifting whatever, at least none from which inconvenience can result. There have been instances, indeed, where this method of screwing has resulted in the most lamentable consequences, arising from a cause altogether distinct from the danger attendant upon a shifting of cargo. A load of cotton, for example, tightly screwed while in certain conditions, has been known, through the expansion of its bulk, to rend a vessel asunder at sea. There can be no doubt, either, that the same result would ensue in the case of tobacco, while undergoing its usual course of fermentation, were it not for the interstices consequent upon the rotundity of the hogsheads.

It is when a partial cargo is received that danger is chiefly to be apprehended from shifting, and that precautions should be always taken to guard against such misfortune. Only those who have encountered a violent gale of wind, or, rather, who have experienced the rolling of a vessel in a sudden calm after the gale, can form an idea of the tremendous force of the plunges, and of the consequent terrible impetus given to all loose articles in the vessel. It is then that the necessity of a cautious stowage, when there is a partial cargo, becomes obvious. When lying to (especially with a small head sail), a vessel which is not properly modelled in the bows is frequently thrown upon her beamends; this occurring even every fifteen or twenty minutes upon an average, yet without any serious consequences resulting, *provided there be a proper stowage*. If this, however, has not been strictly attended to, in the first of these heavy lurches the whole of the cargo tumbles over to the side of the vessel which lies upon the water, and, being thus prevented from regaining her equilibrium, as she would otherwise necessarily do, she is certain to fill in a few seconds and go down. It is not too much to say that at least one half of the instances in which vessels have foundered in heavy gales at sea may be attributed to a shifting of cargo or of ballast.

When a partial cargo of any kind is taken on board, the whole, after being first stowed as compactly as may be, should be covered with a layer of stout shifting-boards, extending completely across the vessel. Upon these boards strong temporary stanchions should be erected, reaching to the timbers above, and thus securing everything in its place. In cargoes consisting of grain, or any similar matter, additional precautions are requisite. A hold filled entirely with grain upon leaving port will be found not more than three fourths full upon reaching its destination—this, too, although the freight, when measured bushel by bushel by the consignee, will overrun by a vast deal (on account of the swelling of the grain) the quantity consigned. This result is occasioned by *settling* during the voyage, and is the more perceptible in proportion to the roughness of the weather experienced. If grain loosely thrown in a vessel, then, is ever so well secured by shifting-boards and stan-

chions, it will be liable to shift in a long passage so greatly as to bring about the most distressing calamities. To prevent these, every method should be employed before leaving port to *settle* the cargo as much as possible; and for this there are many contrivances, among which may be mentioned the driving of wedges into the grain. Even after all this is done, and unusual pains taken to secure the shifting-boards, no seaman who knows what he is about will feel altogether secure in a gale of any violence with a cargo of grain on board, and, least of all, with a partial cargo. Yet there are hundreds of our coasting vessels, and, it is likely, many more from the ports of Europe, which sail daily with partial cargoes, even of the most dangerous species, and without any precautions whatever. The wonder is that no more accidents occur than do actually happen. A lamentable instance of this heedlessness occurred to my knowledge in the case of Captain Joel Rice of the schooner Firefly, which sailed from Richmond, Virginia, to Madeira, with a cargo of corn, in the year 1825. The captain had gone many voyages without serious accident, although he was in the habit of paying no attention whatever to his stowage, more than to secure it in the ordinary manner. He had never before sailed with a cargo of grain, and on this occasion had the corn thrown on board loosely, when it did not much more than half fill the vessel. For the first portion of the voyage he met with nothing more than light breezes; but when within a day's sail of Madeira there came on a strong gale from the N. N. E. which forced him to lie to. He brought the schooner to the wind under a double-reefed foresail alone, when she rode as well as any vessel could be expected to do, and shipped not a drop of water. Towards night the gale somewhat abated, and she rolled with more unsteadiness than before, but still did very well, until a heavy lurch threw her upon her beam-ends to starboard. The corn was then heard to shift bodily, the force of the movement bursting open the main hatchway. The vessel went down like a shot. This happened within hail of a small sloop from Madeira, which picked up one of the crew (the only person saved), and which rode out the gale in perfect security, as indeed a jollyboat might have done under proper management.

The stowage on board the Grampus was most clumsily done, if stowage that could be called which was little better than a promiscuous huddling together of oil-casks[9] and ship furniture. I have already spoken of the condition of articles in the hold. On the orlop deck there was space enough for my body (as I have stated) between the oil-casks and the upper deck; a space was left open around the main hatchway; and several other large spaces were left in the stowage. Near the hole cut through the bulkhead by Augustus there was room enough for an entire cask, and in this space I found myself comfortably situated for the present.

By the time my friend had got safely into the berth, and readjusted his handcuffs and the rope, it was broad daylight. We had made a nar-

9. Pym adds the following note: "Whaling vessels are usually fitted with iron oil-tanks—why the Grampus was not I have never been able to ascertain."

row escape indeed; for scarcely had he arranged all matters, when the mate came below, with Dirk Peters and the cook. They talked for some time about the vessel from the Cape Verds, and seemed to be excessively anxious for her appearance. At length the cook came to the berth in which Augustus was lying, and seated himself in it near the head. I could see and hear everything from my hiding-place, for the piece cut out had not been put back, and I was in momentary expectation that the negro would fall against the pea-jacket, which was hung up to conceal the aperture, in which case all would have been discovered, and our lives would, no doubt, have been instantly sacrificed. Our good fortune prevailed, however; and although he frequently touched it as the vessel rolled, he never pressed against it sufficiently to bring about a discovery. The bottom of the jacket had been carefully fastened to the bulkhead, so that the hole might not be seen by its swinging to one side. All this time Tiger was lying in the foot of the berth, and appeared to have recovered in some measure his faculties, for I could see him occasionally open his eyes and draw a long breath.

After a few minutes the mate and cook went above, leaving Dirk Peters behind, who, as soon as they were gone, came and sat himself down in the place just occupied by the mate. He began to talk very sociably with Augustus, and we could now see that the greater part of his apparent intoxication, while the two others were with him, was a feint. He answered all my companion's questions with perfect freedom; told him that he had no doubt of his father's having been picked up, as there were no less than five sail in sight just before sundown on the day he was cut adrift; and used other language of a consolatory nature, which occasioned me no less surprise than pleasure. Indeed, I began to entertain hopes, that through the instrumentality of Peters we might be finally enabled to regain possession of the brig, and this idea I mentioned to Augustus as soon as I found an opportunity. He thought the matter possible, but urged the necessity of the greatest caution in making the attempt, as the conduct of the hybrid appeared to be instigated by the most arbitrary caprice alone; and, indeed, it was difficult to say if he was at any moment of sound mind. Peters went upon deck in about an hour, and did not return again until noon, when he brought Augustus a plentiful supply of junk beef and pudding. Of this, when we were left alone, I partook heartily, without returning through the hole. No one else came down into the forecastle during the day, and at night I got into Augustus's berth, where I slept soundly and sweetly until nearly daybreak, when he awakened me upon hearing a stir upon deck, and I regained my hiding-place as quickly as possible. When the day was fully broke, we found that Tiger had recovered his strength almost entirely, and gave no indications of hydrophobia, drinking a little water that was offered him with great apparent eagerness. During the day he regained all his former vigour and appetite. His strange conduct had been brought on, no doubt, by the deleterious quality of the air of the hold, and had no connexion with canine madness. I could not sufficiently rejoice that I had per-

sisted in bringing him with me from the box. This day was the thirtieth of June, and the thirteenth since the Grampus made sail from Nantucket.

On the second of July the mate came below, drunk as usual, and in an excessively good-humour. He came to Augustus's berth, and, giving him a slap on the back, asked him if he thought he could behave himself if he let him loose, and whether he would promise not to be going into the cabin again. To this, of course, my friend answered in the affirmative, when the ruffian set him at liberty, after making him drink from a flask of rum which he drew from his coat-pocket. Both now went on deck, and I did not see Augustus for about three hours. He then came below with the good news that he had obtained permission to go about the brig as he pleased anywhere forward of the mainmast, and that he had been ordered to sleep, as usual, in the forecastle. He brought me, too, a good dinner, and a plentiful supply of water. The brig was still cruising for the vessel from the Cape Verds, and a sail was now in sight which was thought to be the one in question. As the events of the ensuing eight days were of little importance, and had no direct bearing upon the main incidents of my narrative, I will here throw them into the form of a journal, as I do not wish to omit them altogether.

July 3. Augustus furnished me with three blankets, with which I contrived a comfortable bed in my hiding-place. No one came below, except my companion, during the day. Tiger took his station in the berth just by the aperture, and slept heavily, as if not yet entirely recovered from the effects of his sickness. Towards night a flaw of wind struck the brig before sail could be taken in, and very nearly capsized her. The puff died away immediately, however, and no damage was done beyond the splitting of the foretopsail. Dirk Peters treated Augustus all this day with great kindness, and entered into a long conversation with him respecting the Pacific Ocean, and the islands he had visited in that region. He asked him whether he would not like to go with the mutineers on a kind of exploring and pleasure voyage in those quarters, and said that the men were gradually coming over to the mate's views. To this Augustus thought it best to reply that he would be glad to go on such an adventure, since nothing better could be done, and that anything was preferable to a piratical life.

July 4th. The vessel in sight proved to be a small brig from Liverpool, and was allowed to pass unmolested. Augustus spent most of his time on deck, with a view of obtaining all the information in his power respecting the intentions of the mutineers. They had frequent and violent quarrels among themselves, in one of which a harpooner, Jim Bonner, was thrown overboard. The party of the mate was gaining ground. Jim Bonner belonged to the cook's gang, of which Peters was a partisan.

July 5th. About daybreak there came on a stiff breeze from the west, which at noon freshened into a gale, so that the brig could carry nothing more than her trysail and foresail. In taking in the foretopsail, Simms, one of the common hands, and belonging also to the cook's

gang, fell overboard, being very much in liquor, and was drowned—no attempt being made to save him. The whole number of persons on board was now thirteen, to wit: Dirk Peters; Seymour, the black cook; ——— Jones; ——— Greely; Hartman Rogers; and William Allen, of the cook's party; the mate, whose name I never learned; Absalom Hicks; ——— Wilson; John Hunt; and Richard Parker, of the mate's party—besides Augustus and myself.

July 6th. The gale lasted all this day, blowing in heavy squalls, accompanied with rain. The brig took in a good deal of water through her seams, and one of the pumps was kept continually going, Augustus being forced to take his turn. Just at twilight a large ship passed close by us, without having been discovered until within hail. This ship was supposed to be the one for which the mutineers were on the look-out. The mate hailed her, but the reply was drowned in the roaring of the gale. At eleven, a sea was shipped amid-ships, which tore away a great portion of the larboard bulwarks, and did some other slight damage. Towards morning the weather moderated, and at sunrise there was very little wind.

July 7th. There was a heavy swell running all this day, during which the brig, being light, rolled excessively, and many articles broke loose in the hold, as I could hear distinctly from my hiding-place. I suffered a great deal from sea-sickness. Peters had a long conversation this day with Augustus, and told him that two of his gang, Greely and Allen, had gone over to the mate, and were resolved to turn pirates. He put several questions to Augustus which he did not then exactly understand. During a part of this evening the leak gained upon the vessel; and little could be done to remedy it, as it was occasioned by the brig's straining, and taking in the water through her seams. A sail was thrummed, and got under the bows, which aided us in some measure, so that we began to gain upon the leak.

July 8th. A light breeze sprung up at sunrise from the eastward, when the mate headed the brig to the southwest, with the intention of making some of the West India islands, in pursuance of his piratical designs. No opposition was made by Peters or the cook; at least none in the hearing of Augustus. All idea of taking the vessel from the Cape Verds was abandoned. The leak was now easily kept under by one pump going every three quarters of an hour. The sail was drawn from beneath the bows. Spoke two small schooners during the day.

July 9th. Fine weather. All hands employed in repairing bulwarks. Peters had again a long conversation with Augustus, and spoke more plainly than he had done heretofore. He said nothing should induce him to come into the mate's views, and even hinted his intention of taking the brig out of his hands. He asked my friend if he could depend upon his aid in such case, to which Augustus said, "Yes," without hesitation. Peters then said he would sound the others of his party upon the subject, and went away. During the remainder of the day Augustus had no opportunity of speaking with him privately.

Chapter VII

July 10. Spoke a brig from Rio, bound to Norfolk. Weather hazy, with a light baffling wind from the eastward. To-day Hartman Rogers died, having been attacked on the eighth with spasms after drinking a glass of grog. This man was of the cook's party, and one upon whom Peters placed his main reliance. He told Augustus that he believed the mate had poisoned him, and that he expected, if he did not be on the look-out, his own turn would come shortly. There were now only himself, Jones, and the cook belonging to his own gang—on the other side there were five.[1] He had spoken to Jones about taking the command from the mate; but the project having been coolly received, he had been deterred from pressing the matter any further, or from saying anything to the cook. It was well, as it happened, that he was so prudent, for in the afternoon the cook expressed his determination of siding with the mate, and went over formally to that party; while Jones took an opportunity of quarrelling with Peters, and hinted that he would let the mate know of the plan in agitation. There was now, evidently, no time to be lost, and Peters expressed his determination of attempting to take the vessel at all hazards, provided Augustus would lend him his aid. My friend at once assured him of his willingness to enter into any plan for that purpose, and, thinking the opportunity a favourable one, made known the fact of my being on board. At this the hybrid was not more astonished than delighted, as he had no reliance whatever upon Jones, whom he already considered as belonging to the party of the mate. They went below immediately, when Augustus called to me by name, and Peters and myself were soon made acquainted. It was agreed that we should attempt to retake the vessel upon the first good opportunity, leaving Jones altogether out of our councils. In the event of success we were to run the brig into the first port that offered, and deliver her up. The desertion of his party had frustrated Peters's design of going into the Pacific—an adventure which could not be accomplished without a crew, and he depended upon either getting acquitted upon trial on the score of insanity (which he solemnly averred had actuated him in lending his aid to the mutiny), or upon obtaining a pardon, if found guilty, through the representations of Augustus and myself. Our deliberations were interrupted for the present by the cry of "All hands take in sail," and Peters and Augustus ran up on deck.

As usual, the crew were nearly all drunk; and, before sail could be properly taken in, a violent squall laid the brig on her beam-ends. By keeping her away, however, she righted, having shipped a good deal of water. Scarcely was everything secure, when another squall took the vessel, and immediately afterward another—no damage being done. There was every appearance of a gale of wind, which, indeed, shortly came on, with great fury, from the northward and westward. All was made as snug as possible, and we laid to, as usual, under a close-

1. Cf. the list of seven in Chapter VI.

reefed foresail. As night drew on, the wind increased in violence, with a remarkably heavy sea. Peters now came into the forecastle with Augustus, and we resumed our deliberations.

We agreed that no opportunity could be more favourable than the present for carrying our design into effect, as an attempt at such a moment would never be anticipated. As the brig was snugly laid to, there would be no necessity of manœuvring her until good weather, when, if we succeeded in our attempt, we might liberate one, or perhaps two of the men, to aid us in taking her into port. The main difficulty was the great disproportion in our forces. There were only three of us, and in the cabin there were nine. All the arms on board, too, were in their possession, with the exception of a pair of small pistols which Peters had concealed about his person, and the large seaman's knife which he always wore in the waistband of his pantaloons. From certain indications, too, such, for example, as there being no such thing as an axe or a handspike lying in their customary places, we began to fear that the mate had his suspicions, at least in regard to Peters, and that he would let slip no opportunity of getting rid of him. It was clear, indeed, that what we should determine to do could not be done too soon. Still the odds were too much against us to allow of our proceeding without the greatest caution.

Peters proposed that he should go up on deck, and enter into conversation with the watch (Allen), when he would be able to throw him into the sea without trouble, and without making any disturbance, by seizing a good opportunity; that Augustus and myself should then come up, and endeavour to provide ourselves with some kind of weapons from the deck; and that we should then make a rush together, and secure the companion-way before any opposition could be offered. I objected to this, because I could not believe that the mate (who was a cunning fellow in all matters which did not affect his superstitious prejudices) would suffer himself to be so easily entrapped. The very fact of there being a watch on deck at all was sufficient proof that he was upon the alert—it not being usual, except in vessels where discipline is most rigidly enforced, to station a watch on deck when a vessel is lying to in a gale of wind. As I address myself principally, if not altogether, to persons who have never been to sea, it may be as well to state the exact condition of a vessel under such circumstances. Lying to, or, in sea-parlance "laying to," is a measure resorted to for various purposes, and effected in various manners. In moderate weather, it is frequently done with a view of merely bringing the vessel to a stand-still, to wait for another vessel, or any similar object. If the vessel which lies to is under full sail, the manœuvre is usually accomplished by throwing round some portion of her sails so as to let the wind take them aback, when she becomes stationary. But we are now speaking of lying to in a gale of wind. This is done when the wind is ahead, and too violent to admit of carrying sail without danger of capsizing; and sometimes even when the wind is fair, but the sea too heavy for the vessel to be put before it. If a vessel be suffered to scud before the wind in a very heavy sea, much damage is usually done her

by the shipping of water over her stern, and sometimes by the violent plunges she makes forward. This manœuvre, then, is seldom resorted to in such case, unless through necessity. When the vessel is in a leaky condition, she is often put before the wind even in the heaviest seas; for, when lying to, her seams are sure to be greatly opened by her violent straining, and it is not so much the case when scudding. Often, too, it becomes necessary to scud a vessel, either when the blast is so exceedingly furious as to tear in pieces the sail which is employed with a view of bringing her head to the wind, or when, through the false modelling of the frame or other causes, this main object cannot be effected.

Vessels in a gale of wind are laid to in different manners, according to their peculiar construction. Some lie to best under a foresail, and this, I believe, is the sail most usually employed. Large square-rigged vessels have sails for the express purpose, called storm-staysails. But the jib is occasionally employed by itself—sometimes the jib and foresail, or a double-reefed foresail, and not unfrequently the after-sails, are made use of. Foretopsails are very often found to answer the purpose better than any other species of sail. The Grampus was generally laid to under a close-reefed foresail.[2]

When a vessel is to be laid to, her head is brought up to the wind just so nearly as to fill the sail under which she lies, when hauled flat aft, that is, when brought diagonally across the vessel. This being done, the bows point within a few degrees of the direction from which the wind issues, and the windward bow of course receives the shock of the waves. In this situation a good vessel will ride out a very heavy gale of wind without shipping a drop of water, and without any further attention being requisite on the part of the crew. The helm is usually lashed down, but this is altogether unnecessary (except on account of the noise it makes when loose), for the rudder has no effect upon the vessel when lying to. Indeed, the helm had far better be left loose than lashed very fast, for the rudder is apt to be torn off by heavy seas if there be no room for the helm to play. As long as the sail holds, a well-modelled vessel will maintain her situation, and ride every sea, as if instinct with life and reason. If the violence of the wind, however, should tear the sail into pieces (a feat which it requires a perfect hurricane to accomplish under ordinary circumstances), there is then imminent danger. The vessel falls off from the wind, and, coming broadside to the sea, is completely at its mercy: the only resource in this case is to put her quickly before the wind, letting her scud until some other sail can be set. Some vessels will lie to under no sail whatever, but such are not to be trusted at sea.

But to return from this digression. It had never been customary with the mate to have any watch on deck when lying to in a gale of wind, and the fact that he had now one, coupled with the circumstance of the missing axes and handspikes, fully convinced us that the crew were too well on the watch to be taken by surprise in the manner

2. Reefing a sail has been previously mentioned; here, tightly wound; to reef means to tuck in a portion of a sail or roll it around a yardarm to make it smaller.

Peters had suggested. Something, however, was to be done, and that with as little delay as practicable, for there could be no doubt that a suspicion having been once entertained against Peters, he would be sacrificed upon the earliest occasion, and one would certainly be either found or made upon the breaking of the gale.

Augustus now suggested that if Peters could contrive to remove, under any pretext, the piece of chain-cable which lay over the trap in the stateroom, we might possibly be able to come upon them unawares by means of the hold; but a little reflection convinced us that the vessel rolled and pitched too violently for any attempt of that nature.

By good fortune I at length hit upon the idea of working upon the superstitious terrors and guilty conscience of the mate. It will be remembered that one of the crew, Hartman Rogers, had died during the morning, having been attacked two days before with spasms after drinking some spirits and water. Peters had expressed to us his opinion that this man had been poisoned by the mate, and for this belief he had reasons, so he said, which were incontrovertible, but which he could not be prevailed upon to explain to us—this wayward refusal being only in keeping with other points of his singular character. But whether or not he had any better grounds for suspecting the mate than we had ourselves, we were easily led to fall in with his suspicion, and determined to act accordingly.

Rogers had died about eleven in the forenoon, in violent convulsions; and the corpse presented in a few minutes after death one of the most horrid and loathsome spectacles I ever remember to have seen. The stomach was swollen immensely, like that of a man who has been drowned and lain under water for many weeks. The hands were in the same condition, while the face was shrunken, shrivelled, and of a chalky whiteness, except where relieved by two or three glaring red splotches, like those occasioned by the erysipelas:[3] one of these splotches extended diagonally across the face, completely covering up an eye as if with a band of red velvet. In this disgusting condition the body had been brought up from the cabin at noon to be thrown overboard, when the mate getting a glimpse of it (for he now saw it for the first time), and being either touched with remorse for his crime or struck with terror at so horrible a sight, ordered the men to sew the body up in its hammock, and allow it the usual rites of seaburial. Having given these directions he went below, as if to avoid any further sight of his victim. While preparations were making to obey his orders, the gale came on with great fury, and the design was abandoned for the present. The corpse, left to itself, was washed into the larboard scuppers, where it still lay at the time of which I speak, floundering about with the furious lurches of the brig.

Having arranged our plan, we set about putting it in execution as speedily as possible. Peters went upon deck, and, as he had anticipated, was immediately accosted by Allen, who appeared to be sta-

3. Skin rash. Is this another error? Or does Pym see the body after his emergence from the hold and learn of the short time lapse between death and decay from others?

tioned more as a watch upon the forecastle than for any other pur-
pose. The fate of this villain, however, was speedily and silently de-
cided; for Peters, approaching him in a careless manner, as if about to
address him, seized him by the throat, and, before he could utter a
single cry, tossed him over the bulwarks. He then called to us, and we
came up. Our first precaution was to look about for something with
which to arm ourselves, and in doing this we had to proceed with great
care, for it was impossible to stand on deck an instant without holding
fast, and violent seas broke over the vessel at every plunge forward. It
was indispensable, too, that we should be quick in our operations,
for every minute we expected the mate to be up to set the pumps go-
ing, as it was evident the brig must be taking in water very fast. After
searching about for some time, we could find nothing more fit for our
purpose than the two pump-handles, one of which Augustus took, and
I the other. Having secured these, we stripped off the shirt of the
corpse and dropped the body overboard. Peters and myself then went
below, leaving Augustus to watch upon deck, where he took his sta-
tion just where Allen had been placed, and with his back to the cabin
companion-way, so that, if any one of the mate's gang should come up,
he might suppose it was the watch.

As soon as I got below I commenced disguising myself so as to rep-
resent the corpse of Rogers. The shirt which we had taken from the
body aided us very much, for it was of a singular form and character,
and easily recognisable—a kind of smock, which the deceased wore
over his other clothing. It was a blue stockinett, with large white
stripes running across. Having put this on, I proceeded to equip my-
self with a false stomach, in imitation of the horrible deformity of the
swollen corpse. This was soon effected by means of stuffing with some
bedclothes. I then gave the same appearance to my hands by drawing
on a pair of white woolen mittens, and filling them in with any kind of
rags that offered themselves. Peters then arranged my face, first rub-
bing it well over with white chalk, and afterward splotching it with
blood, which he took from a cut in his finger. The streak across the
eye was not forgotten, and presented a most shocking appearance.

Chapter VIII

As I viewed myself in a fragment of looking-glass which hung up in
the cabin, and by the dim light of a kind of battle-lantern, I was so im-
pressed with a sense of vague awe at my appearance, and at the recol-
lection of the terrific reality which I was thus representing, that I was
seized with a violent tremour, and could scarcely summon resolution
to go on with my part. It was necessary, however, to act with decision,
and Peters and myself went upon deck.

We there found everything safe, and, keeping close to the bulwarks,
the three of us crept to the cabin companion-way. It was only partially
closed, precautions having been taken to prevent its being suddenly
pushed to from without, by means of placing billets of wood on the
upper step so as to interfere with the shutting. We found no difficulty

in getting a full view of the interior of the cabin through the cracks where the hinges were placed. It now proved to have been very fortunate for us that we had not attempted to take them by surprise, for they were evidently on the alert. Only one was asleep, and he lying just at the foot of the companion-ladder, with a musket by his side. The rest were seated on several mattresses, which had been taken from the berths and thrown on the floor. They were engaged in earnest conversation; and although they had been carousing, as appeared from two empty jugs, with some tin tumblers which lay about, they were not as much intoxicated as usual. All had knives, one or two of them pistols, and a great many muskets were lying in a berth close at hand.

We listened to their conversation for some time before we could make up our minds how to act, having as yet resolved on nothing determinate, except that we would attempt to paralyze their exertions, when we should attack them, by means of the apparition of Rogers. They were discussing their piratical plans, in which all we could hear distinctly was, that they would unite with the crew of a schooner Hornet, and, if possible, get the schooner herself into their possession preparatory to some attempt on a large scale, the particulars of which could not be made out by either of us.

One of the men spoke of Peters, when the mate replied to him in a low voice which could not be distinguished, and afterward added more loudly, that "he could not understand his being so much forward with the captain's brat in the forecastle, and he thought the sooner both of them were overboard the better." To this no answer was made, but we could easily perceive that the hint was well received by the whole party, and more particularly by Jones. At this period I was excessively agitated, the more so as I could see that neither Augustus nor Peters could determine how to act. I made up my mind, however, to sell my life as dearly as possible, and not to suffer myself to be overcome by any feelings of trepidation.

The tremendous noise made by the roaring of the wind in the rigging and the washing of the sea over the deck prevented us from hearing what was said except during momentary lulls. In one of these we all distinctly heard the mate tell one of the men to "go forward, and order the d——d lubbers to come into the cabin, where he could have an eye upon them, for he wanted no such secret doings on board the brig." It was well for us that the pitching of the vessel at this moment was so violent as to prevent this order from being carried into instant execution. The cook got up from his mattress to go for us, when a tremendous lurch, which I thought would carry away the masts, threw him headlong against one of the larboard stateroom doors, bursting it open, and creating a good deal of other confusion. Luckily, neither of our party was thrown from his position, and we had time to make a precipitate retreat to the forecastle, and arrange a hurried plan of action before the messenger made his appearance, or rather before he put his head out of the companion-hatch, for he did not come on deck. From this station he could not notice the absence of Allen, and

he accordingly bawled out as if to him, repeating the orders of the mate. Peters cried out, "Ay, ay," in a disguised voice, and the cook immediately went below, without entertaining a suspicion that all was not right.

My two companions now proceeded boldly aft and down into the cabin, Peters closing the door after him in the same manner he had found it. The mate received them with feigned cordiality, and told Augustus that, since he had behaved himself so well of late, he might take up his quarters in the cabin, and be one of them for the future. He then poured him out a tumbler half full of rum; and made him drink it. All this I saw and heard, for I followed my friends to the cabin as soon as the door was shut, and took up my old point of observation. I had brought with me the two pump-handles, one of which I secured near the companion-way, to be ready for use when required.

I now steadied myself as well as possible so as to have a good view of all that was passing within, and endeavoured to nerve myself to the task of descending among the mutineers when Peters should make a signal to me as agreed upon. Presently he contrived to turn the conversation upon the bloody deeds of the mutiny, and, by degrees, led the men to talk of the thousand superstitions which are so universally current among seamen. I could not make out all that was said, but I could plainly see the effects of the conversation in the countenances of those present. The mate was evidently much agitated, and presently, when some one mentioned the terrific appearance of Roger's corpse, I thought he was upon the point of swooning. Peters now asked him if he did not think it would be better to have the body thrown overboard at once, as it was too horrible a sight to see it floundering about in the scuppers. At this the villain absolutely gasped for breath, and turned his head slowly round upon his companions, as if imploring some one to go up and perform the task. No one, however, stirred, and it was quite evident that the whole party were wound up to the highest pitch of nervous excitement. Peters now made me the signal. I immediately threw open the door of the companion-way, and, descending without uttering a syllable, stood erect in the midst of the party.

The intense effect produced by this sudden apparition is not at all to be wondered at when the various circumstances are taken into consideration. Usually, in cases of a similar nature, there is left in the mind of the spectator some glimmering of doubt as to the reality of the vision before his eyes; a degree of hope, however feeble, that he is the victim of chicanery, and that the apparition is not actually a visitant from the world of shadows. It is not too much to say that such remnants of doubt have been at the bottom of almost every such visitation, and that the appalling horror which has sometimes been brought about, is to be attributed, even in the cases most in point, and where most suffering has been experienced, more to a kind of anticipative horror, lest the apparition *might possibly be* real, than to an unwavering belief in its reality. But, in the present instance, it will be seen immediately, that in the minds of the mutineers there was not even the shadow of a basis upon which to rest a doubt that the ap-

parition of Rogers was indeed a revivification of his disgusting corpse, or at least its spiritual image. The isolated situation of the brig, with its entire inaccessibility on account of the gale, confined the apparently possible means of deception within such narrow and definite limits, that they must have thought themselves enabled to survey them all at a glance. They had now been at sea twenty-four days, without holding more than a speaking communication with any vessel whatever. The whole of the crew, too, at least all whom they had the most remote reason for suspecting to be on board, were assembled in the cabin, with the exception of Allen, the watch; and his gigantic stature (he was six feet six inches high) was too familiar in their eyes to permit the notion that he was the apparition before them to enter their minds even for an instant. Add to these considerations the awe-inspiring nature of the tempest, and that of the conversation brought about by Peters; the deep impression which the loathsomeness of the actual corpse had made in the morning upon the imaginations of the men; the excellence of the imitation in my person; and the uncertain and wavering light in which they beheld me, as the glare of the cabin lantern, swinging violently to and fro, fell dubiously and fitfully upon my figure, and there will be no reason to wonder that the deception had even more than the entire effect which we had anticipated. The mate sprang up from the mattress on which he was lying, and, without uttering a syllable, fell back, stone dead, upon the cabin floor, and was hurled to the leeward like a log by a heavy roll of the brig. Of the remaining seven there were but three who had at first any degree of presence of mind. The four others sat for some time rooted apparently to the floor, the most pitiable objects of horror and utter despair my eyes ever encountered. The only opposition we experienced at all was from the cook, John Hunt, and Richard Parker; but they made but a feeble and irresolute defence. The two former were shot instantly by Peters, and I felled Parker with a blow on the head from the pump-handle which I had brought with me. In the mean time Augustus seized one of the muskets lying on the floor, and shot another mutineer (———— Wilson) through the breast. There were now but three remaining; but by this time they had become aroused from their lethargy, and perhaps began to see that a deception had been practised upon them, for they fought with great resolution and fury, and, but for the immense muscular strength of Peters, might have ultimately got the better of us. These three men were ———— Jones, ———— Greely, and Absalom Hicks. Jones had thrown Augustus on the floor, stabbed him in several places along the right arm, and would no doubt have soon despatched him (as neither Peters nor myself could immediately get rid of our own antagonists), had it not been for the timely aid of a friend upon whose assistance we surely had never depended. This friend was no other than Tiger. With a low growl he bounded into the cabin, at a most critical moment for Augustus, and throwing himself upon Jones, pinned him to the floor in an instant. My friend, however, was now too much injured to render us any aid whatever, and I was so encumbered with my disguise that I could do but little. The dog would

not leave his hold upon the throat of Jones—Peters, nevertheless, was far more than a match for the two men who remained, and would, no doubt, have despatched them sooner, had it not been for the narrow space in which he had to act, and the tremendous lurches of the vessel. Presently he was enabled to get hold of a heavy stool, several of which lay about the floor. With this he beat out the brains of Greely as he was in the act of discharging a musket at me, and immediately afterward a roll of the brig throwing him in contact with Hicks, he seized him by the throat, and, by dint of sheer strength, strangled him instantaneously. Thus, in far less time than I have taken to tell it, we found ourselves masters of the brig.

The only person of our opponents who was left alive was Richard Parker. This man, it will be remembered, I had knocked down with a blow from the pump-handle at the commencement of the attack. He now lay motionless by the door of the shattered stateroom; but, upon Peters touching him with his foot, he spoke, and entreated for mercy. His head was only slightly cut, and otherwise he had received no injury, having been merely stunned by the blow. He now got up, and, for the present, we secured his hands behind his back. The dog was still growling over Jones; but, upon examination, we found him completely dead, the blood issuing in a stream from a deep wound in the throat, inflicted, no doubt, by the sharp teeth of the animal.

It was now about one o'clock in the morning, and the wind was still blowing tremendously. The brig evidently laboured much more than usual, and it became absolutely necessary that something should be done with a view of easing her in some measure. At almost every roll to leeward she shipped a sea, several of which came partially down into the cabin during our scuffle, the hatchway having been left open by myself when I descended. The entire range of bulwarks to larboard had been swept away, as well as the caboose, together with the jollyboat from the counter. The creaking and working of the mainmast, too, gave indication that it was nearly sprung. To make room for more stowage in the after hold, the heel of this mast had been stepped between decks (a very reprehensible practice, occasionally resorted to by ignorant ship-builders), so that it was in imminent danger of working from its step. But, to crown all our difficulties, we plummed the well, and found no less than seven feet water.

Leaving the bodies of the crew lying in the cabin, we got to work immediately at the pumps—Parker, of course, being set at liberty to assist us in the labour. Augustus's arm was bound up as well as we could effect it, and he did what he could, but that was not much. However, we found that we could just manage to keep the leak from gaining upon us by having one pump constantly going. As there were only four of us, this was severe labour; but we endeavoured to keep up our spirits, and looked anxiously for daybreak, when we hoped to lighten the brig by cutting away the mainmast.

In this manner we passed a night of terrible anxiety and fatigue, and, when the day at length broke, the gale had neither abated in the least, nor were there any signs of its abating. We now dragged the bod-

ies on deck and threw them overboard. Our next care was to get rid of
the mainmast.[4] The necessary preparations having been made, Peters
cut away at the mast (having found axes in the cabin), while the rest
of us stood by the stays and lanyards. As the brig gave a tremendous
lee-lurch, the word was given to cut away the weather-lanyards, which
being done, the, whole mass of wood and rigging plunged into the sea,
clear of the brig, and without doing any material injury. We now found
that the vessel did not labour quite as much as before, but our situa-
tion was still exceedingly precarious, and, in spite of the utmost exer-
tions, we could not gain upon the leak without the aid of both pumps.
The little assistance which Augustus could render us was not really of
any importance. To add to our distress, a heavy sea, striking the brig to
windward, threw her off several points from the wind, and, before she
could regain her position, another broke completely over her, and
hurled her full upon her beam-ends. The ballast now shifted in a mass
to leeward (the stowage had been knocking about perfectly at random
for some time), and for a few moments we thought nothing could save
us from capsizing. Presently, however, we partially righted; but the bal-
last still retaining its place to larboard, we lay so much along that it
was useless to think of working the pumps, which indeed we could not
have done much longer in any case, as our hands were entirely raw
with the excessive labour we had undergone, and were bleeding in the
most horrible manner.

Contrary to Parker's advice, we now proceeded to cut away the fore-
mast, and at length accomplished it after much difficulty, owing to the
position in which we lay. In going overboard the wreck took with it the
bowsprit, and left us a complete hulk.

So far we had had reason to rejoice in the escape of our longboat,
which had received no damage from any of the huge seas which had
come on board. But we had not long to congratulate ourselves; for the
foremast having gone, and, of course, the foresail with it, by which the
brig had been steadied, every sea now made a complete breach over
us, and in five minutes our deck was swept from stem to stern, the
longboat and starboard bulwarks torn off, and even the windlass shat-
tered into fragments. It was, indeed, hardly possible for us to be in a
more pitiable condition.

At noon there seemed to be some slight appearance of the gale's
abating, but in this we were sadly disappointed, for it only lulled for a
few minutes to blow with redoubled fury. About four in the afternoon
it was utterly impossible to stand up against the violence of the blast;
and, as the night closed in upon us, I had not a shadow of hope that
the vessel would hold together until morning.

By midnight we had settled very deep in the water, which was now
up to the orlop deck. The rudder went soon afterward, the sea which
tore it away lifting the after portion of the brig entirely from the water,
against which she thumped in her descent with such a concussion as

4. Here, as in subsequent chapters, Poe makes use of accounts in R. Thomas's *Remarkable
Shipwrecks and Remarkable Events* (1836), as well as passages from Morrell.

would be occasioned by going ashore. We had all calculated that the rudder would hold its own to the last, as it was unusually strong, being rigged as I have never seen one rigged either before or since. Down its main timber there ran a succession of stout iron hooks, and others in the same manner down the stern-post. Through these hooks there extended a very thick wrought-iron rod, the rudder being thus held to the stern-post, and swinging freely on the rod. The tremendous force of the sea which tore it off may be estimated by the fact, that the hooks in the stern-post, which ran entirely through it, being clinched on the inside, were drawn every one of them completely out of the solid wood.

We had scarcely time to draw breath after the violence of this shock, when one of the most tremendous waves I had then ever known broke right on board of us, sweeping the companion-way clear off, bursting in the hatchways, and filling every inch of the vessel with water.

Chapter IX

Really struggling to stay alive

Luckily, just before night, all four of us had lashed ourselves firmly to the fragments of the windlass, lying in this manner as flat upon the deck as possible. This precaution alone saved us from destruction. As it was, we were all more or less stunned by the immense weight of water which tumbled upon us, and which did not roll from above us until we were nearly exhausted. As soon as I could recover breath, I called aloud to my companions. Augustus alone replied, saying, "It is all over with us, and may God have mercy upon our souls." By-and-by both the others were enabled to speak, when they exhorted us to take courage, as there was still hope; it being impossible, from the nature of the cargo, that the brig could go down, and there being every chance that the gale would blow over by the morning. These words inspired me with new life; for, strange as it may seem, although it was obvious that a vessel with a cargo of empty oil-casks would not sink, I had been hitherto so confused in mind as to have overlooked this consideration altogether; and the danger which I had for some time regarded as the most imminent was that of foundering. As hope revived within me, I made use of every opportunity to strengthen the lashings which held me to the remains of the windlass, and in this occupation I soon discovered that my companions were also busy. The night was as dark as it could possibly be, and the horrible shrieking din and confusion which surrounded us it is useless to attempt describing. Our deck lay level with the sea, or rather we were encircled with a towering ridge of foam, a portion of which swept over us every instant. It is not too much to say that our heads were not fairly out of water more than one second in three. Although we lay close together, no one of us could see the other, or, indeed, any portion of the brig itself, upon which we were so tempestuously hurled about. At intervals we called one to the other, thus endeavouring to keep alive hope, and render consolation and encouragement to such of us as stood most in need of

it. The feeble condition of Augustus made him an object of solicitude with us all; and as, from the lacerated condition of his right arm, it must have been impossible for him to secure his lashings with any degree of firmness, we were in momentary expectation of finding that he had gone overboard—yet to render him aid was a thing altogether out of the question. Fortunately, his station was more secure than that of any of the rest of us; for the upper part of his body lying just beneath a portion of the shattered windlass, the seas, as they tumbled in upon him, were greatly broken in their violence. In any other situation than this (into which he had been accidentally thrown after having lashed himself in a very exposed spot) he must inevitably have perished before morning. Owing to the brig's lying so much along, we were all less liable to be washed off than otherwise would have been the case. The heel, as I have before stated, was to larboard, about one half of the deck being constantly under water. The seas, therefore, which struck us to starboard were much broken by the vessel's side, only reaching us in fragments as we lay flat on our faces; while those which came from larboard, being what are called back-water seas, and obtaining little hold upon us on account of our posture, had not sufficient force to drag us from our fastenings.

In this frightful situation we lay until the day broke so as to show us more fully the horrors which surrounded us. The brig was a mere log, rolling about at the mercy of every wave; the gale was upon the increase, if anything, blowing indeed a complete hurricane, and there appeared to us no earthly prospect of deliverance. For several hours we held on in silence, expecting every moment that our lashings would either give way, that the remains of the windlass would go by the board, or that some of the huge seas, which roared in every direction around us and above us, would drive the hulk so far beneath the water that we should be drowned before it could regain the surface. By the mercy of God, however, we were preserved from these imminent dangers, and about midday were cheered by the light of the blessed sun. Shortly afterward we could perceive a sensible diminution in the force of the wind, when, now for the first time since the latter part of the evening before, Augustus spoke, asking Peters, who lay closest to him, if he thought there was any possibility of our being saved. As no reply was at first made to this question, we all concluded that the hybrid had been drowned where he lay; but presently, to our great joy, he spoke, although very feebly, saying that he was in great pain, being so cut by the tightness of his lashings across the stomach, that he must either find means of loosening them or perish, as it was impossible that he could endure his misery much longer. This occasioned us great distress, as it was altogether useless to think of aiding him in any manner while the sea continued washing over us as it did. We exhorted him to bear his sufferings with fortitude, and promised to seize the first opportunity which should offer itself to relieve him. He replied that it would soon be too late; that it would be all over with him before we could help him; and then, after moaning for some minutes, lay silent, when we concluded that he had perished.

As the evening drew on, the sea had fallen so much that scarcely more than one wave broke over the hulk from windward in the course of five minutes, and the wind had abated a great deal, although still blowing a severe gale. I had not heard any of my companions speak for hours, and now called to Augustus. He replied, although very feebly, so that I could not distinguish what he said. I then spoke to Peters and to Parker, neither of whom returned any answer.

Shortly after this period I fell into a state of partial insensibility, during which the most pleasing images floated in my imagination; such as green trees, waving meadows of ripe grain, processions of dancing girls, troops of cavalry, and other phantasies. I now remember that, in all which passed before my mind's eye, *motion* was a predominant idea. Thus, I never fancied any stationary object, such as a house, a mountain, or anything of that kind; but windmills, ships, large birds, balloons, people on horseback, carriages driving furiously, and similar moving objects, presented themselves in endless succession. When I recovered from this state, the sun was, as near as I could guess, an hour high. I had the greatest difficulty in bringing to recollection the various circumstances connected with my situation, and for some time remained firmly convinced that I was still in the hold of the brig, near the box, and that the body of Parker was that of Tiger.[5]

When I at length completely came to my senses, I found that the wind blew no more than a moderate breeze, and that the sea was comparatively calm; so much so that it only washed over the brig amidships. My left arm had broken loose from its lashings, and was much cut about the elbow; my right was entirely benumbed, and the hand and wrist swollen prodigiously by the pressure of the rope, which had worked from the shoulder downward. I was also in great pain from another rope which went about my waist, and had been drawn to an insufferable degree of tightness. Looking round upon my companions, I saw that Peters still lived, although a thick line was pulled so forcibly around his loins as to give him the appearance of being cut nearly in two; as I stirred, he made a feeble motion to me with his hand, pointing to the rope. Augustus gave no indication of life whatever, and was bent nearly double across a splinter of the windlass. Parker spoke to me when he saw me moving, and asked me if I had not sufficient strength to release him from his situation; saying, that if I would summon up what spirits I could, and contrive to untie him, we might yet save our lives; but that otherwise we must all perish. I told him to take courage, and I would endeavour to free him. Feeling in my pantaloons' pocket, I got hold of my penknife, and, after several ineffectual attempts, at length succeeded in opening it. I then, with my left hand, managed to free my right from its fastenings, and afterward cut the other ropes which held me. Upon attempting, however, to move from my position, I found that my legs failed me altogether,

5. Pym's dog is not mentioned again; critics have suggested another authorial lapse in the appearance, disappearance, reappearance, and disappearance of Tiger, though Pym's mental state is such that it is unclear what is real and what is illusion or dream. Cf. Ch. II, p. 447, n. 8 herein.

and that I could not get up; neither could I move my right arm in any direction. Upon mentioning this to Parker, he advised me to lie quiet for a few minutes, holding on to the windlass with my left hand, so as to allow time for the blood to circulate. Doing this, the numbness presently began to die away, so that I could move first one of my legs, and then the other; and, shortly afterward, I regained the partial use of my right arm. I now crawled with great caution towards Parker, without getting on my legs, and soon cut loose all the lashings about him, when, after a short delay, he also recovered the partial use of his limbs. We now lost no time in getting loose the rope from Peters. It had cut a deep gash through the waistband of his woollen pantaloons, and through two shirts, and made its way into his groin, from which the blood flowed out copiously as we removed the cordage. No sooner had we removed it, however, than he spoke, and seemed to experience instant relief—being able to move with much greater ease than either Parker or myself—this was no doubt owing to the discharge of blood.

We had little hope that Augustus would recover, as he evinced no signs of life; but, upon getting to him, we discovered that he had merely swooned from loss of blood, the bandages we had placed around his wounded arm having been torn off by the water; none of the ropes which held him to the windlass were drawn sufficiently tight to occasion his death. Having relieved him from the fastenings, and got him clear of the broken wood about the windlass, we secured him in a dry place to windward, with his head somewhat lower than his body, and all three of us busied ourselves in chafing his limbs. In about half an hour he came to himself, although it was not until the next morning that he gave signs of recognising any of us, or had sufficient strength to speak. By the time we had thus got clear of our lashings it was quite dark, and it began to cloud up, so that we were again in the greatest agony lest it should come on to blow hard, in which event nothing could have saved us from perishing, exhausted as we were. By good fortune it continued very moderate during the night, the sea subsiding every minute, which gave us great hopes of ultimate preservation. A gentle breeze still blew from the N. W., but the weather was not at all cold. Augustus was lashed carefully to windward in such a manner as to prevent him from slipping overboard with the rolls of the vessel, as he was still too weak to hold on at all. For ourselves there was no such necessity. We sat close together, supporting each other with the aid of the broken ropes about the windlass, and devising methods of escape from our frightful situation. We derived much comfort from taking off our clothes and wringing the water from them. When we put them on after this, they felt remarkably warm and pleasant, and served to invigorate us in no little degree. We helped Augustus off with his, and wrung them for him, when he experienced the same comfort.

Our chief sufferings were now those of hunger and thirst, and, when we looked forward to the means of relief in this respect, our hearts sunk within us, and we were induced to regret that we had escaped the less dreadful perils of the sea. We endeavoured, however, to console ourselves with the hope of being speedily picked up by some

vessel, and encouraged each other to bear with fortitude the evils that might happen.

The morning of the fourteenth at length dawned, and the weather still continued clear and pleasant, with a steady but very light breeze from the N. W. The sea was now quite smooth, and as, from some cause which we could not determine, the brig did not lie so much along as she had done before, the deck was comparatively dry, and we could move about with freedom. We had now been better than three entire days and nights without either food or drink, and it became absolutely necessary that we should make an attempt to get up something from below. As the brig was completely full of water, we went to this work despondingly, and with but little expectation of being able to obtain anything. We made a kind of drag by driving some nails which we broke out from the remains of the companion-hatch into two pieces of wood. Tying these across each other, and fastening them to the end of a rope, we threw them into the cabin, and dragged them to and fro, in the faint hope of being thus able to entangle some article which might be of use to us for food, or which might at least render us assistance in getting it. We spent the greater part of the morning in this labour without effect, fishing up nothing more than a few bed-clothes, which were readily caught by the nails. Indeed, our contrivance was so very clumsy, that any greater success was hardly to be anticipated.

We now tried the forecastle, but equally in vain, and were upon the brink of despair, when Peters proposed that we should fasten a rope to his body, and let him make an attempt to get up something by diving into the cabin. This proposition we hailed with all the delight which reviving hope could inspire. He proceeded immediately to strip off his clothes with the exception of his pantaloons; and a strong rope was then carefully fastened around his middle, being brought up over his shoulders in such a manner that there was no possibility of its slipping. The undertaking was one of great difficulty and danger; for, as we could hardly expect to find much, if any provision in the cabin itself, it was necessary that the diver, after letting himself down, should make a turn to the right, and proceed under water a distance of ten or twelve feet, in a narrow passage, to the storeroom, and return, without drawing breath.

Everything being ready, Peters now descended into the cabin, going down the companion-ladder until the water reached his chin. He then plunged in, head first, turning to the right as he plunged, and endeavouring to make his way to the storeroom. In this first attempt, however, he was altogether unsuccessful. In less than half a minute after his going down we felt the rope jerked violently (the signal we had agreed upon when he desired to be drawn up). We accordingly drew him up instantly, but so incautiously as to bruise him badly against the ladder. He had brought nothing with him, and had been unable to penetrate more than a very little way into the passage, owing to the constant exertions he found it necessary to make in order to keep himself from floating up against the deck. Upon getting out he was very

much exhausted, and had to rest full fifteen minutes before he could again venture to descend.

The second attempt met with even worse success; for he remained so long under water without giving the signal, that, becoming alarmed for his safety, we drew him out without it, and found that he was almost at the last gasp, having, as he said, repeatedly jerked at the rope without our feeling it. This was probably owing to a portion of it having become entangled in the balustrade at the foot of the ladder. This balustrade was, indeed, so much in the way, that we determined to remove it, if possible, before proceeding with our design. As we had no means of getting it away except by main force, we all descended into the water as far as we could on the ladder, and, giving a pull against it with our united strength, succeeded in breaking it down.

The third attempt was equally unsuccessful with the two first, and it now became evident that nothing could be done in this manner without the aid of some weight with which the diver might steady himself, and keep to the floor of the cabin while making his search. For a long time we looked about in vain for something which might answer this purpose; but at length, to our great joy, we discovered one of the weather-forechains so loose that we had not the least difficulty in wrenching it off. Having fastened this securely to one of his ancles, Peters now made his fourth descent into the cabin, and this time succeeded in making his way to the door of the steward's room. To his inexpressible grief, however, he found it locked, and was obliged to return without effecting an entrance, as, with the greatest exertion, he could remain under water not more, at the utmost extent, than a single minute. Our affairs now looked gloomy indeed, and neither Augustus nor myself could refrain from bursting into tears, as we thought of the host of difficulties which encompassed us, and the slight probability which existed of our finally making an escape. But this weakness was not of long duration. Throwing ourselves on our knees to God, we implored his aid in the many dangers which beset us; and arose with renewed hope and vigour to think what could yet be done by mortal means towards accomplishing our deliverance.

Chapter X

Shortly afterward an incident occurred which I am induced to look upon as more intensely productive of emotion, as far more replete with the extremes first of delight and then of horror, than even any of the thousand chances which afterward befell me in nine long years,[6] crowded with events of the most startling, and, in many cases, of the most unconceived and unconceivable character. We were lying on the

6. The time period is of interest to critics looking for errors in Poe's text. The title page indicates June 1827 as the date of the mutiny on the *Grampus*; the whole narrative extends only to March 22, 1828, i.e., between eight and nine months later, not nine years. But Pym's retrospective narrative (purporting to be a "true" account) was published in the summer of 1838, or about nine years after the events described (which lasted nine months); rather than an error, the time scheme is consistent and perhaps symbolically suggestive regarding a "rebirth" theme (see following notes).

deck near the companion-way, and debating the possibility of yet making our way into the storeroom, when, looking towards Augustus, who lay fronting myself, I perceived that he had become all at once deadly pale, and that his lips were quivering in the most singular and unaccountable manner. Greatly alarmed, I spoke to him, but he made me no reply, and I was beginning to think that he was suddenly taken ill, when I took notice of his eyes, which were glaring apparently at some object behind me. I turned my head, and shall never forget the ecstatic joy which thrilled through every particle of my frame, when I perceived a large brig bearing down upon us, and not more than a couple of miles off. I sprung to my feet as if a musket bullet had suddenly struck me to the heart; and, stretching out my arms in the direction of the vessel, stood in this manner, motionless, and unable to articulate a syllable. Peters and Parker were equally affected, although in different ways. The former danced about the deck like a madman, uttering the most extravagant rhodomontades, intermingled with howls and imprecations, while the latter burst into tears, and continued for many minutes weeping like a child.

The vessel in sight was a large hermaphrodite brig, of a Dutch build, and painted black, with a tawdry gilt figurehead.[7] She had evidently seen a good deal of rough weather, and, we supposed, had suffered much in the gale which had proved so disastrous to ourselves; for her foretopmast was gone, and some of her starboard bulwarks. When we first saw her, she was, as I have already said, about two miles off and to windward, bearing down upon us. The breeze was very gentle, and what astonished us chiefly was, that she had no other sails set than her foresail and mainsail, with a flying jib—of course she came down but slowly, and our impatience amounted nearly to phrensy. The awkward manner in which she steered, too, was remarked by all of us, even excited as we were. She yawed about so considerably, that once or twice we thought it impossible she could see us, or imagined that, having seen us, and discovered no person on board, she was about to tack and make off in another direction. Upon each of these occasions we screamed and shouted at the top of our voices, when the stranger would appear to change for a moment her intention, and again hold on towards us—this singular conduct being repeated two or three times, so that at last we could think of no other manner of accounting for it than by supposing the helmsman to be in liquor.[8]

No person was seen upon her decks until she arrived within about a quarter of a mile of us. We then saw three seamen, whom by their dress we took to be Hollanders. Two of these were lying on some old sails near the forecastle, and the third, who appeared to be looking at us with great curiosity, was leaning over the starboard bow near the bowsprit. This last was a stout and tall man, with a very dark skin. He

7. A possible allusion to the *Flying Dutchman* (see notes to "Ms. Found in a Bottle," pp. 107, 110–111 herein); the ship has features of both a brigantine and a schooner (thus is an "hermaphrodite brig" combining features of different genera of ships).
8. Scholars have suggested the influence here of Michael Scott's *Tom Cringle's Log*, a popular British sea novel published in 1833.

seemed by his manner to be encouraging us to have patience, nodding to us in a cheerful although rather odd way, and smiling constantly so as to display a set of the most brilliantly white teeth. As his vessel drew nearer, we saw a red flannel cap which he had on fall from his head into the water; but of this he took little or no notice, continuing his odd smiles and gesticulations. I relate these things and circumstances minutely, and I relate them, it must be understood, precisely as they *appeared* to us.

The brig came on slowly, and now more steadily than before, and— I cannot speak calmly of this event—our hearts leaped up wildly within us, and we poured out our whole souls in shouts and thanksgiving to God for the complete, unexpected, and glorious deliverance that was so palpably at hand. Of a sudden, and all at once, there came wafted over the ocean from the strange vessel (which was now close upon us) a smell, a stench, such as the whole world has no name for —no conception of—hellish—utterly suffocating—insufferable, inconceivable. I gasped for breath, and, turning to my companions, perceived that they were paler than marble. But we had now no time left for question or surmise—the brig was within fifty feet of us, and it seemed to be her intention to run under our counter, that we might board her without her putting out a boat. We rushed aft, when, suddenly, a wide yaw threw her off full five or six points from the course she had been running, and, as she passed under our stern at the distance of about twenty feet, we had a full view of her decks. Shall I ever forget the triple horror of that spectacle? Twenty-five or thirty human bodies, among whom were several females, lay scattered about between the counter and the galley, in the last and most loathsome state of putrefaction! We plainly saw that not a soul lived in that fated vessel! Yet we could not help shouting to the dead for help! Yes, long and loudly did we beg, in the agony of the moment, that those silent and disgusting images would stay for us, would not abandon us to become like them, would receive us among their goodly company! We were raving with horror and despair—thoroughly mad through the anguish of our grievous disappointment.

As our first loud yell of terror broke forth, it was replied to by something, from near the bowsprit of the stranger, so closely resembling the scream of a human voice that the nicest ear might have been startled and deceived. At this instant another sudden yaw brought the region of the forecastle for a moment into view, and we beheld at once the origin of the sound. We saw the tall stout figure still leaning on the bulwark, and still nodding his head to and fro, but his face was now turned from us so that we could not behold it. His arms were extended over the rail, and the palms of his hands fell outward. His knees were lodged upon a stout rope, tightly stretched, and reaching from the heel of the bow-sprit to a cathead. On his back, from which a portion of the shirt had been torn, leaving it bare, there sat a huge seagull, busily gorging itself with the horrible flesh, its bill and talons deep buried, and its white plumage spattered all over with blood. As the brig moved further round so as to bring us close in view, the bird, with

much apparent difficulty, drew out its crimsoned head, and, after eying us for a moment as if stupified, arose lazily from the body upon which it had been feasting, and, flying directly above our deck, hovered there a while with a portion of clotted and liver-like substance in its beak. The horrid morsel dropped at length with a sullen splash immediately at the feet of Parker. May God forgive me, but now, for the first time, there flashed through my mind a thought, a thought which I will not mention, and I felt myself making a step towards the ensanguined spot. I looked upward, and the eyes of Augustus met my own with a degree of intense and eager meaning which immediately brought me to my senses. I sprang forward quickly, and, with a deep shudder, threw the frightful thing into the sea.

The body from which it had been taken, resting as it did upon the rope, had been easily swayed to and fro by the exertions of the carnivorous bird, and it was this motion which had at first impressed us with the belief of its being alive. As the gull relieved it of its weight, it swung round and fell partially over, so that the face was fully discovered. Never, surely, was any object so terribly full of awe! The eyes were gone, and the whole flesh around the mouth, leaving the teeth utterly naked. This, then, was the smile which had cheered us on to hope! this the—but I forbear. The brig, as I have already told, passed under our stern, and made its way slowly but steadily to leeward. With her and with her terrible crew went all our gay visions of deliverance and joy. Deliberately as she went by, we might possibly have found means of boarding her, had not our sudden disappointment, and the appalling nature of the discovery which accompanied it, laid entirely prostrate every active faculty of mind and body. We had seen and felt, but we could neither think nor act, until, alas, too late. How much our intellects had been weakened by this incident may be estimated by the fact, that, when the vessel had proceeded so far that we could perceive no more than the half of her hull, the proposition was seriously entertained of attempting to overtake her by swimming!

I have, since this period, vainly endeavoured to obtain some clew to the hideous uncertainty which enveloped the fate of the stranger. Her build and general appearance, as I have before stated, led us to the belief that she was a Dutch trader, and the dresses of the crew also sustained this opinion. We might have easily seen the name upon her stern, and, indeed, taken other observations which would have guided us in making out her character; but the intense excitement of the moment blinded us to everything of that nature. From the saffron-like hue of such of the corpses as were not entirely decayed, we concluded that the whole of her company had perished by the yellow fever, or some other virulent disease of the same fearful kind. If such were the case (and I know not what else to imagine), death, to judge from the positions of the bodies, must have come upon them in a manner awfully sudden and overwhelming, in a way totally distinct from that which generally characterizes even the most deadly pestilences with which mankind are acquainted. It is possible, indeed, that poison, accidentally introduced into some of their sea-stores, may have brought

about the disaster; or that the eating some unknown venomous species of fish, or other marine animal, or oceanic bird, might have induced it—but it is utterly useless to form conjectures where all is involved, and will, no doubt, remain for ever involved, in the most appalling and unfathomable mystery.

Chapter XI

We spent the remainder of the day in a condition of stupid lethargy, gazing after the retreating vessel until the darkness, hiding her from our sight, recalled us in some measure to our senses. The pangs of hunger and thirst then returned, absorbing all other cares and considerations. Nothing, however, could be done until the morning, and, securing ourselves as well as possible, we endeavoured to snatch a little repose. In this I succeeded beyond my expectation, sleeping until my companions, who had not been so fortunate, aroused me at daybreak to renew our attempts at getting up provision from the hull.

It was now a dead calm, with the sea as smooth as I have ever known it—the weather warm and pleasant. The brig was out of sight. We commenced our operations by wrenching off, with some trouble, another of the forechains; and having fastened both to Peter's feet, he again made an endeavour to reach the door of the store-room, thinking it possible that he might be able to force it open, provided he could get at it in sufficient time; and this he hoped to do, as the hulk lay much more steadily than before.

He succeeded very quickly in reaching the door, when, loosening one of the chains from his ankle, he made every exertion to force a passage with it, but in vain, the framework of the room being far stronger than was anticipated. He was quite exhausted with his long stay under water, and it became absolutely necessary that some other one of us should take his place. For this service Parker immediately volunteered; but, after making three ineffectual efforts, found that he could never even succeed in getting near the door. The condition of Augustus's wounded arm rendered it useless for him to attempt going down, as he would be unable to force the room open should he reach it, and it accordingly now devolved upon me to exert myself for our common deliverance.

Peters had left one of the chains in the passage, and I found, upon plunging in, that I had not sufficient ballast to keep me firmly down. I determined, therefore, to attempt no more, in my first effort, than merely to recover the other chain. In groping along the floor of the passage for this I felt a hard substance, which I immediately grasped, not having time to ascertain what it was, but returning and ascending instantly to the surface. The prize proved to be a bottle, and our joy may be conceived when I say that it was found to be full of Port wine.[9]

9. Cf. the swamping of the ship *Lark* in chapter 58 of Irving's *Astoria*, where a Hawaiian crew member swims into the submerged cabin and brings up "a few bottles of wine and a porter" and then another "quarter cask of wine." Alcohol, in addition to affecting the mind, eventually increases one's thirst rather than relieving it.

Giving thanks to God for this timely and cheering assistance, we immediately drew the cork with my penknife, and, each taking a moderate sup, felt the most indescribable comfort from the warmth, strength, and spirits with which it inspired us. We then carefully recorked the bottle, and, by means of a handkerchief, swung it in such a manner that there was no possibility of its getting broken.

Having rested a while after this fortunate discovery, I again descended, and now recovered the chain, with which I instantly came up. I then fastened it on and went down for the third time, when I became fully satisfied that no exertions whatever, in that situation, would enable me to force open the door of the storeroom. I therefore returned in despair.

There seemed now to be no longer any room for hope, and I could perceive in the countenances of my companions that they had made up their minds to perish. The wine had evidently produced in them a species of delirium, which, perhaps, I had been prevented from feeling by the immersion I had undergone since drinking it. They talked incoherently, and about matters unconnected with our condition, Peters repeatedly asking me questions about Nantucket. Augustus, too, I remember, approached me with a serious air, and requested me to lend him a pocket-comb, as his hair was full of fish scales, and he wished to get them out before going on shore. Parker appeared somewhat less affected, and urged me to dive at random into the cabin, and bring up any article which might come to hand. To this I consented, and, in the first attempt, after staying under a full minute, brought up a small leather trunk belonging to Captain Barnard. This was immediately opened in the faint hope that it might contain something to eat or drink. We found nothing, however, except a box of razors and two linen shirts. I now went down again, and returned without any success. As my head came above water I heard a crash on deck, and, upon getting up, saw that my companions had ungratefully taken advantage of my absence to drink the remainder of the wine, having let the bottle fall in the endeavour to replace it before I saw them. I remonstrated with them on the heartlessness of their conduct, when Augustus burst into tears. The other two endeavoured to laugh the matter off as a joke, but I hope never again to behold laughter of such a species: the distortion of countenance was absolutely frightful. Indeed, it was apparent that the stimulus, in the empty state of their stomachs, had taken instant and violent effect, and that they were all exceedingly intoxicated. With great difficulty I prevailed upon them to lie down, when they fell very soon into a heavy slumber, accompanied with loud stertorous breathing.

I now found myself, as it were, alone in the brig, and my reflections, to be sure, were of the most fearful and gloomy nature. No prospect offered itself to my view but a lingering death by famine, or, at the best, by being overwhelmed in the first gale which should spring up, for in our present exhausted condition we could have no hope of living through another.

The gnawing hunger which I now experienced was nearly insupport-

able, and I felt myself capable of going to any lengths in order to appease it. With my knife I cut off a small portion of the leather trunk, and endeavoured to eat it, but found it utterly impossible to swallow a single morsel, although I fancied that some little alleviation of my suffering was obtained by chewing small pieces of it and spitting them out. Towards night my companions awoke, one by one, each in an indescribable state of weakness and horror, brought on by the wine, whose fumes had now evaporated. They shook as if with a violent ague, and uttered the most lamentable cries for water. Their condition affected me in the most lively degree, at the same time causing me to rejoice in the fortunate train of circumstances which had prevented me from indulging in the wine, and consequently from sharing their melancholy and most distressing sensations. Their conduct, however, gave me great uneasiness and alarm; for it was evident that, unless some favourable change took place, they could afford me no assistance in providing for our common safety. I had not yet abandoned all idea of being able to get up something from below; but the attempt could not possibly be resumed until some one of them was sufficiently master of himself to aid me by holding the end of the rope while I went down. Parker appeared to be somewhat more in possession of his senses than the others, and I endeavoured, by every means in my power, to arouse him. Thinking that a plunge in the seawater might have a beneficial effect, I contrived to fasten the end of a rope around his body, and then, leading him to the companion-way (he remaining quite passive all the while), pushed him in, and immediately drew him out. I had good reason to congratulate myself upon having made this experiment; for he appeared much revived and invigorated, and, upon getting out, asked me, in a rational manner, why I had so served him. Having explained my object, he expressed himself indebted to me, and said that he felt greatly better from the immersion, afterward conversing sensibly upon our situation. We then resolved to treat Augustus and Peters in the same way, which we immediately did, when they both experienced much benefit from the shock. This idea of sudden immersion had been suggested to me by reading in some medical work the good effect of the shower-bath in a case where the patient was suffering from *mania a potu.*[1]

Finding that I could now trust my companions to hold the end of the rope, I again made three or four plunges into the cabin, although it was now quite dark, and a gentle but long swell from the northward rendered the hulk somewhat unsteady. In the course of these attempts I succeeded in bringing up two case-knives, a three-gallon jug, empty, and a blanket, but nothing which could serve us for food. I continued my efforts, after getting these articles, until I was completely exhausted, but brought up nothing else. During the night Parker and Peters occupied themselves by turns in the same manner; but nothing coming to hand, we now gave up this attempt in despair, concluding that we were exhausting ourselves in vain.

1. Madness (mania) from drink; i.e., from drinking too much alcohol.

We passed the remainder of this night in a state of the most intense mental and bodily anguish that can possibly be imagined. The morning of the sixteenth at length dawned, and we looked eagerly around the horizon for relief, but to no purpose. The sea was still smooth, with only a long swell from the northward, as on yesterday. This was the sixth day since we had tasted either food or drink, with the exception of the bottle of Port wine, and it was clear that we could hold out but a very little while longer unless something could be obtained. I never saw before, nor wish to see again, human beings so utterly emaciated as Peters and Augustus. Had I met them on shore in their present condition I should not have had the slightest suspicion that I had ever beheld them. Their countenances were totally changed in character, so that I could not bring myself to believe them really the same individuals with whom I had been in company but a few days before. Parker, although sadly reduced, and so feeble that he could not raise his head from his bosom, was not so far gone as the other two. He suffered with great patience, making no complaint, and endeavouring to inspire us with hope in every manner he could devise. For myself, although at the commencement of the voyage I had been in bad health, and was at all times of a delicate constitution, I suffered less than any of us, being much less reduced in frame, and retaining my powers of mind in a surprising degree, while the rest were completely prostrated in intellect, and seemed to be brought to a species of second childhood, generally simpering in their expressions, with idiotic smiles, and uttering the most absurd platitudes. At intervals, however, they would appear to revive suddenly, as if inspired all at once with a consciousness of their condition, when they would spring upon their feet in a momentary flash of vigour, and speak, for a short period, of their prospects, in a manner altogether rational, although full of the most intense despair. It is possible, however, that my companions may have entertained the same opinion of their own condition as I did of mine, and that I may have unwittingly been guilty of the same extravagances and imbecilities as themselves—this is a matter which cannot be determined.

About noon Parker declared that he saw land off the larboard[2] quarter, and it was with the utmost difficulty I could restrain him from plunging into the sea with the view of swimming towards it. Peters and Augustus took little notice of what he said, being apparently wrapped up in moody contemplation. Upon looking in the direction pointed out I could not perceive the faintest appearance of the shore—indeed, I was too well aware that we were far from any land to indulge in a hope of that nature. It was a long time, nevertheless, before I could convince Parker of his mistake. He then burst into a flood of tears, weeping like a child, with loud cries and sobs, for two or three hours, when, becoming exhausted, he fell asleep.

Peters and Augustus now made several ineffectual efforts to swallow portions of the leather. I advised them to chew it and spit it out; but

2. Port (left) side. The term has been used by Pym before, apparently not always with precision. The origin of the term is probably an elision from "loading side."

they were too excessively debilitated to be able to follow my advice. I continued to chew pieces of it at intervals, and found some relief from so doing; my chief distress was for water, and I was only prevented from taking a draught from the sea by remembering the horrible consequences which thus have resulted to others who were similarly situated with ourselves.

The day wore on in this manner, when I suddenly discovered a sail to the eastward, and on our larboard bow. She appeared to be a large ship, and was coming nearly athwart us, being probably twelve or fifteen miles distant. None of my companions had as yet discovered her, and I forbore to tell them of her for the present, lest we might again be disappointed of relief. At length, upon her getting nearer, I saw distinctly that she was heading immediately for us, with her light sails filled. I could now contain myself no longer, and pointed her out to my fellow-sufferers. They immediately sprang to their feet, again indulging in the most extravagant demonstrations of joy, weeping, laughing in an idiotic manner, jumping, stamping upon the deck, tearing their hair, and praying and cursing by turns. I was so affected by their conduct, as well as by what I now considered a sure prospect of deliverance, that I could not refrain from joining in with their madness, and gave way to the impulses of my gratitude and ecstasy by lying and rolling on the deck, clapping my hands, shouting, and other similar acts, until I was suddenly called to my recollection, and once more to the extreme of human misery and despair, by perceiving the ship all at once with her stern fully presented towards us, and steering in a direction nearly opposite to that in which I had at first perceived her.

It was some time before I could induce my poor companions to believe that this sad reverse in our prospects had actually taken place. They replied to all my assertions with a stare and a gesture implying that they were not to be deceived by such misrepresentations. The conduct of Augustus most sensibly affected me. In spite of all I could say or do to the contrary, he persisted in saying that the ship was rapidly nearing us, and in making preparations to go on board of her. Some seaweed floating by the brig, he maintained that it was the ship's boat, and endeavoured to throw himself upon it, howling and shrieking in the most heartrending manner, when I forcibly restrained him from thus casting himself into the sea.

Having become in some degree pacified, we continued to watch the ship until we finally lost sight of her, the weather becoming hazy, with a light breeze springing up. As soon as she was entirely gone, Parker turned suddenly towards me with an expression of countenance which made me shudder. There was about him an air of self-possession which I had not noticed in him until now, and before he opened his lips my heart told me what he would say. He proposed, in a few words, that one of us should die to preserve the existence of the others.[3]

3. Critics have suggested the symbolic relation of cannibalism here with the Christian ritual of communion, perhaps reinforced by the baptismal suggestions of casting oneself into the sea. Whatever the force of such possible symbolism, encounters with instances of cannibalism were literal features of many travel adventures. One of the most famous is Owen Chase's

Chapter XII

I had, for some time past, dwelt upon the prospect of our being re-
duced to this last horrible extremity, and had secretly made up my
mind to suffer death in any shape or under any circumstances rather
than resort to such a course. Nor was this resolution in any degree
weakened by the present intensity of hunger under which I laboured.
The proposition had not been heard by either Peters or Augustus. I
therefore took Parker aside; and mentally praying to God for power to
dissuade him from the horrible purpose he entertained, I expostulated
with him for a long time and in the most supplicating manner, begging
him in the name of everything which he held sacred, and urging him
by every species of argument which the extremity of the case sug-
gested, to abandon the idea, and not to mention it to either of the
other two.

He heard all I said without attempting to controvert any of my argu-
ments, and I had begun to hope that he would be prevailed upon to do
as I desired. But when I had ceased speaking, he said that he knew
very well all I had said was true, and that to resort to such a course
was the most horrible alternative which could enter into the mind of
man; but that he had now held out as long as human nature could be
sustained; that it was unnecessary for all to perish, when, by the death
of one, it was possible, and even probable, that the rest might be fi-
nally preserved; adding that I might save myself the trouble of trying
to turn him from his purpose, his mind having been thoroughly made
up on the subject even before the appearance of the ship, and that
only her heaving in sight had prevented him from mentioning his in-
tention at an earlier period.

I now begged him, if he would not be prevailed upon to abandon his
design, at least to defer it for another day, when some vessel might
come to our relief; again reiterating every argument I could devise,
and which I thought likely to have influence with one of his rough na-
ture. He said, in reply; that he had not spoken until the very last pos-
sible moment; that he could exist no longer without sustenance of
some kind; and that therefore in another day his suggestion would be
too late, as regarded himself at least.

Finding that he was not to be moved by anything I could say in a
mild tone, I now assumed a different demeanour, and told him that he
must be aware I had suffered less than any of us from our calamities;
that my health and strength, consequently, were at that moment far
better than his own, or than that either of Peters or Augustus; in short,
that I was in a condition to have my own way by force if I found it nec-
essary; and that, if he attempted in any manner to acquaint the others
with his bloody and cannibal designs, I would not hesitate to throw
him into the sea. Upon this he immediately seized me by the throat,
and drawing a knife, made several ineffectual efforts to stab me in the

*Narrative of the Most Extraordinary and Distressing Shipwreck of the Whale-Ship Essex of
Nantucket, Which Was Attacked and Finally Destroyed by a Large Spermacetti-Whale in the
Pacific Ocean* (1821), a source for Melville's *Moby-Dick*.

stomach; an atrocity which his excessive debility alone prevented him from accomplishing. In the mean time, being roused to a high pitch of anger, I forced him to the vessel's side, with the full intention of throwing him overboard. He was saved from this fate, however, by the interference of Peters, who now approached and separated us, asking the cause of the disturbance. This Parker told before I could find means in any manner to prevent him.

The effect of his words was even more terrible than what I had anticipated. Both Augustus and Peters, who, it seems, had long secretly entertained the same fearful idea which Parker had been merely the first to broach, joined with him in his design, and insisted upon its being immediately carried into effect. I had calculated that one at least of the two former would be found still possessed of sufficient strength of mind to side with myself in resisting any attempt to execute so dreadful a purpose; and, with the aid of either one of them, I had no fear of being able to prevent its accomplishment. Being disappointed in this expectation, it became absolutely necessary that I should attend to my own safety, as a further resistance on my part might possibly be considered by men in their frightful condition a sufficient excuse for refusing me fair play in the tragedy that I knew would speedily be enacted.

I now told them I was willing to submit to the proposal, merely requesting a delay of about one hour, in order that the fog which had gathered around us might have an opportunity of lifting, when it was possible that the ship we had seen might be again in sight. After great difficulty I obtained from them a promise to wait thus long; and, as I had anticipated (a breeze rapidly coming in), the fog lifted before the hour had expired, when, no vessel appearing in sight, we prepared to draw lots.[4]

It is with extreme reluctance that I dwell upon the appalling scene which ensued; a scene which, with its minutest details, no after events have been able to efface in the slightest degree from my memory, and whose stern recollection will imbitter every future moment of my existence. Let me run over this portion of my narrative with as much haste as the nature of the events to be spoken of will permit. The only method we could devise for the terrific lottery, in which we were to take each a chance, was that of drawing straws. Small splinters of wood were made to answer our purpose, and it was agreed that I should be the holder. I retired to one end of the hulk, while my poor companions silently took up their station in the other with their backs turned towards me. The bitterest anxiety which I endured at any period of this fearful drama was while I occupied myself in the arrangement of the lots. There are few conditions into which man can possibly fall where he will not feel a deep interest in the preservation of his existence; an interest momentarily increasing with the frailness of the tenure by which that existence may be held. But now that the

4. Some critics suggest biblical allusions in the drawing of lots (see Matthew 27:35, Mark 15:24, Luke 23:24; and John 19:23–24. See also Owen Chase's account of surviving the wreck of the *Essex*.

silent, definite, and stern nature of the business in which I was en-
gaged (so different from the tumultuous dangers of the storm or the
gradually approaching horrors of famine) allowed me to reflect on the
few chances I had of escaping the most appalling of deaths—a death
for the most appalling of purposes—every particle of that energy
which had so long buoyed me up departed like feathers before the
wind, leaving me a helpless prey to the most abject and pitiable terror.
I could not, at first, even summon up sufficient strength to tear and fit
together the small splinters of wood, my fingers absolutely refusing
their office, and my knees knocking violently against each other. My
mind ran over rapidly a thousand absurd projects by which to avoid
becoming a partner in the awful speculation. I thought of falling on
my knees to my companions, and entreating them to let me escape
this necessity; of suddenly rushing upon them, and, by putting one of
them to death, of rendering the decision by lot useless—in short, of
everything but of going through with the matter I had in hand. At last,
after wasting a long time in this imbecile conduct, I was recalled to my
senses by the voice of Parker, who urged me to relieve them at once
from the terrible anxiety they were enduring. Even then I could not
bring myself to arrange the splinters upon the spot, but thought over
every species of finesse by which I could trick some one of my fellow-
sufferers to draw the short straw, as it had been agreed that whoever
drew the shortest of four splinters from my hand was to die for the
preservation of the rest. Before any one condemn me for this apparent
heartlessness, let him be placed in a situation precisely similar to my
own.

At length delay was no longer possible, and, with a heart almost
bursting from my bosom, I advanced to the region of the forecastle,
where my companions were awaiting me. I held out my hand with the
splinters, and Peters immediately drew. He was free—his, at least, was
not the shortest; and there was now another chance against my es-
cape. I summoned up all my strength, and passed the lots to Augustus.
He also drew immediately, and he also was free; and now, whether I
should live or die, the chances were no more than precisely even. At
this moment all the fierceness of the tiger possessed my bosom, and I
felt towards my poor fellow-creature, Parker, the most intense, the
most diabolical hatred. But the feeling did not last; and, at length,
with a convulsive shudder and closed eyes, I held out the two remain-
ing splinters towards him. It was full five minutes before he could
summon resolution to draw, during which period of heartrending sus-
pense I never once opened my eyes. Presently one of the two lots was
quickly drawn from my hand. The decision was then over, yet I knew
not whether it was for me or against me. No one spoke, and still I
dared not satisfy myself by looking at the splinter I held. Peters at
length took me by the hand, and I forced myself to look up, when I
immediately saw by the countenance of Parker that I was safe, and
that he it was who had been doomed to suffer. Gasping for breath, I
fell senseless to the deck.

I recovered from my swoon in time to behold the consummation of

the tragedy in the death of him who had been chiefly instrumental in bringing it about. He made no resistance whatever, and was stabbed in the back by Peters, when he fell instantly dead. I must not dwell upon the fearful repast which immediately ensued. Such things may be imagined, but words have no power to impress the mind with the exquisite horror of their reality. Let it suffice to say that, having in some measure appeased the raging thirst which consumed us by the blood of the victim, and having by common consent taken off the hands, feet, and head, throwing them, together with the entrails, into the sea, we devoured the rest of the body, piecemeal, during the four ever memorable days of the seventeenth eighteenth, nineteenth, and twentieth of the month.

On the nineteenth, there coming on a smart shower which lasted fifteen or twenty minutes, we contrived to catch some water by means of a sheet which had been fished up from the cabin by our drag just after the gale. The quantity we took in all did not amount to more than half a gallon; but even this scanty allowance supplied us with comparative strength and hope.

On the twenty-first we were again reduced to the last necessity. The weather still remained warm and pleasant, with occasional fogs and light breezes, most usually from N. to W.

On the twenty-second, as we were sitting close huddled together, gloomily revolving over our lamentable condition, there flashed through my mind all at once an idea which inspired me with a bright gleam of hope. I remembered that, when the foremast had been cut away, Peters, being in the windward chains, passed one of the axes into my hand, requesting me to put it, if possible, in a place of security, and that a few minutes before the last heavy sea struck the brig and filled her I had taken this axe into the forecastle, and laid it in one of the larboard berths. I now thought it possible that, by getting at this axe, we might cut through the deck over the store-room, and thus readily supply ourselves with provisions.

When I communicated this project to my companions, they uttered a feeble shout of joy, and we all proceeded forthwith to the forecastle. The difficulty of descending here was greater than that of going down in the cabin, the opening being much smaller, for it will be remembered that the whole framework about the cabin companion-hatch had been carried away, whereas the forecastle-way, being a simple hatch of only about three feet square, had remained uninjured. I did not hesitate, however, to attempt the descent; and, a rope being fastened round my body as before, I plunged boldly in, feet foremost, made my way quickly to the berth, and, at the very first attempt, brought up the axe. It was hailed with the most ecstatic joy and triumph, and the ease with which it had been obtained was regarded as an omen of our ultimate preservation.

We now commenced cutting at the deck with all the energy of rekindled hope, Peters and myself taking the axe by turns, Augustus's wounded arm not permitting him to aid us in any degree. As we were still so feeble as to be scarcely able to stand unsupported, and could

consequently work but a minute or two without resting, it soon became evident that many long hours would be requisite to accomplish our task—that is, to cut an opening sufficiently large to admit of a free access to the storeroom. This consideration, however, did not discourage us; and, working all night by the light of the moon, we succeeded in effecting our purpose by daybreak on the morning of the twenty-third.

Peters now volunteered to go down; and, having made all arrangements as before, he descended, and soon returned, bringing up with him a small jar, which, to our great joy, proved to be full of olives. Having shared these among us, and devoured them with the greatest avidity, we proceeded to let him down again. This time he succeeded beyond our utmost expectations, returning instantly with a large ham and a bottle of Madeira wine. Of the latter we each took a moderate sup, having learned by experience the pernicious consequences of indulging too freely. The ham, except about two pounds near the bone, was not in a condition to be eaten, having been entirely spoiled by the salt water. The sound part was divided among us. Peters and Augustus, not being able to restrain their appetite, swallowed theirs upon the instant; but I was more cautious, and ate but a small portion of mine, dreading the thirst which I knew would ensue. We now rested a while from our labours, which had been intolerably severe.

By noon, feeling somewhat strengthened and refreshed, we again renewed our attempt at getting up provision, Peters and myself going down alternately, and always with more or less success, until sundown. During this interval we had the good fortune to bring up, altogether, four more small jars of olives, another ham, a carboy containing nearly three gallons of excellent Cape Madeira wine, and, what gave us still more delight, a small tortoise of the Gallipago breed, several of which had been taken on board by Captain Barnard, as the Grampus was leaving port, from the schooner Mary Pitts, just returned from a sealing voyage in the Pacific.

In a subsequent portion of this narrative I shall have frequent occasion to mention this species of tortoise.[5] It is found principally, as most of my readers may know, in the group of islands called the Gallipagos, which, indeed, derive their name from the animal—the Spanish word Gallipago meaning a fresh-water terapin. From the peculiarity of their shape and action they have been sometimes called the elephant tortoise. They are frequently found of an enormous size. I have myself seen several which would weigh from twelve to fifteen hundred pounds, although I do not remember that any navigator speaks of having seen them weighing more than eight hundred. Their appearance is singular, and even disgusting. Their steps are very slow, measured, and heavy, their bodies being carried about a foot from the

5. An inaccuracy apparently (it is called a "fresh-water terapin" in the next sentence), for the Galápagos tortoise is a land, not a marine, animal. The description is partially derived from Morrell's *A Narrative of Four Voyages*. Herman Melville was also fascinated by the tortoise of the Galápagos Islands (which lie approximately six hundred miles west of the Ecuador coast along the Equator). See the ten sketches of Melville's "The Encantadas" (the Enchanted Isles) in Melville's *Piazza Tales* (1856); critics have also found echoes of *Pym* in *Moby-Dick*.

ground. Their neck is long, and exceedingly slender; from eighteen inches to two feet is a very common length, and I killed one, where the distance from the shoulder to the extremity of the head was no less than three feet ten inches. The head has a striking resemblance to that of a serpent. They can exist without food for an almost incredible length of time, instances having been known where they have been thrown into the hold of a vessel and lain two years without nourishment of any kind—being as fat, and, in every respect, in as good order at the expiration of the time as when they were first put in. In one particular these extraordinary animals bear a resemblance to the dromedary, or camel of the desert. In a bag at the root of the neck they carry with them a constant supply of water. In some instances, upon killing them after a full year's deprivation of all nourishment, as much as three gallons of perfectly sweet and fresh water have been found in their bags. Their food is chiefly wild parsley and celery, with purslain, sea-kelp, and prickly pears, upon which latter vegetable they thrive wonderfully, a great quantity of it being usually found on the hillsides near the shore wherever the animal itself is discovered. They are excellent and highly nutritious food, and have, no doubt, been the means of preserving the lives of thousands of seamen employed in the whale-fishery and other pursuits in the Pacific.

The one which we had the good fortune to bring up from the store-room was not of a large size, weighing probably sixty-five or seventy pounds. It was a female, and in excellent condition, being exceedingly fat, and having more than a quart of limpid and sweet water in its bag. This was indeed a treasure; and, falling on our knees with one accord, we returned fervent thanks to God for so seasonable a relief.

We had great difficulty in getting the animal up through the opening, as its struggles were fierce and its strength prodigious. It was upon the point of making its escape from Peters's grasp, and slipping back into the water, when Augustus, throwing a rope with a slip-knot around its throat, held it up in this manner until I jumped into the hole by the side of Peters, and assisted him in lifting it out.

The water we drew carefully from the bag into the jug, which, it will be remembered, had been brought up before from the cabin. Having done this, we broke off the neck of a bottle so as to form, with the cork, a kind of glass, holding not quite half a gill. We then each drank one of these measures full, and resolved to limit ourselves to this quantity per day as long as it should hold out.

During the last two or three days, the weather having been dry and pleasant, the bedding we had obtained from the cabin, as well as our clothing, had become thoroughly dry, so that we passed this night (that of the twenty-third) in comparative comfort, enjoying a tranquil repose, after having supped plentifully on olives and ham, with a small allowance of the wine. Being afraid of losing some of our stores overboard during the night, in the event of a breeze springing up, we secured them as well as possible with cordage to the fragments of the windlass. Our tortoise, which we were anxious to preserve alive as long as we could, we threw on his back, and otherwise carefully fastened.

Chapter XIII

July 24. This morning saw us wonderfully recruited in spirits and strength. Notwithstanding the perilous situation in which we were still placed, ignorant of our position, although certainly at a great distance from land, without more food than would last us for a fortnight even with great care, almost entirely without water, and floating about at the mercy of every wind and wave, on the merest wreck in the world, still the infinitely more terrible distresses and dangers from which we had so lately and so providentially been delivered caused us to regard what we now endured as but little more than an ordinary evil—so strictly comparative is either good or ill.

At sunrise we were preparing to renew our attempts at getting up something from the storeroom, when, a smart shower coming on, with some lightning, we turned our attention to the catching of water by means of the sheet we had used before for this purpose. We had no other means of collecting the rain than by holding the sheet spread out with one of the forechain-plates in the middle of it. The water, thus conducted to the centre, was drained through into our jug. We had nearly filled it in this manner, when, a heavy squall coming on from the northward, obliged us to desist, as the hulk began once more to roll so violently that we could no longer keep our feet. We now went forward, and, lashing ourselves securely to the remnant of the wind-lass as before, awaited the event with far more calmness than could have been anticipated, or would have been imagined possible under the circumstances. At noon the wind had freshened into a two-reef breeze, and by night into a stiff gale, accompanied with a tremendously heavy swell. Experience having taught us, however, the best method of arranging our lashings, we weathered this dreary night in tolerable security, although thoroughly drenched at almost every instant by the sea, and in momentary dread of being washed off. Fortunately, the weather was so warm as to render the water rather grateful than otherwise.

July 25. This morning the gale had diminished to a mere ten-knot breeze, and the sea had gone down with it so considerably that we were able to keep ourselves dry upon the deck. To our great grief, however, we found that two jars of our olives, as well as the whole of our ham, had been washed overboard, in spite of the careful manner in which they had been fastened. We determined not to kill the tortoise as yet, and contented ourselves for the present with a breakfast on a few of the olives, and a measure of water each, which latter we mixed, half and half, with wine, finding great relief and strength from the mixture, without the distressing intoxication which had ensued upon drinking the Port. The sea was still far too rough for the renewal of our efforts at getting up provision from the storeroom. Several articles, of no importance to us in our present situation, floated up through the opening during the day, and were immediately washed overboard. We also now observed that the hulk lay more along than ever, so that we could not stand an instant without lashing ourselves. On this account

we passed a gloomy and uncomfortable day. At noon the sun appeared to be nearly vertical, and we had no doubt that we had been driven down by the long succession of northward and northwesterly winds into the near vicinity of the equator. Towards evening saw several sharks, and were somewhat alarmed by the audacious manner in which an enormously large one approached us. At one time, a lurch throwing the deck very far beneath the water, the monster actually swam in upon us, floundering for some moments just over the companion-hatch, and striking Peters violently with his tail. A heavy sea at length hurled him overboard, much to our relief. In moderate weather we might have easily captured him.

July 26. This morning, the wind having greatly abated, and the sea not being very rough, we determined to renew our exertions in the storeroom. After a great deal of hard labour during the whole day, we found that nothing further was to be expected from this quarter, the partitions of the room having been stove during the night, and its contents swept into the hold. This discovery, as may be supposed, filled us with despair.

July 27. The sea nearly smooth, with a light wind, and still from the northward and westward. The sun coming out hotly in the afternoon, we occupied ourselves in drying our clothes. Found great relief from thirst, and much comfort otherwise, by bathing in the sea; in this, however, we were forced to use great caution, being afraid of sharks, several of which were seen swimming around the brig during the day.

July 28. Good weather still. The brig now began to lie along so alarmingly that we feared she would eventually roll bottom up. Prepared ourselves as well as we could for this emergency, lashing our tortoise, water-jug, and two remaining jars of olives as far as possible over to the windward, placing them outside the hull, below the main-chains. The sea very smooth all day, with little or no wind.

July 29. A continuance of the same weather. Augustus's wounded arm began to evince symptoms of mortification. He complained of drowsiness and excessive thirst, but no acute pain. Nothing could be done for his relief beyond rubbing his wounds with a little of the vinegar from the olives, and from this no benefit seemed to be experienced. We did everything in our power for his comfort, and trebled his allowance of water.

July 30. An excessively hot day, with no wind. An enormous shark kept close by the hulk during the whole of the forenoon. We made several unsuccessful attempts to capture him by means of a noose. Augustus much worse, and evidently sinking as much from want of proper nourishment as from the effect of his wounds. He constantly prayed to be released from his sufferings, wishing for nothing but death. This evening we ate the last of our olives, and found the water in our jug so putrid that we could not swallow it at all without the addition of wine. Determined to kill our tortoise in the morning.

July 31. After a night of excessive anxiety and fatigue, owing to the position of the hulk, we set about killing and cutting up our tortoise. He proved to be much smaller than we had supposed, although in

good condition—the whole meat about him not amounting to more than ten pounds. With a view of preserving a portion of this as long as possible, we cut it into fine pieces, and filled with them our three remaining olive-jars and the wine-bottle (all of which had been kept), pouring in afterward the vinegar from the olives. In this manner we put away about three pounds of the tortoise, intending not to touch it until we had consumed the rest. We concluded to restrict ourselves to about four ounces of the meat per day; the whole would thus last us thirteen days. A brisk shower, with severe thunder and lightning, came on about dusk, but lasted so short a time that we only succeeded in catching about half a pint of water. The whole of this, by common consent, was given to Augustus, who now appeared to be in the last extremity. He drank the water from the sheet as we caught it (we holding it above him as he lay so as to let it run into his mouth), for we had now nothing left capable of holding water, unless we had chosen to empty out our wine from the carboy, or the stale water from the jug. Either of these expedients would have been resorted to had the shower lasted.

The sufferer seemed to derive but little benefit from the draught. His arm was completely black from the wrist to the shoulder, and his feet were like ice. We expected every moment to see him breathe his last. He was frightfully emaciated; so much so that, although he weighed a hundred and twenty-seven pounds upon his leaving Nantucket, he now did not weigh more than *forty or fifty at the farthest*.[6] His eyes were sunk far in his head, being scarcely perceptible, and the skin of his cheeks hung so loosely as to prevent his masticating any food, or even swallowing any liquid, without great difficulty.

August 1. A continuance of the same calm weather, with an oppressively hot sun. Suffered exceedingly from thirst, the water in the jug being absolutely putrid and swarming with vermin. We contrived, nevertheless, to swallow a portion of it by mixing it with wine—our thirst, however, was but little abated. We found more relief by bathing in the sea, but could not avail ourselves of this expedient except at long intervals, on account of the continual presence of sharks. We now saw clearly that Augustus could not be saved; that he was evidently dying. We could do nothing to relieve his sufferings, which appeared to be great. About twelve o'clock he expired in strong convulsions, and without having spoken for several hours.[7] His death filled us with the most gloomy forebodings, and had so great an effect upon our spirits that we sat motionless by the corpse during the whole day, and never addressed each other except in a whisper. It was not until some time after dark that we took courage to get up and throw the body overboard. It was then loathsome beyond expression, and so far decayed that, as Peters attempted to lift it, an entire leg came off in his grasp. As the mass of putrefaction slipped over the vessel's side into the water, the glare of phosphoric light with which it was surrounded plainly discov-

6. Cf. James Riley's *An Authentic Narrative of the American Brig Commerce* (1818).
7. Some critics have attempted to see special autobiographical significance in this date. August 1 is when Poe's brother, William Henry Leonard Poe, died. Cf. p. 527, n. 4 herein.

ered to us seven or eight large sharks, the clashing of whose horrible
teeth, as their prey was torn to pieces among them, might have been
heard at the distance of a mile. We shrunk within ourselves in the ex-
tremity of horror at the sound.

August 2. The same fearfully calm and hot weather. The dawn found
us in a state of pitiable dejection as well as bodily exhaustion. The wa-
ter in the jug was now absolutely useless, being a thick gelatinous
mass; nothing but frightful-looking worms mingled with slime. We
threw it out, and washed the jug well in the sea, afterward pouring a
little vinegar in it from our bottles of pickled tortoise. Our thirst could
now scarcely be endured, and we tried in vain to relieve it by wine,
which seemed only to add fuel to the flame, and excited us to a high
degree of intoxication. We afterward endeavoured to relieve our suf-
ferings by mixing the wine with seawater; but this instantly brought
about the most violent retchings, so that we never again attempted it.
During the whole day we anxiously sought an opportunity of bathing,
but to no purpose; for the hulk was now entirely besieged on all sides
with sharks—no doubt the identical monsters who had devoured our
poor companion on the evening before, and who were in momentary
expectation of another similar feast. This circumstance occasioned
us the most bitter regret, and filled us with the most depressing and
melancholy forebodings. We had experienced indescribable relief in
bathing, and to have this resource cut off in so frightful a manner was
more than we could bear. Nor, indeed, were we altogether free from
the apprehension of immediate danger, for the least slip or false move-
ment would have thrown us at once within reach of these voracious
fish, who frequently thrust themselves directly upon us, swimming up
to leeward. No shouts or exertions on our part seemed to alarm them.
Even when one of the largest was struck with an axe by Peters, and
much wounded, he persisted in his attempts to push in where we
were. A cloud came up at dusk, but, to our extreme anguish, passed
over without discharging itself. It is quite impossible to conceive our
sufferings from thirst at this period. We passed a sleepless night, both
on this account and through dread of the sharks.

August 3. No prospect of relief, and the brig lying still more and
more along, so that now we could not maintain a footing upon deck at
all. Busied ourselves in securing our wine and tortoise-meat, so that
we might not lose them in the event of our rolling over. Got out two
stout spikes from the forechains, and, by means of the axe, drove them
into the hull to windward within a couple of feet of the water; this not
being very far from the keel, as we were nearly upon our beam-ends.
To these spikes we now lashed our provisions, as being more secure
than their former position beneath the chains. Suffered great agony
from thirst during the whole day—no chance of bathing on account of
the sharks, which never left us for a moment. Found it impossible to
sleep.

August 4. A little before daybreak we perceived that the hulk was
heeling over, and aroused ourselves to prevent being thrown off by the
movement. At first the roll was slow and gradual, and we contrived to

clamber over to windward very well, having taken the precaution to leave ropes hanging from the spikes we had driven in for the provision. But we had not calculated sufficiently upon the acceleration of the impetus; for presently the heel became too violent to allow of our keeping pace with it; and, before either of us knew what was to happen, we found ourselves hurled furiously into the sea, and struggling several fathoms beneath the surface, with the huge hull immediately above us.

In going under the water I had been obliged to let go my hold upon the rope; and finding that I was completely beneath the vessel, and my strength utterly exhausted, I scarcely made a struggle for life, and resigned myself, in a few seconds, to die. But here again I was deceived, not having taken into consideration the natural rebound of the hull to windward. The whirl of the water upward, which the vessel occasioned in rolling partially back, brought me to the surface still more violently than I had been plunged beneath. Upon coming up, I found myself about twenty yards from the hulk, as near as I could judge. She was lying keel up, rocking furiously from side to side, and the sea in all directions around was much agitated, and full of strong whirlpools. I could see nothing of Peters. An oil-cask was floating within a few feet of me, and various other articles from the brig were scattered about.

My principal terror was now on account of the sharks, which I knew to be in my vicinity. In order to deter these, if possible, from approaching me, I splashed the water vigorously with both hands and feet as I swam towards the hulk, creating a body of foam. I have no doubt that to this expedient, simple as it was, I was indebted for my preservation; for the sea all around the brig, just before her rolling over, was so crowded with these monsters, that I must have been, and really was, in actual contact with some of them during my progress. By great good fortune, however, I reached the side of the vessel in safety, although so utterly weakened by the violent exertion I had used that I should never have been able to get upon it but for the timely assistance of Peters, who now, to my great joy, made his appearance (having scrambled up to the keel from the opposite side of the hull), and threw me the end of a rope—one of those which had been attached to the spikes.

Having barely escaped this danger, our attention was now directed to the dreadful imminency of another; that of absolute starvation. Our whole stock of provision had been swept overboard in spite of all our care in securing it; and seeing no longer the remotest possibility of obtaining more, we gave way both of us to despair, weeping aloud like children, and neither of us attempting to offer consolation to the other. Such weakness can scarcely be conceived, and to those who have never been similarly situated will, no doubt, appear unnatural; but it must be remembered that our intellects were so entirely disordered by the long course of privation and terror to which we had been subjected, that we could not justly be considered, at that period, in the light of rational beings. In subsequent perils, nearly as great, if not greater, I bore up with fortitude against all the evils of my situation,

and Peters, it will be seen, evinced a stoical philosophy nearly as incredible as his present childlike supineness and imbecility—the mental condition made the difference.

The overturning of the brig, even with the consequent loss of the wine and turtle, would not, in fact, have rendered our situation more deplorable than before, except for the disappearance of the bedclothes by which we had been hitherto enabled to catch rainwater, and of the jug in which we had kept it when caught; for we found the whole bottom, from within two or three feet of the bends as far as the keel, together with the keel itself, *thickly covered with large barnacles, which proved to be excellent and highly nutritious food.* Thus, in two important respects, the accident we had so greatly dreaded proved a benefit rather than an injury; it had opened to us a supply of provisions, which we could not have exhausted, using it moderately, in a month; and it had greatly contributed to our comfort as regards position, we being much more at our ease, and in infinitely less danger, than before.

The difficulty, however, of now obtaining water blinded us to all the benefits of the change in our condition. That we might be ready to avail ourselves, as far as possible, of any shower which might fall, we took off our shirts, to make use of them as we had of the sheets—not hoping, of course, to get more in this way, even under the most favourable circumstances, than half a gill at a time. No signs of a cloud appeared during the day, and the agonies of our thirst were nearly intolerable At night Peters obtained about an hour's disturbed sleep, but my intense sufferings would not permit me to close my eyes for a single moment.

August 5. To-day, a gentle breeze springing up carried us through a vast quantity of seaweed, among which we were so fortunate as to find eleven small crabs, which afforded us several delicious meals. Their shells being quite soft, we ate them entire, and found that they irritated our thirst far less than the barnacles. Seeing no trace of sharks among the seaweed, we also ventured to bathe, and remained in the water for four or five hours, during which we experienced a very sensible diminution of our thirst. Were greatly refreshed, and spent the night somewhat more comfortably than before, both of us snatching a little sleep.

August 6. This day we were blessed by a brisk and continual rain, lasting from about noon until after dark. Bitterly did we now regret the loss of our jug and carboy; for, in spite of the little means we had of catching the water, we might have filled one, if not both of them. As it was, we contrived to satisfy the cravings of thirst by suffering the shirts to become saturated, and then wringing them so as to let the grateful fluid trickle into our mouths. In this occupation we passed the entire day.

August 7. Just at daybreak we both at the same instant descried a sail to the eastward, and *evidently coming towards us!* We hailed the glorious sight with a long, although feeble shout of rapture; and began instantly to make every signal in our power, by flaring the shirts in the

air, leaping as high as our weak condition would permit, and even by halloing with all the strength of our lungs, although the vessel could not have been less than fifteen miles distant. However, she still continued to near our hulk, and we felt that, if she but held her present course, she must eventually come so close as to perceive us. In about an hour after we first discovered her we could clearly see the people on her decks. She was a long, low, and rakish-looking topsail schooner, with a black ball in her foretopsail, and had, apparently, a full crew. We now became alarmed, for we could hardly imagine it possible that she did not observe us, and were apprehensive that she meant to leave us to perish as we were—an act of fiendish barbarity, which, however incredible it may appear, has been repeatedly perpetrated at sea, under circumstances very nearly similar, and by beings who were regarded as belonging to the human species.[8] In this instance, however, by the mercy of God, we were destined to be most happily deceived; for presently we were aware of a sudden commotion on the deck of the stranger, who immediately afterward run up a British flag, and, hauling her wind, bore up directly upon us. In half an hour more we found ourselves in her cabin. She proved to be the Jane Guy, of Liverpool, Captain Guy, bound on a sealing and trading voyage to the South Seas and Pacific.

Chapter XIV

The Jane Guy was a fine-looking topsail schooner of a hundred and eighty tons burden. She was unusually sharp in the bows, and on a wind, in moderate weather, the fastest sailer I have ever seen. Her qualities, however, as a rough sea-boat, were not so good, and her draught of water was by far too great for the trade to which she was destined. For this peculiar service a larger vessel, and one of a light

8. Pym adds a note here: The case of the brig Polly, of Boston, is one so much in point, and her fate, in many respects, so remarkably similar to our own, that I cannot forbear alluding to it here. This vessel, of one hundred and thirty tons burden, sailed from Boston, with a cargo of lumber and provisions, for Santa Croix, on the twelfth of December, 1811, under the command of Captain Casneau. There were eight souls on board besides the captain—the mate, four seamen, and the cook, together with a Mr. Hunt, and a negro girl belonging to him. On the fifteenth, having cleared the shoal of Georges, she sprung a leak in a gale of wind from the southeast, and was finally capsized; but, the mast going by the board, she afterward righted. They remained in this situation, without fire, and with very little provision, for the period of *one hundred and ninety-one days* (from December the fifteenth to June the twentieth) when Captain Casneau and Samuel Badger, the only survivers, were taken off the wreck by the Fame, of Hull, Captain Featherstone, bound home from Rio Janeiro. When picked up they were in latitude 28 N., longitude 13 W., *having drifted above two thousand miles.* On the ninth of July the Fame fell in with the brig Dromeo, Captain Perkins, who landed the two sufferers in Kennebeck. The narrative from which we gather these details ends in the following words.

"It is natural to inquire how they could float such a vast distance, upon the most frequented part of the Atlantic, and not be discovered all this time. *They were passed by more than a dozen sail, one of which came so nigh them that they could distinctly see the people on deck and on the rigging looking at them; but, to the inexpressible disappointment of the starving and freezing men, they stifled the dictates of compassion, hoisted sail, and cruelly abandoned them to their fate.*" [End of Pym's note]

Scholars have identified this note as from the account of "The Loss of the Brig Polly" in Thomas's *Remarkable Shipwrecks;* other passages in this and subsequent chapters seem also to have been influenced by Thomas; meanwhile Morrell continues to be the major source of Poe's details.

proportionate draught, is desirable—say a vessel of from three to three hundred and fifty tons. She should be barque-rigged,[9] and in other respects of a different construction from the usual South Sea ships. It is absolutely necessary that she should be well armed. She should have, say ten or twelve twelve pound carronades, and two or three long twelves, with brass blunderbusses,[1] and water-tight armchests for each top. Her anchors and cables should be of far greater strength than is required for any other species of trade, and, above all, her crew should be numerous and efficient—not less, for such a vessel as I have described, than fifty or sixty able-bodied men. The Jane Guy had a crew of thirty-five, all able seamen, besides the captain and mate, but she was not altogether as well armed or otherwise equipped as a navigator acquainted with the difficulties and dangers of the trade could have desired.

Captain Guy was a gentleman of great urbanity of manner, and of considerable experience in the southern traffic, to which he had devoted a great portion of his life. He was deficient, however, in energy, and, consequently, in that spirit of enterprise which is here so absolutely requisite. He was part owner of the vessel in which he sailed, and was invested with discretionary powers to cruise in the South Seas for any cargo which might come most readily to hand. He had on board, as usual in such voyages, beads, looking-glasses, tinder-works, axes, hatchets, saws, adzes, planes, chisels, gouges, gimlets, files, spokeshaves, rasps, hammers, nails, knives, scissors, razors, needles, thread, crockery-ware, calico, trinkets, and other similar articles.

The schooner sailed from Liverpool on the tenth of July, crossed the Tropic of Cancer on the twenty-fifth, in longitude twenty degrees west, and reached Sal, one of the Cape Verd Islands, on the twenty-ninth, where she took in salt and other necessaries for the voyage. On the third of August she left the Cape Verds and steered southwest, stretching over towards the coast of Brazil so as to cross the equator between the meridians of twenty-eight and thirty degrees west longitude. This is the course usually taken by vessels bound from Europe to the Cape of Good Hope, or by that route to the East Indies. By proceeding thus they avoid the calms and strong contrary currents which continually prevail on the coast of Guinea, while, in the end, it is found to be the shortest track, as westerly winds are never wanting afterward by which to reach the Cape. It was Captain Guy's intention to make his first stoppage at Kerguelen's Land—I hardly know for what reason. On the day we were picked up the schooner was off Cape St. Roque,[2] in longitude 31 W.; so that, when found, we had drifted probably, from north to south, *not less than five-and-twenty degrees.*

9. "Barque": an old-fashioned spelling for *bark*, a sailing ship with three to five masts, all square-rigged (the sails are set at right angles to the length of the ship) except for the aftermast, which is fore and aft rigged (in line with the length of the ship).
1. Short muskets with a wide bore and flaring muzzle, used for short-range scatter shots. "Carronades": short, large-caliber cannons, used at short range.
2. One source for St. Roque may be *Symzonia*; note the connection between Symmes and J. N. Reynolds explained in the headnote on pp. 429–30 herein. There is also general reliance on Morrell in this chapter and over the next several chapters. The journey described here and in the next paragraphs is capable of being fairly precisely plotted.

On board the Jane Guy we were treated with all the kindness our distressed situation demanded. In about a fortnight, during which time we continued steering to the southeast, with gentle breezes and fine weather, both Peters and myself recovered entirely from the effects of our late privation and dreadful suffering, and we began to remember what had passed rather as a frightful dream from which we had been happily awakened, than as events which had taken place in sober and naked reality. I have since found that this species of partial oblivion is usually brought about by sudden transition, whether from joy to sorrow or from sorrow to joy—the degree of forgetfulness being proportioned to the degree of difference in the exchange. Thus, in my own case, I now feel it impossible to realize the full extent of the misery which I endured during the days spent upon the hulk. The incidents are remembered, but not the feelings which the incidents elicited at the time of their occurrence. I only know that, when they did occur, I then thought human nature could sustain nothing more of agony.[3]

We continued our voyage for some weeks without any incidents of greater moment than the occasional meeting with whaling-ships, and more frequently with the black or right whale, so called in contradistinction to the spermaceti. These, however, were chiefly found south of the twenty-fifth parallel. On the sixteenth of September, being in the vicinity of the Cape of Good Hope, the schooner encountered her first gale of any violence since leaving Liverpool. In this neighbourhood, but more frequently to the south and east of the promontory (we were to the westward), navigators have often to contend with storms from the northward which rage with great fury. They always bring with them a heavy sea, and one of their most dangerous features is the instantaneous chopping round of the wind, an occurrence almost certain to take place during the greatest force of the gale. A perfect hurricane will be blowing at one moment from the northward or northeast, and in the next not a breath of wind will be felt in that direction, while from the southwest it will come out all at once with a violence almost inconceivable. A bright spot to the southward is the sure forerunner of the change, and vessels are thus enabled to take the proper precautions.

It was about six in the morning when the blow came on with a white squall, and, as usual, from the northward. By eight it had increased very much, and brought down upon us one of the most tremendous seas I had then ever beheld. Everything had been made as snug as possible, but the schooner laboured excessively, and gave evidence of her bad qualities as a seaboat, pitching her forecastle under at every plunge, and with the greatest difficulty struggling up from one wave before she was buried in another. Just before sunset the bright spot for which we had been on the lookout made its appearance in the southwest, and in an hour afterward we perceived the little headsail we car-

3. Parallels have been noted between this passage and J. N. Reynolds's *Voyage of the United States Frigate Potomac* (1835).

ried flapping listlessly against the mast. In two minutes more, in spite of every preparation, we were hurled on our beam-ends as if by magic, and a perfect wilderness of foam made a clear breach over us as we lay. The blow from the southwest, however, luckily proved to be nothing more than a squall, and we had the good fortune to right the vessel without the loss of a spar. A heavy cross sea gave us great trouble for a few hours after this, but towards morning we found ourselves in nearly as good condition as before the gale. Captain Guy considered that he had made an escape little less than miraculous.

On the thirteenth of October we came in sight of Prince Edward's Island, in latitude 46° 53' S., longitude 37° 46' E.[4] Two days afterward we found ourselves near Possession Island, and presently passed the islands of Crozet, in latitude 42° 59' S., longitude 49° E. On the eighteenth we made Kerguelen's or Desolation Island, in the Southern Indian Ocean, and came to anchor in Christmas Harbour, having four fathoms of water.

This island, or rather group of islands, bears southeast from the Cape of Good Hope, and is distant therefrom nearly eight hundred leagues. It was first discovered in 1772, by the Baron de Kergulen, or Kerguelen, a Frenchman, who, thinking the land to form a portion of an extensive southern continent, carried home information to that effect, which produced much excitement at the time. The government, taking the matter up, sent the baron back in the following year for the purpose of giving his new discovery a critical examination, when the mistake was discovered. In 1777, Captain Cook fell in with the same group, and gave to the principal one the name of Desolation Island, a title which it certainly well deserves. Upon approaching the land, however, the navigator might be induced to suppose otherwise, as the sides of most of the hills, from September to March, are clothed with very brilliant verdure. This deceitful appearance is caused by a small plant resembling saxifrage, which is abundant, growing in large patches on a species of crumbling moss. Besides this plant there is scarcely a sign of vegetation on the island, if we except some coarse rank grass near the harbour, some lichen, and a shrub which bears resemblance to a cabbage shooting into seed, and which has a bitter and acrid taste.

The face of the country is hilly, although none of the hills can be called lofty. Their tops are perpetually covered with snow. There are several harbours, of which Christmas Harbour is the most convenient. It is the first to be met with on the northeast side of the island after passing Cape François, which forms the northern shore, and, by its peculiar shape, serves to distinguish the harbour. Its projecting point terminates in a high rock, through which is a large hole, forming a natural arch. The entrance is in latitude 48° 40' S., longitude 69° 6' E. Passing in here, good anchorage may be found under the shelter of several small islands, which form a sufficient protection from all easterly winds. Proceeding on eastwardly from this anchorage you come to

4. Poe's text relies heavily on Morrell from this point forward.

Wasp Bay, at the head of the harbour. This is a small basin, completely landlocked, into which you can go with four fathoms, and find anchorage in from ten to three, hard clay bottom. A ship might lie here with her best bower ahead all the year round without risk. To the westward, at the head of Wasp Bay, is a small stream of excellent water, easily procured.

Some seal of the fur and hair species are still to be found on Kerguelen's Island, and sea elephants abound. The feathered tribes are discovered in great numbers. Penguins are very plenty, and of these there are four different kinds. The royal penguin, so called from its size and beautiful plumage, is the largest. The upper part of the body is usually gray, sometimes of a lilach tint; the under portion of the purest white imaginable. The head is of a glossy and most brilliant black, the feet also. The chief beauty of the plumage, however, consists in two broad stripes of a gold colour, which pass along from the head to the breast. The bill is long, and either pink or bright scarlet. These birds walk erect, with a stately carriage. They carry their heads high, with their wings drooping like two arms, and, as their tails project from their body in a line with the legs, the resemblance to a human figure is very striking, and would be apt to deceive the spectator at a casual glance or in the gloom of the evening. The royal penguins which we met with on Kerguelen's Land were rather larger than a goose. The other kinds are the macaroni, the jackass, and the rookery penguin. These are much smaller, less beautiful in plumage, and different in other respects.[5]

Besides the penguin many other birds are here to be found, among which may be mentioned seahens, blue peterels, teal, ducks, Port Egmont hens, shags, Cape pigeons, the nelly, seaswallows, terns, seagulls, Mother Carey's chickens, Mother Carey's geese, or the great peterel, and, lastly, the albatross.[6]

The great peterel is as large as the common albatross, and is carnivorous. It is frequently called the break-bones, or osprey peterel. They are not at all shy, and, when properly cooked, are palatable food. In flying they sometimes sail very close to the surface of the water, with the wings expanded, without appearing to move them in the least degree, or make any exertion with them whatever.

The albatross is one of the largest and fiercest of the South Sea birds. It is of the gull species, and takes its prey on the wing, never coming on land except for the purpose of breeding. Between this bird and the penguin the most singular friendship exists. Their nests are constructed with great uniformity, upon a plan concerted between the two species—that of the albatross being placed in the centre of a little square formed by the nests of four penguins. Navigators have agreed in calling an assemblage of such encampments *a rookery*. These rookeries have been often described, but, as my readers may not all have

5. The configuration of the penguin/albatross rookery is described in Morrell ("First Voyage," Chapter III); in the next few paragraphs Poe departs from Morrell here and there, seemingly for symbolic or thematic purposes (e.g., the deceptive effect of their human resemblance).
6. Poe's list of birds is accurate, in part derived from J. N. Reynolds.

seen these descriptions, and as I shall have occasion hereafter to speak of the penguin and albatross, it will not be amiss to say something here of their mode of building and living.

When the season for incubation arrives, the birds assemble in vast numbers, and for some days appear to be deliberating upon the proper course to be pursued. At length they proceed to action. A level piece of ground is selected, of suitable extent, usually comprising three or four acres, and situated as near the sea as possible, being still beyond its reach. The spot is chosen with reference to its evenness of surface, and that is preferred which is the least encumbered with stones. This matter being arranged, the birds proceed, with one accord, and actuated apparently by one mind, to trace out, with mathematical accuracy, either a square or other parallelogram, as may best suit the nature of the ground, and of just sufficient size to accommodate easily all the birds assembled, and no more—in this particular seeming determined upon preventing the access of future stragglers who have not participated in the labour of the encampment. One side of the place thus marked out runs parallel with the water's edge, and is left open for ingress or egress.

Having defined the limits of the rookery, the colony now begin to clear it of every species of rubbish, picking up stone by stone, and carrying them outside of the lines, and close by them, so as to form a wall on the three inland sides. Just within this wall a perfectly level and smooth walk is formed, from six to eight feet wide, and extending around the encampment—thus serving the purpose of a general promenade.

The next process is to partition out the whole area into small squares exactly equal in size. This is done by forming narrow paths, very smooth, and crossing each other at right angles throughout the entire extent of the rookery. At each intersection of these paths the nest of an albatross is constructed, and a penguin's nest in the centre of each square—thus every penguin is surrounded by four albatrosses, and each albatross by a like number of penguins. The penguin's nest consists of a hole in the earth, very shallow, being only just of sufficient depth to keep her single egg from rolling. The albatross is somewhat less simple in her arrangements, erecting a hillock about a foot high and two in diameter. This is made of earth, seaweed, and shells. On its summit she builds her nest.

The birds take especial care never to leave their nests unoccupied for an instant during the period of incubation, or, indeed, until the young progeny are sufficiently strong to take care of themselves. While the male is absent at sea in search of food, the female remains on duty, and it is only upon the return of her partner that she ventures abroad. The eggs are never left uncovered at all—while one bird leaves the nest, the other nestling in by its side. This precaution is rendered necessary by the thievish propensities prevalent in the rookery, the inhabitants making no scruple to purloin each other's eggs at every good opportunity.

Although there are some rookeries in which the penguin and alba-

tross are the sole population, yet in most of them a variety of oceanic birds are to be met with, enjoying all the privileges of citizenship, and scattering their nests here and there, wherever they can find room, never interfering, however, with the stations of the larger species. The appearance of such encampments, when seen from a distance, is exceedingly singular. The whole atmosphere just above the settlement is darkened with the immense number of the albatross (mingled with the smaller tribes) which are continually hovering over it, either going to the ocean or returning home. At the same time a crowd of penguins are to be observed, some passing to and fro in the narrow alleys, and some marching, with the military strut so peculiar to them, around the general promenade-ground which encircles the rookery. In short, survey it as we will, nothing can be more astonishing than the spirit of reflection evinced by these feathered beings, and nothing surely can be better calculated to elicit reflection in every well-regulated human intellect.[7]

On the morning after our arrival in Christmas Harbour the chief mate, Mr. Patterson, took the boats, and (although it was somewhat early in the season) went in search of seal, leaving the captain and a young relation of his on a point of barren land to the westward, they having some business, whose nature I could not ascertain, to transact in the interior of the island. Captain Guy took with him a bottle, in which was a sealed letter, and made his way from the point on which he was set on shore towards one of the highest peaks in the place. It is probable that his design was to leave the letter on that height for some vessel which he expected to come after him.[8] As soon as we lost sight of him we proceeded (Peters and myself being in the mate's boat) on our cruise around the coast, looking for seal. In this business we were occupied about three weeks, examining with great care every nook and corner, not only of Kerguelen's Land, but of the several small islands in the vicinity. Our labours, however, were not crowned with any important success. We saw a great many fur seal, but they were exceedingly shy, and, with the greatest exertions, we could only procure three hundred and fifty skins in all. Sea elephants were abundant, especially on the western coast of the main island, but of these we killed only twenty, and this with great difficulty. On the smaller islands we discovered a good many of the hair seal, but did not molest them. We returned to the schooner on the eleventh, where we found Captain Guy and his nephew, who gave a very bad account of the interior, representing it as one of the most dreary and utterly barren countries in the world. They had remained two nights on the island, owing to some misunderstanding, on the part of the second mate, in regard to the sending a jollyboat from the schooner to take them off.

7. Poe omits Morrell's moralizing comment that the order and regularity of the birds' rookery suggest " 'the Divinity which stirs within' them" ("First Voyage," Chapter III).
8. Leaving a message in a bottle and throwing it into the sea is a convention associated with sea travel and sea stories (cf. Poe's "Ms. Found in a Bottle," pp. 106ff. herein). But leaving the bottle on a hill or other high place was a common practice as well; see, e.g., Captain James Cook and James King, *A Voyage to the Pacific* (1784).

Chapter XV

On the twelfth we made sail from Christmas Harbour, retracing our way to the westward, and leaving Marion's Island, one of Crozet's group, on the larboard.[9] We afterward passed Prince Edward's Island, leaving it also on our left; then, steering more to the northward, made, in fifteen days, the islands of Tristan d'Acunha, in latitude 37° 8' S., longitude 12° 8' W.

This group, now so well known, and which consists of three circular islands, was first discovered by the Portuguese, and was visited afterward by the Dutch in 1643, and by the French in 1767. The three islands together form a triangle, and are distant from each other about ten miles, there being fine open passages between. The land in all of them is very high, especially in Tristan d'Acunha, properly so called. This is the largest of the group, being fifteen miles in circumference, and so elevated that it can be seen in clear weather at the distance of eighty or ninety miles. A part of the land towards the north rises more than a thousand feet perpendicularly from the sea. A tableland at this height extends back nearly to the centre of the island, and from this tableland arises a lofty cone like that of Teneriffe. The lower half of this cone is clothed with trees of good size, but the upper region is barren rock, usually hidden among the clouds, and covered with snow during the greater part of the year. There are no shoals or other dangers about the island, the shores being remarkably bold and the water deep. On the northwestern coast is a bay, with a beach of black sand, where a landing with boats can be easily effected, provided there be a southerly wind. Plenty of excellent water may here be readily procured; also cod, and other fish, may be taken with hook and line.

The next island in point of size, and the most westwardly of the group, is that called the Inaccessible. Its precise situation is 37° 17' S. latitude, longitude 12° 24' W. It is seven or eight miles in circumference, and on all sides presents a forbidding and precipitous aspect. Its top is perfectly flat, and the whole region is steril, nothing growing upon it except a few stunted shrubs.

Nightingale Island, the smallest and most southerly, is in latitude 37° 26' S., longitude 12° 12' W. Off its southern extremity is a high ledge of rocky islets; a few also of a similar appearance are seen to the northeast. The ground is irregular and steril, and a deep valley partially separates it.

The shores of these islands abound, in the proper season, with sea lions, sea elephants, the hair and fur seal, together with a great variety of oceanic birds. Whales are also plenty in their vicinity. Owing to the ease with which these various animals were here formerly taken, the group has been much visited since its discovery. The Dutch and French frequented it at a very early period. In 1790, Captain Patten,

9. Critics have suggested that Poe abruptly changed the course of his whole narrative. But J. G. Kennedy, in his edition of *Pym*, suggests that, after rounding the Cape of Good Hope, the *Jane Guy*'s turning "inexplicably to the west, retracing its own route," may intentionally reflect the confusion and indecisiveness of the captain.

of the ship Industry, of Philadelphia, made Tristan d'Acunha, where he remained seven months (from August, 1790, to April, 1791) for the purpose of collecting sealskins. In this time he gathered no less than five thousand six hundred, and says that he would have had no difficulty in loading a large ship with oil in three weeks. Upon his arrival he found no quadrupeds, with the exception of a few wild goats—the island now abounds with all our most valuable domestic animals, which have been introduced by subsequent navigators.

I believe it was not long after Captain Patten's visit that Captain Colquhoun, of the American brig Betsey, touched at the largest of the islands for the purpose of refreshment. He planted onions, potatoes, cabbages, and a great many other vegetables, an abundance of all which are now to be met with.

In 1811, a Captain Heywood, in the Nereus, visited Tristan. He found there three Americans, who were residing upon the islands to prepare sealskins and oil. One of these men was named Jonathan Lambert, and he called himself the sovereign of the country. He had cleared and cultivated about sixty acres of land, and turned his attention to raising the coffee-plant and sugar-cane, with which he had been furnished by the American minister at Rio Janeiro. This settlement, however, was finally abandoned, and in 1817 the islands were taken possession of by the British government, who sent a detachment for that purpose from the Cape of Good Hope. They did not, however, retain them long; but, upon the evacuation of the country as a British possession, two or three English families took up their residence there independently of the government. On the twenty-fifth of March, 1824, the Berwick, Captain Jeffrey, from London to Van Diemen's Land, arrived at the place, where they found an Englishman of the name of Glass, formerly a corporal in the British artillery. He claimed to be supreme governor of the islands, and had under his control twenty-one men and three women. He gave a very favourable account of the salubrity of the climate and of the productiveness of the soil. The population occupied themselves chiefly in collecting sealskins and sea elephant oil, with which they traded to the Cape of Good Hope, Glass owning a small schooner. At the period of our arrival the governor was still a resident, but his little community had multiplied, there being fifty-six persons upon Tristan, besides a smaller settlement of seven on Nightingale Island. We had no difficulty in procuring almost every kind of refreshment which we required—sheep, hogs, bullocks, rabbits, poultry, goats, fish in great variety, and vegetables were abundant. Having come to anchor close in with the large island, in eighteen fathoms, we took all we wanted on board very conveniently. Captain Guy also purchased of Glass five hundred sealskins and some ivory. We remained here a week, during which the prevailing winds were from the northward and westward, and the weather somewhat hazy. On the fifth of November[1] we made sail to the southward and westward, with the in-

1. Supposedly another of Poe's lapses; the month should apparently be December, but given the increasing mental derangement of the narrator the discrepancy may be thematic. Meanwhile, Poe's general reliance on the Morrell narrative continues.

tention of having a thorough search for a group of islands called the Auroras, respecting whose existence a great diversity of opinion has existed. These islands are said to have been discovered as early as 1762, by the commander of the ship Aurora. In 1790, Captain Manuel de Oyarvido, in the ship Princess, belonging to the Royal Philippine Company, sailed, as he asserts, directly among them. In 1794, the Spanish corvette Atrevida went with the determination of ascertaining their precise situation, and, in a paper published by the Royal Hydrographical Society of Madrid in the year 1809, the following language is used respecting this expedition. "The corvette Atrevida practised, in their immediate vicinity, from the twenty-first to the twenty-seventh of January, all the necessary observations, and measured by chronometers the difference of longitude between these islands and the port of Soledad in the Malninas. The islands are three; they are very nearly in the same meridian; the centre one is rather low, and the other two may be seen at nine leagues distance." The observations made on board the Atrevida give the following results as the precise situation of each island. The most northern is in latitude 52° 37' 24" S., longitude 47° 43' 15" W.; the middle one in latitude 53° 2' 40" S., longitude 47° 55' 15" W.; and the most southern in latitude 53° 15' 22" S., longitude 47° 57' 15" W.

On the twenty-seventh of January, 1820, Captain James Weddel, of the British navy, sailed from Staten Land also in search of the Auroras. He reports that, having made the most diligent search, and passed not only immediately over the spots indicated by the commander of the Atrevida, but in every direction throughout the vicinity of these spots, he could discover no indication of land. These conflicting statements have induced other navigators to look out for the islands; and, strange to say, while some have sailed through every inch of sea where they are supposed to lie without finding them, there have been not a few who declare positively that they have seen them, and even been close in with their shores. It was Captain Guy's intention to make every exertion within his power to settle the question so oddly in dispute.[2]

We kept on our course, between the south and west, with variable weather, until the twentieth of the month, when we found ourselves on the debated ground, being in latitude 53° 15' S., longitude 47° 58' W.—that is to say, very nearly upon the spot indicated as the situation of the most southern of the group. Not perceiving any sign of land, we continued to the westward in the parallel of fifty-three degrees south, as far as the meridian of fifty degrees west. We then stood to the north as far as the parallel of fifty-two degrees south, when we turned to the eastward, and kept our parallel by double altitudes, morning and evening, and meridian altitudes of the planets and moon. Having thus gone eastwardly to the meridian of the western coast of Georgia, we kept

2. Among the vessels which at various times have professed to meet with the Auroras may be mentioned the ship San Miguel, in 1769; the ship Aurora, in 1774; the brig Pearl, in 1779; and the ship Dolores, in 1790. They all agree in giving the mean latitude fifty-three degrees south [Pym's note].

that meridian until we were in the latitude from which we set out. We then took diagonal courses throughout the entire extent of sea circumscribed, keeping a lookout constantly at the masthead, and repeating our examination with the greatest care for a period of three weeks, during which the weather was remarkably pleasant and fair, with no haze whatsoever. Of course we were thoroughly satisfied that, whatever islands might have existed in this vicinity at any former period, no vestige of them remained at the present day. Since my return home I find that the same ground was traced over with equal care in 1822 by Captain Johnson, of the American schooner Henry, and by Captain Morrell, in the American schooner Wasp—in both cases with the same result as in our own.

Chapter XVI

It had been Captain Guy's original intention, after satisfying himself about the Auroras, to proceed through the Strait of Magellan, and up along the western coast of Patagonia; but information received at Tristan d'Acunha induced him to steer to the southward, in the hope of falling in with some small islands said to lie about the parallel of 60° S., longitude 41° 20' W. In the event of his not discovering these lands, he designed, should the season prove favourable, to push on towards the pole. Accordingly, on the twelfth of December, we made sail in that direction. On the eighteenth we found ourselves about the station indicated by Glass, and cruised for three days in that neighbourhood without finding any traces of the islands he had mentioned. On the twenty-first, the weather being unusually pleasant, we again made sail to the southward, with the resolution of penetrating in that course as far as possible. Before entering upon this portion of my narrative, it may be as well, for the information of those readers who have paid little attention to the progress of discovery in these regions, to give some brief account of the very few attempts at reaching the southern pole which have hitherto been made.[3]

That of Captain Cook was the first of which we have any distinct account. In 1772 he sailed to the south in the Resolution, accompanied by Lieutenant Furneaux in the Adventure. In December he found himself as far as the fifty-eighth parallel of south latitude, and in longitude 26° 57' E. Here he met with narrow fields of ice, about eight or ten inches thick, and running northwest and southeast. This ice was in large cakes, and usually it was packed so closely that the vessels had great difficulty in forcing a passage. At this period Captain Cook supposed, from the vast number of birds to be seen, and from other indications, that he was in the near vicinity of land. He kept on to the southward, the weather being exceedingly cold, until he reached the sixty-fourth parallel, in longitude 38° 14' E. Here he had mild weather,

3. In this paragraph is the first definitive indication that the final destination is the South Pole, though there are earlier suggestions of a voyage to the ends of the earth. In the following paragraphs, Poe temporarily veers away from his source in Morrell and sails with J. N. Reynolds, in this case his *Address, on the Subject of a Surveying and Exploring Expedition to the Pacific Ocean and the South Seas* (1836).

with gentle breezes, for five days, the thermometer being at thirty-six. In January, 1773, the vessels crossed the Antarctic circle, but did not succeed in penetrating much farther; for, upon reaching latitude 67° 15', they found all farther progress impeded by an immense body of ice, extending all along the southern horizon as far as the eye could reach. This ice was of every variety—and some large floes of it, miles in extent, formed a compact mass, rising eighteen or twenty feet above the water. It being late in the season, and no hope entertained of rounding these obstructions, Captain Cook now reluctantly turned to the northward.

In the November following he renewed his search in the Antarctic. In latitude 59° 40' he met with a strong current setting to the southward. In December, when the vessels were in latitude 67° 31', longitude 142° 54' W., the cold was excessive, with heavy gales and fog. Here also birds were abundant; the albatross, the penguin, and the peterel especially. In latitude 70° 23' some large islands of ice were encountered, and shortly afterward, the clouds to the southward were observed to be of a snowy whiteness, indicating the vicinity of field ice. In latitude 71° 10', longitude 106° 54' W., the navigators were stopped, as before, by an immense frozen expanse, which filled the whole area of the southern horizon. The northern edge of this expanse was ragged and broken, so firmly wedged together as to be utterly impassable, and extending about a mile to the southward. Behind it the frozen surface was comparatively smooth for some distance, until terminated in the extreme back-ground by gigantic ranges of ice mountains, the one towering above the other. Captain Cook concluded that this vast field reached the southern pole or was joined to a continent. Mr. J. N. Reynolds,[4] whose great exertions and perseverance have at length succeeded in getting set on foot a national expedition, partly for the purpose of exploring these regions, thus speaks of the attempt of the Resolution. "We are not surprised that Captain Cook was unable to go beyond 71° 10', but we are astonished that he did attain that point on the meridian of 106° 54' west longitude. Palmer's Land lies south of the Shetland, latitude sixty-four degrees, and tends to the southward and westward farther than any navigator has yet penetrated. Cook was standing for this land when his progress was arrested by the ice; which, we apprehend, must always be the case in that point, and so early in the season as the sixth of January— and we should not be surprised if a portion of the icy mountains described was attached to the main body of Palmer's Land, or to some other portions of land lying farther to the southward and westward."

4. In his review of Reynolds's 1836 *Address*, Poe tried to promote him as the most estimable advocate of U.S. South Seas exploration. He emphasized Reynolds's ability as a writer, suggesting that the official narrative of the proposed voyage should be written by him. But Reynolds quarreled with Secretary of the Navy Mahlon Dickerson and was not named to the expedition (Poe hints at some such trouble in his review). Lieutenant Charles Wilkes led the South Sea expedition; he too was a problematic figure, but the adventure was successful. In 1845, Wilkes published his five-volume *Narrative of the United States Exploring Expedition during the Years 1838, 1839, 1840, 1841, and 1842*. Poe next returns for a few paragraphs to Morrell.

In 1803, Captains Kreutzenstern and Lisiausky were despatched by Alexander of Russia for the purpose of circumnavigating the globe. In endeavouring to get south, they made no farther than 59° 58', in longitude 70° 15' W. They here met with strong currents setting eastwardly. Whales were abundant, but they saw no ice. In regard to this voyage, Mr. Reynolds observes that, if Kreutzenstern had arrived where he did earlier in the season, he must have encountered ice—it was March when he reached the latitude specified. The winds prevailing, as they do, from the southward and westward, had carried the floes, aided by currents, into that icy region bounded on the north by Georgia, east by Sandwich Land and the South Orkneys, and west by the South Shetland Islands.

In 1822, Captain James Weddell, of the British navy, with two very small vessels, penetrated farther to the south than any previous navigator, and this too, without encountering extraordinary difficulties. He states that although he was frequently hemmed in by ice *before* reaching the seventy-second parallel, yet, upon attaining it, not a particle was to be discovered, and that, upon arriving at the latitude of 74° 15', no fields, and only three islands of ice were visible. It is somewhat remarkable that, although vast flocks of birds were seen, and other usual indications of land, and although, south of the Shetlands, unknown coasts were observed from the masthead tending southwardly, Weddell[5] discourages the idea of land existing in the polar regions of the south.

On the eleventh of January, 1823, Captain Benjamin Morrell, of the American schooner Wasp, sailed from Kerguelen's Land with a view of penetrating as far south as possible. On the first of February he found himself in latitude 64° 52' S., longitude 118° 27' E. The following passage is extracted from his journal of that date. "The wind soon freshened to an eleven-knot breeze, and we embraced this opportunity of making to the west; being however convinced that the farther we went south beyond latitude sixty-four degrees the less ice was to be apprehended, we steered a little to the southward, until we crossed the Antarctic circle, and were in latitude 69° 15' E. In this latitude there was *no field ice*, and very few ice islands in sight."

Under the date of March fourteenth I find also this entry. "The sea was now entirely free of field ice, and there were not more than a dozen ice islands in sight. At the same time the temperature of the air and water was at least thirteen degrees higher (more mild) than we had ever found it between the parallels of sixty and sixty-two south. We were now in latitude 70° 14' S., and the temperature of the air was forty-seven, and that of the water forty-four. In this situation I found the variation to be 14° 27' easterly, per azimuth. . . . I have several times passed within the Antarctic circle on different meridians, and have uniformly found the temperature, both of the air and the water, to become more and more mild the farther I advanced beyond the sixty-fifth degree of south latitude, and that the variation decreases in

5. James Weddell, British navigator, discovered the sea that still bears his name in 1823.

the same proportion. While north of this latitude, say between sixty and sixty-five south, we frequently had great difficulty in finding a passage for the vessel between the immense and almost innumerable ice islands, some of which were from one to two miles in circumference, and more than five hundred feet above the surface of the water."

Being nearly destitute of fuel and water, and without proper instruments, it being also late in the season, Captain Morrell was now obliged to put back, without attempting any farther progress to the southward, although an entirely open sea lay before him. He expresses the opinion that, had not these overruling considerations obliged him to retreat, he could have penetrated, if not to the pole itself, at least to the eighty-fifth parallel. I have given his ideas respecting these matters somewhat at length, that the reader may have an opportunity of seeing how far they were borne out by my own subsequent experience.

In 1831, Captain Briscoe, in the employ of the Messieurs Enderby, whale-ship owners of London, sailed in the brig Lively for the South Seas, accompanied by the cutter[6] Tula. On the twenty-eighth of February, being in latitude 66° 30' S., longitude 47° 31' E., he descried land, and "clearly discovered through the snow the black peaks of a range of mountains running E. S. E." He remained in this neighbourhood during the whole of the following month, but was unable to approach the coast nearer than within ten leagues, owing to the boisterous state of the weather. Finding it impossible to make farther discovery during this season, he returned northward to winter in Van Diemen's Land.

In the beginning of 1832 he again proceeded southwardly, and on the fourth of February land was seen to the southeast in latitude 67° 15', longitude 69° 29' W. This was soon found to be an island near the headland of the country he had first discovered. On the twenty-first of the month he succeeded in landing on the latter, and took possession of it in the name of William IV., calling it Adelaide's Island, in honour of the English queen. These particulars being made known to the Royal Geographical Society of London, the conclusion was drawn by that body "that there is a continuous tract of land extending from 47° 30' E. to 69° 29' W. longitude, running the parallel of from sixty-six to sixty-seven degrees south latitude." In respect to this conclusion Mr. Reynolds observes, "In the correctness of it we by no means concur; nor do the discoveries of Briscoe warrant any such inference. It was within these limits that Weddell proceeded south on a meridian to the east of Georgia, Sandwich Land, and the South Orkney and Shetland Islands." My own experience will be found to testify most directly to the falsity of the conclusion arrived at by the society.

These are the principal attempts which have been made at penetrating to a high southern latitude, and it will now be seen that there remained, previous to the voyage of the Jane, nearly three hundred

6. A single-masted, fore- and aft-rigged vessel (usually with three or more sails), designed for speed.

degrees of longitude in which the Antarctic circle had not been crossed at all. Of course a wide field lay before us for discovery, and it was with feelings of most intense interest that I heard Captain Guy express his resolution of pushing boldly to the southward.[7]

Chapter XVII

We kept our course southwardly for four days after giving up the search for Glass's Islands, without meeting with any ice at all. On the twenty-sixth, at noon, we were in latitude 63° 23' S., longitude 41° 25' W. We now saw several large ice islands, and a floe of field ice, not, however, of any great extent. The winds generally blew from the southeast, or the northeast, but were very light. Whenever we had a westerly wind, which was seldom, it was invariably attended with a rain squall. Every day we had more or less snow. The thermometer, on the twenty-seventh, stood at thirty-five.[8]

January 1, 1828. This day we found ourselves completely hemmed in by the ice, and our prospects looked cheerless indeed. A strong gale blew, during the whole forenoon, from the northeast, and drove large cakes of the drift against the rudder and counter with such violence that we all trembled for the consequences. Towards evening, the gale still blowing with fury, a large field in front separated, and we were enabled, by carrying a press of sail, to force a passage through the smaller flakes into some open water beyond. As we approached this space we took in sail by degrees, and having at length got clear, lay'to under a single reefed foresail.

January 2. We had now tolerably pleasant weather. At noon we found ourselves in latitude 69° 10' S., longitude 42° 20' W., having crossed the Antarctic circle. Very little ice was to be seen to the southward, although large fields of it lay behind us.[9] This day we rigged some sounding gear, using a large iron pot capable of holding twenty gallons, and a line of two hundred fathoms. We found the current setting to the north, about a quarter of a mile per hour. The temperature of the air was now about thirty-three. Here we found the variation to be 14° 28' easterly, per azimuth.

January 5. We had still held on to the southward without any very great impediments. On this morning, however, being in latitude 73° 15' E., longitude 42° 10' W., we were again brought to a stand by an immense expanse of firm ice. We saw, nevertheless, much open water to the southward, and felt no doubt of being able to reach it eventually. Standing to the eastward along the edge of the floe, we at length came to a passage of about a mile in width, through which we warped our way by sundown. The sea in which we now were was thickly covered with ice islands, but had no field ice, and we pushed on boldly as before. The cold did not seem to increase, although we

7. Poe has made use of Reynolds for several lines and the concluding words echo his *Address*.
8. Poe returns to Morrell's text here and continues to do so throughout this chapter.
9. Cf. Symmes's *Symzonia* and Reynolds's "Leaves."

had snow very frequently, and now and then hail squalls of great violence. Immense flocks of the albatross flew over the schooner this day, going from southeast to northwest.

January 7. The sea still remained pretty well open, so that we had no difficulty in holding on our course. To the westward we saw some icebergs of incredible size, and in the afternoon passed very near one whose summit could not have been less than four hundred fathoms from the surface of the ocean. Its girth was probably, at the base, three quarters of a league, and several streams of water were running from crevices in its sides. We remained in sight of this island two days, and then only lost it in a fog.

January 10. Early this morning we had the misfortune to lose a man overboard. He was an American, named Peter Vredenburgh, a native of New-York, and was one of the most valuable hands on board the schooner. In going over the bows his foot slipped, and he fell between two cakes of ice, never rising again. At noon of this day we were in latitude 78° 30', longitude 40° 15' W. The cold was now excessive, and we had hail squalls continually from the northward and eastward. In this direction also we saw several more immense icebergs, and the whole horizon to the eastward appeared to be blocked up with field ice, rising in tiers, one mass above the other. Some driftwood floated by during the evening, and a great quantity of birds flew over, among which were Nellies, peterels, albatrosses, and a large bird of a brilliant blue plumage. The variation here, per azimuth, was less than it had been previously to our passing the Antarctic circle.[1]

January 12. Our passage to the south again looked doubtful, as nothing was to be seen in the direction of the pole but one apparently limitless floe, backed by absolute mountains of ragged ice, one precipice of which arose frowningly above the other. We stood to the westward until the fourteenth, in the hope of finding an entrance.

January 14. This morning we reached the western extremity of the field which had impeded us, and, weathering it, came to an open sea, without a particle of ice. Upon sounding with two hundred fathoms, we here found a current setting southwardly at the rate of half a mile per hour. The temperature of the air was forty-seven, that of the water thirty-four. We now sailed to the southward, without meeting any interruption of moment until the sixteenth, when, at noon, we were in latitude 81° 21', longitude 42° W. We here again sounded, and found a current setting still southwardly, and at the rate of three quarters of a mile per hour. The variation per azimuth had diminished, and the temperature of the air was mild and pleasant, the thermometer being as high as fifty-one. At this period not a particle of ice was to be discovered. All hands on board now felt certain of attaining the pole.

January 17. This day was full of incident. Innumerable flights of birds flew over us from the southward, and several were shot from the deck; one of them, a species of pelican, proved to be excellent eating. About midday a small floe of ice was seen from the masthead off the

1. Cf. Reynolds's description in "Leaves."

So many details on longitude/temperature

larboard bow, and upon it there appeared to be some large animal. As the weather was good and nearly calm, Captain Guy ordered out two of the boats to see what it was. Dirk Peters and myself accompanied the mate in the larger boat. Upon coming up with the floe, we perceived that it was in the possession of a gigantic creature of the race of the Arctic bear, but far exceeding in size the largest of these animals. Being well armed, we made no scruple of attacking it at once. Several shots were fired in quick succession, the most of which took effect, apparently, in the head and body. Nothing discouraged, however, the monster threw himself from the ice, and swam, with open jaws, to the boat in which were Peters and myself. Owing to the confusion which ensued among us at this unexpected turn of the adventure, no person was ready immediately with a second shot, and the bear had actually succeeded in getting half his vast bulk across our gunwale, and seizing one of the men by the small of his back, before any efficient means were taken to repel him. In this extremity nothing but the promptness and agility of Peters saved us from destruction. Leaping upon the back of the huge beast, he plunged the blade of a knife behind the neck, reaching the spinal marrow at a blow. The brute tumbled into the sea lifeless, and without a struggle, rolling over Peters as he fell. The latter soon recovered himself, and a rope being thrown him, he secured the carcass before entering the boat. We then returned in triumph to the schooner, towing our trophy behind us. This bear, upon admeasurement, proved to be full fifteen feet in his greatest length. His wool was perfectly white, and very coarse, curling tightly. The eyes were of a blood red, and larger than those of the Arctic bear—the snout also more rounded, rather resembling the snout of the bulldog. The meat was tender, but excessively rank and fishy, although the men devoured it with avidity, and declared it excellent eating.

Scarcely had we got our prize alongside, when the man at the masthead gave the joyful shout of "*land on the starboard bow!*" All hands were now upon the alert, and, a breeze springing up very opportunely from the northward and eastward, we were soon close in with the coast. It proved to be a low rocky islet, of about a league in circumference, and altogether destitute of vegetation, if we except a species of prickly pear. In approaching it from the northward, a singular ledge of rock is seen projecting into the sea, and bearing a strong resemblance to corded bales of cotton.[2] Around this ledge to the westward is a small bay, at the bottom of which our boats effected a convenient landing.

It did not take us long to explore every portion of the island, but, with one exception, we found nothing worthy of observation. In the southern extremity, we picked up near the shore, half buried in a pile of loose stones, a piece of wood, which seemed to have formed the

2. Some critics point to the approach to the ledge that looks like "bales of cotton," specifically "from the northward," as evidence of a coded allegory of relations between the American South and North. For such critics, the increasing bifurcation of everything into black and white suggests the issues of slavery and racism. But this interpretation is problematic and complicated; for some of the pros and cons, see the introduction to "The South and Slavery," pp. 767ff. herein, and the essay by John Carlos Rowe, pp. 904ff.

prow of a canoe. There had been evidently some attempt at carving upon it, and Captain Guy fancied that he made out the figure of a tortoise, but the resemblance did not strike me very forcibly. Besides this prow, if such it were, we found no other token that any living creature had ever been here before. Around the coast we discovered occasional small floes of ice—but these were very few. The exact situation of this islet (to which Captain Guy gave the name of Bennet's Islet, in honour of his partner in the ownership of the schooner) is 82° 50' S. latitude, 42° 20' W. longitude.

We had now advanced to the southward more than eight degrees farther than any previous navigators, and the sea still lay perfectly open before us. We found, too, that the variation uniformly decreased as we proceeded, and, what was still more surprising, that the temperature of the air, and latterly of the water, became milder. The weather might even be called pleasant, and we had a steady but very gentle breeze always from some northern point of the compass. The sky was usually clear, with now and then a slight appearance of thin vapour in the southern horizon—this, however, was invariably of brief duration. Two difficulties alone presented themselves to our view; we were getting short of fuel, and symptoms of scurvy had occurred among several of the crew. These considerations began to impress upon Captain Guy the necessity of returning, and he spoke of it frequently. For my own part, confident as I was of soon arriving at land of some description upon the course we were pursuing, and having every reason to believe, from present appearances, that we should not find it the steril soil met with in the higher Arctic latitudes, I warmly pressed upon him the expediency of persevering, at least for a few days longer, in the direction we were now holding. So tempting an opportunity of solving the great problem in regard to an Antarctic continent had never yet been afforded to man, and I confess that I felt myself bursting with indignation at the timid and ill-timed suggestions of our commander. I believe, indeed, that what I could not refrain from saying to him on this head had the effect of inducing him to push on. While, therefore, I cannot but lament the most unfortunate and bloody events which immediately arose from my advice, I must still be allowed to feel some degree of gratification at having been instrumental, however remotely, in opening to the eye of science one of the most intensely exciting secrets which has ever engrossed its attention.

Chapter XVIII

January 18. This morning[3] we continued to the southward, with the same pleasant weather as before. The sea was entirely smooth, the air

3. The terms *morning* and *evening*, which I have made use of to avoid confusion in my narrative, as far as possible, must not, of course, be taken in their ordinary sense. For a long time past we had had no night at all, the daylight being continual. The dates throughout are according to nautical time, and the bearings must be understood as per compass. I would also remark in this place, that I cannot, in the first portion of what is here written, pretend to strict accuracy in respect to dates, or latitudes and longitudes, having kept no regular journal until after the period of which this first portion treats. In many instances I have relied altogether upon memory [Pym's note].

tolerably warm and from the northeast, the temperature of the water fifty-three. We now again got our sounding-gear in order, and, with a hundred and fifty fathoms of line, found the current setting towards the pole at the rate of a mile an hour. This constant tendency to the southward, both in the wind and current, caused some degree of speculation, and even of alarm, in different quarters of the schooner, and I saw distinctly that no little impression had been made upon the mind of Captain Guy. He was exceedingly sensitive to ridicule, however, and I finally succeeded in laughing him out of his apprehensions. The variation was now very trivial. In the course of the day we saw several large whales of the right species, and innumerable flights of the albatross passed over the vessel. We also picked up a bush, full of red berries, like those of the hawthorn, and the carcass of a singular-looking land-animal. It was three feet in length, and but six inches in height, with four very short legs, the feet armed with long claws of a brilliant scarlet, and resembling coral in substance. The body was covered with a straight silky hair, perfectly white. The tail was peaked like that of a rat, and about a foot and a half long. The head resembled a cat's, with the exception of the ears—these were flapped like the ears of a dog. The *teeth* were of the same brilliant scarlet as the claws.

January 19.[4] To-day, being in latitude 83° 20', longitude 43° 5' W. (the sea being of an extraordinarily dark colour), we again saw land from the masthead, and, upon a closer scrutiny, found it to be one of a group of very large islands. The shore was precipitous, and the interior seemed to be well wooded, a circumstance which occasioned us great joy. In about four hours from our first discovering the land we came to anchor in ten fathoms, sandy bottom, a league from the coast, as a high surf, with strong ripples here and there, rendered a nearer approach of doubtful expediency. The two largest boats were now ordered out, and a party, well armed (among whom were Peters and myself), proceeded to look for an opening in the reef which appeared to encircle the island. After searching about for some time, we discovered an inlet, which we were entering, when we saw four large canoes put off from the shore, filled with men who seemed to be well armed. We waited for them to come up, and, as they moved with great rapidity, they were soon within hail. Captain Guy now held up a white handkerchief on the blade of an oar, when the strangers made a full stop, and commenced a loud jabbering all at once, intermingled with occasional shouts, in which we could distinguish the words *Anamoo-moo!* and *Lama-Lama!*[5] They continued this for at least half an hour,

4. As indicated, certain critics have read the dates of August 1 (the death of Augustus coinciding with the death of Poe's brother) and January 19 (the arrival at the island of Tsalal on Poe's birthday)—even going so far as to suggest that *Pym* contains a coded autobiographical allegory of figurative death and personal redemption or rebirth.

5. Scholars have been much interested in Poe's use or invention of native words. A concise overview of some of the speculations may be found in Burton R. Pollin's edition of *Pym*, including those of J. V. Ridgely based on Tregear's *Maori-Polynesian Comparative Dictionary*. Among the more interesting suggestions are *ana* (hana) = shine or glow; *mumu* = to gather together or swarm; and *lamalama* = many lights or much light. Robert C. Suggs points out that *ana* in many Polynesian languages means "cave" and that one cannot equate *ana* with *hana*, which in Marquesan means "bay" or "work" or is a causative prefix. He notes that *mumu* might be related to Hawaiian *mumulu*, with the same meaning "to swarm," and that

during which we had a good opportunity of observing their appearance.

In the four canoes, which might have been fifty feet long and five broad, there were a hundred and ten savages in all. They were about the ordinary stature of Europeans, but of a more muscular and brawny frame. Their complexion a jet black, with thick and long woolly hair.[6] They were clothed in skins of an unknown black animal, shaggy and silky, and made to fit the body with some degree of skill, the hair being inside, except where turned out about the neck, wrists, and ankles. Their arms consisted principally of clubs, of a dark, and apparently very heavy wood. Some spears, however, were observed among them, headed with flint, and a few slings. The bottoms of the canoes were full of black stones about the size of a large egg.

When they had concluded their harangue (for it was clear they intended their jabbering for such), one of them who seemed to be the chief stood up in the prow of his canoe, and made signs for us to bring our boats alongside of him. This hint we pretended not to understand, thinking it the wiser plan to maintain, if possible, the interval between us, as their number more than quadrupled our own. Finding this to be the case, the chief ordered the three other canoes to hold back, while he advanced towards us with his own. As soon as he came up with us he leaped on board the largest of our boats, and seated himself by the side of Captain Guy, pointing at the same time to the schooner, and repeating the words *Anamoo-moo!* and *Lama-Lama!* We now put back to the vessel, the four canoes following at a little distance.

Upon getting alongside the chief evinced symptoms of extreme surprise and delight, clapping his hands, slapping his thighs and breast, and laughing obstreperously. His followers behind joined in his merriment, and for some minutes the din was so excessive as to be absolutely deafening. Quiet being at length restored, Captain Guy ordered the boats to be hoisted up, as a necessary precaution, and gave the chief (whose name we soon found to be *Too-wit*) to understand that we could admit no more than twenty of his men on deck at one time. With this arrangement he appeared perfectly satisfied, and gave some directions to the canoes, when one of them approached, the rest remaining about fifty yards off. Twenty of the savages now got on board, and proceeded to ramble over every part of the deck, and scramble about among the rigging, making themselves much at home, and examining every article with great inquisitiveness.

lamalama has the additional meaning of "fair complected." Morrell ("Fourth Voyage," Chapter III) gives the provocative name of the southern island of New Zealand as "Tavi Poënammoo" ("Tavi Poe Nammoo"). Morrell's remarks on "Dusky Bay" are also provocative in the context of Poe's narrative; he observes that Captain Cook, being "unable to reach one of the arms of Dusky Bay, near the western point of the northern island . . . gave it the name of 'Nobody-knows-what' " (Chapter III). In these last portions of *Pym*, Poe mixes Hebrew, Arabic, and other languages with variant Polynesian phonetic transliterations and with rock inscriptions resembling pictographs and hieroglyphs, to suggest an ancient cryptographic "message"; but it is left indefinitive and mysterious. Richard Wilbur (pp. 807ff. herein) suggests a biblical reference for *Lama*: "Eli, eli, lama sabacthani?" (My God, my God why hast thou forsaken me?; Matthew 27:46 and Mark 15:34). Cf. the interpretations of the word *tekeli-li* in the notes to Chapter 22.

6. Some editors have altered the punctuation; here the fragment is left as it appears in the American edition.

It was quite evident that they had never before seen any of the white race—from whose complexion, indeed, they appeared to recoil. They believed the Jane to be a living creature, and seemed to be afraid of hurting it with the points of their spears, carefully turning them up. Our crew were much amused with the conduct of Too-wit in one instance. The cook was splitting some wood near the galley, and, by accident, struck his axe into the deck, making a gash of considerable depth. The chief immediately ran up, and pushing the cook on one side rather roughly, commenced a half whine, half howl, strongly indicative of sympathy in what he considered the sufferings of the schooner, patting and smoothing the gash with his hand, and washing it from a bucket of seawater which stood by. This was a degree of ignorance for which we were not prepared, and for my part I could not help thinking some of it affected.

When the visiters had satisfied, as well as they could, their curiosity in regard to our upper works, they were admitted below, when their amazement exceeded all bounds. Their astonishment now appeared to be far too deep for words, for they roamed about in silence, broken only by low ejaculations. The arms afforded them much food for speculation, and they were suffered to handle and examine them at leisure. I do not believe that they had the least suspicion of their actual use, but rather took them for idols, seeing the care we had of them, and the attention with which we watched their movements while handling them. At the great guns their wonder was redoubled. They approached them with every mark of the profoundest reverence and awe, but forbore to examine them minutely. There were two large mirrors in the cabin, and here was the acme of their amazement. Too-wit was the first to approach them, and he had got in the middle of the cabin, with his face to one and his back to the other, before he fairly perceived them. Upon raising his eyes and seeing his reflected self in the glass, I thought the savage would go mad; but, upon turning short round to make a retreat, and beholding himself a second time in the opposite direction, I was afraid he would expire upon the spot.[7] No persuasions could prevail upon him to take another look; but, throwing himself upon the floor, with his face buried in his hands, he remained thus until we were obliged to drag him upon deck.

The whole of the savages were admitted on board in this manner, twenty at a time, Too-wit being suffered to remain during the entire period. We saw no disposition to thievery among them, nor did we miss a single article after their departure. Throughout the whole of their visit they evinced the most friendly manner. There were, however, some points in their demeanour which we found it impossible to understand: for example, we could not get them to approach several very harmless objects—such as the schooner's sails, an egg, an

7. The village chief in Morrell's narrative, whom he dubs "Nero" ("Fourth Voyage," Chapter V), is shown only one mirror; Poe doubles and redoubles the effect. The description of the visit to the village and farther inland has more parallels with Morrell's account. R. C. Suggs notes that the chief's name, Too-wit, and the name of the village, Klock-Klock (see p. 532) are not Polynesian words (which end in vowels).

open book, or a pan of flour. We endeavoured to ascertain if they had among them any articles which might be turned to account in the way of traffic, but found great difficulty in being comprehended. We made out, nevertheless, what greatly astonished us, that the islands abounded in the large tortoise of the Gallipagos, one of which we saw in the canoe of Too-wit. We saw also some *biche de mer*[8] in the hands of one of the savages, who was greedily devouring it in its natural state. These anomalies, for they were such when considered in regard to the latitude, induced Captain Guy to wish for a thorough investigation of the country, in the hope of making a profitable speculation in his discovery. For my own part, anxious as I was to know something more of these islands, I was still more earnestly bent on prosecuting the voyage to the southward without delay. We had now fine weather, but there was no telling how long it would last; and being already in the eighty-fourth parallel, with an open sea before us, a current setting strongly to the southward, and the wind fair, I could not listen with any patience to a proposition of stopping longer than was absolutely necessary for the health of the crew and the taking on board a proper supply of fuel and fresh provisions. I represented to the captain that we might easily make this group on our return, and winter here in the event of being blocked up by the ice. He at length came into my views (for in some way, hardly known to myself, I had acquired much influence over him), and it was finally resolved that, even in the event of our finding *biche de mer*, we should only stay here a week to recruit, and then push on to the southward while we might. Accordingly we made every necessary preparation, and, under the guidance of Too-wit, got the Jane through the reef in safety, coming to anchor about a mile from the shore, in an excellent bay, completely landlocked, on the southeastern coast of the main island, and in ten fathoms of water, black sandy bottom. At the head of this bay there were three fine springs (we were told) of good water, and we saw abundance of wood in the vicinity. The four canoes followed us in, keeping, however, at a respectful distance. Too-wit himself remained on board, and, upon our dropping anchor, invited us to accompany him on shore, and visit his village in the interior. To this Captain Guy consented; and ten savages being left on board as hostages, a party of us, twelve in all, got in readiness to attend the chief. We took care to be well armed, yet without evincing any distrust. The schooner had her guns run out, her boarding-nettings up, and every other proper precaution was taken to guard against surprise. Directions were left with the chief mate to admit no person on board during our absence, and, in the event of our not appearing in twelve hours, to send the cutter, with a swivel, round the island in search of us.

At every step we took inland the conviction forced itself upon us that we were in a country differing essentially from any hitherto visited by civilized men. We saw nothing with which we had been formerly conversant. The trees resembled no growth of either the torrid,

8. Sea-cucumber. The details are from Morrell.

the temperate, or the northern frigid zones, and were altogether unlike those of the lower southern latitudes we had already traversed. The very rocks were novel in their mass, their colour, and their stratification; and the streams themselves, utterly incredible as it may appear, had so little in common with those of other climates, that we were scrupulous of tasting them, and, indeed, had difficulty in bringing ourselves to believe that their qualities were purely those of nature. At a small brook which crossed our path (the first we had reached) Too-wit and his attendants halted to drink. On account of the singular character of the water, we refused to taste it, supposing it to be polluted; and it was not until some time afterward we came to understand that such was the appearance of the streams throughout the whole group. I am *water* at a loss to give a distinct idea of the nature of this liquid, and cannot do so without many words. Although it flowed with rapidity in all declivities where common water would do so, yet never, except when falling in a cascade, had it the customary appearance of *limpidity*.[9] It was, nevertheless, in point of fact, as perfectly limpid as any limestone water in existence, the difference being only in appearance. At first sight, and especially in cases where little declivity was found, it bore resemblance, as regards consistency, to a thick infusion of gum Arabic in common water. But this was only the least remarkable of its extraordinary qualities. It was *not* colourless, nor was it of any one uniform colour—presenting to the eye, as it flowed, every possible shade of purple, like the hues of a changeable silk. This variation in shade was produced in a manner which excited as profound astonishment in the minds of our party as the mirror had done in the case of Too-wit. Upon collecting a basinful, and allowing it to settle thoroughly, we perceived that the whole mass of liquid was made up of a number of distinct veins, each of a distinct hue; that these veins did not commingle; and that their cohesion was perfect in regard to their own particles among themselves, and imperfect in regard to neighbouring veins. Upon passing the blade of a knife athwart the veins, the water closed over it immediately, as with us, and also, in withdrawing it, all traces of the passage of the knife were instantly obliterated. If, however, the blade was passed down accurately between two veins, a perfect separation was effected, which the power of cohesion did not immediately rectify. The phenomena of this water formed the first definite link in that vast chain of apparent miracles with which I was destined to be at length encircled.

Chapter XIX

We were nearly three hours in reaching the village, it being more than nine miles in the interior, and the path lying through a rugged country. As we passed along, the party of Too-wit (the whole hundred and ten savages of the canoes) was momentarily strengthened by

9. Critics have offered several symbolic or metaphoric interpretations of the striated water of Tsalal, including the idea that it is a self-reflexive reference to textuality (i.e., lines on a page). *Limpid* means transparent clearness.

smaller detachments, of from two to six or seven, which joined us, as if by accident, at different turns in the road. There appeared so much of system in this that I could not help feeling distrust, and I spoke to Captain Guy of my apprehensions. It was now too late, however, to recede, and we concluded that our best security lay in evincing a perfect confidence in the good faith of Too-wit. We accordingly went on, keeping a wary eye upon the manœuvres of the savages, and not permitting them to divide our numbers by pushing in between. In this way, passing through a precipitous ravine, we at length reached what we were told was the only collection of habitations upon the island. As we came in sight of them, the chief set up a shout, and frequently repeated the word *Klock-Klock*; which we supposed to be the name of the village, or perhaps the generic name for villages.

The dwellings were of the most miserable description imaginable, and, unlike those of even the lowest of the savage races with which mankind are acquainted, were of no uniform plan. Some of them (and these we found belonged to the *Wampoos* or *Yampoos*, the great men of the land)[1] consisted of a tree cut down at about four feet from the root, with a large black skin thrown over it, and hanging in loose folds upon the ground. Under this the savage nestled. Others were formed by means of rough limbs of trees, with the withered foliage upon them, made to recline, at an angle of forty-five degrees, against a bank of clay, heaped up, without regular form, to the height of five or six feet. Others, again, were mere holes dug in the earth perpendicularly, and covered over with similar branches, these being removed when the tenant was about to enter, and pulled on again when he had entered. A few were built among the forked limbs of trees as they stood, the upper limbs being partially cut through, so as to bend over upon the lower, thus forming thicker shelter from the weather. The greater number, however, consisted of small shallow caverns, apparently scratched in the face of a precipitous ledge of dark stone, resembling fuller's earth, with which three sides of the village was bounded. At the door of each of these primitive caverns was a small rock, which the tenant carefully placed before the entrance upon leaving his residence, for what purpose I could not ascertain, as the stone itself was never of sufficient size to close up more than a third of the opening.

This village, if it were worthy of the name, lay in a valley of some depth, and could only be approached from the southward, the precipitous ledge of which I have already spoken cutting off all access in other directions. Through the middle of the valley ran a brawling stream of the same magical-looking water which has been described. We saw several strange animals about the dwellings, all appearing to be thoroughly domesticated. The largest of these creatures resembled our common hog in the structure of the body and snout; the tail, however, was bushy, and the legs slender as those of the antelope. Its mo-

1. Critics speculate that the port of Whampoa in *Symzonia* (note the phrase "great men") may be a source for these names. But "Whampoa" seems to have been an English mispronunciation of Huangpu, an actual anchorage at Canton, China, mentioned in Poe's review of Irving's *Astoria*.

tion was exceedingly awkward and indecisive, and we never saw it attempt to run. We noticed also several animals very similar in appearance, but of a greater length of body, and covered with a black wool. There were a great variety of tame fowls running about, and these seemed to constitute the chief food of the natives. To our astonishment we saw black albatross among these birds in a state of entire domestication, going to sea periodically for food, but always returning to the village as a home, and using the southern shore in the vicinity as a place of incubation. There they were joined by their friends the pelicans as usual,[2] but these latter never followed them to the dwellings of the savages. Among the other kinds of tame fowls were ducks, differing very little from the canvass-back of our own country, black gannets, and a large bird not unlike the buzzard in appearance, but not carnivorous. Of fish there seemed to be a great abundance. We saw, during our visit, a quantity of dried salmon, rock cod, blue dolphins, mackerel, blackfish, skate, conger eels, elephantfish, mullets, soles, parrotfish, leather-jackets, gurnards, hake, flounders, paracutas, and innumerable other varieties. We noticed, too, that most of them were similar to the fish about the group of the Lord Auckland Islands, in a latitude as low as fifty-one degrees south. The Gallipago tortoise was also very plentiful. We saw but few wild animals, and none of a large size, or of a species with which we were familiar. One or two serpents of a formidable aspect crossed our path, but the natives paid them little attention, and we concluded that they were not venomous.

As we approached the village with Too-wit and his party, a vast crowd of the people rushed out to meet us, with loud shouts, among which we could only distinguish the everlasting *Anamoo-moo!* and *Lama-Lama!* We were much surprised at perceiving that, with one or two exceptions, these new comers were entirely naked, the skins being used only by the men of the canoes. All the weapons of the country seemed also to be in the possession of the latter, for there was no appearance of any among the villagers. There were a great many women and children, the former not altogether wanting in what might be termed personal beauty. They were straight, tall, and well formed, with a grace and freedom of carriage not to be found in civilized society. Their lips, however, like those of the men, were thick and clumsy, so that, even when laughing, the teeth were never disclosed. Their hair was of a finer texture than that of the males. Among these naked villagers there might have been ten or twelve who were clothed, like the party of Too-wit, in dresses of black skin, and armed with lances and heavy clubs. These appeared to have great influence among the rest, and were always addressed by the title *Wampoo*. These, too, were the tenants of the black skin palaces. That of Too-wit was situated in the centre of the village, and was much larger and somewhat better con-

2. Supposedly another of Poe's errors, since the albatrosses are associated with penguins in the rookery of Chapter XIV. Indeed, Charles Baudelaire changed the word to *penguins* in his 1858 translation; but there is no necessary reason that, on this or other islands, relationships among exactly the same birds should exist, though "as usual" would seem to suggest a lapse on the author's part.

structed than others of its kind. The tree which formed its support was cut off at a distance of twelve feet or thereabout from the root, and there were several branches left just below the cut, these serving to extend the covering, and in this way prevent its flapping about the trunk. The covering, too, which consisted of four very large skins fastened together with wooden skewers, was secured at the bottom with pegs driven through it and into the ground. The floor was strewed with a quantity of dry leaves by way of carpet.

To this hut we were conducted with great solemnity, and as many of the natives crowded in after us as possible. Too-wit seated himself on the leaves, and made signs that we should follow his example. This we did, and presently found ourselves in a situation peculiarly uncomfortable, if not indeed critical. We were on the ground, twelve in number, with the savages, as many as forty, sitting on their hams so closely around us that, if any disturbance had arisen, we should have found it impossible to make use of our arms, or indeed to have risen on our feet. The pressure was not only inside the tent, but outside, where probably was every individual on the whole island, the crowd being prevented from trampling us to death only by the incessant exertions and vociferations of Too-wit. Our chief security lay, however, in the presence of Too-wit himself among us, and we resolved to stick by him closely, as the best chance of extricating ourselves from the dilemma, sacrificing him immediately upon the first appearance of hostile design.

After some trouble a certain degree of quiet was restored, when the chief addressed us in a speech of great length, and very nearly resembling the one delivered in the canoes, with the exception that the *Anamoo-moos!* were now somewhat more strenuously insisted upon than the *Lama-Lamas!* We listened in profound silence until the conclusion of his harangue, when Captain Guy replied by assuring the chief of his eternal friendship and goodwill, concluding what he had to say by a present of several strings of blue beads and a knife. At the former the monarch, much to our surprise, turned up his nose with some expression of contempt; but the knife gave him the most unlimited satisfaction, and he immediately ordered dinner. This was handed into the tent over the heads of the attendants, and consisted of the palpitating entrails of a species of unknown animal, probably one of the slim-legged hogs which we had observed in our approach to the village. Seeing us at a loss how to proceed, he began, by way of setting us an example, to devour yard after yard of the enticing food, until we could positively stand it no longer, and evinced such manifest symptoms of rebellion of stomach as inspired his majesty with a degree of astonishment only inferior to that brought about by the looking-glasses. We declined, however, partaking of the delicacies before us, and endeavoured to make him understand that we had no appetite whatever, having just finished a hearty *déjeuner*.[3]

When the monarch had made an end of his meal, we commenced a series of cross-questioning in every ingenious manner we could devise,

3. Morning or noon meal.

with a view of discovering what were the chief productions of the country, and whether any of them might be turned to profit. At length he seemed to have some idea of our meaning, and offered to accompany us to a part of the coast where he assured us the *biche de mer* (pointing to a specimen of that animal) was to be found in great abundance. We were glad at this early opportunity of escaping from the oppression of the crowd, and signified our eagerness to proceed. We now left the tent, and, accompanied by the whole population of the village, followed the chief to the southeastern extremity of the island, not far from the bay where our vessel lay at anchor. We waited here for about an hour, until the four canoes were brought round by some of the savages to our station. The whole of our party then getting into one of them, we were paddled along the edge of the reef before mentioned, and of another still farther out, where we saw a far greater quantity of *biche de mer* than the oldest seaman among us had ever seen in those groups of the lower latitudes most celebrated for this article of commerce. We stayed near these reefs only long enough to satisfy ourselves that we could easily load a dozen vessels with the animal if necessary, when we were taken alongside the schooner, and parted with Too-wit after obtaining from him a promise that he would bring us, in the course of twenty-four hours, as many of the canvass-back ducks and Gallipago tortoises as his canoes would hold. In the whole of this adventure we saw nothing in the demeanour of the natives calculated to create suspicion, with the single exception of the systematic manner in which their party was strengthened during our route from the schooner to the village.

Chapter XX

The chief was as good as his word, and we were soon plentifully supplied with fresh provision. We found the tortoises as fine as we had ever seen, and the ducks surpassed our best species of wild fowl, being exceedingly tender, juicy, and well-flavoured. Besides these, the savages brought us, upon our making them comprehend our wishes, a vast quantity of brown celery and scurvy grass, with a canoe-load of fresh fish and some dried. The celery was a treat indeed, and the scurvy grass proved of incalculable benefit in restoring those of our men who had shown symptoms of disease. In a very short time we had not a single person on the sick-list. We had also plenty of other kinds of fresh provision, among which may be mentioned a species of shellfish resembling the muscle in shape, but with the taste of an oyster. Shrimps, too, and prawns were abundant, and albatross and other birds' eggs with dark shells. We took in, too, a plentiful stock of the flesh of the hog which I have mentioned before. Most of the men found it a palatable food, but I thought it fishy and otherwise disagreeable. In return for these good things we presented the natives with blue beads, brass trinkets, nails, knives, and pieces of red cloth, they being fully delighted in the exchange. We established a regular market on shore, just under the guns of the schooner, where our bar-

terings were carried on with every appearance of good faith, and a degree of order which their conduct at the village of *Klock-klock* had not led us to expect from the savages.

Matters went on thus very amicably for several days, during which parties of the natives were frequently on board the schooner, and parties of our men frequently on shore, making long excursions into the interior, and receiving no molestation whatever. Finding the ease with which the vessel might be loaded with *biche de mer*, owing to the friendly disposition of the islanders, and the readiness with which they would render us assistance in collecting it, Captain Guy resolved to enter into negotiation with Too-wit for the erection of suitable houses in which to cure the article, and for the services of himself and tribe in gathering as much as possible, while he himself took advantage of the fine weather to prosecute his voyage to the southward. Upon mentioning this project to the chief he seemed very willing to enter into an agreement. A bargain was accordingly struck, perfectly satisfactory to both parties, by which it was arranged that, after making the necessary preparations, such as laying off the proper grounds, erecting a portion of the buildings, and doing some other work in which the whole of our crew would be required, the schooner should proceed on her route, leaving three of her men on the island to superintend the fulfilment of the project, and instruct the natives in drying the *biche de mer*. In regard to terms, these were made to depend upon the exertions of the savages in our absence. They were to receive a stipulated quantity of blue beads, knives, red cloth, and so forth, for every certain number of piculs of the *biche de mer* which should be ready on our return.[4]

A description of the nature of this important article of commerce, and the method of preparing it, may prove of some interest to my readers, and I can find no more suitable place than this for introducing an account of it. The following comprehensive notice of the substance is taken from a modern history of a voyage to the South Seas.[5]

"It is that *mollusca* from the Indian Seas which is known in commerce by the French name *bouche de mer* (a nice morsel from the sea). If I am not much mistaken, the celebrated Cuvier calls it *gasteropeda pulmonifera*. It is abundantly gathered in the coasts of the Pacific Islands, and gathered especially for the Chinese market, where it commands a great price, perhaps as much as their much-talked of edible bird's nests, which are probably made up of the gelatinous matter picked up by a species of swallow from the body of these molluscæ. They have no shell, no legs, nor any prominent part, except an *absorbing* and an *excretory*, opposite organs; but, by their elastic wings,[6] like caterpillars or worms, they creep in shallow waters, in which, when low, they can be seen by a kind of swallow, the sharp bill of which, inserted in the soft animal, draws a gummy and filamentous substance, which, by drying, can be wrought into the solid walls of their nest. Hence the name of *gasteropeda pulmonifera*.

4. The details are from Morrell.
5. Poe is quoting, without specifying his source, Morrell's *Four Voyages*.
6. Probably a printer's error; in Morrell, elastic "rings."

"This mollusca is oblong, and of different sizes, from three to eighteen inches in length; and I have seen a few that were not less than two feet long. They are nearly round, a little flattish on one side, which lies next the bottom of the sea; and they are from one to eight inches thick. They crawl up into shallow water at particular seasons of the year, probably for the purpose of gendering, as we often find them in pairs. It is when the sun has the most power on the water, rendering it tepid, that they approach the shore; and they often go up into places so shallow, that, on the tide's receding, they are left dry, exposed to the heat of the sun. But they do not bring forth their young in shallow water, as we never see any of their progeny, and the full-grown ones are always observed coming in from deep water. They feed principally on that class of zoophytes which produce the coral.

"The *biche de mer* is generally taken in three or four feet water; after which they are brought on shore, and split at one end with a knife, the incision being one inch or more, according to the size of the mollusca. Through this opening the entrails are forced out by pressure, and they are much like those of any other small tenant of the deep. The article is then washed, and afterward boiled to a certain degree, which must not be too much or too little. They are then buried in the ground for four hours, then boiled again for a short time, after which they are dried, either by the fire or the sun. Those cured by the sun are worth the most; but where one picul (133⅓ lbs.) can be cured that way, I can cure thirty piculs by the fire. When once properly cured, they can be kept in a dry place for two or three years without any risk; but they should be examined once in every few months, say four times a year, to see if any dampness is likely to affect them.

"The Chinese, as before stated, consider *biche de mer* a very great luxury, believing that it wonderfully strengthens and nourishes the system, and renews the exhausted system of the immoderate voluptuary. The first quality commands a high price in Canton, being worth ninety dollars a picul; the second quality seventy-five dollars; the third fifty dollars; the fourth thirty dollars; the fifth twenty dollars; the sixth twelve dollars; the seventh eight dollars; and the eighth four dollars; small cargoes, however, will often bring more in Manilla, Singapore, and Batavia."

An agreement having been thus entered into, we proceeded immediately to land everything necessary for preparing the buildings and clearing the ground. A large flat space near the eastern shore of the bay was selected, where there was plenty both of wood and water, and within a convenient distance of the principal reefs on which the *biche de mer* was to be procured. We now all set to work in good earnest, and soon, to the great astonishment of the savages, had felled a sufficient number of trees for our purpose, getting them quickly in order for the framework of the houses, which in two or three days were so far under way that we could safely trust the rest of the work to the three men whom we intended to leave behind. These were John Carson, Alfred Harris, and ——— Peterson (all natives of London, I believe), who volunteered their services in this respect.

By the last of the month we had everything in readiness for departure. We had agreed, however, to pay a formal visit of leavestaking to the village, and Too-wit insisted so pertinaciously upon our keeping the promise, that we did not think it advisable to run the risk of offending him by a final refusal. I believe that not one of us had at this time the slightest suspicion of the good faith of the savages. They had uniformly behaved with the greatest decorum, aiding us with alacrity in our work, offering us their commodities frequently without price, and never, in any instance, pilfering a single article, although the high value they set upon the goods we had with us was evident by the extravagant demonstrations of joy always manifested upon our making them a present. The women especially were most obliging in every respect, and, upon the whole, we should have been the most suspicious of human beings had we entertained a single thought of perfidy on the part of a people who treated us so well. A very short while sufficed to prove that this apparent kindness of disposition was only the result of a deeply-laid plan for our destruction, and that the islanders for whom we entertained such inordinate feelings of esteem were among the most barbarous, subtle, and bloodthirsty wretches that ever contaminated the face of the globe.

It was on the first of February that we went on shore for the purpose of visiting the village. Although, as said before, we entertained not the slightest suspicion, still no proper precaution was neglected. Six men were left in the schooner with instructions to permit none of the savages to approach the vessel during our absence, under any pretence whatever, and to remain constantly on deck. The boarding-nettings were up, the guns double-shotted with grape and canister, and the swivels loaded with canisters of musket-balls. She lay, with her anchor apeak, about a mile from the shore, and no canoe could approach her in any direction without being distinctly seen and exposed to the full fire of our swivels immediately.

The six men being left on board, our shore-party consisted of thirty-two persons in all. We were armed to the teeth, having with us muskets, pistols, and cutlasses, besides each a long kind of seaman's knife, somewhat resembling the Bowie knife now so much used throughout our western and southern country. A hundred of the black skin warriors met us at the landing for the purpose of accompanying us on our way. We noticed, however, with some surprise, that they were now entirely without arms; and, upon questioning Too-wit in relation to this circumstance, he merely answered that *Mattee non we pa pa si*—meaning that there was no need of arms where all were brothers. We took this in good part, and proceeded.

We had passed the spring and rivulet of which I before spoke, and were now entering upon a narrow gorge leading through the chain of soapstone hills among which the village was situated. This gorge[7] was very rocky and uneven, so much so that it was with no little difficulty we scrambled through it on our first visit to Klock-klock. The whole

7. Cf. Stephens's *Incidents of Travel in Arabia Petraea.*

length of the ravine might have been a mile and a half, or probably two miles. It wound in every possible direction through the hills (having apparently formed, at some remote period, the bed of a torrent), in no instance proceeding more than twenty yards without an abrupt turn. The sides of this dell would have averaged, I am sure, seventy or eighty feet in perpendicular altitude throughout the whole of their extent, and in some portions they arose to an astonishing height, overshadowing the pass so completely that but little of the light of day could penetrate. The general width was about forty feet, and occasionally it diminished so as not to allow the passage of more than five or six persons abreast. In short, there could be no place in the world better adapted for the consummation of an ambuscade, and it was no more than natural that we should look carefully to our arms as we entered upon it. When I now think of our egregious folly, the chief subject of astonishment seems to be, that we should have ever ventured, under any circumstances, so completely into the power of unknown savages as to permit them to march both before and behind us in our progress through this ravine. Yet such was the order we blindly took up, trusting foolishly to the force of our party, the unarmed condition of Too-wit and his men, the certain efficacy of our firearms (whose effect was yet a secret to the natives), and, more than all, to the long-sustained pretension of friendship kept up by these infamous wretches. Five or six of them went on before, as if to lead the way, ostentatiously busying themselves in removing the larger stones and rubbish from the path. Next came our own party. We walked closely together, taking care only to prevent separation. Behind followed the main body of the savages, observing unusual order and decorum.

Dirk Peters, a man named Wilson Allen, and myself were on the right of our companions, examining, as we went along, the singular stratification of the precipice which overhung us. A fissure in the soft rock attracted our attention. It was about wide enough for one person to enter without squeezing, and extended back into the hill some eighteen or twenty feet in a straight course, sloping afterward to the left. The height of the opening, as far as we could see into it from the main gorge, was perhaps sixty or seventy feet. There were one or two stunted shrubs growing from the crevices, bearing a species of filbert, which I felt some curiosity to examine, and pushed in briskly for that purpose, gathering five or six of the nuts at a grasp, and then hastily retreating. As I turned, I found that Peters and Allen had followed me. I desired them to go back, as there was not room for two persons to pass, saying they should have some of my nuts. They accordingly turned, and were scrambling back, Allen being close to the mouth of the fissure, when I was suddenly aware of a concussion resembling nothing I had ever before experienced, and which impressed me with a vague conception, if indeed I then thought of anything, that the whole foundations of the solid globe were suddenly rent asunder, and that the day of universal dissolution was at hand.[8]

8. See the notes to "Al Aaraaf" (pp. 22ff. herein), "The Colloquy of Monos and Una" (pp. 279ff.), "The Masque of the Red Death" (pp. 299ff.), "The Power of Words" (pp. 398ff.), and *Eureka* (pp. 568ff.).

Chapter XXI

As soon as I could collect my scattered senses, I found myself nearly suffocated, and grovelling in utter darkness among a quantity of loose earth, which was also falling upon me heavily in every direction, threatening to bury me entirely. Horribly alarmed at this idea, I struggled to gain my feet, and at length succeeded. I then remained motionless for some moments, endeavouring to conceive what had happened to me, and where I was. Presently I heard a deep groan just at my ear, and afterward the smothered voice of Peters calling to me for aid in the name of God. I scrambled one or two paces forward, when I fell directly over the head and shoulders of my companion, who, I soon discovered, was buried in a loose mass of earth as far as his middle, and struggling desperately to free himself from the pressure. I tore the dirt from around him with all the energy I could command, and at length succeeded in getting him out.

As soon as we sufficiently recovered from our fright and surprise to be capable of conversing rationally, we both came to the conclusion that the walls of the fissure in which we had ventured had, by some convulsion of nature, or probably from their own weight, caved in overhead, and that we were consequently lost for ever, being thus entombed alive. For a long time we gave up supinely to the most intense agony and despair, such as cannot be adequately imagined by those who have never been in a similar situation. I firmly believe that no incident ever occurring in the course of human events is more adapted to inspire the supremeness of mental and bodily distress than a case like our own, of living inhumation. The blackness of darkness[9] which envelops the victim, the terrific oppression of lungs, the stifling fumes from the damp earth, unite with the ghastly considerations that we are beyond the remotest confines of hope, and that such is the allotted portion of *the dead*, to carry into the human heart a degree of appalling awe and horror not to be tolerated—never to be conceived.

At length Peters proposed that we should endeavour to ascertain precisely the extent of our calamity, and grope about our prison; it being barely possible, he observed, that some opening might be yet left us for escape. I caught eagerly at this hope, and, arousing myself to exertion, attempted to force my way through the loose earth. Hardly had I advanced a single step before a glimmer of light became perceptible, enough to convince me that, at all events, we should not immediately perish for want of air. We now took some degree of heart, and encouraged each other to hope for the best. Having scrambled over a bank of rubbish which impeded our farther progress in the direction of the light, we found less difficulty in advancing, and also experienced some relief from the excessive oppression of lungs which had tormented us.

9. This phrase occurs in Jude 1:13 as a description of eternal punishment for sinners: "Raging waves of the sea, foaming out their own shame; wandering stars, to whom is reserved the blackness of darkness for ever." Although the phrase has become conventional, it is worth noting that it occurs in Reynolds's "Leaves"; other parallels of language and incident with Reynolds's text are noticeable.

Presently we were enabled to obtain a glimpse of the objects around, and discovered that we were near the extremity of the straight portion of the fissure, where it made a turn to the left. A few struggles more, and we reached the bend, when, to our inexpressible joy, there appeared a long scam or crack extending upward a vast distance, generally at an angle of about forty-five degrees, although sometimes much more precipitous. We could not see through the whole extent of this opening; but, as a good deal of light came down it, we had little doubt of finding at the top of it (if we could by any means reach the top) a clear passage into the open air.

I now called to mind that three of us had entered the fissure from the main gorge, and that our companion, Allen, was still missing; we determined at once to retrace our steps and look for him. After a long search, and much danger from the farther caving in of the earth above us, Peters at length cried out to me that he had hold of our companion's foot, and that his whole body was deeply buried beneath the rubbish, beyond a possibility of extricating him. I soon found that what he said was too true, and that, of course, life had been long extinct. With sorrowful hearts, therefore, we left the corpse to its fate, and again made our way to the bend.

The breadth of the seam was barely sufficient to admit us, and, after one or two ineffectual efforts at getting up, we began once more to despair. I have before said that the chain of hills through which ran the main gorge was composed of a species of soft rock resembling soapstone. The sides of the cleft we were now attempting to ascend were of the same material, and so excessively slippery, being wet, that we could get but little foothold upon them even in their least precipitous parts; in some places, where the ascent was nearly perpendicular, the difficulty was, of course, much aggravated; and, indeed, for some time we thought it insurmountable. We took courage, however, from despair; and what, by dint of cutting steps in the soft stone with our Bowie knives, and swinging, at the risk of our lives, to small projecting points of a harder species of slaty rock which now and then protruded from the general mass, we at length reached a natural platform, from which was perceptible a patch of blue sky, at the extremity of a thickly-wooded ravine. Looking back now, with somewhat more leisure, at the passage through which we had thus far proceeded, we clearly saw, from the appearance of its sides, that it was of late formation, and we concluded that the concussion, whatever it was, which had so unexpectedly overwhelmed us, had also, at the same moment, laid open this path for escape. Being quite exhausted with exertion, and, indeed, so weak that we were scarcely able to stand or articulate, Peters now proposed that we should endeavour to bring our companions to the rescue by firing the pistols which still remained in our girdles—the muskets as well as cutlasses had been lost among the loose earth at the bottom of the chasm. Subsequent events proved that, had we fired, we should have sorely repented it; but, luckily, a half suspicion of foul play had by this time arisen in my mind, and we forbore to let the savages know of our whereabouts.

After having reposed for about an hour, we pushed on slowly up the ravine, and had gone no great way before we heard a succession of tremendous yells. At length we reached what might be called the surface of the ground; for our path hitherto, since leaving the platform, had lain beneath an archway of high rock and foliage, at a vast distance overhead. With great caution we stole to a narrow opening, through which we had a clear sight of the surrounding country, when the whole dreadful secret of the concussion broke upon us in one moment and at one view.

The spot from which we looked was not far from the summit of the highest peak in the range of the soapstone hills. The gorge in which our party of thirty-two had entered ran within fifty feet to the left of us. But, for at least one hundred yards, the channel or bed of this gorge was entirely filled up with the chaotic ruins of more than a million tons of earth and stone that had been artificially tumbled within it. The means by which the vast mass had been precipitated were not more simple than evident, for sure traces of the murderous work were yet remaining. In several spots along the top of the eastern side of the gorge (we were now on the western) might be seen stakes of wood driven into the earth. In these spots the earth had not given way; but throughout the whole extent of the face of the precipice from which the mass *had* fallen, it was clear, from marks left in the soil resembling those made by the drill of the rock-blaster, that stakes similar to those we saw standing had been inserted, at not more than a yard apart, for the length of perhaps three hundred feet, and ranging at about ten feet back from the edge of the gulf. Strong cords of grape vine were attached to the stakes still remaining on the hill, and it was evident that such cords had also been attached to each of the other stakes. I have already spoken of the singular stratification of these soapstone hills; and the description just given of the narrow and deep fissure through which we effected our escape from inhumation will afford a further conception of its nature. This was such that almost every natural convulsion would be sure to split the soil into perpendicular layers or ridges running parallel with one another; and a very moderate exertion of art would be sufficient for effecting the same purpose. Of this stratification the savages had availed themselves to accomplish their treacherous ends. There can be no doubt that, by the continuous line of stakes, a partial rupture of the soil had been brought about, probably to the depth of one or two feet, when, by means of a savage pulling at the end of each of the cords (these cords being attached to the tops of the stakes, and extending back from the edge of the cliff), a vast leverage power was obtained, capable of hurling the whole face of the hill, upon a given signal, into the bosom of the abyss below. The fate of our poor companions was no longer a matter of uncertainty. We alone had escaped from the tempest of that overwhelming destruction. We were the only living white men upon the island.

Chapter XXII

Our situation, as it now appeared, was scarcely less dreadful than when we had conceived ourselves entombed for ever. We saw before us no prospect but that of being put to death by the savages, or of dragging out a miserable existence in captivity among them. We might, to be sure, conceal ourselves for a time from their observation among the fastnesses of the hills, and, as a final resort, in the chasm from which we had just issued; but we must either perish in the long Polar winter through cold and famine, or be ultimately discovered in our efforts to obtain relief.

The whole country around us seemed to be swarming with savages, crowds of whom, we now perceived, had come over from the islands to the southward on flat rafts, doubtless with a view of lending their aid in the capture and plunder of the Jane. The vessel still lay calmly at anchor in the bay, those on board being apparently quite unconscious of any danger awaiting them. How we longed at that moment to be with them! either to aid in effecting their escape, or to perish with them in attempting a defence. We saw no chance even of warning them of their danger without bringing immediate destruction upon our own heads, with but a remote hope of benefit to them. A pistol fired might suffice to apprize them that something wrong had occurred; but the report could not possibly inform them that their only prospect of safety lay in getting out of the harbour forthwith—it could not tell them that no principles of honour now bound them to remain, that their companions were no longer among the living. Upon hearing the discharge they could not be more thoroughly prepared to meet the foe, who were now getting ready to attack, than they already were, and always had been. No good, therefore, and infinite harm, would result from our firing, and, after mature deliberation, we forbore.

Our next thought was to attempt a rush towards the vessel, to seize one of the four canoes which lay at the head of the bay, and endeavour to force a passage on board. But the utter impossibility of succeeding in this desperate task soon became evident. The country, as I said before, was literally swarming with the natives, skulking among the bushes and recesses of the hills, so as not to be observed from the schooner. In our immediate vicinity especially, and blockading the sole path by which we could hope to attain the shore in the proper point, were stationed the whole party of the black skin warriors, with Too-wit at their head, and apparently only waiting for some re-enforcement to commence his onset upon the Jane. The canoes, too, which lay at the head of the bay were manned with savages, unarmed, it is true, but who undoubtedly had arms within reach. We were forced, therefore, however unwillingly, to remain in our place of concealment, mere spectators of the conflict which presently ensued.

In about half an hour we saw some sixty or seventy rafts, or flatboats, with outriggers, filled with savages, and coming round the southern bight of the harbour. They appeared to have no arms except short clubs, and stones which lay in the bottom of the rafts. Immediately af-

terward another detachment, still larger, approached in an opposite direction, and with similar weapons. The four canoes, too, were now quickly filled with natives, starting up from the bushes at the head of the bay, and put off swiftly to join the other parties. Thus, in less time than[1] I have taken to tell it, and as if by magic, the *Jane* saw herself surrounded by an immense multitude of desperadoes evidently bent upon capturing her at all hazards.

That they would succeed in so doing could not be doubted for an instant.[2] The six men left in the vessel, however resolutely they might engage in her defence, were altogether unequal to the proper management of the guns, or in any manner to sustain a contest at such odds. I could hardly imagine that they would make resistance at all, but in this was deceived; for presently I saw them get springs upon the cable, and bring the vessel's starboard broadside to bear upon the canoes, which by this time were within pistol range, the rafts being nearly a quarter of a mile to windward. Owing to some cause unknown, but most probably to the agitation of our poor friends at seeing themselves in so hopeless a situation, the discharge was an entire failure. Not a canoe was hit or a single savage injured, the shots striking short and *ricochêting* over their heads. The only effect produced upon them was astonishment at the unexpected report and smoke, which was so excessive that for some moments I almost thought they would abandon their design entirely, and return to the shore. And this they would most likely have done had our men followed up their broadside by a discharge of small arms, in which, as the canoes were now so near at hand, they could not have failed in doing some execution, sufficient, at least, to deter this party from a farther advance, until they could have given the rafts also a broadside. But, in place of this, they left the canoe party to recover from their panic, and, by looking about them, to see that no injury had been sustained, while they flew to the larboard to get ready for the rafts.

The discharge to larboard produced the most terrible effect. The star and double-headed shot of the large guns cut seven or eight of the rafts completely asunder, and killed, perhaps, thirty or forty of the savages outright, while a hundred of them, at least, were thrown into the water, the most of them dreadfully wounded. The remainder, frightened out of their senses, commenced at once a precipitate retreat, not even waiting to pick up their maimed companions, who were swimming about in every direction, screaming and yelling for aid. This great success, however, came too late for the salvation of our devoted people. The canoe party were already on board the schooner to the number of more than a hundred and fifty, the most of them having succeeded in scrambling up the chains and over the boarding nettings even before the matches had been applied to the larboard guns.

1. Some editions have "corrected" a typographical error of *that* for *than*; but there is no such error in the 1838 American edition, the copy text reprinted here.
2. Poe's description of the attack on the *Jane Guy* is usually attributed to Morrell's description of the attack on the ship *Antarctic*, but the parallels are rather general (see "Fourth Voyage," chapter V).

Nothing could now withstand their brute rage. Our men were borne down at once, overwhelmed, trodden under foot, and absolutely torn to pieces in an instant.

Seeing this, the savages on the rafts got the better of their fears, and came up in shoals to the plunder. In five minutes the Jane was a pitiable scene indeed of havoc and tumultuous outrage. The decks were split open and ripped up; the cordage, sails, and everything moveable on deck demolished as if by magic; while, by dint of pushing at the stern, towing with the canoes, and hauling at the sides, as they swam in thousands around the vessel, the wretches finally forced her on shore (the cable having been slipped), and delivered her over to the good offices of Too-wit, who, during the whole of the engagement, had maintained, like a skilful general, his post of security and reconnoissance among the hills, but, now that the victory was completed to his satisfaction, condescended to scamper down with his warriors of the black skin, and become a partaker in the spoils.

Too-wit's descent left us at liberty to quit our hiding-place and reconnoitre the hill in the vicinity of the chasm. At about fifty yards from the mouth of it we saw a small spring of water, at which we slaked the burning thirst that now consumed us. Not far from the spring we discovered several of the filbert-bushes which I mentioned before. Upon tasting the nuts we found them palatable, and very nearly resembling in flavour the common English filbert. We collected our hats full immediately, deposited them within the ravine, and returned for more. While we were busily employed in gathering these, a rustling in the bushes alarmed us, and we were upon the point of stealing back to our covert, when a large black bird of the bittern species[3] strugglingly and slowly arose above the shrubs. I was so much startled that I could do nothing, but Peters had sufficient presence of mind to run up to it before it could make its escape, and seize it by the neck. Its struggles and screams were tremendous, and we had thoughts of letting it go, lest the noise should alarm some of the savages who might be still lurking in the neighbourhood. A stab with a Bowie knife, however, at length brought it to the ground, and we dragged it into the ravine, congratulating ourselves that, at all events, we had thus obtained a supply of food enough to last us for a week.

We now went out again to look about us, and ventured a considerable distance down the southern declivity of the hill, but met with nothing else which could serve us for food. We therefore collected a quantity of dry wood and returned, seeing one or two large parties of the natives on their way to the village, laden with the plunder of the vessel, and who, we were apprehensive, might discover us in passing beneath the hill.

Our next care was to render our place of concealment as secure as possible, and, with this object, we arranged some brushwood over the

3. Kopley, in his edition of *Pym*, notes that the bittern is a bird associated biblically with the destruction of the cities of Babylon (Isaiah 14:23), Idumea (Isaiah 34:11), and Nineveh (Zephaniah 2:14). He notes also that the bird is mentioned in Dr. Alexander Keith's *Evidence of the Truth of Christianity* (1832), cited by Poe in his review of Stephens's *Incidents*.

aperture which I have before spoken of as the one through which we saw the patch of blue sky, on reaching the platform from the interior of the chasm. We left only a very small opening, just wide enough to admit of our seeing the bay, without the risk of being discovered from below. Having done this, we congratulated ourselves upon the security of the position; for we were now completely excluded from observation, as long as we chose to remain within the ravine itself, and not venture out upon the hill. We could perceive no traces of the savages having ever been within this hollow; but, indeed, when we came to reflect upon the probability that the fissure through which we attained it had been only just now created by the fall of the cliff opposite, and that no other way of attaining it could be perceived, we were not so much rejoiced at the thought of being secure from molestation as fearful lest there should be absolutely no means left us for descent. We resolved to explore the summit of the hill thoroughly, when a good opportunity should offer. In the mean time we watched the motions of the savages through our loophole.

They had already made a complete wreck of the vessel, and were now preparing to set her on fire.[4] In a little while we saw the smoke ascending in huge volumes from her main-hatchway, and, shortly afterward, a dense mass of flame burst up from the forecastle. The rigging, masts, and what remained of the sails caught immediately, and the fire spread rapidly along the decks. Still a great many of the savages retained their stations about her, hammering with large stones, axes, and cannon balls at the bolts and other copper and iron work. On the beach, and in canoes and rafts, there were not less, altogether, in the immediate vicinity of the schooner, than ten thousand natives, besides the shoals of them who, laden with booty, were making their way inland and over to the neighbouring islands. We now anticipated a catastrophe, and were not disappointed. First of all there came a smart shock (which we felt distinctly where we were as if we had been slightly galvanized), but unattended with any visible signs of an explosion. The savages were evidently startled, and paused for an instant from their labours and yellings. They were upon the point of recommencing, when suddenly a mass of smoke puffed up from the decks, resembling a black and heavy thunder-cloud—then, as if from its bowels, arose a tall stream of vivid fire to the height, apparently, of a quarter of a mile—then there came a sudden circular expansion of the flame—then the whole atmosphere was magically crowded, in a single instant, with a wild chaos of wood, and metal, and human limbs—and, lastly, came the concussion in its fullest fury, which hurled us impetuously from our feet, while the hills echoed and re-echoed the tumult, and a dense shower of the minutest fragments of the ruins tumbled headlong in every direction around us.

The havoc among the savages far exceeded our utmost expectation, and they had now, indeed, reaped the full and perfect fruits of their treachery. Perhaps a thousand perished by the explosion, while at least

4. Some scholars have suggested Irving's description in *Astoria* of the destruction of the ship *Tonquin* as the source of this scene.

an equal number were desperately mangled. The whole surface of the bay was literally strewn with the struggling and drowning wretches, and on shore matters were even worse. They seemed utterly appalled by the suddenness and completeness of their discomfiture, and made no efforts at assisting one another. At length we observed a total change in their demeanour. From absolute stupor they appeared to be, all at once, aroused to the highest pitch of excitement, and rushed wildly about, going to and from a certain point on the beach, with the strangest expressions of mingled horror, rage, and intense curiosity depicted on their countenances, and shouting, at the top of their voices, *Tekeli-li!*[5] *Tekeli-li!*

Presently we saw a large body go off into the hills, whence they returned in a short time, carrying stakes of wood. These they brought to the station where the crowd was the thickest, which now separated so as to afford us a view of the object of all this excitement. We perceived something white lying on the ground, but could not immediately make out what it was. At length we saw that it was the carcass of the strange animal with the scarlet teeth and claws which the schooner had picked up at sea on the eighteenth of January. Captain Guy had had the body preserved for the purpose of stuffing the skin and taking it to England. I remember he had given some directions about it just before our making the island, and it had been brought into the cabin and stowed away in one of the lockers. It had now been thrown on shore by the explosion; but why it had occasioned so much concern among the savages was more than we could comprehend. Although they crowded around the carcass at a little distance, none of them seemed willing to approach it closely. By-and-by the men with the stakes drove them in a circle around it, and, no sooner was this arrangement completed, than the whole of the vast assembly rushed into the interior of the island, with loud screams of *Tekeli-li! Tekeli-li!*

Chapter XXIII-a[6]

During the six or seven days immediately following we remained in our hiding-place upon the hill, going out only occasionally, and then

5. Many readers have been struck by the word *tekel* embedded in this cry because of the forewarning of destruction in the apocalyptic handwriting on the wall of Belshazzar's palace in Daniel 5:25: "Mene mene tekel upharsin," with *tekel* translated as "Thou art; weighed in the balances and art found wanting" (verse 27). Several inscriptions in the walls of rock on the island of Tsalal are about to be revealed, and as Pym edges nearer the pole, there is a suggestion of some great judgment, or curse, on the "region of the south."

Particular linguistic-mythic speculations combine the Hebrew *li* with *tekel* and add the meaning of "to me" or "by me" as though from or by a god of some kind. Scholars have also noted Polynesian and Arabic cognates suggesting "shaking with fear" (Polynesian: *tekelili*), especially before a god (Polynesian: *tiki*) who is "angry" (Polynesian: *lili*), in whom one must nevertheless "trust" (Arabic: *tekkela*). Among the more arcane but provocative interpretations of the ancient history that the text vaguely implies are those that connect the mysterious Egyptian, Ethiopian, Arabic, and other rock inscriptions to the myth of the lost tribes of Israel; these clues resonate with the discussion of the curse on the land of Edom by John Stephens in *Incidents of Travel in Arabea Petraea, Egypt, and the Holy Land*, reviewed by Poe just before the publication of *Pym*. Another arresting resonance, less thematic, is that Poe's mother, Elizabeth, performed the role of Christine in Theodore Hook's *Tekeli, or, The Siege of Mongatz* (1806).

6. As indicated in the headnote, there are two chapters numbered XXIII in the American edition. Some scholars have speculated that what is now the first one was added in view of the

with the greatest precaution, for water and filberts. We had made a kind of penthouse on the platform, furnishing it with a bed of dry leaves, and placing in it three large flat stones, which served us for both fireplace and table. We kindled a fire without difficulty by rubbing two pieces of dry wood together, the one soft, the other hard. The bird we had taken in such good season proved excellent eating, although somewhat tough. It was not an oceanic fowl, but a species of bittern, with jet black and grizzly plumage, and diminutive wings in proportion to its bulk. We afterward saw three of the same kind in the vicinity of the ravine, apparently seeking for the one we had captured; but, as they never alighted, we had no opportunity of catching them.

As long as this fowl lasted we suffered nothing from our situation; but it was now entirely consumed, and it became absolutely necessary that we should look out for provision. The filberts would not satisfy the cravings of hunger, afflicting us, too, with severe gripings of the bowels, and, if freely indulged in, with violent headache. We had seen several large tortoises near the seashore to the eastward of the hill, and perceived they might be easily taken, if we could get at them without the observation of the natives. It was resolved, therefore, to make an attempt at descending.

We commenced by going down the southern declivity, which seemed to offer the fewest difficulties, but had not proceeded a hundred yards before (as we had anticipated from appearances on the hill-top) our progress was entirely arrested by a branch of the gorge in which our companions had perished. We now passed along the edge of this for about a quarter of a mile, when we were again stopped by a precipice of immense depth, and, not being able to make our way along the brink of it, we were forced to retrace our steps by the main ravine.

We now pushed over to the eastward, but with precisely similar fortune. After an hour's scramble, at the risk of breaking our necks, we discovered that we had merely descended into a vast pit of black granite, with fine dust at the bottom, and whence the only egress was by the rugged path in which we had come down. Toiling again up this path, we now tried the northern edge of the hill. Here we were obliged to use the greatest possible caution in our manœuvres, as the least indiscretion would expose us to the full view of the savages in the village. We crawled along, therefore, on our hands and knees, and, occasionally, were even forced to throw ourselves at full length, dragging our bodies along by means of the shrubbery. In this careful manner we had proceeded but a little way, when we arrived at a chasm far deeper than any we had yet seen, and leading directly into the main gorge. Thus our fears were fully confirmed, and we found ourselves cut off entirely from access to the world below. Thoroughly exhausted by our exertions, we made the best of our way back to the platform, and, throwing ourselves upon the bed of leaves, slept sweetly and soundly for some hours.

emphasis on the polar theme ("farther, farther South"); but since that theme is developed before this point in the novel, it is perhaps more likely a printer's error.

For several days after this fruitless search we were occupied in exploring every part of the summit of the hill, in order to inform ourselves of its actual resources. We found that it would afford us no food, with the exception of the unwholesome filberts, and a rank species of scurvy grass which grew in a little patch of not more than four rods square, and would be soon exhausted. On the fifteenth of February, as near as I can remember, there was not a blade of this left, and the nuts were growing scarce; our situation, therefore, could hardly be more lamentable.[7] On the sixteenth we again went round the walls of our prison, in hope of finding some avenue of escape, but to no purpose. We also descended the chasm in which we had been overwhelmed, with the faint expectation of discovering, through this channel, some opening to the main ravine. Here, too, we were disappointed, although we found and brought up with us a musket.

On the seventeenth we set out with the determination of examining more thoroughly the chasm of black granite into which we had made our way in the first search. We remembered that one of the fissures in the sides of this pit had been but partially looked into, and we were anxious to explore it, although with no expectation of discovering here any opening.

We found no great difficulty in reaching the bottom of the hollow as before, and were now sufficiently calm to survey it with some attention. It was, indeed, one of the most singular-looking places imaginable, and we could scarcely bring ourselves to believe it altogether the work of nature. The pit, from its eastern to its western extremity, was about five hundred yards in length, when all its windings were threaded; the distance from east to west in a straight line not being more (I should suppose, having no means of accurate examination) than forty or fifty yards. Upon first descending into the chasm, that is to say, for a hundred feet downward from the summit of the hill, the sides of the abyss bore little resemblance to each other, and, apparently, had at no time been connected, the one surface being of the soapstone and the other of marl, granulated with some metallic matter. The average breadth, or interval between the two cliffs, was probably here sixty feet, but there seemed to be no regularity of formation. Passing down, however, beyond the limit spoken of, the interval rapidly contracted, and the sides began to run parallel, although, for some distance farther, they were still dissimilar in their material and form of surface. Upon arriving within fifty feet of the bottom, a perfect regularity commenced. The sides were now entirely uniform in substance, in colour, and in lateral direction, the material being a very black and shining granite, and the distance between the two sides, at all points facing each other, exactly twenty yards. The precise formation of the chasm will be best understood by means of a delineation taken upon the spot; for I had luckily with me a pocketbook and pencil, which I preserved with great care through a long series of subsequent adventure, and to which I am

7. This day was rendered remarkable by our observing in the south several huge wreaths of the grayish vapour I have before spoken of [Pym's note].

indebted for memoranda of many subjects which would otherwise have
been crowded from my remembrance.

Figure 1

This figure (see figure 1) gives the general outlines of the chasm,
without the minor cavities in the sides, of which there were several,
each cavity having a corresponding protuberance opposite. The bot-
tom of the gulf was covered to the depth of three or four inches with a
powder almost impalpable, beneath which we found a continuation of
the black granite. To the right, at the lower extremity, will be noticed
the appearance of a small opening; this is the fissure alluded to above,
and to examine which more minutely than before was the object of
our second visit. We now pushed into it with vigour, cutting away a
quantity of brambles which impeded us, and removing a vast heap of
sharp flints somewhat resembling arrowheads in shape. We were en-
couraged to persevere, however, by perceiving some little light pro-
ceeding from the farther end. We at length squeezed our way for about
thirty feet, and found that the aperture was a low and regularly-
formed arch, having a bottom of the same impalpable powder as that
in the main chasm. A strong light now broke upon us, and, turning a
short bend, we found ourselves in another lofty chamber, similar to
the one we had left in every respect but longitudinal form. Its general
figure is here given. (See figure 2.)

Figure 2.

The total length of this chasm, commencing at the opening *a* and pro-
ceeding round the curve *b* to the extremity *d*, is five hundred and fifty
yards. At *c* we discovered a small aperture similar to the one through
which we had issued from the other chasm, and this was choked up in
the same manner with brambles and a quantity of the white arrow-
head flints. We forced our way through it, finding it about forty feet
long, and emerged into a third chasm. This, too, was precisely like the
first, except in its longitudinal shape, which was thus. (See figure 3.)

Figure 3 *Figure 5*

We found the entire length of the third chasm three hundred and
twenty yards. At the point *a* was an opening about six feet wide, and
extending fifteen feet into the rock, where it terminated in a bed of
marl, there being no other chasm beyond, as we had expected. We
were about leaving this fissure, into which very little light was admit-
ted, when Peters called my attention to a range of singular-looking in-
dentures in the surface of the marl forming the termination of the
cul-de-sac. With a very slight exertion of the imagination, the left, or
most northerly of these indentures might have been taken for the in-
tentional, although rude, representation of a human figure standing
erect, with outstretched arm.[8] The rest of them bore also some little
resemblance to alphabetical characters, and Peters was willing, at all
events, to adopt the idle opinion that they were really such. I con-
vinced him of his error, finally, by directing his attention to the floor of
the fissure, where, among the powder, we picked up, piece by piece,
several large flakes of the marl, which had evidently been broken off
by some convulsion from the surface where the indentures were
found, and which had projecting points exactly fitting the indentures;
thus proving them to have been the work of nature. Figure 4. presents
an accurate copy of the whole.

Figure 4

8. Critics have seen a resemblance to the petrographs of Chapter 6 of Poe's "The Journal of
Julius Rodman," where lines on a cliff are described.

After satisfying ourselves that these singular caverns afforded us no means of escape from our prison, we made our way back, dejected and dispirited, to the summit of the hill. Nothing worth mentioning occurred during the next twenty-four hours, except that, in examining the ground to the eastward of the third chasm, we found two triangular holes of great depth, and also with black granite sides. Into these holes we did not think it worth while to attempt descending, as they had the appearance of mere natural wells, without outlet. They were each about twenty yards in circumference, and their shape, as well as relative position in regard to the third chasm, is shown in figure 5, preceding page.

Chapter XXIII-b

On the twentieth of the month, finding it altogether impossible to subsist any longer upon the filberts, the use of which occasioned us the most excruciating torment, we resolved to make a desperate attempt at descending the southern declivity of the hill. The face of the precipice was here of the softest species of soapstone, although nearly perpendicular throughout its whole extent (a depth of a hundred and fifty feet at the least), and in many places even overarching. After long search we discovered a narrow ledge about twenty feet below the brink of the gulf; upon this Peters contrived to leap, with what assistance I could render him by means of our pocket-handkerchiefs tied together. With somewhat more difficulty I also got down; and we then saw the possibility of descending the whole way by the process in which we had clambered up from the chasm when we had been buried by the fall of the hill—that is, by cutting steps in the face of the soapstone with our knives. The extreme hazard of the attempt can scarcely be conceived; but, as there was no other resource, we determined to undertake it.

Upon the ledge where we stood there grew some filbert-bushes; and to one of these we made fast an end of our rope of handkerchiefs. The other end being tied round Peters's waist, I lowered him down over the edge of the precipice until the handkerchiefs were stretched tight. He now proceeded to dig a deep hole in the soapstone (as far in as eight or ten inches), sloping away the rock above to the height of a foot, or thereabout, so as to allow of his driving, with the butt of a pistol, a tolerably strong peg into the levelled surface. I then drew him up for about four feet, when he made a hole similar to the one below, driving in a peg as before, and having thus a resting-place for both feet and hands. I now unfastened the handkerchiefs from the bush, throwing him the end, which he tied to the peg in the uppermost hole, letting himself down gently to a station about three feet lower than he had yet been, that is, to the full extent of the handkerchiefs. Here he dug another hole, and drove another peg. He then drew himself up, so as to rest his feet in the hole just cut, taking hold with his hands upon the peg in the one above. It was now necessary to untie the handkerchiefs from the topmost peg, with the view of fastening them to the

second; and here he found that an error had been committed in cutting the holes at so great a distance apart. However, after one or two unsuccessful and dangerous attempts at reaching the knot (having to hold on with his left hand while he laboured to undo the fastening with his right), he at length cut the string, leaving six inches of it affixed to the peg. Tying the handkerchiefs now to the second peg, he descended to a station below the third, taking care not to go too far down. By these means (means which I should never have conceived of myself, and for which we were indebted altogether to Peters's ingenuity and resolution) my companion finally succeeded, with the occasional aid of projections in the cliff, in reaching the bottom without accident.[9]

It was some time before I could summon sufficient resolution to follow him; but I did at length attempt it. Peters had taken off his shirt before descending, and this, with my own, formed the rope necessary for the adventure. After throwing down the musket found in the chasm, I fastened this rope to the bushes, and let myself down rapidly, striving, by the vigour of my movements, to banish the trepidation which I could overcome in no other manner. This answered sufficiently well for the first four or five steps; but presently I found my imagination growing terribly excited by thoughts of the vast depth yet to be descended, and the precarious nature of the pegs and soapstone holes which were my only support. It was in vain I endeavoured to banish these reflections, and to keep my eyes steadily bent upon the flat surface of the cliff before me. The more earnestly I struggled *not to think*, the more intensely vivid became my conceptions, and the more horribly distinct. At length arrived that crisis of fancy, so fearful in all similar cases, the crisis in which we begin to anticipate the feelings with which we *shall* fall—to picture to ourselves the sickness, and dizziness, and the last struggle, and the half swoon, and the final bitterness of the rushing and headlong descent. And now I found these fancies creating their own realities, and all imagined horrors crowding upon me in fact. I felt my knees strike violently together, while my fingers were gradually yet certainly relaxing their grasp. There was a ringing in my ears, and I said, "This is my knell of death!" And now I was consumed with the irrepressible desire of looking below. I could not, I would not, confine my glances to the cliff; and, with a wild, indefinable emotion half of horror, half of a relieved oppression, I threw my vision far down into the abyss. For one moment my fingers clutched convulsively upon their hold, while, with the movement, the faintest possible idea of ultimate escape wandered, like a shadow, through my mind—in the next my whole soul was pervaded with a *longing to fall*;[1] a desire, a yearning, a passion utterly uncontrollable. I let go at once my grasp upon the peg, and, turning half round from the precipice, re-

9. Scholars have suggested a parallel in Frederick Marryat's *Peter Simple* (1834), a popular novel of the day. Marryat wrote a number of sea adventure tales, the most famous of which is *Mr. Midshipman Easy* (1836) and the most Poe-like of which is probably *The Phantom Ship* (1837), in which a great cat suddenly manifests itself.
1. See p. 455, n. 3 herein. Cf. "The Imp of the Perverse" (especially pp. 404–05).

mained tottering for an instant against its naked face. But now there came a spinning of the brain; a shrill-sounding and phantom voice screamed within my ears; a dusky, fiendish, and filmy figure stood immediately beneath me; and, sighing, I sunk down with a bursting heart, and plunged within its arms.

I had swooned, and Peters had caught me as I fell. He had observed my proceedings from his station at the bottom of the cliff; and, perceiving my imminent danger, had endeavoured to inspire me with courage by every suggestion he could devise; although my confusion of mind had been so great as to prevent my hearing what he said, or being conscious that he had even spoken to me at all. At length, seeing me totter, he hastened to ascend to my rescue, and arrived just in time for my preservation. Had I fallen with my full weight, the rope of linen would inevitably have snapped, and I should have been precipitated into the abyss; as it was, he contrived to let me down gently, so as to remain suspended without danger until animation returned. This was in about fifteen minutes. On recovery, my trepidation had entirely vanished; I felt a new being, and, with some little further aid from my companion, reached the bottom also in safety.

We now found ourselves not far from the ravine which had proved the tomb of our friends, and to the southward of the spot where the hill had fallen. The place was one of singular wildness, and its aspect brought to my mind the descriptions given by travellers of those dreary regions marking the site of degraded Babylon. Not to speak of the ruins of the disrupted cliff, which formed a chaotic barrier in the vista to the northward, the surface of the ground in every other direction was strewn with huge tumuli, apparently the wreck of some gigantic structures of art; although, in detail, no semblance of art could be detected. Scoria were abundant, and large shapeless blocks of the black granite, intermingled with others of marl,[2] and both granulated with metal. Of vegetation there were no traces whatsoever throughout the whole of the desolate area within sight. Several immense scorpions were seen, and various reptiles not elsewhere to be found in the high latitudes.

As food was our most immediate object, we resolved to make our way to the seacoast, distant not more than half a mile, with a view of catching turtle, several of which we had observed from our place of concealment on the hill. We had proceeded some hundred yards, threading our route cautiously between the huge rocks and tumuli, when, upon turning a corner, five savages sprung upon us from a small cavern, felling Peters to the ground with a blow from a club. As he fell the whole party rushed upon him to secure their victim, leaving me time to recover from my astonishment. I still had the musket, but the barrel had received so much injury in being thrown from the precipice that I cast it aside as useless, preferring to trust my pistols, which had been carefully preserved in order. With these I advanced upon the as-

2. The marl was also black; indeed, we noticed no light-coloured substances of any kind upon the island [Pym's note]. "Marl": a mixture of clay, calcium carbonates, magnesium, and shell fragments.

sailants, firing one after the other in quick succession. Two savages fell, and one, who was in the act of thrusting a spear into Peters, sprung to his feet without accomplishing his purpose. My companion being thus released, we had no further difficulty. He had his pistols also, but prudently declined using them, confiding in his great personal strength, which far exceeded that of any person I have ever known. Seizing a club from one of the savages who had fallen, he dashed out the brains of the three who remained, killing each instantaneously with a single blow of the weapon, and leaving us completely masters of the field.

So rapidly had these events passed, that we could scarcely believe in their reality, and were standing over the bodies of the dead in a species of stupid contemplation, when we were brought to recollection by the sound of shouts in the distance. It was clear that the savages had been alarmed by the firing, and that we had little chance of avoiding discovery. To regain the cliff, it would be necessary to proceed in the direction of the shouts; and even should we succeed in arriving at its base, we should never be able to ascend it without being seen. Our situation was one of the greatest peril, and we were hesitating in which path to commence a flight, when one of the savages whom I had shot, and supposed dead, sprang briskly to his feet, and attempted to make his escape. We overtook him, however, before he had advanced many paces, and were about to put him to death, when Peters suggested that we might derive some benefit from forcing him to accompany us in our attempt at escape. We therefore dragged him with us, making him understand that we would shoot him if he offered resistance. In a few minutes he was perfectly submissive, and ran by our sides as we pushed in among the rocks, making for the seashore.

So far, the irregularities of the ground we had been traversing hid the sea, except at intervals, from our sight, and, when we first had it fairly in view, it was, perhaps, two hundred yards distant. As we emerged into the open beach we saw, to our great dismay, an immense crowd of the natives pouring from the village, and from all visible quarters of the island, making towards us with gesticulations of extreme fury, and howling like wild beasts. We were upon the point of turning upon our steps, and trying to secure a retreat among the fastnesses of the rougher ground, when I discovered the bows of two canoes projecting from behind a large rock which ran out into the water. Towards these we now ran with all speed, and, reaching them, found them unguarded, and without any other freight than three of the large Gallipago turtles and the usual supply of paddles for sixty rowers. We instantly took possession of one of them, and, forcing our captive on board, pushed out to sea with all the strength we could command.

We had not made, however, more than fifty yards from the shore before we became sufficiently calm to perceive the great oversight of which we had been guilty in leaving the other canoe in the power of the savages, who, by this time, were not more than twice as far from the beach as ourselves, and were rapidly advancing to the pursuit. No time was now to be lost. Our hope was, at best, a forlorn one, but we

had none other. It was very doubtful whether, with the utmost exertion, we could get back in time to anticipate them in taking possession of the canoe; but yet there was a chance that we could. We might save ourselves if we succeeded, while not to make the attempt was to resign ourselves to inevitable butchery.

The canoe was modelled with the bow and stern alike, and, in place of turning it round, we merely changed our position in paddling. As soon as the savages perceived this they redoubled their yells, as well as their speed, and approached with inconceivable rapidity. We pulled, however, with all the energy of desperation, and arrived at the contested point before more than one of the natives had attained it. This man paid dearly for his superior agility, Peters shooting him through the head with a pistol as he approached the shore. The foremost among the rest of his party were probably some twenty or thirty paces distant as we seized upon the canoe. We at first endeavoured to pull her into the deep water, beyond the reach of the savages, but, finding her too firmly aground, and there being no time to spare, Peters, with one or two heavy strokes from the butt of the musket, succeeded in dashing out a large portion of the bow and of one side. We then pushed off. Two of the natives by this time had got hold of our boat, obstinately refusing to let go, until we were forced to despatch them with our knives. We were now clear off, and making great way out to sea. The main body of the savages, upon reaching the broken canoe, set up the most tremendous yell of rage and disappointment conceivable. In truth, from everything I could see of these wretches, they appeared to be the most wicked, hypocritical, vindictive, bloodthirsty, and altogether fiendish race of men upon the face of the globe. It is clear we should have had no mercy had we fallen into their hands. They made a mad attempt at following us in the fractured canoe, but, finding it useless, again vented their rage in a series of hideous vociferations, and rushed up into the hills.

We were thus relieved from immediate danger, but our situation was still sufficiently gloomy. We knew that four canoes of the kind we had were at one time in the possession of the savages, and were not aware of the fact (afterward ascertained from our captive) that two of these had been blown to pieces in the explosion of the Jane Guy. We calculated, therefore, upon being yet pursued, as soon as our enemies could get round to the bay (distant about three miles) where the boats were usually laid up. Fearing this, we made every exertion to leave the island behind us, and went rapidly through the water, forcing the prisoner to take a paddle. In about half an hour, when we had gained, probably, five or six miles to the southward, a large fleet of the flat-bottomed canoes or rafts was seen to emerge from the bay, evidently with the design of pursuit. Presently they put back, despairing to overtake us.

Chapter XXIV

We now found ourselves in the wide and desolate Antarctic Ocean, in a latitude exceeding eighty-four degrees,[3] in a frail canoe, and with no provision but the three turtles. The long Polar winter, too, could not be considered as far distant, and it became necessary that we should deliberate well upon the course to be pursued. There were six or seven islands in sight belonging to the same group, and distant from each other about five or six leagues; but upon neither of these had we any intention to venture. In coming from the northward in the Jane Guy we had been gradually leaving behind us the severest regions of ice—this, however little it may be in accordance with the generally-received notions respecting the Antarctic, was a fact experience would not permit us to deny. To attempt, therefore, getting back, would be folly—especially at so late a period of the season. Only one course seemed to be left open for hope. We resolved to steer boldly to the southward, where there was at least a probability of discovering other lands, and more than a probability of finding a still milder climate.

So far we had found the Antarctic, like the Arctic Ocean, peculiarly free from violent storms or immoderately rough water; but our canoe was, at best, of frail structure, although large, and we set busily to work with a view of rendering her as safe as the limited means in our possession would admit. The body of the boat was of no better material than bark—the bark of a tree unknown. The ribs were of a tough osier, well adapted to the purpose for which it was used. We had fifty feet room from stern to stern, from four to six in breadth, and in depth throughout four feet and a half—the boats thus differing vastly in shape from those of any other inhabitants of the Southern Ocean with whom civilized nations are acquainted. We never did believe them the workmanship of the ignorant islanders who owned them; and some days after this period discovered, by questioning our captive, that they were in fact made by the natives of a group to the southwest of the country where we found them, having fallen accidentally into the hands of our barbarians. What we could do for the security of our boat was very little indeed. Several wide rents were discovered near both ends, and these we contrived to patch up with pieces of woollen jacket. With the help of the superfluous paddles, of which there were a great many, we erected a kind of framework about the bow, so as to break the force of any seas which might threaten to fill us in that quarter. We also set up two paddle-blades for masts, placing them opposite each other, one by each gunwale, thus saving the necessity of a yard. To these masts we attached a sail made of our shirts—doing this with some difficulty, as here we could get no assistance from our prisoner whatever, although he had been willing enough to labour in all the other operations. The sight of the linen seemed to affect him in a very singular

3. Since the Antarctic was still unexplored in the 1830s, Poe could not have known that this degree of latitude would be on land.

manner. He could not be prevailed upon to touch it or go near it, shuddering when we attempted to force him, and shrieking out *Tekeli-li!*

Having completed our arrangements in regard to the security of the canoe, we now set sail to the south southeast for the present, with the view of weathering the most southerly of the group in sight. This being done, we turned the bow full to the southward. The weather could by no means be considered disagreeable. We had a prevailing and very gentle wind from the northward, a smooth sea, and continual daylight. No ice whatever was to be seen; *nor did I ever see one particle of this after leaving the parallel of Bennett's Islet.* Indeed, the temperature of the water was here far too warm for its existence in any quantity. Having killed the largest of our tortoises, and obtained from him not only food, but a copious supply of water, we continued on our course, without any incident of moment, for perhaps seven or eight days, during which period we must have proceeded a vast distance to the southward, as the wind blew constantly with us, and a very strong current set continually in the direction we were pursuing.

March 1.[4] Many unusual phenomena now indicated that we were entering upon a region of novelty and wonder. A high range of light gray vapour appeared constantly in the southern horizon, flaring up occasionally in lofty streaks, now darting from east to west, now from west to east, and again presenting a level and uniform summit—in short, having all the wild variations of the Aurora Borealis. The average height of this vapour, as apparent from our station, was about twenty-five degrees. The temperature of the sea seemed to be increasing momentarily, and there was a very perceptible alteration in its colour.

March 2. To-day, by repeated questioning of our captive, we came to the knowledge of many particulars in regard to the island of the massacre, its inhabitants, and customs—but with these how can I *now* detain the reader? I may say, however, that we learned there were eight islands in the group—that they were governed by a common king, named *Tsalemon* or *Psalemoun*,[5] who resided in one of the smallest of the islands—that the black skins forming the dress of the warriors came from an animal of huge size to be found only in a valley near the court of the king—that the inhabitants of the group fabricated no other boats than the flat-bottomed rafts; the four canoes being all of the kind in their possession, and these having been obtained, by mere accident, from some large island to the southwest—that his own name was Nu-Nu—that he had no knowledge of Bennett's Islet—and that the appellation of the island we had left was *Tsalal*.[6] The commencement of the words *Tsalemon* and *Tsalal* was given

4. Pym's note here reads: "For obvious reasons I cannot pretend to strict accuracy in these dates. They are given principally with a view to perspicuity of narration, and as set down in my pencil memoranda."
5. A play on the name of the biblical King Solomon, another vaguely suggested clue to the ancient history of a once great civilization now mysteriously destroyed or disappeared. R. C. Suggs notes that the word can mean "shady"; see next note.
6. See the editorial "Note," pp. 561–63 herein. Suggs observes that *Tsalal* is a root word that can be employed with various prefixes to yield a wide variety of meanings: "to tumble down," "to vibrate," "to hover," "to be shady," "to begin to darken." "Nu-Nu": scholars have suggested that this is a word play on "new" discoveries or possibly an echo of a story by Nathaniel Parker Willis, "The Cherokee's Threat," in his *Inklings of Adventure* (1836), though there the character is female and Poe thought Willis's writings in this style laugh-

with a prolonged hissing sound,[7] which we found it impossible to imitate, even after repeated endeavours, and which was precisely the same with the note of the black bittern we had eaten upon the summit of the hill.

March 3. The heat of the water was now truly remarkable, and its colour was undergoing a rapid change, being no longer transparent, but of a milky consistency and hue. In our immediate vicinity it was usually smooth, never so rough as to endanger the canoe—but we were frequently surprised at perceiving, to our right and left, at different distances, sudden and extensive agitations of the surface—these, we at length noticed, were always preceded by wild flickerings in the region of vapour to the southward.

March 4. To-day, with the view of widening our sail, the breeze from the northward dying away perceptibly, I took from my coat-pocket a white handkerchief. Nu-Nu was seated at my elbow, and the linen accidentally flaring in his face, he became violently affected with convulsions. These were succeeded by drowsiness and stupor, and low murmurings of Tekeli-li! Tekeli-li!

March 5. The wind had entirely ceased, but it was evident that we were still hurrying on to the southward, under the influence of a powerful current. And now, indeed, it would seem reasonable that we should experience some alarm at the turn events were taking—but we felt none. The countenance of Peters indicated nothing of this nature, although it wore at times an expression I could not fathom. The Polar winter appeared to be coming on—but coming without its terrors. I felt a *numbness* of body and mind—a dreaminess of sensation—but this was all.

March 6. The gray vapour had now arisen many more degrees above the horizon, and was gradually losing its grayness of tint. The heat of the water was extreme, even unpleasant to the touch, and its milky hue was more evident than ever. To-day a violent agitation of the water occurred very close to the canoe. It was attended, as usual, with a wild flaring up of the vapour at its summit, and a momentary division at its base. A fine white powder, resembling ashes—but certainly not such—fell over the canoe and over a large surface of the water, as the flickering died away among the vapour and the commotion subsided in the sea. Nu-Nu now threw himself on his face in the bottom of the boat, and no persuasions could induce him to arise.

March 7. This day we questioned Nu-Nu concerning the motives of his countrymen in destroying our companions; but he appeared to be too utterly overcome by terror to afford us any rational reply. He still obstinately lay in the bottom of the boat; and, upon our reiterating the questions as to the motive, made use only of idiotic gesticulations, such as raising with his forefinger the upper lip, and displaying the teeth which lay beneath it. These were black. We had never before seen the teeth of an inhabitant of Tsalal.[8]

able. Suggs notes that *nunu* in Marquesan can mean "to cook" and in Hawaiian "to be greedy," "to extort," or "to be puffed up."

7. Kopley notes Jeremiah 19:8: "And I will make this city desolate, and an hissing." Cf. the curse on Edom in Poe's review of John L. Stephens.

8. Scholars have noted a paragraph on "black teeth" in native societies in the Baltimore *Saturday Visiter* (October 5, 1833), Poe's first publisher. Some critics take this detail to indicate

March 8. To-day there floated by us one of the white animals whose appearance upon the beach at Tsalal had occasioned so wild a commotion among the savages. I would have picked it up, but there came over me a sudden listlessness, and I forbore. The heat of the water still increased, and the hand could no longer be endured within it. Peters spoke little, and I knew not what to think of his apathy. Nu-Nu breathed, and no more.

March 9. The white ashy material fell now continually around us, and in vast quantities. The range of vapour to the southward had arisen prodigiously in the horizon, and began to assume more distinctness of form. I can liken it to nothing but a limitless cataract, rolling silently into the sea from some immense and far-distant rampart in the heaven.[9] The gigantic curtain ranged along the whole extent of the southern horizon. It emitted no sound.

March 21. A sullen darkness now hovered above us—but from out the milky depths of the ocean a luminous glare arose, and stole up along the bulwarks of the boat. We were nearly overwhelmed by the white ashy shower which settled upon us and upon the canoe, but melted into the water as it fell. The summit of the cataract was utterly lost in the dimness and the distance. Yet we were evidently approaching it with a hideous velocity. At intervals there were visible in it wide, yawning, but momentary rents, and from out these rents, within which was a chaos of flitting and indistinct images, there came rushing and mighty, but soundless winds, tearing up the enkindled ocean in their course.

March 22.[1] The darkness had materially increased, relieved only by the glare of the water thrown back from the white curtain before us. Many gigantic and pallidly white birds flew continuously now from beyond the veil, and their scream was the eternal *Tekeli-li!* as they retreated from our vision. Hereupon Nu-Nu stirred in the bottom of the boat; but, upon touching him, we found his spirit departed. And now we rushed into the embraces of the cataract, where a chasm threw itself open to receive us. But there arose in our pathway a shrouded human figure, very far larger in its proportions than any dweller among men. And the hue of the skin of the figure was of the perfect whiteness of the snow.[2]

the racist subtheme of *Pym* or of Poe's own racism; but some South Seas native cultures do make use of the (potentially narcotic) juice of the betel nut, which stains the teeth, an exotic fact noted in newspapers like the *Visiter*.

9. Possibly illuminated by the Antarctic southern lights (*aurora australis*), a parallel to the Arctic northern lights (*aurora borealis*). Scholars have suggested a source in William Scoresby Jr.: *An Account of the Arctic Regions with a History and Description of the Northern Whale-Fishery* (1820). See the headnote (p. 429 herein) on Symmes and the "holes at the poles" theory of the circulation of the ocean currents into one Pole, traveling the interior of the earth, and rushing out to the surface again at the other Pole. Cf. "Ms. Found in a Bottle" (pp. 106ff. herein) and "A Descent into the Maelström" (pp. 266ff.).

1. In the Southern Hemisphere this is the date of the autumn equinox, nine months after the mutiny aboard the *Grampus*.

2. Cf. Daniel 7:9 and Revelation 1:14. The ambiguous conclusion of the narrative and the mysterious figure have generated numerous critical interpretations from the literal to the symbolic and allegorical: e.g., fog, an ice formation, the figurehead of the returning ship *Penguin*, Christ, God, an angel, Death, the Ancient of Days, the last patriarch of an ancient race, the Great Mother, Pym's own (white) shadow, a vision of Void. See the selections on *Pym* in the Criticism section of this volume.

Note[3]

The circumstances connected with the late sudden and distressing death of Mr. Pym are already well known to the public through the medium of the daily press. It is feared that the few remaining chapters which were to have completed his narrative, and which were retained by him, while the above were in type, for the purpose of revision, have been irrecoverably lost through the accident by which he perished himself. This, however, may prove not to be the case, and the papers, if ultimately found, will be given to the public.

No means have been left untried to remedy the deficiency. The gentleman whose name is mentioned in the preface,[4] and who, from the statement there made, might be supposed able to fill the vacuum, has declined the task—this for satisfactory reasons connected with the general inaccuracy of the details afforded him, and his disbelief in the entire truth of the latter portions of the narration. Peters, from whom some information might be expected, is still alive, and a resident of Illinois, but cannot be met with at present. He may hereafter be found, and will, no doubt, afford material for a conclusion of Mr. Pym's account.

The loss of the two or three final chapters (for there were but two or three) is the more deeply to be regretted, as, it cannot be doubted, they contained matter relative to the Pole itself, or at least to regions in its very near proximity; and as, too, the statements of the author in relation to these regions may shortly be verified or contradicted by means of the governmental expedition now preparing for the Southern Ocean.[5]

On one point in the Narrative some remarks may be well offered; and it would afford the writer of this appendix[6] much pleasure if what he may here observe should have a tendency to throw credit, in any degree, upon the very singular pages now published. We allude to the chasms found in the island of Tsalal, and to the whole of the figures upon pages 182, 183, 184, 185.[7]

Mr. Pym has given the figures of the chasms without comment, and speaks decidedly of the *indentures* found at the extremity of the most easterly of these chasms as having but a fanciful resemblance to alphabetical characters, and, in short, as being positively *not such*. This assertion is made in a manner so simple, and sustained by a species of demonstration so conclusive (viz., the fitting of the projections of the fragments found among the dust into the indentures upon the wall),

3. Many accounts of travels to remote places insinuate further revelations—of ultimate mysteries—of a vast connection among seemingly unconnected things. The convention of the appended "Note" promising further discoveries is exemplified for example in Stephens's *Incidents of Travel*.
4. I.e., Edgar A. Poe; see the headnote on p. 429 herein and the Preface (pp. 432–33).
5. The Wilkes Expedition of 1838–42. The expeditionary fleet sailed just after the publication of *Pym*.
6. Yet another narrative layer or frame to the story, presumably by a (fictive) publisher or editor; cf. the Preface.
7. These are the pages in the original American edition; the corresponding pages in the present edition are 550–51.

that we are forced to believe the writer in earnest; and no reasonable reader should suppose otherwise. But as the facts in relation to *all* the figures are most singular (especially when taken in connexion with statements made in the body of the narrative), it may be as well to say a word or two concerning them all—this, too, the more especially as the facts in question have, beyond doubt, escaped the attention of Mr. Poe.

Figure 1, then, figure 2, figure 3, and figure 5, when conjoined with one another in the precise order which the chasms themselves presented, and when deprived of the small lateral branches or arches (which, it will be remembered, served only as means of communication between the main chambers, and were of totally distinct character), constitute an Ethiopian verbal root—the root ᎪᏆᏋ "To be shady"—whence all the inflections of shadow or darkness.[8]

In regard to the "left or most northwardly" of the indentures in figure 4, it is more than probable that the opinion of Peters was correct, and that the hieroglyphical appearance was really the work of art, and intended as the representation of a human form. The delineation is before the reader, and he may, or may not, perceive the resemblance suggested; but the rest of the indentures afford strong confirmation of Peters's idea. The upper range is evidently the Arabic verbal root ᏄᎵᏁ "To be white," whence all the inflections of brilliancy and whiteness. The lower range is not so immediately per-

8. Poe relies here on Edward Robinson, *A Hebrew and English Lexicon of the Old Testament from the Latin of William Gesenius* (1836). Suggs observes that the "verbal root" is not Ethiopian, nor is it Egyptian hieroglyphics. John Lloyd Stephens (1805–1852), in his *Incidents of Travel in Egypt, Arabia Petræa, and the Holy Land* (1835), mentions rock inscriptions in Arabia Petraea and adjoining desert areas. The mountainous region along the eastern border of the Arabah valley from the Dead Sea to the Gulf of Aqaba (Akaba) is known by several names, including Iduma, Idmæa, and Edom (and sometimes sweepingly as Mount Seir). In his long review of Stephens's book (*New York Review*, October 1837), Poe brings in linguistic analyses of Hebrew and other characters in passages from the books of Ezekiel and Isaiah in the Old Testament that he had received from Professor Charles Anthon (1797–1867) of Columbia University. (See Anthon's June 1, 1837, letter to Poe, reprinted in *Works*, ed. Harrison, XVII, 42–43). These glosses (having to do with eternity and the impossibility of traveling through a desolate land) seem in part to explain the mysterious characters written in stone at the end of *Pym*. That is, they appear to be portentously prophetic. But of what?

In chapter 24 of *Incidents*, Stephens refers to Dr. Alexander Keith's arguments for a literal interpretation of biblical predictions (Keith's popular *Evidences of Prophecy* had by then gone through at least fourteen editions). In his review, Poe shows special interest in Stephens's account of the Old Testament curse placed on the land of Edom and focuses on the issue of the accuracy of biblical prophecy. The history of Edom is characterized by hostility and warfare between the descendants of Esau (the Edomites) and the descendants of Jacob (the Jews), as well as with other neighbors like the Assyrians and the Syrians. The Edomites were eventually subdued by the Maccabees, subsumed by the Jews, and conquered by the Romans, who merged the province with Galilee, Samaria, and Judæa. After the destruction of Jerusalem, Edom was included in the province of Arabia Petræa. According to the Old Testament, the strife between the twin brothers Jacob and Esau began in the womb. The descendants of Esau in Edom dedicated themselves to the destruction of the descendants of Jacob in Israel. For this, the God of Israel placed a curse on Edom: the land would be devastated, nothing would grow in it, and no one entering it would return again. The long global working-out of such divine retribution suggests possible allegorical readings of the ending of *Arthur Gordon Pym*.

In insinuating an encrypted message in at least three ancient languages, the "Note" at the end of *Pym* implies a further narrative under the story as presented. Among the more prominent critical speculations is the following suggestion: the natives of Tsalal may be the lost, supposedly black-skinned tribe of Ham mentioned in the Bible; the gigantic figure that rises up may be a representative of an ancient (white) race of beings who have retreated from a scorched and ruined Eden. This mythos plays into the interpretation of the narrative as an allegory of race.

spicuous. The characters are somewhat broken and disjointed; nevertheless, it cannot be doubted that, in their perfect state, they formed the full Egyptian word Π ᎯᲚᎩᎢᏢᎻᏟ, "The region of the south."[9] It should be observed that these interpretations confirm the opinion of Peters in regard to the "most northwardly" of the figures. The arm is outstretched towards the south.

Conclusions such as these open a wide field for speculation and exciting conjecture. They should be regarded, perhaps, in connexion with some of the most faintly-detailed incidents of the narrative; although in no visible manner is this chain of connexion complete. Tekeli-li! was the cry of the affrighted natives of Tsalal upon discovering the carcass of the *white* animal picked up at sea. This also was the shuddering exclamation of the captive Tsalalian upon encountering the *white* materials in possession of Mr. Pym. This also was the shriek of the swift-flying, *white,* and gigantic birds which issued from the vapoury *white* curtain of the South. Nothing *white* was to be found at Tsalal, and nothing otherwise in the subsequent voyage to the region beyond. It is not impossible that "Tsalal," the appellation of the island of the chasms, may be found, upon minute philological scrutiny, to betray either some alliance with the chasms themselves, or some reference to the Ethiopian characters so mysteriously written in their windings.

"I have graven it within the hills, and my vengeance upon the dust within the rock."[1]

9. According to Suggs, this "Egyptian word" is not in hieroglyphics nor is it in Coptic script; the phrase "southern region" is written with a combination of signs including a small bird, a plant, and a couple of geometric signs.
1. Not exactly biblical, but cf. Jeremiah 4:23–27 and Job 19:23–24.

Eureka

In July 1848, *Eureka: A Prose Poem* was published by George P. Putnam (formerly Wiley & Putnam) in New York as a small book of some 140 pages—the source for the selections reprinted here (about one-fifth of the whole). According to James A. Harrison's 1902 edition of *Works*, Poe annotated a copy of *Eureka* in anticipation of a second, revised edition (this text is known as the Bishop Hurst copy, after its owner). These annotations are printed in *Works*, XVI, 319–336; Harrison also prints a number of "addenda" from various sources purporting to be Poe's intended revisions (see *Works*, XVI, 337–346) along with "unpublished notes" from the Griswold collection of Poe's papers (XVI, 347–354). These addenda and variants are omitted from the selected passages reprinted here.

The cry "Eureka!" is by tradition the exclamation of the Syracusan engineer and mathematician Archimedes (287–212 B.C.E.), when, in his overflowing bath, he suddenly understood that the displacement of water by his body was the answer to a problem that he had been given to solve by Hiero II of Syracuse. He had been asked to determine whether a particular crown was pure gold or gold alloyed with silver. Realizing that gold and silver would displace different weights of water, Archimedes is said to have jumped up and run naked from his bath shouting "*Eureka!*": Greek for "I have found it!" He is also famous for another saying: "Give me a place to stand, a fulcrum, and a lever long enough, and I will move the world." His works of mathematics and geometry include studies of spheres and cylinders (see Poe's "A Descent into the Maelström, p. 277 herein), circles and spirals, and other such figures. The title *Eureka* thus indicates Poe's claim to have suddenly discovered a scientific and intuitive answer to the riddle of the universe. Poe's revelation is a combination of mathematics, physics, astronomy, residual Western moralism, and Romantic poetics. He comes close to an Einsteinian conception of curved or warped space and a space-time continuum and posits a pulsating cycle of cosmic expansion and contraction. But Poe is hardly as original in these thoughts as certain scholars have suggested, for in essence he echoes some of the more advanced scientific theories of his day.

His attempt to merge contemporary science with Romanticism is made clear from the outset: the subtitle and preface ask that the book be taken as a prose poem. Moreover, Poe's annotation for a revised conclusion also emphasizes the Romantic agenda under the science of the book:

> NOTE.—The pain of the consideration that we shall lose our individual identity, ceases at once when we further reflect that the process, as above described is, neither more nor less than that of the absorption, by each individual intelligence, of all other intelligences (that is, of the Universe) into its own. That God may be all in all, each must become God. [Harrison, XVI, 336]

As this proposed addition illustrates, Poe, for all his employment of physics and astronomy, insistently merges scientific concepts of the physical construction of the universe with metaphysical musings reflecting the secularized nature religion of Romanticism. Beginning with proposition that annihilation of the individual self is part of creation, he eventually comes to the conclusion that the individual self is all—is part and parcel God (or what Emerson calls the "Oversoul")—a version of that Romantic "self-apotheosis" (making oneself God-like) we find in such writers as Wordsworth, Whitman, and the German and American Transcendentalists. Poe several times outlined his basic argument for friends; his letter to George W. Eveleth (February 29, 1848), is helpful:

I presume you have seen some newspaper notices of my late lecture on the Universe. You could have gleaned, however, no idea of what the lecture was, from what the papers said it was. All praised it—as far as I have yet seen—and all absurdly misrepresented it. The only report of it which approaches the truth, is the one I enclose—from the "Express"—written by E. A. Hopkins—a gentleman of much scientific acquirement—son of Bishop Hopkins of Vermont—but he conveys only my general idea, and his digest is full of inaccuracies. I enclose also a slip from the "Courier & Enquirer":—*please return them.* To eke out a chance of your understanding what I really *did* say, I add a loose summary of my propositions & results:

The General Proposition is this:—Because Nothing was, *therefore* All Things are.

1—An inspection of the *universality* of Gravitation—i.e, of the fact that each particle tends, *not* to any one common point, but to *every other* particle—suggests *perfect* totality, or *absolute* unity, as the source of the phaenomenon.

2—Gravity is but the mode in which is manifested the tendency of all things to return into their original unity; is but the reaction of the first Divine Act.

3—The *law* regulating the return—i.e, the *law* of Gravitation—is but a necessary result of the necessary & sole possible mode of equable *irradiation* of matter through space:—this *equable* irradiation is necessary as a basis for the Nebular Theory of Laplace.

4—The Universe of Stars (contradistinguished from the Universe of Space) is limited.

5—Mind is cognizant of Matter *only* through its two properties, attraction and repulsion: therefore Matter *is* only attraction & repulsion: a finally consolidated globe of globes, being but *one* particle, would be without attraction, ie, gravitation; the existence of such a globe presupposes the expulsion of the separative ether which we know to exist between the particles as at present diffused:—thus the final globe would be matter without attraction & repulsion:—but these *are* matter:—then the final globe would be matter without matter:—i,e, no matter at all:—it must disappear. Thus Unity is *Nothingness.*

6. Matter, springing from Unity, sprang from Nothingness:—i,e, was *created.*

7. All will return to Nothingness, in returning to Unity.

Read these items *after* the Report. As to the Lecture, I am very quiet about it—but, if you have ever dealt with such topics, you will recognize the novelty & *moment* of my views. What I have

propounded will (in good time) revolutionize the world of Physical & Metaphysical Science. I say this calmly—but I say it. I shall not go till I hear from you.

Poe made use of numerous scientific writings in *Eureka*. Among the writers cited in his scientific catalog, the father and son of the prominent eighteenth- and nineteenth-century British family of Herschel especially stand out. Sir William Herschel (1738–1822) was renowned as an astronomer and as a maker of powerful new telescopes; Sir John Herschel (1792–1871) carried on his father's work over a long period of years. Beginning in the 1770s, the elder Herschel surveyed the Orion nebula (which had been discovered in 1610) with his improved telescopes and began a careful mapping of star systems. In 1781, he discovered a new planet, later given the name Uranus. In 1789, he constructed what was then apparently the world's largest telescope; it had a forty-eight-inch mirror and a focal length of forty feet. He discovered the sixth and seventh satellites of Saturn, determined the rotation of Saturn and other planets, and discovered and surveyed double stars (cataloging over eight hundred). From the motions of double stars, he concluded that they move about a common center and are held together by reciprocal gravitation. He expanded the number of known nebulae from about one hundred to some twenty-five hundred and advanced the theory that new stars and planets form out of gaseous material (see the discussion of Laplace's "nebular hypothesis" below). He postulated that the solar system was moving directionally in space and accelerating—a point directly pertinent to Poe's conception not only of the solar system but also of the universe. His son, John, confirmed and extended many of his father's observations and in 1833 presented a star catalog to Britain's most prestigious scientific association, the Royal Society.

In *Eureka*, Poe gives summaries of the Herschels' work (mainly omitted in the selections reprinted here), paraphrasing their theories along with the writings of many other astronomers. These include those of Dr. John Pringle Nichol (1804–1859), a professor of astronomy at Glasgow University, who set about disseminating the theories of the Herschels to a wide lay public. In 1837 Nichol published *Views of the Architecture of the Heavens* as "a series of letters to a lady" (i.e., a popular rather than a technical account), in which he rather closely follows the Herschels in his discussions of the Orion nebula and the "nebular hypothesis." (See Poe's comments on the Herschels and Nichol in "Murders in the Rue Morgue," pp. 245–46 herein, and his "New York Literati" sketch of Richard Adams Locke.)

Another important source for Poe's essay is William Whewell, *The Bridgewater Treatises on the Power, Wisdom and Goodness of God as Manifested in the Creation*, especially Treatise III, "On Astronomy and General Physics" (1834), where he would have found a discussion of the law of universal gravitation. Whewell argues that the attraction of planets to one another varies inversely with the square of their distance and concludes that every particle of matter in the universe attracts every other according to that principle. He also argues that the beauty and order of the physical world corresponds with the same in the moral world.

During the course of *Eureka*, Poe also incorporates ideas and information from the writings of (among others) the following: Sir David Brewster (1781–1868), a Scottish physicist; William Parsons, earl of Ross (1800–1867), who constructed a thirty-six-inch telescope in 1839; George W.

Blunt (1802–1878), an American geographer, celebrated maker of maps of both the earth and the moon; Nevil Maskelyne (1732–1811), a British astronomer, who wrote on the physical attraction of mountains as measured by a plumb line; Henry Cavendish (1731–1810), a British chemist and physicist, who discovered nitric acid and was the first scientist to combine hydrogen and oxygen to make water; Jean Sylvain Bailly (1736–1793), a French astronomer, who wrote *Histoire de l'astronomie* (1775–87); Jacob Bryant (1715–1804), a British antiquary and author of *A New System or Analysis of Antient Mythology* (1774–76), who figures in several of Poe's poems and tales; one Fourier, doubtless not Charles Fourier, the French social philosopher, but rather Jean Baptiste Joseph Fourier (1765–1830), a French mathematician (cf. "Mellonta Tauta"); Friedrich Wilhelm August Argelander (1799–1875), a German astronomer and author of *Über die eigene Bewegung des Sonnensystems* (1837; On the movements of sunsystems); and Johan Heinrich von Mädler (1794–1874), a German astronomer, who theorized on the limits of the universe and claimed to have measured a degree of curvature in the solar system's journey through space.

Central to Poe's vision is the nebular hypothesis, associated primarily with Pierre Simon, marquis de Laplace (1749–1827), a French mathematician and astronomer, who is specifically mentioned in *Eureka* (see p. 576, n. 2 herein). Laplace also figures in Poe's discussion of the two basic methods of applying logical analysis to scientific investigation: the inductive (or Aristotelian) and the deductive (or Baconian). In paragraphs omitted here but found in the fictional futurist satire "Mellonta Tauta," Poe makes fun of the contemporary debate on what constituted the "pure" logical method of science: the inductive (reasoning from observations toward generalization) or the deductive (reasoning from a general theory to explain particular phenomena). Poe sides with neither; instead he argues for a combination of both, as he does in "Murders in the Rue Morgue." In that tale, Poe mentions Laplace's "Calculus of Probabilities," a reference to *Théorie analytique des probablités* (1812) and *Essai philosophique sur les probabilités* (1814), in which Laplace suggests that "unity" and absolute "certainty" must be the same thing, a premise of *Eureka*. Poe seems also to have been influenced by current articles on the place of induction and deduction in scientific method by J. D. Whelpley and Joseph Henry in the *American Journal of Science* and the entry on logic in the *Edinburgh Encyclopaedia* (1830), the last a work that Poe uses for his essay on the automaton (humanoid robot-computer) called Maelzel's Chess-Player. And, as usual, he also cites John Locke (1632–1704), one of the most influential of British philosophers, best known for his empirical system of knowledge and consciousness based on physical sensations (rather than innate ideas), as articulated in *An Essay concerning Human Understanding* (completed in 1690).

From Eureka: An Essay on the Material and Spiritual Universe

WITH VERY PROFOUND RESPECT, THIS WORK IS DEDICATED
TO ALEXANDER VON HUMBOLDT.[1]

Preface

To the few who love me and whom I love—to those who feel rather than to those who think—to the dreamers and those who put faith in dreams as in the only realities—I offer this Book of Truths, not in its character of Truth-Teller, but for the Beauty that abounds in its Truth; constituting it true.[2] To these I present the composition as an Art-Product alone:—let us say as a Romance; or, if I be not urging too lefty a claim, as a Poem.

What I here propound is true:—therefore it cannot die:—or if by any means it be now trodden down so that it die, it will "rise again to the Life Everlasting."

Nevertheless it is as a Poem only that I wish this work to be judged after I am dead.

E. A. P.

Eureka

It is with humility really unassumed—it is with a sentiment even of awe—that I pen the opening sentence of this work: for all conceivable subjects I approach the reader with the most solemn—the most comprehensive—the most difficult—the most august.

What terms shall I find sufficiently simple in their sublimity—sufficiently sublime in their simplicity—for the mere enunciation of my theme?

I design to speak of the *Physical, Metaphysical and Mathematical—of the Material and Spiritual Universe:—of its Essence, its Origin, its Creation, its Present Condition and its Destiny.* I shall be so rash, more-

1. Poe's dedication is to Friedrich Heinrich Alexander, Freiherr von Humboldt (1769–1859), German philosopher, explorer, and naturalist. Alexander and his brother, Wilhelm (1767–1835), were among the most celebrated figures of their time. Wilhelm was minister of education in Prussia and a world-renowned linguist, an expert in the languages of the South Pacific Island cultures (see notes to Poe's *Arthur Gordon Pym*). Alexander was famous for his feats of exploration and voluminous publications, in which he meticulously recorded his scientific observations: notably meteorology, geology, and geography but also biology (focusing on the locations of the flora and fauna found in new lands). Among these are the detailed accounts of his expedition with A. J. A. Bonpland during the years 1799–1804 to the Caribbean and to Central and South America. Humboldt's text is noted for precise measurements of the courses of the Orinoco and Amazon Rivers in Brazil and of the geology and geography of the flora of the Andes Mountains in Ecuador and Peru. His twenty-three-volume magnum opus, published over many years as the *Voyages of Humboldt and Bonpland* (1805–34), is known generally by the title of its first part: *Voyage to the Equinoctial Regions of the New Continent.* Among other things, Humboldt studied the dynamics of volcanoes, plotted the course of tropical storms, and measured the increase of magnetic intensity from the equator toward the poles. His subsequent multivolume work, *Kosmos* (1845–58, 1862), posited a unified theory of natural order.
2. See John Keats, "Ode on a Grecian Urn" (1819), which concludes with a classic Romantic pronouncement: " 'Beauty is truth, truth beauty'—that is all / Ye know on earth, and all ye need to know."

over, as to challenge the conclusions, and thus, in effect, to question the sagacity, of many of the greatest and most justly reverenced of men.

In the beginning, let me as distinctly as possible announce—not the theorem which I hope to demonstrate—for, whatever the mathematicians may assert, there is, in this world at least, *no such thing* as demonstration—but the ruling idea which, throughout this volume, I shall be continually endeavoring to suggest.

My general proposition, then, is this:—*In the Original Unity of the First Thing lies the Secondary Cause of All Things, with the Germ of their Inevitable Annihilation.*

In illustration of this idea, I propose to take such a survey of the Universe that the mind may be able really to receive and to perceive an individual impression.

He who from the top of Ætna[3] casts his eyes leisurely around, is affected chiefly by the *extent* and *diversity* of the scene. Only by a rapid whirling on his heel could he hope to comprehend the panorama in the sublimity of its *oneness*. But as, on the summit of Ætna, *no* man has thought of whirling on his heel, so no man has ever taken into his brain the full uniqueness of the prospect; and so, again, whatever considerations lie involved in this uniqueness, have as yet no practical existence for mankind.

I do not know a treatise in which a survey of the *Universe*—using the word in its most comprehensive and only legitimate acceptation— is taken at all:—and it may be as well here to mention that by the term "Universe," wherever employed without qualification in this essay, I mean to designate *the utmost conceivable expanse of space, with all things, spiritual and material, that can be imagined to exist within the compass of that expanse.* In speaking of what is *ordinarily* implied by the expression, "Universe," I shall take a phrase of limitation—"the Universe of stars." Why this distinction is considered necessary, will be seen in the sequel.

But even of treatises on the really limited, although always assumed as the *un*limited, Universe of *stars*, I know none in which a survey, even of this limited Universe, is so taken as to warrant deductions from its *individuality*. The nearest approach to such a work is made in the "Cosmos" of Alexander Von Humboldt.[4] He presents the subject, however, *not* in its individuality but in its generality. His theme, in its last result, is the law of *each* portion of the merely physical Universe, as this law is related to the laws of *every other* portion of this merely

3. Or Etna; the highest active volcano in Europe (10,700 feet), situated on the east coast of the island of Sicily (part of Italy). Several of its eruptions were notoriously destructive (especially those of 475 B.C.E., 1169 C.E., and 1669 C.E.).

4. In *Kosmos* (1845–1862), Alexander von Humboldt offers a detailed argument for a unity underlying the complex variety of all natural phenomena—providing Poe with a "scientific" validation for another classic Romantic principle ("unity in variety"). "*Cosmos*" is Greek for "order" (as opposed to *chaos*, "disorder"). The first English translations of small parts of the *Kosmos* volumes appeared in the mid-1840s, a matter of some interest since several scholars have suggested that Poe did not know German. See, e.g., Thomas S. Hansen, in *The German Face of Edgar Allan Poe*, a work that should be used with caution since it bases some of its conclusions on reviews and essays attributed to Poe (in the current ongoing edition of Poe's nonfiction prose) that he may not in reality have written.

physical Universe. His design is simply synœretical.[5] In a word, he discusses the universality of material relation, and discloses to the eye of Philosophy whatever inferences have hitherto lain hidden *behind* this universality. But however admirable be the succinctness with which he has treated each particular point of his topic, the mere multiplicity of these points occasions, necessarily, an amount of detail, and thus an involution of idea, which preclude all *individuality* of impression.

It seems to me that, in aiming at this latter effect, and, through it, at the consequences—the conclusions—the suggestions—the speculations—or, if nothing better offer itself, the mere guesses which may result from it—we require something like a mental gyration on the heel. We need so rapid a revolution of all things about the central point of sight that, while the minutiæ vanish altogether, even the more conspicuous objects become blended into one. Among the vanishing minutiæ, in a survey of this kind, would be all exclusively terrestrial matters. The Earth would be considered in its planetary relations alone. A man, in this view, becomes mankind; mankind a member of the cosmical family of Intelligences.

And now, before proceeding to our subject proper, let me beg the reader's attention to an extract or two from a somewhat remarkable letter, which appears to have been found corked in a bottle and floating on the *Mare Tenebrarum*—an ocean well described by the Nubian geographer.[6]

* * *

Here end my quotations from this very unaccountable and, perhaps, somewhat impertinent epistle; and perhaps it would be folly to comment, in any respect, upon the chimerical,[7] not to say revolutionary, fancies of the writer—whoever he is—fancies so radically at war with the well-considered and well-settled opinions of this age. Let us proceed, then, to our legitimate thesis, *The Universe*.

* * *

Let us begin, then, at once, with that merest of words, "Infinity." This, like "God," "spirit," and some other expressions of which the equivalents exist in all languages, is by no means the expression of an idea—but of an effort at one. It stands for the possible attempt at an impossible conception. Man needed a term by which to point out the *direction* of this effort—the cloud behind which lay, forever invisible,

5. *Synæresis* means "drawing together"; the word is usually used of language (e.g., pronouncing two vowels as one), but is also used in chemistry, where the meaning is almost the reverse.
6. See p. 267, n. 4. The next several paragraphs of *Eureka* occur in Poe's satiric story "Mellonta Tauta." Although published in 1849, "Mellonta Tauta" was finished by January 1848, and several passages were revised for a lecture on "the universe" delivered at the New York Society Library on February 3, 1848, and incorporated at this point in *Eureka* (published July 1848). The function of the comic aspects of *Eureka* (including parodies of philosophers like Aristotle, Bacon, Ramus, and Kant) has been a topic of debate among Poe scholars. Is *Eureka* possibly a hoax? Or is the satiric element an elaborate defense against criticism of heartfelt cosmology? Is it a form of Romantic irony? However satiric the presentation, the critique of inductive and deductive logic (Aristotelian vs. Baconian) as individually inadequate is apparently to be taken seriously; also cited as *à priori* (deductive) and *à posteriori* (inductive). After this *jeu d'esprit*, Poe resumes his philosophical argument in what appears to be a more serious vein.
7. Illusory, fantasized; from Chimæra, an ancient mythical beast.

the *object* of this attempt. A word, in fine, was demanded, by means of which one human being might put himself in relation at once with another human being and with a certain *tendency* of the human intellect. Out of this demand arose the word, "Infinity;" which is thus the representative but of the *thought of a thought*.

As regards *that* infinity now considered—the infinity of space—we often hear it said that "its idea is admitted by the mind—is acquiesced in—is entertained—on account of the greater difficulty which attends the conception of a limit." But this is merely one of those *phrases* by which even profound thinkers, time out of mind, have occasionally taken pleasure in deceiving *themselves*. The quibble lies concealed in the word "difficulty." "The mind," we are told, "entertains the idea of *limitless*, through the greater *difficulty* which it finds in entertaining that of *limited*, space." Now, were the proposition but fairly *put*, its absurdity would become transparent at once. Clearly, there is no mere *difficulty* in the case. The assertion intended, if presented *according* to its intention and without sophistry, would run thus:—"The mind admits the idea of limitless, through the greater *impossibility* of entertaining that of limited, space."

It must be immediately seen that this is not a question of two statements between whose respective credibilities—or of two arguments between whose respective validities—the *reason* is called upon to decide:—it is a matter of two conceptions, directly conflicting, and each avowedly impossible, one of which the *intellect* is supposed to be capable of entertaining, on account of the greater *impossibility* of entertaining the other. The choice is *not* made between two difficulties;—it is merely *fancied* to be made between two impossibilities. Now of the former, there *are* degrees—but of the latter, none:—just as our impertinent letter-writer has already suggested.

* * *

We *believe* in a God. We may or may not *believe* in finite or in infinite space; but our belief, in such cases, is more properly designated as *faith*, and is a matter quite distinct from that belief proper— from that *intellectual* belief—which presupposes the mental conception.

The fact is, that, upon the enunciation of any one of that class of terms to which "Infinity" belongs—the class representing *thoughts of thought*—he who has a right to say that he thinks *at all*, feels himself called upon, *not* to entertain a conception, but simply to direct his mental vision toward some given point, in the intellectual firmament, where lies a nebula never to be resolved. To solve it, indeed, he makes no effort; for with a rapid instinct he comprehends, not only the impossibility, but, as regards all human purposes, the *inessentiality*, of its solution. He perceives that the Deity has not *designed* it to be solved. He sees, at once, that it lies *out* of the brain of man, and even *how*, if not exactly *why*, it lies out of it. There *are* people, I am aware, who, busying themselves in attempts at the unattainable, acquire very easily, by dint of the jargon they emit, among those thinkers-that-they-think with whom darkness and depth are synonymous, a kind of

cuttle-fish[8] reputation for profundity; but the finest quality of Thought is its self-cognizance; and, with some little equivocation, it may be said that no fog of the mind can well be greater than that which, extending to the very boundaries of the mental domain, shuts out even these boundaries themselves from comprehension.

It will now be understood that, in using the phrase, "Infinity of Space," I make no call upon the reader to entertain the impossible conception of an *absolute* infinity. I refer simply to the *"utmost conceivable expanse"* of space—a shadowy and fluctuating domain, now shrinking, now swelling, in accordance with the vacillating energies of the imagination.

Hitherto, the Universe of stars has always been considered as coincident with the Universe proper, as I have defined it in the commencement of this Discourse. It has been always either directly or indirectly assumed—at least since the dawn of intelligible Astronomy—that, were it possible for us to attain any given point in space, we should still find, on all sides of us, an interminable succession of stars. This was the untenable idea of Pascal when making perhaps the most successful attempt ever made, at periphrasing the conception for which we struggle in the word "Universe." "It is a sphere," he says, "of which the centre is everywhere, the circumference, nowhere."[9] But although this intended definition is, in fact, *no* definition of the Universe of *stars*, we may accept it, with some mental reservation, as a definition (rigorous enough for all practical purposes) of the Universe *proper*—that is to say, of the Universe of *space*. This latter, then, let us regard as *"a sphere of which the centre is everywhere, the circumference nowhere."* In fact, while we find it impossible to fancy an *end* to space, we have no difficulty in picturing to ourselves any one of an infinity of *beginnings*.

As our starting-point, then, let us adopt the *Godhead*. Of this Godhead, *in itself*, he alone is not imbecile—he alone is not impious who propounds——nothing. *"Nous ne connaissons rien,"* says the Baron de Bielfeld[1]—*"Nous ne connaissons rien de la nature ou de l'essence de Dieu:—pour savoir ce qu'il est, il faut être Dieu même."*—"We know absolutely *nothing* of the nature or essence of God:—in order to comprehend what he is, we should have to be God ourselves."

"We should have to be God ourselves!"—With a phrase so startling as this yet ringing in my ears, I nevertheless venture to demand if this our present ignorance of the Deity is an ignorance to which the soul is *everlastingly* condemned.

By *Him*, however—*now*, at least, the Incomprehensible—by Him— assuming him as *Spirit*—that is to say, as *not Matter*—a distinction

8. A squid-like cephalopod marine mollusk that squirts a dark inky liquid—Poe's image for some philosophers' lack of clarity (inkiness and fogginess), which they hope will be mistaken for wisdom.

9. An adaptation that Blaise Pascal (1623–1662), French scientist and religious philosopher, made of St. Augustine's 5th-century definition of God (rather than the physical universe).

1. One of Poe's favorite encyclopedias was *Les Premiers Traits de L'Erudition Universelle, par M. Le Baron de Bielfeld* (1767), trans. as *The Elements of Universal Erudition* (1770; 1771); Poe seems always to have used the original French version.

which, for all intelligible purposes, will stand well instead of a definition—by Him, then, existing as Spirit, let us content ourselves, to-night, with supposing to have been *created*, or made out of Nothing, by dint of his Volition—at some point of Space which we will take as a centre—at some period into which we do not pretend to inquire, but at all events immensely remote—by Him, then again, let us suppose to have been created——*what?* This is a vitally momentous epoch in our considerations. *What* is it that we are justified—that alone we are justified in supposing to have been, primarily and solely, *created?*

We have attained a point where only *Intuition* can aid us:—but now let me recur to the idea which I have already suggested as that alone which we can properly entertain of intuition. It is but *the conviction arising from those inductions or deductions of which the processes are so shadowy as to escape our consciousness, elude our reason, or defy our capacity of expression.* With this understanding, I now assert—that an intuition altogether irresistible, although inexpressible, forces me to the conclusion that what God originally created—that that Matter which, by dint of his Volition, he first made from his Spirit, or from Nihility, *could* have been nothing but Matter in its utmost conceivable state of——what?—of *Simplicity.*

* * *

Let us now endeavor to conceive what Matter must be, when, or if, in its absolute extreme of *Simplicity*. Here the Reason flies at once to Imparticularity—to a particle—to *one* particle—a particle of *one* kind—of *one* character—of *one* nature—of *one* size—of one form—a particle, therefore, "*without* form and void"—a particle positively a particle at all points—a particle absolutely unique, individual, undivided, and not indivisible only because He who *created* it, by dint of his Will, can by an infinitely less energetic exercise of the same Will, as a matter of course, divide it.

Oneness, then, is all that I predicate of the originally created Matter; but I propose to show that this *Oneness is a principle abundantly sufficient to account for the constitution, the existing phænomena and the plainly inevitable annihilation of at least the material Universe.*

The willing into being the primordial particle, has completed the act, or more properly the *conception*, of Creation. We now proceed to the ultimate purpose for which we are to suppose the Particle created—that is to say, the ultimate purpose so far as our considerations *yet* enable us to see it—the constitution of the Universe from it, the Particle.

This constitution has been effected by *forcing* the originally and therefore normally *One* into the abnormal condition of *Many*. An action of this character implies reaction. A diffusion from Unity, under the conditions, involves a tendency to return into Unity—a tendency ineradicable until satisfied. But on these points I will speak more fully hereafter.

The assumption of absolute Unity in the primordial Particle includes that of infinite divisibility. Let us conceive the Particle, then, to be only not totally exhausted by diffusion into Space. From the one

Particle, as a centre, let us suppose to be irradiated spherically—in all directions—to immeasurable but still to definite distances in the previously vacant space—a certain inexpressibly great yet limited number of unimaginably yet not infinitely minute atoms.

Now, of these atoms, thus diffused, or upon diffusion, what conditions are we permitted—not to assume, but to infer, from consideration as well of their source as of the character of the design apparent in their diffusion? *Unity* being their source, and *difference from Unity* the character of the design manifested in their diffusion, we are warranted in supposing this character to be at least *generally* preserved throughout the design, and to form a portion of the design itself:—that is to say, we shall be warranted in conceiving continual differences at all points from the uniquity and simplicity of the origin. But, for these reasons, shall we be justified in imagining the atoms heterogeneous, dissimilar, unequal, and inequidistant? More explicitly—are we to consider no two atoms as, at their diffusion, of the same nature, or of the same form, or of the same size?—and, after fulfilment of their diffusion into Space, is absolute inequidistance, each from each, to be understood of all of them? In such arrangement, under such conditions, we most easily and immediately comprehend the subsequent most feasible carrying out to completion of any such design as that which I have suggested—the design of variety out of unity—diversity out of sameness—heterogeneity out of homogeneity—complexity out of simplicity—in a word, the utmost possible multiplicity of *relation* out of the emphatically irrelative *One*. Undoubtedly, therefore, we *should* be warranted in assuming all that has been mentioned, but for the reflection, first, that supererogation is not presumable of any Divine Act; and, secondly, that the object supposed in view, appears as feasible when some of the conditions in question are dispensed with, in the beginning, as when all are understood immediately to exist. I mean to say that some are involved in the rest, or so instantaneous a consequence of them as to make the distinction inappreciable. Difference of *size*, for example, will at once be brought about through the tendency of one atom to a second, in preference to a third, on account of particular inequidistance; which is to be comprehended as *particular inequidistances between centres of quantity, in neighboring atoms of different form*—a matter not at all interfering with the generally-equable distribution of the atoms. Difference of *kind*, too, is easily conceived to be merely a result of differences in size and form, taken more or less conjointly:—in fact, since the *Unity* of the Particle Proper implies absolute homogeneity, we cannot imagine the atoms, at their diffusion, differing in kind, without imagining, at the same time, a special exercise of the Divine Will, at the emission of each atom, for the purpose of effecting, in each, a change of its essential nature:—so fantastic an idea is the less to be indulged, as the object proposed is seen to be thoroughly attainable without such minute and elaborate interposition. We perceive, therefore, upon the whole, that it would be supererogatory, and consequently unphilosophical, to predicate of the atoms, in view of their purposes, any

thing more than *difference of form* at their dispersion, with particular inequidistance after it—all other differences arising at once out of these, in the very first processes of mass-constitution:—We thus establish the Universe on a purely *geometrical* basis. Of course, it is by no means necessary to assume absolute difference, even of form, among *all* the atoms irradiated—any more than absolute particular inequidistance of each from each. We are required to conceive merely that no *neighboring* atoms are of similar form—no atoms which can ever approximate, until their inevitable rēunion at the end.

Although the immediate and perpetual *tendency* of the disunited atoms to return into their normal Unity, is implied, as I have said, in their abnormal diffusion; still it is clear that this tendency will be without consequence—a tendency and no more—until the diffusive energy, in ceasing to be exerted, shall leave *it*, the tendency, free to seek its satisfaction. The Divine Act, however, being considered as determinate, and discontinued on fulfilment of the diffusion, we understand, at once, a *rēaction*—in other words, a *satisfiable* tendency of the disunited atoms to return into *One*.

* * *

Discarding now the two equivocal terms, "gravitation" and "electricity," let us adopt the more definite expressions, *"attraction"* and *"repulsion."* The former is the body; the latter the soul: the one is the material; the other the spiritual, principle of the Universe. *No other principles exist. All* phænomena are referable to one, or to the other, or to both combined. So rigorously is this the case—so thoroughly demonstrable is it that attraction and repulsion are the *sole* properties through which we perceive the Universe—in other words, by which Matter is manifested to Mind—that, for all merely argumentative purposes, we are fully justified in assuming that matter *exists* only as attraction and repulsion—that attraction and repulsion *are* matter.

* * *

Some person may here demand:—"Why—since it is to the *One* that the atoms struggle back—do we not find and define Attraction 'a merely general tendency to a centre?'—why, in especial, do not *your* atoms—the atoms which you describe as having been irradiated from a centre—proceed at once, rectilinearly, back to the central point of their origin?"

I reply that *they do*; as will be distinctly shown; but that the cause of their so doing is quite irrespective of the centre *as such*. They all tend rectilinearly towards a centre, because of the sphereicity with which they have been irradiated into space. Each atom, forming one of a generally uniform globe of atoms, finds more atoms in the direction of the centre, of course, than in any other, and in that direction, therefore, is impelled—but is *not* thus impelled because the centre is *the point of its origin*. It is not to any *point* that the atoms are allied. It is not any *locality*, either in the concrete or in the abstract, to which I suppose them bound. Nothing like *location* was conceived as their origin. Their source lies in the principle, *Unity*. This is their lost parent. *This* they seek always—immediately—in all directions—wherever it is

even partially to be found; thus appeasing, in some measure, the in-
eradicable tendency, while on the way to its absolute satisfaction in
the end.

* * *

Thus the two Principles Proper, *Attraction* and *Repulsion*—the Ma-
terial and the Spiritual—accompany each other, in the strictest fellow-
ship, forever. Thus *The Body and The Soul walk hand in hand.*

If now, in fancy, we select *any one* of the agglomerations considered
as in their primary stages throughout the Universal sphere, and sup-
pose this incipient agglomeration to be taking place at that point
where the centre of our Sun exists—or rather where it *did* exist origi-
nally; for the Sun is perpetually shifting his position—we shall find
ourselves met, and borne onward for a time at least, by the most mag-
nificent of theories—by the Nebular Cosmogony of Laplace:[2]—al-
though "Cosmogony" is far too comprehensive a term for what he
really discusses—which is the constitution of our solar system alone—
of one among the myriad of similar systems which make up the Uni-
verse Proper—that Universal sphere—that all-inclusive and absolute
Kosmos which forms the subject of my present Discourse.

* * *

We comprehend, then, the insulation of our Universe. We perceive
the isolation of *that*—of *all* that which we grasp with the senses. We
know that there exists one *cluster of clusters*—a collection around
which, on all sides, extend the immeasurable wildernesses of a Space
to all human perception untenanted. But *because* upon the confines of
this Universe of Stars we are compelled to pause, through want of far-
ther evidence from the senses, is it right to conclude that, in fact,
there *is* no material point beyond that which we have thus been per-
mitted to attain? Have we, or have we not, an analogical right[3] to the
inference that this perceptible Universe—that this cluster of clus-
ters—is but one of *a series* of clusters of clusters, the rest of which are
invisible through distance—through the diffusion of their light being

2 Laplace (cf. p. 567 herein) investigated the eccentric orbits of Jupiter and Saturn, the asym-
 metrical motions of Jupiter's satellites, and the irregularities of the paths of comets. He also
 studied the variations of the moon's motions as affected by the earth's orbit and developed a
 theory of tides. These researches, along with a mathematical confirmation of Sir Isaac New-
 ton's theory of gravity, were published in his *Théorie des attractions des sphéroides et de la fig-
 ure des planètes* (Theory of the attraction of spheroids in the formation of planets, 1785) and
 in the famous *Mécanique céleste* (Celestial mechanics; 1795–1825; trans. 1829–39). The
 latter work also included his history of the science of astronomy. *Exposition du système du
 monde* (Explanation of the system of the world; 1796), and a mathematical demonstration of
 the nebular hypothesis. In brief, Laplace's hypothesis about the origin of the solar system
 (other versions of which had been suggested by Emanuel Swedenborg and Immanuel Kant)
 is that it began as an incredibly hot, rotating swirl of gas (the nebula) that gradually cooled,
 thereby contracting and thus rotating ever faster. This process eventuated in a series of
 events in which gravity and centrifugal force came into equilibrium, throwing off separate
 rings of matter that whirled around the condensed center; these rings or orbits in turn con-
 densed into planets and other bodies. (The theory is discounted by most modern physicists
 and astronomers.)
3. *Analogy* can mean a correspondence in some respects of the function, structure, position, or
 appearance of otherwise dissimilar things or the inference that if (two) things are alike in
 some ways they may be alike in other ways or have a general metaphoric likeness. Poe's point
 appears to be that even though human beings do not have the power fully to comprehend
 the actual nature of the universe, we may still approximate it by imaginative metaphor or
 analogy.

so excessive, ere it reaches us, as not to produce upon our retinas a light-impression—or from there being no such emanation as light at all, in these unspeakably distant worlds—or, lastly, from the mere interval being so vast, that the electric tidings of their presence in Space, have not yet—through the lapsing myriads of years—been enabled to traverse that interval?

Have we any right to inferences—have we any ground whatever for visions such as these? If we have a right to them in *any* degree, we have a right to their infinite extension.

The human brain has obviously a leaning to the *"Infinite"* and fondles the phantom of the idea.[4] It seems to long with a passionate fervor for this impossible conception, with the hope of intellectually believing it when conceived. What is general among the whole race of Man, of course no individual of that race can be warranted in considering abnormal; nevertheless, there *may* be a class of superior intelligences, to whom the human bias alluded to may wear all the character of monomania.[5]

My question, however, remains unanswered:—Have we any right to infer—let us say, rather, to imagine—an interminable succession of the "clusters of clusters," or of "Universes" more or less similar?

I reply that the "right," in a case such as this, depends absolutely upon the hardihood of that imagination which ventures to claim the right. Let me declare, only, that, as an individual, I myself feel impelled to the *fancy*—without daring to call it more—that there *does* exist a *limitless* succession of Universes, more or less similar to that of which we have cognizance—to that of which *alone* we shall ever have cognizance—at the very least until the return of our own particular Universe into Unity. *If* such clusters of clusters exist, however—*and they do*—it is abundantly clear that, having had no part in our origin, they have no portion in our laws. They neither attract us, nor we them. Their material—their spirit is not ours—is not that which obtains in any part of our Universe. They could not impress our senses or our souls. Among them and us—considering all, for the moment, collectively—there are no influences in common. Each exists, apart and independently, *in the bosom of its proper and particular God.*[6]

In the conduct of this Discourse, I am aiming less at physical than at metaphysical order. The clearness with which even material phænomena are presented to the understanding, depends very little, I have long since learned to perceive, upon a merely natural, and almost altogether upon a moral, arrangement. If then I seem to step somewhat too discursively from point to point of my topic, let me suggest that I do so in the hope of thus the better keeping unbroken that chain of *graduated impression*[7] by which alone the intellect of Man

4. See the previous note.
5. Poe may be referring to the world's sense of geniuses as madmen fixed on a particular idea, or the reference may be to the idea of superior beings in a gradated universe (say, from humans to angels) accessible only to human beings whose sensibilities border on madness; see the notes to Poe's poems herein.
6. See p. 583, n. 9 herein.
7. See n. 5 above; and p. 204 n. 6 herein.

can expect to encompass the grandeurs of which I speak, and, in their majestic totality, to comprehend them.

* * *

Space and Duration are one. That the Universe might *endure* throughout an æra [era] at all commensurate with the grandeur of its component material portions and with the high majesty of its spiritual purposes, it was necessary that the original atomic diffusion be made to so inconceivable an extent as to be only not infinite. It was required, in a word, that the stars should be gathered into visibility from invisible nebulosity—proceed from nebulosity to consolidation—and so grow grey in giving birth and death to unspeakably numerous and complex variations of vitalic development:—it was required that the stars should do all this—should have time thoroughly to accomplish all these Divine purposes—*during the period* in which all things were effecting their return into Unity with a velocity accumulating in the inverse proportion of the squares of the distances at which lay the inevitable End.

Throughout all this we have no difficulty in understanding the absolute accuracy of the Divine *adaptation.* The density of the stars, respectively, proceeds, of course, as their condensation diminishes; condensation and heterogeneity keep pace with each other; through the latter, which is the index of the former, we estimate the vitalic and spiritual development. Thus, in the density of the globes, we have the measure in which their purposes are fulfilled. As density proceeds—*as* the divine intentions *are* accomplished—*as* less and still less remains *to be* accomplished—so—in the same ratio—should we expect to find an acceleration of *the End:*—and thus the philosophical mind will easily comprehend that the Divine designs in constituting the stars, advance *mathematically* to their fulfilment:—and more; it will readily give the advance a mathematical expression; it will decide that this advance is inversely proportional with the squares of the distances of all created things from the starting-point and goal of their creation.

Not only is this Divine adaptation, however, mathematically accurate, but there is that about it which stamps it *as divine*, in distinction from that which is merely the work of human constructiveness. I allude to the complete *mutuality* of adaptation. For example; in human constructions a particular cause has a particular effect; a particular intention brings to pass a particular object; but this is all; we see no reciprocity. The effect does not re-act upon the cause; the intention does not change relations with the object. In Divine constructions the object is either design or object as we choose to regard it—and we may take at any time a cause for an effect, or the converse—so that we can never absolutely decide which is which.

* * *

The pleasure which we derive from any display of human ingenuity is in the ratio of *the approach* to this species of reciprocity. In the construction of *plot*, for example, in fictitious literature, we should aim at so arranging the incidents that we shall not be able to determine, of any one of them, whether it depends from any one other or upholds it.

In this sense, of course, *perfection of plot* is really, or practically, unattainable—but only because it is a finite intelligence that constructs. The plots of God are perfect. The Universe is a plot of God.[8] And now we have reached a point at which the intellect is forced, again, to struggle against its propensity for analogical inference—against its monomaniac grasping at the infinite. Moons have been seen *revolving* about planets; planets about stars; and the poetical instinct of humanity—its instinct of the symmetrical, if the symmetry be but a symmetry of surface:—this *instinct*, which the Soul, not only of Man but of all created beings, took up, in the beginning, from the *geometrical* basis of the Universal irradiation—impels us to the fancy of an endless extension of this system of *cycles*. Closing our eyes equally to *de*duction and *in*duction, we insist upon imagining a *revolution* of all the orbs of the Galaxy about some gigantic globe which we take to be the central pivot of the whole. Each cluster in the great cluster of clusters is imagined, of course, to be similarly supplied and constructed; while, that the "analogy" may be wanting at no point, we go on to conceive these clusters themselves, again, as *revolving* about some still more august sphere;—this latter, still again, *with* its encircling clusters, as but one of a yet more magnificent series of agglomerations, *gyrating* about yet another orb central *to them*—some orb still more unspeakably sublime—some orb, let us rather say, of infinite sublimity endlessly multiplied by the infinitely sublime. Such are the conditions, continued in perpetuity, which the voice of what some people term "analogy" calls upon the Fancy to depict and the Reason to contemplate, if possible, without becoming dissatisfied with the picture.

* * *

Humboldt, whose generalizing powers have never, perhaps, been equalled, has the following observation:

"When we regard the real, proper, or non-perspective motions of the stars, we find *many groups of them moving in opposite directions;* and the data as yet in hand render it not necessary, at least, to conceive that the systems composing the Milky Way, or the clusters, generally, composing the Universe, are revolving about any particular centre unknown, whether luminous or non-luminous. It is but Man's longing for a fundamental First Cause, that impels both his intellect and his fancy to the adoption of such an hypothesis."[9]

8. Some critics note an analogy to Poe's whole theory of unity and structure in writing. See "The Philosophy of Composition" (pp. 675ff. herein) and Poe's review of Hawthorne's *Twice-told Tales* (pp. 643ff.); see also the essays by Richard Wilbur (pp. 807ff.) and Joseph J. Moldenhauer (pp. 829ff.).

9. Betrachtet man die nicht perspectivischen eigenen Bewegungen der Sterne, so scheinen viele gruppenweise in ihrer Richtung entgegengesetzt; und die bisher gesammelten Thatsachen machen es auf's wenigste nicht nothwendig, anzunehmen, dass alle Theile unserer Sternenschicht oder gar der gesammten Sterneninseln, welche den Weltraum füllen, sich um einen grossen, unbekannten, leuchtenden oder dunkeln Centrolkörper bewegen. Das Streben nach den letzten und höchsten Grundursachen macht freilich die reflectirende Thätigkeit des Menschen, wie seine Phantasie, zu einer solchen Annahme geneigt [Poe's note]. Thomas S. Hansen explores some of the possible sources for Poe's translation of this passage from Humboldt's *Kosmos*; these include a sixty-six-page pamphlet published by Harper & Brothers from a London translation. A translation of the passage similar to Poe's appears on page 46, and Hansen accuses Poe of merely substituting a few words to make it look as if the translation were his own.

Recurring, then, to a previous suggestion, let us understand the systems—let us understand each star, with its attendant planets—as but a Titanic atom existing in space with precisely the same inclination for Unity which characterized, in the beginning, the actual atoms after their irradiation throughout the Universal sphere. As these original atoms rushed towards each other in generally straight lines, so let us conceive as at least generally rectilinear, the paths of the system-atoms towards their respective centres of aggregation:—and in this direct drawing together of the systems into clusters, with a similar and simultaneous drawing together of the clusters themselves while undergoing consolidation, we have at length attained the great *Now*—the awful[1] Present—the Existing Condition of the Universe.

Of the still more awful Future a not irrational analogy may guide us in framing an hypothesis. The equilibrium between the centripetal and centrifugal forces of each system, being necessarily destroyed upon attainment of a certain proximity to the nucleus of the cluster to which it belongs, there must occur, at once, a chaotic or seemingly chaotic precipitation, of the moons upon the planets, of the planets upon the suns, and of the suns upon the nuclei; and the general result of this precipitation must be the gathering of the myriad now-existing stars of the firmament into an almost infinitely less number of almost infinitely superior spheres. In being immeasurably fewer, the worlds of that day will be immeasurably greater than our own. Then, indeed, amid unfathomable abysses, will be glaring unimaginable suns. But all this will be merely a climacic[2] magnificence foreboding the great End. Of this End the new genesis described, can be but a very partial postponement. While undergoing consolidation, the clusters themselves, with a speed prodigiously accumulative, have been rushing towards their own general centre—and now, with a thousand-fold electric velocity, commensurate only with their material grandeur and with the spiritual passion of their appetite for oneness, the majestic remnants of the tribe of Stars flash, at length, into a common embrace. The inevitable catastrophe is at hand.

But this catastrophe—what is it? We have seen accomplished the ingathering of the orbs. Henceforward, are we not to understand *one material globe of globes* as constituting and comprehending the Universe? Such a fancy would be altogether at war with every assumption and consideration of this Discourse.

I have already alluded to that absolute *reciprocity of adaptation* which is the idiosyncrasy of the divine Art—stamping it divine. Up to this point of our reflections, we have been regarding the electrical influence as a something by dint of whose repulsion alone Matter is enabled to exist in that state of diffusion demanded for the fulfilment of its purposes:—so far, in a word, we have been considering the influence in question as ordained for Matter's sake—to subserve the ob-

1. Here meaning awesome, full of awe. A good deal of American Romanticism focuses on the "Present Moment" as opposed to dwelling on the past; e.g., see Emerson's *Nature* (1836) or Thoreau's *Walden* (1854). The differences with Poe's "awful Present" are instructive.
2. Presumably a printer's error for *climactic*.

jects of matter. With a perfectly legitimate reciprocity, we are now permitted to look at Matter, as created *solely for the sake of this influence*—solely to serve the objects of this spiritual Ether.[3] Through the aid—by the means—through the agency of Matter, and by dint of its heterogeneity—is this Ether manifested—is *Spirit individualized.* It is merely in the development of this Ether, through heterogeneity, that particular masses of Matter become animate—sensitive—and in the ratio of their heterogeneity;—some reaching a degree of sensitiveness involving what we call *Thought* and thus attaining Conscious Intelligence.

In this view, we are enabled to perceive Matter as a Means—not as an End. Its purposes are thus seen to have been comprehended in its diffusion; and with the return into Unity these purposes cease. The absolutely consolidated globe of globes would be *objectless:*—therefore not for a moment could it continue to exist. Matter, created for an end, would unquestionably, on fulfilment of that end, be Matter no longer. Let us endeavor to understand that it would disappear, and that God would remain all in all.

That every work of Divine conception must cŏexist and cŏexpire with its particular design, seems to me especially obvious; and I make no doubt that, on perceiving the final globe of globes to be *objectless*, the majority of my readers will be satisfied with my "*therefore* it cannot continue to exist." Nevertheless, as the startling thought of its instantaneous disappearance is one which the most powerful intellect cannot be expected readily to entertain on grounds so decidedly abstract, let us endeavor to look at the idea from some other and more ordinary point of view:—let us see how thoroughly and beautifully it is corroborated in an *à posteriori* consideration of Matter as we actually find it.

I have before said that "Attraction and Repulsion being undeniably the sole properties by which Matter is manifested to Mind, we are justified in assuming that Matter *exists* only as Attraction and Repulsion—in other words that Attraction and Repulsion *are* Matter; there being no conceivable case in which we may not employ the term Matter and the terms 'Attraction' and 'Repulsion' taken together, as equivalent, and therefore convertible, expressions in Logic." * * *

Now the very definition of Attraction implies particularity—the existence of parts, particles, or atoms; for we define it as the tendency of "each atom &c. to every other atom" &c. according to a certain law. Of course where there are *no* parts—where there is absolute Unity—where the tendency to oneness is satisfied—there can be no Attraction:—this has been fully shown, and all Philosophy admits it. When, on fulfilment of its purposes, then, Matter shall have returned into its original condition of *One*—a condition which presupposes the expulsion of the separative ether, whose province and whose capacity are limited to keeping the atoms apart until that great day when, this

3. Apparently connecting the ancient idea of the impalpable gaseous "ether" between the planetary orbits with the 18th-century "nebular" hypothesis, Poe suggests that matter is merely a manifestation of the ethereal as it becomes individualized.

ether being no longer needed, the overwhelming pressure of the finally collective Attraction shall at length just sufficiently predominate[4] and expel it:—when, I say, Matter, finally, expelling the Ether, shall have returned into absolute Unity,—it will then (to speak paradoxically for the moment) be Matter without Attraction and without Repulsion—in other words, Matter without Matter—in other words, again, *Matter no more*. In sinking into Unity, it will sink at once into that Nothingness which, to all Finite Perception, Unity must be—into that Material Nihility from which alone we can conceive it to have been evoked—to have been *created* by the Volition of God.

I repeat then—Let us endeavor to comprehend that the final globe of globes will instantaneously disappear, and that God will remain all in all.

But are we here to pause? Not so. On the Universal agglomeration and dissolution, we can readily conceive that a new and perhaps totally different series of conditions may ensue—another creation and irradiation, returning into itself—another action and rēaction of the Divine Will. Guiding our imaginations by that omniprevalent law of laws, the law of periodicity, are we not, indeed, more than justified in entertaining a belief—let us say, rather, in indulging a hope—that the processes we have here ventured to contemplate will be renewed forever, and forever, and forever; a novel Universe swelling into existence, and then subsiding into nothingness, at every throb of the Heart Divine?

And now—this Heart Divine—what is it? *It is our own*.[5]

Let not the merely seeming irreverence of this idea frighten our souls from that cool exercise of consciousness—from that deep tranquillity of self-inspection—through which alone we can hope to attain the presence of this, the most sublime of truths, and look it leisurely in the face.

The *phænomena* on which our conclusions must at this point depend, are merely spiritual shadows, but not the less thoroughly substantial.[6]

We walk about, amid the destinies of our world-existence, encompassed by dim but ever present *Memories* of a Destiny more vast—very distant in the by-gone time, and infinitely awful.[7]

We live out a Youth peculiarly haunted by such dreams; yet never mistaking them for dreams. As Memories we *know* them. *During our Youth* the distinction is too clear to deceive us even for a moment.[8]

So long as this Youth endures, the feeling *that we exist*, is the most natural of all feelings. We understand it *thoroughly*. That there was a period at which we did *not* exist—or, that it might so have happened

4. Gravity therefore must be the strongest of forces * * * [Poe's note], quoting a sentence early in *Eureka*.
5. Poe's version of Romantic "self-apotheosis"; being one with the cycle of creation and destruction of the universe, we are ourselves God.
6. Poe's version of neoplatonism makes the earthly "shadows" an actual part of the spiritual or ideal real.
7. Awesome. Cf. the Romantic poems of Shelley and Wordsworth, especially the latter's ode "Intimations of Immortality" (1802–04).
8. See the notes to Poe's early poems reprinted herein.

that we never had existed at all—are the considerations, indeed, which *during this youth*, we find difficulty in understanding. Why we should *not* exist, is, *up to the epoch of our Manhood*, of all queries the most unanswerable. Existence—self-existence—existence from all Time and to all Eternity—seems, up to the epoch of Manhood, a normal and unquestionable condition:—*seems, because it is.*

But now comes the period at which a conventional World-Reason awakens us from the truth of our dream. Doubt, Surprise and Incomprehensibility arrive at the same moment. They say:—"You live and the time was when you lived not. You have been created. An Intelligence exists greater than your own; and it is only through this Intelligence you live at all." These things we struggle to comprehend and cannot:— *cannot*, because these things, being untrue, are thus, of necessity, incomprehensible.

No thinking being lives who, at some luminous point of his life of thought, has not felt himself lost amid the surges of futile efforts at understanding, or believing, that anything exists *greater than his own soul*. The utter impossibility of any one's soul feeling itself inferior to another; the intense, overwhelming dissatisfaction and rebellion at the thought;—these, with the omniprevalent aspirations at perfection, are but the spiritual, coincident with the material, struggles towards the original Unity—are, to my mind at least, a species of proof far surpassing what Man terms demonstration, that no one soul *is* inferior to another—that nothing is, or can be, superior to any one soul—that each soul is, in part, its own God—its own Creator:—in a word, that God—the material *and* spiritual God—*now* exists solely in the diffused Matter and Spirit of the Universe; and that the regathering of this diffused Matter and Spirit will be but the re-constitution of the *purely* Spiritual and Individual God.

In this view, and in this view alone, we comprehend the riddles of Divine Injustice—of Inexorable Fate. In this view alone the existence of Evil becomes intelligible; but in this view it becomes more—it becomes endurable. Our souls no longer rebel at a *Sorrow* which we ourselves have imposed upon ourselves, in furtherance of our own purposes—with a view—if even with a futile view—to the extension of our own *Joy*.

I have spoken of *Memories* that haunt us during our youth. They sometimes pursue us even in our Manhood:—assume gradually less and less indefinite shapes:—now and then speak to us with low voices; saying:

"There was an epoch in the Night of Time, when a still-existent Being existed—one of an absolutely infinite number of similar Beings that people the absolutely infinite domains of the absolutely infinite space.[9] It was not and is not in the power of this Being—any more than it is in your own—to extend, by actual increase, the joy of his Existence; but just as it *is* in your power to expand or to concentrate your pleasures (the absolute amount of happiness remaining always the

9. See * * * Paragraph commencing "I reply that the right," and ending "proper and particular God" [Poe's note]. (See p. 577 herein.)

same) so did and does a similar capability appertain to this Divine Be-
ing, who thus passes his Eternity in perpetual variation of Concen-
trated Self and almost Infinite Self-Diffusion. What you call The
Universe is but his present expansive existence. He now feels his life
through an infinity of imperfect pleasures—the partial and pain-
intertangled pleasures of those inconceivably numerous things which
you designate as his creatures, but which are really but infinite indi-
vidualizations of Himself. All these creatures—*all*—those which you
term animate, as well as those to whom you deny life for no better rea-
son than that you do not behold it in operation—*all* these creatures
have, in a greater or less degree, a capacity for pleasure and for
pain:—*but the general sum of their sensations is precisely that amount
of Happiness which appertains by right to the Divine Being when con-
centrated within Himself.* These creatures are all, too, more or less
conscious Intelligences; conscious, first, of a proper identity; con-
scious, secondly and by faint indeterminate glimpses, of an identity
with the Divine Being of whom we speak—of an identity with God. Of
the two classes of consciousness, fancy that the former will grow
weaker, the latter stronger, during the long succession of ages which
must elapse before these myriads of individual Intelligences become
blended—when the bright stars become blended—into One. Think
that the sense of individual identity will be gradually merged in the
general consciousness—that Man, for example, ceasing imperceptibly
to feel himself Man, will at length attain that awfully triumphant
epoch when he shall recognize his existence as that of Jehovah. In the
meantime bear in mind that all is Life—Life—Life within Life—the
less within the greater, and all within the *Spirit Divine*.

THE END.

BACKGROUNDS
AND CONTEXTS

Letters, Prefaces, Essays, and Reviews

Unless otherwise indicated, the texts in this section were written by Poe. In addition to the letters, essays, and reviews by Poe, the section contains letters to Poe as well as contemporary reviews of his works, biographical sketches, and memorials. The letters are reprinted from the edition of John Ward Ostrom (see Selected Bibliography, p. 955 herein), reprinted by permission of Harvard University Press. They are indentified by Ostrom's numbering system: for example, "(Letter 13)." Ostrom's symbols indicating cancellations, additions, and speculations on blurred words have in general been omitted. Nineteenth-century spelling, punctuation, and individual eccentricities have been preserved wherever possible.

To John Allan (Letter 13)[1]

Baltimore May 29th 1829,

Dear Pa,

I am now going to make a request different from any I have ever yet made.

As I wrote you, some time since, I have been several times to visit Mr Wirt, who has treated me with great kindness & attention. I sent him, for his opinion, a day or two ago, *a poem* which I have written since I left home—& in the letter which I now enclose you have his opinion upon its merits—From such a man as Mr Wirt the flattering character he has given of the work, will surely be to you a recommendation in its favor.

In the conclusion of the letter you will see that he advises me to "get a personal introduction to Mr Walsh" the editor of the American Quarterly Review & get his interest in my favor—that interest, and his highest encomiums on the poem are already obtained—as Editor of the Review he promises to notice it which will assure it, if not of popularity, of success—

Under these circumstances, I have thought it my duty to write to you on the subject—Believing you to be free from prejudice, I think you will aid me, if you see cause; At my time of life there is much in being *before the eye of the world*—if once noticed I can easily cut out a path

1. Poe had quarreled with John Allan after his removal from the University of Virginia (see biographical introduction, pp. xxi–xxii herein); after several stormy arguments, Poe was ordered out of Allan's house in 1827; yet two years later he felt that he could seek Allan's help in publishing a volume of poems.

to reputation—It can certainly be of no disadvantage as it will not, even for a moment, interfere with other objects which I have in view.

I am aware of the difficulty of getting a poem published in this country—Mr Wirt & Mr Walsh have advised me of that—but the *difficulty* should be no object, with a proper aim in view.

If Mssrs Carey, Lea, & Carey, should decline publishing (as I have no reason to think they will not—they having invariably declined it with all our American poets) that is upon their *own risk* the request I have to make is this—that you will give me a letter to Mssrs Carey, Lea, & Carey saying that if in publishing the poem "Al Aaraaf" they shall incur any *loss*—you will make it good to them.

The cost of publishing the work, in a style equal to any of our American publications, will at the extent be $100— This then, of course, must be the limit of any loss supposing not a single copy of the work to be sold—It is more than probable that the work will be profitable & that I may gain instead of lose, even in a pecuniary way—

I would remark, in conclusion that I have long given up *Byron* as a model—for which, I think, I deserve some credit.

If you will help me in this matter I will be always grateful for your kindness.

If you conclude upon giving me a *trial* please enclose me the letter to Messrs Carey, Lea, & Carey—I shall wait anxiously for your answer—

Give my love to Miss Valentine & all

> I remain Yours affecty:
> E A. Poe

Letter to B——[1]

IT HAS BEEN SAID that a good critique on a poem may be written by one who is no poet himself. This, according to *your* idea and *mine* of poetry, I feel to be false—the less poetical the critic, the less just the critique, and the converse. On this account, and because there are but few B——'s in the world, I would be as much ashamed of the world's good opinion as proud of your own. Another than yourself might here observe, "Shakspeare is in possession of the world's good opinion, and yet Shakspeare is the greatest of poets. It appears then that the world judge correctly, why should you be ashamed of their favorable judgment?" The difficulty lies in the interpretation of the word "judgment" or "opinion." The opinion is the world's, truly, but it may be called theirs as a man would call a book his, having bought it; he did not

1. The text was prefaced by the following note: [These detached passages form part of the preface to a small volume printed some years ago for private circulation. They have vigor and much originality—but of course we shall not be called upon to endorse all the writer's opinions.—*Ed.*] It is unclear whether the footnote to the title is by T. W. White, owner and at that time editor of the *Messenger*, or by Poe himself. The text here is that reprinted in the *Southern Literary Messenger* in 1836.

 Letter to B—— was first published as the preface to *Poems* (1831) under the title "Letter to Mr. —— ——." The identity of "B" is uncertain, though the publisher of the volume, Elam Bliss, is a strong likelihood. The asterisks in the text are Poe's.

write the book, but it is his; they did not originate the opinion, but it is theirs. A fool, for example, thinks Shakspeare a great poet—yet the fool has never read Shakspeare. But the fool's neighbor, who is a step higher on the Andes of the mind, whose head (that is to say his more exalted thought) is too far above the fool to be seen or understood, but whose feet (by which I mean his every-day actions) are sufficiently near to be discerned, and by means of which that superiority is ascertained, which *but* for them would never have been discovered—this neighbor asserts that Shakspeare is a great poet—the fool believes him, and it is henceforward his *opinion*. This neighbor's own opinion has, in like manner, been adopted from one above *him*, and so, ascendingly, to a few gifted individuals, who kneel around the summit, beholding, face to face, the master spirit who stands upon the pinnacle. * * * *

You are aware of the great barrier in the path of an American writer. He is read, if at all, in preference to the combined and established wit of the world. I say established; for it is with literature as with law or empire—an established name is an estate in tenure, or a throne in possession. Besides, one might suppose that books, like their authors, improve by travel—their having crossed the sea is, with us, so great a distinction. Our antiquaries abandon time for distance; our very fops glance from the binding to the bottom of the title-page, where the mystic characters which spell London, Paris, or Genoa, are precisely so many letters of recommendation.

* * *

I mentioned just now a vulgar error as regards criticism. I think the notion that no poet can form a correct estimate of his own writings is another. I remarked before, that in proportion to the poetical talent, would be the justice of a critique upon poetry. Therefore, a bad poet would, I grant, make a false critique, and his self-love would infallibly bias his little judgment in his favor; but a poet, who is indeed a poet, could not, I think, fail of making a just critique. Whatever should be deducted on the score of self-love, might be replaced on account of his intimate acquaintance with the subject; in short, we have more instances of false criticism than of just, where one's own writings are the test, simply because we have more bad poets than good. There are of course many objections to what I say: Milton is a great example of the contrary; but his opinion with respect to the Paradise Regained, is by no means fairly ascertained. By what trivial circumstances men are often led to assert what they do not really believe! Perhaps an inadvertent word has descended to posterity. But, in fact, the Paradise Regained is little, if at all, inferior to the Paradise Lost, and is only supposed so to be, because men do not like epics, whatever they may say to the contrary, and reading those of Milton in their natural order, are too much wearied with the first to derive any pleasure from the second.

I dare say Milton[2] preferred Comus to either—if so—justly. * * * * * * * * *

2. John Milton (1608–1679). His works *Paradise Lost* (1667), *Paradise Regained* (1671), and *Comus* (1634) are referred to in order of decreasing length.

As I am speaking of poetry, it will not be amiss to touch slightly upon the most singular heresy in its modern history—the heresy of what is called very foolishly, the Lake School.[3] Some years ago I might have been induced, by an occasion like the present, to attempt a formal refutation of their doctrine; at present it would be a work of supererogation. The wise must bow to the wisdom of such men as Coleridge and Southey, but being wise, have laughed at poetical theories so prosaically exemplified.

Aristotle, with singular assurance, has declared poetry the most philosophical of all writing[4]—but it required a Wordsworth to pronounce it the most metaphysical. He seems to think that the end of poetry is, or should be, instruction—yet it is a truism that the end of our existence is happiness; if so, the end of every separate part of our existence—every thing connected with our existence should be still happiness. Therefore the end of instruction should be happiness; and happiness is another name for pleasure;—therefore the end of instruction should be pleasure: yet we see the above mentioned opinion implies precisely the reverse.

To proceed: ceteris paribus,[5] he who pleases, is of more importance to his fellow men than he who instructs, since utility is happiness, and pleasure is the end already obtained which instruction is merely the means of obtaining.

I see no reason, then, why our metaphysical poets should plume themselves so much on the utility of their works, unless indeed they refer to instruction with eternity in view; in which case, sincere respect for their piety would not allow me to express my contempt for their judgment; contempt which it would be difficult to conceal, since their writings are professedly to be understood by the few, and it is the many who stand in need of salvation. In such case I should no doubt be tempted to think of the devil in Melmoth,[6] who labors indefatigably through three octavo volumes, to accomplish the destruction of one or two souls, while any common devil would have demolished one or two thousand.

* * *

Against the subtleties which would make poetry a study—not a passion—it becomes the metaphysician to reason—but the poet to protest. Yet Wordsworth and Coleridge are men in years; the one imbued in contemplation from his childhood, the other a giant in intellect and learning. The diffidence, then, with which I venture to dispute their authority, would be over-whelming, did I not feel, from

3. Reference to the British Romantic poets, especially William Wordsworth (1770–1850) and Samuel Taylor Coleridge (1772–1834), but also including Robert Southey (1774–1843) and others.
4. Spoudiotaton kai philosophikotaton genos [Poe's note]. From Aristotle's *Poetics*, IX.3. The phrase is taken out of context. Aristotle writes that poetry is more philosophical than history, for poetry tends to express the universal, history the particular. Poe follows the lead of Wordsworth in the Preface to *Lyrical Ballads* (1800): "Aristotle, I have been told, has said, that Poetry is the most philosophic of all writings."
5. Other things being equal (Latin).
6. Charles Maturin's *Melmoth the Wanderer* (1820).

the bottom of my heart, that learning has little to do with the imagi-
nation—intellect with the passions—or age with poetry. * * * * *

> "Trifles, like straws, upon the surface flow,
> He who would search for pearls must dive below,"[7]

are lines which have done much mischief. As regards the greater
truths, men oftener err by seeking them at the bottom than at the top;
the depth lies in the huge abysses where wisdom is sought—not in the
palpable palaces where she is found. The ancients were not always
right in hiding the goddess in a well:[8] witness the light which Bacon
has thrown upon philosophy; witness the principles of our divine
faith—that moral mechanism by which the simplicity of a child may
overbalance the wisdom of a man.

We see an instance of Coleridge's liability to err, in his Biographia
Literaria—professedly his literary life and opinions, but, in fact, a trea-
tise *de omni scibili et quibusdam aliis.*[9] He goes wrong by reason of his
very profundity, and of his error we have a natural type in the contem-
plation of a star. He who regards it directly and intensely sees, it is
true, the star, but it is the star without a ray—while he who surveys it
less inquisitively is conscious of all for which the star is useful to us
below—its brilliancy and its beauty.

* * *

As to Wordsworth, I have no faith in him. That he had, in youth, the
feelings of a poet I believe—for there are glimpses of extreme delicacy in
his writings—(and delicacy is the poet's own kingdom—his *El Do-
rado*)—but they have the appearance of a better day recollected; and
glimpses, at best, are little evidence of present poetic fire—we know that
a few straggling flowers spring up daily in the crevices of the glacier.

He was to blame in wearing away his youth in contemplation with
the end of poetizing in his manhood. With the increase of his judg-
ment the light which should make it apparent has faded away. His
judgment consequently is too correct. This may not be understood,—
but the old Goths of Germany would have understood it, who used to
debate matters of importance to their State twice, once when drunk,
and once when sober—sober that they might not be deficient in for-
mality—drunk lest they should be destitute of vigor.

The long wordy discussions by which he tries to reason us into ad-
miration of his poetry, speak very little in his favor: they are full of
such assertions as this—(I have opened one of his volumes at ran-
dom)[1] "Of genius the only proof is the act of doing well what is worthy
to be done, and what was never done before"—indeed! then it follows
that in doing what is *un*worthy to be done, or what *has* been done be-
fore, no genius can be evinced: yet the picking of pockets is an unwor-
thy act, pockets have been picked time immemorial, and Barrington,

7. Slight misquotation from the Prologue (11.25–26) of *All for Love* (1677) by John Dryden
 (1631–1700). For "trifles" read *errors.*
8. Democritus (c. 470–c. 370 B.C.E.) was alleged to have said that truth lies at the bottom of a
 well; see Diogenes Laertius, *Pyrrho,* IX.72.
9. Concerning all that can be known and certain other things (Latin).
1. Wordsworth's "Essay Supplementary to the Preface" in his *Collected Poems* (1815).

the pick-pocket, in point of genius, would have thought hard of a comparison with William Wordsworth, the poet.

Again—in estimating the merit of certain poems, whether they be Ossian's or M'Pherson's, can surely be of little consequence, yet, in order to prove their worthlessness, Mr. W. has expended many pages in the controversy. *Tantæne animis?*[2] Can great minds descend to such absurdity? But worse still: that he may bear down every argument in favor of these poems, he triumphantly drags forward a passage, in his abomination of which he expects the reader to sympathize. It is the beginning of the epic poem *"Temora."*[3] "The blue waves of Ullin roll in light; the green hills are covered with day; trees shake their dusky heads in the breeze." And this—this gorgeous, yet simple imagery— where all is alive and panting with immortality—this—William Wordsworth, the author of Peter Bell, has *selected* for his contempt. We shall see what better he, in his own person, has to offer. Imprimis:

> "And now she's at the pony's head,
> And now she's at the pony's tail,
> On that side now, and now on this,
> And almost stifled her with bliss—
> A few sad tears does Betty shed,
> She pats the pony where or when
> She knows not: happy Betty Foy!
> O Johnny! never mind the Doctor!"[4]

Secondly:

> "The dew was falling fast, the—stars began to blink,
> I heard a voice, it said——drink, pretty creature, drink;
> And looking o'er the hedge, be—for me I espied
> A snow-white mountain lamb with a—maiden at its side,
> No other sheep were near, the lamb was all alone,
> And by a slender cord was—tether'd to a stone."[5]

Now we have no doubt this is all true; we *will* believe it, indeed we will, Mr. W. Is it sympathy for the sheep you wish to excite? I love a sheep from the bottom of my heart.

<p style="text-align:center">* * *</p>

But there *are* occasions, dear B——, there are occasions when even Wordsworth is reasonable. Even Stamboul, it is said, shall have an end, and the most unlucky blunders must come to a conclusion. Here is an extract from his preface—

"Those who have been accustomed to the phraseology of modern writers, if they persist in reading this book to a conclusion (*impossible!*) will, no doubt, have to struggle with feelings of awkwardness; (ha! ha! ha!) they will look round for poetry (ha! ha! ha! ha!) and will

2. I.e., Why such anger? (Latin); from Virgil's *Aeneid*, I.ɪɪ.
3. One of the "Ossian" poems of James Macpherson that Wordsworth alludes to in "Essay Supplementary."
4. From Wordsworth's "The Idiot Boy" (1798). The first two lines are reversed and two lines are omitted.
5. Wordsworth's "The Pet Lamb" (1800), with dashes added by Poe.

be induced to inquire by what species of courtesy these attempts have been permitted to assume that title."[6] Ha! ha! ha! ha! ha!

Yet let not Mr. W. despair; he has given immortality to a wagon, and the bee Sophocles has transmitted to eternity a sore toe, and dignified a tragedy with a chorus of turkeys.[7]

* * *

Of Coleridge I cannot speak but with reverence. His towering intellect! his gigantic power! He is one more evidence of the fact "que la plupart des sectes ont raison dans une bonne partie de ce qu'elles avancent, mais non pas en ce qu'elles nient."[8] He has imprisoned his own conceptions by the barrier he has erected against those of others. It is lamentable to think that such a mind should be buried in metaphysics, and, like the Nyctanthes,[9] waste its perfume upon the night alone. In reading his poetry I tremble—like one who stands upon a volcano, conscious, from the very darkness bursting from the crater, of the fire and the light that are weltering below.

* * *

What is Poetry?—Poetry!—that Proteus-like idea, with as many appellations as the nine-titled Corcyra![1] Give me, I demanded of a scholar some time ago, give me a definition of poetry? "Tres-volontiers,"[2]—and he proceeded to his library, brought me a Dr. Johnson, and overwhelmed me with a definition. Shade of the immortal Shakspeare! I imagined to myself the scowl of your spiritual eye upon the profanity of that scurrilous Ursa Major. Think of poetry, dear B—, think of poetry, and then think of—Dr. Samuel Johnson![3] Think of all that is airy and fairy-like, and then of all that is hideous and unwieldy; think of his huge bulk, the Elephant! and then—and then think of the Tempest—the Midsummer Night's Dream—Prospero—Oberon—and Titania![4]

* * *

A poem, in my opinion, is opposed to a work of science by having, for its *immediate* object, pleasure, not truth; to romance, by having for its object an *indefinite* instead of a *definite* pleasure, being a poem only so far as this object is attained; romance presenting perceptible images with definite, poetry with *in*definite sensations, to which end music is an *essential*, since the comprehension of sweet sound is our most indefinite conception. Music, when combined with a pleasurable idea, is

6. From the preface to *Lyrical Ballads*.
7. A series of playful allusions: Wordsworth wrote a work called "The Waggoner" (1819). "Sore toe": a reference to *Oedipus* ("swollen foot"). Sophocles was called "the Attic Bee" (see A. W. Schlegel, *Lectures on Dramatic Art and Literature*, 1808, lecture VII). He was said by Pliny (*Natural History*, XXXVII.40) to have used a chorus of guinea fowls to lament the death of Meleager in one of his plays.
8. For the most part, most sects are right in what they advance, but not in what they deny (French). Quoted by Coleridge in chapter II of the *Biographia Literaria* (1817).
9. Night-blooming jasmine.
1. I.e., Corfu, frequently renamed throughout history.
2. Very willingly (French).
3. The "literary dictator" of London in his time (1709–1784), author of essays in literary taste, of *Lives of the Poets* (1779–81), and of the famous *Dictionary of the English Language* (1755); he was corpulent to the extreme.
4. Magical, dreamlike, and fairy characters in Shakespeare's *The Tempest* (1611–12) and *A Midsummer Night's Dream* (1595–96).

poetry; music without the idea is simply music; the idea without the music is prose from its very definitiveness.

What was meant by the invective against him who had no music in his soul?

* * *

To sum up this long rigmarole, I have, dear B——, what you no doubt perceive, for the metaphysical poets, *as* poets, the most sovereign contempt. That they have followers proves nothing—

> No Indian prince has to his palace
> More followers than a thief to the gallows.[5]

To Joseph T. and Edwin Buckingham (Letter 37)[1]

Baltimore May 4th 1833

Gentlemen,

I send you an original tale in hope of your accepting it for the N. E. Magazine. It is one of a number of similar pieces which I have contemplated publishing under the title of 'Eleven Tales of the Arabesque'. They are supposed to be read at table by the eleven members of a literary club, and are followed by the remarks of the company upon each. These remarks are intended as a burlesque upon criticism. In the whole, originality more than any thing else has been attempted. I have said this much with a view of offering you the entire M.S. If you like the specimen which I have sent I will forward the rest at your suggestion—but if you decide upon publishing all the tales, it would not be proper to print the one I now send until it can be printed in its place with the others. It is however optional with you either to accept them all, or publish 'Epimanes' and reject the rest—if indeed you do not reject them altogether.

* * *

5. From Samuel Butler's *Hudibras*, part II (1664), I.272ff.
1. Along with this letter about his collection of "arabesque" tales, Poe sent his political satire "Epimanes" (later titled "Four Beasts in One") to the *New-England Magazine*. This journal was new, having been founded in 1831 by Joseph T. Buckingham and his son, Edwin. The Buckinghams did not accept the tale, and the magazine folded in December 1835. Poe's story was published March 1836 in the *Southern Literary Messenger*, one of the most enduring of antebellum magazines. For a discussion of the meanings of *arabesque* and the developing theory of the framed tale cycle, see the Tales and Sketches introduction (pp. 77ff. herein). For Poe's further attempts to publish a collection of arabesques, see "The Folio Club" (pp. 595–96) and the letter from John P. Kennedy (p. 602) and Poe's reply (p. 603). Also see the March 1836 letter from James Kirk Paulding to Thomas White, publisher of the *Messenger*, in which Paulding tries to explain why the publishing house of Harper's was skeptical about the marketability of Poe's collection of tales (p. 603) and Poe's 1840 preface to *Tales of the Grotesque and Arabesque* (pp. 620–21). For further comments on the "book-unity" of his collected tales, see Poe's letter to Philip P. Cooke (pp. 684–85).

The Folio Club[1]

There is a Machiavelian plot
Though every nare olfact it not.

Butler[2]

The Folio Club is, I am sorry to say, a mere Junto of *Dunderheadism*. I think too the members are quite as ill-looking as they are stupid. I also believe it their settled intention to abolish Literature, subvert the Press, and overturn the Government of Nouns and Pronouns. These are my private opinions which I now take the liberty of making public.

Yet when, about a week ago, I first became one of this diabolical association, no person could have entertained for it more profound sentiments of admiration and respect. Why my feelings in this matter have undergone a change will appear, very obviously, in the sequel. In the meantime I shall vindicate my own character, and the dignity of Letters.

I find, upon reference to the records, that the Folio Club was organized as such on the——day of——in the year——. I like to begin with the beginning, and have a partiality for dates. A clause in the Constitution then adopted forbade the members to be otherwise than erudite and witty: and the avowed objects of the Confederation were 'the instruction of society, and the amusement of themselves.' For the latter purpose a meeting is held monthly at the house of some one of the association, when each individual is expected to come prepared with a 'Short Prose Tale' of his own composition. Each article thus produced is read by its author to the company assembled over a glass of wine at dinner. Much rivalry will of course ensue—more particularly as the writer of the 'Best Thing' is appointed President of the Club *pro tem:*, an office endowed with many dignities and little expence, and which endures until its occupant is dispossessed by a superior *morceau*. The father of the Tale held, on the contrary, to be the least meritorious, is bound to furnish the dinner and wine at the next similar meeting of the Society. This is found an excellent method of occasionally supplying the body with a new member, in the place of some unfortunate who, forfeiting two or three entertainments in succession, will naturally decline, at the same time, the 'supreme honour' and the association. The number of the Club is limited to eleven. For this there are many good reasons which it is unnecessary to mention, but which will of course suggest themselves to every person of reflection. One of them, however, is that on the first of April, in the year three hundred and fifty before the Deluge, there are said to have been just eleven spots upon the sun. It will be seen that, in giving these rapid outlines of the Society, I have so far restrained my indignation as

1. This "preface" was to serve as an introduction to a collection of about a dozen tales, for which Poe was still trying to find a publisher in 1834 (see letter 37 directly above). The text is that of the original manuscript at Harvard University, reprinted in Mabbott, II.203–06.
2. The motto is from Samuel Butler's *Hudibras* (1663 ff.), I.i.741–42. In the 1902 Harrison edition, the word *nare* in the motto (Latin, "nostrils") was misprinted as *hare* (rabbit). A favorite game of scholars is trying to determine the "authors" to particular tales.

to speak with unusual candour and liberality. The *exposé* which it is my intention to make will be sufficiently effected by a mere detail of the Club's proceedings on the evening of Tuesday last, when I made my *debût* as a member of that body, having been only chosen in place of the Honourable Augustus Scratchaway, resigned.

At five P.M. I went by appointment to the house of Mr. Rouge-et-Noir who admires Lady Morgan, and whose Tale was condemned at the previous monthly meeting. I found the company already assembled in the dining-room, and must confess that the brilliancy of the fire, the comfortable appearance of the apartment, and the excellent equipments of the table, as well as a due confidence in my own abilities, contributed to inspire me, for the time, with many pleasant meditations. I was welcomed with great show of cordiality, and dined with much self-congratulation at becoming one of so wise a Society.

The members, generally, were most remarkable men. There was, first of all, Mr. Snap, the President, who is a very lank man with a hawk nose, and was formerly in the service of the Down-East Review.

Then there was Mr. Convolvulus Gondola, a young gentleman who had travelled a good deal.

Then there was De Rerum Naturâ, Esqr., who wore a very singular pair of green spectacles.

Then there was a very little man in a black coat with very black eyes.

Then there was Mr. Solomon Seadrift who had every appearance of a fish.

Then there was Mr. Horribile Dictû, with white eyelashes, who had graduated at Gottingen.

Then there was Mr. Blackwood Blackwood who had written certain articles for foreign Magazines.

Then there was the host, Mr. Rouge-et-Noir, who admired Lady Morgan.

Then there was a stout gentleman who admired Sir Walter Scott.

Then there was Chronologos Chronology who admired Horace Smith, and had a very big nose which had been in Asia Minor.

Upon the removal of the cloth Mr. Snap said to me 'I believe there is little need of my giving you any information, Sir, in regard to the regulations of our Club. I think you know we intend to instruct society, and amuse ourselves. To night however we propose doing the latter solely, and shall call upon you in turn to contribute your quota. In the meantime I will commence operations.' Here Mr. Snap, having pushed the bottle, produced a M.S. and read as follows. ["Epimanes."]

To Thomas W. White (Letter 42)

[Baltimore, April 30, 1835]

* * *

A word or two in relation to Berenice. Your opinion of it is very just. The subject is by far too horrible, and I confess that I hesitated in

sending it you especially as a specimen of my capabilities. The Tale originated in a bet that I could produce nothing effective on a subject so singular, provided I treated it seriously. But what I wish to say relates to the character of your Magazine more than to any articles I may offer, and I beg you to believe that I have no intention of giving you *advice*, being fully confident that, upon consideration, you will agree with me. The history of all Magazines shows plainly that those which have attained celebrity were indebted for it to articles *similar in nature—to Berenice*—although, I grant you, far superior in style and execution. I say similar in *nature*. You ask me in what does this nature consist? In the ludicrous heightened into the grotesque: the fearful coloured into the horrible: the witty exaggerated into the burlesque: the singular wrought out into the strange and mystical. You may say all this is bad taste. I have my doubts about it. Nobody is more aware than I am that simplicity is the cant of the day—but take my word for it no one cares any thing about simplicity in their hearts. Believe me also, in spite of what people say to the contrary, that there is nothing easier in the world than to be extremely simple. But whether the articles of which I speak are, or are not in bad taste is little to the purpose. To be appreciated you must be *read*, and these things are invariably sought after with avidity. They are, if you will take notice, the articles which find their way into other periodicals, and into the papers, and in this manner, taking hold upon the public mind they augment the reputation of the source where they originated. Such articles are the "M.S. found in a Madhouse" and the "Monos and Daimonos" of the London New Monthly—the "Confessions of an Opium-Eater" and the "Man in the Bell" of Blackwood. The two first were written by no less a man than Bulwer—the *Confessions* [*illegible*] universally attributed to Coleridge—although unjustly.[1] Thus the first men in [England] have not thought writings of this nature unworthy of their talents, and I have go[od] reason to believe that some very high names valued themselves *principally* upon this species of literature. To be sure originality is an essential in these things—great attention must be paid to style, and much labour spent in their composition, or they will degenerate into the tugid or the absurd. If I am not mistaken you will find Mr Kennedy, whose writings you admire, and whose Swallow-Barn is unrivalled for purity of style and thought of my opinion in this matter. It is unnecessary for you to pay much attention to the many who will no doubt favour you with their critiques. In respect to Berenice individually I allow that it approaches the very verge of bad taste—but I will not sin quite so egregiously again. I propose to furnish you every month with a Tale of the nature which I have alluded to. The effect—if any—will be estimated better by the circulation of the Magazine than by any comments upon its

1. "MS. Found in a Madhouse" is by Charles Dickens. Edward Bulwer-Lytton is in fact the author of "Monos and Daimonos." "The Man in the Bell is by William Maginn (see pp. 762ff. herein). "Confessions of an English Opium Eater" was at first widely attributed to Samuel Taylor Coleridge but is actually by Thomas DeQuincey.

contents. This much, however, it is necessary to premise, that no two of these Tales will have the slightest resemblance one to the other either in matter or manner—still however preserving the character which I speak of.

* * *

From Theodore S. Fay[1]

Norman Leslie. A Tale of the Present Times.
New York: Published by Harper and Brothers.

Well!—here we have it! This is *the* book—*the* book *par excellence*—the book bepuffed, beplastered, and be-*Mirrored*: the book "attributed to" Mr. Blank, and "said to be from the pen" of Mr. Asterisk: the book which has been "about to appear"—"in press"—"in progress"—"in preparation"—and "forthcoming:" the book "graphic" in anticipation— "talented" *a priori*—and God knows what *in prospectu*. For the sake of every thing puffed, puffing, and puffable, let us take a peep at its contents!

Norman Leslie, gentle reader, a Tale of the Present Times, is, after all, written by nobody in the world but Theodore S. Fay, and Theodore S. Fay is nobody in the world but "one of the Editors of the New York Mirror." The book commences with a Dedication to Colonel Herman Thorn, in which that worthy personage, whoever he may be, is held up, in about a dozen lines, to the admiration of the public, as "hospitable," "generous," "attentive," "benevolent," "kind-hearted," "liberal," "highly-esteemed," and withal "a patron of the arts." But the less we say of this matter the better.

In the Preface Mr. Fay informs us that the most important features of his story are founded on fact—that he has availed himself of certain poetical licenses—that he has transformed character, and particularly the character of a young lady, (oh fi! Mr. Fay—oh, Mr. Fay, fi!) that he has sketched certain peculiarities with a mischievous hand—and that the art of novel writing is as dignified as the art of Canova, Mozart or Raphael,—from which we are left to infer, that Mr. Fay himself is as dignified as Raphael, Mozart, and Canova—all three. Having satisfied us on this head, he goes on to say something about an humble student, with a feeble hand, throwing groupings upon a canvass, and standing behind a curtain: and then, after perpetrating all these impertinences, thinks it best "frankly to bespeak the indulgence of the solemn and sapient critics." Body of Bacchus! *we*, at least, are neither solemn nor sapient, and, therefore, do not feel ourselves bound to show him a shadow of mercy. But will any body tell us what is the object of Prefaces in general, and what is the meaning of Mr. Fay's Preface in particular?

1. Poe's review was originally published in the *Southern Literary Messenger* of December 1835.

* * *

Thus ends the Tale of the Present Times, and thus ends the most inestimable piece of balderdash with which the common sense of the good people of America was ever so openly or so villainously insulted.

We do not mean to say that there is positively *nothing* in Mr. Fay's novel to commend—but there is indeed very little. One incident is tolerably managed, in which, at the burning house of Mr. Temple, Clairmont anticipates Leslie in his design of rescuing Flora. A cotillon scene, too, where Morton, a simple fop, is frequently interrupted in his attempts at making love to Miss Temple, by the necessity of forward-twoing and *sachezing*, (as Mr. Fay thinks proper to call it) is by no means very bad, although savoring too much of the farcical. A duel story told by Kreutzner is really good, but unfortunately not original, there being a Tale in the *Diary of a Physician*,² from which both its matter and manner are evidently borrowed. And here we are obliged to pause; for we can positively think of nothing farther worth even a qualified commendation. The plot, as will appear from the running outline we have given of it, is a monstrous piece of absurdity and incongruity. The characters *have no character*; and, with the exception of Morton, who is, (perhaps) amusing, are, one and all, vapidity itself. No attempt seems to have been made at individualization. All the good ladies and gentlemen are demi-gods and demi-goddesses, and all the bad are—the d—l. The hero, Norman Leslie, "that young and refined man with a leaning to poetry," is a great coxcomb and a great fool. What else must we think of a *bel-esprit* who, in picking up a rose just fallen from the curls of his lady fair, can hit upon no more appropriate phrase with which to make her a presentation of the same, than "Miss Temple, you have dropped your rose—allow me!"— who courts his mistress with a "Dear, dear Flora, how I love you!"— who calls a *buffet* a *bufet*, an *improvisatore* an *improvisitore*—who, before bestowing charity, is always ready with the canting question if the object be *deserving*—who is everlastingly talking of his foe "sleeping in the same red grave with himself," as if American sextons made a common practice of burying two people together—and, who having not a sous in his pocket at page 86, pulls out a handful at page 87, although he has had no opportunity of obtaining a copper in the interim?

As regards Mr. Fay's *style*, it is unworthy of a school-boy. The "Editor of the New York Mirror" has either never seen an edition of Murray's Grammar, or he has been a-Willising so long as to have forgotten his vernacular language. Let us examine one or two of his sentences at random. Page 28, vol. i. "He was doomed to wander through the *farthest* climes alone and branded." Why not say at once *farthererther-est*? Page 150, vol. i. "Yon kindling orb should be hers; and that faint spark close to its side should teach her how dim and yet how near my soul was to her own." What is the meaning of all this? Is Mr. Leslie's

2. *Passages from the Diary of a Late Physician* by Samuel Warren (1807–1877) was serialized in *Blackwood's Edinburgh Magazine* from 1830 to 1837.

soul dim to her own, as well as near to her own?—for the sentence implies as much. Suppose we say "should teach her how dim was my soul, and yet how near to her own." Page 101, vol. i. "You are both right and both wrong—you, Miss Romain, to judge so harshly of all men who are not versed in the easy elegance of the drawing room, and your father in too great lenity towards men of sense, &c." This is really something new, but we are sorry to say, something incomprehensible. Suppose we translate it. "You are both right and both wrong—you, Miss Romain, *are both right and wrong* to judge so harshly of all not versed in the elegance of the drawing-room, &c.; and your father *is both right and wrong* in too great lenity towards men of sense."—Mr. Fay, have you ever visited Ireland in your peregrinations? But the book is full to the brim of such absurdities, and it is useless to pursue the matter any farther. There is not a single page of Norman Leslie in which even a school-boy would fail to detect at least two or three gross errors in Grammar, and some two or three most egregious sins against common-sense.

We will dismiss the "Editor of the Mirror" with a few questions. When did you ever know, Mr. Fay, of any prosecuting attorney behaving so much like a bear as *your* prosecuting attorney in the novel of Norman Leslie? When did you ever hear of an American Court of Justice objecting to the testimony of a witness on the ground that the said witness *had an interest* in the cause at issue? What do you mean by informing us at page 84, vol. i, "that you *think* much faster than you write?" What do you mean by "*the wind roaring in the air?*" see page 26, vol. i. What do you mean by "an *unshadowed* Italian girl?" see page 67, vol. ii. Why are you always talking about "stamping of feet," "kindling and flashing of eyes," "plunging and parrying," "cutting and thrusting," "passes through the body," "gashes open in the cheek," "sculls cleft down," "hands cut off," and blood gushing and bubbling, and doing God knows what else—all of which pretty expressions may be found on page 88, vol. i.? What "mysterious and inexplicable destiny" compels you to the so frequent use, in all its inflections, of that euphonical dyssyllable *blister*? We will call to your recollection some few instances in which you have employed it. Page 185, vol. i. "But an arrival from the city brought the fearful intelligence in all its *blistering* and naked details." Page 193, vol. i. "What but the glaring and *blistering* truth of the charge would select him, &c." Page 39, vol. ii. "Wherever the winds of heaven wafted the English language, the *blistering* story must have been echoed." Page 150, vol. ii. "Nearly seven years had passed away, and here he found himself, as at first, still marked with the *blistering* and burning brand." Here we have a *blistering* detail, a *blistering* truth, a *blistering* story, and a *blistering* brand, to say nothing of innumerable other blisters interspersed throughout the book. But we have done with Norman Leslie,—if ever we saw as silly a thing, may we be—blistered.

From Morris Mattson[1]

Paul Ulric: Or the Adventures of an Enthusiast. New York:
Published by Harper & Brothers.

These two volumes are by Morris Mattson, Esq. of Philadelphia, and
we presume that Mr. Mattson is a very young man. Be this as it may,
when we called Norman Leslie the silliest book in the world we had
certainly never seen Paul Ulric. *One* sentence in the latter, however, is
worthy of our serious attention. "We want a few faithful laborers in
the vineyard of literature, to root out the noxious weeds which infest
it." See page 116, vol. ii.

In itself, the book before us is too purely imbecile to merit an ex-
tended critique—but as a portion of our daily literary food—as
an American work published by the Harpers—as one of a class of
absurdities with an inundation of which our country is grievously
threatened—we shall have no hesitation, and shall spare no pains, in
exposing fully before the public eye its four hundred and forty-three
pages of utter folly, bombast, and inanity.

"My name," commences Mr. Mattson, "is Paul Ulric. Thus much,
gentle reader, you already know of one whose history is about to be
recorded for the benefit of the world. I was always an enthusiast, but
of this I deem it inexpedient to say much at present. I will merely re-
mark that I possessed by nature a wild and adventurous spirit which
has led me on blindly and hurriedly, from object to object, without any
definite or specific aim. My life has been one of continual excitement,
and in my wild career I have tasted of joy as well as of sorrow. [Oh re-
markable Mr. Ulric!] At one moment I have been elevated to the very
pinnacle of human happiness, at the next I have sunk to the lowest
depths of despair. Still I fancied there was always an equilibrium. This
may seem a strange philosophy to some, but is it the less true? The
human mind is so constituted as always to seek a level—if it is de-
pressed it will be proportionately elevated, if elevated it will be propor-
tionately depressed. But" says Mr. U., interrupting himself, "I am
growing metaphysical!" We had thought he was only growing absurd.

* * *

Our hero himself was born, we are told, on the borders of the
Thames, not far from Greenwich. When a well grown lad he accom-
panies his father to the continent. In Florence he falls in love with a
Countess in her thirty-fifth year, who curls his hair and gives him
sugar-plums. The issue of the adventure with the Countess is thus
told.

> "You have chosen them with much taste," said the Countess; "a
> beautiful flower is this!" she continued, selecting one from among
> the number, "its vermillion is in your cheeks, its blue in your eyes,
> and for this pretty compliment I deserve a—— you resist eh! My
> pretty, pretty lad, I will! There! Another, and you may go free. Still

1. Poe's review was originally published in the *Southern Literary Messenger* of February 1836.

perverse? Oh, you stubborn boy! How can you refuse? One—
two—three! I shall devour you with kisses!"

We have printed the passage precisely as we find it in the book—notes
of admiration—dashes—Italics—and all. Two rows of stars wind up the
matter, and stand for the catastrophe—for we hear no more of the
Countess. Now if any person over curious should demand why Morris
Mattson, Esq. has mistaken notes of admiration for sense—dashes,
kisses, stars and Italics for sentiment—the answer is very simple indeed.
The author of Vivian Grey made the same mistake before him.

Indeed we have made up our minds to forward Ben D'Israeli[2] a copy
of Paul Ulric. He will read it, and if he do not expire upon the spot, it
will do him more real service than the crutch. Never was there a more
laughable burlesque of any man's manner. Had Mr. Mattson only *in-
tended it* as a burlesque we would have called him a clever fellow. But
unfortunately this is not the case. No jackdaw was ever more soberly
serious in fancying herself a peacock, than our author in thinking
himself D'Israeli the second.

* * *

In summing up an opinion of Paul Ulric, it is by no means our
intention to mince the matter at all. The book is despicable in every re-
spect. Such are the works which bring daily discredit upon our national
literature. We have no right to complain of being laughed at abroad
when so villainous a compound, as the thing we now hold in our hand,
of incongruous folly, plagiarism, immorality, inanity, and bombast, can
command at any moment both a puff and a publisher.

* * *

John P. Kennedy to Poe

[Baltimore, February 9, 1836]

* * *

I am greatly rejoiced at your success not only in Richmond, but
every where. My predictions have been more than fulfilled in regard to
the public favour for your literary enterprises. Let me beg you to set
down this praise at its value, as nothing, but an incentive to the ut-
most care and labour for improvement. You are strong enough now to
be criticized. Your fault is your love of the extravagant. Pray beware of
it. You find a hundred *intense* writers for one *natural* one. Some of
your *bizarreries* have been mistaken for satire—and admired too in
that character. They deserved it, but *you* did not, for you did not in-
tend them so. I like your grotesque—it is of the very best stamp, and I
am sure you will do wonders for yourself in the comic, I mean the
serio tragi comic. Do you easily keep pace with the demands of
the magazine? Avoid, by all means, the appearance of flagging. I like

2. Benjamin Disraeli (1804–1881), first earl of Beaconsfield, British statesman and novelist,
 twice prime minister of England, and author of *Vivian Grey* (1831) and other novels of the
 "Silver Fork School." He was frequently lampooned by Poe. Later in the review Poe also ac-
 cuses Mattson of plagiarizing Disraeli's father, Isaac D'Israeli.

the critical notices very well. By the by, I wish you would tell White that he never sent me the Nov^r. number.

* * *

Yours truly

John P. Kennedy.

To John P. Kennedy (Letter 57)

[Richmond, February 11, 1836]

D^r Sir,

* * *

You are nearly, but not altogether right in relation to the satire of some of my Tales. Most of them were *intended* for half banter, half satire—although I might not have fully acknowledged this to be their aim even to myself. "Lionizing" and "Loss of Breath" were satires properly speaking—at least so meant—the one of the rage for Lions and the facility of becoming one—the other of the extravagancies of Blackwood.

* * *

J. K. Paulding to T. W. White

New York, March 3, 1836.

Dear Sir,—I duly received the Book containing the Tales by Mr. Poe heretofore published in the "Messenger," and have delayed writing to you on the subject until I could communicate the final decision of the Messrs. Harpers as to their republication.

* * *

The[y] have finally declined republishing it for the following reasons: They say that the stories have so recently appeared before the Public in the "Messenger" that they would be no novelty—but most especially they object that there is a degree of obscurity in their application, which will prevent ordinary readers from comprehending their drift, and consequently from enjoying the fine satire they convey. It requires a degree of familiarity with various kinds of knowledge which they do not possess, to enable them to relish the joke: the dish is too refined for them to banquet on. They desire me, however, to state to Mr. Poe that if he will lower himself a little to the ordinary comprehension of the generality of readers, and prepare a series of original Tales, or a single work, and send them to the Publishers, previous to their appearance in the "Messenger," they will make such arrangements with him as will be liberal and satisfactory.

I regret this decision of the Harpers, though I have not opposed it, because I do not wish to lead them into any measure that might be accompanied by a loss, and felt as I would feel for myself in a similar case. I would not press a work of my own on them, nor do I think Mr. Poe would be gratified at my doing so with one of his.

I hope Mr. Poe will pardon me if the interest I feel in his success should prompt me to take this occasion to suggest to him to apply his fine humor, and his extensive acquirements, to more familiar subjects of satire; to the faults and foibles of our own people, their peculiarities of habits and manners, and above all to the ridiculous affectations and extravagancies of the fashionable English Literature of the day, which we copy with such admirable success and servility. His quiz on Willis, and the Burlesque of "Blackwood," were not only capital, but what is more, were understood by all. For Satire to be relished, it is necessary that it should be leveled at something with which readers are familiar. My own experience has taught me this, in the failure of some efforts of my own formerly.

Be good enough to let me know what disposition I shall make of the work.

<div style="text-align: right">

I am respectfully,
Your friend and Servant,
J. K. PAULDING.

</div>

From Joseph Rodman Drake—Fitz-Greene Halleck[1]

The Culprit Fay, and other Poems, by Joseph Rodman Drake. New York: George Dearborn.

Alnwick Castle, with other Poems, by Fitz-Greene Halleck. New York: George Dearborn.

Before entering upon the detailed notice which we propose of the volumes before us, we wish to speak a few words in regard to the present state of American criticism.

It must be visible to all who meddle with literary matters, that of late years a thorough revolution has been effected in the censorship of our press. That this revolution is infinitely for the worse we believe. There was a time, it is true, when we cringed to foreign opinion—let us even say when we paid a most servile deference to British critical dicta. That an American book could, by any possibility, be worthy perusal, was an idea by no means extensively prevalent in the land; and if we were induced to read at all the productions of our native writers, it was only after repeated assurances from England that such productions were not altogether contemptible. But there was, at all events, a shadow of excuse, and a slight basis of reason for a subserviency so grotesque. Even now, perhaps, it would not be far wrong to assert that such basis of reason may still exist. Let us grant that in many of the abstract sciences—that even in Theology, in Medicine, in Law, in Oratory, in the Mechanical Arts, we have no competitors whatever, still nothing but the most egregious national vanity would assign us a place, in the matter of Polite Literature, upon a level with the elder

1. Poe's review is reprinted from *Southern Literary Messenger* of April 1836.

and riper climes of Europe, the earliest steps of whose children are among the groves of magnificently endowed Academics, and whose innumerable men of leisure, and of consequent learning, drink daily from those august fountains of inspiration which burst around them every where from out the tombs of their immortal dead, and from out their hoary and trophied monument of chivalry and song. In paying then, as a nation, a respectful and not undue deference to a supremacy rarely questioned but by prejudice or ignorance, we should, of course, be doing nothing more than acting in a rational manner. The *excess* of our subserviency was blameable—but, as we have before said, this very excess might have found a shadow of excuse in the strict justice, if properly regulated, of the principle from which it issued. Not so, however, with our present follies. We are becoming boisterous and arrogant in the pride of a too speedily assumed literary freedom. We throw off, with the most presumptuous and unmeaning hauteur, *all* deference whatever to foreign opinion—we forget, in the puerile inflation of vanity, that *the world* is the true theatre of the biblical histrio—we get up a hue and cry about the necessity of encouraging native writers of merit—we blindly fancy that we can accomplish this by indiscriminate puffing of good, bad, and indifferent, without taking the trouble to consider that what we choose to denominate encouragement is thus, by its general application, rendered precisely the reverse. In a word, so far from being ashamed of the many disgraceful literary failures to which our own inordinate vanities and misapplied patriotism have lately given birth, and so far from deeply lamenting that these daily puerilities are of home manufacture, we adhere pertinaciously to our original blindly conceived idea, and thus often find ourselves involved in the gross paradox of liking a stupid book the better, because, sure enough, its stupidity is American.[2]

* * *

Who will deny that in regard to individual poems no definitive opinions can exist, so long as to Poetry in the abstract we attach no definitive idea? Yet it is a common thing to hear our critics, day after day, pronounce, with a positive air, laudatory or condemnatory sentences, *en masse*, upon metrical works of whose merits and demerits they have, in the first place, virtually confessed an utter ignorance, in confessing ignorance of all determinate principles by which to regulate a decision. Poetry has never been defined to the satisfaction of all parties. Perhaps, in the present condition of language it never will be. Words cannot hem it in. Its intangible and purely spiritual nature refuses to be bound down within the widest horizon of mere sounds. But it is not, therefore, misunderstood—at least, not by all men is it misunderstood. Very far from it. If, indeed, there be any one circle of thought distinctly and palpably marked out from amid the jarring and tumultuous chaos of human intelligence, it is that evergreen and radi-

2. This charge of indiscriminate puffing will, of course, only apply to the *general* character of our criticism—there are some noble exceptions. We wish also especially to discriminate between those *notices* of new works which are intended merely to call public attention to them, and deliberate criticism on the works themselves [Poe's note].

ant Paradise which the true poet knows, and knows alone, as the limited realm of his authority—as the circumscribed Eden of his dreams. But a definition is a thing of words—a conception of ideas. And thus while we readily believe that Poesy, the term, it will be troublesome, if not impossible to define—still, with its image vividly existing in the world, we apprehend no difficulty in so describing Poesy, the Sentiment, as to imbue even the most obtuse intellect with a comprehension of it sufficiently distinct for all the purposes of practical analysis.

To look upwards from any existence, material or immaterial, to its *design*, is, perhaps, the most direct, and the most unerring method of attaining a just notion of the nature of the existence itself. Nor is the principle at fault when we turn our eyes from Nature even to Nature's God. We find certain faculties implanted within us, and arrive at a more plausible conception of the character and attributes of those faculties, by considering, with what finite judgment we possess, the *intention* of the Deity in so implanting them within us, than by any actual investigation of their powers, or any speculative deductions from their visible and material effects. Thus, for example, we discover in all men a disposition to look with reverence upon superiority, whether real or supposititious. In some, this disposition is to be recognized with difficulty, and, in very peculiar cases, we are occasionally even led to doubt its existence altogether, until circumstances beyond the common routine bring it accidentally into development. In others again it forms a prominent and distinctive feature of character, and is rendered palpably evident in its excesses. But in all human beings it is, in a greater or less degree, finally perceptible. It has been, therefore, justly considered a primitive sentiment. Phrenologists call it Veneration. It is, indeed, the instinct given to man by God as security for his own worship. And although, preserving its nature, it becomes perverted from its principal purpose, and although, swerving from that purpose, it serves to modify the relations of human society—the relations of father and child, of master and slave, of the ruler and the ruled—its primitive essence is nevertheless the same, and by a reference to primal causes, may at any moment be determined.

Very nearly akin to this feeling, and liable to the same analysis, is the Faculty of Ideality—which is the sentiment of Poesy. This sentiment is the sense of the beautiful, of the sublime, and of the mystical.[3] Thence spring immediately admiration of the fair flowers, the fairer forests, the bright valleys and rivers and mountains of the Earth—and love of the gleaming stars and other burning glories of Heaven—and, mingled up inextricably with this love and this admiration of Heaven and of Earth, the unconquerable desire—*to know*. Poesy is the sentiment of Intellectual Happiness here, and the Hope of a higher Intellectual Happiness hereafter.[4] Imagination is its

3. We separate the sublime and the mystical—for, despite of high authorities, we are firmly convinced that the latter *may* exist, in the most vivid degree, without giving rise to the sense of the former [Poe's note].
4. The consciousness of this truth was possessed by no mortal more fully than by Shelley, although he has only once especially alluded to it. In his *Hymn to Intellectual Beauty* we find these lines [Poe's note]. Poe here quotes the poem.

Soul.[5] With the *passions* of mankind—although it may modify them greatly—although it may exalt, or inflame, or purify, or control them— it would require little ingenuity to prove that it has no inevitable, and indeed no necessary co-existence. We have hitherto spoken of Poetry in the abstract: we come now to speak of it in its every-day acceptation—that is to say, of the practical result arising from the sentiment we have considered.

And now it appears evident, that since Poetry, in this new sense, *is* the practical result, expressed in language, of this Poetic Sentiment in certain individuals, the only proper method of testing the merits of a poem is by measuring its capabilities of exciting the Poetic Sentiment in others. And to this end we have many aids—in observation, in experience, in ethical analysis, and in the dictates of common sense. Hence the *Poeta nascitur*,[6] which is indisputably true if we consider the Poetic Sentiment, becomes the merest of absurdities when we regard it in reference to the practical result. We do not hesitate to say that a man highly endowed with the powers of Causality—that is to say, a man of metaphysical acumen—will, even with a very deficient share of Ideality,[7] compose a finer poem (if we test it, as we should, by its measure of exciting the Poetic Sentiment) than one who, without such metaphysical acumen, shall be gifted, in the most extraordinary degree, with the faculty of Ideality. For a poem is not the Poetic faculty, but *the means* of exciting it in mankind. Now these means the metaphysician may discover by analysis of their effects in other cases than his own, without even conceiving the nature of these effects— thus arriving at a result which the unaided Ideality of his competitor would be utterly unable, except by accident, to attain. It is more than possible that the man who, of all writers, living or dead, has been most successful in writing the purest of all poems—that is to say, poems which excite most purely, most exclusively, and most powerfully the imaginative faculties in men—owed his extraordinary and almost magical pre-eminence rather to metaphysical than poetical powers. We allude to the author of Christabel, of the Rime of the Auncient Mariner, and of Love—to Coleridge—whose head, if we mistake not its character, gave no great phrenological tokens of Ideality, while the organs of Causality and Comparison were most singularly developed.

Perhaps at this particular moment there are no American poems held in so high estimation by our countrymen, as the poems of Drake, and of Halleck.

* * *

It is more than probable that from among ten readers of the *Culprit Fay*, nine would immediately pronounce it a poem betokening the most extraordinary powers of imagination, and of these nine, perhaps five or six, poets themselves, and fully impressed with the truth

5. Imagination is, possibly, in man, a lesser degree of the creative power in God. What the Deity imagines, *is*, but *was not* before. What man imagines, *is*, but *was* also. The mind of man cannot imagine what *is not*. This latter point may be demonstrated.—*See Les Premiers Traits de L'Erudition Universelle, par M. Le Baron de Bielfield, 1767* [Poe's note].
6. Born poet (Latin). The traditional phrase is *poeta nascitur, non fit* (a poet is born, not made).
7. See Sciences of the Mind (pp. 742ff. herein).

of what we have already assumed, that Ideality is indeed the soul of the Poetic Sentiment, would feel embarrassed between a half-consciousness that they *ought* to admire the production, and a wonder that they *do not*. This embarrassment would then arise from an indistinct conception of the results in which Ideality is rendered manifest. Of these results some few are seen in the *Culprit Fay*, but the greater part of it is utterly destitute of any evidence of imagination whatever. The general character of the poem will, we think, be sufficiently understood by any one who may have taken the trouble to read our foregoing compendium of the narrative. It will be there seen that what is so frequently termed the imaginative power of this story, lies especially—we should have rather said is thought to lie—in the passages we have quoted, or in others of a precisely similar nature. These passages embody, principally, mere specifications of qualities, of habiliments, of punishments, of occupations, of circumstances &c, which the poet has believed in unison with the size, firstly, and secondly with the nature of his Fairies. To all which may be added specifications of other animal existences (such as the toad, the beetle, the lance-fly, the fire-fly and the like) supposed also to be in accordance. An example will best illustrate our meaning upon this point—we take it from page 20.

> He put his acorn helmet on;
> It was plumed of the silk of the thistle down;
> The corslet plate that guarded his breast
> Was once the wild bee's golden vest;
> His cloak of a thousand mingled dyes,
> Was formed of the wings of butterflies;
> His shield was the shell of a lady-bug queen,
> Studs of gold on a ground of green,
> And the quivering lance which he brandished bright,
> Was the sting of a wasp he had slain in fight.

We shall now be understood. Were any of the admirers of the *Culprit Fay* asked their opinion of these lines, they would most probably speak in high terms of the *imagination* they display. Yet let the most stolid and the most confessedly unpoetical of these admirers only try the experiment, and he will find, possibly to his extreme surprise, that he himself will have no difficulty whatever in substituting for the equipments of the Fairy, as assigned by the poet, other equipments equally comfortable, no doubt, and equally in unison with the preconceived size, character, and other qualities of the equipped. Why we could accoutre him as well ourselves—let us see.

> His blue-bell helmet, we have heard,
> Was plumed with the down of the humming-bird,
> The corslet on his bosom bold
> Was once the locust's coat of gold,
> His cloak, of a thousand mingled hues,
> Was the velvet violet, wet with dews,
> His target was the crescent shell

Of the small sea Sidrophel,
And a glittering beam from a maiden's eye
Was the lance which he proudly wav'd on high.

The truth is, that the only requisite for writing verses of this nature, *ad libitum*,[8] is a tolerable acquaintance with the qualities of the objects to be detailed, and a very moderate endowment of the faculty of Comparison—which is the chief constituent of *Fancy* or the powers of combination. A thousand such lines may be composed without exercising in the least degree the Poetic Sentiment, which is Ideality, Imagination, or the creative ability. And, as we have before said, the greater portion of the *Culprit Fay* is occupied with these, or similar things, and upon such, depends very nearly, if not altogether, its reputation.

* * *

But if these things evince no Ideality in their author, do they not excite it in others?—if so, we must conclude, that without being himself imbued with the Poetic Sentiment, he has still succeeded in writing a fine poem—a supposition as we have before endeavored to show, not altogether paradoxical. Most assuredly we think not. In the case of a great majority of readers the only sentiment aroused by compositions of this order is a species of vague wonder at the writer's *ingenuity*, and it is this indeterminate sense of wonder which passes but too frequently current for the proper influence of the Poetic power. For our own parts we plead guilty to a predominant sense of the ludicrous while occupied in the perusal of the poem before us—a sense whose promptings we sincerely and honestly endeavored to quell, perhaps not altogether successfully, while penning our compend of the narrative. That a feeling of this nature is utterly at war with the Poetic Sentiment, will not be disputed by those who comprehend the character of the sentiment itself. This character is finely shadowed out in that popular although vague idea so prevalent throughout all time, that a species of melancholy is inseparably connected with the higher manifestations of the beautiful. But with the numerous and seriously-adduced incongruities of the Culprit Fay, we find it generally impossible to connect other ideas than those of the ridiculous. We are bidden, in the first place, and in a tone of sentiment and language adapted to the loftiest breathings of the Muse, to imagine a race of Fairies in the vicinity of West Point. We are told, with a grave air, of their camp, of their king, and especially of their sentry, who is a wood-tick. We are informed that an Ouphe of about an inch in height has committed a deadly sin in falling in love with a mortal maiden, who may, very possibly, be six feet in her stockings. The consequence to the Ouphe is—what? Why, that he has "dyed his wings," "broken his elfin chain," and "quenched his flame-wood lamp." And he is therefore sentenced to what? To catch a spark from the tail of a falling star, and a drop of water from the belly of a sturgeon. What are his equipments for the first adventure? An acorn helmet, a thistle-down plume, a butterfly cloak, a lady-

8. As one wishes; with freedom (Latin). Cf. the term *ad lib*, "to improvise."

bug shield, cockle-seed spurs, and a fire-fly horse. How does he ride to the second? On the back of a bull-frog. What are his opponents in the one? "Drizzly mists," "sulphur and smoke," "shadowy hands" and "flame-shot tongues." What in the other? "Mailed shrimps," "prickly prongs," "blood-red leeches," "jellied quarls," "stony star fishes," "lancing squabs" and "soldier crabs." Is that all? No—Although only an inch high he is in imminent danger of seduction from a "sylphid queen," dressed in a mantle of "rolled purple," "tied with threads of dawning gold," "buttoned with a sparkling star," and sitting under a rainbow with "beamlet eyes" and a countenance of "lily roon." In our account of all this matter we have had reference to the book—and to the book alone. It will be difficult to prove us guilty in any degree of distortion or exaggeration. Yet such are the puerilities we daily find ourselves called upon to admire, as among the loftiest efforts of the human mind, and which not to assign a rank with the proud trophies of the matured and vigorous genius of England, is to prove ourselves at once a fool, a maligner, and no patriot.[9]

* * *

In a world where evil is a mere consequence of good, and good a mere consequence of evil—in short where all of which we have any conception is good or bad only by comparison—we have never yet been fully able to appreciate the validity of that decision which would debar the critic from enforcing upon his readers the merits or demerits of a work by placing it in juxta-position with another. It seems to us that an adage based in the purest ignorance has had more to do with this popular feeling than any just reason founded upon common sense. Thinking thus, we shall have no scruple in illustrating our opinion in regard to what *is not* Ideality or the Poetic Power, by an example of what *is*.[1]

* * *

It will be seen that the Fairy of Shelley is not a mere compound of incongruous natural objects, inartificially put together, and unaccompanied by any *moral* sentiment—but a being, in the illustration of whose nature some physical elements are used collaterally as adjuncts, while the main conception springs immediately *or thus apparently springs*, from the brain of the poet, enveloped in the moral sentiments of grace, of color, of motion—of the beautiful, of the mystical, of the august—in short of *the ideal.*

* * *

9. A review of Drake's poems, emanating from one of our proudest Universities, does not scruple to make use of the following language in relation to the *Culprit Fay.* "It is, to say the least, an elegant production, the purest specimen of Ideality we have ever met with, sustaining in each incident a most bewitching interest. Its very title is enough," &c. &c. We quote these expressions as a fair specimen of the general unphilosophical and adulatory tenor of our criticism [Poe's note].
1. As examples of entire poems of the purest ideality, we would cite the *Prometheus Vinctus* of Æschylus, the *Inferno* of Dante, Cervantes' *Destruction of Numantia*, the *Comus* of Milton, Pope's *Rape of the Lock*, Burns' *Tam O' Shanter*, the *Ancient Mariner*, the *Christabel*, and the *Kubla Khan* of Coleridge; and most especially the *Sensitive Plant* of Shelley, and the *Nightingale* of Keats. We have seen American poems evincing the faculty in the highest degree. [Poe's note]. Poe goes on to compare Drake's poem with Shelly's *Queen Mab* (1812–13).

Halleck's poetical powers appear to us essentially inferior, upon the whole, to those of his friend Drake.

[Poe continues for several paragraphs to list Halleck's weaknesses as a poet.]

But we must bring our notice to a close. It will be seen that while we are willing to admire in many respects the poems before us, we feel obliged to dissent materially from that public opinion (perhaps not fairly ascertained) which would assign them a very brilliant rank in the empire of Poesy. That we have among us poets of the loftiest order we believe—but we do *not* believe that these poets are Drake and Halleck.

To Harrison Hall (Letter 74)[1]

Richmond Sep: 2. 1836.

Dr Sir,

* * *

At different times there has appeared in the Messenger a series of Tales, by myself—in all seventeen. They are of a bizarre and generally whimsical character, and were originally written to illustrate a large work "On the Imaginative Faculties." I have prepared them for republication, in book form, in the following manner. I imagine a company of 17 persons who call themselves the Folio Club. They meet once a month at the house of one of the members, and, at a late dinner, each member reads aloud a short prose tale of his own composition. The votes are taken in regard to the merits of each tale. The author of the worst tale, for the month, forfeits the dinner & wine at the next meeting. The author of the best, is President at the next meeting. The seventeen tales which appeared in the Messr are supposed to be narrated by the seventeen members at one of these monthly meetings. As soon as <one> each tale is read—the other 16 members criticise it in turn—and these criticisms are intended as a burlesque upon criticism generally. The author of the tale adjudged to be the worst demurs from the general judgment, seizes the seventeen M.SS. upon the table, and, rushing from the house, determines to appeal, by printing the whole, from the decision of the Club, to that of the public. The critical remarks, *which have never been published*, will make about ¼ of the whole—the whole will form a volume of about 300 close pages. oct.

I refer you for the reputation of these tales to the covers of the 1rst & 2d vols. Lit. Messr—A mass of eulogy, in the way of extracts from papers, might be appended if necessary, *such as have never appeared to any volume in the country*. I mention this merely as a matter of business.

1. Harrison Hall was a Philadelphia printer who had acted as publisher of the magazine *Port-Folio* (1816–27). Poe, writing to him on behalf of T. W. White regarding business matters for the *Messenger*, took the opportunity to promote his collection of stories, now expanded from eleven to seventeen. Text in angle brackets had been canceled.

My object in stating the nature of these tales &c is to ascertain if you, or any bookseller of your acquaintance, would feel willing to undertake the publication. I make you the first offer. In regard to remuneration, as ¾ of the book will have been published before, I shall expect none beyond a few copies of the work. My interest with the press throughout the U.S. is perhaps as extensive as that of any man in the country, and would aid the sale, no doubt. Please write me, as soon as possible, on this head. I shall be happy to review, fully, any books you may be pleased to forward.

* * *

From Robert M. Bird[1]

Sheppard Lee: written by himself. New York: Harper and Brothers.

* * *

We must regard "Sheppard Lee," upon the whole, as a very clever, and not altogether unoriginal, *jeu d'esprit*. Its incidents are well conceived, and related with force, brevity, and a species of *directness* which is invaluable in certain cases of narration—while in others it should be avoided. The language is exceedingly unaffected and (what we regard as high praise) exceedingly well adapted to the varying subjects. Some fault may be found with the conception of the metempsychosis which is the basis of the narrative. There are two general methods of telling stories such as this. One of these methods is that adopted by the author of Sheppard Lee. He conceives his hero endowed with some idiosyncracy beyond the common lot of human nature, and thus introduces him to a series of adventures which, under ordinary circumstances, could occur only to a plurality of persons. The chief source of interest in such narrative is, or should be, the contrasting of these varied events, in their influence upon a character *unchanging*—except as changed by the events themselves. This fruitful field of interest, however, is neglected in the novel before us, where the hero, very awkwardly, partially loses, and partially does not lose, his identity, at each transmigration. The sole object here in the various metempsychoses seem to be, merely the depicting of seven different conditions of existence, and the enforcement of the very doubtful moral that every person should remain contented with his own. But it is clear that both these points could have been more forcibly shown, without any reference to a confused and jarring system of transmigration, by the mere narrations of seven different individuals. All deviations, especially wide ones, from nature, should be justified to the author by some specific object—the object, in the present case, might have been found, as above-mentioned, in the opportunity afforded of depicting widely-different conditions of existence actuating *one* individual.

1. Poe's text is reprinted from *Southern Literary Messenger* for September 1836. Poe begins with a very long and detailed plot summary of Robert Montgomery Bird's psycho-supernatural novel, which involves among other things metempsychosis or the transmigration of souls.

A second peculiarity of the species of novel to which Sheppard Lee belongs, and a peculiarity which is *not* rejected by the author, is the treating the whole narrative in a jocular manner throughout (inasmuch as to say "I know I am writing nonsense, but then you must excuse me for the very reason that I know it") or the solution of the various absurdities by means of a dream, or something similar. The latter method is adopted in the present instance—and the idea is managed with unusual ingenuity. Still—having read through the whole book, and having been worried to death with incongruities (allowing such to exist) until the concluding page, it is certainly little indemnification for our sufferings to learn that, in truth, the whole matter was a dream, and that we were very wrong in being worried about it at all. The damage is done, and the apology does not remedy the grievance. For this and other reasons, we are led to prefer, in this kind of writing, the *second* general method to which we have alluded. It consists in a variety of points—principally in avoiding, as may easily be done, that *directness* of expression which we have noticed in Sheppard Lee, and thus leaving much to the imagination—in writing as if the author were firmly impressed with the truth, yet astonished at the immensity, of the wonders he relates, and for which, professedly, he neither claims nor anticipates credence—in minuteness of detail, especially upon points which have no immediate bearing upon the general story—this minuteness not being at variance with indirectness of expression—in short, by making use of the infinity of arts which give verisimilitude to a narration—and by leaving the result as a wonder not to be accounted for. It will be found that *bizzarreries* thus conducted, are usually far more effective than those otherwise managed. The attention of the author, who does not depend upon explaining away his incredibilities, is directed to giving them the character and the luminousness of truth, and thus are brought about, unwittingly, some of the most vivid creations of human intellect. The reader, too, readily perceives and falls in with the writer's humor, and suffers himself to be borne on thereby. On the other hand what difficulty, or inconvenience, or danger can there be in leaving us uninformed of the important facts that a certain hero *did not* actually discover the elixir vitæ, *could not* really make himself invisible, and *was not* either a ghost in good earnest, or a bonâ fide Wandering Jew?

Baron de la Motte Fouqué Poe's review was originally published in *Burton's Gentleman's Magazine* in September 1839. Friedrich Heinrich Karl, Baron de la Motte Fouqué (1777–1843), German poet and novelist, popular author of romances, is best known for the fairy tale love story *Undine* (1811). It was frequently translated and republished; Poe's review was occasioned by its new publication in English in Colman's Library of Romance in 1839. After the opening paragraph of the review, Poe gives a detailed summary. In brief, one Sir Huldbrand seeks the favors of the Lady Bertalda, who sends him on a quest into an enchanted forest. On a wooded peninsula jutting out into a mysterious lake, the knight encoun-

ters an old fisherman, his wife, and their "daughter," Undine. The knight falls in love with the girl, who is actually a water sprite, one of a race of "other" beings who have no immortal soul and who vanish completely at death. Undine, in love, desires a soul—which she can attain only by union with an earthly mortal. The couple marries, but little by little the knight's love for Undine ebbs—especially when they leave the forest and arrive at the court of the Lady Bertalda. It turns out that Bertalda is actually the stolen mortal daughter of the fisherman and that a ruling water god had "replaced" her with Undine. Broken hearted, Undine returns to the world of water spirits. Sir Huldbrand eventually marries Lady Bertalda—despite a dream in which it is revealed that by the laws of the water-spirit world Undine will be forced to destroy him if he remarries—which she does.

From Baron de la Motte Fouqué

Undine: A Miniature Romance, from the German of Baron de la Motte Fouqué. Colman's Library of Romance. Edited by Grenville Mellen. Samuel Colman. New York.

The re-publication of such a work as "Undine," in the very teeth of our anti-romantic national character, is an experiment well adapted to excite interest, and in the crisis caused by this experiment—for a crisis it is—it becomes the duty of every lover of literature for its own sake and spiritual uses, to speak out, and speak boldly, against the untenable prejudices which have so long and so unopposedly enthralled us. It becomes, we say, his plain duty to show, with what ability he may possess, the full value and capacity of that species of writing generally, which, as a people, we are too prone to discredit.

* * *

This is an exceedingly meagre outline of the leading events of the story; which, although brief, is crowded with incident. Beneath all, there runs a mystic or under-current of meaning, of the simplest and most easily intelligible, yet of the most richly philosophical character. From internal evidence afforded by the book itself, we gather that the author has deeply suffered from the ills of an ill-assorted marriage— and to the bitter reflections induced by these ills, we owe the conception and peculiar execution of "Undine."

In the contrast between the artless, thoughtless, and careless character of Undine before possessing a soul, and her serious, enwrapped, and anxious, yet happy condition after possessing it—a condition which, with all its multiform cares and disquietudes, she still feels to be preferable to her original fate—M. Fouqué has beautifully painted the difference between the heart unused to love, and the heart which has received its inspiration.

The jealousies which follow the marriage, arising from the conduct of Bertalda, are the natural troubles of love—but the persecutions of Kuhleborn and the other water-spirits, who take umbrage at Huldbrand's treatment of his wife, are meant to picture certain difficulties

from the interference of relations in conjugal matters—difficulties which the author has himself experienced. The warning of Undine to Huldbrand—"reproach me not upon the waters, or we part for ever"— is meant to embody the truth that quarrels between man and wife, are seldom or never irremediable unless when taking place in the presence of third parties. The second wedding of the knight, with his gradual forgetfulness of Undine and Undine's intense grief beneath the waters—are dwelt upon so pathetically and so passionately—that there can be no doubt of the personal opinions of the author on the subject of such marriages—no doubt of his deep personal interest in the question. How thrillingly are these few and simple words made to convey his belief that the *mere death* of a beloved wife does not imply a final separation so complete as to justify an union with another— "The fisherman had loved Undine with exceeding tenderness, and it was a doubtful conclusion to his mind, that the mere disappearance of his beloved child could be properly viewed as her death!" This is where the old man is endeavoring to dissuade the knight from wedding Bertalda.

We have no hesitation in saying that this portion of the design of the romance—the portion which conveys an under-current of meaning—does not afford the fairest field to the romanticist—does not appertain to the higher regions of ideality. Although, in this case, the plan is essentially distinct from Allegory, yet it has too close an affinity to that most indefensible species of writing—a species whose gross demerits we cannot now pause to examine. That M. Fouqué was well aware of the disadvantage under which he labored—that he well knew the field he traversed not to be the fairest—and that a personal object alone induced him to choose it—we cannot and shall not doubt. For the hand of the master is visible in every line of his beautiful fable. "Undine" is a model of models, in regard to the high artistical talent which it evinces. We could write volumes in a detailed commentary upon its various beauties in this respect. Its unity is absolute—its keeping unbroken. Yet every minute point of the picture fills and satisfies the eye. Every thing is attended to, and nothing is out of time or out of place.

We say that some private and personal design to be fulfilled has thrown M. Fouqué upon that objectionable under-current of meaning which he has so elaborately managed. Yet his high genius has nearly succeeded in turning the blemish into a beauty. At all events he has succeeded, in spite of a radical defect, in producing what we advisedly consider the finest romance in existence. We say this with a bitter kind of half-consciousness that only a very few will fully agree with us—yet these few are our all in such matters. They will stand by us in a just opinion.

Were we to pick out *points* for admiration in Undine, we should pick out the greater portion of the story. We cannot say whether the novelty of its conception, or the loftiness of its ideality, or its intense pathos, or its rigorous simplicity, or that high artistical talent with which all are combined, is the particular to be chiefly admired. Addressing those

who have read the book, we may call attention to the delicacy and grace of transition from subject to subject—a point which never fails to test the power of the writer—as, for example, at page 128, when, for the purposes of the story, it becomes necessary that the knight, with Undine and Bertalda, shall proceed down the Danube. An ordinary novelist would have here tormented both himself and his readers, in his search for a sufficient *motive* for the voyage. But, in connexion with a fable such as Undine, how all-sufficient seems the simple motive assigned by Fouqué!—"In this grateful union of friendship and affection winter came and passed away; and spring, with its foliage of tender green, and its heaven of softest blue, succeeded to gladden the hearts of the three inmates of the castle. The season was in harmony with their minds, and their minds imparted their own hues to the season. *What wonder, then, that its storks and swallows inspired them also with a disposition to travel!*"

Again, we might dwell upon the exquisite *management of imagination*, which is so visible in the passages where the brooks are waterspirits, and the water-spirits brooks—neither distinctly either. What can be more ethereally ideal than the frequent indeterminate glimpses caught of Kuhleborn—or than his singular and wild lapses into shower and foam?—or than the evanishing of the white wagoner and his white horses into the shrieking and devouring flood?—or than the gentle melting of the passionately-weeping bride into the chrystal waters of the Danube? What can be more divine than the character of the soul-less Undine?—what more august than her transition into the soul-possessing wife? What can be more intensely beautiful than the whole book? We calmly think—yet cannot help asserting with enthusiasm—that the whole wide range of fictitious literature embraces nothing comparable in loftiness of conception, or in felicity of execution, to those final passages of the volume before us which embody the uplifting of the stone from the fount by the order of Bertalda, the sorrowful and silent re-advent of Undine, and the rapturous death of Sir Huldbrand in the embraces of his spiritual wife.

To Philip P. Cooke (Letter 82)[1]

Philadelphia
Sep. 21rst. 1839.

My Dear Sir,

* * *

I say that I read your letter with delight. In fact, I am aware of *no* delight greater than that of feeling one's self appreciated (in such wild matters as Ligeia) by those in whose judgment one has faith. You read my most intimate spirit "like a book"—and, with the single exception of D'Israeli, I have had communication with no other person who

1. The text reprinted here is the corrected version added to a later edition of Poe's *Letters* by John Ward Ostrom. Poe's claims of laudatory remarks by Washington Irving and others seem to be either false or suspect.

does. Willis had a glimpse of it—Judge Tucker[2] saw about ½ way through—but your ideas are the very echo of my own. I am very far from meaning to flatter—I am flattered, and honored. Beside me is now lying a letter from Washington Irving in which he speaks with enthusiasm of a late Tale of mine "The Fall of the House of Usher"—and in which he promises to make his opinion public upon the first good opportunity—but, from the bottom of my heart I assure you, I regard his best word as but dust in the balance, when weighed with those discriminating opinions of your own which teach me that you feel and perceive.

Touching Ligeia, you are right—all right—throughout. The *gradual* perception of the fact that Ligeia lives again in the person of Rowena, is a far loftier and more thrilling idea than the one I have embodied. It offers, in my opinion, the widest possible scope to the imagination—it might be rendered even sublime. And this idea was mine—had I never written before I should have adopted it—but then there is Morella. Do you remember, there, the *gradual* conviction on the part of the parent that the spirit of the first Morella tenants the person of the second? It was necessary, since Morella was written, to modify Ligeia. I was forced to be content with a sudden half-consciousness, on the part of the narrator, that Ligeia stood before him. One point I have not fully carried out—I should have intimated that the *will* did not perfect its intention—there sh[d] have been a relapse—a final one—and Ligeia (who had only succeeded in so much as to convey an idea of the truth to the narrator) should be at length entombed as Rowena—the bodily alterations having gradually faded away.

But since Morella is upon record, I will suffer Ligeia to remain as it is. Your word that it is "intelligible" suffices—and your commentary sustains your word. As for the mob—let them talk on. I should be grieved if I thought they comprehended me here.

* * *

From Thomas Moore[1]

Alciphron, a Poem. By Thomas Moore, Esq., author of Lalla Rookh, etc., etc. Carey and Hart, Philadelphia.

Amid the vague mythology of Egypt, the voluptuous scenery of her Nile, and the gigantic mysteries of her pyramids, Anacreon Moore has found all of that striking *materiel* which he so much delights in working up, and which he has embodied in the poem before us. The design of the story (for plot it has none) has been a less consideration than its facilities, and is made subservient to its execution. The subject is comprised in five epistles. In the first, Alciphron, the head of the Epi-

2. I.e., Nathaniel Beverley Tucker (1784–1851). Benjamin Disraeli (1804–1881) was prime minister of England and a popular novelist, whose works Poe had satirized several times.
1. Poe's review was originally published in *Burton's Gentleman's Magazine*, January 1840. Cf. notes on Moore in "Al Aaraaf" (pp. 22ff. herein).

curean sect at Athens, writes, from Alexandria, to his friend Cleon, in the former city. He tells him (assigning a reason for quitting Athens and her pleasures) that, having fallen asleep one night after protracted festivity, he beholds, in a dream, a spectre, who tells him that, beside the sacred Nile, he, the Epicurean, shall find that Eternal Life for which he had so long been sighing. In the second, from the same to the same, the traveller speaks, at large, and in rapturous terms, of the scenery of Egypt; of the beauty of her maidens; of an approaching Festival of the Moon; and of a wild hope entertained that amid the subterranean chambers of some huge pyramid lies the secret which he covets, the secret of Life Eternal. In the third letter, he relates a love adventure at the Festival. Fascinated by the charms of one of the nymphs of a procession, he is first in despair at losing sight of her, then overjoyed at again seeing her in Necropolis, and finally traces her steps until they are lost near one of the smaller pyramids. In epistle the fourth, (still from the same to the same,) he enters and explores the pyramid, and, passing through a complete series of Eleusinian mysteries, is at length successfully initiated into the secrets of Memphian priestcraft; we learning this latter point from letter the fifth, which concludes the poem, and is addressed by Orcus, high priest of Memphis, to Decius, a prætorian prefect.[2]

A new poem from Moore calls to mind that critical opinion respecting him which had its origin, we believe, in the dogmatism of Coleridge—we mean the opinion that he is essentially the poet of *fancy*—the term being employed in contradistinction to *imagination*. "The fancy," says the author of the "Auncient Mariner," in his *Biographia Literaria*, "the fancy combines, the imagination creates." And this was intended, and has been received, as a distinction. If so at all, it is one without a difference; without even a difference of *degree*. The fancy as nearly creates as the imagination; and neither creates in any respect. All novel conceptions are merely unusual combinations. The mind of man can *imagine* nothing which has not really existed; and this point is susceptible of the most positive demonstration—see the Baron de Bielfeld, in his *Premiers Traits de L'Erudition Universelle*, 1767. It will be said, perhaps, that we can imagine a *griffin*, and that a griffin does not exist. Not the griffin certainly, but its component parts. It is a mere compendium of known limbs and features—of known qualities. Thus with all which seems to be *new*—which appears to be a *creation* of intellect. It is resoluble into the old. The wildest and most vigorous effort of mind cannot stand the test of this analysis.

We might make a distinction, *of degree*, between the fancy and the imagination, in saying that the latter is the former *loftily employed*. But experience proves this distinction to be unsatisfactory. What we *feel* and *know* to be fancy, will be found still only *fanciful*, whatever be the theme which engages it. It retains its idiosyncrasy under all circumstances. No *subject* exalts it into the ideal. We might exemplify this by reference to the writings of one whom our patriotism, rather

2. For glosses on Poe's occultism, see Barton Levi St. Armand on pp. 873ff. herein.

than our judgment, has elevated to a niche in the Poetic Temple which he does not becomingly fill, and which he cannot long uninterruptedly hold. We allude to the late Dr. Rodman Drake, whose puerile abortion, "The Culprit Fay," we examined, at some length, in a *critique* elsewhere;[3] proving it, we think, beyond all question, to belong to that class of the pseudo-ideal, in dealing with which we find ourselves embarrassed between a kind of half-consciousness that we ought to admire, and the certainty that we do not.

* * *

The truth is that the just distinction between the fancy and the imagination (and which is still but a distinction *of degree*) is involved in the consideration of the *mystic*. We give this as an idea of our own, altogether. We have no authority for our opinion—but do not the less firmly hold it. The term *mystic* is here employed in the sense of Augustus William Schlegel, and of most other German critics.[4] It is applied by them to that class of composition in which there lies beneath the transparent upper current of meaning, an under or *suggestive* one. What we vaguely term the *moral* of any sentiment is its mystic or secondary expression. It has the vast force of an accompaniment in music. This vivifies the air; that spiritualizes the *fanciful* conception, and lifts it into the *ideal*.

This theory will bear, we think, the most rigorous tests which can be made applicable to it, and will be acknowledged as tenable by all who are themselves imaginative. If we carefully examine those poems, or portions of poems, or those prose romances, which mankind have been accustomed to designate as *imaginative*, (for an instinctive feeling leads us to employ properly the term whose full import we have still never been able to define,) it will be seen that all so designated are remarkable for the *suggestive* character which we have discussed. They are strongly *mystic*—in the proper sense of the word. We will here only call to the reader's mind, the *Prometheus Vinctus* of Æschylus; the *Inferno* of Dante; the *Destruction of Numantia* by Cervantes; the *Comus* of Milton; the *Auncient Mariner*, the *Christabel*, and the *Kubla Khan*, of Coleridge; the *Nightingale* of Keats; and, most especially, the *Sensitive Plant* of Shelley, and the *Undine* of De La Motte Fouqué.[5] These two latter poems (for we call them both such) are the finest possible examples of the purely *ideal*. There is little of fancy here, and every thing of imagination. With each note of the lyre is heard a ghostly, and not always a distinct, but an august and soul-exalting *echo*. In every glimpse of beauty presented, we catch, through long and wild vistas, dim bewildering visions of a far more ethereal beauty *beyond*. But not so in poems which the world has always persisted in terming *fanciful*. Here the upper current is often exceedingly brilliant and beautiful; but then men *feel* that this upper current *is all*. No Naiad voice addresses them *from below*. The notes of the air of the song do not tremble with the according tones of the accompaniment.

3. See the selections from this review on pp. 604ff. herein.
4. See the selections from Schlegel and other German critics in the Transcendentalism and Alternative Romanticism section on pp. 717ff. herein.
5. See the selections from Poe's review of Fouqué's *Undine* on pp. 613ff. herein.

It is the failure to perceive these truths which has occasioned that embarrassment which our critics experience while discussing the topic of Moore's station in the poetic world—that hesitation with which we are obliged to refuse him the loftiest rank among the most noble.

* * *

We proceed with a few random observations upon Alciphron. The poem is distinguished throughout by a very happy facility which has never been mentioned in connection with its author, but which has much to do with the reputation he has obtained. We allude to the facility with which he recounts a poetical story in a *prosaic* way. By this is meant that he preserves the tone and method of arrangement of a prose relation, and thus obtains great advantages over his more stilted compeers. His is no poetical *style*, (such, for example, as the French have—a distinct style for a distinct purpose,) but an easy and ordinary prose manner, *ornamented into poetry.* * * *

While Moore does not reach, except in rare snatches, the height of the loftiest qualities of some whom we have named, yet he has written finer poems than any, of equal length, by the greatest of his rivals. His radiance, not always as bright as some flashes from other pens, is yet a radiance of equable glow, whose total amount of light exceeds, by very much, we think, that total amount in the case of any co[n]temporary writer whatsoever. A vivid fancy; an epigrammatic spirit; a fine taste; vivacity, dexterity and a musical ear; have made him very easily what he is, the most popular poet now living—if not the most popular that ever lived—and, perhaps, a slight modification at birth of that which phrenologists have agreed to term *temperament*, might have made him the truest and noblest votary of the muse of any age or clime. As it is, we have only casual glimpses of that *mens divinior*[6] which is assuredly enshrined within him.

Preface

(Tales of the Grotesque and Arabesque—1840)

The Epithets "Grotesque" and "Arabesque" will be found to indicate with sufficient precision the prevalent tenor of the tales here published. But from the fact that, during a period of some two or three years, I have written five-and-twenty short stories whose general character may be so briefly defined, it cannot be fairly inferred—at all events it is not truly inferred—that I have, for this species of writing, any inordinate, or indeed any peculiar taste or prepossession. I may have written with an eye to this republication in volume form, and may, therefore, have desired to preserve, as far as a certain point, a certain unity of design. This is, indeed, the fact; and it may even happen that, in this manner, I shall never compose anything again. I speak of these things here, because I am led to think it is this prevalence of the "Arabesque" in my serious tales, which has induced one

6. Divine mind or heart (Latin).

or two critics to tax me, in all friendliness, with what they have been pleased to term "Germanism" and gloom. The charge is in bad taste, and the grounds of the accusation have not been sufficiently considered. Let us admit, for the moment, that the "phantasy-pieces" now given *are* Germanic, or what not. Then Germanism is "the vein" for the time being. To morrow I may be anything but German, as yesterday I was everything else. These many pieces are yet one book. My friends would be quite as wise in taxing an astronomer with too much astronomy, or an ethical author with treating too largely of morals. But the truth is that, with a single exception, there is no one of these stories in which the scholar should recognise the distinctive features of that species of pseudo-horror which we are taught to call Germanic, for no better reason than that some of the secondary names of German literature have become identified with its folly. If in many of my productions terror has been the thesis, I maintain that terror is not of Germany, but of the soul,—that I have deduced this terror only from its legitimate sources, and urged it only to its legitimate results.

There are one or two of the articles here, (conceived and executed in the purest spirit of extravaganza,) to which I expect no serious attention, and of which I shall speak no farther. But for the rest I cannot conscientiously claim indulgence on the score of hasty effort. I think it best becomes me to say, therefore, that if I have sinned, I have deliberately sinned. These brief compositions are, in chief part, the results of matured purpose and very careful elaboration.

Prospectus of *The Penn Magazine*[1]

A Monthly Literary Journal, to be Edited and Published in the City of Philadelphia.

To THE PUBLIC.—Since resigning the conduct of The Southern Literary Messenger, at the commencement of its third year, I have had always in view the establishment of a Magazine which should retain some of the chief features of that Journal, abandoning or greatly modifying the rest. Delay, however, has been occasioned by a variety of causes, and not until now have I found myself at liberty to attempt the execution of the design.

I will be pardoned for speaking more directly of The Messenger. Having in it no proprietary right, my objects too being at variance in many respects with those of its very worthy owner, I found difficulty in stamping upon its pages that *individuality* which I believe essential to the full success of all similar publications. In regard to their perma-

1. Privately printed in 1840 as a broadside; i.e., a large sheet of paper printed on one side (also called a broadsheet). Cf. Poe's second attempt three years later to create his own magazine closely parallel to the lines suggested here; see "Prospectus of the Stylus" (published in the *Philadelphia Saturday Museum*, March 4, 1843). In both, Poe is punning on the word for a writer's pen (*The Penn Magazine* suggests Pennsylvania, and *stylus* is an archaic word for a sharp-pointed pen).

nent influence, it appears to me that a continuous, definite character, and a marked certainty of purpose, are desiderata of vital importance, and only attainable where one mind alone has the general direction of the undertaking. Experience has rendered obvious, what might indeed have been demonstrated *a priori*;[2] that in founding a Magazine of my own lies my sole chance of carrying out to completion whatever peculiar intentions I may have entertained.

To those who remember the early days of the Southern periodical in question it will be scarcely necessary to say that its main feature was a somewhat overdone causticity in its department of Critical Notices of new books. The Penn Magazine will retain this trait of severity in so much only as the calmest yet sternest sense of justice will permit. Some years since elapsed may have mellowed down the petulance without interfering with the rigor of the critic. Most surely they have not yet taught him to read through the medium of a publisher's will, nor convinced him that the interests of letters are unallied with the interests of truth. It shall be the first and chief purpose of the Magazine now proposed to become known as one where may be found at all times, and upon all subjects, an honest and a fearless opinion. It shall be a leading object to assert in precept, and to maintain in practice the rights, while in effect it demonstrates the advantages, of an absolutely independent criticism—a criticism self-sustained; guiding itself only by the purest rules of Art; analyzing and urging these rules as it applies them; holding itself aloof from all personal bias; acknowledging no fear save that of outraging the right; yielding no point either to the vanity of the author, or to the assumptions of antique prejudice, or to the involute and anonymous cant of the Quarterlies, or to the arrogance of those organized *cliques* which, hanging like nightmares upon American literature, manufacture, at the nod of our principal booksellers, a pseudo-public-opinion by wholesale. These are objects of which no man need be ashamed. They are purposes, moreover, whose novelty at least will give them interest. For assurance that I will fulfil them in the best spirit and to the very letter, I appeal with confidence to the many thousands of my friends, and especially of my Southern friends, who sustained me in the Messenger, where I had but a very partial opportunity of completing my own plans.

In respect to the other features of the Penn Magazine, a few words here will suffice. It will endeavour to support the general interests of the republic of letters, without reference to particular regions; regarding the world at large as the true audience of the author. Beyond the precincts of literature, properly so called, it will leave in better hands the task of instruction upon all matters of *very* grave moment. Its aim chiefly shall be *to please*; and this through means of versatility, originality, and pungency. It may be as well here to observe that nothing said in this Prospectus should be construed into a design of sullying the Magazine with any tincture of the buffoonery, scurrility, or profan-

2. Here meaning beforehand, deductively.

ity, which are the blemish of some of the most vigorous of the European prints. In all branches of the literary department, the best aid, from the highest and purest sources, is secured.

To the mechanical execution of the work the greatest attention will be given which such a matter can require. In this respect it is proposed to surpass, by very much; the ordinary Magazine style. The form will nearly resemble that of The Knickerbocker; the paper will be equal to that of The North American Review; the pictorial embellishments will be numerous, and by the leading artists of the country, but will be introduced only in the necessary illustration of the text.

The Penn Magazine will be published in Philadelphia, on the first of each month, and will form, half-yearly, a volume of about 500 pages. The price will be $5 per annum, payable in advance, or upon the receipt of the first number, which will be issued on the first of January, 1841. Letters addressed to the Editor and Proprietor,

EDGAR A. POE.
1840

To William E. Burton (Letter 93)

[Philadelphia, June 1, 1840]
Sir:

* * *

As for the rest, you do me gross injustice; and you know it. As usual you have wrought yourself into a passion with me on account of some imaginary wrong; for no real injury, or attempt at injury, have you ever received at my hands. As I live, I am utterly unable to say why you are angry, or what true grounds of complaint you have against me. You are a man of <high passions>[1] impulses; have made yourself, in consequence, some enemies; have been in many respects ill treated by those whom you had looked upon as friends—and these things have rendered you suspicious. You once wrote in your magazine [a sharp critique] upon a book of mine—a [very silly book—Pym. Had I written a simi]lar critici[sm] upon a book of yours, you feel that you would [have been] my enemy for life, and you therefore ima[gine in my] bosom a latent hostility towards yourself. This has been a mainspring in your whole conduct towards me since our first acquaintance. It has acted to prevent all cordiality. In a general view of human nature your idea is just—but you will find yourself puzzled in judging me by ordinary motives. Your criticism was essentially correct and therefore, although severe, it did not occasion in me one solitary emotion either of anger or dislike.

* * *

1. Text in angle brackets had been canceled.

From Edward Lytton Bulwer[1]

Night and Morning. A Novel. By the author of
Pelham, Rienzi, Eugene Aram, &c. 2 vols. Re-published by
Harper & Brothers, New York.

*　*　*

The word "plot," as commonly accepted, conveys but an indefinite meaning. Most persons think of it as of simple *complexity*; and into this error even so fine a critic as Augustus William Schlegel has obviously fallen, when he confounds its idea with that of the mere *intrigue* in which the Spanish dramas of Cervantes and Calderon[2] abound. But the greatest involution of incident will not result in plot; which, properly defined, is *that in which no part can be displaced without ruin to the whole.* It may be described as a building so dependently constructed, that to change the position of a single brick is to overthrow the entire fabric. In this definition and description, we of course refer only to that infinite perfection which the true artist bears ever in mind—that unattainable goal to which his eyes are always directed, but of the possibility of attaining which he still endeavors, if wise, to cheat himself into the belief. The reading world, however, is satisfied with a less rigid construction of the term. It is content to think that plot a good one, in which none of the *leading* incidents can be *removed* without *detriment* to the mass. Here indeed is a material difference; and in this view of the case the plot of "Night and Morning" is decidedly excellent. Speaking comparatively, and in regard to stories similarly composed, it is one of the best. This the author has evidently designed to make it. For this purpose he has taxed his powers to the utmost. Every page bears marks of excessive elaboration, all tending to one point—a perfect adaptation of the very numerous atoms of a very unusually involute story. The better to attain his object he has resorted to the expedient of writing his book backwards. This is a simple thing in itself, but may not be generally understood. * * * What appears first in the published book, was last in the original MS. Many of the most striking portions of the novel were *interleaved* in the same manner—thus giving to after-thought that air of premeditation which is so pleasing. Effect seems to follow cause in the most natural and in the most provident manner, but, in the true construction, the cause (and here we commit no bull) is absolutely brought about by the effect. The many brief, and seemingly insulated chapters met with in the course of the narrative, are the interposed after-thoughts in question.

1. Poe's text is reprinted from *Graham's Magazine*, April 1841. He begins with a careful summary of the plot of Bulwer's *Night and Morning* (1841); he then launches into a mini-essay on the necessary importance and unnecessary excesses of plot in narrative fiction.
2. Pedro Calderón de la Barca (1600–1681), one of the most famous of Spanish Renaissance playwrights, is best known for *La Vida es Sueño* (Life is a dream). Miguel de Cervantes (1547–1616), author of the classic novel *Don Quixote* (part I 1605; part II 1615), also wrote dramas that are still read today.

So careful has been our author in this working-up of his story—in this nice dovetailing of its constituent parts—that it is difficult to detect a blemish in any portion. What he has intended to do he has done well; and his main intention, as we have before hinted, was *perfection of plot*. A few defects, indeed, we note; and note them chiefly to show the skill with which that narrative is wrought, where such blemishes are the sole ones.

* * *

We have defined the word "plot," in a definition of our own to be sure, but in one which we do not the less consider substantially correct; and we have said that it has been a main point with Mr. Bulwer in this his last novel, "Night and Morning," to work up his plot as near perfection as possible. We have asserted, too, that his design is well accomplished; but we do not the less assert that it has been conceived and executed in error.

The interest of plot, referring, as it does, to cultivated thought in the reader, and appealing to considerations analogous with those which are the essence of sculptural taste, is by no means a popular interest; although it has the peculiarity of being appreciated in its atoms by all, while in its totality of beauty it is comprehended but by the few. The pleasure which the many derive from it is disjointed, ineffective, and evanescent; and even in the case of the critical reader it is a plea-sure which may be purchased too dearly. A good tale may be written without it. Some of the finest fictions in the world have neglected it altogether. We see nothing of it in Gil Blas, in the Pilgrim's Progress, or in Robinson Crusoe.[3] Thus it is not an essential in story-telling at all; although, well-managed, within proper limits, it is a thing to be desired. At best it is but a secondary and rigidly artistical merit, for which no merit of a higher class—no merit founded in nature—should be sacrificed. But in the book before us *much* is sacrificed for its sake, and every thing is rendered subservient to its purposes. So excessive is, here, the involution of circumstances, that it has been found impossible to dwell for more than a brief period upon any particular one. The writer seems in a perpetual flurry to accomplish what, in autorical[4] parlance, is called "bringing up one's time." He flounders in the vain attempt to keep all his multitudinous incidents at one and the same moment before the eye. His ability has been sadly taxed in the effort—but more sadly the time and temper of the reader. No sooner do we begin to take some slight degree of interest in some cursorily-sketched event, than we are hurried off to some other, for which a new feeling is to be built up, only to be tumbled down, forthwith, as before. And thus, since there is no sufficiently continuous scene in the whole novel, it results that there is not a strongly effective one. Time not being given us in which to become absorbed, we are only permitted to admire, while we are not the less chilled, tantalised, wearied, and displeased. Nature, with natural

3. *Robinson Crusoe* (1719), a novel by Daniel Defoe. *Gil Blas* (1749), an episodic novel by Alain René Le Sage. *Pilgrim's Progress* (part I, 1678; part II, 1684), an allegorical narrative by John Bunyan.
4. Authorial (archaic).

interest, has been given up a bond-maiden to an elaborate, but still to a misconceived, perverted, and most unsatisfactory Art.

Very little reflection might have sufficed to convince Mr. Bulwer that narratives, even one fourth so long as the one now lying upon our table, are *essentially* inadapted to that nice and complex adjustment of incident at which he has made this desperate attempt. In the wire-drawn romances which have been so long fashionable, (God only knows how or why) the pleasure we derive (if any) is a composite one, and made up of the respective sums of the various pleasurable sentiments experienced in perusal. Without excessive and fatiguing exertion, inconsistent with legitimate interest, the mind cannot comprehend at one time, and in one survey, the numerous individual items which go to establish the whole. Thus the high ideal sense of the *unique* is sure to be wanting:—for, however absolute in itself be the unity of the novel, it must inevitably fail of appreciation. We speak now of that species of unity which is alone worth the attention of the critic—the unity or totality *of effect.*

But we could never bring ourselves to attach any idea of merit to mere *length* in the abstract. A long story does not appear to us necessarily twice as good as one only half so long. The ordinary talk about "continuous and sustained effort" is pure twaddle and nothing more.

* * *

From Lambert A. Wilmer[1]

The Quacks of Helicon: A Satire. By L. A. Wilmer, Philadelphia: Printed by J. W. Macclefield.

A SATIRE, professedly such, at the present day, and especially by an American writer, is a welcome novelty, indeed. We have really done very little in the line upon this side of the Atlantic—nothing, certainly, of importance—Trumbull's clumsy poem and Halleck's "Croakers"[2] to the contrary notwithstanding. Some things we have produced, to be sure, which were excellent in the way of burlesque, without intending a syllable that was not utterly solemn and serious. Odes, ballads, songs, sonnets, epics, and epigrams, possessed of this unintentional excellence, we could have no difficulty in designating by the dozen; but, in the matter of directly-meant and genuine satire, it cannot be denied that we are sadly deficient. Although, as a literary people, how-

1. Poe's review is reprinted from *Graham's Magazine* of August 1841. Lambert A. Wilmer (c. 1805–1863), a friend of Poe, was a journalist and author in Baltimore and Philadelphia. The *Quacks of Helicon* was a verse satire on the literati of the day. Although Poe begins and ends with some remarks on Wilmer's book, the bulk of the "review" is actually a scathing attack on the literary and publishing cliques who overpraised members of their own set and more or less controlled the publishing industry in Philadelphia, New York, and Boston. It is one of the most trenchant and vigorous assessments of the American literary scene written in the 19th century.
2. With Joseph Rodman Drake, Fitz-Greene Halleck (1790–1867) wrote *The Croaker Papers* (1819), a series of humorous accounts, in verse, of Broadway and its environs. See Poe's review of their more serious poetry on pp. 604ff. herein. John Trumbull (1750–1831) wrote a long satiric poem called *The Progress of Dullness* (1772–73).

ever, we are not exactly Archilocuses—although we have no pretensions to the ηχεηντες ιαμβοι[3]—although, in short, we are no satirists ourselves, there can be no question that we answer sufficiently well as subjects for satire.

We repeat, that we are glad to see this book of Mr. Wilmer's; first, because it is something new under the sun; secondly, because, in many respects, it is well executed; and, thirdly, because, in the universal corruption and rigmarole amid which we gasp for breath, it is really a pleasant thing to get even one accidental whiff of the unadulterated air of *truth*.[4]

* * *

We repeat it:—*it is* the truth which he has spoken, and who shall contradict us? He has said unscrupulously what every reasonable man among us has long known to be "as true as the Pentateuch"[5]—that, as a literary people, we are one vast perambulating humbug. He has asserted that we are *clique*-ridden, and who does not smile at the obvious truism of that assertion? He maintains that chicanery is, with us, a far surer road than talent to distinction in letters. Who gainsays this? The corrupt nature of our ordinary criticism has become notorious. Its powers have been prostrated by its own arm. The intercourse between critic and publisher, as it now almost universally stands, is comprised either in the paying and pocketing of black mail, as the price of a simple forbearance, or in a direct system of petty and contemptible bribery, properly so called— a system even more injurious than the former to the true interests of the public, and more degrading to the buyers and sellers of good opinion, on account of the more positive character of the service here rendered for the consideration received. We laugh at the idea of any denial of our assertions upon this topic; they are infamously true. In the charge of general corruption there are undoubtedly many noble exceptions to be made. There are, indeed, some very few editors, who, maintaining an entire independence, will receive no books from publishers at all, or who receive them with a perfect understanding, on the part of these latter, that an unbiassed *critique* will be given. But these cases are insufficient to have much effect on the popular mistrust: a mistrust heightened by late exposure of the machinations of *coteries* in New York—*coteries* which, at the bidding of leading booksellers, manufacture, as required from time to time, a pseudo-public opinion by wholesale, for the benefit of any little hanger on of the party, or pettifogging protector of the firm.

We speak of these things in the bitterness of scorn. It is unnecessary to cite instances, where one is found in almost every issue of a book. It is needless to call to mind the desperate case of Fay[6]—a case where

3. Echoing iambics (Greek). The ancient Greek satirist Archilocus (flourished 700–650 B.C.E.) was supposedly the first to write in iambic meter.
4. Poe goes on in paragraphs omitted here to compare Wilmer with the great Neoclassic satirists (John Dryden, Alexander Pope, Jonathan Swift, and others), mildly charging him with excessive "imitation." He predicts that Wilmer will suffer "persecution" from the literary quacks (humbug artists) of Boston, New York, and Philadelphia because he has spoken the truth about them.
5. The first five books of the Old Testament.
6. See Poe's searing review of Theodore S. Fay's *Norman Leslie*, pp. 598ff. herein. Fay was a member of the New York *Mirror* clique.

the pertinacity of the effort to gull—where the obviousness of the attempt at forestalling a judgment—where the wofully over-done be-Mirrorment of that man-of-straw, together with the pitiable platitude of his production, proved a dose somewhat too potent for even the well-prepared stomach of the mob. We say it is supererogatory to dwell upon "Norman Leslie," or other by-gone follies, when we have, before our eyes, hourly instances of the machinations in question. To so great an extent of methodical assurance has the *system* of puffery arrived, that publishers, of late, have made no scruple of keeping on hand an assortment of commendatory notices, prepared by their men of all work, and of sending these notices around to the multitudinous papers within their influence, done up within the fly-leaves of the book. The grossness of these base attempts, however, has not escaped indignant rebuke from the more honorable portion of the press; and we hail these symptoms of restiveness under the yoke of unprincipled ignorance and quackery (strong only in combination) as the harbinger of a better era for the interests of real merit, and of the national literature as a whole.

It has become, indeed the plain duty of each individual connected with our periodicals, heartily to give whatever influence he possesses, to the good cause of integrity and the truth. The results thus attainable will be found worthy his closest attention and best efforts. We shall thus frown down all conspiracies to foist inanity upon the public consideration at the obvious expense of every man of talent who is not a member of a *clique* in power. We may even arrive, in time, at that desirable point from which a distinct view of our men of letters may be obtained, and their respective pretensions adjusted, by the standard of a rigorous and self-sustaining criticism alone. That their several positions are as yet properly settled; that the posts which a vast number of them now hold are maintained by any better tenure than that of the chicanery upon which we have commented, will be asserted by none but the ignorant, or the parties who have best right to feel an interest in the "good old condition of things." No two matters can be more radically different than the reputation of some of our prominent *litterateurs*, as gathered from the mouths of the people, (who glean it from the paragraphs of the papers,) and the same reputation as deduced from the private estimate of intelligent and educated men. We do not advance this fact as a new discovery. Its truth, on the contrary, is the subject, and has long been so, of every-day witticism and mirth.

Why not? Surely there can be few things more ridiculous than the general character and assumptions of the ordinary critical notices of new books! An editor, sometimes without the shadow of the commonest attainment—often without brains, always without time—does not scruple to give the world to understand that he is in the *daily* habit of critically reading and deciding upon a flood of publications one tenth of whose title-pages he may possibly have turned over, three fourths of whose contents would be Hebrew to his most desperate efforts at comprehension, and whose entire mass and amount, as might be

mathematically demonstrated, would be sufficient to occupy, in the most cursory perusal, the attention of some ten or twenty readers for a month! What he wants in plausibility, however, he makes up in obsequiousness; what he lacks in time he supplies in temper. He is the most easily pleased man in the world. He admires everything, from the big Dictionary of Noah Webster to the last diamond edition of Tom Thumb. Indeed his sole difficulty is in finding tongue to express his delight. Every pamphlet is a miracle—every book in boards is an epoch in letters. His phrases, therefore, get bigger and bigger every day, and, if it were not for talking Cockney, we might call him a "regular swell."

Yet in the attempt at getting definite information in regard to any one portion of our literature, the merely general reader, or the foreigner, will turn in vain from the lighter to the heavier journals. But it is not our intention here to dwell upon the radical, antique, and systematized rigmarole of our Quarterlies. The articles here are anonymous. Who writes?—who causes to be written? Who but an ass will put faith in tirades which *may* be the result of personal hostility, or in panegyrics which nine times out of ten may be laid, directly or indirectly, to the charge of the author himself? It is in the favor of these saturnine pamphlets that they contain, now and then, a good essay *de omnibus rebus et quibusdam aliis*,[7] which may be looked into, without decided somnolent consequences, at any period not immediately subsequent to dinner. But it is useless to expect criticism from periodicals called "Reviews" from never reviewing. Besides, all men know, or should know, that these books are sadly given to verbiage. It is a part of their nature, a condition of their being, a point of their faith. A veteran reviewer loves the safety of generalities, and is therefore rarely particular. "Words, words, words" are the secret of his strength. He has one or two ideas of his own, and is both wary and fussy in giving them out. His wit lies with his truth, in a well,[8] and there is always a world of trouble in getting it up. He is a sworn enemy to all things simple and direct. He gives no ear to the advice of the giant Moulineau—*"Belier, mon ami, commencez au commencement."*[9] He either jumps at once into the middle of his subject, or breaks in at a back door, or sidles up to it with the gait of a crab. No other mode of approach has an air of sufficient profundity. When fairly into it, however, he becomes dazzled with the scintillations of his own wisdom, and is seldom able to see his way out. Tired of laughing at his antics, or frightened at seeing him flounder, the reader at length shuts him up, with the book. "What song the Syrens sang," says Sir Thomas Browne, "or what name Achilles assumed when he hid himself among women, though puzzling questions, are not beyond *all* conjecture"[1]—but it

7. Concerning all things and certain other things as well (Latin).
8. A reference to the old saying, ascribed to Democritus (c. 460–c. 370 B.C.E.), that truth lies deep at the bottom of a well.
9. Belier, my friend, begin at the beginning (French).
1. From *Hydriotaphia, or Urn-Burial* (1658), chapter V, para. 3, by Sir Thomas Browne (1605–1682). The Sirens ("Syrens") were beautiful female creatures who lured sailors to their deaths on the rocks of their island by means of their otherworldly songs. Poe used the passage on at least four occasions, most notably as the motto for "The Murders in the Rue Morgue."

would puzzle Sir Thomas, backed by Achilles and all the Syrens in Heathendom, to say, in nine cases out of ten, *what is the object* of a thorough-going Quarterly Reviewer.

Should the opinions promulgated by our press at large be taken, in their wonderful aggregate, as an evidence of what American literature absolutely is, (and it may be said that, in general, they are really so taken,) we shall find ourselves the most enviable set of people upon the face of the earth. Our fine writers are legion. Our very atmosphere is redolent of genius; and we, the nation, are a huge, well-contented chameleon, grown pursy by inhaling it. We are *teretes et rotundi*—enwrapped in excellence.[2] All our poets are Miltons, neither mute nor inglorious; all our poetesses are "American Hemanses;"[3] nor will it do to deny that all our novelists are great Knowns or great Unknowns, and that every body who writes, in every possible and impossible department, is the admirable Crichton,[4] or at least the admirable Crichton's ghost. We are thus in a glorious condition, and will remain so until forced to disgorge our ethereal honors. In truth, there is some danger that the jealousy of the Old World will interfere. It cannot long submit to that outrageous monopoly of "all the decency and all the talent" in which the gentlemen of the press give such undoubted assurance of our being so busily engaged.

But we feel angry with ourselves for the jesting tone of our observations upon this topic. The prevalence of the spirit of puffery is a subject far less for merriment than for disgust. Its truckling, yet dogmatical character—its bold, unsustained, yet self-sufficient and wholesale laudation—is becoming, more and more, an insult to the common sense of the community. Trivial as it essentially is, it has yet been made the instrument of the grossest abuse in the elevation of imbecility, to the manifest injury, to the utter ruin, of true merit. Is there any man of good feeling and of ordinary understanding—is there one single individual among all our readers—who does not feel a thrill of bitter indignation, apart from any sentiment of mirth, as he calls to mind instance after instance of the purest, of the most unadulterated quackery in letters, which has risen to a high post in the apparent popular estimation, and which still maintains it, by the sole means of a blustering arrogance, or of a busy wriggling conceit, or of the most barefaced plagiarism, or even through the simple immensity of its assumptions—assumptions not only unopposed by the press at large, but absolutely supported in proportion to the vociferous clamor with which they are made—in exact accordance with their utter baselessness and untenability? We should have no trouble in pointing out, to-

2. Pursy: presumably, puckered at the mouth. *Teretes et rotundi*: smooth and rounded. Cf. *teres atque rotundus* (Latin); *totus teres atque rotundus*: wise, completed, rounded; someone rolling smoothly through the world; see Horace, *Satires*, II, vii, 86.
3. Probably a reference to women poets such as Mrs. L. H. Sigourney, whose verses Poe gently suggested shared a number of qualities with those of Mrs. Felicia Hemans.
4. James Crichton (1560–1585?), Scottish traveler, adventurer, and scholar, noted for knowing over a dozen languages and for having a prodigious memory; he was killed in a street fight in Italy. His reputation comes mainly from the lavish praise bestowed on him in a biography by Sir Thomas Urquhart, who called him the "Admirable Crichton."

day, some twenty or thirty so-called literary personages, who, if not idiots, as we half think them, or if not hardened to all sense of shame by a long course of disingenuousness, will now blush, in the perusal of these words, through consciousness of the shadowy nature of that purchased pedestal upon which they stand—will now tremble in thinking of the feebleness of the breath which will be adequate to the blowing it from beneath their feet. With the help of a hearty good will, even *we* may yet tumble them down.

So firm, through a long endurance, has been the hold taken upon the popular mind (at least so far as we may consider the popular mind reflected in ephemeral letters) by the laudatory system which we have deprecated, that what is, in its own essence, a vice, has become endowed with the appearance, and met with the reception of a virtue. Antiquity, as usual, has lent a certain degree of speciousness even to the absurd. So continuously have we puffed, that we have at length come to think puffing the duty, and plain speaking the dereliction. What we began in gross error, we persist in through habit. Having adopted, in the earlier days of our literature, the untenable idea that this literature, as a whole, could be advanced by an indiscriminate approbation bestowed on its every effort—having adopted this idea, we say, without attention to the obvious fact that praise of all was bitter although negative censure to the few alone deserving, and that the only result of the system, in the fostering way, would be the fostering of folly—we now continue our vile practices through the supineness of custom, even while, in our national self-conceit, we repudiate that necessity for patronage and protection in which originated our conduct. In a word, the press throughout the country has not been ashamed to make head against the very few bold attempts at independence which have, from time to time, been made in the face of the reigning order of things. And if, in one, or perhaps two, insulated cases, the spirit of severe truth, sustained by an unconquerable will, was not to be so put down, then, forthwith, were private chicaneries set in motion; then was had resort, on the part of those who considered themselves injured by the severity of criticism, (and who were so, if the just contempt of every ingenuous man is injury,) resort to arts of the most virulent indignity, to untraceable slanders, to ruthless assassination in the dark. We say these things were done, while the press in general looked on, and, with a full understanding of the wrong perpetrated, spoke not against the wrong. The idea had absolutely gone abroad—had grown up little by little into toleration—that attacks however just, upon a literary reputation however obtained, however untenable, were well retaliated by the basest and most unfounded traduction of personal fame. But is this an age—is this a day—in which it can be necessary even to advert to such considerations as that the book of the author is the property of the public, and that the issue of the book is the throwing down of the gauntlet to the reviewer—to the reviewer whose duty is the plainest; the duty not even of approbation, or of censure, or of silence, at his own will, but at the sway of those sentiments and of those opinions which are derived from the author himself, through the

medium of his written and published words? True criticism is the reflection of the thing criticised upon the spirit of the critic.

* * *

Exordium to Critical Notices[1]

In commencing, with the New Year, a New Volume, we shall be permitted to say a very few words by way of *exordium* to our usual chapter of Reviews, or, as we should prefer calling them, of Critical Notices. Yet we speak *not* for the sake of the *exordium*, but because we have really something to say, and know not when or where better to say it.

That the public attention, in America, has, of late days, been more than usually directed to the matter of literary criticism, is plainly apparent. Our periodicals are beginning to acknowledge the importance of the science (shall we so term it?) and to disdain the flippant *opinion* which so long has been made its substitute.

Time was when we imported our critical decisions from the mother country. For many years we enacted a perfect farce of subserviency to the *dicta* of Great Britain. At last a revulsion of feeling, with self-disgust, necessarily ensued. Urged by these, we plunged into the opposite extreme. In throwing *totally* off that "authority," whose voice had so long been so sacred, we even surpassed, and by much, our original folly. But the watchword now was, "a national literature!"—as if any true literature *could be* "national"—as if the world at large were not the only proper stage for the literary *histrio*.[2] We became, suddenly, the merest and maddest *partizans* in letters. Our papers spoke of "tariffs" and "protection." Our Magazines had habitual passages about that "truly native novelist, Mr. Cooper," or that "staunch American genius, Mr. Paulding."[3] Unmindful of the spirit of the axioms that "a prophet has no honor in his own land" and that "a hero is never a hero to his *valet-de-chambre*"—axioms founded in reason and in truth—our reviews urged the propriety—our booksellers the necessity, of strictly "American" themes. A foreign subject, at this epoch, was a weight more than enough to drag down into the very depths of critical damnation the finest writer owning nativity in the States; while, on the reverse, we found ourselves daily in the paradoxical dilemma of liking, or pretending to like, a stupid book the better because (sure enough) its stupidity was of our own growth, and discussed our own affairs.

It is, in fact, but very lately that this anomalous state of feeling has

1. Poe's essay was published in the first issue (January) of *Graham's Magazine* for 1842, the "New Volume" referred to in the opening sentence. "Exordium": introductory part of a text (a speech, lecture, essay, etc.). Poe apparently intended to expand his criticisms of the contemporary state of criticism and publishing into a longer work.
2. Actor, performer.
3. James Kirke Paulding (1778–1860), New York novelist sympathetic to Southern causes (see the South and Slavery section (pp. 767ff. herein) and the Paulding-Drayton review ("Slavery," pp. 772ff.). James Fenimore Cooper (1789–1851): author of the "Leatherstocking" novels and other popular romances.

shown any signs of subsidence. Still it *is* subsiding. Our views of liter-
ature in general having expanded, we begin to demand the use—to in-
quire into the offices and provinces of criticism—to regard it more as
an art based immoveably in nature, less as a mere system of fluctuat-
ing and conventional dogmas. And, with the prevalence of these ideas,
has arrived a distaste even to the home-dictation of the book-seller-
coteries. If our editors are not as yet *all* independent of the will of a
publisher, a majority of them scruple, at least, *to confess* a sub-
servience, and enter into no positive combinations against the minor-
ity who despise and discard it. And this is a *very* great improvement of
exceedingly late date.

Escaping these quicksands, our criticism is nevertheless in some
danger—some very little danger—of falling into the pit of a most
detestable species of cant—the cant of *generality.* This tendency has
been given it, in the first instance, by the onward and tumultuous
spirit of the age. With the increase of the thinking-material comes the
desire, if not the necessity, of abandoning particulars for masses. Yet in
our individual case, as a nation, we seem merely to have adopted this
bias from the British Quarterly Reviews, upon which our own Quar-
terlies have been slavishly and pertinaciously modelled. In the foreign
journal, the review or criticism properly so termed, has gradually yet
steadily degenerated into what we see it at present—that is to say into
anything but criticism. Originally a "review," was not so called as *lucus
a non lucendo.*[4] Its name conveyed a just idea of its design. It re-
viewed, or surveyed the book whose title formed its text, and, giving an
analysis of its contents, passed judgment upon its merits or defects.
But, through the system of anonymous contribution, this natural
process lost ground from day to day. The name of a writer being
known only to a few, it became to him an object not so much to write
well, as to write fluently, at so many guineas per sheet. The analysis of
a book is a matter of time and of mental exertion. For many classes of
composition there is required a deliberate perusal, with notes, and
subsequent generalization. An easy substitute for this labor was found
in a digest or compendium of the work noticed, with copious ex-
tracts—or a still easier, in random comments upon such passages as
accidentally met the eye of the critic, with the passages themselves
copied at full length. The mode of reviewing most in favor, however,
because carrying with it the greatest *semblance* of care, was that of dif-
fuse essay upon the subject matter of the publication, the reviewer (?)
using the facts alone which the publication supplied, and using them
as material for some theory, the sole concern, bearing, and intention
of which, was mere difference of opinion with the author. These came
at length to be understood and habitually practised as the customary
or conventional *fashions* of review; and although the nobler order of
intellects did not fall into the full heresy of these fashions—we may
still assert that even Macaulay's nearest approach to criticism in its

4. A grove is dark because it has no light (Latin; loose trans.). The phrase is used to indicate
silly derivations of words or fatuous observations; here the meaning is that the word *review*
originally meant something and was not the ridiculous misnomer it has become.

legitimate sense, is to be found in his article upon Ranke's "History of the Popes"—an article in which the whole strength of the reviewer is put forth *to account* for a single fact—the progress of Romanism— which the book under discussion has established.

Now, while we do not mean to deny that a good essay is a good thing, we yet assert that these papers on general topics have nothing whatever to do with that *criticism* which their evil example has nevertheless infected *in se*. Because these dogmatising pamphlets, which *were once* "Reviews," have lapsed from their original faith, it does not follow that the faith itself is extinct—that "there shall be no more cakes and ale"[5]—that criticism, in its old acceptation, does not exist. But we complain of a growing inclination on the part of our lighter journals to believe, on such grounds, that such is the fact—that because the British Quarterlies, through supineness, and our own, through a degrading imitation, have come to merge all varieties of vague generalization in the one title of "Review," it therefore results that criticism, being everything in the universe, is, consequently, nothing whatever in fact. For to this end, and to none other conceivable, is the tendency of such propositions, for example, as we find in a late number of that very clever monthly magazine, Arcturus.[6]

"But *now*" (the emphasis on the *now* is our own)—"But *now*," says Mr. Mathews, in the preface to the first volume of his journal, "criticism has a wider scope and a universal interest. It dismisses errors of grammar, and hands over an imperfect rhyme or a false quantity to the proof-reader; it looks *now* to the heart of the subject and the author's design. It is a test of opinion. Its acuteness is not pedantic, but philosophical; it unravels the web of the author's mystery to interpret his meaning to others; it detects his sophistry, because sophistry is injurious to the heart and life; it promulgates his beauties with liberal, generous praise, because this is its true duty as the servant of truth. Good criticism may be well asked for, since it is the type of the literature of the day. It gives method to the universal inquisitiveness on every topic relating to life or action. A criticism, *now*, includes every form of literature, except perhaps the imaginative and the strictly dramatic. It is an essay, a sermon, an oration, a chapter in history, a philosophical speculation, a prose-poem, an art-novel, a dialogue; it admits of humor, pathos, the personal feelings of autobiography, the broadest views of statesmanship. As the ballad and the epic were the productions of the days of Homer, the review is the native characteristic growth of the nineteenth century."

We respect the talents of Mr. Mathews, but must dissent from nearly all that he here says. The species of "review" which he designates as the "characteristic growth of the nineteenth century" is only

5. As phrased here, the "quotation" is from Shakespeare's *Twelfth Night* (c. 1600); but the phrase goes back to Aesop (c. 620–560 B.C.E.): it is better to have beans and bacon in peace than cakes and ale in fear.
6. A magazine (1840–42) edited by Cornelius Mathews (1817–1889) and Evert Augustus Duyckinck (1816–1878). Poe at first made fun of Mathews's work (see, e.g., *Graham's* for February 1842) but later tried to enlist him as an ally.

the growth of the last twenty or thirty years *in Great Britain*. The French Reviews, for example, which are *not* anonymous, are very different things, and preserve the *unique* spirit of true criticism. And what need we say of the Germans?—what of Winkelmann, of Novalis, of Schelling, of Göethe, of Augustus William, and of Frederick Schlegel?—that their magnificent *critiques raisonnées*[7] differ from those of Kaimes, of Johnson, and of Blair, in principle not at all, (for the principles of these artists will not fail until Nature herself expires,) but solely in their more careful elaboration, their greater thoroughness, their more profound analysis and application of the principles themselves. That a criticism "*now*" should be different in spirit, as Mr. Mathews supposes, from a criticism at any previous period, is to insinuate a charge of variability in laws that cannot vary—the laws of man's heart and intellect—for these are the sole basis upon which the true critical art is established. And this art "*now*" no more than in the days of the "Dunciad,"[8] can, without neglect of its duty, "dismiss errors of grammar," or "hand over an imperfect rhyme or a false quantity to the proof-reader." What is meant by a "test of opinion" in the connexion here given the words by Mr. M., we do not comprehend as clearly as we could desire. By this phrase we are as completely enveloped in doubt as was Mirabeau in the castle of *If*.[9] To our imperfect appreciation it seems to form a portion of that general vagueness which is the *tone* of the whole philosophy at this point:—but all that which our journalist describes a criticism to be, is all that which we sturdily maintain it is *not*. Criticism is *not*, we think, an essay, nor a sermon, nor an oration, nor a chapter in history, nor a philosophical speculation, nor a prose-poem, nor an art novel, nor a dialogue. In fact, it *can be* nothing in the world but—a criticism. But if it were all that Arcturus imagines, it is not very clear why it might not be equally "imaginative" or "dramatic"—a romance or a melo-drama, or both. That it would be a farce cannot be doubted.

It is against this frantic spirit of *generalization* that we protest. We have a word, "criticism," whose import is sufficiently distinct, through long usage, at least; and we have an art of high importance and clearly-ascertained limit, which this word is quite well enough understood to represent. Of that conglomerate science to which Mr.

7. Reasoned critiques (French). The list is composed of German and British critics, rhetoricians, and philosophers. The Germans: Johann Joachim Winckelmann (1717–1716), archaeologist and historian of ancient art. Novalis, the pseudonym of Friedrich von Hardenberg (1772–1801), German Romantic poet and fiction writer. Friedrich Wilhelm Joseph von Schelling (1775–1854) German philosopher. Johann Wolfgang von Goethe (1749–1832), scientist, musician, and author (the "Shakespeare of German literature"). August Wilhelm von Schlegel (1767–1845), critic and historian (pp. 732ff. herein). Friedrich von Schlegel (1772–1829), critic, historian, and literary theorist (pp. 727ff. herein). The British: Henry Home, Lord Kames (1696–1792), jurist, author of works on logical thinking. Samuel Johnson (1709–1784), poet, novelist, critic, author of the famous *Dictionary of the English Language* (1755), the novel *Rasselas* (1759), and the *Lives of the Poets* (1779–81). Hugh Blair, author of *Lectures on Rhetoric* (1783).
8. The *Dunciad* (1728, followed by several revisions; final version 1743) is a long verse satire of the British literati by Alexander Pope.
9. The Chateau D'If, constructed in 1524 on the Island of If in the Mediterranean, was for a while used as a prison. It is most famous as the prison of the fictional Edmond Dantès in Alexandre Dumas's *The Count of Monte Cristo* (1844). Honoré Gabriel Victor Riqueti Mirabeau (1749–1791), French orator, pamphleteer, and revolutionary.

Mathews so eloquently alludes, and of which we are instructed that it is anything and everything at once—of this science we know nothing, and really wish to know less; but we object to our contemporary's appropriation in its behalf, of a term to which we, in common with a large majority of mankind, have been accustomed to attach a certain and very definitive idea. Is there no word but "criticism" which may be made to serve the purposes of "Arcturus?" Has it any objection to Orphicism, or Dialism, or Emersonism,[1] or any other pregnant compound indicative of confusion worse confounded?

Still, we must not pretend a total misapprehension of the idea of Mr. Mathews, and we should be sorry that he misunderstood *us*. It may be granted that we differ only in terms—although the difference will yet be found not unimportant in effect. Following the highest authority, we would wish, in a word, to limit literary criticism to comment upon *Art*. A book is written—and it is only *as the book* that we subject it to review. With the opinions of the work, considered otherwise than in their relation to the work itself, the critic has really nothing to do. It is his part simply to decide upon *the mode* in which these opinions are brought to bear. Criticism is thus no "test of opinion." For this test, the work, divested of its pretensions as an *art-product*, is turned over for discussion to the world at large—and first, to that class which it especially addresses—if a history, to the historian—if a metaphysical treatise, to the moralist. In this, the only true and intelligible sense, it will be seen that criticism, the test or analysis of *Art*, (*not* of opinion,) is only properly employed upon productions which have their basis in art itself, and although the journalist (whose duties and objects are multiform) may turn aside, at pleasure, from the *mode* or vehicle of opinion to discussion of the opinion conveyed—it is still clear that he is *"critical"* only in so much as he deviates from his true province not at all.

And of the critic himself what shall we say?—for as yet we have spoken only the *proem* to the true *epopea*.[2] What *can* we better say of him than, with Bulwer,[3] that "he must have courage to blame boldly, magnanimity to eschew envy, genius to appreciate, learning to compare, an eye for beauty, an ear for music, and a heart for feeling." Let us add, a talent for analysis and a solemn indifference to abuse.

Henry Wadsworth Longfellow The history and context of Poe's reviews of Henry Wadsworth Longfellow (1807–1882) are too diffuse and complicated to detail here. Suffice it to say that Poe, regarding Longfellow as an overrated clique writer, repeatedly attacked the immensely popular (indeed, beloved) Harvard professor. Poe's principal criticisms involved what he considered Longfellow's lack of originality, and he even went to far as to accuse him of various plagiarisms (including thefts from Poe's

1. References to Bronson Alcott's "Orphic Sayings" and to *The Dial*, the magazine of the New England Transcendentalists, whose most famous spokesperson was Ralph Waldo Emerson.
2. I.e., a beginning to the real work of criticism (which would be epical).
3. Edward Bulwer-Lytton (1803–1873), popular British novelist who figures prominently in Poe's works (see, e.g., Poe's review of Bulwer's *Night and Morning* pp. 624ff. herein).

own works). Poe created quite a stir, and insofar as his purpose was to draw attention to himself, he succeeded, but it was often to the detriment of his own reputation for fairness and acumen.

Poe initially gave a brief notice, in *Graham's Magazine*, of Longfellow's *Hyperion, a Romance* in October of 1839, and then reviewed his *Voices of the Night* in *Burton's Gentleman's Magazine* in February 1840. He gave a brief notice of *Ballads and Other Poems* in *Graham's* in March 1842, then printed a long review of the same work in *Graham's* for April 1842 (reprinted here). About two and a half years later, he reviewed Longfellow's *The Waif* in the *New York Weekly Mirror* (January 25, 1845), which contained Poe's reply to a defense of Longfellow by one "H." (probably Henry Hewitt). With this review, Poe initiated what he soon called the "Little Longfellow War." The first countershot was an attack on Poe by one "Outis" (Greek for "nobody"), to which Poe replied at length in five installments in the *Broadway Journal* from March 8, 1845 to April 5, 1845, augmented by one more salvo in the *Aristidean* for April 1845. For details of the Longfellow War, see the biographical introduction on p. xxxviii herein.

Reprinted here are only those sections of Poe's 1842 review of *Ballads* that deal specifically with Romantic poetic theory rather than with the literary warfare. The long sequence of charges and replies of the Longfellow War may be found in *Essays and Reviews* (pp. 671–777), ed. G. R. Thompson. For a thorough account of Poe's wars with the Northern literati, see Sidney P. Moss, *Poe's Literary Battles: The Critic in the Context of His Literary Milieu* (1963), which reads like a novel. Of special note in the theoretical part of Poe's review of Longfellow's *Ballads* is his vigorous denunciation of didacticism (moral instruction) as an aim of poetry and his formulation of a Kantian triad of cognitive, aesthetic, and moral faculties of the mind with the imaginative (aesthetic) faculty in the middle mediating between the other two.

From Henry Wadsworth Longfellow

Ballads and Other Poems. By Henry Wadsworth Longfellow.
Author of "Voices of the Night," "Hyperion," &c. Second Edition.
John Owen: Cambridge.

In our last number we had some hasty observations on these "Ballads"—observations which we now propose, in some measure, to amplify and explain.

It may be remembered that, among other points, we demurred to Mr. Longfellow's *themes*, or rather to their general character. We found fault with the too obtrusive nature of their *didacticism*.

* * *

We have said that Mr. Longfellow's conception of the *aims* of poesy is erroneous; and that thus, laboring at a disadvantage, he does violent wrong to his own high powers; and now the question is, what *are* his ideas of the aims of the Muse, as we gather these ideas from the *general* tendency of his poems?

* * *

[D]idacticism is the prevalent *tone* of his song. His invention, his imagery, his all, is made subservient to the elucidation of some one or more points (but rarely of more than one) which he looks upon as *truth*. And that this mode of procedure will find stern defenders should never excite surprise, so long as the world is full to overflowing with cant and conventicles. There are men who will scramble on all fours through the muddiest sloughs of vice to pick up a single apple of virtue. There are things called men who, so long as the sun rolls, will greet with snuffling huzzas every figure that takes upon itself the semblance of truth, even although the figure, in itself only a "stuffed Paddy," be as much out of place as a toga on the statue of Washington, or out of season as rabbits in the days of the dog-star.

Now with as deep a reverence for "the true" as ever inspired the bosom of mortal man, we would limit, in many respects, its modes of inculcation. We would limit to enforce them. We would not render them impotent by dissipation. The demands of truth are severe. She has no sympathy with the myrtles. All that is indispensible in song is all with which she has nothing to do. To deck her in gay robes is to render her a harlot. It is but making her a flaunting paradox to wreathe her in gems and flowers. Even in stating this our present proposition, we verify our own words—we feel the necessity, in enforcing this *truth*, of descending from metaphor. Let us then be simple and distinct. To convey "the true" we are required to dismiss from the attention all inessentials. We must be perspicuous, precise, terse. We need concentration rather than expansion of mind. We must be calm, unimpassioned, unexcited—in a word, we must be in that peculiar mood which, as nearly as possible, is the exact converse of the poetical. He must be blind indeed who cannot perceive the radical and chasmal difference between the truthful and the poetical modes of inculcation. He must be grossly wedded to conventionalisms who, in spite of this difference, shall still attempt to reconcile the obstinate oils and waters of Poetry and Truth.

Dividing the world of mind into its most obvious and immediately recognisable distinctions, we have the pure intellect, taste, and the moral sense. We place *taste* between the intellect and the moral sense, because it is just this intermediate space which, in the mind, it occupies. It is the connecting link in the triple chain. It serves to sustain a mutual intelligence between the extremes. It appertains, in strict appreciation, to the former, but is distinguished from the latter by so faint a difference, that Aristotle has not hesitated to class some of its operations among the Virtues themselves. But the *offices* of the trio are broadly marked. Just as conscience, or the moral sense, recognises duty; just as the intellect deals with *truth*; so is it the part of taste alone to inform us of BEAUTY. And Poesy is the handmaiden but of Taste. Yet we would not be misunderstood. This handmaiden is not forbidden to moralise—in her own fashion. She is not forbidden to depict—but to reason and preach, of virtue. As, of this latter, conscience recognises the obligation, so intellect teaches the expediency, while taste contents herself with displaying the beauty: waging war with vice

merely on the ground of its inconsistency with fitness, harmony, proportion—in a word with τo χαλον.[1]

An important condition of man's immortal nature is thus, plainly, the sense of the Beautiful. This it is which ministers to his delight in the manifold forms and colors and sounds and sentiments amid which he exists. And, just as the eyes of Amaryllis[2] are repeated in the mirror, or the living lily in the lake, so is the mere *record* of these forms and colors and sounds and sentiments—so is their mere oral or written repetition a duplicate source of delight. But this repetition is not Poesy. He who shall merely sing with whatever rapture, in however harmonious strains, or with however vivid a truth of imitation, of the sights and sounds which greet him in common with all mankind—he, we say, has yet failed to prove his divine title. There is still a longing unsatisfied, which he has been impotent to fulfil. There is still a thirst unquenchable, which to allay he has shown us no crystal springs. This burning thirst belongs to the *immortal* essence of man's nature. It is equally a consequence and an indication of his perennial life. It is the desire of the moth for the star. It is not the mere appreciation of the beauty before us. It is a wild effort to reach the beauty above. It is a forethought of the loveliness to come. It is a passion to be satiated by no sublunary sights, or sounds, or sentiments, and the soul thus athirst strives to allay its fever in futile efforts at *creation*. Inspired with a prescient ecstasy of the beauty beyond the grave, it struggles by multiform novelty of combination among the things and thoughts of Time, to anticipate some portion of that loveliness whose very elements, perhaps, appertain solely to Eternity. And the result of such effort, on the part of souls fittingly constituted, is alone what mankind have agreed to denominate Poetry.

We say this with little fear of contradiction. Yet the spirit of our assertion must be more heeded than the letter. Mankind have *seemed* to define Poesy in a thousand, and in a thousand conflicting definitions. But the war is one only of words. Induction is as well applicable to this subject as to the most palpable and utilitarian; and by its sober processes we find that, in respect to compositions which have been really received as poems, the *imaginative*, or, more popularly, the creative portions *alone* have ensured them to be so received. Yet these works, on account of these portions, having once been so received and so named, it has happened, naturally and inevitably, that other portions totally unpoetic have not only come to be regarded by the popular voice as poetic, but have been made to serve as false standards of perfection, in the adjustment of other poetical claims. Whatever has been found in whatever has been received as a poem, has been blindly regarded as *ex statû*[3] poetic. And this is a species of gross error which scarcely could have made its way into any less intangible topic. In fact

1. Beauty [*to kalon*] (Greek).
2. The fair shepherdess in Virgil's *Eclogues* (c. 37 B.C.E.). The amaryllus is the name for a family of lily-like perennial flowers (lilies, jonquils, daffodils, etc.), including the South African beladonna lily and the narcissus. One variety is called the century plant because it blooms at very long intervals (from five to one hundred years).
3. By decree (Latin).

that license which appertains to the Muse herself, it has been thought decorous, if not sagacious to indulge, in all examination of her character.

Poesy is thus seen to be a response—unsatisfactory it is true—but still in some measure a response, to a natural and irrepressible demand. Man being what he is, the time could never have been in which Poesy was not. Its first element is the thirst for supernal BEAUTY—a beauty which is not afforded the soul by any existing collocation of earth's forms—a beauty which, perhaps, *no possible* combination of these forms would fully produce. Its second element is the attempt to satisfy this thirst by *novel* combinations among those forms of beauty which already exist—or by novel combinations *of those combinations which our predecessors, toiling in chase of the same phantom, have already set in order.* We thus clearly deduce the *novelty*, the *originality*, the *invention*, the *imagination*, or lastly the *creation* of BEAUTY, (for the terms as here employed are synonimous) as the essence of all Poesy. Nor is this idea so much at variance with ordinary opinion as, at first sight, it may appear. A multitude of antique dogmas on this topic will be found, when divested of extrinsic speculation, to be easily resoluble into the definition now proposed. We do nothing more than present tangibly the vague clouds of the world's idea. We recognize the idea itself floating, unsettled, indefinite, in every attempt which has yet been made to circumscribe the conception of "Poesy" in words. A striking instance of this is observable in the fact that no definition exists, in which either "the beautiful," or some one of those qualities which we have above designated synonimously with "creation," has not been pointed out as the *chief* attribute of the Muse. "Invention," however, or "imagination," is by far more commonly insisted upon. The word ποιησις itself (creation) speaks volumes upon this point. Neither will it be amiss here to mention Count Bielfeld's definition of poetry as *"L'art d'exprimer les pensées par la fiction."*[4] With this definition (of which the philosophy is profound to a certain extent) the German terms *Dichtkunst*, the art of fiction, and *Dichten*,[5] to feign, which are used for *"poetry"* and *"to make verses,"* are in full and remarkable accordance. It is, nevertheless, in the *combination* of the two omniprevalent ideas that the novelty and, we believe, the force of our own proposition is to be found.

So far, we have spoken of Poesy as of an abstraction alone. As such, it is obvious that it may be applicable in various moods. The sentiment may develop itself in Sculpture, in Painting, in Music, or otherwise. But our present business is with its development in words—that development to which, in practical acceptation, the world has agreed to limit the term. And at this point there is one consideration which induces us to pause. We cannot make up our minds to admit (as some

4. The art of expressing thoughts by fiction (French); from Poe's favorite reference work: Baron Jacob de Bielfeld, *Les premiers traits de l'erudition universelle* (1767; trans. London, 1770 as *The Elements of Universal Erudition*).
5. To write poetry. A *Dichter* is a poet. The proper word for "to feign" is *vortäuschen*, which also means to simulate.

have admitted) the inessentiality of rhythm. On the contrary, the universality of its use in the earliest poetical efforts of all mankind would be sufficient to assure us, not merely of its congeniality with the Muse, or of its adaptation to her purposes, but of its elementary and indispensible importance. But here we must, perforce, content ourselves with mere suggestion; for this topic is of a character which would lead us too far. We have already spoken of Music as one of the moods of poetical development. It is in Music, perhaps, that the soul most nearly attains that end upon which we have commented—the creation of supernal beauty. It may be, indeed, that this august aim is here even partially or imperfectly attained, *in fact*. The *elements* of that beauty which is felt in sound, *may be* the mutual or common heritage of Earth and Heaven. In the soul's struggles at combination it is thus not impossible that a harp may strike notes not unfamiliar to the angels. And in this view the wonder may well be less that all attempts at defining the character or sentiment of the deeper musical impressions, has been found absolutely futile. Contenting ourselves, therefore, with the firm conviction, that music (in its modifications of rhythm and rhyme) is of so vast a moment in Poesy, as *never* to be neglected by him who is truly poetical—is of so mighty a force in furthering the great aim intended that he is mad who rejects its assistance—content with this idea we shall not pause to maintain its absolute essentially, for the mere sake of rounding a definition. We will but add, at this point, that the highest possible development of the Poetical Sentiment is to be found in the union of song with music, in its popular sense. The old Bards and Minnesingers possessed, in the fullest perfection, the finest and truest elements of Poesy; and Thomas Moore, singing his own ballads, is but putting the final touch to their completion as poems.

To recapitulate, then, we would define in brief the Poetry of words as the *Rhythmical Creation of Beauty*. Beyond the limits of Beauty its province does not extend. Its sole arbiter is Taste. With the Intellect or with the Conscience it has only collateral relations. It has no dependence, unless incidentally, upon either Duty or *Truth*. That our definition will necessarily exclude much of what, through a supine toleration, has been hitherto ranked as poetical, is a matter which affords us not even momentary concern. We address but the thoughtful, and heed only their approval—with our own. If our suggestions are truthful, then "after many days" shall they be understood as truth, even though found in contradiction of *all* that has been hitherto so understood. If false shall we not be the first to bid them die?

<p style="text-align:center">* * *</p>

Of the poets who have appeared most fully instinct with the principles now developed, we may mention *Keats* as the most remarkable. He is the sole British poet who has never erred in his themes. Beauty is always his aim.

We have thus shown our ground of objection to the general *themes* of Professor Longfellow. In common with all who claim the sacred title of poet, he should limit his endeavors to the creation of novel moods of

beauty, in form, in color, in sound, in sentiment; for over all this wide range has the poetry of words dominion. To what the world terms *prose* may be safely and properly left all else. The artist who doubts of his thesis, may always resolve his doubt by the single question—"might not this matter be as well or better handled in *prose?*" If it *may*, then is it no subject for the Muse. In the general acceptation of the term *Beauty* we are content to rest; being careful only to suggest that, in our peculiar views, it must be understood as inclusive of *the sublime*.

Of the pieces which constitute the present volume, there are not more than one or two thoroughly fulfilling the idea above proposed; although the volume as a whole is by no means so chargeable with didacticism as Mr. Longfellow's previous book. We would mention as poems *nearly true*, "The Village Blacksmith;" "The Wreck of the Hesperus" and especially "The Skeleton in Armor." In the first-mentioned we have the *beauty* of simple-mindedness as a genuine thesis; and this thesis is inimitably handled until the concluding stanza, where the spirit of legitimate poesy is aggrieved in the pointed antithetical deduction of a *moral* from what has gone before. In "The Wreck of the Hesperus" we have the *beauty* of child-like confidence and innocence, with that of the father's stern courage and affection. But, with slight exception, those particulars of the storm here detailed are not poetic subjects. Their thrilling *horror* belongs to prose, in which it could be far more effectively discussed, as Professor Longfellow may assure himself at any moment by experiment. There *are* points of a tempest which afford the loftiest and truest poetical themes—points in which pure beauty is found, or, better still, beauty heightened into the sublime, by terror. But when we read, among other similar things, that

> The salt sea was frozen on her breast,
> The salt tears in her eyes,

we feel, if not positive disgust, at least a chilling sense of the inappropriate. In the "Skeleton in Armor" we find a pure and perfect thesis artistically treated. We find the beauty of bold courage and self-confidence, of love and maiden devotion, of reckless adventure, and finally of life-contemning grief. Combined with all this we have numerous *points* of beauty apparently insulated, but all aiding the main effect or impression. The heart is stirred, and the mind does not lament its mal-instruction. The metre is simple, sonorous, well-balanced and fully adapted to the subject. Upon the whole, there are fewer truer poems than this. It has but one defect—an important one. The prose remarks prefacing the narrative are really *necessary*. But every work of art should contain within itself all that is requisite for its own comprehension. And this remark is especially true of the ballad. In poems of magnitude the mind of the reader is not, at all times, enabled to include, in one comprehensive survey, the proportions and proper adjustment of the whole. He is pleased, if at all, with particular passages; and the sum of his pleasure is compounded of the sums of the pleasurable sentiments inspired by these individual passages in the progress of perusal. But, in pieces of less extent, the pleasure is

unique, in the proper acceptation of this term—the understanding is employed, without difficulty, in the contemplation of the picture *as a whole*; and thus its effect will depend, in great measure, upon the perfection of its finish, upon the nice adaptation of its constituent parts, and especially, upon what is rightly termed by Schlegel *the unity or totality of interest*. But the practice of prefixing explanatory passages is utterly at variance with such unity. By the prefix, we are either put in possession of the subject of the poem; or some hint, historic fact, or suggestion, is thereby afforded, not included in the body of the piece, which, without the hint, is incomprehensible. In the latter case, while perusing the poem, the reader must revert, in mind at least, to the prefix, for the necessary explanation. In the former, the poem being a mere paraphrase of the prefix, the interest is divided between the prefix and the paraphrase. In either instance the totality of effect is destroyed.

Of the other original poems in the volume before us, there is none in which the aim of instruction, or *truth*, has not been too obviously substituted for the legitimate aim, *beauty*. In our last number, we took occasion to say that a didactic moral might be happily made the *under-current* of a poetical theme, and, in "Burton's Magazine," some two years since, we treated this point at length, in a review of Moore's "Alciphron;"[6] but the moral thus conveyed is invariably an ill effect when obtruding beyond the upper current of the thesis itself.

* * *

Nathaniel Hawthorne[1]

Twice-Told Tales. By Nathaniel Hawthorne.
James Munroe & Co.: Boston.

We have always regarded the *Tale* (using this word in its popular acceptation) as affording the best prose opportunity for display of the highest talent. It has peculiar advantages which the novel does not admit. It is, of course, a far finer field than the essay. It has even points of superiority over the poem. An accident has deprived us, this month, of our customary space for review; and thus nipped in the bud a design long cherished of treating this subject in detail; taking Mr. Hawthorne's volumes as a text. In May we shall endeavor to carry out our intention. At present we are forced to be brief.

With rare exception—in the case of Mr. Irving's "Tales of a Traveller" and a few other works of a like cast—we have had no American tales of high merit. We have had no skilful compositions—nothing which could bear examination as works of art. Of twattle called talewriting we have had, perhaps, more than enough. We have had a superabundance of the Rosa-Matilda effusions—gilt-edged paper all

6. See Poe's review of Moore on pp. 617ff. herein.
1. The initial notice (reprinted from *Graham's Magazine*, April 1842) of three of Hawthorne by Poe. Poe was one of the earliest critics to recognize Hawthorne's talent. The second notice begins on p. 645 herein. The third review—much cooler, though still positive—begins on p. 685.

couleur de rose:[2] a full allowance of cut-and-thrust blue-blazing melo-dramaticisms; a nauseating surfeit of low miniature copying of low life, much in the manner, and with about half the merit, of the Dutch herrings and decayed cheeses of Van Tuyssel—of all this, *eheu jam satis!*[3]

Mr. Hawthorne's volumes appear to us misnamed in two respects. In the first place they should not have been called "Twice-Told Tales"—for this is a title which will not bear *repetition*. If in the first collected edition they were twice-told, of course now they are thrice-told.—May we live to hear them told a hundred times! In the second place, these compositions are by no means *all* "Tales." The most of them are essays properly so called. It would have been wise in their author to have modified his title, so as to have had reference to all included. This point could have been easily arranged.

But under whatever titular blunders we receive this book, it is most cordially welcome. We have seen no prose composition by any American which can compare with *some* of these articles in the higher merits, or indeed in the lower; while there is not a single piece which would do dishonor to the best of the British essayists.

"The Rill from the Town Pump" which, through the *ad captandum* nature of its title, has attracted more of public notice than any one other of Mr. Hawthorne's compositions, is perhaps, the *least* meritorious. Among his best, we may briefly mention "The Hollow of the Three Hills;" "The Minister's Black Veil;" "Wakefield;" "Mr. Higginbotham's Catastrophe;" "Fancy's Show-Box;" "Dr. Heidegger's Experiment;" "David Swan;" "The Wedding Knell;" and "The White Old Maid." It is remarkable that all these, with one exception, are from the first volume.

The style of Mr. Hawthorne is purity itself. His *tone* is singularly effective—wild, plaintive, thoughtful, and in full accordance with his themes. We have only to object that there is insufficient diversity in these themes themselves, or rather in their character. His *originality* both of incident and of reflection is very remarkable; and this trait alone would ensure him at least *our* warmest regard and commendation. We speak here chiefly of the tales; the essays are not so markedly novel. Upon the whole we look upon him as one of the few men of indisputable genius to whom our country has as yet given birth. As such, it will be our delight to do him honor; and lest, in these undigested and cursory remarks, without proof and without explanation, we should appear to do him *more* honor than is his due, we postpone all farther comment until a more favorable opportunity.

2. Under the pseudonym "Rosa Matilda," Charlotte Dacre (1782–1840?) wrote sentimental gothic novels, such as *Zafloya, the Moor* (1806) and *The Libertine* (1807), which gave rise to the phrase "the Rose Matilda School" of fiction. Thus pages of *"couleur de rose"* (the color of rose).
3. Ah now, enough! (Latin). Van Tuyssel: a reference to Washington Irving's popular Dutch stories of New Amsterdam (New York).

Twice-Told Tales: By Nathaniel Hawthorne.
Two Volumes, Boston: James Munroe and Co.[4]

We said a few hurried words about Mr. Hawthorne in our last number, with the design of speaking more fully in the present. We are still, however, pressed for room, and must necessarily discuss his volumes more briefly and more at random than their high merits deserve.

The book professes to be a collection of *tales,* yet is, in two respects, misnamed. These pieces are now in their third republication, and, of course, are thrice-told. Moreover, they are by no means *all* tales, either in the ordinary or in the legitimate understanding of the term. Many of them are pure essays, for example, "Sights from a Steeple," "Sunday at Home," "Little Annie's Ramble," "A Rill from the Town-Pump," "The Toll-Gatherer's Day," "The Haunted Mind," "The Sister Years," "Snow-Flakes," "Night Sketches," and "Foot-Prints on the Sea-Shore." We mention these matters chiefly on account of their discrepancy with that marked precision and finish by which the body of the work is distinguished.

Of the Essays just named, we must be content to speak in brief. They are each and all beautiful, without being characterised by the polish and adaptation so visible in the tales proper. A painter would at once note their leading or predominant feature, and style it *repose.* There is no attempt at effect. All is quiet, thoughtful, subdued. Yet this repose may exist simultaneously with high originality of thought; and Mr. Hawthorne has demonstrated the fact. At every turn we meet with novel combinations; yet these combinations never surpass the limits of the quiet. We are soothed as we read; and withal is a calm astonishment that ideas so apparently obvious have never occurred or been presented to us before. Herein our author differs materially from Lamb or Hunt or Hazlitt[5]—who, with vivid originality of manner and expression, have less of the true novelty of thought than is generally supposed, and whose originality, at best, has an uneasy and meretricious quaintness, replete with startling effects unfounded in nature, and inducing trains of reflection which lead to no satisfactory result. The Essays of Hawthorne have much of the character of Irving, with more of originality, and less of finish; while, compared with the Spectator,[6] they have a vast superiority at all points. The Spectator, Mr. Irving, and Mr. Hawthorne have in common that tranquil and subdued manner which we have chosen to denominate *repose*; but, in the case of the two former, this repose is attained rather by the absence of novel combination, or of originality, than otherwise, and consists chiefly in the calm, quiet, unostentatious expression of commonplace thoughts, in an unambitious unadulterated Saxon. In them, by strong

4. Poe's second notice of Hawthorne, an elaboration of the first, was printed in *Graham's* in May 1842.
5. British essayists: Charles Lamb (1775–1834), Leigh Hunt (1784–1859), William Hazlitt (1778–1830).
6. A periodical (March 1711–December 1712) composed of a series of essays by Joseph Addison (1672–1719) and Richard Steele (1672–1729), noted for their elegance of style and social satire. Washington Irving was as well known for sketches and essays as for tales.

effort, we are made to conceive the absence of all. In the essays before us the absence of effort is too obvious to be mistaken, and a strong undercurrent of *suggestion* runs continuously beneath the upper stream of the tranquil thesis. In short, these effusions of Mr. Hawthorne are the product of a truly imaginative intellect, restrained, and in some measure repressed, by fastidiousness of taste, by constitutional melancholy and by indolence.

But it is of his tales that we desire principally to speak. The tale proper, in our opinion, affords unquestionably the fairest field for the exercise of the loftiest talent, which can be afforded by the wide domains of mere prose. Were we bidden to say how the highest genius could be most advantageously employed for the best display of its own powers, we should answer, without hesitation—in the composition of a rhymed poem, not to exceed in length what might be perused in an hour. Within this limit alone can the highest order of true poetry exist. We need only here say, upon this topic, that, in almost all classes of composition, the unity of effect or impression is a point of the greatest importance. It is clear, moreover, that this unity cannot be thoroughly preserved in productions whose perusal cannot be completed at one sitting. We may continue the reading of a prose composition, from the very nature of prose itself, much longer than we can persevere, to any good purpose, in the perusal of a poem. This latter, if truly fulfilling the demands of the poetic sentiment, induces an exaltation of the soul which cannot be long sustained. All high excitements are necessarily transient. Thus a long poem is a paradox. And, without unity of impression, the deepest effects cannot be brought about. Epics were the offspring of an imperfect sense of Art, and their reign is no more. A poem *too* brief may produce a vivid, but never an intense or enduring impression. Without a certain continuity of effort—without a certain duration or repetition of purpose—the soul is never deeply moved. There must be the dropping of the water upon the rock. De Béranger has wrought brilliant things—pungent and spirit-stirring—but, like all immassive bodies, they lack *momentum*, and thus fail to satisfy the Poetic Sentiment. They sparkle and excite, but, from want of continuity, fail deeply to impress. Extreme brevity will degenerate into epigrammatism; but the sin of extreme length is even more unpardonable. *In medio tutissimus ibis.*[7]

Were we called upon however to designate that class of composition which, next to such a poem as we have suggested, should best fulfil the demands of high genius—should offer it the most advantageous field of exertion—we should unhesitatingly speak of the prose tale, as Mr. Hawthorne has here exemplified it. We allude to the short prose narrative, requiring from a half-hour to one or two hours in its perusal. The ordinary novel is objectionable, from its length, for reasons already stated in substance. As it cannot be read at one sitting, it deprives itself, of course, of the immense force derivable from *totality*. Worldly interests intervening during the pauses of perusal, modify, an-

7. You will travel with the greatest safety in the middle (Latin), from Ovid, *Metamorphoses*, II.137.

nul, or counteract, in a greater or less degree, the impressions of the book. But simple cessation in reading would, of itself, be sufficient to destroy the true unity. In the brief tale, however, the author is enabled to carry out the fulness of his intention, be it what it may. During the hour of perusal the soul of the reader is at the writer's control. There are no external or extrinsic influences—resulting from weariness or interruption.

A skilful literary artist has constructed a tale. If wise, he has not fashioned his thoughts to accommodate his incidents; but having conceived, with deliberate care, a certain unique or single *effect* to be wrought out, he then invents such incidents—he then combines such events as may best aid him in establishing this preconceived effect. If his very initial sentence tend not to the outbringing of this effect, then he has failed in his first step. In the whole composition there should be no word written, of which the tendency, direct or indirect, is not to the one pre-established design. And by such means, with such care and skill, a picture is at length painted which leaves in the mind of him who contemplates it with a kindred art, a sense of the fullest satisfaction. The idea of the tale has been presented unblemished, because undisturbed; and this is an end unattainable by the novel. Undue brevity is just as exceptionable here as in the poem; but undue length is yet more to be avoided.

We have said that the tale has a point of superiority even over the poem. In fact, while the *rhythm* of this latter is an essential aid in the development of the poem's highest idea—the idea of the Beautiful— the artificialities of this rhythm are an inseparable bar to the development of all points of thought or expression which have their basis in *Truth*. But Truth is often, and in very great degree, the aim of the tale. Some of the finest tales are tales of ratiocination. Thus the field of this species of composition, if not in so elevated a region on the mountain of Mind, is a table-land of far vaster extent than the domain of the mere poem. Its products are never so rich, but infinitely more numerous, and more appreciable by the mass of mankind. The writer of the prose tale, in short, may bring to his theme a vast variety of modes or inflections of thought and expression—(the ratiocinative, for example, the sarcastic or the humorous) which are not only antagonistical to the nature of the poem, but absolutely forbidden by one of its most peculiar and indispensable adjuncts; we allude of course, to rhythm. It may be added, here, *par parenthèse*,[8] that the author who aims at the purely beautiful in a prose tale is laboring at great disadvantage. For Beauty can be better treated in the poem. Not so with terror, or passion, or horror, or a multitude of such other points. And here it will be seen how full of prejudice are the usual animadversions against those *tales of effect* many fine examples of which were found in the earlier numbers of Blackwood. The impressions produced were wrought in a legitimate sphere of action, and constituted a legitimate although sometimes an exaggerated interest. They were relished by every man

8. By way of parenthesis (French).

of genius: although there were found many men of genius who condemned them without just ground. The true critic will but demand that the design intended be accomplished, to the fullest extent, by the means most advantageously applicable.

We have very few American tales of real merit—we may say, indeed, none, with the exception of "The Tales of a Traveller" of Washington Irving, and these "Twice-Told Tales" of Mr. Hawthorne. Some of the pieces of Mr. John Neal[9] abound in vigor and originality; but in general, his compositions of this class are excessively diffuse, extravagant, and indicative of an imperfect sentiment of Art. Articles at random are, now and then, met with in our periodicals which might be advantageously compared with the best effusions of the British Magazines; but, upon the whole, we are far behind our progenitors in this department of literature.

Of Mr. Hawthorne's Tales we would say, emphatically, that they belong to the highest region of Art—an Art subservient to genius of a very lofty order. We had supposed, with good reason for so supposing, that he had been thrust into his present position by one of the impudent *cliques* which beset our literature, and whose pretensions it is our full purpose to expose at the earliest opportunity; but we have been most agreeably mistaken. We know of few compositions which the critic can more honestly commend then these "Twice-Told Tales." As Americans, we feel proud of the book.

Mr. Hawthorne's distinctive trait is invention, creation, imagination, originality—a trait which, in the literature of fiction, is positively worth all the rest. But the nature of originality, so far as regards its manifestation in letters, is but imperfectly understood. The inventive or original mind as frequently displays itself in novelty of *tone* as in novelty of matter. Mr. Hawthorne is original at *all* points.

It would be a matter of some difficulty to designate the best of these tales; we repeat that, without exception, they are beautiful. "Wakefield" is remarkable for the skill with which an old idea—a well-known incident—is worked up or discussed. A man of whims conceives the purpose of quitting his wife and residing *incognito*, for twenty years, in her immediate neighborhood. Something of this kind actually happened in London. The force of Mr. Hawthorne's tale lies in the analysis of the motives which must or might have impelled the husband to such folly, in the first instance, with the possible causes of his perseverance. Upon this thesis a sketch of singular power has been constructed.

"The Wedding Knell" is full of the boldest imagination—an imagination fully controlled by taste. The most captious critic could find no flaw in this production.

"The Minister's Black Veil" is a masterly composition of which the sole defect is that to the rabble its exquisite skill will be *caviare*. The *obvious* meaning of this article will be found to smother its insinuated one. The *moral* put into the mouth of the dying minister will be supposed to convey the *true* import of the narrative; and that a crime of

9. John Neal (1793–1876), American critic and fiction writer.

dark dye, (having reference to the "young lady") has been committed, is a point which only minds congenial with that of the author will perceive.

"Mr. Higginbotham's Catastrophe" is vividly original and managed most dexterously.

"Dr. Heidegger's Experiment" is exceedingly well imagined, and executed with surpassing ability. The artist breathes in every line of it.

"The White Old Maid" is objectionable, even more than the "Minister's Black Veil," on the score of its mysticism. Even with the thoughtful and analytic, there will be much trouble in penetrating its entire import.

"The Hollow of the Three Hills" we would quote in full, had we space;—not as evincing higher talent than any of the other pieces, but as affording an excellent example of the author's peculiar ability. The subject is common-place. A witch subjects the Distant and the Past to the view of a mourner. It has been the fashion to describe, in such cases, a mirror in which the images of the absent appear; or a cloud of smoke is made to arise, and thence the figures are gradually unfolded. Mr. Hawthorne has wonderfully heightened his effect by making the ear, in place of the eye, the medium by which the fantasy is conveyed. The head of the mourner is enveloped in the cloak of the witch, and within its magic folds there arise sounds which have an all-sufficient intelligence. Throughout this article also, the artist is conspicuous— not more in positive than in negative merits. Not only is all done that should be done, but (what perhaps is an end with more difficulty attained) there is nothing done which should not be. Every word *tells*, and there is not a word which does *not* tell.

In "Howe's Masquerade" we observe something which resembles a plagiarism—but which *may be* a very flattering coincidence of thought. We quote the passage in question.

"*With a dark flush of wrath* upon his brow they saw the general *draw his sword* and *advance to meet* the figure *in the cloak* before the latter had stepped one pace upon the floor.

" '*Villain, unmuffle yourself,*' cried he, 'you pass no farther!'

"The figure, without blenching a hair's breadth from the sword which was pointed at his breast, made a solemn pause, and *lowered the cape of the cloak* from his face, yet not sufficiently for the spectators to catch a glimpse of it. But Sir William Howe had evidently seen enough. The sternness of his countenance gave place to a look of wild amazement, if not horror, while he recoiled several steps from the figure, *and let fall his sword* upon the floor."—See vol. 2, page 20.

The idea here is, that the figure in the cloak is the phantom or reduplication of Sir William Howe,[1] but in an article called "William

1. A British general (1729–1814); after several stunning but inconclusive successes against George Washington and the Continental Armies, he resigned in protest over lack of home support. Hawthorne's story (1838) portrays a ghostly procession at a masquerade ball as Howe prepares to abandon the Old Province House in Boston.

Wilson," one of the "Tales of the Grotesque and Arabesque," we have not only the same idea, but the same idea similarly presented in several respects. We quote two paragraphs, which our readers may compare with what has been already given. We have italicized, above, the immediate particulars of resemblance.

"The brief moment in which I averted my eyes had been sufficient to produce, apparently, a material change in the arrangement at the upper or farther end of the room. A large mirror, it appeared to me, now stood where none had been perceptible before: and as I stepped up to it in extremity of terror, mine own image, but with features all pale and dabbled in blood, *advanced* with a feeble and tottering gait to meet me.

"Thus it appeared I say, but was not. It was Wilson, who then stood before me in the agonies of dissolution. Not a line in all the marked and singular lineaments of that face which was not even identically mine own. *His mask and cloak lay where he had thrown them, upon the floor.*"—Vol. 2. p. 57.

Here it will be observed that, not only are the two general conceptions identical, but there are various *points* of similarity. In each case the figure seen is the wraith or duplication of the beholder. In each case the scene is a masquerade. In each case the figure is cloaked. In each, there is a quarrel—that is to say, angry words pass between the parties. In each the beholder is enraged. In each the cloak and sword fall upon the floor. The "villain, unmuffle yourself;" of Mr. H. is precisely paralleled by a passage at page 56 of "William Wilson."

In the way of objection we have scarcely a word to say of these tales. There is, perhaps, a somewhat too general or prevalent *tone*—a tone of melancholy and mysticism. The subjects are insufficiently varied. There is not so much of *versatility* evinced as we might well be warranted in expecting from the high powers of Mr. Hawthorne. But beyond these trivial exceptions we have really none to make. The style is purity itself. Force abounds. High imagination gleams from every page. Mr. Hawthorne is a man of the truest genius. We only regret that the limits of our Magazine will not permit us to pay him that full tribute of commendation, which, under other circumstances, we should be so eager to pay.

To Joseph Evans Snodgrass (Letter 137)[1]

Philadelphia—June 4. 1842.

My Dear Snodgrass,

*　*　*

I have a proposition to make. You may remember a tale of mine published about a year ago in "Graham" and entitled the "Murders in the

1. In the first two paragraphs of his letter (omitted here), Poe complains that he has not heard from Snodgrass for some time; then he suggests that they join in a magazine project (the collaboration never came to pass). Text in angle brackets had been canceled.

Rue Morgue". Its *theme* was the exercise of ingenuity in detecting a murderer. I am just now putting the concluding touch to a similar article, which I shall entitle "The Mystery of Marie Rogêt—a Sequel to 'The Murders in the Rue Morgue'." The story is based upon that of the real murder of Mary Cecilia Rogers, which created so vast an excitement, some months ago, in New-York. I have handled the design in a very singular and entirely *novel* manner. I imagine a series of nearly exact *coincidences* occurring in Paris. A young grisette, one *Marie Rogêt*, has been murdered under precisely similar circumstances with *Mary Rogers*. Thus under pretence of showing how Dupin (the hero of the Rue Morgue) unravelled the mystery of Marie's assassination, I, in fact, enter into a very rigorous analysis of the *real* tragedy in New-York. *No point* is omitted. I examine<d>, each by each, the opinions and arguments of our press on the subject, and show (I think satisfactorily) that this subject has never yet been *approached*. The press has been entirely on a wrong scent. In fact, I really believe, not only that I have demonstrated the falsity of the idea that the girl was <not> the victim of a gang <as supposed>, but have *indicated the assassin*. My main object, however, as you will readily understand, is the analysis of the *principles of investigation* in cases of like character. Dupin *reasons* the matter throughout.

* * *

To James R. Lowell (Letter 179)[1]

New-York, July 2. 44.

My Dear Mr Lowell,

I can feel for the "constitutional indolence" of which you complain—for it is one of my own besetting sins. I am excessively slothful, and wonderfully industrious—by fits. There are epochs when any kind of mental exercise is torture, and when nothing yields me pleasure but solitary communion with the "mountains & the woods"—the "altars" of Byron. I have thus rambled and dreamed away whole months, and awake, at last, to a sort of mania for composition. Then I scribble all day, and read all night, so long as the disease endures. This is also the temperament of P. P. Cooke,[2] of Va the author of "Florence Vane", "Young Rosalie Lee", & some other sweet poems—and I should not be surprised if it were your own. Cooke writes and thinks as you—and I have been told that you resemble him personally.

I am *not* ambitious—unless negatively. I, now and then feel stirred up to excel a fool, merely because I hate to let a fool imagine that he may excel me. Beyond this I feel nothing of ambition. I really perceive that vanity about which most men merely prate—the vanity of the

1. This letter seems, in part, to have been written with an eye to influencing James Russell Lowell's biographical sketch of Poe, which appeared in *Graham's* for February 1845 (pp. 656ff. herein). Text in angle brackets had been canceled.
2. Philip Pendleton Cooke (1816–1850), a Virginia poet, wrote several critically appreciative letters to Poe (e.g., see references pp. 616–17 herein).

human or temporal life. I live continually in a reverie of the future. I have no faith in human perfectibility. I think that human exertion will have no appreciable effect upon humanity. Man is now only more active—not more happy—nor more wise, than he was 6000 years ago. The result will never vary—and to suppose that it will, is to suppose that the foregone man has lived in vain—that the foregone time is but the rudiment of the future—that the myriads who have perished have not been upon equal footing with ourselves—nor are we with our posterity. I cannot agree to lose sight of man the individual, in man the mass.—I have no belief in spirituality. I think the word a *mere* word. No one has really a conception of spirit. We cannot imagine what is not. We deceive ourselves by the idea of infinitely rarefied matter. Matter escapes the senses by degrees—a stone—a metal—a liquid—the atmosphere—a gas—the luminiferous ether. Beyond this there are other modifications more rare. But to all we attach the notion of a constitution of particles—atomic composition. For this reason only, we think spirit different; for spirit, we say is unparticled, and *therefore* is not matter. But it is clear that if we proceed sufficiently far in our ideas of rarefaction, we shall arrive at a point where the particles coalesce; for, although the particles be infinite, the infinity of littleness in the spaces between them, is an absurdity.—The unparticled matter, permeating & impelling, all things, is God. Its activity is the thought of God—which creates. Man, and other thinking beings, are individualizations of the unparticled matter. Man exists as a "person", by being clothed with matter (the particled matter) which individualizes him. Thus habited, his life is rudimental. What we call "death" is the painful metamorphosis. The stars are the habitations of rudimental beings. But for the necessity of the rudimental life, there would have been no worlds. At death, the worm is the butterfly—still material, but of a matter unrecognized by our organs—recognized, occasionally, perhaps, by the sleep-waker, directly—without organs—through the mesmeric medium. Thus a sleep-waker may see ghosts. Divested of the rudimental covering, the being inhabits *space*—what we suppose to be the immaterial universe—passing every where, and acting all things, by mere volition—cognizant of all secrets but that of the nature of God's volition—the motion, or activity, of the unparticled matter.

You speak of "an estimate of my life"—and, from what I have already said, you will see that I have none to give. I have been too deeply conscious of the mutability and evanescence of temporal things, to give any continuous effort to anything—to be consistent in anything. My life has been *whim*—impulse—passion—a longing for solitude—a scorn of all things present, in an earnest desire for the future.

I am profoundly excited by music, and by some poems—those of Tennyson especially—whom, with Keats, Shelley, Coleridge (occasionally) and a few others of like thought and expression, I regard as the *sole* poets. Music is the perfection of the soul, or idea, of Poetry. The *vagueness* <and> of exultation arous[ed by] a sweet air (which should be strictly indefinite & never too strongly suggestive) is precisely what

we should aim at in poetry. Affectation, within bounds, is thus no blemish.

I still adhere to Dickens as either author, or dictator, of the review.[3] My reasons would convince you, could I give them to you—but I have left myself no space. I had two long interviews with Mr D. when here. Nearly every thing in the critique, I heard from <D> him or suggested to him, personally. The poem of Emerson I read to him.

I have been so negligent as not to preserve copies of any of my volumes of poems—nor was either worthy preservation. The best passages were culled in Hirst's article.[4] I think my best poems, "The Sleeper", "The Conqueror Worm", "The Haunted Palace", "<A Paen">" "Lenore", "Dreamland" & "The Coliseum"—but all have been hurried & unconsidered. My best tales are "Ligeia"; The "Gold-Bug"; The "Murders in the Rue Morgue", "The Fall of the House of Usher", The "Tell-Tale Heart", The "Black Cat", "William Wilson", & "The Descent into the Maelström." "The Purloined Letter," forthcoming in the "Gift", is, perhaps, the best of my tales of ratiocination. I have lately written, for Godey, "The Oblong-Box", and "Thou art the Man"—as yet unpublished. With this, I mail you "The Gold-Bug", which is the only one of my tales I have on hand.

* * *

From Marginalia[1]

In getting my books, I have been always solicitous of an ample margin; this not so much through any love of the thing in itself, however agreeable, as for the facility it affords me of pencilling suggested thoughts, agreements and differences of opinion, or brief critical comments in general. Where what I have to note is too much to be included within the narrow limits of a margin, I commit it to a slip of paper, and deposit it between the leaves; taking care to secure it by an imperceptible portion of gum tragacanth paste.

All this may be whim; it may be not only a very hackneyed, but a very idle practice;—yet I persist in it still; and it affords me plea-

3. Poe attributed to Charles Dickens a recent article on "American Poetry" in the *London Foreign Quarterly*, in which Poe was called "an imitator of Tennyson" (see Poe's letter to Lowell—Letter 175—of May 28, 1844; not printed here). Lowell thought it by John Forster, who was to become Dickens's biographer.
4. Henry B. Hirst (1817–1874) published a biographical sketch of Poe in the *Saturday Museum* (February 25–March 4, 1843).
1. Reprinted from the *Democratic Review* for November 1844. In November 1844, Poe began a series of what he called marginal notes to various books and articles he said he had read and annotated. Appearing in different periodicals, the series extended to September 1849, for a total of seventeen installments. Some of the notes were reproduced from his reviews and articles and previous notations (some were cribbed from encyclopedias); others were new. Poe had begun publishing such "notes," "brevities," or "random thoughts" from what he called his commonplace notebook in the *Southern Literary Messenger* as early as 1836 with a sequence he called "Pinakidia" (or "Tablets"). Similar jottings can be found in "A Chapter of Suggestions" (1845); in the "Editorial Miscellanies" (1846–47), which includes random gossip; and in "Fifty Suggestions" (1849). These later sequences, along with the "Marginalia," can be found entire in *Essays and Reviews* (1984) edited by G. R. Thompson. Cf. the *Fragments* of Friedrich Schlegel (pp. 727–30 herein).

sure; which is profit, in despite of Mr. Bentham with Mr. Mill[2] on his back.

This making of notes, however, is by no means the making of mere *memoranda*—a custom which has its disadvantages, beyond doubt. "*Ce que je mets sur papier,*" says Bernardin de St. Pierre, "*je remets de ma mémoire, et par consequence je l'oublie,*"[3]—and, in fact, if you wish to forget anything upon the spot, make a note that this thing is to be remembered.

But the purely marginal jottings, done with no eye to the Memorandum Book, have a distinct complexion, and not only a distinct purpose, but none at all; this it is which imparts to them a value. They have a rank somewhat above the chance and desultory comments of literary chit-chat—for these latter are not unfrequently "talk for talk's sake," hurried out of the mouth; while the *marginalia* are deliberately pencilled, because the mind of the reader wishes to unburthen itself of a *thought*;—however flippant—however silly—however trivial—still a thought indeed, not merely a thing that might have been a thought in time, and under more favorable circumstances. In the *marginalia*, too, we talk only to ourselves; we therefore talk freshly—boldly—originally—with *abandonnement*—without conceit—much after the fashion of Jeremy Taylor, and Sir Thomas Browne, and Sir William Temple, and the anatomical Burton, and that most logical analogist, Butler,[4] and some other people of the old day, who were too full of their matter to have any room for their manner, which, being thus left out of question, was a capital manner, indeed,—a model of manners, with a richly marginalic air.

The circumscription of space, too, in these pencillings, has in it something more of advantage than of inconvenience. It compels us (whatever diffuseness of idea we may clandestinely entertain), into Montesquieu-ism, into Tacitus-ism (here I leave out of view the concluding portion of the "Annals")—or even into Carlyle-ism[5]—a thing which, I have been told, is not to be confounded with your ordinary affectation and bad grammar. I say "bad grammar," through sheer obsti-

2. Jeremy Bentham (1748–1842) and James Mill (1773–1836), British economic theorists dedicated to the philosophy of "utilitarianism" (in essence, the greatest good for the greatest number).
3. That which I put on paper . . . I remove from my memory, and consequently I forget it—from Jacques Henri Bernadin de Saint-Pierre (1737–1814), French naturalist and author of the Romantic nature novel *Paul and Virginia* (1788).
4. Probably Samuel Butler (1612–1680), British satiric poet, author of the rambling mock-epic *Hudibras* (1663–78). "*Abandonnement*": abandonment, wildness, shamelessness. Jeremy Taylor (1613–1667), English clergyman known for eloquence and religious passion. Sir Thomas Browne (1605–1682), English physician and essayist, the author of *Religio Medici* (1643), *Hydriotaphia, or Urn-Burial* (1658), and *The Garden of Cyrus* (1658). Sir William Temple (1628–1699), English diplomat, statesman, and author, who involved himself in the "battle of the books" (ancient vs. modern values). Robert Burton (1557–1640) put together a voluminous compendium of thoughts and jottings he called the *Anatomy of Melancholy* (1621).
5. More or less random references to ancient, 18th-century, and 19th-century essayists and wits. Baron de La Brède et de Montesquieu (1689–1755) was the author of a series of witty *Personal Letters* (1721). Cornelius Tacitus (55?–117? C.E.) was a Roman historian, noted for cleverness and elegance. Thomas Carlyle (1795–1881) was a Romantic-Victorian historian, satirist, translator, and fiction writer, best remembered for his study of *The French Revolution* (3 vols., 1837) and the satiric, ironic, yet serious *Sartor Resartus* (1833–34).

nacy, because the grammarians (who should know better) insist upon it that I should not. But then grammar is not what these grammarians will have it; and, being merely the analysis of language, with the result of this analysis, must be good or bad just as the analyst is sage or silly—just as he is a Horne Tooke or a Cobbett.[6]

But to our sheep. During a rainy afternoon, not long ago, being in a mood too listless for continuous study, I sought relief from *ennui* in dipping here and there, at random, among the volumes of my library— no very large one, certainly, but sufficiently miscellaneous; and, I flatter myself, not a little *recherché*.[7]

Perhaps it was what the Germans call the "brain-scattering" humor of the moment; but, while the picturesqueness of the numerous pencil-scratches arrested my attention, their helter-skelter-iness of commentary amused me. I found myself at length, forming a wish that it had been some other hand than my own which had so bedevilled the books, and fancying that, in such case, I might have derived no inconsiderable pleasure from turning them over. From this the transition-thought (as Mr. Lyell, or Mr. Murchinson, or Mr. Featherstonhaugh[8] would have it) was natural enough:—there might be something even in *my* scribblings which, for the mere sake of scribbling, would have interest for others.

The main difficulty respected the mode of transferring the notes from the volumes—the context from the text—without detriment to that exceedingly frail fabric of intelligibility in which the context was imbedded. With all appliances to boot, with the printed pages at their back, the commentaries were too often like Dodona's oracles—or those of Lycophron Tenebrosus—or the essays of the pedant's pupils, in Quintillian,[9] which were "necessarily excellent, since even he (the pedant) found it impossible to comprehend them:"—what, then, would become of it—this context—if transferred?—if translated? Would it not rather be *traduit* (traduced) which is the French synonym, or *overzezet* (turned topsy-turvy) which is the Dutch one?

I concluded, at length, to put extensive faith in the acumen and imagination of the reader:—this as a general rule. But, in some instances, where even faith would not remove mountains, there seemed no safer plan than so to re-model the note as to convey at least the ghost of a conception as to what it was all about. Where, for such conception, the text itself was absolutely necessary, I could quote it;

6. William Cobbett (1762–1835), author of the once famous *Rural Rides* (1830), a description of the changing conditions of the English countryside, was a political writer who, while in America, wrote (under the name of "Peter Porcupine") several pro-British, more or less anti-American pamphlets. [John] Horne Tooke (1736–1812), English radical politician.
7. Obscure, arcane, excessively erudite (French).
8. Scientists. Sir Roderick Imprey Murchison (1792–1871) and Charles Lyell (1797–1875) were English geologists. Lyell's public engagements with the controversy over the earth's origin (uniformian development vs. catastrophic change) helped pave the way for the later arguments over Darwinian theories of evolution.
9. Quintilianus (c. 35–c. 99 C.E.), a Spanish-born rhetorician noted for eloquence and cleverness. Dodona was an oracle in the Greek village of Epirus; the prophecies, associated with the rustling of leaves, were "delivered" from the tops of trees. Sometimes brass pots were tied to the branches of the trees; their rattling gave rise to the connotation of "Dodonian" as "babbling." Lycophron (early 3rd century B.C.E.), Greek poet noted for obscurity.

where the title of the book commented upon was indispensable, I could name it. In short, like a novel-hero dilemma'd, I made up my mind "to be guided by circumstances," in default of more satisfactory rules of conduct.

As for the multitudinous opinion expressed in the subjoined *far-rago*[1]—as for my present assent to all, or dissent from any portion of it—as to the possibility of my having, in some instances, altered my mind—or as to the impossibility of my not having altered it often—these are points upon which I say nothing, because upon these there can be nothing cleverly said. It may be as well to observe, however, that just as the goodness of your true pun is in the direct ratio of its intolerability, so is nonsense the essential sense of the Marginal Note.

JAMES RUSSELL LOWELL

From Our Contributors.—No. XVII. Edgar Allan Poe[1]

With A Portrait.

The situation of American literature is anomalous. It has no centre, or, if it have, it is like that of the sphere of Hermes.[2] It is divided into many systems, each revolving round its several sun, and often presenting to the rest only the faint glimmer of a milk-and-watery way.

* * *

Mr. Poe is at once the most discriminating, philosophical, and fearless critic upon imaginative works who has written in America. It may be that we should qualify our remark a little, and say that he *might be*, rather than that he always *is*, for he seems sometimes to mistake his phial of prussic-acid for his inkstand. If we do not always agree with him in his premises, we are, at least, satisfied that his deductions are logical, and that we are reading the thoughts of a man who thinks for himself, and says what he thinks, and knows well what he is talking about. His analytic power would furnish forth bravely some score of ordinary critics. We do not know him personally, but we suspect him for a man who has one or two pet prejudices on which he prides himself. These sometimes allure him out of the strict path of criticism,[3] but, where they do not interfere, we would put almost entire confidence in his judgments. Had Mr. Poe had the control of a magazine of his own, in which to display his critical abilities, he would have been as autocratic, ere this, in America, as Professor Wilson[4] has been in

1. A compendium, a random mixture.
1. Lowell's review of Poe is reprinted from *Graham's Magazine* for February 1845.
2. Called Mercury in Roman myth: preeminently the messenger of the gods, he was also the god of fortunate windfalls; the god of flocks and shepherds; the patron god of eloquence and cunning and of rogues; the guide of travelers; as well as the guide of souls to the underworld (as Hermes Psychopompus).
3. We cannot but think that this was the case in his review of W. E. Channing's poems, in which we are sure that there is much which must otherwise have challenged Mr. Poe's hearty liking [Lowell's note].
4. John Wilson, editor of *Blackwood's Edinburgh Magazines*.

England; and his criticisms, we are sure, would have been far more profound and philosophical than those of the Scotsman. As it is, he has squared out blocks enough to build an enduring pyramid, but has left them lying carelessly and unclaimed in many different quarries.

Remarkable experiences are usually confined to the inner life of imaginative men, but Mr. Poe's biography displays a vicissitude and peculiarity of interest such as is rarely met with. The offspring of a romantic marriage, and left an orphan at an early age, he was adopted by Mr. Allan, a wealthy Virginian, whose barren marriage-bed seemed the warranty of a large estate to the young poet. Having received a classical education in England, he returned home and entered the University of Virginia, where, after an extravagant course, followed by reformation at the last extremity, he was graduated with the highest honors of his class. Then came a boyish attempt to join the fortunes of the insurgent Greeks, which ended at St. Petersburg, where he got into difficulties through want of a passport, from which he was rescued by the American consul and sent home?[5] He now entered the military academy at West Point, from which he obtained a dismissal on hearing of the birth of a son to his adopted father, by a second marriage, an event which cut off his expectations as an heir. The death of Mr. Allan, in whose will his name was not mentioned, soon after relieved him of all doubt in this regard, and he committed himself at once to authorship for a support. Previously to this, however, he had published (in 1827) a small volume of poems, which soon ran through three editions, and excited high expectations of its author's future distinction in the minds of many competent judges.[6]

* * *

Mr. Poe's early productions show that he could see through the verse to the spirit beneath, and that he already had a feeling that all the life and grace of the one must depend on and be modulated by the will of the other. We call them the most remarkable boyish poems that we have ever read. We know of none that can compare with them for maturity of purpose, and a nice understanding of the effects of language and metre. Such pieces are only valuable when they display what we can only express by the contradictory phrase of *innate experience*. We copy one of the shorter poems written when the author was only *fourteen!* There is a little dimness in the filling up, but the grace and symmetry of the outline are such as few poets ever attain. There is a smack of ambrosia about it.

[Quotes "To Helen."]

It is the *tendency* of the young poet that impresses us. Here is no "withering scorn," no heart "blighted" ere it has safely got into its teens, none of the drawing-room sansculottism[7] which Byron had

5. Poe made up these details to make his biography more interesting in the mode of Lord Byron.
6. Lowell here briefly compares the early signs of genius or talent in writers like Shakespeare, Milton, Pope, Collins, Burns, Coleridge, Byron, Wordsworth, Southey, Shelley, and others.
7. In the manner of a revolutionary extremist. From French *sans* + *culottes*, "without breeches," referring to the republican extremists during the French Revolution, who wore pantaloons rather than upper-class knee-breeches.

brought into vogue. All is limpid and serene, with a pleasant dash of the Greek Helicon[8] in it. The melody of the whole, too, is remarkable. It is not of that kind which can be demonstrated arithmetically upon the tips of the fingers. It is of that finer sort which the inner ear alone can estimate. It seems simple, like a Greek column, because of its perfection. In a poem named "Ligeia," under which title he intended to personify the music of nature, our boy-poet gives us the following exquisite picture:

> *Ligeia! Ligeia!*
> *My beautiful one,*
> *Whose harshest idea*
> *Will to melody run,*
> *Say, is it thy will*
> *On the breezes to toss,*
> *Or capriciously still,*
> *Lik[e] the lone albatross,*
> *Incumbent on night,*
> *As she on the air,*
> *To keep watch with delight*
> *On the harmony there?*

John Neal,[9] himself a man of genius, and whose lyre has been too long capriciously silent, appreciated the high merit of these and similar passages, and drew a proud horoscope for their author. The extracts which we shall presently make from Mr. Poe's later poems, fully justify his predictions.

Mr. Poe has that indescribable something which men have agreed to call *genius*. No man could ever tell us precisely what it is, and yet there is none who is not inevitably aware of its presence and its power. Let talent writhe and contort itself as it may, it has no such magnetism. Larger of bone and sinew it may be, but the wings are wanting. Talent sticks fast to earth, and its most perfect works have still one foot of clay. Genius claims kindred with the very workings of Nature herself, so that a sunset shall seem like a quotation from Dante or Milton, and if Shakspeare be read in the very presence of the sea itself, his verses shall but seem nobler for the sublime criticism of ocean. Talent may make friends for itself, but only genius can give to its creations the divine power of winning love and veneration. Enthusiasm cannot cling to what itself is unenthusiastic, nor will he ever have disciples who has not himself impulsive zeal enough to be a disciple. Great wits are allied to madness only inasmuch as they are possessed and carried away by their demon, while talent keeps him, as Paracelsus[1] did, securely prisoned in the pommel of its sword. To the eye of genius, the veil of the spiritual world is ever rent asun-

8. Mount Helicon was often referred to as the home of the Muses (goddesses of the sciences and arts). *Helicon* (from *helix*) means "winding," as in a winding willow vine or branch.
9. American poet, novelist, and critic (1793–1876).
1. Philippus Aureolus Paracelcus (Theophrastus Bombastus von Hohenheim; 1493?–1541), Swiss chemist and physician, who wrote many tracts on alchemy and the occult in relation to medicine.

der, that it may perceive the ministers of good and evil who throng
continually around it. No man of mere talent ever flung his inkstand
at the devil. When we say that Mr. Poe has genius, we do not mean to say that
he has produced evidence of the highest. But to say that he possesses
it at all is to say that he needs only zeal, industry, and a reverence for
the trust reposed in him, to achieve the proudest triumphs and the
greenest laurels.

* * *

Mr. Poe has two of the prime qualities of genius, a faculty of vigor-
ous yet minute analysis, and a wonderful fecundity of imagination.
The first of these faculties is as needful to the artist in words, as a
knowledge of anatomy is to the artist in colors or in stone. This en-
ables him to conceive truly, to maintain a proper relation of parts, and
to draw a correct outline, while the second groups, fills up, and colors.
Both of those Mr. Poe has displayed with singular distinctness in his
prose works, the last predominating in his earlier tales, and the first in
his later ones. In judging of the merit of an author, and assigning him
his niche among our household gods, we have a right to regard him
from our own point of view, and to measure him by our own standard.
But, in estimating his works, we must be governed by his own design,
and, placing them by the side of his own ideal, find how much is want-
ing. We differ with Mr. Poe in his opinions of the objects of art. He es-
teems that object to be the creation of Beauty, * * * and perhaps it
is only in the definition of that word that we disagree with him. But in
what we shall say of his writings we shall take his own standard as our
guide. The temple of the god of song is equally accessible from every
side, and there is room enough in it for all who bring offerings, or seek
an oracle.

In his tales, Mr. Poe has chosen to exhibit his power chiefly in that
dim region which stretches from the very utmost limits of the probable
into the weird confines of superstition and unreality. He combines in a
very remarkable manner two faculties which are seldom found united;
a power of influencing the mind of the reader by the impalpable shad-
ows of mystery, and a minuteness of detail which does not leave a pin
or a button unnoticed. Both are, in truth, the natural results of the
predominating quality of his mind, to which we have before alluded,
analysis. It is this which distinguishes the artist. His mind at once
reaches forward to the effect to be produced. Having resolved to bring
about certain emotions in the reader, he makes all subordinate parts
tend strictly to the common centre. Even his mystery is mathematical
to his own mind. To him χ is a known quantity all along. In any
picture that he paints, he understands the chemical properties of all
his colors. However vague some of his figures may seem, however
formless the shadows, to him the outline is as clear and distinct as
that of a geometrical diagram. For this reason Mr. Poe has no sympa-
thy with *Mysticism*. The Mystic dwells *in* the mystery, is enveloped
with it; it colors all his thoughts; it effects his optic nerve especially,
and the commonest things get a rainbow edging from it. Mr Poe, on

the other hand, is a spectator *ab extrà*.[2] He analyzes, he dissects, he watches

> ——"with an eye serene,
> The very pulse of the machine,"

for such it practically is to him, with wheels and cogs and piston-rods all working to produce a certain end. It is this that makes him so good a critic. Nothing baulks him, or throws him off the scent, *except now and then a prejudice.*

This analyzing tendency of his mind balances the poetical, and by giving him the patience to be minute, enables him to throw a wonderful reality into his most unreal fancies. A monomania he paints with great power. He loves to dissect these cancers of the mind, and to trace all the subtle ramifications of its roots.

In raising images of horror, also, he has a strange success; conveying to us sometimes by a dusky hint some terrible *doubt* which is the secret of all horror. He leaves to imagination the task of finishing the picture, a task to which only she is competent. * * *

We have hitherto spoken chiefly of Mr. Poe's *collected* tales, as by them he is more widely known than by those published since in various magazines, and which we hope soon to see collected. In these he has more strikingly displayed his analytic propensity. * * *

Beside the merit of conception, Mr. Poe's writings have also that of form. His style is highly finished, graceful and truly classical. It would be hard to find a living author who had displayed such varied powers. As an example of his style we would refer to one of his tales, "The House of Usher," in the first volume of his "Tales of the Grotesque and Arabesque." It has a singular charm for us, and we think that no one could read it without being strongly moved by its serene and sombre beauty. Had its author written nothing else it would alone have been enough to stamp him as a man of genius, and the master of a classic style. In this tale occurs one of the most beautiful of his poems. It loses greatly by being taken out of its rich and appropriate setting, but we cannot deny ourselves the pleasure of copying it here. We know no modern poet who might not have been justly proud of it.

[Quotes "The Haunted Palace."]

Was ever the wreck and desolation of a noble mind so musically sung? A writer in the London Foreign Quarterly Review, who did some faint justice to Mr. Poe's poetical abilities, speaks of his resemblance to Tennyson. The resemblance, if there be any, is only in so sensitive an ear to melody as leads him sometimes into quaintness, and the germ of which may be traced in his earliest poems, published several years before the first of Tennyson's appeared.

We copy one more of Mr. Poe's poems, whose effect cannot fail of being universally appreciated.

2. From the outside (Latin).

[Quotes "Lenore."]

Beside his "Tales of the Grotesque and Arabesque," and some works unacknowledged, Mr. Poe is the author of "Arthur Gordon Pym," a romance, in two volumes, which has run through many editions in London; of a system of Conchology,[3] of a digest and translation of Lemmonnier's Natural History,[4] and has contributed to several reviews in France, in England, and in this country. He edited the Southern Literary Messenger during its novitiate, and by his own contributions gained it most of its success and reputation. He was also, for some time, the editor of this magazine, and our readers will bear testimony to his ability in that capacity.

Mr. Poe is still in the prime of life, being about thirty-two years of age, and has probably as yet given but an earnest of his powers. As a critic, he has shown so superior an ability that we cannot but hope that he will collect his essays of this kind and give them a more durable form. They would be a very valuable contribution to our literature, and would fully justify all we have said in his praise. We could refer to many others of his poems than those we have quoted, to prove that he is the possessor of a pure and original vein. His tales and essays have equally shown him a master in prose. It is not for us to assign him his definite rank among contemporary authors, but we may be allowed to say that we know of *none* who has displayed more varied and striking abilities.

[In 1850 Lowell added a new ending, omitting "The Haunted Palace" and the last paragraphs.]

The great masters of imagination have seldom resorted to the vague and the unreal as sources of effect. They have not used dread and horror alone, but only in combination with other qualities, as means of subjugating the fancies of their readers. The loftiest muse has ever a household and fireside charm about her. Mr. Poe's secret lies mainly in the skill with which he has employed the strange fascination of mystery and terror. In this his success is so great and striking as to deserve the name of art, not artifice. We cannot call his materials the noblest or purest, but we must concede to him the highest merit of construction.

As a critic, Mr. Poe was aesthetically deficient. Unerring in his analysis of dictions, meters, and plots, he seemed wanting in the faculty of perceiving the profounder ethics of art. His criticisms are, however, distinguished for scientific precision and coherence of logic. They have the exactness, and, at the same time, the coldness of mathematical demonstrations. Yet they stand in strikingly refreshing contrast with the vague generalisms and sharp personalities of the day. If deficient in warmth, they are also without the heat of partisanship. They are especially valuable as illustrating the great truth, too generally overlooked, that analytic power is a subordinate quality of the critic.

3. Poe lent his name to a pirated edition of a book on seashells (see the biographical introduction on p. xxxi herein).
4. Presumably Pierre Charles Lemonnier (1715–1799), French astronomer.

On the whole, it may be considered certain that Mr. Poe has attained an individual eminence in our literature, which he will keep. He has given proof of power and originality. He has done that which could only be done once with success or safety, and the imitation or repetition of which would produce weariness.

Henry Wadsworth Longfellow An anonymous review of several volumes of Henry Wadsworth Longfellow's poems appeared in the April 1845 issue of the *Aristidean* magazine—just after the Little Longfellow War installments in Poe's *Broadway Journal* (see p. xxxviii and p. 637 herein). This review continues the campaign initiated by Poe to impugn Longfellow as a representative of *coterie* politics; Poe regarded Longfellow as a charter member of the literary cliques nefariously controlling the publishing and reviewing business in America. The *Aristidean* was edited by Thomas Dunn English (1819–1902), Poe's on-again off-again friend; and it may be that Poe made a deal with English to "plant" the review to bolster his case against Longfellow. The extracts reprinted here give a good idea of the vituperation and acrimony of the literary combatants at the time. With the exception of the comments on Longfellow's *Poems on Slavery*, the criticisms of particular volumes and poems are omitted; the remarks on the slavery poems are offered as pertinent to the racism and slavery issues raised by recent cultural critics (see The South and Slavery section on pp. 767ff. herein). The *Slavery* volume was Longfellow's somewhat suspiciously expedient response to the criticism of his abolitionist friends in the North that he (like Emerson) had distanced himself too much from the great political issues facing the nation. Others were angered by what they thought were ill-considered attacks on the South. Some scholars think that English wrote the majority of the piece, while others claim it as Poe's—though the authorship of neither is absolutely certain. In the opinion of several scholars, the review's crudely vituperative tone, awkward style, and grammatical errors are not quite characteristic of Poe. But whoever wrote it, the gibes are representative of the substantial antiabolitionist feeling, not only in the South but across the nation at the time.

From Henry Wadsworth Longfellow

"*Poems on Slavery*. By Henry Wadsworth Longfellow. Second edition, Cambridge: Published by John Owen. 1842." 12mo, pp. 31.
"*Voices of the Night*. By Henry Wadsworth Longfellow. Tenth edition. Cambridge: Published by John Owen. 1844." 12mo, pp. 144.
"*Ballads and other Poems*. By Henry Wadsworth Longfellow, author of 'Voices of the Night,' 'Hyperion,' &c. Eighth edition. Cambridge: Published by John Owen. 1844." 12mo, pp. 132.
"*The Waif: a collection of Poems*.
 'A waif the which by fortune came
 Upon your seas, he claimed as property;
 And yet nor his, nor his in equity, but
 Yours the waif by high perogative.'—*The Fairie Queene*.
Second edition. Cambridge. Published by John Owen. 1845." 12mo, pp. 144

The poetical reputation of Mr. Longfellow is, no doubt, in some measure well-deserved; but it may be questioned whether, without the adventitious influence of his social position as Professor of Modern Languages and Belles Lettres at HARVARD, and an access of this influence by marriage with an heiress, he would even have acquired his present celebrity—such as it is.

We really feel no little shame in being forced, not into the expression, but into the entertainment of opinions such as these—the only shame we feel in respect to the matter of their expression, is shame for others and not for ourselves—shame that we in the infancy of our journalism, should have been permitted to take the lead in the utterance of a thought so long common with the *literati* of the land. In no literary circle out of BOSTON—or, indeed, out of the small coterie of abolitionists, transcendentalists and fanatics in general, which is the Longfellow junto—have we heard a seriously dissenting voice on this point. It is universally, in private conversation—out of the knot of rogues and madmen aforesaid—admitted that the poetical claims of Mr. LONGFELLOW have been vastly overrated, and that the individual himself would be esteemed little without the accessaries of wealth and position. It is usually said, that he has a sufficient scholarship, a fine taste, a keen appreciation of the beautiful, a happy memory, a happier tact at imitation or transmutation, felicity of phrase and some fancy. A few insist on his imagination—thus proving the extent of their own—and showing themselves to be utterly unread in the old English and modern German literature, to one or other of which, the author of "Outre Mer" is unquestionably indebted for whatever imagination or traces of invention his works may display. No phrenologist,[1] indeed, would require to be told that Mr. LONGFELLOW was not the man of genius his friends would have us believe him—his head giving no indication of ideality. Nor, when we speak of phrenologists, do we mean to insist on implicit faith in the marvels and inconsistencies of the FOWLERS *et id genus omne.*[2] Common observation, independently of either GALL or SPURZHEIM, would suffice to teach all mankind that very many of the salient points of phrenological science are undisputable truths—whatever falsity may be detected in the principles kindly furnished to the science by hot-headed and asinine votaries. Now, one of these salient points, is the fact that what men term "poetical genius," and what the phrenologists generally term the organ of ideality, are always found co-existent in the same individual. We should as soon expect to see our old friend, SATAN, presiding at a temperance meeting, as to see a veritable poem—of his own—composed by a man whose head was flattened at the temples, like that of Professor LONGFELLOW. Holding these views, we confess that we were not a little surprised to hear Mr. POE, in a late lecture, on the Poetry of AMERICA, claim for the Professor a pre-eminence over all poets of this

1. Phrenology is the reading of the contours of the skull in an effort to determine the development of mental "organs" of the brain underneath. See Sciences of the Mind section on pp. 742ff. herein.
2. And all persons of that hype (*Hoc genus omne*; Horace, *Satires*, I.ii.2).

country on the score of the "loftiest poetical quality—imagination." There is no doubt in our minds, that an opinion so crude as this, must arise from a want of leisure or inclination to compare the works of the writer in question with the sources from which they were stolen. A defensive letter written by an unfortunate wight who called himself "OUTIS," seems to have stirred up the critic to make the proper examination, and we will make an even wager of a pound avoirdupois of nothing against LONGFELLOW's originality, that the rash opinion would not be given again. The simple truth is, that, whatever may be the talents of Professor LONGFELLOW, he is the GREAT MOGUL of the Imitators. There is, perhaps, no other country than our own, under the sun, in which it would have been possible for him to have attained his present eminence; and no other, certainly, in which, after having attained it by accident or chicanery, he would not have been hurled from it in a very brief period after its attainment.

We have now before us all the collected poems of Mr. LONGFELLOW; and the first question which forces itself upon us as we look at them, is, how much of their success may be attributed to the luxurious manner in which, as merely physical books, they have been presented to the public. Of course we cannot pretend to answer our own question with precision; but that the *physique* has had vast influence upon the *morale*, no reflecting person of common honesty will be willing to deny.

* * *

The first volume is entitled "Poems on Slavery," and is intended for the especial use of those negrophilic[3] old ladies of the north, who form so large a part of Mr. LONGFELLOW's friends. The first of this collection is addressed to WILLIAM ELLERY CHANNING,[4] the great essayist, and not the very little poet of the same name.

* * *

In the second poem—"The Slave's Dream"—there is also a particularly beautiful close to one of the stanzas:—

> "At night he heard the lion roar,
> And the hyæna scream,
> And the river-horse as he crushed the reeds
> Beside some hidden stream;
> And it passed *like a glorious roll of drums*,
> *Through the triumph of his dream*."

This is certainly very fine; although we do do not exactly understand *what* is like the glorious roll of drums, whether it be the stream, or the various sounds aforesaid. This embarrassment in future will be pre-

3. Negro-loving.
4. William Ellery Channing (1780–1842) was an anti-Calvinist Unitarian clergyman and abolitionist propagandist. He wrote several abolitionist tracts, including *Slavery* (1835), *The Abolitionist* (1836), *Emancipation* (1840), and *The Duty of the Free States* (1842). His nephew of the same name (1818–1901) was a minor Transcendentalist poet, for whose talents Poe had nothing but contempt. It is easy to confuse the various Channings. A cousin, William Henry Channing (1810–1884), was also involved in the Transcendentalist movement (and the experiment in communal living at Brook Farm); Ralph Waldo Emerson's famous "Ode" of 1847, defending what at the time was his own elitist antipolitical position (especially his lack of interest in the issue of the war with Mexico) is inscribed to him.

vented, if the poet will only affix a note to the next edition, declaring what he does mean, if he know himself.

The third poem—"The Good Part that shall not be taken away"—has two very effective lines:—

> "And musical as silver bells
> Their falling chains shall be."

The whole poem is in praise of a certain lady, who

> "——— was rich and gave up all
> To break the iron bands
> Of those who waited in her hall
> And labored in her lands."

No doubt, it is a very commendable and very comfortable thing, in the Professor, to sit at ease in his library chair, and write verses instructing the southerners how to give up their all with a good grace, and abusing them if they will not; but we have a singular curiosity to know how much of his own, under a change of circumstances, the Professor himself would be willing to surrender. Advice of this character looks well only in the mouth of those who have entitled themselves to give it, by setting an example of the self-sacrifice.

The fourth is "The Slave in the Dismal Swamp." This is a shameless medley of the grossest misrepresentation. When did Professor LONGFELLOW ever *know* a slave to be hunted with bloodhounds in the DISMAL SWAMP? Because he has heard that runaway slaves are so treated in CUBA, he has certainly no right to change the locality, and by insinuating a falsehood in lieu of a fact, charge his countrymen with barbarity. What makes the matter worse, he is one of those who insist upon truth as one of the elements of poetry.

The fifth—"The Slave singing at midnight," embodies some good and novel rhymes—for example—

> "In that hour when night is *calmest*,
> Sang he from the Hebrew *psalmist*."

"Angel" and "evangel," however, are inadmissible because identical—just as "excision" and "circumcision" would be—that is to say: the ear, instead of being gratified with a variation of a sound—the principle of rhyme—is positively displeased by its bare repetition. The commencement of the rhyming words, or—equally—of the rhyming portions of words, must always be different.

The sixth is "The witnesses," and is exceedingly feeble throughout. We cannot conceive how any artist could in two distinct stanzas of so brief a poem, admit such a termination as "witness*es*"—rhyming it too with "abyss."

The seventh, "The Quadroon Girl," is the old abolitionist story—worn threadbare—of a slaveholder selling his own child—a thing which may be as common in the South as in the East, is the infinitely worse crime of making matrimonial merchandise—or even less legitimate merchandise—of one's daughter.

The eighth—"The Warning," contains at least one stanza of absolute truth—as follows.

> "There is a poor, blind Sampson in this land,
> Shorn of his strength and bound in bonds of steel,
> Who may, in some grim revel, raise his hand,
> And shake the pillars of the common weal,
> Till the vast temple of our Liberties,
> A shapeless mass of wreck and rubbish lies."

One thing is certain:—if this prophecy be *not* fulfilled, it will be through no lack of incendiary doggrel on the part of Professor LONGFELLOW and his friends. We dismiss this volume with no more profound feeling than that of contempt.

* * *

[The review proceeds through the other volumes listed, with repeated charges of plagiarisms by Longfellow, especially from the works of Poe, before concluding.]

It is, indeed, for that whereas, Mr. LONGFELLOW has stolen so much from Mr. POE, that we have alluded so much to the *exposé* of the latter; for it appeared to us, our course was but just. The latter, driven to it by a silly letter of Mr. LONGFELLOW's friends, has exposed the knavery of the Professor, and any one who reads the "Broadway Journal," will acknowledge he has done it well.

There are other plagiarisms of Mr. LONGFELLOW which we might easily expose; but we have said enough. There can be no reasonable doubt in the mind of any, out of the little clique, to which we at first alluded, that the author of "Outre Mer," is not only a servile imitator, but a most insolent literary thief. Commencing his literary life he began, struck with his quiet style, to imitate BRYANT. As he pored over the pages of the Spanish, and then of the great Northern writers, his imitation took a new direction. Soon, to save labor, he began to filch a little here and a little there—some straw to make his bricks, something to temper his own heavy clay. Finding he was not detected, he stole with more confidence, until stealing became habit, and so second nature. At this time we doubt whether he could write without helping himself to the ideas and style of other people. Indeed, if he were by chance to perpetrate an original idea, he would be as much astonished as the world around; and would go about cackling and "making a fuss in general," like a little bantam hen, who by a strange freak of nature, had laid a second egg on the same day.

From Thomas Hood[1]

Wiley and Putnam's Library of Choice Reading No. XVI.
Prose and Verse. By Thomas Hood. Part I. New York:
Willey and Putnam.

* * *

In especial, whatever merit *may* accidentally be discovered in a pun, arises altogether from *unexpectedness*. This is its element, and is twofold. First, we demand that the combination of the pun be unexpected, and secondly, we demand the most entire unexpectedness in the pun *per se*. A rare pun, rarely appearing, is, to a certain extent, a pleasurable effect—but to no mind, however debased in taste, is a continuous effort at punning otherwise than unendurable. The man who maintains that he derives gratification from any such chapters of punnage as Hood was in the daily habit of putting to paper, has no claim to be believed upon his oath.

* * *

The continuous and premediated puns of Hood, however, are to be regarded as the weak points of the man. Independently of their ill effect, in a literary view, as mere puns, they leave upon us a painful impression; for too evidently they are the hypochondriac's struggles at mirth—they are the grinnings of the death's-head. No one can read his Literary Reminiscences without being convinced of his habitual despondency—and the species of pseudo wit in question, is precisely of that character which would be adopted by an author of Hood's temperament and cast of intellect, when compelled to write, at an emergency. That his heart had no interest in these *niaiseries*,[2] is clear. We allude, of course, to his *mere* puns for the pun's sake—a class of letters by which he attained his most extensive renown. That he did *more* in this way than in any other, would follow as a corollary from what we have already said—for, generally, he was unhappy, and, almost continually, he was obliged to write, *invitá Minerva*.[3] But his true element was a very rare and ethereal class of *humor*, in which the *mere* pun was left altogether out of sight, or took the character of the richest *grotesquerie*, impressing the imaginative reader with very remarkable force, as if by a new phase of the ideal. It is in this species of brilliant *grotesquerie*, uttered with a rushing *abandon* which wonderfully aided its effect, that Hood's marked originality of manner consisted; and it is this which fairly entitles him, at times, to the epithet "great;"—we say fairly so entitles him; for *that* undeniably may be considered *great*—(of

1. British editor and writer Thomas Hood (1799–1845) was noted for his combination of odd humor, melancholy, and social protest. Poe took the occasion of the American publication of Hood's *Prose and Poetry* in Wiley and Putnam's series, the Library of Choice Reading, to discuss the relation of and discriminations among fancy, imagination, fantasy, and humor as well as offering observations on wit, sarcasm, and the grotesque—the portion of the review from *Broadway Journal* (August 9, 1845) reprinted here.
2. Sillinesses, foolishness.
3. Literally when Minerva, the goddess of wisdom, is "unwilling"; i.e., a writer lacks natural talent (see Horace, *Art of Poetry*, 385).

whatever seeming littleness in itself) which has the capability of producing intense emotion in the minds of those who are themselves undeniably great.

When we said, however, that Hood wrought profound impressions upon imaginative men, we spoke only of what is imagination in the popular acceptance of the term. His true province—that is to say the field in which he is distinctive—is a kind of border land between the Fancy and the Fantasy—but in this region he reigns supreme. That we may be the more clearly understood on this head, we will venture to quote a few passages of definition which were used by ourselves on a former occasion—while commenting on the prose style of Mr. Willis;[4]—it is indeed too much the custom to employ at absolute random such words as Wit, Humor, Fantasy, the Fancy, and the Imagination.

In the style of Mr. Willis we easily detect this idiosyncrasy. We have no trouble in tracing it home—and when we reach it and look it fairly in the face, we recognize it on the instant.—It is Fancy.

To be sure there is quite a tribe of Fancies—although one half of them never suspected themselves to be such until so told by the metaphysicians—but the one of which we speak has never yet been accredited among men, and we beg pardon of Mr. Willis for the liberty we take in employing the topic of his *style*, as the best possible vehicle and opportunity for the introduction of this, our *protégé*, to the consideration of the literary world.

"Fancy," says the author[5] of "Aids to Reflection" (who aided Reflection to much better purpose in his "Genevieve")—"Fancy combines—Imagination creates." This was intended, and has been received, as a distinction; but it is a distinction without a difference—without even a difference of degree. The Fancy as nearly creates as the imagination, and neither at all. Novel conceptions are merely unusual combinations. The mind of man can imagine nothing which does not exist:—if it could, it would create not only ideally, but substantially—as do the thoughts of God. It may be said—"We imagine a griffin, yet a griffin does not exist." Not the griffin certainly, but its component parts. It is no more than a collation of known limbs—features—qualities. Thus with all which claims to be new—which appears to be a *creation* of the intellect:—it is re-soluble into the old. The wildest effort of the mind cannot stand the test of the analysis.

We might make a distinction of *degree* between the fancy and the imagination, in calling the latter the former loftily employed. But experience would prove this distinction to be unsatisfactory. What we *feel* to be fancy, will be found still fanciful, whatever be the theme which engages it. No *subject* exalts it into imagination. When Moore[6] is termed a fanciful poet, the epithet is precisely applied; he *is*. He is

4. Nathaniel Parker Willis (1806–1867), American editor and author; an on-again off-again friend of Poe.
5. Samuel Taylor Coleridge (1772–1834).
6. Thomas Moore (1779–1852), Irish writer who figures repeatedly in Poe's works (see, e.g., the Poems introduction on pp. 3ff. herein; notes to "Al Aaraaf," pp. 22ff.; and Poe's review of Moore, pp. 617ff.).

fanciful in "Lalla Rookh," and had he written the "Inferno,"[7] there he would have been fanciful still: for not only is he essentially fanciful, but he has no ability to be any thing more, unless at rare intervals—by snatches—and with effort. What we say of him at this point, moreover, is equally true of all little frisky men, personally considered.

The fact seems to be that Imagination, Fancy, Fantasy, and Humor, have in common the elements, Combination, and Novelty. The Imagination is the artist of the four. From novel arrangements of old forms which present themselves to it, it selects only such as are harmonious:—the result, of course, is *beauty* itself—using the term in its most extended sense, and as inclusive of the sublime. The pure imagination chooses, *from either beauty or deformity*, only the most combinable things hitherto uncombined;—the compound, as a general rule, partaking (in character) of sublimity or beauty, in the ratio of the respective sublimity or beauty of the things combined—which are themselves still to be considered as atomic—that is to say, as previous combinations. But, as often analogously happens in physical chemistry, so not unfrequently does it occur in this chemistry of the intellect, that the admixture of two elements will result in a something that shall have nothing of the quality of one of them—or even nothing of the qualities of either. The range of Imagination is therefore, unlimited. Its materials extend throughout the Universe. Even out of deformities it fabricates that *beauty* which is at once its sole object and its inevitable test. But, in general, the richness or force of the matters combined—the facility of discovering combinable novelties worth combining—and the absolute "chemical combination" and proportion of the completed mass—are the particulars to be regarded in our estimate of Imagination. It is this thorough harmony of an imaginative work which so often causes it to be under-valued by the undiscriminating, through the character of *obviousness* which is super-induced. We are apt to find ourselves asking "*why is it* that these combinations have never been imagined before?"

Now, when this question *does not occur*—when the harmony of the combination is comparatively neglected, and when in addition to the element of novelty, there is introduced the sub-element of *unexpectedness*—when, for example, matters are brought into combination which not only have never been combined but whose combination strikes us *as a difficulty happily overcome*—the result then appertains to the FANCY—and is, to the majority of mankind more grateful than the purely harmonious one—although, absolutely, it is less beautiful (or grand) for the reason that *it is* less harmonious.

Carrying its errors into excess—for, however enticing, they *are* errors still, or Nature lies,—Fancy is at length found impinging upon the province of *Fantasy*. The votaries of this latter delight not only in novelty and unexpectedness of combination, but in the *avoidance* of proportion. The result is therefore abnormal, and to a healthy mind affords less of pleasure through its novelty, than of pain through its

7. The first part of Dante's *Divine Comedy* (c. 1300–1320).

incoherence. When, proceeding a step farther, however, Fantasy seeks not merely disproportionate but incongruous or antagonistical elements, the effect is rendered more pleasurable from its greater positiveness;—there is a merry effort of Truth to shake from her that which is no property of hers;—and we laugh outright in recognizing *Humor*.

The four faculties in question appear to me all of their class;—but when either Fancy or Humor is expressed to gain an end—is pointed at a purpose—whenever either becomes objective in place of subjective—then it becomes, also, pure Wit or Sarcasm, just as the purpose is well-intentioned or malevolent.

These, we grant, are entirely new views, but we do not consider them as the less surely deduced. At all events their admission for the present will enable us to be lucid on the topic of Hood. When we speak of his province as a border ground between Fantasy and Fancy, of course we do not mean rigorously to confine him to this province. He has made very successful and frequent incursions into the dominions of Humor (in general he has been too benevolent to be witty), and there have been one or two occasions—(those, for instance, of his "Eugene Aram" and "Bridge of Sighs,") in which he has stepped boldly, yet vacillatingly, into the realm of Imagination herself. We mean to say, however, that he is never truly imaginative for more than a paragraph at a time.

In a word, the genius of Hood is the result of vivid Fancy impelled, or controlled,—certainly tinctured, at all points, by hypochondriasis.

* * *

Edgar Allan Poe[1]

Tales by Edgar A. Poe. New York: Wiley and Putnam,
161 Broadway. 1845. 18 mo. pp. 228.

The great fault of American and British authors is imitation of the peculiarities of thought and diction of those who have gone before them. They tread on a beaten track because it is well trodden. They follow as disciples, instead of being teachers. Hence it is that they denounce all novelty as a culpable variation from standard rules, and think all originality to be incomprehensible. To produce something which has not been produced before, in their estimation, is equal to six, at least, of the seven deadly sins—perhaps, the unpardonable sin itself—and for this crime they think the author should atone here in the purgatory of false criticism, and hereafter by the hell of oblivion. The odor of originality in a new book is "a savor of death unto death" to their productions, unless it can be destroyed. So they cry aloud—"Strange! incomprehensible! what is it about?" even though its idea may be

1. Most scholars believe that Poe wrote a good deal of this review and planted it with Thomas Dunn English for the latter's magazine, the *Aristidean*, for October 1845.

plainly developed as the sun at noon-day. Especially, we are sorry to say, does this prevail in this country. Hence it is, that we are chained down to a wheel, which ever monotonously revolves round a fixed centre, progressing without progress.

Yet that we are beginning to emancipate ourselves from this thraldom, is seen in the book before us, and in the general appreciation of its merits, on both sides of the Atlantic. It has sold well: and the press has praised it, discriminately and yet with no stint. "The British Critic," and other English literary journals laud it most handsomely. Though, as a general rule, we do not care a fig for British criticism—conducted as it mostly is, we *do* prize a favorable review, when it is evidently wrung from the reviewer by a high admiration and a strong sense of justice—as in the case before us. And all this, as we have said, proves that we are escaping the shackles of imitation. There is just as much chance of originality at this day, as at any other—all the nonsense of the sophists to the contrary, notwithstanding. "There is nothing new under the sun," said SOLOMON. In the days of his many-wived majesty the proverb might apply—it is a dead saying now. The creative power of the mind is boundless. There is no end to the original combinations of words—nor need there be to the original combination of ideas.

The first tale in Mr. POE's book is called "The Gold Bug." If we mistake not, it was written in competition for a large premium, some years since—a premium which it obtained. It made a great noise when first issued, and was circulated to a greater extent than any American tale, before or since. The intent of the author was evidently to write a popular tale: money, and the finding of money being chosen as the most popular thesis. In this he endeavoured to carry out his idea of the perfection of the plot, which he defines as—that, in which nothing can be disarranged, or from which nothing can be removed, without ruin to the mass—as that, in which we are never able to determine whether any one point depends upon or sustains any one other. We pronounce that he has perfectly succeeded in his perfect aim. There is a marked peculiarity, by-the-by, in it, which is this. The bug, which gives title to the story, is used only in the way of mystification, having throughout a seeming and no real connection with the subject. Its purpose is to seduce the reader into the idea of supernatural machinery, and keeping him so mystified until the last moment. The ingenuity of the story cannot be surpassed. Perhaps it is the most *ingenious* story Mr. POE has written; but in the higher attributes—a great invention—an invention proper—it is not at all comparable to the "Tell-tale Heart"—and more especially to "Ligeia," the most extraordinary, of its kind, of his productions. The characters are well-drawn. The reflective qualities and steady purpose, founded on a laboriously obtained conviction of LEGRAND, is most faithfully depicted. The negro is a perfect picture. He is drawn accurately—no feature overshaded, or distorted. Most of such delineations are caricatures.[2]

2. We see, by-the-by, that Willis, in one of his letters, talks about the tales having to encounter an obstacle in England, because of the word "bug." This is a mere affectation—but were it

The materials of which the "Gold Bug" is constructed are, apparently, of the simplest kind. It is the mode of grouping them around the main idea, and their absolute necessity of each to the whole—note Mr. POE's definition of plot before given—in which the perfection of their use consists. The solution of the mystery is the most curious part of the whole, and for this, which is a splendid specimen of analysis, we refer the reader to the book.

"The Black Cat" is the next tale. In our last number we found fault with this, as a reproduction of the "Tell-tale Heart." On further examination, we think ourselves in error, somewhat. It is rather an amplification of one of its phases. The *dénôuement* is a perfect printed *tableau*.

"Mesmeric Revelations" [*sic*], which comes next, has excited much discussion. A large number of the mesmerists, queerly enough, take it all for gospel. Some of the Swedenborgians,[3] at PHILADELPHIA, wrote word to POE, that at first they doubted, but in the end became convinced, of its truth. This was excruciatingly and unsurpassably funny—in spite of the air of *vraisemblance*[4] that pervades the article itself. It is evidently meant to be nothing more than the vehicle of the author's views concerning the DEITY, immateriality, spirit, &c., which he apparently believes to be true, in which belief he is joined by Professor BUSH.[5] The matter is most rigorously condensed and simplified. It might easily have been spread over the pages of a large octavo.

"Lionizing," which PAULDING,[6] and some others regard with great favor, has been overlooked, in general. It is an extravaganza, composed by rules—and the laws of extravaganza is as much and clearly defined as those of any other species of composition.

"The Fall of the House of Usher," was stolen by BENTLEY, who copied it in his "Miscellany,"[7] without crediting the source from whence he derived it. The thesis of this tale, is the revulsion of feeling consequent upon discovering that for a long period of time we have been mistaking sounds of agony, for those of mirth or indifference. It is an elaborate tale—surpassed only by "Ligeia," in our judgment. IRVING's[8] view of it—and he speaks of it, in italics, as *powerful*, is correct. The *dénôuement*, where the doors open, and the figure is found standing without the door, as USHER had foretold, is grand and impressive. It appears to be better liked than the rest of Mr. Poe's productions, among literary people—though with the mass, the "Gold-bug," and "Murders in the Rue Morgue," are more popular, be-

not, the junction with "gold" saves it. Look at the other compounds in common English use—"*bugbear*," for instance. "Gold-bug" is peculiarly an English—not an American word [Reviewers' note].

3. Emanuel Swedenborg (1688–1772), Swedish theologian, scientist, and philosopher. He underwent a spiritual crisis between 1743 and 1745. After his death, his followers founded the New Church or New Jerusalem Church. Swedenborg's accounts of his mystical visions influenced a number of writers. Franz Anton Mesmer (1734–1815), Austrian physician who developed a method of medical treatment by hypnosis that he called animal magnetism.
4. Appearance of reality.
5. George Bush (1796–1859), professor of Hebrew at the University of New York.
6. James Kirke Paulding (1778–1860), American novelist.
7. Bentley's *Miscellany*, British magazine.
8. Washington Irving (1783–1859), American author.

cause of their unbroken interest, novelty of the combination of ordinary incident, and faithful minuteness of detail. "The Haunted Palace," from which we stated in our late review of his poems, LONGFELLOW had stolen, all, that was worth stealing, of his "BELEAGUERED CITY," and which is here introduced with effect, was originally sent to O'SULLIVAN,[9] of the "Democratic Review," and by him rejected, because "he found it impossible to comprehend it." In connection with the subject of rejections, there is a good thing concerning TUCKERMAN,[1] which would show—if it needed to show the very palpable— his utter lack of discrimination, and his supreme self-esteem. When he edited the "Boston Miscellany," POE, under the impression that the work was still conducted by HALE,[2] sent him "The Tell-tale Heart," a most extraordinary, and very original composition. Whereon Master TUCKERMAN, in noting its rejection, chose to say, through his publishers, that "if Mr. POE would condescend to be more quiet, he would be a valuable contributor to the press." POE rejoined, that TUCKERMAN was the King of the Quietists, and in three months would give a quietus to the "Miscellany." The author was mistaken in time—it only took two months to finish the work. LOWELL[3] afterwards published the "Tell-tale Heart," in the "Pioneer."

"A [D]escent into the Maelström," is chiefly noted for the boldness of its subject—a subject never dreamed of before—and for the clearness of its descriptions.

"Monos and Una," is one of a series of *post-mortem* reveries. The style, we think, is good. Its philosophy is damnable; but this does not appear to have been a point with the author, whose purpose, doubtless, was novelty of effect—a novelty brought about by the tone of the colloquy. The reader feels as though he were listening to the talk of spirits. In the usual imaginary conversations—LANDOR's,[4] for instance—he is permitted to see a tone of banter. He feels that the author is not in earnest. He understands that spirits have been invented for the purpose of introducing their supposed opinions.

"The [M]an of the Crowd," is the last sketch in the work. It is peculiar and fantastic, but contains little worthy of special note, after what has been said of others.

The three tales before the last, are "Murders in the Rue Morgue"— "Mystery of Marie Roget"—and "The Purloined Letter." They are all of the same class—a class peculiar to Mr. POE. They are inductive—tales of ratiocination—of profound and searching analysis. "The Mystery of Marie Roget"—although in this, the author appears to have been hampered by facts—reveals the whole secret of their mode of construction. It is true that there the facts were before him—so that it is not

9. John Louis O'Sullivan (1813–1895), editor of the *Democratic Review*. See notes to Poe's review of Henry Wadsworth Longfellow's *Ballads* (pp. 636ff. herein). In what he called the Little Longfellow War, Poe charged Longfellow with various plagiarisms, including this one.
1. Henry Theodore Tuckerman (1813–1871), American author.
2. Sarah Josepha Hale (1788–1879), American journalist and editor.
3. James Russell Lowell (1819–1891), American author and editor (see his review of Poe on pp. 656ff. herein).
4. Walter Savage Landor (1775–1864), British poet, author of *Imaginary Conversations* (1824–53).

fully a parallel—but the *rationale* of the process is revealed by it. The author, as in the case of "Murders in the Rue Morgue," the first written, begins by imagining a deed committed by such a creature, or in such a manner, as would most effectually mislead inquiry. Then he applies analysis to the investigation.

There is much made of nothing in "The Purloined Letter,"—the story of which is simple; but the reasoning is remarkably clear, and directed solely to the required end. It first appeared in the "Gift," and was thence copied into CHAMBERS' "Edinburgh Journal," as a most notable production. We like it less than the others, of the same class. It has not their continuous and absorbing interest.

"The Mystery of Marie Roget" has a local, independent of any other, interest. Every one, at all familiar with the internal history of NEW YORK, for the last few years, will remember the murder of MARY ROGERS, the segar-girl. The deed baffled all attempts of the police to discover the time and mode of its commission, and the identity of the offenders. To this day, with the exception of the light afforded by the tale of Mr. POE, in which the faculty of analysis is applied to the facts, the whole matter is shrouded in complete mystery. We think, he has proven, very conclusively, that which he attempts. At all events, he has dissipated in our mind, all belief that the murder was perpetrated by more than one.

The incidents in the "Murder [sic] in the Rue Morgue" are purely imaginary. Like all the rest, it is written backwards.

We have thus noticed the entire collection—and have only to say, by way of close, that the collection embraces by no means the best of Mr. POE's productions that we have seen; or rather is not totally so good, as might have been made, though containing some of the best.

The style of Mr. POE is clear and forcible. There is often a minuteness of detail; but on examination it will always be found that this minuteness was necessary to the development of the plot, the effect, or the incidents. His style may be called, strictly, an earnest one. And this earnestness is one of its greatest charms. A writer must have the fullest belief in his statements, or must simulate that belief perfectly, to produce an absorbing interest in the mind of his reader. That power of stimulation can only be possessed by a man of high genius. It is the result of a peculiar combination of the mental faculties. It produces earnestness, minute, not profuse detail, and fidelity of description. It is possessed by Mr. POE, in its full perfection.

The evident and most prominent aim of Mr. POE is originality, either of idea, or the combination of ideas. He appears to think it a crime to write unless he has something novel to write about, or some novel way of writing about an old thing. He rejects every word not having a tendency to develope the effect. Most writers get their subjects first, and write to develope it. The first inquiry of Mr. POE is for a novel effect— then for a subject; that is, a new arrangement of circumstance, or a new application of tone, by which the effect shall be developed. And he evidently holds whatever tends to the furtherance of the effect, to be legitimate material. Thus it is that he has produced works of the

most notable character, and elevated the mere "tale," in this country, over the larger "novel"—conventionally so termed.

Preface

(The Raven and Other Poems—1845)

These trifles are collected and republished chiefly with a view to their redemption from the many improvements to which they have been subjected while going at random "the rounds of the press." If what I have written is to circulate at all, I am naturally anxious that it should circulate as I wrote it. In defence of my own taste, nevertheless, it is incumbent upon me to say, that I think nothing in this volume of much value to the public, or very creditable to myself. Events not to be controlled have prevented me from making, at any time, any serious effort in what, under happier circumstances, would have been the field of my choice. With me poetry has been not a purpose, but a passion; and the passions should be held in reverence; they must not—they cannot at will be excited with an eye to the paltry compensations, or the more paltry commendations, of mankind.

E. A. P.

The Philosophy of Composition[1]

Charles Dickens, in a note now lying before me, alluding to an examination I once made of the mechanism of "Barnaby Rudge," says—"By the way, are you aware that Godwin[2] wrote his 'Caleb Williams' backwards? He first involved his hero in a web of difficulties, forming the second volume, and then, for the first, cast about him for some mode of accounting for what had been done."

I cannot think this the *precise* mode of procedure on the part of Godwin—and indeed what he himself acknowledges, is not altogether in accordance with Mr. Dickens' idea—but the author of "Caleb Williams" was too good an artist not to perceive the advantage derivable from at least a somewhat similar process. Nothing is more clear than that every plot, worth the name, must be elaborated to its *dénouement* before any thing be attempted with the pen. It is only with the *dénouement* constantly in view that we can give a plot its indispensable air of consequence, or causation, by making the incidents, and especially the tone at all points, tend to the development of the intention.

There is a radical error, I think, in the usual mode of constructing a story. Either history affords a thesis—or one is suggested by an incident of the day—or, at best, the author sets himself to work in the

1. Poe's essay on how he composed "The Raven" is reprinted from *Graham's* of April 1846.
2. William Godwin (1756–1836), British writer and philosopher who wrote *Caleb Williams* (1794) as a mystery novel.

combination of striking events to form merely the basis of his narrative—designing, generally, to fill in with description, dialogue, or autorial comment, whatever crevices of fact, or action, may, from page to page, render themselves apparent.

I prefer commencing with the consideration of an *effect*. Keeping originality *always* in view—for he is false to himself who ventures to dispense with so obvious and so easily attainable a source of interest—I say to myself, in the first place, "Of the innumerable effects, or impressions, of which the heart, the intellect, or (more generally) the soul is susceptible, what one shall I, on the present occasion, select?" Having chosen a novel, first, and secondly a vivid effect, I consider whether it can best be wrought by incident or tone—whether by ordinary incidents and peculiar tone, or the converse, or by peculiarity both of incident and tone—afterward looking about me (or rather within) for such combinations of event, or tone, as shall best aid me in the construction of the effect.

I have often thought how interesting a magazine paper might be written by any author who would—that is to say, who could—detail, step by step, the processes by which any one of his compositions attained its ultimate point of completion. Why such a paper has never been given to the world, I am much at a loss to say—but, perhaps, the autorial vanity has had more to do with the omission than any one other cause. Most writers—poets in especial—prefer having it understood that they compose by a species of fine frenzy—an ecstatic intuition—and would positively shudder at letting the public take a peep behind the scenes, at the elaborate and vacillating crudities of thought—at the true purposes seized only at the last moment—at the innumerable glimpses of idea that arrived not at the maturity of full view—at the fully matured fancies discarded in despair as unmanageable—at the cautious selections and rejections—at the painful erasures and interpolations—in a word, at the wheels and pinions—the tackle for scene-shifting—the step-ladders and demon-traps—the cock's feathers, the red paint and the black patches, which, in ninety-nine cases out of the hundred, constitute the properties of the literary *histrio*.[3]

I am aware, on the other hand, that the case is by no means common, in which an author is at all in condition to retrace the steps by which his conclusions have been attained. In general, suggestions, having arisen pell-mell, are pursued and forgotten in a similar manner.

For my own part, I have neither sympathy with the repugnance alluded to, nor, at any time, the least difficulty in recalling to mind the progressive steps of any of my compositions; and, since the interest of an analysis, or reconstruction, such as I have considered a *desideratum*, is quite independent of any real or fancied interest in the thing analyzed, it will not be regarded as a breach of decorum on my part to show the *modus operandi*[4] by which some one of my own works was put together. I select "The Raven," as the most generally known. It is

3. Performer, actor (Latin).
4. Method of operation (M.O.; Latin).

my design to render it manifest that no one point in its composition is referrible either to accident or intuition—that the work proceeded, step by step, to its completion with the precision and rigid consequence of a mathematical problem.

Let us dismiss, as irrelevant to the poem *per se*, the circumstance— or say the necessity—which, in the first place, gave rise to the intention of composing a poem that should suit at once the popular and the critical taste.

We commence, then, with this intention.

The initial consideration was that of extent. If any literary work is too long to be read at one sitting, we must be content to dispense with the immensely important effect derivable from unity of impression— for, if two sittings be required, the affairs of the world interfere, and every thing like totality is at once destroyed. But since, *ceteris paribus*,[5] no poet can afford to dispense with *any thing* that may advance his design, it but remains to be seen whether there is, in extent, any advantage to counterbalance the loss of unity which attends it. Here I say no, at once. What we term a long poem is, in fact, merely a succession of brief ones—that is to say, of brief poetical effects. It is needless to demonstrate that a poem is such, only inasmuch as it intensely excites, by elevating, the soul; and all intense excitements are, through a psychal necessity, brief. For this reason, at least one half of the "Paradise Lost"[6] is essentially prose—a succession of poetical excitements interspersed, *inevitably*, with corresponding depressions— the whole being deprived, through the extremeness of its length, of the vastly important artistic element, totality, or unity, of effect.

It appears evident, then, that there is a distinct limit, as regards length, to all works of literary art—the limit of a single sitting—and that, although in certain classes of prose composition, such as "Robinson Crusoe,"[7] (demanding no unity,) this limit may be advantageously overpassed, it can never properly be overpassed in a poem. Within this limit, the extent of a poem may be made to bear mathematical relation to its merit—in other words, to the excitement or elevation—again in other words, to the degree of the true poetical effect which it is capable of inducing; for it is clear that the brevity must be in direct ratio of the intensity of the intended effect:—this, with one proviso—that a certain degree of duration is absolutely requisite for the production of any effect at all.

Holding in view these considerations, as well as that degree of excitement which I deemed not above the popular, while not below the critical, taste, I reached at once what I conceived the proper *length* for my intended poem—a length of about one hundred lines. It is, in fact, a hundred and eight.

My next thought concerned the choice of an impression, or effect, to be conveyed: and here I may as well observe that, throughout the

5. All things being equal (Latin).
6. By John Milton (1608–1674). Poe repeatedly makes the point that there is no such thing as a *long* poem elsewhere.
7. A novel (1719–20) by Daniel Defoe (1660–1731).

construction, I kept steadily in view the design of rendering the work *universally* appreciable. I should be carried too far out of my immediate topic were I to demonstrate a point upon which I have repeatedly insisted, and which, with the poetical, stands not in the slightest need of demonstration—the point, I mean, that Beauty is the sole legitimate province of the poem. A few words, however, in elucidation of my real meaning, which some of my friends have evinced a disposition to misrepresent. That pleasure which is at once the most intense, the most elevating, and the most pure, is, I believe, found in the contemplation of the beautiful. When, indeed, men speak of Beauty, they mean, precisely, not a quality, as is supposed, but an effect—they refer, in short, just to that intense and pure elevation of *soul*—*not* of intellect, or of heart—upon which I have commented, and which is experienced in consequence of contemplating "the beautiful." Now I designate Beauty as the province of the poem, merely because it is an obvious rule of Art that effects should be made to spring from direct causes—that objects should be attained through means best adapted for their attainment—no one as yet having been weak enough to deny that the peculiar elevation alluded to, is *most readily* attained in the poem. Now the object, Truth, or the satisfaction of the intellect, and the object Passion, or the excitement of the heart, are, although attainable, to a certain extent, in poetry, far more readily attainable in prose. Truth, in fact, demands a precision, and Passion, a *homeliness* (the truly passionate will comprehend me) which are absolutely antagonistic to that Beauty which, I maintain, is the excitement, or pleasurable elevation, of the soul. It by no means follows from any thing here said, that passion, or even truth, may not be introduced, and even profitably introduced, into a poem—for they may serve in elucidation, or aid the general effect, as do discords in music, by contrast—but the true artist will always contrive, first, to tone them into proper subservience to the predominant aim, and, secondly, to enveil them, as far as possible, in that Beauty which is the atmosphere and the essence of the poem.

Regarding, then, Beauty as my province, my next question referred to the *tone* of its highest manifestation—and all experience has shown that this tone is one of *sadness*. Beauty of whatever kind, in its supreme development, invariably excites the sensitive soul to tears. Melancholy is thus the most legitimate of all the poetical tones.

The length, the province, and the tone, being thus determined, I betook myself to ordinary induction, with the view of obtaining some artistic piquancy which might serve me as a key-note in the construction of the poem—some pivot upon which the whole structure might turn. In carefully thinking over all the usual artistic effects—or more properly *points*, in the theatrical sense—I did not fail to perceive immediately that no one had been so universally employed as that of the *refrain*. The universality of its employment sufficed to assure me of its intrinsic value, and spared me the necessity of submitting it to analysis. I considered it, however, with regard to its susceptibility of improvement, and soon saw it to be in a primitive condition. As

commonly used, the *refrain*, or burden, not only is limited to lyric verse, but depends for its impression upon the force of monotone—both in sound and thought. The pleasure is deduced solely from the sense of identity—of repetition. I resolved to diversify, and so vastly heighten, the effect, by adhering, in general, to the monotone of sound, while I continually varied that of thought: that is to say, I determined to produce continuously novel effects, by the variation *of the application* of the *refrain*—the *refrain* itself remaining, for the most part, unvaried.

These points being settled, I next bethought me of the *nature* of my *refrain*. Since its application was to be repeatedly varied, it was clear that the *refrain* itself must be brief, for there would have been an insurmountable difficulty in frequent variations of application in any sentence of length. In proportion to the brevity of the sentence, would, of course, be the facility of the variation. This led me at once to a single word as the best *refrain*.

The question now arose as to the *character* of the word. Having made up my mind to a *refrain*, the division of the poem into stanzas was, of course, a corollary: the *refrain* forming the close to each stanza. That such a close, to have force, must be sonorous and susceptible of protracted emphasis, admitted no doubt: and these considerations inevitably led me to the long *o* as the most sonorous vowel, in connection with *r* as the most producible consonant.

The sound of the *refrain* being thus determined, it became necessary to select a word embodying this sound, and at the same time in the fullest possible keeping with that melancholy which I had predetermined as the tone of the poem. In such a search it would have been absolutely impossible to overlook the word "Nevermore." In fact, it was the very first which presented itself.

The next *desideratum* was a pretext for the continuous use of the one word "nevermore." In observing the difficulty which I at once found in inventing a sufficiently plausible reason for its continuous repetition, I did not fail to perceive that this difficulty arose solely from the pre-assumption that the word was to be so continuously or monotonously spoken by *a human* being—I did not fail to perceive, in short, that the difficulty lay in the reconciliation of this monotony with the exercise of reason on the part of the creature repeating the word. Here, then, immediately arose the idea of a *non*-reasoning creature capable of speech; and, very naturally, a parrot, in the first instance, suggested itself, but was superseded forthwith by a Raven, as equally capable of speech, and infinitely more in keeping with the intended *tone*.

I had now gone so far as the conception of a Raven—the bird of ill omen—monotonously repeating the one word, "Nevermore," at the conclusion of each stanza, in a poem of melancholy tone, and in length about one hundred lines. Now, never losing sight of the object *supremeness*, or perfection, at all points, I asked myself—"Of all melancholy topics, what, according to the *universal* understanding of mankind, is the *most* melancholy?" Death—was the obvious reply.

"And when," I said, "is this most melancholy of topics most poetical?" From what I have already explained at some length, the answer, here also, is obvious—"When it most closely allies itself to *Beauty*: the death, then, of a beautiful woman is, unquestionably, the most poetical topic in the world—and equally is it beyond doubt that the lips best suited for such topic are those of a bereaved lover."

I had now to combine the two ideas, of a lover lamenting his deceased mistress and a Raven continuously repeating the word "Nevermore"—I had to combine these, bearing in mind my design of varying, at every turn, the *application* of the word repeated; but the only intelligible mode of such combination is that of imagining the Raven employing the word in answer to the queries of the lover. And here it was that I saw at once the opportunity afforded for the effect on which I had been depending—that is to say, the effect of the *variation of application*. I saw that I could make the first query propounded by the lover—the first query to which the Raven should reply "Nevermore"—that I could make this first query a commonplace one—the second less so—the third still less, and so on—until at length the lover, startled from his original *nonchalance* by the melancholy character of the word itself—by its frequent repetition—and by a consideration of the ominous reputation of the fowl that uttered it—is at length excited to superstition, and wildly propounds queries of a far different character—queries whose solution he has passionately at heart—propounds them half in superstition and half in that species of despair which delights in self-torture—propounds them not altogether because he believes in the prophetic or demoniac character of the bird (which, reason assures him, is merely repeating a lesson learned by rote) but because he experiences a phrenzied pleasure in so modeling his questions as to receive from the *expected* "Nevermore" the most delicious because the most intolerable of sorrow. Perceiving the opportunity thus afforded me—or, more strictly, thus forced upon me in the progress of the construction—I first established in mind the climax, or concluding query—that to which "Nevermore" should be in the last place an answer—that in reply to which this word "Nevermore" should involve the utmost conceivable amount of sorrow and despair.

Here then the poem may be said to have its beginning—at the end, where all works of art should begin—for it was here, at this point of my preconsiderations, that I first put pen to paper in the composition of the stanza:

> "Prophet," said I, "thing of evil! prophet still if bird or devil!
> By that heaven that bends above us—by that God we both adore,
> Tell this soul with sorrow laden, if within the distant Aidenn,
> It shall clasp a sainted maiden whom the angels name Lenore—
> Clasp a rare and radiant maiden whom the angels name Lenore."
> Quoth the raven "Nevermore."

I composed this stanza, at this point, first that, by establishing the climax, I might the better vary and graduate, as regards seriousness and importance, the preceding queries of the lover—and, secondly,

that I might definitely settle the rhythm, the metre, and the length and general arrangement of the stanza—as well as graduate the stanzas which were to precede, so that none of them might surpass this in rhythmical effect. Had I been able, in the subsequent composition, to construct more vigorous stanzas, I should, without scruple, have purposely enfeebled them, so as not to interfere with the climacteric effect.

And here I may as well say a few words of the versification. My first object (as usual) was originality. The extent to which this has been neglected, in versification, is one of the most unaccountable things in the world. Admitting that there is little possibility of variety in mere *rhythm*, it is still clear that the possible varieties of metre and stanza are absolutely infinite—and yet, *for centuries, no man, in verse, has ever done, or ever seemed to think of doing, an original thing.* The fact is, originality (unless in minds of very unusual force) is by no means a matter, as some suppose, of impulse or intuition. In general, to be found, it must be elaborately sought, and although a positive merit of the highest class, demands in its attainment less of invention than negation.

Of course, I pretend to no originality in either the rhythm or metre of the "Raven." The former is trochaic—the latter is octameter acatalectic, alternating with heptameter catalectic repeated in the *refrain* of the fifth verse, and terminating with tetrameter catalectic.[8] Less pedantically—the feet employed throughout (trochees) consist of a long syllable followed by a short: the first line of the stanza consists of eight of these feet—the second of seven and a half (in effect two-thirds)—the third of eight—the fourth of seven and a half—the fifth the same—the sixth three and a half. Now, each of these lines, taken individually, has been employed before, and what originality the "Raven" has, is in their *combination into stanza*; nothing even remotely approaching this combination has ever been attempted. The effect of this originality of combination is aided by other unusual, and some altogether novel effects, arising from an extension of the application of the principles of rhyme and alliteration.

The next point to be considered was the mode of bringing together the lover and the Raven—and the first branch of this consideration was the *locale.* For this the most natural suggestion might seem to be a forest, or the fields—but it has always appeared to me that a close *circumscription of space* is absolutely necessary to the effect of insulated incident:—it has the force of a frame to a picture. It has an indisputable moral power in keeping concentrated the attention, and, of course, must not be confounded with mere unity of place.

I determined, then, to place the lover in his chamber—in a chamber rendered sacred to him by memories of her who had frequented it. The room is represented as richly furnished—this in mere pursuance of the ideas I have already explained on the subject of Beauty, as the sole true poetical thesis.

8. These technical verse terms are explained in Poe's next sentences.

The *locale* being thus determined, I had now to introduce the bird—and the thought of introducing him through the window, was inevitable. The idea of making the lover suppose, in the first instance, that the flapping of the wings of the bird against the shutter, is a "tapping" at the door, originated in a wish to increase, by prolonging, the reader's curiosity, and in a desire to admit the incidental effect arising from the lover's throwing open the door, finding all dark, and thence adopting the half-fancy that it was the spirit of his mistress that knocked.

I made the night tempestuous, first, to account for the Raven's seeking admission, and secondly, for the effect of contrast with the (physical) serenity within the chamber.

I made the bird alight on the bust of Pallas, also for the effect of contrast between the marble and the plumage—it being understood that the bust was absolutely *suggested* by the bird—the bust of *Pallas* being chosen, first, as most in keeping with the scholarship of the lover, and, secondly, for the sonorousness of the word, Pallas, itself.

About the middle of the poem, also, I have availed myself of the force of contrast, with a view of deepening the ultimate impression. For example, an air of the fantastic—approaching as nearly to the ludicrous as was admissible—is given to the Raven's entrance. He comes in "with many a flirt and flutter."

Not the *least obeisance made he*—not a moment stopped or stayed he,
But with mien of lord or lady, perched above my chamber door.

In the two stanzas which follow, the design is more obviously carried out:—

Then this ebony bird beguiling my sad fancy into smiling
By the *grave and stern decorum of the countenance it wore,*
"Though thy *crest be shorn and shaven* thou," I said, "art sure no craven,
Ghastly grim and ancient Raven wandering from the nightly shore—
Tell me what thy lordly name is on the Night's Plutonian shore!"
 Quoth the Raven "Nevermore."

Much I marvelled *this ungainly fowl* to hear discourse so plainly,
Though its answer little meaning—little relevancy bore;
For we cannot help agreeing that no living human being
Ever yet was blessed with seeing bird above his chamber door—
Bird or beast upon the sculptured bust above his chamber door,
 With such name as "Nevermore."

The effect of the *dénouement* being thus provided for, I immediately drop the fantastic for a tone of the most profound seriousness:—this tone commencing in the stanza directly following the one last quoted, with the line,

But the Raven, sitting lonely on that placid bust, spoke only, etc.

From this epoch the lover no longer jests—no longer sees any thing even of the fantastic in the Raven's demeanor. He speaks of him as a

"grim, ungainly, ghastly, gaunt, and ominous bird of yore," and feels the "fiery eyes" burning into his "bosom's core." This revolution of thought, or fancy, on the lover's part, is intended to induce a similar one on the part of the reader—to bring the mind into a proper frame for the *dénouement*—which is now brought about as rapidly and as *directly* as possible.

With the *dénouement* proper—with the Raven's reply, "Nevermore," to the lover's final demand if he shall meet his mistress in another world—the poem, in its obvious phase, that of a simple narrative, may be said to have its completion. So far, every thing is within the limits of the accountable—of the real. A raven, having learned by rote the single word "Nevermore," and having escaped from the custody of its owner, is driven, at midnight, through the violence of a storm, to seek admission at a window from which a light still gleams— the chamber-window of a student, occupied half in poring over a volume, half in dreaming of a beloved mistress deceased. The casement being thrown open at the fluttering of the bird's wings, the bird itself perches on the most convenient seat out of the immediate reach of the student, who, amused by the incident and the oddity of the visiter's demeanor, demands of it, in jest and without looking for a reply, its name. The raven addressed, answers with its customary word, "Nevermore"—a word which finds immediate echo in the melancholy heart of the student, who, giving utterance aloud to certain thoughts suggested by the occasion, is again startled by the fowl's repetition of "Nevermore." The student now guesses the state of the case, but is impelled, as I have before explained, by the human thirst for self-torture, and in part by superstition, to propound such queries to the bird as will bring him, the lover, the most of the luxury of sorrow, through the anticipated answer "Nevermore." With the indulgence, to the utmost extreme, of this self-torture, the narration, in what I have termed its first or obvious phase, has a natural termination, and so far there has been no overstepping of the limits of the real.

But in subjects so handled, however skilfully, or with however vivid an array of incident, there is always a certain hardness or nakedness, which repels the artistical eye. Two things are invariably required— first, some amount of complexity, or more properly, adaptation; and, secondly, some amount of suggestiveness—some under current, however indefinite of meaning. It is this latter, in especial, which imparts to a work of art so much of that *richness* (to borrow from colloquy a forcible term) which we are too fond of confounding with *the ideal*. It is the *excess* of the suggested meaning—it is the rendering this the upper instead of the under current of the theme—which turns into prose (and that of the very flattest kind) the so called poetry of the so called transcendentalists.

Holding these opinions, I added the two concluding stanzas of the poem—their suggestiveness being thus made to pervade all the narrative which has preceded them. The under current of meaning is rendered first apparent in the lines—

"Take thy beak from out *my heart*, and take thy form from off my door!"
Quoth the Raven "Nevermore!"

It will be observed that the words, "from out my heart," involve the first metaphorical expression in the poem. They, with the answer, "Nevermore," dispose the mind to seek a moral in all that has been previously narrated. The reader begins now to regard the Raven as emblematical—but it is not until the very last line of the very last stanza, that the intention of making him emblematical of *Mournful and Never-ending Remembrance* is permitted distinctly to be seen:

And the Raven, never flitting, still is sitting, still is sitting,
On the pallid bust of Pallas just above my chamber door;
And his eyes have all the seeming of a demon's that is dreaming,
And the lamplight o'er him streaming throws his shadow on the floor;
And my soul *from out that shadow* that lies floating on the floor
Shall be lifted—nevermore.

To Philip P. Cooke (Letter 240)

New-York—August 9, 1846.

My Dear Sir,

* * *

You are right about the hair-splitting of my French friend:—that is all done for effect. These tales of ratiocination owe most of their popularity to being something in a new key. I do not mean to say that they are not ingenious—but people think them more ingenious than they are—on account of their method and *air* of method. In the "Murders in the Rue Morgue", for instance, where is the ingenuity of unravelling a web which you yourself (the author) have woven for the express purpose of unravelling? The reader is made to confound the ingenuity of the supposititious Dupin with that of the writer of the story.

* * *

Should you undertake the work for me, there is one topic—there is one particular in which I have had wrong done me—and it may not be indecorous in me to call your attention to it. The last selection of my Tales was made from about 70, by Wiley & Putnam's reader, Duyckinck.[1] He has what he thinks a taste for ratiocination, and has accordingly made up the book mostly of analytic stories. But this is not *representing* my mind in its various phases—it is not giving me fair play. In writing these Tales one by one, at long intervals, I have kept the book-unity always in mind—that is, each has been composed with reference to its effect as part of *a whole*. In this view, one of my chief aims has been the widest diversity of subject, thought, & especially *tone* & manner of handling. Were all my tales now before me in a large volume and as the composition of another—the merit which would principally arrest my attention would be the wide *diversity and* variety.

1. Evert Augustus Duyckinck (1816–1878).

You will be surprised to hear me say that (omitting one or two of my first efforts) I do not consider any one of my stories *better* than another. There is a vast variety of kinds and, in degree of value, these kinds vary—but each tale is equally good *of its kind*. The loftiest kind is that of the highest imagination—and, for this reason only, "Ligeia" may be called my *best* tale. I have much improved this last since you saw it and I mail you a copy, as well as a copy of my best specimen of analysis—"The Philosophy of Composition."

* * *

Nathaniel Hawthorne[1]

Twice-Told Tales. By Nathaniel Hawthorne.
James Munroe & Co., Boston, 1842.

Mosses from an Old Manse. By Nathaniel Hawthorne.
Wiley & Putnam, New York, 1846.

In the preface to my sketches of New York Literati, while speaking of the broad distinction between the seeming public and real private opinion respecting our authors, I thus alluded to Nathaniel Hawthorne:—

"For example, Mr. Hawthorne, the author of 'Twice-Told Tales,' is scarcely recognized by the press or by the public, and when noticed at all, is noticed merely to be damned by faint praise. Now, my own opinion of him is, that although his walk is limited and he is fairly to be charged with mannerism, treating all subjects in a similar tone of dreamy *innuendo*, yet in this walk he evinces extraordinary genius, having no rival either in America or elsewhere; and this opinion I have never heard gainsaid by any one literary person in the country. That this opinion, however, is a spoken and not a written one, is referable to the facts, first, that Mr. Hawthorne *is* a poor man, and, secondly, that he *is not* an ubiquitous quack."

The reputation of the author of "Twice-Told Tales" has been confined, indeed, until very lately, to literary society; and I have not been wrong, perhaps, in citing him as *the* example, *par excellence*, in this country, of the privately-admired and publicly-unappreciated man of genius. Within the last year or two, it is true, an occasional critic has been urged, by honest indignation, into very warm approval. Mr. Webber,[2] for instance, (than whom no one has a keener relish for that kind of writing which Mr. Hawthorne has best illustrated,) gave us, in a late number of "The American Review," a cordial and certainly a full tribute to his talents; and since the issue of the "Mosses from an Old

1. *Godey's Lady's Book* (November 1847). Cf. Poe's 1842 review of Hawthorne in *Graham's* (pp. 643ff. herein).
2. Charles Wilkens Webber (1819–1856), a writer of Westerns, was the author of a story Poe admired, mentioned at the end of the review.

Manse," criticisms of similar tone have been by no means infrequent in our more authoritative journals. I can call to mind few reviews of Hawthorne published *before* the "Mosses." One I remember in "Arcturus" (edited by Matthews and Duyckinck) for May, 1841; another in the "American Monthly" (edited by Hoffman and Herbert) for March, 1838; a third in the ninety-sixth number of the "North American Review."[3] These criticisms, however, seemed to have little effect on the popular taste—at least, if we are to form any idea of the popular taste by reference to its expression in the newspapers, or by the sale of the author's book. It was never the fashion (until lately) to speak of him in any summary of our best authors. The daily critics would say, on such occasions, "Is there not Irving and Cooper, and Bryant and Paulding, and—Smith?" or, "Have we not Halleck and Dana, and Longfellow and—Thompson?" or, "Can we not point triumphantly to our own Sprague, Willis, Channing, Bancroft, Prescott and—Jenkins?" but these unanswerable queries were never wound up by the name of Hawthorne.[4]

Beyond doubt, this inappreciation of him on the part of the public arose chiefly from the two causes to which I have referred—from the facts that he is neither a man of wealth nor a quack;—but these are insufficient to account for the whole effect. No small portion of it is attributable to the very marked idiosyncrasy of Mr. Hawthorne himself. In one sense, and in great measure, to be peculiar is to be original, and than the true originality there is no higher literary virtue. This true or commendable originality, however, implies not the uniform, but the continuous peculiarity—a peculiarity springing from ever-active vigor of fancy—better still if from ever-present force of imagination, giving its own hue, its own character to everything it touches, and, especially, *self impelled to touch everything.*

It is often said, inconsiderately, that very original writers always fail in popularity—that such and such persons are too original to be comprehended by the mass. "Too peculiar," should be the phrase, "too idiosyncratic." It is, in fact, the excitable, undisciplined and child-like popular mind which most keenly feels the original. The criticism of the conservatives, of the hackneys, of the cultivated old clergymen of the "North American Review," is precisely the criticism which condemns and alone condemns it. "It becometh not a divine," saith Lord Coke, "to be of a fiery and salamandrine spirit."[5] Their conscience allowing them to move nothing themselves, these dignitaries have a holy horror of being moved. "Give us *quietude,*" they say. Opening their mouths with proper caution, they sigh forth the word "*Repose.*" And this is, indeed, the one thing they should be permitted to enjoy, if only upon the Christian principle of give and take.

3. The most prestigious of the quarterly magazines, edited by a distinguished series of intellectuals. The magazine *Arcturus* was edited by Cornelius Mathews and Evert A. Duyckinck. The *American Monthly* was edited by Charles Fenno Hoffman.
4. In this series of three joking questions, Poe names several of the most distinguished writers in America, ending each list with a common name that would have no recognition (thus—Hawthorne).
5. Salamanders were believed to be able to live comfortably in fire and fireplaces. Sir Edward Coke (1552–1634), famous English jurist.

The fact is, that if Mr. Hawthorne were really original, he could not fail of making himself felt by the public. But the fact is, he is *not* original in any sense. Those who speak of him as original, mean nothing more than that he differs in his manner or tone, and in his choice of subjects, from any author of their acquaintance—their acquaintance not extending to the German Tieck,[6] whose manner, in *some* of his works, is absolutely identical with that *habitual* to Hawthorne. But it is clear that the element of the literary originality is novelty. The element of its appreciation by the reader is the reader's sense of the new. Whatever gives him a new and insomuch a pleasurable emotion, he considers original, and whoever frequently gives him such emotion, he considers an original writer. In a word, it is by the sum total of these emotions that he decides upon the writer's claim to originality. I may observe here, however, that there is clearly a point at which even novelty itself would cease to produce the legitimate originality, if we judge this originality, as we should, by the effect designed: this point is that at which *novelty becomes nothing novel*; and here the artist, *to preserve his originality*, will subside into the common-place. No one, I think, has noticed that, merely through inattention to this matter, Moore[7] has comparatively failed in his "Lalla Rookh." Few readers, and indeed few critics, have commended this poem for originality—and, in fact, the effect, originality, is not produced by it—yet no work of equal size so abounds in the happiest originalities, individually considered. They are so excessive as, in the end, to deaden in the reader all capacity for their appreciation.

These points properly understood, it will be seen that the critic (unacquainted with Tieck) who reads a single tale or essay by Hawthorne, may be justified in thinking him original; but the tone, or manner, or choice of subject, which induces in this critic the sense of the new, will—if not in a second tale, at least in a third and all subsequent ones—not only fail of inducing it, but bring about an exactly antagonistic impression. In concluding a volume, and more especially in concluding all the volumes of the author, the critic will abandon his first design of calling him "original," and content himself with styling him "peculiar."

With the vague opinion that to be original is to be unpopular, I could, indeed, agree, were I to adopt an understanding of originality which, to my surprise, I have known adopted by many who have a right to be called critical. They have limited, in a love for mere words, the literary to the metaphysical originality. They regard as original in letters, only such combinations of thought, of incident, and so forth, as are, in fact, absolutely novel. It is clear, however, not only that it is the novelty of *effect* alone which is worth consideration, but that this effect is *best* wrought, for the end of all fictitious composition, plea-

6. Ludwig Tieck (1773–1852), prominent Romantic German author of avant-garde novels, tales, and plays; editor and translator of Shakespeare.
7. Thomas Moore (1779–1852), Irish poet who figures prominently in Poe's writings; see especially notes to "Al Aaraaf" (pp. 22ff. herein), "The Assignation" (pp. 116ff.), and to Poe's review of Moore (pp. 617ff.).

sure, by shunning rather than by seeking the absolute novelty of combination. Originality, thus understood, tasks and startles the intellect, and so brings into undue action the faculties to which, in the lighter literature, we least appeal. And thus understood, it cannot fail to prove unpopular with the masses, who, seeking in this literature amusement, are positively offended by instruction. But the true originality—true in respect of its purposes—is that which, in bringing out the half-formed, the reluctant, or the unexpressed fancies of mankind, or in exciting the more delicate pulses of the heart's passion, or in giving birth to some universal sentiment or instinct in embryo, thus combines with the pleasurable effect of *apparent* novelty, a real egotistic delight. The reader, in the case first supposed, (that of the absolute novelty,) is excited, but embarrassed, disturbed, in some degree even pained at his own want of perception, at his own folly in not having himself hit upon the idea. In the second case, his pleasure is doubled. He is filled with an intrinsic and extrinsic delight. He feels and intensely enjoys the seeming novelty of the thought, enjoys it as really novel, as absolutely original with the writer—*and* himself. They two, he fancies, have, alone of all men, thought thus. They two have, together, created this thing. Henceforward there is a bond of sympathy between them, a sympathy which irradiates every subsequent page of the book.

There is a species of writing which, with some difficulty, may be admitted as a lower degree of what I have called the true original. In its perusal, we say to ourselves, not "how original this is!" nor "here is an idea which I and the author have alone entertained," but "here is a charmingly obvious fancy," or sometimes even, "here is a thought which I am not sure has ever occurred to myself, but which, of course, has occurred to all the rest of the world." This kind of composition (which still appertains to a high order) is usually designated as "the natural." It has little external resemblance, but strong internal affinity to the true original, if, indeed, as I have suggested, it is not of this latter an inferior degree. It is best exemplified, among English writers, in Addison, Irving and *Hawthorne*.[8] The "ease" which is so often spoken of as its distinguishing feature, it has been the fashion to regard as ease in appearance alone, as a point of really difficult attainment. This idea, however, must be received with some reservation. The natural style is difficult only to those who should never intermeddle with it— to the unnatural. It is but the result of writing with the understanding, or with the instinct, that the *tone*, in composition, should be that which, at any given point or upon any given topic, would be the tone of the great mass of humanity. The author who, after the manner of the North Americans, is merely at *all* times *quiet*, is, of course, upon *most* occasions, merely silly or stupid, and has no more right to be thought "easy" or "natural" than has a cockney exquisite or the sleeping beauty in the wax-works.

The "peculiarity" or sameness, or monotone of Hawthorne, would, in its mere character of "peculiarity," and without reference to what *is*

8. Apparently Poe means that the style of Hawthorne and Washington Irving is like that of the famous English essayist Joseph Addison (1672–1719).

the peculiarity, suffice to deprive him of all chance of popular appreciation. But at his failure to be appreciated, we can, *of course*, no longer wonder, when we find him monotonous at decidedly the worst of all possible points—at that point which, having the least concern with Nature, is the farthest removed from the popular intellect, from the popular sentiment and from the popular taste. I allude to the strain of allegory which completely overwhelms the greater number of his subjects, and which in some measure interferes with the direct conduct of absolutely all.

In defense of allegory, (however, or for whatever object, employed,) there is scarcely one respectable word to be said. Its best appeals are made to the fancy—that is to say, to our sense of adaptation, not of matters proper, but of matters improper for the purpose, of the real with the unreal; having never more of intelligible connection than has something with nothing, never half so much of effective affinity as has the substance for the shadow. The deepest emotion aroused within us by the happiest allegory, *as* allegory, is a very, very imperfectly satisfied sense of the writer's ingenuity in overcoming a difficulty we should have preferred his not having attempted to overcome. The fallacy of the idea that allegory, in any of its moods, can be made to enforce a truth—that metaphor, for example, may illustrate as well as embellish an argument—could be promptly demonstrated: the converse of the supposed fact might be shown, indeed, with very little trouble—but these are topics foreign to my present purpose. One thing is clear, that if allegory ever establishes a fact, it is by dint of over-turning a fiction. Where the suggested meaning runs through the obvious one in a *very* profound under-current, so as never to interfere with the upper one without our own volition, so as never to show itself unless *called* to the surface, there only, for the proper uses of fictitious narrative, is it available at all. Under the best circumstances, it must always interfere with that unity of effect which, to the artist, is worth all the allegory in the world. Its vital injury, however, is rendered to the most vitally important point in fiction—that of earnestness or verisimilitude. That "The Pilgrim's Progress"[9] is a ludicrously over-rated book, owing its seeming popularity to one or two of those accidents in critical literature which by the critical are sufficiently well understood, is a matter upon which no two thinking people disagree; but the pleasure derivable from it, in any sense, will be found in the direct ratio of the reader's capacity to smother its true purpose, in the direct ratio of his ability to keep the allegory out of sight, or of his *in*ability to comprehend it. Of allegory properly handled, judiciously subdued, seen only as a shadow or by suggestive glimpses, and making its nearest approach to truth in a not obtrusive and therefore not unpleasant *appositeness*, the "Undine" of De La Motte Fouqué[1] is the best, and undoubtedly a very remarkable specimen.

The obvious causes, however, which have prevented Mr. Haw-

9. A Christian (Puritan) allegory by John Bunyan (1628–1688).
1. See Poe's review of Fouqué's *Undine* (pp. 613ff. herein).

thorne's *popularity*, do not suffice to condemn him in the eyes of the few who belong properly to books, and to whom books, perhaps, do not quite so properly belong. These few estimate an author, not as do the public, altogether by what he does, but in great measure—indeed, even in the greatest measure—by what he evinces a capability of doing. In this view, Hawthorne stands among literary people in America much in the same light as did Coleridge in England. The few, also, through a certain warping of the taste, which long pondering upon books as books merely never fails to induce, are not in condition to view the errors of a scholar as errors altogether. At any time these gentlemen are prone to think the public not right rather than an educated author wrong. But the simple truth is, that the writer who aims at impressing the people, is *always* wrong when he fails in forcing that people to receive the impression. How far Mr. Hawthorne has addressed the people at all, is, of course, not a question for me to decide. His books afford strong internal evidence of having been written to himself and his particular friends alone.

There has long existed in literature a fatal and unfounded prejudice, which it will be the office of this age to overthrow—the idea that the mere bulk of a work must enter largely into our estimate of its merit. I do not suppose even the weakest of the Quarterly reviewers weak enough to maintain that in a book's size or mass, abstractly considered, there is anything which especially calls for our admiration. A mountain, simply through the sensation of physical magnitude which it conveys, does, indeed, affect us with a sense of the sublime, but we cannot admit any such influence in the contemplation even of "The Columbiad."[2] The Quarterlies themselves will not admit it. And yet, what else are we to understand by their continual prating about "sustained effort?" Granted that this sustained effort has accomplished an epic—let us then admire the effort, (if this be a thing admirable,) but certainly not the epic on the effort's account. Common sense, in the time to come, may possibly insist upon measuring a work of art rather by the object it fulfils, by the impression it makes, than by the time it took to fulfil the object, or by the extent of "sustained effort" which became necessary to produce the impression. The fact is, that perseverance is one thing and genius quite another; nor can all the transcendentalists in Heathendom confound them.

Full of its bulky ideas, the last number of the "North American Review," in what it imagines a criticism on Simms,[3] "honestly avows that it has little opinion of the mere tale;" and the honesty of the avowal is in no slight degree guarantied by the fact that this Review has never yet been known to put forth an opinion which was *not* a very little one indeed.

The tale proper affords the fairest field which can be afforded by the wide domains of mere prose, for the exercise of the highest genius. Were I bidden to say how this genius could be most advantageously

2. A long American epic poem (1807)—perhaps the longest poem in American literature—by Joel Barlow (1754–1812).
3. William Gilmore Simms (1806–1870), Southern epic novelist.

employed for the best display of its powers, I should answer, without hesitation, "in the composition of a rhymed poem not to exceed in length what might be perused in an hour." Within this limit alone can the noblest order of poetry exist. I have discussed this topic elsewhere, and need here repeat only that the phrase "a long poem" embodies a paradox. A poem must intensely excite. Excitement is its province, its essentiality. Its value is in the ratio of its (elevating) excitement. But all excitement is, from a psychal necessity, transient. It cannot be sustained through a poem of great length. In the course of an hour's reading, at most, it flags, fails; and then the poem is, in effect, no longer such. Men admire, but are wearied with the "Paradise Lost;" for platitude follows platitude, *inevitably*, at regular interspaces, (the depressions between the waves of excitement,) until the poem, (which, properly considered, is but a succession of brief poems,) having been brought to an end, we discover that the sums of our pleasure and of displeasure have been very nearly equal. The absolute, ultimate or aggregate effect of any epic under the sun is, for these reasons, a nullity. "The Iliad," in its form of epic, has but an imaginary existence; granting it real, however, I can only say of it that it is based on a primitive sense of Art. Of the modern epic nothing can be so well said as that it is a blindfold imitation of a "come-by-chance." By and by these propositions will be understood as self-evident, and in the meantime will not be essentially damaged as truths by being generally condemned as falsities.

A poem *too* brief, on the other hand, may produce a sharp or vivid, but never a profound or enduring impression. Without a certain continuity, without a certain duration or repetition of the cause, the soul is seldom moved to the effect. There must be the dropping of the water on the rock. There must be the pressing steadily down of the stamp upon the wax. De Béranger[4] has wrought brilliant things, pungent and spirit-stirring, but most of them are too immassive to have *momentum*, and, as so many feathers of fancy, have been blown aloft only to be whistled down the wind. Brevity, indeed, may degenerate into epigrammatism, but this danger does not prevent extreme length from being the one unpardonable sin.

Were I called upon, however, to designate that class of composition which, next to such a poem as I have suggested, should best fulfil the demands and serve the purposes of ambitious genius, should offer it the most advantageous field of exertion, and afford it the fairest opportunity of display, I should speak at once of the brief prose tale. History, philosophy, and other matters of that kind, we leave out of the question, of course. *Of course*, I say, and in spite of the graybeards. These graver topics, to the end of time, will be best illustrated by what a discriminating world, turning up its nose at the drab pamphlets, has agreed to understand as *talent*. The ordinary novel is objectionable, from its length, for reasons analogous to those which render length objectionable in the poem. As the novel cannot be read at one sitting,

4. Pierre Jean de Béranger (1780–1857), French Romantic poet; see the epigraph to "The Fall of the House of Usher" (p. 199 herein).

it cannot avail itself of the immense benefit of *totality*. Worldly interests, intervening during the pauses of perusal, modify, counteract and annul the impressions intended. But simple cessation in reading would, of itself, be sufficient to destroy the true unity. In the brief tale, however, the author is enabled to carry out his full design without interruption. During the hour of perusal, the soul of the reader is at the writer's control.

A skillful artist has constructed a tale. He has not fashioned his thoughts to accommodate his incidents, but having deliberately conceived a certain *single effect* to be wrought, he then invents such incidents, he then combines such events, and discusses them in such tone as may best serve him in establishing this preconceived effect. If his very first sentence tend not to the outbringing of this effect, then in his very first step has he committed a blunder. In the whole composition there should be no word written of which the tendency, direct or indirect, is not to the one pre-established design. And by such means, with such care and skill, a picture is at length painted which leaves in the mind of him who contemplates it with a kindred art, a sense of the fullest satisfaction. The idea of the tale, its thesis, has been presented unblemished, because undisturbed—an end absolutely demanded, yet, in the novel, altogether unattainable.

Of skillfully-constructed tales—I speak now without reference to other points, some of them more important than construction—there are very few American specimens. I am acquainted with no better one, upon the whole, than the "Murder Will Out" of Mr. Simms,[5] and this has some glaring defects. The "Tales of a Traveler," by Irving,[6] are graceful and impressive narratives—"The Young Italian" is especially good—but there is not one of the series which can be commended as a whole. In many of them the interest is subdivided and frittered away, and their conclusions are insufficiently *climacic*. In the higher requisites of composition, John Neal's[7] magazine stories excel—I mean in vigor of thought, picturesque combination of incident, and so forth—but they ramble too much, and invariably break down just before coming to an end, as if the writer had received a sudden and irresistible summons to dinner, and thought it incumbent upon him to make a finish of his story before going. One of the happiest and best-sustained tales I have seen, is "Jack Long; or, The Shot in the Eye," by Charles W. Webber, the assistant editor of Mr. Colton's "American Review." But in general skill of construction, the tales of Willis, I think, surpass those of any American writer—with the exception of Mr. Hawthorne.

I must defer to the better opportunity of a volume now in hand, a full discussion of his individual pieces, and hasten to conclude this paper with a summary of his merits and demerits.

He is peculiar and *not* original—unless in those detailed fancies and detached thoughts which his want of general originality will deprive of

5. William Gilmore Simms's story is actually titled "Greyling; or Murder Will Out" (1845–46).
6. Irving's *Tales of a Traveler* (1824) contains four integrated story sequences.
7. American novelist, poet, and critic (1793–1876).

the appreciation due to them, in preventing them forever reaching the *public* eye. He is infinitely too fond of allegory, and can never hope for popularity so long as he persists in it. This he will not do, for allegory is at war with the whole tone of his nature, which disports itself never so well as when escaping from the mysticism of his Goodman Browns and White Old Maids into the hearty, genial, but still Indian-summer sunshine of his Wakefields and Little Annie's Rambles. Indeed, *his* spirit of "metaphor run-mad" is clearly imbibed from the phalanx and phalanstery atmosphere in which he has been so long struggling for breath. He has not half the material for the exclusiveness of authorship that he possesses for its universality. He has the purest style, the finest taste, the most available scholarship, the most delicate humor, the most touching pathos, the most radiant imagination, the most consummate ingenuity; and with these varied good qualities he has done *well* as a mystic. But is there any one of these qualities which should prevent his doing doubly as well in a career of honest, upright, sensible, prehensible and comprehensible things? Let him mend his pen, get a bottle of visible ink, come out from the Old Manse, cut Mr. Alcott, hang (if possible) the editor of "The Dial,"[8] and throw out of the window to the pigs all his odd numbers of "The North American Review."

From James Russell Lowell[1]

A Fable for the Critics. New York: George P. Putnam.

What have we Americans accomplished in the way of Satire? "The Vision of Rubeta," by Laughton Osborn,[2] is probably our best composition of the kind: but, in saying this, we intend no excessive commendation. Trumbull's clumsy and imitative work is scarcely worth mention—and then we have Halleck's[3] "Croakers," local and ephemeral—but what is there besides? Park Benjamin has written a clever address, with the title "Infatuation," and Holmes[4] has an occasional scrap, piquant enough in its way—but we can think of nothing more that can be fairly called "satire." Some matters we have produced, to be sure, which were excellent in the way of burlesque—(the Poems of William Ellery Channing,[5] for example)—without meaning a syllable that was not utterly solemn and serious. Odes, ballads, songs,

8. Bronson Alcott (1799–1888) was associated with the American Transcendentalist magazine, the *Dial*, edited by Ralph Waldo Emerson and Margaret Fuller.
1. Poe's review is reprinted from the *Southern Literary Messenger* for March 1849. The reader should remember that Poe was less than pleased with Lowell's jab at him in this book (quoted in this review), which may have influenced the tone of the review.
2. Laughton Osborn (c. 1809–1878), American poet (1809–1878); see Poe's dismissive review of his *Confessions of a Poet* (*Southern Literary Messenger*, April 1835).
3. Fitz-Greene Halleck (1790–1867); see Poe's review on pp. 604ff. herein. John Trumbell (1750–1831), one of the "Hartford Wits," a group of late-18th-century writers given to satirizing the pretensions of the New Republic.
4. Oliver Wendell Holmes (1809–1894), physician and influential essayist, poet, and novelist. Park Benjamin (1809–1864), editor of the *New World*, a New York weekly paper.
5. American poet (1780–1842); see p. 664, n.4 herein.

sonnets, epics and epigrams, possessed of this unintentional excellence, we should have no difficulty in designating by the dozen; but in the particular of direct and obvious satire, it cannot be denied that we are unaccountably deficient.

It has been suggested that this deficiency arises from the want of a suitable field for satirical display. In England, it is said, satire abounds, because the people there find a proper target in the aristocracy, whom they (the people) regard as a distinct race with whom they have little in common; relishing even the most virulent abuse of the upper classes with a gusto undiminished by any feeling that they (the people) have any concern in it. In Russia, or Austria, on the other hand, it is urged, satire is unknown; because there is danger in touching the aristocracy, and self-satire would be odious to the mass. In America, also, the people who write are, it is maintained, the people who read:—thus in satirizing the people we satirize only ourselves and are never in condition to sympathize with the satire.

All this is more verisimilar than true. It is forgotten that no individual considers himself as one of the mass. Each person, in his own estimate, is the pivot on which all the rest of the world spins round. We may abuse *the people* by wholesale, and yet with a clear conscience so far as regards any compunction for offending any one from among the multitude of which that "people" is composed. Every one of the crowd will cry "*Encore!*—give it to them, the vagabonds!—it serves them right." It seems to us that, in America, we have refused to encourage satire—not because what we have had touches us too nearly—but because it has been too pointless to touch us at all. Its namby-pambyism has arisen, in part, from the general want, among our men of letters, of that minute *polish*—of that skill in details—which, in combination with natural sarcastic power, satire, more than any other form of literature, so imperatively demands. In part, also, we may attribute our failure to the colonial sin of imitation. We content ourselves—at this point not less supinely than at all others—with doing what not only has been done before, but what, however well done, has yet been done *ad nauseam*.

* * *

"The Vision" is bold enough—if we leave out of sight its anonymous issue—and bitter enough, and witty enough, if we forget its pitiable punning on names—and long enough (Heaven knows) and well constructed and decently versified; but it fails in the principal element of all satire—*sarcasm*—because the *intention* to be sarcastic (as in the "English Bards and Scotch Reviewers,"[6] and in all the more classical satires) is permitted to render itself manifest. The malevolence *appears*. The author is never very severe, because he is at no time particularly cool. We laugh not so much at his victims as at himself for letting them put him in such a passion. And where a deeper sentiment than mirth is excited—where it is pity or contempt that we are made to feel—the feeling is too often reflected, in its object, from the satirized to the satirist—with whom we sympathize in the discomfort of

6. A scathing satire (1809) on the British literary establishment by Lord Byron.

his animosity. Mr. Osborn has not many superiors in downright invective; but this is the awkward left arm of the satiric Muse. *That* satire alone is worth talking about which at least *appears* to be the genial, good humored outpouring of irrepressible merriment.

"The Fable for the Critics," just issued, has not the name of its author on the title-page; and but for some slight fore-knowledge of the literary opinions, likes, dislikes, whims, prejudices and crotchets of Mr. *James Russell Lowell*, we should have had much difficulty in attributing so very *loose* a brochure to *him*. The "Fable" is essentially "loose"—ill conceived and feebly executed, as well in detail as in general. Some good hits and some sparkling witticisms do not serve to compensate us for its rambling plot (if plot it can be called) and for the want of artistic finish so particularly noticeable throughout the work—especially in its versification. In Mr. Lowell's prose efforts we have before observed a certain *disjointedness*, but never, until now, in his verse—and we confess some surprise at his putting forth so unpolished a performance. The author of "The Legend of Brittany" (which is decidedly the noblest poem, of the same length, written by an American) could not do a better thing than to take the advice of those who mean him well, in spite of his fanaticism, and leave prose, with satiric verse, to those who are better able to manage them; while he contents himself with that class of poetry for which, and for which alone, he seems to have an especial vocation—the poetry of *sentiment*. This, to be sure, is *not* the very loftiest order of verse; for it is far inferior to either that of the imagination or that of the passions—but it is the loftiest region in which Mr. Lowell can get his breath without difficulty.

Our primary objection to this "Fable for the Critics" has reference to a point which we have already touched in a general way. "The malevolence appears." We laugh not so much at the author's victims as at himself for letting them put him in such a passion. The very title of the book shows the want of a due sense in respect to the satiric essence, *sarcasm*. This "fable"—this severe lesson—is meant *"for the Critics."* "Ah!" we say to ourselves at once—"we see how it is. Mr. L. is a poor-devil poet, and some critic has been reviewing him, and making him feel very uncomfortable; whereupon, bearing in mind that Lord Byron, when similarly assailed, avenged his wrongs in a satire which he called 'English Bards and Scotch Reviewers,' he (Mr. Lowell) imitative as usual has been endeavoring to get redress in a parallel manner—by a satire with a parallel title—'A Fable for the Critics.' "

All this the reader says to himself; and all this tells *against* Mr. L. in two ways—first, by suggesting unlucky comparisons between Byron and Lowell, and, secondly, by reminding us of the various criticisms, in which we have been amused (rather ill-naturedly) at seeing Mr. Lowell "used up."

The title starts us on this train of thought and the satire sustains us in it. Every reader versed in our literary gossip, is at once put *dessous des cartes*[7] as to the particular provocation which engendered the

7. The underside of the cards (French, literal trans.); here, in the know.

"Fable." Miss Margaret Fuller,[8] some time ago, in a silly and conceited piece of Transcendentalism which she called an "Essay on American Literature," or something of that kind, had the consummate pleasantry, after *selecting* from the list of American poets, *Cornelius Mathews* and *William Ellery Channing*, for especial commendation, to speak of *Longfellow*[9] as a booby and of *Lowell* as so wretched a poetaster "as to be disgusting even to his best friends." All this Miss Fuller *said*, if not in our precise words, still in words quite as much to the purpose. *Why* she said it, Heaven only knows—unless it was because she was Margaret Fuller, and wished to be taken for nobody else. Messrs. Longfellow and Lowell, so pointedly picked out for abuse as the *worst* of our poets, are, upon the whole, perhaps, our best—although Bryant, and one or two others are scarcely inferior. As for the two favorites, selected just as pointedly for laudation, by Miss F.—it is really difficult to think of them, in connexion with poetry, without laughing. Mr. Mathews once wrote some sonnets "On Man," and Mr. Channing some lines on "A Tin Can," or something of that kind—and if the former gentleman be not the very worst poet that ever existed on the face of the earth, it is only because he is not quite so bad as the latter. To speak algebraically:—Mr. M. is *ex*ecrable, but Mr. C. is x plus I-ecrable.

Mr. Lowell has obviously aimed his "Fable" at Miss Fuller's head, in the first instance, with an eye to its ricochêt-ing so as to knock down Mr. Mathews in the second. Miss F. is first introduced as Miss F——, rhyming to "cooler," and afterwards as "Miranda;" while poor Mr. M. is brought in upon all occasions, head and shoulders; and now and then a sharp thing, although never very original, is said *of* them or *at* them; but all the true satiric *effect* wrought, is that produced by the satirist against himself. The reader is all the time smiling to think that so unsurpassable a—(*what* shall we call her?—we wish to be civil,) a transcendentalist as Miss Fuller, should, by *such* a criticism, have had the power to put a respectable poet in *such* a passion.

As for the plot or conduct of this Fable, the less we say of it the better. It is so weak—so flimsy—so ill put together—as to be not worth the trouble of understanding:—something, as usual, about Apollo and Daphne.[1] Is there *no* originality on the face of the earth? Mr. Lowell's total want of it is shown at all points—very especially in his Preface of rhyming verse written without distinction by lines or initial capitals, (a hackneyed matter, originating, we believe, with Frazer's Magazine:)— very especially also, in his long continuations of some particular rhyme—a fashion introduced, if we remember aright, by Leigh Hunt,[2] more than twenty-five years ago, in his "Feast of the Poets"—which, by the way, has been Mr. L's model in many respects.

8. Author, editor, feminist (1810–1850).
9. Authors: Cornelius Mathews (1817–1889), William Ellery Channing (1780–1842), Henry Wadsworth Longfellow (1807–1882).
1. Daphne, daughter of the river god Peneus, was pursued by Apollo, the sun god. Fleeing him, she pled with the gods to save her and so they changed her into a laurel tree (the favorite tree of Apollo).
2. British poet, journalist, and essayist (1784–1859).

Although ill-temper has evidently engendered this "Fable," it is by no means a satire throughout. Much of it is devoted to panegyric—but our readers would be quite puzzled to know the grounds of the author's laudations, in many cases, unless made acquainted with a fact which we think it as well they should be informed of at once. Mr. Lowell is one of the most rabid of the Abolition fanatics; and no Southerner who does not wish to be insulted, and at the same time revolted by a bigotry the most obstinately blind and deaf, should ever touch a volume by this author.[3] His fanaticism about slavery is a mere local outbreak of the same innate wrong-headedness which, if he owned slaves, would manifest itself in atrocious ill-treatment of them, with murder of any abolitionist who should endeavor to set them free. A fanatic of Mr. L's species, is simply a fanatic for the sake of fanaticism, and *must* be a fanatic in whatever circumstances you place him.

His prejudices on the topic of slavery break out every where in his present book. Mr. L. has not the common honesty to speak well, even in a literary sense, of any man who is not a ranting abolitionist. With the exception of Mr. Poe, (who has written some commendatory criticisms on his poems,) no Southerner is mentioned *at all* in this "Fable." It is a fashion among Mr. Lowell's set to affect a belief that there is *no such thing* as Southern Literature. Northerners—people who have really nothing to speak of as men of letters,—are cited by the dozen and lauded by this candid critic without stint, while Legaré, Simms, Longstreet,[4] and others of equal note are passed by in contemptuous silence. Mr. L. cannot carry his frail honesty of opinion even so far South as New York. All whom he praises are Bostonians. Other writers are barbarians and satirized accordingly—if mentioned at all.

To show the general *manner* of the Fable, we quote a portion of what he says about Mr. Poe:

> Here comes Poe with his Raven, like Barnaby Rudge—
> Three-fifths of him genius, and two-fifths sheer fudge;
> Who talks like a book of iambs and pentameters,
> In a way to make all men of common sense d—n metres;
> Who has written some things far the best of their kind;
> But somehow the heart seems squeezed out by the mind.[5]

We may observe here that *profound* ignorance on any particular topic is always sure to manifest itself by some allusion to "common sense" as an all-sufficient instructor. So far from Mr. P's talking "like a

3. This "Fable *for the Critics*"—this *literary* satire—this benevolent *jeu d'esprit* is disgraced by such passages as the following:

> Forty fathers of Freedom, of whom twenty bred
> Their sons for the rice swamps at so much a head,
> And their daughters for—faugh! [Poe's note].

This passage is a key one in the discussion of the racial subtext of some of Poe's works (see the South and Slavery section on pp. 767ff.; and the essays by John Carlos Rowe on pp. 904ff. herein) and Terence Whalen (pp. 920ff.).
4. James Matthewes Legaré (1823–1859), William Gilmore Simms (1806–1870), and Augustus Baldwin Longstreet (1790–1870), all Southern writers.
5. We must do Mr. L. the justice to say that his book was in press before he could have seen Mr. Poe's "*Rationale of Verse*" published in this Magazine for November and December last [Poe's note].

book" on the topic at issue, his chief purpose has been to demonstrate that there exists *no* book on the subject worth talking *about*; and "common sense," after all, has been the basis on which *he* relied, in contradistinction from the *un*common nonsense of Mr. L. and the small pedants.

* * *

Two-thirds of the force of the "Dunciad"[6] may be referred to its exquisite finish; and had "The Fable for the Critics" been, (what it is *not*,) the quintessence of the satiric spirit itself, it would nevertheless, in so slovenly a form, have failed. As it is, no failure was ever more complete or more pitiable. By the publication of a book at once so ambitious and so feeble—so malevolent in design and so harmless in execution—a work so roughly and clumsily yet so weakly constructed—so very different, in body and spirit, from anything that he has written before—Mr. Lowell has committed an irrevocable *faux pas* and lowered himself at least fifty per cent in the literary public opinion.

From The Poetic Principle[1]

In speaking of the Poetic Principle, I have no design to be either thorough or profound. While discussing, very much at random, the essentiality of what we call Poetry, my principal purpose will be to cite for consideration, some few of those minor English or American poems which best suit my own taste, or which, upon my own fancy, have left the most definite impression. By "minor poems" I mean, of course, poems of little length. And here, in the beginning, permit me to say a few words in regard to a somewhat peculiar principle, which, whether rightfully or wrongfully, has always had its influence in my own critical estimate of the poem. I hold that a long poem does not exist. I maintain that the phrase, "a long poem," is simply a flat contradiction in terms.

I need scarcely observe that a poem deserves its title only inasmuch as it excites, by elevating the soul. The value of the poem is in the ratio of this elevating excitement. But all excitements are, through a psychal necessity, transient. That degree of excitement which would entitle a poem to be so called at all, cannot be sustained throughout a composition of any great length. After the lapse of half an hour, at the very utmost, it flags—fails—a revulsion ensues—and then the poem is, in effect, and in fact, no longer such.

There are, no doubt, many who have found difficulty in reconciling the critical dictum that the "Paradise Lost"[2] is to be devoutly admired throughout, with the absolute impossibility of maintaining for it, during perusal, the amount of enthusiasm which that critical dictum

6. *The Dunciad* (1728; 1743) by Alexander Pope, a satire on "dullness."
1. Published posthumously in *Sartain's Union Magazine* (October 1850); Poe makes extensive use of his review of Longfellow's *Ballads* (pp. 636ff. herein).
2. *Paradise Lost* (1667) by John Milton (1608–1674) is in twelve books, averaging a thousand lines each.

would demand. This great work, in fact, is to be regarded as poetical, only when, losing sight of that vital requisite in all works of Art, Unity, we view it merely as a series of minor poems. If, to preserve its Unity—its totality of effect or impression—we read it (as would be necessary) at a single sitting, the result is but a constant alternation of excitement and depression. After a passage of what we feel to be true poetry, there follows, inevitably, a passage of platitude which no critical pre-judgment can force us to admire; but if, upon completing the work, we read it again, omitting the first book—that is to say, commencing with the second—we shall be surprised at now finding that admirable which we before condemned—that damnable which we had previously so much admired. It follows from all this that the ultimate, aggregate, or absolute effect of even the best epic under the sun, is a nullity:—and this is precisely the fact.

In regard to the Iliad, we have, if not positive proof, at least very good reason for believing it intended as a series of lyrics; but, granting the epic intention, I can say only that the work is based in an imperfect sense of art. The modern epic is, of the supposititious ancient model, but an inconsiderate and blindfold imitation. But the day of these artistic anomalies is over. If, at any time, any very long poem *were* popular in reality, which I doubt, it is at least clear that no very long poem will ever be popular again.

That the extent of a poetical work is, *cæteris paribus*,[3] the measure of its merit, seems undoubtedly, when we thus state it, a proposition sufficiently absurd—yet we are indebted for it to the Quarterly Reviews. Surely there can be nothing in mere *size*, abstractly considered—there can be nothing in mere *bulk*, so far as a volume is concerned, which has so continuously elicited admiration from these saturnine pamphlets! A mountain, to be sure, by the mere sentiment of physical magnitude which it conveys, *does* impress us with a sense of the sublime—but no man is impressed after *this* fashion by the material grandeur of even "The Columbiad."[4] Even the Quarterlies have not instructed us to be so impressed by it. *As yet*, they have not *insisted* on our estimating Lamartine by the cubic foot, or Pollock[5] by the pound—but what else are we to *infer* from their continual prating about "sustained effort?" If, by "sustained effort," any little gentleman has accomplished an epic, let us frankly commend him for the effort—if this indeed be a thing commendable—but let us forbear praising the epic on the effort's account. It is to be hoped that common sense, in the time to come, will prefer deciding upon a work of art, rather by the impression it makes, by the effect it produces, than by the time it took to impress the effect, or by the amount of "sustained effort" which had been found necessary in effecting the impression. The fact is, that perseverance is one thing, and genius quite another;

3. All things being equal (Latin).
4. Long epic poem (1807) of America by Joel Barlow (1754–1812).
5. Robert Pollock, Scots poet and author of *The Course of Time* (1827), a long, didactic religious poem. The French poet Alphonse Marie Louis de Lamartine (1790–1869) was notoriously long-winded.

nor can all the Quarterlies in Christendom confound them. By and by, this proposition, with many which I have been just urging, will be received as self-evident. In the mean time, by being generally condemned as falsities, they will not be essentially damaged as truths.

On the other hand, it is clear that a poem may be improperly brief. Undue brevity degenerates into mere epigrammatism. A *very* short poem, while now and then producing a brilliant or vivid, never produces a profound or enduring effect. There must be the steady pressing down of the stamp upon the wax. De Béranger has wrought innumerable things, pungent and spirit-stirring; but, in general, they have been too imponderous to stamp themselves deeply into the public attention; and thus, as so many feathers of fancy, have been blown aloft only to be whistled down the wind.

* * *

While the epic mania—while the idea that, to merit in poetry, prolixity is indispensable—has, for some years past, been gradually dying out of the public mind, by mere dint of its own absurdity—we find it succeeded by a heresy too palpably false to be long tolerated, but one which, in the brief period it has already endured, may be said to have accomplished more in the corruption of our Poetical Literature than all its other enemies combined. I allude to the heresy of *The Didactic*. It has been assumed, tacitly and avowedly, directly and indirectly, that the ultimate object of all Poetry is Truth. Every poem, it is said, should inculcate a moral; and by this moral is the poetical merit of the work to be adjudged. We Americans, especially, have patronised this happy idea; and we Bostonians, very especially, have developed it in full. We have taken it into our heads that to write a poem simply for the poem's sake, and to acknowledge such to have been our design, would be to confess ourselves radically wanting in the true Poetic dignity and force:—but the simple fact is, that, would we but permit ourselves to look into our own souls, we should immediately there discover that under the sun there neither exists nor *can* exist any work more thoroughly dignified—more supremely noble than this very poem—this poem *per se*—this poem which is a poem and nothing more—this poem written solely for the poem's sake.

With as deep a reverence for the True as ever inspired the bosom of man, I would, nevertheless, limit, in some measure, its modes of inculcation. I would limit to enforce them. I would not enfeeble them by dissipation. The demands of Truth are severe. She has no sympathy with the myrtles. All *that* which *is* so indispensable in Song, is precisely all *that* with which *she* has nothing whatever to do. It is but making her a flaunting paradox; to wreathe her in gems and flowers. In enforcing a truth, we need severity rather than efflorescence of language. We must be simple, precise, terse. We must be cool, calm, unimpassioned. In a word, we must be in that mood which, as nearly as possible, is the exact converse of the poetical. *He* must be blind, indeed, who does not perceive the radical and chasmal differences between the truthful and the poetical modes of inculcation. He must be

theory-mad beyond redemption who, in spite of these differences, shall still persist in attempting to reconcile the obstinate oils and waters of Poetry and Truth.

Dividing the world of mind into its three most immediately obvious distinctions, we have the Pure Intellect, Taste, and the Moral Sense.[6] I place Taste in the middle, because it is just this position, which, in the mind, it occupies. It holds intimate relations with either extreme; but from the Moral Sense is separated by so faint a difference that Aristotle has not hesitated to place some of its operations among the virtues themselves. Nevertheless, we find the *offices* of the trio marked with a sufficient distinction. Just as the Intellect concerns itself with Truth, so Taste informs us of the Beautiful while the Moral Sense is regardful of Duty. Of this latter, while Conscience teaches the obligation, and Reason the expediency, Taste contents herself with displaying the charms:—waging war upon Vice solely on the ground of her deformity—her disproportion—her animosity to the fitting, to the appropriate, to the harmonious—in a word, to Beauty.

An immortal instinct, deep within the spirit of man, is thus, plainly, a sense of the Beautiful. This it is which administers to his delight in the manifold forms, and sounds, and odours, and sentiments amid which he exists. And just as the lily is repeated in the lake, or the eyes of Amaryllis in the mirror,[7] so is the mere oral or written repetition of these forms, and sounds, and colours, and odours, and sentiments, a duplicate source of delight. But this mere repetition is not poetry. He who shall simply sing, with however glowing enthusiasm, or with however vivid a truth of description, of the sights, and sounds, and odours, and colours, and sentiments, which greet *him* in common with all mankind—he, I say, has yet failed to prove his divine title. There is still a something in the distance which he has been unable to attain. We have still a thirst unquenchable, to allay which he has not shown us the crystal springs. This thirst belongs to the immortality of Man. It is at once a consequence and an indication of his perennial existence. It is the desire of the moth for the star. It is no mere appreciation of the Beauty before us—but a wild effort to reach the Beauty above. Inspired by an ecstatic prescience of the glories beyond the grave, we struggle, by multiform combinations among the things and thoughts of Time, to attain a portion of that Loveliness whose very elements, perhaps, appertain to eternity alone. And thus when by Poetry—or when by Music, the most entrancing of the Poetic moods—we find ourselves melted into tears—we weep then—not as the Abbaté Gravina[8] supposes—through excess of pleasure, but through a certain, petulant, impatient sorrow at our inability to grasp *now*, wholly, here on earth, at once and for ever, those divine and rapturous joys, of

6. This is the tripartite paradigm of the German philosopher Immanuel Kant (1724–1804), in the *Critique of Judgment* (1793); see the Transcendentalism and Alternative Romanticism section (p. 717ff. herein).
7. Amaryllis, the shepherdess in Virgil's *Ecologues*, gave her name to the species of flower also known as narcissus. In Ovid's *Metamorphoses*, the young man Narcissus, in love with his own reflection, is changed into the flower that habitually bends over its reflection in a pool.
8. See *Marginalia, Southern Literary Messenger*, April 1849.

which *through* the poem, or *through* the music, we attain but brief and indeterminate glimpses.

The struggle to apprehend the supernal Loveliness—this struggle, on the part of souls fittingly constituted—has given to the world all *that* which it (the world) has ever been enabled at once to understand and *to feel* as poetic.

The Poetic Sentiment, of course, may develop itself in various modes—in Painting, in Sculpture, in Architecture, in the Dance—very especially in Music—and very peculiarly, and with a wide field, in the composition of the Landscape Garden. Our present theme, however, has regard only to its manifestation in words. And here let me speak briefly on the topic of rhythm. Contenting myself with the certainty that Music, in its various modes of metre, rhythm, and rhyme, is of so vast a moment in Poetry as never to be wisely rejected—is so vitally important an adjunct, that he is simply silly who declines its assistance, I will not now pause to maintain its absolute essentiality. It is in Music, perhaps, that the soul most nearly attains the great end for which, when inspired with the Poetic Sentiment, it struggles—the creation of supernal Beauty. It *may* be, indeed, that here this sublime end is, now and then, attained *in fact*. We are often made to feel, with a shivering delight, that from an earthly harp are stricken notes which *cannot* have been unfamiliar to the angels. And thus there can be little doubt that in the union of Poetry with Music in its popular sense, we shall find the widest field for the Poetic development. The old Bards and Minnesingers had advantages which we do not possess—and Thomas Moore,[9] singing his own songs, was, in the most legitimate manner, perfecting them as poems.

To recapitulate, then:—I would define, in brief, the Poetry of words as *The Rhythmical Creation of Beauty*. Its sole arbiter is Taste. With the Intellect or with the Conscience, it has only collateral relations. Unless incidentally, it has no concern whatever either with Duty or with Truth.

A few words, however, in explanation. *That* pleasure which is at once the most pure, the most elevating, and the most intense, is derived, I maintain, from the contemplation of the Beautiful. In the contemplation of Beauty we alone find it possible to attain that pleasurable elevation, or excitement, *of the Soul*, which we recognise as the Poetic Sentiment, and which is so easily distinguished from Truth, which is the satisfaction of the Reason, or from Passion, which is the excitement of the Heart. I make Beauty, therefore—using the word as inclusive of the sublime—I make Beauty the province of the poem, simply because it is an obvious rule of Art that effects should be made to spring as directly as possible from their causes:—no one as yet having been weak enough to deny that the peculiar elevation in question is at least *most readily* attainable in the poem. It by no means follows, however, that the incitements of Passion, or the precepts of

9. Thomas Moore (1779–1852), Irish poet to whom Poe makes frequent reference. The Minnesingers were the lyric poets of the 12th- and 13th-century German courts; they sang of love, religion, and politics.

Duty, or even the lessons of Truth, may not be introduced into a poem, and with advantage; for they may subserve, incidentally, in various ways, the general purposes of the work:—but the true artist will always contrive to tone them down in proper subjection to that *Beauty* which is the atmosphere and the real essence of the poem.

* * *

Thus, although in a very cursory and imperfect manner, I have endeavoured to convey to you my conception of the Poetic Principle. It has been my purpose to suggest that, while this Principle itself is, strictly and simply, the Human Aspiration for Supernal Beauty, the manifestation of the Principle is always found in *an elevating excitement of the Soul*—quite independent of that passion which is the intoxication of the Heart—or of that Truth which is the satisfaction of the Reason. For, in regard to Passion, alas! its tendency is to degrade, rather than to elevate the Soul. Love, on the contrary—Love— the true, the divine Eros—the Uranian, as distinguished from the Dionæan Venus[1]—is unquestionably the purest and truest of all poetical themes. And in regard to Truth—if, to be sure, through the attainment of a truth, we are led to perceive a harmony where none was apparent before, we experience, at once, the true poetical effect—but this effect is referable to the harmony alone, and not in the least degree to the truth which merely served to render the harmony manifest.

We shall reach, however, more immediately a distinct conception of what the true Poetry is, by mere reference to a few of the simple elements which induce in the Poet himself the true poetical effect. He recognises the ambrosia which nourishes his soul, in the bright orbs that shine in Heaven—in the volutes of the flower—in the clustering of low shrubberies—in the waving of the grain-fields—in the slanting of tall, Eastern trees—in the blue distance of mountains—in the grouping of clouds—in the twinkling of half-hidden brooks—in the gleaming of silver rivers—in the repose of sequestered lakes—in the star-mirroring depths of lonely wells. He perceives it in the songs of birds—in the harp of Æeolus[2]—in the sighing of the night wind—in the repining voice of the forest—in the surf that complains to the shore—in the fresh breath of the woods—in the scent of the violet— in the voluptuous perfume of the hyacinth—in the suggestive odour that comes to him, at eventide, from far-distant, undiscovered islands, over dim oceans, illimitable and unexplored. He owns it in all noble thoughts—in all unworldly motives—in all holy impulses—in all chivalrous, generous, and self-sacrificing deeds. He feels it in the beauty of woman—in the grace of her step—in the lustre of her eye— in the melody of her voice—in her soft laughter—in her sigh—in the harmony of the rustling of her robes. He deeply feels it in her winning

1. References to mythology. Urania was the Muse (goddess) of astronomy. Milton referred to Urania as the spirit of the loftiest poetry. Dione, a female Titan, was the mother of Aphrodite (Roman Venus).
2. God of the winds, which he kept imprisoned in the Aeolian islands.

endearments—in her burning enthusiasms—in her gentle charities—in her meek and devotional endurances—but above all—ah, far above all—he kneels to it—he worships it in the faith, in the purity, in the strength, in the altogether divine majesty—of her *love*.

* * *

[WALTER G. BOWEN]

A Reviewer Reviewed[1]

As we rode along the valley we saw a herd of *asses* on the top of one
of the mountains—how they viewed and *reviewed* us!
Sterne—"Letter from France."[2]

Mr editor—In a late number of your widely circulated Magazine I had the satisfaction of reading an epigram which appeared to me, and to your subscribers generally, if I am not very much mistaken, to be not less well aimed and fairly driven home to the mark, than righteously deserved. It was in these words,

On P—, the Versifier, reviewing his own Verses.

When critics scourged him there was scope
 For self-amendment and for hope;
Reviewing his own verses, he
 Has done the deed—*felo de se*.[3]

I am glad to perceive that there is at least one editor of a Magazine who is not so tied up in Mr Poe's interest as to be afraid of expressing an honest opinion of him as a literary man, but I do assure you that not only myself but a great many others were astonished beyond measure at finding that you had the courage to insert the epigram, good as it was. Your putting it in however, has elevated you not a little in the public opinion, and has encouraged me to hope that you will do me the favor of publishing this Review of the Reviewer, especially as what I ask is merely in the way of perfectly fair and above board retaliation for what Mr P. upon one or two occasions has seen fit to say of some unpretending poems of mine, as well as of a novel by my brother-in-law. And as for the truth and justice of what I shall write, I trust that on that score there will be no one to offer objection, as I do not intend to say a single word that shall not be accompanied *by the proof*. Mr Poe, to say nothing of my own case, has done little else than "ride rough shod" over what he is in the facetious habit of denominating the "poor devil authors" of the land, and I presume that neither you nor any body else will think it unreasonable that, sooner or later, he

1. The unfinished manuscript of this hoax review, in Poe's handwriting, was found in Poe's trunk after his death.
2. Actually from Laurence Sterne's *Tristram Shandy* (1759–67), but Poe seems to have taken the epigraph, as quoted, from Horace Binney Wallace's *Stanley* (1838).
3. A felon upon himself (Anglo-Latin); i.e., a person who kills himself.

should have the bitter chalice of criticism returned to his own lip—provided always and of course that the thing is done fairly, honorably, and with no trick or subterfuge—in a word, provided that the criticism be *just*.

To follow Mr Poe's own apparently frank mode of reviewing, I will begin by putting the merits of my author "in the fairest light." I shall not pretend to deny then that he has written several pieces of very considerable merit, and that some of these pieces have attracted, partly of their own accord and partly through the puffing of his friends, an unusual degree of notoriety. Among these I feel called upon to mention his Tales published by Wiley & Putnam, and especially the one called "The Murder in the Rue Morgue," which I learn has been reprinted and highly complimented in Paris, and "The Gold Bug" which Martin Farquhar Tupper justly praises, as well as the "Descent into the Maelstroom,"[4] and several other stories, all of which I am willing to admit display great power of analysis and imagination. "The Facts in the Case of Mr Valdemar" have perhaps made a greater "sensation" than anything else he has written, and has, I understand, not only gone the complete rounds of the London press, from the Morning Post down, but has been printed in pamphlet form in London, Paris and Vienna. The ingenuity and general merit of his "Raven" I do not wish to detract from, although I certainly do not think quite so highly of it as Miss Barrett or as Mr Willis professes to do; nor as Mr P himself does,[5] if we are to judge by the laudatory criticism on it which he lately published in "Graham," a criticism which displayed, perhaps, more analysis than modesty. Some of his shorter poems are also praiseworthy, and his "Sleeper" and "Dreamland" are in my opinion better than the Raven, although in a different way. Of his criticisms I have not so much to observe in the way of commendation. They show scholarship, and the peculiar analytic talent which is the ruling feature in everything he writes. They are also remarkable for that Quixotic kind of courage which induces people of Mr P's temperament to be perpetually tilting at something—although it too often happens that the something is a windmill;[6] and there is one good point about them which it would be unjust to omit; and that is, they show no respect for persons. They are seldom aimed at small game. On the other hand they seem to me bitter in the extreme, captious, fault-finding, and unnecessarily severe. Mr. P. has been so often complimented for his powers of sarcasm that he thinks it incumbent upon him to keep up his reputation in that line by sneers upon all occasions and downright abuse. As for the beauties of a work, he appears to have

4. The misspellings are apparently intentional (in support of the hoax). Pirated adaptations of "The Murders in the Rue Morgue" by two rival French journalists led to a lawsuit between them in 1846 that helped bring Poe to the attention of the French public. His "The Gold-Bug" was widely pirated. Tupper's review, titled "American Romance," appeared in the London *Literary Gazette* on January 31, 1846.
5. Elizabeth Barrett wrote to Poe complimenting him on "The Raven." Nathaniel Parker Willis praised the poem in the New York *Evening Mirror* of January 29, 1845. Poe's own "review" of the poem is in "The Philosophy of Composition" (pp. 675ff. herein).
6. In Cervantes's *Don Quixote* (part I, 1605; part II, 1615), the crazed "knight" attacks windmills that he thinks are many-armed giants.

made up his mind to neglect them altogether, or when he condescends to point one out, or to quote it, his compliments, however well they begin, are always sure to end with a point, or barb, which it is easy to mistake for satire in disguise. Real, honest, heartfelt praise is a thing not to be looked for in a criticism by Mr Poe. Even when it is his evident intention to be partial, to compliment in an extravagant manner some of his *lady* friends (for he never compliments a gentleman) there always seems to be something constrained, and shall I say malicious, at the bottom of the honey cup. These blemishes render his critical judgments of little value. They may be read for their pungency, but all the honesty they ever contain may be placed upon the point of a cambric needle.

Before proceeding with some very serious literary accusations which I have to make on my own part against Mr Poe, it may be as well, perhaps, to call his attention to something which has been said about him in the "London Literary Gazette." I wish to see if he will vouchsafe a reply to it. Mr P. has pointed out, in his late "Literati", a number of *scientific* blunders on the part of Mr. Richard Adams Locke,[7] and perhaps the public may have some curiosity to know how he will account for his own. The "Gazette" referred to is of the date of March 14th 1846.

"*To the Editor of the Literary Gazette*—Sir, Having just read a review of Edgar Poe's Romances in the *Literary Gazette* of January p 101, allow me to advert to a curious misconception in a scientific point of view which the author has fallen into. In describing his whirling in the Maelstroom he says—'On looking out when half way down, the boat appeared *hanging* as if by magic *upon the interior surface* of a funnel of vast circumference and prodigious depth' &c. . . . 'My gaze fell instinctively *downwards* The smack hung on the *inclined surface of the pool which sloped at an angle* of more than forty-five degrees; so that we *seemed* to be lying on our beam ends.' &c.

Now, with all deference I would submit, first, That our only notions of *up* or *down* are derived from the direction of gravity; when therefore the direction of gravity is changed by centrifugal force, *that* direction will still *appear* to be down. 2d. That our only sense of motion is relative; when therefore all that is visible is rotating along with ourselves, we shall have no sense of motion; and in few cases do we ever *ourselves* appear to be the moving objects (witness the case of railway travelling). The only apparent motion will be the slight *difference of motion* between the various objects and ourselves. Whence it appears that the gentleman in the predicament described would, on looking about him, see a vast funnel of water apparently *laid on its side*, with its lower side horizontal, at which lower part his boat would *always appear to be lying*; the heavens appearing *at one end horizontally* and *apparently rotating*; while the chaotic abyss and foam would be at the

7. In "The Literati of New York City" (*Godey's*, October 1846), Poe gives an account of the "Moon-Hoax" (as it came to be called) of Richard Adams Locke (1800–1871), published over a decade before (in 1835)—a circumstance he claimed dissuaded him from continuing his own moon narrative(s) begun in "Hans Phaall" (or "Hans Pfaall"; 1835, 1840).

opposite end; the waters appearing (full of local currents no doubt) stretching in a miraculous archway or tunnel, almost motionless, about and over the boat, and apparently supported by nothing; and objects nearer the entrance would appear to rotate vertically in a *slowly* retrograde direction; while objects would appear to have an opposite rotation, more and more rapid, towards the misty tumultuous end; the real velocity of the whole being unperceived, except by the contrary apparent rotation of the heavens. This would, indeed, be a wondrous spectacle, though scarcely sufficing to induce a personal experiment by your humble servant,

<div align="right">

William Petrie."

</div>

So much for Mr Petrie, and leaving Mr Poe to reply to him, I will just here put in a point for myself, although I confess it has been suggested to me by a friend at my elbow. It is this—In accounting for his hero's escape from the Maelstrom, Mr P. quotes Archimedes *"De Incidentibus in Fluido"*[8] lib 2. for the following fact, viz: that "a cylinder swimming in a vortex, offers more resistance to its suction and is drawn in with greater difficulty than an equally bulky body of any form whatsoever." Now the friend at my elbow asserts roundly, first, that the fact stated is no fact at all and is contrary to known laws, and secondly that there is no such passage in the second book of Archimedes as the one referred to. Thirdly he says that *no such passage, nor any resembling it, is in Archimedes at all, and that he defies Mr Poe to point it out.*

With Mr Poe's general *style* no great fault can be justly found. He has the rare merit of distinctness and simplicity, and can be forcible enough upon occasion; but as he has a most unmannerly habit of picking flaws in the grammar of other people, I feel justified in showing him that he is far from being immaculate himself. Not long ago I remember his sneering at some one for using the verb "drop" in an active sense, but at page 14 of his Tales (Wiley & Putnam edition) he commits the very same blunder—e.g—"As sure as you *drop* that beetle I'll break your neck." Again at page 18—"Was it this eye or that through which you *dropped* the beetle?" "As sure as you *let fall* that beetle" would be proper. An apple drops, but we let an apple fall. At page 34 he uses "except," with gross impropriety, for "unless"—a common error. E.g—"I found that it was impossible to retain a seat *upon* it *except* in one particular position." *"Upon"* in this sentence is also improperly employed for *"on."* This error is very usual with Mr Poe. At page 25 there are no less than five instances of it—e.g—"I doubted not that heat had been the agent in bringing to light *upon* the parchment the skull which I saw designed *upon* it." The *up* is properly used only where *action* appears. An apple, for instance, lies *on* a table; but we place an apple *up*on a table. Even in the Preface to his Poems, where we are forced to suppose him careful if ever, he is guilty of inaccurate construction. For example—"If what I have written is to circulate at all, I am naturally anxious that it should circulate as I wrote it." Now here the sentence

8. See notes to "A Descent into the Maelström" (pp. 266ff. herein).

should obviously be—"I am naturally anxious that what I have written should circulate as I wrote it, if it circulate at all." Or—"I am naturally anxious that what I have written, if it is to circulate at all, should circulate as I wrote it." But a truce with these trifles—and yet they are the very kind of *trifles* which Mr P. is so fond of exposing in other people.[9]

The truth is, I have something more serious to speak of. The great *point* which Mr Poe has become notorious for making is that of *plagiarism*, and in his elaborate reply to *"Outis"* in the earlier numbers of the "Broadway Journal,"[1] he was at great pains to demonstrate what a plagiarism is, and by what chain of reasoning it could be established. My own purpose at present is simply to copy a few parallel passages, leaving it for the public to decide whether they do or do not come properly under the head of *wilful and deliberate literary theft.*

At page 24 of Mr P's last volume of Poems (Wiley & Putnam's edition) in a song called Eulalie, is the passage,

> Now Doubt—now Pain
> Come never again
> For her soul *gives me sigh for sigh.*

In Tom Moore's "Last Rose of Summer" we find it thus,

> No flower of her kindred,
> No rose-bud is nigh,
> To reflect back her blushes
> *Or give sigh for sigh.*

The author of the lines which follow I cannot *name* just now, but I give them because there are doubtless many of my readers who can. *Some* poet, however, is speaking of a traitor to his country and wishes him doomed

> *to dwell*
> Full in the sight of Paradise
> *Beholding Heaven yet feeling Hell.*[2]

In "Al Aaraaf," at page 69 of the Poems, we read

> And there oh may my weary spirit *dwell*
> *Apart from Heaven's eternity, and yet how far from Hell!*

One of Mr Poe's most admired passages is this, forming the conclusion of the poem called "The City in the Sea," and to be found at page 22—

> And when, amid no earthly moans
> Down, down, that town shall settle hence
> *Hell rising from a thousand thrones*
> *Shall do it reverence.*

9. Mabbott points out that these constructions were marked by Poe for correction in his copy of *Tales.*
1. See the notes to Poe's review of Longfellow's *Ballads* (pp. 636ff.). The self-irony of the present review seems to strengthen the argument of some critics that Outis was Poe himself.
2. Also from Thomas Moore; "The Fire Worshippers" section of *Lalla Rookh* (see notes to Poe's "Al Aaraaf, pp. 22ff. herein).

But unfortunately Mrs Sigourney,[3] in a little poem called "Musing Thoughts," first published in "The Token," for 1829, has the lines,

> *Earth slowly rising from her thousand thrones*
> *Did homage* to the Corsican.

Mr Poe has also been much praised for these lines, found at page 63 of the Poems,

> A dome by linked light from Heaven let down
> Sat gently on these columns as a crown.

Every classical scholar however must remember the Gods' Council of Homer, beginning Ἠὼς μὲν κροκόπεπλος ἐκίδνατο πᾶσαν ἐπ᾽ αἶαν, and the lines which Pope translates (I have not the original by me)

> Let down our golden everlasting chain
> Whose strong embrace holds Heaven and Earth and Main.[4]

That Mr Poe has in many cases obtained *help* from the more obscure classics is, I fancy, no more than a legitimate inference from so glaringly obvious an *imitation* as this, which we find at page 20.

SONNET TO ZANTE

Fair isle that, from the fairest of all flowers,
 Thy gentlest of all gentle names dost take!
How many memories of what radiant hours
 At sight of thee and thine at once awake!
How many scenes of what departed bliss!
 How many thoughts of what entombed hopes
How many visions of a maiden that is
 No more—no more upon thy verdant slopes!
No more! alas that magical sad sound
 Transforming all! Thy charms shall please no more—
Thy memory *no more*! Accursed ground
 Henceforth I hold thy flower-enamelled shore,

O hyacinthine isle! O purple Zante!
Isola d'oro! Fior di Levante!

Here I might safely pause; but it would not be quite proper to omit all mention of this critic's facility at *imitation!* in prose as well as verse. In his story of "Hans Phaall" published in his "Tales of the Grotesque and Arabesque," but originally appearing in the first volume of the "Southern Literary Messenger"

[The manuscript breaks off.]

3. Lydia Howard Huntley Sigourney (1791–1865), American poet.
4. Alexander Pope's translation of Homer's *Iliad*, book VIII.1. The Greek actually means: "Dawn yellow-robed spread over all the earth" (translation from Mabbott). See Poe's "Al Aaraaf" (II.20–21; p. 33 herein) for the vague parallel.

The Late Edgar Allan Poe Reprinted from *Graham's Magazine* (March 1850), for which George Rex Graham (1813–1894), the owner and editor, wrote a column titled "The Editor's Table." Graham employed Poe from 1841 to 1842. In this obituary review, he uses Nathaniel Parker Willis (1806–1867), the first-named editor on the title page of the 1850 Redfield edition of Poe's *Works*, as his addressee in what is actually an "open letter" to Poe's detractors. It is in fact a rejoinder to the negative remarks of the "Reverend" Rufus Wilmot Griswold (1815–1857), one of the editors of the Poe edition. Griswold had met Poe in the spring of 1841. His anthology *The Poets and Poetry of America* (1842) was quite popular, but Poe made criticisms of it in his lectures, for which Griswold seems never to have forgiven him. Although Griswold commented favorably on Poe's works in his anthology *The Prose Writers of America* (1847), his obituary, signed "Ludwig" (New York *Daily Tribune*, October 9, 1849), was vindictive; he denigrated both Poe's achievements and his character. He begins: "Edgar Poe is dead. He died in Baltimore the day before yesterday. This announcement will startle many, *but few will be grieved by it . . . he had few or no friends.*" This pronouncement outraged many, like Willis, Evert Duyckinck, Sarah Helen Whitman, George Graham, and others. Griswold's piece was widely reprinted; and his "Memoir" for Poe's *Works* is even more malicious—and false—than his original "Ludwig" obituary. The "Memoir" skews the facts of Poe's life, distorts their contexts, and even adds fictitious passages to Poe's letters to make him look bad. Unfortunately, these pieces set the tone for the posthumous evaluation of Poe the man for decades, despite several corrective defenses by Poe's contemporaries. It was not until the publication of Arthur Hobson Quinn's biography in 1941 that Griswold's perfidy became fully clear, for Quinn printed Poe's original letters side by side with Griswold's versions and revealed his forgeries. Neither the "Ludwig" article nor the "Memoir" seems fit to be perpetuated in the present volume; Graham's rebuttal presents the basic controversy.

GEORGE R. GRAHAM

From The Late Edgar Allan Poe

* * *

MY DEAR WILLIS,—in an article of yours, which accompanies the two beautiful volumes of the writings of Edgar Allan Poe,[1] you have spoken with so much truth and delicacy of the deceased, and with the magical touch of genius have called so warmly up before me the memory of our lost friend, as you and I both seem to have known him, that I feel warranted in addressing to you the few plain words I have to say in defense of his character, as set down by Dr. Rufus W. Griswold. Although the article, it seems, appeared originally in the New York Tribune, it met my eye for the first time in the volumes before me.[2] I now purpose to

1. *The Works of the Late Edgar Allan Poe: With Notices of His Life and Genius, by N. P. Willis, J. R. Lowell, and R. W. Griswold. In Two Volumes. New York: J. S. Redfield, Clinton Hall* [Graham's note].
2. See the headnote (above). For further discussion, see the biographical introduction on p. xlvff.

take exception to it in the most public manner. I knew Mr. Poe well—
far better than Mr. Griswold; and by the memory of old times, when he
was an editor of "Graham," I pronounce this exceedingly ill-timed and
unappreciative estimate of the character of our lost friend *unfair and
untrue.* It must have been made in a moment of spleen, written out and
laid aside, and handed to the printer, when his death was announced,
with a sort of chuckle. It is Mr. Poe, as seen by the writer while labor-
ing under a fit of the nightmare; but so dark a picture has no resem-
blance to the *living* man. Accompanying these beautiful volumes, it is
an immortal infamy—the death's head over the entrance to the garden
of beauty—a horror that clings to the brow of mo[u]rning, whispering
of murder. It haunts the memory through every page of his writings,
leaving upon the heart a sensation of utter gloom, a feeling almost of
terror. The only relief we feel, is in knowing that it is not true—that it
is a fancy sketch of a perverted, jaundiced vision. The man who could
deliberately say of Edgar Allan Poe, in a notice of his life and writings,
prefacing the volumes which were to become a priceless souvenir to all
who loved him—that his death might startle many, *"but that few would
be grieved by it"*—and blast the whole fame of the man by such a para-
graph as follows, is a judge dishonored. He is not Mr. Poe's peer, and I
challenge him before the country, even as a juror in the case.[3]

* * *

Now, this is dastardly, and, what is worse, it is false. It is very
adroitly done, with phrases very well turned and with gleams of truth
shining out from a setting so dusky as to look devilish. Mr. Griswold
does not feel the worth of the man he has undervalued—he had no
sympathies in common with him, and has allowed old prejudices and
old enmities to steal, insensibly perhaps into the coloring of his pic-
ture. They were for years totally uncongenial, if not enemies, and dur-
ing that period Mr. Poe, in a scathing lecture upon The Poets of
America gave Mr. Griswold some raps over the knuckles of force suffi-
cient to be remembered. He had, too, in the exercise of his functions
as critic, put to death, summarily, the literary reputation of some of
Mr. Griswold's best friends and their ghosts cried in vain for him to
avenge them during Poe's life-time—and it almost seems, as if the
present hacking at the cold remains of him who struck them down, is
a sort of compensation for duty long delayed—for reprisal long desired
but defer[r]ed. But without this—the opportunities afforded Mr. Gris-
wold to estimate the character of Poe occurred, in the main, after his
stability had been wrecked, his whole nature in a degree changed and
with all his prejudices aroused and active. Nor do I consider Mr. Gris-
wold *competent*—with all the opportunities he may have cultivated or
acquired—to act as his judge—to dissect that subtle and singularly
fine intellect—to probe the motives and weigh the actions of that
proud heart. His whole nature—that distinctive presence of the de-
parted which now stands impalpable, yet in strong outline before me,

3. Graham here quotes (with minor errors) Griswold's "quotation" from Bulwer-Lytton's *The
Caxtons.* This passage, describing an unsavory fictional character, was applied directly to Poe
by Griswold.

as I knew him and *felt* him to be—eludes the rude grasp of a mind so warped and uncongenial as Mr. Griswold's.

* * *

But my object in throwing together a few thoughts upon the character of Edgar All[a]n Poe, was not to attempt an elaborate criticism, but to say what might palliate[4] grave faults that have been attributed to him, and to meet by facts, unjust accusation—in a word, to give a mere outline of the man as he lived before me. I think I am warranted in saying to Mr. Griswold, that he must review his decision. It will not stand the calm scrutiny of his own judgment, or of time, while it must be regarded by all the friends of Mr. Poe as an ill-judged and misplaced calumny upon that gifted Son of Genius.

Yours truly,

GEO. R. GRAHAM.

To N. P. WILLIS, Esq.
Philadelphia, Feb. 2, 1850.

CHARLES BAUDELAIRE

From Edgar Allan Poe: His Life and His Works[1]

Introduction to *Les Histoires Extraordinaires*

* * *

Does there, then, exist some diabolic Providence which prepares misery from the cradle; which throws, and throws with premeditation, these spiritual and angelic natures into hostile ranks, as martyrs were once hurled into the arena? Can there, then, be holy souls destined to the sacrificial altar, compelled to march to death and glory across the very ruins of their lives? Will the nightmare of gloom eternally besiege these chosen souls? Vainly they may struggle, vainly conform themselves to the world, to its foresight, to its cunning; let them grow perfect in prudence, batten up every entry, nail down every window, against the shafts of Fate; still the Demon will enter by a key-hole; some fault will arise from the very perfection of their breastplate; some superlative quality will be the germ of their damnation:

> L'aigle, pour le briser, du haut du firmament,
> Sur leur front découvert lâchera la torture,
> Car ils doivent périr inévitablement.[2]

4. To make something seem less serious or offensive, to extenuate.
1. Charles Baudelaire (1821–1867) first published "Edgar Allan Poe, *sa vie et ses ouvrages*" (Edgar Allan Poe: His life and his works) in the *Revue de Paris* in 1852. He had translated Poe's "Mesmeric Revelation" in 1848; he then began a series of additional translations, *Les histoires extraordinaires* (Extraordinary stories), which appeared in five volumes from 1856 to 1865. The 1856 volume contained a revision of Baudelaire's 1852 essay, the version reprinted here. The translation is that of Henry Curwen, which stood as an introduction to an edition of the selected works of Poe published by J. C. Hotten (1872), as presented and abridged by I. M. Walker in *Poe: The Critical Heritage*; additional cuts have been made for the present edition. Reprinted by permission of the publisher.
2. From "Ténèbres" [Darkness] by Théophile Gautier (1811–1872):

Their destiny is written in their very constitution; sparkling with a sinister brilliancy in their looks and in their gestures; circulating through their arteries in every globule of their blood.

<center>* * *</center>

A lamentable tragedy this Life of Edgar Poe! His death a horrible unravelling of the drama, where horror is besmutched with trivialities! All the documents I have studied strengthen me in the conviction that the United States was for Poe only a vast prison through which he ran, hither and thither, with the feverish agitation of a being created to breathe in a purer world—only a wild barbarous country—barbarous and gas-lit—and that his interior life, spiritual as a poet, spiritual even as a drunkard, was but one perpetual effort to escape the influence of this anti-pathetical atmosphere. There is no more pitiless dictator than that of 'Public Opinion' in democratic societies; beseech it not for charity, indulgence, nor any elasticity whatsoever, in the application of its laws to the varied and complex cases of moral life. We might say that from the impious love of liberty has been born a new tyranny of fools—which in its insensible ferocity, resembles the idol of Juggernaut.[3]

<center>* * *</center>

Poe, feeling, perhaps, the sinister foreboding of a sudden death, had nominated Griswold and Willis as his literary executors, to set his papers in order, to write his life and to restore his memory. The first—the *pedagogue vampire*[4]—has defamed his friend at full length in an enormous article—wearisome and crammed with hatred—which was fixed to the posthumous edition of Poe's works; are there then no regulations in America to keep the curs out of the cemeteries? Mr Willis, however, has proved, on the contrary, that kindliness and respect go hand in hand with true wit, and that charity, which is ever a moral duty, is also one of the dictates of good taste.

Talk of Poe with an American—he will, perhaps, confess his genius, perhaps even show a personal pride in it; but, with that sardonic superiority which betokens your positive man, he will tell you of the poet's disordered life; of his alcoholized breath, ready to have taken light at any candle-flame; of his vagabond habits; he will reiterate that the poet was an erratic and strange being, an orbitless planet, rolling incessantly from Baltimore to New York, from New York to Philadelphia, from Philadelphia to Boston, from Boston to Baltimore, from Baltimore to Richmond; and, if deeply moved by these preludes of a grievous history, you try to make him understand that the individual was not alone blameworthy, that it must have been difficult to write or think at ease in a country where there are a million sovereigns, a country without, strictly speaking, a metropolis, and without an aris-

The eagle, in order to shatter it, will from the vault of heaven
Loose torture upon their naked brow—
For they must ultimately perish.
[Trans. Elizabeth Boyd Thompson.]
3. In an annual procession, a statue of the Hindu god Krishna was carried on an enormous wagon, under which worshipers threw themselves to be crushed sacrificially.
4. Blood-sucking academic.

tocracy, his eyes will open fiercely, and sparkling with rage, drivel of suffering patriotism will foam to his lips and America, by his mouth, will hurl curses at its old mother, Europe, and at the philosophy of ancient days.

I repeat once more my firm conviction that Edgar Poe and his country were never upon a level. The United States is a gigantic and infantine country, not unnaturally jealous of the old continent. Proud of its material development, abnormal and almost monstrous, this new comer into history has a *naive* faith in the all-powerfulness of industry, being firmly convinced, moreover, like some unfortunates among ourselves, that it will finish by devouring the devil himself. Time and money are there held in such extraordinary esteem; material activity, exaggerated almost to the proportions of a national mania, leaves room in their minds for little that is not of the earth.

* * *

No man, I repeat, has told with greater magic the *exceptions* of human life and nature, the ardours of the curiosities of convalescence, the close of seasons charged with enervating splendours, sultry weather, humid and misty, where the south wind softens and distends the nerves, like the chords of an instrument; where the eyes are filled with tears that come not from the heart; hallucination at first giving place to doubt, soon convinced and full of reasons as a book; absurdity installing itself in the intellect, and governing it with a crushing logic; hysteria usurping the place of will, a contradiction established between the nerves and the mind, and mien out of all accord expressing grief by laughter. He analyses them where they are most fugitive; he poises the imponderable, and describes in that minute and scientific manner, whose effects are terrible, all that imaginary world which floats around the nervous man, and conducts him on to evil.

The very ardour with which he threw himself into the grotesque, out of love for the grotesque, and into the horrible, out of love for the horrible, seems to verify the sincerity of his work, and the accord of the poet with the man. I have already remarked that in many men this ardour was often the result of a vast unoccupied vital energy, sometimes of a self-promoted chastity, and also of a profound back-driven sensibility. The supernatural delight that a man can experience in watching his own blood flow—sudden, violent, useless movements, loud cries thrown into the air, without any mental will—are phenomena of the same order.

* * * Edgar Poe loves to move his figures upon a ground of green or violet, where the phosphorescence of putrefaction, and the odour of the hurricane, reveal themselves. Nature inanimate, so styled, participates of the nature of living beings, and, like it, trembles with a shiver, supernatural and galvanic. Space is fathomed by opium; for opium gives a magic tinge to all the hues, and causes every noise to vibrate with the most sonorous magnificence. Sometimes glorious visions, full of light and colour, suddenly unroll themselves in its landscape; and on the furthest horizon-line we see oriental cities and

palaces, mist covered, in the distance, which the sun floods with golden showers.

* * *

WALT WHITMAN

From Edgar Poe's Significance[1]

Jan. 1, '80.
IN DIAGNOSING this disease called humanity—to assume for the nonce what seems a chief mood of the personality and writings of my subject—I have thought that poets, somewhere or other on the list, present the most mark'd indications. Comprehending artists in a mass, musicians, painters, actors, and so on, and considering each and all of them as radiations or flanges of that furious whirling wheel, poetry, the centre and axis of the whole, where else indeed may we so well investigate the causes, growths, tally-marks of the time—the age's matter and malady?

By common consent there is nothing better for man or woman than a perfect and noble life, morally without flaw, happily balanced in activity, physically sound and pure, giving its due proportion, and no more, to the sympathetic, the human emotional element—a life, in all these, unhasting, unresting, untiring to the end. And yet there is another shape of personality dearer far to the artist-sense, (which likes the play of strongest lights and shades) where the perfect character, the good, the heroic, although never attain'd, is never lost sight of, but through failures, sorrows, temporary downfalls, is return'd to again and again, and while often violated, is passionately adhered to as long as mind, muscles, voice, obey the power we call volition. This sort of personality we see more or less in Burns, Byron, Schiller, and George Sand. But we do not see it in Edgar Poe. (All this is the result of reading at intervals the last three days a new volume of his poems—I took it on my rambles down by the pond, and by degrees read it all through there.) While to the character first outlined the service Poe renders is certainly that entire contrast and contradiction which is next best to fully exemplifying it.

Almost without the first sign of moral principle, or of the concrete or its heroisms, or the simpler affections of the heart, Poe's verses illustrate an intense faculty for technical and abstract beauty, with the rhyming art to excess, an incorrigible propensity toward nocturnal themes, a demoniac undertone behind every page—and, by final judgment, probably belong among the electric lights of imaginative literature, brilliant and dazzling, but with no heat. There is an indescribable magnetism about the poet's life and reminiscences, as well as the poems. To one who could work out their subtle retracing and retrospect,

1. From *Specimen Days and Collect* (1882–83).

the latter would make a close tally no doubt between the author's birth and antecedents, his childhood and youth, his physique, his so-call'd education, his studies and associates, the literary and social Baltimore, Richmond, Philadelphia and New York, of those times—not only the places and circumstances in themselves, but often, very often, in a strange spurning of, and reaction from them all.

The following from a report in the Washington *Star* of November 16, 1875, may afford those who care for it something further of my point of view toward this interesting figure and influence of our era. There occurr'd about that date in Baltimore a public reburial of Poe's remains, and dedication of a monument over the grave:

"Being in Washington on a visit at the time, 'the old gray'[2] went over to Baltimore, and though ill from paralysis, consented to hobble up and silently take a seat on the platform, but refused to make any speech, saying, 'I have felt a strong impulse to come over and be here today myself in memory of Poe, which I have obey'd, but not the slightest impulse to make a speech, which, my dear friends, must also be obeyed.' In an informal circle, however, in conversation after the ceremonies, Whitman said: 'For a long while, and until lately, I had a distaste for Poe's writings. I wanted, and still want for poetry, the clear sun shining, and fresh air blowing—the strength and power of health, not of delirium, even amid the stormiest passions—with always the background of the eternal moralities. Non-complying with these requirements, Poe's genius has yet conquer'd a special recognition for itself, and I too have come to fully admit it, and appreciate it and him.

" 'In a dream I once had, I saw a vessel on the sea, at midnight, in a storm. It was no great full-rigg'd ship, nor majestic steamer, steering firmly through the gale, but seem'd one of those superb little schooner yachts I had often seen lying anchor'd, rocking so jauntily, in the waters around New York, or up Long Island sound—now flying uncontroll'd with torn sails and broken spars through the wild sleet and winds and waves of the night. On the deck was a slender, slight, beautiful figure, a dim man, apparently enjoying all the terror, the murk, and the dislocation of which he was the center and the victim. That figure of my lurid dream might stand for Edgar Poe, his spirit, his fortunes, and his poems—themselves all lurid dreams.' "

* * *

2. Whitman was known as "the good gray poet" and "the old gray poet."

Transcendentalism and
Alternative Romanticism

One way of understanding Romanticism is to see it as having two complementary aspects, one positive or optimistic (symbolized by light and organic growth), one negative or skeptical (symbolized by darkness and decay). The British poet and critic William Wordsworth and his American counterpart Ralph Waldo Emerson perhaps best represent the aesthetics of light. The classic statement of Romantic poetics is voiced in Wordsworth's Preface to the second edition of *Lyrical Ballads* in 1800 (the first edition of 1798, a volume of original poetry written in collaboration with Samuel Taylor Coleridge, had enormous influence on shaping the new Romantic lyric). In his preface Wordsworth contends that the new poetry should be written in the language of ordinary people rather than in the heightened "poetic diction" of the eighteenth-century Neoclassic writers, that poetry should reflect the harmony of man and nature, and that the best poetry is the result of the "spontaneous overflow of powerful feelings" recollected in tranquility as the poet meditates on, mediates, and re-creates the experience. Emerson in his essay "The Poet" (1844) carries Wordsworth's aesthetic to mythic heights, echoing Percy Bysshe Shelley's claim in "Defence of Poetry" (1821) that poets, as the "unacknowledged legislators of the world," modulate political and moral affairs; Emerson in fact casts the poet as the new Messiah. Behind and within all this new speculation is one central idea—that physical Nature is also the World Spirit—a force that is orderly, harmonious, progressive, and benign. By rediscovering human kinship with the patterns of physical and spiritual nature and conjoining them in the Self, human beings can find their own inner divinity. The path of such natural divinity is through Art (characterized by intuition and imagination), especially the art of poetry. Emerson, Henry David Thoreau, and Walt Whitman are the major representatives of American Transcendental nature philosophy (*Transcendentale Naturphilosophie*) and the Romantic cult of the Apotheosis of the Self.

Another, darker, skeptical, alternative Romantic aesthetic also exists, but the division of the Romantics into the light and the dark is not simple; aspects of the affirmative and the skeptical crisscross in their writings, creating disturbing mixtures of transcendental optimism and gothic and grotesque apprehensiveness. This mixture is especially obvious in Wordsworth's co-author, Coleridge, and of course in Poe himself. Coleridge, who was a student of German Transcendental

717

philosophers and writers, heavily influenced Poe (both pro and con). The combination of visionary revelation and awesome doubt is also found in British Romantic poets like Keats and Shelley. A key poem by Shelley, the very Poesque "Hymn to Intellectual Beauty" (1816), invokes the "awful shadow" of "some unseen Power" amid "life's unquiet dream." This poem is referenced and quoted by Poe several times.

The selections reprinted in this section exemplify some of the more important literary and philosophical contexts for understanding Poe via the conflicted Romanticism emanating out of Germany. The first is from a popular American anthology, *Prose Writers of Germany* (1847; reprinted several times through 1870), edited and introduced by Frederic Henry Hedge, one of the founders of the American Transcendental Club in Concord, Massachusetts. Emerson was a key member of the club and in fact produced for it his own distillation of German Romantic thinking in *Nature* (1836), a book that has been called the "Bible of American Transcendentalism." Noting the centrality in the English-speaking world of the "German" aesthetics of Coleridge, Hedge offers summaries, interpretations, and selections from the "four great Transcendental philosophers" of Germany: Immanuel Kant (1724–1804), Johann Gottlieb Fichte (1762–1814), Friedrich Wilhelm Joseph von Schelling (1775–1854), and Georg Wilhelm Friedrich Hegel (1770–1831). Since space permits the inclusion only of Hedge's concise overview of Kant, it will be well here to contextualize Kant in terms of the materialistic philosophy that preceded his as well as in terms of the other three German Transcendental writers Hedge presents.

Kant set the tone for Transcendentalism as *the* new philosophy in reaction to the materialism of John Locke (1632–1704) and the Scottish Common-Sense school. Locke had denied the existence of innate ideas and argued that the mind is a blank slate (*tabula rasa*) on which physical experience writes. The mind assembles sense impressions (sensations) according to the order of the physical world. The Common Sense philosophers of Enlightenment Scotland—Thomas Reid (1710–1796), Dugald Stewart (1753–1828), and others—followed Locke and incorporated the "associational psychology" of David Hartley (1705–1757), who located mental activity in the connection of the spinal chord and the brain via "vibrations" stimulated by physical sensations.

Kant, on the other hand, argued among other things that there is a "transcendent" realm (beyond the world of objects) that we can know only indirectly via subjective intuition or instinct and that this instinct (or higher Reason) was the combination of the contradictory realms of the objective and the subjective. The rational aspect of mind was limited and could not apprehend this transcendent reality directly or objectively. Schelling argued that there is a mental or ideational realm behind and within physical nature and that nature was evolving toward greater and greater consciousness of itself. Hegel, picking up on the correlative themes of freedom and duty in Kant, Schelling, and Fichte (not to mention the celebrated poet and dramatist Friedrich

Schiller), argued for a dialectical progress from the oppositions of thesis/antithesis to a higher synthesis that would eventuate in *Humanität*, an ideal state of humanity and society.

Aspects of the theories of these three philosophers are relevant in one degree or another to Poe's worldview and theory of art; but Fichte seems to have a special pertinence. Fichte argued that the transcendent was not a realm beyond logical comprehension but a "power" residing in the mind that enabled it to transcend earthly limitations. His *Bestimmung des Menschen* (Destination of man, 1800) moves in three books from "Doubt" to "Knowledge" to "Faith" in a manner suggestive of Thomas Carlyle (1795–1881), who was one of the most influential Germanists writing in the English language. (Another was Thomas De Quincey, 1785–1859.) In Carlyle's seriocomic philosophical narrative *Sartor Resartus* (1833–34), a German professor, Herr Dr. Teufelsdröck (Dr. Devilsdung) goes through the "Everlasting Nay," to "The Centre of Indifference," and finally comes to the "Everlasting Yea." If one charts Poe's philosophical themes from the beginning of his career to *Eureka* (1848), a similar pattern of the quest for the Absolute— through idealist despair, nightmarish doubt, and qualified affirmation—can be seen. And as in Carlyle, the affirmation is sent through the alembic of skepticism and dark humor.

In addition to Hedge's introduction of Kant as the foremost of the Big Four Transcendentalist philosophers, three German literary critics are represented in this section by selections from their writings on myth, poetry, and the new fiction—with special attention to theories of humor and irony—all matters important for a full understanding of Poe. The brothers Friedrich and August Wilhelm Schlegel were for a time everywhere cited in American publications; and Poe frequently mentions and borrows from them. Moreover, the metafictional novelist "Jean Paul" Friedrich Richter, in a treatise called the "Pre-School for Aesthetics" (1804), offers among many other things a theory of irony similar to that of the Schlegels in terms of "humoristic totality," "annihilating humor," "humoristic subjectivity," and the like.

To complement this foray into German Romanticism is a retrospective assessment by Floyd Stovall (pp. 789ff. herein) of the influence of Coleridge's aesthetics on Poe. Stovall's overview includes discussion of the famous distinction between imagination and fancy that so perplexed and vexed Poe, the difference between objective and subjective in Transcendentalist thinking, and the dialectical and dialogical processes of the creative mind with physical perception as Coleridge understood them from German philosophy. The interrelation of philosophical and moral speculation with psychological (and neurological) interests is a striking feature of the time (cf. the Sciences of the Mind section, pp. 742–53). And Poe's concern with the mental processes of the relationship of sound and rhythm, particularly meter, in Romantic poetry is explored by another twentieth-century critic, Robert C. McLean (pp. 798ff.). In his essay of the aesthetics of George Tucker (1775–1861), one of Poe's instructors at the University of Virginia, McLean demonstrates that the nearly forgotten Tucker provides an-

other perspective on Romantic poetics; many of his ideas are derived from the rhetoricians and psychologists of the School of Scottish Common-Sense philosophy (notably Hugh Blair, George Campbell, Lord Kames, Adam Smith, and Dugald Stewart). It was from Tucker's Virginia lectures, McLean claims, that Poe probably first entered the debate on the difference between the sublime and the beautiful (one of the most hotly contended aesthetic issues of the early Romantic period) and developed his antididactic stance in art. In sum, Tucker's Scottish aesthetics complemented the ideas Poe would find in the writings of the English and German Romantics. It is recommended that the reader follow the reading of the German writers reprinted in this section with a look at the two later essays.

FREDERIC HENRY HEDGE

Frederic Henry Hedge (1805–1890) was a Unitarian minister and a professor of German and ecclesiastical history at Harvard University. He is generally acknowledged to have been the founder of the seminal Transcendental Club in Maine and Massachusetts (known at first as the Hedge Club). Introducing Americans to a variety German Romantic writings, he translated and commented on a number of their philosophical and literary works. In the March 1833 *Christian Examiner*, he published an essay ostensibly on the literary and philosophical thinking of Samuel Taylor Coleridge (1772–1834), who was arguably the most famous and respected literary critic in the English-speaking world. Rather than giving a detailed explication of Coleridge's thought, however, he focused on the German background of Transcendentalism and organic literary theory that had influenced him. Hedge's essay attracted the notice of Ralph Waldo Emerson, who excitedly called the work "a living leaping Logos." The essay prompted Emerson to begin writing *Nature* (1836), the early seminal work of American Transcendentalism.

In 1847, Hedge compiled a very popular anthology, representing the interests of the time, *Prose Writers of Germany* (1870). In this massive book (580 double-columned oversize pages), he offered a fuller discussion of what he called the "illustrious four" German philosophers of Transcendentalism: Kant, Fichte, Schelling, and Hegel (see pp. 718–19 herein). The book contains a large number of expertly selected and translated extracts not only from these philosophers and aestheticians but also from many other German prose writers, including fiction writers like Ludwig Tieck, E. T. A. Hoffmann, and Adelbert von Chamisso. Reprinted here is Hedge's introduction to Immanuel Kant (1724–1804), in which he emphasizes Kant's conception of "antimonies" or necessary contradictions of objective and subjective knowledge. The point is relevant to all of Poe's creative work but perhaps most especially to the angelic after-death visions of "Al Aaraaf," "The Colloquy of Monos and Una," and "The Power of Words," along with the prose-poem on the nature of the universe, *Eureka*.

[On Immanuel Kant and German Transcendentalism]

* * *

In reading Kant's writings, the observation often forces itself upon us, that the words will very well bear a construction quite opposite to that he himself seems to put upon them; and we discover that they are equally intelligible and harmonious from two entirely distinct points of view. It is true, indeed, of all honest and thorough discussion of principles, that its application is infinitely wider than the particular intent of the writer. Thus a profound remark in Morals is equally applicable to Physics, Art, and Politics. But in Kant, born to represent an important step in the progress of Modern Philosophy, this double meaning, passing easily into open contradiction, accompanied too by the most entire earnestness and strictness of inquiry, is particularly remarkable, and has given occasion to much difference of opinion as to the whole scope and fundamental character of his philosophy.

Thus he is commonly cited as the founder of modern Transcendentalism, which in the popular estimate is equivalent to Mysticism; yet where the aim is rather to find fault than to understand, it is easy to make him out a materialist and a skeptic. This peculiarity, allied to and resulting from the very nature of his system, as we shall hereafter see, must be understood and kept in view in the study of his writings, and particularly in the Critique of the Judgment,[1] (from which the longest of our extracts is taken); which it renders one of the most interesting, but most difficult of his writings.

Kant's starting-point is altogether with the Materialists, or as they call themselves of late, the Common-sense, or Inductive Philosophers.[2] In common with all the world of his time, and with most persons of the present day, he assumes that our knowledge is limited, both in extent and in degree; that we know in part, and parts only.

Nevertheless, the fact that we have Experience, of some kind, whatever be its value, remains unshaken; and with this he commences his examination of our Cognitive Faculty; having for his aim to discover, and after the rigidest scrutiny, set down, as Knowledge, only what we certainly know; leaving all that belongs to Opinion, Faith or Feeling, to stand on its own basis.

1. Kant's most famous works include three "critiques": the Critique of Pure Reason (Kritik der reinen Vernunft, 1781), the Critique of Practical Reason (Kritik der praktischen Vernunft, 1788), and the Critique of Judgment (Kritik der Urteilskraft, 1790). In the first, he maintains that our experience, though rational, can understand a thing considered only as an object of that experience but not the intrinsic thing in itself (Ding an sich). In the second, he sets forth ethical and moral propositions based on the existence of human free will (practical reason) in tension with universal moral law, which he calls the "categorical imperative"; knowledge of the spirit (or God) comes from moral-ethical intuition, not mere reason. In the third, he argues that the aesthetic realm, the artistic representation of a thing (object), provides an approximation of the thing in itself. The last in particular seems to be an idea that is shared by Poe. Thus in the overall Kantian system, the aesthetic faculty mediates between the understanding (or cognitive) faculty and the moral sense—again a paradigm found in Poe.
2. For the Scottish school of common-sense, see the comments on p. 718 herein and the notes to Robert C. McLean's essay on pp. 798ff.

As his Test of Certainty, he appeals directly to the private intuition, or consciousness, not relying on Experience, however often repeated; for, as he says, this, though it may be amply sufficient for the uses of everyday life, is yet easily distinguishable from absolute and original certainty. This latter he calls Knowledge *à priori*, by which is to be understood, not a knowledge preceding Experience, but deriving its support from something prior to and independent of Experience. For example, our conception of a triangle, though suggested by the actual figure, cannot be derived from it; for there is no perfect triangle; none perfectly adequate to the conception.

It is obvious that on the strict application of this test, most of our so-called Knowledge must take another name; and the inquiry occurs: whether there be anything in Experience deserving to be called Knowledge.

Kant answers that there is: viz.[3] That in all our perceptions of outward things, they must appear as existing in Space and Time. This is not the result of Experience; for all Experience must presuppose it; and whatever validity we may allow our knowledge of phenomena, of this at least we are certain, that they can appear to us only in Space and Time.

These, then, are the *forms* of our perceptions, not indicating anything in the nature of the objects perceived, but mere subjective forms.

Accordingly, he divides Knowledge into two kinds; Knowledge of Forms, (subjective Knowledge); and Knowledge of subject-matter, (objective Knowledge); and he says that of the latter we not only have nothing, but cannot even conceive of the possibility of our ever having any knowledge of things *as they are in themselves*.

It would not be possible for us in the brief space devoted to this sketch of Kant's philosophy, to give even a general account of his development of his theory of Perception, nor of his critique of the Understanding. Suffice it to say that on this principle of the subjectiveness of all Knowledge, he proceeds to construct a system of subjective Knowledge, (Understanding); embracing, according to him, all our proper cognitive faculty.

It is evident, however, from what has already been said, that as Knowledge relates only to the forms and conditions of Experience, it must depend entirely upon the possibility of Experience; and where this is impossible, Knowledge must also be impossible. Now, Kant finds certain conceptions in the mind, not only unconnected with, but, by their very nature, transcending all possibility of Experience. For example, our conceptions of God, Freedom, and Immortality, to which no possible sensuous experience can be adequate. Such conceptions Kant calls *Transcendental Ideas;* and the faculty conceiving them, *Reason.* The Transcendental Ideas lay claim to absolute certainty and objectivity, without reference to Experience. This is evidently in contradiction to the theory of Knowledge according to the

3. Namely.

Understanding. Finite perception is deceptive, and must appeal to Experience as the test of its correctness. The claims of the Transcendental Ideas to theoretic Knowledge, therefore, must be considered as an overweening pretence, and they should rather be called transcendent, than transcendental. They cannot give us any information as to the nature of any object; but, at most, like empirical conceptions, declare some law of the subject. And in support of this he shows that every Transcendental Idea contains a contradiction; that is, when we endeavour to give it a theoretic application, to declare what it asserts concerning its object, two opposite propositions of equal apparent truth are the result. Thus our idea as to the extent of the Universe,— it is equally easy to maintain that it is infinite, or that it is finite; eternal, or having originated in Time, and so on. And these *Antinomies*[4] *of Pure Reason*, as he calls, them, he shows are inherent in all Ideas.

* * *

All Knowledge must presuppose some connection between the Subject and the Object; the mind and the thing; and whichever it may be that acts on the other, there is at all events a communication between them. And moreover this empirical communication must depend upon an original and essential connection. If we could imagine two essentially and primarily distinct kinds of Matter, they could not act upon each other, nor could there be any communication between them. For Matter can act or be acted upon only according to its laws. But the laws of Matter are its essence, and if they act according to the same laws they must be identical. It is necessary, therefore, and an antecedent condition of the perception of things, that both they and we should be parts of one identical nature. So too in proceeding beyond mere sensuous perception,—the abstract rules formed by the Understanding, e.g. the common hypotheses in Physics, presuppose a like identity, for they are formed by generalization, and this is impossible without at least a dim idea of a common centre of all things. The reason why animals, or men reduced to a mere animal existence, do not generalize nor form rules, except to a very limited extent, is that this Idea is not present in their consciousness, (or only very dimly,) but exists *outside* of them, as Instinct.

So that the simplest Experience presupposes an entire continuity throughout the Universe as its fundamental condition. This series or continuity, considered abstractly, is Space. Space is not the *idea*, but the *abstraction* of the material Universe; for it belongs to subjective perception and Understanding, which have nothing to do with Ideas; but it is a sufficient recognition, by the sensuous faculty, of what the Reason afterwards comes to know as concrete Truth. Thus we cannot imagine a limitation of Space, nor of a place where it is not. The edge, or boundary of Space, or a vacuum where there is Extension without Space, is an absurdity. And it is equally impossible to imagine an object not in Space.

4. Oppositions, contradictions; especially between ideas that seem equally rational and necessary.

Space is in fact the abstraction of the Infinite displayed in the Finite. For Matter, though necessarily connected with and supported by Spirit, is yet its direct opposite. Every one of the qualities of Matter is antagonistic to the corresponding spiritual quality. Thus Spirit is infinite and eternal; Matter finite and transitory. Or rather, Matter, if it could be considered by itself, would be a mere negation, and is incapable of being expressed without its opposite. For transience, for example, implies a certain duration. The material Universe, therefore, is an embodied contradiction, and Space of course a mere suspension or abstraction of this. Thus Space is both the affirmative condition and the negation of Extension; for there is no unlimited Extension, and limitation is equivalent to negation.

So of Time. It differs from Space only as quality from quantity; Intension from Extension; the inward from the outward sense, so called. As Matter is limited in extent, so also it is transient in substance; and as Space contains both extension and limitation, so Time is embodied Change, i.e. persistence and transience: we cannot arrest any particle of it, as the Present, for as we pause, it is already Past. Every-day experience shows us that our notion of Time depends upon the number of events that have successively impressed us and then given place to others. Amid a rapid succession of interesting events, a week, when past, seems a month, and a month a year, for we date from each succeeding event. On the other hand, to measure Time for economic purpose, we employ astronomic changes, since here the succession is unvarying.

It is the profound remark of an ancient Hindoo book, that Time is the connection of Matter and Spirit. And the same is true of Space.

The interesting point here, and that to which the preceding inquiries tend, is this: That not the Transcendental Ideas alone, but the commonest and simplest experience must necessarily contain a contradiction, to the Understanding. Time is the contradiction of Eternity, yet also of the moment, or point in Time; Space is the opposition of Unity, yet also of the point in Space. And it is also very remarkable that Kant in the table which he gives of the different classes of possible judgments, and also in his table of Categories, or classes under which all pure conceptions of the Understanding may be reduced, has in each instance distributed them under various heads, *by threes*, of which two are contraries and the third their result; without giving any deduction, or reason for so doing. Thus under the head of Quantity, in judgment, he gives: Universal, Particular, and Special; and under the same head in the Categories, he gives: Unity, Multiplicity, and Totality; and so on through the whole. The truth is that each of these classes contains, not only three kinds of judgment, or of conceptions, but also the three elements necessary to every judgment and every conception; viz. the contradiction and its result. Thus if I say: This paper is white, here we have the general attribute, *white*, the limitation, to this piece of paper, (negation of other paper); and the result, this special piece of paper. So of all conceptions, and so of all knowledge; there is no possible act of cognition that does not embrace this element of con-

tradiction. It is the combination of outside and inside, light and darkness, extent and limitation, requisite to every sensuous impression; and it is the puzzle in the highest problems that employ the mind of man Thus in Civil Government, the cöexistence of personal freedom, (which supposes each individual supreme and unlimited), with Society in which he is only a part. So in Religion, the fierce disputes that have agitated the world now for eighteen centuries, arise solely from the impossibility, and at the same time the ever-recurring necessity, of conceiving Man to be at once human and divine, finite and infinite; and the difficulty of reconciling the doctrine of Immortality and possible perfection, with the common views of humanity, on any other ground. A finite immortal is the most tremendous of contradictions. This is the cause of the horror with which the doctrine of the mere humanity of Jesus Christ is looked upon by most persons.

But these contradictions and these impossibilities are such only to the Understanding; that is, the mind employed only with particulars. The contradiction truly exists in the Universe, and to him who does not transcend it, does not see it and its contrary united in an harmonious synthesis, it is final. But in reality it is superficial, and Reason, or the mind contemplating things as a Whole, readily resolves it. Then it is no longer contradiction, but the necessary organism of the Idea.

Kant, from his point of view, was quite right in making knowledge subjective only, for he confines his inquiries as to the Cognitive faculty entirely to the Understanding, or subjective Reason, to the very nature of which, this antagonism of the subjective and objective, and their absolute separation, is altogether essential.

There is another branch of Kant's enquiry, touched upon in the beginning of these remarks, but which our limits forbid our discussing at much length; leading, however, to the same point. This is the distinction he makes between the *phenomenon*, or *appearance of a thing*, and *the thing itself*, and his doctrine that we can know nothing of the latter, but that all our perception and knowledge is confined to the former. This evidently follows from his premises.

For if all our intercourse with things is that of one thing with another, it must evidently be merely outward, like all relations of things to each other.

If we bring two bodies together, they touch only their outer surfaces; an inward union is impossible. Modern Chemistry has shown experimentally that the transformations of Matter are merely apparent, and consist solely of various combinations of the same particles. Bodies apparently the most distinct, for example starch, gum, sugar, fat, and the woody fibre of plants are the same or nearly so, in composition. For Matter, as has been well said, has no inside, but only outside, and is capable only of outward relations.

This Kant shows, psychologically, in our sensuous perceptions. For what do we after all mean, when we say we perceive a thing, for instance a tree? Plainly nothing more than that we see certain colours and outlines apparently connected and belonging to some thing.

But whether there is anything really existing in that place, or whether it be only something within myself, or the effect of another thing, I cannot (with absolute certainty) tell. For our senses are our only evidence, and they pretend to nothing more than a perception of appearances. To another intelligence, or to differently constructed senses, the object may appear quite different. At first sight, indeed, it might seem that we do entirely rely upon the report of our senses; but let any one compare his knowledge of any outward fact with his perception of a mathematical truth, and he will find the former much the weaker. We may admit the possibility of our being persuaded to change our notions as to the colour; shape, and other qualities of any object; but we cannot for an instant admit the possibility of being convinced that two and two do not make four. Now evidently there are no degrees of certainty; we either know, or we do not know.

Kant accordingly comes to the conclusion that we cannot, properly speaking, *know* anything of the real nature or substance of objects: and that all we can hope to know about them is their effect upon ourselves; or at the most, the forms and rules of this subjective effect.

Nevertheless our claim of objective knowledge continues: in spite of the contradiction of the Understanding; there is an instinctive feeling that it is not absolute, but only the different sides of one truth. And in truth the contradiction here too belongs only to the Understanding, transcending its province. It is true, that of anything absolutely objective, really foreign to our nature, we can know nothing objectively; and more than this, as we have seen above, we could not have even subjective knowledge of an absolute object; it would be for us a mere nonentity.

But this antithesis of Subject and Object is entirely subordinate and belongs wholly to the Understanding. Reflection and consciousness indeed by nature require it, and depend upon it; but it is the prerogative of Reason to see through and reconcile all distinctions and oppositions, not indeed annihilating them, but appointing to them their proper sphere.

So that this contradiction to the Understanding is so far from interfering with the validity of the Transcendental Ideas (conceptions of the Reason) that it is essential to their nature. Knowledge is not rendered impossible by it, but all knowledge, down to the merest sensuous perception, is shown by Kant himself (properly understood), to contain and require it.

Kant is not the only philosopher who has arrived at these contradictions. They are necessarily present in the Understanding; and in all empirical philosophy, logically carried out, this is made evident. The only escape is either in the feebleness that cannot understand its own results; or in wilfully ignoring them, which is the course pursued by Cousin,[5] and more avowedly by the "Scotch School."

5. Victor Cousin (1792–1867), French educator and philosopher, sought to combine recent "psychological" speculation with the idealism of Hegel and Schelling and the common-sense philosophy of the Scottish empiricists. He introduced the history of philosophy into the

But the interesting feature in Kant's inquiry, and that which gives it its place in the History of Philosophy, arises from the faithfulness with which it is made. His rigid and faithful examination of facts of consciousness brought him to principles, which his adherence to the common point of view made him reject or overlook, but which in fact involved a revolution in Philosophy. His close analysis revealed the contradiction contained in those propositions which seem most solid and certain to the Understanding, and this showed the true province and the limitations of this faculty (or rather this direction of the mind), by pushing to their necessary consequences the common principles. It is not sufficient to contradict or refute Error; it is requisite moreover to show that it is an embodied self-contradiction and self-refutation, and to see this the repugnant elements must be displayed. It is this dialectic that makes the value of Kant's Critique, and it is not the less interesting for being unconscious.

* * *

FRIEDRICH SCHLEGEL

Fragments[1]

From *Lyceum*

26. Novels are the Socratic dialogues of our time. And this free form has become the refuge of common sense in its flight from pedantry.

30. In modern tragedy, fate is sometimes replaced by God the Father, more often by the devil himself. How is it that this hasn't yet inspired some scholar to formulate a theory of the diabolic genre?

42. Philosophy is the real homeland of irony, which one would like to define as logical beauty: for wherever philosophy appears in oral or written dialogues—and is not simply confined into rigid systems—there irony should be asked for and provided. And even the Stoics considered urbanity a virtue. Of course, there is also a rhetorical species

French educational system. Among his works are *Fragments philosophiques* (1826), *Cours de l'histoire de la philosophie* (8 vols., 1815–29), and *Du vrai, du beau et du bien* (1836, Of the True, the Beautiful and the Good).

1. The "Fragments" were published principally in two magazines from 1797 to 1798; Friedrich Schlegel was the major author, but at least four others (including A. W. Schlegel) made contributions. The selections printed here are all by Friedrich Schlegel. The "Fragments" series purported to be the "sky-rocketing" (brain-storming) ideas of the moment—short notations made by the new Romantic writers as though in the margins of their books. These marginalia were deliberately open-ended and suggestive, in opposition to what they considered stultifying attempts at conclusive aesthetic analysis by the older generation of Neoclassicists. The "Fragments" included comments on the imagination, on the origin of poetry in myth and the unconscious, on the form of the Romance novel (the *Roman*), on Romanticism, on the grotesque and arabesque, on the higher poetic unity of the Romantic text, and on the transformative vision of the new (Romantic) artist. The *Lyceum* and *Athenæm* fragments printed here are from *Friedrich Schlegel's Lucinde and the Fragments*, translated with an introduction by Peter Firchow (Minneapolis: University of Minneapolis Press, 1971), used by permission of the publisher.

of irony which, sparingly used, has an excellent effect, especially in polemics; but compared to the sublime urbanity of the Socratic muse, it is like the pomp of the most splendid oration set over against the noble style of an ancient tragedy. Only poetry can also reach the heights of philosophy in this way, and only poetry does not restrict itself to isolated ironical passages, as rhetoric does. There are ancient and modern poems that are pervaded by the divine breath of irony throughout and informed by a truly transcendental buffoonery. Internally: the mood that surveys everything and rises infinitely above all limitations, even above its own art, virtue, or genius; externally, in its execution: the mimic style of an averagely gifted Italian *buffo*.[2]

48. Irony is the form of paradox. Paradox is everything simultaneously good and great.

108. Socratic irony is the only involuntary and yet completely deliberate dissimulation. It is equally impossible to feign it or divulge it. To a person who hasn't got it, it will remain a riddle even after it is openly confessed. It is meant to deceive no one except those who consider it a deception and who either take pleasure in the delightful roguery of making fools of the whole world or else become angry when they get an inkling they themselves might be included. In this sort of irony, everything should be playful and serious, guilelessly open and deeply hidden. It originates in the union of *savoir vivre*[3] and scientific spirit, in the conjunction of a perfectly instinctive and a perfectly conscious philosophy. It contains and arouses a feeling of indissoluble antagonism between the absolute and the relative, between the impossibility and the necessity of complete communication. It is the freest of all licenses, for by its means one transcends oneself; and yet it is also the most lawful, for it is absolutely necessary. It is a very good sign when the harmonious bores are at a loss about how they should react to this continuous self-parody, when they fluctuate endlessly between belief and disbelief until they get dizzy and take what is meant as a joke seriously and what is meant seriously as a joke.

* * *

From *Athenaeum*

116. Romantic poetry is a progressive, universal poetry. Its aim isn't merely to reunite all the separate species of poetry and put poetry in touch with philosophy and rhetoric. It tries to and should mix and fuse poetry and prose, inspiration and criticism, the poetry of art and the poetry of nature; and make poetry lively and sociable, and life and society poetical; poeticize wit and fill and saturate the forms of art with every kind of good, solid matter for instruction, and animate them

2. A male opera singer, but suggesting a windbag (Italian, "puff of wind"), related to *buffoon*, a clown. Schlegel here begins the transformation of "irony" from a limited rhetorical trope to a concept of irony as pervading the whole of a work embodying a sequence of antinomies (see Hedge on Kant, p. 723, n. 4 herein).
3. Breeding, good manners, polish (French).

with the pulsations of humor. It embraces everything that is purely poetic, from the greatest systems of art, containing within themselves still further systems, to the sigh, the kiss that the poetizing child breathes forth in artless song. It can so lose itself in what it describes that one might believe it exists only to characterize poetical individuals of all sorts; and yet there still is no form so fit for expressing the entire spirit of an author: so that many artists who started out to write only a novel ended up by providing us with a portrait of themselves. It alone can become, like the epic, a mirror of the whole circumambient world, an image of the age. And it can also—more than any other form— hover at the midpoint between the portrayed and the portrayer, free of all real and ideal self-interest, on the wings of poetic reflection, and can raise that reflection again and again to a higher power, can multiply it in an endless succession of mirrors. It is capable of the highest and most variegated refinement, not only from within outwards, but also from without inwards; capable in that it organizes—for everything that seeks a wholeness in its effects—the parts along similar lines, so that it opens up a perspective upon an infinitely increasing classicism. Romantic poetry is in the arts what wit is in philosophy, and what society and sociability, friendship and love are in life. Other kinds of poetry are finished and are now capable of being fully analyzed. The romantic kind of poetry is still in the state of becoming; that, in fact, is its real essence: that it should forever be becoming and never be perfected. It can be exhausted by no theory and only a divinatory criticism would dare try to characterize its ideal. It alone is infinite, just as it alone is free; and it recognizes as its first commandment that the will of the poet can tolerate no law above itself. The romantic kind of poetry is the only one that is more than a kind, that is, as it were, poetry itself: for in a certain sense all poetry is or should be romantic.

121. An idea is a concept perfected to the point of irony, an absolute synthesis of absolute antitheses, the continual self-creating interchange of two conflicting thoughts. An ideal is at once idea and fact. If ideals don't have as much individuality for the thinker as the gods of antiquity do for the artist, then any concern with ideas is no more than a boring and laborious game of dice with hollow phrases, or, in the manner of the Chinese boxes, a brooding contemplation of one's own nose. Nothing is more wretched and contemptible than this sentimental speculation without any object. But one shouldn't call this mysticism, since this beautiful old word is so very useful and indispensable for absolute philosophy, from whose perspective the spirit regards everything as a mystery and a wonder, while from other points of view it would appear theoretically and practically normal. Speculation *en detail* is as rare as abstraction *en gros*,[4] and yet it is these that beget the whole substance of scientific wit, these that are the principles of higher criticism, the highest rungs of spiritual cultivation. The great practical abstraction is what makes the ancients—among whom this

4. Large, sweeping. "*En detail*": in detail or at the smallest point.

was an instinct—actually ancients. In vain did individuals express the ideal of their species completely, if the species themselves, strictly and sharply isolated, weren't freely surrendered, as it were, to their originality. But to transport oneself arbitrarily now into this, now into that sphere, as if into another world, not merely with one's reason and imagination, but with one's whole soul; to freely relinquish first one and then another part of one's being, and confine oneself entirely to a third; to seek and find now in this, now in that individual the be-all and end-all of existence, and intentionally forget everyone else: of this only a mind is capable that contains within itself simultaneously a plurality of minds and a whole system of persons, and in whose inner being the universe which, as they say, should germinate in every monad,[5] has grown to fullness and maturity.

305. Intention taken to the point of irony and accompanied by the arbitrary illusion of its self-destruction is quite as naive as instinct taken to the point of irony. Just as the naive plays with the contradictions between theory and practice, so the grotesque plays with the wonderful permutations of form and matter, loves the illusion of the random and the strange and, as it were, coquettes with infinite arbitrariness. Humor deals with being and nonbeing, and its true essence is reflection. Hence its closeness to the elegy and to everything transcendental; and hence its arrogance and its bent for the mysticism of wit. Just as genius is necessary to naiveté, so too an earnest, pure beauty is a requisite of humor. Most of all humor likes to hover about the gently and clearly flowing rhapsodies of philosophy or poetry, and abhors cumbersome masses and disconnected parts.

429. Just as the novella has to be new and striking at every point of its substance and development, so perhaps the poetical tale and especially the romance has to be infinitely bizarre. For the romance tries not only to interest the imagination, but also to enchant the mind and stimulate the feelings; and the essence of the bizarre seems to consist precisely in certain arbitrary and strange connections and confusions of the processes of thinking, poetizing, and acting. There is a kind of bizarreness of enthusiasm that is compatible with the greatest refinement and freedom, and that not only intensifies tragedy but makes it beautiful and, as it were, deifies it: like Goethe's *Bride of Corinth*,[6] which is an epoch in the history of poetry. What moves one in that work lacerates and nevertheless is seductively fascinating. Some parts could almost be called burlesque, and it is precisely in these parts that the horrible seems overwhelmingly great.

5. In the metaphysics of the German philosopher Gottfried Wilhelm Leibniz (1646–1716), the smallest building block of existence, conceived as psychical rather than physical. His *Monadology* was published in 1714 (see notes to "The Fall of the House of Usher," (esp. p. 204, n. 6 herein).
6. A ballad written in 1797.

From Dialogue on Poetry[1]

* * *

Mythology is * * * a work of art created by nature. In its texture, the sublime is really formed; everything is relation and metamorphosis, conformed and transformed, and this conformation and transformation is its peculiar process, its inner life and method, if I may say so.

Here I find a great similarity with the marvelous wit of romantic poetry, which does not manifest itself in individual conceptions but in the structure of the whole, and which was so often pointed out by our friend for the works of Cervantes[2] and Shakespeare. Indeed, this artfully ordered confusion, this charming symmetry of contradictions, this wonderfully perennial alternation of enthusiasm and irony, which lives even in the smallest parts of the whole, seem to me to be an indirect mythology themselves. The organization is the same, and certainly the arabesque is the oldest and most original form of human imagination. Neither this wit nor a mythology can exist without something original and inimitable that is absolutely irreducible, and in which after all the transformations its original character and creative energy are still dimly visible, where the naive profundity permits the semblance of the absurd and of madness, of simplicity and foolishness, to shimmer through. For this is the beginning of all poetry, to cancel the progression and laws of rationally thinking reason, and to transplant us once again into the beautiful confusion of imagination, into the original chaos of human nature, for which I know as yet no more beautiful symbol than the motley throng of the ancient gods.

* * *

Letter about the Novel[3]

. . . In my historical research, I came upon several fundamental forms that are not further reducible. Thus, in the sphere of romantic

1. Friedrich Schlegel's "Dialogue on Poetry" (Gespräch über Poesie) appeared in 1800. The English text is the edited translation of Ernst Behler and Roman Struc, from *German Romantic Criticism*, edited by A. Leslie Willson (New York: Continuum, 1982). Originally published by the Pennsylvania State University Press. Reprinted by permission of the publisher. The essay is set up as a conversation among several people and an exchange of letters, especially as an epistolary dialogue between the narrator and a lady of his acquaintance. The first section, "Epochs of Literature," traces the history of poetry and romance from ancient Greek epics, lyric poems, and tragic drama through the European Middle Ages and the Renaissance to the late eighteenth century (the author's own time). Schlegel presents a vision of human experience and literature as "formed chaos," including the ideas of returning to humankind's "original" roots and the intertwining of the serious and the comic, the tragic and the satiric, and the mixing of genres. In the "Mythology" section Schlegel further particularizes his mythopoeic sense of history and art as a continuum of ancient and modern, the idealistic and the realistic, which leads him to his final section on the modern novel or new Romance, which recaptures the original form of human imagination, the "arabesque."
2. Miguel de Cervantes Saavedra (1547–1616), author of *Don Quixote* (Part I, 1605; Part II 1615), has the same stature in Spanish literature as Goethe in German literature and Shakespeare in English literature. Schlegel and others saw *Don Quixote* as the progenitor of the modern novel.
3. This is the most famous part of the "Dialogue on Poetry"; the translation of the word *Roman* as "novel" is inadequate, for Schlegel's concept of modern (Romantic) fiction is an amalgamation of both novel and romance, realism and fantasy. His concept of individual and col-

poetry, for instance, novellas and fairy tales seem to me, if I may say so, infinitely contrasted. I only wish that an artist would rejuvenate each of these genres by restoring them to their original character.

If such examples became known, then I would have the courage for a *theory of the novel*, which would be a theory in the original sense of the word: a spiritual viewing of the subject with calm and serene feeling, as it is proper to view in solemn joy the meaningful play of divine images. Such a theory of the novel would have to be itself a novel that would reflect imaginatively every eternal tone of the imagination and would again confound the chaos of the world of knights. The things of the past would live in it in new forms; Dante's sacred shadow would arise from the lower world, Laura would hover heavenly before us, Shakespeare would converse intimately with Cervantes, and there Sancho would jest with Don Quixote again.[4]

These would be true arabesques that, together with confessions, as I claimed at the outset of my letter, are the only romantic products of nature in our age.

It will no longer appear strange to you that I include confessions here, when you have admitted that true story is the foundation of all romantic poetry; and you will—if you wish to reflect on it—easily remember and be convinced that what is best in the best of novels is nothing but a more or less veiled confession of the author, the profit of his experience, the quintessence of his originality.

<p style="text-align:center">* * *</p>

AUGUST WILHELM SCHLEGEL

August Wilhelm Schlegel (1767–1845) was better known in English-speaking countries than his brother Friedrich—probably because his writing was more carefully organized and clearer—though many readers find his steady step-by-step work somewhat less exciting than the early works of his "sky-rocketing" brother. Both of the Schlegels were gifted linguists and historians, with a keen interest in Far Eastern and Middle Eastern cultures. A. W. Schlegel's history and analysis of the drama from its origins to contemporary times was enormously popular in England and America. His *Course of Lectures on Dramatic Art and Literature* was reprinted numerous times from 1815 through the 1840s. The critical writings of "the brothers Schlegel," as they were known, were featured or described in a number of American periodicals and had great influence on Poe's ideas of that "unity of effect" that he and others were coming to regard as essential to the highest art. Poe refers to the Schlegels several times in his critical

lective mythology is augmented by his concept of modern literature as an expression of the totality of the mind of the creative artist; in this, Schlegel is quintessentially representative of a mainstream of Romantic thinking.

4. For Schlegel, the Renaissance writers who most captured—indeed, set the foundation for—modern literature are Cervantes and Shakespeare. Sancho Panza is the realist companion to the mad but idealistic Don Quixote in Cervantes's great novel. The great Italian poet, Dante Alighieri (1265–1321), casts himself as the protagonist in his journey to Hell, Purgatory, and Heaven in the *Divine Comedy* (at first called simply the *Commedia*, 1321). Another great Italian poet of the same general era, Petrarch (Francesco Petrarca, 1304–1374), addresses a series of love lyrics to an idealized woman he names Laura; the songs develop psychological moods and themes almost like a lyric novel.

writings. The selections printed here represent some of the older brother's key ideas on artistic unity in terms of tragic and comic elements in a single work. Of particular interest is his analysis of the multiple functions of the Greek chorus—especially the ideas of "parabasis" or "parekbasis"— that is, casually or deliberately interruptive addresses to the audience, sometimes as self-referential commentary on dramatic action. In a review in the *Southern Literary Messenger* (September 1835) of a new translation of the works of the Greek tragedian, Euripides, Poe extensively quotes "Augustus William" Schlegel (even lifting substantial passages without full acknowledgment). The text of Schlegel's "Dramatic Lectures" reprinted here is from A. J. W. Morrison's 1846 revision of the first English translation by John Black in 1815.

From Dramatic Lectures

From *Lecture III*

* * *

[T]he *tragic* and *comic* bear the same relation to one another as *earnest* and *sport*. Every man, from his own experience, is acquainted with both these states of mind; but to determine their essence and their source would demand deep philosophical investigation.

* * *

Man alone, of all the animals with which we are acquainted, is capable of looking back towards the past, and forward into futurity; and he has to purchase the enjoyment of this noble privilege at a dear rate. Earnestness, in the most extensive signification, is the direction of our mental powers to some aim. But as soon as we begin to call ourselves to account for our actions, reason compels us to fix this aim higher and higher, till we come at last to the highest end of our existence: and here that longing for the infinite which is inherent in our being, is baffled by the limits of our finite existence. All that we do, all that we effect, is vain and perishable; death stands everywhere in the back ground, and to it every well or ill-spent moment brings us nearer and closer; and even when a man has been so singularly fortunate as to reach the utmost term of life without any grievous calamity, the inevitable doom still awaits him to leave or to be left by all that is most dear to him on earth. There is no bond of love without a separation, no enjoyment without the grief of losing it. When, however, we contemplate the relations of our existence to the extreme limit of possibilities: when we reflect on its entire dependence on a chain of causes and effects, stretching beyond our ken: when we consider how weak and helpless, and doomed to struggle against the enormous powers of nature, and conflicting appetites, we are cast on the shores of an unknown world, as it were, shipwrecked at our very birth; how we are subject to all kinds of errors and deceptions, any one of which may be our ruin; that in our passions we cherish an enemy in our bosoms; how every moment demands from us, in the name of the most sacred duties, the sacrifice of our dearest inclinations, and how at one blow

we may be robbed of all that we have acquired with much toil and difficulty; that with every accession to our stores, the risk of loss is proportionately increased, and we are only the more exposed to the malice of hostile fortune: when we think upon all this, every heart which is not dead to feeling must be overpowered by an inexpressible melancholy, for which there is no other counter-poise than the consciousness of a vocation transcending the limits of this earthly life. This is the tragic tone of mind; and when the thought of the possible issues out of the mind as a living reality, when this tone pervades and animates a visible representation of the most striking instances of violent revolutions in a man's fortunes, either prostrating his mental energies or calling forth the most heroic endurance—then the result is *Tragic Poetry*. We thus see how this kind of poetry has its foundation in our nature, while to a certain extent we have also answered the question, why we are fond of such mournful representations, and even find something consoling and elevating in them? This tone of mind we have described is inseparable from strong feeling; and although poetry cannot remove these internal dissonances, she must at least endeavour to effect an ideal reconciliation of them.

As earnestness, in the highest degree, is the essence of tragic representation; so is sport of the comic. The disposition to mirth is a forgetfulness of all gloomy considerations in the pleasant feeling of present happiness. We are then inclined to view every thing in a sportive light, and to allow nothing to disturb or ruffle our minds. The imperfections and the irregularities of men are no longer an object of dislike and compassion, but serve, by their strange inconsistencies, to entertain the understanding and to amuse the fancy. The comic poet must therefore carefully abstain from whatever is calculated to excite moral indignation at the conduct, or sympathy with the situations of his personages, because this would inevitably bring us back again into earnestness. He must paint their irregularities as springing out of the predominance of the animal part of their nature, and the incidents which befal them as merely ludicrous distresses, which will be attended with no fatal consequences. This is uniformly what takes place in what we call Comedy, in which, however, there is still a mixture of seriousness, as I shall show in the sequel. The oldest comedy of the Greeks was, however, entirely sportive, and in that respect formed the most complete contrast to their tragedy. Not only were the characters and situations of individuals worked up into a comic picture of real life, but the whole frame of society, the constitution, nature, and the gods, were all fantastically painted in the most ridiculous and laughable colours.

* * *

From *Lecture XI*

* * *

Plato towards the end of his *Symposium* * * * tells us that, after the other guests were dispersed or had fallen asleep, Socrates was left awake with Aristophanes and Agathon, and that while he drank with

them out of a large cup, he forced them to confess, however unwillingly, that it is the business of one and the same man to be equally master of tragic and comic composition, and that the tragic poet is, in virtue of his art, comic poet also. This was not only repugnant to the general opinion, which wholly separated the two kinds of talent, but also to all experience, inasmuch as no tragic poet had ever attempted to shine in Comedy, nor conversely; his remark, therefore, can only have been meant to apply to the inmost essence of the things. Thus at another time, the Platonic Socrates says, on the subject of comic imitation: "All opposites can be fully understood only by and through each other; consequently we can only know what is serious by knowing also what is laughable and ludicrous." If the divine Plato by working out that dialogue had been pleased to communicate his own, or his master's thoughts, respecting these two kinds of poetry, we should have been spared the necessity of the following investigation.

One aspect of the relation of comic to tragic poetry may be comprehended under the idea of *parody*.

* * *

The comic poet, as well as the tragic, transports his characters into an ideal element: not, however, into a world subjected to necessity, but one where the caprice of inventive wit rules without check or restraint, and where all the laws of reality are suspended. He is at liberty, therefore, to invent an action as arbitrary and fantastic as possible; it may even be unconnected and unreal, if only it be calculated to place a circle of comic incidents and characters in the most glaring light. In this last respect, the work should, nay, must, have a leading aim, or it will otherwise be in want of *keeping*. * * * But then, to preserve the comic inspiration, this aim must be made a matter of diversion, and be concealed beneath a medley of all sorts of out-of-the-way matters.

But as the contrast between the matter and form is here in its proper place, and nothing can be more thoroughly opposite to the ludicrous form of exhibition than the most important and serious concerns of men, public life and the state naturally became the peculiar subject-matter of the Old Comedy. It is, therefore, altogether political; and private and family life, beyond which the new never soars, was only introduced occasionally and indirectly, in so far as it might have a reference to public life. The Chorus is therefore essential to it, as being in some sort a representation of the public. * * * The most remarkable peculiarity of the comic chorus is the *Parabasis*,[1] an address to the

1. The usual or preferred English word, the meaning of which is exactly as A. W. Schlegel defines it: the coming forward of the chorus to address the audience—thus breaking the dramatic illusion—which, in comedy, may not *necessarily* have any relevance to the theme or plot of the play, but instead may refer to the author's general concerns and personal conditions or difficulties with artistic execution. Cf. Poe's review of a new edition of Euripides in which he lifts, sometimes word for word, A. W. Schlegel's text on this point. Friedrich Schlegel more often uses the term *parekbasis*, which means deviation or separation. This word suggests deviation or separation of the artist from accepted artistic, social, or moral norms—and/or a self alongside another self. The difference between the Schlegel brothers' understanding of this "breaking of illusion" technique is suggestive; the latter is more in line with Friedrich's complex concept of overall Romantic irony.

spectators by the chorus, in the name, and as the representative of the poet, but having no connexion with the subject of the piece. Sometimes he enlarges on his own merits, and ridicules the pretensions of his rivals; at other times, availing himself of his right as an Athenian citizen, to speak on public affairs in every assembly of the people, he brings forward serious or ludicrous motions for the common good. The Parabasis must, strictly speaking, be considered as incongruous with the essence of dramatic representation; for in the drama the poet should always be behind his dramatic personages, who again ought to speak and act as if they were alone, and to take no perceptible notice of the spectators. Such intermixtures, therefore, destroy all tragic impression, but to the comic tone these intentional interruptions or intermezzos are welcome, even though they be in themselves more serious than the subject of the representation.

* * *

From *Lecture XVII*

The external sense perceives in objects only an indefinite plurality of distinguishable parts; the judgement, by which we comprehend these into an entire and perfect unity, is in all cases founded on a reference to a higher sphere of ideas. Thus, for example, the mechanical unity of a watch consists in its aim of measuring time; this aim, however, exists only for the understanding, and is neither visible to the eye, nor palpable to the touch: the organic unity of a plant or an animal consists in the idea of life; but the inward intuition of life, which, in itself uncorporeal, nevertheless manifests itself through the medium of the corporeal world, is brought by us to the observation of the individual living object, otherwise we could not obtain it from that object.

The separate parts of a work of art, and * * * the separate parts, consequently, of a tragedy, must not be taken in by the eye and ear alone, but also comprehended by the understanding. Collectively, however, they are all subservient to one common aim, namely, to produce a joint impression on the mind. Here, therefore, as in the above examples, the Unity lies in a higher sphere, in the feeling or in the reference to ideas. This is all one; for the feeling, so far as it is not merely sensual and passive, is our sense, our organ for the Infinite, which forms itself into ideas for us.

* * *

From *Lecture XXIII*

SHAKSPEARE

* * *

Shakspeare makes each of his principal characters the glass in which the others are reflected, and by like means enables us to discover what could not be immediately revealed to us. What in others is most profound, is with him but surface. Ill-advised should we be were

we always to take men's declarations respecting themselves and others for sterling coin. Ambiguity of design with much propriety he makes to overflow with the most praiseworthy principles; and sage maxims are not unfrequently put in the mouth of stupidity, to show how easily such common-place truisms may be acquired. Nobody ever painted so truthfully as he has done the facility of self-deception, the half self-conscious hypocrisy towards ourselves, with which even noble minds attempt to disguise the almost inevitable influence of selfish motives in human nature. This secret irony of the characterization commands admiration as the profound abyss of acuteness and sagacity; but it is the grave of enthusiasm. We arrive at it only after we have had the misfortune to see human nature through and through; and when no choice remains but to adopt the melancholy truth, that "no virtue or greatness is altogether pure and genuine," or the dangerous error that "the highest perfection is attainable." Here we therefore may perceive in the poet himself, notwithstanding his power to excite the most fervent emotions, a certain cool indifference, but still the indifference of a superior mind, which has run through the whole sphere of human existence and survived feeling.

The irony in Shakspeare has not merely a reference to the separate characters, but frequently to the whole of the action. Most poets who [portray] human events in a narrative or dramatic form take themselves a part, and exact from their readers a blind approbation or condemnation of whatever side they choose to support or oppose. The more zealous this rhetoric is, the more certainly it fails of its effect. In every case we are conscious that the subject itself is not brought immediately before us, but that we view it through the medium of a different way of thinking. When, however, by a dexterous manœuvre, the poet allows us an occasional glance at the less brilliant reverse of the medal, then he makes, as it were, a sort of secret understanding with the select circle of the more intelligent of his readers or spectators; he shows them that he had previously seen and admitted the validity of their tacit objections; that he himself is not tied down to the represented subject, but soars freely above it; and that, if he chose, he could unrelentingly annihilate the beautiful and irresistibly attractive scenes which his magic pen has produced.

* * *

JEAN PAUL FRIEDRICH RICHTER

The German novelist and critic Johann Paul Friedrich Richter (1763–1825), although now largely forgotten, is still better known by his pseudonym "Jean Paul." He was at one time quite popular—despite the often bewildering complexity of his works and the dense allusiveness of his pervasive word play. His novels include *Die unsichtbare Loge* (1793, The invisible lodge), *Hesperus* (1795), *Leben des Quintus Fixlein* (1796, The life of Quintus Fixlein), *Siebenkäs* (1796–97, the full title of which is The Married Life, Death, and Wedding of the Advocate of the Poor Mr.

Firmian Siebenkäs), *Titan* (1800–03), and *Flegeljahre* (1804–05, The fledgling years). These works combine artistic and social criticism with sentimentality, humor, and a pervasive irony; they are characterized by a playful metafictional self-reflexivity in the manner of Cervantes's *Don Quixote* and Sterne's *Tristram Shandy*. In the English-speaking world his best-known work is the novella *Das Leben des vergnügten Schulmeisterlein Maria Wutz in Auental* (The life of the self-satisfied schoolmaster Maria Wutz of Auental). *Maria Wutz*, which was originally an "appendix" to the never quite finished *Invisible Lodge*, is a story that antedates the bewildering epistemological, narratival, and temporal dislocations of modernist/postmodernist writers like Jorge Luis Borges and John Barth.

The fictions of Jean Paul, along with his introductory dissertation on aesthetics, *Vorschule für Aesthetik* (1804, literally, Preschool for Aesthetics), were instrumental in the foundation of one aspect of international Romanticism, and some of the basic ideas of the *Vorschule* treatise are represented here by selections on humor and irony. The text is the translation by Erika Casey in *Jean Paul: A Reader*, edited by Timothy J. Casey (Baltimore: Johns Hopkins University Press, 1992), pp. 251, 253, 254, 255–56, 258–59. Copyright © 1991. Reprinted by permission of the publisher.

From Preschool for Aesthetics

The Seventh Program. On Humoristic Poetry

§ 32

* * *

If Schlegel rightly maintains that the romantic is not a genre of poetry but that poetry must itself be romantic: then the same goes even more for the comic; that is to say, everything must become romantic, i.e., humoristic. The disciples of the new aesthetic Lyceum[1] display a superior comic universal spirit in their burlesques, dramas, parodies, and the like, without becoming denouncer and gallows chaplain of the individual fool. * * *

§ 33

This is the second component of humor, as an inverse sublime. Just as Luther calls our will in a bad sense a lex inversa:[2] so humor is one in the good sense; and its descent into hell paves the way for its ascent into heaven. It resembles the merops, the bird that turns its tail up to heaven, while rising in that very direction, the little juggler who sips its nectar topsy-turvy and *upwards*.

If man, like the old theology, regards our mortal world from the celestial one: it passes by in its orbit, small and vain; but if, like humor, he measures the infinite world by the humble one: then that laughter is born, which yet contains greatness and pain. Therefore, just as Greek poetry, as opposed to the present day, made serene: so humor,

1. A place for concerts, exhibitions, lectures, debates, and the exchange of ideas—or the general organization sponsoring such events. *Lyceum* is the name that the Schlegels gave to one of their magazines at the end of the eighteenth century (see p. 727, n. 1 herein).
2. Inverse law (Latin). Martin Luther (1483–1546), German theologian, leader of the Protestant Reformation.

in contrast to the old jest, makes partly serious; it walks on the lower soccus[3] while frequently bearing the tragic mask, at least in its hand. Therefore, not only were great humorists very serious, as we just said, but we have to thank a melancholy people for the greatest of them. The ancients enjoyed their life far too much to hold it in humoristic disdain. * * * I can well imagine the devil being the true inverse of the divine world, the great world shadow, setting off the form of the luminous body, as the greatest humorist and "whimsical man," who as the *moresque*[4] of a *moresque* would, however, be far, too unaesthetical; for his laugh would have too much pain in it; it would be like the gaily flowering gown of the—guillotined.

After each pathetic strain, man desires a comic relaxing; as, however, no sensation can desire its opposite but only its scaling downward: the joke sought by pathos must contain a reductive seriousness. And this is inherent in humor. Hence there is, as in Shakespeare a court jester, Madhawya in the Sakontala.[5] Hence Socrates finds in the disposition toward the tragic in Plato's Symposion the comic as well. Hence the English offer a humorous epilogue and a comedy after a tragedy, in the Greek tradition, where *after* the threefold seriousness the tetralogy will conclude with a satire, * * * and where the parodists raised their voice after the rhapsodes.[6] And in French mystery plays, whenever Christ or a martyr was about to be flogged, the old tender kindheartedness would advise in brackets: "Let Harlequin here enter and speak and cheer us up a little."[7]

* * *

A heroic epos is easy to parody and to topple into its counterpart—; but woe betide tragedy if it does not continue to work even through parody! One can travesty Homer but never Shakespeare; for while the trivial does with annihilatory force oppose the sublime, it does not so oppose the pathetic.

* * *

In the heading of this §, I called the idea annihilating. This is evident everywhere. As reason generally dazzles the intellect, strikes and transports it by force (with the idea of an infinite godhead for instance), as a god does a mortal: likewise humor, which, unlike persiflage, turns its back on reason and falls down in worship of the idea. That is why humor oftentimes revels in its own contradictions and impossibilities, for example in Tieck's Zerbino,[8] where the characters

3. The slipper or sandal worn by actors in classical comedy ("sock").
4. Literally, a Moor (North African Arab); here Jean Paul apparently means a redoubled caricature of the *moresque* in the sense of the *arabesque* as a literary work or in the style of multiple frames and perspectives, including mixtures of humor and seriousness.
5. Or *Shakuntala*, a classic Sanskrit play by Kalidasa (5th century), Indian poet.
6. Entranced people, who speak, sing, and/or dance in an uncontrolled exuberant manner (cf. "rhapsody" in music).
7. Flögel's History of the Comic Grotesque [Jean Paul's note]. "Harlequin": the clown figure in the *commedia dell'arte* of the 17th and 18th centuries. Karl Friedrich Flögel (1729–1788) bases his remarks on Justus Möser's pamphlet *Harlekin oder die Verteidigung des Grotesk-Komischen* (1761, Harlequin, or the defense of the grotesquely comic), an important early treatment of the subject.
8. Among the plays of Ludwig Tieck (1773–1853), a translator, dramatist, and fiction writer who was a major force in the transition of the late Neoclassic period in German literature (the Storm and Stress era) to Romanticism per se, is *Prince Zerbino* (1798), in which stan-

take themselves in the end to be nothing but figures on paper and nonsense, hauling the readers on stage and the stage itself under the impress. * * * Hence humor's predilection for the most vacuous ending, while seriousness concludes epigrammatically with the most weighty. * * * Thus *Sterne* for instance several times deliberates assiduously on certain occurrences only finally to decide: there was not a word of truth in it anyway.

Something similar to the boldness of this annihilating humor, an expression of disdain for the world, may be discerned in certain music, like Haydn's, for instance, where whole series may be annihilated by one alien one and that rushes pell-mell between pianissimo and fortissimo, presto and andante[9] by turns. A second similarity is the skepticism that * * * comes into being when the mind reviews the awful throng of belligerent beliefs by which it is surrounded; a vertigo of the soul, as it were, suddenly turning *our* rapid motion into the *alien* one of the whole static world.

And a third similarity are the humorous Feasts of Fools of the Middle Ages, which with an untrammeled hysteron proteron,[1] with an inner spiritual masquerade, but without any impure intention, turn topsy-turvy the worldly and spiritual, caste and custom, in the great liberty and equality of Joy. But for such a vigorous humor our taste is not so much too delicate as our disposition is too poor.

§ 34

Comic Romanticism, no less than serious, is—by contrast with classical objectivity—the sovereign of subjectivity. For if the comic consists of the interchange of subjective and objective maxims, I cannot, since according to the above, the objective maxim must be a wished-for infinity, think and posit this *outside* myself, but only within myself, where I base it upon the subjective. Consequently, I myself put myself into this quandary—albeit not externally, as happens in comedy—dividing myself into finite and infinite factors and letting the latter derive from the former. This is when man will laugh and cry: "Impossible! This is too crazy by half!" To be sure! That is why Self plays first fiddle with every humorist; if at all possible, he will put even his personal circumstances on his comic stage if only to annihilate them poetically. He being his own court jester and Commedia dell'arte quarter as well as the regent and régisseur[2] to go with it: the reader is asked

dard literary and theatrical conventions are turned inside out and the dramatic illusion of real life is repeatedly broken. A few sentences later Jean Paul compares the works of Tieck to those of the British writer Laurence Sterne (1713–1768); in his novel *Tristam Shandy* (1760–67), Sterne does much the same thing that Tieck does in his plays and prose fictions.

9. Terms for the pace and style of a musical passage; Franz Joseph Haydn (1732–1809), Austrian composer. Jean Paul's point is that a writer may, like the musican Haydn, effortlessly but breathtakingly vary the effects of the text.

1. Basically a figure of speech in which the logical (or natural) order of terms (as in presumed cause and effect) seems backwards. In logic, it is the fallacy of assuming as a premise something yet to be proved (i.e., reverse order). "Feasts of Fools": part of Carnival, when sensuous impulses are allowed the night before the fleshly renunciations of Lent in Catholic tradition (see notes to "The Cask of Amontillado," pp. 415–16, esp. n. 5 herein). "Untrammeled": unshackled, unrestricted.

2. Director of a ballet or other musical theatrical performance. "Commedia dell'arte": a somewhat sinister burlesque form of theater in which the players wore grotesque masks and made wild, unnatural movements and gestures; especially associated with Italy in the 17th century and after.

to contribute a measure of goodwill, or at the least no ill will, toward the writing self and not to make his semblance reality; it would have to be the best reader of the best author who could fully relish a satire on himself. * * * A Cervantes, for instance, had to attack and denigrate his own Don Quixote in the initial doldrums, so that the crowd should rate it more highly, writing a hostile review called: "el buscapiè," or the rocket, lest he himself should scatter into the sky.

§ 35

* * *

The prodigal presentation through images and contrasts of wit and imagination alike, i.e., through groupings and colorings, should charge the soul through sensuousness and fire it with that dithyrambic song[3] that holds up the world of the senses, distorted and angular in its concave mirror, to face the idea. Insofar as such a Doomsday plunges the world of the senses into a second chaos—merely in order to sit in divine judgment—, while the intellect can only dwell in an orderly universe, although reason, like God, is not even contained in the amplest temple—: insofar humor might seem to border on madness, which takes leave of its senses naturally, as the philosopher artificially, but like the latter, keeping its reason; humor is, as the ancients dubbed Diogenes, a raving Socrates.—[4]

3. The deeper into Tristram the more humoristic lyrical Sterne becomes. Thus his magnificent journey in volume 7; the humoristic dithyrambic song in Volume 8, c. 11, 12 etc. [Jean Paul's note]. I.e., Sterne becomes ever more so in these scenes in his novel *Tristram Shandy*. "Dithyramb": a frenzied choral hymn and dance in honor of the ancient Greek god of fertility, Dionysus.

4. Socrates (469–399 B.C.E.), known from the *Dialogues* of Plato, is the most famous "wise man" of the ancient intellectual inquirers. Of the two or three well-known figures named Diogenes in classical times, the likely reference is to the eccentric Greek philosopher Diogenes of Athens (c. 412–323 B.C.E.), who is said to have lived in a tub and to have walked the streets at night, holding up a lantern in people's faces, looking for an honest man. Both figures have been symbolic for centuries as questers after truth and honesty. Humor here is personified as a mad seeker after truth, a Socrates gone over the edge.

Sciences of the Mind

Attempts to locate various mental faculties and personal characteristics in the features of the human head date from ancient times. Narrowly defined, *physiognomy* means the study of the face, particularly in regard to external physical links with internal moral character and personality. The modern pseudo-science of physiognomy may be said to begin with Johann Kasper Lavater (1741–1801), a Swiss theologian, whose work in this field stimulated another related pseudo-science: *phrenology*, or the study of the contours and general shape (morphology) of the skull. From 1775 forward, Lavater, with the collaboration of the eminent German writer Johann Wolfgang von Goethe, produced the series of volumes called *Physiognomical Fragments for the Promotion of the Knowledge and Love of Man.* Lavater's works were readily available in translation in Britain and America. *Essays on Physiognomy* was printed in Boston in 1794; and citizens found *The Pocket Lavater, or, The Science of Physiognomy* (New York, 1817) useful for carrying about with them as they observed their contemporaries.

The aim of phrenology was similar to that of physiognomy—to connect external physical characteristics (the bone structures and bumps of the skull) with mental abilities and with proclivities and moral tendencies of internal character. The two words continued to be used more or less interchangeably (along with *physiology*) throughout the nineteenth century, though the Austrian physician, Franz Joseph Gall (1758–1828), in *Anatomy and Physiology of the Nervous System in General* (1810–19), tried to use them with more precise distinction. Among Gall's basic principles are the following: the brain is the center of all mental and neurological activity; the brain is composed of several different neurological organs (the faculties) controlling different abilities, behaviors, and sentiments; the form of the cranium mimics the form and size of the brain and thus provides an external map or model of a person's mental characteristics. Gall concluded that the brain could be divided into over thirty different organs, such as "ideality," "destructiveness," "alimentiveness" (heavy feeding), and "secretiveness." By studying the skull's external evidence of the relative development of these organs, a person could take advantage of innate gifts indicated by larger bony swells and protrusions of the head and ameliorate poorer performance and behavior by awareness of underdeveloped areas. It became one of the great self-improvement fads in American history, with over forty phrenological societies established by the 1830s and scores of self-proclaimed readers of heads (also known as "bump doctors") traveling from town to town across the nation.

JOHANN G. SPURZHEIM

A student and collaborator of Franz Gall, Dr. Johann G. Spurzheim (1776–1832), edited, translated, rewrote, augmented, and in general popularized his mentor's works, especially in Great Britain and the United States. Indeed, in the United States, the names Gall and Spurzheim are almost invariably linked. Spurzheim expanded and revised the nomenclature and descriptions of such organs or propensities as amativeness, philoprogenitiveness, adhesiveness, combativeness, destructiveness, covetiveness, secretiveness, and ideality. Reprinted here are selections from *The Physiognomical System of Drs. Gall and Spurheim*, 2nd ed. (London: Baldwin, Cradock, and Joy, 1815).

From The Physiognomical System of Drs. Gall and Spurzheim

VI. Organ of the Propensity to Destroy, or of Destructiveness

A difference in the skulls of carnivorous and herbivorous animals gave the first idea of the existence of this organ. If we place a skull of any carnivorous animal horizontally, and trace a vertical line through the external meatus auditorius,[1] a great portion of the cerebral mass is situated behind that line; and the more an animal is carnivorous, the more considerable is the portion of the cerebral mass situated there.

* * *

In man this propensity presents different degrees of activity, from a mere indifference to the pain of animals, to the pleasure of seeing them killed, or even to the most irresistible desire to kill. This doctrine may shock sensibility, but it is not the less true. Whoever endeavours to study nature and judge of its phenomena must admit the existence of things as they are. It may be observed that in children as well as in adults, among the uncultivated as well as among the polite and well bred classes of society, certain individuals are sensible, and others indifferent, to the suffering of others. Some persons feel a pleasure in tormenting animals and in seeing them tortured or killed, even when it is impossible to ascribe this disposition to bad habit or bad education.

* * *

We may also determine the existence of this propensity, and its diversities, by the impressions which different spectators receive from public executions. The view of them is insupportable to some individuals and delightful to others.

* * *

Certain madmen are alienated only in respect to the propensity to murder.

1. The opening of the ear.

* * *

[There was] one who did not show any mark of alienation in respect to memory, imagination and judgment, but who confessed that, in his narrow seclusion, his propensity to murder was quite involuntary and utterly irresistible, and that his wife, notwithstanding his tenderness for her, was near being immolated, he having time only to warn her to fly.

* * *

[M]any similar examples, observed in the healthy and diseased state of man—in idiots and madmen—prove evidently that the propensity to kill and destroy is innate, not only in animals but in man. Does not, indeed, the whole history of mankind confirm this assertion? In all ages the earth has been drenched with blood.

* * *

It remains still that we should examine what is the essential nature of this faculty? I think that its sphere of activity is more extended than the instinct to kill. It seems to me that this faculty produces the propensity to destroy in general, without denoting any object. Destruction may be applied to inanimate things, to animals, or to man; and in this signification, this faculty may be necessary and destined from creation. It must certainly be granted that throughout all nature one being lives upon another, that violent death is an institution of nature, and that there are animals of prey among all orders of animals.

* * *

This faculty then produces the propensity to destroy, in general, without determining the object to be destroyed, or the manner of destroying it: it gives the propensity to pinch, scratch, bite, cut, break, pierce, devastate, demolish, ravage, burn, massacre, strangle, butcher, suffocate, drown, kill, poison, murder and assassinate. Gall formerly called the organ of this faculty the organ of murder, because he found it much developed in two murderers; but it is evident that a name cannot be given to any faculty according to its abuse. This misnomer arose from the circumstance that the organs can be discovered only when they are extremely developed: but in the highest state of developement many faculties produce abuses. Such was the origin of this too limited term, erroneously derived from the abuse of a faculty of which the well regulated employment is, like that of all other faculties, essential to life. I think that the name, organ of the propensity to destroy, or of destructiveness, is the most general and the most conformable to the sphere of activity of this faculty. We are convinced, by a great number of observations, that the seat of this organ is on the side of the head immediately above the ears.

* * *

It is a proverb that a poet must be born; and it is also certain that the heads of great poets, though not necessarily of versificators, are enlarged above the temples in an arched direction. * * * Now it is impossible that poetry, in general, should be confined to one single organ; and I therefore think that the name organ of poetry, given by Gall to this organ, does not indicate its essential faculty, but that it is necessary to determine what is essential to all kinds of poetry: for this

common faculty of all poets then must be the special faculty of this organ, and the combination of this with the other faculties must determine the species of poetry which each poet may produce. It can neither be the faculty of versification, nor that of rhyming; for some authors write in prose, and yet their expressions are really poetical; while others make verses which however contain no poetical thought. Rhyme is still less essential to poetry, for among the ancients it was entirely unknown, and among the moderns poetry is not always rhythmic. It seems to me that in every kind of poetry the sentiments are exalted, the expressions warm, and that there must be rapture, inspiration—what is commonly called imagination or fancy. I observe moreover, that in all persons this faculty gives a peculiar tinge to all other faculties: it makes them in every thing aspire to ideality. It is a sentiment, and, if I may so speak, the opposite of circumspection: it renders us enthusiasts, while circumspection stops our career by saying, Take care. I call this organ that of Ideality.

I have here to mention certain curious observations without being capable of determining their peculiar nature.—We have observed that if the part of the head, above the organ of ideality and a little backward from it, be very much developed, the persons are disposed to mysticism, to have visions, to see ghosts, demons and phantoms, and to believe in astrology, magic and sorcery. I cannot say whether this is a particular organ, or a greater developement of the organ of hope, or of that of ideality, or of both together.

* * *

ORSON S. FOWLER

Other major figures associated with phrenology include two sets of brothers. The Scottish brothers George Combe (1788–1858) and Andrew Combe (1797–1847) had a great influence on the American brothers Lorenzo Niles Fowler (1811–1896) and Orson Squire Fowler (1809–1887). George Combe's *Constitution of Man* (1828) was popular in both Europe and the United States; he established the Phrenological Society in Britain along with the *Phrenological Journal*. In America, the Fowlers imitated Combe's success by establishing the *American Phrenological Journal* and the New York–based American Phrenological Institute. Like Combe, the Fowlers traveled widely across the United States, giving lectures and consultations, and they produced an extensive series of revised versions of their books. One of the most popular was *The Illustrated Self-Instructor in Phrenology and Physiology*; published in 1849, it was reprinted some twenty times before the end of the century. Reprinted here is the section on the faculty of ideality from *Fowler's Practical Phrenology* of 1846 and a phrenological chart of the human head from the 1886 edition of O. S. Fowler's *Life: Its Factors, Science, and Culture*, Vol. 1: *Mind, Organism, and Health by Hygiene; Or Phrenology and Physiology Applied to the Laws, Preservation, and Restoration of Health.*

From Fowler's Practical Phrenology

21. Ideality

IMAGINATION—FANCY—LOVE OF THE EXQUISITE, THE BEAUTIFUL, THE
SPLENDID, THE TASTEFUL, AND THE POLISHED—THAT IMPASSIONED
ECSTASY AND RAPTURE OF FEELING WHICH GIVE INSPIRATION TO POETRY
AND ORATORY, AND A CONCEPTION OF THE SUBLIME.

That there exists in the human mind some faculty, the function of
which is to inspire man with a love of the beautiful and the exqui-
site—a fondness for the sublime, the elegant, and the tasteful, will ap-
pear evident when we compare man with the lower order of animals,
or civilized man with the savage, or the refined inhabitants of a city
with the common population of the country. Were it not for the influ-
ence of this faculty, these things would be held in no higher estima-
tion by man than by the brute, or by one man than by another. Were it
not for its influence, mankind would have no higher relish for the ex-
quisite, the tasteful, the beautiful, and the sublime, than for the in-
sipid, the dull, the homely, and the vulgar. Were it not for this faculty,
we should no more highly prize the bold images, the glowing flights of
fancy, the daring thoughts, and the impassioned bursts of eloquence
which characterize the productions of Homer, of Shakspeare, of Mil-
ton, of Byron, of Addison, of Irving, of Chalmers, of Patrick Henry,
and of Daniel Webster, than we do the plainer and dryer style of
Locke, Dean Swift, William Cobbett, and many other still more
homely writers. Without ideality, the splendid productions of a Ra-
phael, a Corregio, a Canova, a Phidias, and a Praxiteles,[1] would find
no more favour in our eyes than the rudest paintings, and the rough-
est carvings, of the most uncivilized nations.

Although poetry is one form in which this faculty manifests itself,
yet it is by no means exclusively confined to a relish for the inspira-
tions of the muses. Though essential to the poet, it takes a wider
range. It adds to the delight we take in viewing an elegant statue, an
exquisite painting, a splendid temple, or any other finished production
of art. It causes and increases the glow and rapture experienced in be-
holding the beautiful landscape, the rugged cliff, the bold promontory,
and the lofty mountain.

* * *

LOCATION.—Ideal. is located upon the *sides* of the head, about the
spot in which the hair begins to appear, upwards and backwards of
construct., beneath the temporal ridge, and near its union with the
parietal bone, and nearly in a line with compar., caus., and mirth.
When large or very large, the sides of the head, where the hair makes
its appearance, are widened and heightened, but when it is small, they
are narrow and depressed.

1. Fowler's list begins with famous writers and proceeds through orators and politicians to
painters and sculptors from the European Renaissance to classical Greece.

Phrenological chart of the human head. Reprinted from O.S. Fowler, *Life: Its Factors, Science, and Culture*, Vol. 1: *Mind, Organism, and Health by Hygiene; Or Phrenology and Physiology Applied to the Laws, Preservation, and Restoration of Health* (1886).

VITATION: Hardihood, longevity, constitution.

APPETITE: Feeding, relish, greed, heartiness.

BIBATION: Fondness for liquids, drink and bathing.

SLEEP: Mental heaviness, dullness or lethargy

SMELL: Love of fragrant, odors, aromas, perfumes.

GENDER: Love, the creating power.

MATING: Conjugality, constancy, fidelity to mate.

PARENTAL LOVE: Love of own children, pets, etc.

FORCE: Energy, puck, courage, vim, push defense, attack, valor.

DESTRUCTION: Severity, cruelty, wrath, killing.

SECRECY: Tact, strategy, craft, policy, intrigue.

ACQUISITION: Love of getting and boarding, grasping, miserly.

CAUTION: Care, anxiety, safety, prudence.

CONSTRUCTION: Ingenuity, manual dexterity, working, knack.

APPLICATION: Continuing, finishing what is begun.

FRIENDSHIP: Sociability, affection, co-operation.

HABITATION: Love of home, patriotism.

AGRICULTRE: Love of tillage, pomology, etc.

EMULATION: Ambition, rivalry, honor, show, pride, display.

DOMINATION: Self-assertion, authority.

FIRMNESS: Stability, wilfulness, stubbornness.

BEAUTY: Taste, finish, elegance, poetry.

GRANDEUR: Admiration of the boundless, infinite, eternal, sublime and awful.

IMITATION: Mimicing, patterning after, copying.

MIRTH: Fun, ridicule, laughter, joking.

URBANITY: Politeness, courtesy, flattery.

OBSERVATION: Scrutiny, desire to see and examine.

FORM: Memory of faces, shapes, looks.

MEASUREMENT: Estimation of quantity, proportions, levels, etc.

GRAVITATION: Muscular control, balancing, marksmanship.

COLOR: Love of colors in painting, flowers, etc.

SYSTEM: Order, keeping things in their places, method.

NUMBERATION: Mental arithmetic, cyphering.

AUDITION: Hearing, perception and memory of sounds.

TIME: The mental clock, periodicity.

MUSIC: Tune, learning tunes by rote, musical knack.

LOCATION: Remembering places, love of traveling.

EVENTUATION: Scholarship, smartness in acquiring and using knowledge and facts.

EXPRESSION: Loquacity, talking and committing talent.

CAUSATION: Deduction, sense, originality, foresight.

INDUCTION: Criticism, analysis, comparison.

INTUITION: Reading character by minor signs.

KINDNESS: Sympathy, pity, goodness, charity.

ADORATION: Worship, awe, deference, obedience, humility, solemnity.

INSPIRATION: Prophetic foresight, spiritual guidance.

HOPE: Expectation, looking on the bright side.

CONSCIENCE: Integrity, love of right, truth and duty.

THOMAS C. UPHAM

Thomas C. Upham was, beginning in 1824, a professor of metaphysics and moral philosophy at Bowdoin College in Massachusetts, where Nathaniel Hawthorne was his student. Upham's poetry has been forgotten, but his treatises on the structures of the mind and on mental illness were well known in America from the 1820s through the 1860s. These include *The Elements of Human Intellectuality* (1827), which was revised in two volumes as *Elements of Mental Philosophy* (1831) and expanded with a third volume, *Philosophical and Practical Treatises on the Will* (1834); these works were followed by *Outlines of Imperfect and Disordered Mental Action* (1840, rev. 1868), *Principles of the Interior or Hidden Life* (1843), and others.

Because his writings contain psychological analyses of the Salem Witch Trials of 1692, he is sometimes confused with the clergyman, politician, and historian, Charles Wentworth Upham (1802–75), a resident of Salem with Hawthorne and author of *Salem Witchcraft* (1867). Hawthorne seems not to have had much respect for this other Upham, either as a historian or as a human being, partially because he conspired to have Hawthorne removed from the Customs House appointment in Salem and then maliciously spread stories of the Hawthornes' poverty. (Charles Wentworth Upham is supposed to be the model for the unflattering portrait of the younger Judge Pyncheon in *The House of the Seven Gables*.)

Thomas Upham, on the other hand, in his systematic analyses of human motives, desires, and instabilities, influenced not only Hawthorne but also other writers of the American Romantic period. The selections printed here are from the 1868 revision of his *Outlines of Imperfection and Disordered Mental Action* (Harper and Brothers, 1840). Following other writers like David Hartley, Thomas Reid, Benjamin Rush, and Dugald Stewart, Upham tried to systematize the physical configurations of mental (and eventually moral) thought. Upham's model of the mind is divided into three basic parts: the intellect, the sensibilities, and the will. The first two parts are further subdivided. The first is composed of "Intellectual States of External Origin," "Intellectual States of Internal Origin," and the "Pathology of the Intellect." Sensibilities is subdivided into "Natural or Pathematic . . . Emotions and Desires," "Moral . . . Emotions of Approval and Disapproval . . . Feelings of Moral Obligation," and the "Pathology of the Affections." These shape the progression of the many anecdotes of mental aberrations that Upham presents.

In giving examples of mental "alienation," Upham paraphrases and quotes from, among others, the so-called case histories described in Sir Walter Scott's enormously popular *Letters on Demonology and Witchcraft* (1830). This book contains not only stories and anecdotes of the supernatural, but also analyses of the psychological aspects of ghostly superstition and the witchcraft hysteria of the 16th and 17th centuries.

From Outlines of Imperfection and Disordered Mental Action

Introduction.

CHAPTER I.

OUTLINES OF MENTAL PHILOSOPHY.

§ 1. *Extent and importance of the subject to be examined.*

The reader will notice that I have entitled this Treatise, Imperfect and Disordered Mental Action. A title designedly made thus general, in order to include all the varieties of imperfect and alienated action of which (and they are almost without number) the human mind is the subject. Our inquiries are not meant to be limited to those more aggravated forms of mental disorder which infringe upon moral accountability, and which are commonly had in view, when what is called Insanity or Madness comes under discussion. We propose to take a more extensive view of the subject.

* * *

We refer to those instances of mental disorder where the mind is not merely discomposed, not merely temporarily set ajar, but in ruins. No sight is so afflicting, so overwhelming, as that of a mind fundamentally, and, perhaps, permanently unsettled. What, then, can be more important than to understand the facts and causes of its ruin, and the principles on which a restoration may be possible.

* * *

§ 14. *Remarks on the Imagination.*

Another leading power which, when we accurately consider its nature, seems properly to be arranged under the general head of the Intellect, is the Imagination. We shall have occasion hereafter to recur again to the nature and intellectual process of imaginative action, when it comes in place to consider the disorders to which this important faculty is subject. All we propose to do here is briefly to point out the relation existing between the imagination and the reasoning power.

* * *

Some of the particulars, in which the imaginative and deductive powers are closely related, are these. They both imply the antecedent exercise of the power of abstraction; they are both employed in framing new combinations of thought from the elements already in possession; they both put in requisition, and in precisely the same way, the powers of association and relative suggestion. Nevertheless, they are separated from each other, and characterized by the two circumstances, that they operate in part on different materials, and that their objects are different. Reasoning, as it aims to give us a knowledge of

the truth, deals exclusively with facts more or less probable. Imagination, as it aims chiefly to give pleasure, is at liberty to transcend the limits of the world of reality, and, consequently, often deals with the mere conceptions of the mind, whether they correspond to reality or not. Accordingly, the one ascertains what is true, the other what is possible; the office of the one is to inquire, of the other to create.

* * *

§ 23. *Shown also from the effects of stimulating drugs and gases.*

If there be not a close connexion between the body and mind, and if there be not various influences propagated from one to the other, how does it happen that many things of a stimulating nature, such as ardent spirits and opium, strongly affect the mind when taken into the system in considerable quantities? But, without delaying upon the effects of drugs of this description, which, unhappily, can hardly fail to be noticed every day, we would instance particularly the results which are found to follow from the internal use of the nitrous oxyde gas. This gas, when it is received into the system, operates, in the first instance, on the body. The effect is a *physical* one. In particular, it quickens the circulation of the blood and also, as is commonly supposed, increases the volume of that fluid. But its effects, which are first felt in the body, are afterward experienced in the mind, and generally in a high degree. When it is inhaled in a considerable quantity, the sensations are more acute; the conceptions of absent objects are more vivid; associated trains of thought pass through the mind with increased rapidity; and emotions and passions, generally of a pleasant kind, are excited, corresponding in strength to the increased acuteness of sensations and the increased vividness of conceptions.

There is another gas, the FEBRILE MIASMA,[1] which is found, on being inhaled, to affect the mind also, by first affecting the sanguineous fluid. But this gas diminishes, instead of increasing the volume of blood; as is indicated by a small, contracted pulse, and an increasing constriction of the capillaries. As in the case of the nitrous oxyde gas, the mental exercises are rendered intense and vivid by the febrile miasma; but the emotions which are experienced, instead of being pleasant, are gloomy and painful. The trains of thought which are at such times suggested, and the creations of the imagination, are all of an analogous character, strange, spectral, and terrifying.

* * *

§ 57. *Illustrations of the Subject from the use of Opium.*

There are some articles, such as ardent spirits in their various forms, opium, and the febrile miasma gas, as we have already had occasion to remark in a former chapter, which, on being introduced into the system, and especially when taken repeatedly and in considerable

1. "Febrile": fever. "Miasma": heavy vapor, often supposed to be toxic and capable of producing hallucinations. See notes to "The Fall of the House of Usher" (esp. p. 201, n.1 herein).

quantities, are found powerfully to affect the mind. And the effect on the mind appears to be produced by means of an intermediate influence, as we should naturally expect it would be, upon the sensorial organ. All the various sensations and perceptions, those which originate in the sense of sight no less than others, may be more or less disordered in this way.

It appears from the work entitled the Confessions of an English Opium-eater,[2] that the author of it was inordinately addicted to the use of opium; so that, in the end, not only his health was affected, but his intellect was thrown into an unnatural and disorderly posture. The nerve of vision became so disordered that it at once assumed the position which his thoughts indicated, whatever that might be. So that his eye, in discordance with its natural laws of action, constantly peopled the surrounding vacant space with visions and phantasms of terror or of beauty. He informs us, among other things, that at night, when he lay in bed, vast processions passed along in mournful pomp. But his visions do not appear to have been limited to representations of a mournful character. Whatever he happened to think upon, whether it were landscapes, or palaces, or armies in battle array; in a word, whatever was a subject of thought, and was capable of being visually represented, formed themselves into images or phantasms of the eye, and swept before him in order and distinctness, no less marked and imposing than if the real objects themselves had been present.

* * *

§ 211. Of the mental disease termed Hypochondriasis.

The seat of the well-known mental disease termed Hypochondriasis is to be sought for in a disordered state of the Sensibilities. It is, in fact, nothing more or less than a state of deep depression, gloom, or melancholy.[3] This is the fact; and we never apply the term hypochondriasis to a state of the mind where such gloom or melancholy does not exist; but it is nevertheless true, that the occasion or basis of the fact may sometimes be found in a disordered condition of some other part of the mind. One or two concise statements will illustrate what we mean.

One of the slighter forms of hypochondriasis can, perhaps, be traced to inordinate workings of the Imagination. The mind of the sufferer is fixed upon some unpromising and gloomy subject; probably one which has particular relation either to his present or future

2. A lurid autobiographical account (1821–22) of drug-induced dreams and visions by Thomas De Quincey (1785–1859). First published anonymously, it was misattributed to Samuel Taylor Coleridge (1772–1834); see Poe's satiric treatment of the work in "How to Write a Blackwood Article" (p. 176 herein).

3. Today, hypochondria normally indicates that someone chronically believes that he or she is ill without a physical basis. Its earlier meanings are, as Upham indicates, depression and melancholy along with obsessive self-absorption. An article in vol. 18 of Rees's Cyclopedia for 1819 defines it as "listlessness, or want of resolution and activity," as "lowness of spirits, sadness, and timidity," and attributes it to a "deranged state of bodily health," especially involving the digestive organs. Pollin, commenting on the term morbid sensibility, observes that in Poe's day, "hypochondria was thought to be a male counterpart, often hereditary, of the female 'hysteria' and cognate with 'melancholia' " (Collected Writings of Poe, I.583).

prospects. He gives it an undue place in his thoughts, dwelling upon it continually. His imagination hovers over it, throwing a deeper shade on what is already dark. Thus the mind becomes disordered; it is broken off from its ordinary and rightful mode of action, and is no longer what it was, nor what nature designed it should be.

§ 212. Of other forms of Hypochondriasis.

There is another and still more striking form of hypochondriasis, which is connected in its origin with an alienation of the power of belief. As in all other cases of hypochondriasis, the subject of it suffers much mental distress. He is beset with the most gloomy and distressing apprehensions, occasioned, not by exaggerated and erroneous notions in general, but by some fixed and inevitable false belief.—One imagines that he has no soul; another, that his body is gradually but rapidly perishing; and a third, that he is converted into some other animal, or that he has been transformed into a plant. * * * [T]his last idea once took possession of the mind of one of the princes of Bourbon. So deeply was he infected with this notion, that he often went into his garden, and insisted on being watered in common with the plants around him. Some have imagined themselves to be transformed into glass, and others have fallen into the still stranger folly of imagining themselves dead.—What has been said confirms our remark, that although hypochondriasis is, in itself considered, seated in the sensibilities, yet its origin may sometimes be found in a disordered state of some other part of the mind.

* * *

§ 215. Disordered action of the passion of Fear.

The passion of FEAR, inasmuch as there are various objects around us which are or may be dangerous, is obviously implanted in us for wise purposes. But it not unfrequently exhibits an irregular or disordered action. This disordered state of the affection may discover itself, when considered either in reference to the occasion on which it exists, or in reference to the degree in which it exists. In some cases, for instance, it is connected with objects which, in the view of reason and common sense, ought not to excite it. Some persons are afraid to be alone in the dark; it is exceedingly distressing to them. Others are afraid (so much so, perhaps, as to be thrown into convulsions by their presence) of a mouse, or a squirrel, or an insect.

* * *

§ 216. Other illustrations of the disordered action of this passion.

Again, fear may exist with such an intensity as essentially to affect the very structure of the mind, and even cause insanity in the higher sense of the term. Probably the power of this passion is not well understood. Certain it is, that terrible results have often followed from the attempts of persons, particularly of children, to excite it in others,

even in sport. Many instances are on record of individuals who have been permanently and most seriously injured, either in mind or body, or both, by a sudden fright. * * *

Sometimes, especially when connected with permanent causes, it gradually expands and strengthens itself, till it is changed into DESPAIR. The distinctive trait of Despair, in distinction from all other modifications of fear, is, that it excludes entirely the feeling of hope.

* * *

Popular Fiction: *Blackwood's* and the Sensation Tale

Within the parameters of personal preoccupation and the general taste of the Romantic era, Poe's fiction exhibits surprising variety and experimentation. He tried several different forms of the short story, the sketch, the philosophical dialogue, literary parody, social satire, travel-adventure narrative, landscape narrative, detective fiction, science fiction—and above all the modes and genres of the gothic, the grotesque, and the arabesque. (For a discussion of these matters, see the Tales and Sketches introduction on pp. 77ff. herein.) But of particular significance in assessing Poe's work and his worldview is his deployment of certain kinds and forms of best-selling magazine fiction, especially the formula stories of *Blackwood's Edinburgh Magazine*, founded in 1817–18.

Readers will have to determine for themselves how serious Poe was in his emulation or imitation of the types of sensational fiction that *Blackwood's* made famous. In his early satiric works, Poe was, he said, "hitting right and left" at things in general—for example, fatuous scenes in popular literature, "purple prose," philosophical posturing, and literary politics—and one of his major targets, as the subtitles to a couple of his tales indicate, is *Blackwood's*. The *Blackwood's* specialty was the "sensation tale," in which protagonists get into a predicament (such as getting trapped in an enormous heated copper vat or being buried alive) and then minutely describe and analyze their physical and psychological sensations, all the while moralizing on the human condition and philosophizing on the mysteries of the universe. Poe caricatures the aspiring author-narrators of such tales, satirizes hack writers, and burlesques the various formulaic conventions of the sensation subgenre. He satirizes not only the recurrent absurd situations and incidents but also the overwrought tone, fake learning, philosophical pretension, recondite allusions, overused foreign phrases, and inappropriate figures of speech typical of many of these pieces (elements that some critics have suggested characterize Poe's own style in his serious tales).

Poe's "Loss of Breath" (pp. 89ff. herein), for example, begins with a literalization of the phrase: the narrator actually loses his breath in cursing his wife; and the tale plays out some of the comic consequences. This work and other of Poe's earliest tales may be most fully appreciated when read in conjunction with the selections from *Blackwood's* reprinted in this section and Poe's overt metafictional satires on such fiction, especially "How to Write a Blackwood Article" (pp. 173ff.) and its companion piece "A Predicament." One should also read the Preface to the never published "Tales of the Folio Club" (pp. 595–96). Other tales that the reader will recognize as satiric or parodic are "Lionizing" (pp. 128ff.), "King Pest" (pp. 148ff.), "Never Bet the Devil Your Head" (pp. 286ff.), "The Premature Burial" (pp. 356ff.), and "Some Words with a Mummy" (pp. 382ff.). Other works in a similar vein of adventure, predicament, and sensation

may not be parodic at all. But Michael Allen, in *Poe and the British Magazine Tradition*, posits a complex "Blackwood's pattern" in which writers like Poe and his British contemporaries addressed a "dual audience" simultaneously. One audience was composed of the mass of ordinary readers who saw only the surface horror-adventure gothic elements; the other audience was composed of the intellectual cognoscenti, the literary ingroup who could see the additional layers of parody and irony. (Think of movie-goers today.) Whether works like "Metzengerstein" and "The Assignation"—or, more distantly, "Ligeia" and "The Fall of the House of User" or "The Pit and the Pendulum"—are satiric or ironic is a matter of critical debate. The selections from *Blackwood's* should contribute to that debate.

The three stories reprinted here follow the original texts in *Blackwood's*. The author of "Extracts from Gosschen's Diary" (1818) is anonymous, as is the author of "The Buried Alive" (1821). The first exemplifies the confessional narrative in which a man recounts his murder of a woman as obsessive love object—a subject supposed by some biographical critics to be a wish-fulfillment fantasy of Poe's. The second exemplifies the premature burial theme that is also supposed by some critics to be a psychological obsession of Poe's. Both tales are typical of dozens of such stories in the best-selling magazines of the time. The third story, "The Man in the Bell" (1821), mentioned by Poe in "How to Write a Blackwood Article," exemplifies the predicament narrative in which the protagonists minutely analyze or record their sensations. The author, William Maginn (1793–1842), is the best-remembered of the magazine writers specializing in such fiction; several of his stories appeared in *Blackwood's*; and in 1830, he established *Fraser's Magazine*, which, though publishing a good deal of formula fiction and other highly conventional works, became a major influence on the British periodical scene.

ANONYMOUS

Extracts from Gosschen's Diary

[The following striking narrative is translated from the MS. Memoirs of the late Rev. Dr. Gottlieb Michael Gosschen, a Catholic clergyman of great eminence in the city of Ratisbonne. It was the custom of this divine to preserve, in the shape of a diary, a regular account of all the interesting particulars which fell in his way, during the exercise of his sacred profession. Two thick small quartos, filled with these strange materials, have been put into our hands by the kindness of Count Frederick von Lindenbäumenberg, to whom the worthy father bequeathed them. Many a dark story, well fitted to be the groundwork of a romance,—many a tale of guilty love and repentance,—many a fearful monument of remorse and horror, might we extract from this record of dungeons and confessionals. We shall from time to time do so, but sparingly, and what is still more necessary, with selection.]

EDITOR.[1]

1. The introductory "editorial" frame was a popular device in presenting a fiction as possibly "real" in order to intensify the effect of the odd or bizarre or of madness; these included pretended extracts from letters, journals, diaries, medical records, official reports, newspapers,

Never had a murder so agitated the inhabitants of this city as that of Maria von Richterstein. No heart could be pacified till the murderer was condemned. But no sooner was his doom sealed, and the day fixed for his execution, than a great change took place in the public feeling. The evidence, though conclusive, had been wholly circumstantial. And people who, before his condemnation, were as assured of the murderer's guilt as if they had seen him with red hands, began now to conjure up the most contradictory and absurd reasons for believing in the possibility of his innocence. His own dark and sullen silence seemed to some, an indignant expression of that innocence which he was too proud to avow;—some thought they saw in his imperturbable demeanour, a resolution to court death; because his life was miserable, and his reputation blasted,—and others, the most numerous, without reason or reflection, felt such sympathy with the criminal, as almost amounted to a negation of his crime. The man under sentence of death was, in all the beauty of youth, distinguished above his fellows for graceful accomplishments, and the last of a noble family. He had lain a month in his dungeon, heavily laden with irons. Only the first week he had been visited by several religionists, but he then fiercely ordered the jailor to admit no more "men of God,"—and till the eve of his execution, he had lain in dark solitude, abandoned to his own soul.

It was near midnight when a message was sent to me by a magistrate, that the murderer was desirous of seeing me. I had been with many men in his unhappy situation, and in no case had I failed to calm the agonies of grief, and the fears of the world to come. But I had known this youth—had sat with him at his father's table—I knew also that there was in him a strange and fearful mixture of good and evil—I was aware that there were circumstances in the history of his progenitors not generally known—nay, in his own life—that made him an object of awful commiseration—and I went to his cell with an agitating sense of the enormity of his guilt, but a still more agitating one of the depth of his misery, and the wildness of his misfortunes.

I entered his cell, and the phantom struck me with terror. He stood erect in his irons, like a corpse that had risen from the grave. His face, once so beautiful, was pale as a shroud, and drawn into ghastly wrinkles. His black-matted hair hung over it with a terrible expression of wrathful and savage misery. And his large eyes, which were once black, glared with a light in which all colour was lost, and seemed to fill the whole dungeon with their flashing. I saw his guilt—I saw what was more terrible than his guilt—his insanity—not in emaciation only— not in that more than death-like whiteness of his face—but in *all* that stood before me—*the figure*, round which was gathered the agonies of so many long days and nights of remorse and phrenzy—and of a despair that had no fears of this world or its terrors, but that was plunged in the abyss of eternity.

For a while the figure said nothing. He then waved his arm, that

and so forth—the more exotic (foreign) and faraway the better. Most of the German names in this piece are made up.

made his irons clank, motioning me to sit down on the iron frame-
work of his bed; and when I did so, the murderer took his place by my
side.

A lamp burned on a table before us—and on that table there had
been drawn by the maniac—for I must indeed so call him—a decapi-
tated human body—the neck as if streaming with gore—and the face
writhed into horrible convulsions, but bearing a resemblance not to be
mistaken to that of him who had traced the horrid picture. He saw
that my eyes rested on this fearful mockery—and, with a recklessness
fighting with despair, he burst out into a broken peal of laughter, and
said, "To-morrow will you see that picture drawn in blood!"

He then grasped me violently by the arm, and told me to listen to
his confession,—and then to say what I thought of God and his eter-
nal Providence.

"I have been assailed by idiots, fools, and drivellers, who could un-
derstand nothing of me nor of my crime,—men who came not here
that I might confess before God, but reveal myself to them,—and I
drove the tamperers with misery and guilt out of a cell sacred to in-
sanity. But my hands have played in infancy, long before I was a mur-
derer, with thy gray hairs, and now, even that I am a murderer, I can
still touch them with love and with reverence. Therefore my lips, shut
to all beside, shall be opened unto thee.

"I murdered her. Who else loved her so well as to shed her innocent
blood? It was I that enjoyed her beauty—a beauty surpassing that of
the daughters of men,—it was I that filled her soul with bliss, and with
trouble,—it was I alone that was privileged to take her life. I brought
her into sin—I kept her in sin—and when she would have left her sin,
it was fitting that I, to whom her heart, her body, and her soul be-
longed, should suffer no divorcement of them from my bosom, as long
as there was blood in hers—and when I saw that the poor infatuated
wretch was resolved—I slew her;—yes, with this blessed hand I
stabbed her to the heart.

"Do you think there was no pleasure in murdering her? I grasped
her by that radiant, that golden hair,—I bared those snow-white
breasts,—I dragged her sweet body towards me, and, as God is my wit-
ness, I stabbed, and stabbed her with this very dagger, ten, twenty,
forty times, through and through her heart. She never so much as gave
one shriek, for she was dead in a moment,—but she would not have
shrieked had she endured pang after pang, for she saw my face of
wrath turned upon her,—she knew that my wrath was just, and that I
did right to murder her who would have forsaken her lover in his in-
sanity.

"I laid her down upon a bank of flowers,—that were soon stained
with her blood. I saw the dim blue eyes beneath the half-closed lids,—
that face so changeful in its living beauty was now fixed as ice, and the
balmy breath came from her sweet lips no more. My joy, my happi-
ness, was perfect. I took her into my arms—madly as I did on that
night when first I robbed her of what fools called her innocence—but
her innocence has gone with her to heaven—and there I lay with her

bleeding breasts prest to my heart, and many were the thousand kisses that I gave those breasts, cold and bloody as they were, which I had many million times kissed in all the warmth of their loving loveliness, and which none were ever to kiss again but the husband who had murdered her.

"I looked up to the sky. There shone the moon and all her stars. Tranquility, order, harmony, and peace, glittered throughout the whole universe of God. 'Look up, Maria, your favourite star has arisen.' I gazed upon her, and death had begun to change her into something that was most terrible. Her features were hardened and sharp,—her body stiff as a lump of frozen clay,—her fingers rigid and clenched,— and the blood that was once so beautiful in her thin blue veins was now hideously coagulated all over her corpse. I gazed on her one moment longer, and, all at once, I recollected that we were a family of madmen. Did not my father perish by his own hand? Blood had before been shed in our house. Did not that warrior ancestor of ours die raving in chains? Were not those eyes of mine always unlike those of other men? Wilder—at times fiercer—and oh! father, saw you never there a melancholy, too woful for mortal man, a look sent up from the darkness of a soul that God never visited in his mercy?

"I knelt down beside my dead wife. But I knelt not down to pray. No: I cried unto God, if God there be—"Thou madest me a madman! Thou madest me a murderer! Thou foredoomedst me to sin and to hell! Thou, thou, the gracious God whom we mortals worship. There is the sacrifice! I have done thy will,—I have slain the most blissful of all thy creatures;—am I a holy and commissioned priest, or am I an accursed and infidel murderer?"

"Father,[2] you start at such words! You are not familiar with a madman's thoughts. Did I make this blood to boil so? Did I form this brain? Did I put that poison into my veins which flowed a hundred years since in the heart of that lunatic, my heroic ancestor? Had I not my being imposed, forced upon me, with all its red-rolling sea of dreams; and will you, a right holy and pious man, curse me because my soul was carried away by them as a ship is driven through the raging darkness of a storm? A thousand times, even when she lay in resigned love in my bosom, something whispered to me, 'Murder her!' It may have been the voice of Satan—it may have been the voice of God. For who can tell the voice of heaven from that of hell? Look on this blood-crusted dagger—look on the hand that drove it to her heart, and then dare to judge of me and of my crimes, or comprehend God and all his terrible decrees!

"Look not away from me. Was I not once confined in a madhouse? Are these the first chains I ever wore? No. I remember things of old, that others may think I have forgotten. Dreams will disappear for a long, long time, but they will return again. It may have been some one like me that I once saw sitting chained, in his black melancholy, in a

2. The narrator-visitor to the murderer's cell is a priestly confessor, a typical situation for a number of these narratives; cf. Poe's "The Cask of Amontillado" (pp. 415ff. herein).

madhouse. I may have been only a stranger passing through that wild world. I know not. The sound of chains brings with it a crowd of thoughts, that come rushing upon me from a dark and far-off world. But if it indeed be true, that in my boyhood I was not as other happy boys, and that even then the clouds of God's wrath hung around me,—that God may not suffer my soul everlastingly to perish.

"I started up. I covered the dead body with bloody leaves, and tufts of grass, and flowers. I washed my hands from blood—I went to bed—I slept—yes. I slept—for there is no hell like the hell of sleep, and into that hell God delivered me. I did not give myself up to judgment. I wished to walk about with the secret curse of the murder in my soul. What could men do to me so cruel as to let me live? How could God curse me more in black and fiery hell than on this green and flowery earth? And what right had such men as those dull heavy-eyed burghers to sit in judgment upon me, in whose face they were afraid to look for a moment, lest one gleam of it should frighten them into idiocy? What right have they, who are not as I am, to load me with their chains, or to let their villain executioner spill my blood? If I deserve punishment—it must rise up in a blacker cloud under the hand of God in my soul.

"I will not kneel—a madman has no need of sacraments. I do not wish the forgiveness nor the mercy of God. All that I wish is the forgiveness of her I slew; and well I know that death cannot so change the heart that once had life, as to obliterate from THINE the merciful love of me! Spirits may in heaven have beautiful bosoms no more; but thou, who art a spirit; wilt save him from eternal perdition, whom thou now knowest God created subject to a terrible disease. If there be mercy in heaven, it must be with thee. Thy path thither lay through blood: so will mine. Father! thinkst thou that we shall meet in heaven. Lay us at least in one grave on earth."

In a moment he was dead at my feet. The stroke of the dagger was like lightning, and—[3]

ANONYMOUS

The Buried Alive

I had been for some time ill of a low and lingering fever. My strength gradually wasted, but the sense of life seemed to become more and more acute as my corporeal powers became weaker. I could see by the looks of the doctor that he despaired of my recovery; and the soft and whispering sorrow of my friends, taught me that I had nothing to hope.

One day towards the evening, the crisis took place.—I was seized with a strange and indescribable quivering,—a rushing sound was in my ears—, I saw around my couch innumerable strange faces; they

3. The abrupt ending (purporting to be the actual breaking off of the narrative at an emotional high point in real life) was a standard device of many of these narratives.

were bright and visionary, without bodies. There was light, and solemnity, and I tried to move, but could not.—For a short time a terrible confusion overwhelmed me,—and when it passed off, all my recollection returned with the most perfect distinctness, but the power of motion had departed.—I heard the sound of weeping at my pillow—and the voice of the nurse say, "He is dead."—I cannot describe what I felt at these words—I exerted my utmost power of volition to stir myself, but I could not move even an eyelid. After a short pause my friend drew near; and sobbing, and convulsed with grief, drew his hand over my face, and closed my eyes. The world was then darkened, but I could still hear, and feel, and suffer.

When my eyes were closed, I heard by the attendants that my friend had left the room, and I soon after found, the undertakers were preparing to habit me in the garments of the grave. Their thoughtlessness was more awful than the grief of my friends. They laughed at one another as they turned me from side to side, and treated what they believed a corpse, with the most appalling ribaldry.

When they had laid me out, these wretches retired, and the degrading formality of affected mourning commenced. For three days, a number of friends called to see me.—I heard them, in low accents, speak of what I was; and more than one touched me with his finger. On the third day, some of them talked of the smell of corruption in the room.

The coffin was procured—I was lifted and laid in—My friend placed my head on what was deemed its [last] pillow, and I felt his tears drop on my face.

When all who had any peculiar interest in me, had for a short time looked at me in the coffin, I heard them retire; and the undertaker's men placed the lid on the coffin, and screwed it down. There were two of them present—one had occasion to go away before the task was done. I heard the fellow who was left begin to whistle as he turned the screw-nails; but he checked himself, and completed his work in silence.

I was the[n] left alone,—every one shunned the room.—I knew, however, that I was not yet buried; and though darkened and motionless, I had still hope:—but this was not permitted long. The day of internment arrived—I felt the coffin lifted and borne away—I heard and felt it placed in the hearse.—There was a crowd of people around; some of them spoke sorrowfully of me. The hearse began to move—I knew that it carried me to the grave. It halted, and the coffin was taken out—I felt myself carried on the shoulders of men, by the inequality of the motion—A pause ensued—I heard the cords of the coffin moved—I felt it swing as dependent by them—It was lowered, and rested on the bottom of the grave—The cords were dropped upon the lid—I heard them fall.—Dreadful was the effort I then made to exert the power of action, but my whole frame was immoveable.

Soon after, a few handfuls of earth were thrown upon the coffin—Then there was another pause—after which the shovel was employed,

and the sound of the rattling mould, as it covered me, was far more tremendous than thunder. But I could make no effort. The sound gradually became less and less, and by a surging revolution in the coffin, I knew that the grave was filled up, and that the sexton was treading in the earth, slapping the grave with the flat of his spade. This too ceased, and then all was silent.

I had no means of knowing the lapse of time; and the silence continued. This is death, thought I, and I am deemed to remain in the earth till the resurrection. Presently the body will fall into corruption, and the epicurean worm, that is only satisfied with the flesh of man, will come to partake of the banquet that has been portrayed for him with so much solicitude and care. In the contemplation of this hideous thought, I heard a low and under-sound in the earth over me, and I fancied that the worms and the reptiles of death were coming— that the mole and the rat of the grave would soon be upon me. The sound continued to grow louder and nearer. Can it be possible, I thought, that my friends suspect they have buried me too soon? The hope was truly like light bursting through the gloom of death.

The sound ceased, and presently I felt the hands of some dreadful being working about my throat. They dragged me out of the coffin by the head, I felt again the living air, but it was piercingly cold; and I was carried swiftly away—I thought to judgment, perhaps perdition.

When borne to some distance, I was the thrown like a clod—it was not upon the ground. A moment after I found myself on a carriage; and, by the interchange of two or three brief sentences, I discovered that I was in the hands of two of those robbers who live by plundering the grave, and selling the bodies of parents, and children, and friends. One of the men sung snatches and scraps of obscene songs, as the cart rattled over the pavement of the streets.

When it halted, I was lifted out, and I soon perceived, by the closeness of the air, and the change of temperature, that I was carried into a room; and, being rudely stripped of my shroud, was placed naked on a table. By the conversation of the two fellows with the servant who admitted them, I learnt that I was that night to be dissected.

My eyes were still shut, I saw nothing; but in a short time I heard, by the bustle in the room, that the students of anatomy were assembling. Some of them came round the table and examined me minutely. They were pleased to find that so good a subject had been procured. The demonstrator himself at last came in.

Previous to the beginning of the dissection, he proposed to try on me some galvanic experiment—and an apparatus[1] was arranged for that purpose. The first shock vibrated through all my nerves; they rung and jangled like the strings of a harp. The students expressed their admiration at the convulsive effect. The second shock threw my eyes open, and the first person I saw was the doctor who had attended me.

1. A chemical battery; see notes to Poe's "Loss of Breath" (pp. 89ff. herein) and "Some Words with a Mummy" (p. 382ff. herein).

But still I was as dead: I could, however, discover among the students the faces of many with whom I was familiar; and when my eyes were opened, I heard my name pronounced by several of the students, with an accent of awe and compassion, and a wish that it had been some other subject.

When they had satisfied themselves with the galvanic phenomena, the demonstrator took the knife, and pierced on the bosom with the point. I felt a dreadful crackling, as it were, throughout my whole frame—a convulsive shuddering instantly followed, and a shriek of horror rose from all present. The ice of death was broken up—my trance ended. The utmost exertions were made to restore me, and in the course of an hour I was in the full possession of all my faculties.

WILLIAM MAGINN

The Man in the Bell

In my younger days, bell-ringing was much more in fashion among the young men of ———, than it is now. Nobody, I believe, practises it there at present except the servants of the church, and the melody has been much injured in consequence. Some fifty years ago, about twenty of us who dwelt in the vicinity of the Cathedral, formed a club, which used to ring every peal that was called for; and, from continual practice and a rivalry which arose between us and a club attached to another steeple, and which tended considerably to sharpen our zeal, we became very Mozarts on our favourite instruments. But my bell-ringing practice was shortened by a singular accident, which not only stopt my performance, but made even the sound of a bell terrible to my ears.

One Sunday, I went with another into the belfry to ring for noon prayers, but the second stroke we had pulled shewed us that the clapper of the bell we were at was muffled. Some one had been buried that morning, and it had been prepared, of course, to ring a mournful note. We did not know of this, but the remedy was easy. "Jack," said my companion, "step up to the loft, and cut off the hat"; for the way we had of muffling was by tying a piece of an old hat, or of cloth (the former was preferred) to one side of the clapper, which deadened every second toll. I complied, and mounting into the belfry, crept as usual into the bell, where I began to cut away. The hat had been tied on in some more complicated manner than usual, and I was perhaps three or four minutes in getting it off; during which time my companion below was hastily called away, by a message from his sweetheart I believe, but that is not material to my story. The person who called him was a brother of the club, who, knowing that the time had come for ringing for service, and not thinking that any one was above, began to pull. At this moment I was just getting out, when I felt the bell moving; I guessed the reason at once—it was a moment of terror; but by a

hasty, and almost convulsive effort, I succeeded in jumping down, and throwing myself on the flat of my back under the bell.

The room in which it was, was little more than sufficient to contain it, the bottom of the bell coming within a couple of feet of the floor of lath. At that time I certainly was not so bulky as I am now, but as I lay it was within an inch of my face. I had not laid myself down a second, when the ringing began.—It was a dreadful situation. Over me swung an immense mass of metal, one touch of which would have crushed me to pieces; the floor under me was principally composed of crazy laths, and if they gave way, I was precipitated to the distance of about fifty feet upon a loft, which would, in all probability, have sunk under the impulse of my fall, and sent me to be dashed to atoms upon the marble floor of the chancel, an hundred feet below. I remembered—for fear is quick in recollection—how a common clock-wright, about a month before, had fallen, and bursting through the floors of the steeple, driven in the ceilings of the porch, and even broken into the marble tombstone of a bishop who slept beneath. This was my first terror, but the ringing had not continued a minute, before a more awful and immediate dread came on me. The deafening sound of the bell smote into my ears with a thunder which made me fear their drums would crack.—There was not a fibre of my body it did not thrill through: it entered my very soul; thought and reflection were almost utterly banished; I only retained the sensation of agonizing terror. Every moment I saw the bell sweep within an inch of my face; and my eyes—I could not close them, though to look at the object was bitter as death—followed it instinctively in its oscillating progress until it came back again. It was in vain I said to myself that it could come no nearer at any future swing than it did at first; every time it descended, I endeavoured to shrink into the very floor to avoid being buried under the down-sweeping mass; and then reflecting on the danger of pressing too weightily on my frail support, would cower up again as far as I dared.

At first my fears were mere matter of fact. I was afraid the pulleys above would give way, and let the bell plunge on me. At another time, the possibility of the clapper being shot out in some sweep, and dashing through my body, as I had seen a ramrod glide through a door, flitted across my mind. The dread also, as I have already mentioned, of the crazy floor, tormented me, but these soon gave way to fears not more unfounded, but more visionary, and of course more tremendous. The roaring of the bell confused my intellect, and my fancy soon began to teem with all sort of strange and terrifying ideas. The bell pealing above, and opening its jaws with a hideous clamour, seemed to me at one time a ravening monster, raging to devour me; at another, a whirlpool ready to suck me into its bellowing abyss. As I gazed on it, it assumed all shapes; it was a flying eagle, or rather a roc of the Arabian story-tellers, clapping its wings and screaming over me. As I looked upward into it, it would appear sometimes to lengthen into indefinite extent, or to be twisted at the end into the spiral folds of the tail of a flying-dragon. Nor was the flaming breath, or fiery glance of that

fabled animal, wanting to complete the picture. My eyes inflamed, bloodshot, and glaring, invested the supposed monster with a full proportion of unholy light.

It would be endless were I to merely hint at all the fancies that possessed my mind. Every object that was hideous and roaring presented itself to my imagination. I often thought that I was in a hurricane at sea, and that the vessel in which I was embarked tossed under me with the most furious vehemence. The air, set in motion by the swinging of the bell, blew over me, nearly with the violence, and more than the thunder of a tempest; and the floor seemed to reel under me, as under a drunken man. But the most awful of all the ideas that seized on me were drawn from the supernatural. In the vast cavern of the bell hideous faces appeared, and glared down on me with terrifying frowns, or with grinning mockery, still more appalling. At last, the devil himself, accoutred, as in the common description of the evil spirit, with hoof, horn, and tail, and eyes of infernal lustre, made his appearance, and called on me to curse God and worship him, who was powerful to save me. This dread suggestion he uttered with the fulltoned clangour of the bell. I had him within an inch of me, and I thought on the fate of the Santon Barsisa.[1] Strenuously and desperately I defied him, and bade him be gone. Reason, then, for a moment, resumed her sway, but it was only to fill me with fresh terror, just as the lightning dispels the gloom that surrounds the benighted mariner, but to shew him that his vessel is driving on a rock, where she must inevitably be dashed to pieces. I found I was becoming delirious, and trembled lest reason should utterly desert me. This is at all times an agonizing thought, but it smote me then with tenfold agony. I feared lest, when utterly deprived of my senses, I should rise, to do which I was every moment tempted by that strange feeling which calls on a man, whose head is dizzy from standing on the battlement of a lofty castle, to precipitate himself from it, and then death would be instant and tremendous. When I thought of this, I became desperate. I caught the floor with a grasp which drove the blood from my nails; and I yelled with the cry of despair. I called for help, I prayed, I shouted, but all the efforts of my voice were, of course, drowned in the bell. As it passed over my mouth, it occasionally echoed my cries, which mixed not with its own sound, but preserved their distinct character. Perhaps this was but fancy. To me, I know, they then sounded as if they were the shouting, howling, or laughing of the fiends with which my imagination had peopled the gloomy cave which swung over me.

You may accuse me of exaggerating my feelings; but I am not. Many a scene of dread have I since passed through, but they are nothing to the self-inflicted terrors of this half hour. The ancients have doomed one of the damned, in their Tartarus,[2] to lie under a rock, which every

1. A reference to the Islamic ascetic Barsisa, who, according to legend, gave in to the temptations of Satan and proceeded to seduce and kill one woman after another; after his compact with the devil he was continuously barraged with words from the Koran in mockery of his former faith.
2. The deepest, darkest hole of Hell in Greek myth, as far below Hades as the abode of the gods was above the earth.

moment seems to be descending to annihilate him,—and an awful punishment it would be. But if to this you add a clamour as loud as if ten thousand furies were howling about you—a deafening uproar banishing reason, and driving you to madness, you must allow that the bitterness of the pang was rendered more terrible. There is no man, firm as his nerves may be, who could retain his courage in this situation.

In twenty minutes the ringing was done. Half of that time passed over me without power of computation,—the other half appeared an age. When it ceased, I became gradually more quiet, but a new fear retained me. I knew that five minutes would pass without ringing, but, at the end of that short time, the bell would be rung a second time, for five minutes more. I could not calculate time. A minute and an hour were of equal duration. I feared to rise, lest the five minutes should have elapsed, and the ringing be again commenced, in which case I should be crushed, before I could escape, against the walls or framework of the bell. I therefore still continued to lie down, cautiously shifting myself, however, with a careful gliding, so that my eye no longer looked into the hollow. This was of itself a considerable relief. The cessation of the noise had, in a great measure, the effect of stupefying me, for my attention, being no longer occupied by the chimeras[3] I had conjured up, began to flag. All that now distressed me was the constant expectation of the second ringing, for which, however, I settled myself with a kind of stupid resolution. I closed my eyes, and clenched my teeth as firmly as if they were screwed in a vice. At last the dreaded moment came, and the first swing of the bell extorted a groan from me, as they say the most resolute victim screams at the sight of the rack, to which he is for a second time destined. After this, however, I lay silent and lethargic, without a thought. Wrapt in the defensive armour of stupidity, I defied the bell and its intonations. When it ceased, I was roused a little by the hope of escape. I did not, however, decide on this step hastily, but, putting up my hand with the utmost caution, I touched the rim. Though the ringing had ceased, it still was tremulous from the sound, and shook under my hand, which instantly recoiled as from an electric jar.[4] A quarter of an hour probably elapsed before I again dared to make the experiment, and then I found it at rest. I determined to lose no time, fearing that I might have lain then already too long, and that the bell for evening service would catch me. This dread stimulated me, and I slipped out with the utmost rapidity, and arose. I stood, I suppose, for a minute, looking with silly wonder on the place of my imprisonment, penetrated with joy at escaping, but then rushed down the stony and irregular stair with the velocity of lightning, and arrived in the bell-ringer's room. This was the last act I had power to accomplish. I leant against the wall, motionless and deprived of thought, in which posture my companions found me, when, in the course of a couple of hours, they returned to their occupation.

3. Illusions; in myth a fantastic creature of the imagination.
4. Chemical battery.

They were shocked, as well they might, at the figure before them. The wind of the bell had excoriated my face, and my dim and stupefied eyes were fixed with a lack-lustre gaze in my raw eye-lids. My hands were torn and bleeding; my hair dishevelled; and my clothes tattered. They spoke to me, but I gave no answer. They shook me, but I remained insensible. They then became alarmed, and hastened to remove me. He who had first gone up with me in the forenoon, met them as they carried me through the church-yard, and through him, who was shocked at having, in some measure, occasioned the accident, the cause of my misfortune was discovered. I was put to bed at home, and remained for three days delirious, but gradually recovered my senses. You may be sure the bell formed a prominent topic of my ravings, and if I heard a peal, they were instantly increased to the utmost violence. Even when the delirium abated, my sleep was continually disturbed by imagined ringings, and my dreams were haunted by the fancies which almost maddened me while in the steeple. My friends removed me to a house in the country, which was sufficiently distant from any place of worship, to save me from the apprehensions of hearing the church-going bell; for what Alexander Selkirk, in Cowper's[5] poem, complained of as a misfortune, was then to me as a blessing. Here I recovered; but, even long after recovery, if a gale wafted the notes of a peal towards me, I started with nervous apprehension. I felt a Mahometan hatred to all the bell tribe, and envied the subjects of the Commander of the Faithful the sonorous voice of their Muezzin.[6] Time cured this, as it does the most of our follies; but, even at the present day, if, by chance, my nerves be unstrung, some particular tones of the Cathedral bell have power to surprise me into a momentary start.

5. William Cowper (1731–1800) wrote a celebrated poem, "The Castaway" (1803), based on the incident described in *A Voyage Round the World* (1748) by the explorer George Anson (1697–1762). Alexander Selkirk (1676–1721) was a Scots sailor marooned in the San Fernández Islands, where he lived essentially alone on the island of Más Atierra; finally rescued by a British vessel after four years and four months, he became the inspiration for Daniel Defoe's novel, *Robinson Crusoe* (1719).
6. Islamic crier who calls the faithful to prayers five times a day from atop a minaret.

The South and Slavery

Recent Poe criticism has been almost obsessed with finding racist or racialist issues in his writings, often charging previous critics with sweeping Poe's racism under the carpet in an effort to "de-historicize" him (the presumption being that critics who do not focus on racism in some way have a conservative political agenda or suffer from a "modernist elitism" that eschews social and political issues). Readers should consider what *historical context* means—is it only politics and socioeconomic matters or does it include ethical systems, morals, religion, and the like? What about philosophy, aesthetics, and literary traditions? Ultimately, readers will decide for themselves how cogent the arguments about historicizing, de-historicizing, re-historicizing Poe are. In this section, a few basic historical documents and findings relevant to such cultural-political issues as provincial regionalism and racism in Poe are reprinted. Critical interpretations focusing on (but not confined to) the *Narrative of Arthur Gordon Pym*, the main test case for Poe's racism, will be found later in this volume.

Of particular importance is the debate on the disputed authorship of the "Paulding-Drayton" review, an article in the *Southern Literary Messenger* for April 1836 defending two books on the "peculiar institution" of slavery in the American South. Some critics have assumed, and others vigorously argued, that Poe was the author. Others have pointed out that a letter from Poe to Nathaniel Beverley Tucker (May 2, 1836) indicates that Tucker was the author, not Poe. At one time the claims that Poe was *not* the author seemed shrill; later the reverse seemed true, especially after the publication of J. V. Ridgely's 1992 review of the known facts.

Reprinted here are the review in the 1836 *Messenger*, Poe's 1836 letter to Tucker, and Ridgely's assessment. In addition, an excerpt is reprinted from a letter to Joseph Evans Snodgrass (June 17, 1840), indicating that Poe had written a lengthy review of John L. Carey's book *Domestic Slavery* (1838) but that the review had not been published because of a quarrel with William Burton after Poe left Burton's *Gentleman's Magazine*. Modern racialist critics take this claim as further evidence of Poe's racism, but the claim rests on a presumption that the review would have been positive. Other critics are doubtful about whether the review was ever actually written (see, e.g., Terence Whalen, pp. 934–35 herein) and what this possibility implies.

Readers interested in the issues of Southern regionalism and racism in Poe will want to look at an unsigned review of Longfellow's poetry in the *Aristidean* for April 1845 (pp. 652ff. herein). In this review (long presumed to have been co-authored by Poe and Thomas Dunn English), Longfellow's *Poems on Slavery* is criticized for its misrepresentations of the South and the slavery issue. Also pertinent is Poe's March 1849 review of James R. Lowell's *A Fable for Critics* (pp. 693ff.). For further discussion, see the essays by John Carlos Rowe (pp. 904ff.) and Terence Whalen (pp. 920ff.).

In order to give readers a regionalist overview of some of the cultural issues felt by the South, this section begins with a representative essay

calling for a "Southern Literature" by one of the editors of the *Southern Literary Messenger*.

JAMES E. HEATH

James Ewell Heath (1792–1862) of Richmond Virginia edited the first seven numbers of the *Southern Literary Messenger* (August 1834–March 1835), which was founded and owned by Thomas Willis White (1788–1843). Not having the educational background of the usual literary editor, White sought the assistance of Southern writers like Heath and Edward Vernon Sparhawk (1798–1838), who edited four issues (April–May 1835). In August 1835, Poe became the de facto editor of the *Messenger*, working (and chafing) under White's proprietorship; the relationship between Poe and White steadily worsened until on January 3, 1837, White fired him. Heath once again helped out at the *Messenger*, again under the strict proprietorship of White. The editorial reprinted here is typical of the Old South in the 1830s; it appeared in the first issue of the *Messenger* (August 1834).

Southern Literature

It is understood that the first number of the "Messenger," will be sent forth by its Publisher, as a kind of pioneer, to spy out the land of literary promise, and to report whether the same be fruitful or barren, before he resolves upon future action. It would be a mortifying discovery, if instead of kindness and good will, he should be repulsed by the coldness and neglect of a Virginia public. Hundreds of similar publications thrive and prosper north of the Potomac, sustained as they are by the liberal hand of patronage. *Shall not one be supported in the whole south?* This is a question of great importance;—and one which ought to be answered with sober earnestness by all who set any value upon public character, or who are in the least degree jealous of that individual honor and dignity which is in some measure connected with the honor and dignity of the state. Are we to be doomed forever to a kind of vassalage to our northern neighbors—a dependance for our literary food upon our brethren, whose superiority in all the great points of character,—in valor—eloquence and patriotism, we are no wise disposed to admit? Is it not altogether extraordinary that in this extensive commonwealth, containing a white population of upwards of six hundred thousand souls—a vast deal of agricultural wealth, and innumerable persons of both sexes, who enjoy both leisure and affluence—there is not one solitary periodical exclusively literary? What is the cause? We are not willing to borrow our political,—religious, or even our agricultural notions from the other side of Mason and Dixon's line, and we generously patronize various domestic journals devoted to those several subjects. Why should we consider the worthy descendants of the pilgrims—of the Hollanders of Manhattan, or the German adventurers of Pennsylvania, as exclusively entitled to cater for us in our choicest intellectual aliment? Shall it be said that the empire of literature has no

geographical boundaries, and that local jealousies ought not to disturb its harmony? To this there is an obvious answer. If we continue to be *consumers* of northern productions, we shall never ourselves become *producers*. We may take from them the fabrics of their looms, and give in exchange without loss our agricultural products—but if we depend exclusively upon their *literary* supplies, it is certain that the spirit of invention among our own sons, will be damped, if not entirely extinguished. The value of a *domestic* publication of the kind, consists in its being at once accessible to all who choose to venture into the arena as rivals for renown. It imparts the same energy, and exercises the same influence upon mental improvement, that a rail road does upon agricultural labor, when passing by our doors and through our estates. The literary spirit which pervades some portions of New England and the northern cities, would never have existed, at least in the same degree, if the journals and repositories designed to cherish and promote it, had been derived exclusively from London and Edinburgh. In like manner, if we look entirely to Boston, New York or Philadelphia, for that delightful mental enjoyment and recreation, which such publications afford, we must con-tent ourselves with being the readers and admirers of other men's thoughts, and lose all opportunity of stirring up our own minds, and breathing forth our own meditations. In other words, we must be satisfied to partake of the feast, as it is set before us by our more industrious and enterprising countrymen, and if peradventure, the cookery should not be altogether to our taste, we must, nevertheless, with our characteristic courtesy, be thankful,—and like honest Sancho, "bid God bless the giver."

It is not intended to be intimated that the aristarchy [*sic*] of the north and east, cherish any unkind feelings towards the literary claims of the south. Oh no! In truth, they have no cause whatsoever, either for unkindness or jealousy. If we only continue to patronize their multitudinous magazines, they will pocket our money and praise us as a very generous and chivalrous race; or if, perchance, some juvenile drama, or poem, or some graver duodecimo of southern manufacture, should find its way to the seats of learning and criticism beyond the Susquehanna, it is an even chance, that in order to preserve the monopoly of the southern market, they will dole out to us a modicum of praise, and render some faint tribute to rising merit. Without therefore intending any thing invidious, or without cherishing any unkind or unmanly sentiment towards our political confederates, we ought forthwith to buckle on our armour, and assert our mental independence. All their own lofty and generous spirits will approve the resolution, and be among the first to welcome the dawn of a brighter era in a region of comparative twilight. Their Irvings and Pauldings, their Everetts and Neals, their Coopers and Verplancks, their Kennedys and Flints, their Hallecks and Bryants, their Sedgewicks and Sigourneys,[1]

1. A list of contemporary American literary luminaries—all Northern (with the partial exception of the Baltimore novelist J. P. Kennedy, who sometimes wrote of Virginia plantation life). Washington Irving (1783–1859), New York humorist and satirist, short-story writer, essayist, historian, and biographer, was perhaps the most famous American author of the time,

will rejoice in the emancipation of the south, from the shackles which either indolence, indifference, or the love of pleasure, have imposed upon us. We are too old, and ought to be too proud to lag behind even some of our younger sisters, in the cultivation of one of the most attractive departments of human knowledge. It is folly to boast of political ascendancy, of moral influence, of professions eminence, or unrivalled oratory, when, in all the Corinthian[2] graces which adorn the structure of mind, we are lamentably deficient. It is worse than folly to talk of this "ancient and unterrified commonwealth"—if we suffer ourselves to be *terrified* at the idea of supporting one poor periodical, devoted to letters and mental improvement. It would be an indelible reproach to us, that whilst we waste so many thousands annually in luxury—whilst we squander our means in expensive tours of recreation and pleasure,—and even impoverish our resources in indulgences too gross to be mentioned—we should be unwilling to contribute a single mite towards building up a character of our own, and providing the means of imbodying and concentrating the neglected genius of our country. Let the hundreds of our gifted sons, therefore, who have talents and acquirements, come forth to this work of patriotism, with a firm resolution to persevere until victory is achieved. Let them dismiss their apprehensions,—that because as yet they are unpractised in composition—and the highway to literary eminence is already thronged with competitors—that, therefore, the most vigorous effort will be vanquished in the contest. In the race

having scored international successes with "Diedrich Knickerbocker's" *History of New York* (1809) and the *Sketch-Book* of "Geoffrey Crayon" (1818–20). James Kirke Paulding (1778–1860), New York novelist, dramatist, and historian, collaborated with Irving on a satiric series of sketches, *Salmagundi* (1807–08); among his novels are *Konigsmarke* (1823) and the *Dutchman's Fireside* (1831). The reference to Everett is most likely to Edward Everett (1794–1865), a Massachusetts clergyman, statesman, biographer, and Harvard professor (president of the college, 1846–49); he later served as U.S. secretary of state (1852–53) and as a U.S. senator (1853–54). He was editor of the *North American Review*, the most influential of the serious American reviews (1820–24). John Neal (1793–1876), Maine lawyer, poet, novelist, and critic, was well known for the novels *Logan* (1818), which included stringent attacks on U.S. political and social policies, and *Rachel Dyer* (1828), which tells the story of a Salem witch; he also published a series of sketches of U.S. authors in *Blackwood's Edinburgh Magazine*, thus increasing international awareness of the growing body of American literature. In 1824 with *The Pioneers*, James Fenimore Cooper (1789–1851) of New Jersey and New York published the first of five interlinked historical romances—the popular "Leatherstocking Tales," featuring the archetypal frontier hero Natty Bumppo. After Irving, Cooper was the best-known American fiction writer abroad. Gulian Commelin Verplanck (1786–1870), New York politician, author, Shakespeare scholar, and editor, was one of the founders of the *New York American* magazine. Two novels of John Pendleton Kennedy (1795–1870), a Baltimore lawyer, satirist, and historical novelist, were especially admired in his time: *Swallow Barn* (1832), and *Horse-Shoe Robinson* (1835). He befriended Poe and tried to advance his literary career. Timothy Flint (1780–1840), Massachusetts novelist, historian, and editor, wrote a number of historical frontier romances. Fitz-Greene Halleck (1790–1867), Connecticut poet and businessman, was co-author with Joseph Rodman Drake of *The Croaker Papers* (1819 ff.); see Poe's review (pp. 604ff. herein). Beginning in 1817, William Cullen Bryant (1794–1878), Massachusetts poet, critic, editor, and classicist, produced a long series of what were to become some of the best-loved poems of the American people (e.g., "Thanatopsis," "To a Waterfowl," "A Forest Hymn," and a number of Indian poems). He also published important essays on the nature and function of poetry. Catharine Maria Sedgwick (1789–1867), Massachusetts novelist and biographer, is best known for her historical novel *Hope Leslie* (1827). The poems of the Connecticut writer Lydia Howard Huntley Sigourney (1791–1865) were treated rather gently by the often otherwise acerbic Poe in his reviews.

2. Ornate elegance, as in the Corinthian style of Greek architecture, especially the thin fluted columns adorning temples.

for political or professional distinction, who is influenced by such timid suggestions? In that noble strife, which animates southern bosoms to control by the magic of oratory the passions of the multitude, or in a more learned arena "the applause of listening senates to command"—who ever heard of discouragements and difficulties sufficient to chill their ardor, or restrain their aspirations? And yet is it less difficult to attain the prize of eloquence—to rival the fame of a Henry, or a Wirt,[3] than to achieve the task of vigorous and graceful composition?

To our lovely and accomplished countrywomen, may not a successful appeal be also addressed, to lend their aid in this meritorious task. Their influence upon the happiness and destiny of society, is so extensively felt and acknowledged, that to dwell upon its various bearings and relations, would be altogether superfluous. It is to the watchful care of a mother's love, that those first principles of moral wisdom are implanted in childhood, which ripen into the blossoms and fruit of maturer years; and it is to the reproving virtues and refining tenderness of the sex, through all its mutations, from blooming sixteen to the matronly grace of forty—that man is indebted for all that is soft, and for much that is noble and wise, in his own character. It is true that there is another side to this picture. If a woman's education has itself been neglected; if she has been trained up in the paths of folly and vanity—and been taught to ornament the casket in preference to the celestial jewel which it contains,—she will neither be a fit companion for the sterner sex, nor be qualified to assume the divine responsibility of maternal instruction. To diffuse therefore not only the benefits of moral but intellectual culture, among those whom heaven has given to restore in part the blessings of a lost Eden—to withdraw their minds from vain and unprofitable pursuits—to teach them to emulate the distinguished names of their own sex, who have given lustre to literature, and scattered sweets in the paths of science—is a duty not only of paramount importance on our part, but claims the united and cordial support of the fair and interesting objects of our care.

Let no one therefore presume to disparage this humble effort to redeem our country's escutcheon[4] from the reproach which has been cast upon it. Let the miser open his purse—the prodigal save a pittance from his health-wasting and mind-destroying expenditures—the lawyer and physician, spare a little from their fees—the merchant and mechanic, from their speculations and labor—and the man of fortune, devote a part, a very small part of his abundance, towards the creation of a new era in the annals of this blessed Old Dominion. It may possibly be the means of effecting a salutary reform in public taste and individual habits; of overcoming that tendency to mental repose and luxurious indulgence supposed to be peculiar to southern latitudes;

3. Patrick Henry (1736–1799), the famous Virginia statesman and orator, was the subject of a biography by William Wirt (1772–1834), a Virginia lawyer and essayist, and later U.S. attorney general. Wirt's writing, modeled after that of the British essayist Joseph Addison, was noted for its 18th-century elegance of style. His most celebrated work was *The Letters of a British Spy* (1803), a collection of witty observations on Southern culture and social style.
4. Here, a family crest (indicating noble birth).

and of awakening a spirit of inquiry and a zeal for improvement, which cannot fail ultimately to exalt and adorn society.

[NATHANIEL BEVERLEY TUCKER]

Nathaniel Beverley Tucker (1784–1851) was one of the staunchest defenders of the culture of the Old South and of the "peculiar institution" of slavery. As a professor of law at the College of William and Mary and as an essayist and novelist, Tucker offered political opinions on the necessary disunion of the United States and warned against Northern assaults on the cultural and intellectual integrity of the "Southron Country." In 1836, he published two historically important novels. *George Balcombe*, which condones slavery, idealizes plantation life and defends states' rights, is basically a mystery story involving the recovery of a will. It was praised by Poe, who went so far as to call it *"the best* American novel"* to date—but for aesthetic reasons rather than political or regional ones. Tucker's other novel of 1836 was much more celebrated. *The Partisan Leader: A Tale of the Future* bears the fictive publication date of 1856 and tells the retrospective story of events set thirteen years into the future: thus, in 1849, the South has seceded from the union without armed conflict; but Virginia, caught in the middle, is in danger of being subverted by Northern infiltrators. The book is notable for its vehement attacks on Andrew Jackson and Martin Van Buren. Tucker wrote a third novel, *Gertrude*, which was published serially in the *Southern Literary Messenger* from 1844 to 1845. Tucker is important in Poe studies primarily because of his probable or possible authorship of a favorable review in the *Messenger* (April 1836, II.336–39) of two books defending slavery. The "Paulding-Drayton" review has been attributed to Poe and taken by a number of critics as prima facie evidence of Poe's racism. But as J. V. Ridgely demonstrates in a 1992 article (pp. 779ff. herein), the case for Poe's authorship is weak.

Slavery

Slavery in the United States. By J. K. Paulding. New York: Harper and Brothers.

The South Vindicated from the Treason and Fanaticism of the Northern Abolitionists. Philadelphia: Published by H. Manly.

It is impossible to look attentively and understandingly on those phenomena that indicate public sentiment in regard to the subject of these works, without deep and anxious interest. *"Nulla vestigia retrorsum,"*[1] is a saying fearfully applicable to what is called the "march of mind." It is unquestionable truth. The absolute and palpable impossibility of ever unlearning what we know, and of returning, even by forgetfulness, to the state of mind in which the knowledge of it first found us, has always afforded flattering encouragement to the hopes of him who dreams about the perfectibility of human nature. Sometimes one scheme, and sometimes another is devised for accom-

1. No stepping back again (Latin), from Horace's *Epistles* I (c. 20 B.C.E.).

plishing this great end; and these means are so various, and often so opposite, that the different experiments which the world has countenanced would seem to contradict the maxim we have quoted. At one time human nature is to be elevated to the height of perfection, by emancipating the mind from all the restrains imposed by Religion. At another, the same end is to be accomplished by the universal spread of a faith, under the benign influence of which every son of Adam is to become holy, "even as God is holy." One or the other of these schemes has been a cardinal point in every system of perfectibility which has been devised since the earliest records of man's history began. At the same time the progress of knowledge (subject indeed to occasional interruptions) has given to each successive experiment a seeming advantage over that which preceded it.

But it is lamentable to observe, that let research discover, let science teach, let art practice what it may, man, in all his mutations, never fails to get back to some point at which he has been before. The human mind seems to perform, by some invariable laws, a sort of cycle, like those of the heavenly bodies. We may be unable, (and, for ourselves, we profess to be so) to trace the *causes* of these changes; but we are not sure that an accurate observation of the history of various nations at different times, may not detect the *laws* that govern them. However eccentric the orbit, the comet's place in the heavens enables the enlightened astronomer to anticipate its future course, to tell when it will pass its perihelion,[2] in what direction it will shoot away into the unfathomable abyss of infinite space, and at what period it will return. But what especially concerns us, is to mark its progress through our planetary system, to determine whether in coming or returning it may infringe upon us, and prove the messenger of that dispensation which, in the end of all things, is to wrap our earth in flames.

Not less eccentric, and far more deeply interesting to us, is the orbit of the human mind. If, as some have supposed, the comet in its upward flight is drawn away by the attraction of some other sun, around which also it bends its course, thus linking another system with our own, the analogy will be more perfect. For while man is ever seen rushing with uncontrollable violence toward one or the other of his opposite extremes, fanaticism and irreligion—at each of these we find placed an attractive force identical in its nature and in many of its effects. At each extreme, we find him influenced by the same prevailing interest—devoting himself to the accomplishment of the same great object. Happiness is his purpose. The sources of that, he may be told, are within himself—but his eye will fix on the external means, and these he will labor to obtain. Foremost among these, and the equivalent which is to purchase all the rest, is property. At this all men aim, and their eagerness seems always proportioned to the excitement, which, from whatever cause, may for the time prevail. Under such excitement, the many who want, band themselves together against the

2. Point nearest the sun in the orbit of a planet, asteroid, etc.

few that possess; and the lawless appetite of the multitude for the property of others calls itself the spirit of liberty.

In the calm, and, as we would call it, the healthful condition of the public mind, when every man worships God after his own manner, and Religion and its duties are left to his conscience and his Maker, we find each quietly enjoying his own property, and permitting to others the quiet enjoyment of theirs. Under that state of things, those modes and forms of liberty which regulate and secure this enjoyment, are preferred. Peace reigns, the arts flourish, science extends her discoveries, and man, and the sources of his enjoyments, are multiplied. But in this condition things never rest. We have already disclaimed any knowledge of the causes which forbid this—we only know that such exist. We know that men are always passing, with fearful rapidity, between the extremes of fanaticism and irreligion, and that at either extreme, property and all the governmental machinery provided to guard it, become insecure. "Down with the Church! Down with the Altar!" is at one time the cry. "Turn the fat bigots out of their styes, sell the property of the Church and give the money to the poor!" "Behold our turn cometh," says the Millenarian.[3] "The kingdoms of this world are about to become the kingdoms of God and of his Christ. Sell what you have and give to the poor, and let all things be in common!"

It is now about two hundred years since this latter spirit showed itself in England with a violence and extravagance which accomplished the overthrow of all the institutions of that kingdom. With that we have nothing to do; but we should suppose that the striking resemblance between the aspect of a certain party in that country then and now, could hardly escape the English statesman. Fifty years ago, in France, this eccentric comet, "public sentiment," was in its opposite node. Making allowance for the difference in the characters of the two people, the effects were identical, the apparent causes were the opposites of each other. In the history of the French Revolution, we find a sort of symptomatic phenomenon, the memory of which was soon lost in the fearful exacerbation of the disease. But it should be remembered now, that in that war against property, the first object of attack was property in slaves; that in that war on behalf of the alleged right of man to be discharged from all control of law, the first triumph achieved was in the emancipation of slaves.

The recent events in the West Indies, and the parallel movement here, give an awful importance to these thoughts in our minds. They superinduce a something like despair of success in any attempt that may be made to resist the attack on all our rights, of which that on Domestic Slavery (the basis of all our institutions) is but the precursor. It is a sort of boding that may belong to the family of superstitions. All vague and undefined fears, from causes the nature of which we know not, the operations of which we cannot stay, are of that character. Such apprehensions are alarming in proportion to our estimate

3. Pertains to the number one thousand; here, a specific reference to a believer in the coming of the Millennium in Christian doctrine.

of the value of the interest endangered; and are excited by every thing which enhances that estimate. Such apprehensions have been awakened in our minds by the books before us. To Mr. Paulding,[4] as a Northern man, we tender our grateful thanks for the faithful picture he has drawn of slavery as it appeared to him in his visit to the South, and as exhibited in the information he has carefully derived from those most capable of giving it. His work is executed in the very happiest manner of an author in whom America has the greatest reason to rejoice, and will not fail to enhance his reputation immeasurably as a writer of pure and vigorous English, as a clear thinker, as a patriot, and as a man. The other publication, which we take to be from a Southern pen,[5] is more calculated to excite our indignation against the calumnies which have been put forth against us, and the wrongs meditated by those who come to us in the names of our common Redeemer and common country—seeking our destruction under the mask of Christian Charity and Brotherly Love. This too is executed with much ability, and may be read with pleasure as well as profit. While we take great pleasure in recommending these works to our readers, we beg leave to add a few words of our own. We are the more desirous to do this, because there is a view of the subject most deeply interesting to us, which we do not think has ever been presented, by any writer, in as high relief as it deserves. We speak of the moral influences flowing from the relation of master and slave, and the moral feelings engendered and cultivated by it. A correspondent of Mr. Paulding's justly speaks of this relation as one partaking of the patriarchal character, and much resembling that of clanship. This is certainly so. But to say this, is to give a very inadequate idea of it, unless we take into consideration the peculiar character (I may say the peculiar nature) of the negro. Let us reason upon it as we may, there is certainly a power, in causes inscrutable to us, which works essential changes in the different races of animals. In their physical constitution this is obvious to the senses. The color of the negro no man can deny, and therefore, it was but the other day, that they who will believe nothing they cannot account for, made this manifest fact an authority for denying the truth of holy writ. Then comes the opposite extreme— they are, like ourselves, the sons of Adam, and must therefore, have like passions and wants and feelings and tempers in all respects. This, we deny, and appeal to the knowledge of all who know. But their authority will be disputed, and their testimony falsified, unless we can devise something to show how a difference might and should have been brought about. Our theory is a short one. It was the will of God it should be so. But the means—how was this effected? We will give the answer to any one who will develop the causes which might and should have blackened the negro's skin and crisped his hair into

4. James Kirk Paulding (1778–1860), New York novelist, dramatist, and historian, sympathetic to Southern culture and its problems.
5. *The South Vindicated* is attributed to William Drayton (1776–1846), who attained the rank of colonel in the War of 1812 (see J. V. Ridgely, p. 780, n. 3 herein).

wool. Until that is done, we shall take leave to speak, as of things *in esse*,[6] of a degree of loyal devotion on the part of the slave to which the white man's heart is a stranger, and of the master's reciprocal feeling of parental attachment to his humble dependant, equally incomprehensible to him who drives a bargain with the cook who prepares his food, the servant who waits at his table, and the nurse who doses over his sick bed. That these sentiments in the breast of the negro and his master, are stronger than they would be under like circumstances between individuals of the white race, we believe. That they belong to the class of feelings "by which the heart is made better," we know. How come they? They have their rise in the relation between the infant and the nurse. They are cultivated between him and his foster brother. They are cherished by the parents of both. They are fostered by the habit of affording protection and favors to the younger offspring of the same nurse. They grow by the habitual use of the word "my," used as the language of affectionate appropriation, long before any idea of value mixes with it. It is a term of endearment. That is an easy transition by which he who is taught to call the little negro "his," in this sense and *because he loves him*, shall love him *because he is his*. The idea is not new, that our habits and affections are reciprocally cause and effect of each other.

But the great teacher in this school of feeling is sickness. In this school we have witnessed scenes at which even the hard heart of a thorough bred philanthropist would melt. But here, we shall be told, it is not humanity, but interest that prompts. Be it so. Our business is not with the cause but the effect. But is it interest, which, with assiduous care, prolongs the life of the aged and decrepid negro, who has been, for years, a burthen? Is it interest which labors to rear the crippled or deformed urchin, who can never be any thing but a burthen—which carefully feeds the feeble lamp of life that, without any appearance of neglect, might be permitted to expire? Is not the feeling more akin to that parental στοργη,[7] which, in defiance of reason, is most careful of the life which is, all the time, felt to be a curse to the possessor. Are such cases rare? They are as rare as the occasions; but let the occasion occur, and you will see the case. How else is the longevity of the negro proverbial? A negro who does no work for thirty years! (and we know such examples) is it interest which has lengthened out his existence?

Let the philanthropist think as he may—by the negro himself, his master's care of him in sickness is not imputed to interested feelings. We know an instance of a negress who was invited by a benevolent lady in Philadelphia to leave her mistress. The lady promised to secrete her for a while, and then to pay her good wages. The poor creature felt the temptation and was about to yield. "You are mighty good, madam," said she "and I am a thousand times obliged to you. And if I am sick, or any thing, I am sure you will take care of me, and nurse me, like my good mistress used to do, and bring me something warm

6. In existence (Latin).
7. Affection, tenderness (Greek; *storge*).

and good to comfort me, and tie up my head and fix my pillow." She spoke in the simplicity of her heart, and the tempter had not the heart to deceive her. "No," said she "all *that* will come out of your wages—for you will have money enough to hire a nurse." The tears had already swelled into the warm hearted creature's eyes, at her own recital of her mistress's kindness. They now gushed forth in a flood, and running to her lady who was a lodger in the house, she threw herself on her knees, confessed her fault, was pardoned, and was happy.

But it is not by the bedside of the sick negro that the feeling we speak of is chiefly engendered. They who would view it in its causes and effects must see him by the sick bed of his master—must see *her* by the sick bed of her *mistress*. We have seen these things. We have seen the dying infant in the lap of its nurse, and have stood with the same nurse by the bed side of her own dying child. Did mighty nature assert her empire, and wring from the mother's heart more and bitterer tears than she had shed over her foster babe? None that the eye of man could distinguish. And he who sees the heart—did he see dissimulation giving energy to the choking sobs that *seemed* to be rendered more vehement by her attempts to repress them? *Philanthropy* may think so if it pleases.

A good lady was on her death bed. Her illness was long and protracted, but hopeless from the first. A servant, (by no means a favorite with her, being high tempered and ungovernable) was advanced in pregnancy, and in bad health. Yet she could not be kept out of the house. She was permitted to stay about her mistress during the day, but sent to bed at an early hour every night. Her reluctance to obey was obvious, and her master found that she evaded his order, whenever she could escape his eye. He once found her in the house late at night, and kindly reproving her, sent her home. An hour after, suddenly going out of the sick room, he stumbled over her in the dark. She was crouched down at the door, listening for the groans of the sufferer. She was again ordered home, and turned to go. Suddenly she stopped, and bursting into tears, said, "Master it aint no use for me to go to bed, Sir. It don't do me no good, I cannot sleep, Sir."

Such instances prove that in reasoning concerning the moral effect of slavery, he who regards man as a unit, the same under all circumstances, leaves out of view an important consideration. The fact that he is not so, is manifest to every body—but the application of the fact to this controversy is not made. The author of "The South Vindicated" quotes at page 228, a passage from Lamartine,[8] on this very point, though he only uses it to show the absurdity of any attempt at amalgamation. The passage is so apt to our purpose that we beg leave to insert it.

> The more I have travelled, the more I am convinced *that the races of men form the great secret of history and manners.* Man is not so capable of education as philosophers imagine. The influence of

8. Alphonse Marie Louis de Lamartine (1790–1869), French poet, dramatist, and political activist, noted for the musical effects of his lyric verses.

governments and laws has less power, radically, than is supposed, over the manners and instincts of any people, while the primitive constitution and the blood of the race have always their influence, and manifest themselves, thousands of years afterwards, in the physical formations and moral habits of a particular family or tribe. Human nature flows in rivers and streams into the vast ocean of humanity; but its waters mingle but slowly, sometimes never; and it emerges again, like the Rhone from the Lake of Geneva, with its own taste and color. Here is indeed an abyss of thought and meditation, and at the same time a grand secret for legislators. As long as they keep the spirit of the race in view they succeed; but they fail when they strive against this natural predisposition: nature is stronger than they are. This sentiment is not that of the philosophers of the present time, but it is evident to the traveller; and there is more philosophy to be found in a caravan journey of a hundred leagues, than in ten years' reading and meditation.

There is much truth here, though certainly not what passes for truth with those who study human nature wholly in the closet, and in reforming the world address themselves exclusively to the faults of *others*, and the evils of which they know the least, and which least concern themselves.

We hope the day has gone by when we are to be judged by the testimony of false, interested, and malignant accusers alone. We repeat that we are thankful to Mr. Paulding for having stepped forward in our defence. Our assailants are numerous, and it is indispensable that we should meet the assault with vigor and activity. Nothing is wanting but manly discussion to convince our own people at least, that in continuing to command the services of their slaves, they violate no law divine or human, and that in the faithful discharge of their reciprocal obligations lies their true duty. Let these be performed, and we believe (with our esteemed correspondent Professor Dew)[9] that society in the South will derive much more of good than of evil from this much abused and partially-considered institution.

To Beverley Tucker (Letter 62)[1]

Richmond May 2, 1836.

Dear Sir,

At M^r White's request I write to apologise for the omission of your verses "To a Coquette" in the present number of the Messenger. Upon making up the *form* containing them it was found impossible to get

9. Thomas Roderick Dew (1802–1846) was professor of economics at the College of William and Mary.
1. This letter by Poe is a key text in the ongoing debate over his racism and the interpretation of several of his works. It seems to identify Tucker as the author of the unsigned review defending the institution of slavery rather than Poe himself; see the article by J. V. Ridgely (pp. 779ff. herein), which addresses certain ambiguities of Poe's references to "alterations" in Tucker's text.

both the pieces in, and their connection one with the other rendered it desirable not to separate them—they were therefore left for the May number.

I must also myself beg your pardon for making a few immaterial alterations in your article on Slavery, with a view of so condensing it as to get it in the space remaining at the end of the number. One very excellent passage in relation to the experience of a sick bed has been, necessarily, omitted altogether.

It would give me great pleasure to hear your opinion of the *February*, and of the *April* number of the Messenger—I mean of the Editorial articles. It is needless for me to say that I value your good opinion, and wish to profit by your counsel.

* * *

J. V. RIDGELY

The Authorship of the "Paulding-Drayton Review"[1]

Emory Elliott, gen. ed. *The Columbia History of the American Novel.* New York: Columbia Univ. Press, 1991. xviii + 905 pp. $59.95.
Dana D. Nelson. *The Word in Black and White: Reading "Race" in American Literature 1638–1867.* New York: Oxford Univ. Press, 1992, xvi + 189 pp. $35.[2]

Both of these wide-ranging studies contain sections on Poe, with particular attention to the ways in which his views on race and slavery may be reflected in his fiction. In the first, Joan Dayan, writing a chapter on "Romance and Race," traces her interpretation of his racial views through several tales and the *Narrative of Arthur Gordon Pym.* In "Ethnocentrism Decentered," a section of her study which focuses on *Pym*, Dana D. Nelson sees a "recent trend to sweep Poe's politics under the rug" and considers how such a "trend toward a depoliticized and dehistoricized reading of the Poe oeuvre concomitantly 'saves' Poe for a canon increasingly skeptical of texts that support human oppression." She adds: "I am not suggesting that acknowledging the racist

1. This article appeared in the *PSA Newsletter* [Poe Studies Association Newsletter], 20, no. 2 (Fall 1992), 1–3, 6. Reprinted by permission of the Poe Studies Association and the author.
2. Begun as a review, the essay is headed with these references. The following editorial note was published in the same issue:

> *Editor's Note: With the appearance of recent studies that assume Poe's authorship of a controversial defense of slavery in the 1836* Southern Literary Messenger, *we thought it an opportune time to review the conflicting claims and evidence for and against ascribing this review to Poe. We therefore asked J. V. Ridgely, currently at work on an edition of Poe's contributions to the* Messenger, *to address once more the matter of Poe's authorship. Professor Ridgely, rather than writing a conventional review of the two books under discussion, focuses on the issue of attribution. Readers of the newsletter should note that since the solicitation of Professor Ridgely's essay, other publications have appeared that bear relevance to the discussion below: a reprinting of Sidney Kaplan's introduction to* The Narrative of Arthur Pym *in his* American Studies in Black and White: Selected Essays *(Amherst: Univ. of Massachusetts Press, 1991) and essays by John Carlos Rowe and G. R. Thompson in the recently published proceedings of the 1988 conference, "Arthur Gordon Pym and Contemporary Criticism."*

dimension of Poe's work should remove his works from the canon; but I think we must at least consider the cultural work performed now by masking that aspect of his work."

What both Dayan and Nelson see as among the acts of "masking" is the disinclination by most scholars to accept as Poe's the review of two books on slavery which appeared in the April 1836 *Southern Literary Messenger* (*SLM* 2: 336–39), of which he was editor. Why is assigning to Poe authorship of this review so crucial to them? Clearly it is because, accepted as evidence, it can provide the critic with a more extended, more theoretical, and more emotional defense of racism and slavery than can be found in the few comments that are unquestionably his. For Dayan, who has no doubt about Poe's authorship, this review, emphasizing the master-slave bond, is revelatory because it is "what could be called Poe's most disturbing, because most authentic, 'love poem' . . ." As support for the attribution to Poe, both critics cite approvingly an article by Bernard Rosenthal, "Poe, Slavery, and the *Southern Literary Messenger*: A Reexamination," published in the December 1974 *Poe Studies* (7: 29–38). Before the persuasions of Dayan and Nelson lead us toward a new orthodoxy, it would be well to look again at the strength of Rosenthal's "reexamination."

The review in question is headed simply "Slavery"; below this caption are listed two works: James K. Paulding's *Slavery in the United States* and the anonymous *The South Vindicated* . . ., now attributed to William Drayton.[3] A reader of the "Paulding-Drayton Review" (Rosenthal's title) quickly sees that this is less a book review than it is an excuse for a proslavery essay. As Rosenthal notes, it was printed as Poe's by James A. Harrison in his Virginia edition (8: 265–75); but, after the publication in 1924 of a letter from Poe to the prominent proslavery spokesman Beverley Tucker (to which I will return), it was credited to Tucker by William Doyle Hull in his 1941 dissertation on the Poe canon. Rosenthal's apparently inclusive article is devoted to rebutting this widely accepted attribution and to returning authorship to Poe.

Rosenthal is concerned first with demonstrating that the proslavery ideas expressed by Poe in other notices are compatible with those in "Paulding-Drayton." He cites four, all in the *SLM*: those of (1) Joseph H. Ingraham's *The South-West* (2: 122–23); (2) Anne Grant's *Memoirs* (2: 511–12); (3) R. M. Bird's *Sheppard Lee* (2: 662–67); (4) Thomas R. Dew's *Address* (2: 721–22). (He also instances a later unpublished review by Poe of John L. Carey's *Domestic Slavery*; the text does not survive.) Now, there should be no doubt that Poe shared in the racism and proslavery sentiment of his time and place; he also expressed contempt for abolitionists. But Rosenthal's extrapolations—his quotations

3. William Drayton (1776–1846), a colonel in the War of the 1812, a judge, and U.S. congressman (1825–1833) from South Carolina, befriended and assisted Poe during his Philadelphia years: Poe dedicated *Tales of the Grotesque and Arabesque* (1840) to him. James Kirk Paulding (1778–1860), a New York writer, described people, places, and customs he saw on an 1816 trip to Virginia in *Letters from the South* (1817). He supported the growth of Southern letters and the founding of the *Southern Literary Messenger*, and came to the aid of Poe. Paulding was sympathetic to Southern causes and defended the "peculiar institution" in his *Slavery in the United States* (1836). He later became the secretary of the U.S. Navy.

from the texts reviewed—have the effect of obscuring the actual extent of Poe's remarks. In (1) there is most of one paragraph; in (2) one sentence, introducing a quotation; in (3) one paragraph, referring to abolitionist activities; in (4) praise for Dew, a leading proslavery spokesman and president of William and Mary; the review deals with the College's curriculum, and there is no reference to slavery except in a quoted excerpt from Dew's address. In short, all of Poe's printed comments on slavery would fill no more than a longish paragraph. But the issue here is not the fact of Poe's racist attitudes. And it is not whether Poe *could* have written "Paulding-Drayton," unique though such a long piece promoting the "positive good" theory of slavery would be in his canon. It is, simply, what proof is there that he did?

There is only one piece of documentary evidence, and it is one which Rosenthal must convincingly challenge if the rest of his brief for Poe is to have any weight. This is a letter from Poe to Tucker, dated May 2, 1836 (full text in John Ward Ostrom, ed., *Letters* [New York, 1966] 1: 90–91). Two paragraphs are relevant. In the first, Poe, speaking for the owner of the *SLM*, Thomas W. White, writes: "At Mr. White's request I write to apologise for the omission of your verses 'To a Coquette' in the present [i.e., April] number of the *Messenger*. Upon making up the *form* containing them it was found impossible to get both the pieces in, and their connection one with the other rendered it desirable not to separate them—they were therefore left for the May number." In the second paragraph, Poe refers to his own editorial duties: "I must also myself beg your pardon for making a few immaterial alterations in your article on Slavery, with a view of so condensing it as to get it in the space remaining at the end of the number. One very excellent passage in relation to the experience of a sick bed has been, necessarily, omitted altogether." As Rosenthal notes, both Hull and Tucker's biographer, Percy W. Turrentine, assigned "Paulding-Drayton" to Tucker on the basis of this comment, but both had problems. Turrentine observed that it does not come at the end of the number (it is followed by another review and a long supplement of notices of the the *SLM*). Both also felt that Poe's remarks about "a sick bed" were inconsistent with what is printed in the text; he must, therefore, have changed his mind about about omission of the passage just before publication. Rosenthal seizes upon this last point. He argues that by the date of the letter the April *SLM* had already *already* been been issued, since it was reviewed in the *New Yorker* for May 7; for Hull's and Turrentine's suggestions of last-minute changes to be valid, a harried Poe, after quickly resetting forms to alter the text, would have needed incredible luck with mail-carrying boats for the *SLM* to have arrived in New York in time for this review. We should be aware of what Rosenthal has done here; with a kind of patter about timetables he has diverted our attention from Poe's own words and has refocused it on Hull's and Turrentine's mistaken interpretations of them. He then caps his verbal legerdemain with an unwarranted conclusion: he triumphantly announces that, with "the basic explanation of the inconsistencies found by Hull and Turrentine rendered implausible, if

not impossible, there is scarcely anything left to suggest that Tucker wrote the Paulding-Drayton review."

What is *actually* left, however, is the plain sense of Poe's letter. Of course, it was written after the April *SLM* had appeared; Poe is telling Tucker not what he plans to do but what, as makeup editor, he has already done: he has made "a few immaterial alterations in your article on Slavery," including omitting a "passage in *relation* to the *experience* of a sick bed," "with a view of so condensing it as to get it in *the space remaining* at the end of the number" (italics added). In the the printed text there are, as Hull and Turrentine noted, two anecdotes about "sick beds." But there are also four other unelaborated allusions to sick beds; Poe's cut could have been made in material "in relation to" any of these "experiences."

A fuller understanding of Poe's explanation to Tucker requires some knowledge about the physical makeup of the March and April issues of the *SLM*. An "Advertisement" on the cover of the March number informed readers that its publication had been delayed because of the Proprietor's (i.e., White's) desire to get in a long address by Thomas R. Dew (2: 261–82), which is on the "Federative Republican System of Government." (It is is not, as Rosenthal misleadingly calls it, "an essay on slavery.") The notice continues: "To counterbalance this delay, 16 pages of *extra* matter are given. The April Number . . . will contain, therefore, 16 pages less than usual." (italics in original; full text given in Dwight Thomas and David K. Jackson, *The Poe Log* [Boston, 1987], p. 196). This is accurate: the March issue consisted of ten eight-page (quarto) signatures; the April issue had only six, the last being a self-contained (and self-puffing) "Supplement" of critical notices of the *SLM*. (The point is that the supplement has no *textual* connection to the preceding signature and was probably set before it.) Space was thus tight in April, but Poe managed nevertheless to get in his own "A Tale of Jerusalem" (a reprint), "Maelzel's Chess-Player," and the long "Drake-Halleck" review. The latter led off the final section of "Critical Notices"; the space now "remaining at the end of the number" (i.e., in the last eight-page signature which he had to fill) was slightly more than four pages. What Poe placed in the form were the "Paulding-Drayton review" (captioned with the single word "Slavery") and another headed "Brunnens of Nassau." Rosenthal points to a puzzle here: why would Poe have made cuts in a review by Tucker when Tucker could see that the final notice is largely quotation and therefore a better candidate for shortening if space was limited? The question is unanswerable: we can guess but we cannot know why Poe resolved his space problems as he did. But is our lack of explanation grounds for canceling out his unambiguous statement to Tucker?

Rosenthal, of course, wants to argue that it does, but his tactic is so weak that even he admits its inadequacy. He speculates that what Poe is talking about may be an earlier *SLM* article by Tucker refuting Blackstone's views on slavery. Perhaps Tucker wanted Poe to have copies of this article reprinted as a pamphlet. Or perhaps it's some other essay. But Rosenthal's own comment leaves us little to debate:

"My own speculation has the serious weakness of postulating that an offprint would be called a 'number,' and I am not ready to defend a guess as a fact. Nor have I been able to locate an actual offprint."

In the rest of his long essay, Rosenthal dodges further mention of Poe's letter and goes on to present what he takes to be other evidence for Poe's authorship. He also makes a brief (and unproductive) attempt to show specific parallels between "Paulding-Drayton" and passages in Poe's works. He does not tell us whether he made the same sort of comparison for Tucker beyond the weak claim that Tucker's prose shows a heavy reliance on colons and semicolons and the review does not. I have space here only to suggest what a more enterprising (and necessary) demonstration for Tucker would show. Confining myself to what Tucker had published thus far in the *SLM*, I would instance first his "Note to Blackstone's Commentaries . . . on the Subject of Domestic Slavery . . ." (1: 227–31; identified as Tucker's in the volume index). This article and "Paulding-Drayton" share these specific points (first page reference to "Blackstone," second to "Paulding-Drayton"): (1) masters' care of sick slaves (1: 230; 2: 338–39); (2) reference to slaves as "property" (1: 231; 2: 337); (3) citation of Edmund Burke on emancipation (direct in 1: 231; inferentially in 2: 337, in a discussion of the French Revolution); (4) attacks on "philanthropy" (i.e., the movement for ending slavery on humanitarian grounds) (1: 231; 2: 338–39); (5) allusion to recent events in the West Indies (i.e., slave revolts) (1: 231; 2: 337). Not one of these references can be found anywhere in Poe's known comments on slavery. I would add one more point—a small and curious item, but one which offers a link between Tucker and "Paulding-Drayton." This is the background: In December 1834, before Poe had any connection with the journal, the *SLM* published the text of a "Law Lecture" given by Tucker (1: 145–54). This was directly followed by a short anonymous piece entitled "The March of Mind," a conservative's discussion of human progress (1: 154–56). Tucker makes a direct allusion to it in his *SLM* review of George Bancroft's *History of the United States* (1: 587–91; attributed to Tucker by Poe in 2: 283). A second allusion occurs at the very beginning of "Paulding-Drayton" (2: 396).

Here is the sequence of relevant quotations: (1) "The March of Mind": "nearly approaching the idolatrous reverence of a Hindoo, for the fabled virtues of his bloody Juggernaut" (1: 154). (2) Tucker's Bancroft review: "How long it shall be before '*the march of mind,*' as it is called, in its Juggernaut car, shall pass over us . . ." (1: 587–88; italics in original). (3) "Paulding-Drayton": "*Nulla vestigia retrorsum,*" is a saying fearfully applicable to what is called the 'march of mind' " (2: 336). The Latin phrase, derived from Horace, *Epistles*, I, means "no stepping back again"; it introduces a turgid disquisition on the vagaries of human progress that echoes the "March of Mind" piece. Tucker's concern with "The March of Mind" is obvious. That Poe on his own would have decided to refer directly to the same obscure article seems to me beyond probability.

Other strong arguments against Poe's authorship of the review could

be adduced in regard to its rhetoric and vocabulary. But I have offered enough information to show that Rosenthal's thesis is, at best, deeply flawed. Future critics should ponder this contradictory evidence before proclaiming his article an "excellent argument" (Dayan) or "impressively thorough" (Nelson).

To Joseph Evans Snodgrass (Letter 95)[1]

Philadelphia June 17 [1840]

My dear Snodgrass,

* * *

Mr. Carey's book on slavery was received by me not very long ago, and in last month's number I wrote, at some length, a criticism upon it, in which I endeavored to do justice to the author, whose talents I highly admire. But this critique, as well as some six or seven others, were refused admittance into the Magazine by Mr. Burton, upon his receiving my letter of resignation. [I] allude to the number for June— the one last issued. I fancy, moreover, that he has some private pique against Mr. Carey (as he has against every honest man) for not long ago he refused admission to a poetical address of his which I was anxious to publish.

Herewith you have my Prospectus.[2] You will see that I have given myself sufficient time for preparation. I have every hope of success. As yet I have done nothing more than send a few Prospectuses to the Philadelphia editors, and it is rather early to strike—six months in anticipation. My object, at present, is merely to call attention to the contemplated design. In the meantime be assured that I am not idle—and that if there is any impossibility about the matter, it is the impossibility of *not* succeeding. The world is fond of novelty, and in being absolutely *honest*, I shall be utterly novel.

If you would show the Prospectus to Mr. Carey, or any other editorial friend, when you have done with it, I would be obliged to you.

* * *

1. Snodgrass was a frequent correspondent with Poe on both professional and personal matters. A section on the Poe–Snodgrass correspondence, extracted and summarized in the *New York Herald* (March 27, 1881), appears in the Harrison edition of Poe's *Works* (XVII.68–80). These along with the fuller letters from Poe to Snodgrass in the Ostrom edition present a vivid picture of Poe's situation at mid-career. His letters excusing and/or denying his drinking are of particular biographical interest. Also intriguing is Poe's reference in this letter of June 17, 1840, to his review of John L. Carey's *Domestic Slavery* (1838), which he says William Burton refused to publish. The review (if it ever existed) is lost; see the introduction to this section on p. 767 herein. Snodgrass also wrote a reminiscence of Poe's death: "Death and Burial of Edgar A. Poe," *New York Life Illustrated* (May 17, 1856).
2. For the *Penn Magazine* (see pp. 621ff. herein).

CRITICISM

Selecting essays to represent modern criticism on Poe was especially difficult. The Bibliography to this Norton Critical Edition lists a large number of books, and it is not complete. The number of essays in critical journals, not to mention book chapters in works not focused directly on Poe, is enormous. Of course, among the three thousand or so essays that have been published are many that are slipshod, uninformed, unscholarly, or critically naive. There are also a great many eccentric, downright quirky studies in which authors ride various hobbyhorses (many of which, however, are quite fascinating). One of the problems of selection is that much of the best work on Poe is devoted to careful readings of individual works, and to collect a representative group that does justice to the many excellent analyses of particular poems and tales is well nigh impossible in less than a thousand pages.

Limiting the current selections to a dozen or so was guided by several considerations. First (and unfortunately), a number of more or less classic essays from the end of the nineteenth century through the middle of the twentieth century are not included: essays by Paul Valéry, D. H. Lawrence, T. S. Eliot, Allen Tate, and Yvor Winters, for example, which have been many times reprinted in collections on Poe. So the first stratagem of selectivity was chronological: to begin at mid-century and come forward to the end of the century. Next, the essays were selected for their *overall* usefulness in the classroom, for students exploring Poe on their own, or for the literate general reader. A corollary to this concern is how representative the essays are of various critical approaches (and not just current ones). Finally, they were selected, in general, for readability—that is, even though intellectually demanding, how accessible they are to the nonspecialist.

Almost all of the essays have had to be shortened; thus the reprint of an essay originally using, say, "The Fall of the House of Usher," *Eureka*, and "The Purloined Letter" may contain only the analysis of one of these works (a decision made in consultation with the authors and publishers). As it turned out, the recurrent texts in the essays that follow are principally "Usher," *Arthur Gordon Pym*, and "The Purloined Letter"—though a large number of other works are dealt with.

A brief description of the essays suggests some of the thematic strands that weave in and out. Floyd Stovall's older essay on poetics and cosmic philosophy (revised in 1960) connects Poe's ideas about the universe and art with those of the most influential English-speaking critic of the nineteenth century, Samuel Taylor Coleridge, and points to Poe's sources in the German critics who essentially founded the international Romantic movement. Robert C. McLean's essay on the Virginian George Tucker's influence on Poe shows specific connections between Poe's poetics, Coleridge, the Scottish commonsense school of philosophy, and the relation of associationist mental theory to theories of poetry in the antebellum

South. Richard Wilbur's "The House of Poe" remains one of the most seminal essays ever written on Poe's grand symbols, connecting them to his cosmology and to his characters' mythic and psychological descent into a "hypnagogic state." James W. Gargano offers a succinct treatment of the mental states and therefore suspect narrative reliability of Poe's story-tellers from a different perspective. Joseph J. Moldenhauer explores Poe's peculiar "inverse Transcendentalism" in his "Murder as a Fine Art" and suggests basic connections among Poe's aesthetics, psychology, and moral vision. Paul John Eakin, in "Poe's Sense of an Ending," observes that ambiguous endings embody what may be called the "Lazarus plot" of Poe's cosmos. Grace Farrell examines the descent into Hell motif of *Arthur Gordon Pym* and other works in conjunction with a voyage into the collective unconscious. Liahna Armstrong lucidly discusses Poe's characters as Doppelgängers and reveals "doubling" structures in a classic detective story, "The Purloined Letter," which has become a psychoanalytic and deconstructive battleground.

Barton Levi St. Armand offers an overview of the presence of the occult—especially Egyptian occultism—in Poe's works in terms of the quest for a gothic monomyth, with special attention to "The Fall of the House of Usher." As edited for the present volume, the focus of Joseph N. Riddel's "The 'Crypt' of Edgar Poe" is also on "Usher"; more comprehensively, Riddel's is a poststructuralist essay about self-consuming symbols on the level of both the individual story and the national narrative that provides the reader with an introduction to the main deconstructive readings and psychoanalytic issues in Poe studies. J. Gerald Kennedy, in the process of pursuing a thematic analysis of four principal paradigms of gothic fiction as seen in Poe's fiction, also provides an illuminating historical contextualization of rites and fears of sepulture in Poe's America.

John Carlos Rowe attempts to restore our sense of Poe as a Southern writer, in part by reexamining Poe's disputed authorship of a notorious *Southern Literary Messenger* review defending the institution of slavery, and then links "modernism" with an "elitist" avoidance of retrograde political motifs in Poe and Poe criticism. Terence Whalen, in "Average Racism: Poe, Slavery, and the Wages of Literary Nationalism," acknowledges racism in Poe's works but suggests that he was probably no more racist than the average white Northerner; in the process of making this argument, Whalen looks at important issues of regionalism and nationalism. John T. Irwin, in "Detective Fiction as High Art: Lacan, Derrida, and Johnson on 'The Purloined Letter,' " succinctly lays out the famous poststructuralist/deconstructionist readings of the tale; in defining a new postmodernist way of looking at Poe and the detective story, Irwin discusses the contestatory readings of the story by Lacan, Derrida, and Johnson in relation to an occult, mathematical, geometric "iconography" in Poe's fiction. Thus, in addition to offering insights into individual works, the modern critical selections address the aesthetic, the cosmic and mythic, the psychological and and psychoanalytic—along with problems of genre and issues of deconstruction and historicism.

FLOYD STOVALL

From Poe's Debt to Coleridge†

* * *

Poe was ambitious to establish himself as a critic and a literary leader in America, but he realized that to do so he must be familiar with the literature and thought of other times than his own. He was a journalist, however, with the journalist's bias for all that is contemporary, and, besides, had scant time for general reading in the literature of the past. In his search for the knowledge he needed he was therefore constrained to make the most of such handbooks, encyclopedias, and other similar short cuts as he could lay his hands on. Coleridge's *Biographia Literaria* was to him a treasure, for it not only contained a digest of an entire school of philosophy and criticism, but also made reference to a variety of sources to which he might not otherwise have been introduced. After a careful reading of this book he could discourse with some assurance on A. W. Schlegel's theories of criticism, for instance, or on Schelling's system of identity with but little firsthand acquaintance with the writings of these authors. The question arises, then, whether an idea which Poe held in common with both Coleridge and Schlegel was borrowed, if borrowed at all, from one or the other.

* * *

[I]t seems to me probable that Poe owed most to Coleridge for such ideas as he held in common with Coleridge and Schlegel, even though in the development of those ideas he ultimately had recourse to the latter. The same is true of Schelling. Some of Poe's philosophical ideas that came to him through Coleridge are to be found most fully developed in the writings of Schelling. Poe had no opportunity to read Schelling unless he read him in the original German, for practically nothing of Schelling's work was translated until long after Poe's death.[1] It may be, as one writer has said,[2] that Coleridge is indebted to Schlegel for most of his principles of criticism; and he himself readily

† "Poe's Debt to Coleridge," an essay evaluating Coleridge's pervasive influence on Poe, was first published in 1930; it was revised for *Edgar Poe the Poet: Essays Old and New on the Man and His Work* (Charlottesville, University Press of Virginia, 1969), the text used here by permission of the publisher. Only a brief tabulated overview along with some concise concluding comments on the parallels between Poe's *Eureka* and Coleridge's posthumously printed *Theory of Life* (1848) are reprinted from this long essay; specific footnote references to the 1902 edition of Poe's *Works* have been omitted (Stovall's remaining notes are so indicated) and the notes renumbered and integrated with those of the editor.

1. According to Bayard Quincy Morgan, *A Bibliography of German Literature in English Translation*, University of Wisconsin *Studies in Language and Literature*, No. 16, 1922. In seeking in Coleridge's writing the source of Poe's ideas, I take no account of those works which were not published until after Poe's death [Stovall's note].

2. Anna Augusta Helmholtz, *The Indebtedness of Samuel Taylor Coleridge to August Wilhelm von Schlegel*, Bulletin of the University of Wisconsin, Philology and Literature Series, III, No. 4, 1907 [Stovall's note].

admitted that his philosophical principles were largely identical with Schelling's, though he denied that he had borrowed, explaining that their theories were the same because they learned them from the same masters.[3] It will thus be practically impossible to prove that in a given case Poe was influenced by Coleridge to the exclusion of others whose ideas corresponded so closely to his, nor shall I attempt to offer such proof. I wish merely to make my own position clear. Poe's first and chief debt was to Coleridge; to Schlegel and Schelling he probably owed little directly, having been drawn to them through Coleridge. If he appeared sometimes to give credit to Schlegel and Schelling that might have belonged to Coleridge, it was because of a desire to appear and to be a man of erudition; and if as he grew older he became less enthusiastic in his admiration of Coleridge, it was because of an abnormal desire to appear and to be an original critic, and, consequently, a growing reluctance to admit, even to himself, perhaps, his obligation to the author of the *Biographia Literaria*.

Let me say at the very beginning that the theories which Poe and Coleridge held in common—or perhaps it would be more correct to say the theories which Poe developed from suggestions found in the writings of Coleridge—are almost wholly concerned with poetry. Poe's criticism of the short story derives from Coleridge only in so far as it embodies the same general principles that constitute his theory of poetry. What, then, is Poe's theory of poetry? * * *

1. The immediate object of poetry is pleasure, not truth.
2. The pleasure derived from the poem differs from that derived from the romance in being indefinite, not definite.
3. Music is an essential element in poetry.
4. Beauty is the sole province of the poem.
5. Poetic Beauty has the quality of strangeness or novelty.
6. The poem must have unity or totality of effect or interest (the terms are variously combined).
7. The true poem must be brief.
8. Passion and poetry are discordant.
9. The tone of the poem should be sadness or melancholy.

[Stovall here elaborates on each of these "constituent ideas" for several pages and then comes to the issues of the imagination, fancy, and allegory.]

F. C. Prescott points out that Poe derived from Coleridge the distinction between fancy and imagination, and "attempted to analyze and clarify it."[4] I agree with the first part of this opinion, but not altogether with the last part, which implies that Poe approved Coleridge's distinction. As a matter of fact, he opposed it, sought to refute it, and

3. *Biographia Literaria*, ed. J. Shawcross (2 vols.; London, 1907), I, 102–103. All citations of *Biographia Literaria* are made to this edition [Stovall's note].
4. F. C. Prescott, *Selections from the Critical Writings of Edgar Allan Poe* (New York, 1909), pp. xxxi [Stovall's note].

set up various theories in its place. In the end, however, he agreed substantially with Coleridge in all except a few terms.

In an early definition of "poesy," Poe includes this sentence, making it a separate paragraph for emphasis: "Imagination is its soul."[5] As a footnote to this statement, he adds:

> Imagination is, possibly in man, a lesser degree of the creative power in God. What the Deity imagines *is*, but *was not* before. What man imagines, *is*, but *was* also. The mind of man cannot imagine what *is not*.

He defines "the Poetic Sentiment" as "Ideality, Imagination, or the creative ability." The first open disagreement with Coleridge occurs four years afterwards in a lengthy discussion of the poems of Moore, of which the following passage must be quoted at length:

> "The fancy," says the author of the "Ancient Mariner," in his *Biographia Literaria*, "the fancy combines, the imagination creates." And this was intended, and has been received, as a distinction. If so at all, it is one without a difference; without even a difference of *degree*. The fancy as nearly creates as the imagination; and neither creates in any respect. All novel conceptions are merely unusual combinations. The mind of man can imagine nothing which has not really existed. . . . It will be said, perhaps, that we can imagine a *griffin*, and that a griffin does not exist. Not the griffin certainly, but its component parts. It is a mere compendium of known limbs and features—of known qualities. Thus with all which seems to be *new*—which appears to be a *creation* of intellect. It is resoluble into the old. The wildest and most vigorous effort of mind cannot stand the test of this analysis.[6]

He then attempts a distinction of his own, according to which an imaginative work, unlike a work of the fancy, is one in which "the main conception springs immediately, *or thus apparently springs*, from the brain of the poet, enveloped in the moral sentiments of grace, of colour, of motion—of the beautiful, of the mystical, of the august—in short, of the ideal." He continues by way of conclusion:

> The truth is that the just distinction between the fancy and the imagination (and which is still but a distinction of *degree*) is involved in the consideration of the *mystic*. We give this as an idea of our own, altogether. We have no authority for our opinion—but do not the less firmly hold it. The term *mystic* is here employed in the sense of Augustus William Schlegel, and of most other German critics. It is applied by them to that class of composition in which there lies beneath the transparent upper current of meaning an under or *suggestive* one. What we vaguely term the *moral* of any sentiment is its mystic or secondary expression.

5. Review of the poems of Drake and Halleck, *Southern Literary Messenger*, April 1836 [Stovall's note]. The present volume contains selections from this review and from the other of Poe's works that Stovall references in notes 6 and 7 below; note 4, page 794; notes 5, 6, and 8, page 795; and *Eureka*, pp. 795–96 [Editor].
6. Review of Moore's *Alciphron: A Poem, Burton's Gentleman's Magazine*, Jan. 1840 [Stovall's note].

This new opinion in which the "mystic" was made to explain the imagination was apparently soon abandoned, for he does not insist on it afterwards, but continues to use Coleridge's terms. * * *

> Its second element is the attempt to satisfy this thirst by *novel* combinations, *of those combinations which our predecessors, toiling in chase of the same phantom, have already set in order*. We thus clearly deduce the *novelty*, the *originality*, the *invention*, the *imagination*, or lastly the *creation* of Beauty, (for the terms as here employed are synonymous) as the essence of all poesy. . . .
>
> "Invention," however, or "imagination," is by far more commonly insisted upon. The word ποιησις itself (creation) speaks volumes upon the point.[7]
>
> Poe's next attempt to formulate a distinction between fancy and imagination appears in a long comparison and analysis of imagination, fancy, fantasy, and humor, which, he says, "have in common the elements Combination and Novelty."

* * *

For the sake of a fair comparison it will be necessary to quote several passages from the writings of Coleridge. In an article first published with Southey's *Omniana* (1812) he names among the human faculties "the imagination, or shaping and modifying power; the fancy, or the aggregative and associative power."[8] The statement of Coleridge's theory which Poe alluded to is probably the following:

> The imagination then I consider either as primary, or secondary. The primary imagination I hold to be the living power and prime agent of all human perception, and as a repetition in the finite mind of the eternal act of creation in the infinite I Am. The secondary I consider as an echo of the former, co-existing with the conscious will, yet still as identical with the primary in the kind of its agency, and differing only in degree, and in the mode of its operation. It dissolves, diffuses, dissipates, in order to recreate; or where this process is rendered impossible, yet still, at all events, it struggles to idealize and to unify. It is essentially *vital*, even as all objects (as objects) are essentially fixed and dead.
>
> Fancy, on the contrary, has no other counters to play with, but fixities and definites. The Fancy is indeed no other than a mode of memory emancipated from the order of time and space; and blended with, and modified by that empirical phenomenon of the will, which we express by the word choice. But equally with the ordinary memory, it must receive all its materials ready made from the law of association.[9]

The distinction here made between the primary and the secondary imagination occurs nowhere else in Coleridge's writings; it may therefore be concluded, I think, that it was not very important. Most of his

7. Review of Longfellow's *Ballads and Other Poems*, *Graham's Magazine*, April 1842 [Stovall's note].
8. *Omniana* (bound with *Table Talk*), p. 383. The passage is repeated in *Biographia Literaria*, I, 193 [Stovall's note].
9. *Biographia Literaria*, I, 202 [Stovall's note].

other definitions conform to the definition here made of the secondary imagination. He further describes the imagination as a "synthetic" power.

> This power, first put in action by the will and understanding, and retained under their irremissive, though gentle and unnoticed, control (*laris effertur habenis*) reveals itself in the balance or reconciliation of opposite or discordant qualities; of sameness, with difference; of the general, with the concrete; the idea, with the image; the individual, with the representative; the sense of novelty and freshness, with old and familiar objects; a more than usual state of emotion, with more than usual order; judgment ever awake and steady self-possession, with enthusiasm and feeling profound or vehement; and while it blends and harmonizes the natural and the artificial, still subordinates art to nature; the manner to the matter; and our admiration of the poet to our sympathy with the poetry [II.12].

Summing up this part of his discussion, he says:

> Finally, good sense is the body of poetic genius, fancy its drapery, motion its life, and imagination the soul that is every where, and in each; and forms all into one graceful and intelligent whole [II.13].

Elsewhere he calls imagination "that reconciling and mediatory power, which incorporating the reason in images of the sense . . . gives birth to a system of symbols, harmonious in themselves, and consubstantial with the truths of which they are the conductors."[1] To understand this definition we must know that his distinction between reason and understanding is somewhat like that between imagination and fancy. The understanding he calls "the science of phenomena"; the reason, "the science of the universal, having the ideas of oneness and allness as its two elements or primary factors."[2] Finally he says:

> The Fancy brings together images which have no connection natural or moral, but are yoked together by the poet by means of some accidental coincidence. . . . The Imagination modifies images, and gives unity to variety; it sees all things in one, *il piu nell' uno.*[3]

A casual examination of these passages reveals that Poe and Coleridge are agreed on the following points at least:

1. Imagination is the soul of poetry.
2. It harmonizes diverse matters and gives unity to variety.
3. It is analogous to the creative power of God.
4. Of two elements known and unlike it can create a third element different from either.

1. *The Statesman's Manual: A Lay Sermon* (London, 1816), p. 35 [Stovall's note].
2. *Ibid.*, Appendix C, pp. v–vi [Stovall's note].
3. *Table Talk*, p. 291 [Stovall's note].

They differ, or seem to differ, in one point only: the meaning of the word "create." Coleridge says the imagination dissolves and diffuses in order to recreate; it creates, therefore, in the sense of bringing order out of chaos. Poe says creation by the imagination is merely the combination of whole parts of known objects in a new way. But in reality Poe means by combination exactly what Coleridge means by creation. For if one asks how small these combinable parts may be, the reply is obviously that they may be as small in their world, the ideal, as the atom in the physical world. He actually mentions physical chemistry as an aid to the understanding of imaginative creation, which he calls the "chemistry of the intellect." In the light of this analogy his example of the griffin as an object created imaginatively is absurd. As a matter of fact, I feel confident that he agreed with Coleridge in every respect; but, impelled by the desire to be original, and painfully conscious of his obligation to Coleridge, he sought to avoid the obligation by opposing him. To this end he first conceived the theory that the idea of the mystic is involved in that of the imagination, but gave that up. It was only then that he began to quibble over the words "creation" and "combination." He often used the word "create" in Coleridge's sense, and undoubtedly applied Coleridge's theory, not his own, in all his best poems.

Poe was vigorously and consistently opposed to didacticism in poetry. His love of sweeping generalization and of striking metaphor sometimes betrayed him, however, into saying more than he really intended, as it did, for example, in the famous phrase about "the obstinate oils and waters of Poetry and Truth," often repeated. His ambiguity consists in his using the word "truth" in a special sense, yet permitting the reader to suppose it used in a general sense. In the "Letter to B——" he opposes "the heresy of what is called very foolishly, the Lake School," but thinks it would be a work of supererogation to refute their doctrine. This doctrine is doubtless the same that afterwards in "The Poetic Principle" he attacks as "the heresy of *The Didactic*," which he identifies with the doctrine that "the ultimate object of all Poetry is Truth." He makes no clear distinction between philosophical poetry, such as that of Wordsworth, and poetry that is frankly didactic.

<p style="text-align:center">*　*　*</p>

On the very page with the phrase referred to above about "the obstinate oils and waters of Poetry and Truth," we find the following:

> Just as conscience, or the moral sense, recognizes duty; just as the intellect deals with truth; so is it the part of taste alone to inform us of BEAUTY. And Poesy is the handmaiden but of Taste. Yet we would not be misunderstood. This handmaiden is not forbidden to moralize—in her own fashion. She is not forbidden to depict—but to reason and preach, of virtue. As, of this latter, conscience recognizes the obligation, so intellect teaches the expediency, while taste contents herself with displaying the beauty: waging war with vice merely on the ground of its inconsistency with fitness, harmony, proportion—in a word with τo καλov.[4]

4. Review of Longfellow's *Ballads and Other Poems*, *Graham's Magazine*, April 1842 [Stovall's note]. To *kalon*: beauty (Greek).

Thus poetry becomes didactic, and so objectionable, only when it seeks to convey truth by preaching or reasoning. Not only may poetry depict truth; it may also insinuate or suggest truth. Poe objects to Hawthorne's story "The Minister's Black Veil" because "the *obvious* meaning of this article will be found to smother its insinuated one."[5] In the following passage he distinguishes between pure didacticism and poetic suggestion:

> The defects observable in the "Legend of Brittany" are, chiefly, consequent upon the error of *didacticism*. After every few words of narration, comes a page of morality. Not that the morality, *here*—not that the reflections deduced from the incidents, are peculiarly exceptionable, but that they are too obviously, intrusively, and artificially introduced. The story might have been rendered more *unique*, and altogether more in consonance with the true poetic sentiment, by suffering the morality to be *suggested*; as it is, for example, in the "Old Curiosity Shop," of Dickens—or in that superb *poem*, the "Undine" of De la Motte Fouqué.[6]

Other references to *Undine* will further explain Poe's meaning. "How thoroughly—how radically—how wonderfully," he exclaims, "has 'Undine' been misunderstood! Beneath its obvious meaning there runs an under-current, simple, quite intelligible, artistically managed, and richly philosophical."[7] Again he writes:

> Of allegory properly handled, judiciously subdued, seen only as a shadow or by suggestive glimpses, and making its nearest approach to truth in a not obtrusive and therefore not unpleasant *appositeness*, the "Undine" of De La Motte Fouqué is the best, and undoubtedly a very remarkable specimen.[8]

Poe would agree with Coleridge that depth and energy of thought are an aid to the poet, and if not antagonized he would admit, too, I believe, that truth in the higher, ideal sense of the word, is of concern to the poet. But he would perhaps limit more strictly than Coleridge the means to be used in conveying truth in poetry. Both would exclude any method which would jeopardize the immediate aim of poetry, which is to give pleasure.

[For several pages Stovall suggests step-by-step correspondences between Poe's aesthetic theories and the cosmic philosophy that culminates in *Eureka*.]

Eureka is Poe's attempt to explain the universe, material and spiritual. It is a queer mixture of mathematical calculation and transcen-

5. Review of *Twice-Told Tales*, *Graham's Magazine*, May 1842 [Stovall's note].
6. Review of Lowell's *Poems*, *Graham's Magazine*, March 1844 [Stovall's note].
7. *Marginalia*, *Democratic Review*, Dec. 1844 (*Works*, XVI, 48) [Stovall's note].
8. Notice of Nathaniel Hawthorne, *Godey's Lady's Book*, Nov. 1847. In a review of *Undine: A Miniature Romance*, in *Burton's Gentleman's Magazine*, Sept. 1839, he calls it "the finest romance in existence"; he also says, "What can be more divine than the character of the soulless Undine?" (*Works*, X, 37–39) See also "Marginalia," XVI, 51, for a repetition of this question. Poe may have been influenced here by Coleridge's opinion. "Undine," says Coleridge, "is a most exquisite work. . . . Undine's character, before she receives a soul, is marvellously beautiful" (*Table Talk*, p. 88) [Stovall's note].

dental speculation. He begins his treatise * * * with the assertion that intuition is a surer road to truth than either induction or deduction. His theory may be briefly summarized as follows. There are two contending forces in the universe, attraction, or gravitation, and repulsion, or electricity. Gravitation is the physical principle, and electricity is the spiritual principle. Matter exists only by reason of the conflict of these two forces, and through matter spirit is individualized, reaching its highest development in the conscious intelligence of man. Originally God existed in spirit only and individually. Now He exists variously in the diffused matter and spirit of the universe. The diffusion originates in the Thought of God; but when diffusion is completed, God's Thought is withdrawn. Then commences the reaction, and the consequent conflict of the powers of attraction and repulsion. * * * Eventually, by its tendency to draw to a single center, matter and spirit will be perfectly unified again.

> The absolutely consolidated globe of globes would be *objectless*,—therefore not for a moment could it continue to exist. Matter, created for an end, would unquestionably, on fulfilment of that end, be matter no longer. Let us endeavor to understand that it would disappear, and that God would remain all in all.

Conflict having ceased, with the consequent annihilation of matter as such, God, now existing variously as matter and spirit, will be again as He was at first, purely spiritual and individual—that is to say, Unity.

> God—the material *and* spiritual God—*now* exists solely in the diffused Matter and Spirit of the Universe; and . . . the regathering of this diffused Matter and Spirit will be but the reconstitution of the *purely* Spiritual and Individual God.

Eventually the "inconceivably numerous things which you designate as his creatures, but which are really but infinite individualizations of Himself, will become blended into one, and then will commence a new diffusion and a new cycle of life.

> Think that the sense of individual identity will be gradually merged in the general consciousness—that Man, for example, ceasing imperceptibly to feel himself Man, will at length attain that awfully triumphant epoch when he shall recognize his existence as that of Jehovah. In the meantime bear in mind that all is Life—Life—Life within Life—the less within the greater, and all within the *Spirit* Divine.

For purposes of comparison let me now summarize with like brevity the significant ideas of Coleridge's posthumous essay, *Hints Towards the Formation of a More Comprehensive Theory of Life*. To begin with, he objects to the division "of all that surrounds us into things with life, and things without life" as an "arbitrary assumption."[9] He himself de-

9. *Theory of Life* [American edition] (Philadelphia, 1848, p. 21 [Stovall's note].

fines life as "*the principle of individuation*, or the power which unites a given *all* into a *whole* that is presupposed by all its parts." The mere act of growth, then; does not constitute the idea of life; in fact, he conceives of metals as having a low order of life, as evidenced by the irritability which they manifest to galvanism. After establishing the tendency to individuation, he finds that the law or most general form under which this tendency acts is "*polarity*," or the essential dualism of Nature, arising out of its productive unity, and still tending to reaffirm it, either as equilibrium, indifference, or identity. He affirms that the "one great end of Nature, her ultimate object, is a tendency to the ultimate production of the highest and most comprehensive individuality. Continuing, he says:

> Life, then, we consider as the copula, or the unity of thesis and antithesis, position and counterposition,—Life itself being the positive of both; as, on the other hand, the two counterpoints are the necessary conditions of the *manifestations* of *Life*. These, by the same necessity, unite in a synthesis; which again, by the law of dualism, essential to all actual existence, expands, or *produces* itself, from the point into the *line*, in order to again converge, as the initiation of the same productive process in some intenser form of reality. Thus, in the identity of the two counterpowers, Life *sub*sists; in their strife, it *con*sists; and in their reconciliation it at once dies and is born again into a new form, either falling back into the life of the whole, or starting anew in the process of individuation.

Here we find a suggestion of the cyclic process of creation and annihilation of matter and life which Poe likens to the rhythmic throb of the Heart Divine. In the following passage [from Coleridge] we have precisely Poe's idea of creation through the conflicting powers of attraction and repulsion:

> If we pass to the construction of matter, we find it as the product, or *tertium aliud*,[1] of antagonist powers of repulsion and attraction. Remove these powers, and the conception of matter vanishes into space—conceive repulsion only, and you have the same result. For infinite repulsion, uncounteracted and alone, is tantamount to infinite, dimensionless diffusion, and this again to infinite weakness; viz., to space. Conceive attraction alone, and as an infinite contraction, its product amounts to the absolute point, viz., to time.

Coleridge objects to Milton's idea of a heterogeneous chaos, adding:

> The requisite and only serviceable fiction, therefore, is the representation of Chaos as one vast homogeneous drop! In this sense

1. This Latin phrase may be best understood in terms of another—*tertium quid*—which means a "third" position for two categories considered to be exhaustive and that cannot be contained within each other. The phrase *tertium quid* is used to indicates an intermediate or tentative position, whereas *tertium aliu* (completed) means a "third" position that is all inclusive or final; see the block quotation from Coleridge beginning "as something must," below [Editor].

it may be even justified, as an appropriate symbol of the great fundamental truth that all things spring from, and subsist in, the endless strife between indifference and difference.

Here is a suggestion of Poe's definition of spirit or God in unity as unparticled matter. * * * *Eureka* was published in March, 1848. It is hardly possible, therefore, that Poe could have derived much benefit from the *Theory of Life*, supposing that he had an opportunity to read it. Yet he might have been influenced materially by Coleridge without having read his *Theory of Life*, for the germ from which this essay grew is to be found in the *Biographia Literaria* * * * [in] the passage which defines intelligence as "an indestructible power with two opposite and counteracting forces." In another place Coleridge says more specifically:

> . . . grant me a nature having two contrary forces, the one of which tends to expand indefinitely, while the other strives to apprehend or find itself in this infinity, and I will cause the world of intelligences with the whole system of their representations to rise up before you. [*Biographia*, I.196].

Further he says that

> as something must be the result of these two forces, both alike infinite, and both alike indestructible; and as rest or neutralization cannot be this result; no other conception is possible, but that the product must be a *tertium aliquid*, or finite generation. Consequently this conception is necessary. Now this *tertium aliquid* can be no other than an inter-penetration of the counteracting powers, partaking of both.

These passages alone, with their connotation, might have been sufficient to set Poe to work on a train of thinking that would produce such a theory as that of *Eureka*.

* * *

ROBERT COLIN McLEAN

George Tucker (1775–1861) was a Virginia politician, economist, writer, and teacher. As McLean points out, Poe, as Tucker's student at the University of Virginia, would have been exposed to his Scottish common-sense school of philosophy and aesthetics as well as to associational psychology. Born in Bermuda to a well-to-do family, Tucker was privately tutored with an emphasis on law. In 1795, he came to the United States and became a protégé of his kinsman St. George Tucker (father of Nathaniel Beverley Tucker). He attended the College of William and Mary, graduating in 1797. In 1800, he opened a law practice in Richmond, Virginia, where he sought to combine his legal vocation with his interests in literature and political journalism. He wrote verse, letters, and articles for newspapers, magazine essays, and political pamphlets. In 1801, he published a *Letter to a Member of the General Assembly of Virginia, on the Subject of the Late*

Conspiracy of the Slaves: With a Proposal for Their Colonization, in which he suggested that the federal government purchase land west of the Mississippi for freed slaves. The theme of the ultimate withering away of slavery would recur in his works for the rest of his life. (In this view he differed from Nathaniel Beverley Tucker, a staunch proslavery advocate; see pp. 772 ff. herein.)

George Tucker left Richmond in 1806 to live in the Shenandoah Valley and two years later moved back to southern Virginia. In 1814–15, he serially published a collection of essays as "Thoughts of a Hermit" in the Philadelphia magazine, the *Port Folio*; these essays were later incorporated into *Essays on Various Subjects of Taste, Morals, and National Policy* (1822), which followed *Speech of Mr. Tucker, of Virginia, on the Penetration of Slavery in Missouri* (1820). Tucker became increasingly interested not only in economics and philosophy but also in public service. In 1815, he was elected to the Virginia House of Burgesses and in 1819 to the U.S. House of Representatives.

His literary interests continued as well. In 1824, he published his first novel, *The Valley of Shenandoah*, a picture of planter life in the Old South. In 1824–25, he became professor of moral philosophy at the University of Virginia, a position he held for two decades. In 1830–31, he gave an important series of lectures on rhetoric and belles lettres to the students and faculty of the University of Virginia. In 1827, he published a satiric science-fiction novel, *A Voyage to the Moon: With Some Account of the Manners and Customs, Science and Philosophy, of the People of Morosofia and Other Lunarians*, a book that may have influenced Poe's own moon writings. In 1841, he wrote another futuristic narrative, *A Century Hence: Or a Romance of 1941*, which, however, was not published until the later twentieth century. Meanwhile, he continued his prolific output of works of biography, history, economics, and political science. A personal friend of Thomas Jefferson and James Madison, he wrote the first authorized *Life of Thomas Jefferson*, 2 vol. (1837). The same year also saw *The Laws of Wages, Profits, and Rent Investigated* and *Theory of Money and Banks Investigated*. For several years, he worked on *A History of the United States*, which was published in 4 vols (1856–57). He quickly followed this landmark study with *Political Economy for the People* (1859) and the collection *Essays, Moral and Metaphysical* (1860).

Of special literary interest, in addition to his "Lectures on Rhetoric and Belles Lettres," are Tucker's reflections on the relation of neuropsychology and the creative process—especially his 1804 essay "On the Illusions of Fancy" (from the edited volume of essays by members of the Rainbow Club in Richmond) and the later piece "On Beauty" (in *Essays, Moral and Metaphysical*). Also of interest are Tucker's comments on the relation of horror and madness to sublime Beauty. For further discussion see Robert Colin McLean's *George Tucker*, pp. 118ff. These works link him both with the philosophers and aestheticians represented in this volume and with theories of mental process and its aberrations. The selection reprinted here is a portion, "Poetic Theory," from "Aesthetics and Literature," chapter 9 of McLean's book on Tucker; the notes have been shortened, deleted, or integrated into the main text in brackets and renumbered; added material by the editor is labeled as such.

From Poetic Theory†

In poetic theory, as in aesthetics and philosophy, Tucker derived many ideas from the literature of the immediate past. His lectures reveal, in a general way, the influence of those critical and creative writings of the late eighteenth and early nineteenth centuries which stressed the significance for poetry of man's feelings and passions to the neglect of his rational endowments. More specifically, Tucker's theory of poetry reflects his eclectic use of eighteenth-century philosophy to propound a view of the nature and function of poetry. Although he never believed that all of man's experience could be explained in terms of the mechanical operation of the mind, Tucker did hold that the doctrine of associational psychology helped elucidate the nature of poetic creation and communication.

* * *

In an effort to define poetry, Tucker distinguished it from other forms of expression, conveniently summarizing what he believed were its "outward characteristics." It differs from prose in having "greater melody of diction," inversion of word order, greater brevity or greater amplification, "greater dignity of language," "more varied & more abundant imagery," and, most importantly, "a more elevated tone of feeling & *wilder enthusiasm*." Prose, he admitted, possesses "more or less" these same traits but lacks "perfect regularity" of structure, never exhibits all six attributes concurrently as does poetry, and uses each only as an "auxiliary" to address "the will or the understanding." In the same fashion, eloquence differs not only in wanting "regularity of diction" but in its intent: oratory, like poetry, "addresses itself to the feelings," but it does so "with a view to persuasion, whilst poetry addresses them only for the purpose of producing pleasure and kindling the same enthusiasm as that which excited it" [Lecture XXXIX].

Tucker thought so highly of the emotional aspect of poetry that, though he carefully covered the material in Blair and Campbell, he labeled the rhetorical aspects of poetry as superficial ornaments of the art [Lecture XLII]. His major interest was to explain how the poet utilizes the raw materials of experience to write verse which sympathetically arouses in his audience the same emotions and feelings which occasioned him to write.

* * *

Basic to Tucker's theory is the tenet that great poetry, which serves as a vehicle for the emotions, cannot be didactic. His belief that the end of poetry is pure pleasure, unalloyed with any attempt to persuade or instruct, rests upon the philosophic premise "that the strength & beauty of all metaphysical experience have their foundation in our

† From *George Tucker: Moral Philosopher and Man of Letters* (Chapel Hill: University of North Carolina Press, 1961) by Robert Colin McLean, copyright © 1961 by the University of North Carolina Press, renewed 1989 by Robert Colin McLean, reprinted by permission of the publisher and the author.

pleasures & pains—those having the greatest effect which refer to our liveliest emotions."[1] Because Tucker assumed all emotional excitement to be enjoyable, he said that it is the duty of the poet "to awaken our sympathy by giving touching & natural exhibitions of human passions & sentiments" and to "exhibit to our imaginations lively & faithful delineations of the most interesting forms of nature."[2]

That portion of the lectures which may have dealt in detail with the poet's description of human passions is missing.[3] What remains on that subject is Tucker's assertion that the "emotions of the heart" are manifested by "sentiments of love and pity and horror and disgust [Lecture XLIV]. Tucker's definition of the "essence" or "soul" of poetry, however, suggests the nature of human passions and their relationship in poetry to the operations of the fancy:

> This consists either in the elevation of the thought, or a fervid glow of feeling by which the poet seems to be hurried away by his subject—and which never fails to impart to the hearer or reader somewhat of the same animating warmth, which inspired it. Of all the qualities of poetry there is none to which it so much owes its success as this, or which so truly marks the genius of the poet. The rapturous feelings to which he gives utterance find a sympathetic tho' fainter response in every bosom to whom [sic] they are addressed, for his language is a faithful echo to his feelings. It is emotion, then, warm, generous, lofty emotion, such as the perception of the beautiful and the grand may inspire!—such as seems to raise him who feels it above the sordidness & petty concerns of ordinary life,—which seems to be the essence of poetry. . . . It is emotion which calls forth the electric spark of the mind, & the past & the future stand before him with the freshness & distinctness of a present picture or landscape & reendows every object of the scene with life & thot [sic] & passion—and objects of his lively sympathy [Lecture XL].

The balance of Tucker's discussion of poetic theory is found in his elaboration on the importance of the beautiful and sublime "in composition." He treated both concepts somewhat confusingly, first, in terms of physical objects or emotional states which inspire the poet and, second, as effects to be created by him. In so doing Tucker followed the Scottish critics in holding that the imagination and the "sensibility" work together to bring about the effect of "warm emotion," and in delineating the manner in which the poet evokes the sympathetic participation of his audience.

When Tucker discussed "beauty, as applied to composition," he insisted that the poet should not be limited to the "function of representing beautiful objects" [Lecture LXVI] a practice which, he said, gives so much charm to descriptive poetry that some poets, such as

1. "Lectures on Rhetoric and Belles Lettres," Lecture IX [McLean's note].
2. Lecture XXXIX [McLean's note].
3. Lecture XXXVIII. Part of Lecture IX is also missing [McLean's note].

Erasmus Darwin, "by considering all poetry whatever to be merely a 'speaking picture' have precluded themselves from excelling in its higher species, the pathetic and sublime."[4]

* * *

Tucker's denigration of Darwin's poetical theory did not result from a denial that beautiful physical objects are subject matter for poetry. On the contrary, Tucker felt that "the most copious sources of materials to the poet" are to be found in the "two species of beauty in the physical world." Poets address themselves forcibly and agreeably to the imagination by representing, first, "soft & agreeable colours, melodious & symphonious sounds, gentle & graceful motions, symmetrical proportions and the numerous items which constitute personal beauty, and which make a world of itself," and, second, "the agreeable associations to which all these objects give rise."[5] But, as Tucker explained in exalting the role of the poet in arousing the emotion of the beautiful, there could be a great heightening of the effect of beauty. When the poet merely describes beautiful objects, said Tucker, there is in the poem a weakening of the force of beauty, since "the immediate perception or sensation more powerfully excites the mind than the mere conception." But, he pointed out, in the best poetry there are more than adequate compensations for this loss. Poems, more than any other composition or "any physical object whatever," "directly & forcibly" create in the mind that "moral beauty" which consists of those "softer & more amiable virtues" which are "so similar to the mixt feelings of love & admiration we experience for physical beauty." This is so, said Tucker, because "words are more perfect signs of thoughts & feelings than any mere combinations of form & colour": melody, rhythm, and rhyme, which "impart the character of music to articulate language," provide a desirable and gratifying sensual impact upon the ears, thus compensating for that loss of the direct sensual pleasure which occurs in the translation of a beautiful object from the physical through the mental realm into poetry; and the attributes of language also simultaneously excite "our minds" so as to stimulate the associating activity. In much the same fashion of musical verse, figures of speech—the products of the fancy—are inherently pleasurable and also contribute to the over-all effect of the poem. Indeed, said Tucker, when the poet contemplates the "beautiful or grand," he is moved to a state of "high wrought feeling," and when his mind is agitated, he sees and is able to utilize in language "analogies & resemblances which are

4. "On Beauty," *Essays* (1860), p. 189 [McLean's note]. "Pathetic": in ordinary use, inadequacy or unmerited self-pity; as a literary term, *pathos* (from the Greek word for feeling) indicates the sorrow or pity associated with suffering (and perhaps purgation of grief) in Greek tragedy. "Sublime": noble, majestic, grand; as a literary term the word indicates a psychological-aesthetic reaction to that which is awesome, stupendous, vast, lofty, spiritually enlarging—as high mountains, vast oceans, infinite space, and the like. The Greek critic Longinus (flourished 1st century? B.C.E.) wrote the treatise *On the Sublime*, which has been the subject of debate for two thousand years. Erasmus Darwin (1731–1802), English physician, scientist, and poet (grandfather of Charles Darwin), wrote poetry and prose on botanical and evolutionary themes, including *The Botanic Garden* (1789, 1791) and *Zoönomia* (1794–96) [Editor].
5. This quotation and the balance of the discussion on beauty "in composition" are taken from Lecture LXVI, "Lectures on Rhetoric and Belles Lettres" [McLean's note].

not perceived by a mind in a state of quiescence." And, said Tucker, explaining how "sensibility" unites with the imagination in the creation of poetry, "according to the mechanism of the mind, the fancy & feelings mutually act upon one another, & whatever excites the one, has a tendency to lend new strength & activity to the other." The poet is inspired by a sort of Longinian[6] frenzy and, because of the power of figurative and musical language, transfers by a kind of emotional chemistry his feelings to his audience.

Before concluding his lecture on beauty and poetry, Tucker emphasized that a poem not only is "the vehicle of transmitting conceptions of beauty & the various emotions which accompany these conceptions" but in and of itself is "capable of having beauty—and that of the same two kinds," both of which are independent of its subject matter. It has, first of all, a "direct sensitive beauty" of ordered, melodious language which produces "the same sort of pleasure as the sound of a musical instrument," and, more importantly, there is awakened a feeling of beauty which is aroused by the "excellence of style" as well as a recognition that the poet, by the handling of language, meter, and plan, has succeeded in exciting the emotions of his readers.

Like many critics of his age, Tucker thought highly of poetry which evoked the emotion of sublimity [Lecture LXV, from "Rhetoric and Belles Lettres"]. He pointed out that this feeling always "arises from a reference to ourselves & our species" of such physical attributes as power and magnitude or such moral qualities as virtue and evil. Citing Shakespeare, Milton, and Byron as writers who reached the heights of sublimity, Tucker said that the poet could arouse the emotion in two ways. On the one hand, he could represent such sights as storm-tossed oceans or thunder storms, or, in the other, he could delineate such human beings as Robespierre, Medea, Timon of Athens, or Coriolanus,[7] who, indifferent or invulnerable to those frailties and calamities common to humanity, are either utterly vicious or virtuous.

Although Tucker expressed the view that any excitement of emotion tended to be gratifying, he recognized, he said, that in real life the experience of observing such phenomena as inspired the sublime might become "unmingled pain." But, he said, emphasizing that successful artists create "as lively & impressive representations" as possible,

6. I.e., like Longinus [Editor].
7. All "villains" in history and literature. Maximilien Marie Isadore Robespierre (1758–1794) was one of the principal figures of the French Revolution; he called for the execution of the king of France and led the citizens' committee that inaugurated the Reign of Terror. In mythology, Medea is a sorceress married to the Greek hero Jason, leader of the Argonauts who carried away the Golden Fleece. In the tragedy *Medea* by Euripides (480?–405 B.C.E.), Jason decides he wants a new wife, whereupon Medea kills their children, along with the woman Jason fancies. *Timon of Athens* (c. 1607), a tragedy by Shakespeare and others, depicts the outrage and misanthropy of a generous patron, set in motion when his so-called friends fail to help when he runs into financial difficulties; cursing humankind, Timon retreats to a cave to live as a hermit. Finding a treasure of gold, he plots a siege of the city of Athens; after some political intrigue Timon is found dead in his cave, his last words a denunciation of the human race. Shakespeare's *The Tragedy of Coriolanus* (c. 1608) portrays the inconstancy of loyalty and the ambiguities of treason in the story of the overweening ambition of Caius Martius, who was given his honorific name after his military victory at Corioli; after being denied the consulship of Rome, Coriolanus attacks the city and is ultimately murdered [Editor].

when "sublime objects are represented to us through the imagination" they are always agreeable, and the sublime when but "a copy" may become "an object of beauty & admiration." Because of this softening effect of art, the writer who seeks to win the greatest admiration should portray the "most terrible and odious" phenomena and even "such horrible crimes as would produce abhorrence & disgust" in real life. Rather than attempting to diminish the effect of their material, then, "poets & those writers who would address themselves to the imagination" should do all possible to heighten the intensity of their works, only taking care not to over-exaggerate so as to pass beyond the sublime to the ridiculous, the distinction between which is "a very nice one." For the sublime, obscurity is an asset, said Tucker, "whenever it favors the operation of the sense of danger & gives more play to our fears." Lastly and most importantly, the composition "should have a certain degree of singleness, since a variety of objects by exciting many ideas & emotions would prevent any one from having that force which concentration would give."

Tucker's poetic theory, as well as his discussions of prose, suggests the interesting possibility that he influenced the early Poe, indeed, helped to form some of Poe's most characteristic aesthetic doctrines and practices. Poe's theory of the unity of effect, generally thought to have its origins in the writings of A. W. von Schlegel,[8] but also * * * traced by Robert Jacobs to Archibald "Alison's demand for a unity of emotion,"[9] seems to have been adumbrated by Tucker's postulate that each composition "have a certain degree of singleness." Other of Tucker's lectures which discuss the technical skills needed by a writer suggest Poe's stress upon a necessary unity of tone in a work of art and his theory of causal arrangement. In Lectures XXIV to XXVI, * * * Tucker said that all prose writings could be classified into three groups, according to their primary appeals to the understanding, the imagination, and the feelings. In addressing successfully any of these faculties, it was the writer's task, said Tucker in Lecture XXVII, to advance in logical steps, though carefully concealing his method from his readers. He should "begin in the tone with which he means to proceed," and should arrange his materials "so that one part may seem to rise naturally out of another," as in a "chain of cause & effect," thus skillfully leading the reader "by easy gradations to the conclusion."

Poe's famous attack upon didacticism has been traced to his reading of Coleridge's *Biographia Literaria*,[1] but perhaps it was first suggested by Tucker. Tucker emphasized in a number of ways that poetry's aim is

8. The influence of Schlegel has been documented by many Poe scholars. A * * * work which stresses the influence of Schlegel and other German Romantics on Poe is Albert J. Lubell, "Poe and A. W. Schlegel," *JEGP* [*Journal of English and Germanic Philology*], 52 (1953), 1–12. See also George Kelly, "Poe's Theory of Beauty," *American Literature* 27 (1956), 521–536 [McLean's note]. See the selections from A. W. Schlegel, Friedrich Schlegel, and other German Romantic writers reprinted herein [Editor].
9. See "Poe's Heritage from Jefferson's Virginia" (Johns Hopkins University diss., 1953), pp. 133–134 and *passim* [McLean's note].
1. See Floyd Stovall, "Poe's Debt to Coleridge," *University of Texas Studies in English*, 10 (1930), 85 [McLean's note]. See pp. 789–98 herein [Editor].

pure pleasure, free from any taint of instruction or persuasion. Related to this hedonistic view of poetry is Tucker's tenet that music is an intrinsic element of poetry. Taken together, these statements might well culminate in Poe's famous definition of poetry as "the rhythmical creation of beauty." In his review of Joseph Rodman Drake's *The Culprit Fay*, Poe distinguished between two aspects of poetry.[2] First, "poesy" or "the Poetic Sentiment" he associated with the inspiration which evokes the poet's love of the beautiful and his sense of the sublime. For Poe this mood is "one in which the poet is impassioned and excited and has expansion of mind," corresponding "to . . . excitement or elevation of soul."[3] Second, Poe was concerned with the merits of the poem itself, that is, with the "*means*" by which the poet affects the minds and emotions of his audience. In Tucker's lectures is set forth a similar distinction. There Tucker defined the "essence" or "soul" of poetry as that which is called forth by "the perception of the beautiful and the grand"—that "fervent glow of feeling" which lifts the artist "above the sordidness & petty concerns of ordinary life." At the same time, however, Tucker, too, was concerned with the poem itself, as a means by which the poet conveys a sense of the beautiful and sublime to his readers, using carefully ordered, musical language, which, through the sensual pleasure it provides, more than compensates for that loss of pleasure that takes place when a beautiful object or experience undergoes a translation from the physical world into the world of art. Like Poe,[4] Tucker felt that the mere recording of "poetic" materials, though capable of providing a degree of pleasure, does not result in great poetry, which needs to be inspired and to be carefully arranged. It was for this reason that he emphasized the importance of approximating music in poetry by means of melody, rhythm, rhyme, and onomatopoeia.

Several examples of onomatopoeia provided by Tucker to illustrate the naturalness and universality of imitation suggest the possible use of his ideas by Poe in two famous poems.[5] The title of Poe's "Ulalume" seems to mean "wailing" or "light of or in sorrow" and comes from the Latin word *ululare*.[6] In Tucker's lecture appears an illustration of how words, by their sounds, designate actions: "ὀλολύξω, *ululare, heulen, hurler*, to howl." The reason for Poe's puzzling spelling of "Yaanek" in the same poem as a name for Mount Erebus, down which "restlessly

2. *Edgar Allan Poe [Representative Selections, with Introduction, Bibliography, and Notes]*, ed. Margaret Alterton and Hardin Craig (New York, 1925), pp. xxix–xxx [McLean's note].
3. Stovall, "Poe's Debt to Coleridge," p. 97. Stovall's point was to distinguish "between the softened emotion succeeding an outburst of passion and the outburst itself," to show that, for Poe, the poetic mood "grows out of passion frequently, but composition never begins until the passion is tranquilized or transmuted into a spiritual exaltation" * * * [McLean's note]. Cf. Wordsworth's idea of the spontaneous overflow of powerful emotions recollected in tranquility [Editor].
4. See Poe's review of Longfellow's *Ballads and Other Poems*. * * * [McLean's note]. Reprinted on pp. 637ff. herein [Editor].
5. "Lectures on Rhetoric and Belles Lettres," Lecture XIII. Tucker apparently took his illustrations from an encyclopedia, which he did not identify [McLean's note]. "Onomatopoeia": words that echo or sound like what they describe, e.g., *snap, crack, pop, bubble, murmur, whisper* [Editor].
6. Thomas O. Mabbott, *Explicator*, 1 (Feb., 1943), Item 25. See also *Selected Writings of Edgar Allan Poe*, ed. Edward H. Davidson (Boston, 1956), p. 497 n. [McLean's note].

roll" the "scoriac rivers," is made clearer by another entry in the same Tucker lecture, in which he explained how vowel sounds, requiring "nothing but the simple opening of the mouth," offer "no obstacle to the emission of sound" and approximate the nature of the idea to be expressed. "Now," said Tucker, "we . . . see the probable origin of the Danish word *aa*, which signifies *river*. This generic term has in use become the name of three rivers in the Low Countries, of three in Switzerland, and of five in Westphalia—the vowels running without obstacle like the river." A third example, cited to show the close relationship between sounds and ideas, suggests a source for Poe's use of "tintinnabulation" in "The Bells," a problem which has concerned many critics.[7] "Ringing (tintinement), tinnitus, tintinnabulum, are words," said Tucker, "whose common radical *tin*, exactly imitates the clear, sharp & continued sound which is heard to diminish gradually when a metallic vessel is struck."

In Tucker's lectures, furthermore, Poe could have found the germ and justification for his belief that the beautiful could include the horrible; his utilization of the obscure in stories to heighten the effect of terror; and his assumption that "sensation" (horror) stories are legitimate forms of artistic expression, that, as Poe said, "even out of deformities" the imagination "fabricates . . . *Beauty*."[8] Margaret Alterton has plausibly suggested that in his review of Hawthorne's *Twice-Told Tales* Poe's defense of the horror story rests on the grounds that "it satisfied a human craving for excitement" [*Poe*, p. XIX n]. Similarly, Tucker defended the portrayal of the "most terrible and odious," such "crimes as would produce abhorrence & disgust" in real life, by arguing, first of all, that emotional excitement is as basic to man as physical exercise and, second, that what is horrible in life is tempered by the artist to satisfy aesthetically this fundamental drive of man [Lecture LXV].

Other possible influences on Poe's aesthetic theory, less specific, if not less important, may be traced in Tucker's work. Tucker perhaps provided Poe with a rationale for the treatment of purely "poetic" subjects for poetry—beautiful and sublime sentiments and objects. And, in a more general way, Tucker's philosophical theory may have stimulated Poe's interest in abnormal psychology. It is admittedly a long step from Tucker's delineation of Julia Moncrief's irrational father to Poe's treatment of Roderick Usher; but Tucker's belief, stated as early as 1804, that "delirium and madness, though remotely caused by corporeal disease, are the *immediate* effects of an imagination stimulated to preternatural vigour"[9] may well have interested Poe.

Although it has long been felt that Poe's thinking was strongly af-

7. See, for examples, Fred A. Dudley, "Tintinnabulation: And a Source of Poe's 'The Bells,' " *American Literature* 4 (1933), 296–300; Kills Campbell, *Poems of Edgar Allan Poe* (Boston, 1917), pp. 281–282 [McLean's note].
8. Quoted by Jay Hubbell, *The South in American Literature, 1607–1900* (Durham, N.C., 1954), p. 532 [McLean's note].
9. Tucker's statement appears in *The Rainbow*, p. 53 [McLean's note]. Twenty-five essays on political and social issues, mostly by members of the Rainbow Club, were published in the Richmond *Enquirer*. The first ten were published as a book in 1804 [Editor].

fected by his year at the University of Virginia in 1826, no convincing case has ever been made for his literary theory having been formed there. Poe studied modern and classical languages and is not known to have attended Tucker's lectures, though it is possible that he audited Tucker's classes, looked at the notes of Tucker's students, or, perhaps, talked to Tucker about literature and aesthetics, since the two shared many tastes, especially that for Byron's poetry.[1] Establishment of a direct relationship between Poe and Tucker must await more concrete evidence; yet it seems not improbable that Tucker's interpretation of Scottish aesthetics aroused Poe's literary interests and provided him with several basic critical ideas which he developed and changed as he read further in the writings of German and English romantics.

RICHARD WILBUR

From The House of Poe†

A few weeks ago, in the *New York Times Book Review*, Mr. Saul Bellow expressed impatience with the current critical habit of finding symbols in everything. No self-respecting modern professor, Mr. Bellow observed, would dare to explain Achilles' dragging of Hector around the walls of Troy by the mere assertion that Achilles was in a bad temper. That would be too drearily obvious. No, the professor must say that the circular path of Achilles and Hector relates to the theme of circularity which pervades *The Iliad*.

In the following week's *Book Review*, a pedantic correspondent corrected Mr. Bellow, pointing out that Achilles did not, in Homer's *Iliad*, drag Hector's body around the walls of Troy; this perhaps invalidates the Homeric example, but Mr. Bellow's complaint remains, never-

1. [Hervey] Allen, *Israfel: The Life and Times of Edgar Allan Poe* (New York: Rinehart, 1934)], I, 179, speculates that William Wertenbaker and Poe passed part of Poe's last night at Charlottesville as guests of Tucker or Professor Blaetterman. [Arthur Hobson] Quinn, *Edgar Allan Poe*, p. 102, believes that Poe "would probably have gained most from intercourse with Tucker," of all the faculty members. Several scholars have suggested that Poe knew and was influenced by Tucker. J. O. Bailey in "Sources for Poe's *Arthur Gordon Pym*, 'Hans Pfaal,' and Other Pieces," *PMLA*, 57 (1942), 513–535, thinks that Poe probably knew Tucker well; that for "Hans Pfaal," as well as for *Eureka*, Poe read Tucker's *A Voyage to the Moon*, either in manuscript or in printed form; and that Meredith Niel Posey ("Notes on Hans Pfaal," *Modern Language Notes*, 45 (1930), 501–507) is wrong in thinking that Dr. Robley Dunglison's review of Tucker's book (*American Quarterly Review*, 3 [1828], 61–88) provided enough information for Poe's story of a voyage to the moon. Second, Alterton asserts that Poe's political theories were very similar to Tucker's. It should be pointed out that Alterton misinterprets Tucker's political and social ideas and could have made a much stronger case for Tucker's possible influence had she known that Tucker, like the Poe she describes, held more in common with the early Federalists than with the Jeffersonians. It seems certain that Poe knew Tucker's views, since he joined the *Southern Literary Messenger* only three months after Tucker published in it an article outlining some of his extremely conservative political and social theories ("A Discourse on the Progress of Philosophy and its Influence on the Intellectual and Moral Character of Man," 1 [1835], 405–421). Like Poe, Tucker opposed perfectibilian reforms, especially those based upon *a priori* reasoning; distrusted the "ignorant rabble" of democracies; preferred the life of cities to the joys of rural life * * * See Alterton, pp. lxxii–lxviii * * * [McLean's note].

† Originally presented as a lecture at the Library of Congress under the auspices of the Gertrude Clarke Whittall Poetry and Literature Fund in 1959. From *Anniversary Lectures 1959.* Copyright © 1966 by Richard Wilbur. Reprinted by permission of the author.

theless, a very sensible one. We are all getting a bit tired, I think, of that laboriously clever criticism which discovers mandalas in Mark Twain, rebirth archetypes in Edwin Arlington Robinson, and fertility myths in everybody.

Still, we must not be carried away by our impatience, to the point of demanding that no more symbols be reported. The business of the critic, after all, is to divine the intention of the work, and to interpret the work in the light of that intention; and since some writers are intentionally symbolic, there is nothing for it but to talk about their symbols. If we speak of Melville, we must speak of symbols. If we speak of Hawthorne, we must speak of symbols. And as for Edgar Allan Poe, whose sesquicentennial year we are met to observe, I think we can make no sense about him until we consider his work—and in particular his prose fiction—as deliberate and often brilliant allegory.

Not everyone will agree with me that Poe's work has an accessible allegorical meaning. Some critics, in fact, have refused to see any substance, allegorical or otherwise, in Poe's fiction, and have regarded his tales as nothing more than complicated machines for saying "boo." Others have intuited undiscoverable meanings in Poe, generally of an unpleasant kind: I recall one Freudian critic declaring that if we find Poe unintelligible we should congratulate ourselves, since if we *could* understand him it would be proof of our abnormality.

It is not really surprising that some critics should think Poe meaningless, or that others should suppose his meaning intelligible only to monsters. Poe was not a wide-open and perspicuous writer; indeed, he was a secretive writer both by temperament and by conviction. He sprinkled his stories with sly references to himself and to his personal history. He gave his own birthday of January 19 to his character William Wilson; he bestowed his own height and color of eye on the captain of the phantom ship in "Ms. Found in a Bottle"; and the name of one of his heroes, Arthur Gordon Pym, is patently a version of his own. He was a maker and solver of puzzles, fascinated by codes, ciphers, anagrams, acrostics, hieroglyphics, and the Kabbala. He invented the detective story. He was fond of aliases; he delighted in accounts of swindles; he perpetrated the famous Balloon Hoax of 1844; and one of his most characteristic stories is entitled "Mystification." A man so devoted to concealment and deception and unraveling and detection might be expected to have in his work what Poe himself called "undercurrents of meaning."

And that is where Poe, as a critic, said that meaning belongs: not on the surface of the poem or tale, but below the surface as a dark undercurrent. If the meaning of a work is made overly clear—as Poe said in his "Philosophy of Composition"—if the meaning is brought to the surface and made the upper current of the poem or tale, then the work becomes bald and prosaic and ceases to be art. Poe conceived of art, you see, not as a means of giving imaginative order to earthly experience, but as a stimulus to unearthly visions. The work of literary art does not, in Poe's view, present the reader with a provisional arrangement of reality; instead, it seeks to disengage the reader's mind

from reality and propel it toward the ideal. Now, since Poe thought the function of art was to set the mind soaring upward in what he called "a wild effort to reach the Beauty above," it was important to him that the poem or tale should not have such definiteness and completeness of meaning as might contain the reader's mind within the work. Therefore Poe's criticism places a positive value on the obscuration of meaning, on a dark suggestiveness, on a deliberate vagueness by means of which the reader's mind may be set adrift toward the beyond.

Poe's criticism, then, assures us that his work does have meaning. And Poe also assures us that this meaning is not on the surface but in the depths. If we accept Poe's invitation to play detective, and commence to read him with an eye for submerged meaning, it is not long before we sense that there *are* meanings to be found, and that in fact many of Poe's stories, though superficially dissimilar, tell the same tale. We begin to have this sense as we notice Poe's repeated use of certain narrative patterns; his repetition of certain words and phrases; his use, in story after story, of certain scenes and properties. We notice, for instance, the recurrence of the *spiral* or *vortex*. In "Ms. Found in a Bottle," the story ends with a plunge into a whirlpool; the "Descent into the Maelström" also concludes in a watery vortex; the house of Usher, just before it plunges into the tarn, is swaddled in a whirlwind; the hero of "Metzengerstein," Poe's first published story, perishes in "a whirlwind of chaotic fire"; and at the close of "King Pest," Hugh Tarpaulin is cast into a puncheon of ale and disappears "amid a whirlpool of foam." That Poe offers us so many spirals or vortices in his fiction, and that they should always appear at the same terminal point in their respective narratives, is a strong indication that the spiral had some symbolic value for Poe. And it did: What the spiral invariably represents in any tale of Poe's is the loss of consciousness, and the descent of the mind into sleep.

I hope you will grant, before I am through, that to find spirals in Poe is not so silly as finding circles in Homer. The professor who finds circles in Homer does so to the neglect of more important and more provable meanings. But the spiral or vortex is a part of that symbolic language in which Poe said his say, and unless we understand it we cannot understand Poe.

But now I have gotten ahead of myself, and before I proceed with my project of exploring one area of Poe's symbolism, I think I had better say something about Poe's conception of poetry and the poet.

Poe conceived of God as a poet. The universe, therefore, was an artistic creation, a poem composed by God. Now, if the universe is a poem, it follows that the one proper response to it is aesthetic, and that God's creatures are attuned to Him in proportion as their imaginations are ravished by the beauty and harmony of his creation. Not to worship beauty, not to regard poetic knowledge as divine, would be to turn one's back on God and fall from grace.

The planet Earth, according to Poe's myth of the cosmos, has done just this. It has fallen away from God by exalting the scientific reason

above poetic intuition, and by putting its trust in material fact rather than in visionary knowledge. The Earth's inhabitants are thus corrupted by rationalism and materialism; their souls are diseased; and Poe sees this disease of the human spirit as having contaminated physical nature. The woods and fields and waters of Earth have thereby lost their first beauty, and no longer clearly express God's imagination; the landscape has lost its original perfection of composition, in proportion as men have lost their power to perceive the beautiful.

Since Earth is a fallen planet, life upon Earth is necessarily a torment for the poet: neither in the human sphere nor in the realm of nature can he find fit objects for contemplation, and indeed his soul is oppressed by everything around him. The rationalist mocks at him; the dull, prosaic spirit of the age damps his imaginative spark; the gross materiality of the world crowds in upon him. His only recourse is to abandon all concern for Earthly things, and to devote himself as purely as possible to unearthly visions, in hopes of glimpsing that heavenly beauty which is the thought of God.

Poe, then, sees the poetic soul as at war with the mundane physical world; and that warfare is Poe's fundamental subject. But the war between soul and world is not the only war. There is also warfare within the poet's very nature. To be sure, the poet's nature was not always in conflict with itself. Prior to his earthly incarnation, and during his dreamy childhood, Poe's poet enjoyed a serene unity of being; his consciousness was purely imaginative, and he knew the universe for the divine poem that it is. But with his entrance into adult life, the poet became involved with a fallen world in which the physical, the factual, the rational, the prosaic are not escapable. Thus, compromised, he lost his perfect spirituality, and is now cursed with a divided nature. Though his imagination still yearns toward ideal beauty, his mortal body chains him to the physical and temporal and local; the hungers and passions of his body draw him toward external objects, and the conflict of conscience and desire degrades and distracts his soul; his mortal senses try to convince him of the reality of a material world which his soul struggles to escape; his reason urges him to acknowledge everyday fact, and to confine his thought within the prison of logic. For all these reasons it is not easy for the poet to detach his soul from earthly things, and regain his lost imaginative power—his power to commune with that supernal beauty which is symbolized, in Poe, by the shadowy and angelic figures of Ligeia, and Helen, and Lenore.

These, then, are Poe's great subjects: first, the war between the poetic soul and the external world; second, the war between the poetic soul and the earthly self to which it is bound. All of Poe's major stories are allegorical presentations of these conflicts, and everything he wrote bore somehow upon them.

How does one wage war against the external world? And how does one release one's visionary soul from the body, and from the constraint of the reason? These may sound like difficult tasks; and yet we all accomplish them every night. In a subjective sense—and Poe's thought is wholly subjective—we destroy the world every time we close our

eyes. If *esse est percipi*, as Bishop Berkeley said—if to be is to be perceived—then when we withdraw our attention from the world in somnolence or sleep, the world ceases to be. As our minds move toward sleep, by way of drowsiness and reverie and the hypnagogic state, we escape from consciousness of the world, we escape from awareness of our bodies, and we enter a realm in which reason no longer hampers the play of the imagination: we enter the realm of dream.

Like many romantic poets, Poe identified imagination with dream. Where Poe differed from other romantic poets was in the literalness and absoluteness of the identification, and in the clinical precision with which he observed the phenomena of dream, carefully distinguishing the various states through which the mind passes on its way to sleep. A large number of Poe's stories derive their very structure from this sequence of mental states: "Ms. Found in a Bottle," to give but one example, is an allegory of the mind's voyage from the waking world into the world of dreams, with each main step of the narrative symbolizing the passage of the mind from one state to another—from wakefulness to reverie, from reverie to the hypnagogic state, from the hypnagogic state to the deep dream. The departure of the narrator's ship from Batavia represents the mind's withdrawal from the waking world; the drowning of the captain and all but one of the crew represents the growing solitude of reverie; when the narrator is transferred by collision from a real ship to a phantom ship, we are to understand that he has passed from reverie, a state in which reality and dream exist in a kind of equilibrium, into the free fantasy of the hypnagogic state. And when the phantom ship makes its final plunge into the whirlpool, we are to understand that the narrator's mind has gone over the brink of sleep and descended into dreams.

What I am saying by means of this example is that the scenes and situations of Poe's tales are always concrete representations of states of mind. If we bear in mind Poe's fundamental plot—the effort of the poetic soul to escape all consciousness of the world in dream—we soon recognize the significance of certain scenic or situational motifs which turn up in story after story. The most important of these recurrent motifs is that of *enclosure* or *circumscription*; perhaps the latter term is preferable, because it is Poe's own word, and because Poe's enclosures are so often more or less circular in form. The heroes of Poe's tales and poems are violently circumscribed by whirlpools, or peacefully circumscribed by cloud-capped Paradisal valleys; they float upon circular pools ringed in by steep flowering hillsides; they dwell on islands, or voyage to them; we find Poe's heroes also in coffins, in the cabs of balloons, or hidden away in the holds of ships; and above all we find them sitting alone in the claustral and richly furnished rooms of remote and mouldering mansions.

Almost never, if you think about it, is one of Poe's heroes to be seen standing in the light of common day; almost never does the Poe hero breathe the air that others breathe; he requires some kind of envelope in order to be what he is; he is always either enclosed or on his way to an enclosure. The narrative of William Wilson conducts the hero from

Stoke Newington to Eton, from Eton to Oxford, and then to Rome by way of Paris, Vienna, Berlin, Moscow, Naples, and Egypt: and yet, for all his travels, Wilson seems never to set foot out-of-doors. The story takes place in a series of rooms, the last one locked from the inside.

Sometimes Poe emphasizes the circumscription of his heroes by multiple enclosures. Roderick Usher dwells in a great and crumbling mansion from which, as Poe tells us, he has not ventured forth in many years. This mansion stands islanded in a stagnant lake, which serves it as a defensive moat. And beyond the moat lies the Usher estate, a vast barren tract having its own peculiar and forbidding weather and atmosphere. You might say that Roderick Usher is defended in depth; and yet at the close of the story Poe compounds Roderick's inaccessibility by having the mansion and its occupant swallowed up by the waters of the tarn.

What does it mean that Poe's heroes are invariably enclosed or circumscribed? The answer is simple: circumscription, in Poe's tales, means the exclusion from consciousness of the so-called real world, the world of time and reason and physical fact; it means the isolation of the poetic soul in visionary reverie or trance. When we find one of Poe's characters in a remote valley, or a claustral room, we know that he is in the process of dreaming his way out of the world.

Now, I want to devote the time remaining to the consideration of one kind of enclosure in Poe's tales: the mouldering mansion and its richly furnished rooms. I want to concentrate on Poe's architecture and décor for two reasons: first, because Poe's use of architecture is so frankly and provably allegorical that I *should* be able to be convincing about it; second, because by concentrating on one area of Poe's symbolism we shall be able to see that his stories are allegorical not only in their broad patterns, but also in their smallest details.

Let us begin with a familiar poem, "The Haunted Palace." The opening stanzas of this poem, as a number of critics have noted, make a point-by-point comparison between a building and the head of a man. The exterior of the palace represents the man's physical features; the interior represents the man's mind engaged in harmonious imaginative thought.

* * *

I expect you observed that the two luminous windows of the palace are the eyes of a man, and that the yellow banners on the roof are his luxuriant blond hair. The "pearl and ruby" door is the man's mouth—ruby representing red lips, and pearl representing pearly white teeth. The beautiful Echoes which issue from the pearl and ruby door are the poetic utterances of the man's harmonious imagination, here symbolized as an orderly dance. The angel-guarded valley in which the palace stands, and which Poe describes as "the monarch Thought's dominion," is a symbol of the man's exclusive awareness of exalted and spiritual things. The valley is what Poe elsewhere called "that evergreen and radiant paradise which the true poet knows . . . as the limited realm of his authority, as the circumscribed Eden of his dreams."

As you all remember, the last two stanzas of the poem describe the

physical and spiritual corruption of the palace and its domain, and it was to this part of the poem that Poe was referring when he told a correspondent, "By the 'Haunted Palace' I mean to imply a mind haunted by phantoms—a disordered brain."

* * *

The domain of the monarch Thought, in these final stanzas, is disrupted by civil war, and in consequence everything alters for the worse. The valley becomes barren, like the domain of Roderick Usher; the eye-like windows of the palace are no longer "luminous," but have become "red-litten"—they are like the bloodshot eyes of a madman or a drunkard. As for the mouth of our allegorized man, it is now "pale" rather than "pearl and ruby," and through it come no sweet Echoes, as before, but the wild laughter of a jangling and discordant mind.

The two states of the palace—before and after—are, as we can see, two states of mind. Poe does not make it altogether clear *why* one state of mind has given way to the other, but by recourse to similar tales and poems we can readily find the answer. The palace in its original condition expresses the imaginative harmony which the poet's soul enjoys in early childhood, when all things are viewed with a tyrannical and unchallenged subjectivity. But as the soul passes from childhood into adult life, its consciousness is more and more invaded by the corrupt and corrupting external world: it succumbs to passion, it develops a conscience, it makes concessions to reason and to objective fact. Consequently, there is civil war in the palace of the mind. The imagination must now struggle against the intellect and the moral sense; finding itself no longer able to possess the world through a serene solipsism, it strives to annihilate the outer world by turning in upon itself; it flees into irrationality and dream; and all its dreams are efforts both to recall and to simulate its primal, unfallen state. "The Haunted Palace" presents us with a possible key to the general meaning of Poe's architecture; and this key proves, if one tries it, to open every building in Poe's fiction. Roderick Usher, as you will remember, declaims "The Haunted Palace" to the visitor who tells his story, accompanying the poem with wild improvisations on the guitar. We are encouraged, therefore, to compare the palace of the poem with the house of the story; and it is no surprise to find that the Usher mansion has "vacant eye-like windows," and that there are mysterious physical sympathies between Roderick Usher and the house in which he dwells. The House of Usher *is*, in allegorical fact, the physical body of Roderick Usher, and its dim interior *is*, in fact, Roderick Usher's visionary mind.

The House of Usher, like many edifices in Poe, is in a state of extreme decay. The stonework of its facade has so crumbled and decomposed that it reminds the narrator, as he puts it, "of the specious totality of old wood-work which has rotted for long years in some neglected vault." The Usher mansion is so eaten away, so fragile, that it seems a breeze would push it over; it remains standing only because the atmosphere of Usher's domain is perfectly motionless and dead. Such is the case also with the "time-eaten towers that tremble not" in

Poe's poem "The City in the Sea"; and likewise the magnificent architecture of "The Domain of Arnheim" is said to "sustain itself by a miracle in mid-air." Even the detective Dupin lives in a perilously decayed structure: the narrator of "The Murders in the Rue Morgue" tells how he and Dupin dwelt in a "time-eaten and grotesque mansion, long deserted through superstitions into which we did not enquire, and tottering to its fall in a retired and desolate portion of the Faubourg St. Germain." (Notice how, even when Poe's buildings are situated in cities, he manages to circumscribe them with a protective desolation.)

We must now ask what Poe means by the extreme and tottering decay of so many of his structures. The answer is best given by reference to "The Fall of the House of Usher," and in giving the answer we shall arrive, I think, at an understanding of the pattern of that story.

"The Fall of the House of Usher" is a journey into the depths of the self. I have said that all journeys in Poe are allegories of the process of dreaming, and we must understand "The Fall of the House of Usher" as a dream of the narrator's, in which he leaves behind him the waking, physical world and journeys inward toward his *moi intérieur*, toward his inner and spiritual self. That inner and spiritual self is Roderick Usher.

Roderick Usher, then, is a part of the narrator's self, which the narrator reaches by way of reverie. We may think of Usher, if we like, as the narrator's imagination, or as his visionary soul. Or we may think of him as a *state of mind* which the narrator enters at a certain stage of his progress into dreams. Considered as a state of mind, Roderick Usher is an allegorical figure representing the hypnagogic state.

The hypnagogic state, about which there is strangely little said in the literature of psychology, is a condition of semi-consciousness in which the closed eye beholds a continuous procession of vivid and constantly changing forms. These forms sometimes have color, and are often abstract in character. Poe regarded the hypnagogic state as the visionary condition *par excellence*, and he considered its rapidly shifting abstract images to be—as he put it—"glimpses of the spirit's outer world." These visionary glimpses, Poe says in one of his *Marginalia*, "arise in the soul . . . only . . . at those mere points of time where the confines of the waking world blend with those of the world of dreams." And Poe goes on to say: "I am aware of these 'fancies' only when I am upon the very brink of sleep, with the consciousness that I am so."

Roderick Usher enacts the hypnagogic state in a number of ways. For one thing, the narrator describes Roderick's behavior as inconsistent, and characterized by constant alternation: he is alternately vivacious and sullen; he is alternately communicative and rapt; he speaks at one moment with "tremulous indecision," and at the next with the "energetic concision" of an excited opium-eater. His conduct resembles, in other words, that wavering between consciousness and subconsciousness which characterizes the hypnagogic state. The trembling of Roderick's body, and the floating of his silken hair, also bring to mind the instability and underwater quality of hypnagogic images. His improvisations on the guitar suggest hypnagogic experience

in their rapidity, changeableness, and wild novelty. And as for Usher's paintings, which the narrator describes as "pure abstractions," they quite simply *are* hypnagogic images. The narrator says of Roderick, "From the paintings over which his elaborate fancy brooded, and which grew, touch by touch, into vaguenesses at which I shuddered the more thrillingly because I shuddered without knowing why—from these paintings (vivid as their images now are before me) I would in vain endeavor to educe more than a small portion which should lie within the compass of merely written words." That the narrator finds Roderick's paintings indescribable is interesting, because in that one of the *Marginalia* from which I have quoted, Poe asserts that the only things in human experience which lie "beyond the compass of words" are the visions of the hypnagogic state.

Roderick Usher stands for the hypnagogic state, which as Poe said is a teetering condition of mind occurring "upon the very brink of sleep." Since Roderick is the embodiment of a state of mind in which *falling*—falling asleep—is imminent, it is appropriate that the building which symbolizes his mind should promise at every moment to fall. The House of Usher stares down broodingly at its reflection in the tarn below, as in the hypnagogic state the conscious mind may stare into the subconscious; the house threatens continually to collapse because it is extremely easy for the mind to slip from the hypnagogic state into the depths of sleep; and when the House of Usher *does* fall, the story ends, as it must, because the mind, at the end of its inward journey, has plunged into the darkness of sleep.

We have found one allegorical meaning in the tottering decay of Poe's buildings; there is another meaning, equally important, which may be stated very briefly. I have said that Poe saw the poet as at war with the material world, and with the material or physical aspects of himself; and I have said that Poe identified poetic imagination with the power to escape from the material and the materialistic, to exclude them from consciousness and so subjectively destroy them. Now, if we recall these things, and recall also that the exteriors of Poe's houses or palaces, with their eye-like windows and mouth-like doors, represent the physical features of Poe's dreaming heroes, then the characteristic dilapidation of Poe's architecture takes on sudden significance. The extreme decay of the House of Usher—a decay so extreme as to approach the atmospheric—is quite simply a sign that the narrator, in reaching that state of mind which he calls Roderick Usher, has very nearly dreamt himself free of his physical body, and of the material world with which that body connects him.

This is what decay or decomposition mean everywhere in Poe; and we find them almost everywhere. Poe's preoccupation with decay is not, as some critics have thought, an indication of necrophilia; decay in Poe is a symbol of visionary remoteness from the physical, a sign that the state of mind represented is one of almost pure spirituality. When the House of Usher disintegrates or dematerializes at the close of the story, it does so because Roderick Usher has become all soul. "The Fall of the House of Usher," then, is not really a horror story; it

is a triumphant report by the narrator that it *is* possible for the poetic soul to shake off this temporal, rational, physical world and escape, if only for a moment, to a realm of unfettered vision.

We have now arrived at three notions about Poe's typical building. It is set apart in a valley or a sea or a waste place, and this remoteness is intended to express the retreat of the poet's mind from worldly consciousness into dream. It is a tottery structure, and this indicates that the dreamer within is in that unstable threshold condition called the hypnagogic state. Finally, Poe's typical building is crumbling or decomposing, and this means that the dreamer's mind is moving toward a perfect freedom from his material self and the material world. Let us now open the door—or mouth—of Poe's building and visit the mind inside.

As we enter the palace of the visionary hero of "The Assignation," or the house of Roderick Usher, we find ourselves approaching the master's private chamber by way of dim and winding passages, or a winding staircase. There is no end to dim windings in Poe's fiction: there are dim and winding woods paths, dim and winding streets, dim and winding watercourses—and, whenever the symbolism is architectural, there are likely to be dim and winding passages or staircases. It is not at all hard to guess what Poe means by this symbol. If we think of waking life as dominated by reason, and if we think of the reason as a daylight faculty which operates in straight lines, then it is proper that reverie should be represented as an obscure and wandering movement of the mind. There are other, and equally obvious meanings in Poe's symbol of dim and winding passages: to grope through such passages is to become confused as to place and direction, just as in reverie we begin to lose any sense of locality, and to have an infinite freedom in regard to space. In his description of the huge old mansion in which William Wilson went to school, Poe makes this meaning of winding passages very plain:

> But the house!—how quaint an old building was this!—to me how veritable a palace of enchantment! There was no end to its windings—to its incomprehensible subdivisions. It was difficult, at any given time, to say with certainty upon which of its two stories one happened to be. From each room to every other there were sure to be found three or four steps either in ascent or descent. Then the lateral branches were innumerable—inconceivable—and so returning in upon themselves, that our most exact ideas in regard to the whole mansion were not very far different from those with which we pondered on infinity.

Dim windings indicate the state of reverie; they point toward that infinite freedom in and from space which the mind achieves in dreams; also, in their curvature and in their occasional doubling-back, they anticipate the mind's final spiralling plunge into unconsciousness. But the immediate goal of reverie's winding passages is that magnificent chamber in which we find the visionary hero slumped in a chair or lolling on an ottoman, occupied in purging his consciousness of everything that is earthly.

Since I have been speaking of geometry—of straight lines and curves and spirals—perhaps the first thing to notice about Poe's dream rooms is their shape. It has already been said that the enclosures of Poe's tales incline to a curving or circular form. And Poe himself, in certain of his essays and dialogues, explains this inclination by denouncing what he calls "the harsh mathematical reason of the schools," and complaining that practical science has covered the face of the earth with "rectangular obscenities." Poe quite explicitly identifies regular angular forms with everyday reason, and the circle, oval, or fluid arabesque with the otherworldly imagination. Therefore, if we discover that the dream chambers of Poe's fiction are free of angular regularity, we may be sure that we are noticing a pointed and purposeful consistency in his architecture and décor.

The ball-room of the story "Hop-Frog" is circular. The Devil's apartment in "The Duc de l'Omelette" has its corners "rounded into niches," and we find rounded corners also in Poe's essay "The Philosophy of Furniture." In "Ligeia," the bridal chamber is a pentagonal turret room; however, the angles are concealed by sarcophagi, so that the effect is circular. The corners of Roderick Usher's chamber are likewise concealed, being lost in deep shadow. Other dream rooms are either irregular or indeterminate in form. For example, there are the seven rooms of Prince Prospero's imperial suite in "The Masque of the Red Death." As Poe observes, "in many palaces . . . such suites form a long and straight vista"; but in Prince Prospero's palace, as he describes it, "the apartments were so irregularly disposed that the vision embraced but little more than one at a time. There was a sharp turn at every twenty or thirty yards, and at each turn a novel effect." The turret room of *The Oval Portrait* is not defined as to shape; we are told, however, that it is architecturally "bizarre," and complicated by a quantity of unexpected nooks and niches. Similarly, the visionary's apartment in "The Assignation" is described only as dazzling, astounding and original in its architecture; we are not told in what way its dimensions are peculiar, but it seems safe to assume that it would be a difficult room to measure for wall-to-wall carpeting. The room of "The Assignation," by the way—like that of "Ligeia"—has its walls enshrouded in rich figured draperies which are continually agitated by some mysterious agency. The fluid shifting of the figures suggests, of course, the behavior of hypnagogic images; but the agitation of the draperies would also produce a perpetual ambiguity of architectural form, and the effect would resemble that which Pevsner ascribes to the interior of San Vitale in Ravenna: "a sensation of uncertainty [and] of a dreamlike floating."

Poe, as you see, is at great pains to avoid depicting the usual squarish sort of room in which we spend much of our waking lives. His chambers of dream either approximate the circle—an infinite form which is, as Poe somewhere observes, "the emblem of Eternity"—or they so lack any apprehensible regularity of shape as to suggest the changeableness and spatial freedom of the dreaming mind. The exceptions to this rule are few and entirely explainable. I will grant, for

instance, that the iron-walled torture chamber of "The Pit and the Pendulum" portrays the very reverse of spatial freedom, and that it is painfully angular in character, the angles growing more acute as the torture intensifies. But there is very good allegorical reason for these things. The rooms of "Ligeia" or "The Assignation" symbolize a triumphantly imaginative state of mind in which the dreamer is all but free of the so-called "real" world. In "The Pit and the Pendulum," the dream is of quite another kind; it is a nightmare state, in which the dreamer is imaginatively impotent, and can find no refuge from reality, even in dream. Though he lies on the brink of the pit, on the very verge of the plunge into unconsciousness, he is still unable to disengage himself from the physical and temporal world. The physical oppresses him in the shape of lurid graveyard visions; the temporal oppresses him in the form of an enormous and deadly pendulum. It is altogether appropriate, then, that this particular chamber should be constricting and cruelly angular.

But let us return to Poe's typical room, and look now at its furnishings. They are generally weird, magnificent, and suggestive of great wealth. The narrator of "The Assignation," entering the hero's apartment, feels "blind and dizzy with luxuriousness," and looking about him he confesses, "I could not bring myself to believe that the wealth of any subject in Europe could have supplied the princely magnificence which burned and blazed around." Poe's visionaries are, as a general thing, extremely rich; the hero of "Ligeia" confides that, as for wealth, he possesses "far more, very far more, than ordinarily falls to the lot of mortals"; and Ellison, in "The Domain of Arnheim," is the fortunate inheritor of 450 million dollars. Legrand, in "The Gold Bug," with his treasure of 450 *thousand*, is only a poor relation of Mr. Ellison; still, by ordinary standards, he seems sublimely solvent.[1]

Now, we must be careful to take all these riches in an allegorical sense. As we contemplate the splendor of any of Poe's rooms, we must remember that the room is a state of mind, and that everything in it is therefore a thought, a mental image. The allegorical meaning of the costliness of Poe's décor is simply this: that his heroes are richly imaginative. And since imagination is a gift rather than an acquisition, it is appropriate that riches in Poe should be inherited or found, but never earned.

Another thing we notice about Poe's furnishings is that they are eclectic in the extreme. Their richness is not the richness of Tiffany's and Sloan's, but of all periods and all cultures. Here is a partial inventory of the fantastic bridal-chamber in "Ligeia": Egyptian carvings and sarcophagi; Venetian glass; fretwork of a semi-Gothic, semi-Druidical character; a Saracenic chandelier; Oriental ottomans and candelabra; an Indian couch; and figured draperies with Norman motifs. The same defiance of what interior decorators once called "keeping" is found in the apartment of the visionary hero of "The Assignation," and one of

1. In writing the above, I misremembered the amount of Legrand's treasure. The sum mentioned is the estimated value of the coins only, whereas the treasure's total value was in excess of "a million and a half of dollars" [Wilbur's note, 1966].

that hero's speeches hints at the allegorical meaning of his jumbled décor:

> To dream [says the hero of "The Assignation"]—to dream has been the business of my life. I have therefore framed for myself, as you see, a bower of dreams. In the heart of Venice could I have erected a better? You behold around you, it is true, a medley of architectural embellishments. The chastity of Ionia is offended by antediluvian devices, and the sphynxes of Egypt are outstretched upon carpets of gold. Yet the effect is incongruous to the timid alone. Proprieties of place, and especially of time, are the bugbears which terrify mankind from the contemplation of the magnificent.

That last sentence, with its scornful reference to "proprieties of place, and . . . time," should put us in mind of the first stanza of Poe's poem "Dream-Land."

* * *

In dream-land, we are "out of SPACE—out of TIME," and the same is true of such apartments or "bowers of dreams" as the hero of "The Assignation" inhabits. His eclectic furnishings, with their wild juxtapositions of Venetian and Indian, Egyptian and Norman, are symbolic of the visionary soul's transcendence of spatial and temporal limitations. When one of Poe's dream-rooms is *not* furnished in the fashion I have been describing, the idea of spatial and temporal freedom is often conveyed in some other manner: Roderick Usher's library, for instance, with its rare and precious volumes belonging to all times and tongues, is another concrete symbol of the timelessness and placelessness of the dreaming mind.

We have spoken of the winding approaches to Poe's dream chambers, of their curvilinear or indeterminate shape, and of the rich eclecticism of their furnishings. Let us now glance over such matters as lighting, soundproofing, and ventilation. As regards lighting, the rooms of Poe's tales are never exposed to the naked rays of the sun, because the sun belongs to the waking world and waking consciousness. The narrator of "The Murders in the Rue Morgue" tells how he and his friend Dupin conducted their lives in such a way as to avoid all exposure to sunlight. "At the first dawn of the morning," he writes, "we closed all the massy shutters of our old building; lighting a couple of tapers which, strongly perfumed, threw out only the ghastliest and feeblest of rays. By the aid of these we then busied our souls in dreams . . ."

In some of Poe's rooms, there simply are no windows. In other cases, the windows are blocked up or shuttered. When the windows are not blocked or shuttered, their panes are tinted with a crimson or leaden hue, so as to transform the light of day into a lurid or ghastly glow. This kind of lighting, in which the sun's rays are admitted but transformed, belongs to the portrayal of those half-states of mind in which dream and reality are blended. Filtered through tinted panes, the sunlight enters certain of Poe's rooms as it might enter the half-

closed eyes of a daydreamer, or the dream-dimmed eyes of someone awakening from sleep. But when Poe wishes to represent that deeper phase of dreaming in which visionary consciousness has all but annihilated any sense of the external world, the lighting is always artificial and the time is always night.

Flickering candles, wavering torches, and censers full of writhing varicolored flames furnish much of the illumination of Poe's rooms, and one can see the appropriateness of such lighting to the vague and shifting perceptions of the hypnagogic state. But undoubtedly the most important lighting-fixture in Poe's rooms—and one which appears in a good half of them—is the chandelier. It hangs from the lofty ceiling by a long chain, generally of gold, and it consists sometimes of a censer, sometimes of a lamp, sometimes of candles, sometimes of a glowing jewel (a ruby or a diamond), and once, in the macabre tale "King Pest," of a skull containing ignited charcoal. What we must understand about this chandelier, as Poe explains in his poem "Al Aaraaf," is that its chain does not stop at the ceiling: it goes right on through the ceiling, through the roof, and up to heaven. What comes down the chain from heaven is the divine power of imagination, and it is imagination's purifying fire which flashes or flickers from the chandelier. That is why the immaterial and angelic Ligeia makes her reappearance directly beneath the chandelier; and that is why Hop-Frog makes his departure for dream-land by climbing the chandelier chain and vanishing through the skylight.

The dreaming soul, then, has its own light—a light more spiritual, more divine, than that of the sun. And Poe's chamber of dream is autonomous in every other respect. No breath of air enters it from the outside world: either its atmosphere is dead, or its draperies are stirred by magical and intramural air currents. No earthly sound invades the chamber: either it is deadly still, or it echoes with a sourceless and unearthly music. Nor does any odor of flower or field intrude: instead, as Poe tells in "The Assignation," the sense of smell is "oppressed by mingled and conflicting perfumes, reeking up from strange convolute censers."

The point of all this is that the dreaming psyche separates itself wholly from the bodily senses—the "rudimental senses," as Poe called them. The bodily senses are dependent on objective stimuli—on the lights and sounds and odors of the physical world. But the sensuous life of dream is self-sufficient and immaterial, and consists in the imagination's Godlike enjoyment of its own creations.

I am reminded, at this point, of a paragraph of Santayana's, in which he describes the human soul as it was conceived by the philosopher Leibniz. Leibniz, says Santayana, assigned

> a mental seat to all sensible objects. The soul, he said, had no windows and, he might have added, no doors; no light could come to it from without; and it could not exert any transitive force or make any difference beyond its own insulated chamber. It was a *camera obscura*, with a universe painted on its impene-

trable walls. The changes which went on in it were like those in a dream, due to the discharge of pent-up energies and fecundities within it . . .

Leibniz' chamber of the soul is identical with Poe's chamber of dream: but the solipsism which Leibniz saw as the normal human condition was for Poe an ideal state, a blessed state, which we may enjoy as children or as pre-existent souls, but can reclaim in adult life only by a flight from everyday consciousness into hypnagogic trance.

The one thing which remains to be said about Poe's buildings is that cellars or catacombs, whenever they appear, stand for the irrational part of the mind; and that is so conventional an equation in symbolic literature that I think I need not be persuasive or illustrative about it. I had hoped, at this point, to discuss in a leisurely way some of the stories in which Poe makes use of his architectural properties, treating those stories as narrative wholes. But I have spoken too long about other things; and so, if you will allow me a few minutes more, I shall close by commenting briskly on two or three stories only.

The typical Poe story occurs *within* the mind of a poet; and its characters are not independent personalities, but allegorical figures representing the warring principles of the poet's divided nature. The lady Ligeia, for example, stands for that heavenly beauty which the poet's soul desires; while Rowena stands for that earthly, physical beauty which tempts the poet's passions. The action of the story is the dreaming soul's gradual emancipation from earthly attachments—which is allegorically expressed in the slow dissolution of Rowena. The result of this process is the soul's final, momentary vision of the heavenly Ligeia. Poe's typical story presents some such struggle between the visionary and the mundane; and the duration of Poe's typical story is the duration of a dream.

There are two tales in which Poe makes an especially clear and simple use of his architectural symbolism. The first is an unfamiliar tale called "The System of Dr. Tarr and Prof. Fether," and the edifice of that tale is a remote and dilapidated madhouse in southern France. What happens, in brief, is that the inmates of the madhouse escape from their cells in the basement of the building, overpower their keepers, and lock them up in their own cells. Having done this, the lunatics take possession of the upper reaches of the house. They shutter all the windows, put on odd costumes, and proceed to hold an uproarious and discordant feast, during which there is much eating and drinking of a disgusting kind, and a degraded version of Ligeia or Helen does a strip tease. At the height of these festivities, the keepers escape from their cells, break in through the barred and shuttered windows of the dining room, and restore order.

Well: the madhouse, like all of Poe's houses, is a mind. The keepers are the rational part of that mind, and the inmates are its irrational part. As you noticed, the irrational is suitably assigned to the cellar. The uprising of the inmates, and the suppression of the keepers, symbolizes the beginning of a dream, and the mad banquet which follows

is perhaps Poe's least spiritual portrayal of the dream state: *this* dream, far from being an escape from the physical, consists exclusively of the release of animal appetites—as dreams sometimes do. When the keepers break in the windows, and subdue the revellers, they bring with them reason and the light of day, and the wild dream is over.

"The Masque of the Red Death" is a better-known and even more obvious example of architectural allegory. You will recall how Prince Prospero, when his dominions are being ravaged by the plague, withdraws with a thousand of his knights and ladies into a secluded, impregnable and windowless abbey, where after a time he entertains his friends with a costume ball. The weird décor of the seven ballrooms expresses the Prince's own taste, and in strange costumes of the Prince's own design the company dances far into the night, looking, as Poe says, like "a multitude of dreams." The festivities are interrupted only by the hourly striking of a gigantic ebony clock which stands in the westernmost room; and the striking of this clock has invariably a sobering effect on the revellers. Upon the last stroke of twelve, as you will remember, there appears amid the throng a figure attired in the blood-dabbled graveclothes of a plague-victim. The dancers shrink from him in terror. But the Prince, infuriated at what he takes to be an insolent practical joke, draws his dagger and pursues the figure through all of the seven rooms. In the last and westernmost room, the figure suddenly turns and confronts Prince Prospero, who gives a cry of despair and falls upon his own dagger. The Prince's friends rush forward to seize the intruder, who stands now within the shadow of the ebony clock; but they find nothing there. And then, one after the other, the thousand revellers fall dead of the Red Death, and the lights flicker out, and Prince Prospero's ball is at an end.

In spite of its cast of one thousand and two, "The Masque of the Red Death" has only one character. Prince Prospero is one-half of that character, the visionary half; the nameless figure in grave clothes is the other, as we shall see in a moment.

More than once, in his dialogues or critical writings, Poe describes the earth-bound, time-bound rationalism of his age as a *disease*. And that is what the Red Death signifies. Prince Prospero's flight from the Red Death is the poetic imagination's flight from temporal and worldly consciousness into dream. The thousand dancers of Prince Prospero's costume ball are just what Poe says they are—"dreams" or "phantasms," veiled and vivid creatures of Prince Prospero's rapt imagination. Whenever there is a feast, or carnival, or costume ball in Poe, we may be sure that a dream is in progress.

But what is the gigantic ebony clock? For the answer to that, one need only consult a dictionary of slang: we call the human heart a *ticker*, meaning that it is the clock of the body; and that is what Poe means here. In sleep, our minds may roam beyond the temporal world, but our hearts tick on, binding us to time and mortality. Whenever the ebony clock strikes, the dancers of Prince Prospero's dream grow momentarily pale and still, in half-awareness that they and their revel

must have an end; it is as if a sleeper should half-awaken, and know that he has been dreaming, and then sink back into dreams again.

The figure in blood-dabbled graveclothes, who stalks through the terrified company and vanishes in the shadow of the clock, is waking temporal consciousness, and his coming means the death of dreams. He breaks up Prince Prospero's ball as the keepers in "Dr. Tarr and Prof. Fether" break up the revels of the lunatics. The final confrontation between Prince Prospero and the shrouded figure is like the terrible final meeting between William Wilson and his double. Recognizing his adversary as his own worldly and mortal self, Prince Prospero gives a cry of despair which is also Poe's cry of despair: despair at the realization that only by self-destruction could the poet fully free his soul from the trammels of this world.

Poe's aesthetic, Poe's theory of the nature of art, seems to me insane. To say that art should repudiate everything human and earthly, and find its subject matter at the flickering end of dreams, is hopelessly to narrow the scope and function of art. Poe's aesthetic points toward such impoverishments as *poésie pure* and the abstract expressionist movement in painting. And yet, despite his aesthetic, Poe is a great artist, and I would rest my case for him on his prose allegories of psychic conflict. In them, Poe broke wholly new ground, and they remain the best things of their kind in our literature. Poe's mind may have been a strange one; yet all minds are alike in their general structure; therefore we can understand him, and I think that he will have something to say to us as long as there is civil war in the palaces of men's minds.

JAMES W. GARGANO

The Question of Poe's Narrators†

Part of the widespread critical condescension toward Edgar Allan Poe's short stories undoubtedly stems from impatience with what is taken to be his "cheap" or embarrassing Gothic style. Finding turgidity, hysteria, and crudely poetic overemphasis in Poe's works, many critics refuse to accept him as a really serious writer. Lowell's flashy indictment of Poe as "two-fifths sheer fudge"[1] agrees essentially with Henry James's magisterial declaration that an "enthusiasm for Poe is the mark of a decidedly primitive stage of reflection."[2] T. S. Eliot seems to be echoing James when he attributes to Poe "the intellect of a highly gifted young person before puberty."[3] Discovering in Poe one of the

† From *College English*, 25 (December 1963), 177–81. Copyright © 1963 by James W. Gargano. Reprinted by permission of The National Council of Teachers of English.
1. "A Fable for Critics," *The Complete Poetical Works of James Russell Lowell* (Cambridge, 1896), p. 140 [Gargano's note]. All notes to this selection are Gargano's [Editor].
2. Henry James, "Charles Baudelaire," *French Poets and Novelists* (London, 1878), p. 76.
3. T. S. Eliot, *From Poe to Valéry* (New York, 1948), p. 28.

fountainheads of American obscurantism, Ivor Winters condemns the incoherence, puerility, and histrionics of his style. Moreover, Huxley's charge that Poe's poetry suffers from "vulgarity" of spirit, has colored the views of critics of Poe's prose style.[4]

Certainly, Poe has always had his defenders. One of the most brilliant of modern critics, Allen Tate finds a variety of styles in Poe's works; although Tate makes no high claims for Poe as stylist, he nevertheless points out that Poe could, and often did, write with lucidity and without Gothic mannerisms.[5] Floyd Stovall, a long time and more enthusiastic admirer of Poe, has recently paid his critical respects to "the conscious art of Edgar Allan Poe."[6] Though he says little about Poe's style, he seems to me to suggest that the elements of Poe's stories, style for example, should be analyzed in terms of Poe's larger artistic intentions. Of course, other writers, notably Edward H. Davidson, have done much to demonstrate that an intelligible rationale informs Poe's best work.[7]

It goes without saying that Poe, like other creative men, is sometimes at the mercy of his own worst qualities. Yet the contention that he is fundamentally a bad or tawdry stylist appears to me to be rather facile and sophistical. It is based, ultimately, on the untenable and often unanalyzed assumption that Poe and his narrators are identical literary twins and that he must be held responsible for all their wild or perfervid utterances; their shrieks and groans are too often conceived as emanating from Poe himself. I believe, on the contrary, that Poe's narrators possess a character and consciousness distinct from those of their creator. These protagonists, I am convinced, speak their own thoughts and are the dupes of their own passions. In short, Poe understands them far better than they can possibly understand themselves. Indeed, he often so designs his tales as to show his narrators' limited comprehension of their own problems and states of mind; the structure of many of Poe's stories clearly reveals an ironical and comprehensive intelligence critically and artistically ordering events so as to establish a vision of life and character which the narrator's very inadequacies help to "prove."

What I am saying is simply that the total organization or completed form of a work of art tells more about the author's sensibility than does the report or confession of one of its characters. Only the most naïve reader, for example, will credit as the "whole truth" what the narrators of Barry Lyndon, Huckleberry Finn, and The Aspern Papers will divulge about themselves and their experiences. In other words, the "meaning" of a literary work (even when it has no narrator) is to be found in its fully realized form; for only the entire work achieves the

4. Aldous Huxley, "Vulgarity in Literature," Music at Night and Other Essays (London, 1949), pp. 297–309.
5. Allen Tate, "Our Cousin, Mr. Poe," The Man of Letters in the Modern World, Meridian Books, pp. 132–145.
6. Floyd Stovall, "The Conscious Art of Edgar Allan Poe," College English, 24 (March 1963), 417–21.
7. Davidson, Poe: A Critical Study (Cambridge, 1957).

resolution of the tensions, heterogeneities, and individual visions which make up the parts. The Romantic apologists for Milton's Satan afford a notorious example of the fallacy of interpreting a brilliantly integrated poem from the point of view of its most brilliant character.

The structure of Poe's stories compels realization that they are more than the effusions of their narrators' often disordered mentalities. Through the irony of his characters' self-betrayal and through the development and arrangement of his dramatic actions, Poe suggests to his readers ideas never entertained by the narrators. Poe intends his readers to keep their powers of analysis and judgment ever alert; he does not require or desire complete surrender to the experience of the sensations being felt by his characters. The point of Poe's technique, then, is not to enable us to lose ourselves in strange or outrageous emotions, but to see these emotions and those obsessed by them from a rich and thoughtful perspective. I do not mean to advocate that, while reading Poe, we should cease to feel; but feeling should be "simultaneous" with an analysis carried on with the composure and logic of Poe's great detective, Dupin. For Poe is not merely a Romanticist; he is also a chronicler of the consequences of the Romantic excesses which lead to psychic disorder, pain, and disintegration.

Once Poe's narrative method is understood, the question of Poe's style and serious artistry returns in a new guise. Clearly, there is often an aesthetic compatibility between his narrators' hypertrophic language and their psychic derangement; surely, the narrator in "Ligeia," whose life is consumed in a blind rage against his human limitations, cannot be expected to consider his dilemma in coolly rational prose. The language of men reaching futilely towards the ineffable always runs the risk of appearing more flatulent than inspired. Indeed, in the very breakdown of their visions into lurid and purple rhetoric, Poe's characters enforce the message of failure that permeates their aspirations and actions. The narrator in "Ligeia" blurts out, in attempting to explain his wife's beauty in terms of its "expression": "Ah, words of no meaning!" He rants about "incomprehensible anomalies," "words that are impotent to convey," and his inability to capture the "inexpressible." He raves because he cannot explain. His feverish futility of expression, however, cannot be attributed to Poe, who with an artistic "control," documents the stages of frustration and fantastic desire which end in the narrator's madness. The completed action of "Ligeia," then, comments on the narrator's career of self-delusion and exonerates Poe from the charge of lapsing into self-indulgent, sentimental rodomantade.

In "The Tell-Tale Heart" the cleavage between author and narrator is perfectly apparent. The sharp exclamations, nervous questions, and broken sentences almost too blatantly advertise Poe's conscious intention; the protagonist's painful insistence [on] "proving" himself sane only serves to intensify the idea of his madness. Once again Poe presides with precision of perception at the psychological drama he describes. He makes us understand that the voluble murderer has been tortured by the nightmarish terrors he attributes to his victim. "He was

sitting up in bed listening;—just as I have done, night after night, harkening to the death watches in the wall"; further the narrator interprets the old man's groan in terms of his own persistent anguish: "Many a night, just at midnight, when all the world slept, it has welled up from my own bosom, deepening, with its dreadful echo, the terrors that distracted me." Thus, Poe, in allowing his narrator to disburden himself of his tale, skillfully contrives to show also that he lives in a haunted and eerie world of his own demented making.

Poe assuredly knows what the narrator never suspects and what, by the controlled conditions of the tale, he is not meant to suspect—that the narrator is a victim of his own self-torturing obsessions. Poe so manipulates the action that the murder, instead of freeing the narrator, is shown to heighten his agony and intensify his delusions. The watches in the wall become the ominously beating heart of the old man, and the narrator's vaunted self-control explodes into a frenzy that leads to self-betrayal. I find it almost impossible to believe that Poe has no serious artistic motive in "The Tell-Tale Heart," that he merely revels in horror and only inadvertently illuminates the depths of the human soul. I find it equally difficult to accept the view that Poe's style should be assailed because of the ejaculatory and crazy confession of his narrator.

For all of its strident passages, "William Wilson" once again exhibits in its well-defined structure a sense of authorial poise which contrasts markedly with the narrator's confusion and blindness. Wilson's story is organized in six parts: a rather "over-written" *apologia* for his life; a long account of his early student days at Dr. Bransby's grammar school, where he is initiated into evil and encounters the second Wilson; a brief section on his wild behavior at Eton; an episode showing his blackguardly conduct at Oxford; a nondramatic description of his flight from his namesake-pursuer; and a final, climactic scene in which he confronts and kills his "double." The incidents are so arranged as to trace the "development" of Wilson's wickedness and moral blindness. Moreover, Poe's conscious artistic purpose is evident in the effective functioning of many details of symbolism and setting. "Bright rays" from a lamp enable Wilson to see his nemesis "vividly" at Dr. Bransby's; at the critical appearance of his double at Eton, Wilson's perception is obscured by a "faint light"; and in the scene dealing with Wilson's exposé at Oxford, the darkness becomes almost total and the intruder's presence is "felt" rather than seen. Surely, this gradual extinction of light serves to point up the darkening of the narrator's vision. The setting at Dr. Bransby's school, where it was impossible to determine "upon which of its two stories one happened to be," cleverly enforces Poe's theme of the split consciousness plaguing Wilson. So, too, does the portrait of the preacher-pastor:

> This reverend man, with countenance so demurely benign, with robes so glossy and so clerically flowing, with wig so minutely powdered, so rigid and so vast,—could this be he who, of late, with sour visage and in snuffy habiliments, administered, ferule

in hand, the Draconian laws of the academy? Oh, gigantic paradox, too utterly monstrous for solution!

Finally, the masquerade setting in the closing scene of the tale ingeniously reveals that Wilson's whole life is a disguise from his own identity.

To maintain that Poe has stumbled into so much organization as can be discovered in "William Wilson" and his other tales requires the support of strong prejudice. There seems little reason for resisting the conclusion that Poe knows what ails Wilson and sees through his narrator's lurid self-characterization as a "victim to the horror and the mystery of the wildest of all sublunary visions." Assuredly, a feeling for the design and subtlety of Poe's "William Wilson" should exorcise the idea that he is as immature and "desperate" as his protagonist. After all, Poe created the situations in which Wilson confronts and is confronted by his *alter ego*; it is Wilson who refuses to meet, welcome, and be restrained by him.

Evidence of Poe's "seriousness" seems to me indisputable in "The Cask of Amontillado," a tale which W. H. Auden has belittled.[8] Far from being his author's mouthpiece, the narrator, Montresor, is one of the supreme examples in fiction of a deluded rationalist who cannot glimpse the moral implications of his planned folly. Poe's fine ironic sense makes clear that Montresor, the stalker of Fortunato, is both a compulsive and pursued man; for in committing a flawless crime against another human being, he really (like Wilson and the protagonist in "The Tell-Tale Heart") commits the worst of crimes against himself. His reasoned, "cool" intelligence weaves an intricate plot which, while ostensibly satisfying his revenge, despoils him of humanity. His impeccably contrived murder, his weird mask of goodness in an enterprise of evil, and his abandonment of all his life energies in one pet project of hate convict him of a madness which he mistakes for the inspiration of genius. The brilliant masquerade setting of Poe's tale intensifies the theme of Montresor's apparently successful duplicity; Montresor's ironic appreciation of his own deviousness seems further to justify his arrogance of intellect. But the greatest irony of all, to which Montresor is never sensitive, is that the "injuries" supposedly perpetrated by Fortunato are illusory and that the vengeance meant for the victim recoils upon Montresor himself. In immolating Fortunato, the narrator unconsciously calls him the "noble" Fortunato and confesses that his own "heart grew sick." Though Montresor attributes this sickness to "the dampness of the catacombs," it is clear that his crime has begun to "possess" him. We see that, after fifty years, it remains the obsession of his life; the meaning of his existence resides in the tomb in which he has, symbolically, buried himself. In other words, Poe leaves little doubt that the narrator has violated his own mind and humanity, that the external act has had its destructive inner consequences.

The same artistic integrity and seriousness of purpose evident in

8. Auden, "Introduction" to *Edgar Allan Poe: Selected Prose and Poetry*, Rinehart Editions, p. v.

"The Cask of Amontillado" can be discovered in "The Black Cat." No matter what covert meanings one may find in this much-discussed story, it can hardly be denied that the nameless narrator does not speak for Poe. Whereas the narrator, at the beginning of his "confession," admits that he cannot explain the events which overwhelmed him, Poe's organization of his episodes provides an unmistakable clue to his protagonist's psychic deterioration. The tale has two distinct, almost parallel parts: in the first, the narrator's inner moral collapse is presented in largely symbolic narrative; in the second part, the consequence of his self-violation precipitate an act of murder, punishable by society. Each section of the story deals with an ominous cat, an atrocity, and an exposé of a "crime." In the first section, the narrator's house is consumed by fire after he has mutilated and subsequently hanged Pluto, his pet cat. Blindly, he refuses to grant any connection between his violence and the fire; yet the image of a hanged cat on the one remaining wall indicates that he will be haunted and hag-ridden by his deed. The sinister figure of Pluto, seen by a crowd of neighbors, is symbolically both an accusation and a portent, an enigma to the spectators but an infallible sign to the reader.

In the second section of "The Black Cat," the reincarnated cat goads the narrator into the murder of his wife. As in "William Wilson," "The Tell-Tale Heart," and "The Cask of Amontillado," the narrator cannot understand that his assault upon another person derives from his own moral sickness and unbalance. Like his confreres, too, he seeks psychic release and freedom in a crime which completes his torture. To the end of his life, he is incapable of locating the origin of his evil and damnation within himself.

The theme of "The Black Cat" is complicated for many critics by the narrator's dogged assertion that he was pushed into evil and self-betrayal by the "imp of the perverse." This imp is explained, by a man who, it must be remembered, eschews explanation, as a radical, motiveless, and irresistible impulse within the human soul. Consequently, if his self-analysis is accepted, his responsibility for his evil life vanishes. Yet, it must be asked if it is necessary to give credence to the words of the narrator. William Wilson, too, regarded himself as a "victim" of a force outside himself and Montresor speaks as if he has been coerced into his crime by Fortunato. The narrator in "The Black Cat" differs from Wilson in bringing to his defense a well-reasoned theory with perhaps a strong appeal to many readers. Still, the narrator's pat explanation is contradicted by the development of the tale, for instead of being pushed into crime, he pursues a life which makes crime inevitable. He cherishes the intemperate self-indulgence which blunts his powers of self-analysis; he is guided by his delusions to the climax of damnation. Clearly, Poe does not espouse his protagonist's theory any more than he approves of the specious rationalizations of his other narrators. Just as the narrator's well-constructed house has a fatal flaw, so the theory of perverseness is flawed because it really explains nothing. Moreover, even the most cursory reader must be struck by the fact that the narrator is most "possessed and maddened" when he

most proudly boasts of his self-control. If the narrator obviously cannot be believed at the end of the tale, what argument is there for assuming that he must be telling the truth when he earlier tries to evade responsibility for his "sin" by slippery rationalizations?

A close analysis of "The Black Cat" must certainly exonerate Poe of the charge of merely sensational writing. The final frenzy of the narrator, with its accumulation of superlatives, cannot be ridiculed as an example of Poe's style. The breakdown of the shrieking criminal does not reflect a similar breakdown in the author. Poe, I maintain, is a serious artist who explores the neuroses of his characters with probing intelligence. He permits his narrator to revel and flounder into torment, but he sees beyond the torment to its causes.

In conclusion, then, the five tales I have commented on display Poe's deliberate craftsmanship and penetrating sense of irony. If my thesis is correct, Poe's narrators should not be construed as his mouthpieces; instead they should be regarded as expressing, in "charged" language indicative of their internal disturbances, their own peculiarly nightmarish visions. Poe, I contend, is conscious of the abnormalities of his narrators and does not condone the intellectual ruses through which they strive, only too earnestly, to justify themselves. In short, though his narrators are often febrile or demented, Poe is conspicuously "sane." They may be "decidedly primitive" or "wildly incoherent," but Poe, in his stories at least, is mature and lucid.

JOSEPH J. MOLDENHAUER

From Murder as a Fine Art: Basic Connections between Poe's Aesthetics, Psychology, and Moral Vision†

Not only in *Eureka*, his late cosmological treatise, but throughout his literary career, Edgar Allan Poe pursued a unitary theory of metaphysics, nature, art, and the human mind. He conducted his search with astounding vitality and persistence, and surely, by the time he had written *Eureka*, he believed he had arrived at the goal. Yet his writings, both imaginative and discursive, exhibit extreme contradictions of thought and feeling. Between and sometimes even within individual works Poe appears as a Shelleyan romantic and as an eighteenth-century rationalist, as a neurotic escapist and as a broadly social figure, as a neo-Platonic visionary and as a severe logician or a commonsense realist, as a selfless devotee to artistic ideals and as a calculating exploiter of literary fads. It has therefore been the challenge of his critics, particularly in recent years, in turn to seek the essential Poe, the central principle of his art and thought, amid the welter of attitudes his writings display.

† From *PMLA* 83 (1968): 284–97. Reprinted by permission of the Modern Language Association of America and the author.

I

His sensibility seems to me divided between two distinct phases. The first might be labelled the "active," "self-assured," or "manic" phase, and is most clearly represented by the tales of ratiocination and the literary criticism. The protagonist-persona of these works, whether detective or landscape architect or litterateur, masters every enigma and places every discordant fragment of his experience into a coherent design, no less satisfying to the taste than to the reason. The governing impulse here is what Allen Tate describes, in an essay appropriately subtitled "Poe as God," as hypertrophy of intellect, "the intellect moving in isolation from both love and the moral will, whereby it declares itself independent of the human situation in the quest of essential knowledge."[1] The mind of the hero or persona in this mode displays a genius for creating formal order, a controlling and shaping power, which strikes us as "archangelic" or "divine." As reviewer of the works of other artists he is always imperious and often cruel; as the "ideal author" in the more theoretical essays he looms as a mesmerist or medicine man, a supreme magician and inquisitor, who manipulates at his pleasure the undefended emotions of his audience, pressing the "stamp" onto the reader's passive "wax,"[2] or consciously dreaming into the reader his own special wish-fulfillment or his own peculiar *cauchemar*.

In the second group of works, including the most famous poems and almost all the tales of terror, Poe's imagination exhibits its "submissive," "self-pitying," or "depressive" phase. Hypertrophy of feeling constitutes, for Tate, the essential character of the terror tales: in them, he writes, "A nightmare of paranoia, schizophrenia, necrophilism, and vampirism supervenes, in which the natural affections are perverted by the will to destroy."[3] Such poems as "The Sleeper," "Annabel Lee," "Ulalume," "The Raven," and "Lenore" display the same exaggeration of emotion and dramatize the same aberrations.

In the creations of this phase the protagonist is all feeling: his sensibility is so narrowly channeled, his emotions honed to so keen an edge, that his mind cannot be violated by a normal idea. Reflecting on these fictions, Paul Elmer More called Poe the writer "of unripe boys and unsound men," and Henry James asserted that "to take him with more than a certain degree of seriousness is to lack seriousness one's self."[4] The protagonist, who is also typically the narrator of the piece, is driven by inner compulsions or beset by horrific external forces, or both; he seems to assert no control over his acts, and moves inexorably

1. "The Angelic Imagination," currently reprinted in *The Man of Letters in the Modern World* (New York, 1955), p. 115 [Moldenhauer's note]. All notes to this selection are Moldenhauer's unless otherwise indicated [Editor].
2. *The Complete Works of Edgar Allan Poe*, ed. James A. Harrison, 17 vols. (New York, 1902), XIII, 152. Quotations from Poe will hereafter be drawn from this edition and will be identified parenthetically in the text.
3. Tate, p. 115. See also D. H. Lawrence, "Edgar Allan Poe," in *Studies in Classic American Literature* (New York, 1923).
4. More, "A Note on Poe's Method," in *The Demon of the Absolute*, New Shelburne Essays, I (Princeton, N.J., 1928), 86; James, *French Poets and Novelists* (London, 1893), p. 60.

toward destruction. "Going down," the concluding words of one of Poe's earliest tales, is an apt figure for that destiny: the hero descends into swoon or coma or death; or he is sucked into a vortex or an antarctic Symmes' Hole; or he is placed living into the grave or some coffin-like enclosure. Sometimes his catastrophe is associated with the death of a beautiful woman—an unworldly and compelling creature to whom the protagonist stands in something of the relation of an infant to its mother, or of the minute and dependent male of certain insect species to the dominant female, destined finally to be absorbed and digested by her.

The recurrent and conspicuous convergence in his writings of the morbid and the beautiful—the inseparability or even identity, for Poe, of the conditions of art and those of death—suggests a center of meaning or a unified design underlying these polar modes of imagination. It is my purpose here to explore the implications of this art-death "complex," drawing upon Poe's works as a whole,[5] and to present a coherent view of his literary motives which will in turn illuminate that astonishing assemblage of symbolic acts, his prose romances, his poems, his criticism, and *Eureka*. My analysis embodies several basic convictions about Poe's writings: first, that his critical essays point to the fundamental themes and techniques of his creative productions—though not in the mechanical way that "The Philosophy of Composition" purports to explain "The Raven"; next, that the recurrent terms of Poe's aesthetic themselves comprise a symbolic structure, grounded in the same attitudes as the symbols, motifs, and patterns of characterization in his poetry and tales; and, finally, that Poe's extraordinary anticipation of modern psychology in his dramatization of irrational drives sanctions the critic's availing himself of psychological approaches.[6] Terms like "normal," "perverse," and "aberration," which I have offered without qualification in the foregoing paragraphs, will not be particularly useful as this study proceeds, for, as I hope to demonstrate, Poe's singularly self-consistent vision is based on norms foreign to commonplace life. To comprehend his vision we must at least provisionally yield to it, tentatively espousing the norms to which Poe was so fervently committed. Because the theory of value which informs all his works is brought forward most openly in his aesthetic essays, it is with these that my analysis will begin.

II

The notion that Poe somehow shares the moralistic inclinations of his countrymen, if ventured in literate company, is likely to be dismissed as impertinent. Leaving aside the retort biographical (namely,

5. I have avoided reference to Poe's life in developing this argument; but I believe that my conclusions about his works—the life of his imagination—will not prove inconsistent with serious biographical interpretation.
6. Although Marie Bonaparte's *The Life and Works of Edgar Allan Poe: A Psycho-Analytic Interpretation*, tr. John Rodker (London, 1949), distorts Poe's works in subordinating them to a preconceived conceptual formula, a less dogmatic application of Freud's psychology to Poe has obvious and widely tested merit.

that the author's shortcomings of character preclude any moral dimension in his works), it will surely be pointed out that Poe banished "the didactic" from the proper sphere of art. Nevertheless, it might not be entirely whimsical to isolate one level of meaning on which Poe can be called a conventional moralist.

It may well be this "didactic" level which has accounted for the acceptability of Poe's tales to the framers of school curricula, and which in part explains their popularity among juvenile readers. For all the monstrosity and morbidity they record, these stories are free from the taint of "impurity." At least after his early "grotesques," Poe observed his own dictum, "let nothing vulgar be *ever* said, or conceived" (x, 184).[7] No exposures of flesh, no overt sexual encounters mar the relationship of the hero and heroine—even when they are wed under the law. Poe's women are remote, virginal, asexual—as asexual, indeed, as the cameo or marble bust with which they are often compared. Moreover, the outcome of each tale invites, from the childish mind, a pat moral summary. Thus, "The Black Cat" can be construed to mean something like *Be kind to dumb animals—or else!* "The Tell-Tale Heart" and "William Wilson" yield the maxim *Crime does not pay* or *The wages of sin is death*. Pride goeth before a fall in "The Masque of the Red Death," "Metzengerstein," and "Hop-Frog." "The Fall of the House of Usher," appealing to the adolescent imagination, might be summed up in the apothegm, *Each man kills the thing he loves the most*—still a "moral," though a sentimental and fatalistic one. And the seemingly Hawthornesque "Oval Portrait" teaches that life should not be sacrificed to artistic perfectionism. Such moralistic responses seem further encouraged by Poe's use, in "William Wilson," "The Imp of the Perverse," "The Black Cat," and other tales, of confessional rhetoric: the narrator-protagonist introduces or concludes his account with elaborate gestures of self-condemnation, and with dire forecasts of eternal disgrace for his name or perpetual torment for his soul. In these aspects of Poe's art even a puritan conscience might find comfort.

We cannot, however, long maintain so naive a perspective on Poe's fictions, nor will he, in his statements on the nature of literature, allow us to do so at all. In "The Poetic Principle" and the last review essay on Hawthorne's tales, to specify only the most famous critical documents, Poe ridicules the "heresy of *The Didactic*," the idea that moral edification is a valid object of the imaginative writer. * * *

Predictably, Poe has no patience with allegory, the literary form most explicitly in the service of moral "inculcation"; in its defense, he writes, "there is scarcely one respectable word to be said." His antagonism is firmly grounded in his theory of the separateness of aesthetic and didactic ends: "The fallacy of the idea that allegory, in any of its moods, can be made to enforce a truth—that metaphor, for example, may illustrate as well as embellish an argument—could be promptly

7. Edward H. Davidson examines the ill-disguised obscenity of the "grotesques" in *Poe: A Critical Study* (Cambridge, Mass., 1957), pp. 137–155.

demonstrated . . . One thing is clear, that if allegory ever establishes a fact, it is by dint of overturning a fiction" (XIII, 148).

According to Poe, the supreme criterion for the literary performance is not truthfulness, moral or otherwise, but rather unity (sometimes called totality): a condition in which every portion of the work is indispensable for the "effect" which the artist chooses to induce, and, at the same time, indispensable for the structural completeness, symmetry, "proportion," or "harmony" of the composition. "Equalities" of rhyme and meter in poetry, mutual adaptation of plot elements in fiction and the drama, and consistency of tone in both prose and verse are among the devices by which unity of effect or impression may be achieved.[8] Subordinate to unity are the quantitative criterion of brevity and the qualitative one of originality—both terms addressing the proper management or direction of audience psychology toward unity of impression. Repeatedly—almost to the point of tedium—Poe stresses unity as the major formal aim of the "skilful artist" in prose or verse.[9]

In addition to the implicit triad of Unity-Brevity-Originality, two other important "trios" are presented in the aesthetic essays. In a well-known passage from "The Poetic Principle," Poe anatomizes the mind into the aesthetic, the rational, and the ethical faculties. * * * Of these faculties Poe regards Taste as preeminent: it stands at the center, or at the apex of the triangle. In its active role as imagination, or in its receptive role as "the susceptibility to impressions of beauty," it is the highest of all human powers (XVI, 121).

The objects of the three mental capacities are likewise distinct and threefold: "Just as the Intellect concerns itself with Truth [here meaning propositional or discursive knowledge, "science" in the wide sense], so Taste informs us of the Beautiful while the Moral Sense is regardful of Duty" (XVI, 273). The poet's legitimate province is beauty; and to beauty the other two objects stand in no more than an accessory relationship.[1] * * * An "undercurrent" of moral or intellectual meaning may indeed, Poe concedes, be acceptable in the art work, and may even contribute to its "ideality"; but should this thematic material intrude into the "upper current" or fictive content, appealing on its own terms to the reader's mind and distracting him from the imagina-

8. Poe's equivocations about "effect" betray a certain vagueness, if not confusion, in the concept. The poet *chooses* an effect; yet "Beauty" is the only valid effect of the poem (XIV, 194, 197–198). In some contexts Poe seems to refer to the mere mood which the work induces; in others to a total response of emotions, intellect, and "soul," caused in part by its "leading idea"—though the validity of this central theme has no bearing on the work's artistic worth (XI, 83–84). *Unity* of effect, moreover, I take to mean not simple *concentration* of a mood (or mood-colored idea), but rather the *completion* or *exhaustion* of the effect which the work generates. Poe's affective unity consists practically in his carrying an intense effect *through* to a state of emotional and intellectual rest.

9. For studies of the relationship of unity, originality, beauty, "indefinitiveness," "ideality," and other key concepts, see George Kelly, "Poe's Theory of Beauty," *AL*, XXVII (1956), 521–536, and "Poe's Theory of Unity," *PQ*, XXXVII (1958), 34–44.

1. With other students of Poe's poetics, I take seriously his distinction between the "severe" language and "mode of inculcation" of "Truth" and the language and impressive mode of literature (XIV, 272). With them also—and with Poe himself (e.g., XIII, 151–152)—I regard his theory of "Poetry" as his essential aesthetics, applicable in its broad outlines to his practice of the prose tale.

tive experience *per se*, the unique aesthetic unity and pleasure are dispelled, and the work ceases immediately to be artistic. Poe categorically distinguishes didactic from legitimately artistic interests. * * *

What, we must now inquire, does Poe mean by "Beauty"? The term can be approached, and Poe approaches it, within several frames of reference: the formal, the spiritual, and the psychological. These contexts are interrelated, and Poe's definitions are mutually supporting, but they are marked by a "sufficient distinction" (to borrow a phrase from the author) which permits us to examine them separately. Beauty, in each context, seems synonymous with Unity. Formally, of course, beauty resides in the "nice adaptation" and perfect interdependence of constituent parts in a verbal (or musical or physical) structure (xi, 79). To the technical instruments by which formal beauty may be created Poe devotes great stretches of his criticism. Far more interesting is Poe's concept of Beauty as the focus of an apocalyptic religion. It is God's "purest . . . attribute," which "alone proves his existence" (xi, 256); and the poet or "man of genius"—Poe uses the terms interchangeably—is at once the high priest and the most devout worshipper of this "supernal Loveliness." The apprehension of beauty is thus a condition of the soul, a state of rapt rightness or harmony with the divine which we might term an artistic nirvana. * * * The "Poetic Sentiment," this "Human Aspiration for Supernal Beauty" (xiv, 290), is even more urgent in the poet than in his audience; and the longing of the soul is what inspires his creative effort. The artist's works are attempts, necessarily imperfect in some degree, to seize or approximate this supersensuous beauty through "novel combinations" of the forms of natural beauty (xi, 73, 80, 256; xiv 274).[2] In the beauties of this world, including human features and sentiments, the artist recognizes intimations of heavenly beauty. These realities stimulate his aspiration for the ideal and offer themselves as "forms" for the "collocation" by which he attempts to grasp it; the higher loveliness they adumbrate is the "ambrosia which nourishes his soul" (xiv, 290). The supernal beauty which the poet strives to express lies beyond even the most engaging shapes of mundane experience, beyond description in the language which names those shapes. Clearly, therefore, the artist should aim not for truthfulness—verisimilitude—so much as for *ideality*. Neither should he dwell upon or seek to excite the "passions of the heart," even the noblest, for the yearning which is the Poetic Sentiment has no earthly object for its satisfaction.[3] It pertains to man's "immortal existence," while the passions are always "homely." Both the creative enthusiasm of the poet and the responsive excitement of his audience are properly spiritual,

2. Poe believed that the highest earthly beauty was always touched with strangeness, and he was fond of quoting Bacon to that effect. Further, he found "beauty heightened into the sublime, by terror" perferable even to "pure beauty" (xi, 77–78). The "ideality" of a literary work was also intensified by "grotesquerie" (xvi, 178), as "The pure Imagination chooses, *from either beauty or deformity*, only the most combinable things hitherto uncombined . . . Even out of deformities it fabricates that *Beauty* which is at once its sole object and its inevitable test" (xii, 38–39).

3. This point is made repeatedly throughout Poe's criticism; see esp. xi, 256, 277; xiii, 131; xiv, 198; xv, 117.

unprofaned by bodily heat and palpitations of "the heart." An ethereal indefiniteness and suggestive power, like that of music, pervades the loftiest order of poetry (XIV, 220; XVI, 29).

Considered psychologically, Beauty, like Unity, refers to the attainment, however fleeting, of a state of perfect satisfaction. It is the completion not only of the demands of form, but of the impulses of the poet and his audience. Poe's aesthetic scheme, even in its religious dimension, is fundamentally affective or rhetorical rather than objective or formalistic; and that which in the spiritual vocabulary is "ambrosia," in the psychological vocabulary is "pleasure." In "The Philosophy of Composition" Poe quite explicitly speaks of beauty not as "a quality" but as "an effect" (XIV, 197). * * * He adopts and closely paraphrases Coleridge's definition of literature as the expressive mode whose immediate object is pleasure, in contrast to science and history, whose primary aim is truth, in his first critical essay, "Letter to B———" (VII, xliii; cf. *Biographia Literaria*, Ch. XIV). Thereafter, throughout his criticism, he insists on the priority of pleasure in art. * * * Indeed, "pleasure" and related terms appear as regularly in Poe's generalizations on artistic response as "sacred" and "divine" occur in his considerations of the poet.

But to gain the paradise of Beauty, or the apprehension of that Unity which constitutes the "god-term" of Poe's aesthetic, man must suffer the bitter frustration of groping toward the ideal with intractable, earth-bound materials.[4] * * * [As] *process* poetry involves "struggle," nervous tension, dislocation from the familiar patterns of experience.[5] Artist and audience alike must suffer to earn their beatitude—must lose their life to find it.[6]

* * *

[Moldenhauer here explores the place of Taste and Beauty "in their respective triads."]

The materials of moral experience are rendered beautiful, in the ratiocinative tales, by the detective's superhuman, and acutely aesthetic, intelligence. Conspicuous in Poe's observations on Taste and Beauty is a vocabulary more appropriate, we might at first think, to moral praise; and in his attacks upon didacticism in art he employs a didactic and polemical diction which betrays a huge investment of moral energy. He writes in "The Poetic Principle," for instance, that "the epic mania . . . [has been] succeeded by a heresy too palpably false to be long tolerated, but one which . . . may be said to have accomplished more in

4. See "The Poetic Principle," XIV, 273–274 [Editor].
5. A similar distinction between process and end underlies Poe's analysis of the cosmos in *Eureka*. The material universe ("plot of God") is by definition "a difference from the normal— from the right" (XVI, 233–234), and the inevitable reaction to unitary spirituality "is the return from the condition of *as it is and ought not to be* into the condition of *as it was, originally, and therefore ought to be*" (XVI, 234).
6. Davidson makes what I regard as an equivalent point as he describes the movement of the poem in Poe's theory destructively "through" the "rational intelligible world" toward "ultimate meaning" located figuratively on the "other side" (p. 100; see also pp. 150–151, 258).

the corruption of our Poetical Literature than all its other enemies combined. I allude to the heresy of *The Didactic*" (xiv, 271).

Clearly, what Poe has done is to elevate artistic values into the sphere of a morality; ordinary ethical factors are demoted to a secondary ("incidental") place, and have value only insofar as they subserve the aesthetic supermorality. In the establishment of art as religion and morality lies Poe's mysticism—though he used the word to demean and ridicule Hawthorne, Emerson, Carlyle, and other moral idealists, never suspecting that his own aesthetic idealism was equally, if not more, mystical, and that it represented only a realignment of the moral idealists' terms.

* * *

Just as for Emerson the man of Reason was a man exercising his divinity, the Poet for Poe was a god, or at least a god-in-the-making. Conversely, God was the supreme "poet." In *Eureka: A Prose Poem*, Poe explains the origin of the universe in terms of the self-dissemination or "radiation" of God throughout space. In the beginning, he argues, was a *condition*: Unity, or God, or the divine Mind; this Deity manifested Himself as a gigantic "single particle," which then He diffused, by great pulsations of energy, outwardly from its center in the form of innumerable separate atoms (xvi, 207, 230–231). The resulting vast globe of atoms—and Poe regarded it as both spherical and limited—is the cosmos. But it might more fairly be defined as a planned chaos, since its characteristics are division, alienation, fragmentation, and frustrated desire—in sum, "*difference from Unity*" (xvi, 208).

* * *

III

* * *

Near the end of *Eureka* Poe calls the universe the "plot of God," which, like a perfect tale or poem, "spring[s] out of the bosom of the thesis—out of the heart of the ruling idea" (xvi, 292, 306). Simplicity and economy are observed throughout the cosmic plan. The materials of the universe—the "elements" of the "design"—are to be understood as a means, and not as the end, of the "divine Art" (xvi, 308–309). Poe's final staggering revelation is that the "Heart Divine" is our own; since "soul" exists in all beings, "each soul is, *in part*, its own God—its own Creator" (xvi, 311, 313).[7]

* * *

Like Poe the critical theorist, the protagonist of the ratiocinative tales is a God or demigod. As Richard Wilbur reminds us, the mental operations of the great investigator C. Auguste Dupin are less logical calculations than they are intuitions or visions.[8] In Dupin, reason is so intense and lofty as to constitute a "creative" faculty, and the detective

7. Italics mine; until the universal collapse, the divinity of any individual can only be partial, just as the Poetic Sentiment is satisfied only in "glimpses" of supernal loveliness through art.
8. Wilbur, Introduction to Poe selections in *Major Writers of America*, ed. Perry Miller (New York. 1962), i, 379.

can "dream" a solution to the most tangled mystery without so much as stirring from his armchair. He is, then, a master artist, dictating or imagining—i.e., imaging—a coherent order for discordant experience. Like the poet, he imposes upon life, or abstracts from it, a perfect unity. And Poe the critic, while in fact dogmatically making aesthetic laws of his own temperamental necessities, projects himself as an artist of the rules of art, or a "detective" discovering "the whole truth" about literature. The analogies between Poe's literal detectives and the Poe-persona of the critical essays are numerous and provocative.[9] Just as Dupin's friend, at the outset of "The Murders in the Rue Morgue," toys with the idea that the detective possesses a dual "soul," the "resolvent" or analytic and the "creative" (IV, 152), Poe represents the ideal critic as both a rational philosopher of art and a person endowed generously with the "Poetic Sentiment" or creative *vision* of the artist, whether or not he also enjoys the actual combinative skill by which the creative genius translates vision into form (XVI, 66–67). * * * Though Poe will not yet, in the first of the ratiocinative tales, grant that extraordinary mental powers such as Dupin's are intuitional (IV, 146–149), he locates them "among recesses of thought altogether inaccessible to the ordinary understanding" (IV, 148) and asserts that they are closely associated with imagination: "the ingenious are always fanciful, and the *truly* imaginative never otherwise than analytic" (IV, 150). The equation between lofty truth and the intuitional poetic vision is made even more overt in the review of Horne's *Orion* (XI, 257) and "A Chapter of Suggestions" (XIV, 187, 189–190), and, as we have seen, in *Eureka*.[1] Poe's declaration that the critic must understand true philosophical and poetic *principles*, through whose application he cannot fail to arrive at a proper critical practice in evaluating any particular work (XVI, 81, 69; XI, 39–40; XII, 240), is echoed in Dupin's predominantly theoretical approach to problems of criminology. Poe's critic is the conservator of the poetic ideal, an absolute criterion of excellence, against which he measures the concrete poetic performance, concentrating more upon failures than upon successes, since the latter can speak for themselves (XIV, 281; XI, 41–42). Likewise, Dupin studies the logic of policemen and of the witness-interpreters of a crime, gauging this logic against the highest norms of thought and exposing its fallacies. * * *

Just as the critic explicates printed or written texts, the detective is far less concerned with physical evidence than with difficult, faulty, or incomplete verbal materials; and the most crucial phases of his investigation are these "critical readings" of his "texts." * * *

Dupin, Legrand [of "The Gold-Bug"], and the Poe-persona of the critiques resemble majestic, Apollonian deities. But what can be said of the protagonists or narrator-protagonists of the tales of terror? Cringing, driven by compulsions, at the mercy of natural and supernatural powers, are they even household gods? They prove, in any event, to be artists. Consider the painter in "The Oval Portrait," who vampirizes his beautiful bride into a "perfect" art object, at whose completion she expires. Con-

9. Cf. Robert Daniel, "Poe's Detective God," *Furioso*, VI (Summer 1951), 47.
1. Cf. Vincent Buranelli, *Edgar Allan Poe* (New York, 1961), pp. 46–50.

sider Roderick Usher—a musical genius, a painter of surrealistic canvases, the author of "The Haunted Palace." Consider Prince Prospero in "The Masque of the Red Death"—a superb interior decorator and deviser of scenarios. Consider the lugubrious husband of Ligeia, whose "philosophy of furniture" is equally exquisite, and whose artistry (though he is seemingly ignorant of its intention and effect) serves to transform his second wife, Rowena, into her beloved predecessor, by debilitating and finally destroying her. Before Ligeia's own death, the protagonist had consistently described her in the language of the fine arts (particularly sculpture), revealing that her value resides largely in her loveliness as an aesthetic object, and that his "appreciation" of her is essentially that of the critic. The list of objects and sensations which stimulate in him the same "sentiment" as Ligeia's eyes arouse is almost interchangeable with the catalogue of stimuli to the Poetic Sentiment in "The Poetic Principle" (II, 252; XIV, 290–291). Other art critics in the tales of terror include the Baron Metzengerstein and the narrator of "The Fall of the House of Usher." In the tales or prose poems on taste artists and connoisseurs are naturally abundant: Ellison in "The Domain of Arnheim" and his companion the narrator are conspicuous examples, as are the personae of "Landor's Cottage" and "The Philosophy of Furniture."

Even when Poe's perverse characters are not artists in language, paint, or music, they bend to murder or to suicide all the craftsmanship of the fine artist. Further, their impulse to destroy is as intuitive or unconsciously compulsive as a *furor poeticus*: they are "inspired to kill" and practice a fine art of killing. Ligeia's husband once more affords a fascinating illustration in his tasteful extermination of Rowena; but the suicide of "The Assignation," the murderers of "The Imp of the Perverse," "The Tell-Tale Heart," and "The Black Cat," the grave-robbing hero of "Berenice," the husband and father of "Morella," and William Wilson, who over a period of years eradicates his moral sensibility in elaborate contrivances of debauchery and who finally kills his *Doppelgänger* at a masked ball—all are accomplished artists. And so is Hop-Frog, the monkey-shaped but essentially kingly and chivalrous jester. * * *

For these artful murderers in Poe's fiction, even the most perverse and ghastly assassination is a technique for the attainment of that blissful Unity which we have identified with the perfect artistic work. Obsessed with their separateness—whatever has caused it—from others, they slay; and to kill the other, the thing or person outside, is both symbolically and finally to give up one's own life. The destruction of the victim means the union with him in death.[2] * * * Murder con-

2. It is noteworthy that Poe rarely specifies a reasonable, concrete motive for his characters' destructive urges. He sometimes offers a vague allusion to an "offense" done the protagonist by his enemy, or allows the "cause" to be a simple object (e.g., the filmed eye or Berenice's teeth) behind which, for the criminal, lurks some obscure and unnamed abstract conception. A phrase from *Eureka* helps us to understand this motivational vacuum and to see the general condition of human separateness as the real source of these desires: "wrongfulness implies *relation*" (XVI, 233). Conversely, relation—which exists everywhere outside total Unity—implies wrongfulness. Also in *Eureka*, Poe declares that clusters of particles seek Unity "wherever it is even partially to be found," namely, in other masses, and that in the final cataclysm they will realize their most intense wish—to be "even *more than together*" (XVI, 219–220).

stitutes a radical but fundamentally aesthetic solution to the problem of disunity and separateness in a fragmented universe.

In "The Tell-Tale Heart," which like Poe's other first-person tales of terror should be regarded less as a *study of* the deranged mind than as a controlled *exercise in* madness,[3] an enactment of a view of experience remote from our common view, the analogies between the two main figures are again remarkable. The narrator announces that his obsession to kill the old man was not rooted in passion, greed, or hatred; in fact, he says, "I loved the old man." * * * Having projected his own nature upon the innocuous old man, the narrator had violently destroyed him; then, believing him still alive, in the house or symbolically "within himself," he betrays himself to the authorities and insures his fatal punishment. By a slight further extension, the story may be read as a fantasy-account of an entirely internal self-annihilation, in which both the old man who is slain and the calm authorities empowered to retaliate are equally projections, personae, of the disturbed and suicidal mind of the persona.[4]

Although the aristocrat Montresor, protagonist of "The Cask of Amontillado," murders his enemy Fortunato with impunity, the tale still provides a happy illustration of the principle of doubling. Most obviously, both men are connoisseurs of wines, and it is this common expertise which affords the main device of the revenge-plot. * * * A particularly striking instance of "ironic identification" occurs as the drunken Fortunato makes a masonic gesture after emptying a bottle of wine en route to the supposed Amontillado. When he explains the gesture to his curious host, the latter declares that he too is of the brotherhood, "a mason," and draws from beneath his cloak the trowel which he will later use to wall in his enemy. Moreover, in the dialogue of the tale, the men constantly echo one another's language and repeat themselves. * * * While on the conscious level Montresor is untouched by sympathy for his entombed companion, his malaise betrays at least a bodily "kinship" with Fortunato and suggests a psychological identification as well. The last irony of the tale is Montresor's prayer, "*In pace requiescat,*" half a century after the murder. Yet this irony, like the others, has its candid dimension: Fortunato's undisturbed rest has doubly assured his assassin's peace of mind. The two requisites of a perfect revenge "plot," which Montresor identified at the beginning of the tale, have been satisfied. The family honor has been boldly avenged, with the full knowledge of the victim, and the act of revenge has gone unredressed.[5] But to speak of the characters as enemies, or as avenger and

3. Even though our suspicions to the contrary are *confirmed* by Poe's heroes' protestations of sanity, we find it difficult to view their acts from a "clinical" perspective. The mode of narration forces us to adopt the persona's outlook as the norm. See, in this connection, XVI, 165.
4. For a similar "psychomachic" reading of this tale see Patrick F. Quinn, *The French Face of Edgar Poe* (Carbondale, Ill., 1957), pp. 233–236.
5. An item in the "Fifty Suggestions" sheds further light on Montresor's personality: "An artist *is* an artist only by dint of his exquisite sense of Beauty—a sense affording him rapturous enjoyment, but at the same time implying, or involving, an equally exquisite sense of Deformity or disproportion. Thus a wrong—an injustice—done a poet who is really a poet, excites him to a degree which, to ordinary apprehension, appears disproportionate with the wrong. . . . the man who is *not* 'irritable' . . . is *no poet*" (XIV, 175–176).

victim, is to blur an important symbolic pattern in the tale. The wine cellar and the family tomb are one and the same; the "treasure" which Montresor's name implies is at once the honor of those revered dead, the rare wines in the catacombs and especially the prized Amontillado which Fortunato expects to find, and, finally, the dead Fortunato himself. On all three the satisfied Montresor reposes; all three are his "possessions," his secrets, his mementos, functions of his mind. The identity of Fortunato has become internalized in Montresor, forming no small part of his "buried" store of values.

<div align="center">*　*　*</div>

In the tales of ratiocination the principle of the double is advanced as a philosophical method. I have suggested that Dupin imposes upon the violence and horror of crime his own lucid, perfect, and ideal order; in this sense he "orders the world" as the artist of unified experience.[6] But is Dupin an artist only in this rationalistic or "resolvent" manner? His real genius, as he explains to the narrator in "The Purloined Letter" and "The Murders in the Rue Morgue," inheres in his ability to enter into the mind of, to *identify with*, the other person (VI, 40–41; IV, 152–156). He is therefore capable of reenacting the thoughts and feelings of the criminal; imaginatively and vicariously, he *is* the criminal, participating in the artistry that is crime as well as the artistry that is solution. * * * As Poe's critic is soul-brother to the poet, Poe's detective is the double of the criminal; he lacks, it may be, the "constructive" volition literally to perform a crime himself, but he partakes wholly in the psychology of crime—the Criminal-Poetic Sentiment of the blackmailer or murderer.

Poe's most compelling works are those in which the death, or seeming death, of a woman provokes the hero to acts of despair. "The death . . . of a beautiful woman," Poe insists in "The Philosophy of Composition," "is, unquestionably, the most poetical topic in the world" (XIV, 201). It might be suggested that Poe as artist murders, or "wishes into death," the beautiful women who people his fictions, so as to avail himself of the "most poetical topic"; or, alternatively, that in the choice of the most poetic subject—*in the service of the art-religion and the art-morality*—Poe perforce becomes, symbolically, a killer of beautiful women. His protagonist-artists might similarly be seen to "murder" their beloved and lovely women, who already resemble works of art, in order to further their perfection as *objets de virtu*. If the "supernally" beautiful lady is symbolic of an ideal,[7] shadowing it forth in corporeal form, her departure from the mortal sphere is as inevitable as it is appropriate. It was noted earlier that no erotic contact takes place between the protagonist and the lady; dying, the latter becomes a "still unravish'd bride of quietness" in every literal and figurative sense. But the *final* completion or perfection of their "love" requires that the hero himself join, merge with, and utterly possess or be possessed by the soul of the beautiful dead virgin. In so doing he achieves unity with

6. For another consideration of Dupin as resolvent artist see Davidson, pp. 216–222.
7. See Wilbur, pp. 375–378.

his "creation" and dissolves the vestigial separateness, becomes all mind, becomes, as it were, God in the state of rest.

Regarded dramatically and symbolically, each of Poe's tales of terror contains no more than two characters: the protagonist and his "victim," "enemy," or "beloved." The death of the latter is the requirement for his own death; it precedes and foreshadows his own withdrawal from life. When Poe uses an "independent narrator," as in "The Fall of the House of Usher" and several lesser tales, the narrator seems only *technically* separate from the protagonist—a voice, alone returned to tell us, but emotionally identified with the mournful or demented prime agent of the tale. The voice of the ratiocinative tales is that of an apprentice figure, temperamentally associated with the detective and endowed, though to a lesser degree, with the protagonist's tastes and talents. Poe's murdering narrator-protagonists, having dispatched the victim, are typically soon betrayed by an overwhelming perversity. As they confess to the authorities, and thus guarantee their own death, they pass through extraordinary physical and nervous states, usually ending in a "swoon." This swoon, the final vertigo or "going down," is properly the conclusion of the tale, for it marks the long-awaited surrender of the murderer's separate identity. Should he continue to narrate—as he does in "The Imp of the Perverse"—the added lines, though few, ring false, for the voice of the tale no longer really exists; both his experience and the reader's have already been perfected. Both speaker and audience are fictively dead to the world, having realized the extinction of appetite, of tension, of "electricity." Even the reader has attained, if only temporarily, the condition of God. Thus the "spirit of PERVERSENESS," which Poe defines in "The Black Cat" as an "unfathomable longing of the soul *to vex itself*" (v, 146), and elsewhere as a "radical, primitive, irreducible" impulse to oppose one's own conscious and realistic best interests (vi, 145), is at bottom not an evil sentiment but a beneficent one. Like imagination, it triumphs over reason and conscience. Sadomasochism and the death-wish (technical synonyms for Poe's "imp of the perverse") are a saving grace in the eschatology and psychology to which Poe is committed. Only superficially does the imp work against man's welfare. Fundamentally his best interests lie in a world outside that of normal humanity, of social intercourse, and of nature, and to this realm of Unity the imp, more daimon than demon, is his spiritual guide.[8]

IV

Perfection, then, involves the reduction of all divided and opposed things into single wholes or unities. This concept underlies almost

8. Poe's attitude toward real nature is by no means appreciative. In "The Domain of Arnheim" he expresses a distinct preference for the artificial over the natural garden: the irregularity of "primitive" nature is indicative of the fragmented, mortal state of the world (vi, 183–184). The true landscape artist regularizes his materials, evoking from or imposing on them an aura of the strange and unearthly. "Ideality," as induced by remoteness, exotic weirdness, and abstract design, is what Poe values in nature. See also iv, 238–239; vi, 190–196, 255–271; xiv, 291. His two catchwords for his tales, "grotesque" and "arabesque," denote just this avoidance of verisimilitude and subordination of natural shapes to formal designs.

everything of importance that Poe wrote, and in the mature tales and criticism and *Eureka* it dominates his imagination. * * * The theme is nowhere more effectively dramatized than in "The Fall of the House of Usher," with its repeated doublings on the literal and symbolic planes. These include (1) the house and its mirror image in the tarn; (2) the Usher family and the Usher mansion, both "houses"; (3) the physical house and the sole male survivor, Roderick—a doubling developed symbolically in the descriptions of the mansion and of Roderick's features, and presented allegorically in Roderick's emblem poem; (4) Roderick and Madeline—twins, both ill of nervous diseases, between whom "sympathies of a scarcely intelligible nature had always existed" (iii, 289);[9] (5) the left side and the right side of the house, the two halves being separated by a fissure and symbolizing the two surviving Ushers, or the ambivalent, indeed schizophrenic mental state of Roderick as the life-urge and the death-wish compete within him; and, finally, (6) if the narrator is seen as an adjunct to Roderick, introduced for merely technical purposes, the doubling of Madeline on the one hand and "us" on the other. That is, to exploit a pun in the hero's name, the story deals with the fall and completion of the house of "Us-her." And indeed the tale concludes with the merging of these complementary images and figures in the unity of death.

* * *

The "going down" of Poe's protagonists symbolizes a return to the mother, to soporific warmth and darkness, to the womb. But this is no more than, and perhaps finally less than, the achievement of an artistic perfection in death. Incidentally, this loss of personal identity and separateness as the protagonist swoons, or descends into the grave, or falls toward the pit, or utters the admission which seals his doom, is rendered in images of constriction and loss of breath: sensations felt, it would seem, by the infant at birth.

* * *

"Going down" into the aesthetic death state is surely fraught with terrific anxieties and physical torments. But madness and pain are the necessary stages of the protagonist's progress toward Unity, just as the poet must suffer frustration and anguish in striving to perfect his poem. Death, for Poe's haunted heroes, is truly a well-wrought urn: simultaneously a poem, a tomb, and a bridal chamber—a private place for souls finally joined after long and agonizing alienation. * * *

We are now prepared to discover, at the symbolic hub of Poe's works, an ethical structure. Poe's holy war upon the didactic in art notwithstanding, this pattern of values controls his critical, philosophical, and imaginative writings. The highest value, Unity, is the characteristic of both death and art. Hence, all that conduces to Unity—to blissful completion whether in imaginative or direct experience—is a

9. Despite the biological absurdity, Poe suggests (iii, 288) that they are *identical* twins; and in two earlier versions of the tale, he writes that Madeline's figure, air, and features were "all, in their very minutest development . . . identically those" of Roderick (iii, 339–340). The notion of identical kinship is, of course, powerfully indicative of the theme under discussion in this essay.

"good"; and all that perpetuates diversity is "evil." Yet, since the inten-
sification of separateness provokes violent reactions like the urge to
kill, even division can be understood as instrumental to goodness. Dis-
ease, decay, mental "alienation"—all the apparent antitheses to the
state of harmonious rest—are, in this view, the threshold to Unity. All
horror eventuates as pleasure; all crime issues in a "supernal" virtue.[1]

Poe's special version of Romantic diabolism can best be compre-
hended in terms of this longing for union. The simple moral formulas
which I considered earlier are, in fact, inverted on the deepest levels
of Poe's symbolism. He effects, within the single short work, a drastic
conversion of values. "Be kind to dumb animals" becomes "Extermi-
nate the brutes!" because sadism will result in one's own destruction.
"Crime doesn't pay" becomes "Crime pays handsomely, in the richest
of spiritual coin." "Each man kills the thing he loves the most" be-
comes "Each man *must* kill the thing he loves in order to make it
loveliest and most lovable," or, more tersely, "The only good woman is
a dead woman." And murder, for all the bombast of self-damnation
which Poe's confessional protagonists spout, is a signal virtue, a route
to the aesthetic heaven of death. The perversions in Poe's fiction fi-
nally defy any judgment or even comprehension in conventional moral
terms. In addition to the reasons already given, the social rank of
many artist-murderers among Poe's heroes "justifies" their behavior;
they are "aristocrats," even if "ruined" ones, and with an exquisite aes-
thetic and moral license they place themselves above the norms of so-
ciety. Further, the exaggerated confessional quality of tales like "The
Black Cat" and "William Wilson" does not actually presuppose normal
ethical criteria: the protagonist's admission no less than his crime is
compulsively motivated; and his self-accusations have rather the effect
of sharing or "socializing" his anxieties, as Kenneth Burke might say,
with the audience. The confessor "infects" the reader with the very
torments of mind which beset himself, until confessor and reader are
mutually released by the dissolution of identity which concludes the
tale.

Unlike Hawthorne and Melville, Poe refuses to provide an external
vantage point from which the reader can scrutinize the action of the
tale and the motivations of its hero. No appeal by the author to the
community of ordinary men, with ordinary values, relieves the intense
and solipsistic privacy of these works; we have no means of bridging
our commonplace world and the strange realm of his art. We are
thrust entirely within that realm as, during the "hour of perusal," the
author manipulates our "souls" (xiii, 153). No witness figures from a
world like ours move in his plots; we can look to no Ishmael or Geor-
giana Aylmer to expose the excesses of the protagonist; we have no
omniscient narrator (as in Hawthorne's tales) to measure his obsessed

1. It is the usual view of critics, expressed directly in Joseph M. Garrison, Jr.'s, "The Function
of Terror in the Works of Edgar Allan Poe," AQ, xviii (1966), 136–150, that madness, per-
versity, and terror are Poe's revelations by contrast, by antithesis, of supernal beauty. Accord-
ing to these readings, man's condition is diametrically opposed to the harmonious condition
of art, and death is the ultimate human *dis*harmony.

behavior against a common norm by overt judgment or by the covert judgment of irony. Rather, as Poe's rhetorical theory of "effect" demands, the hero's values and psychology are induced in ourselves. This is what makes Poe's tales so permanently and authentically horrific, as the line between spectator and perverse actor imaginatively dissolves. Poe's protagonists are never ethically accountable to mankind for their deeds, being compelled by profound intuitive reserves within themselves to do that which is at once an outrage upon life and a salvation from life. Life in its customary categories—time, space, matter, the body, sex, birth, motion, variety, change—life is, in Poe's vision, the thing to be defeated, to be transcended, or to be evaded in acts of an aesthetic character. These acts are simultaneously the destruction of the self and the creation of the perfect poem.

PAUL JOHN EAKIN

From Poe's Sense of an Ending†

[*The Lazarus Plot*]

* * *

I

In a well-known passage from the "Marginalia" (*Graham's American Monthly Magazine*, March, 1846) Poe claimed for his own a complex of concerns that inform the group of fictions to be studied in the later sections of this essay. Here he reports his personal experience of the farthest reach of consciousness, nothing less than "a glimpse of the spirit's outer world."[1] The passage is, in effect, his most elaborate account of his sense of an ending, an anatomy of the special "psychal impressions" that transmit such visionary experience. "They arise in the soul," he writes, "where the confines of the waking world blend with those of the world of dreams, . . . upon the very brink of sleep." This evanescent dream-state induces an ecstasy of vision remarkable for its "*absoluteness of novelty*," for in these "psychal impressions" "there is really nothing even approximate in character to impressions ordinarily received." Poe and his heroes pursue these "fancies" because they allow a rare and privileged anticipation of the soul's destination *outre-tombe*, what Georges Poulet has so aptly termed "posthumous consciousness."[2] The revelation of "the spirit's outer

† From *American Literature* 45 (1973): 1–22. Reprinted by permission of Duke University Press and the author.

1. *The Complete Works of Edgar Allan Poe*, ed. James A. Harrison (New York, 1902), XVI, 89. All citations from Poe refer to this edition unless otherwise noted [Eakin's note]. All notes to this selection are Eakin's [Editor].
2. "Poe," in *The Recognition of Edgar Allan Poe: Selected Criticism Since 1829*, ed. Eric W. Carlson (Ann Arbor, Mich., 1966), p. 233. D. H. Lawrence speaks, similarly, of Poe as the master of "inorganic consciousness" in *Studies in Classic American Literature* (New York, 1955), p. 88.

world" is registered by five senses somehow "alien to mortality"; had man the power to prolong such experience he could compel "the Heaven into the Earth." So great is Poe's faith in "the *power of words*," nevertheless, that he believes he can, at least, capture his transcendent visions in language.

As Poe proceeds in the "Marginalia" passage to describe "experiments" designed to demonstrate the possibility of an accurate mortal record of "posthumous consciousness," a basic plot for the pursuit of such knowledge begins to emerge: a movement of approach and entry, in his claim that he can make this special state of consciousness supervene; and a movement of withdrawal and return, in his claim that he can startle himself from this "condition" into wakefulness in order to effect its transfer into his conscious memory. To this fundamental motion of approach to and return from a "supernal" realm of "vision" or "ecstasy" the "Marginalia" passage adds one more clarification: the moment of revelation itself, that is, the climax of this plot, can be but "an inappreciable *point* of time," and hence it is rather in terms of an image than as some paraphrase or other exposition that its content can be rendered (XVI, 88–89).[3]

Richard Wilbur has argued that the movement toward and entry into this state of visionary consciousness (which he terms "the hypnagogic state") provides the plot structure of a central group of Poe's narratives which he calls "dream-voyages."[4] His analysis of "the mind's progress into unconsciousness" focuses on the final descent or plunge into "the one truly paradisal state, . . . the suspended death-in-life or life-in-death of reverie."[5] Poe himself, however, in "The Power of Words," suggests important corrections to the basic thrust of Wilbur's formulation of the archetypal soul-plot of the Poe story. Here he defines the motive for the dream-journey as "the thirst *to know*" (VI, 140). Thus the drive toward insensibility or "death-wish," as Harry Levin has pointed out, is always accompanied in these stories by an insatiable and morbid curiosity which takes the form of a will to survive in order to know all.[6] The Poe protagonist either resists the end to which he is irresistibly drawn, defying it like Ligeia, surviving it like Pym; or else he discovers that the end is somehow not final, learning like Monos that to die is to be "born again."

The mortal "thirst *to know*," then, is not fulfilled in the journey out, as Wilbur's one-way formulation might seem to imply, but in the jour-

3. Thus the abruptness of the ending of *Pym* accords completely with Poe's own sense of the dynamics of the transcendent order of perceptions he is attempting to capture in words. Walter E. Bezanson comments, "Poe's most important gift is in psychological projection from the mind of a troubled sleeper who wakes and then drops back into the self's midnight. . . . The question in Poe is how much flummery one will endure in exchange for his special vision." "The Troubled Sleep of Arthur Gordon Pym," in *Essays in Literary History Presented to J. Milton French*, ed. Rudolf Kirk and C. F. Main (New Brunswick, N.J., 1960), p. 173.
4. "In 'Arnheim,' as in all of his dream-voyage tales, Poe deliberately derives his basic structure from the typical stages of the mind's approach to sleep." "Introduction" to the Laurel *Poe* (New York, 1959), p. 22.
5. Wilbur, pp. 25, 31.
6. Levin, *The Power of Blackness* (New York, 1960), p. 101. Roderick Usher, for example, one of Wilbur's exemplary dream-travelers, suffers characteristically from "a morbid acuteness of the senses" (III, 280).

ney out and back. Further, this vital principle of the soul, which creates the dramatic tension in the dream-voyage between surrender and survival, determines Poe's paradoxical conception of the journey's end. Mortals may dream, he writes, that in the attainment of final knowledge the soul would achieve supreme felicity; the angels recognize such knowledge for what it is, the ultimate threat.

* * *

II

In his own uncanny way, in tale after tale, Poe managed to explore his sense of an ending while following to the letter his burlesque recipe for "a genuine Blackwood article of the sensation stamp." "Get yourself into such a scrape as no one ever got into before," he instructs, and report it with "the actual fact to bear you out," for "nothing so well assists the fancy, as an experimental knowledge of the matter in hand." The ending of such a story is both its point and its point of departure: "Should you ever be drowned or hung, be sure and make a note of your sensations" (II, 274). It is in Poe's angelic colloquies, however, rather than his tales in the *Blackwood* manner, that the aspirations of the "Marginalia" program receive their total, wishful fulfillment: here the novel sensations of life beyond the grave are reported *viva voce* by the angels themselves, obviating the mortal necessity of cataleptic fits, premature burials, bottled messages, and the like. The "psychal impressions" of the "Marginalia" passage become the substance for narrative in the colloquies; further, the same analogy between sleep and death obtains but reversed, death now understood as a kind of sleep. "The Colloquy of Monos and Una" provides an explicit and extended definition of the matter and the form of the root Poe story.

* * *

In "The Conversation of Eiros and Charmion," the root Poe story defined by Monos and Una is extended into an apocalyptic dimension, in which the end of the individual soul merges with the end of the world.[7] Eiros's account of his final days on earth, which recapitulates the plot of Monos's story phase by phase, is especially remarkable for his formulation of the end. Since some or all of its characteristics are to be found in many of Poe's endings, it may serve as the prototype for them all:

> Let me be brief—brief as the ruin that overwhelmed. For a moment there was a wild lurid light alone, visiting and penetrating all things. Then let us bow down, Charmion, before the excessive majesty of the great God!—then, there came a shouting and pervading sound, as if from the mouth itself of HIM; while the whole incumbent mass of ether in which we existed, burst at once into a

7. John Lynen writes, "For Poe the final catastrophe is implicit in all experience: the more an experience is understood, the more clearly it is seen in relation to universal history, the more, in consequence, emotion crystallizes into the terror of death, and the more the percipient's view approximates a vision of annihilation." *The Design of the Present: Essays on Time and Form in American Literature* (New Haven, 1969), p. 222.

species of intense flame, for whose surpassing brilliancy and all-fervid heat even the angels in the high Heaven of pure knowledge have no name. Thus ended all.

The end is striking, first of all, in its brevity: the "inappreciable *point of time*" is but a point, and its rendering, consequently, must be highly concentrated. Second, the violence of the catastrophe is explicitly apocalyptic, "the entire fulfillment, in all their minute and terrible details, of the fiery and horror-inspiring denunciations of the prophecies of the Holy Book" (IV, 8). This ultimate moment is heralded by a sudden influx of light accompanied by an outpouring of sound, which Eiros has likened to the "voice of many waters" at the opening of his relation and which he now identifies as the voice of God himself. Poe invariably uses these motifs of light and sound to indicate the acceleration of history that brings the soul to the threshold of final knowledge: not merely is it to know all but specifically to know the end, which for Poe is itself the symbol of total knowledge. Finally, it is crucial that the Poe hero be in a position to witness the end *and to relate* the wonder of what he has seen. The ingenuity of Poe's solution to this problem in these narratives of Monos and Eiros is that the angelic stance permits the transcendence of the otherwise insuperable limitations of mortality (which seemed to say to Una, "thus far, and no farther"): from his privileged location beyond the veil, the hero as angel, "overburdened with the majesty of all things—of the unknown now known" (IV, 2), can utter the words which seal both the literary and the eschatological completion of the Poe story: "Thus ended all."

The angelic colloquies, however, fail by definition to offer a human solution to the pursuit of final knowledge; they do not provide for communication with the world of the living. In his pieces inspired by mesmerism, "A Tale of the Ragged Mountains," "Mesmeric Revelation," and "The Facts in the Case of M. Valdemar," Poe explores the riddle of final knowledge in terms of the human rather than the angelic condition. Mesmerism seemed to offer a means by which the barrier between the angelic and the mortal realms might be crossed by a living man. Poe values mesmeric revelation, in the piece with that title, precisely because it constitutes an anticipation of angelic experience, and the eschatological drift and the dialogue format of this narrative heighten its resemblance to the form and content of the angelic colloquies.[8] The ending of the tale makes clear, however, that Poe, in his quest for final knowledge, required something more, finally, than either conversation with the living in a mesmerist trance or colloquies between the angels could offer. When "P" rouses his mesmerized subject at the last, the "sleep-waker" expires, his body assuming the condition ordinarily to be observed in the dead "only after long

8. The resemblance between "Mesmeric Revelation" and the "Marginalia" passage, between the mesmerist trance of the one and the dream-state of the other, is equally striking. The opening of the tale emphasizes man's power to induce visionary consciousness by an act of will and his power, subsequently, to effect the transfer of the preview of "the ultimate life" (V, 251) to mortal waking consciousness. In his letters Poe invites his correspondents to interpret "Mesmeric Revelation" as a statement of his own ideas. *The Letters of Edgar Allan Poe*, ed. John Ward Ostrom (Cambridge, Mass., 1948), I, 259–261, 273.

pressure from Azrael's hand. Had the sleep-waker, indeed, during the latter portion of his discourse, been addressing me from out the region of the shadows?" (V, 254). These final words of the story manifest the desire of the living for direct communication with those who have been truly dead; no mere similitude of death will do. Given the intransigence of this desire, nothing less would serve than a hero who could, like Lazarus, return from the dead to tell all, an old man of the Maelström, a Ligeia, and, as we shall see, an Arthur Gordon Pym.

"The Facts in the Case of M. Valdemar" show what mesmerism could and could not do to satisfy this need. In this last of his mesmerist fictions, Poe tortures the pseudo-science to extract the ultimate confession, producing what is surely the most grisly avatar of the Lazarus figure in all of Poe. As with "Berenice," however, the horror of this story, especially the loathsomeness of certain of its "facts," has worked to deny it the central place in the Poe canon which, from the nature of its concerns, it deserves. Allen Tate, though, has not allowed the matter of the tale to interfere with his keen perception of its significance. "All of Poe's characters," he writes, "represent one degree or another in a movement towards an archetypal condition: the survival of the soul in a dead body; but only in 'The Facts in the Case of M. Valdemar' is the obsessive subject explicit."[9] The narrator relates that his primary motive in his experiment with M. Valdemar, namely to mesmerize his subject "*in articulo mortis*," was to arrest "the encroachments of Death" (VI, 155) for as long a period as possible, thus going one better than the dreamer of the "Marginalia" passage who could not prolong the point of his condition. The upshot of the experiment is that M. Valdemar, dying in the course of his trance, is privileged to relate, "I *have been* sleeping—and now—now—*I am dead*" (VI, 163).

The Lazarus-Valdemar figure, however, unlike the angel Monos, rarely presumes to give a more detailed account of his condition—for obvious reasons. If Poe valued the analogy between sleep and death operative in the mesmeric trance insofar as it permitted a preview of angelic experience, the premise of that angelic experience was, he argued, that death was but some sleep. But the case of M. Valdemar does not allow for the fiction—so important elsewhere—that the end is anything other than final. The extraordinary conclusion of the story reads as follows:

> As I rapidly made the mesmeric passes, amid ejaculations of "dead! dead!" absolutely *bursting* from the tongue and not from the lips of the sufferer, his whole frame at once—within the space of a single minute, or even less, shrunk—crumbled—absolutely *rotted* away beneath my hands. Upon the bed, before that whole company, there lay a nearly liquid mass of loathsome—of detestable putridity. (VI, 166)

It is death that speaks here, literally, and not some benign angelic condition in the disguise of transcendent sleep or dream. D. H. Lawrence

9. "Our Cousin, Mr. Poe," in *Poe: A Collection of Critical Essays*, ed. Robert Regan (Englewood Cliffs, N.J., 1967), p. 42.

knew that the quest of the Poe hero was doomed: "There is no end. There is only the rupture of death. That's where men, and women, are 'had.' Man is always sold, in his search for final KNOWLEDGE."[1] And it may well be that a large share of the horror with which Poe invites us to contemplate the facts in the case of M. Valdemar stems from his own reluctant if unshrinking recognition in this instance of the defeat of his ultimate aspiration. "Quoth the Raven, 'Nevermore.' "

III

* * *

There is, however, a considerable body of stories in which Poe, adopting what I have chosen to call a Lazarus plot, manages to provide for his hero's venture into the great unknown a round-trip ticket, steering a precarious middle course between death and immortality. I have selected "A Descent into the Maelström" and "Ligeia" as illustrations of the two principal varieties of Lazarus fictions in Poe, the tales of miraculous voyage in which the hero charts strange and unknown realms and the tales of the grave itself in which "the posthumous heroine"[2] descends into the mystery of the tomb and returns to the world of the living.

The opening of "A Descent into the Maelström" announces this story as a tale of the *Blackwood* stamp: "about three years past," the old man observes, "there happened to me an event such as never happened before to mortal man—or at least such as no man ever survived to tell of " (II, 225). As these words suggest, the old man's special destiny has made of him a man as rare as Lazarus, for the descent into the whirlpool is in fact a classic version of the drama of final experience in Poe. The preliminary manifestations of the old man's adventure present the familiar cluster of motifs that Poe invariably employs to signal the imminence of the end. A violent acceleration in the speed of his fishing-boat throws him to the deck, and a sudden influx of light and outpouring of sound usher in the "singular change" (II, 237) that follows. Discovering that his watch has run down, he flings it into the ocean, for he has reached the end of time, poised, apocalyptically, between one world and the next. His account of his state of mind here on the threshold of the Maelström expresses precisely the ambition to know all and yet survive that Poe's Lazarus fictions are designed to gratify: "I positively felt a *wish* to explore its depths, even at the sacrifice I was going to make; and my principal grief was that I should never be able to tell my old companions on shore about the mysteries I should see" (II, 240). Rushing "headlong into the abyss," the old man crosses intact the barrier that seemed to stand between him and the secrets of "the gulf beyond": "I still lived" (II, 241). The ensuing imagery of revelation overwhelms him with its sublimity as he beholds with "awe, horror, and admiration" "the rays of the full moon" that "streamed in a flood of golden glory along the black walls, and far

1. Lawrence, p. 81.
2. Levin, p. 156.

away down into the inmost recesses of the abyss" (II, 242). This vision of the ultimate dimension transforms him and it is in his new guise as one of Poe's elect, returned from the grave, that he is rescued at the last: "Those who drew me on board were my old mates and daily companions—but they knew me no more than they would have known a traveller from the spirit-land" (II, 247).

It is in the elaborate narrative frame, to which Poe devotes the first third of the tale, that the significance of the contrast between the sublime Lazarus and the ordinary mortal is made clear. The old man himself insists on the importance of the frame, leading the narrator to the top of a cliff overlooking the Maelström in order to tell him "the whole story with the spot just under your eye" (II, 226). When the narrator presently beholds the whirlpool as it takes shape and throws himself on the ground in the prone and clinging posture which the old man will assume on board the boat in his story, it becomes clear that he is reenacting in the frame situation an experience of the end that closely resembles that of the old man himself.[3] For all these carefully worked-out parallels between the narrator and the old man, however, the fundamental difference between their experiences is decisive. The narrator recoils from the brink, desirous of full knowledge yet fearful, while the old man willingly plunges over the rim to get to the bottom of it all. The narrator, as I think Poe would have us see, is what men mostly are, and the old man what men dream of being.

Even as "A Descent into the Maelström" would seem to offer the satisfaction of transcending mortal limitations, it reasserts them, for the old man's experience of the end is, in fact, strangely inconclusive. First, his initial headlong rush into the abyss proves to be only the prelude to a second and final plunge that apparently awaits all things in the whirlpool at the bottom. Then, as to the revelation itself, even though he beholds the very bottom of the gulf, his vision is incomplete: "I could make out nothing distinctly, on account of a thick mist in which everything there was enveloped" (II, 243). Endings following endings, revelations withheld in revelations granted—man's mortal limitations abide for all the ingenious doubling of final experience in the story and its frame. Poe must content himself with the fact of the old man's return in place of the final revelation finally deferred. The old man returns *as though* he were "a traveller from the spirit-land," *as though* he descended to the bottom of the abyss, whereas only his unfortunate brother, no Lazarus he, did that and was heard from no more.

The kinship of the Lady Ligeia with the old man of the Maelström will be immediately obvious, for she is what he had merely seemed, "a

3. "The wild bewildering sense of *the novel*" which confounds the narrator as he beholds the Maelström here is invariably the hallmark of final experience in Poe: "The mountain trembled to its very base, and the rock rocked." Interestingly, he identifies the impact of "the magnificence" and "the horror" which this scene inspires as an experience of the American sublime, comparing the sudden outpouring of sound to "the moaning of a vast herd of buffaloes upon an American prairie," "an appalling voice, half shriek, half roar, such as not even the mightly cataract of Niagara ever lifts up in its agony to Heaven" (II, 228–229). In Poe's sense of an ending the novel and the sublime are frequently linked.

traveller from the spirit-land." The dying Ligeia, in "her wild desire for life,—for life—*but* for life" (II, 255), aspires to conquer "the Conqueror Worm" (II, 257), and she succeeds. She dies, only to rise once more, a monument to the vigor of the will, to man's refusal to yield himself—in the words from Joseph Glanvill ever on her lips—"unto death utterly." The narrative frame in "Ligeia" is even more elaborate than in "A Descent into the Maelström," and makes an analogous contribution to narrative design. In both tales the frame doubles thematically and structurally the story it surrounds; the result is an obsessive reenactment of the paradigm of final experience, of the moment in which all knowledge is to be revealed. Thus the drama of recollection in the first part of "Ligeia," the narrator's attempt to "bring before mine eyes in fancy the image of her who is no more" (II, 249), becomes no less than a literal calling back in the second part: "I would call aloud upon her name . . . as if, through the wild eagerness, the solemn passion, the consuming ardor of my longing for the departed, I could restore her to the pathway she had abandoned—ah, *could* it be for ever?—upon the earth" (II, 261).

To examine the narrator's preoccupation with the image of Ligeia, however, is to recognize that his drive to recall her is not merely the counterpart of her ambition to triumph over death but the expression as well of his own desire for ultimate knowledge. "The beauty of beings either above or apart from the earth" is, he believes, incarnate in her, and she functions, accordingly, as the medium for his aspiration to transcend his "ignorance of so much of the spiritual" (II, 251). Standing in her presence he beholds the promise of the angelic condition, "that delicious vista by slow degrees expanding before me, down whose long, gorgeous, and all untrodden path, I might at length pass onward to the goal of a wisdom too divinely precious not to be forbidden!" (II, 254). Since it is, above all, in "the *expression*" of Ligeia's eyes that the riddle of the universe resides, they become the narrator's fixation. He reports that their special aura of significance is peculiarly noticeable "in moments of intense excitement" (II, 251) (his or her own?), and, further, that this excitement betrays the intensity of her "gigantic volition," accompanied as it is by her "wild words" (II, 253) which express the urgency of her determination to master her mortality. The same passage from Glanvill on the will links the meaning of Ligeia's eyes with the meaning of her words, confirming the twinship of the narrator's quest and that of his beloved.

This likeness is instructive. If the "Marginalia" passage, in its description of the entry into and withdrawal from special states of mind, contains the latent germ of the tales of the miraculous voyage and "the posthumous heroine," conversely, such journeys into the unknown, into the grave, are always, finally, properly regarded as an objectification of a drama of consciousness. The metaphoric nature of the Lazarus plot in Poe is nowhere more clearly set forth than in the parallel relationship between the narrator and Ligeia. Further, the figure adopted by the narrator to dramatize the ebb and flow of his consciousness in its meditations on Ligeia bears this out:

There is no point, among the many incomprehensible anomalies of the science of mind, more thrillingly exciting than the fact— never, I believe, noticed in the schools—that in our endeavors to recall to memory something long forgotten, we often find ourselves *upon the very verge* of remembrance, without being able, in the end, to remember. And thus how frequently, in my intense scrutiny of Ligeia's eyes, have I felt approaching the full knowledge of their expression—felt it approaching—yet not quite be mine—and so at length entirely depart!

The loss and recovery of the image mirrors the departure and return of the beloved. *"Upon the very verge"*—this is the critical posture of the Lazarus figure in Poe. Ligeia's "large and luminous orbs" (II, 252) are to the narrator what the whirlpool is to the old man of the Maelström, a symbol of the ultimate significance.[4] As the eyes of Ligeia slowly open at the close of the story, the narrator is restored to his longed-for contemplation of the Alpha and the Omega; the departed spirit has returned, the lost image has been recaptured.

In a revealing exchange of letters with Philip Pendleton Cooke about "Ligeia," Poe offered a criticism of the ending which sets the twin Lazarus quests of the tale in a new perspective. "One point I have not fully carried out—I should have intimated that the *will* did not perfect its intention—there should have been a relapse—a final one— and Ligeia (who had only succeeded in so much as to convey an idea of the truth to the narrator) should be at length entombed as Rowena—the bodily alterations having gradually faded away" (XVII, 52). In the face of his opportunity to allow the ambitions of the "Marginalia" program to succeed, I would argue, Poe decided not to let on that "the *will* did not perfect its intention." In any case, Poe's comment, which points up the ambiguity of Ligeia's apparent triumph at the last, applies with equal justice to the narrator's success as well. Even though—*mirabile dictu*—he beholds Ligeia's eyes once more, the content of his symbolic experience of revelation remains, finally, as inscrutable as "the very bottom" of the Maelström wrapped in mist. "What was it—that something more profound than the well of Democritus—which lay far within the pupils of my beloved?" (II, 251). The answer to the question of questions is never disclosed.

* * *

IV

So completely realized is Poe's pretense that Arthur Gordon Pym's narrative is incomplete that many unreflecting readers have been content to assume that Poe's story is unfinished as well, that Poe had

4. Wilbur points up the connection between the two stories, noting that the same lines from Joseph Glanvill which Poe has the narrator associate with the mystery of Ligeia's eyes serve as the epigraph for "A Descent into the Maelström." He argues, further, that the similarity of the endings of the two narratives (whirling movement and plunge) confirms his view that they are, in effect, parallel versions of the familiar dream-journey in so much of Poe's fiction. "Edgar Allan Poe," in *Major Writers of America*, ed. Perry Miller (New York, 1962), pp. 375–376, 379.

more work to do and that he left that work undone. Given the logic of this misconception, it was probably inevitable that someone would eventually presume to write the rest of the story, and Jules Verne obliged with a lengthy sequel, *Le Sphinx des Glaces*, in 1897. Given Poe's strategies for ending his tales, however, there is every indication that *The Narrative of Arthur Gordon Pym* is a completed fiction.

In the last chapter, once Poe has set his hero and his friend, Dirk Peters, together with their captive, the savage Nu-Nu, adrift "in the wide and desolate Antarctic Ocean . . . in a frail canoe" (III, 236), he signals the approaching end of the story in his customary fashion. In his first dated entry in many a chapter Pym himself stresses the point of transition: "Many unusual phenomena now indicated that we were entering upon a region of novelty and wonder" (III, 238). There is a "rapid change" (III, 239) in the color and temperature of the water, and the southerly current suddenly takes on a "hideous velocity," carrying the canoe inexorably toward "a limitless cataract, rolling silently into the sea from some immense and far-distant rampart in the heaven" (III, 241). "Rushing and mighty, but soundless" winds arise. The ebbing life of Pym and Peters, the death of Nu-Nu, the prophetic cries of the birds "from beyond the veil"—all confirm that Pym and his companions have reached the boundary between this world and the next. Not content to mark the advent of revelation by despatching his hero headlong into the abyss, Poe boldly supplies an image of the revelation itself: "And now we rushed into the embraces of the cataract, where a chasm threw itself open to receive us. But there arose in our pathway a shrouded human figure, very far larger in its proportions than any dweller among men. And the hue of the skin of the figure was of the perfect whiteness of the snow" (III, 242). Here final knowledge is confronted directly in the mysterious white figure rather than at one remove in the person of the Lazarus hero who has looked upon it. * * * Here Pym's narrative concludes, but Poe lets on instead that it has been merely interrupted, that the end is not the end.

The lengthy editorial note to the ending proper announces that Pym survived his ordeal and returned from the end of the world with knowledge of "the Pole itself, or at least to regions in its very near proximity." Lazarus lived to tell his tale—but the man and the "two or three final chapters" of his story were destroyed in an unfortunate accident following his safe return. And then, as if "to fill the vacuum" (III, 243) left by the "missing" chapters and their account, presumably, of the world "beyond the veil," the note proceeds to decipher the mysterious "*indentures*" that Pym encountered in his wanderings on the island of Tsalal. In the light of the apocalyptic utterance of the final line of the note, which reads, "*I have graven it within the hills, and my vengeance upon the dust within the rock*" (III, 245), the decoded message about "the region of the south" purports to be nothing less than revelation divine.

Pym survived—but he died. The key to the mystery is lost—but here it is. Clearly we are in the presence of an elaborate sleight-of-hand, designed to establish Pym's extraordinary adventure as a genuine

Lazarus fiction. The balance of recent critical opinion, however, emphatically rejects the editorial note and its instructions for the interpretation of Pym's narrative. Thus J. V. Ridgely and Iola S. Haverstick observe, "the 'Note' remains a curious, almost contemptuous, treatment of the credulity of the reader." Their piece on *Pym*, a massively documented and carefully researched investigation of the vicissitudes of the writing of the tale, brings to a culmination the lively interest in this subject in recent years. While their account of the facts is unlikely to be superseded, their sense of the fits and starts of Poe's composition of the story has led them, strangely, to the position that the story cannot be interpreted.

* * *

Now the upshot of the editorial note is an argument in favor of narrative design: although Pym's narrative seems to be incomplete, it is based on a completed manuscript unfortunately lost; the apparently meaningless "figures" of the chasms on the island of Tsalal have a meaning after all, "especially when taken in connection with statements made in the body of the narrative" (III, 244). Sidney Kaplan, for one, has interpreted these figures literally, with that "minute philological scrutiny" (III, 245) the note prescribes. Translating the message that they spell in ancient letters as a key to the concluding portions of *Pym*, he reads in Pym's adventures on Tsalal a fundamentalist allegory on race which damns the black man to the end of time.[5] This is not, however, what the figures signify when they are first encountered in the text. Only one of the series bears "some little resemblance to alphabetical characters" (III, 225); the others denote the course of Pym's wanderings in the labyrinthine chasms. That is to say that Poe establishes the figures in the text itself as symbols of the shape of Pym's experience, the configuration made by the path of the embattled self as it moves tortuously through a threatening nature. Thus the dual angle of vision permitted by text and note allows the figures to function both allegorically and symbolically, allegorically (as Kaplan persuades) in the sequence on Tsalal, symbolically in the narrative as a whole. The figures are at once the letters of ancient alphabets and the characters of a primordial language of experience, "the awful Chaldee," as it were, "of the Sperm Whale's brow." If we are to learn this second language, in the belief that the meaning of Pym's adventures is in some fundamental way expressed in the very shape of his experience itself, it is to the pattern of the adventures and to the strategies of fiction devoted to the creation of such patterns, rather than to the "editor's" fancy show of Ethiopian, Arabic, and Egyptian, that we must turn.

Pym's initial adventure, his madcap, nearly fatal, escapade with his friend Augustus on board the *Ariel*, offers a paradigm for all that follows: the approach to a seemingly inevitable death followed by a miraculous return to life. Pym tastes the zenith and the nadir of sensation in brief compass when the two young men, intoxicated with drink and

5. "An Introduction to *Pym*," in Regan, pp. 145–163.

power, embark in a gale at night; for the intensity of heightened con-
sciousness, that ecstasy which man's capacity to attain the ultimate
reach of experience inspires, and the numbness of insensibility when
this "mental energy" gives way, are always yoked in Poe, who would live
the life of the dead. Poe resuscitates Pym "from a state bordering very
nearly upon death" (III, 16) in the aftermath of the wreck of the *Ariel*
only to restore him to it at greater length in the episode that follows.
Buried alive in an ironbound box in the labyrinthine hold of the *Gram-
pus*, Pym is subjected to cycle after punishing cycle of the loss and re-
covery of consciousness as hunger, thirst, and suffocation push him
over the edge of sanity into nightmare and impending annihilation.
"Those only who have been suddenly redeemed from the jaws of the
tomb" (III, 46) possess the knowledge that is his upon his rescue.

From this point forward in the narrative Poe pursues a systematic ex-
ploration of every imaginable form of human extremity: what counts is
the isolated consciousness and its sensations in the face of the ultimate
calamity. True child of *Blackwood's*, Pym identifies himself at the outset
as the melancholy man whose imaginative life is consecrated to visions
of death and disaster. The urgency of his sense of an ending, which
functions, somewhat paradoxically, as the vital principle of his existence,
is most strikingly displayed in the celebrated passage of his penultimate
plunge, his "*longing to fall*" (III, 230) into the Tsalalian abyss. This cen-
tral fact of Pym's character governs the design of Poe's fiction; the hero
and his author collaborate to act it out at the expense of narrative itself,
for no single story can suffice but rather a seemingly endless series of
tales that constitute a tale without an end. Thus Poe's strategies are de-
signed to repeat Pym's longed-for confrontation with the end, and each
new situation is reduced accordingly to fit this final shape.

* * *

Is Poe's treatment irresponsible or, worse, insulting, or does he give
us a haunting double view of the possibilities of his hero's Lazarus
quest? To recognize the presence of an equivocation on so central an
issue as this is to confront the question of the meaning of Pym's expe-
riences once and for all. If the diagrams of the chasms of Tsalal may
be taken to represent the shape of Pym's experience, and if this shape
is invariably that of an ending obsessively reenacted in each and every
episode of this episodic narrative, has this shape any significance at
all? Poe's presentation of the figures themselves provides a clue, for it
shares in the very doubleness that I take them to symbolize. For Pym's
"editor," stationed as he is at a privileged, indeed "angelic," vantage
point looking down on the chasms from above, the figures have a
meaning, they spell out a message. Pym's position in the earth, how-
ever, his stance within the figures, does not permit transcendence; he
inhabits a significance that he fails to fathom.

The reader who would press such experience for greater certitude is
certain to encounter a critical ambivalence at its very core, for the dou-
ble ending of this tale states baldly what the more richly ambiguous
"Ligeia" and "A Descent into the Maelström" imply, that Poe's attitude
toward the experience of meaning is divided. Taking the text and the

note together, the conclusion of *Pym* presents in a single extravagant
and contradictory package the range of possible endings devised by
Poe: either the hero is arrested in tantalizing proximity at the very
threshold of revelation, as in "MS. Found in a Bottle" or "The Man of
the Crowd"; or he attains the vision of "the spirit's outer world" and re-
turns transfigured to the world of the living, like Ligeia or the old man
of the Maelström: sometimes even the revelation itself is supplied, as in
the angelic colloquies or the transcripts of mesmerist trances. Of these
alternatives in the case of *Pym*, it is to the first that the imagination
most readily assents for reasons which some consideration of the psy-
chology of endings will supply. First, we want to believe that we could
know all, but the urgency of our wanting is directly proportionate to
our conviction of the impossibility of our knowing. Second, we believe
that the knowledge we seek is by its very nature incommunicable,
hence any translation of the ineffable into the language of the tribe
could only prove unsatisfactory. Thus we prefer our Lazarus at one re-
move to the too-familiar Pym, better the sublimity of a figure rare and
strange, resplendent with the aura of last things beheld but unspoken,
than the inevitable banality of an editor's intrusive explication.

* * *

What the equivocation of *Pym* reveals, finally, is that Poe in pushing
his hero to the limits of experience was pushing himself to the limits
of fiction as well. While we would surrender to the sublime bravado of
the headlong plunge into the abyss, Poe compels us most when we
linger upon the very verge. The epigraph from Joseph Glanvill that
heads "A Descent into the Maelström" may serve as an epitaph to
Poe's daring attempts to construct a fiction commensurate to final
knowledge: "The ways of God in Nature, as in Providence, are not as
our ways; nor are the models that we frame in any way commensurate
to the vastness, profundity, and unsearchableness of His works, *which
have a depth in them greater than the well of Democritus*" (II, 225).

GRACE FARRELL

From The Quest of Arthur Gordon Pym†

Focusing upon the apparent lack of any sustained linear movement in
Edgar Allan Poe's *The Narrative of Arthur Gordon Pym of Nantucket*,
several critics have concluded that the tale is a yoking of two or more
disassociated sea adventures.[1] Critics who have analyzed the tale's var-

† From the *Southern Literary Journal* 4 (1972): 22–33. Reprinted by permission of the *South-
 ern Literary Journal* and the author; slightly revised for the present volume.
1. L. Moffitt Cecil, "The Two Narratives of Arthur Gordon Pym," *Texas Studies in Literature
 and Language*, V (Summer, 1963), first declared *Pym* to be two disjointed, superficially fused
 tales: "The *Grampus* story wants climax and conclusion, and the *Jane Guy* story, so placed
 that it might be expected to serve for both, can really supply neither" (p. 63).
 Supporting Cecil's conclusions, Joseph V. Ridgely and Iola H. Haverstick, "Chartless Voy-
 age: The Many Narratives of Arthur Gordon Pym," Texas Studies in Literature and Lan-
 guage, VIII (Spring, 1966), through extensive use of biographical data delineated five stages
 of Pym's development as well as noting numerous discrepancies within the text. They con-

ious themes have accomplished little in presenting the structural vehicle of these themes as any kind of cohesive entity.[2] The evidence that Poe composed the work in several stages and under various economic pressures is quite conclusive. Yet such evidence does not preclude the existence of a structural principle underlying the successive stages of the story, nor does it necessitate the implication that Poe had little serious intent in his production of *Pym*, for even under extreme pressure and in great haste this master story-teller was attempting to explore, in fictive form, a phenomenon fundamental to his human experience.

Arthur Gordon Pym revitalizes an archetype found throughout religious mythology, the descent into Hell, and utilizes the structure of a sea voyage, a familiar post-Jungian image of the collective unconscious, to voyage into the recesses of the human psyche and to journey backward in time to the origins of creation. *Pym* is a two-pronged dream quest into the unknown where the terror of the universe and of man's confrontation with primal nature is reawakened.

The mythological and psychological directions of Pym's quest are not divergent, for, to use Jungian terms, myth symbolizes unconscious psychic action which is made available to the conscious mind through projections onto the natural world. Thus, myth arises from the depths of the unconscious. There also, in the deepest layers of the psyche, in the collective unconscious, lies the universal. There the cosmic and the psychic meet. Thus, by surging inward upon himself via his dream experiences, Pym can propel himself backward in time to his primordial origins and to the universality of all existence.

The archetype for the descent into Hell in pagan mythology assumes the form of a journey by the dead to Hades. In Christian documents, especially in the Gospel of Nicodemus, a parallel may be discovered in

cluded, ". . . the story lacks a controlling theme and has no uncontrovertible serious meaning No amount of straining can bring all its disparate elements into a consistent interpretation" (p. 80).

 Sidney Moss, "*Arthur Gordon Pym* or the Fallacy of Thematic Interpretation," *University Review*, XXXIII (Summer, 1967), contends that those who find unity of theme within *Pym* have merely discovered a thematic relation between two tales, a not uncommon occurrence among the works of Poe [Farrell's note].

2. Several critics, including Sidney Kaplan, "An Introduction to *Pym*," *Poe: A Collection of Critical Essay*, ed. Robert Regan (Englewood Cliffs, 1967), and Harry Levin, *The Power of Blackness* (New York, 1958), have ignored structural problems to concentrate on an analysis of the Jane Guy section of the tale.

 Other critics have isolated themes which are sustained through a structural principle of repetition. However, as Moss contends, a pattern of repetition could easily occur in separate tales. Patrick Quinn, *The French Face of Edgar Poe* (Carbondale, 1957), discusses a recurring pattern of revolt integrated with the theme of deception. Marie Bonaparte, *The Life and Works of Edgar Allan Poe* (London, 1949), presents a psychoanalytic view of the tale as a series of revolts against father figures in an effort to return to the womb of the mother. Walter Bezanson, "The Troubled Sleep of Arthur Gordon Pym," *Essays in Literary History*, ed. Rudolph Kirk and C. F. Main (New York, 1965), posits a eseries of deaths and rebirths as the underlying pattern of the work. As the Grampus section ends, ". . . we see that it has provided us two sustained episodes which meet the promise of the Prologue: one, burial in the hold and birth into a mutinous world; the other a cycle of primal deprivations on the wrecked hull, culminating in the feeding of man on man. The power of each lies in its literary evocation of dream forms" (p. 167). In the Jane Guy section Pym is again buried, in the island chasm, and again marooned. As is evident in my article, I concur with Bezanson's analysis, although I do not feel that he presents the structural vehicle by which Poe conveyed the rebirth motif [Farrell's note].

the descent of Christ into Hell. *Pym* combines the two, pagan and Christian elements, to create a structure for his quest.

Poe's tale does not allegorize or paraphrase the descent myths. Rather, it is an attempt to express the most fundamental of phenomena, to search for some "deep axis of reality." As a probe into the depths of the self and of the universe, the use of myth may be an unconscious expression of a psychic phenomenon. *Pym* does not imitate myth; rather, it *is* myth, a verbal structure imposed upon psychic phenomena for the purpose of making such phenomena accessible to consciousness. Furthermore, it is a verbal structure imposed upon the same sorts of phenomena as are those of the myths to the underworld and the Christian descent story. Thus, the mythology of *Pym* does not depend upon other mythologies for its viability. Rather, all are structures which express a fundamental psychic phenomenon, the return to sources. All partake, as it were, of the "mythological unconscious."

Traditional techniques for affecting the archetypal return described by Mircea Eliade correspond to the situations depicted in *A. Gordon Pym*:

> First and foremost, there is the well-known symbolism of initiation rituals implying a *regressus ad uterum* A large number of myths feature (1) a hero being swallowed by a sea monster and emerging victorious after breaking through the monster's belly; (2) initiatory passage through a *vagina dentata*, or the dangerous descent into a cave or crevice assimilated to the mouth or the uterus of Mother Earth. All these adventures are in fact initiatory ordeals, after accomplishing which the victorious hero acquires a new mode of being.[3]

Both of these common, mythological features are expressed in *Pym*, the first in the hold episode aboard the Grampus and the second in the cave incident on Tsalal. The hold of the ship is the mythic equivalent of the belly of the sea monster. Walter Benzanson, agreeing with Marie Bonaparte that Pym's hideaway box is womblike, views the cord leading from it to the secret trapdoor of the stateroom as umbilical. I would add that by means of the cord, in a sort of difficult birth process through the labyrinths created by piles of lumber, Pym finally emerges reborn. The process is similarly experienced in the island cave.

Each time Pym undergoes the rebirth ordeal he emerges at a deeper level in his descent. Pym begins his return to his source through dream, begun in the Ariel episode and intensified in the stupefaction and prolonged sleep of the hold sequence, where Pym dreams within his dream. His rebirth from the hold constitutes not an awakening, but rather a movement which passes right through dream into a realm of being once more removed from consciousness. The rebirth sequence in the Tsalalian cave takes Pym still deeper within himself and still farther backward until he reaches the very origins of creation.

The hold episode introduces the mythic pattern of descent by the dead into the underworld. Numerous critics have taken note of the

3. Mircea Eliade, *Myth and Reality* (New York, 1963), pp. 79, 81 [Farrell's note].

death-like aspects of this sequence. Pym's box is described as coffin-shaped and is regally outfitted, as were the coffins of ancient kings set off on their journey of death:

> It was nearly four feet high, and full six long, but very narrow
> A mattress from one of the cabin berths covered the whole of its bottom, and it contained almost every article of mere comfort which could be crowded into so small a space, allowing me, at the same time, sufficient room for my accommodation, either in a sitting position or lying at full length.[4]

In addition, Augustus describes Pym as being buried, and Pym himself speaks in terms of entombment and calls his rescue a redemption "from the jaws of the tomb" (p. 748). His incarceration in the hold of the ship is reminiscent of Jonah's imprisonment in the belly of the whale. The associations with death are embodied in the object of the ship, which is a familiar image of the vehicle of the soul on its journey to the underworld. The image arises from the custom of boat burials which implies belief in the necessity of crossing the sea to reach the underworld. Throughout literature, in Homer, Virgil, Dante, this primitive belief has left vestiges in the images of some sort of water barrier which must be crossed before a mortal is permitted entry into the world of spirit.[5] Thus, not only is water the psychological medium through which Pym enters his unconscious, but also it is the mythical substance through which he travels to reach the underworld.

The water imagery accrues further mythological implications with the introduction of the scenes of diving into the waterfilled hold of the Grampus. Here men who forage for food become the "earth divers" of mythology, who, in the beginnings of time, when the earth was entirely covered by water, attempted to discover the world by diving underwater and grasping soil in their hands[6] This ritualistic action, which begins immediately after the retaking of the Grampus by Pym and Peters and continues until the cannibalistic feast, is symbolic of the entire tale as a movement through water to discover reality.

As the narrator describes them as immersions, the divings are further infused with Biblical overtones, and the action begins to resemble various baptismal rites in which a believer is immersed in water. Early Christian thought associated baptisms with the descent into Hell. "The starting-point is the word 'abyss'—the underwaters and so the underworld to which Christ descended."[7] Thus, the ritual of the divings accrues Biblical associations, which also imply descent into Hell.

The appearance of the Dutch brig creates further implications of a movement toward the underworld. The ship is quite literally a ship of death, in many ways similar to that of the "Ancient Mariner."[8]

4. Edgar Allan Poe, *The Complete Poems and Stories*, ed. Arthur Hobson Quinn and Edward H. O'Neill (New York, 1967), p. 735. All subsequent quotations from the works of Poe are taken from this source [Farrell's note].
5. L. C. Wimberly, *Folklore in the English and Scottish Ballads* (Chicago, 1928), p. 108 [Farrell's note].
6. *Ibid* [Farrell's note].
7. J. A. MacCulloch, *The Harrowing of Hell* (Edinburgh, 1930), pp. 133–34 [Farrell's note].
8. Farrell here quotes from chapter X of *Pym* (see pp. 489–90 herein) [Editor].

* * *

The appearance of the Ship of Death is important to the structure of the tale. It accomplishes more than the creation of yet another horror in Pym's world. Rather, it functions as a catalyst for his mythical voyage, giving direction to its movement. The black brig enchants those aboard the hull of the Grampus as its appearance focuses upon it all the dispersed energy of the survivors. It becomes a powerful mesmeric force as the sailor at the bowsprit beckons encouragingly, casting over the survivors of the Grampus a state of stupefaction. When finally the gull makes the symbolic offering of human flesh, the narrative focus zeroes in on the splashed morsel. Attention rivets to it. The implications of the offering escape none of the survivors, for it is accepted in the cannibalistic rite which follows. Their acceptance seals their fate and insures the direction of their voyage, for as folklore relates, anyone who eats food offered by the dead cannot return to the world of living men [Wimberly, p. 280].

The cannibalistic feast exemplifies the transforming power of Poe's narrative gaze whose hypnotic concentration extracts details from their proper contexts and recreates them grotesquely exaggerated and fragmented. His parodic vision creates a mock communion from a scene of cannibalism by interfusing it with allusions to the Last Supper of Christ. The cannibalistic rite is imbued with a confusion of Biblical overtones, and the language with Biblical cadences. Bezanson notes, "Pym intones: 'we devoured the rest of the body piecemeal, during the four ever memorable days of the seventeenth, eighteenth, nineteenth, and twentieth of the month.' The solemn rhythm of these phrases, and the religious quality of the terms Pym used earlier when protesting the sacrifice, suggest a savage communion" [Bezanson, p. 166].

The Biblical allusions are not presented in any cohesive temporal sequence, rather they are interspersed throughout the scene, and only as they are experienced through a process of accumulation do they accrue significance and meaning as an aggregate. Words are transformed from references to material reality to become mobile, reverberating against one another in space, forming clusters of meaning within the linguistic structure of the tale. The port, drunk in common, is associated with such words as "species," "immersion," "Peter," "fish-scales," "consummation," all of which create great ramifications of innuendo surrounding the word *port* to suggest communion wine, St. Peter, and the fishermen apostles.

The religious is continually transmuted into the macabre as the Sacrificial rite is transported, like Pym himself, to a primitive, subliminal realm where the sacred can make linkage with the most degraded of human actions, and where the cannibalistic innuendos of the Gospel account are parodied into high relief. Parker, who proposes ". . . that one of us should die to preserve the existence of the others" (789), is portrayed as the most willing of sacrificial lambs, ". . . who had been doomed to suffer . . . [and who] made no resistance whatever" (792). The casting of lots to determine who must be the victim echoes both the Biblical scene in which the garments of Christ are di-

vided and the story of Jonah in which lots are cast to determine who will be thrown overboard to appease the wrath of God and, thus, to save the other lives aboard ship. The Last Supper is again conjured up as the dead Parker makes the same offering, rendered in bizarre literality, as did Christ, that of his body to be eaten and his blood to be drunk, "Let it suffice to say that, having in some measure appeased the raging thirst which consumed us by the blood of the victim, and having by common consent taken off the hands, feet, and head, throwing them together with the entrails, into the sea, we devoured the rest of the body . . ." (792). Later, vinegar is applied to the wounds of Augustus, as it was once forced into the wounded mouth of Christ.

As in the Jonah narrative, after lots are cast and the human sacrifice is performed, the ship is saved. In Pym's voyage relief comes in the shape of the Jane Guy out of Liverpool. However, the survivors of the Grampus have been enchanted by the Ship of Death. They must proceed to the underworld. Thus it is not an accident that it is Pym who convinces Captain Guy to set course for the Polar regions where they arrive at the island of Tsalal.

Tsalal is easily recognized as an imaginative portrayal of Hell. In many folktales and myths the underworld is coextensive with this world [MacCulloch, p. 300; Wimberly, p. 139], as is Tsalal, situated near to the South Pole. Moreover, it is a place of unusual warmth; Pym marvels at the absence of icebergs or any other indication of a polar region. The fire and explosion on board ship, which turns the entire inlet into flame, is a more vivid portrayal of the traditional Hell's fire.

The darkness of Hell is quite recognizable in the total blackness of the island and of its inhabitants, whose very teeth are black. The purplish veined rivers have been explained by Bezanson as fantasies on Negro blood. However, in much English and Scottish folklore the underworld contains rivers of blood [Wimberly, p. 128]. In addition, as Sidney Kaplan also points out, the water of Dante's *Inferno* is depicted as purple; "Tsalal is Hell; its water is Styx, a kind of dirty, imperfect blood flowing thickly 'in distinct veins, each of a distinct hue,' which do not commingle. The color of the water is 'every possible shade of purple'—'persa,' as Dante . . . describes it in the *Inferno*" [Kaplan, p. 157].

Tsalal, and the total Jane Guy section, is indeed a fitting climax to the Grampus episodes. The mythical structure of an enchanted descent of the dead into Hades finds its completion on the island. The fragmentary ending of *Pym* has produced much speculation as to its relationship to the rest of the work. Marie Bonaparte's conclusion that the ending depicts a return to an immersion in mother's milk is supported by Bezanson and Harry Levin, while others, notably Henry James, conclude that the ending means nothing and connects with nothing else in the fiction. However, it does complete the mythical structure of enchantment and movement into the underworld, for it was impossible to return from Hell without affecting some mode of disenchantment, one of which was immersion in water or milk to

effect a transformation from non-human to human form, or to redeem one from another realm of being [Wimberly, pp. 388–90].

The Jane Guy section is also a fitting climax to the Biblical innuendoes of the death and descent into Hell of Christ, the Prince of Light who came to conquer Darkness. The Gospel of Nicodemus, which relates the descent, concludes as two brethren ascend from the underworld, are baptized, and clothed in white robes, "transfigured, exceedingly white, and were no more seen" [MacCulloch, p. 170]. Therefore, the ending, in which Pym and Peters disappear when enveloped in whiteness, provides a conclusion to the mythic-Biblical framework of death and descent to the underworld; and the whole provides a structure from which Poe may descend into the unconscious and may move backwards to his primal origins.

The intent of his voyage is to confront the real by breaking through the structures created by man to alleviate the awesomeness of his vision. The action is a reversal of the process of civilization, which seeks to construct an artifice of order, and then to impose it upon the chaos. Poe was very much aware of the notion that what a man normally sees as real is only what he has been taught to see. His perceptions are determined more by what he is as a creature rooted in a certain historical and physical context, than by what may exist distinct from him. This concern is evident in Poe's play with Pym, who constantly attempts to synchronize what he experiences with his expectations and preconceived notions of the situations. Pym's voyage is an attempt to disintegrate the structured world in order to approach a fundamental reality which lies behind all time and within the minds of all men. As Davidson suggests, "The movement toward simplicity and opaqueness is one of the curiosities of the book . . . the farther it moves the more it tends to reduce external objects and events to their simplest forms."[9] Pym moves to the very beginnings of creation where, on the island of Tsalal, the light brought forth in creation confronts in everlasting opposition the black.

Tsalal embodies the basic reduction of all into the eternal conflict of black and white. While Bezanson, Levin, and Kaplan have cast this conflict in racial terms, my mythic reading emphasizes blackness and whiteness as the stuff of reality, separated in the course of creation and symbolizing, for Poe, the basic forces of attraction and repulsion of which the universe consists. *Pym* is Poe's fictive manipulation of the ideas that were later to be crystallized in his philosophical treatise *Eureka*, in which the antagonism of opposites becomes the basic principle of the universe.

Throughout the tale Pym plays with darkness and light. His first adventure takes place in the dead of night interfused with the full moon, onboard the Ariel. Darkness pervades the hold of the Grampus and the black Dutch brig. Most of Pym's voyage takes place not only in water, but also in gloom, signifying the return of the outcast forces of blackness into his world. The blackness becomes increasingly threat-

9. Edward H. Davidson, *Poe: A Critical Study* (Cambridge, Mass., 1957), p. 173 [Farrell's note].

ening with the appearance of the Ship of Death and in the death of Augustus, whose black rotted arm eats away at his living flesh.

The world of Tsalal is, as Kaplan writes, ". . . black to its core—so quintessentially black that it is divided by 'chasmal differences' from whiteness in any form. * * *

Pym has reached the foundation of reality in the opposition of these forces. Their conflict sets off the apocalyptic fire on the Jane Guy which annihilates the island, its inhabitants, and every force of blackness. In *Eureka* Poe expressed belief that all matter arises from an original unity and attempts to return to that unity. This reverse motion leads the universe to contract into its center and thus to destroy itself. Here in Pym's voyage all matter is subsumed into unity as he and Peters are swallowed up by the perfect whiteness of the chasm. Pym's quest within himself has taken him into the supra-reality of what Poe would term "fancies"; it has taken him back to the universal essence of being. Poe's fictive probe of "fancies" has enabled him to sight a force similar to what another romantic, Wordsworth, had intuited in "Tintern Abbey," although Poe's sighting is void of Wordsworthian consolation; the fundamental reality of his vision is one of conflict, rather than one of peace.

* * *

Poe consciously and even cautiously led his reader into a descent into the unconscious realm of "fancies" by means of a voyage which took his fictional characters to an imaginative Hell to confront the primal elements of reality. The tale is a philosophical exploration of ideas essential to Poe's entire work. The significance of the mythic structure may be unconscious, but whether Poe was aware of the significance of his episodes or not matters little. The structure exists, and it arose from his imagination. It mirrors the intent of Poe's philosophy as later concretized in *Eureka*, for it returns him to the "source of sources," which Eliade cites as the goal of most mythologies, and to the awareness of the essence of all. His structure and his meaning are the same thing, and, contrary to the conclusions of several critics, they do exist.

LIAHNA ARMSTRONG

The Shadow's Shadow: The Motif of the Double in Edgar Allan Poe's "The Purloined Letter"†

In 1845, Edgar Allan Poe published "The Purloined Letter," his third contribution to the form he had himself invented. While critics of the work have generally recognized its superiority to Poe's other detective stories, particularly in light of its additions to the new genre, few have attributed its merit to factors other than skillful handling of the

† From *The Mystery and Detection Annual* (1972): 21–32. Reprinted by permission of the author (formerly Liahna Klenman Babener); slightly revised for the present volume.

"ratiocinative" method, or effective rendering of structural unity.[1] But these qualities do not sufficiently account for the distinctive achievement of the work. The author himself admonished against overvaluing his detective tales merely "on account of their method or *air* of method,"[2] and encouraged the prudent reader to discover meaning beneath the surface as "an undercurrent of suggestion."

One aspect of the work, often noticed but as yet unexplained, is the pervasive doubling motif[3] which underlies the structure of the tale as a whole and characterizes particularly the relationship between M. Dupin and his rival, the Minister D——. Poe's insistent use of doublings in the story considerably exceeds that which is necessary for presenting Dupin's method of investigation, which in this case stresses detection through psychological identification with an adversary. Rather, the prominent pattern of doubles suggests that the protagonist and his foil are moral duplicates and may ultimately be two phases of the same mind.

The double principle informs the basic action of the story, the major event of which is Dupin's retrieval of the purloined letter and consequent triumph over the resourceful D——. The action revolves around

1. For example, in her introduction to *The Omnibus of Crime* (New York: Harcourt Brace, 1929), p. 16, Dorothy L. Sayers praises the story for its contributions to the new detective story genre (the "method of *psychological deduction* and solution by the formula of the *most obvious place*"), but her analysis does not extend much beyond this. Brander Matthews states the commonly held attitude that the tale (and all Poe's detective fiction) is noteworthy for its process of analytical deduction, rather than for any intrinsic interest in the mystery itself. "Poe and the Detective Story," *The Recognition of Edgar Allan Poe*, ed. Eric Carlson (Ann Arbor: Univ. of Michigan Press, 1966), p. 85. See also Ellery Queen, "Introduction," in Michael Harrison, *The Exploits of the Chevalier Dupin* (Sauk City, Wisconsin: Arkham House, 1968), p. ix; T. O. Mabbott in his introduction to *The Selected Poetry and Prose of Edgar Allan Poe* (New York: Modern Library, 1951), p. xiv; Arthur Hobson Quinn, *Edgar Allan Poe: A Critical Biography* (New York: Appleton-Century, 1941), p. 421, all of whom evaluate "The Purloined Letter" as Poe's best detective tale, but do little to defend or explain their assessments [Armstrong's note]. All notes to this selection are Armstrong's [Editor].
2. *The Letters of Edgar Allan Poe*, ed. John Ward Ostrom, 2nd ed. (New York: Gordian Press, 1966), II, 328.
3. Although scholars have frequently observed Poe's propensity for the "double" image in fiction, few have noticed its operation in "The Purloined Letter." Those who mention the idea do little to develop the point. See Howard Haycraft, "Murder for Pleasure," in *The Art of the Mystery Story: A Collection of Critical Essays*, ed. Howard Haycraft (New York: Simon and Schuster, 1946), p. 174: attempting to identify the historical model for Dupin as one of two illustrious brothers surnamed Dupin, Haycraft comments on the similarity between the fictional Dupin and the Minister D——, and suggests that "in the dual circumstances of Poe's . . . adaptation of the characteristics of the real brothers Dupin," one will readily "scent a highly logical, if possibly unconscious 'transference,' " between hero and foe. See also Alice Chandler, " 'The Visionary Race': Poe's Attitude Toward His Dreamers," *Emerson Society Quarterly*, No. 60 (1970), Pt. II, 73–81; Joseph Moldenhauer, "Murder as a Fine Art: Basic Connections Between Poe's Aesthetics, Psychology and Moral Vision," *PMLA*, 83 (1968), 294; Patrick Quinn in *The French Face of Edgar Poe* (Carbondale: Southern Illinois Univ. Press, 1957), especially pp. 223–56; and Richard Wilbur, "The Poe Mystery Case," *New York Review of Books* (13 July 1967), 16, 25–28. Wilbur deals primarily with "The Murders in the Rue Morgue," which he attempts to explicate as a study in the multiple nature of the personality and accounts for parallels between Dupin and the other main characters "allegorically as elements of one person." He does not extend his study to "The Purloined Letter." Although the now infamous reading of "The Purloined Poe" by French psychoanalyst Jacques Lacan was presented as part of his weeklong seminar in April 1955 and published as an essay in 1956, it was not until the burgeoning interest in poststructuralism that Lacan's reading began to have a major impact on criticism of the story. While most responsible critical treatments of "The Purloined Letter" since the 1980s address in one way or another the issues raised by Lacan, there is one indispensable source on the Lacanian interpretation: *The Purloined Poe: Lacan, Derrida, and Psychoanalytic Reading*, ed. John P. Muller and William J. Richardson (Baltimore and London: The Johns Hopkins University Press, 1988).

Dupin's method of detection, which is based primarily on two logical premises from which he will eventually reason forth the solution to the mystery. One is that the cunning investigator must achieve an "identification of the reasoner's intellect with that of his opponent."[4] The other is the recognition that the truth "may escape observation by dint of being excessively obvious." Both axioms are exemplified by means of an analogy to game strategy. For the first, Dupin describes the familiar schoolboys' game of "even and odd." "One player holds in his hand a number of . . . [marbles], and demands of another whether that number is even or odd. If the guess is right, the guesser wins one; if wrong, he loses one." The shrewder player wins by anticipating the strategy of the other competitor. Dupin illustrates his second postulate with the old sport of locating place names printed on a map. While "a novice in the game generally seeks to embarrass his opponents by giving them the most minutely lettered names . . . the adept selects such words as stretch, in large characters, from one end of the chart to the other." The prudent player correctly presumes that the other will overlook the larger and more diffused letters in favor of the smaller, more compact words, and wins by subverting the expectations of his opponent. It is significant that both of these illustrations incorporate the use of parallel reasoning between contenders, and both epitomize in miniature the primary action of the tale as a whole. Dupin's casual game analogies thus serve as metaphors for the more consequential rivalry between him and D—.

Acting upon these paired axioms, the detective approaches the twofold problem of the missing letter and the astute thief. Dupin knows that the Minister, who has purportedly stolen the document for purposes of political extortion, must fulfill two requirements if he is ever to utilize his spoils. He must be able to produce the letter at momentary notice, and he must protect it from frequent searches by the police. Given these circumstances, the sleuth reasons that the letter must be secreted on the premises of D—'s lodgings, despite the failure of the Prefect's men to find it. At this point, Dupin applies the first supposition of his method on the basis of a prior knowledge of the character of his adversary, and proceeds to recreate the Minister's reasoning in the current situation:

> Such a man, I considered, could not fail to be aware of the ordinary policial modes of action. He could not have failed to anticipate . . . the waylaying to which he was subjected. He must have foreseen, I reflected, the secret investigations of his premises. . . . I felt also, that the whole train of thought, which I was at some pains in detailing to you just now . . . would necessarily pass through the mind of the Minister. It would imperatively lead him to despise all the ordinary *nooks* of concealment. . . . I saw, in fine, that he would be driven, as a matter of course, to *simplicity*, if not deliberately induced to it as a matter of choice.

4. "The Purloined Letter," *The Complete Works of Edgar Allan Poe*, ed. James A. Harrison (New York: Crowell, 1902). All citations from the text of this story are from the 1902 edition.

In this extract, Dupin is actually reproducing the Minister's own method of reasoning: he "admeasures" the mind of his competitor (as D— has appraised the intelligence of his police assailants) and predicts his tactics (as D— has anticipated the tactics of his pursuers). In this way, the detective deduces D—'s plan for concealment of the letter—the paradoxical scheme of the conspicuous hiding place—which is the practical embodiment of Dupin's own axiom about the difficulty of perceiving the obvious. Like the game players' strategy in his analogies, Dupin's is to outguess his antagonist.

It remains for Dupin, having unriddled the mystery, to verify his solution and to retrieve the letter. He makes an unsolicited visit to the Minister's apartment, where, camouflaged behind a "pair of green spectacles," he scans the room for the letter which he locates, revamped and resealed, in a letter rack in plain view of the observer. A second visit, on a spurious excuse, furnishes the occasion for a surreptitious exchange of letters, where Dupin, repeating the method used initially by D— to steal the letter, replaces the original document with a counterfeit one. Dupin describes his replica as "a *fac-simile*, (so far as regards externals) which I had carefully prepared at my lodgings; imitating the D— cipher, very readily, by means of a seal formed of bread." The vital letter itself is present in two guises. Dupin, studying the one in D—'s letter rack, recognizes that though "it was, to all appearance, radically different from the one of which the Prefect has read us so minute a description," nevertheless this document is the one sought. "It was torn nearly in two, across the middle" and it "had been turned, as a glove, inside out, re-directed and re-sealed." So the purloined letter becomes a double of itself. Thus, the entire process of crime solution incorporates a series of noticeable doublings and parallelings: the twin analytical axioms, the pair of game analogies, the two successive intellectual gambols between the police and D— and between D— and Dupin, the sequence of mimicked stratagems by which Dupin trips up his enemy, and the twofold nature of the chief clue.

While Poe unquestionably sets up the tale to enable Dupin to demonstrate his imitative method of detection against an antagonist of equal powers, this explanation does not sufficiently account for other insistent uses of the double pattern in the story.

This doubling technique appears especially in the portraits of the two major characters. Dupin's own reasoning processes are frequently depicted by means of coupled thoughts and parallel ideas. He is particularly fond of elaborate, point by point analogies. "The material world," he observes, "abounds with very strict analogies to the immaterial." He is fascinated by semblances and correspondences and often uses them as indirect means of communication. In one occurrence, Dupin induces the Prefect to acknowledge and reward his assistance in the present case by means of the "Abernethy" anecdote. The sleuth recounts the fable of a miser who uses hypothetical questions to maneuver advice from a doctor, and the Prefect, inferring Dupin's point, properly sees in the analogy an image of his own avarice. " 'But,' said the Prefect, a little discomposed, 'I am *perfectly* willing to take advice,

and to pay for it. I would *really* give fifty thousand francs to any one who would aid me in the matter,' " and Dupin correspondingly interprets the Prefect's allusion as a reluctant offer of compensation. Dupin's anecdote illustrates again the gaming psychology and emphasizes his tendency to devise fictional doubles as means of expression. Moreover, Dupin himself is often described in terms of paired images. He is first pictured to us relaxing in his secluded quarters, "au troisième, No. 33, Rue Dunôt," (note the repetition of the numbers and the echo of the protagonist's name in that of his street) where he and the nameless narrator enjoy the "twofold luxury of meditation and a meerschaum." Correspondingly, the Minister D— is frequently depicted by means of yoked images. The Prefect portrays him as a man who "dares all things, those unbecoming as well as those becoming a man." He practices a thievery "not less ingenious than bold." Dupin knows him as poet and mathematician, courier and intrigant. D—'s residence, the D— Hotel, is also a reverberation of his name.

These parallelisms and mated adjectives used to describe the major characters are compounded by an almost compulsive duplication of structural elements in the tale. Nearly every major movement of plot occurs twice. There are two consultations between the Prefect and Dupin. On the occasion of the second call, we are told by the narrator that the Prefect "found us occupied very nearly as before." Both visits are at night and both times the caller is supplied with pipe and chair. There are two interviews as well between Dupin and D—, and on each occasion they discuss the same subject. There are two major searches of the Minister's apartment by the police. (When the Prefect expresses bewilderment after the first fruitless inspection, Dupin's advice is "to make a thorough re-search of the premises.") Similarly, we are informed that D— "has been twice waylaid" in the streets by the inspector's men; both times the men are costumed as thugs, both times the search is executed under the covert supervision of the Prefect himself, and both times D— is found without the stolen document. There are also two instances of "blackmail": the Minister's against "a personage of most exalted station," and Dupin's of the Prefect to obtain payment for his assistance. There are two rewards paid for the recovery of the letter—both are "very liberal." (The Prefect notes that the prize offered "has been lately doubled.") In addition, there are two instances of papers being purloined, both involving the furtive substitution of the original with a facsimile. Finally, there are two political power struggles, both involving the high deputies of state and both associated with possession of the letter. In the first, D— plots, and nearly accomplishes, the political collapse of the royal lady; in the second, Dupin extricates the same lady from the grip of her enemies and arranges the downfall of D—.

These numerous and striking instances of mirroring all underscore the paramount doubling in the tale—that between Dupin and the Minister D—. From the perspective of the detective story genre, the two function respectively as sleuth and criminal, protagonist and antagonist. Dupin traps his quarry by adopting his rationale and dupli-

cating his method. But the resemblance between the two far exceeds that which results from Dupin's conscious imitation of his foil, and renders inapplicable the conventional moral separation between detective and culprit.

The doubling which links Dupin and D— is readily exhibited by the astonishing similarity of their minds. Both possess the same intellectual capacities and interests. The Minister, author of a treatise on "the differential Calculus," has gained some fame as a mathematician, a subject for which Dupin also demonstrates fondness by his frequent use of mathematical models to illustrate abstract ideas and by his fascination with probabilities. D— has also "acquired renown as a poet," and Dupin admits to the same talent: "I have been guilty of certain doggerel myself." Dupin clearly recognizes D— as a like mind: "I knew him . . . as both mathematician and poet," a man of equal mental make-up and a perfect peer.

If Dupin and D— are intellectual counterparts, they are more significantly moral equivalents, whose motives and methods are equally dubious from an ethical standpoint. While D—'s villainy is never questioned by critics, few regard Dupin as other than an artist, who solves crimes for sheer aesthetic pleasure and hence is exempt from moral scrutiny, or else as a representative of the forces of morality. Neither appraisal is appropriate. Unquestionably, Dupin displays his characteristic preoccupation with sophisticated epistemological puzzles. In this sense, his interest in the case at hand is "artistic," though it does *not* distinguish him from D—, who shares an attraction to the artistic dimension of the problem.

Dupin cannot be regarded simplistically as a moral agent whose able solution of the crime represents a triumph for the cause of virtue. Dupin's mode of procedure, while successful, is nevertheless ethically suspicious; he does, after all, imitate D—'s own tactics which are clearly pernicious. Both men employ ingenious forms of trickery to execute their plans and to deceive their antagonists. The Minister's talent for duplicity is plain. The letter was first pirated by means of one clever deception, and secreted by another "to delude the beholder into an idea of the worthlessness of the document." Once the letter is "hidden," the Minister uses an elaborate ruse to safeguard it. He arranges to be regularly absent from his residence during the evenings in order to facilitate what he knows will be a futile search by the police, and thus to convince the Prefect that the letter is not secreted there. During Dupin's visit, the Minister enacts the role of the unsuspecting innocent in order to discourage speculation that he has anything to hide.

Dupin likewise employs deception to confound his opponent. His ostensibly "accidental" call upon D— is really calculated to gain him entry into the man's lodgings, and once there, he resorts to a series of crafty pretenses to promote his search: he pretends a sight handicap to disguise his survey of the room; he diverts D— with conversation in order to prolong his inspection; he purposefully leaves behind a snuff box to provide an excuse for a second visit; he stages a commotion

outside the D— Hotel to distract the Minister's attention and he sub-
stitutes a fraudulent letter for the real one in the precise manner that
D— had once used to purloin it himself. He practices a similar kind of
deception against the Prefect. Clearly, then, Dupin is not above using
the same kind of duplicity practiced by his rival.

While Dupin's methods do not differ materially from those of his
adversary, neither, in fact, do his motives. It may be argued that, like
D—, Dupin is moved to participate in the affair for reasons which are
morally dubious. First, there is the submerged but abiding rivalry with
the Prefect, a lesser instance of the more momentous competition
with D—. While the Prefect assuredly admires Dupin, he regards the
detective as an eccentric and scoffs at his attitudes. For example, he
ridicules Dupin's preference for meditation in the dark as "another of
your odd notions," and disdainfully equates poets with fools, though
he knows Dupin to be a poet himself. His contempt for Dupin's idio-
syncracies induces a subtle competitiveness in Dupin to vindicate
himself and to deflate the arrogant inspector. The subdued rivalry be-
tween them often takes the form of a flippant banter with a belligerent
undercurrent, where the Prefect is frequently outclassed. At the con-
clusion of one verbal bout between them, heavily interspersed with
Dupin's sarcasm, the Prefect laughs, "'Oh, Dupin, you will be the
death of me yet!' " Beneath the superficial levity of the remark is the
suggestion of ferocity and violence, and a veiled allusion to the more
consequential enmity between Dupin and D—.

Second, there is the matter of the reward. We are told by the "Rue
Morgue" narrator that Dupin is a man deprived of his fortune by a "va-
riety of untoward events" and allowed to subsist only "by courtesy of
his creditors." The Prefect repeatedly mentions the prize offered for
the return of the letter, and each time stresses that it is "enormous"—
"I don't like to say how much, precisely." The vagueness of the amount
of course augments its value to the hearer. Dupin employs the letter
for his own financial intrigue. He promptly demands a large check
from the Prefect and witholds the twice stolen document until the
sum is paid. Although it may be considered fair recompense, neverthe-
less Dupin's little machination is a form of extortion and looks very
much like one of D—'s habits.

Third, there is the political turmoil unleashed by the affair of the
letter. The Minister has taken it to gain political advantage over the
unnamed owner and the interests she represents. The power asso-
ciated with possession of the letter is frequently underlined by the
Prefect as he reveals the story of the theft to Dupin. D— has been
wielding this power "for some months past" "to a dangerous extent,"
by blackmailing its recipient. This political advantage is not lost upon
Dupin, who employs the document for that very purpose when he
plots the downfall of D— and the deliverance of the "illustrious per-
sonage" from the hold of her enemies: "You know my political prepos-
sessions. In this matter, I act as a partisan of the lady concerned."
Hence, Dupin (like D—) uses the letter to obtain influence and (like
D—) to further partisan ends. Moreover, even his ostensibly chivalric

rescue of the royal lady in distress is not free from moral ambiguity
and possible impropriety since he is, in effect, assisting her to shelter
an illicit romance and to deceive the "other personage from whom it
was her wish to conceal it."

Finally, there is the motive of personal revenge against the Minister
who "once did [him] an evil turn." Dupin has apparently long nur-
tured a private vendetta against D—; although he depicts the matter
as a kind of amicable contest ("I told him, quite good humoredly, that
I should remember"), there is an edge of compulsiveness to his
vengeance which is intimated by the epigraph attributed to Seneca:
"*Nil sapientiae odiosius acumine nimio.*"—"Nothing is so hateful to
wisdom as too much sharpness." This implication, that the rivalry is
tinged with an element of hate, is reinforced by further evidence of
Dupin's vindictiveness, for example his near glee at the prospect of
D—'s downfall and his willingness to expose himself to possible injury,
even death, to assure such a consequence:

> "D—," replied Dupin, "is a desperate man, and a man of nerve.
> His hotel, too, is not without attendants devoted to his interests.
> Had I made the wild attempt you suggest [seizing the letter
> openly], I might never have left the Ministerial presence alive."

The extremity of the danger present, and Dupin's unusual daring in
the face of it, emphasize the viciousness which underlies the personal
competition between them. Furthermore, Dupin feels the need to
make himself known conclusively to his victim and to invite further
reprisals. He inserts tauntingly into the substitute letter an excerpt
from Crébillon's *Atrée*, a play which dramatizes the fatal opposition
between two brothers. Dupin's quotation recalls the excessive and
bloody retaliation of Atreus against the affronts of his brother
Thyestes, and implies the truly malicious quality of the present re-
venge.

> —Un dessein si funeste,
> S'il n'est digue d'Atrée, est digne de Thyeste.

> —A design so deadly,
> If it's not worthy of Atreus, it's worthy of Thyestes.

The two characters in the play alluded to are paired by their like
capacity for malice and brutality and are implicit counterparts of the
detective and his adversary.

Dupin pursues his scheme to promote D—'s downfall in part be-
cause he believes the Minister to be a "*monstrum horrendum*, an un-
principled man of genius." He sees in D—'s example the hazards
which may attend the ascendency of one of exceptional intelligence
who uses his talents for unscrupulous ends. But what really differenti-
ates Dupin from his opponent? The two are virtual surrogates. Except
for the fact that Dupin is on the side of the established order (and
even this is perplexing, since it is not clear whether he represents the
"queen" or royal figure *against* her husband, presumably then the
"king," or both of them together against common conspirators), his

own motives are not less suspect than those of D——, and his methods are as cunning and often as reprehensible as those of his rival. For Dupin, in instigating the overthrow of such a reprobate as D——, becomes an ethical replica of his enemy, a *monstrum horrendum* in his own right.

The pattern of the double suggests further possibilities. There is some implication, for example, that the enigmatic relationship between Dupin and the Minister may be fraternal. A close personal intimacy between them is clearly alluded to several times. Dupin knows D——'s private and official dealings almost better than does the Prefect, who has been following the Minister for several months. It is apparent that the detective has been acquainted with D—— for a considerable time. Dupin remarks specifically upon a prior encounter "at Vienna, once," and others are implied. Moreover, the two men are familiar enough that Dupin's unexpected arrival at D——'s dwelling causes the latter no evident surprise. Dupin relates that he "maintained a most animated discussion with the Minister, upon a topic which I knew well had never failed to interest and excite him." The sleuth knows the idiosyncrasies of his rival well; there is ample suggestion that some unusual affinity exists between them. Dupin is so intimate with the workings of D——'s mind that he anticipates the Minister's thoughts with an almost deterministic certainty and intuits D——'s reasoning patterns in their exact order. Dupin is also able to penetrate the Minister's various dissemblings. He perceives that D——'s nightly excursions are calculated "ruses" to fool the police, and he recognizes that the crumpled letter visible in the letter rack is "so inconsistent with the *true* methodical habits of D——" that it must be a disguise for the missing one. This uncanny perceptivity exceeds the kind of shrewdness which is requisite for detective work.

Poe drops several clues that this strong affiliation between the two characters is fraternal. Certainly Dupin's choice of the Crébillon quotation referring to the fatal competition between brothers invites such speculation. The narrator also invokes conjecture that Dupin and D—— may be brothers by his confusion about the reputed accomplishments of the Minister. " 'But is this really the poet?' I asked. 'There are two brothers, I know; and both have attained reputation in letters.' " Who is the second brother? He is never identified, for Dupin conspicuously fails to acknowledge the remark. The mention of an unnamed relation who mirrors his brother's achievements certainly suggests Dupin. We are also struck by the fact that Monsieur Dupin and Minister D—— share phonetically similar names and surnames which begin with the same letter; the obscurity surrounding the pointedly undisclosed last name invites some inference that it may be "Dupin."

But Poe's persistent duplication suggests yet another possibility: that the two characters somehow constitute a single person. Although biographical details in this story are few, those given do tend to underscore this notion of unanimity. Both men live in relatively secluded quarters. Dupin's lodgings are located in "a retired and desolate portion of the Faubourg St. Germain," and the Minister, despite his emi-

nence at Court, prefers a solitary apartment and houses his servants "at a distance." Also important is the way that the two characters are counterpoised in time in the story. Dupin, at least in this tale, stays home at night. The Prefect arranges his visits in the evenings, "just after dark," because he knows Dupin prefers to deliberate in the dark. Conversely, the Minister has a habit of being "frequently absent from home all night." In fact, "for three months a night has not passed" that he has not disappeared to some unstated and unknown location. Dupin's only outings in the course of the story (his two visits to D—) both occur in the morning. Significantly, on both occasions he finds the Minister at home, "yawning, lounging and dawdling as usual." One goes out only at night and the other leaves only in the daytime. It is almost as if the two participate cooperatively in some sort of phased existence and one half of the twosome ceases to exist after nightfall. It is notable that the Minister's presence in the tale is related only by hearsay. We are apprised of his activities by the Prefect and by Dupin, but they are *never* directly depicted in the story. There is some implication that D— may not exist as a separate, independent being at all. D— figures immediately in only one episode of the plot, and that is reported, after the fact, solely by Dupin. Dupin's account of the meeting is sketchy and suspiciously vague. No dialogue is recorded; for that matter, we are never made to hear any verbatim statement by D—. Dupin's report focuses almost entirely on his own undercover inspection of the apartment. The single reference to D—'s physical appearance is more mystifying than informative: Dupin depicts D— in a state of pretended languor and then remarks: "He is, perhaps, the most really energetic human being now alive—but that is only when nobody sees him." What does this statement mean? Dupin seems to imply that the Minister is a different person when he is not being observed, a man with a divided identity which changes aspect depending on the viewer. Perhaps the comment by Dupin is a concealed reference to himself. Importantly, the same kind of observation has been made about the detective. The narrator of the "Rue Morgue" tale observes a potential second self resident within the personality of the detective and often "amused [himself] with the fancy of a double Dupin." Hence, like D—, Dupin also has been portrayed as a person of fluctuating identity, and in still another sense is interchangeable with D—. All of these factors, then, tend to interfuse the two figures into one singular character whole and point ultimately to the suggestion that the tale is, in its deepest implications, a study in the oneness of pursuer and pursued.

Poe's use of the double in "The Purloined Letter" is so pervasive that it deserves serious scrutiny. I have attempted to demonstrate that Poe employs the doubling in the tale chiefly to expose a deep affinity between Dupin and his arch-rival, one which equates them morally and calls into question the customary ethical norms of the detective tale. Further, the emphatic double pattern encourages the inference that Dupin and D— may be brothers, and suggests finally that the two may constitute a singular composite being. In this ultimate sense,

then, "The Purloined Letter" explores the composition of the self, and the double becomes a metaphor for the variant phases—hunter and hunted—of the human mind.

BARTON LEVI ST. ARMAND

From The "Mysteries" of Edgar Poe: The Quest for a Monomyth in Gothic Literature†

In exploring the mysteries of Gothic taste, it is easy for the critic to forget that the whole genre was, first and foremost, a fashion, a style, and a mode of interior decoration. That the particular interior being redecorated was human consciousness itself is ancillary to the nature of Gothic as primarily an aesthetic revival which somehow managed to provide Romanticism with its first full set of swaddling clothes. The remarkable thing about this taste is that we can chart its serpentine course almost from work to work in terms of the development of theme, character, and popularity of novel modes and means of decoration. The Wandering Jew, who plays only a minor walk-on part in Lewis' *The Monk*, for example, emerges as the main character type of Maturin's *Melmoth*. Mrs. Radcliffe's Appenines somehow contribute both to Shelley's *Mont Blanc* and to the frozen Arctic landscapes of his wife's *Frankenstein*. The Venetian segment of *The Mysteries of Udolpho* becomes the whole focus of a tale like Poe's deliberately Byronic "The Assignation"; we cannot fully understand the rationale of its conclusion or the presence of "the cracked and blackened goblet" clutched in the marble hand of Poe's dead voluptuary unless we know that Radcliffe's hero-villain Montoni avoided death by using a special type of Venetian glass which splintered and bubbled when poison was poured into it. In such ways, both major and minor, one can chart the growth of Gothic romance from the first appearance of the species in the *Otranto* of 1764 to such late examples as Faulkner's *Absalom, Absalom!*

Yet, even considering Gothicism as a particular formal structure or burgeoning type, the extreme left-wing or avant-garde of Romanticism, with a curious organic vitality seemingly built into it, certain problems arise. These problems are those continuing ones of device and depth, control and connotation, adaptability and meaning. A mode can evolve so fast that, in an attempt to utilize the best of what the recent past has been as well as what the present is still yearning to be, it reaches a point of critical mass which collapses from within and leaves only an empty eclecticism. In the case of the Gothic genre, in all its manifestations—architectural and social as well as literary—this circumstance becomes doubly true. For the Gothic was an alien revival which took root in an age devoted to one supreme mode—that of

† From *The Gothic Imagination: Essays in Dark Romanticism*, ed. G. R. Thompson (Pullman: Washington State University Press, 1974), pp. 65–93. Reprinted by permission of Washington State University Press and the author. All rights reserved.

Classicism, with its fidelity to decorum, uniformity, and the rule of law. To preserve its vitality, the Gothic always needed some new exotic quality, some as-yet-untapped antiquarian element, to grow and to flourish. Hence its frank sensationalism, its fantastic "outreaching comprehensiveness of sweep," to quote the American Gothicist, Herman Melville. The Gothic was nothing if not new and varied; yet at the same time, there was an unexpected mental growth as well, a dimensional growth in acuity of intelligence and refinement of consciousness. The problem was to impose or synthesize a style which would control, deepen, and extend the mode's previous line of development. In specific literary terms, it was the same process which led William Blake to purify the experimental chaos of the *Poetical Sketches* by utilizing the ingenuous hymns of Dr. Watts and so produce at last the *Songs of Innocence* and the *Songs of Experience*. Later, Blake was similarly to transmute the pseudo-Celtic meters of James Macpherson's *Ossian* (1762) into the bardic thunder of the *Prophetic Books*, proving that the mode, the style, the species bred in the unlikeliest places and consorted with the most disreputable models in order to bring forth a superior type.

In our own century, William Butler Yeats, emerging from that same Celtic twilight and its peculiar conjunctions of primal myth and Romantic fustian, of Blake and Macpherson, was to speak of "masterful images" that grew out of pure mind yet began in a "mound of refuse or the sweepings of a street."[1] What remains important, however, is the fact that the Celtic and the Druidical were both manifestations of the taste for barbaric revivals which was to become known generally as "Gothic." The variety and adaptability of the style, from William Beckford's Oriental Gothic in *Vathek* to Herman Melville's remarkable cetological sub-species in *Moby-Dick*, masked an underlying search for a monomyth which could exploit the possibilities of this fanciful interior decoration while it unified Romantic multiplicity and became at the same time a paradigm for expressing fundamental human experience. The nature of this experience was in most cases (surprisingly enough given the Gothic's stiff anti-clerical and anti-Catholic bias) profoundly inward, even "religious" in the broadest sense. It may have begun in Walpole's antiquarian fascination with a lost world of Medieval superstition as a means of relieving the boredom of eighteenth-century social realities, but the religious impulse in Gothicism soon galloped from a concern with talking pictures and bleeding nuns to a consideration of man's position in a terrifying and inscrutable universe, an obsession with individual destiny and damnation, and a determined exploration of the mysteries of the soul itself.

"Mystery" is a word which we automatically associate with the Gothic genre since it found its way over and over again into so many Gothic titles, the most famous, of course, being *The Mysteries of Udolpho* (1794) by Ann Radcliffe. But the dimensions of the idea of

1. William Butler Yeats, "The Circus Animals' Desertion," in *Selected Poems*, ed. by M. L. Rosenthal (New York: Collier Books, 1962), p. 185 [St. Armand's note]. All notes to this selection are St. Armand's [Editor].

Gothic mystery can lead us into a consideration of just what the control of the genre by an underlying monomyth entails. At the primary level, for example, the "mysteries" of Udolpho are common detective-story mysteries involving the solution of a contrived puzzle: what was the hideous thing behind the black veil which caused the sensitive Emily to swoon so plaintively and so frequently during her incarceration within the dark battlements of Udolpho? It was, we discover at the end of this monumental romance, only a Medieval remnant of monkish superstition, a waxen votary object left as a penance by a long-vanished ancestor of the House of Udolpho. Yet Emily's timid lifting of the black veil has much deeper psychic resonances when, in later Romantic fiction, that veil becomes the Veil of Isis which, as Esther Harding explains, is also "the ever-changing form of nature, whose beauty and tragedy veil the spirit from our eyes. . . ."[2] Shelley develops this symbol in his "A Defense of Poetry" and deepens the connotations of the metaphor even further when he remarks that "Poetry lifts the veil from the hidden beauty of the world, and makes familiar objects be as if they were not familiar." Similarly, it is not Mrs. Radcliffe's invention of a trick ending to the Gothic tale which insures her a place in the larger chronicles of literary culture and the history of Romanticism in particular. To be sure, the wild voices heard in the night are found to be the wind whipping through eroded battlements and the mysterious nocturnal melodies are always traced to a very real but concealed musician; yet this is not what caused De Quincey to call her a "great enchantress" or Keats to acknowledge her as "Mother Radcliffe." Rather, to paraphrase Poe, Radcliffe's terror is not of Italy but of the soul, and her horror is only a small part of the larger landscape of sensibility—of limitless spiritual and psychological "mystery"—which she was the first to enter and explore. Through her heroine Emily, Mrs. Radcliffe helped to spread suddenly open the gorgeous fan of the Romantic consciousness and accomplish what Wordsworth called "widening the sphere of human sensibility." Emily's voyage through the Alps and Appenines toward Udolpho becomes, then, another metaphor for that quest which the Romantics themselves cultivated and often internalized.[3] This was a journey on which the Neo-Classic sensibility was unwilling to embark, as it kept strictly within the limits of a Reason which feared excesses of the imagination and an over-stimulation of the faculties of the soul. Indeed, Emily's unfortunate father, M. St. Aubert, a figure of melancholy common sense who warns Emily about the "evils of susceptibility" at the beginning of the *Mysteries*, actually has to alight from the coach when it pauses on its magic journey in order to renew his contact with the earth. Ostensibly, he crawls so intently over the landscape because, as a typical rationalist, he has a botanical passion for classifying (and so limiting the possibilities of) natural phenomena. Eventually, however,

2. M. Esther Harding, *Woman's Mysteries: Ancient and Modern* (1935; rpt. ed., New York: G. P. Putnam's Sons, 1971), p. 181.
3. Cf. Harold Bloom, "The Internalization of Quest-Romance," in *Romanticism and Consciousness: Essays in Criticism*, ed. by H. Bloom (New York: W. W. Norton, 1970), pp. 3–24.

St. Aubert dies of the effects of the journey itself, a journey in which as it continues "the mountains seemed to multiply, as they went, and what was the summit of one eminence proved to be only the base of another," or, "the scene seemed perpetually changing, and its features to assume new forms, as the winding road brought them to the eye in different attitudes while the shifting vapours, now partially concealing their minuter beauties and now illuminating them with splendid tints, assisted in the illusions of the sight."[4] It is of this constantly shifting confusion of the real and the ideal, of noumena and phenomena, of the dazzle of the veil, that M. St. Aubert finally expires, and, in truth, it can be said that he died, like the Age of Reason itself, of an overexposure to Romanticism. What Mrs. Radcliffe has done, with her pages and pages of landscape description which never seem to end (in which more and more sublime vistas continue to unveil themselves through the rolling mists and rainbow fogs), is to make the momentous connection between the life of nature and the life of the mind which made Romanticism itself into a true revolution of the human consciousness. Emily does not merely contemplate these sublime scenes, but she actually helps to create, through the ever-expansive faculties of her Romantic imagination, the mountains beyond mountains and the plains behind plains. Her mediumistic powers of reverie and feminine weaving of the warp of landscape with the woof of dreamscape are halted only by a traumatic confrontation with the dark and limiting male reality of Udolpho itself:

> Emily gazed with melancholy awe upon the castle, which she understood to be Montoni's; for, though it was now lighted up by the setting sun, the gothic greatness of its features, and its mouldering walls of dark grey stone, rendered it a gloomy and sublime object. As she gazed, the light died away on its walls, leaving a melancholy purple tint, which spread deeper and deeper, as the thin vapour crept up the mountain, while the battlements above were still tipped with splendour. From these, too, the rays soon faded, and the whole edifice was invested with the solemn duskiness of evening. Silent, lonely and sublime, it seemed to stand the sovereign of the scene, and to frown defiance upon all, who dared to invade its solitary reign. As the twilight deepened, its features became more awful in obscurity, and Emily continued to gaze, till its clustering towers were alone seen, rising over the tops of the woods, beneath whose thick shade the carriages soon after began to ascend. (*Mysteries of Udolpho*, pp. 226–227)

From a conveniently modern Jungian perspective, we could say that the Anima has here met the Shadow. Yet it was not for Mrs. Radcliffe to follow the profound implications of her method, for those implications were at once too dangerous and disturbing for her own retiring sensibility to sustain. Rather, it was for others, like Edgar Allan Poe (who, in his tale "The Oval Portrait," described the chateau to which

4. Ann Radcliffe, *The Mysteries of Udolpho*, ed. by Bonamy Dobrée (London: Oxford Univ. Press, 1966), p. 226.

the wounded narrator is brought as "one of those piles of commingled gloom and grandeur which have so long frowned among the Appenines, not less in fact than in the fancy of Mrs. Radcliffe")[5] to explore fully those novel elements implicit in *Udolpho*, which were in fact the mysteries of the progress, experience, and destiny of the Romantic soul. In undertaking this quest, Poe also had to solve the problem which had eluded Mrs. Radcliffe in her own attempt to embody such a pilgrimage, for finally *The Mysteries of Udolpho* is subverted by its own freedom and eclecticism. The romance disintegrates from and succumbs to an imitative fallacy, an overindulgence in openness and limitlessness, as Emily becomes supplanted by another heroine, the Lady Blanche, and Mrs. Radcliffe's own interests turn from the adventures offered by a picaresque travel narrative to the more genteel enchantments of a sentimental and well-bred fairy tale. This eclecticism and lack of definition, springing from the eternal process of Romantic reverie, was to plague as well such artists as Shelley, whose conflict of Demogorgan and Jupiter in *Prometheus Unbound* is a similar struggle of freedom with tyranny, as is the opposition between the Los and Urizen of Blake's late epics. The common Romantic problem remained the synthesis of an archetypal monomyth which would not destroy the surface mix and float of those novel elements which preserved the beauty and majesty of the free Romantic temperament. In specifically Gothic works of a less epic character, the further dilemma was to preserve the novelty, variety, and dark sensationalism which composed the fabric of the genre while also suggesting a profound spiritual and emotional depth. This is the enigma which challenged Poe when, in describing the effect of the sight of the House of Usher upon the narrator of his most famous tale, he wrote that, "It was a mystery all insoluble; nor could I grapple with the shadowy fancies that crowded upon me as I pondered" (*Works*, III, 274).

Poe confronted this mystery in a typically "Gothic" way; that is, in spite of the fact that, as an anatomist of the imagination, he had mastered all of the genre's obvious popular elements and even felt some condescension toward it as a set of counters which he could manipulate at will, he decided to utilize in "The Fall of the House of Usher" its most radical manifestation for his own particular purposes. The most avant-garde of the Romantic revivals when he was writing the tale in 1839 was the Egyptian mode, and it is my contention that, in experimenting with a daring mixture of the Gothic and the Egyptian, Poe managed to create a work of art which fulfilled the search of the Romantics for a monomyth which functions at two distinct levels: the surface level of the picturesque, or the decorative, and the subterranean level of the subliminal and the archetypal. For, in resurrecting the Egyptian mode as part of the dramatic stage setting of his tale, Poe also revived the pattern of initiation ritual which underlaid the symbols of the Egyptian Mysteries, the Mysteries of Isis and Osiris, as

5. Edgar Allan Poe, "The Oval Portrait," *The Complete Works*, ed. by James A. Harrison (New York: Thomas Y. Crowell, 1902), IV, 245. Hereafter, all references to Poe's works will appear in the text.

they were understood by his own age. That ritual had already found its way into the ceremonies of the countless secret societies (such as the Masons and the Odd Fellows) which abounded in the America of the early ninteenth century. In *The Modern Eleusinia, or The Principles of Odd Fellowship Explained by a Brother of the Order* (published in Nashua, New Hampshire, in 1844) the anonymous author, speaking of the Eleusinian Mysteries, expresses both a Romantic eclecticism and the fascination of his age at all levels with these "secrets of the soul":

> Their object seemed to be to teach the doctrine of one God, the resurrection of the good to eternal life, the dignity of the human soul, and to lead the people to see the Shadow of the Deity, in the beauty, magnificence, and splendour of the universe. The Mysteries of Isis . . . varied in some of their forms, from the Eleusinian, yet they all had one common design; namely, by the most solemn and impressive ceremonies, to lead the minds of the Neophytes, to meditate, seriously, the great problems of human duty and destiny, to imbue them with a living sense of the vanity and brevity of life, and of the certainty of a future state of retribution, to set forth, in marked contrast, the beauty of Virtue and Truth, and the deep bitterness, and tormenting darkness of Vice and Error;— and, lastly, to enjoin on them, by the most binding obligations, charity, brotherly love, and inflexible honor, as the greatest of all duties, the most beneficial to the world, and the most pleasing to the Gods. By their rites, many of which we should now think rude and childish, rites commencing in gloom and sorrow, and ending in light and glory,—they dimly shadowed forth, the transition of man from the savage to the civilized state, from ignorance to science, and his constant progress, onward and upward through the Ages, to still sublimer revelations. By them, they also signified, that the soul's exaltation, and highest good, were to be approached, only by the way of tears, and sacrifice, and toil.[6]

Here we have, optimistically and floridly, the outline of the same monomyth which is being enacted in the cavernous glooms of "The House of Usher." As Kathleen Raine notes in her *Blake and Tradition*, "The Eleusinian Mysteries were in fashion in and about 1790,"[7] and they soon merged with a general interest in things Eastern, Oriental, and especially Egyptian.

Little of the physical evidence of this Egyptian Revival remains with us today, though there were famous architectural examples such as "The Tombs" (a New York prison in Egyptian style in which Melville's Bartleby found his undeserved end) and we still have the towering obelisk of the Washington Monument as a witness to its brief but powerful influence on public taste. A popular interest in Egyptology

6. Anonymous, *The Modern Eleusinia, or The Principles of Odd Fellowship Explained by a Brother of the Order* (Nashua, New Hampshire: Murray and Kimball, 1844). pp. 29–30.
7. Kathleen Raine, *Blake and Tradition* (Princeton, New Jersey: Princeton Univ. Press, 1968), I, p. 124.

had been spurred with the finding of the Rosetta Stone in 1799 by Napoleon's armies, and, after its cession to the British in 1801, it became, along with other Egyptian antiquities, almost as curious and sensational an exhibit as the Elgin Marbles were to be in 1807. The deciphering of hieroglyphics became the rage among antiquarians, and researches were carried on by a host of eminent scholars. Besides prison buildings, cemetery gates and entrances were done in a pylonic form copied from Nile temples, for, while the Gothic style of architecture was naturally associated with religious ideas of spiritual aspiration (hence its use for ecclesiastical and college buildings), the Egyptian mode was considered to be more suited for the contemplation of darker, more impenetrable mysteries. As Frances Lichten writes of this revival:

> The first decorative inspirations derived from the contemplation of these archeological wonders seem weighted with immense solemnity—the Victorian architect, if not the Victorian designer, was sensitive to the portentousness of Egyptian art and used it for equally serious purposes, calculated to move the beholder to thoughts of death. Nor did he miss the correspondence of catacombs with the idea of prisons; therefore prisons styled in the Egyptian manner breathed forth their gloomy implications, even in the United States.[8]

In American literature, as in American art and architecture, the Egyptian Revival produced no really lasting monuments and so always remained something of an underground style. But the Egyptian mode carried with it, as we have seen, a whole host of complex and intricate mythic associations, and it is my contention, to repeat, that many of these associations inform and help to shape the over-all design of the Gothic castle or manor house of literature, which, like much of the architecture of its time, mixes Gothic arches with Egyptian obelisks. The haunted castles and mansions of such tales as Poe's "The Fall of the House of Usher" are, I believe, eclectic structures in which a Gothic frame is supported by a basically Egyptian foundation, and the mystery all insoluble of their effect has a direct relation to the larger Mysteries of Initiation into temple secrets concerned with the exaltation of the soul and its torturous rebirth.

The exact nature of these Egyptian Mysteries, meant to be imparted in the labyrinths of temple and pyramid, springs from the ancient religion which was practiced in Dynastic Egypt from an almost immemorial time until it was adopted, first by the Greeks, and then by the Romans. Finally, it reached an apex in the cult of Isis, which flourished in the world capitals of the early Christian era. Alexandria (the site of the Great Library whose volumes of sacred lore were later used by Arab invaders to fire the waters of the public bath) became the center for this mystery cult and the perpetuation of its ritual, as the sun

8. Frances Lichten, *Decorative Art of Victoria's Era* (New York: Bonanza Books, 1950), p. 71.

god, Osiris, sacred to the Pharohs, was transformed into the more cosmopolitan and eclectic deity, Serapis. As Harold Willoughby summarizes in his study of Mystery initiations in the Graeco-Roman world, *Pagan Regeneration*:

> The ancient system had centered in the god, Osiris; but in the reformed cult of Hellenistic times he was replaced to a considerable extent by a new divinity, Serapis, and popular interest was transferred to the more appealing personality of Isis. She dominated the Hellenistic cult quite as Demeter held the supreme place in the Eleusinian mysteries, or the *Magna Mater* in those that emanated from Phrygia. In the ancient Osirian religion, the public ritual with its strong appeal to the masses was important. In the Hellenized worship of Isis, the significant ceremonials were those secret rites that had such deep meaning for the individual. These were only some of the ways in which the new cult showed adaptation to the very personal needs of individual religionists in the Hellenized world.[9]

So in the first and second centuries A.D. the Mysteries of Egypt became the Mysteries of Isis, just as in the Dark Ages they were to become the Mysteries of Hermes, centering on alchemy and the transmutation of lead into gold as a means of symbolizing the tenets of basically the same esoteric ritual and philosophy. The Mysteries always involved a hieratic initiation into an arcane knowledge of immortality, knowledge achieved by a purification of the soul and a rite of passage through various prescribed trials and tests. It is a tribute to the truly sacred and secret character of this ritual that we know of its details only in fragments salvaged from ancient classical historians and a few Doctors of the Church. Even Herodotus, speaking of the performance of the Egyptian Mysteries at Saïs, felt constrained to tell his readers that "I could speak more exactly of these matters, for I know the truth, but I will hold my peace." What we do know, then, comes mainly from a handful of authors who are themselves the fathers of the occult tradition known generally as Hermeticism, which includes later alchemical and mystical commentaries as well as the few original texts which survived the wreck of the ancient world and the apparent extinction of learning during the early Middle Ages.

Poe's works, for example, contain learned references not only to Herodotus, Diodorus, and Plutarch, but also to Lucius Apuleius, who included in his *Metamorphoses* (better known in English as *The Golden Ass*) the most famous description of Isiac ritual which we possess. Apuleius, a Neo-Platonic philosopher of the second century A.D., followed Plutarch's model in holding back the most sacred details of the initiation rite as "things too holy for utterance," for "both tongue and ear would be infected with like guilt did I gratify such rash curiousity." Poe also mentions such authors as Tertullian and Iamblichus,

9. Harold R. Willoughby, *Pagan Regeneration: A Study of Mystery Initiations in the Graeco-Roman World* (Chicago: University of Chicago Press, 1929), pp. 176–177.

both of whom discussed the Mysteries in one form or another, and he makes further reference to Demeter and Isis, who were considered by Diodorus to be interchangeable forms of the same goddess (the reform of the Osiris cult merged many aspects of the native Greek Eleusinian Mysteries with the Mysteries of Egypt). In "A Descent into the Maelström" there is even a reference by Poe to the seventeenth-century Jesuit occultist, Athanasius Kircher. Kircher's most famous work was the massive *Oedipus Aegyptiacus* (1652), a compendium of Egyptian, alchemical, and kabbalistic lore which contained in its final volume a description of the Mensa Isiaca, a hieroglyphic stone tablet once thought to describe in detail the full process of initiation, which Kircher relates to the *De Mysteriis Aegyptiorum* of Iamblichus, among others. There were, too, already in existence literary transmutations of these sources, such as Jean Terrasson's eighteenth-century romance, *Sethos*, and Novalis' *The Novices of Saïs* (1798). Coming closer to the time of Poe, we could say, as H. Bruce Franklin says of Melville's knowledge of Egyptian myth, "For contemporaneous versions and explanations [he] could have opened the pages of innumerable magazines, travel books, encyclopedias, and polemical tracts."[1]

But, for Poe, there is firm evidence of a more specific contemporary source for his acquaintance with a highly romanticized narrative of initiation into the Mysteries of Isis. In 1840, a year after "Usher" was published, Poe reviewed *Alciphron: A Poem* (1839) by the Irish poet, Thomas Moore, who had already caught the public fancy for things exotic with his long Oriental fantasy *Lalla Rookh. Alciphron*, however, was only a redoing in verse of what Moore had already done in his short prose romance, *The Epicurean* (first published in 1827) with which Poe was undoubtedly familiar, for in his review of *Alciphron* he mentions that the narrator is head of the Epicurean sect at Athens, a fact that is mentioned only in the romance and not in the poem. Burton R. Pollin has already traced the influence of *Alciphron* and *The Epicurean* on Poe's prose fantasy, "Shadow—A Parable,"[2] but no one has yet considered its influence on "The Fall of the House of Usher." For Moore's work provided not only that Romantic-Gothic eclecticism which gives the tale a novel and even sensational character, but also the underlying monomyth of initiation ritual which secretly unifies and deepens its metaphysical dimension.

* * *

The quest for a monomyth involving the trials and progress of the soul was to become, as we have mentioned, more and more of a secular rather than a literary endeavor, as the eclecticism in which Romanticism began at last exhausted and subverted the Romantic consciousness itself. Beginning with the attempt of Athanasius Kircher to produce a compendium of occult knowledge in his *Oedipus Aegyptiacus* (1652–

1. H. Bruce Franklin, *The Wake of the Gods: Melville's Mythology* (Stanford: Stanford University Press, 1963), p. 73.

2. Burton R. Pollin, "Light on 'Shadow' and Other Pieces by Poe; Or, More of Thomas Moore," *ESQ: A Journal of the American Renaissance*, 18 (No. 3, 3rd Quarter, 1972), 166–172.

1655), the scholarly synthesis of ancient religious history and the Mysteries of myth continued in * * * the enormously influential *A New System, or An Analysis of Ancient Mythology* (published by Jacob Bryant in three volumes from 1774 to 1776). Poe was undoubtedly familiar with this work, for he refers to Bryant's "very learned 'Mythology'" in "The Purloined Letter," and in *Eureka* he quotes with approval Bryant's declaration that "Although the Pagan fables are not believed, yet we forget ourselves continually and make inferences from them as from existing realities" (*Works*, XVI, 217). Bryant proceeded to reduce all antique mythologies to one grand monomyth, which could be traced to the primal event of the Flood, so that "All the mysteries of the Gentile world seem to have been memorials of the Deluge." Bryant's syncretism was continued by disciples such as George Stanley Faber, whose *Dissertation on the Mysteries of the Cabiri* (1803) bore the typically fulsome and self-explanatory subtitle: *Being an Attempt to Deduce the Several Orgies of Isis, Ceres, Mithras, Bacchus, Rhea, Adonis, and Hecate, from an Union of the Rites Commemorative of the Deluge with the Adoration of the Host of Heaven.* The historical quest, then, subsumed particular concerns with the nature and destiny of the individual soul in a general interest in mythology. The goal became the elusive monomyth that tied all myths together as a fossilized "epic of humanity" which portrayed the evolution from sympathetic magic to sophisticated religion. Sir James George Frazer climaxed this search in 1890 with the publication of the first two volumes of *The Golden Bough*, which was the virtuoso attempt of a trained classicist to solve the seemingly insoluble Mysteries of the Grove of Nemi.

* * *

[Jessie Weston's] *From Ritual to Romance* * * * attempts to prove that the Grail romances are derived from the vegetation rites of those same Mystery religions and that the main features of the Grail story—the Waste Land, the Fisher King, the Hidden Castle with its solemn Feast, and the Mysterious Feeding Vessel, the Bleeding Lance and Cup—are elements transmuted from the original monomyth of initiation ceremonies. Under this rubric, Usher, with his obscure illness and impotence, is also of course another kind of Fisher King, while the House itself becomes the Hidden Castle or sinister Chapel Perilous and its surrounding landscape of decayed and noxious vegetation is the Perilous Cemetery or Waste Land. The "Mad Trist" of Sir Launcelot Canning (the title of which is reminiscent of *The Geste of Syr Gawaine*, another Grail romance mentioned by Miss Weston) continues the chivalric imagery, for the trencher or ringing brass shield that Poe's hero Ethelred must win is very like the sacred vessel of the Attis rite, which, as she points out, was both tympanum and cymbal. Weston concludes that the Grail romances are veiled accounts of Mystery initiations and she deduces that:

> The earliest version of the Grail story, represented by our Blerheris form, relates the visit of a wandering knight to one of these hidden temples; his successful passing of the test into the lower

grade of Life initiation, his failure to attain to the highest degree. It matters little whether it were the record of an actual, or of a possible, experience; the casting into romantic form of an event which the story-teller knew to have happened, had, perchance, actually witnessed; or the objective recital of what he knew *might* have occurred; the essential fact is that the *mise-en-scène* of the story, the nomenclature, the march of incident, the character of the tests, correspond to what we know from independent sources of the details of this Nature Ritual. The Grail Quest was actually possible then, it is actually possible to-day, for the indication of two of our romances as to the final location of the Grail is not imagination, but the record of actual fact.[3]

[The] narrator [of "Usher"], too, passes, or at least beholds, the first trials of initiation like the wandering knight at the threshold of the hidden temple, but his failure to recognize the full significance of the esoteric symbolism and ritual displayed by the hierophant loses him his chance for the highest degree. Indeed, the whole ambiguous narrative technique of "The Fall of the House of Usher" is implicit in Weston's description of this earliest of the Grail romances.

* * *

What remains important is the fact that, while the unifying legend of the Grail romance and its occult meaning, uncovered by Frazer and Weston, made the quest for a monomyth possible again for Eliot in 1922, it was also possible for Poe in 1839. Ultimately, Poe and Eliot have the same sources and the same concerns, for, like all modern seekers for that myth (whether literary or anthropological), they try to reverse the direction of the quest away from romance and back toward ritual, that task which Jacob Bryant defined in his subtitle of *A New System, or An Analysis of Ancient Mythology* as the attempt "to divest Tradition of Fable; and to reduce the Truth to its Original Purity." An awareness of this tradition, in turn, may force us to realize that, given its antecedents, *The Waste Land* is more truly "Gothic" in character than its first readers ever imagined. But the tradition also demonstrates that Poe, in successfully using the monomyth of initiation ritual to structure and to deepen the vital eclecticism of "The Fall of the House of Usher," was not only an adept of Gothic prestidigitation, but that he had mastered as well the most complex thaumaturgies of Romantic art.

3. Jessie L. Weston, *From Ritual to Romance* (1920; rpt. ed., Garden City, New York: Doubleday and Company, 1957), pp. 204–205.

JOSEPH N. RIDDEL

From The "Crypt" of Edgar Poe†

I

If Poe did not exist, he would have had to be invented. One authoritative critical view holds that he is, after all, a French creation; or even that he invented, by a series of extravagant displacements, French symbolist poetics. T. S. Eliot has provided one account of this curious genealogy: "Poe's influence is . . . puzzling. In France the influence of his poetry and of his poetic theories has become immense. In England and America it seems almost negligible. Can we point to any poet whose style appears to have been formed by a study of Poe? The only one whose name immediately suggests itself is—Edward Lear."[1] In English, Poe is Emerson's jingle man; transcribed into French, he inaugurates the revolution of the word, as in the radical modernism of Borges' Pierre Menard, the "Symbolist from Nimes" who was a "devoté of Poe, who engendered Baudelaire, who engendered Mallarmé, who engendered Valéry, who engendered Edmond Teste."[2] Nearly a quarter of a century before Eliot's short history of this detour from American nonsense to Gallic *nouvelle vague*, Williams plotted another genealogy for Poe in *In the American Grain*. The French, Williams argued, had misread Poe's "scrupulous originality." They failed to understand his "re-awakened genius of *place*," his clearing of the "ground" for the "*beginning*" of a "juvenescent *local* literature" (216–17). Eliot's Poe, who had the mind of a "pre-pubescent adolescent," becomes Williams' forger of a "new" language. The one point of agreement: any in-mixing of Poe and Continental poetics produces an interesting hybrid, a graft and a graph sometimes called by the double name of "modernism."

Eliot's reading of Poeisme, the symbolist quest for a "purity" in which the word is refined of its worldliness, both its referentiality and its materiality, is an attack upon "amoral" modernism, which at the same time he reluctantly praises for its "craft." The fate of modernism, which in Eliot's view led inexorably to the narcissism of Paul Valéry, was to be entrapped in the machinery of its own operations, to exhaust itself in pale fire. The abandonment of "subject matter," of referentiality and at least the illusion of representation (as in a proper symbolist linkage of earth and sky), has produced the twofold vertigo and paralysis of modern poetry. "That Poe had a powerful intellect," Eliot writes, "is undeniable":

† From *Purloined Letters: Originality and Repetition in American Literature*, ed. Mark Bauerlein (Baton Rouge: Louisiana State University Press, 1995), pp. 121–48. This essay was first printed in 1979 and was revised for the 1995 publication. Reprinted by permission of Louisiana State University Press.

1. T. S. Eliot, *To Criticize the Critic* (New York, 1965), 27 [Riddell's note]. All notes to this selection are Riddell's [Editor].
2. Jorge Luis Borges, "Pierre Menard, Author of the Quixote," in *Labyrinths*, trans. James E. Irby (New York, 1962), 40–41.

but it seems to me the intellect of a highly gifted young person before puberty. The forms which his lively curiosity takes are those in which a pre-adolescent mentality delights: wonders of nature and of mechanics and of the supernatural, cryptograms and cyphers, puzzles and labyrinths, mechanical chess-players and wild flights of speculation. The variety and ardour of his curiosity delight and dazzle; yet in the end the eccentricity and lack of coherence of his interests tire. There is just that lacking which gives dignity to the mature man: a consistent view of life.[3]

Poeisme/modernism marks an "eccentricity" in the order of things; it is aberrational, nonteleological, a stylistic machine. An interest in cryptograms, cyphers, puzzles, labyrinths—they are the obsessions of the child and the pure intellect, and will lead symptomatically to the incoherence of writing.

Poe or Valéry—in Eliot's view both signify the excess and the impasse of a language turned from the world upon itself: "with Poe and Valéry, extremes meet, the immature mind playing with ideas because it had not developed to the point of convictions, and the very adult mind playing with ideas because it was too sceptical to hold convictions" (40). Skepticism, Eliot adds, is a healthy quality of the "mature intellect," but the extreme, as in Valéry, leads to "intellectual narcissism." Poe's "Philosophy of Composition" provided Valéry with "a method and an occupation—that of observing himself write." The "penetration of the poetic by the introspective critical activity," says Eliot, produced the fore-structure and the fore-play of a modernist crisis, a poetics that can neither be rejected nor appropriated, a poetics that dissolves the traditional "ground" of a "real" world (whether subjective or objective) and suggests a recuperation of the barbarously romantic dream of spontaneous, irreflective expression (41). Eliot presents the most recent modernist crisis as an impossible choice between the mutually exclusive illusions of vitalism and formalism, barbarous paganism and civilized restraint, evident in the "extreme awareness of and concern for language which we find in Valéry," a condition "which must ultimately break down, owing to an increasing strain against which the human mind and nerves will rebel" (42).

Williams, to the contrary, claimed that Poe "struck to lay low the 'niaiseries' of form and content with which his world abounded."[4] He called Poe's writing an "attack" on representation or "colonial imitation," an attack "from the center out": "With Poe words were not hung by usage with associations, the pleasing wraiths of former masteries, this is the sentimental trap-door to beginnings. With Poe words were figures; an old language truly, but one from which he carried over only the most elemental qualities to his new purpose. . . . Sometimes he used words so playfully his sentences seem to fly away from sense, the destructive! with the conserving abandon, foreshadowed, of a Gertrude Stein" (219, 221). And Williams describes the method of

3. Eliot, To Criticize the Critic, 35.
4. William Carlos Williams, In the American Grain (1925; rpr. New York, 1956), 221.

this "immaculate attack" as a strategic chiasmus: "He has a habit, bor-
rowed perhaps from algebra, of balancing sentences in the middle, or
of reversing them in the later clauses, a sense of play, as with objects,
or numerals which he *has* in the original, disassociated, that is, from
other literary habit; separate words" that do not " 'belong properly to
books' " (221–22). Poe has little interest in "supernatural mysteries"
or the "extraordinary eccentricity of fate," but is preoccupied with
"writing": "Method, punctuation, grammar—" (227). Thus, Williams
continues, the French mistook a rhetorical inversion for a representa-
tion of the "bizarre," when they should have recognized, as in their
own avant-garde experiment, the necessity of negative or destructive
writing: "On him is FOUNDED A LITERATURE—typical; an anger
to sweep out the unoriginal, that became ill-tempered; a monomania-
cal driving to destroy, to annihilate the copied, the slavish, the FALSE
literature about him" (223). America's imported literary tradition had
denied its writers a "natural landscape"; thus Poe could only imitate
the "field of cold logic . . . to which his work must still present a natu-
ral *appearance*" (228). Language displaces "nature" as the object of
language, as the "place" or "local" of the "beginning," its own extraor-
dinary "scene."

Two Poes, two modernisms, at least—Eliot and Williams agree that
an abyss has opened up between word and world, and hence in the
word itself; but if for Eliot that abyss is the consequence of a skepti-
cism become nihilism, for Williams it is the "desire" for "originality"
that compels all writing and marks indelibly the aporia of every mod-
ernist strategy to "make it new" or to "begin again" in a field of lan-
guage without origin or end. Poe's canon, as Eliot sees it, becomes the
fractured mirror of the modern, forestructuring a literature of moral
exhaustion, of purely surface play. In the hollow reverberations of
Poesque language the word functions only in an endless play of dis-
placements that is literature. Every beginning is already a beginning
inter-text, in a "field of cold logic" which, we have forgotten, is
metaphorical, already always—like Nietzsche's truths that are the
vestiges of fictions (figures) whose origins are either forgotten or re-
pressed. The word becomes its own broken reflection, and as in the
image of the "House of Usher," the "barely perceptible fissure" disori-
ents even the illusion of a stable if submerged origin/ground. The nat-
ural world dissolves in its own image, to become the image of nature's
absence. There is no accessible point of departure but only a second-
ary and heterogeneous world, as he describes it in *Eureka*, hence a
world or cosmology that can only be revealed as two irreducible
plots—God's ideal plot and man's imperfect plot, itself doubled, com-
plex, unnatural. Poe abandons nature for the image. His world be-
comes a text, or a library of multiple texts.

As Eliot and, later, Allen Tate were to see, though they interpreted it
as a moral deficiency, the secondary, heterogeneous realm in Poe's the-
ory was nothing other than a world of words, dispersed and material-
ized into disrelated atoms. In Poe the images of nature are already
metonymic substitutions for words—or substitutions for substitutions.

It is all the more strange that Eliot and Tate, those fathers of New Critical formalism, would be enchanted by the force of his madness, and equally repelled by it. Tate saw Poe as "our cousin," the exemplum of a peculiar variety of American, essentially southern, moral guilt.[5] Yet Tate, like Eliot, was equally attentive to what he called Poe's "angelic imagination" or the obsession with "verbal magic," a belief in the "power of words" (to revert to one of Poe's titles) that characterized the extreme thrust of a romantic will to signification. Eliot's concern with the impasse of a language turned upon itself reflects Tate's disturbance over the romantic displacement of language upon the abyss, upon what Tate called the "zero" of "unity." In either case, Poe is indicted for a poetics which erases that secure zone in which formalist criticism situated language, that uninterrogated margin where a "poetic language" may freely play between its dual obligation to represent the world and trace a shadow of the universal, or mediate between an outside and an inside. For the fathers of New Critical formalism, Poe (and Poeisme) is culpable of removing poetic language from that sanctuary where its power or its impotence need not be questioned.

But it is just this violation of the taboo of literary language to which Williams drew an early attention. It should call our attention, here, to the strategies by which Poe constructed metaphorical puzzles out of metaphorical fragments, or built a house of fiction out of the "crypts" of outmoded structures, those mausoleums of a philosophical (and therefore, if we follow Nietzsche, a metaphorical) history. "The Power of Words," which Tate claims to be the essay most clearly evidencing Poe's drift toward "angelic" madness, dissolves the privileged difference between a discursive and an imaginative text that it seems most intent on confirming. In fact, as a fable, and as a parody of the philosophical dialogue, this "colloquy" tends to erase the margin between a poetic or creative language and an analytical or scientific discourse that seems to be its theme. Rather than displacing language upon the void, as Tate argues, it is a meditation upon the problematics of a reverse displacement, of the abyss that has opened up on the sign, so that the world of words signifies the absence of the world, or signifies absence. Poe's so-called colloquy reflects on a romantic commonplace, the provisional non-presence of language and the possibility of the recuperation of presence in the poetic "void." In the words of one speaker in "The Conversation of Eiros and Charmion": "Let us converse of familiar things, in the old familiar language of the world which has so fearfully perished."[6] The event of the creation is a "fall," as in the dispersal and materialization of the word, leaving the poet with (and within) a medium that only traces, in a "nebulous light," the original and unrepeated creative moment, which is also a destructive moment.

It is a theme familiar in poems like "Israfel" or even "The Bells": the

5. See Allen Tate, "Our Cousin, Mr. Poe," in Tate, *Essays of Four Decades* (Chicago, 1969), 385–400. The essay was a lecture delivered in 1949.
6. Edgar Allan Poe, *Complete Works*, ed. James A. Harrison (16 vols.; New York, 1902), IV, 2. Hereinafter cited parenthetically in the text by volume and page number.

increasing loss of power in words, which are dispersed from the zero degree of unity and also turned from themselves, becoming materialized and leaden. Language is a shadow light, at best, the vestiges of an annihilated universe. The text of the world—for the world has perished and only its language remains—is a non-presence. Yet, a poetic, or should one call it scriptive, hope derives from this negative, for while the poet is deprived of true originality, he may be endowed with an "algebraic" sense, through which his belated representations, which are only "tracing(s)" of "every impulse given the air" (V, 142), may vibrate across the void. Thus the "power of words" rests in their original displacement and dispersal, a fall marked by a fissure in the image. The poet's work, like the angels', is always retrograde and decadent; the power of words is a physical representation of the metaphysical, and the poet's secondary creative power functions wholly within a physical ether (language), which he modulates by setting "impulses" in motion. Poe's colloquy "The Power of Words" concludes with a figure of fabulous imitation, or fabulist invention, in which the two angels recall their own imitation of the divine creation as a loss. The angelic Oinos asks his fellow Agathos why he weeps and his wings droop as they hover over the "fair-star—which is the greenest and yet most terrible of all we have encountered in our flight" (V, 143). The star, which Agathos calls a "wild star," is a figural repetition of the Earth, or the Divine creation that can never be repeated. It is, therefore, a text, spoken into existence by Agathos' "impulse," his physical speech. Here are his concluding words: "This wild star—it is now three centuries since, with clasped hands, and with streaming eyes, at the feet of my beloved, I spoke it, with a few passionate sentences—into birth. Its brilliant flowers *are* the dearest of all unfulfilled dreams, and its raging volcanoes *are* the passions of the most turbulent and unhallowed of hearts" (V, 143–44). Agathos' creation is a figure of figure, a repetition of the original creation and a mocking sign of the absence that is angelic or poetic repetition. The power of words is no more than a power to move other words. Words are already secondary, and they repeat only an original abysm that marks their distance from any "first law." Ironically, their naturalness, or materiality, like the increasing dullness in the poem "The Bells," signifies at once their "power" and their death. In Poe there is no natural language, and no nature. Nature is not an origin but a rundown trope. This is a fable Poe obsessively retells, the wearying struggle to purify language through language, the poetic repetition of some idea of "absolute perfection" or some idea of purity that in the same gesture reveals the mark of its own discontinuity with any original form, idea, truth, reality. The Poesque realm of dream, which is the realm of language, is always a realm of the "unfulfilled." The poetic repetition can never represent "perfection," but only a "difference" of perfection, a turbulence and passion. Poetry is textuality that can only reflect an absence of the ideal.

In what follows, I would like to explore a patchwork of metaphors that nets together much of the Poe canon, weaving discursive and imaginative texts and at the same time erasing the generic margins be-

tween the so-called tales of the grotesque and the tales of ratiocina-
tion. The metaphors, of course, derive from a double sense of "the
power of words" that generates so much of the obscurity and, Eliot
might have said, prepubescent melodrama of the tales, and ineffec-
tively conceals the plagiarisms in a quasi-scientific text like *Eureka*. I
am referring to the metaphors of "house" and "tomb," of "crypt" and
"cryptographer," and therefore the figure of poet-author-analyst whose
writing is always an "impulse on the air," a retranscription of some an-
tique manuscript or misplaced letter. The "letter," then, in the double
sense of alphabetic character and enveloped message, is related to
each of the other figures, each of which, whether library, labyrinth,
pyramid, tomb, or house, prefigures the question of the letter's proper
location and its eccentric movement, like a manuscript in a bottle or a
story within a story. At the same time, however, these metaphors,
which have a metaphysical and a literary history, have become dis-
placed from that history and are situated, or rather are floating, in a
space between two senses or orders of history, between two notions of
literature. In the case of a discursive text like *Eureka*, most of which is
openly appropriated from the cosmology of Alexander von Humboldt
and Laplace, and hence from the mechanics of Newton, it may be
praised by Paul Valéry for anticipating Einstein's law of relativity and
the entropic destiny of the second law of thermodynamics. The pseu-
doscience of *Eureka*, however, is clearly not a proleptic text—not so
much prophetic of the new science as it is a critique of the logic that
cements the old. It is therefore a critique of the notion of closure
(Newtonian and/or poetic); and it perhaps justifies Poe's own claim
that it is a poem and is to be judged as a poem after his death, not so
much in its curious formulation of an imaginary cosmology as in its
marking of the limits of the imaginary. It thus signifies the excess—in-
deed the literariness—in the enclosed universes of science and the
lack or absence in the imaginary and human plots of literature—or
what one might call literature's scientificity, referentiality, or natural-
ness.

Earlier I claimed that what makes American literature extraordinary
is that it is a literature without a history, and that its obsession with
beginning anew manifests itself in repeated but failing attacks upon
the notion of representation. There is another sense in which Ameri-
can literature is exemplary. If we borrow from the French revisionists
and not from our own uninterrogated historical periods, we must ad-
mit that what we call the beginning of a "native" style or voice is co-
incidental with what the French consider a break between the
"classical" and the "modern," a rupture in the linguistic history of the
sign. Charles Feidelson suggested that American literature of the nine-
teenth century (which he called symbolistic) could finally be read with
the advent of modernism, since it was modern in its self-referential
preoccupation with being new. The French appropriation of Poe, as
against our own history of trying to accommodate him to the literary
tradition, is only the most obvious example of his eccentric displace-
ment into what is called modernism. Poe is in two senses the deca-

dent: the end of a progressively degraded literary history; the sign of some grotesque perturbation in romantic thought, perhaps a doubling and a deconstruction, hence an allegorization of that particularly modern appropriation of romanticism as "natural supernaturalism." Perhaps Poe's "uses of incoherence," as Valéry defined generative style, is only his remarking of the madness inhabiting the image, a madness aggravated by every poetic attempt to close the play opened up by even the "barely perceptible fissure" traced out in every style.

In the befogged, miasmic atmosphere of Poe's house of fiction, his subject matter is, as Williams suggests, "cold logic." Newton and Laplace's cosmic machine, which represents the universal perfection in its capacity for inexhaustible repetition, is a plot of narrative closure that deprives the poet of originality but not of truth. Criticism as a reversal of this order, as a retelling of its teleology (for example, Poe's critical recounting of the creation of a poem from its completion back toward the unity of conception where it originates), becomes, however, a perturbation that intervenes in this closure. Poe introduces what Schlegel had foreseen as the inevitability for a new literature, a self-critical or self-annihilating textual performance—the poem/story and even the critical essay (as performance) that deconstructs itself. This is Poe's ironic theme in "The Philosophy of Composition" and "The Poetic Principle"—and the thematizing of the poem as the inseparability of Beauty and Death, of the image that re-marks its own absence, thematizes the notion of writing as displacement, supplementation, and radical theft. Beauty as the difference of Truth is neither an image of Truth nor reversible into Truth. The figure of beauty, the dead woman, is the figure of the text in Poe—not of the word that substitutes for truth but of the word that absents itself, or is the material sign of a double absence. Poe introduces a theme that "American" literature obsessively retells—of purloined letters and de-constructed architecture. Like Stevens' lament in "The Rock" that it is an "illusion" we were ever alive and lived in the "houses" of mothers,[7] Poeisme "cures" a "ground" for literature by constructing a deconstruction, by erecting one house upon the remnants of another, like a book, say, made out of the books of some incomplete library, a library never composed except in a fiction. Poe constructs a mausoleum (text) to contain his sign of Beauty/Death.

II

As the narrator approaches the "House of Usher," he feels himself engulfed in its "melancholy" and "insufferable gloom." The natural order of things is inverted: day seems like night, and the house reflects "a wild inconsistency between the still perfect adaptation of parts, and the crumbling condition of the individual stones." The house is a "specious totality," an "extraordinary dilapidation," marked by a "barely perceptible fissure" that runs a "zigzag direction" down its exterior to disappear in the "sullen waters of the tarn." The origin of the fissure is

7. Wallace Stevens, *Collected Poems* (New York, 1954), 248.

erased in a series of reflections that has no scrutable beginning or end. The narrator is disoriented and overcome with a "melancholy" that is "unrelieved by any of that half-pleasurable, because poetic, sentiment, with which the mind usually receives even the sternest natural images of the desolate or terrible" (III, 273). Everything is a "scene" or "picture" but not a coherent representation. It is like the "after-dream of the reveller upon opium—the bitter lapse into everyday life—the hideous dropping off of the veil." The primary inversion at the beginning of "The Fall of the House of Usher" lies in the beginning of narrative itself, a grotesque "lapse" or fall into a world of images where words and things no longer coincide. The narrator ponders a failure of creative perception, of poetic images, to mediate a scene of vacant nature: "I was forced to fall back upon the unsatisfactory conclusion, that while, beyond doubt, there *are* combinations of very simple natural objects which have the power of thus affecting us, still the analysis of this power lies among considerations beyond our depth. It was possible, I reflected, that a mere different arrangement of the particulars of the scene, of the details of the picture, would be sufficient to modify, or perhaps to annihilate its capacity for sorrowful impression" (III, 274). Nature, it seems, is either a text or a chaos. Either or both. Double like an afterdream. As problematic as language.

The narrator first views the "house" as a grotesque reflection in the "lurid tarn," in "remodelled and inverted images." And when he lifts his gaze from the image to the house itself he is almost overwhelmed by the atmosphere or estrangement that, as he puts it, "had no affinity with the air of heaven." Natural order and expectancy is suspended and inverted. Nature and culture, landscape and house, reflect each other without difference. The Usher family, now reduced to twins without "collateral issue," inhabit an estate that bears the "quaint and equivocal appellation of the 'House of Usher'" (III, 275), erasing in the minds of the peasantry any difference between the family and its residence. All differences, natural or cultural, are in a state of collapse or degeneration. But in the narrator's mind, the most ominous disruption in the order of things is signified by a failure of language, of the poetic sentiment to mediate and hence to restore and maintain the priority of spiritual or ideal harmony to natural heterogeneity or randomness. Nature is either in a state of irreparable decay or is a stormy "whirlwind." In either case, it signifies an obliteration of all those hierarchal differences and genealogical fictions upon which the privilege of the Usher family has been founded.

It is little wonder, then, that the narrator's reflections move from the image of the "house," whose architecture reflects a "specious totality" of related differences, to the figure of the "ancient family" that is now without "collateral issue" and is represented by asexual twins who are the last of an "ancient family" that lies in "the direct line of descent and had always, with very trifling and very temporary variation, so lain" (III, 274). This "deficiency," as the narrator twice calls it, signifies the end of both the family and history and reveals that both are problematical metaphors based on a questionable analogy between a

biological and a genealogical order. The "quaint and equivocal appellation of the 'House of Usher' " signifies the irreversible direction of exhaustion and decay that predicates a final collapse of the distinctions between nature and culture, or material and spiritual, in the collapse of proper signification itself. It is the idea of the "direct" unbroken "line" of a teleological (and hence a narrational) order that is broken in this incompatible "house." The house of fiction reflects the "malady" in the fiction of the house.

The narrator finds himself directly confronting a "family" that exemplifies a history he cannot understand, but which we, along with Valéry, might suggest to be the entropic history predicated in the "second law of thermodynamics," or in the romantic appropriation of the transnatural law.[8] Poe's own metaphysical preoccupation with energetics, which supplants materialism or naturalism, anticipates this displacement of one notion of history by another. As in *Eureka*, where he plagiarizes and emends the Newtonian cosmos of von Humboldt and Laplace, the end of the creation in material dispersion and extreme heterogeneity must either lead to an inert, stable universe, in which the discrete particulars offer no clue of their origin, or there must be some radical supplementation in the nature of things, an overcoming of this deadly trend toward non-difference by some "different arrangement." Thus Poe will not accept the unidirectional, entropic sense of history that his demystification of the old metaphors reveals to him, but will attempt to reverse them, which means he must allegorize the fiction once again. It is the inevitability of closure, in either Laplace's cosmos or any reversal of it, that aggravates Poe's desire to imagine a new text of the world.

The interior of the Usher house repeats its exterior. It is a clutter of antiquated styles and disrelated objects, a bric-a-brac that can no longer signify the stability of the family's estate in a meaningful order of things or suggest its continuing "line." Like Usher, the narrator is resigned to a desperate hope that by a "mere different arrangement of the particulars" he can overcome the evidence of random distribution and defer the death signified by the collapse of a symbolic system. Yet the narrator, who has been summoned to "Usher" by an agitated "letter" from his boyhood friend, can no more superintend the scene from the outside than he can regenerate it from the inside. The interior disorder of the "house" is as irreversible as the decay of the carefully arranged stones that characterize its archi-texture. When the narrator and Usher turn as a last resort to a hope that through art they may delay, if not reverse, the degeneration, they resort inevitably to the very metaphors or debris in which they are entombed. The hope that art will restore the spirit, by recuperating a generative origin, can only be prefigured in the metaphors of improvised, or non-representational, art, an art that by analysis restores some sign of an orderly scene, an ideal or centered scene, albeit a scene that unveils the artifice of its in-

8. See Paul Valéry's essay on *Eureka*, in *Leonardo, Poe, Mallarmé*, trans. Malcolm Cowley and James R. Lawler (Princeton, N.J., 1972), 161–76, Vol. VIII of Valéry, *Collected Works*, 15 vols.

stituted center: "We painted or read together, or I listened, as if in a
dream, to the wild improvisations of his speaking guitar" (III, 282).

Usher improvises music, paints feverishly, and writes poems, one of
which, a so-called ballad, "The Haunted Palace," reduplicates the
paintings which in their turn are pure renderings (hence allegories) of
"an idea." Usher's allegorical art becomes the phantasmagoria of a de-
sire, an "incoherence—an inconsistency" (like the house) that reflects
at the same time an unseen but recoverable unity and the lawlessness
of life. Each of his works, however, is inadequate: they render a desire
without an object. The "wild fantasias" of his music shatter the norms
of harmony but recuperate no sensible structure. His poem repeats
the allegory of a green world or happy consciousness, figured in the
metaphor of the "stately palace" of "Thought's dominion" situated in a
"happy valley" that is suddenly afflicted by motion, time, and decay,
the exhaustion of its radiance and the degeneration of its "well-tuned
law" into "discordant melody" (III, 284–85). And the one painting that
beyond all others entrances the narrator is an abstract or phantas-
magorical rendering of a "vault" or a "tunnel," an abyssal structure
suggesting some subterranean realm illuminated by a "ghastly" light
that is without natural origin, a fictional light inscribed there as a sign
that marks the absence of both nature and origin.

Despite the narrator's concern over their perverse and wild air,
each of Usher's works represents a rather ordinary desire for a self-
sustaining, self-present inside, an inexhaustible presence that can dis-
tribute itself effectively through every outside or image. But each can
render the idea only by suggesting its opposite, that the artist can only
fictionalize this center as a provisional loss; therefore, the images dis-
tributed about this center, or dispersed from it, are shadows doubling
its absence. In Usher's painting, then, the light becomes the sign of a
fiction subject to at least two contrary interpretations, which the nar-
rator indicates in his protests that words describing the picture are in-
adequate to the "spirit of abstraction," that they render only a "ghostly
and inappropriate splendour" (III, 283). In Usher's art, every sign in-
dicates a radical secondariness, a discontinuity between image and im-
aged. At the circumference of each of his productions there is entropic
non-difference—noise, shadow, cold death, random distribution.

Nothing in Usher's house, however, is more inappropriate than his
very exclusive library, a bibliography largely made up of an authentic
list of pseudoscientific, mystical, and quasi-theological texts, each in
one way or another devoted to the idea of "the sentience of all veg-
etable things" (III, 286). Usher's paintings and writings are repeated
by his library, in which each text betokens an animistically centered or
unified world, a unity reflected in all the stable differences of a natu-
ral world. As the narrator states, Usher's library is another testimony
to his faith in the priority of inside to outside, of the one to the many.
The collection reduplicates, in Usher's mind, the conception of his
"forefathers" in their arranging the "gray stones of the home." The
sentience of matter, the orderly distribution of differences in an archi-
tecture, would suggest not only the sustaining arche of the family line

but would give the material evidence of decay and degeneration an informing myth, a reversed teleology.

Yet rather than alleviating Usher's hypochondria, his art and study aggravate his neurosis. The library, then, is not simply a collection and totalization of books representing and authenticating the family history, thereby situating man securely in the order of nature. The exclusiveness of the library, on the contrary, calls attention to its own arbitrariness. Like the family, the library produces no "collateral issue" or ideas, but reproduces a monomania. Just as it excludes other fictions, it reveals only the "phantasm," the malady and deficiency, of its originator. The obsession of the family with its destiny has generated a sterile fiction, of which the library with its single idea is the primary metaphor. The library reduplicates the "specious totality" and "wild inconsistency" of the "house"—an outside of disrelated stones repeated in an inside that is a specious totality of texts. Moreover, the library is not only a central room, but another closure that stands outside or over the central tomb. The texts that stand for one idea signify its absence. They are signs of death.

Of all its listed books, only one, the romantic melodrama "Mad Trist," which the narrator chooses to read to Usher during the time of his most extreme hysteria, is purely fictional—except, of course, Usher's own works of art. But this produces yet another exception, since "The Haunted Palace" is Poe's own poem, previously published. House and library repeat the *mise en abîme* of fiction-within-fiction: like Don Quixote's library, which contains one of Cervantes' books. The narrator condemns "Mad Trist" for its "uncouth and unimaginative prolixity" (III, 292), but it of all the texts in Usher's library is a simulacrum of a master book, the central image. "Mad Trist," according to the narrator, was "the only book immediately at hand," and though it is unworthy of Usher's "lofty and spiritual ideality," the narrator uses it as a distraction for his friend's increasing incoherence. The romance narrates a knightly quest that includes the slaying of a dragon and the winning of a "shield." It is read against the background of a "whirlwind" that swirls up around the house coincidentally with Usher's hysteria, while both he and the narrator listen to the "muffled reverberations" from the sister's crypt. Again, inside and outside collapse, and nature (whether vegetable or human) is signified as unnameable force, an in-coherence.

"Mad Trist" is employed by the narrator to defer both his and Usher's sense of the torment, the question, encrypted at the center of the house. Yet it can only amplify the question of the tomb. Ultimately, the story's own fictional center, the "brazen shield" of enchantment that attracts the Knight, must be approached, the last sign at the interior of a receding tunnel of fictions, an image that doubles all the rest. But as soon as it is won, and the dragon dispatched, the shield falls to the ground, metal ringing against metal with a dissonance that repeats every other center in the house/tale. The narrative within the narrative reduplicates the fictional labyrinth of the house; the "romance" reflects the fictional center of all the other texts of the library, the shield

of enchantment that forever defers any direct look into the abyss. Usher's desperate repression of the question, his dispatching of his sister to the tomb, is a last futile gesture to maintain the structure of "house" and "family," a last will to signification, a final attempt to preserve presence or life by a reinstallation of some sign of presence there where the center is absented. The body remanded to the tomb is alive; yet like a body or sign that stands for life, it is dead. For Usher, his repression of death conceals the absence of life in the house, but in the same gesture reveals the death or nothingness that has always inhabited the "house"/"family"/"direct line." The house's crypt, like Usher's art, conceals the secret of the center, that it is neither a presence nor an absence but a place constructed to install a sign of presence or absence.

Everything in "The Fall of the House of Usher" is a metaphorical detour, a delay in the course of a narrative that pushes toward its own tautological conclusion. For the thrust of every narrative reduplicates Usher's madness: the need to sustain differences yet the desire to realize the ideal of some final, ultimate unity. The double fault of the house of fiction must inevitably fall inward upon itself. Still, every narrative is at the same time a deferral of the center, of that "enshrouded figure" (Usher's sister) or "brazen shield" that is only another sign of the sense of an ending. As the narrator retreats from the house, he passes along the "old causeway" by which he entered, amid a storm that obscures and shadows every detail. His last view is of some "wild light" that has its source in a "blood-red moon" radiating through the "barely perceptible fissure" of the house. As the fissure widens, the house collapses inward upon itself, reduplicating the collapse of the twins upon one another. The airing of the crypt exposes the secret that sustains all such structures of difference, including narratives: "While I gazed, this fissure rapidly widened—there came a fierce breath of the whirlwind— the entire orb of the satellite burst at once upon my sight—my brain reeled as I saw the mighty walls rushing asunder—there was a long tumultuous shouting sound like the voice of a thousand waters—and the deep and dank tarn at my feet closed sullenly and silently over the fragments of the 'House of Usher' " (III, 297). The fragments of the narrative collapse upon themselves and are enclosed in a final metaphor that contains the figure of the house, the family, and the story itself—an infinitely refracted series of fictions without origin or end, without the sustaining center of the crypt. The metaphors of "family," "house," and "library," or of art as the rendering or expression of "idea," are all figures concealing a tomb at the center. Poe's renowned aesthetic ideal of a "unity of effect" is itself a meta-phor, of an architecture elaborately constructed upon the zero metaphor, the arche that is neither present nor absent. The "House of Usher" is built out of old books, the fragments of legends, romances, superstitions, and quasi-scientific metaphors, all erected upon a "hollow coffin" that must be protected even as it is ultimately opened and revealed as the place of just another missing body, another simulacrum of a simulacrum.

* * *

J. GERALD KENNEDY

From Phantasms of Death in Poe's Fiction†

* * *

Under the ostensible influence of Walpole, Radcliffe, Brockden Brown, Coleridge, Irving, and the German Romantics Tieck and Hoffmann, Poe assimilated the conventions of Gothic horror. His gravitation toward that mode was probably inevitable, for its narrative configuration seems to have embodied his fundamental perception of the human condition.[1] In his preface to *Tales of the Grotesque and Arabesque* (1840), he described the "terror . . . of the soul" as his essential "thesis."[2] The supernatural paraphernalia of the Gothic, particularly phantasms of death and destruction, afforded a means of articulating this primal fear. In a broad sense, Poe's "terror of the soul" bears traces of the historical and intellectual crisis that produced the Gothic novel; indeed, we cannot make sense of his preoccupation with madness, violence, perverseness, disease, death, and decomposition without recognizing the cultural drama inherent in what David Punter has called the "literature of terror."[3] It is a commonplace notion that the Gothic emerged from the rupture in Western thought between rationalism and Romanticism that occurred in the latter half of the eighteenth century. This formulation, however crude, contains an important truth: Gothic fiction enacts the radical uncertainty of an epoch of revolution in which nearly all forms of authority—neoclassicism, Right Reason, religious orthodoxy, and aristocracy—came to be seen as constricting systems. Ghosts and crumbling castles, wicked lords and diabolical monks served as fictive emblems of a collapsing order. Alone in a landscape of nightmare, the Gothic hero experienced the dark side of Romantic freedom: existential disorientation, wrought by the loss of defining structures. The Gothic paradigm dramatized for the first time the quintessential modern predicament—the plight of an alienated being whose rational skepticism had vitiated his capacity for belief, while paralyzing dread had betrayed the insufficiency of science and logic. It was the peculiar achievement of the Gothic (and, one imagines, the basis of its appeal) to express in playful, imaginative terms the latent fears of Western culture in an urban, industrial, post-rational, and post-Christian era. If this species of fiction presented a

† From *The Haunted Dusk: American Supernatural Fiction, 1820–1920*, ed. Howard Kerr, John W. Crowley, and Charles L. Crow (Athens: University of Georgia Press, 1983), pp. 37–65. Reprinted by permission of the University of Georgia Press and the author.
1. An idea ably developed by Stephen L. Mooney, "Poe's Gothic Waste Land," in *The Recognition of Edgar Allan Poe*, ed. Eric W. Carlson (Ann Arbor: University of Michigan Press, 1966), pp. 278–97 [Kennedy's note]. All notes to this selection are Kennedy's [Editor].
2. Preface to the *Collected Works of Edgar Allan Poe*, ed. Thomas Ollive Mabbott (Cambridge: Harvard University Press, 1978), 2: 473. All subsequent references to Poe's poetry and fiction correspond to the Mabbott edition, cited parenthetically by volume and page.
3. David Punter, *The Literature of Terror: A History of Gothic Fictions from 1765 to the Present Day* (London: Longman, 1980).

search for answers, an elucidation of mysteries, its real force lay, as
Punter observes, in the evocation of doubt, in its capacity for "remov-
ing the illusory halo of certainty from the so-called 'natural' world."[4]
Through its own illogic, Gothic supernaturalism exposed the limits
of reason as an explanatory model. The proliferation of occult themes
in eighteenth-century literature amounted, in the view of Patricia
Meyer Spacks, to a recognition that "the mind of man is naturally sub-
ject to secret terrors and apprehensions" and that supernatural motifs
possess a "real and universal" validity.[5] Writers of Gothic fiction, even
those like Ann Radcliffe who were committed to an ultimately rational
vision, felt the need to widen the range of narrative possibility and draw
upon the imagery of dreams. But the insurgence of literary supernatu-
ralism expressed more than a resistance to Augustan aesthetic con-
straints; it also manifested a curious response to the rationalizing of
religious thought in the eighteenth century. In effect, writers of Gothic
novels salvaged elements of popular belief—devils, curses, and spiritual
visitations—that had been jettisoned by Christian humanist thought.
And their use of supernatural imagery appears to have one other major
implication: as a response to death in the face of religious skepticism.
Glen St. John Barclay has argued that "any story which in any sense
refers to the intervention of the supernatural in human affairs neces-
sarily affirms that the supernatural exists. It holds out the reality of al-
ternative modes or realms of existence beyond the physical limitations
of our material life. In doing so, it responds directly to what is certainly
man's most abiding concern, the prospect of his own personal annihila-
tion and oblivion in death."[6] One must question the inference that any
literary representation of the supernatural affirms its existence in the
experiential world—a blatant confusion of art and life—but Barclay's
perception of the uncanny in fiction as a response to the fear of "per-
sonal annihilation" seems astute. When we consider that the Gothic
movement derived much of its impetus from the graveyard school of
poetry, we perceive that in the midst of other revolutions in taste, be-
lief, and thought in the eighteenth century, a wholly new and powerful
consciousness of death had begun to emerge. In place of the calm ac-
ceptance of mortality we might expect in the verse of a clergyman-poet,
we find in Young's *Night Thoughts on Death* and Blair's *The Grave* a
deepening anxiety about extinction. Such poetry excited curiosity about
death and decomposition; it introduced dreams and fantasies about dy-
ing; and it conferred upon the tomb and the cemetery a peculiar new

4. Punter, p. 404. I have characterized the modern age as "post-Christian" in the sense defined
by Alan D. Gilbert: "A post-Christian society is not one from which Christianity has de-
parted, but one in which it has become marginal. It is a society where to be irreligious is to
be normal, where to think and act in secular terms is to be conventional, where neither sta-
tus nor respectability depends upon the practice or profession of religious faith." See *The
Making of Post-Christian Britain: A History of the Secularization of Modern Society* (London:
Longman, 1980), p. ix.
5. Patricia Meyer Spacks, *The Insistence of Horror: Aspects of the Supernatural in Eighteenth-
Century Poetry* (Cambridge: Harvard University Press, 1962), pp. 196, 200.
6. Glen St. John Barclay, *Anatomy of Horror: The Masters of Occult Fiction* (New York: St. Mar-
tin's Press, 1978), p. 9.

importance. The abode of death became associated with preternatural phenomena, as instanced by Blair's depiction of a weird procession:

> Roused from their slumbers,
> In grim array the grisly spectres rise,
> Grin horrible, and obstinately sullen
> Pass and repass, hushed as the foot of night. (ll. 39–42)

Such images proliferated in the mid-eighteenth century as a funeral sensibility infused popular literature; death was no longer simply an event or moment in writing but its very object.

The association of supernaturalism and mortality acquires broader significance in light of the monumental study of Philippe Ariès, *The Hour of Our Death*. Through research into the burial practices, wills, and memorial sculpture of France (and Western culture generally) since the Middle Ages, Ariès demonstrates that, far from being a universal and static phenomenon, our conception of mortality has undergone vast changes, from the serene, public leave-taking of the medieval "tame death" to the lonely despair of our contemporary "invisible death"—the institutional concealment of the final hour.[7] Perhaps the most striking of Ariès's general conclusions is the observation that before the end of the seventeenth century, "human beings as we are able to perceive them in the pages of history [had] never really known the fear of death" (p. 405). Initially this seems a baseless proposition, for the phrase "fear of death" involves an apparent conflation of several distinct responses—to the idea of death, its imminence, its bodily effects, and its psychic consequences. As a historical judgment, this also seems doubtful; we know, for example, that the deadly plagues of the late Middle Ages inspired terror throughout Europe. But we must bear in mind that the medieval fear of an immediate threat and its spiritual corollary fear of eternal judgment are both quite different from the modern dread of mortality, the crux of the general claim. Ariès associates the onset of contemporary death-anxiety with three broad developments: the secularization of death and the erosion of belief in an afterlife; the growth of self-consciousness and individualism, which diminished the communal aspect of death and made it a private, personal experience; and the advent of science and modern medicine, which converted the corpse into an object of study and death into a physiological process. As indices of these changes, we see in the eighteenth century the appearance of public cemeteries and the abandonment of services once provided by the church; the practice of erecting funerary monuments to commemorate the existence of the common folk; the exhuming of bodies for experimental purposes; and, as noted earlier, the appearance of literary and artistic productions concerned with mortality and grief.

One result of scientific attention to the physiology of death was a mounting curiosity about the connection between the body and the soul. The medieval idea of the *homo toto*, the whole and indissoluble

7. Philippe Ariès, *The Hour of Our Death*, trans. Helen Weaver (New York: Alfred A. Knopf, 1981). Subsequent references to Ariès all derive from this work, with page references noted parenthetically.

man, was supplanted during the Enlightenment by the concept of a self that divided at death. But what part did the soul play in the agony of dying, and where did it go at the moment of extinction? Ariès notes that "this question, which is at the heart of the medical interest in death, is also one of the central preoccupations of the age" (p. 354). Investigations of cadavers exerted a "profound impact on the imagination of the time" (p. 367), feeding speculation about residual sentience in the corpse and about the prospect of galvanic reanimation. Such research demanded fresh anatomical specimens and thus gave rise to the atrocity of grave-robbing. This clandestine industry swiftly generated a folklore of violated tombs and reviving corpses; it must have contributed to the appearance, about 1740, of a terror hitherto unexpressed in Western culture—the fear of premature burial (p. 397).

III

This upheaval in attitudes touches almost every facet of cultural experience. With respect to Gothic fiction, the ubiquity of corpses (often bleeding preternaturally) reminds us, as Freud would much later, that the ultimate source of all terror is death itself. In effect, the haunted castle, the subterranean passageway, the secret vault, and the sealed room—all the conventional scenes of Gothic mystery—evoke anxiety because they pose the implicit threat of fatal enclosure. In an age that witnessed what Ariès calls "the first manifestation of the great modern fear of death" (p. 403), we discover a literary form given over to the recurrent staging of ultimate vulnerability. But the Gothic did not remain a static form; when we come upon its recognizable contours in the fiction of Poe, we also encounter new resonances and motifs indicative of changes in the cultural consciousness of death.

Perhaps in reaction to the eighteenth century's prolonged contemplation of the unshrouded corpse and the gaping grave, the dark imaginings once poetically associated with death had shaded into a bland sentimentality about time and transience, about loss and separation. By the early nineteenth century, as Ariès points out, the sense of mortality as "pure negativity" accompanied a fascination with the idea of a spiritual reunion beyond the grave. The ghastly image of death created by the procurement and dissection of cadavers yielded to an extravagant, romanticized vision of "the beautiful death"—a tender, well-planned departure, in which the prospect of an other-worldly rendezvous loomed large. Religious sentiment enjoyed a superficial resurgence in consolation literature, as the hour of death became a fetishized event. Ann Douglas has called attention to the necrolatry inherent in these works: "Such writings inflated the importance of dying and the dead by every possible means; they sponsored elaborate methods of burial and commemoration, communication with the next world, and microscopic viewings of a sentimentalized afterlife."[8] The poetry of Felicia Hemans and her American admirer, Lydia Huntley Sigourney,

8. Ann Douglas, *The Feminization of American Culture* (New York: Alfred A. Knopf, 1977), pp. 201–2.

epitomized the movement in popular culture toward an ethereal image of mortality, purged of gross physical detail. Ariès summarizes the prevailing attitude: "Since death is not the end of the loved one, however bitter the grief of the survivor, death is neither ugly nor fearful. On the contrary, death is beautiful, as the dead body is beautiful. Presence at the deathbed in the nineteenth century is more than a customary participation in a social ritual; it is an opportunity to witness a spectacle that is both comforting and exalting" (p. 473). But this new perception involves aesthetic contrivance: "This death [was] no longer death, it [was] an illusion of art." Indeed, the preoccupation with mortality so evident in magazines, annuals, and contemporary engravings betrays massive cultural self-deception: "In life as well as in art and literature, death [was] concealing itself under the mask of beauty" (p. 473).

What these shifts in sensibility reveal most clearly is the essential instability of Western ideas about mortality since roughly 1700. The reassuring model of "familiar and tame" death, prevalent until the late seventeenth century, vanished with the rise of the modern, industrialized, secular city. In its place emerged a multiplicity of conflicting attitudes and assumptions, producing radical confusion about the nature and meaning of death. The Christian message of resurrection continued to be heard, but clergymen as frequently extolled the beauty of dying, outlined the spiritual benefits of grief, or described the amenities of a domesticated heaven. Proponents of spiritualism grew numerous and by the mid-nineteenth century had established an organized movement. Those still influenced by a deistic or pantheistic perspective saw death as Bryant had painted it in "Thanatopsis": a beatific return to the bosom of nature, that "mighty sepulchre" of humanity. Attitudes originating in eighteenth-century graveyard verse continued to obtrude upon the popular consciousness; as I have shown in another essay, the fear of premature burial sustained a flourishing fictional subgenre in contemporary periodicals.[9] Medical experiments upon corpses still excited a horrified fascination, as the popularity of Mary Shelley's *Frankenstein* (1819) suggests. The rise of scientific positivism prompted widespread doubts about the existence of an immaterial soul, to the chagrin of ministers and spiritualists alike.

But amid the welter of contending viewpoints, David Stannard has discerned the "overriding national treatment of death" between the Revolution and the Civil War: "In large measure, if not entirely in response to the growing individual anonymity brought on by changes in their social world, Americans sought a return to their lost sense of community in the graveyard and the heavenly world of the dead; in the process, paradoxically, they effectively banished the reality of death from their lives by a spiritualistic and sentimentalized embracing of it."[1] That is, the death fetish of the early nineteenth century grew from a need to reestablish bonds of commitment in an increasingly imper-

9. J. Gerald Kennedy, "Poe and Magazine Writing on Premature Burial," *Studies in the American Renaissance* I (1977): 165–78.
1. David Stannard, *The Puritan Way of Death* (New York: Oxford University Press, 1977), p. 185.

sonal, urban society. But in order for death to become the great Meeting Place, it had to be disinfected and prettified. The effort to invest death with sentimentalized beauty drew the support of many leading writers; Washington Irving's tales "The Pride of the Village" and "The Broken Heart" (in *The Sketch-Book*) epitomize the tearful fare that flooded the publishing scene, promoting the Beautiful Death. This was the very society that, in Mark Twain's *Huckleberry Finn*, produced the lachrymose Emmeline Grangerford: "She warn't particular, she could write about anything you choose to give her to write about, just so it was sadful. Every time a man died, or a woman died, or a child died, she would be on hand with her 'tribute' before he was cold." With respect to popular gift book poetry, there is less exaggeration in Twain's caricature than one would suppose.

IV

Such was the literary and cultural environment in which Poe endeavored to sustain himself as a writer in the early 1830s. That he found the funereal sentimentality of the day a valid rhetorical mode may be surmised from his appreciative regard for Mrs. Sigourney, Letitia E. Landon, Mrs. E. Clementine Stedman, and other purveyors of maudlin stuff. In 1842 he did score the "namby-pamby character" of *Graham's Magazine* in a moment of pique,[2] but there is no evidence that he found the cultural preoccupation with mortality unhealthy, inappropriate, or laughable. By temperament and mournful personal experience, Poe was drawn into the contemporary cult of death. But if he respected the muse of sentiment, he avoided in his tales the conventional sad-but-joyful departure, and he clearly saw through the "mask of beauty" that concealed the grim features of human dissolution. In his "Marginalia" series Poe observed trenchantly: "Who ever *really* saw anything but horror in the smile of the dead? We so earnestly *desire* to fancy it 'sweet'—that is the source of the mistake; if, indeed, there ever was a mistake in the question."[3] Unlike his contemporaries, he refused to soften or idealize mortality and kept the essential "horror" in view; but he also moved beyond the Gothic formula to explore divergent conceptions of death.

[Kennedy here specifies four principal paradigms of death in gothic fiction as seen in Poe's works: Annihilation ("Ligeia," "Shadow," "The Masque of the Red Death"; Compulsion ("The Imp of the Perverse," *Arthur Gordon Pym*, "The Tell-Tale Heart," "The Black Cat," "The Cask of Amontillado," "Metzengerstein," "The Assignation," "Ms. Found in a Bottle"); Separation ("The Oval Portrait," "Morella," "The Fall of the House of Usher"); and Transformation ("The Premature Burial," "Monos and Una," "Mesmeric Revelation").]

* * *

2. Letter to Frederick W. Thomas, 25 May 1842, in *The Letters of Edgar Allan Poe*, ed. John Ward Ostrom (1948; rpt. New York: Gordian Press, 1966), I: 197. A vexed Poe thus rationalized his break with the journal.
3. "Marginala," in *The Complete Works of Edgar Allan Poe*, ed. James A. Harrison (1902; rpt. New York: AMS Press, 1965), 16: 42.

V

Among Poe's manifold representations of death and dying, we discern no single formulation that might confidently be described as the essential design. His object as a writer was not, of course, to construct a programmatic analysis of human fate; his thematic diversity and penchant for irony complicate even further an identification of his "real" conceptual matrix. Nevertheless, the imagery of death recurs with such insistence that its imaginative priority seems self-evident. Edward Davidson once described Poe as a "verbal landscapist of death,"[4] and in an early poem, "The City in the Sea," we encounter the characteristic scene of silence and desolation, upon which "Death looks gigantically down" (I: 202). For Poe, death was indeed gigantic, not in crude physical terms but as a ubiquitous and oppressive presence. Personal experience, popular culture, and intellectual history conspired to make it so. The pathetic facts of his own life—the successive deaths of his parents, his surrogate mother (Mrs. Jane Stith Stanard), his foster mother (Mrs. Allan), and his child bride, Virginia—describe a pattern of loss that must have haunted him like a specter. His inveterate melancholy also fed upon the funereal spirit of the age, as manifested in the sentimental offerings of the gift books and ladies' magazines. And his fear and trembling (to use the phrase of his contemporary, Kierkegaard) further derived from the crisis of authority and understanding that shook Western culture in the eighteenth century. Among other consequences, this crisis seriously challenged or destroyed traditional ways of accepting death and introduced a welter of new, secular conceptions that necessarily contributed further uncertainty. To use the phrase of Becker, it was at this moment that the "eclipse of secure communal ideologies of redemption"[5] produced the anxiety characteristic of the modern age. Since 1700 rapidly changing conceptions of death, symptomatic of a decentered culture, have failed to mitigate or resolve the underlying dread. It is a mark of Poe's genius that he perceived the central problem of death and sensed in his own dubiety the confusion of our existential plight. As Sarah Helen Whitman shrewdly perceived in 1859, the "unrest and faithlessness of the age culminated in him"; Poe was the saddest and loneliest writer of his generation because he "came to sound the very depths of the abyss," to plumb the nature of modern despair.[6]

No story in the Poe canon sounds the depths more effectively than "The Facts in the Case of M. Valdemar." * * *

Despite the fact that Poe in correspondence acknowledged the tale to be a "hoax," "Valdemar" demands serious attention as a conceptualization of death. With excruciating precision, it records the grotesque "facts" of the protagonist's apparent demise:

4. Edward Davidson, *Poe: A Critical Study* (Cambridge: Harvard University Press, 1957), p. 115.
5. Ernest Becker, *The Denial of Death* (New York: Free Press, 1973), p. 193.
6. Sarah Helen Whitman, *Edgar Poe and His Critics* (New York: Rudd and Carleton, 1860), p. 6.

The eyes rolled themselves slowly open, the pupils disappearing upwardly; the skin generally assumed a cadaverous hue, resembling not so much parchment as white paper; and the circular hectic spots which, hitherto, had been strongly defined in the center of each check, *went out* at once. . . . The upper lip, at the same time, writhed itself away from the teeth, which it had previously covered completely; while the lower jaw fell open with an audible jerk, leaving the mouth widely extended, and disclosing in full view the swollen and blackened tongue. (3: 1239)

The disappearance of the "hectic spots" brings to mind, appropriately, the sudden extinction of the sun in "MS. Found in a Bottle," while the revelation of the writhing lip recalls "Metzengerstein," "Berenice," and other Poe tales in which teeth function as a sign of death. This moment of apparent decease has its counterpart in the tale's unforgettable final image, the instantaneous decomposition of Valdemar: "Upon the bed, before that whole company, there lay a nearly liquid mass of loathsome—of detestable putridity" (3: 1243). Apart from effecting our revulsion, these details serve a figurative purpose, for "Valdemar" dramatizes the scientific effort—undertaken in the eighteenth century and continuing in our era of medical technology—to understand, control, and perhaps finally conquer the major causes of death. From an empirical viewpoint, cessation of life results from physiological processes that can theoretically be halted or reversed. Even aging has proved susceptible to retardation, and recent developments in genetic engineering and organ replacement bring ever closer the possibility of a technologically guaranteed immortality. However improbable or undesirable this idea seems, one can scarcely deny that the great dream of our scientific utopia lies in the direction of extending life beyond its traditional limits and converting death into a manageable, discretionary experience. Like Hawthorne's Dr. Rappaccini, the narrator of "Valdemar" uses scientific (or pseudoscientific) methods to control the processes of life artificially. His ultimate object is to determine "to what extent, or for how long a period, the encroachments of Death might be arrested" (3: 1233) by mesmerism. The stratagem succeeds in postponing Valdemar's dissolution, but when the man is awakened from his vegetative stupor, the grotesque final scene betrays the limitation of human efficacy and reaffirms the sovereignty of death. In effect, the illusion of a scientifically insured immortality disintegrates with Valdemar.

Another key to the symbolic ramifications of the tale lies in the supernatural voice, the "harsh, and broken and hollow" sound that seems to emanate from some deep or distant source, producing a "gelatinous" impression. When the voice declares, "I *have been* sleeping—and now—now—*I am dead*" (3: 1240), it perpetrates what Roland Barthes has called a "scandal of language, . . . the coupling of the first person (*I*) and of the attribute '*dead*' "; it "asserts two contraries at the same time (Life, Death)"; and it effects a "scandalous return to the literal" when "Death, as primordial repressed, erupts

directly into language."[7] The last point seems especially pertinent: the tale violates language, logic, and cultural taboo, allowing the unspeakable to speak, the unbearable sight to be seen. It compels us to confront death in all of its visceral repulsiveness, unsoftened by the effusion of sentiment or the prospect of a spiritual afterlife.

As noted earlier, Poe rejected the illusion of "the Beautiful Death" which beguiled his generation, and through the preternatural voice in "Valdemar" he expresses the hard physical and psychological truth at the core of modern consciousness. In this work as in so many others, supernaturalism intrudes upon the world of reason and experience to deliver the message of mortality. The uncanny produces a disruption, shatters the illusion of one's control over the flow of existence; it rivets the consciousness of Poe's protagonists like the first undeniable sign of a mortal illness. It arrives as a threat to the quest for knowledge, beauty, and godlike dominance, driving home a perception of the existential paradox summarized by Becker: "Man is literally split in two: he has an awareness of his own splendid uniqueness in that he sticks out of nature with a towering majesty, and yet he goes back into the ground a few feet in order blindly and dumbly to rot and disappear forever. It is a terrifying dilemma to be in and to have to live with" (p. 26). While Poe could entertain visions of transcendence, he was finally too much the victim of our own crisis of death to exorcise its dread. Yet he faced the "terrifying dilemma" with remarkable tenacity and acuity, producing a literature that seems, in our age of "invisible death," more than ever disturbing and menacing. Little wonder that for many, Poe cannot be taken seriously: to do so is to confront the fearful yet vitalizing truth that our century has done its best to deny.

JOHN CARLOS ROWE

From Antebellum Slavery and Modern Criticism: Edgar Allan Poe's *Pym* and "The Purloined Letter"†

My argument is on the face of it simple: Poe was a proslavery Southerner and should be reassessed as such in whatever approach we take to his life and writings. This is by no means an original claim. From Ernest Marchand in the 1930s to Bernard Rosenthal in the 1970s, the pro-slavery case against Poe has been argued again and again, usually on the very specific grounds of the infamous review of pro-slavery books by James Kirke Paulding and William Drayton published in 1836 in *The Southern Literary Messenger* while Poe was an assistant editor under Thomas Wylkes White, the general editor.[1] For these ear-

7. Roland Barthes, "Textual Analysis of a Tale by Edgar Poe," trans. Donald G. Marshall, *Poe Studies* 10 (June 1977): 10.

† From *At Emerson's Tomb: The Politics of Classic American Literature* (New York: Columbia University Press, 1997), pp. 42–62; reprinted by permission of Columbia University Press and the author. First published in 1992; revised in 1997.

1. The historical focus of this essay on Poe's proslavery sympathies does not depend exclusively on new arguments favoring Poe's authorship of the disputed review of James Kirke Pauld-

lier critics, Poe's sympathies with the Southern aristocracy, plantation life, and the institution of slavery have been treated as personal prejudices, which are not consistently displayed in his literary writings. Marchand, F. O. Matthiessen, and Rosenthal, among others, have found elements of Poe's racism at the heart of certain key works, notably *The Narrative of Arthur Gordon Pym*, but in most cases have treated the literary work as an allegory of Poe's antebellum prejudices. My own argument is that Poe's proslavery sentiments are fundamental to his literary production and thus demand a searching reconsideration of his aesthetic canon. Of equal interest, I think, is the history of Poe's twentieth-century canonization as modernist and the ways it has compounded the problem. Thus the reinterpretation of Poe's writings in terms of his pro-slavery sentiments involves an equally comprehensive reconsideration of twentieth-century critical approaches to Poe, as well as their theoretical assumptions.

My thesis is complicated by several factors that cannot always be kept clear and distinct, so I shall simply make a preliminary effort to identify them and then let these factors play throughout the rest of this chapter. First, the critical neglect of the historical circumstances surrounding Poe's literary production has been the work both of traditional literary historians and critical theorists. Ironically, the only literary historians who seem to have been *right* about Poe's complicity with antebellum Southern legitimists are those who have been demonstrated to have been factually *wrong* on several scores. In a similarly ironic manner, the vigorous efforts of poststructuralist theorists to modernize Poe and thus remove him (and his writings) from any historical context other than our own has had the effect of complementing what I contend was precisely Poe's racist strategy of literary production in the antebellum period. Second, Poe's racism is inextri-

ing's *Slavery in the United States* and [William Drayton's] *The South Vindicated from the Treason and Fanaticism of the Northern Abolitionists.* This unsigned review of two proslavery "histories" appeared in the April 1836 issue of the *Southern Literary Messenger* and was included in the James A. Harrison edition of *The Complete Works of Edgar Allan Poe*, 17 vols., ed. James A. Harrison (1902; New York: AMS Press, 1979), vol. 8, pp. 265–75. William Doyle Hull II argued in his doctoral dissertation, "A Canon of the Critical Works of Edgar Allan Poe with a Study of Poe as Editor and Reviewer" (Ph.D. dissertation, University of Virginia, 1941), that the surviving evidence did not support Poe's authorship but rather that of Judge Beverly Tucker, a proslavery advocate. Both before and after Hull's thesis appeared, however, scholars and critics have argued that Poe's writings and his personal beliefs were compatible with Southern aristocratic values, including the defense of the institution of and laws pertaining to chattel slavery. In this essay, this tradition of Poe criticism is best represented by Ernest Marchand's "Poe as Social Critic," *American Literature*, 6 (1934), 28–43; F. O. Matthiessen's "Edgar Allan Poe" entry in *The Literary History of the United States*, 3 vols., edited by Robert Spiller et al. (New York: Macmillan, 1947), vol. I, pp. 321–42; Bernard Rosenthal's "Poe, Slavery, and the *Southern Literary Messenger*: A Re-Examination," *Poe Studies* 7 (1974): 29–38. Sidney Kaplan's "Introduction" to *The Narrative of Arthur Gordon Pym of Nantucket* (New York: Hill and Wang, 1960) discusses Poe's racism and explicitly refers to the disputed review, but without apparent knowledge that Poe's authorship had been disputed by Hull. Harold Beaver's "Introduction" to *Pym* (Baltimore, MD.: Penguin Books, 1975) is the fullest treatment of *Pym* as an allegory of Southern racism in the antebellum period. This tradition of Poe criticism has been strong enough, albeit marginalized by both literary historians (in part, as a consequence of Hull's thesis) and modern critical theorists, that it deserves renewed attention as a tradition that tells us much more about Poe. Whether or not such new attention will lead to new scholarly discoveries that will revise Hull's thesis regarding the disputed review is less important, however, than continuing discussion of the ways in which Poe's major literary works are structured around racist, sexist, and aristocratic themes.

cably entangled with his attitudes toward women and his conception of the literary author as the new aristocrat. Racism, sexism, and aristocratic pretensions, of course, often go hand-in-hand, but in the case of Poe these prejudices are finely woven into the fabric of his art.

I will entangle Poe's name and thus meaning in contemporary debates about the psychoanalytical dimensions of literature (or the inevitable literariness of psychoanalysis) with a much-needed review of the historical study of Poe's proslavery sentiments, even as I warn against a narrow reliance on strictly empirical evidence. Such documentary evidence as the review of Paulding and Drayton in the 1836 *Messenger* and the possible sale of a slave by Poe in Baltimore[2] should not be ignored, but they should not be treated in purely archival and historical terms. Treated in a strictly positivist manner, they can be easily enough refuted or ignored, as has been the case with these two significant "details" from Poe's life. The ruses by which willful critics separate and discriminate "life" from "letters" are sufficiently familiar to all of us, and the text-bound myopia of literary criticism is by no means restricted to that brief historical moment we have so obsessively monumentalized in the ominous name "Anglo-American New Criticism." Textualists have often done the same work, trivializing biographical and historical facts, even when they know well enough that such facts ought to be incorporated into rhetorical history, rather than conveniently forgotten.

The stakes of my argument are by no means exclusively concerned with Poe's reading by modern scholars and critics. In his own time, Poe enjoyed a reputation as a poetic extremist who challenged the transcendentalists' confidence in the correspondence between natural and supernatural realms. Writing as an avowedly anti-Emersonian idealist, Poe advocated a seemingly more radical, posttheological idealism that often uses scientific rhetoric and pseudoscientific evidence to legitimate its concepts. In these respects, Poe was often judged in his own times as a radical and even "revolutionist," insofar as what has been termed his "romantic irony" criticized the established values of "the New England transcendentalist clique he would dub the 'Frogpondians.'"[3] Joan Dayan interprets Poe as a nineteenth-century alternative to Emerson and thus to "the Emersonian strain of American literary history, best represented by Charles Feidelson's *Symbolism and American Literature* and Sacvan Bercovitch's *The Puritan Origins of the American Self*" (Dayan, 5).

Yet even as the nineteenth-century Poe seems to offer an idealist alternative to American transcendentalism and Continental romanticism, he ends up representing simply a more systematic or logical idealism: "Poe is not interested in any simple opposition between 'scientific reason' and 'poetic intuition' or 'material fact' and 'visionary

2. John C. Miller, "Did Edgar Allan Poe Really Sell a Slave?," *Poe Studies* 9 (1976): 52–53.
3. Joan Dayan, *Fables of Mind: An Inquiry into Poe's Fiction* (New York: Oxford University Press, 1987), p. 3. Dayan quotes an 1856 review in the *North American Review* of Poe as a subversive author "who was 'like other revolutionists, desirous mainly of decapitating the sovereign, and debasing all the blood royal.'" Further references in the text as: Dayan.

knowledge.' He works his language so that such oppositions become convertible. Instead of arguing against materialism and rationalism, Poe shows how the arch-rationalist can engender the most amazing fanaticism, how the facts of matter can be turned into suppositions of mind" (Dayan, 9). In my view, this qualifies the nineteenth-century Poe as the obverse of the Emersonian coin, the unconscious of a transcendentalist idealism that would overtly endorse liberal progressive ideals and still be liable to a philosophical "imperialism" isomorphic with nineteenth-century social and economic hierarchies. In the case of Emerson and the New England transcendentalists, I have argued that their views often reproduced the social system they criticized: the entreprenuerial expansion of Jacksonian-era capitalism and its general tendency toward Manifest Destiny. In the case of Poe, philosophical and aesthetic idealism props up reactionary politics that reject any sign of liberal progressivism for the sake of a "radical" retreat to feudal hiearchies, albeit redefined to survive in Poe's nineteenth century (Dayan, 9).

The marginal, eccentric, supercilious nineteenth-century Poe has thus done specific cultural work in legitimating the American Self, even if Dayan is right to argue that he has more often seemed to represent the opposite or negative of the Emersonian "self-reliant man." The attenuated, gnostic, even obliterated self is often enough Poe's literary theme, and it is the necessary other of Emerson's "man thinking" (Dayan, 5–6). The construction of such a "Poe," pushed to the margins of American culture and yet nonetheless a figure who continues to exert an obsessive fascination for interpreters of nineteenth-century America, must be considered part of the cultural work that made Emersonianism such an enduring and defining legacy of American identity. Enduring as an "exile" of this tradition, thereby serving to frame it, Poe has also escaped reconsideration in terms of the central political issues of his age: abolition and women's rights. Protected by his aesthetic supernaturalism, hiding behind his pose as poetic rebel, Poe has realized his own grandest ambition: to escape history.

Literary historians have also played a part in this work of historically reconstructing, if not outright protecting Edgar Allan Poe from his own Southern identity. In this regard, let me turn to the fate of the review of Paulding and Drayton in the twentieth century. The misattribution of that infamous review to Poe seemed to be settled decisively by William Doyle Hull's 1941 doctoral dissertation at the University of Virginia, "A Canon of the Critical Reviews of Edgar Allan Poe."[4] Arraying an impressive variety of circumstantial evidence, Hull argued that the review was most likely written by Judge Beverly Tucker, the proslavery advocate. Hull's scholarship is in no way concerned with Poe's literary writings, except in their connection with the literary taste demonstrated in his reviews. Hull equally ignores the wider cultural context in which proslavery works appeared in the antebellum period. "Authorship" for Hull is not a theoretical matter; it is simply a ques-

4. William Doyle Hull, "A Canon of the Critical Works of Edgar Allan Poe."

tion of assessing the surviving empirical evidence to determine the authorship of an unsigned work.

Yet as the scandal about Paul de Man's wartime writings for *Het Vlaamsche Land* and *Le Soir* has once again taught us, the moral responsibilities of writing are hardly covered by conventional notions of historical "authorship." Those defending de Man's writings on the grounds that they display only occasional and then debatable anti-Semitic and pro-Nazi sentiments can do so only by ignoring or trivializing the virulent anti-Semitic and vigorously pro-Nazi views published along with de Man's "cultural" reviews in *Le Soir* during the German occupation of Belgium. Wary as we should be of the dangers of charging "guilt by association," we must acknowledge that the association of publication in the same newspaper or journal can be the basis for a substantial case.[5]

In the case of Poe, such an association with the likes of Judge Beverly Tucker, should he in fact be the author of the disputed review, is made even more invidious when we consider Poe's "heavy correspondence" with Tucker in the spring of 1836 while Poe was working as an assistant editor for Thomas Wylkes White of *The Southern Literary Messenger*. Although there is no evidence that Poe commissioned the review by Tucker, Poe was serving effectively as the "review editor" when the review of Paulding and Drayton's books was published.[6] In 1974, responding in part to criticism that his *Race and the American Romantics* (1971) had mistakenly included the Paulding-Drayton review as the work of *Poe*, thus ignoring the evidence of Hull's doctoral dissertation, Bernard Rosenthal carefully argued both the "guilt by association" thesis and challenged the circumstantial evidence of Hull's thesis in "Poe, Slavery, and the *Southern Literary Messenger*: A Reexamination."[7] In that essay, Rosenthal argues the case in historically concrete terms, but he includes as part of that history Poe's deferential correspondence with Judge Tucker, his great admiration for and gratitude to Paulding himself, and Poe's undisputed admiration for Thomas R. Dew in his October 1836 review of Dew's address to the students at William and Mary—the Thomas R. Dew, who Rosenthal calls "the ar-

5. In "Paul de Man's Past," Christopher Norris argues in de Man's defense that "The articles have been mined for passages that show him up in the worst possible light, often by being juxtaposed with other items from *Le Soir* whose content bears no relation to anything that de Man wrote" (6). Yet it is just this latter point I would make about both de Man's wartime writings *and* Poe's work as assistant editor (primarily responsible for reviews) of the *Southern Literary Messenger*. Newspapers and journals are written by the authors of their different articles, but they nevertheless have a certain *corporate* authority that is familiar to even the most casual reader. Although this corporate authority sometimes takes the explicit form of an editorial, it is normally communicated by the *dominant political tone* of the periodical. Periodicals that encourage a wide range of opinions and subjects are not exceptions to this rule; they generally reflect a political attitude of liberal pluralism. For contributors, of course, this means that they must share responsibility with the other contributors for that corporate authority. For an editor of a periodical, that responsibility is even more binding. The political rhetoric of *Le Soir* during the German Occupation of Belgium is unmistakable: shrill German nationalism punctuated by the ugliest anti-Semitic and racist rancor. The *Southern Literary Messenger* is just as propagandistic when its anti-Northern, pro-Southern, and proslavery attitudes are added up.
6. Hervey Allen, *Israfel: The Life and Times of Edgar Allan Poe*, 2d ed. (New York: Farrar and Rinehart, 1934), p. 317.
7. Bernard Rosenthal, "Poe, Slavery, and the *Southern Literary Messenger*: A Re-Examination," pp. 29–38.

chitect of the South's intellectual position in defense of slavery" and who subsequently became president of William and Mary (Rosenthal, 30).

Yet, since Rosenthal reopened the debate concerning the authorship of the infamous Paulding-Drayton review, there has been very little scholarly discussion of Poe and slavery, with the exception of interpretations of *Pym* as a "fantasy of white slaveholding paranoia" that have followed the leads of Walter Bezanson and Rosenthal himself.[8] The "modern" or "postmodern" Poe hardly lends himself to this debate, which turns so crucially on historical details and the very regional identification that Poe himself seemed to do everything possible to disavow in his major literary productions. Rosenthal made an understandable, albeit strategic, error in framing his 1974 argument primarily in historical terms. Although he broadened the historical context of Hull's argument, he kept the argument primarily in an archival context at the very moment Poe was about to reemerge as a major figure in what has come to be termed "Deconstruction in America."

Rosenthal's arguments were virtually ignored, even by Poe scholars. One notable exception was the distinguished Poe scholar G. R. Thompson, who reviewed Rosenthal's argument in *American Literary Scholarship* for 1974 and concluded: "Although his argument depends on a number of ambiguities and a few improbabilities, he does a good job of showing greater improbability that the review is Tucker's."[9] Such grudging acknowledgement of Rosenthal's challenge to Hull, appearing as it did in the annual *ALS* review of Poe scholarship, was not likely to have much impact on poststructuralists working on Poe, especially since their interest derived hardly from the study of Poe as an American author but from the study of Poe primarily in the context of comparative literature and Continental theory.

Thompson himself seems to have forgotten what he wrote in 1975 about Rosenthal, because in his contribution to the new *Columbia Literary History of the United States*, Thompson argues in "Poe and the Writers of the Old South" that "Poe's conception of letters is virtually devoid of regionalist sentiment" and that: "(The notorious review of two books defending slavery in the *Messenger* in 1836, upon which some critical interpretations of Poe's *Narrative of Arthur Gordon Pym* have been based, was written not by Poe but in all likelihood by Beverly Tucker)."[1] Acknowledging that "Poe's Southernness" remains a

8. See Bezanson, "The Troubled Sleep of Arthur Gordon Pym," in *Essays in Literary History Presented to J. Milton French*, eds. Rudolf Kirk and C. F. Main (New Brunswick, N.J.: Rutgers University Press, 1960), pp. 149–75. See especially p. 169 on the curious water of Tsalal: "Even fresh water runs purple, and the use of the word 'veins' to describe its peculiar structure suggests a fantasy on negro blood."

9. G. R. Thompson, "Edgar Allan Poe," *American Literary Scholarship: An Annual/1974*, ed. James Woodress (Durham, N.C.: Duke University Press, 1976), p. 33.

1. G. R. Thompson, "Poe and the Writers of the Old South," *Columbia Literary History of the United States*, ed. Emory Elliott (New York: Columbia University Press, 1988), pp. 268–69. Given Poe's well-documented correspondence with Tucker (especially in the spring of 1836, when the disputed review was published), the disassociation of Poe from the proslavery sentiments in the Paulding-Drayton review seems even more improbable. In his edition of Poe's *Essays and Reviews* for the Library of America, Thompson includes Poe's review of Beverly Tucker's *George Balcombe, A Novel*, which appeared in the January 1837 *Messenger*, only

question "of recurrent critical debate," Thompson judges Poe's "high formalism of prose style, . . . idealization of women, . . . scorn for democracy and the idea of progress, and an uneasiness about the age of the machine" as "not . . . specifically Southern" (269). Further, in his volume for the Library of America, *Poe's Criticism and Reviews*, Thompson pays little attention in his "Notes" to Poe's Southern sentiments, despite his inclusion of Poe's long, admiring review of Beverly Tucker's chivalric romance, *Balcombe*. Throughout the reviews and criticism that Thompson selects for this volume, there is frequent evidence of Poe's preferences for Southern literature and the chivalric romance, including Poe's praise for William Gilmore Simms' melodramatic novel about Southern honor and romance, *Beauchamp*. In his introduction to the notes for this volume, Thompson cites Hull's dissertation as one of his sources for establishing the canon of Poe's reviews and criticism, which seems to explain why Thompson makes no reference to the Paulding-Drayton review.[2]

In *The Word in Black and White*, Dana Nelson has woven together a number of the same strands in this critical reception of Rosenthal's 1974 essay to conclude that Thompson's version of Poe in the *Columbia Literary History of the United States* "most directly voices the recent trend to sweep Poe's politics under the rug."[3] Nelson is careful not to decide hastily the question of Poe's racism, appealing instead for a reconsideration of how "a depoliticized and dehistoricized reading of the Poe oeuvre concomitantly 'saves' Poe for a canon increasingly skeptical of texts that support human oppression."[4] What Nelson's approach enables us to do is judge not merely Poe's Southern sentiments and racist values, but also reexamine political conse-

nine months after the Paulding-Drayton review. *George Balcombe* is an utterly conventional Southern chivalric romance, rendered thinly contemporary by setting the usual plot of misplaced wills and elusive fortunes primarily in the Missouri frontier. Poe judges it with his typical critical hyperbole as "upon the whole, . . . *the best* American novel. There have been few books of its peculiar kind, we think, written in *any* country, much its superior" (978). One of the few "philosophical" points that Poe challenges in the novel is Balcombe's (and, for Poe, the author's) view that "When truth and honor abound, they are most prized. They depreciate as they become rare." Poe responds in the manner of a Southern aristocrat: "But it is clear that were *all* men true and honest, then truth and honor, *beyond their intrinsic*, would hold no higher value, than would wine in a Paradise where all the rivers were Johannisberger, and all the duck-ponds Vin de Margaux" (978).

2. Thompson, *Poe: Essays and Reviews*, p. 1483. Although Poe's critical evaluations of Simms' works vary throughout the reviews collected in Thompson's *Essays and Reviews*, he is one of the most frequently cited writers and, like Tucker, receives one of Poe's longest reviews (for *The Partisan: A Tale of the Revolution*). In his review of Simms' *The Wigwam and the Cabin*, Poe writes, "The fiction of Mr. Simms gave indication . . . of genius, and that of no common order. Had he been even a Yankee, this genius would have been rendered *immediately* manifest to his countrymen" (p. 904).

3. Dana Nelson, *The Word in Black and White: Reading "Race" in American Literature, 1638–1867* (New York: Oxford University Press, 1992), p. 91. Dana Nelson's and my own interests in the history of the academic reception of Bernard Rosenthal's essay have had independent origins in our respective interests in Poe's critical revaluation, but they coincided when both of us contacted Professor Rosenthal about his essay. I called Bernie in 1988 while I was preparing an original version of this chapter as a lecture ("Poe's *Narrative of Arthur Gordon Pym* and Modern Theories of Psychoanalysis") at a conference on *Pym* sponsored by Pennsylvania State University and held on the island of Nantucket in May 1988. Professor Rosenthal directed Cathy Davidson's doctoral dissertation, and Cathy in turn directed Dana Nelson's doctoral dissertation. Both Nelson and I thus benefited from Rosenthal's generous account of this interesting controversy, and I wish to acknowledge here my thanks to him (as Nelson does in *The Word in Black and White*, p. 162n2).

4. Ibid., pp. 91–92.

quences of the several critical traditions from the New Critics and phenomenological critics to post-structuralists that have canonized Poe by depoliticizing his writings.

* * *

Thompson's assessment of Poe in the *Columbia Literary History* as a protomodern cosmopolitan writer without "specifically Southern" identity in his writings is the place to begin reinterpreting Poe's significance for our own time as well as in the antebellum South. Rosenthal's mistake, like Marchand's and Matthiessen's before him, was to treat the historical Poe and the modernist Poe as different figures, involving drastically different intellectual issues. The consequence has been that the rise of the "modernist Poe" has left the historical Poe in the archives, virtually ignored in our generation and, unfortunately, for the next generation reading the *Columbia Literary History of the United States.*

Let me now try to weave together some of these specific historical questions, including Poe's critical reception in the twentieth century, together with the theoretical Poe, whose circulation in the past twenty years has given him a new currency, but one that has strategically ignored his nineteenth-century political affiliations. Since the recovery of Poe by the French Symbolistes, "Poe" has been treated as an invention or an occasion for a wide variety of different language games—Symbolist poetry, psychobiography, psychoanalysis, deconstruction—that would seem to have little to do with the historical Poe. Edgar Allan Poe, of course, would have loved this transcendence; he himself never much cared to live in his own age. The translation of his literary works into the language game of psychoanalysis has accomplished precisely what Edgar Allan Poe had hoped: the substitution of an immaterial world for the threatening world of material history. The immaterial poetic world of the language game that Poe worked so hard to distinguish from ordinary reality is in no way an "unreal" or purely "fictional" world. The very appropriateness of post-Freudian psychoanalytical and textualist approaches to Poe's writings argue just the opposite, and I have no intention of attacking their claims according to some specious criteria for "truth" and "falsehood." My contention is that there is a rhetorical and psychoanalytical relation between the immaterial, poetic world of Poe's writing and the material history from which it flees. It is just this differential relation between the material and the immaterial that modern psychoanalytical theories using Poe's writings have missed—not only in Poe, but also in themselves.

[Rowe next reviews the psychoanalytic-deconstructive debate over "The Purloined Letter" as especially represented by Lacan, Derrida, and Johnson; for a concise overview in a different context, see John T. Irwin, "Detective Fiction as High Art," pp. 941ff. herein.]

* * * *Pym*, written twenty-four years before the American Civil War, yet addresses all the fears that the Southerner would revolve in the turbulent years leading to the necessity of battle. I make no claim

for originality here; the interpretation of *Pym* as a thinly disguised al-
legory of Poe's manifesto, "Keep the South white," belongs to others.[5]
I add only a few touches, delicate strokes, as it were, not the least of
which involves the entanglement of scholarly debates over historical,
psychoanalytical, and theoretical issues.

The date of *Pym*'s first appearance in *The Southern Literary Messen-
ger* is 1837, but the date of the voyage on the *Grampus* is "June 1827."
Poe probably got the idea for *Pym* from James Kirke Paulding's sugges-
tion in a letter of March 1836 that Poe "undertake a Tale in a couple
of volumes, for that is the magical number." Paulding was trying to
soften the blow Poe certainly felt when Paulding had notified him two
weeks earlier that Harpers had turned down Poe's manuscript, *Tales of
the Folio Club*.[6] This is the same period of Poe's work as assistant edi-
tor at the *Southern Literary Messenger*, his correspondence with Bev-
erly Tucker, and weeks before the proslavery review was published in
the *Messenger*. The significant event on board the *Grampus* is a
mutiny, which seems distinguished for its extraordinary brutality and
its utter irrationality. Emancipation in the British West Indies was for-
mally declared on August 1, 1834. Three years earlier, Nat Turner's
Rebellion—the Southampton Insurrection—occurred in August 1831,
in Southampton County in southeastern Virginia.

Following the much-publicized trial and execution of Nat Turner in
November 1831, much stricter laws regulating Southern slaves (espe-
cially laws regarding travel passes) were passed in most Southern
states. Just as the earlier slave revolts by Gabriel Prosser and Denmark
Vesey had fueled Southern white paranoia, so Turner's revolt had the
effect of what Eric Sundquist judges an instance of nineteenth-
century terrorism: "The white paranoia that followed the revolt bred
distortions that in turn heightened apprehension—accounts suggest-
ing that the rebels wore outfits ceremoniously dyed red in their vic-
tims' blood or, more strikingly, that they drank the blood of the
slaveholders."[7] Poe writes this long narrative in the historical context
of decades of Southern white anxieties regarding the possibility of
widespread slave revolts, recently made real in Turner's revolt. As Nel-
son points out in *The Word in Black and White*, this Southern cultural
anxiety is complemented by wider nineteenth-century Anglo-European

5. In addition to Sidney Kaplan's and Harold Beaver's interpretations of *Pym* as an allegory of
Southern white fears regarding slave insurrections and Dana Nelson's interpretation of the
narrative as a Eurocentric colonialist fantasy, Kenneth Alan Hovey's "Critical Provincialism:
Poe's Poetic Principle in Antebellum Context" (*American Quarterly* 4 [1987]: 341–54) com-
plements my own approach to Poe's writings. Focusing on Poe's criticism of Longfellow and
other Northeastern writers, Hovey argues that Poe endorsed an aesthetic formalism as a re-
action to Northern artists' "double error of didacticism and progressivism." For Hovey, Poe
"formulated a poetic principle which eliminated messages altogether. A 'poem written solely
for the poem's "sake" ' could have no social implications. It might be morbid, but it could
never be incendiary or fanatical" (350). The combination of Kaplan, Beaver, and Hovey's
readings presents a convincing case that Poe's antebellum values are integral to his major
writings and not just a matter for scholars deciding his authorship of an objectionable re-
view. This is what I mean by recognizing anew the *tradition* of critical interpretation of Poe
as Southern writer.
6. Allen, *Israfel*, p. 317.
7. Eric Sundquist, *To Wake the Nations: Race in the Making of American Literature* (Cam-
bridge: Harvard University Press, 1993), p. 69.

defenses of "Anglo racial superiority," arguments that helped support various imperialist projects as well as the more specific ideology of Southern slavery.[8]

The Narrative of Arthur Gordon Pym of Nantucket is thus not a mere allegory of proslavery values; in this regard, the historical interpretations have been too crude, rather than simply "inaccurate" or falsely "historical," as defenders of Poe against proslavery charges have argued. Poe's own repressed fears regarding slave rebellions in the South and the deeper fear that Southern aristocratic life itself might be passing are the psychic *contents* that provoke the poetic narrative. The defense of the poetic narrative against just these fears is its argument that language, the essence of reason, is the basis of all reality and thus the only proper "property." As the "enlightened ruler" of language, its rational governor, the poet works to recontain savagery—the mob, the black, the lunatic—within poetic form.

In *Beneath the American Renaissance*, David Reynolds shows how Poe "had learned from America's pioneering penny newspaper a lesson in conscious manipulation of sensational themes through a double-sided fiction that possessed both novelty and tact, excitement and control." For Reynolds, *Pym* combines the irrational sensationalist and the pseudoscientific in a narrative that, if "not altogether successful," nonetheless constitutes a defensive parody of such popular styles.[9] Nat Turner's Southampton Insurrection provoked sensationalist journalism of the most hysterical kind, often focusing on Turner's gory use of a broad-axe to murder his master and the master's wife.

Poe's defensive fantasy about savage, rebellious blacks is not exclusively enacted on the island of Tsalal. The first outbreak of such savagery is on board the *Grampus* during the mutiny. As I argued in "Writing and Truth in *The Narrative of Arthur Gordon Pym*," it is during the mutiny that *writing* assumes the virtual bodily character of the blood Augustus desperately uses to send his warning to Pym in the hold.[1] From this point on, writing will become the primary referent for reality, and it will be represented commonly in metaphors of the body and/or physical reality. Chief among the savages of the crew is the Black Cook, who is a virtual "demon" and executes bound seamen who have not joined the mutiny by "striking each victim on the head as he was forced over the side of the vessel" (P 1:86). The Black Cook tells Augustus "that he should never put his foot on deck again 'until the brig was no longer a brig' " (P 1:89). As Reynolds points out, piracy was a common topic for sensational literature of the time. In Poe's narrative, this conventional subject is poetically, perversely metaphorized to cross "piracy" as a literary topic with the historical threat of the "theft" of property posed by slave insurrection and Abolition in general. Like Nat Turner, the Black Cook strikes his victims on the head,

8. Dana Nelson, *The Word in Black and White*, p. 93.
9. David Reynolds, *Beneath the American Renaissance: The Subversive Imagination in the Age of Emerson and Melville* (New York: Knopf, 1988), pp. 241, 242.
1. John Carlos Rowe, *Through the Custom-House: Nineteenth-Century American Fiction and Modern Theory* (Baltimore: Johns Hopkins University Press, 1982), pp. 99–102.

testifying to the symbolic danger to reason posed by the emergence of irrational savagery so many Southern whites imagined would accompany slave rebellion or even legal emancipation.[2]

The mutiny unleashes a terrible savagery that belongs for Poe to the uncivilized state. The providential "storm" that saves Augustus and Pym from butchery seems to argue against Poe's thesis that the "savagery" of the pirate or the black belongs to a "state of Nature" that civilization must control. In the Paulding-Drayton review, the reviewer endorses the extended "family" of the Southern slaveowner as the basis for "the moral influences flowing from the relation of master and slave, and the moral feeling engendered and cultivated by it." In a perfectly conventional manner, the reviewer argues for the happy patriarchal character" and the essential "clanship" in the extended "family" of the black's childlike relation to his/her benign master. These are typical proslavery views, certainly more compatible with Tucker, Paulding, and Dew on that subject than the subtler, more ambivalent Poe.

Even so, in *Pym* nature is nothing but the site of savagery and precisely what the unnatural family of master and slave, and thus of the institution of slavery itself, are designed to control. The providential storm arrives, however, at precisely the moment that the *Narrative of Arthur Gordon Pym* has been transformed from the pseudo-realism of either sensational or scientific voyages and travels into the *poetic* voyage constituted by Augustus' and Pym's writing and reading. It is the very moment, in fact, when Pym learns to *impersonate* the dead mutineer, Hartman Rogers. This impersonation will be followed by the *ingestion* of the other surviving mutineer, Richard Parker.

The scene of cannibalism enacted by the survivors on the drifting hulk of the *Grampus* only appears to identify them with the savagery they have miraculously escaped. The "horrible purpose," "the most horrible alternative which could enter the mind of man," is proposed initially by Parker, who becomes the victim of his own plan. Although Pym's efforts to convince Parker to "abandon his design" or "at least . . . defer it for another day" seem motivated by Pym's reason and humanity, Pym's arguments have the consequence of turning Parker's savage instinct for survival into a rational, even democratic "lottery." In short, Pym tricks Parker into agreeing to a rational choice of victim. Once he is chosen in this manner, Parker is utterly unmanned, mastered by Pym's trick, no less than the mutineers were mastered by the ghostly apparition of Hartman Rogers: "He made no resistance whatever, and was stabbed in the back by Peters, when he fell instantly dead."

Translated into the rhetoric of the poetic voyage, such cannibalism figures doubly. On the one hand, as empirical event, it represents the savagery exploited by sensationalist literature. Read as poetic enactment, it is the *internalization* of white power, the transformation of

2. Throughout my re-reading of *Pym*, I am indebted to the work of Scott Bradfield's revisionary reading of Poe in *Dreaming Revolution: Transgression in the Development of the American Romance* (Iowa City: University of Iowa Press, 1993), esp. pp. 68–82.

the "blood" of Augustus' message into the perverse Transubstantiation of Poe's Poetic Mystery. As Poe's version of the Southern white reaction to the Turner revolt, such figurative "cannibalism" appropriates the "savagery" attributed to Turner and his rebels, such as the myth that they drank the blood of their victims. The cannibalism in *Pym*, however, is not simply a defensive enactment of the savage custom of eating an enemy to defeat his spirit, although it certainly partakes of that ritual. Internalizing his power, consuming his own body, the poet transforms the threatened body of the White Master into the rhetoric of the White Poet. Without offering a full analysis, I shall merely note here the curious rhetoric of *inversion*, of a *topsy-turvy* world, that characterizes the experiences of the survivors on the capsized *Grampus*.

There is yet one more touch that, speculative as it must remain, I cannot help adding to this account. Of the six judges signing the November 5, 1831, order for Nat Turner's execution, one was "James W. Parker." Conventional as the name is, the association of these "Parkers" is at least suggestive. Judge Parker, of course, can hardly be identified with a "mutineer" in league with that savage executioner with his hatchet, the Black Cook, but the wayward tracks of condensation and displacement hardly meet the requirements of logic. Even so, if the "Parker" eaten by Pym is not just his threatening enemy but also the authority of the Court in Jerusalem, Virginia, that condemned Nat Turner, then Pym is invested with the power of the Law, now transposed into the fictional frame.[3]

In *Pym*, the narrative begins in Nantucket as Augustus enchants Pym with stories of romantic adventure at sea, not unlike, we might guess, the sensational stories of pirates that appeared contemporaneously in the popular press. Reborn first in the accident of the *Ariel*, then again from the mutiny and shipwreck of the *Grampus*, Pym and Augustus leave behind the nuclear family of Pym's own family of lawyers and Augustus' family of sea-captains. In the place of those conventional forms of bourgeois control and civilization, Augustus and Pym substitute their own friendship, which is based on their adolescent rebellion against family authority (especially various father figures for Pym and Augustus). This friendship is repeatedly linked with story-telling and writing, as if to suggest that this, rather than the bourgeois family, is the real source of social authority. Augustus' wounded arm, which rots disgustingly as they drift on the *Grampus*, has its obvious sexual suggestiveness, which few critics have missed. The threat of castration that Augustus makes sensuously present to Pym provokes Pym's own narrative of compensation. Insofar as the "savagery" of the mutineers and, above all, the Black Cook threaten the powers of reason represented by Augustus and Pym, the pencil that Pym wields as he keeps that soggy diary of events following the

3. See the statement by members of the court, Jerusalem, Virginia, in the preface to *The Confessions of Nat Turner*, the twenty-page pamphlet published in Richmond in 1832, the year following Nat Turner's Southampton Insurrection. This document is conveniently reproduced in the section, "To the Public," in William Styron's *The Confessions of Nat Turner, A Novel* (New York: Random House, 1966).

mutiny becomes his best defense. But so does his subsequent companion, Dirk Peters.

As a "half-breed," Peters offers an alternative to the "savagery" of the Black Cook. Like the black slaves who would serve their masters faithfully and often to the death during the Civil War, Dirk Peters is Poe's fantasy of the faithful and grateful servant. It is Peters, of course, who embodies the "fierceness of the tiger" that grips Pym when the decision is made to sacrifice Parker to save the others from starvation. Peters' savagery is of a fundamentally different character than the Black Cook's, because it enacts what has already been conceptualized by Pym, who is from this moment on Peters' white master. Peters both resembles and is distinguished from the natives of Tsalal, who "were among the most barbarous, subtle, and bloodthirsty wretches that ever contaminated the face of the globe." In his July 1835 review of Theodore Irving's *The Conquest of Florida, by Hernando De Soto*, Poe observes that "the Floridian savage was a more formidable foe than his Mexican brother—more hardy of frame, and more implacable in his revenge." In his favorable review of James Hall's *Sketches of History, Life, and Manners in the West* in the December 1835 *Messenger*, Poe praises Hall's "undoubted abilities as a writer" and claims that he is "excellently qualified to write precisely such a book as he has written," which includes "the policy of our government in regard to the Aborigines."

Peters is from a Missouri tribe, his father a fur-trapper, but he resembles these Floridians and the "Aborigines" William Henry Harrison, old "Tippecanoe," helped subdue by defeating Tecumseh in 1811. Let us not forget that Poe would campaign vigorously for Harrison in the 1840 Election, along with his friend Frederick W. Thomas. Peters reenacts the fate of the faithful crewmen on the *Grampus* met at the hands of the Black Cook: "We had proceeded some hundred yards, threading our route cautiously between the huge rocks and tumuli, when, upon turning a corner, five savages sprung upon us from a small cavern, felling Peters to the ground with a blow from a club." With pistols in hand, Pym kills two "savages" and frees Peters, who promptly "seizing a club from one of the savages who had fallen . . . dashed out the brains of the three who remained, killing each instantaneously with a single blow of the weapon, and leaving us *completely masters of the field*" (emphasis added). Like Native Americans who scouted for and fought with the American Cavalry against tribal foes in the course of Manifest Destiny, like the East Indian Sepoys who fought faithfully for the British in India, Dirk Peters exemplifies one common "colonial solution" to the problem of a native population: subjugation by way of ideological conversion. As "half-breeds," either biologically or ideologically, such colonized people are indentured to the colonizer's values. It is an "art" never raised to a higher level than that of the British in their vast Empire, practiced more crudely in the American West and in our ventures in Southeast Asia.

The black prisoner, Nu-Nu, whom Peters and Pym take along on their escape from the savagery of Tsalal, wastes away as they advance

toward the whiteness of the Pole. As Orlando Patterson and Toni Morrison have interpreted respectively the sociology of slavery and the cultural rhetoric of "blackness," the social death of the slave and the destruction of the racially marked other are crucial strategies in the invention of "white" authority.[4] The incomplete "family" of Augustus and Pym is here fully constituted, albeit in appropriately *masculine* form. With the help of the servile half-breed, the white master affirms his mastery and takes possession of the savagery that so threatens him. He does so not by means of legal and economic domination, but in and through the poetic domination that is figured in the *writing* in the interior of the island of Tsalal. Like Nantucket, the poeticized Tsalal now becomes a place of civilization, thanks to the powers of reading and, above all, the power of *writing* that has helped insinuate this fiction—*The Narrative of Arthur Gordon Pym of Nantucket*—into reality. It should not surprise us that the author of the "Note" tells us that "Peters, from whom some information might be expected, is still alive, and a resident of Illinois, but cannot be met with at present. He may hereafter be found, and will, no doubt, afford material for the conclusion of Mr. Pym's account." I shall not belabor this passage, although I am tempted to do so. Suffice it to say that Illinois is a free-state, and the convenience of Peters' status as "half-breed" (Native American and white) allows Poe's Pym to liberate a "savage" without succumbing to the Southern heresy of liberating a perfectly good piece of property, that is, a slave. Having served his murderous purposes—the murder of Parker, the vengeful murder of the natives on Tsalal, the indirect cause of Nu-Nu's death, Peters has earned his just desserts: the "free-state" that only the white slave master, now turned poet and parodist, can award for service against the savagery that threatens him and his kind. That Peters remains a potential authority able to verify the authenticity of Pym's posthumous narration only underscores this point.

Much could still be said of the translation of black and white oppositions into the manageable black letters and white field of Poe/Pym's written text. Even Poe's apparent anticipation of Freud's thesis about the "antithetical sense of primal words" (in his review of Karl Abel's philological work of the same title) seems to confirm Pym's will-to-power in this instance. If the psychic script has the power to transform opposites into uncanny relations, if black is nothing but the repression of *white* (and, of course, vice versa), then the psychic nar-

4. Orlando Patterson, *Slavery and Social Death: A Comparative Study* (Cambridge: Harvard University Press, 1982), p. 338: "The ideological inversion of reality was the creation of the slaveholder class, so it is not surprising that few of them expressed reservations about its veracity; almost all masters, in fact, genuinely believed that they cared and provided for their slaves and that it was the slaves who, in the words of one southern ex-slave owner, had 'been raised to depend on others.'" Toni Morrison, *Playing in the Dark: Whiteness and the Literary Imagination* (New York: Random House, 1993), pp. 32–33, reads brilliantly the cultural significance of this penultimate episode in *Pym*: "The images of the white curtain and the 'shrouded human figure' with skin 'the perfect whiteness of snow' both occur after the narrative has encountered blackness. The first white image seems related to the expiration and erasure of the serviceable and serving black figure, Nu-Nu. Both are figurations of impenetrable whiteness that surface in American literature whenever an Africanist presence is engaged. These closed white images are found frequently, but not always, at the end of the narrative."

rative is little more than a confirmation of Poe's own thesis: that the transformation of material history into poetic history will save the reign of Reason from the savage intrusions of the real. Freud would not stop at such a conclusion, but reveal, as we have crudely attempted to do, how the "black savagery" so frightening to both Pym and Poe is little other than the repressed contents of their own white psyches. Such an interpretation would matter little to Poe, however, for it would depend crucially upon a reading in which the Ego would read the authority of its own unconscious. In fact, Poe has constituted a narrative in which the reader is by no means the Ego of Poe/Pym, but yet another Dirk Peters, the faithful "half-breed" who discovers only the authority of the white master.

I return at the end to those twentieth-century narratives of psychoanalysis provoked by Poe's *Narrative*. In his reading of the uncanny relation between black and white in *Pym*, John Irwin concludes: "For though Pym says that they 'noticed no light-colored substance of any kind on the island' and though the anonymous author of the note adds that 'nothing *white* was to be found at Tsalal, and nothing otherwise in the subsequent voyage to the region beyond,' Pym himself points out the white arrowhead flints in the chasm. And just as whiteness lies at the core of the dark realm of Tsalal, so darkness must be present in the white realm of Tekeli-li, otherwise there would be no color boundary, no figure/ground differentiation, no signification. The shadow image haunts the lone regions of Tekeli-li—whether Pym recognizes it or not. . . . What the ending of *Pym* acts out, then, is 'a certain *tendency* of the human intellect' (inscribed within it by the very structure of its birth) to try to survive death by projecting an image of itself (the self as image) into the infinite void of the abyss."[5] In the subtle optical reading he offers of the appearance of the white figure at the Pole, Irwin contends that it is the shadow cast by Pym that establishes the figure/ground relation. Irwin has already made clear that such an optical scene is always already a psychic scene of representation, that the "shadow" of Pym is nothing other than his fear of death, the ghostly double of Freud's Uncanny. Without for a moment disagreeing with this reading, I would supplement that shadow—the shadow of the White Man as Poet—with the corpse of Nu-Nu: the black body that as slave chattel or as "soulless" corpse is the necessary shadow for the poetic representation of *Pym*. The "whiteness" found at the heart of the chasms is, after all, that of "arrowhead flints," which are instruments of the kill. As images of the savage threat posed by the black natives and by black slaves, they are metonymies for their targets: not animals of the hunt, but the whites tabooed in the cry, "Tekeli-li!" Poetically repossessed both by the white poet and the "half-breed" with whom arrowhead flints are so conventionally identified, the "white arrowhead flints" become the "invisible bullets" of Poe's poetic mastery, his poetic colonialism.

5. John Irwin, *American Hieroglyphics: The Symbol of the Egyptian Hieroglyphics in the American Renaissance* (New Haven: Yale University Press, 1980), pp. 204–5.

Such a reading is thus not the radical "other" of the psychoanalytical debate occasioned by Poe's writings between Jacques Lacan and Jacques Derrida, unless that other is the uncanny double of just what psychoanalysis threatens to consolidate as the "law" of psychic signification. In her account of that debate, Barbara Johnson summarizes the consequences for the reader of the Poe text and the psychic Signifier of the Unconscious:

> The reader is comprehended by the letter: there is no place from which he can stand back and observe *it*. Not that the latter's meaning is subjective rather than objective, but that the letter is precisely that which subverts the polarity subjective/objective, that which makes subjectivity into something whose position in a structure is situated by the passage through it of an object. The letter's destination is thus *wherever it is read*, the place it assigns to its reader as his own partiality.[6]

The "letter" thus quite by design "takes dominion everywhere," so constituting the reader's relation to his psychic text that he can find nothing but the letter's dominion, its specular *shadowing-forth* of his own identity. In this way, Lacan, Derrida, Barbara Johnson, and I myself (among other textualist readers of Poe) would institutionalize the domain of language, both as psychic and literary landscape, as the ineluctable field of our historical acts. The appropriateness of these gestures to Poe's own intentions is thus perfect; the textualist has read, even as he/she has disregarded Poe's own historical situation, in a manner that perfectly realizes Poe's very contemporary poetic purpose. Johnson continues:

> The opposition between the "phallus" [Lacan] and "dissemination" [Derrida] is not between two theoretical objects but between two interested positions. And if sender and receiver are merely the two poles of a reversible message, then Lacan's *substitution* of "destin" for "dessein" in the Crébillon quotation—a misquotation that Derrida finds revealing enough to end his analysis upon—*is* in fact the quotation's message. The sender (*dessein*) and the receiver (*destin*) of the violence that passes between Atreus and Thyestes are *equally* subject to the violence the letter *is*.[7]

Once again, we can find no fault with this reading, insofar as we stay within the frame of psycholinguistic reference. The revenge-cycle of the ancient struggle between Atreus and Thyestes, which turns upon the subtle arts by which each attempts to destroy the lineage of the other's house, is precisely the incestuous violence initiated by this postmodern poetic: that of Poe's art and of psychoanalysis itself. Internalizing the violence of material history, the immaterial history of poetry and psychoanalysis transforms such violence into the very principle of its perverse power.

6. Barbara Johnson, *The Purloined Poe: Lacan, Derrida and Psychoanalytic Reading*, ed. John P. Muller and William J. Richardson (Baltimore: Johns Hopkins University Press, 1988), p. 248.
7. Ibid.

* * *

However powerless, irrelevant, or insignificant the institutions of academic criticism might seem in the larger context of our postindustrial age of information, they have helped legitimate hierarchies of language use that are today the structural foundations for what I would term a "hermeneutics of class." The calls for "cultural literacy" are only the most recent echoes of this modern appeal for the reorganization of human activity along the lines of signifying authority. Abolitionists like Frederick Douglass knew well enough that the postbellum fight for genuine economic and social freedom would have to be conducted at all levels in terms of verbal authority—in politics, in the courts, in the press, as well as in literature. Those with *access* to language, both in terms of their educations (the capabilities to speak in technically proper ways) and the availability to them of actual media (who controls the presses of the papers, journals, and publishing industry), control the political economy. The rest constitute the "mob," which Poe fears as profoundly as any of his literate contemporaries. Like Poe's "Man of the Crowd," the mob represents all that which "does not permit itself to be read," a fearful collective unconscious.

* * *

Poe's insistence upon a new *authority* capable of reading what remains profoundly unconscious either to the malevolent Tsalalian native or to the London mob becomes his warrant for a new class system predicated on linguistic competency. The new property of words may have seemed to have little practical value for the Poe harassed by money worries and dependent on his Southern patrons, whose capital was counted in human beings and acreage. But today we may conclude, as we so often have, that Poe was profoundly clairvoyant, even if we must insist that his was a perverse vision. Today one's class identification and one's virtual earning power are tied intimately to the "Power of Words." If we hope to revive the important historical question of Poe's antebellum politics, then we will have to reconsider its continuity with the postbellum politics of aesthetic language and its powerful hierarchies of verbal competency and cultural literacy, which is to say we must rethink the entanglement of the antebellum Southern writer with his shadowy other: the modern, cosmopolitan trickster, Edgar Allan Poe.

TERENCE WHALEN

From Average Racism: Poe, Slavery, and the Wages of Literary Nationalism†

* * *

In recent years the political and racial meaning of Poe's work has been the focus of intense critical debate, and undoubtedly the positions generated from this debate will have enduring consequences, not only for Poe scholars, but for all those investigating the importance of race in American culture. * * * Poe's lifelong struggle with the publishing industry constitutes a kind of deep politics that should matter more than his awkward and infrequent forays into partisan rhetoric. Poe, that is to say, should be distinguished from the public-spirited intellectuals of his age, for whereas these intellectuals embraced a wide variety of civic and political causes, Poe's political agenda was conspicuously confined to problems of production, ranging from the poverty of authors to the corruption of publishers to the emergence of a vaguely ominous mass audience. To put such a theory to the test, it is necessary to consider what is conventionally seen as the single most important political struggle of antebellum America, namely the struggle over slavery that divided North from South and that culminated, a dozen years after Poe's death, in a catastrophic civil war. * * * [A]ny investigation into Poe's racial views should begin by acknowledging that in the 1830s, there were multiple racisms and multiple positions on slavery even in the South. In order to understand the complex relation between race and literature, moreover, it is also necessary to account for the pressures of literary nationalism and a national literary market, because these pressures put constraints on commercial writers in all regions and contributed to the always unfinished formation of what might be called average racism. For Poe and other antebellum writers, average racism was not a sociological measurement of actual beliefs but rather a strategic construction designed to overcome political dissension in the emerging mass audience. In other words, publishers and commercial writers were seeking a form of racism acceptable to white readers who were otherwise divided over the more precise issue of slavery.

Fredric Jameson's admonition about the textual nature of history * * * suggests the general difficulty of unraveling such political intricacies of the past. In the case of Poe and race, this task has been

† From *Poe and the Masses: The Political Economy of Literature in Antebellum America* (Princeton, N.J.: Princeton University Press, 1999), pp. 111–40, 293–302. Copyright © 1999 by Princeton University Press. Reprinted by permission of the publisher and the author. The argument is complexly modulated, and the chapter is long and richly detailed; the interested reader is urged to consult the original for a mass of historical details. The notes have been selected and renumbered to fit the excerpted passages; additions made by the editor are so indicated.

rendered doubly difficult by the texts themselves, because most are ambiguous, some are unsigned, and at least one does not even exist. Of all these real and imaginary texts, none is more controversial than the so-called Paulding-Drayton review, an anonymous proslavery essay published in the April 1836 *Southern Literary Messenger*. On one side of the controversy stand those who attribute the review to Poe and who use it to document his "Southern" attitudes or, more explicitly, his virulent and flagrant racism. Many of these critics share some broad assumptions, not only about regionalism and ideology in antebellum America, but also about the *aberrance* of discredited doctrines from the past. It's not that they find racism literally unthinkable. Instead, it might be said that for these and other critics, racism is only thinkable as the thought of a Southerner. On the other side of the dispute stand those who attribute the review to Beverley Tucker, law professor at the College of William and Mary and author of the first secessionist novel. The group favoring Tucker's authorship comprises both literary critics who seek to defend Poe from charges of racism, and historians who, apparently oblivious to the whole controversy, seek only to clarify Tucker's famous—or infamous—position on slavery and secession. As shall become clear, this ostensibly simple case of attribution raises fundamental questions about the meaning of authorship, questions that no interpretive approach can answer without recourse to history itself.

The nature of the controversy is best illustrated by the glaring contradiction between two literary histories recently issued by Columbia University Press. In the *Columbia Literary History of the United States*, G. R. Thompson disavows Poe's authorship and then argues that an 1849 review of James Russell Lowell is "the only instance of Poe's taking any kind of stance on the issue of slavery" (269). In the *Columbia History of the American Novel*, Joan Dayan identifies Poe as the author of the Paulding-Drayton review, calling it "five of the most disturbing pages Poe ever wrote," and relying upon it to expose his "ugly" theory that "the enslaved want to be mastered, for they *love*—and this is the crucial term for Poe—to serve, to be subservient" (98).

Even by the most traditional definition of authorship, Thompson and Dayan are both wrong. As I shall demonstrate in this chapter, Thompson is in error because Poe did make several statements about slavery, and Dayan is wrong because her interpretation is based on a review that Poe did not write.[1] In order to explore all of the relevant evidence, I initially reserve judgment about the legitimacy of "author" and "authorial intent," for by holding the fate of these concepts in abeyance, I am free to pose some basic questions: What can one know

1. Neither Thompson nor Dayan, I hasten to add, is completely culpable for these mistakes. Thompson was making a quick point with a bit of hyperbole, and Dayan was basing her arguments on a persuasive but flawed article by Bernard Rosenthal (see note 4). In addition, both writers were prevented from qualifying or justifying their arguments in footnotes. For complete texts, see G. R. Thompson, "Poe and the Writers of the Old South," *Columbia Literary History of the United States*, ed. Emory Elliott (New York: Columbia University Press, 1988), 262–77; and Joan Dayan, "Romance and Race," *The Columbia History of the American Novel* (New York: Columbia University Press, 1991). 89–109 [Whalen's note]. All notes are Whalen's unless otherwise indicated [Editor].

about Poe's racial views? In what sense are Poe's expressed views properly his own? What, if anything, can be deduced from Poe's silences? And how should an author's "racism" influence the interpretation of a literary text? Although these questions lead to further inquiries into authorship and literary nationalism, my ultimate aim in this essay is to lay the groundwork for a more historically informed criticism of race, a criticism that surpasses the prevailing rhetoric of praise and denunciation. In doing so I often find myself contending against those who, like myself, stress the social ramifications of Poe's work; but if political criticism is to be more than politics as usual, it must fulfill a special burden of proof when it turns outward to the unconverted and the undecided.

I. The Resilience of Error

In April 1836 the *Southern Literary Messenger* published "Slavery," an unsigned essay purporting to review two recent books: *Slavery in the United States* by James Kirke Paulding and *The South Vindicated from the Treason and Fanaticism of the Northern Abolitionists*, an anonymous work generally attributed to William Drayton. The author of the review devotes only a few laudatory sentences to these works, reserving the bulk of the essay to develop an alternative justification for slavery. Instead of treating slavery as a necessary evil, the reviewer defends slavery as a positively beneficial institution that fulfills God's will by creating a bond of sympathy between the inferior black slave and the superior white master. * * *

After James A. Harrison included the Paulding-Drayton review in *The Complete Works of Edgar Allan Poe* (1902), many literary historians relied upon it to document Poe's relation to his social and political surroundings. Later, however, an 1836 letter from Poe to Beverley Tucker raised important questions about the authorship of the review and the validity of interpretations that relied on it. In the letter, dated and postmarked 2 May 1836, Poe refers to "your article on Slavery" and then apologizes for having made some editorial alterations.[2] First published in 1924 and later reprinted in John W. Ostrom's 1948 edition of Poe's correspondence, the letter seemed to provide conclusive proof that Tucker had written the review and that Harrison had committed a major editorial blunder.

As illustrated by "The Purloined Letter," however, investigators often overlook the most obvious evidence, and many critics continued to attribute the Paulding-Drayton review to Poe long after Ostrom had displayed the letter in plain view. In their anthology *Race and the American Romantics*, for example, Vincent Freimarck and Bernard Rosenthal used the review to prove that Poe was "certainly the most blatant racist among the American Romantics."[3] Later, amid charges that he had perpetuated Harrison's error, Rosenthal defended his

2. Poe to Beverley Tucker, *Letters*, 1:90–91. The original is in the Tucker-Coleman collection.
3. Vincent Freimarck and Bernard Rosenthal, eds., *Race and the American Romantics* (New York: Schocken Books, 1971), 3. Rosenthal selected and introduced the material on Poe.

choice by claiming that Poe's letter to Tucker must be referring to a still undiscovered article or pamphlet rather than the Paulding-Drayton review.[4] Rosenthal did not provide any definitive proof of Poe's authorship, but he did raise enough doubts to excuse the continued depiction of Poe as a brazen advocate of slavery. In the *Columbia History of the American Novel*, Dayan accordingly mentions Rosenthal's "excellent argument for Poe's authorship" and then relies on the Paulding-Drayton review to demonstrate "how much Poe's politics concerning slavery, social status, and property rights owed to the conservative tradition of the Virginia planter aristocracy" (96). Dayan does not explain how this planter ideology was assimilated by the child of itinerant actors and foster-son of a Scottish-born tobacco merchant; like many other literary critics, she implies that all white Southerners—even transplanted and temporary Southerners—held identical views on slavery.

Significantly, even those dubious of the review tend to make similar generalizations. Kenneth Alan Hovey, for example, argues that Poe and Tucker held identical views on slavery, and that Poe may have written at least some of the essay.[5] His support for this position rests on three rather questionable grounds: Poe apologized for making alterations; the review was anonymous; and the first five paragraphs "sound very much like Poe." The last two points seem insufficient to overturn Poe's own letter acknowledging Tucker's authorship of an "article on Slavery." The primary argument, concerning Poe's apology for making "a few immaterial alterations," is misleading. Hovey claims that "these alterations may not be so immaterial" because "Poe felt called upon to apologize for them, something he did not do for any other of his editings in the *Southern Literary Messenger*" (353). On the contrary, Poe did apologize for altering articles, especially articles written by the *Messenger's* more esteemed contributors. Furthermore, Hovey implies that Poe was apologizing for *additions* to Tucker's article, when in fact the young editor was apologizing for *deletions*.

* * *

Even when critics repudiate the Paulding-Drayton review altogether, they nevertheless seem rather eager to contain or enclose Poe's views within a comfortably monolithic definition of racism. In a long chapter on *The Narrative of Arthur Gordon Pym*, A. Robert Lee argues that "Poe's Southern, racially phobic, imagination also plays into this Antarctica, a displaced Deep South and fantasy Eden despoiled and hexed by brute, carbon tribesmen."[6] Lee does some displacing of his own: first he depicts racism as a pathology peculiar to a Deep South which shall never rise again, and then he implies that this historical

4. Bernard Rosenthal, "Poe, Slavery, and the *Southern Literary Messenger*: A Reexamination," *Poe Studies* 7 (December 1974): 29–38.
5. Kenneth Alan Hovey, "Critical Provincialism: Poe's Poetic Principle in Antebellum Context," *American Quarterly* 39 (fall 1987): 347, 353 n. 40.
6. A. Robert Lee, " 'Impudent and ingenious fiction': Poe's *The Narrative of Arthur Gordon Pym of Nantucket*," in *Edgar Allan Poe: The Design of Order* (New York: Barnes and Noble, 1987), 128. For further speculations on Poe's racial fears, see Louis D. Rubin, Jr., *The Edge of the Swamp: A Study in the Literature and Society of the Old South* (Baton Rouge: Louisiana State University Press, 1989).

racism resided less in social practice than in what might be termed the Mind of the South. John Carlos Rowe offers a more complex argument about race and literature, but he too sees Poe's racial views as a regional phenomenon. Attempting to emphasize Poe's "Southern sentiments" and his "complicity with antebellum Southern legitimists," Rowe states his case succinctly: "Poe was a proslavery Southerner and should be reassessed as such in whatever approach we take to his life and writings."[7] As I shall contend throughout, this position exonerates the North while it forestalls any further inquiry into the nature and complexity of race politics in the South. Approaches that restrict racism to the past have a similar effect. By depicting Poe's racism as a universal antebellum trait that has forever vanished from existence, such accounts dismiss precisely what should be specified. Craig Werner, for example, locates Poe within prevailing antebellum conventions, arguing that his racism was "shared with the vast majority of his contemporaries, northern and southern." Referring specifically to *Race and the American Romantics*, Werner then contends that "although there has been much discussion of Poe's authorship of the [Paulding-Drayton] review, there seems little reason to doubt the general conclusions drawn by Freimarck and Rosenthal."[8]

Rosenthal's general conclusions, however, are far from clear. At times, he suggests that Poe's literary works reflect the widely disseminated proslavery positions of John C. Calhoun and Thomas R. Dew, apologists who depicted slavery as a happy combination of political and biological law. At other times, he suggests that Poe viewed slavery as something altogether more insidious and terrifying. Rosenthal's interpretation of *The Narrative of Arthur Gordon Pym* in fact emphasizes the horror of race relations in the South:

> Once comprehended, the ending of that novel reads as a potpourri of every racial cliché and of every racial nightmare that characterized the South. The blacks reflect the sustaining paradox underlying the southern mythology of Poe's day. They are at once stupidly childlike and demonically monstrous. . . . Blacks impotently fear whites and possess the power to destroy them. The very existence of blacks evokes apocalyptic events, and the feared conflagration between the races destroys both black and white society. (*Race and the American Romantics*, 3)

Such a portrayal flatly contradicts the image of black-white relations in the Paulding-Drayton review. There, the author describes "a degree of loyal devotion on the part of the slave . . . and of the master's reciprocal feeling of parental attachment to his humble dependent." Far from depicting a climate of fear and distrust, the author claims that "these sentiments in the breast of the negro and his master are

7. John Carlos Rowe, "Poe, Antebellum Slavery, and Modern Criticism," in *Poe's Pym: Critical Explorations*, ed. Richard Kopley (Durham: Duke University Press, 1992), p. 117. [See pp. 904–20 herein—Editor.]
8. Craig Werner, "The Insurrection of Subjugated Knowledge: Poe and Ishmael Reed," in *Poe and Our Times: Influences and Affinities*, ed. Benjamin Franklin Fisher IV (Baltimore: The Edgar Allan Poe Society, 1986), 155.

stronger than they would be under like circumstances between indi-
viduals of the white race."⁹ Rosenthal simply ignores this contradic-
tion. Instead of acknowledging the difference between a paternalistic
defense of slavery and Poe's "racial nightmare," he asserts that "the
recognition of [Poe's] views does not necessarily require a reassess-
ment," because "there are no jarring incongruities between his politics
and his art" (3).

There are, however, many jarring incongruities between the
Paulding-Drayton review and the body of work known to be by Poe. And
until we can properly establish authorship, we shall also see jarring in-
congruities between those who attribute the review to Tucker and those
who still cling to the notion that Poe wrote it. * * * [I]instead of of-
fering a point-by-point refutation of Rosenthal, I shall focus on the ide-
ological and stylistic similarities between the review and works known to
be by Tucker. Even if there were no other corroborating evidence, these
similarities would be enough to acquit Poe of the accusation, thereby
expediting his arraignment on charges still pending.

II. The Case For Tucker's Authorship

As a rule, those who attribute the Paulding-Drayton review to Poe have
a hard time even imagining that it was written by Beverley Tucker.
Rosenthal claims that the May 1836 letter from Poe to Tucker repre-
sents "the sum total of evidence for Tucker's authorship." Dana Nelson
reiterates this position; although she carefully avoids basing her inter-
pretation of Poe on the review, she nevertheless reports that "Rosenthal
traces the impossibility of attributing the essay to Tucker on the basis
of extant evidence."¹ As demonstrated by a close examination of the ev-
idence, however, Tucker is in fact the most likely of suspects.

Nathaniel Beverley Tucker is today remembered as one of several
proslavery advocates at the College of William and Mary, but he was in
addition a judge, novelist, and active member of the group of South-
ern intellectuals which Drew Gilpin Faust has dubbed "the Sacred
Circle." From 1835 to 1837, Beverley Tucker also performed numer-
ous offices for the *Southern Literary Messenger*, which was published
just fifty miles away from Williamsburg in Richmond, Virginia. Aside
from contributing lectures, poetry, and editorial material. Tucker as-
sisted the magazine by writing favorable notices, selecting appropriate
articles for publication, and even by correcting proof-sheets. Signifi-
cantly, Tucker wrote eleven book reviews during this period. All of
them appear as unsigned critical notices, all of them employ the edi-

9. Cited in *Race and the American Romantics*, 30. Tucker makes a similar argument in an
 1844 essay for the *Messenger*, providing further evidence that he is in fact the author of the
 Drayton-Paulding review. Contrasting the different course of paternalism in Europe and the
 United States, Tucker argues that "the bond of sympathy that once connected the landed
 proprietor with all who lived upon his land is severed, while a like sympathy has been en-
 gendered between the white man and his negro slave." See "On the Moral and Political Ef-
 fect of the Relation between the Caucasian Master and the African Slave," *Southern Literary
 Messenger* 10 (June 1844): 333.
1. Dana D. Nelson, *The Word in Black and White: Reading "Race" in American Literature,
 1638–1867* (New York: Oxford University Press, 1992), 91.

torial "we," and many of them are intermingled with reviews written by Poe.[2] When the Paulding-Drayton review was published in April of 1836, Tucker was also busy writing *The Partisan Leader*, the first secessionist novel in the United States. Because of his standing as law professor, Tucker issued the controversial book under a pseudonym in a vain attempt to conceal his authorship. As Tucker directed the publisher, "Keep dark. I do not wish to be known as the author of these things." In the same letter, Tucker also discussed plans to secure the assistance of Thomas W. White, proprietor of the *Messenger*. "I could, if I would, make White praise it to the skies, but I must not give him any clue to me. He is incapable of secrecy."[3] Tucker's situation, then, can be summarized as follows: 1) He contributed filler as well as numerous unsigned book reviews to the *Messenger*. 2) He had written several proslavery articles for the magazine and was in the midst of writing a proslavery novel. 3) He wanted to maintain a good relationship with the *Messenger*. 4) He wanted to protect the secrecy of at least some of his writings on slavery. Given these circumstances, it is certainly possible that Tucker turned some of his background reading for *The Partisan Leader* into a hastily written book review that Poe had to shorten—either for editorial or ideological reasons.

Before examining the most direct evidence, however, it is important to recognize the strong political affinity between the Paulding-Drayton review and Tucker's known works, especially since there is no such affinity between the review and texts by Poe. As shall become clear, Tucker's proslavery writings contain numerous stock arguments and tropes that are duplicated in the Paulding-Drayton review. These include sentimental descriptions of sickbed scenes, the use of animal comparisons to explain human racial diversity, charges of Northern meddling followed by a Southern call to arms, the characterization of slavery as a positive good rather than a necessary evil, the invocation of Divine will to justify racial subordination, and (sophistical) resolutions of the conflict between equality and difference.[4] Significantly,

2. The use of the editorial voice explains why the author of the Paulding-Drayton review refers to Thomas Dew as a "correspondent" rather than a colleague. For a more detailed account of the magazine, see David K. Jackson, *Poe and the Southern Literary Messenger* (Richmond: Dietz Press, 1934). Recent evidence indicates that Tucker may have had much more to do with the *Messenger* than previously suspected. A newly discovered letter reveals that, in addition to all of his other contributions, Tucker also wrote anonymous short pieces or filler for the *Messenger*; his anecdote in the February 1836 issue entitled "Gibbon and Fox" had been erroneously attributed to Poe. See my "Correcting the Poe Canon: Beverley Tucker's Anecdote on Gibbon and Fox," *Nineteenth-Century Literature* 48.1 (June 1993): 89–92. Rosenthal argues that Tucker "had very little to do with the *Messenger* during Poe's reign, even as a contributor" (Reexamination," 35), but the date of publication for "Gibbon and Fox" (February 1836) suggests otherwise. If we count the Paulding-Drayton review, Tucker contributed to the January, February, April, and May issues of the *Messenger*. Based on internal evidence, it is also possible that Tucker wrote an essay on "The Classics" for the March 1836 issue of the *Messenger* (221–36).

3. Tucker to Duff Green, 20 April 1836, Duff Green Papers, Library of Congress. Typescript in Noma Lee Goodwin, "The Published Works of Nathaniel Beverley Tucker, 1784–1851," unpublished M.A. Thesis, Duke University, 1947, 212–15.

4. For sickbed scenes, compare "Slavery" (338) and "Blackstone" (230); on animal metaphors, compare "Slavery" (338) and *The Partisan Leader* (156); on northern meddling and southern defense, see "Slavery" (339) and "Blackstone" (228); on slavery as a positive good, see "Slavery" (339) and "Blackstone" (227); for appeals to Divine will, see "Slavery" (338) and "Effect" (330, 333); on the paradox of equality and difference, see "Slavery" (338) and "Effect" (330).

Tucker represented some of these arguments as his own unique or distinctive contributions to the proslavery position. In the Paulding-Drayton review, the author suggests that the beneficial "moral influence" of slavery has never been presented "by any writer, in as high relief as it deserves" (338). Tucker makes a similar claim in his "Essay on the Moral and Political Effect of the Relation between the Caucasian Master and the African Slave." After characterizing slavery as "that beautiful system of domestic harmony, which, more than any thing else, foreshadows the blissful state in which love is to be the only law," he adds: "They to whom these ideas are new may think they savor of paradox and extravagance. I am not aware that they have ever been publicly proclaimed by any one" (339).

These ideas may not be as unusual as Tucker claims, but they do lend weight to the more specific stylistic and ideological similarities. Significantly, some of the most striking correspondences are the ones between the Paulding-Drayton review and the novel that Tucker was in the midst of composing.

* * *

A survey of other works by Tucker reveals further correspondences in style and phrasing. The Paulding-Drayton review contains a short history of "the war against property" in England and France (337); in an essay on the commercial profession, Tucker likewise declares that "a war against property, in all its forms, has been openly proclaimed."[5] The author of the Paulding-Drayton review contends that "men are always passing, with fearful rapidity, between the extremes of fanaticism and irreligion" (337); in an 1835 review for the *Southern Literary Messenger*, Tucker remarks that at the commencement of the Restoration, the English people "wished no more" of Charles II than that he oppose "irreligion to fanaticism."[6]

Two other phrases, common in Tucker's writing and uncommon elsewhere, provide additional evidence. In many of his writings, Tucker raises an issue and then refrains from discussing it, presumably because he wants to keep to his central theme. Tucker generally avoids these potential digressions by saying "with that we have nothing to do."

* * *

The other phrase, common in Tucker and uncommon elsewhere, is "the march of mind." In December 1834, long before Poe had returned to Richmond, Tucker published "A Lecture on the Study of the Law" in the *Southern Literary Messenger*. Immediately following his piece there appears an anonymous article called "The March of Mind," which attacks, through irony and sarcasm, the prevalent faith

5. Tucker, "The Nature and Function of the Commercial Profession," 410. Tucker makes similar claims in "The Present State of Europe." There, he notes that "First and last, property is the real object of controversy in strife between the orders of society" (285); and that "Property, then, of old, as now, was at the bottom of all the revolutionary movements of England" (286).

6. Tucker, Review of "An Oration on the Life and Character of Gilbert Motier de Lafayette" by John Quincy Adams and "Eulogy on La Fayette" by Edward Everett, *Southern Literary Messenger* 1 (February 1835): 309.

in social and scientific progress.[7] Tucker, likewise doubtful of all theo-
ries of human perfectibility, later made extensive use of the expression;
to indicate his own skepticism toward progress, he generally put the
phrase in quotations or italics.

* * *

Combine all of the internal stylistic and ideological evidence with the
1836 letter acknowledging his article on "Slavery," and the case for
Tucker's authorship is incontrovertible. What Poe said about the
novel *George Balcombe* must also be said here, for the author of the
Paulding-Drayton review "thinks, speaks, and acts, as no person . . .
but Judge Beverley Tucker, ever precisely thought, spoke, or acted be-
fore" (*ER*, 979).

III. Poe and Slavery Reconsidered

The resilience of the misattribution raises a number of important is-
sues, not only about Poe's racism, but also about the peculiar function
that the concept of racism plays in critical discourse today. As noted
above, some critics tend to identify racism as a collection of proslavery
assumptions held primarily by antebellum Southerners. More recently,
critics have emphasized the similarities between antebellum texts and
current political struggles, but the discourse on race and literature con-
tinues to suffer from several limitations. Due in part to the continuing
urgency of the issue, many neglect the historical context of race and in-
stead resort to moralizing apologies, blanket denunciations, or full-
blown jeremiads. These approaches, however, present fewer difficulties
than the pervasive view of racism as a private sin or psychological mal-
ady rather than a longstanding, systemic condition perpetuated by
powerful political and economic forces. In keeping with this personal-
izing tendency, most interpretations of Poe's racism share some com-
mon assumptions: that he chose his racial attitudes freely or at least
knowingly; that his attitudes could be expressed without constraint;
and, by extension, that his expressions constitute a "true" record of his
thoughts or feelings. These assumptions are open to attack from many
theoretical positions, but I would like to proceed with a more basic in-
vestigation of the scene of literary creation. Aside from specifying the
social determinations of racism, this investigation should help to clarify
one of the most neglected issues in all of Poe criticism, namely the po-
litical and economic constraints on his writing.

In order to understand these constraints, it is necessary to recall
Poe's predicament as editor or editorial assistant for the *Southern Lit-
erary Messenger*. Since this was also Poe's first full-time editorial job, it
cast a powerful shadow over his entire career in the industry of letters.
Thomas Willis White, proprietor of the *Messenger*, conceived of his
magazine as both a catalyst and beneficiary of a mass literary market

7. "The March of Mind," signed "V." (Lynchburg, 30 October 1834), *Southern Literary Mes-
senger* 1 (December 1834): 154–56. This connection is also noted by J. V. Ridgely in "The
Authorship of the 'Paulding-Drayton Review,' " *Poe Studies Association Newsletter* 20.2 (fall
1992): 2. [Reprinted on pp. 779–84 herein—Editor.]

in the South, but he also worked hard to cultivate a reputation as a national periodical. This reputation had little to do with actual demand, because the Lists of Payments * * * reveal, for the first time, that White relied almost entirely on the South for revenue. In 1838, the middle year of White's proprietorship, 90 percent of paid subscriptions were sent to slave states or areas, leaving only 10 percent for paid delivery in free states. The *Messenger* did not travel far even within the South, for of all paying subscribers, 48.9 percent lived in Virginia, with 18.2 percent residing in Richmond alone. Why, then, did White portray the *Messenger* as a national magazine? For one thing, he depended on the North for exchanges, contributions, and editorial favors, which helps to explains why the parsimonious proprietor mailed so many free copies to the offices of Northern newspapers and magazines.[8] Notices in the Northern press enhanced the *Messenger*'s prestige, and since many Southern readers subscribed to Northern journals, this was also an effective (albeit circuitous) way to reach the target audience. For these reasons, White seldom passed up an opportunity to drop intimations of the *Messenger*'s "national" following. During a steamer ride up the James River, for example, White managed to convince antislavery travel writer J. S. Buckingham that although the *Messenger* was published in Richmond, it was "read extensively in every State in the Union."

This marketing strategy sometimes left White straddling both sides of the Mason-Dixon Line. In the *Messenger* Prospectus, for example, White first affirms and then denies any sectional bias. On the one hand, he bemoans the lack of Southern periodicals:

> In all the Union, south of Washington, there are but two Literary periodicals! Northward of that city, there are probably at least twenty-five or thirty! Is this contrast justified by the wealth, the leisure, the native talent, or the actual literary taste, of the Southern people, compared with those of the Northern? No: for in wealth, talents, and taste, we may justly claim at least an *equality* with our brethren; and a domestic institution exclusively our own, beyond all doubt affords us, if we choose, twice the leisure for reading and writing, which they enjoy.[9]

Immediately after making this oblique and approving reference to slavery, the Prospectus disavows all sectional animosity:

> It was from a deep sense of this *local* want, that the word Southern was engrafted on the name of this periodical; and not with

8. Statistics are derived from the Lists of Payments for 1838 (the middle year of White's proprietorship). These show the economic predominance of the South, but since White exchanged with other magazines, and since he canvassed the entire nation for new subscribers, many free copies of the *Messenger* were distributed in the North. See the announcement on the July 1838 cover: "A large distribution of the current volume of the Messenger, having been made in every part of the Union, as specimens of the work, the Editor is unable to furnish new subscribers with the entire volume" ("Wanted Immediately," *Southern Literary Messenger* 4.7 [July 1838]: ii). In addition, White counted on Northern writers for copy and for favorable reviews.

9. This version of the Prospectus appeared on the cover of the December 1838 *Southern Literary Messenger*.

any design to nourish local prejudices, or to advocate supposed local interests. Far from any such thought, it is the Editor's fervent wish, to see the North and South bound endearingly together forever, in the silken bands of mutual kindness and affection. Far from meditating *hostility* to the north, he has already drawn, and he hopes hereafter to draw, much of his choicest matter thence; and happy indeed will he deem himself, should his pages, by making each region know the other better, contribute in any essential degree to dispell the lowering clouds that now threaten the peace of both, and to brighten and strengthen the sacred ties of fraternal love.

On the surface, these comments seem directed solely toward the North, but sectionalism—not to mention nullification—was also a highly charged issue within the South. In other words, White knew that many of his Southern readers were troubled by the growing sectional conflict, and he undoubtedly hoped to mollify these readers with a declaration of nationalist sentiments. The Prospectus accordingly exploits fears of Northern dominance, but at the same time it allows liberal or cosmopolitan readers to identify themselves with the image—if not the reality—of a progressive Southern intelligentsia.

To maintain and expand his share of the Southern market, White therefore had to please an audience that was much less homogeneous than generally assumed, at least in regard to political affairs. The *Messenger's* status as a literary magazine obviously made this task easier, for one of the preeminent ideological attributes of literature is its ability to present itself as a discourse free of ideology. Not surprisingly, White exploited the ostensible neutrality of literature in the Prospectus, claiming that "*Party Politics* and controversial *Theology*, as far as possible, are jealously excluded. They are sometimes so blended with discussions in literature or in moral science, otherwise unobjectionable, as to gain admittance for the sake of the more valuable matter to which they adhere; but whenever that happens, they are *incidental* only; not *primary*." White, however, had so little confidence in his literary judgments that he generally deferred to Poe, and when he could not count on Poe, he begged advice from trusted supporters like Beverley Tucker and Lucian Minor. Perhaps because of his uncertainty about literary quality, White often assumed the role of censor, and he paid special attention to inflammatory political issues which might give offense and thereby drive off subscribers.

<p style="text-align:center">* * *</p>

Articles in this Southern magazine did not uphold a single, consistent position on slavery; nor was the *Messenger* a forum for abolitionists and fire-eaters alike. Instead, the political spectrum of the magazine was bounded by gradualists or colonizationists at one extreme and positive-good secessionists at the other. White, moreover, only allowed these extremist positions to be defended by a few privileged contributors, and then only grudgingly. This policy, it should be emphasized, did not arise from any moral aversion toward slavery, but from White's belief that controversial issues were bad for literary business. As indicated

above, he had no desire "to jeopardize the fair prospects of the Messenger, by involving it in the strife of party politics."[1]

The strictures on "party politics" applied to Poe as well, especially since he was not a privileged contributor but merely a paid assistant to White. It was Poe's job, moreover, to implement and articulate the *Messenger's* editorial policies, and on one occasion he found himself explaining that "the pages of our Magazine are open, and have ever been, to the discussion of all general questions in Political Law, or Economy—never to questions of mere party."[2] Obviously, then, there were implicit and explicit constraints on what Poe could say about slavery. Even if he had been a ranting abolitionist or a rabid secessionist, he would never have been able to express these views in the *Southern Literary Messenger*. White's fear of political controversy called for positions that were less progressive than Minor's and less reactionary than Tucker's, and in fact all of Poe's remarks on slavery for the *Messenger* fall between these two extremes.

* * *

In Joseph Holt Ingraham's *The South-West. By a Yankee,* Poe found another Northerner who was willing to pardon the peculiar institution. In an account of his travels through Louisiana and Mississippi, Ingraham pauses on several occasions to excuse, if not to defend, Southern slavery. After passing a group of slaves purchased in Virginia and bound for a plantation outside New Orleans, Ingraham remarks that "they all appeared contented and happy, and highly elated at their sweet anticipations." "Say not," Ingraham continues, "that the slavery of the Louisiana negroes is a *bitter* draught." Such pronouncements inspired the following comment, which remains Poe's most explicit statement on slavery.[3]

> The "Yankee," in travelling Southward, has evidently laid aside the general prejudices of a Yankee—and, viewing the book of Professor Ingraham, as representing, in its very liberal opinions, those of a great majority of well educated Northern gentlemen, we are inclined to believe it will render essential services in the way of smoothing down a vast deal of jealousy and misconception. The traveller from the North has evinced no disposition to look with a jaundiced eye upon the South—to pervert its misfortunes into crimes—or distort its necessities into sins of volition. He has spoken of slavery as he found it—and it is almost needless to say that he found it a very different thing from the paintings he had seen of it in red ochre. He has discovered, in a word, that while the *physical* condition of the slave is *not* what it has been represented, the slave himself is utterly incapable to feel the *moral* galling of his chain.[4]

1. *Richmond Enquirer,* 22 May 1835.
2. Poe, "Editorial: Right of Instruction," *Southern Literary Messenger* 2 (June 1836): 445.
3. This review, here attributed to Poe, does not appear in the Harrison edition of Poe's *Works* or in *Essays and Reviews*; authenticity of Poe's reviews is a matter of ongoing debate—e.g., the authorship of the Paulding-Drake review; see the article by J. V. Ridgely mentioned on p. 928, n. 6 [Editor].
4. Poe, review of Joseph H. Ingraham's *The South-West. By a Yankee. Southern Literary Messenger* 2 (January 1836): 122. The next sentence suggests that Poe had read (though he did

Poe here follows a double strategy. He obviously seeks to defend the South from Yankee "prejudices," but at the same time he attempts to "smooth down" the growing sectional divide by appealing to the liberal opinions of "the great majority of well educated Northern gentlemen." His position on slavery likewise seems directed toward a racist majority. Without advocating any specific policy, he first concedes the "misfortunes" of slavery and then assures his readers that these misfortunes cause little injury to the slaves themselves. In other words, Poe dodges the slavery question by shifting the argument to common ground—only in this case the common ground is racism.

* * *

The rest of Poe's reviews in the *Southern Literary Messenger* have little or nothing to add to these brief statements, indicating that he avoided taking a specific position on slavery and instead attempted to embrace an average racism that would appeal to a majority of subscribers. Despite this evidence, many critics nevertheless accuse Poe of sharing the views of the most extreme proslavery advocates. Kenneth Alan Hovey, for example, contends that Poe's social views "are essentially identical" to those expressed by Beverley Tucker in the Paulding-Drayton review ("Critical Provincialism," 347). Others identify Poe with the proslavery, anti-colonization position of Thomas Dew, political economist and President of the College of William and Mary. Joan Dayan notes that Poe corresponded with Dew and wrote the introduction to his "Address" for the *Southern Literary Messenger*.[5] John Carlos Rowe refers to Poe's "undisputed admiration" for Dew, and Dana Nelson observes that Poe revealed his true sentiments "particularly in his stance on works by the noted Southern defender of slavery, Thomas R. Dew." All of these critics echo Bernard Rosenthal's claim that "Perhaps the most telling fact about Poe's position on slavery is his record of public admiration for Thomas R. Dew, the man most fully identified with the extreme and articulate slavery apologetics of Poe's day."[6]

Aside from insinuating guilt by association, this position rests upon

not review) Paulding's *Slavery in the United States*: "Indeed, we strongly agree with a distinguished Northern contemporary and friend, that the Professor's strict honesty, impartiality, and unprejudiced common sense, on the trying subject which has so long agitated our community, is the distinguishing and the most praiseworthy feature of his book." Paulding—the Northern contemporary and friend—quotes extensively from Ingraham. The longest excerpt (*Slavery in the United States*, 221–26) is immediately followed by a passage discussing the "*galling bonds*" of slavery (227), which probably inspired Poe's phrase about "the *moral* galling of his chain." In another passage echoed by Poe, Paulding refers to "Professor Ingraham" as "the candid and intelligent author of 'The South West' " (293), Poe's reference to "galling chains," it should be noted, puts him more in line with those who depicted slavery as a necessary evil than those—Tucker included—who defended slavery as a positive good.

5. "Romance and Race," 96. Dayan insinuates that Poe is guilty by association. She does not, of course, insinuate that Poe was an abolitionist because he corresponded with Lowell and Longfellow, or because he favorably reviewed the work of Lydia Maria Child. In addition, Dayan identifies Dew as author of *Vindication of Perpetual Slavery*, a book that—if one by that title even exists—no one else attributes to Dew. Dew actually wrote an essay called "Abolition of Negro Slavery," *American Quarterly Review* 12 (1832): 189–265; this was later expanded and published by Thomas W. White as the *Review of the Debate in the Virginia legislature of 1831–1832* (Richmond: T. W. White, 1832), and subsequently reprinted many times, most notably in a collection called *The Pro-slavery Argument* (Charleston: Walker, Richards, & Co., 1852).

6. Rowe, "Poe, Antebellum Slavery, and Modern Criticism," 119–20; Nelson, *The Word in Black and White*, 91; Rosenthal, "Reexamination," 30.

a fundamental misconception of Poe's work and work-related constraints at the *Messenger*. Thomas Dew was an important supporter of the magazine, for in addition to contributing articles directly, he was also in a position to influence many other subscribers and potential subscribers. And since he was president of the College of William and Mary, the *Messenger* could not offend Dew without imperiling the substantial patronage of college faculty, students, and alumni. Even if Poe had wanted to express disapproval of Dew, White would never have permitted it. Moreover, the particular text upon which this whole argument rests was originally composed not by Poe but by Dew himself, a fact overlooked by nearly everyone. The text in question is Poe's October 1836 review of Dew's welcoming address to the entering class. In order to write the review, Poe asked Dew for a copy of the address (published in the next issue of the *Messenger*) and for general information about the college. Dew responded with what we would today call a press release, and Poe merely revised it for his review. Dew's letter was reprinted in the standard edition of Poe's works, and it is a simple matter to identify the blatant similarities between Poe's review and Dew's press release. In a 1941 dissertation on the canon of Poe's critical works, which Rosenthal explicitly cites, William Hull in fact demonstrates that the six basic points in Poe's review are all derived, nearly verbatim, from the letter by Dew. * * * Rosenthal claims that Hull's dissertation "gives meticulous evidence establishing Poe's authorship" of the review in question, but Hull in fact gives meticulous evidence which confounds the very concept of authorship by demonstrating Poe's reliance on a text he couldn't refuse.[7]

Further arguments about Poe's racism have been based on his alleged review of John L. Carey's *Domestic Slavery*. The problem here concerns not authorship but existence, for the review was never published, and no manuscript copy has ever been located. Rosenthal and Nelson nevertheless contend that the review demonstrates Poe's "proslavery sympathies."[8] This claim merits special consideration, because it is one of the most egregious examples of the guilt-by-association strategy practiced by Rosenthal and theoretically justified by Rowe. Reports about the purported content of the review are based on Poe's June 1840 letter to Joseph E. Snodgrass, editor of the *American Museum* and later of the Baltimore *Saturday Visiter*. Snodgrass had sent Poe a copy of Carey's book so that he might review it for Burton's *Gentleman's Magazine*. In a letter to Snodgrass, Poe explained why the review did not appear.[9]

<p style="text-align:center">* * *</p>

7. Rosenthal continues the guilt-by-association argument when he identifies Poe with the brief extract of Dew's address that appeared in the October 1836 *Messenger*. Rosenthal fails to mention that Poe breaks off the extract in mid-sentence and thereby avoids printing a more explicit statement on slavery. In the three sentences following the extract (not quoted by Poe), Dew calls upon students to defend the slave South: "I hope—yes, I know, that at this moment a worthier and a nobler impulse actuates every one of you. And you must recollect too, that you are generally members of that portion of our confederacy whose domestic institutions have been called in question by the meddling spirit of the age. You are slaveholders, or the sons of slaveholders, and as such your duties and responsibilities are greatly increased." Thomas R. Dew, "An Address," *Southern Literary Messenger* 2 (November 1836): 765.
8. See Rosenthal, "Reexamination," 30; and Nelson, *The Word in Black and White*, 91.
9. Actually June 1842; reprinted on pp. 650–51 herein [Editor].

There are several reasons to question the sincerity of this letter. First, Poe was eager to tarnish the reputation of his former employer. * * * Second, Poe was caught up in a network of puffing and promotion that included both Carey and Snodgrass. * * * Poe may have felt that a disparaging review would appear ungrateful to both Carey and Snodgrass—editors whose support Poe still wanted. He would therefore have been inclined to express a favorable opinion of Carey's book, and since the review was not published, this approval—whether feigned or genuine—cost him nothing. This in turn raises the possibility that Poe never reviewed Carey's book at all. If Poe had written a review, Snodgrass would certainly have been willing to publish it in the *Visiter*; as indicated below, Snodgrass ultimately went on to publish several reviews of Carey's works. In other words, it is entirely possible that conclusions about Poe's racism are being drawn from a review that never existed, for Poe may have responded to Snodgrass's inquiry with a complete, yet plausible, fabrication.

Disregarding these considerations, Rosenthal nevertheless claims that "even a review *mildly* sympathetic to Carey's views would place one in a position of sympathy with the South's pro-slavery orthodoxy" ("Reexamination," 30). Aside from its scanty foundation in fact, this argument suffers from two additional weaknesses which are characteristic of regionalist reasoning. First, it collapses the differences between a union-loving colonizationist like Carey and a positive-good secessionist like Tucker.

* * *

Second and most importantly, images of a monolithic South falsify the true political terrain of the region. We have already seen some of the ideological dissension and diversity that characterized the *Messenger* in the 1830s; such diversity was even more pronounced in border states such as Maryland.

* * *

In 1845, Poe had become one of the editors of the *Broadway Journal*. For the March 22 issue, he wrote an extremely favorable notice of the *Southern Literary Messenger*, claiming that under his editorship it had enjoyed "a success quite unparalleled in the history of our five dollar Magazines." The *Messenger's* subscribers, Poe continued, "are almost without exception the *élite*, both as regards wealth and intellectual culture, of the Southern aristocracy, and its corps of contributors are generally men who control the public opinion of the Southerners on *all* topics.[1] Poe's 1845 notice raised doubts about the political neutrality of both the *Messenger* and the *Broadway Journal*. It also aroused the anger of antislavery activists, who were disturbed to see such a notice in a paper that was supposedly friendly to their cause. * * * Briggs claimed to be "unqualifiedly opposed to slavery in every shape,[2] but despite constant prodding from his friend James

1. *Broadway Journal* 1 (March 22, 1845): 183.
2. Briggs to Lowell, 22 January 1845; quoted in Bette S. Weidman, "*The Broadway Journal* (2): A Casualty of Abolition Politics," *Bulletin of the New York Public Library* 73 (February 1969): 106.

Russell Lowell, he was unwilling to turn the *Broadway Journal* into an abolitionist paper. If the paper were to espouse such a position openly, reasoned Briggs, it would lose the very readers most in need of reform. * * * "I cannot afford to publish a radical reform paper, for I could get no readers if I did."[3]

* * *

After this period, Poe made only two conspicuous statements about slavery, and unfortunately the context of these statements has been universally neglected. The references to slavery appear in reviews of Longfellow and Lowell,[4] but in each case Poe made the remarks anonymously, or under cover of what we would today call plausible deniability. The first statement occurs in an unsigned review of Longfellow published in the April 1845 *Aristidean*. * * * The review begins by disparaging Longfellow's Boston supporters, a group identified as "the small coterie of abolitionists, transcendentalists, and fanatics in general," or more pointedly as "the knot of rogues and madmen." Then commences an attack on Longfellow's latest poetic works. Referring specifically to *Poems on Slavery*, the reviewer accuses Longfellow of pandering to "those negrophilic old ladies of the north" with "a shameless medley of the grossest misrepresentation." Noting how easily a Northern professor can "write verses instructing the southerners how to give up their all with a good grace," the reviewer charges that Longfellow has confused slavery in the South with the treatment of slaves in Cuba. Longfellow, the reviewer continues, has "no right to change the locality, and by insinuating a falsehood in lieu of a fact, charge his countrymen with barbarity."

* * * This review, however, must be used with caution, for it is evidently a collaborative production by Poe and Thomas Dunn English, editor of the *Aristidean*. Most passages seem to come directly from Poe, but there are enough inconsistencies to indicate the work of a second author. In all likelihood, Poe provided a rough draft, which English altered to suit his own designs.[5] This arrangement apparently satisfied both parties, for Poe wanted the piece to look as if it had been written by another hand. The Longfellow review contains many third-person references to "Mr. Poe," and in a subsequent notice of the *Aristidean*, Poe with some impudence attempts to maintain this illusion:

> Some of the papers are exceedingly good—precisely what Magazine papers should be—vigorous, terse, and independent. . . . There is a long review or rather running commentary on Longfellow's poems. It is, perhaps, a little coarse, but we are not disposed to call it unjust; although there are in it some opinions which, by implication, are attributed to ourselves individually, and with which we cannot altogether coincide.[6]

3. Briggs to Lowell, 19 March 1845 and 10 April 1845; quoted in Weidman, "*The Broadway Journal*," 108, 110.
4. Both are reprinted herein; see pp. 662ff. and 693ff. [Editor].
5. For a more conservative estimate of Poe's contribution to the review, see Dwight Thomas and David K. Jackson, *Poe Log*, 529.
6. "The Aristidean," *Broadway Journal* 1 (3 May 1845): 285.

It is therefore difficult to decide whether to blame Poe or English for such phrases as "negrophilic old ladies of the north."[7] But two points are clear. First, the defense of the South is presented as a reaction to a Northern attack, specifically an attack by a Boston gentleman who could—without financial risk—turn poetry into a vehicle for political criticism. Second, whether or not Poe "coincided" with the *Aristidean* review, he certainly recognized that it might arouse some outcry, and he accordingly sought to distance himself from any "horrifying because unprofitable doctrines."

Poe repeated this strategy in his 1849 attack on James Russell Lowell's A *Fable for Critics*. In a review written expressly for the *Southern Literary Messenger*, Poe denounces Lowell as "one of the most rabid of the Abolition fanatics." Posing as a guardian of Southern sensibility, he attempts to shield prospective readers from Lowell's "prejudices on the topic of slavery." "No Southerner," Poe warns, "who does not wish to be insulted, and at the same time revolted by a bigotry the most obstinately blind and deaf, should ever touch a volume by this author."

As with the Longfellow review, Poe intended this to be anonymous. On several occasions, the writer refers to "Mr. Poe" in the third person, and in his private correspondence, Poe stresses that he had the review published "editorially" (*Letters*, 2:449). For the first time in years, then, Poe was in a position to write anonymously for a Southern audience. But instead of unleashing a pent-up defense of slavery, Poe uses the opportunity to discuss the perils of fanaticism in general: "His fanaticism about slavery is a mere local outbreak of the same innate wrongheadedness which, if he owned slaves, would manifest itself in atrocious ill-treatment of them, with murder of any abolitionist who should endeavor to set them free. A fanatic of Mr. L's species, is simply a fanatic for the sake of fanaticism, and *must* be a fanatic in whatever circumstances you place him." In other words, fanaticism is a national problem which merely expresses itself differently in different regions. But as indicated in the succeeding paragraph, what most disturbs Poe is the power of fanaticism to aggravate the cultural division between North and South, for this effectively deprives Southern writers of access to the national literary market: "It is a fashion among Mr. Lowell's set to affect a belief that there is no such thing as Southern Literature. Northerners—people who have really nothing to speak of as men of letters,—are cited by the dozen . . . Other writers are barbarians and are satirized accordingly—if mentioned at all" (*ER*, 819–20). Even when writing anonymously, Poe found it easier to denounce abolitionism than to justify slavery, and when he did defend the South, he showed greater concern for Southern writers than for Southern institutions.

There are other stray references to race, ranging from a comment on African-American speech in his review of Sedgwick's *The Linwoods*

7. Kenneth Silverman speculates that English may be the author of the phrase because he spoke derogatorily of blacks on other occasions. See Silverman, *Edgar A. Poe* (New York: Harper Collins, 1991), pp. 254, 491. To my ear, however, the alliterative slur sounds like the work of Poe, and the rest of the review seems perfectly consistent with Poe's other critical writings.

to a matter-of-fact description of a slave uprising in his review of Bird's *Sheppard Lee*.[8] But given the vast bulk of his writings, these references are conspicuously few. Unable and unwilling to bear the risks of political speech, Poe succumbed to the pressures of a national literary market either by falling silent on controversial issues, or by searching for an average racism that could take the place of unprofitable doctrines about slavery. There were of course writers who rejected this strategy and profited nevertheless, but as G. R. Thompson has pointed out, Poe generally shied away from the literary sectionalism of such writers as Simms, Longfellow, and Harriet Beecher Stowe.[9] Of Poe's sixty-five tales, only two—"The Gold-Bug" and "A Tale of the Ragged Mountains"—are set in the South, and many of the rest seem to be set nowhere at all. Thompson attributes this antiregional stance to Poe's professionalism, but it should be noted that professional calculations are not necessarily honorable or just. For Poe, admission to the national literary market meant turning his back on the momentous political and social struggles of the day, except when such struggles impinged directly upon the material interests of a commercial writer. So if there is little cause to denounce Poe for his statements on slavery, there is likewise no reason to praise him for his professional silence. Patriotism may be the *last* refuge of scoundrels, but professionalism is oftentimes the first.

IV. Conclusion: The Wages of Nationalism

All of this suggests that Poe, far from being "the most blatant racist among the American romantics," was arguably among the most discreet. * * *

* * * Curiously, Poe's most virulent pronouncements on race are contained in *The Narrative of Arthur Gordon Pym*, a book more or less consciously written for a national audience. The book was published by the New York firm of Harper & Brothers in 1838. Two years prior to publication, James Kirke Paulding had quietly urged Poe to "lower himself a little to the ordinary comprehension of the generality of readers." In another letter, Harper & Brothers advised Poe that "Readers in this country have a decided and strong preference for works (especially fiction) in which a single and connected story occupies the whole volume." In response to this advice about the national literary market, Poe composed what would be his only novel; at the end of this novel, Poe describes the black natives of Tsalal as "the most wicked, hypocritical, vindictive, bloodthirsty, and altogether fiendish race of men upon the face of the globe." Modern critics have pointed to the

8. Poe's review of *The Linwoods* appeared in the *Southern Literary Messenger* 1 (December 1835); 57–59; rpt. in *Complete Works*, 8:94–101. His review of Robert Montgomery Bird's *Sheppard Lee* appeared in the *Southern Literary Messenger* 2 (September 1836): 662–67; rpt. in *ER*, 389–403.

9. Thompson argues that Poe lacked the "regionalist sentiment" of other Southern writers ("Poe and the Writers of the Old South," 268–69). Stowe's *Uncle Tom's Cabin* was of course a phenomenal success, but a Boston publisher, accepting the logic of political and regional neutrality, turned it down because "it would not sell in the South" (William Charvat, *The Profession of Authorship in America 1800–1870*, 301).

political implications of this, but in the rush to denounce Poe's racism, the peculiar formal and historical determinants of *Pym* have been obscured. First, Poe clearly borrowed from widely circulated travel narratives of Africa and the South Seas, many of which contain similar denunciations of the ignorance and backwardness of "barbarous" nonwestern peoples, including the dark-skinned aborigines of Australia, New Zealand, and Tasmania. Second, the natives on Tsalal take on an allegorical quality because of their extreme blackness, a blackness that includes not only the eyes and teeth of the natives, but much of the natural environment as well. As the fictitious "editor" emphasizes, "Nothing *white* was to be found at Tsalal, and nothing otherwise in the subsequent voyage to the region beyond." Third, there is no obvious link between this racist representation and a specific position on slavery, especially since abolitionists and colonizationists were themselves prone to accept and repeat racist stereotypes.

These points are crucial to understanding why Poe, whose personal and editorial writings seem relatively muted on the issue of slavery, should make what now appears as his most blatant statement in the most public—and the most national—forum he could find. * * * The lurid description of Tsalal therefore demonstrates the difference between a racist representation—especially one conforming to the orders of average racism—and a statement calling for a specific action on slavery. But this is only part of the story. As suggested at the start of this chapter, average racism arose less from an essential American bigotry than from the historically specific conjunction of an emerging national culture and an emerging national market. In this regard the example of Poe is particularly revealing, for his attempt to construct or exploit an average racism was in many ways a deliberate strategy designed to unify sections divided by slavery. Antebellum nationalism, far from being a simple expression of solidarity, should instead be seen as a product of the growing antagonism between North and South, and Poe's literary nationalism should likewise be understood as an attempt to escape from the realm of unprofitable political strife into the more lucrative *neutral territory* of mass culture.

* * *

[Whalen at this point discusses "A Predicament" and "The Gold-Bug" as the only tales containing extensive depictions of African Americans.]

Poe's calculating approach to the mass literary market complicates the political meaning of *Pym* and his other fictional writings. Based upon what we know of these calculations, it is misguided to conceive of his racism as an attitude or sentiment somehow separable from the constraints and pressures of the prevailing modes of production, especially in a nation that suffered antagonistic modes to coexist until the advent of civil war. By extension, it is misguided to conceive of literary production as occurring in some fantastic realm of freedom apart from the ideological and material forces that characterize a social formation. If nothing else, the recognition of these forces makes it possible to move beyond interpretations that are informed by hindsight but not

by history. For example, the paucity of comments about race in Poe's private correspondence, along with the offhanded disparagement of abolitionist poets in his anonymous critical reviews, should cast doubt on interpretations of the final chapters of *Pym* as divine retribution for "the known offense of slavery" (Dayan, "Romance and Race," 109). I must also question Dayan's claim that "Poe remained haunted, as did Jefferson, by the terrible disjunction between the ideology of slavery . . . and the concrete realities of mutilation, torture, and violation" (102). If anything, Poe seems to have conjured up the haunting portrait of blackness as a means of appealing to multiple segments of the white literary audience. And as soon as the audience is described in these terms, it becomes clear that his racist representations have less to do with black-white relations than with the way white people relate to each other.

The way white people relate to each other: this is what haunts Poe, this is what motivates his fantasies of a neutral culture, and this, to an extent seldom acknowledged, is what burdens the current critical discourse on race. What matters about Poe is not so much his reticence on slavery, nor even his use of racist stereotypes—which are as infrequent as they are offhanded. Instead, the case of Poe matters because his utterances and silences were both part of a coherent strategy to expel politics from the literary commodity. This is why attempts to read politics back into Poe's work have proven so vexing. To make this task easier, critics still turn to the Paulding-Drayton review as the smoking gun that will convict Poe once and for all. When this doesn't succeed, blame is sometimes placed upon conspiratorial Poe scholars, who are seen as withholding or covering up incriminating evidence.[1]

* * * I do hope that I have demonstrated two things: First, although Poe left behind a clear trail of what might be called circumstantial racism, he avoided—by habit and design—the kind of political speech practiced by fire-breathing secessionists like Beverly Tucker and by antislavery moralists like James E. Heath (both of whom Poe knew during his connection with the *Southern Literary Messenger*). From this follows the second point, namely that the "depoliticized" Poe is only partly the work of his interpreters. Observing the dictates of the "cash rule," Poe sometimes played to the average racism of the national audience, but more frequently he avoided altogether those "horrifying because unprofitable doctrines" about slavery. In other words, Poe's work was not simply depoliticized by modern critics; it was in many ways depoliticized from the start. This, I would suggest, must be the basis for all future political criticism of Poe. Paradoxically, this insight also justifies the ideological interpretations of Poe that I have been attacking throughout this chapter. Though there may be flaws in the evidence and assumptions of critics such as Rosenthal, Nelson, and

1. John Carlos Rowe, for example, accuses Poe critics of repressing "the subtle complicity of literary Modernism with racist ideology," and Dana Nelson complains of "the recent trend to sweep Poe's politics under the rug" (Rowe, 136; Nelson, *The Word in Black and White*, 91). Curiously, Rowe himself is one of the critics Nelson accuses of depoliticizing Poe, although she bases her argument on *Through the Custom House*, published ten years before "Poe, Antebellum Slavery, and Modern Criticism."

Rowe, the case of Poe nevertheless demonstrates the importance of race in determining what literature is—the form and meaning of its sentences, the form and meaning of its silences.

Taken in context, the example of Poe reveals the error of viewing racism as a private demon to be exorcised through simple denunciation, or as a Southern disease to be eradicated through a liberal dose of enlightenment. All too frequently, such views lead to the creation of an interpretive procedure that merely diagnoses texts as being racism-positive or racism-negative. When the texts themselves resist such a diagnosis, critics sometimes resort to *ad hominem* arguments, which resolve textual ambiguity by invoking the alleged beliefs of the alleged author. Given the divergent political agendas of such writers as Tucker, Emerson, and even Lydia Maria Child, it is at least necessary to consider the motives and pressures determining their respective representations of race. And given the peculiar circumstances surrounding Poe, it is also worthwhile to recall that the relation between literature and politics is itself historically determined—so much so that a strategy originally designed to avoid controversy now provokes it. To resolve the current tangle of error and simplifi-cation, it is necessary to step back from the purity of ahistorical criticism and to delve into the complexities of a painful and uncompleted past. * * *

JOHN T. IRWIN

Detective Fiction as High Art: Lacan, Derrida, and Johnson on "The Purloined Letter"†

Let me start with a simple-minded question: How does one write analytic detective fiction as high art when the genre's central narrative mechanism seems to discourage the unlimited rereading associated with serious writing? That is, if the point of an analytic detective story is the deductive solution of a mystery, how does the writer keep that solution from exhausting the reader's interest in the story? How does he write a work that can be reread by people other than those with poor memories? I use the term *analytic detective fiction* here to distinguish the genre invented by Poe in the Dupin tales of the 1840s from stories whose main character is a detective but whose main concern is not analysis but adventure, stories whose true genre is less detective fiction than the quest romance, as one of the masters of the adventure mode, Raymond Chandler, implicitly acknowledged when he gave the name Mallory to an early prototype of his detective Philip Marlowe. For Chandler, the private investigator represents a plausible form of modern knight-errant. In "The Simple Art of Murder" he says that the detective story is the detective's "adventure in search of a hidden

† From *The Mystery to a Solution: Poe, Borges, and the Analytic Detective Story* (Baltimore: Johns Hopkins University Press, 1994), pp. 1–13. Reprinted by permission of the Johns Hopkins University Press and the author.

truth, and it would be no adventure if it did not happen to a man fit for adventure."[1] The emphasis in Chandler's remarks, as in his fiction, is on the detective's character and his adventures, with the revelation of a hidden truth simply serving as a device to illuminate the former and motivate the latter. But in the analytic detective story the situation is different. As a character, Dupin is as thin as the paper he's printed on, and his adventures amount to little more than reading newspaper accounts of the crime and talking with the prefect of police and the narrator in the privacy of his apartment.

What gives the analytic detective genre its special appeal is that quality the Goncourt brothers noted on first reading Poe. In an 1856 journal entry they described Poe's stories as "a new literary world" bearing "signs of the literature of the twentieth century—love giving place to deductions . . . the interest of the story moved from the heart to the head . . . from the drama to the solution."[2] Precisely because it is a genre that grows out of an interest in deductions and solutions rather than in love and drama, the analytic detective story shows little interest in character, managing at best to produce caricatures—monsters of idiosyncrasy from Holmes to Poirot. In its purest form it puts all its eggs in the basket of plot, and a specialized kind of plot at that. The problem is that this basket seems to be one that can be tipped out in a single reading.

Related to this difficulty is another. If the writer does his work properly, if he succeeds in building up a sense of the mysterious, of some dark secret or intricately knotted problem, then he has to face the fact that there exists no hidden truth or guilty knowledge whose revelation will not seem anticlimactic compared to an antecedent sense of mystery and the infinite speculative possibilities it permits. Borges, a contemporary master of the analytic detective genre, explicitly acknowledges this difficulty in his story "Ibn Hakkan al-Bokhari, Dead in His Labyrinth." He notes that one of his characters, "steeped in detective stories, thought that the solution of a mystery is always less impressive than the mystery itself. Mystery has something of the supernatural about it, and even of the divine; its solution, however, is always tainted by sleight of hand."[3] In a similar vein, Borges praises Chesterton's detective stories because "Chesterton always performs the tour de force of proposing a supernatural explanation and then replacing it, losing nothing, with another one from this world," a procedure that provides, in Borges's terms, a rational solution at the same time that it conserves a suprarational aura of mystery.[4] But, as Borges notes, the case is different with Poe who, though writing "stories of

1. Raymond Chandler, "The Simple Art of Murder," in *Detective Fiction: Crime and Compromise*, ed. Dick Allen and David Chacko (New York: Harcourt Brace Jovanovich, 1974), 398 [Irwin's note]. Unless otherwise indicated, all notes to this selection are Irwin's [Editor].
2. Edgar Allan Poe, *Collected Works of Edgar Allan Poe*, 3 vols., ed. Thomas Ollive Mabbott (Cambridge: Harvard University Press, 1969–78), 2:521n. All subsequent quotations from Poe's fiction and poetry are taken from this edition unless otherwise noted.
3. Jorge Luis Borges, "Ibn Hakkan al-Bokhari, Dead in His Labyrinth," in *The Aleph and Other Stories, 1933–1969*, trans. and ed. Norman Thomas di Giovanni (New York: Dutton, 1978), 123. Subsequent citations of this volume in text as *A*.
4. Jorge Luis Borges, "Chesterton and the Labyrinths of the Detective Story," in *Borges: A Reader*, ed. Emir Rodríguez Monegal and Alastair Reid (New York: Dutton, 1981), 72–73. Subsequent citations of this volume in text as *BR*.

pure, fantastic horror" as well as detective stories, "never combined the two genres" (*BR*, 89). Poe "never invoked the help of the sedentary French gentleman Auguste Dupin . . . to determine the precise crime of 'The Man of the Crowd' " (*BR*, 89).

But if in the analytic detective story the solution is always in some sense an anticlimax that in dissipating the mystery exhausts the story's interest for us, an interest in speculative reasoning that the mystery empowers, how does one write this kind of story as a serious (i.e., rereadable) literary form? How does one both present the analytic solution of a mystery and at the same time conserve the sense of the mysterious on which analysis thrives?

Obviously, if I didn't consider Poe's Dupin stories to be, on the one hand, archetypes of analytic detective fiction, and on the other, serious literary works that demand and repay rereading, there would be no sense in my evoking at this length the apparent incompatibility of these modes and thus the writer's problem in reconciling them. All of which brings me to the task of uncrumpling that much-crumpled thing, "The Purloined Letter," in order to consider the way that this problem of a mystery with a repeatable solution, a solution that conserves (because it endlessly re-figures) the sense of the mysterious, lies at the very origin of the genre.

My approach to "The Purloined Letter" will be along what has become in recent years a well-worn path. I want to look briefly at three readings of the story that form a cumulative series of interpretations, each successive reading commenting both on the story and on the previous reading(s) in the series. They are Jacques Lacan's "Seminar on 'The Purloined Letter' " (1957), Jacques Derrida's "The Purveyor of Truth" (1975), and Barbara Johnson's "The Frame of Reference: Poe, Lacan, Derrida" (1978). Each of these essays presents a lengthy, complex argument in which "The Purloined Letter" is treated as a pretext, read as a parable of the act of analysis. However, I am not so much interested here in following the convolutions of their individual arguments as in isolating a thread that runs through all three, a clue to conduct us through labyrinthine passages. And that thread is the position that each essay takes on what we might call the numerical/geometrical structure of the story.

Let us begin with Lacan. He says that the story consists of "two scenes, the first of which we shall straightway designate the primal scene, and by no means inadvertently, since the second may be considered its repetition."[5] The first, or primal, scene takes place in "the royal *boudoir*" (41), the second scene in "the Minister's office" (42). And according to Lacan, each of these scenes has a triangular structure, composed of "three logical moments" (43) "structuring three glances, borne by three subjects, incarnated each time by different characters":

5. Jacques Lacan, "Seminar on 'The Purloined Letter,' " trans. Jeffrey Mehlman, *Yale French Studies* 48 (1972): 41. Unless otherwise noted, all subsequent quotations from the "Seminar on 'The Purloined Letter' " are taken from this edition.

The first is a glance that sees nothing: the King and the police.

The second, a glance which sees that the first sees nothing and deludes itself as to the secrecy of what it hides: the Queen, then the Minister.

The third sees that the first two glances leave what should be hidden exposed to whomever would seize it: the Minister, and finally Dupin. (44)

Thus in the royal boudoir the king doesn't see the incriminating letter which the queen in her haste has hidden in the open, leaving it with its address uppermost in plain sight on a table; and the queen, seeing that the king doesn't see the letter, mistakes his blindness for the letter's concealment, thus leaving herself vulnerable to the minister who sees both the king's glance and the queen's and realizes that the letter can be seized before the queen's very eyes precisely because she dare not do anything to attract the king's attention to it.

Similarly, in the second scene at the minister's residence, the letter, having been turned inside out and readdressed in a female hand, is once again hidden in plain sight in a card rack on the mantelpiece. And this time the police, who have searched the minister's quarters repeatedly without noticing the letter, represent that first glance that sees nothing; while the minister, who mistakes the blindness of the police for the concealment of the letter, represents the second glance, and Dupin represents the third glance that sees what the first two miss, that the letter hidden in the open is his for the taking. The figure who participates in both these triangular scenes is the minister, and his shifting from the position of the third glance in the initial scene to that of the second glance in its repetition exhibits the special vulnerability to self-delusion, to a blind spot, which the possession of the letter conveys.

In considering Derrida's critique of this reading in his essay "The Purveyor of Truth," bear in mind that Derrida is motivated less by an interest in Poe or "The Purloined Letter" than by a desire to score points off Lacan. As Johnson points out, Derrida, in a lengthy footnote in his book *Positions*, sketches out the argument that will become "The Purveyor of Truth" and in this note he explicitly refers to Lacan's multiple "*acts of aggression*" against him since the publication of *De la grammatologie* in *Critique* in 1965.[6] Thus Derrida takes the case of "The Purloined Letter" for one of the same reasons Dupin did—the minister once did Dupin "an evil turn" (3:993) at Vienna, and Dupin sees the affair of the letter as an opportunity to get even. The wit of Derrida's essay lies in the way that it uses Lacan's reading of "The Purloined Letter" against itself, for if Lacan believes that with his interpretation of the story he has gained possession of Poe's "Purloined Letter," has made its meaning his own, then Derrida will show him that the possession of the letter, as Lacan himself pointed out, brings with it a blind spot. In his essay Derrida sets out to repeat the en-

6. Barbara Johnson, "The Frame of Reference: Poe, Lacan, Derrida," in *The Critical Difference* (Baltimore: Johns Hopkins University Press, 1980), 118. All subsequent quotations from Johnson are taken from this edition.

counter between Dupin and the minister with himself in the role of Dupin and Lacan in the role of the minister.

Derrida attacks Lacan's reading of the story on a variety of points, but the one that concerns us is Lacan's notion of the triangular structure of each of the tale's two scenes. Derrida agrees that the story consists of two scenes, but not the two on which Lacan focuses. He points out that the scene in the royal boudoir and the subsequent one at the minister's residence are two narrated scenes within the framing artifice of the story, but that the story itself consists of two scenes of narration—the first being the prefect's initial visit to Dupin during which the prefect recounts the events in the royal boudoir, and the second the prefect's subsequent visit during which Dupin recounts the events at the minister's residence. While the narrators of the *two narrated scenes* in the royal boudoir and at the minister's residence are respectively the prefect and Dupin, the narrator of the *two scenes of narration* at Dupin's lodgings is Dupin's unnamed companion. Thus, according to Derrida, Lacan reduces the four-sided structure of the scene of narration—what Derrida calls "the scene of writing"—to the three-sided structure of the narrated scene "by overlooking the narrator's position, the narrator's involvement in the content of what he seems to be recounting.[7] In ignoring the presence of the narrator of "The Purloined Letter," Lacan cuts "a fourth side" out of the narrated figure "to leave merely triangles" (54). And he does this, says Derrida, precisely because as a psychoanalyst Lacan projects upon Poe's story the structure of the Oedipal triangle in his desire to read "The Purloined Letter" as an allegory of psychoanalysis or an *"allegory of the signifier"* (Johnson, 115).

Since in his critique of Lacan's interpretation of "The Purloined Letter" Derrida aims to get even with him by being "one up," and since Lacan in his reading of the numerical structure of the tale has already played the numbers one, two, and three (the tale is composed of two scenes, the second of which, by repeating the triangular structure of the first, creates a sameness or oneness between the two), then being one up means playing the next open number (four), hence Derrida's contention that the structure of the scenes is not triangular but quadrangular. However, whether Derrida arrives at this quadrangular structure by adding one to three or by doubling two is a problematic point, a point on which Johnson focuses in her critique of Lacan's and Derrida's readings of the tale.

As Johnson notes, Derrida objects to the triangular configuration that Lacan sees in the repeated scenes because this structure, derived from the Oedipal triangle, represents in Derrida's opinion a characteristic psychoanalytic attempt to dismiss or absorb the uncanny effects of doubling, a doubling Derrida maintains is everywhere present in the tale. Doubling tends, of course, to be a standard element of the analytic detective story, in that the usual method of apprehending

7. Jacques Derrida, "The Purveyor of Truth," trans. W. Domingo, J. Hulbert, M. Ron, and M.-R. Logan, *Yale French Studies* 52 (1975): 100. All subsequent quotations from "The Purveyor of Truth" are taken from this edition.

the criminal involves the detective's doubling the criminal's thought processes so as to anticipate his next move and end up one jump ahead of him. And the number associated with doubling is usually four rather than two, for what we refer to as doubling is almost always splitting and doubling. Which is to say, the figure of the double externally duplicates an internal division in the protagonist's self (but with the master/slave polarity of that division characteristically reversed), so that doubling tends to be a structure of four halves problematically balanced across the inner/outer limit of the self rather than a structure of two separate, opposing wholes. Thus in the first Dupin story, "The Murders in the Rue Morgue," the narrator says that while observing Dupin in the exercise of his "peculiar analytic ability" (2:533), he entertained "the fancy of a double Dupin—the creative and the resolvent" in accordance with "the old philosophy of the Bi-Part Soul" (2:533). And in "The Purloined Letter" the minister, as both poet and mathematician, is represented as having this same dual intellectual power. In matching wits with the minister, Dupin first doubles his opponent's thought processes—a mental operation that Dupin illustrates by telling the story of the schoolboy who always won at the game of even and odd—and he then replays, in effect temporally doubles, the scene in which the minister originally seized the letter, but with himself now in the minister's role, thus shifting the minister into the role played by the queen in the original event and evoking the destabilizing reversal-into-the-opposite inherent in doubling.

As Johnson notes, Derrida thinks that

> the problem with psychoanalytical triangularity . . . is not that it contains the wrong number of terms, but that it presupposes the possibility of a successful dialectical mediation and harmonious normalization, or *Aufhebung*, of desire. The three terms in the Oedipal triad enter into an opposition whose resolution resembles the synthetic moment of a Hegelian dialectic. (122)

But that synthetic moment, that successful dialectical mediation of desire is precisely what the destabilizing effect of doubling constantly subverts, for in the Oedipal triangle each of the three positions functions as one pole of a mutually constitutive opposition with one of the other positions and thus each position is subject to being reversed into its opposite. There exists in the Oedipal triangle, then, no privileged position that is above or outside the uncanny effects of doubling, no exempt, objective position from which to mediate or regularize the subjective interaction of the other two.

As with Derrida's reading of Lacan, the wit of Johnson's reading of Derrida lies in the way that she doubles Derrida's own insights back upon themselves to make them problematic. Thus in dealing with Derrida's attempt to be one up on Lacan by playing the number four to Lacan's three, Johnson assimilates their opposed readings of the tale's numerical structure to the game of even and odd. Derrida opts for a quadrangular structure (he plays the even number four) in order to evoke the uncanniness, the oddness of doubling, while Lacan opts

for a triangular structure by playing the odd number three, in order to enforce the regularizing or normalizing effect of the dialectical triad. In this game of even and odd, Derrida and Lacan end up as reciprocal opposites, as specular doubles of one another: Derrida asserts the oddness of evenness, while Lacan affirms the evenness of oddness. Given the destabilizing reversal-into-the-opposite inherent in doubling, Johnson sees the opposition between Derrida's and Lacan's interpretations as an "oscillation" between the former's "unequivocal statements of undecidability" and the latter's "ambiguous assertions of decidability" (146).

As to Johnson's own position on "The Purloined Letter," her reading of Lacan and Derrida is meant to free her from having to take a position on the tale's numerical structure, or more exactly, to free her from having to take a *numerical* position on that structure. Johnson's strategy is to call into question the whole concern with numbers. At one point she asks, "But can what is at stake here really be reduced to a mere numbers game?" (121), and a bit later she answers, "Clearly, in these questions, the very notion of a number becomes problematic, and the argument on the basis of numbers can no longer be read literally" (121). As Johnson sees it, taking a position on the numerical structure of the tale means, for Lacan and Derrida, taking a numerical position, choosing a number, but that means playing the game of even and odd, the game of trying to be one up on a specular, antithetical double. And playing that game means endlessly repeating the structure of "The Purloined Letter" in which being one up inevitably leads to being one down. For if the structure created by the repeated scenes in the tale involves doubling the thought processes of one's opponent in order to use his own methods against him—as Dupin does with the minister, as Derrida does with Lacan, and as Johnson does with Derrida—then the very method by which one outwits one's opponent is the same method that will be used against oneself by the next player in the game, the next interpreter in the series, in order to leave the preceding interpreter one down.

Is it possible, then, to interpret "The Purloined Letter" without duplicating in the interpretive act that reversal-into-the-opposite inherent in the mechanism of seizing the letter as it is described in the tale? Is it possible to generate an insight without a blind spot, without a flaw that allows the insight subsequently to be turned against itself? Clearly, the desire for such an invulnerable insight is at work in Johnson's essay and accounts for the disconcerting level of self-consciousness she maintains regarding her own methodological stance, her own critical assumptions. For Johnson the refusal to take a numerical position on the structure of the tale, to play the next open number (five), for example, is an effort to avoid the game of trying to be one up by adding one to the opponent's numerical position, as Derrida does in playing the number four to Lacan's three; for that game will simply turn into an oscillation between even and odd running to infinity. But is it possible for Johnson to avoid becoming involved in this numbers game simply by refusing to choose a specific number

with which to characterize the geometrical/numerical structure of the tale? Doesn't the very form of her essay—as a critique of Derrida's critique of Lacan's reading of "The Purloined Letter"—involve her in the numbers game? In situating her essay as the third of three critical readings following those of Lacan and Derrida, Johnson places herself in that third position which, in the structure governing the wandering of the purloined letter, is the position of maximum insight, but also the position in which the observer is subject to mistaking his insight concerning the subjective interaction of the other two glances for an objective viewpoint above such interaction. Indeed, how are we to describe the relationship between Johnson's interpretation and those of Lacan and Derrida? Are they linked in a triangular structure in which Lacan and Derrida face off as antithetical doubles, while Johnson, by refusing to become involved in the game of even and odd, occupies a position of "successful dialectical mediation" above them, a Hegelian synthesis of their positions? Or are they involved in a quadrangular structure in which Lacan and Derrida are reciprocal halves of one pole of a mutually constitutive opposition (i.e., the pole of trying to be one up on a specular double), while Johnson occupies the other pole of this opposition by doubling back Lacan's and Derrida's methods against them in order to avoid this game of one up? Johnson's final comment on her own methodology invokes the image of Derrida's quadrangular frame: "My own theoretical 'frame of reference' is precisely, to a very large extent, the writings of Lacan and Derrida. The frame is thus framed again by part of its content; the sender again receives his own message backward from the receiver" (146).

Johnson's essay is at odds with itself, as she would be the first to admit. Indeed, it is precisely her strategy to present the opposing aspects of her essay—its explicit refusal to take a numerical position on the structure of the tale coupled with its implicit assumption of a numerical position in representing its relationship to the two earlier essays— as an aporia,[8] a trope of undecidability not unlike the one Paul de Man describes in the passage Johnson uses as the epigraph to her book *The Critical Difference*, whose final chapter is her essay on Derrida and Lacan. In that epigraph de Man evokes the aporia between grammar and rhetoric by citing as an example the case in which Edith Bunker asks her husband Archie if he wants his bowling shoes laced over or under—to which the irascible Archie replies, "What's the difference?" In terms of grammar Archie's reply asks for the difference between two alternatives, but in terms of rhetoric his reply means "Whatever the difference is, it's not important enough to make a difference to me." De Man remarks, "The same grammatical pattern engenders two meanings that are mutually exclusive: the literal meaning asks for the concept (difference) whose existence is denied by the figurative meaning" (Johnson, v). It is in this same vein that Johnson at

8. In logic, an impasse resulting from indecision or uncertainty; in rhetoric often indicating an ironic uncertainty (i.e., expressing doubt but not really intending it). Derrida uses the term to indicate incompatible meanings that are not decidable, so that a text undermines its own grounds, structure, terms—thus deconstructing itself [Editor].

the end of her essay, after having described the opposition between Derrida's and Lacan's position as "the oscillation between unequivocal statements of undecidability and ambiguous assertions of decidability," concludes,

> "Undecidability" can no more be used as a last word than "destination." . . . The "undeterminable" is not opposed to the determinable; "dissemination" is not opposed to repetition. If we could be sure of the difference between the determinable and the undeterminable, the undeterminable would be comprehended within the determinable. What is undecidable is whether a thing is decidable or not. (146)

What are we to make of these words? By which I mean not just what do these words say grammatically but what do they convey rhetorically, for what purpose are they being said in this context? I think the key lies in Johnson's statement that " 'Undecidability' can no more be used as a last word than 'destination.' " At the point she says this, Johnson is nearing her own destination, the end of her essay, and is faced with the formal requirement of saying a last word and thus with the question of whether a last word can be said in the oft-renewed critical discussion of "The Purloined Letter." Having to say a last word, she says in effect, "The last word is that there is no last word." This type of statement, which says one thing grammatically and means its opposite rhetorically, occurs again and again in her essay. As we noted, it is the strategy at work when Johnson refuses to take a numerical position on the structure of the tale at the same time that she implicitly assumes a numerical position in relation to the two earlier readings, which her own essay retrospectively groups into a series along with itself. It is at work again when she turns Derrida's insights on doubling back upon themselves to tell Derrida that it is impossible to be one up on his specular double Lacan, for though what she says on a grammatical level is that it is impossible to be one up in such an encounter, the rhetorical effect of her statement is to leave her one up on her specular double Derrida. And this strategy is at work once again when she decisively concludes, "What is undecidable is whether a thing is decidable or not."

These instances of an aporia between grammar and rhetoric occur in statements that are in one way or another self-reflexive, statements that are themselves included in the class of things to which they refer. A simple example of a self-including statement is the sentence "All statements containing seven words are false." Because the sentence is itself a statement made up of seven words, we are faced with a paradox: if this statement is true, it is false, and if it is false, it is true. Similarly, in an aporia between grammar and rhetoric we are faced, as de Man notes, with a single grammatical pattern that engenders two mutually exclusive meanings. By very reason of the fact that they include themselves in the class of things to which they refer, such statements double back upon themselves and exhibit the uncanny reversal-into-the-opposite inherent in doubling.

One thinks in this connection of Russell's paradox. Distinguishing between two kinds of classes (those that do not include themselves as members and those that do), Russell calls the first class "normal" and the second "non-normal," and he then doubles back upon itself this distinction between nonself-including and self-including classes by asking whether *the class of all normal classes* is a normal or a non-normal class. By definition *the class of all normal classes* includes within itself all normal classes. Consequently, if it is itself a normal class, it must be included in itself. But self-inclusion is the distinguishing characteristic of a non-normal class. *The class of all "normal" classes* is, then, a concept whose form and content are at odds: the concept involves, on the one hand, a formal notion of *class* as absolutely inclusive, which is to say, as ultimately self-inclusive (*the class of all*), that is contradicted, on the other hand, by the content, by the specific definition of the "*classes*" which the former is to include completely within itself. As a result, the class of all normal classes is normal only if it is non-normal, and non-normal only if it is normal. Part of the endless fascination of paradoxes of self-inclusion is, of course, that they seem to reflect in the facing mirrors of language and logic the mysterious nature of self-consciousness as that which seeks to include wholly within itself an exact representation of that which, by its very essence, cannot wholly include itself.

At the very start of her essay Johnson sets the tone for all the self-including statements that are to follow when she remarks that in Poe's tale, Lacan's reading, and Derrida's critique,

> It is the *act of analysis* which seems to occupy the center of the discursive stage, and the *act of analysis of the act of analysis* which in some way disrupts that centrality. In the resulting asymmetrical, abyssal structure, no analysis—including this one—can intervene without transforming and repeating other elements in the sequence, which is thus not a stable sequence, but which nevertheless produces certain regular effects. (110)

The key phrase, of course, is "no analysis—including this one." It has about it the brisk American quality of Mark Twain's "No general statement is worth a damn—including this one"—a general statement that is worth a damn only if general statements aren't worth a damn. The very fact that Johnson makes an analytic statement that includes itself, which is to say, an analysis of her own analysis, in the sentence immediately following her statement that it is the act of analysis of the act of analysis that skews analysis in Poe's tale, Lacan's reading, and Derrida's critique, is her way of announcing her strategy at the start. It is not that Johnson will do anything different in her essay from what Lacan and Derrida have done in theirs. Indeed, it is not clear that she thinks anything different can be done at this point inasmuch as Lacan and Derrida have already replayed the tale's structure in a critical register by acting out the game of even and odd in their opposing positions. What will be different in her version is that these positions will

be repeated with a complete awareness of their implications, a total critical self-consciousness that aims to create an insight without a blind spot. For what is at issue here is not so much whether one's critical argument is logically true or false, or one's reading of the tale perceptive or dull, but whether one's interpretive stance is methodologically self-aware or methodologically naive. In its translation from fiction to criticism, the project of analyzing the act of analysis becomes in effect the program of being infinitely self-conscious about self-consciousness. Or put another way, if the structure that we find in "The Purloined Letter" involves doubling an opponent's thought processes in order to turn his own methods against him, then the only defense against having the same strategy repeated against oneself by the next player is to produce an insight or take a position that is already self-consciously doubled back upon itself, as is the case with the type of self-including statement that says one thing grammatically but conveys its opposite rhetorically. For a position that includes itself and its opposite seems to leave no ground on which it can be undermined.

The commitment to an increasingly self-conscious analytic posture that animates this cumulative series of interpretations produces at last a kind of intellectual vertigo, a not uncharacteristic side effect of thought about thought—the rational animal turning in circles trying to catch itself by a tale it doesn't have. And certainly no one enjoyed producing this vertiginous effect more than did Poe, an effect that he imaged as a dizziness experienced at the edge of a vortex or on the brink of a precipice. That the dizzying, self-dissolving effect of thought about thought—what Johnson calls the "asymmetrical, abyssal structure" of analyzing the act of analysis—forms the continuing theme of the Dupin stories is announced in the opening sentence of the first tale, "The Murders in the Rue Morgue." The story begins with the narrator's lengthy prefatory remarks on the nature of the analytical power, remarks that conclude by presenting the narrative as a "commentary upon the propositions just advanced" (2:531). But those prefatory remarks start with this curious proposition: "The mental features discoursed of as the analytical are, in themselves, but little susceptible of analysis" (2:527). Inasmuch as this statement initiates the narrator's own brief analysis of the analytical power, it is self-reflexive: as an analytic statement about the nonsusceptibility of analysis to being analyzed, it is included in the class of things to which it refers, but what it says in effect is that analytic statements cannot wholly include themselves. In analyzing the act of analysis, self-conscious thought turns back upon itself to find that it cannot absolutely coincide with itself. This insight about the nature of thought is at least as old in our tradition as the philosophies of Zeno and Parmenides and as new as Gödel's proof and Borges's (and Carroll's) map of natural size. It is the paradoxical insight that if one considers the act of thinking and the content of thought as two distinguishable things—as it seems one must in dealing with self-consciousness, with thought that is able to represent itself to itself, able to take itself as its own object—then the

attempt to analyze the act of analysis, to include wholly the act of thinking within the content of thought, will be a progression of the order $n + 1$ to infinity. Which is to say that there will always be one more step needed in order to make the act of thinking and the content of thought coincide.

Selected Bibliography

Some of the categories are chronologically arranged, others alphabetically. Because editions and biographies particularly reflect information available at the times in which they were written, and because more information has gradually come to light over the years, they are listed in chronological order. This arrangement enables one to see how Poe studies have changed—or how certain themes and ideas persist. Critical studies are listed alphabetically by author for ease of reference, and in the case of edited volumes by title as well. Authors, editors, and titles are cross-referenced through the appropriate categories below. The scholarship and criticism of Poe studies is vast; listed here are useful book-length works; from the hundreds upon hundreds of articles only a handful of the most important have been included.

• indicates a work included or excerpted in this Norton Critical Edition.

BOOKS PUBLISHED DURING POE'S LIFETIME

Tamerlane and Other Poems. By A Bostonian. Boston: Calvin F. S. Thomas Printer, 1827.
[Preface, Tamerlane, To ——— ("I saw thee on the bridal day"), Dreams, Visit of the Dead, Evening Star, Imitation, Stanzas ("In youth have I known one with whom the Earth"), Untitled ("A wilder'd being from my birth"), Untitled ("The happiest day—the happiest hour"), The Lake, Notes.]
Al Aaraaf, Tamerlane, and Minor Poems. By Edgar A. Poe. Baltimore: Hatch & Dunning, 1829.
[Untitled ("Science! Meet daughter of old Time thou art!"), Al Aaraaf—Part I, Al Aaraaf—Part II, Tamerlane, Preface ("Romance who loves to nod and sing"), To ——— ("Should my early life seem"), To ——— ("I saw thee on thy bridal day"), To ——— ("The bowers whereat, in dreams, I see"), To the River—, The Lake— To ———, Spirits of the Dead, A Dream, To M—— ("O! I care not that my earthly lot"), Fairyland.]
Poems by Edgar A. Poe. "Second Edition." New York: Elam Bliss, 1831.
[Letter to Mr. ———. Introduction, To Helen, Israfel, The Doomed City, Fairyland, Irene, A Paean, The Valley Nis, Proem ("Science! meet daughter of old Time thou art"), Al Aaraaf, Tamerlane.]
The Narrative of Arthur Gordon Pym of Nantucket. New York: Harper & Brothers, 1838. London: Wiley and Putnam, 1838.
Tales of the Grotesque and Arabesque. By Edgar A. Poe. 2 vols. Philadelphia: Lea and Blanchard, 1840.
[Vol. I: Preface, Morella, Lionizing, William Wilson, The Man That Was Used Up, The Fall of the House of Usher, The Duc de L'Omelette, Ms. Found in a Bottle, Bon-Bon, Shadow, The Devil in the Belfry, King Pest, The Signora Zenobia, The Scythe of Time.
Vol. II: Advertisement, Epimanes, Siope, Hans Phaall, A Tale of Jerusalem, Von Jung, Loss of Breath, Metzengerstein, Berenice, Why the Little Frenchman Wears His Hand in a Sling, The Visionary, The Conversation of Eiros and Charmion, Appendix.]
The Prose Romances of Edgar Allan Poe. Uniform Serial Edition. No. 1. Philadelphia: William H. Graham, 1843.
[Contains "The Murders in the Rue Morgue" and "The Man That Was Used Up"; no further numbers were issued.]

Tales by Edgar A. Poe. New York: Wiley and Putnam, 1845.
[The Gold-Bug, The Black Cat, Mesmeric Revelation, Lionizing, The Fall of the House of Usher, A Descent into the Maelström, The Colloquy of Monos and Una, The Conversation of Eiros and Charmion, The Murders in the Rue Morgue, The Mystery of Marie Roget, The Purloined Letter, The Man of the Crowd.]
The Raven and Other Poems. By Edgar A. Poe. New York and London: Wiley and Putnam, 1845.
[The Raven, The Valley of Unrest, Bridal Ballad, The Sleeper, The Coliseum, Lenore, Catholic Hymn, Israfel, Dream-land, Sonnet—to Zante, The City in the Sea, To One in Paradise, Eulalie—A Song, To F——s S. O——d, To F——, Sonnet—Silence, The Conqueror Worm, The Haunted Palace, Scenes from Politian. POEMS WRITTEN IN YOUTH: Sonnet—to Science, Al Aaraaf, Tamerlane, A Dream, Romance, Fairy-land, To ——, To the River ——, The Lake— To ——, Song, To Helen.]
Eureka. A Prose Poem. By Edgar A. Poe. New York: Geo. P. Putnam, 1848.

EARLY EDITIONS

Works of Edgar Allan Poe, with Notices of his Life and Genius. Ed. Rufus Wilmot Griswold *et al.* (see p. 710, n.1 herein). 4 vols. New York: J. S. Redfield, 1850–56.
The Works of Edgar Allan Poe. Ed. E. C. Stedman and G. E. Woodberry. 10 vols. Chicago: Stone & Kimball, 1894–95.
The Complete Works of Edgar Allan Poe. Ed. James A. Harrison. "Virginia" edition. 17 vols. New York: Thomas Y. Crowell & Co., 1902.
The Poems of Edgar Allan Poe. Ed. Killis Campbell. Boston: Ginn, 1917.
Doings of Gotham, as described in a series of letters to the editors of the "Columbia Spy," together with various editorial comments and criticisms by Poe now first collected. Comp. Jacob E. Spannuth. With an introduction by Thomas Ollive Mabbott. Pottsville, PA: Jacob E. Spannuth, 1929.

LATER COLLECTED EDITIONS

Collected Works of Edgar Allan Poe. Ed. Thomas Ollive Mabbott. 3 vols. Cambridge: Belknap Press of Harvard University Press, 1969–78.
 i. *Poems.*
 ii. *Tales and Sketches, 1831–1842.*
 iii. *Tales and Sketches, 1843–1849.*
Collected Writings of Edgar Allan Poe. Ed. Burton R. Pollin, et al. New York: Twayne and Gordian Press, 1981– . Continues the "Collected Works" initiated by Mabbott:
 i. *The Imaginary Voyages: The Narrative of Arthur Gordon Pym; The Unparalleled Adventure of One Hans Pfaall; The Journal of Julius Rodman*
 ii. *The Brevities: Pinakidia, Marginalia, Fifty Suggestions, and Other Works*
 iii. *The Broadway Journal: Nonfictional Prose. The Text.*
 iv. *The Broadway Journal: Nonfictional Prose. The Annotations.*
 v. *Writings in The Southern Literary Messenger: Nonfictional Prose.*

ANNOTATED POPULAR EDITIONS

The Poems of Edgar Allan Poe. Ed. Killis Campbell. First pub. 1917 (see above); reprint ed., New York: Russell & Russell, 1962.
Selected Writings of Edgar Allan Poe. Ed. Edward H. Davidson. Boston: Houghton Mifflin, Riverside Edition, 1956.
Poems of Edgar Allan Poe. Ed. Richard Wilbur. New York: Dell Laurel, 1959.
Edgar Allan Poe: Representative Selections. Ed. Margaret Alterton and Hardin Craig. New York: Hill and Wang, 1935; 1962.
The Poems of Edgar Allan Poe. Ed. Floyd Stovall. Charlottesville: University Press of Virginia, 1965.
The Short Fiction of Edgar Allan Poe: An Annotated Edition. Ed. Stuart Levine and Susan Levine. Indianapolis: Bobbs-Merrill, 1976. Revised ed., Urbana: University of Illinois Press, 1990.
The Annotated Tales of Edgar Allan Poe. Ed. Stephen Peithman. New York: Avenell Books, 1981.
Edgar Allan Poe: Poetry and Tales. Ed. Patrick Quinn. New York: Library of America, 1984.
Edgar Allan Poe: Essays and Reviews. Ed. G. R. Thompson. New York: Library of America, 1984.

ANNOTATED POPULAR EDITIONS OF *ARTHUR GORDON PYM*

The Narrative of Arthur Gordon Pym. Ed. Sidney Kaplan. New York: Hill & Wang, 1960.
The Narrative of Arthur Gordon Pym. Ed. Harold Beaver. New York: Penguin, 1975.
The Narrative of Arthur Gordon Pym. Ed. J. Gerald Kennedy. New York: Oxford University Press, 1994.
The Narrative of Arthur Gordon Pym. Ed. Richard Kopley. New York: Penguin, 1999.

CONCORDANCES AND INDEXES

A *Concordance to the Poetical Works of Edgar Allan Poe*. Comp. Bradford A. Booth and Claude E. Jones. Baltimore: Johns Hopkins Press, 1941.
An Index to Poe's Critical Vocabulary. Comp. J. Lasley Dameron and Louis Charles Stagg. Hartford, CT: Transcendental Books, 1966.
Dictionary of Names and Titles in Poe's Collected Works. Comp. Burton R. Pollin. New York: Da Capo Books, 1968.
Word Index to Poe's Fiction. Comp. Burton R. Pollin. New York: Gordian, 1982.
Concordance to the Poetry of Edgar Allan Poe. Comp. Elizabeth Wiley. Selinsgrove: Susquehanna University Press, 1989.

LETTERS AND PAPERS

Poe and His Friends: Letters Relating to Poe. Vol. XVII of *The Complete Works of Edgar Allan Poe*. Ed. James A. Harrison. (See editions above.)
The Letters of Edgar Allan Poe, ed. John Ward Ostrom. 2 vols. Cambridge, Massachusetts: Harvard University Press, 1948. Republished with three supplements (New York: Gordian Press, 1966); fourth supplement, *American Literature*, 45 (January 1974): 513–36. [A new edition integrating all supplements is in progress under the supervision of Burton R. Pollin and Roger Texier.]

Poe's papers are widely scattered. Among the more important collections are the following: Beinecke Rare Book and Manuscript Library, Yale University; Boston Public Library (Griswold Collection); Enoch Pratt Free Library, Baltimore; Harvard College Library and the Houghton Library, Harvard University; Henry E. Huntington Library and Art Gallery, San Marino, CA; J. K. Lilly Library, Indiana University (Poe and Griswold Collections); Library of Congress (Ellis and Allan Papers); New York Public Library (Manuscript Division and Berg Collection); Pierpont Morgan Library, New York; M. L. Stark Library and Humanities Research Center, University of Texas, Austin (Koester Collection); Valentine Museum, Richmond, VA. (Ellis and Allan Papers); the State Library of Virginia (Poe Foundation of Richmond); University of Virginia (Ingram Collection).

Two private collections are described in " 'Quoth the Raven': An Exhibition of the work of Edgar Allan Poe . . . from the collections of H. Bradley Martin and Colonel Richard Gimbel," *Yale University Library Gazette*, 33 (April 1959): 138–89.

Guides to the following collections are available: Arthur Hobson Quinn and Richard H. Hart, *Edgar Allan Poe: Letters and Documents in the Enoch Pratt Free Library* (New York: Scholars Facsimiles and Reprints, 1941); John D. Gordan, *Edgar Allan Poe . . . A Catalogue of First Editions, Manuscripts, Autograph Letters, from the Berg Collection* (New York: New York Public Library, 1949); John Carl Miller, *John Henry Ingram's Poe Collection at the University of Virginia: A Calendar* . . . (Charlottesville: University Press of Virginia, 1960); David A. Randall, "The J. K. Lilly Collection of Edgar Allan Poe," *Indiana University Bookman*, no. 4 (March 1960): 46–58; Randall, *The J. K. Lilly Collection of Edgar Allan Poe: An Account of Its Formation* (Bloomington: Lilly Library of Indiana University, 1964); Joseph J. Moldenhauer, *A Descriptive Catalog of Edgar Allan Poe Manuscripts in The Humanities Research Center Library, The University of Texas at Austin* (Austin: Texas Quarterly Supplement, Distributed by the University of Texas Press, 1973).

BIBLIOGRAPHIES
[in chronological order]

Robertson, John W. *Bibliography of the Writings of Edgar A. Poe and Commentary on the Bibliography of Edgar A. Poe*. San Francisco: Russian Hill Private Press, Edwin & Robert Grabhorn Publishers, 1934.
Hull, William D. "A Canon of the Critical Works of Edgar Allan Poe with a Study of Edgar Allan Poe the Magazinist." Ph.D. dissertation, University of Virginia, 1941.
Wylie, John Cook. "A List of the Texts of Poe's Tales," in *Humanistic Studies in Honor of John Calvin Metcalf*. New York: Columbia University Press, 1941. 322–38.
Heartman, Charles F., and James R. Canny. *A Bibliography of First Printings of the Writings of Edgar Allan Poe*. Revised ed. Hattiesburg, MS: The Book Farm, 1943.
Braddy, Haldeen. *Glorious Incense: The Fulfillment of Edgar Allan Poe*. New York: Scarecrow, 1953.
Hubbell, Jay B. "Poe," in *Eight American Authors: A Review of Research and Criticism*. Ed. Floyd Stovall. New York: Modern Language Association, 1956. 1–46.
Todd, William B. "The Early Issues of Poe's Tales (1845)," *Library Chronicle of the University of Texas* 7 (Fall 1961): 13–17.
Tanselle, G. Thomas. "The State of Poe Bibliography," *Poe Newsletter* 2 (Jan. 1969): 1–3.
Hubbell, Jay B. "Poe," in *Eight American Authors: A Review of Research and Criticism*. Revised ed., ed. James Woodress. New York: Norton, 1971. 3–36.
Dameron, J. Lasley. "Thomas Ollive Mabbott on the Canon of Poe's Reviews," *Poe Studies* 5 (Dec. 1972): 56–57.

Hyneman, Esther K. *Edgar Allan Poe: An Annotated Bibliography of Books and Articles in English, 1827–1973.* Boston: G. K. Hall, 1974.
Dameron, J. Lasley, and Irby B. Cauthen Jr. *Edgar Allan Poe: A Bibliography of Criticism 1827–1967.* Charlottesville: University of Press of Virginia, 1974.

OTHER REFERENCE WORKS

An Edgar Allan Poe Companion: A Guide to the Short Stories, Romances and Essays. By J. R. Hammond. London: Macmillan, 1981.
Edgar Allan Poe: The Critical Heritage. Ed. I. M. Walker. London: Routledge, 1986.
Edgar Allan Poe: Critical Assessments. Ed. Graham Clarke. 4 vols. London: Routledge, 1992.
A Companion to Poe Studies. Ed. Eric W. Carlson. Westport, CT: Greenwood, 1996.
The Poe Encyclopedia. Ed. Frederick S. Frank and Anthony Magistrale. Westport, CT: Greenwood, 1997.
The Poe Cinema: A Critical Filmography of Theatrical Releases Based on the Works of Edgar Allan Poe. By Don G. Smith. Jefferson, NC: McFarland, 1999.
The Baltimore Poe Society, the Enoch Pratt Free Library, and the University of Baltimore have conjoined in publishing annual pamphlet-monographs on Poe for over three decades; the subjects are wide ranging, including textual scholarship, biography, criticism of specific works, analysis of cultural contexts, and so forth. Some are listed under "Selected Criticism."
American Literary Scholarship (Durham, NC: Duke University Press) has published annual reviews of select Poe scholarship since 1963.
Poe Studies was initiated in 1968 as *Poe Newsletter*; the title was changed in 1970 and the journal was published twice a year until the mid-1980s; its successor, *Poe Studies/Dark Romanticism*, is published irregularly.
The Poe Studies Association regularly published the *PSA Newsletter* several times a year, including reviews and bibliographical updates of Poe studies. It has been expanded as the *Edgar Allan Poe Review* (2000–).
Heywood Ehrlich maintains a Poe Web Site: *A Poe Webliography: Edgar Allan Poe on the Internet* (andromeda/rutgers~erhlich/poesites.html).

POE'S LIFE AND TIMES

Included here, chronologically arranged, are biographies and studies focusing on the historical conditions (literary, economic, and sociopolitical) of Poe's times. Since many biographical studies are also critical interpretations, some authors are cross-referenced in "Selected Criticism."

Griswold, Rufus Wilmot. "Memoir of the Author," in *The Works of the Late Edgar Allan Poe.* New York: J. S. Redfield, 1850. III: vii–xxxix.
Whitman, Sarah Helen. *Edgar Poe and His Critics.* New York: Rudd & Carleton, 1860.
Gill, William Fearing. *The Life of Edgar Allan Poe.* New York: Dillingham, 1877.
Ingram, John H. *Edgar Allan Poe: His Life, Letters and Opinions.* 2 vols. London: John Hogg, 1880.
Woodberry, George Edward. *The Life of Edgar Allan Poe, Personal and Literary.* 2 vols. Boston: Houghton, Mifflin, 1909.
Allen, Hervey. *Israfel: The Life and Times of Edgar Allan Poe.* 2 vols. New York: Doran, 1926.
Krutch, Joseph Wood. *Edgar Allan Poe: A Study in Genius.* New York: Knopf, 1926.
Phillips, Mary E. *Edgar Allan Poe, the Man.* 2 vols. Chicago: John C. Winston, 1926.
Bonaparte, Marie. *The Life and Works of Edgar Allan Poe: A Psycho-Analytic Interpretation.* Vienna: Internationaler Psychoanalytischer Verlag, 1934. Trans. John Rodker, London: Imago, 1949.
Pope-Hennessy, Una. *Edgar Allan Poe, 1809–1849: A Critical Biography.* London: Macmillan, 1934.
Quinn, Arthur Hobson. *Edgar Allan Poe: A Critical Biography.* New York: D. Appleton-Century, 1941.
Miller, Perry. *The Raven and the Whale: The War of Words and Wits in the Era of Poe and Melville.* New York: Harcourt, Brace, 1956.
Winwar, Frances [pseud.]. *The Haunted Palace: A Life of Edgar Allan Poe.* New York: Harpers, 1959.
• McLean, Robert Colin. *George Tucker: Moral Philosopher and Man of Letters* (Chapel Hill: University of North Carolina Press).
Bittner, William. *Poe: A Biography.* Boston: Little, Brown, 1962.
Wagenknecht, Edward. *Edgar Allan Poe: The Man Behind the Legend.* New York: Oxford University Press, 1963.
Moss, Sidney P. *Poe's Literary Battles: The Critic in the Context of His Literary Milieu.* Durham, NC: Duke University Press, 1963.

Walsh, John E. *Poe the Detective: The Curious Circumstances Behind "The Mystery of Marie Ro-get."* New Brunswick, NJ: Rutgers University Press, 1967.

The Recognition of Edgar Allan Poe: Selected Criticism Since 1829 (1970). See Eric W. Carlson in *Collections.*

Moss, Sidney P. *Poe's Major Crisis: His Libel Suit and New York's Literary World.* Durham, NC: Duke University Press, 1970.

Forclaz, Roger. *Le Monde d'Edgar Poe.* Berne: Herbert Lang; and Frankfurt: Peter Lang, 1974.

Miller, John C. *Building Poe Biography.* Baton Rouge: Louisiana State University Press, 1977.

Symons, Julian. *The Tell-Tale Heart: The Life and Works of Edgar Allan Poe.* New York: Harper & Row, 1978.

Thompson, G. R. "Edgar Allan Poe: Life and Works." In *Dictionary of Literary Biography.* Vol. 3: *Antebellum Writers in New York and the South.* Ed. Joel Myerson. Detroit, MI: Gale, 1979. Revised and enlarged as "Edgar Allan Poe." In *Dictionary of Literary Biography.* Vol. 248: *Antebellum Writers in the South.* 2nd series. Ed. Kent Ljungquist. Detroit, San Francisco, London, Boston, Woodbridge, CT: Gale, 2001.

Miller, John C. *Poe's Helen Remembers.* Charlottesville: University of Virginia Press, 1979.

Edgar Allan Poe: The Critical Heritage (1986). See I. M. Walker in "Other Reference Works."

Thomas, Dwight, and David K. Jackson. *The Poe Log: A Documentary Life of Edgar Allan Poe 1809–1849.* Boston: G. K. Hall, 1987.

Ketterer, David. *Edgar Allan Poe: Life, Work, and Criticism.* York, UK: York University Press, 1989.

Deas, David J. *The Portraits and Daguerreotypes of Edgar Allan Poe.* Charlottesville: University of Virginia Press, 1989.

Silverman, Kenneth. *Edgar A. Poe: Mournful and Never-Ending Remembrance.* New York: HarperCollins, 1991.

Meyers, Jeffrey. *Edgar Allan Poe: His Life and Legacy.* New York: Scribner, 1992.

Rosenheim, Shawn. *The Cryptographic Imagination: Secret Writing from Edgar Poe to the Internet.* Baltimore: Johns Hopkins University Press, 1997.

Hammond, J. R. *An Edgar Allan Poe Chronology.* New York: Macmillan, 1998.

• Whalen, Terence. *Poe and the Masses: The Political Economy of Literature in Antebellum America.* Princeton, NJ: Princeton University Press, 1999.

Kennedy, J. Gerald, ed. *A Historical Guide to Edgar Allan Poe.* New York: Oxford University Press, 2001. [Also listed in "Collections of Critical Essays."]

SELECTED CRITICISM

Many of these studies have strong biographical and cultural elements; they are included here if they are predominately aesthetic, critical, and interpretative; some are cross-referenced to other categories.

Alexander, Jean, ed. *Affidavits of Genius: Edgar Allan Poe and the French Critics, 1847–1924.* Port Washington, NY: Kennikat, 1971.

Allen, Michael. *Poe and the British Magazine Tradition.* New York: Oxford University Press, 1969.

Alterton, Margaret. *The Origins of Poe's Critical Theory.* Iowa City: University of Iowa, 1925.

Anderson, Carl L. *Poe in Northlight: The Scandinavian Response to His Life and Work.* Durham, NC: Duke University Press, 1973.

• Armstrong, Liahna. "The Shadow's Shadow: The Motif of the Double in Edgar Allan Poe's 'The Purloined Letter,' " *The Mystery and Detection Annual* (1972): 21–32.

Baudelaire, Charles. *Baudelaire on Poe: Critical Papers.* Ed. Lois and Francis Hyslop. State College, PA: Bald Eagle Press, 1952.

———. *Edgar Allan Poe, sa vie et ses ouvrages.* Ed. W. T. Bandy. Toronto: University of Toronto Press, 1973.

Benton, Richard P., ed. *New Approaches to Poe. A Symposium.* Hartford, CT: Transcendental Books, 1970.

———, ed. *Poe as Literary Cosmologer: Studies on Eureka. A Symposium.* Hartford, CT: Transcendental Books, 1975.

Bloom, Clive. *Reading Poe Reading Freud: The Romantic Imagination in Crisis.* New York: St. Martin's Press, 1988.

Budd, Louis J., and Edwin H. Cady. *On Poe: The Best from American Literature.* Durham, NC: Duke University Press, 1993.

Buranelli, Vincent. *Edgar Allan Poe.* Boston: Twayne, 1961. Rev. ed., 1977.

Burduck, Michael L. *Grim Phantasms: Fear in Poe's Fiction.* New York: Garland, 1992.

Cambiaire, Célestin P. *The Influence of Edgar Allan Poe in France.* New York: G. E. Stechert, 1927.

Campbell, Killis. *The Mind of Poe and Other Studies.* Cambridge: Harvard University Press, 1933.

Carlson, Eric W., ed. *The Recognition of Edgar Allan Poe: Selected Criticism Since 1829.* Ann Arbor: University of Michigan Press, 1970.

————, ed. *Critical Essays on Poe*. Boston and New York: G. K. Hall, 1987.

Davidson, Edward H. *Poe: A Critical Study*. Cambridge: Harvard University Press, 1957.

Dayan, Joan. *Fables of Mind: An Inquiry into Poe's Fiction*. New York: Oxford University Press, 1987.

Derrida, Jacques. *The Post Card: From Socrates to Freud and Beyond*. Trans. Alan Bass. Chicago: University of Chicago Press, 1987. See "Le Facteur de la Vérité," pp. 411–96; reprinted in *The Purloined Poe*, ed. Muller and Richardson, 173–212.

De Shell, Jeffrey. *The Peculiarity of Literature: An Allegorical Approach to Poe's Fiction*. Cranbury/Rutherford, NJ: Fairleigh Dickinson University Press, 1997.

• Eakin, Paul John. "Poe's Sense of an Ending." *American Literature* 45 (1973): 1–22.

Eddings, Dennis W., ed. *The Naiad Voice: Essays on Poe's Satiric Hoaxing*. Port Washington, NY: Associated Faculty Press, 1983.

Elmer, Jonathan *Reading at the Social Limit: Affect, Mass Culture, and Edgar Allan Poe*. Stanford, CA: Stanford University Press, 1995.

Fagin, N. Bryllion. *The Histrionic Mr. Poe*. Baltimore: Johns Hopkins Press, 1949.

• Farrell, Grace. "The Quest of Author Gordon Pym." *Southern Literary Journal* 4 (1972): 22–33.

Fisher, Benjamin Franklin, IV, ed. *Poe at Work: Seven Textual Studies*. Baltimore: The Edgar Allan Poe Society, 1978.

Fletcher, Richard M. *The Stylistic Development of Edgar Allan Poe*. The Hague: Mouton, 1973.

Forclaz, Roger. *Le Monde d' Edgar Poe*. Berne: Herbert Lang; Frankfurt: Peter Lang, 1974. [See "Poe's Life and Times."]

Fruit, John Phelps. *The Mind and Art of Poe's Poetry*. New York: A. S. Barnes, 1899.

• Gangano, James W. "The Question of Poe's Narrators." *College English* 25 (Dec. 1963): 177–81.

Halliburton, David. *Edgar Allan Poe: A Phenomenological View*. Princeton, NJ: Princeton University Press, 1973.

Hansen, Thomas. *The German Face of Edgar Allan Poe*. Columbia, SC: Camden House, 1995.

Harvey, Ronald. *The Critical History of Edgar Allan Poe's* The Narrative of Arthur Gordon Pym: *A Dialogue with Unreason*. New York: Garland, 1998.

Hoffman, Daniel. *Poe Poe Poe Poe Poe Poe Poe*. Garden City: Doubleday, 1972.

Irwin, John T. *American Hieroglyphics: The Symbol of Egyptian Hieroglyphics in the American Renaissance*. New Haven, CT: Yale University Press, 1980.

• ————. *The Mystery to a Solution: Poe, Borges, and the Analytic Detective Story*. Baltimore: Johns Hopkins University Press, 1994.

Jacobs, Robert. *Poe: Journalist and Critic*. Baton Rouge: Louisiana State University Press, 1969.

Johnson, Barbara. *The Critical Difference: Essays in the Contemporary Rhetoric of Reading*. Baltimore: Johns Hopkins University Press, 1980. See "The Frame of Reference: Poe, Lacan, Derrida," pp. 110–146. Reprinted in *The Purloined Poe*, ed. Muller and Richardson, 213–51.

Kaplan, Sidney. Introduction to Poe's *Narrative of Arthur Gordon Pym*, ed. Kaplan. New York: Hill & Wang, 1960. vii–xxv.

Kennedy, J. Gerald. *Poe, Death, and the Life of Writing*. New Haven, CT: Yale University Press, 1987.

————. *"The Narrative of Arthur Gordon Pym" and the Abyss of Interpretation*. New York: Twayne, 1995.

• ————. "Phantasms of Death in Poe's Fiction." In Howard Kerr et al., eds., *The Haunted Dusk: American Supernatural Fiction, 1820–1920* (Athens: University of Georgia Press, 1983), pp. 37–65.

Ketterer, David. *The Rationale of Deception in Poe*. Baton Rouge: Louisiana State University Press, 1979.

Kopley, Richard, ed. *Poe's "Pym": Critical Explorations*. Durham, NC: Duke University Press, 1992.

Lacan, Jacques. *Écrits I* (Paris: Éditions du Seuil, 1966); see "Le Séminaire sur 'La Lettre volée,'" pp 7–75; abridged and trans. in *The Purloined Poe*, ed. Muller and Richardson, 28–54.

Lee, A. Robert, ed. *Edgar A. Poe: The Design of Order*. New York: Barnes & Noble, 1987.

Levin, Harry. *The Power of Blackness: Hawthorne, Poe, Melville*. New York: Knopf, 1958.

Levine, Stuart G. *Edgar Poe: Seer and Craftsman*. Deland, FL.: Everett/Edwards, 1972.

Link, Franz H. *Edgar Allan Poe: Ein Dichter zwischen Romantik und Moderne*. Frankfurt am Main: Athenaum Verlag, 1968.

Ljungquist, Kent P. *The Grand and the Fair: Poe's Landscape Aesthetics and Pictorial Techniques*. Potomac, MD: Scripta Humanistica, 1984.

May, Charles. *Edgar Allan Poe: A Study of the Short Fiction*. Boston: Twayne, 1991.

• Moldenhauer, Joseph J. "Murder as a Fine Art: Basic Connections between Poe's Aesthetics, Psychology, and Moral Vision." *PMLA* 83 (1968): 284–97.

Moss, Sidney P. See "Poe's Life and Times."

Muller, John P., and William J. Richardson, eds. *The Purloined Poe: Lacan, Derrida and Psychoanalytic Reading*. Baltimore: Johns Hopkins University Press, 1988.

Papers on Poe: Essays in Honor of John Ward Ostrom, ed. Richard P. Veler. Springfield, OH: Chantry Music Press at Wittenberg University, 1972.

Parks, Edd Winfield. *Edgar Allan Poe As A Literary Critic*. Athens: University of Georgia Press, 1964.
Peeples, Scott. *Edgar Allan Poe Revisited*. New York: Twayne, 1998.
Phillips, Elizabeth. *Edgar Allan Poe, An American Imagination: Three Essays*. Port Washington, NY: Kennikat, 1979.
Pollin, Burton R. *Discoveries in Poe*. South Bend, IN: University of Notre Dame Press, 1970.
Quinn, Patrick. *The French Face of Edgar Allan Poe*. Carbondale: Southern Illinois University Press, 1957.
Ramakrishna, D., ed. *Perspectives on Poe*. New Delhi, India: APC Publications, 1996. [Also listed in "Collections of Critical Essays."]
Rans, Geoffrey. *Edgar Allan Poe*. Edinburgh and London: Oliver and Boyd, 1965.
Ransome, Arthur. *Edgar Allan Poe: A Critical Study*. London: Stephen Swift, 1912.
Richard, Claude, ed. *Edgar Allan Poe*. Paris: Editions de l'Herne, 1974.
———. *Edgar Allan Poe journaliste et critique*. Paris: Klincksieck, 1978.
———. *Edgar Allan Poe écrivain*. Ed. Henri Justin. Montpellier, France: Delta, 1990.
• Riddel, Joseph N. "The 'Crypt' of Edgar Poe." Mark Bauerlein, ed., *Purloined Letters: Originality and Repetition in American Literature*. (Baton Rouge: Louisiana State University Press, 1995), pp. 121–48.
Rosenheim, Shawn, and Stephen Rachman, eds. *The American Face of Edgar Allan Poe*. Baltimore: Johns Hopkins University Press, 1995.
• St. Armand, Barton Levi. "The 'Mysteries' of Edgar Poe: The Quest for a Monomyth in Gothic Literature." In G. R. Thompson, ed., *The Gothic Imagination: Essays in Dark Romanticism* (Pullman: Washington State University Press, 1974), pp. 65–93.
• Rowe, John Carlos. *At Emerson's Tomb: The Politics of Classic American Literature* (New York: Columbia University Press, 1997). 42–62.
Saliba, David R. *The Psychology of Fear: The Nightmare Formula of Edgar Allan Poe*. Lanham, MD: University Press of America, 1980.
Silverman, Kenneth, ed. *New Essays on Poe's Major Tales*. New York: Cambridge University Press, 1993.
• Stovall, Floyd. *Edgar Poe the Poet. Essays Old and New on the Man and His Work*. Charlottesville: University Press of Virginia, 1969.
Thompson, G. R. *Poe's Fiction: Romantic Irony in the Gothic Tales*. Madison: University of Wisconsin Press, 1973.
———, and Virgil L. Lokke, eds. *Ruined Eden of the Present: Hawthorne, Melville, Poe*. West Lafayette, IN: Purdue University Press, 1981.
———. *Circumscribed Eden of Dreams: Dreamvision and Nightmare in Poe's Early Poetry*. Baltimore: Enoch Pratt Free Library, the Library of the University of Baltimore, and the Poe Society, 1984.
———. *Romantic Arabesque, Contemporary Theory, and Postmodernism: The Example of Poe's "Narrative."* *ESQ: A Journal of the American Renaissance*, Special Issue, nos. 3–4 (1989).
———, and Eric Carl Link. *Neutral Ground: New Traditionalism and the American Romance Controversy*. Baton Rouge: Louisiana State University Press, 1999.
———. Also see "Annotated Popular Editions" and "Poe's Life and Times."
Veler, Richard P., ed. *Papers on Poe: Essays in Honor of John Ward Ostrom*. Springfield, OH: Chantry Music Press at Wittenberg University, 1972.
Walsh, John. See "Poe's Life and Times."
Whalen, Terence. See "Poe's Life and Times."
• Wilbur, Richard. "The House of Poe," in *Anniversary Lectures 1959*. Washington, D.C.: Reference Department of the Library of Congress, 1959.
———. "Introduction" and "Notes" to *Poe*. The Laurel Poetry Series. New York: Dell, 1959.
———. *Responses: Prose Pieces 1953–1976*. New York: Harcourt Brace Jovanovich, 1976.
Williams, Michael J. S. *A World of Words: Language and Displacement in the Fiction of Edgar Allan Poe*. Durham, NC: Duke University Press, 1988.

COLLECTIONS OF CRITICAL ESSAYS

For convenience of reference (especially in writing research papers), selected anthologies of criticism on Poe are collected here. Changing standards of taste and ideas of cultural significance are reflected in the variety of critical selections editors have made over the decades. The following are arranged chronologically.

The Enigma of Poe. Ed. Warren U. Ober, Paul S. Burtness, and William R. Seat Jr. Boston: D. C. Heath, 1960.
The Recognition of Edgar Allan Poe: Selected Criticism Since 1829. Ed. Eric W. Carlson. Ann Arbor: University of Michigan Press, 1970.
New Approaches to Poe. A Symposium. Ed. Richard P. Benton. Hartford, CT: Transcendental Books, 1970.

Affidavits of Genius. Edgar Allan Poe and the French Critics, 1847–1924. Ed. Jean Alexander. Port Washington, NY: Kennikat, 1971.

Papers on Poe: Essays in Honor of John Ward Ostrom. Ed. Richard P. Veler. Springfield, OH: Chantry Music Press at Wittenberg University, 1972.

Edgar Allan Poe. Ed. Claude Richard. Paris: Edition de l'Herne, 1974.

Poe as Literary Cosmologer: Studies on Eureka. A Symposium. Ed. Richard P. Benton. Hartford, CT: Transcendental Books, 1975.

Poe at Work: Seven Textual Studies. Ed. Benjamin Franklin Fisher IV. Baltimore: The Edgar Allan Poe Society, 1978.

Ruined Eden of the Present: Hawthorne, Melville, Poe. Ed. G. R. Thompson and Virgil L. Lokke. West Lafayette, IN: Purdue University Press, 1981.

The Naiad Voice: Essays on Poe's Satiric Hoaxing. Ed. Dennis W. Eddings. Port Washington, NY: Associated Faculty Press, 1983.

Critical Essays on Poe. Ed. Eric W. Carlson. Boston: G. K. Hall, 1987.

Edgar A. Poe: The Design of Order. Ed. A. Robert Lee. New York: Barnes & Noble, 1987.

The Purloined Poe: Lacan, Derrida and Psychoanalytic Reading. Ed. John P. Muller and William J. Richardson. Baltimore: Johns Hopkins University Press, 1988.

Poe's "Pym": Critical Explorations. Ed. Richard Kopley. Durham, NC: Duke University Press, 1992.

On Poe: The Best from American Literature. Ed. Louis J. Budd and Edwin H. Cady. Durham, NC: Duke University Press, 1993.

New Essays on Poe's Major Tales. Ed. Kenneth Silverman. New York: Cambridge University Press, 1993.

The American Face of Edgar Allan Poe. Ed. Shawn Rosenheim and Stephen Rachman. Baltimore: Johns Hopkins University Press, 1995.

Perspectives on Poe. Ed. D. Ramakrishna. New Delhi, India: APC Publications, 1996.

A Historical Guide to Edgar Allan Poe. Ed. J. Gerald Kennedy. New York: Oxford University Press, 2001.

The Cambridge Companion to Edgar Allan Poe. Ed. Kevin J. Hayes. Cambridge: Cambridge University Press, 2002.

Index of Titles and First Lines